Online Resources for Criminal Justice

Careers in Criminal Justice Website
www.cjinaction.com

Helping students investigate and focus on criminal justice career choices that are right for them, the site includes:

▶ *Career Profiles:* video testimonials from a variety of practicing professionals
▶ *Interest Assessment:* helping students decide which CJ careers are suited for them
▶ *Career Planner:* resumé writing tips and successful job search strategies
▶ *Links for Reference* to federal, state, and local agencies (where students can get contact information)

Wadsworth Criminal Justice Resource Center
www.thomsonedu.com/criminaljustice

Designed with both instructors and students in mind, this Web site features information about Thomson Wadsworth's technology and teaching solutions, as well as several features created specifically for today's criminal justice student. Supreme Court updates, timelines, and hot-topic polling can all be used to supplement in-class assignments and discussions. You'll also find a wealth of links to careers and news in criminal justice, book-specific sites, and much more.

Learn about criminal justice with these intriguing developments . . . straight from the headlines:

Homeland security and the new challenges it presents to CJ professionals

This book's entirely new Chapter 16, "Homeland Security," helps you to better understand terrorism, as well as counterterrorism challenges and strategies, border security, and more. **See page 523.**

Debunking myths about women in police work

Chapter 6's *Myth versus Reality* box puts to rest the myth that policing is primarily men's work. **See page 148.**

The Supreme Court reconsiders the rules of search and seizure

A new chapter-opening vignette focuses on *Georgia v. Randolph*, an intriguing 2006 case with major implications for police searches. **See pages 204 and 205.**

The latest developments in the use of DNA evidence

The new chapter-ending *Criminal Justice in Action* activity in Chapter 6 gets you thinking critically about the controversial practice of collecting DNA evidence from those arrested but not yet convicted of crimes. **See page 199.**

The deadliest shooting rampage in American history

A new chapter-opening account examines the murder of 32 students and professors at Virginia Tech and what it reveals to you about police strategies, gun control issues, and more. **See page 4.**

The latest methods for reducing recidivism

Chapter 14 gives you an up-to-the minute look at reentry concerns, the most effective methods for reducing recidivism, and the challenges posed by a phenomenon know as the "relapse process." **See pages 472 to 475.**

These are just a few of the many real-life developments in this book that will give you an inside look at important issues and concepts in criminal justice.

Criminal Justice in Action

Fifth Edition

Larry K. Gaines
California State University
San Bernardino

Roger LeRoy Miller
Institute for University Studies
Arlington, Texas

THOMSON

WADSWORTH

Australia • Canada • Mexico • Singapore • Spain • United Kingdom • United States

Criminal Justice in Action
Fifth Edition
Larry K. Gaines and Roger LeRoy Miller

Editor-in-Chief: Eve Howard
Publisher/Executive Editor: Marcus Boggs
Senior Acquisitions Editor: Carolyn Henderson-Meier
Senior Developmental Editor: Robert Jucha
Assistant Editor: Meaghan Banks
Editorial Assistant: Beth McMurray
Marketing Manager: Terra Schultz
Marketing Assistant: Emily Elrod
Marketing Communications Manager: Tami Strang
Technology Project Manager: Lauren Keyes
Manufacturing Coordinator: Becky Cross
Senior Content Project Manager: Ann Borman

Photo Researcher: Anne Sheroff, Ann Hoffman
Copyeditor: Pat Lewis
Proofreader: Martha Ghent
Indexer: Bob Marsh
Interior Designer: Ellen Pettengill
Cover Designer: RHDG
Cover images: bullet: © Colin Anderson/Brand X/Corbis; security officer with dog: Getty Images; female police officer: Masterfile; man being searched: Getty Images; DNA: Photodisc
Text & Cover Printer: Transcontitnental, Beauceville
Compositor: Parkwood Composition Service

Library of Congress Control Number: 2007908774
Student Edition ISBN-13: 978-0-495-50545-7
Student Edition ISBN-10: 0-495-50545-5
Instructor's Edition ISBN-13: 978-0-495-50546-4
Instructor's Edition ISBN-10: 0-495-50546-3

Thomson Higher Education
10 Davis Drive
Belmont, CA 94002-3098
USA

For more information about our products, contact us at
Thomson Learning Academic Resource Center
1-800-423-0563
For permission to use material from this text or product, submit a request online at
www.thomsonrights.com. Any additional questions about permissions can be submitted by e-mail to
thomsonrights@thomson.com.

Chapter Opening Credits:

Ch. 1 © UPI Photo/Monika Graff/Landov
Ch. 2 © Jim Richardson/Corbis
Ch. 3 © AP Photo/Mel Evans
Ch. 4 © Chris Rank/Bloomberg News/Landov
Ch. 5 © AP Photo/The Roanoke Times/Matt Gentry
Ch. 6 © Stephanie Chan/Creative Commons
Ch. 7 © REUTERS/Shannon Stapleton /Landov
Ch. 8 © Stuart Westmorland/Corbis
Ch. 9 © Robert Nickelsberg/Getty Images
Ch.10 © Fred Prouser-Pool/Getty Images
Ch.11 © David Paul Morris/Getty Images
Ch. 12 © AP Photo/Rogelio Solis
Ch. 13 © AP Photo/Ben Margot
Ch. 14 © AP, Steve Yeater
Ch. 15 © AP Photo/Stevbe Yeater
Ch. 16 © AP Photo/Aaron Marron
Ch. 17 © iStockphoto

Printed in Canada
1 2 3 4 5 6 7 8 11 10 09 08 07

Contents in Brief

Contents

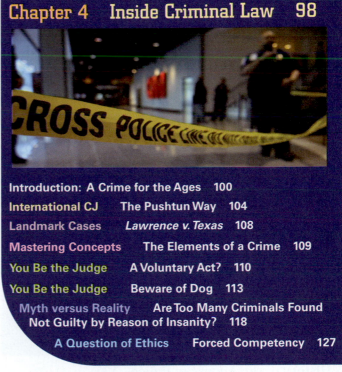

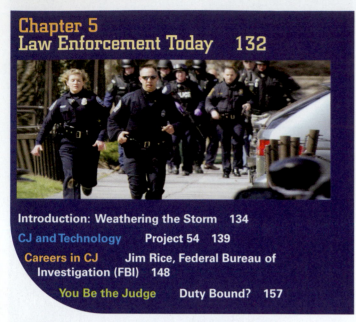

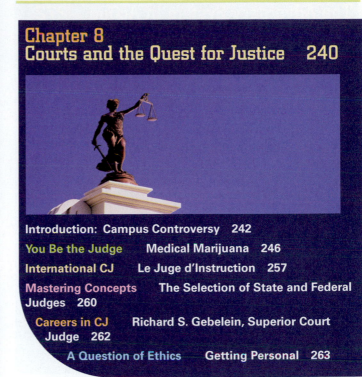

Chapter 9 Pretrial Procedures: The Adversary System in Action 272

Chapter 10 The Criminal Trial 306

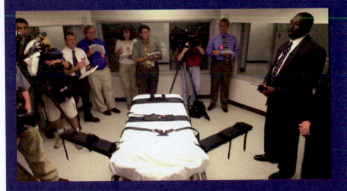

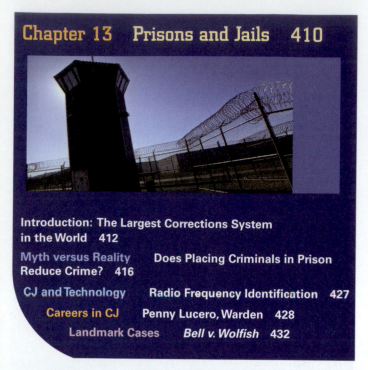
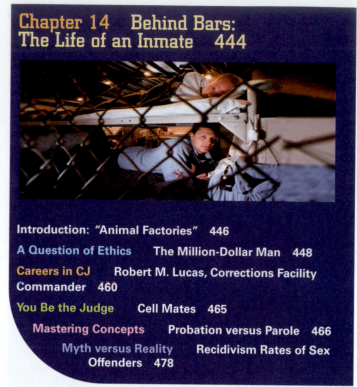

Preface to the Fifth Edition

More than any other subject a student will take on during his or her academic career, criminal justice saturates our daily existence. Issues of crime and justice dominate American culture, from the halls of Congress, to prime-time television, to the blogosphere. A single criminal act, be it a terrorist attack or a lone gunman's shooting spree, will monopolize media coverage for days, months, and sometimes years. Fear of crime, justified or not, influences even the smallest decisions, such as what route to take home or whether to leave the hall light on overnight.

More than any other hardcover in the field, the fifth edition of *Criminal Justice in Action* captures the whirlwind of real-world crime and integrates it with the solid pedagogy professors and students expect. Over the previous four editions of this series, we have, with a great deal of help and advice, constructed a best-selling introductory criminal justice textbook on the basis of three precepts:

1. *Immediacy.* We have always made every possible effort to keep *Criminal Justice in Action* as up to date as possible, and this edition is no exception. Each chapter begins with a recent "ripped from the headlines" example that introduces the themes to be covered in the pages that follow. Hundreds of statistical measures of crime have undergone revision to assure their timeliness, as have the many figures, features, and photos that add insight to the text.
2. *The bedrock principles of criminal justice.* The United States is a nation of laws, and criminal justice is a discipline of rules. To a certain extent, every act taken by a member of the criminal justice system has been prescribed by a politician's pen, a judge's gavel, or the practice of centuries that has been molded into a requirement. We assign these rules the detail and discussion they deserve, providing students with the best possible means of understanding the seemingly helter-skelter existence of the American criminal justice system on the streets, in the courts, and in the prisons and jails.
3. *The first step on the career path.* We know that many students using this text are planning to pursue a career in criminal justice. As a result, each chapter of this textbook includes a feature containing words of wisdom from a criminal justice professional. Furthermore, supplements such as an interactive CD-ROM and a dedicated Web site will help students get their feet in the CJ door, whether their interest is in law enforcement, the courts, the corrections system, or any other aspect of crime and justice in the United States.

For this fifth edition of *Criminal Justice in Action,* we have, at the urging of many of our adopting partners, strengthened our focus on a fourth fundamental: *critical thinking.*

Major Changes to the Fifth Edition

Put simply, *Criminal Justice in Action,* Fifth Edition, provides students with more tools to think critically and then prompts them to do so. These new tools include:

- **Learning Objectives.** At the beginning of each chapter, students are introduced to up to ten *learning objectives* for that chapter. For example, in Chapter 6, "Challenges to Effective Policing," Learning Objective 8 (LO8) asks students to "Determine when police officers are justified in using deadly force." The area of text that furnishes the information required to make this determination is marked with a circular LO8 graphic, and, finally, the correct answer is found in the chapter-ending materials. This constant *active* learning will greatly expand students' understanding of dozens of crucial criminal justice topics.

- **Self Check Boxes.** Students are not, however, required to wait until they have finished reading the chapter to engage in self-assessment. We have placed a new *Self Check* box at the end of each major section of each chapter. Three to five sentences long, these items require students to fill in the blanks, thereby reinforcing the most important points in the section they have just read. (All answers are found at the end of each chapter.)

- **Revised Criminal Justice in Action Features.** Professors are given the ultimate opportunity to assess their students' comprehension levels in the *revised chapter-ending Criminal Justice in Action features*. Each of the new features introduces students to a controversial topic from the chapter and provides them with "for" and "against" arguments related to that topic. Then, using information and knowledge gained from the chapter, the student is asked to write a short essay giving her or his opinion on the controversy. These restructured features not only help students improve their writing and critical-thinking skills, but they also act as a review. Before beginning the assignment, students are advised to return to certain sections of the chapter (page numbers are indicated) that will be helpful in formulating their own arguments.

New Chapter: Homeland Security

Even as the events of September 11, 2001, recede into the past, their influence on the American criminal justice system has remained considerable. In recognition of this situation, we have decided to add a new chapter to the Fifth Edition of *Criminal Justice in Action*. Entitled "Homeland Security," the new Chapter 16 begins with a brief introduction to the historical and social forces behind international terrorism before moving into an in-depth discussion of the terrorist threat to the United States and the steps that our government is taking to protect its citizens against that threat. The chapter ends with a close look at the question, "How many freedoms are Americans willing to give up to further the war against terrorism?" We strongly believe that issues of homeland security will continue to challenge and change our criminal justice system in the years to come and, therefore, consider this new chapter a necessary improvement to this edition and many editions to come.

Chapter-by-Chapter Organization of the Text

This edition's seventeen chapters blend the principles of criminal justice with current research and high-interest examples of what is happening in the world of crime and crime prevention right now. What follows is a summary of each chapter, along with a description of some of the revisions to the Fifth Edition.

PART 1: THE CRIMINAL JUSTICE SYSTEM

Chapter 1 provides an *introduction* to the criminal justice system's three major institutions: law enforcement, the courts, and corrections. The chapter also answers conceptual questions such as "what is crime?" and "what are the values of the American criminal justice system?"

- A **new** A Question of Ethics feature ("Death of a Cowgirl") highlights the importance of discretion in the criminal justice system by asking the student to put himself or herself in the place of a prosecutor forced to make a tough decision.

- The chapter closes with a section entitled **"Criminal Justice Today,"** which has been revised to reflect the unfortunate new reality that after years of decline, violent crime rates in the United States have begun to head upward.

Chapter 2 focuses on *criminology*, giving students insight into why crime occurs before shifting their attention toward how society goes about fighting it. The chapter addresses the most widely accepted and influential criminological hypotheses, including choice theories, trait theories, sociological theories, social process theories, social conflict theories, and life course theories.

- Students will also become acquainted with **emerging, controversial theories in criminology;** for the first time, this edition contains discussions of racial threat theory, which places crime in the context of race relations, and environmental criminology, which considers crime a matter of place.

- In its final pages, the chapter examines the **role of the victim** in the criminal equation, including a new analysis of theories that attempt to explain why some members of society are more likely than others to be targets of crimes.

Chapter 3 furnishes students with an understanding of two areas fundamental to criminal justice: (1) the *practical definitions* of crime, such as the difference between felonies and misdemeanors and different degrees of criminal conduct, and (2) the various modes of *measuring* crime, including the FBI's Uniform Crime Reports and the U.S. Department of Justice's National Crime Victimization Survey.

- To give students an idea of how crime statistics shape our perception of crime in the United States, the chapter includes a section entitled **"Crime Trends Today,"** which has been **significantly expanded** to show the impact that guns, gangs, and drugs have had on escalating violent crime rates.

- The **new** chapter-ending Criminal Justice in Action feature ("Legalizing Drugs") asks students to determine whether the legalization of illicit drugs has any benefits to offer society or would only make an already bad situation worse.

Chapter 4 lays the foundation of *criminal law*. It addresses constitutional law, statutory law, and other sources of American criminal law before shifting its focus to the legal framework that allows the criminal justice system to determine and punish criminal guilt.

- A **new** International CJ feature ("The Pushtun Way") explains the *Pushtunwalli* codes that dominate criminal law in northwestern Afghanistan and asks students to critique the practice of "passing judgment" on foreign customs.

- A **new** You Be the Judge feature ("Beware of Dog") requires students to choose the proper punishment for a woman whose pit bulls have committed homicide.

PART 2: THE POLICE AND LAW ENFORCEMENT

Chapter 5 acts as an *introduction to law enforcement* in the United States today. This chapter offers a detailed description of the country's numerous local, state, and federal law enforcement agencies and examines the responsibilities and duties that come with a career in law enforcement.

- As part of a discussion of the **reorganization of federal law enforcement** brought about by the September 11, 2001, terrorist attacks, students will learn about the **new** U.S. Customs and Border Protection and U.S. Immigration and Customs Enforcement agencies.

- A **new** CJ and Technology feature ("Car 54") describes the latest generation of computerized police vehicles.

- The important issue of police discretion is addressed with **an updated look** at two areas in which such discretion is under attack: domestic violence arrests and high-speed pursuits.

Chapter 6 puts students on the streets and gives them a gritty look at the many *challenges of being a law enforcement officer*. It starts with a rundown of the steps in becoming a police officer and then moves on to policing strategies and issues in modern policing, such as use of force, corruption, and the "thin blue line."

- A **new** section entitled **"Police Strategies: What Works"** gives a comprehensive and critical look at the various crime-fighting methods favored by police departments.

- A **new** A Question of Ethics feature ("Testilying") directs students to contemplate the practical and ethical questions raised by the police practice of misleading judges and juries to ensure that guilty suspects do not go free.

Chapter 7 examines the sometimes uneasy *relationship between law enforcement and the U.S. Constitution* by explaining the rules of being a police officer. Particular emphasis is placed on the Fourth, Fifth, and Sixth Amendments, giving students an understanding of crucial concepts such as probable cause, reasonableness, and custodial interrogation.

- The difference between probable cause sufficient to support a warrantless arrest and a "mere hunch" is illuminated by a **new** You Be the Judge feature ("The Wrong-Handed Beer Drinker"). The exercise transports students behind a bar on the wrong side of the tracks and asks them to judge a police officer's behavior.

- The chapter's **new** Criminal Justice in Action feature requires students to analyze the controversial practice of racial profiling. Are there any circumstances, whether on a highway or in the security corridor of an airport, under which law enforcement officers can use a suspect's race or ethnicity to establish probable cause?

PART 3: CRIMINAL COURTS

Chapter 8 takes a big-picture approach in describing the *American court system*, giving students an overview of the basic principles of our judicial system, the state and federal court systems, and the role of judges in the criminal justice system.

- The court system's ability to live up to societal expectations of truth and justice, a running theme of the third part of this textbook, is explored in the context of the so-called Duke rape case. This chapter's **new** opening vignette concerns the charges brought against three Duke University lacrosse players and the ignominious manner in which the charges were eventually dropped.

- A **new** A Question of Ethics feature ("Getting Personal") highlights the difficult position of judges whose religious beliefs affect the manner in which they decide certain cases.

Chapter 9 provides students with a rundown of *pretrial procedures* and highlights the role that these procedures play in America's *adversary system*. Thus, pretrial procedures such as establishing bail and plea bargaining are presented as part of the larger "battle" between the prosecution and the defense.

- A **new** Myth versus Reality feature ("Are Fingerprint Matches Foolproof?") explains how defense attorneys are starting to gain an edge in this "battle" by raising questions about the infallibility of fingerprinting matches.

- The discussion of attorney-client privilege in this chapter has undergone **a significant expansion,** with a particular focus on the theoretical and practical reasons behind the privilege and its few but important exceptions.

Chapter 10 puts the student in the courtroom and gives her or him a strong understanding of the steps of the *criminal trial.* The chapter also attempts to answer the fascinating but ultimately frustrating question, "Are criminal trials in this country fair?"

- The **"finality" of a verdict** has long been one of the cherished values of the criminal trial. In this chapter, students will learn how growing media coverage of wrongful verdicts, many uncovered by improved DNA technology, has weakened the primacy of finality in our criminal justice system.

- The student's understanding of the rules of evidence is tested by the **new** Criminal Justice in Action feature, which deals with the subject of rape shield laws. The writing assignment of this feature asks the student to determine whether these laws properly balance the rights of the accuser and the rights of the accused.

Chapter 11 links the many different *punishment options* for those who have been convicted of a crime with the theoretical justifications for those punishments. The chapter also examines punishment in the policy context, weighing the public's desire for ever-harsher criminal sanctions against the consequences of such governmental strategies.

- In the face of increased calls for "get tough" sentencing, a countermovement known as **restorative justice,** based on apologies and restitution, is gaining support and is becoming an increasingly popular option for judges and legislatures.

- The chapter's **extensive discussion** of capital punishment has been **updated,** with new discussions concerning the deterrent effect of the death penalty and the legal and ethical issues surrounding the practice of lethal injection.

PART 4: CORRECTIONS

Chapter 12 makes an important point, and one that is often overlooked in the larger discussion of the American corrections system: not all of those who are punished need to be placed behind bars. This chapter explores the *community corrections* options, from probation to intermediate sanctions such as intensive supervision and home confinement.

- A **new** You Be the Judge feature ("What's the Sentence?") concerns the case of a fraternity brother whose hazing methods went too far and requires students to determine the proper punishment for his transgressions.

- The past few years have seen significant advances in the technology of electronic monitoring, and this chapter's discussion of the subject includes an **updated** CJ and Technology feature on the use of global positioning systems (GPS) to track probationers.

Chapter 13 focuses on *prisons and jails.* Record-high rates of incarceration have pushed these institutions to the forefront of the criminal justice system, and this chapter explores the various issues—such as the emergence of private prisons—that have resulted from the prison population boom.

- Endemic overcrowding has disturbing consequences for American jails, as a **new** section in the chapter makes clear.

■ The chapter's **new** Criminal Justice in Action feature addresses a particular sort of prison punishment known as solitary confinement, or "the Hole," and asks the student to decide whether the U.S. Constitution should be interpreted to prohibit this harsh sanction.

Chapter 14 is another example of our efforts to get students "into the action" of the criminal justice system, this time putting them in the uncomfortable position of being behind bars. It also answers the question, "What happens when the inmate is released back into society?"

■ In addition to issues of prison violence covered in previous editions, in this edition we include a **new discussion of prison gangs and security-threat groups (STGs),** and their growing influence on everyday prison life.

■ A **new** section on the **"special case of sex offenders"** explores the many issues pertaining to this controversial segment of America's ex-con population; it includes a **new** Myth versus Reality feature ("Recidivism Rates of Sex Offenders") that presents evidence contradicting the widely held belief that sex offenders are more likely to repeat their crimes than are other criminals.

PART 5: SPECIAL ISSUES

Chapter 15 examines the *juvenile justice system,* giving students a comprehensive description of the path taken by delinquents from first contact with police to trial and punishment. The chapter contains a strong criminological component as well, scrutinizing the various theories of why certain juveniles turn to delinquency and what steps society can take to stop them from doing so before it is "too late."

■ A **new** section on **school violence** looks at the public perception of such violence, efforts to curtail it, and contributing factors such as the so-called bully problem. The section contains a CJ and Technology feature on Safewatch, a real-time video monitoring system that allows the police to "see into" schools during emergencies.

■ The **new** chapter-ending Criminal Justice in Action feature requires students to give their opinion on the practice of transferring juveniles to the adult criminal justice system.

Chapter 16, as noted earlier in this Preface, is a new chapter on *homeland security.* The chapter includes:

■ A **new** International CJ feature ("The Jihad Loophole") that describes an aspect of Yemeni law that recognizes "the right of jihad" among its citizens.

■ A **new** CJ and Technology feature that describes Project Chloe, an antimissile system being developed by the Department of Homeland Security to protect airplanes against future terrorist attacks.

Chapter 17 concludes the text by taking an expanded look at *cyber crime,* a subject whose importance in the criminal justice system is growing as quickly as the reach of the technology that spawns it.

■ The transformation of money laundering into a largely online activity is covered, as well as the **emergence of cyberterrorism** as a major concern for homeland security officials.

■ The last section of the chapter, entitled "Criminal Justice: Looking to the Future," provides students with a **preview of emerging issues in the criminal justice field,** including increased data mining and a new generation of ID cards for U.S. citizens.

Special Features

Supplementing the main text of *Criminal Justice in Action*, Fifth Edition, are nearly ninety eye-catching, instructive, and penetrating special features. These features, described below with examples, have been designed to enhance the student's understanding of a particular criminal justice issue.

Careers in CJ: As stated before, many students reading this book are planning a career in criminal justice. We have provided them with an insight into some of these careers by offering first-person accounts of what it is like to work as a criminal justice professional.

- In Chapter 1, Patrick Connolly, a supervisory special agent with the FBI, gives advice on how to become a federal law enforcement agent and describes his position as coordinator of a joint terrorism task force.
- In Chapter 6, Lois Perillo provides an inside look at life as the San Francisco Police Department's first bicycle community policing officer.

Mastering Concepts: Some criminal justice topics require additional explanation before they become crystal clear in the minds of students. This feature helps students to master many of the essential concepts in the textbook.

- In Chapter 7, these features help students understand the legal differences between a police stop and a police frisk, and the various exceptions to the requirement that a police officer must have a warrant before making an arrest.
- In Chapter 15, the feature compares and contrasts the juvenile justice system with the criminal justice system.

You Be the Judge: Students are put into the position of a judge in a hypothetical criminal case that is based on an actual court case. The facts of the case are presented with alternative possible outcomes, and the student is asked to "be the judge" and make a ruling as if he or she were the judge. Students can compare their own judgment to that of the judge or jury in the real-life case by consulting the actual dispositions in Appendix B at the end of the text.

- "A Voluntary Act?" (Chapter 4) presents the case of Emil, who was driving down a street in Buffalo, New York, when he had an epileptic seizure and lost control of his automobile, which struck and killed four schoolgirls. Students are asked to determine whether he committed a voluntary act and, therefore, is guilty of murder.
- "Should She Stay or Should She Go?" (Chapter 9) requires students to determine whether a suspect should go free on bail before her trial for a single count of child abuse with death or serious injury likely to occur. Reina, the suspect in question, did nothing while her boyfriend physically abused and eventually killed her two young children.

CJ and Technology: Advances in technology are constantly transforming the face of criminal justice. In these features, which appear in nearly every chapter, students learn of one such emergent technology and are asked to critically evaluate its effects.

- This feature in Chapter 1 explores biometrics, or the science of identifying a person through his or her unique physical characteristics, such as the face, eyes, or vein patterns of the hand.
- This feature in Chapter 13 deals with radio frequency identification (RFID), which can use radio waves to track the movements of all inmates and corrections officers in a prison.

International CJ: The world offers a dizzying array of different criminal customs and codes, many of which are in stark contrast to those accepted in the United

States. This feature provides dramatic and sometimes perplexing examples of foreign criminal justice practices in order to give students a better understanding of the domestic way.

- "The World's Oldest Profession" (Chapter 3) presents this startling fact: in Belgium, on any given day, more people are legally paying for sex than are going to the movies. What does this say about the American tradition of criminalizing prostitution?
- "The Great Firewall of China" (Chapter 17) describes China's efforts to limit and control the use of the Internet through criminal laws to an extent that is unimaginable to most Americans.

A Question of Ethics: Ethical dilemmas occur in every profession, but the challenges facing criminal justice professionals often have repercussions beyond their own lives and careers. In this feature, revised for the fifth edition, students are asked to place themselves in the shoes of police officers, prosecutors, defense attorneys, and other criminal justice actors facing ethical dilemmas: Will they do the right thing?

- In "The 'Dirty Harry' Problem" (Chapter 7), a police detective is trying to save the life of a young girl who has been buried alive with only enough oxygen to survive for a few hours. Is he justified in torturing the one person—the kidnapper—who knows where the girl is buried?
- In "Keeping a Secret" (Chapter 9), a client confesses to his defense attorney that he committed a crime for which another man has been convicted. The rules of attorney-client privilege hold that defense attorneys may not divulge such confidences. Should those rules always be followed?

Landmark Cases: Rulings by the United States Supreme Court have shaped every area of the criminal justice system. In this feature, students learn about and analyze the most influential of these cases.

- In Chapter 10's *Batson v. Kentucky* (1986), the Supreme Court rejected the notion that attorneys could, under any circumstances, deny citizens a seat on a jury because of their race or ethnicity.
- In Chapter 15's *In re Gault* (1967), the Supreme Court held that juveniles are entitled to many of the same due process rights granted to adult offenders—a decision that caused a seismic shift in America's juvenile justice system.

Myth versus Reality: Nothing endures like a good myth. In this feature, we try to dispel some of the more enduring myths in the criminal justice system while at the same time asking students to think critically about their consequences.

- "Race Stereotyping and Crime" (Chapter 3) challenges the perceived wisdom that members of certain minority groups, particularly African Americans, are prone to violence and therefore more likely to be criminals than other racial or ethnic groups.
- "Are Too Many Criminals Found Not Guilty by Reason of Insanity?" (Chapter 4) dispels the notion that the criminal justice is "soft" because it lets scores of "crazy" defendants go free due to insanity.

Extensive Study Aids

Criminal Justice in Action, Fifth Edition, includes a number of pedagogical devices designed to complete the student's active learning experience. These devices include:

- Concise **chapter outlines** at the beginning of each chapter. The outlines give students an idea of what to expect in the pages ahead, as well as a quick source of review when needed.
- Dozens of **key terms** and a **running glossary** focus students' attention on major concepts and help them master the vocabulary of criminal justice.

The chosen terms are boldfaced in the text, allowing students to notice their importance without breaking the flow of reading. On the same page that a key term is highlighted, a margin note provides a succinct definition of the term. For further reference, a glossary at the end of the text provides a full list of all the key terms and their definitions. **More than one hundred new key terms were added for the *fifth edition.***

- Each chapter has at least six **figures,** which include graphs, charts, and other forms of colorful art that reinforce a point made in the text.

- Hundreds of **photographs** add to the overall readability and design of the text. Each photo has a caption, and **most of these captions include a critical-thinking question** dealing with the topic at hand.

- At the end of each chapter, students will find up to ten **Questions for Critical Analysis.** These questions will help the student assess his or her understanding of the just-completed chapter, as well as develop critical-thinking skills.

- Our teaching/learning package offers numerous opportunities for using online technology in the classroom. In the margins of each chapter, students will find **links to various Web sites** that illuminate a particular subject in the corresponding text.

- Co-author Larry K. Gaines has contributed his **Stories from the Street** to each chapter. These audio features, accessible from the textbook's Web site, offer a short commentary from Professor Gaines, drawing on his many years of service and unparalleled knowledge of the criminal justice system.

Ancillary Materials

Wadsworth provides a number of supplements to help instructors use *Criminal Justice in Action,* Fifth Edition, in their courses and to aid students in preparing for exams. Supplements are available to qualified adopters. Please consult your local sales representative for details.

FOR THE INSTRUCTOR

- **Instructor's Resource Manual with Test Bank.** This fully updated resource includes teaching aids, a guide to assist you in making use of the supplement package available for this text, and test questions coded according to learning objectives.

- **ExamView® Computerized Testing.** This assessment and tutorial system allows you to create, deliver, and customize tests and study guides in minutes, using the test questions provided in the Instructor's Resource Manual.

- **JoinIn™.** Spark discussion and assess your students' comprehension of chapter concepts with interactive classroom quizzes and background polls developed specifically for use with this edition of *Criminal Justice in Action.*

- **PowerLecture CD.** This instructor resource includes Microsoft® PowerPoint® lecture slides, the JoinIn and ExamView testing software.

- **WebTutor™ ToolBox on Blackboard® and WebCT®.** Easy-to-use course-management tools for whichever course-management program you use combined with content from this text's rich companion Web site.

- **The Wadsworth Criminal Justice Video Library.** So many exciting videos in our library—so many great ways to enrich your lectures and spark discussion of the material in this text!
  - *ABC® Videos:* Short, high-interest clips from current news events specially developed for courses including Introduction to Criminal Justice, Criminology, Corrections, Terrorism, and White-Collar Crime.
  - *The Wadsworth Custom Videos for Criminal Justice:* Produced by Wadsworth and Films for the Humanities, these videos include short (five- to ten-minute) segments that encourage classroom discussion.

- *Court TV Videos:* These one-hour videos present aspects of seminal and high-profile cases, as well as crucial and current issues such as cyber crime, double jeopardy, and the management of the prison on Riker's Island.
- *A&E American Justice:* Instructors can choose from forty videos on topics such as deadly force, women on death row, juvenile justice, strange defenses, and Alcatraz.
- *Films for the Humanities:* These include nearly 200 videos on a variety of topics such as elder abuse, supermax prisons, suicide and the police officer, the making of an FBI agent, domestic violence, and more.
- *Oral History Project:* Compiled over the last several years, each video features a set of Guest Lecturers—scholars whose thinking has helped to build the foundation of present ideas in the discipline.

- **Classroom Activities for Criminal Justice.** This valuable booklet contains both tried-and-true favorites and exciting new projects; activities are drawn from across the spectrum of criminal justice subjects and can be customized to fit any course.

- **Internet Activities for Criminal Justice.** This useful booklet helps familiarize students with Internet resources and allows instructors to integrate resources into their course materials.

- **The Wadsworth Criminal Justice Resource Center: academic.cengage. com/criminaljustice**. Designed with the instructor in mind, this Web site features information about Wadsworth's technology and teaching solutions, as well as several features created specifically for today's criminal justice student.

FOR THE STUDENT

- **TNOW™.** This unique, interactive online resource has the student take a chapter pre-test and then offers him or her a personalized study plan. Once the student has completed the personalized study plan, a posttest evaluates her or his improved comprehension of chapter content.

- **Study Guide.** The updated study guide features outlines and summaries, major terms, and worksheets and self-tests.

- **Audio Study Tools.** Our exclusive audio content, which can be downloaded to any MP3 player, includes practice quizzes as well as reviews of key terms.

- **Lecture Outlines: Notetaking in Action.** This supplement includes images of the PowerPoint slides for each text chapter with plenty of room for students' notes, so they can focus on your lecture rather than on copying slides during class.

- **Careers in Criminal Justice Web Site: academic.cengage.com/ criminaljustice/careers**. This unique Web site gives students information on a wide variety of career paths, including requirements, salaries, training, contact information for key agencies, and employment outlooks. Several important tools help students investigate the criminal justice career choices that are right for them.
  - *Career Profiles:* Video testimonials from a variety of practicing professionals in the field as well as information on many criminal justice careers, including job descriptions, requirements, training, salary and benefits, and the application process.
  - *Interest Assessment:* Self-assessment tool to help students decide which careers suit their personalities and interests.
  - *Career Planner:* Résumé-writing tips and worksheets, interviewing techniques, and successful job search strategies.
  - *Links for Reference:* Direct links to federal, state, and local agencies where students can get contact information and learn more about current job opportunities.

- **Handbook of Selected Supreme Court Cases, Third Edition.** This supplementary handbook covers almost forty landmark cases, with a full case citation, an introduction, a summary from WestLaw, and excerpts and the decision for each case.

- **Current Perspectives: Readings from InfoTrac® College Edition.** These readers, designed to give students a deeper taste of special topics in criminal justice, include free access to InfoTrac College Edition. They include:
  - *Terrorism and Homeland Security*
  - *Cyber Crime*
  - *Juvenile Justice*
  - *Public Policy and Criminal Justice*
  - *Crisis Management and National Emergency Response*
  - *Racial Profiling*
  - *New Technologies and Criminal Justice*
  - *White-Collar Crime*

- **Terrorism: An Interdisciplinary Perspective.** Available for bundling, this eighty-page booklet discusses terrorism in general and the issues surrounding the events of September 11, 2001.

- **Crime Scenes 2.0: An Interactive Criminal Justice CD-ROM.** Recipient of several *New Media Magazine Invision Awards,* this interactive CD-ROM allows your students to take on the roles of investigating officer, lawyer, parole officer, and judge in excitingly realistic scenarios.

- **Mind of a Killer CD-ROM** *(bundle version).* Voted one of the top 100 CD-ROMs by an annual *PC Magazine* survey, *Mind of a Killer* gives students a chilling glimpse into the realm of serial killers, with more than eighty minutes of video *and* 3D simulations, an extensive mapping system, a library, and much more.

- **Internet Guide for Criminal Justice, Second Edition.** Intended for the novice user, this guide provides students with a wealth of criminal justice Web sites and Internet project ideas.

Acknowledgments

Throughout the creation of the five editions of this text, we have been aided by literally hundreds of experts in various criminal justice fields and by professors throughout the country, as well as by numerous students who have used the text. We list below the reviewers for this Fifth Edition, followed by the class-test participants and reviewers for the first three editions. We sincerely thank all who participated on the revision of *Criminal Justice in Action.* We believe that the Fifth Edition is even more responsive to the needs of today's criminal justice instructors and students alike because we have taken into account the constructive comments and criticisms of our reviewers and the helpful suggestions of our survey respondents.

REVIEWERS FOR THE FIFTH EDITION

We are grateful for the participation of the reviewers who read and reviewed portions of our manuscript throughout its development, and for those who gave us valuable insights through their responses to our survey.

Gaylene Armstrong
Southern Illnois University

Lee Roy Black
California University of Pennsylvania

Chuck Brawne
Heartland Community College

Timothy M. Bray
University of Texas–Dallas

Theodore Byrne
California State University, Dominquez Hills

Ellen G. Cohn
Florida International University

Corey Colyer
West Virginia University

Theodore Darden
College of Du Page

Richard H. De Lung
Wayland Baptist University

Frank J. Drummond
Modesto Junior College

Linda L. Fleischer
The Community College of Baltimore
County

Pati Hendrickson
Tarleton State University

Robert Jerin
Endicott College

David Kotajarvi
Lakeshore Technical College

James G. Larson
National University

Larry Linville
Northern Virginia Community College

Ellyn Ness
Mesa Community College

Melinda Schlager
University of Texas at Arlington

Larry Snyder
Herkimer County Community College

Domenick Stampone
Raritan Valley Community College

Amy B. Thistlethwaite
Northern Kentucky University

Class-Test Participants

We also want to acknowledge the participation of the professors and their students
who agreed to class-test portions of the text. Our thanks go to:

Tom Arnold
College of Lake County

Paula M. Broussard
University of Southwestern Louisiana

Mike Higginson
Suffolk Community College

Andrew Karmen
John Jay College of Criminal Justice

Fred Kramer
John Jay College of Criminal Justice

Anthony P. LaRose
Western Oregon University

Anne Lawrence
Kean University

Jerry E. Loar
Walters State Community College

Phil Reichel
University of Northern Colorado

Albert Sproule
Allentown College

Gregory B. Talley
Broome Community College

Karen Terry
John Jay College of Criminal Justice

Angelo Tritini
Passaic County Community College

Gary Uhrin
Westmoreland County Community College

Robert Vodde
Fairleigh Dickinson University

Thanks to the Career Education Criminal Justice Advisory Board for their valuable inputs and contributions to the Wadsworth Criminal Justice Team:

Vincent Benincasa
Hesser College

Terry Campbell
Kaplan University

Megan Cole
Brown College

Frank DiMarino
Kaplan University

Don Josi
South University

Scott Moline
Hamilton College

Adell Newman
Kaplan University

Nancy Oesch
Corinthian Colleges

Barbara Parnell
West Wood College Online

Mike Pittaro
Lehigh Valley College

CarieAnn Potenza
Rasmussen College

Gene Scaramella
Kaplan University

Don Sebo
High Tech Institute

Kathryn Sellers
Virginia College

Luis Velez
Colorado Technical University

Jim Walney
ICM School of Business & Medical
Careers

Robert Winters
Kaplan University

REVIEWERS OF THE FIRST, SECOND, THIRD, AND FOURTH EDITIONS

We appreciate the assistance of the following reviewers whose guidance helped
create the foundation for this best seller. We are grateful to all.

Angela Ambers-Henderson
Montgomery County Community College

Judge James Bachman
Bowling Green State University

Tom Barclay
University of South Alabama

Julia Beeman
University of North Carolina at Charlotte

Anita Blowers
University of North Carolina at Charlotte

John Bower
Bethel College

Steven Brandl
University of Wisconsin–Milwaukee

Charles Brawner III
Heartland Community College

Susan Brinkley
University of Tampa

Paula Broussard
University of Southwestern Louisiana

Michael Brown
Ball State College

Joseph Bunce
Montgomery College–Rockville

James T. Burnett
SUNY, Rockland Community College

Ronald Burns
Texas Christian University

Paul Campbell
Wayne State College

Dae Chang
Wichita State University

Steven Chermak
Indiana University

Charlie Chukwudolue
Northern Kentucky University

Monte Clampett
Asheville-Buncome Community College

John Cochran
University of South Florida

Mark Correia
University of Nevada–Reno

John del Nero
Lane Community College

John Dempsey
Suffolk County Community College

Tom Dempsey
Christopher Newpoint University

Joyce Dozier
Wilmington College

M. G. Eichenberg
Wayne State College

Frank L. Fischer
Kankakee Community College

Frederick Galt
Dutchess Community College

James Gilbert
University of Nebraska–Kearney

Dean Golding
West Chester University of Pennsylvania

Debbie Goodman
Miami-Dade Community College

Donald Grubb
Northern Virginia Community College

Sharon Halford
Community College of Aurora

Michael Hallett
Middle Tennessee State University

Mark Hansel
Moorhead State University

Michelle Heward
Weber State University

Dennis Hoffman
University of Nebraska–Omaha

Richard Holden
Central Missouri State University

Ronald Holmes
University of Louisville

Marilyn Horace-Moore
Eastern Michigan University

Matrice Hurrah
Shelby State Community College

Nicholas Irons
County College of Morris

Michael Israel
Kean University

J. D. Jamieson
Southwest Texas State University

James Jengeleski
Shippensburg University

Paul Johnson
Weber State University

Casey Jordan
Western Connecticut State University

Matthew Kanjirathinkal
Texas A & M University–Commerce

Bill Kelly
University of Texas–Austin

John H. Kramer
Pennsylvania State University

Kristen Kuehnle
Salem State University

Karl Kunkel
Southwest Missouri State

Barry Latzer
John Jay College of Criminal Justice

Deborah Laufersweiler-Dwyer
University of Arkansas at Little Rock

Paul Lawson
Montana State University

Nella Lee
Portland State University

Walter Lewis
St. Louis Community College–Meramec

Faith Lutze
Washington State University

Richard Martin
Elgin Community College

Richard H. Martin
University of Findlay

William J. Mathias
University of South Carolina

Janet McClellan
Southwestern Oregon Community College

Pat Murphy
State University of New York–Geneseo

Rebecca Nathanson
Housatonic Community Technical College

Michael Palmiotto
Wichita State University

Rebecca D. Petersen
University of Texas, San Antonio

Gary Prawel
Monroe Community College

Mark Robarge
Mansfield University

Matt Robinson
Appalachian State University

Debra Ross
Buffalo State College

William Ruefle
University of South Carolina

Gregory Russell
Washington State University

John Scheb II
University of Tennessee–Knoxville

Ed Selby
Southwestern College

Ronald Sopenoff
Brookdale Community College

Katherine Steinbeck
Lakeland Community College

Kathleen M. Sweet
St. Cloud State University

Gregory Talley
Broome Community College

Karen Terry
John Jay College of Criminal Justice

Lawrence F. Travis III
University of Cincinnati

Kimberly Vogt
University of Wisconsin–La Crosse

Robert Wadman
Weber State University

Ron Walker
Trinity Valley Community College

John Wyant
Illinois Central College

Others were instrumental in bringing this Fifth Edition to fruition. We continue to appreciate the extensive research efforts of Shawn G. Miller and the additional legal assistance of William Eric Hollowell. Robert Jucha, our developmental editor, provided equal parts elbow grease and creative energy; it was a pleasure to work with him. Editor Carolyn Hendersen-Meier supplied crucial guidance to the project through her suggestions and recommendations. At the production end, we once again feel fortunate to have enjoyed the services of our tireless production manager, Ann Borman, who oversaw virtually all aspects of this book. How she was able to make all of the schedules on time never ceased to amaze us. Additionally, we wish to thank the designer of this new edition, Ellen Pettengell, who has created what we believe to be the most dazzling and student-friendly design of any text in the field. Photo researchers Anne Sheroff and Ann Hoffman went to great lengths to satisfy our requests, and we sincerely appreciate their efforts. We are also thankful for the services of all those at Parkwood Composition who worked on the Fifth Edition, particularly Debbie Mealey. The eagle eyes of Pat Lewis, who did expert double duty as copy editor and proofreader, and Martha Ghent, proofer extraordinaire, were invaluable.

A special word of thanks must also go to the team responsible for the extensive multimedia package included in this project, including technology project manager Lauren Keyes, writers Robert C. De Lucia of John Jay College of Criminal Justice and Kelli Stevens of Texas Christian University, Larry Bassi of SUNY Brockport, and Carolyn Dennis of Mount Olive College. In addition, we appreciate the work of Julia Campbell of the University of Nebraska–Kearney, who created teaching and discussion tips for the *Annotated Instructor's Edition,* as well as revising the *Instructor's Resource Manual* and *Student Study Guide.* We are also grateful for the aid of assistant editor Meaghan Banks, who ensured the timely publication of supplements, and editorial assistant Jill Nowlin, who assisted with the core text. A final thanks to all of the great people in marketing and advertising who helped to get the word out about the book, including marketing manager Terra Schultz, who has been tireless in her attention to this project; Joy Westberg, for her excellent writing skills; and advertising project manager Tami Strang, for keeping everything on track.

Any criminal justice text has to be considered a work in progress. We know that there are improvements that we can make. Therefore, write us with any suggestions that you may have.

L. K. G.
R. L. M.

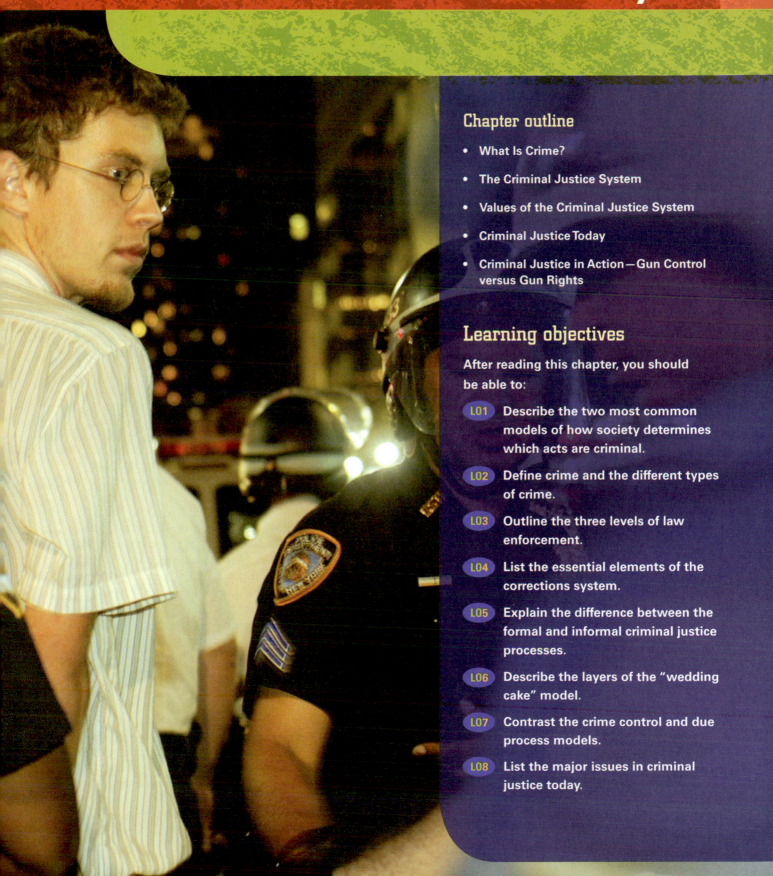

Criminal Justice Today

Chapter outline

- What Is Crime?
- The Criminal Justice System
- Values of the Criminal Justice System
- Criminal Justice Today
- Criminal Justice in Action—Gun Control versus Gun Rights

Learning objectives

After reading this chapter, you should be able to:

L01 Describe the two most common models of how society determines which acts are criminal.

L02 Define crime and the different types of crime.

L03 Outline the three levels of law enforcement.

L04 List the essential elements of the corrections system.

L05 Explain the difference between the formal and informal criminal justice processes.

L06 Describe the layers of the "wedding cake" model.

L07 Contrast the crime control and due process models.

L08 List the major issues in criminal justice today.

The deadliest shooting rampage in American history started just after 7 A.M. on April 16, 2007, in Blacksburg, Virginia. Cho Seung Hui, a twenty-three-year-old English major armed with a Glock 19 9mm pistol and a Walther P22 .22-caliber handgun, started his violent morning by killing two students at West Ambler Johnston dormitory on the campus of Virginia Polytechnic Institute (Virginia Tech). He then stopped by his dorm room before heading to a local post office, where he mailed a package to the headquarters of the NBC television network in New York City. The parcel contained 28 self-made video clips, a 23-page written statement, and more than 40 still photographs of himself, some of which showed him posing menacingly with the two firearms.

Cho was far from finished. He returned to campus and headed for Norris Hall. After chaining the doors to the building shut, he continued upstairs. "He stepped in and assumed the shooting position and took aim," remembered Guillermo Colman, who was sitting in the first row of his Advanced Hydrology class at the time. "His face was a completely blank stare. It seemed very mechanical." Cho opened fire in four different classrooms, methodically shooting each of his victims two or three times. Law enforcement officials believe that he did not stop until he heard the sound of the shotguns that campus police were using to break the chains on the doors. Cho then put one of his weapons to his head and committed suicide.

Including himself, Cho killed thirty-one people in Norris Hall that morning. No motive for the massacre has been uncovered, save for the obvious and unsatisfying conclusion that Cho was a severely mentally ill young man fed by a great delusional anger. "You had a hundred billion chances and ways to have avoided today," he said in one of the video clips sent to NBC. "But you decided to spill my blood. You forced me into a corner and gave me only one option. When the time came, I did it. I had to."

AP Photo/Steve Helber

▲ Students console each other at a memorial service for thirty-two people killed at Virginia Tech on April 16, 2007.

Criminal Justice ⚖ Now™

Maximize your study time by using ThomsonNOW's Personalized Study plan to help you review this chapter and prepare for examination. The Study Plan will

- Help you identify areas on which you should concentrate

- Provide interactive exercises to help you master the chapter concepts; and

- Provide a post-test to confirm you are ready to move on to the next chapter information.

I n retrospect, the red flags concerning Cho Seung Hui seem too numerous to have been overlooked. His writing assignments were laced with gory and violent imagery. "[His] plays had really twisted, macabre violence that used weapons I wouldn't have even thought of," remembered one classmate, adding that he and his friends had "serious worry about whether [Cho] could be a school shooter."[1] Eventually, Cho's manner became so disruptive that his creative writing professor removed him from her class. During the fall of 2005, two female students complained to Virginia Tech police that Cho was harassing them. That same semester, a doctor at nearby Carilion St. Albans Psychiatric Hospital determined that Cho was "mentally ill" but not an imminent threat to himself or anyone else.[2]

For all his menacing and disturbing behavior, Cho had broken no law, and therefore Virginia Tech had no grounds to remove him from school. In Chapter 2, we will learn how difficult it is for law enforcement agents and other crime experts to predict future criminal activity. The rampage at Virginia Tech raised a number of other concerns as well. Why was Cho, whom a physician had determined to be mentally ill, nonetheless able to purchase firearms from a local gunshop and pawnbroker? We will address the controversial topic of gun control later in this chapter and throughout the textbook. Why did the police fail to identify Cho as a suspect and warn the Virginia Tech community during the two-hour window between shooting incidents? We will examine police strategy and other law enforcement topics in

Chapters 5, 6, and 7. Finally, was the tragedy in any way linked to the bullying that apparently was directed at Cho throughout his childhood because of his Korean heritage and a speech impediment? In Chapter 15, we will discuss the causes of school violence and the efforts being made to protect American students.

As you proceed through this textbook, you will see that few aspects of the criminal justice system are ever simple, even though you may have clear opinions about them. In this first chapter, we will introduce you to the criminal justice system by discussing its structure, the values that it is designed to promote, and the most challenging issues it faces today.

What Is Crime?

Under Virginia criminal law, a person is guilty of "stalking" when he or she engages in conduct directed at another person with the knowledge that the conduct places the other person in reasonable fear of "death, criminal sexual assault, or bodily injury."[3] On two separate occasions, female Virginia Tech students had complained to campus officials that Cho Seung Hui was "stalking" them. One of the students reported that Cho had been following her and bothering her with unwelcome telephone calls. The other accused Cho of barraging her with instant messages. Ultimately, because neither woman felt herself to be in danger of bodily harm, no charges were ever brought.[4]

When does this kind of behavior cross the line from "annoying" to "dangerous"? At what point does activity that is merely "wrong" become criminal? There is no easy answer to these questions, but in general an act becomes a *crime* when it meets the legal definitions that designate it as such—which Cho's harassment failed to do with regard to Virginia's definition of "stalking." Therefore, a **crime** can be defined as a wrong against society proclaimed by law and, if committed under certain circumstances, punishable by society. The problem with this definition, however, is that it obscures the complex nature of societies. A society is not static—it evolves and changes, and its concept of criminality evolves and changes as well. Different societies can have vastly different ideas of what constitutes a crime. In several European countries, including France and Germany, it is a criminal offense to deny that the Holocaust—the systematic extermination of millions of Jewish men, women, and children during World War II (1939–1945)—took place. Such legislation would not be allowed in the United States because of our country's long tradition of free speech.

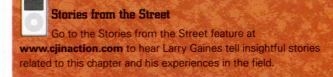

Stories from the Street
Go to the Stories from the Street feature at **www.cjinaction.com** to hear Larry Gaines tell insightful stories related to this chapter and his experiences in the field.

L01 To more fully understand the concept of crime, it will help to examine the two most common models of how society "decides" which acts are criminal: the consensus model and the conflict model.

THE CONSENSUS MODEL

The **consensus model** assumes that as people gather together to form a society, its members will naturally come to a basic agreement with regard to shared norms and values. Those individuals whose actions deviate from the established norms and values are considered to pose a threat to the well-being of society as a whole and must be sanctioned (punished). The society passes laws to control and prevent deviant behavior, thereby setting the boundaries for acceptable behavior within the group.[5] Use of the term *consensus* implies that a majority of the citizens agree on what activities should be outlawed and punished as crimes.

The consensus model, to a certain extent, assumes that a diverse group of people can have similar *morals;* that is, they share an ideal of what is "right" and "wrong." Consequently, as public attitudes toward morality change, so do laws. In colonial times, those found guilty of adultery were subjected to corporal punishment; a century ago, one could walk into a pharmacy and purchase heroin.

Crime An act that violates criminal law and is punishable by criminal sanctions.

Consensus Model A criminal justice model in which the majority of citizens in a society share the same values and beliefs. Criminal acts are those acts that conflict with these values and beliefs and are deemed harmful to society.

In 2001, the Netherlands became the first nation to legalize physician-assisted suicide and euthanasia ("mercy killing"). The new law simply formalized practices that had been taking place since 1973, when this European nation's courts decided that doctors can help terminate a patient's life if certain conditions are met: the patient must explicitly request such an action, the request must be voluntary, and the patient's suffering must be unbearable and without any hope of improvement. The law requires youths aged twelve to sixteen to obtain parental consent before requesting assisted suicide. From the age of sixteen, all patients have the right to discuss the matter with their doctors of their own volition.

In explaining why the Netherlands accepts actions that many other countries would consider objectionable, observers point to several characteristics of Dutch society. First, doctors hold exalted positions, and their actions are rarely questioned. Not only are doctors authorized to terminate "meaningless" lives, but they are also expected to do so. Second, the country lacks a strong religious influence, which might place the question of assisted suicide in a different moral perspective. As it is, hopelessly ill patients who fail to request euthanasia are seen as adhering to outdated ethical values. Third, and most important, is the Dutch emphasis on personal autonomy; the choice to die is considered the responsibility of the individual, not of the state.

In 1998, an elderly Oregon woman whose breast cancer left her unable to breathe easily became the first American to legally commit suicide with the aid of a doctor. Oregon's Death

▲ On April 10, 2000, thousands of protesters gather outside the Upper House of Parliament in The Hague, Netherlands, as Dutch government officials debate the legalization of euthanasia.

with Dignity Act—which is modeled in many respects after the Dutch system—was upheld by the United States Supreme Court in 2006 in a decision that reconfirmed each state's authority to legalize assisted suicide. As of April 2007, 292 people have ended their lives with a physician's help in Oregon, which is still the only state that allows such a practice.

FOR CRITICAL ANALYSIS

What social attitudes make it unlikely that physician-assisted suicide and euthanasia will become widely accepted in this country?

Today, social attitudes have shifted to consider adultery a personal issue, beyond the purview of the state, and to consider the sale of heroin a criminal act. When a consensus does not exist as to whether a certain act falls within the parameters of acceptable behavior, a period of uncertainty ensues as society struggles to formalize its attitudes as law. (For an example of the consensus model at work, see the feature *International CJ—Doctor-Assisted Death and the Dutch*.)

THE CONFLICT MODEL

Those who reject the consensus model do so on the ground that moral attitudes are not absolute. In large, democratic societies such as the United States, different segments of society will inevitably have different value systems and shared norms. According to the **conflict model,** these different segments—separated by social class, income, age, and race—are engaged in a constant struggle with each other for control of society. The victorious groups exercise their power by codifying their value systems into criminal laws.[6]

Consequently, what is deemed criminal activity is determined by whichever group happens to be holding power at any given time. Because certain groups do not have access to political power, their interests are not served by the criminal justice system. To give one example, the penalty (five years in prison) for possession of 5 grams of crack cocaine is the same as for possession of 500 grams of powder cocaine. This 1:100 ratio has had widespread implications for inner-city African Americans, who are statistically more likely to get caught using crack cocaine than are white suburbanites, who appear to favor the illicit drug in its powdered form.[7]

Conflict Model A criminal justice model in which the content of criminal law is determined by the groups that hold economic, political, and social power in a community.

1940s   1950s   1960s   19

v. Alabama: Limited
o counsel in capital cases
shed

Miller: Right to bear
mited to militia

1956 ***Giffin v. Illinois:*** Indigents entitled to court appointed attorney for first appeal

1961 ***Mapp v. Ohio:*** Exclusionary rule required in state courts

1972

1963 ***Fay v. Noia:*** Right to *habeas corpus* expanded
Brady v. Maryland: Prosecutors must turn over evidence favorable to defense
Gideon v. Wainwright: Indigents have right to counsel

1975

1976

1966 ***Sheppard v. Maxwell:*** Conviction reversed based on prejudicial pretrial publicity
Miranda v. Arizona: Suspects must be advised of rights before interrogation

1979

1967 ***In Re Gault:*** Requires counsel for juveniles

Evans Hughes becomes
ustice

al Commission on Law
ance and Enforcement—
sham commission

tion ends

ecutions in U.S.; highest
20th century

court packing plan defeat-

strative Office of U.S.
created

1941 Harlan Stone becomes Chief Justice
1946 Fred Vinson becomes Chief Justice

1953 Earl Warren becomes Chief Justice

1966 Bail Reform Act favors pretrial release
1967 President's Commission on Law Enforcement and Administration of Justice
1969 Warren Burger becomes Chief Justice

1970
1971
1972
1973

1973
1977

---

o mobster Al Capone
of income tax
n

Hauptman convicted
napping Charles
ergh's young son

boss "Lucky"
o guilty of
lsory prostitution

1941 Murder, Inc. trials
1948 Caryl Chessman sentenced to death for kidnapping and robbery
1949 Alger Hiss guilty of perjury in the onset of the Cold War

1951 Julius and Ethel Rosenberg sentenced to death for espionage
1954 Dr. Samuel Sheppard convicted of murder
1958 Daughter of movie actress Lana Turner not guilty of killing mom's hoodlum lover

1964 Teamster President Jimmy Hoffa guilty
1966 Dr. Sam Sheppard acquitted in second trial
1968 Black Panther Huey Newton guilty of voluntary manslaughter
1969 Chicago 7 guilty of incitement to riot and conspiracy

197
197
197

---

e and Clyde killed
aby Face" Nelson
retty Boy" Floyd

1945 Bank robber Willie Sutton escapes from prison
1947 Hollywood hopeful Black Dahlia's mutilated body found

1950 Brinks armored car robbery in Boston
1957 George Metesky confesses to a string of New York City bombings
1959 Murder of Kansas farm couple becomes basis of *In Cold Blood*

1962 French Connection drug bust
1963 President Kennedy assassinated
1964 Boston Strangler arrested
1966 Richard Speck kills eight Chicago nurses
1968 Martin Luther King, Jr. and Robert Kennedy assassinated
1969 Manson family commits Helter Skelter murders

197
197
197
197

Timeline contents courtesy David W. Neubauer, **America's Courts and the Criminal Justice System**, 7th Edition. ©2002 Thomson/Wadsworth.

1970s | 1980s | 1990s | 2000s

Furman v. Georgia: Declares state death penalty laws unconstitutional
Barker v. Wingo: Adopts flexible approach to speedy trial
Gerstein v. Pugh: Arrestee entitled to a prompt hearing
Gregg v. Georgia: Upholds death penalty
North v. Russell: Non-lawyer judges are upheld
Burch v. Louisiana: Six member juries must be unanimous

1986 **Baston v. Kentucky:** Jurors cannot be excluded because of race
1987 **U.S. v. Salerno:** Preventive detention upheld
1989 **Mistretta v. U.S.:** U.S. sentencing guidelines upheld

1991 **Payne v. Tennessee:** Victim impact statements admissible during sentencing
Burns v. Reed: Prosecutors have qualified immunity in civil lawsuits
Chisom v. Roemer: Voting Rights Act applies to elected judges
1995 **U.S. v. Lopez:** Federal law barring guns in school unconstitutional

2002 **Virginia v. Black:** The First Amendment does not bar laws criminalizing cross burning
2004 **Hamdi v. Rumsfeld:** US citizens, seized overseas during anti-terror military operations, must be given access to US courts
2007 **Uttecht v. Brown:** Makes it easier for prosecutors to ensure that all jurors serving on capital punishment cases are pro-death penalty

---

Organized Crime Control Act
Prison riot in Attica, New York
Break-in at Watergate
National Advisory Commission on Criminal Justice Standards and Goals
Nixon declares war on drugs
Determinate sentencing enacted in 4 states

1982 Victim and Witness Protection Act
1984 Bail Reform Act: Judge may consider if defendant is a danger to the community
1985 DNA first used in criminal case
1986 William Rehnquist becomes Chief Justice
1987 U.S. Sentencing Guidelines begin

1993 Three strikes laws gain currency
1994 New Jersey passes Megan's Law
1995 U.S. prison population tops one million
1996 Antiterrorism and Effective Death Penalty Act limits habeas petitions in federal court

2002 The Patriot Act enacted into law; Department of Homeland Security established
2004 U.S. government begins program to classify every airplane passenger according to security risk
2006 Louisiana becomes the fifteenth state to pass a "stand your ground" law allowing greater use of deadly force in self-defense
2007 The United States prison and jail population reaches a record 2.4 million

---

Lt. William Calley guilty of murder in My Lai massacre
Heiress Patty Hearst guilty of bank robbery
Maryland governor Marvin Mandel guilty of mail fraud

1980 John Wayne Gacey convicted of killing 33 boys
1982 Automaker John DeLorean acquitted of cocaine trafficking
1984 Mayflower Madam pleads guilty to misdemeanor of promoting prostitution
1987 Subway vigilante Bernhard Goetz acquitted of attempted murder
1989 Televangelist Jim Baker guilty of fraud

1993 L.A. police officers guilty in federal court of civil rights violations against Rodney King
1996 Menendez brothers guilty of killing wealthy parents during second trail
1997 Timothy McVeigh sentenced to death in Oklahoma City bombing
> O.J. Simpson civil trial

2000 NYPD officers acquitted for killing Amadou Diallo
2003 Washington state's Gary Ridgway sentenced as worst serial killer in U.S. history
2007 California trial of music producer Phil Spector for murder ends in a mistrial

---

Skyjacker D.B. Cooper disappears
Heiress Patty Hearst kidnapped by terrorists
Jimmy Hoffa disappears
Serial murderer Son of Sam arrested in New York
Jonestown massacre

1980 Headmistress Jean Harris kills Scarsdale Diet Doctor
1981 President Ronald Reagan survives John Hinckley assassination attempt
1984 21 killed at San Diego McDonalds
1987 Savings and loan mogul Charles Keating accused of millions in fraud
1989 Junk bond king Michael Milken pays $600 million fine

1992 Boxer Mike Tyson charged with rape
1994 Fire in Waco kills Branch Dividians
1995 Oklahoma City bombing
1997 Nanny in Boston charged with child murder

2001 Terrorists strike and destroy World Trade Center in New York City
2002 John Allen Muhammed and juvenile Lee Boyd Malvo kill ten and injure four others during a month-long sniper spree in the Washington, D.C., area.
2007 Student Cho Seung Hui murders five faculty members and twenty-seven students on the campus of Virginia Tech in Blacksburg, Virginia.

AN INTEGRATED DEFINITION OF CRIME

L02 Considering both the consensus and conflict models, we can construct a definition of crime that will be useful throughout this textbook. For our purposes, crime is an action or activity that is:

1. Punishable under criminal law, as determined by the majority or, in some cases, a powerful minority.
2. Considered an *offense against society as a whole* and prosecuted by public officials, not by victims and their relatives or friends.
3. Punishable by statutorily determined sanctions that bring about the loss of personal freedom or life.

At this point, it is important to understand the difference between crime and **deviance,** or behavior that does not conform to the norms of a given community or society. Deviance is a subjective concept; some segments of society may think that smoking marijuana or killing animals for clothing and food is deviant behavior. Deviant acts become crimes only when a majority is willing to accept that those acts should be punished—as is the situation today in the United States with using illegal drugs but not with eating meat. Furthermore, not all crimes are considered particularly deviant; little social disapprobation is attached to those who fail to follow the letter of parking laws. In essence, criminal law reflects those acts that we, as a society, agree are so unacceptable that steps must be taken to prevent them from occurring.

Deviance Behavior that is considered to go against the norms established by society.

Murder The unlawful killing of one human being by another.

Sexual Assault Forced or coerced sexual intercourse (or other sexual act) against the will of the victim.

Assault The threat or the attempt to do violence to another person, provided that the other person is aware of the danger.

Battery The act of physically contacting another person with the intent to do harm, even if the resulting injury is insubstantial.

Robbery The act of taking property from another person through force, threat of force, or intimidation.

TYPES OF CRIME

The manner in which crimes are classified depends on their seriousness. Federal, state, and local legislation has provided for the classification and punishment of hundreds of thousands of different criminal acts, ranging from jaywalking to first degree murder. For general purposes, we can group criminal behavior into six categories: violent crime, property crime, public order crime, white-collar crime, organized crime, and high-tech crime.

Violent Crime Crimes against persons, or *violent crimes,* have come to dominate our perspectives on crime. There are four major categories of violent crime:

- **Murder,** or the unlawful killing of a human being.
- **Sexual assault,** or *rape,* which refers to coerced actions of a sexual nature against an unwilling participant.
- **Assault** and **battery,** two separate acts that cover situations in which one person physically attacks another (battery) or, through threats, intentionally leads another to believe that he or she will be physically harmed (assault).
- **Robbery,** or the taking of funds, personal property, or any other article of value from a person by means of force or fear.

As you will see in Chapter 4, these violent crimes are further classified by *degree,* depending on the circumstances surrounding the criminal act. These circumstances include the intent of the person committing the crime, whether a weapon was used, and (in cases other than murder) the level of pain and suffering experienced by the victim.

AP Photo/Joel Page

▶ The small town of Newry, Maine, best known for its fall foliage, suffered a shock when Christian Nielsen, left, went on a murder spree over Labor Day weekend, 2006. Nielsen cut three of his victims into pieces and set the fourth on fire. The region's tourist industry worried that intense media attention—including newspaper headlines such as "Beast at the B&B [bed and breakfast]"—would scare away visitors. Why do violent crimes seem to hold such a fascination for the American public?

Property Crime The most common form of criminal activity is *property crime*, or those crimes in which the goal of the offender is some form of economic gain or the damaging of property. Pocket picking, shoplifting, and the stealing of any property that is not accomplished by force are covered by laws against **larceny**, also known as *theft*. **Burglary** refers to the unlawful entry of a structure with the intention of committing a serious crime such as theft. *Motor vehicle theft* describes the theft or attempted theft of a motor vehicle, including all cases in which automobiles are taken by persons not having lawful access to them. The willful and malicious burning of a home, automobile, commercial building, or any other construction, known as *arson*, is also a property crime.

Public Order Crime The concept of **public order crimes** is linked to the consensus model discussed earlier. Historically, societies have always outlawed activities that are considered contrary to public values and morals. Today, the most common public order crimes include public drunkenness, prostitution, gambling, and illicit drug use. These crimes are sometimes referred to as *victimless crimes* because they often harm only the offender. As you will see throughout this textbook, however, that term is rather misleading. Public order crimes may create an environment that gives rise to property and violent crimes.

White-Collar Crime Business-related crimes are popularly referred to as **white-collar crimes.** The term *white-collar crime* is broadly used to describe an illegal act or series of acts committed by an individual or business entity using some nonviolent means to obtain a personal or business advantage. ■ Figure 1.1 lists various types of white-collar crime; note that certain property crimes fall into this category when committed in a corporate context.

■ **Figure 1.1** White-Collar Crime

Embezzlement
Embezzlement is a form of employee fraud in which an individual uses his or her position within a corporation to *embezzle*, or steal, the corporation's funds, property, or other assets. Pilferage is a less serious form of employee fraud in which the individual steals items from the workplace.

Tax Evasion
Tax evasion occurs when taxpayers underreport (or do not report) their taxable income or otherwise purposely attempt to evade a tax liability.

Credit-Card and Check Fraud
This form of white-collar crime involves obtaining credit-card numbers through a variety of schemes (such as stealing them from the Internet) and using the numbers for personal gain. Check fraud includes writing checks that are not covered by bank funds, forging checks, and stealing traveler's checks.

Mail and Wire Fraud
This umbrella term covers all schemes to intentionally deceive in a business environment that involve the use of mail, radio, television, Internet, or a telephone.

Securities Fraud
This area covers illegal activity in the stock market. It includes stockbrokers who steal funds from their clients and those who engage in *insider trading*, which is the illegal trading in a stock by someone (or on behalf of someone) who has inside knowledge about the company in question.

Bribery
Also known as *influence peddling*, bribery occurs in the business world when somebody within a company sells influence, power, or information to a person outside the company who can benefit. A county official, for example, could give a construction company a lucrative county contract to build a new jail. In return, the construction company would give a sum of money, also known as a *kickback*, to the official.

Consumer Fraud
This term covers a wide variety of activities designed to defraud consumers, from selling counterfeit art to offering "free" items, such as electronic devices or vacations, that include a number of hidden charges.

Insurance Fraud
Insurance fraud involves making false claims in order to collect insurance payments under false pretenses. Faking an injury in order to receive payments from a workers' compensation program, for example, is a form of insurance fraud.

Although the extent of this criminal activity is difficult to determine within any certainty, the Association of Certified Fraud Examiners estimates that white-collar crime costs U.S. corporations as much as $652 billion a year.[8]

Traditionally, penalties for white-collar crime have been light. Between 1991 and 2001, the average sentence for a white-collar crime was around twenty months, about a quarter of the average sentence for a drug offense.[9] In the early 2000s, however, four of the six largest corporate bankruptcies in U.S. history took place, fueled by a frenzy of management misconduct. Public attitudes toward business-related crimes hardened, and, consequently, prosecutors began seeking, and getting, harsher punishments for white-collar criminals. In 2005, sixty-three-year-old Bernard J. Ebbers of WorldCom received a twenty-five-year prison term for overseeing an $11 billion fraud at the telephone company he founded. Then, in 2006, a judge sentenced former Enron chief Jeffrey Skilling to twenty-four years behind bars for his role in fraudulent business deals that destroyed more than $2 billion worth of employee pension plans. Enron's chairman Kennth Lay died from heart disease before he could be sentenced to a similar punishment. (See the feature *You Be the Judge—The Party's Over*.)

Organized Crime White-collar crime involves the use of legal business facilities and employees to commit illegal acts. For example, a bank teller can't embezzle unless she is hired first as a legal employee of the bank. In contrast, **organized crime** describes illegal acts by illegal organizations, usually geared toward satisfying the public's demand for unlawful goods and services. Organized crime broadly implies a conspiratorial and illegal relationship among any number of persons engaged in unlawful acts. More specifically, groups engaged in organized crime employ criminal tactics such as violence, corruption, and intimidation for economic gain. The hierarchical structure of organized crime operations often mirrors that of legitimate businesses, and, like any corporation, these

Organized Crime A conspiratorial relationship among any number of persons engaged in the market for illegal goods or services, such as illicit drugs or firearms.

See the **Computer Crime and Intellectual Property Section** of the U.S. Department of Justice for a wealth of information on cyber crimes. Find this Web site by clicking on *Web Links* under *Chapter Resources* at **www.cjinaction.com**.

■ **Figure 1.2** Types of Cyber Crime

Cyber Crimes against Persons

- *Obscene Material and Pornography:* The selling, posting, and distributing of obscene material such as pornography, indecent exposure, and child pornography.
- *Cyberstalking:* The act of using a computer and the Internet to continually attempt to contact and/or intimidate another person.
- *Cyber Harassment:* The harassment of a person through electronic mail, on chat sites, or by posting information about the person on Web sites.

Cyber Crimes against the Government

- *Cyberterrorism:* The use of a computer and/or the Internet to further political goals of terrorism against a country and its citizens.

Cyber Crimes against Persons

- *Hacking:* The act of using programming abilities with malicious intent.
- *Cracking:* The act of using programming abilities in an attempt to gain unauthorized access to a computer or network.
- *Piracy:* Copying and distributing software or other items belonging to someone else over the Internet.
- *Viruses:* The creation and distribution of harmful computer programs.

Source: Susan Brenner and Rebecca Cochran, University of Dayton School of Law at **www.cybercrimes.net**.

groups attempt to capture a sufficient percentage of any given market to make a profit. For organized crime, the traditional preferred markets are gambling, prostitution, illegal narcotics, and loan sharking (lending money at higher-than-legal interest rates), along with more recent ventures into counterfeiting and credit-card scams.

High-Tech Crime The newest typology of crime is directly related to the increased presence of computers in everyday life. The Internet, with approximately 1.1 billion users worldwide, is the site of numerous *cyber crimes,* such as selling pornographic materials, soliciting minors, and defrauding consumers with bogus financial investments. The dependence of businesses on computer operations has left corporations vulnerable to sabotage, fraud, embezzlement, and theft of proprietary data. (See ■ Figure 1.2 for a description of several types of cyber crimes.)

Self Check Fill in the Blanks

A criminal act is a wrong against _____ and therefore is "avenged," or prosecuted, by _____, not by the individual victims of a crime. A crime is not the same as an act of _____, the term for behavior that is nonconformist but not necessarily criminal. Murder, assault, and robbery are labeled _____ crimes because they are committed against persons. The category of crime that includes larceny, motor vehicle theft, and arson is called _____ crime. When a criminal acts to gain an illegal business advantage, he or she has committed what is commonly known as a _____ crime. Check your answers on page 31.

The Criminal Justice System

Defining which actions are to be labeled "crimes" is only the first step in safeguarding society from criminal behavior. Institutions must be created to apprehend alleged wrongdoers, determine whether these persons have indeed committed crimes, and punish those who are found guilty according to society's wishes. These institutions combine to form the **criminal justice system.** As we begin our examination of the American criminal justice system in this introductory chapter, it is important to have an idea of its purpose.

THE PURPOSE OF THE CRIMINAL JUSTICE SYSTEM

In 1967, the President's Commission on Law Enforcement and Administration of Justice stated that the criminal justice system is obliged to enforce accepted standards of conduct so as to "protect individuals and the community."[10] Given this general mandate, we can further separate the purpose of the modern criminal justice system into three general goals:

1. To control crime
2. To prevent crime
3. To provide and maintain justice

Controlling and Preventing Crime Though many observers differ on the precise methods of reaching them, the first two goals are fairly straightforward. By arresting, prosecuting, and punishing wrongdoers, the criminal justice system attempts to *control* crime. In the process, the system also hopes to *prevent* new crimes from taking place. The prevention goal is often used to justify harsh punishments for wrongdoers, which some see as deterring others from committing similar criminal acts.

Maintaining Justice The third goal—of providing and maintaining justice—is more complicated, largely because *justice* is a difficult concept to define. Broadly stated, justice means that all citizens are equal before the law and that they are free from arbitrary arrest or seizure as defined by the law. In other words, the idea of justice is linked with the idea of fairness. Above all, we want our laws and the means by which they are carried out to be fair.

Justice and fairness are subjective terms; different people may have different concepts of what is just and fair. If a woman who has been beaten by her husband retaliates by killing him, what is her just punishment? Reasonable persons could disagree, with some thinking that the homicide was justified and she should be treated leniently, and others insisting that she should not have taken the law into her own hands. Police officers, judges, prosecutors, prison administrators, and other employees of the criminal justice system must decide what is "fair." Sometimes, their course of action is obvious; often, as we shall see, it is not.

Society places the burden of controlling crime, preventing crime, and determining fairness on those citizens who work in the three main institutions of the criminal justice system: law enforcement, courts, and corrections. In the next section, we take an introductory look at these institutions and their role in the criminal justice system as a whole.

THE STRUCTURE OF THE CRIMINAL JUSTICE SYSTEM

To understand the structure of the criminal justice system, one must understand the concept of **federalism,** which means that government powers are shared by the national (federal) government and the states. The framers of the U.S. Constitution, fearful of tyranny and a too-powerful central government, chose the system of federalism as a compromise. The appeal of federalism was that it allowed for state powers and local traditions while establishing a strong national government capable of handling large-scale problems.

The Constitution gave the national government certain express powers, such as the power to coin money, raise an army, and regulate interstate commerce.

Criminal Justice System The interlocking network of law enforcement agencies, courts, and corrections institutions designed to enforce criminal laws and protect society from criminal behavior.

Federalism A form of government in which a written constitution provides for a division of powers between a central government and several regional governments. In the United States, the division of powers between the federal government and the fifty states is established by the Constitution.

All other powers were left to the states, including police power, which allows the states to enact whatever laws are necessary to protect the health, morals, safety, and welfare of their citizens. As the American criminal justice system has evolved, the ideals of federalism have ebbed somewhat; in particular, federal involvement has expanded significantly. Crime is still, however, for the most part a local concern, and the majority of all employees in the criminal justice system work for local government (see ■ Figure 1.3).

Law Enforcement The ideals of federalism can be clearly seen in the local, state, and federal levels of law enforcement. Though agencies from the different levels will cooperate if the need arises, they have their own organizational structures and tend to operate independently of one another. In addition to this brief introduction, each level of law enforcement will be covered in more detail in Chapters 5, 6, and 7.

L03

Local Law Enforcement On the local level, the duties of law enforcement agencies are split between counties and municipalities. The chief law enforcement officer of most counties is the county sheriff. The sheriff is usually an elected post, with a two- or four-year term. In some areas, where city and county governments have merged, there is a county police force, headed by a chief of police. The bulk of local police officers—nearly 580,000—are employed by municipalities. The majority of these forces consist of fewer than ten officers, though a large city such as New York can have a police force of more than 35,000.

Local police are responsible for the "nuts and bolts" of law enforcement work. They investigate most crimes and attempt to deter crime through patrol activities. They apprehend criminals and participate in trial proceedings, if necessary. Local police are also charged with "keeping the peace," a broad set of duties that includes crowd and traffic control and the resolution of minor conflicts between citizens. In many areas, local police have the added obligation of providing social services such as dealing with domestic violence and child abuse.

State Law Enforcement Hawaii is the only state that does not have a state law enforcement agency. Generally, there are two types of state law enforcement agencies, those designated simply as "state police" and those designated as "highway patrols." State highway patrols concern themselves mainly with infractions on public highways and freeways. Other state law enforcers include fire marshals, who investigate suspicious fires and educate the public on fire prevention; and fish, game, and watercraft wardens, who police a state's natural resources and often oversee its firearms laws. Some states also have alcoholic beverage control officers, as well as agents who investigate welfare and food stamp fraud.

■ **Figure 1.3** **Local, State, and Federal Employees in Our Criminal Justice System**

Source: Bureau of Justice Statistics, *Justice Expenditure and Employment in the United States, 2003* (Washington, D.C.: U.S. Department of Justice, April 2006), Table 5.

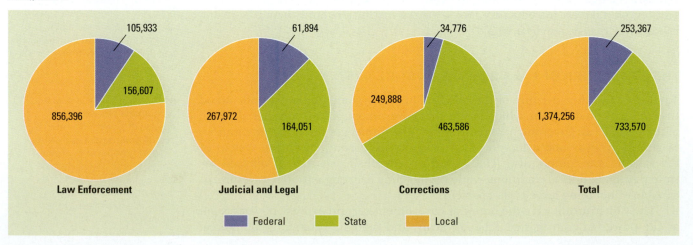

◄ Louisiana State Police officers patrol the streets of New Orleans following the destruction caused by Hurricane Katrina in late August 2005. State-level law enforcement agencies are often among the first responders to natural disasters and other emergencies. What are some of the other common duties of state law enforcement agencies?

Federal Law Enforcement The enactment of new national gun, drug, and violent crime laws over the past thirty years has led to an expansion in the size and scope of the federal government's participation in the criminal justice system. Federal agencies with police powers include the Federal Bureau of Investigation (FBI), the Drug Enforcement Administration (DEA), the U.S. Secret Service, and the Bureau of Alcohol, Tobacco, Firearms and Explosives (ATF). In fact, almost every federal agency, including the postal and forest services, has some kind of police power. On November 25, 2002, President George W. Bush created the Department of Homeland Security, which combines the police powers of twenty-two federal agencies in order to protect the United States from terrorist attacks. The crucial law enforcement role of this new department will be examined in detail in Chapters 5 and 16.

The Courts The United States has a *dual court system;* that is, we have two independent judicial systems, one at the federal level and one at the state level. In practice, this translates into fifty-two different court systems: one federal court system and fifty different state court systems, plus that of the District of Columbia. The federal system consists of district courts, circuit courts of appeals, and the United States Supreme Court. The state systems include trial courts at the local and state levels, intermediate courts of appeals, and state supreme courts.

The *criminal court* and its work group—the judge, prosecutors, and defense attorneys—are charged with the weighty responsibility of determining the innocence or guilt of criminal suspects. We will cover these important participants, their roles in the criminal trial, and the court system as a whole in Chapters 8, 9, 10, and 11.

Corrections Once the court system convicts and sentences an offender, she or he is delegated to the corrections system. Depending on the seriousness of the crime and their individual needs, offenders are placed on probation, incarcerated, or transferred to community-based corrections facilities.

- *Probation,* the most common correctional treatment, allows the offender to return to the community and remain under the supervision of an agent of the court known as a probation officer. While on probation, the offender must follow certain rules of conduct. If probationers fail to follow these rules, they may be incarcerated.
- If the offender's sentence includes a period of incarceration, he or she will be remanded to a corrections facility for a certain amount of time. *Jails* hold those convicted of minor crimes with relatively short sentences, as well as those awaiting trial or involved in certain court proceedings.

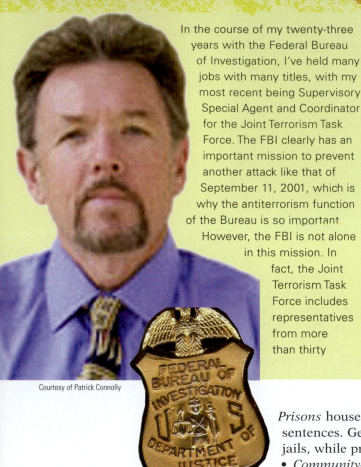

Courtesy of Patrick Connolly

In the course of my twenty-three years with the Federal Bureau of Investigation, I've held many jobs with many titles, with my most recent being Supervisory Special Agent and Coordinator for the Joint Terrorism Task Force. The FBI clearly has an important mission to prevent another attack like that of September 11, 2001, which is why the antiterrorism function of the Bureau is so important. However, the FBI is not alone in this mission. In fact, the Joint Terrorism Task Force includes representatives from more than thirty agencies—including federal, state, and local intelligence and law enforcement agencies.

FROM QUANTICO TO GUANTÁNAMO The training of the FBI members selected for the task force is not different from the standard training. The Special Agents go through fifteen to sixteen weeks of training at the FBI Academy at the U.S. Marine Corps base at Quantico, Virginia. I went through the Academy early in my career but now the training has been refocused to increase the emphasis on international terrorism. There is also a great deal of emphasis on providing timely and relevant training on current terrorism issues to all members of the task force.

In my work with the Bureau, I've been responsible for investigations in every area of FBI jurisdiction—including terrorism, organized crime, drugs/alien smuggling, violent crime, white-collar crime, and civil rights. Most of these investigations were long term and targeted criminal enterprises. We used sophisticated investigative techniques, such as wiretaps and undercover operations. In addition, I've served as a hostage negotiator, police instructor, legal adviser, and crisis management coordinator.

Prisons house those convicted of more serious crimes with longer sentences. Generally speaking, counties and municipalities administer jails, while prisons are the domain of federal and state governments.

• *Community-based corrections* have increased in popularity as jails and prisons have been plagued with problems of funding and overcrowding. Community-based correctional facilities include halfway houses, residential centers, and work-release centers; they operate on the assumption that all convicts do not need, and are not benefited by, incarceration in jail or prison.

The majority of those inmates released from incarceration are not finished with the correctional system. The most frequent type of release from a jail or prison is *parole*, in which an inmate, after serving part of his or her sentence in a correctional facility, is allowed to serve the rest of the term in the community. Like someone on probation, a parolee must conform to certain conditions of freedom, with the same consequences if these conditions are not followed. Issues of probation, incarceration, community-based corrections, and parole will be covered in Chapters 12, 13, and 14.

THE CRIMINAL JUSTICE PROCESS

In its 1967 report, the President's Commission on Law Enforcement and Administration of Justice asserted that the criminal justice system

> is not a hodgepodge of random actions. It is rather a continuum—an orderly progression of events—some of which, like arrest and trial, are highly visible and some of which, though of great importance, occur out of public view.[11]

The commission's assertion that the criminal justice system is a "continuum" is one that many observers would challenge.[12] Some liken the criminal justice system to a sports team, which is the sum of an indeterminable number of decisions,

Coordinator, Joint Terrorism Task Force

I also oversaw our FBI Detainee operation at the military prison at the U.S. Naval Base at Guantánamo Bay, Cuba. There, hundreds of individuals who had been involved with the Taliban and the war in Afghanistan were detained for questioning. Working at Guantánamo made it especially clear to me how important the FBI's role was in preventing attacks in the United States, although there has since been controversy over the appropriateness of detaining so many for so long. A key challenge in the area of antiterrorism is to balance individual liberties with national security. This is always a fine line but I feel that the FBI in general and the Joint Terrorism Task Force in particular have been very successful at achieving that balance.

WORKING FOR THE FBI My background includes a law degree (J.D.) and experience working as a prosecutor in Howard County, Maryland. Before that, I had spent about seven years in other jobs and two years in the Army. All of these experiences helped me in making the career switch from attorney to FBI Special Agent.

What advice would I give a job seeker looking for a position in the FBI? Get a college degree in any subject that interests you because the FBI is looking for individuals with expertise in a wide range of areas. For example, if you're interested in fields that range from criminal justice, to biology, to psychology, to business administration, there are relevant jobs in the FBI. Also, if you're especially interested in terrorism, you can access much unclassified information to educate yourself. For example, just exploring the Web will yield much information about terrorist groups, ideologies, and tactics. Of course, it's necessary to evaluate this material carefully and to use a variety of resources.

Most positions in the FBI now require at least a bachelor's degree and three years of full-time related experience. Given the number of applicants for each position, however, you would have a better chance with a master's degree. You must also have the highest ethics, not only because that's a core value, but you may end up testifying under oath at a trial.

Go to the **Careers in Criminal Justice Interactive CD** for a video of Patrick Connolly discussing his career and more profiles in the field of criminal justice. Also check the list at the end of the table of contents for career profiles in the book.

relationships, conflicts, and adjustments.[13] Such a volatile mix is not what we generally associate with a "system." For most, the word *system* indicates a certain degree of order and discipline. That we refer to our law enforcement agencies, courts, and correctional facilities as part of a "system" may reflect our hopes rather than reality.

The Assembly Line Just as there is an idealized image of the criminal justice system as a smooth continuum, there also exists an idealized version of the *criminal justice process*, or the procedures through which the criminal justice system meets the expectations of society. Professor Herbert Packer, for example, compared the idealized criminal justice process to an assembly line,

> down which moves an endless stream of cases, never stopping, carrying the cases to workers who stand at fixed stations and who perform on each case as it comes by the same small but essential operation that brings it one stop closer to being a finished product, or, to exchange the metaphor for the reality, a closed file.[14]

"What is legal is not necessarily—not even usually—about what is right, just, or ethical. It is about order. Similarly, 'justice' is a process that makes things work, not necessarily a result that is good or moral or ethical."

—*Charles R. Gregg, President, Houston Bar Association*

As Packer himself was wont to point out, the daily operations of criminal justice are not nearly so perfect. In this textbook, the criminal justice process will be examined as the end product of literally thousands of decisions made by the police, courtroom workers, and correctional administrators. It should become clear that, in fact, the criminal justice process functions as a continuous balancing act between its formal and informal nature, both of which are discussed in the following subsections.

The Formal Criminal Justice Process In Packer's image of assembly-line justice, each step of the process "involves a series of routinized operations whose success is gauged primarily by their tendency to pass the case along to a

Discretion The ability of individuals in the criminal justice system to make operational decisions based on personal judgment instead of formal rules or official information.

successful conclusion."[15] These "routinized" steps are detailed in the foldout exhibit in this chapter.

The Informal Criminal Justice Process Each step described in the foldout exhibit is the result of a series of decisions that must be made by those who work in the criminal justice system. This **discretion**—which can be defined as the authority to choose between and among alternative courses of action—leads to the development of the informal criminal justice process, discussed below.

Discretionary Basics One New York City public defender called his job "a pressure cooker." That description could apply to the entire spectrum of the criminal justice process. Law enforcement agencies do not have the staff or funds to investigate *every* crime; they must decide where to direct their restricted resources. Increasing caseloads and a limited amount of time in which to dispose of them constrict many of our nation's courts. Overcrowding in prisons and jails affects both law enforcement agencies and the courts—there is simply not enough room for all convicts.

The criminal justice system uses discretion to alleviate these pressures. Police decide whether to arrest a suspect; prosecutors decide whether to prosecute; magistrates decide whether there is sufficient probable cause for a case to go to a jury; and judges decide on sentencing, to mention only some of the occasions when discretion is used. (See ■ Figure 1.4 for a rundown of some of the most important discretionary decisions.) Collectively, these decisions are said to produce an *informal criminal justice system* because discretion is informally exercised by the individual and is not enclosed by the rigid confines of the law. Even if prosecutors believe that a suspect is guilty, they may decide not to prosecute if the case is weak or if they know that the police erred in the investigative process. In most instances, prosecutors will not squander the scarce resource of court time on a case they might not win. Some argue that the informal process has made our criminal justice system more just. Given the immense pressure of limited resources, the argument goes, only rarely will an innocent person end up before a judge and jury.[16]

Discretionary Values Of course, not all discretionary decisions are dictated by the scarcity of resources. Sometimes, discretion is based on political considerations, such as when a police administrator orders a crackdown on public order crimes because of citizen complaints. Furthermore, employees of the criminal justice system may make decisions based on their personal values or morality, which, depending on what those personal and moral values are, may make the system less just in the eyes of some observers. For that reason, discretion is closely connected to questions of *ethics* in criminal justice and will be discussed in that context throughout this textbook. (For an early look at the role that personal values play in the criminal justice system, see the feature *A Question of Ethics—Death of a Cowgirl.*)

■ **Figure 1.4 Discretion in the Criminal Justice System**

Criminal justice officials must use discretion every day. The officials listed below rely heavily on discretion when meeting the following responsibilities.

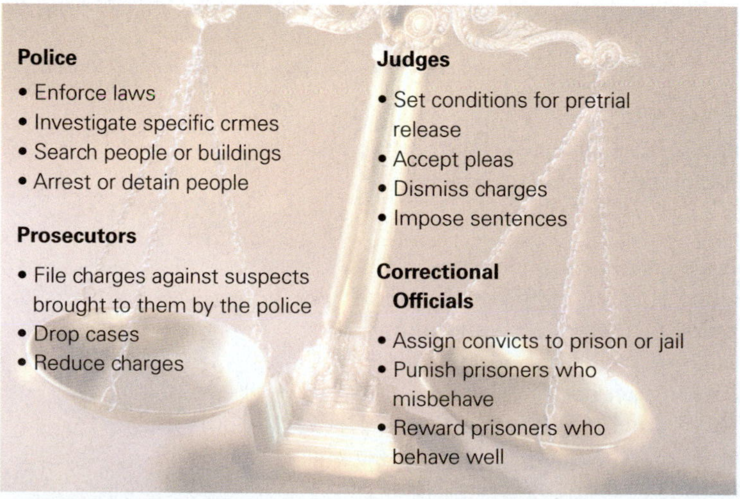
Police
• Enforce laws
• Investigate specific crmes
• Search people or buildings
• Arrest or detain people
Prosecutors
• File charges against suspects brought to them by the police
• Drop cases
• Reduce charges
Judges
• Set conditions for pretrial release
• Accept pleas
• Dismiss charges
• Impose sentences
Correctional Officials
• Assign convicts to prison or jail
• Punish prisoners who misbehave
• Reward prisoners who behave well

Source: U.S. Department of Justice, Bureau of Justice Statistics, *Report to the Nation on Crime and Justice,* 2d ed. (Washington, D.C.: Government Printing Office, 1988), 59. Photo credit: Corbis

The "Wedding Cake" Model of Criminal Justice Some believe that the prevailing informal approach to criminal justice creates a situation in which all cases are not treated equally. As anecdotal evidence, they point to a cultural landmark in the American criminal justice system—the highly publicized O. J. Simpson trial of 1994, during which the wealthy, famous defen-

LO6

dant had a different experience from that of most double-murder suspects. To describe this effect, criminal justice researchers Lawrence M. Friedman and Robert V. Percival came up with a **"wedding cake" model** of criminal justice.[17] This model posits that discretion comes to bear depending on the relative importance of a particular case to the decision makers. Like any wedding cake, Friedman and Percival's model has the smallest layer at the top and the largest at the bottom (see ■ Figure 1.5).

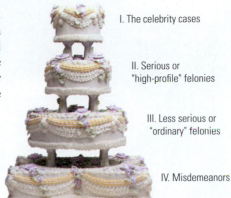

I. The celebrity cases

II. Serious or "high-profile" felonies

III. Less serious or "ordinary" felonies

IV. Misdemeanors

■ **Figure 1.5** The Wedding Cake Model

1. The "top" layer consists of a handful of "celebrity" cases that attract the most attention and publicity. Recent examples of top level cases include the trials of John Evander Couey, convicted of kidnapping, raping, and murdering nine-year-old Jessica Lunsford in Florida; Phil Spector, the famed music producer charged with murdering a female companion; and Mary Winkler, found guilty of voluntary manslaughter in the death of her husband, a small-town Tennessee pulpit minister.

2. The second layer consists of "high-profile" felonies. A *felony* is a serious crime such as murder, rape, or burglary that in most states is punishable either by death or by incarceration for a period longer than one year. This layer includes crimes committed by persons with criminal records, crimes in which the victim was seriously injured, and crimes in which a weapon was used, as well as crimes in which the offender and victim were strangers. These types of felonies are considered "high profile" because they usually draw a certain amount of public attention, which puts pressure on the prosecutors to bring the case to trial instead of accepting a guilty plea for a lesser sentence.

3. The third layer consists of "ordinary" felonies, which include less violent crimes such as burglaries and thefts or even robberies in which no weapon was used. Because of the low profile of the accused—usually a first-time offender who has had a prior relationship with his or her victim—these "ordinary" felonies often do not receive the full formal process of a trial.

> **"Wedding Cake" Model** A wedding cake–shaped model that explains why different cases receive different treatment in the criminal justice system. The cases at the "top" of the cake receive the most attention, while those cases at the "bottom" are disposed of quickly and virtually ignored by the media.

A Question of Ethics Death of a Cowgirl

THE SITUATION During the annual "Wild West Days" celebration, a homeless man named Bert ignored signs labeled "No Disrupting of Parade Route" and crossed Main Street. In doing so, he unintentionally spooked a horse carrying ten-year-old "cowgirl" Katy. The horse bolted, and Katy was thrown to her death. Parade rules stipulate that no person under the age of twelve years may ride a horse, but Katy's mother, an important businesswoman and community leader, managed to circumvent these regulations on her daughter's behalf. Now, Katy's mother is insisting that District Attorney Patty Lopez, who is facing a tough reelection battle, bring murder charges against Bert.

THE ETHICAL DILEMMA Following the letter of the law, District Attorney Lopez could charge Bert with involuntary manslaughter, which, as you will learn in Chapter 3, requires that the offender's carelessness cause a death that he or she did not intend. Lopez realizes, however, that hundreds of people cross Main Street during the parade every year

and that Bert was more unlucky than careless. At the same time, Lopez is well aware that the support of Katy's mother is crucial to her reelection campaign. If she fails to bring charges against Bert, she might well lose the election.

WHAT IS THE SOLUTION? What do you think District Attorney Lopez should do? She knows that, legally, she can charge Bert with involuntary manslaughter. But murder trials take up considerable resources that might be better spent prosecuting more dangerous offenders who are charged with more serious crimes. Lopez also knows that, under most circumstances, she would have very little chance of convincing a jury that such an obvious accident requires punishment. In this situation, though, Katy is a very sympathetic victim and Bert is a very unsympathetic suspect. How will District Attorney Lopez's personal values, and her political considerations, affect her discretion in this matter?

▲ Mary Winkler, followed by a member of her defense team, leaves a Selma, Tennessee, courtroom. On April 20, 2007, Winkler was convicted of voluntary manslaughter for shooting her husband in the back with a shotgun as he lay in bed. The trial, with its titillating plot of the small-town minister's wife fighting back against physical and mental abuse, received "gavel-to-gavel" television coverage. Why do such high-profile cases give the public an unrealistic view of the criminal trial?

4. Finally, the fourth layer consists of *misdemeanors,* or crimes less serious than felonies. Misdemeanors include petty offenses such as shoplifting, disturbing the peace, and violations of local ordinances; they are usually punishable by fines, probation, or short jail times. More than three-quarters of all arrests made by police are for misdemeanors.

The irony of the wedding cake model is that the cases on the top level come closest to meeting our standards of ideal criminal justice. In these celebrity trials, we get to see committed (and expensive) attorneys argue minute technicalities of the law, sometimes for days on end. The further one moves down the layers of the cake, the more informal the process becomes. Though many of the cases in the second layer are brought to trial, only rarely does this occur for the less serious felonies in the third level of the wedding cake. By the fourth level, cases are dealt with almost completely informally, and the end goal appears to be speed rather than what can be called "justice."

Public fascination with celebrity cases obscures a truth of the informal criminal justice process: trial by jury is relatively rare (only about 5 percent of those arrested for felonies go to trial), and most cases are disposed of with an eye more toward convenience than ideals of justice or fairness. Consequently, the summary of the criminal justice system provided by the wedding cake model is much more realistic than the impression many Americans have obtained from the media.

Self Check Fill in the Blanks

To protect against a too-powerful central government, the framers of the U.S. Constitution relied on the principle of _____ to balance power between the national government and the states. Consequently, the United States has a ____ court system—one at the federal level and one at the _____ level. At every level, the criminal justice system relies on the _____ of its employees to keep it from being bogged down by formal rules. Some critics think that this freedom to make decisions leads to the _____ model of court proceedings, in which only the "top" layer of criminal court cases meets ideal standards. Check your answers on page 31.

Values of the Criminal Justice System

If the general conclusion of the wedding cake model—that some defendants are treated differently than others—bothers you, then you probably question the values of the system. Just as individuals have values—a belief structure governing individual conduct—our criminal justice system can be said to have values, too. These values form the foundation for Herbert Packer's two models of the criminal justice system.

CRIME CONTROL AND DUE PROCESS: TO PUNISH OR PROTECT?

In his landmark book, *The Limits of the Criminal Sanction,* Packer introduced two models for the American criminal justice system: the crime control model and the due process model.[18] The underlying value of the crime control model is that the most important function of the criminal justice process is to punish and repress criminal conduct. Though not in direct conflict with crime control, the underlying values of the due process model focus more on protecting the **civil rights,** or those rights guaranteed to all Americans in the U.S. Constitution, of the accused through legal constraints on police, courts, and corrections.

The Crime Control Model Under the **crime control model,** law enforcement must be counted on to control criminal activity. "Controlling" criminal activity is at best difficult, and probably impossible. For the crime control model to operate successfully, Packer writes, it

> must produce a high rate of apprehension and conviction, and must do so in a context where the magnitudes being dealt with are very large and the resources for dealing with them are very limited.[19]

In other words, the system must be quick and efficient. In the ideal crime control model, any suspect who most likely did not commit a crime is quickly jettisoned from the system, while those who are transferred to the trial process are convicted as quickly as possible. It was in this context that Packer referred to the criminal justice process as an assembly line.

The crime control model also assumes that the police are in a better position than the courts to determine the guilt of arrested suspects. Therefore, not only should judges operate on a "presumption of guilt" (that is, any suspect brought before the court is more likely guilty than not), but as few restrictions as possible should be placed on police investigative and fact-gathering activities. The crime control model relies on the informality in the criminal justice system, as discussed earlier.

The Due Process Model Packer likened the **due process model** to an obstacle course instead of an assembly line. Rather than expediting cases through the system, as is preferable in the crime control model, the due process model strives to make it more difficult to prove guilt. It rests on the belief that it is more desirable for society that ninety-nine guilty suspects go free than that a single innocent person be condemned.[20]

The due process model is based on the assumption that the absolute efficiency that is the goal of the crime control model can be realized only if the power of the state is absolute. Because fairness, and not efficiency, is the ultimate goal of the due process model, it rejects the idea of a criminal justice system with unlimited powers. As a practical matter, the model also argues that human error in any process is inevitable; therefore, the criminal justice system should recognize its own fallibility and take all measures necessary to ensure that this fallibility does not impinge on the rights of citizens.

Finally, whereas the crime control model relies heavily on the police, the due process model relies just as heavily on the courts and their role in upholding the legal procedures of establishing guilt. The due process model is willing to accept that a person who is factually guilty will go free if the criminal justice system does not follow legally prescribed procedures in proving her or his culpability.[21] Therefore, the due process model relies on formality in the criminal justice system. *Mastering Concepts* on the following page compares and contrasts the two models.

Civil Rights The personal rights and protections guaranteed by the Constitution, particularly the Bill of Rights.

Crime Control Model A criminal justice model that places primary emphasis on the right of society to be protected from crime and violent criminals. Crime control values emphasize speed and efficiency in the criminal justice process; the benefits of lower crime rates outweigh any possible costs to individual rights.

Due Process Model A criminal justice model that places primacy on the right of the individual to be protected from the power of the government. Due process values hold that the state must prove a person's guilt within the confines of a process designed to safeguard personal liberties as enumerated in the Bill of Rights.

CRIME CONTROL MODEL

DUE PROCESS MODEL

Goals of the Criminal Justice System
- Deter crime.
- Protect the public from crime.
- Incapacitate criminals.
- Provide quick and efficient justice.

Goals Can Best Be Met by:
- Promoting discretion and limiting bureaucratic red tape in criminal justice institutions.
- Making it easier for police to arrest criminals.
- Reducing legal restrictions on proving guilt in a criminal trial.

Favored Policies:
- More police
- More jails and prisons.
- Harsher penalties (including increased use of the death penalty) and longer sentences.

View of Criminality:
- Wrongdoers are responsible for their own actions.
- Wrongdoers have violated the social contract and can therefore be deprived of many of the rights afforded to law-abiding citizens.

Case in Point:
- *Ohio v. Robinette* (519 U.S. 33 [1996]), which allows police greater freedom to search the automobile of a driver stopped for speeding.

Goals of the Criminal Justice System
- Protect the individual against the immense power of the state.
- Rehabilitate those convicted of crimes.

Goals Can Best Be Met by:
- Limiting state power by assuring the constitutional rights of the accused.
- Providing even guilty offenders with full protection of the law, and allowing those offenders to go free if due process procedures are not followed.
- Assuring that all accused criminals receive the same treatment from the law, regardless of class, race, gender, or sexual orientation.
- Protecting the civil rights of prisoners.

Favored Policies:
- Open the criminal justice process to public scrutiny.
- Abolish the death penalty.
- Limit police powers to arbitrarily search, interrogate, and seize criminal suspects.
- Limit discretion and formalize criminal justice procedures so that all suspects and convicted offenders receive the same treatment.
- Increase funding for rehabilitation and education programs in jails and prisons.

View of Criminality:
- Criminal behavior can be attributed to social and biological factors.
- Criminals can be rehabilitated and returned to the community after incarceration.

Case in Point:
- *Mapp v. Ohio* (367 U.S. 643 [1961]), which invalidates evidence improperly gathered by the police, even if the evidence proves the suspect's guilt.

WHICH MODEL PREVAILS TODAY?

Though both the crime control and the due process models have always been present to a certain degree, during different time periods one has taken precedence over the other. The twentieth century saw such an ebb and flow. The influx of immigrants and problems of urbanization in the early 1900s caused somewhat of a panic within the American upper class. Considering that most, if not all, politicians and legal theorists were members of this class, it is not surprising that crime control principles prevailed during the first half of the last century.

The Pendulum Swings As the nation became more secure and prosperous in the 1950s and 1960s, a "due process revolution" took place. Under the leadership of Chief Justice Earl Warren, the United States Supreme Court significantly expanded the rights of the accused. Following a series of landmark cases that will be referred to throughout this textbook (some of which are featured in the timeline on the back of the foldout exhibit in this chapter), suspected offenders were guaranteed, among other things, that an attorney would be provided to them by the state if they could not afford one[22] and that they would be notified of their right to remain silent and retain counsel on being arrested.[23] The 1960s also saw severe limits placed on the power of the police, as the Court required law enforcement officers to strictly follow specific guidelines on gathering evidence or risk having that evidence invalidated.[24]

Rising crime rates in the late 1970s and early 1980s led to increased pressure on politicians and judges to get "tough on crime." These attitudes slowed down the due process revolution and returned the principles of the crime control model to our criminal justice system. In 1984, for example, three Supreme Court cases restored to police some of the freedoms they had enjoyed in the first half of the century. Even if evidence was obtained illegally, the Court ruled, it could be admitted at trial if the police officers could prove they would have obtained the evidence legally anyway.[25] Furthermore, in two separate cases the Court created the "good faith" exception to evidence-gathering rules, which basically allowed illegally obtained evidence to be admitted if the police officers were unaware that they were acting unconstitutionally.[26] According to many criminal law experts, this trio of cases resulted in the values of crime control gaining undue leverage.[27] (The role of the Bill of Rights in determining police power will be covered in Chapter 7.)

Responding to Terrorism The values of the criminal justice system are reflected not only in court decisions, but also in public policy. On September 11, 2001, terrorists hijacked four commercial airliners and used the planes to kill 3,021 people in New York City, northern Virginia, and rural Pennsylvania. Broadly defined as the random use of staged violence to achieve political goals, **terrorism** suddenly became a crucial issue in criminal justice, as will be evident throughout this textbook. Six weeks after the attacks, President George W. Bush signed the Patriot Act into law.[28] In an effort to prevent future strikes, the law strengthened the ability of federal law enforcement agencies to investigate and incarcerate suspects; thus, it represented a dramatic shift toward the crime control model (see ■ Figure 1.6).

Even though many Americans recognize that the government must take strong steps to protect the United States from terrorist attacks, the Patriot Act has been intensely criticized for "going too far" in infringing on individual civil rights. Several incidents have intensified this backlash. First, in 2005, the National Security Agency admitted that it had been eavesdropping on Americans without first obtaining a court order (a topic we will discuss in Chapter 7) since the September 11 attacks. Then, as we will see in Chapter 16, in 2007 the FBI conceded that its agents had been misusing the Patriot Act to gather records on customers from telephone companies and Internet service providers. Although President Bush has expressed "concern" over civil rights abuses connected with antiterrorism efforts, he has also signaled that his administration remains

> **Terrorism** The use or threat of violence to achieve political objectives.

> ⊘ See **Foundations of Inquiry: Terrorism** for information concerning federal, state, local, and international efforts to combat terrorism. Find this Web site by clicking on *Web Links* under *Chapter Resources* at **www.cjinaction.com**.

■ **Figure 1.6 Key Provisions of the Patriot Act**

The 342-page Patriot Act of 2001 is designed to strengthen the hand of law enforcement in its efforts to deter terrorism on American soil. Some of the law's most important provisions are listed below.

- **Creates a new crime of " domestic terrorism,"** defined as acts that "appear to be intended . . . to influence the policy of a government by intimidation or coercion."

- **Expands the definition of "engage in terrorist activity"** to include not only the use of weapons but also the provision of material support by such activities as fund-raising for suspected terrorist organizations.

- **Allows for easier detention and removal** of noncitizens suspected of terrorist activities.

- **Gives law enforcement agents greater ability** to use surveillance and wiretap methods, conduct seaches, track Internet use, and access private records when investigating terrorist activity.

- **Reduces the amount of suspicion law enforcement agents need** before apprehending a terrorist suspect.

Source: USA PATRIOT Act of 2001. Photo credit: PhotoDisc/Getty Images

committed to the values of crime control in the post 9/11 criminal justice landscape.

Criminal Justice Today

On the morning of January 29, 2007, a commuter noticed a suspicious-looking electronic device on the underside of an overpass on Boston's Interstate 93. Within an hour, a bomb squad was on the scene, and authorities had blocked off the highway and closed part of the city's public transportation system. By noon, several more similar-looking devices had been found, leading to the closure of two more bridges and part of the Charles River.

"The fear of burglars is not only the fear of being robbed, but also the fear of a sudden and unexpected clutch out of the darkness."

—Elias Canetti, Austrian novelist (1962)

Much to the anger and embarrassment of Boston officials, the devices turned out to be battery-powered advertisements for a movie based on the animated television series *Aqua Teen Hunger Force*. Facing harsh criticism, city law enforcement officers defended their actions. "Just a little over a mile away from the placement of the first device, a group of terrorists boarded airplanes and launched an attack on New York City," said Boston Police Commissioner Edward Davis. "The city clearly did not overreact. Had we taken any other steps, we would have been endangering the public."[29]

Many Americans would support this stance. A poll taken on the fifth anniversary of September 11, 2001 (the "attack" to which Commissioner Davis was referring), revealed that about 46 percent of those questioned still felt "uneasy" or "in danger" from terrorist activities.[30] The issue of how to keep the United States safe from such attacks continues to dominate public discourse in this country. In closing this introductory chapter with a brief overview of the state of the American criminal justice system, we shall see that terrorism concerns have had a profound impact on crime prevention and control as well.

REALITY CHECK: VIOLENT CRIME

L08 According to the Centers for Disease Control and Prevention, the odds of an American dying from a terrorist attack are 1 in 88,000.[31] In fact, a person is about as likely to die from an accidental fall as to be killed by any type of violent crime.[32] Nevertheless, most people have a greater fear of getting in an airplane or walking down a dark alleyway than climbing up a stepladder. When it comes to fear of crime, researchers have established that "perceived vulnerability" is more persuasive than actual risk. The power of this perception can be seen in our society's somewhat misguided notions about crime. As we will discuss in Chapter 3, the 1990s saw the largest decreases in violent crime in this country since the 1940s, and the rates continued to decline well into the 2000s. Yet, when asked, "Is there more crime in the United States than there was a year ago?" a majority of Americans have answered, "yes," in most years since 1990.[33]

Unfortunately, that answer now would be correct. For the first time since the early 1990s, violent crime is on the rise in the United States. Between 2004 and 2006, the nation's violent crime rate rose 2.2 percent, reflecting a 3.6 percent increase in murders and a 9.3 increase in robberies.[34] Crime experts known as *criminologists,* discussed in the next chapter, believe that these rates are mostly influenced by biological, economic, and social factors beyond the control of the police, courts, or prisons. A number of other observers contend, however, that the recent spike in violent crime is the result of complacency in the criminal justice system, brought on by years of successes. Today, they claim, we are doing a worse job than we were a decade ago in combating the leading indicators of violent crime.[35]

▲ Los Angeles police officers detain a member of the 18th Street gang in the city's Rampart district for questioning. Over twenty-five street gangs compete for Rampart's lucrative drug trade, burdening the predominantly Hispanic neighborhood with one of the highest violent crime rates in the region.

The Gang Problem "Outside of New York, al Qaeda isn't killing people [in the United States]; gang violence is."[36] The speaker, Los Angeles Police Chief William Bratton, has reason to be frustrated. His city experienced 269 gang-related murders in 2006, reflecting a wave of *street gang* violence that is washing over the entire country.[37] (The term **street gang** refers to any group of people who engage in violent, unlawful, or criminal activity.) According to the most recent data available, there are now 21,500 gangs in the United States with nearly 750,000 members.[38] In communities across the United States, law enforcement agencies report high levels of gang involvement in firearm possession and trafficking, vandalism and graffiti, auto theft, and illegal drug sales.[39]

The Gun Problem After David Gavin shot three people to death in Greenwich Village, New York, on March 14, 2007, law enforcement agencies immediately began investigating his guns. They found that each of his firearms—a Ruger P-89 9-millimeter pistol, a Taurus .357-Magnum revolver, and a Russian-made Imez .380-caliber pistol—had been purchased illegally. In all, about 30,000 Americans are killed by gunfire each year, and illegally obtained firearms are a constant concern for law enforcement officials. At the same time, legal gun ownership is widespread in the United States; almost one-third of the households in this country possess at least one gun.[40] The topic of **gun control,** or how to keep guns out of the hands of people like David Gavin and Cho Seung Hui, discussed in the first pages of the textbook, is a divisive one, and we will take a closer look at it in the *Criminal Justice in Action* feature at the end of this chapter.

The Illegal Drugs Problem Many observers blamed the explosion of violent crime that shook this country in the late 1980s and early 1990s on the widespread use and sale of crack cocaine at the time.[41] Today, about 27 percent of victims of violent crimes report that the offender was under the influence of drugs or alcohol.[42] Actually, alcohol falls under the broadest possible definition of a **drug,** which is any substance that modifies biological, psychological, or social behavior. In popular terminology, however, the word *drug* has a more specific connotation. When people speak of the "drug" problem, or the war on "drugs," or "drug" abuse, they are referring specifically to illegal **psychoactive drugs,** which affect the brain and alter consciousness or perception. Almost all of the drugs that we will be discussing in this textbook, such as marijuana, cocaine, heroin, and amphetamines, are illegal and psychoactive.

The main source of drug use data is the National Survey on Drug Use and Health, conducted annually by the National Institute on Drug Abuse (see ■ Figure 1.7 on the following page). According to the survey, only 8.1 percent of those questioned had used an illegal drug in the past month. Even so, this means that a significant number of Americans—almost 20 million—are regularly using illegal drugs, and the figure mushrooms when users of legal substances such as alcohol (126 million users) and tobacco (71.5 million users) are included.[43] The good news is that illegal drug use appears to be

Street Gang A group of people, usually three or more, who share a common identity and engage in illegal activities.

Gun Control Efforts by a government to regulate or control the sale of guns.

Drug Any substance that modifies biological, psychological, or social behavior; in particular, an illegal substance with those properties.

Psychoactive Drugs Chemicals that affect the brain, causing changes in emotions, perceptions, and behavior.

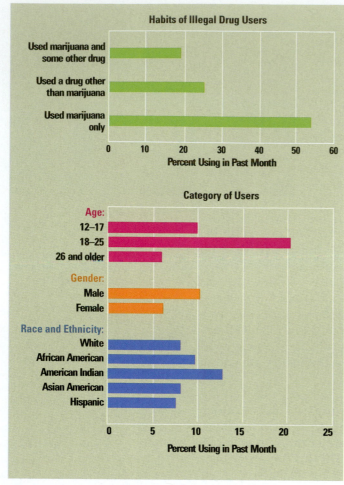

Habits of Illegal Drug Users

Category of Users

■ **Figure 1.7** **Drug Use in the United States**

According to the National Survey on Drug Use and Health, approximately 19.7 million Americans, or 8.1 percent, can be considered "illicit drug users." As you can see, most of these people used marijuana instead of other, stronger drugs. Furthermore, eighteen- to twenty-five-year-olds were more likely to have used drugs than any other segment of the population.

Source: National Survey on Drug Use and Health, 2006.

declining among those under the age of seventeen years, a topic we shall address when we look at the juvenile justice system in Chapter 15.

CRIME AND PUNISHMENT

In this textbook, you will be exposed to a great deal of statistical data. While each figure should help your understanding of the criminal justice system, it is best to keep in mind the warning of the writer William W. Watt, who said, "Do not put your faith in what statistics say until you have carefully considered what they do not say." What, for example, are we to make of the following? From 1991 to 2006, the violent crime rate in the United States fell an impressive 38 percent, even with the recent upswing.[44] During the same time period, however, the number of people in American prisons and jails grew by an astounding 108 percent.[45] If fewer people are committing crimes, why are so many more winding up in prison?

The Growing Prison Population We will take a closer look at this question in Chapter 3. For now, though, it may help to know that the present criminal justice landscape has been greatly influenced by a number of "get tough on crime" laws passed by federal, state, and local politicians in response to the crime wave of the late 1980s and early 1990s. These sentencing laws—discussed in Chapter 11—made it more likely that a person arrested for a crime would wind up behind bars and that, once there, he or she would not be back in the community for a very long while. As a result, the incarcerated population has been growing steadily for more than two decades, reaching yet another new high of 2,245,189 in 2006 (see ■ Figure 1.8).[46] More stringent drug laws have had a particularly large impact. In fact, drug offenders now represent more than half of all inmates in federal prisons.

Our drug laws have had particularly disastrous consequences for African Americans and women. Even though African Americans make up only 13 percent of the general population in the United States, the number of black men in state and federal prisons (577,100) is significantly larger than the number of white men (505,500).[47] According to the U.S. Department of Justice, 60 percent of those African Americans in federal prisons were locked up for drug offenses.[48] The question of whether these figures reflect purposeful bias on the part of certain members of the criminal justice community will be addressed at various points in this textbook. The incarceration rate of women, which is growing faster than that for men, is also fueled by drug abuse. Sixty-five percent of white women and 63 percent of African American women behind bars were arrested on drug charges.[49]

Diversion and Execution Naturally, this expansion of the prison population has come at a cost. In 2003, the last year for which figures are available, state governments spent nearly $37 billion on their prisons and jails.[50] For some states, corrections is the most expensive item on the budget, outpacing important services such as education and health care. Consequently, many states are looking for ways to bring corrections spending under control. One method of doing this is to grant

■ Figure 1.8 Prison and Jail Populations in the United States, 1985–2006

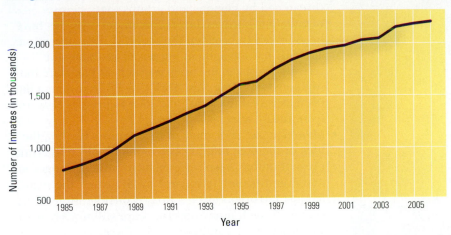

Sources: Bureau of Justice Statistics, *Correctional Populations in the United States, 1995* (Washington, D.C.: U.S. Department of Justice, June 1997), Table 1.1, page 12; and Bureau of Justice Statistics, *Prisoners in 2006* (Washington, D.C.: U.S. Department of Justice, 2007), 2.

early release to nonviolent offenders. Another is the diversion of offenders from correctional facilities through special courts that promote rehabilitation rather than punishment for drug offenses, domestic violence, and other specific crimes. We will examine these policies and their ramifications on the nation's prisons and jails in Chapters 13 and 14.

Attitudes also seem to be changing on the other end of the punishment spectrum. Alone among Western nations, the United States continues to rely on the death penalty as punishment for the most heinous crimes. By April 2007, the states and the federal government had executed 468 convicts in the new century. In two recent cases, however, the United States Supreme Court abolished the death penalty for mentally ill[51] and juvenile offenders.[52] Due in part to these decisions, the number of people sentenced to death in 2006 fell to the lowest level in nearly thirty years, a situation we will explore in Chapter 11.

NEW DIRECTIONS IN LAW ENFORCEMENT

Another reason that so many offenders are finding themselves locked away may be the performance of law enforcement. The crime wave of the late 1980s and early 1990s forced police departments to be more creative, resulting in a crackdown on "quality of life" crimes, such as public urination and vandalism, and a recommitment to a strategy known as "community policing." In Chapter 6, we will take a closer look at the successes of these efforts, as well as their failures.

Changing Tactics The events of September 11, 2001, to a certain extent also served as a "wake-up call" for those agencies and individuals whose duty is to thwart future attacks while at the same time fighting conventional crime. Law enforcement agencies are searching for new strategies to help them become more efficient at fighting domestic and international crime. Increasingly, officials are turning to the following three approaches to achieve that goal:

- *Cooperation.* One of the greatest hindrances to effective crime fighting has been the unwillingness of federal, state, and local law enforcement agencies to cooperate with each other. In the past several years, however, federal agencies such as the FBI and the Central Intelligence Agency (CIA) have begun sharing information to a much greater extent, and "antiterrorist task forces" combining federal, state, and local police agents have become common. Databases have allowed agencies to share important information with each other as well.

▲ The moment of impact as United Airlines Flight 175 crashes into the World Trade Center south tower at 9:03 on the morning of September 11, 2001. To the left, the World Trade Center north tower burns after being hit by American Airlines Flight 11 approximately fifteen minutes earlier. This attack, along with a simultaneous one on the Pentagon in Washington, D.C., cost almost three thousand lives and brought the horrors of terrorism into the lives of all Americans. What freedoms do you think the nation would be willing to give up to prevent such attacks in the future?

- *Globalization.* With American security being threatened by persons and groups that operate outside our borders, law enforcement agencies have been forced to broaden the scope of their operations. The FBI has engaged in numerous searches for terrorist suspects in countries such as Pakistan and Afghanistan, while New York City police officers have been assigned to the Middle East to protect New York from future attacks.

- *Militarization.* For most of this nation's history, the idea of the U.S. military becoming involved in crime prevention has been rejected as improper, dangerous, and even unconstitutional. Now, however, the "war" against terrorism has led to a reconsideration of this stance, though many observers are still uneasy with the prospect of a military police force.

DNA Profiling Police investigators are also enjoying the benefits of perhaps the most effective new crime-fighting tool since fingerprint identification became available a century ago: DNA profiling. This technology allows law enforcement agents to identify a suspect from body fluid evidence, such as blood, saliva, or semen, or biological evidence, such as hair strands or fingernail clippings. By collecting DNA from persons convicted of certain felonies and storing that information in databases, investigators have been able to reach across hundreds of miles and back through time to catch wrongdoers. In 2007, for example, Bridgeport, Connecticut, law enforcement agents ran a random DNA check of blood found under the fingernails of a 1993 murder victim named Maxine Gandy. The evidence led them to Emanuel Lovell Webb, whose DNA had been collected and stored in a national data bank after a Georgia conviction for involuntary manslaughter in the mid-1990s. Further DNA testing linked Webb to the unsolved murders of three other women that occurred in the same Bridgeport neighborhood and time period as Gandy's death.

For many observers, however, DNA profiling raises troubling privacy issues. How far are we as a society willing to go, they ask, in allowing the government to collect personal information for crime control purposes? Seven states (California, Kansas, Louisiana, Minnesota, New Mexico, Texas, and Virginia) and the federal government require all suspects arrested—not necessarily convicted—for felony crimes to provide their DNA to national data banks. We will discuss concerns that civil rights advocates have raised about this practice in Chapter 6. Closer to the end of the textbook, in Chapter 17, we will investigate the federal government's plans to create a high-tech driver's license that would be issued to Americans as their current driver's licenses expire. The card would include a chip containing information verifying a person's identity and would be required for those who want to board or enter airplanes, trains, courthouses, parks, monuments, and other areas under government control. (To learn more about identification methods and crime control, see the feature *CJ and Technology—Biometrics.*)

HOMELAND SECURITY

In 2006, Congress passed a law that permits the federal government to collect DNA samples from all immigrants found to be in this country illegally.[53] This legislation is one example of the recent merger between criminal law and immigration law, which traditionally were separate in the United States. Another is the enhanced ability of law enforcement agents to enforce immigration law by

26 Criminal Justice in Action

WHAT ARE BIOMETRICS?

The science of biometrics involves identifying a person through his or her unique physical characteristics. In the criminal justice context, the term refers to the various technological devices that read these characteristics and report the identity of the subject to authorities.

WHAT DO BIOMETRICS DO?

The most common biometric is the human face. Computerized face-recognition systems use a camera to record from thirty to eighty "markers" on a subject's face, such as cheekbone formations, the width of the nose bridge, and the space between the eyes. Earlier biometric systems examined the hand—measuring shape, size, and other characteristics such as the palm's vein patterns—but today the technology is more likely to focus on a single finger and its print. Another popular method is eye scanning, in which the minute details of the retina or the iris provide a very reliable biometric.

Criminal justice experts think that this technology may eventually be our most effective way to control access to sensitive security sites such as airports, power plants, and computer networks. With biometrics, it seems, the question is not *if* but *when* the technology will become an accepted part of everyday life. At some point, for example, face-recognition systems will allow hidden cameras to check the identities of thousands of people shopping in a mall or taking a stroll in a city park. Police officers will be able to take a photo of a suspect and

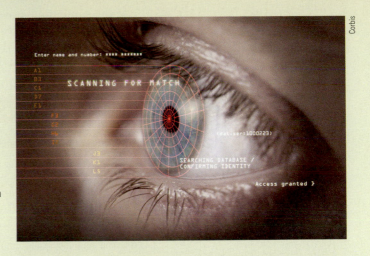

instantaneously check the biometric markers against a database of millions of people.

THINKING ABOUT BIOMETRICS

Biometrics force us to consider how much privacy we are willing to give up to be safer. What would be some of the positives and negatives of a widespread biometrics network in this country, considering both crime-fighting and civil rights issues?

For more information on biometrics and other CJ technologies, click on *Crime and Technology* under *Book Resources* at **www.cjinaction.com.**

---

assisting in the deportation of illegal immigrants who have committed no crime. Police officers in Alabama, Arizona, California, Florida, and North Carolina have taken on these duties, a situation we will address in Chapter 5.

This "crimmigration" trend is only one aspect of the broader **homeland security** movement in the criminal justice system. The goal of this campaign is to focus the efforts of law enforcement, the courts, and corrections on protecting America from foreign and domestic terrorism. The Patriot Act, mentioned on page 21, is a crucial element of homeland security in the context of criminal law. As we will see in Chapter 5, terrorism concerns have inspired the most significant reorganization of the federal departments involved in crime prevention since World War II. The reach of national security goes far beyond even these significant changes, however, and the implications of this new reality are the subject of Chapter 16.

TECHNOLOGY: FIGHTING AND FUELING CRIME

Finally, as technology has become more advanced, high-tech crime has become big business. Although experts have been unable to determine the precise amount of damage caused by computer crimes, estimates put the yearly loss in the United States alone in the billions of dollars.[54] The Internet has become a veritable web of criminal activity, as users have learned to take advantage of the anonymity and access it provides as cover for illegal drug and weapon sales, terrorist activity, gambling, and child pornography. *Identity theft*, in which an imposter steals personal information such as a Social Security number or a credit-card number and uses that information for personal monetary gain, is a major new crime concern

Homeland Security A concerted national effort to prevent terrorist attacks within the United States and reduce the country's vulnerability to terrorism.

for law enforcement in the United States. The Better Business Bureau estimates that almost 9 million Americans were victims of identity theft in 2006, with losses approaching $50 billion.[55]

At the same time, however, technology offers law enforcement agents a wealth of crime-fighting devices to combat both high-tech and conventional crime. Almost every chapter of this textbook will contain some information on the use of technology in the criminal justice system, and we will explore the subject in great depth in Chapter 17.

Self Check Fill in the Blanks

Law enforcement officials blame _____, or groups of people that engage in criminal activity, along with illegal drugs and guns, for the _____ in violent crime over the past few years. As a response to skyrocketing costs, many state corrections agencies are trying to _____ criminals from prison and toward programs that promote _____ instead of punishment. The recent trend of law enforcement agencies enforcing _____ laws is part of the _____ security movement, which is geared toward protecting the United States from terrorist attacks. Check your answers on page 31.

GUN CONTROL VERSUS GUN RIGHTS

For many Americans, gun ownership provides a comforting feeling of safety. In the six-month period following the terrorist attacks of September 11, 2001, for example, handgun sales increased by 455,000 over the same period the year before.[56] The vast majority of Americans who own guns are law-abiding citizens who keep their firearms at home for self-protection. This chapter's *Criminal Justice in Action* feature deals with the thorny issue of how best to protect the rights of this group while at the same time limiting the immense harm done by the illegal or improper use of firearms in the United States.

AS AMERICAN AS . . .

The Second Amendment to the U.S. Constitution states, "A well regulated Militia, being necessary to the security of a free State, the right of the people to keep and bear Arms, shall not be infringed." Forty-four states have added similar guarantees to their constitutions, as well as conferring various rights on gun owners—such as to carry a concealed weapon and to shoot at intruders—not found in the original document.[57] Law enforcement efforts in this area are mostly concerned with keeping guns out of the hands of those, such as children, the mentally ill, and criminals, who might use guns to harm themselves or others.

Critics of our nation's relatively lax gun laws argue for greater restrictions on ownership. They consider gun use to be a public health problem with disastrous consequences for American society. According to government data, on an average day in the United States firearms are used to kill about 80 people and wound 160 more.[58] Nevertheless, in the entire country, only the cities of Washington, D.C., and Chicago, Illinois, can be said to "ban" firearms.

The Case for More Restrictive Gun Laws

- Guns kill. A recent survey found that homicide rates are highest in states with the highest levels of gun ownership.[59]
- Guns in a household are more likely to harm the occupants than protect them. Households that contain guns are three times more likely to be the site of a fatal shooting and five times more likely to experience a suicide than those that have no firearms.[60]

Furthermore, according to the federal government, guns are used for defensive purposes only about 108,000 times each year—a figure that is dwarfed by the 1.3 million gun crimes occurring each year.[61]

- The Second Amendment protects the rights of states to maintain militias without federal government interference, not the rights of individual citizens to have guns.

The Case against More Restrictive Gun Laws

- Gun control laws do not decrease crime, for the simple reason that someone who is going to commit a crime with a gun is probably going to obtain that firearm illegally. So, for example, fifteen years after Washington, D.C.'s "ban" went into effect in 1977, the city's murder rate had increased 300 percent.[62] In 2006, District police confiscated more than 2,600 guns. As one observer points out, "the D.C. gun control laws irrationally prevent only law-abiding citizens from owning handguns."[63]
- Handguns offer protection from criminal attacks beyond that provided by public law enforcement.
- About a quarter of a billion handguns are privately and legally owned in this country. Putting restrictions on that ownership would create a huge new criminal class in this country, not to mention the anger toward the government that such measures would provoke.

Your Opinion—Writing Assignment

In 2007, a federal appeals court struck down Washington, D.C.'s handgun ban, ruling that the law infringed on the constitutional right of an individual to bear arms.[64] The court ruled that while the government can regulate and require registration of handguns, it cannot prevent private ownership in the home, as the D.C. statute did. The city of Washington, D.C., has appealed this decision, making it likely that the issue will find itself before the United States Supreme Court in the near future.

PhotoDisc/Getty Images

How difficult do you think the Supreme Court should make it for government authorities to restrict gun ownership and use? Would our society benefit from stricter gun control? How much leeway should local governments have to pass gun laws that may differ from the norm? Before responding, you can review our discussions in this chapter concerning:

- Consensus and conflict models of crime (pages 5–6).
- Federalism and the structure of the criminal justice system (pages (11–14).
- Guns and violent crime (pages 22–23).

Your answer should take at least three full paragraphs.

Chapter Summary

L01 Describe the two most common models of how society determines which acts are criminal. The consensus model argues that the majority of citizens will agree on which activities should be outlawed and punished as crimes; it rests on the assumption that a diverse group of people can have similar morals. In contrast, the conflict model argues that in a diverse society, the dominant groups exercise power by codifying their value systems into criminal laws.

L02 Define crime and the different types of crime. Crime is any action punishable under criminal statutes and is considered an offense against society. Therefore, alleged criminals are prosecuted by the state rather than by victims. Crimes are punishable by sanctions that bring about a loss of personal freedom or, in some cases, fines. There are six groups of crimes: (a) violent crimes—murder, rape, assault, battery, robbery; (b) property crimes—pocket picking, shoplifting, larceny/theft, burglary, and arson; (c) public order crimes—public drunkenness, prostitution, gambling, and illicit drug use; (d) white-collar crime—fraud and embezzlement; (e) organized crime—crime undertaken by a number of persons who operate their activities much as legal businesses do; and (f) high-tech crime—sabotage, fraud, embezzlement, and theft of proprietary data from computer systems as well as cyber crimes, such as selling child pornography over the Internet.

L03 Outline the three levels of law enforcement. Because we have a federal system of government, law enforcement occurs at the (a) federal and the (b) state levels and within the states at (c) local levels. Because crime is mostly a local concern, most employees in the criminal justice system work for local governments. Agencies at the federal level include the FBI, the DEA, and the U.S. Secret Service, among others.

L04 List the essential elements of the corrections system. Criminal offenders are placed on probation, incarcerated in a jail or prison, transferred to community-based corrections facilities, or released on parole.

L05 Explain the difference between the formal and informal criminal justice processes. The formal criminal justice process involves procedures such as booking, setting bail, and the like. For every step in the formal process, though, someone has discretion, and such discretion leads to an informal process. Even when prosecutors believe that a suspect is guilty, they have the discretion not to prosecute, for example.

L06 Describe the layers of the "wedding cake" model. The top layer consists of celebrity cases, which are most highly publicized; the second layer involves high-profile felonies, such as rape and murder; the third layer consists of property crimes such as larcenies and burglaries; the fourth layer consists of misdemeanors.

L07 Contrast the crime control and due process models. The crime control model assumes that the criminal justice system is designed to protect the public from criminals; thus, its most important function is to punish and repress criminal conduct. The due process model presumes that the accused are innocent and provides them with the most complete safeguards, usually within the court system.

L08 List the major issues in criminal justice today. (a) The rise in violent crime; (b) the proliferation of gangs, guns, and drugs; (c) the ever-expanding prison and jail population; (d) possible bias against minorities and women in the criminal justice system; (e) the diversion of nonviolent offenders from incarceration; (f) the death penalty; (g) new law enforcement tactics; (h) a focus on homeland security; and (i) the role of technology.

Key Terms

assault 7
battery 7
burglary 8
civil rights 19
conflict model 6
consensus model 5
crime 5
criminal justice system 11
deviance 7
discretion 16
drug 23
due process model 19
federalism 11
gun control 23
homeland security 27
larceny 8
organized crime 9
psychoactive drugs 23
public order crime 8
murder 7
robbery 7
sexual assault 7
street gang 23
terrorism 21
"wedding cake" model 16
white-collar crime 8

Questions for Critical Analysis

1. How is it possible to have a consensus about what should or should not be illegal in a country with several hundred million adults from all races, religions, and walks of life?

2. Why are criminals prosecuted by the state, through its public officials, rather than by the victims themselves?

3. Why are public order crimes sometimes referred to as victimless crimes?

4. At what political level is most law enforcement carried out? Relate your answer to the concept of federalism.

5. Assume that all of the officials involved in the criminal justice process were deprived of most of the discretion they now have. What might some of the results be?

6. What is the name of the federal legislation passed in 2001 to aid the federal government's efforts to combat terrorism? What are some of the "tools" this law gives to law enforcement officers to aid their antiterrorism efforts?

7. Using the broadest definition, what is a "drug"? More specifically, what are people usually referring to when they use the word *drug* in the criminal justice context?

8. Although DNA profiling has been a boon for law enforcement, why are some observers concerned about its widespread use?

Maximize Your Best Possible Outcome for Chapter 1

1. **Maximize Your Best Chance for Getting a Good Grade on the Exam.** ThomsonNOW Personalized Study is a diagnostic study tool containing valuable text-specific resources—and because you focus on just what you don't know, you learn more in less time to get a better grade. How do you get ThomsonNOW? If your textbook does not include an access code card, go to **thomsonedu.com** to get ThomsonNOW before your next exam!

2. **Get the Most Out of Your Textbook** by going to the book companion Web site at **www.cjinaction.com** to access one of the tutorial quizzes, use the flash cards to master key terms, and check out the many other study aids you'll find there. Under chapter resources you will also be able to access the Stories from the Street feature and Web links mentioned in the textbook.

3. **Learn about Potential Criminal Justice Careers** discussed in this chapter by exploring careers online at **www.cjinaction.com**. You will find career descriptions and information about job requirements, training, salary and benefits, and the application process. You can also watch video profiles featuring criminal justice professionals.

Notes

1. Quoted in Robert O'Harrow, Jr., "Gunman's Writings 'Out of a Nightmare,'" *Washington Post* (April 18, 2007), A10.
2. Shaila Dewan and Marc Santora, "Killer Showed Troubled State in Fall of 2005," *New York Times* (April 19, 2007), A1.
3. Virginia Code Annotated Section 18.2-60.3(A).
4. Dewan and Santora, A18.
5. Herman Bianchi, *Justice as Sanctuary: Toward a New System of Crime Control* (Bloomington: Indiana University Press, 1994), 72.
6. George B. Vold, *Theoretical Criminology* (New York: Oxford Press, 1994), 72.
7. U.S. Sentencing Commission, *Special Report to Congress: Cocaine and Federal Sentencing Policy* (Washington, D.C.: Government Printing Office, 1995), 184–187.
8. *2006 Report to the Nation: Occupational Fraud and Abuse* (Austin, TX: Association of Certified Fraud Examiners, 2006), 4.
9. U.S. Sentencing Commission, "Monitoring Data Files 1995–2002," at **www.ussc.gov/linktop.htm**.
10. President's Commission on Law Enforcement and Administration of Justice, *The Challenge of Crime in a Free Society* (Washington, D.C.: Government Printing Office, 1967), 7.

11. *Ibid.*
12. John Heinz and Peter Manikas, "Networks among Elites in a Local Criminal Justice System," *Law and Society Review* 26 (1992), 831–861.
13. James Q. Wilson, "What to Do about Crime: Blaming Crime on Root Causes," *Vital Speeches* (April 1, 1995), 373.
14. Herbert Packer, *The Limits of the Criminal Sanction* (Stanford, CA: Stanford University Press, 1968), 154–173.
15. *Ibid.*
16. Daniel Givelber, "Meaningless Acquittals, Meaningful Convictions: Do We Reliably Acquit the Innocent?" *Rutgers Law Review* 49 (Summer 1997), 1317.
17. Lawrence M. Friedman and Robert V. Percival, *The Roots of Justice* (Chapel Hill, NC: University of North Carolina Press, 1981).
18. Packer, 154–173.
19. *Ibid.*
20. Givelber, 1317.
21. Guy-Uriel E. Charles, "Fourth Amendment Accommodations: (Un)Compelling Public Needs, Balancing Acts, and the Fiction of Consent," *Michigan Journal of Race and Law* (Spring 1997), 461.
22. *Gideon v. Wainwright*, 372 U.S. 335 (1963). Many United States Supreme Court cases will be cited in this book, and it is important to understand these citations. *Gideon v. Wainwright* refers to the parties in the case that the Court is reviewing. "U.S." is the abbreviation for United States Reports, the official publication of United States Supreme Court decisions. "372" refers to the volume of the *United States Reports* where the case appears, and "335" refers to the page number. The citation ends with the year the case was decided in parentheses. Most, though not all, case citations in this book will follow this formula. For general information on how to read case citations and find court decisions, see the appendix at the end of this chapter.
23. *Miranda v. Arizona*, 384 U.S. 436 (1966).
24. *Mapp v. Ohio*, 367 U.S. 643 (1961).
25. *Nix v. Williams*, 467 U.S. 431 (1984).
26. *Massachusetts v. Sheppard*, 468 U.S. 981 (1984); and *United States v. Leon*, 468 U.S. 897 (1984).
27. James P. Fleissner, "Glide Path to an 'Inclusionary Rule,'" *Mercer Law Review* 48 (Spring 1997), 1023.
28. Uniting and Strengthening America by Providing Appropriate Tools Required to Intercept and Obstruct Terrorism (USA PATRIOT) Act of 2001, Pub. L. No. 107-56, 115 Stat. 272 (2001).
29. Quoted in Denise Lavoie and Jay Lindsay, "Boston Officials Defend Actions," *Providence (R.I.) Journal Bulletin* (February 2, 2007), A1.
30. Robin Toner and Marjorie Connelly, "9/11 Polls Find Lingering Fears in New York City," *New York Times* (September 7, 2006), A1.
31. "American Indicators," at **www.prorev.com/statshealth.htm**.
32. National Security Council, "What Are the Odds of Dying?" at **www.nsc.org/lrs/statinfo/odds.htm**.
33. *Sourcebook of Criminal Justice Statistics Online*, available at **www.albany.edu/sourcebook/pdf/t2332005.pdf**.
34. Federal Bureau of Investigation, *Crime in the United States, 2006* (Washington, D.C.: U.S. Department of Justice, 2007), at **www.fbi.gov/ucr/cius2006/data/table_01.html**.
35. Mark Sherman, "Violent Crime Up for 1st Time in Five Years," *Associated Press* (June 12, 2006).
36. Quoted in Chris Ragavan and Monika Guttman, "Terror on the Streets," *U.S. News and World Report* (December 13, 2004), 22.
37. Daniel B. Wood, "Spike in Gang Murders Prods L.A. Toward Action," *Christian Science Monitor* (January 19, 2007), 1.
38. Office of Juvenile Justice and Delinquency Prevention, *Highlights of the 2002 National Youth Gang Survey* (Washington, D.C.: U.S. Department of Justice, April 2004), 1.
39. Bureau of Justice Assistance, *2005 National Gang Threat Assessment* (Washington, D.C.: U.S. Department of Justice, 2005).
40. James Lindgren, "Fall from Grace: Arming America and the Bellesiles Scandal," *Yale Law Journal* 111 (2002), 2203.
41. James Alan Fox and Jack Levin, *The Will to Kill: Making Sense of Senseless Murder* (Needham, MA: Allyn & Bacon, 2001), 33–37.
42. Bureau of Justice Statistics, "Drug Use and Crime," at **www.ojp.usdoj.gov/bjs/dcf/duc.htm**.
43. Substance Abuse and Mental Health Services Administration, *Results from the 2005 National Survey on Drug Use and Health: National Findings* (Washington, D.C.: National Institute on Drug Abuse, 2006), 27, 37.
44. *Crime in the United States, 2006*, at **www.fbi.gov/ucr/cius2006/data/table_01.html**.
45. Bureau of Justice Statistics, *Prisons and Jail Inmates at Midyear 2006* (Washington, D.C.: U.S. Department of Justice, June 2007), 2.
46. *Ibid.*, 1.
47. Bureau of Justice Statistics, *Prisoners in 2005* (Washington, D.C.: U.S. Department of Justice, November 2006) Table 10, page 8.
48. See **www.albany.edu/sourcebook/pdf/t653.pdf**.
49. *Ibid.*
50. See **www.albany.edu/sourcebook/pdf/t192003.pdf**.
51. *Atkins v. Virginia*, 536 U.S. 304 (2002).
52. *Roper v. Simmons*, 543 U.S. 551 (2005).
53. 42 U.S.C. Section 3793(a)(18) (2006).
54. *Third Annual BSA and IOC Global Software Piracy Study* (Washington, D.C.: Business Software Alliance, May 2006).
55. Mary T. Monaham, *2007 Identity Fraud Survey Report* (Pleasanton, CA: Javelin Strategy and Research, February 2007).
56. Robert J. Spitzer, *The Politics of Gun Control*, 3d ed. (Washington, D.C.: CQ Press, 2004), viii.
57. Nicholas J. Johnson, "A Second Amendment Thought," *Brooklyn Law Review* (Winter 2005), 715–796.
58. National Centers for Injury Prevention and Control, at **www.cdc.gov/ncipc/wisqars**.
59. Matthew Miller, David Hemenway, and Deborah Azrael, "State-Level Homicide Victimization Rates in the U.S. in Relation to Survey Measures of Household Firearm Ownership, 2001–2003," *Social Science and Medicine* (February 2007), 656–664.
60. David Kairys, "The Origin and Development of the Governmental Handgun Cases," *Connecticut Law Review* (2000), 1166.
61. Johns Hopkins University Center for Gun Policy and Research, "Fact Sheet: Guns in the Home," at **www.jhsph.edu/gunpolicy/Guns_in_Home.pdf**.
62. Paul H. Blackman, "Effects of Restrictive Handgun Laws," *New England Journal of Medicine* (1992), 1157.
63. Quoted in David Nakamura and Robert Barnes, "Appeals Court Rules D.C. Handgun Ban Unconstitutional," *Washington Post* (March 10, 2007), A1.
64. *Parker v. District of Columbia*, 478 F.3d 370 (D.C. Cir. 2007).

Chapter One Appendix

HOW TO READ CASE CITATIONS AND FIND COURT DECISIONS

Many important court cases are discussed throughout this book. Every time a court case is mentioned, you will be able to check its citation using the endnotes on the final pages of the chapter. Court decisions are recorded and published on paper and on the Internet. When a court case is mentioned, the notation that is used to refer to, or to *cite*, the case denotes where the published decision can be found.

State courts of appeals decisions are usually published in two places, the state reports of that particular state and the more widely used *National Reporter System* published by West Group. Some states no longer publish their own reports. The *National Reporter System* divides the states into the following geographic areas: Atlantic (A. or A.2d), North Eastern (N.E. or N.E.2d), North Western (N.W. or N.W.2d), Pacific (P., P.2d, or P.3d), Southern (So. or So.2d), and South Western (S.W., S.W.2d, or S.W.3d). The *2d* and *3d* in these abbreviations refer to the *Second Series* and *Third Series*, respectively.

Federal trial court decisions are published unofficially in West's *Federal Supplement* (F.Supp. or F.Supp.2d), and opinions from the circuit courts of appeals are reported unofficially in West's *Federal Reporter* (F., F.2d, or F.3d). Opinions from the United States Supreme Court are reported in the *United States Reports* (U.S.), the *Lawyers' Edition of the Supreme Court Reports* (L.Ed.), West's *Supreme Court Reporter* (S.Ct.), and other publications. The *United States Reports* is the official publication of United States Supreme Court decisions. It is published by the federal government. Many early decisions are missing from these volumes. The citations of the early volumes of the *United States Reports* include the names of the actual reporters, such as Dallas, Cranch, or Wheaton. *McCulloch v. Maryland*, for example, is cited as 17 U.S. (4 Wheat.) 316. Only after 1874 did the present citation system, in which cases are cited based solely on their volume and page numbers in the *United States Reports*, come into being. The *Lawyers' Edition of the Supreme Court Reports* is an unofficial and more complete edition of Supreme Court decisions. West's *Supreme Court Reporter* is an unofficial edition of decisions dating from October 1882. These volumes contain headnotes and numerous brief editorial statements of the law involved in the case.

State courts of appeals decisions are cited by giving the name of the case; the volume, name, and page number of the state's official report (if the state publishes its own reports); and the volume, unit, and page number of the *National Reporter*. Federal court citations are also listed by giving the name of the case and the volume, name, and page number of the reports. In addition to the citation, this textbook lists the year of the decision in parentheses. Consider, for example, the case *Miranda v. Arizona*, 384 U.S. 436 (1966). The Supreme Court's decision in this case may be found in volume 384 of the *United States Reports* on page 436. The case was decided in 1966.

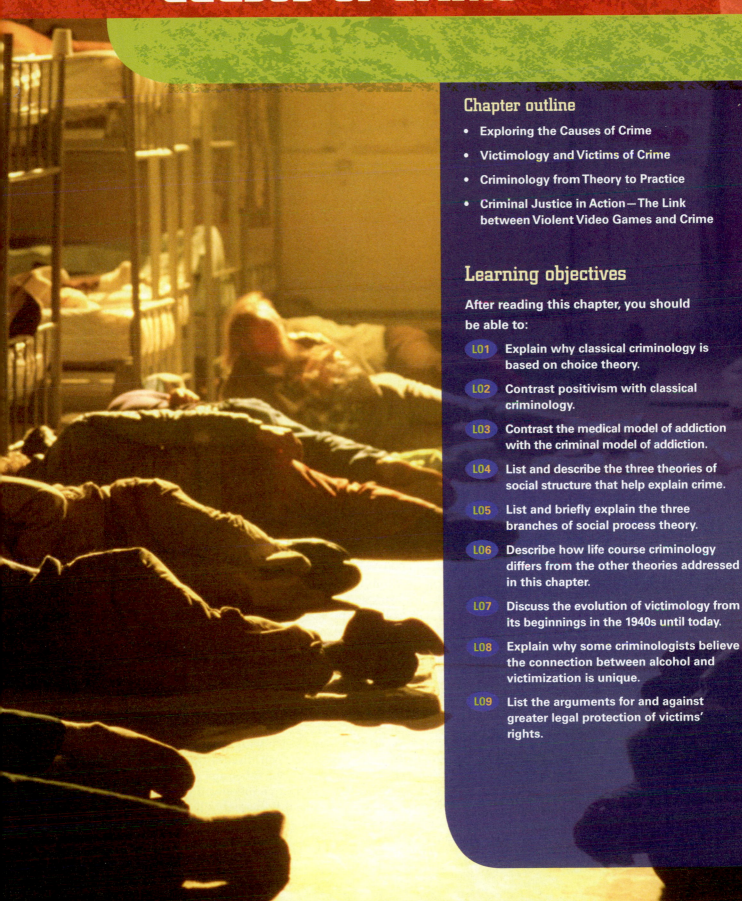

Causes of Crime

Learning objectives

After reading this chapter, you should be able to:

L01   Explain why classical criminology is based on choice theory.

L02   Contrast positivism with classical criminology.

L03   Contrast the medical model of addiction with the criminal model of addiction.

L04   List and describe the three theories of social structure that help explain crime.

L05   List and briefly explain the three branches of social process theory.

L06   Describe how life course criminology differs from the other theories addressed in this chapter.

L07   Discuss the evolution of victimology from its beginnings in the 1940s until today.

L08   Explain why some criminologists believe the connection between alcohol and victimization is unique.

L09   List the arguments for and against greater legal protection of victims' rights.

The Grudge

Like most Americans, the employees of the National Aeronautics and Space Administration (NASA) were horrified and saddened by the deaths of thirty-two people at Virginia Tech on April 16, 2007 (discussed in the introduction to Chapter 1). They could hardly have expected that three days later, tragedy would strike closer to home at NASA's Johnson Space Center in Houston, Texas. This time, the shooter was William Phillips, a sixty-year-old contract worker who had been affiliated with NASA for more than a decade. That Friday in Houston, Phillips sneaked a snub-nosed revolver past security, walked into the office of engineer David Beverly, and killed him with shots to the leg and chest. Phillips then bound Fran Crenshaw, who happened to be in the office, to a chair; taped her mouth shut; and watched televised news reports of the standoff for more than three hours before killing himself.

Unlike Cho Seung Hui, the Virginia Tech gunman, Phillips's motives were clear. Just over a month earlier, Phillips, who lived alone, had received an e-mail from superiors detailing deficiencies in his job performance. Two days later, he purchased a .38 caliber revolver and twenty rounds of ammunition. Before killing Beverly, Phillips said, "You're the one that's going to get me fired." He never had any intention of harming Crenshaw and only taped her mouth so that she would not scream and alarm the police officers outside the room when he shot himself.

Ironically, the Johnson Space Center's security team had reviewed the center's procedures earlier in the week because of the Virginia Tech incident. As a NASA staffer, however, Phillips still had little trouble getting his gun into the building. "When an employee has decided that he wishes to avenge a grudge . . . and is willing to die in the process, it is virtually impossible to stop that person," said NASA administrator Mike Griffin. "[Phillips] was determined that he was going to die."

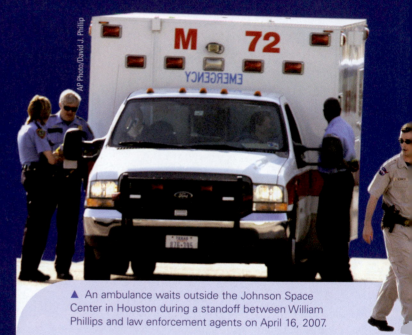

▲ An ambulance waits outside the Johnson Space Center in Houston during a standoff between William Phillips and law enforcement agents on April 16, 2007.

Criminology The scientific study of crime and the causes of criminal behavior.

Criminal Justice ⚖ Now™

Maximize your study time by using ThomsonNOW's Personalized Study plan to help you review this chapter and prepare for examination. The Study Plan will

- Help you identify areas on which you should concentrate
- Provide interactive exercises to help you master the chapter concepts; and
- Provide a post-test to confirm you are ready to move on to the next chapter information.

The carnage at the Johnson Space Center in Houston was hardly uncommon. In an average year, more than 600 employees are murdered while on the job.[1] One out of every six violent crimes committed in the United States occurs in the workplace.[2] In one respect, though, workplace violence is atypical: it seems to follow a pattern. According to data collected by James Alan Fox of Northeastern University in Boston, 73 percent of those persons convicted for workplace homicide are white, more than half are over age thirty-five, and almost all are male.[3] These criminals tend to be hypersensitive to criticism and often respond violently when disciplined. Researchers also note that usually several "trigger" events lead up to a workplace murder, which, in most instances, is carried out with a firearm.[4] Do these factors provide us with any clues as to the underlying causes of William Phillips's behavior?

The study of crime, or **criminology**, is rich with different theories as to why people commit crimes. In this chapter, we will discuss the most influential of these theories, some of which complement each other and some of which do not. We will also look at the various factors most commonly, if not always correctly, associated with criminal behavior. Finally, this chapter will address the question of relevance: What effect do theories of why wrongdoing occurs have on efforts to control and prevent crime?

Exploring the Causes of Crime

Criminologists, or researchers who study the causes of crime, warn against using models to predict violent behavior. After all, not every middle-aged white man who has a grudge against his employers and owns a gun is a potential criminal, and it would be wrong to treat them as such. Studies may show a *correlation* between these factors and workplace violence, but very few criminologists would go as far as to claim that these factors *cause* such violent behavior. Correlation between two variables means that they tend to vary together. Causation, in contrast, means that one variable is responsible for the change in the other. Research shows, for example, that ice cream sales and crime rates both rise in the summer. Thus, there is a correlation between ice cream sales and crime. Nobody would seriously suggest, though, that increased sales of ice cream cause the boost in crime rates.

This is the quandary in which criminologists find themselves. One can say that there is a correlation between violent workplace crime and certain characteristics of the lives of violent workplace criminals. But we cannot say what actually caused William Phillips to kill David Beverly without knowing much more about his background and environment, and possibly not even then. Consequently, the question that is the underpinning of criminology—what causes crime?—has yet to be fully answered.

THE ROLE OF THEORY

Criminologists have, however, uncovered a wealth of information concerning a different, and more practically applicable, inquiry: Given a certain set of circumstances, why do individuals commit criminal acts? This information has allowed criminologists to develop a number of *theories* concerning the causes of crime. For our purposes, a theory is an explanation of a happening or circumstance that is based on observation, experimentation, and reasoning. Scientific and academic researchers observe facts and their consequences to develop theories about what will occur when a similar fact pattern is present in the future. Researchers then test these theories to determine whether they are valid. Criminological theories are primarily concerned with determining the reasons behind criminal behavior, but they can also provide practical guidance for law enforcement, court, and corrections officials. In the following sections, we will examine the most widely recognized theories: choice theories, trait theories, sociological theories, social process theories, social conflict theories, and life course theories.

CRIME AND FREE WILL: CHOICE THEORIES OF CRIME

For the purposes of the American criminal justice system, the answer to why a person commits a crime is rather straightforward: because that person **LO1** chooses to do so. This application of **choice theory** to criminal law is not absolute; if a defendant can prove that she or he lacked the ability to make a rational choice, in certain circumstances the defendant will not be punished as harshly for a crime as would normally be the case. But such allowances are relatively recent. From the early days of this country, the general presumption in criminal law has been that behavior is a consequence of free will.

Theories of Classical Criminology An emphasis on free will and human rationality in the realm of criminal behavior has its roots in **classical criminology.** Classical theorists believed that crime was an expression of a person's rational decision-making process: before committing a crime, a person would weigh the benefits of the crime against the costs of being apprehended. Therefore, if punishments were stringent enough to outweigh the benefits of crime, they would dissuade people from committing the crime in the first place.

Criminologist A specialist in the field of crime and the causes of criminal behavior.

Theory A testable method of explaining certain behavior or circumstances, based on observation, experimentation, and reasoning.

Choice Theory A school of criminology that holds that wrongdoers act as if they weigh the possible benefits of criminal or delinquent activity against the expected costs of being apprehended. When the benefits are greater than the expected costs, the offender will make a rational choice to commit a crime or delinquent act.

Classical Criminology A school of criminology based on the belief that individuals have free will to engage in any behavior, including criminal behavior. To deter criminal behavior, society must hold wrongdoers responsible for their actions by punishing them.

▶ After admitting to their part in an arson spree that destroyed nine churches in rural Alabama during the winter of 2006, college students Russell DeBusk, left, and Ben Moseley claimed that they set the fires as "a joke." According to choice theory, why should criminal law deter most rational people from making these kinds of "jokes"?

The earliest popular expression of classical theory came in 1764 when the Italian Cesare Beccaria (1738–1794) published his *Essays on Crime and Punishments*. Beccaria criticized existing systems of criminal law as irrational and argued that criminal procedures should be more consistent with human behavior. He believed that, to be just, criminal law should reflect three truths:

1. All decisions, including the decision to commit a crime, are the result of rational choice.
2. Fear of punishment can have a deterrent effect on the choice to commit crime.
3. The more swift and certain punishment is, the more effective it will be in controlling crime.[5]

Beccaria believed that any punishment that purported to do anything other than deter crime was cruel and arbitrary. This view was shared by his contemporary, Britain's Jeremy Bentham (1748–1832). In 1789, Bentham pronounced that "nature has placed man under the governance of two sovereign masters, *pain* and *pleasure*." Bentham applied his theory of **utilitarianism** to the law by contending that punishment should use the threat of pain against criminal individuals to assure the pleasure of society as a whole. As a result, Bentham felt that punishment should have four goals:

1. To prevent all crime.
2. When it cannot prevent crime, to assure that a criminal will commit a lesser crime to avoid a harsher punishment.
3. To give the criminal an incentive not to harm others in the pursuit of crime.
4. To prevent crime at the least possible cost to society.[6]

Positivism and Modern Rational Theory

By the end of the nineteenth century, the positivist school of criminologists had superseded classical criminology. According to **positivism**, criminal behavior is determined by biological, psychological, and social forces and is beyond the control of the individual. The Italian physician Cesare Lombroso (1835–1909), an early adherent of positivism who is known as the "Father of Criminology," believed that criminals were throwbacks to the savagery of early humankind and could therefore be identified by certain physical characteristics such as sharp teeth and large jaws. He also theorized that criminality was similar to mental illness and could be genetically passed down from generation to generation in families that had cases of insanity,

L02

Utilitarianism An approach to ethical reasoning in which the "correct" decision is the one that results in the greatest amount of good for the greatest number of people affected by that decision.

Positivism A school of the social sciences that sees criminal and delinquent behavior as the result of biological, psychological, and social forces. Because wrongdoers are driven to deviancy by external factors, they should not be punished but treated to lessen the influence of those factors.

syphilis, epilepsy, and even deafness. Such individuals, according to Lombroso and his followers, had no free choice when it came to wrongdoing—their criminality had been predetermined at birth.

Positivist theory lost credibility as crime rates began to climb in the 1970s. If crime was caused by external factors, critics asked, why had the proactive social programs of the 1960s not brought about a decrease in criminal activity? An updated version of classical criminology, known as *rational choice theory*, found renewed acceptance. James Q. Wilson, one of the most prominent critics of the positivist school, sums up rational choice theory as follows:

> At any given moment, a person can choose between committing a crime and not committing it. The consequences of committing a crime consist of rewards (what psychologists call "reinforcers") and punishments; the consequences of not committing the crime also entail gains and losses. The larger the ratio of the net rewards of crime to the net rewards of [not committing a crime], the greater the tendency to commit a crime.[7]

According to rational choice theory, we can hypothesize that criminal actions, including acts of violence and drug abuse, are committed *as if* individuals had this ratio in mind.

The Seduction of Crime   In expanding on rational choice theory, sociologist Jack Katz has stated that the "rewards" of crime may be sensual as well as financial. The inherent danger of criminal activity, according to Katz, increases the "rush" a criminal experiences on successfully committing a crime. Katz labels the rewards of this "rush" the *seduction of crime*.[8] For example, serial killer John Wayne Gacy claims to have "realized that death was the ultimate thrill" after murdering the first of his more than thirty victims.[9] Katz believes that seemingly "senseless" crimes can be explained by rational choice theory only if the intrinsic reward of the crime itself is considered.

Choice Theory and Public Policy   The theory that wrongdoers choose to commit crimes is a cornerstone of the American criminal justice system. Because crime is seen as the end result of a series of rational choices, policymakers have reasoned that severe punishment can deter criminal activity by adding another variable to the decision-making process. Supporters of the death penalty—now used by thirty-eight states and the federal government—emphasize its deterrent effects, and legislators have used harsh mandatory sentences to control illegal drug use and trafficking. (To get a better idea of how a convicted criminal's ability to choose might affect his or her punishment, see the feature *You Be the Judge—The Tumor Made Me Do It* on the following page.)

"BORN CRIMINAL": BIOLOGICAL AND PSYCHOLOGICAL THEORIES OF CRIME

As we have seen, Cesare Lombroso believed in the "criminal born" man and woman and was confident that he could distinguish criminals by their apelike physical features. Such far-fetched notions have long been relegated to scientific oblivion. Nevertheless, many criminologists do believe that *trait theories* have validity. These theories suggest that certain *biological* or *psychological* traits in individuals could incline them toward criminal behavior given a certain set of circumstances. **Biology** is a very broad term that refers to the scientific study of living organisms, while **psychology** pertains more specifically to the study of the mind. "All behavior is biological," points out geneticist David C. Rowe of the University of Arizona. "All behavior is represented in the brain, in its biochemistry, electrical activity, structure, and growth and decline."[10]

Biology   The science of living organisms, including their structure, function, growth, and origin.

Psychology   The scientific study of mental processes and behavior.

Biochemical Conditions and Crime   One trait theory is that *biochemistry*, or the chemistry of living matter, can influence criminal behavior. The most famous, or

You Be the Judge The Tumor Made Me Do It

THE FACTS Philip, a forty-year-old schoolteacher with no history of deviant behavior, suddenly became obsessed with sex. He began collecting child pornography, soliciting prostitutes, and making sexual advances to young girls, including his stepdaughter. Eventually, Philip's wife reported his behavior, and he was tried and found guilty of child molestation. The judge ruled that Philip must complete a rehabilitation program or face jail time. When Philip was expelled from the program for lewdly propositioning the nurses, the judge had no choice but to order him to jail. The evening before his sentence was to begin, Philip checked himself into a hospital complaining of headaches and an urge to rape his landlady. Doctors removed an egg-sized tumor from Philip's brain, and the overpowering sexual urges disappeared.

THE LAW The ability to choose is an important element in determining punishment under American law. If a person has no control over his or her actions, then no "choice" to commit a crime has been made, and a court will often hand down a lesser punishment or no punishment at all if the defendant agrees to seek medical treatment.

YOUR DECISION There is no doubt that Philip committed the crimes of which he was convicted. The presence of the tumor, however, suggests that he failed to choose to be a sexual deviant, and therefore he might reasonably escape blame for his actions. In light of his dramatic personality change following removal of the tumor, should Philip be required to serve his jail term? How does the basic premise of rational choice theory inform your decision?

[To see how a Virginia judge ruled in a case with similar facts, go to Example 2.1 in Appendix B.]

The **American Society of Criminology** will keep you updated on the hot issues in criminology. Find its Web site by clicking on *Web Links* under *Chapter Resources* at **www.cjinaction.com**.

Hormone A chemical substance, produced in tissue and conveyed in the bloodstream, that controls certain cellular and bodily functions such as growth and reproduction.

Testosterone The hormone primarily responsible for the production of sperm and the development of male secondary sex characteristics such as the growth of facial and pubic hair and the change of voice pitch.

infamous, example of biochemistry's influence on criminal justice occurred in 1979, when Dan White was accused of murdering San Francisco Mayor George Moscone and Supervisor Harvey Milk. White successfully pleaded the "Twinkie defense"—that he should not be held accountable for his actions because he had suffered a major "mood disturbance" caused in part by an addiction to high-sugar junk food.[11]

Hormones and Aggression While the "Twinkie defense" is generally seen as a courtroom fluke, criminologists have paid more serious attention to other possible biochemical factors in criminal behavior. To give one example, chemical messengers known as **hormones** have been the subject of much criminological study. Criminal activity in males has been linked to hormones—specifically, **testosterone**, which controls secondary sex characteristics and has been associated with traits of aggression. Testing of inmate populations shows that those incarcerated for violent crimes exhibit higher testosterone levels than other prisoners.[12] Elevated testosterone levels have also been used to explain the age-crime relationship, as the average testosterone level of men under the age of twenty-eight is double that of men between thirty-one and sixty-six years old.[13]

A very specific form of female violent behavior is also believed to stem from hormones. In 2004, a North Carolina judge found that Yvonne Chapman was not guilty of murder for drowning her six-month-old son because she was suffering from *postpartum psychosis* at the time of her actions. This temporary illness, believed to be partly caused by the hormonal changes that women experience after childbirth, triggers abnormal behavior in a small percentage of new mothers.[14]

Brain Activity and Aggression The study of brain activity, or *neurophysiology,* has also found a place in criminology. Cells in the brain known as *neurons* communicate with each other by releasing chemicals called **neurotransmitters**. Criminologists have isolated three neurotransmitters that seem to be particularly related to criminal behavior:

1. Serotonin, which regulates moods, appetite, and memory.
2. Norepinephrine, which regulates sleep-wake cycles and controls how we respond to anxiety, fear, and stress.
3. Dopamine, which regulates perceptions of pleasure and reward.[15]

Researchers have found that, under certain circumstances, low levels of serotonin and high levels of norepinephrine are correlated with aggressive behavior.[16] Dopamine, as we shall soon see, plays a crucial role in the biochemistry of drug addiction.

Many scientists also think that criminal behavior can be influenced by neurological defects that are acquired early in life. This theory relies on *electroencephalographic* (EEG) scans of brain activity. An EEG records the electric oscillations, or waves, given off by the part of the brain that controls functions such as learning and memory. These brain waves are measured according to their frequency and strength, and certain patterns can be associated with criminal behavior. One study of a sample of 333 EEG subjects found that those who exhibited lifelong patterns of violence had an incidence of EEG abnormality three times higher than the same trait in those who had been charged with only one violent offense.[17] (For more information on "mapping crime" in the brain, see the feature *CJ and Technology—Neuroimaging* on the next page.)

Genetics and Crime Some criminologists might contend that Katz's "seduction of crime" (see page 39) provides more support for a modern, gene-based, evolutionary theory of crime than for rational choice theory. In other words, the seduction of crime represents an ancestral urge—which is stronger in some people than others—to commit acts that are considered crimes only in modern society. When scientists study ancestral or evolutionary developments, they are engaging in **genetics**, a branch of biology that deals with traits that are passed from one generation to another through genes.

Behavioral Genes Psychologist Leda Cosmides and anthropologist John Tooby have advocated a "Swiss army knife model" to explain how genetics influences brain activity. According to this model, humans have evolved special modules and networks in their brains that dispose them toward certain behavioral patterns.[18] Criminologists such as Lee Ellis and Anthony Walsh have suggested that some of these behavior patterns, which at one time were beneficial to human survival, have now become antisocial and have had sanctions imposed on them by society. In prehistoric eras, for example, extreme sexual aggressiveness in males toward a large number of females would have diversified a community's gene pool. Now laws against sexual assault and rape restrict such behavior.[19]

The "Crime Gene" Another theory suggests that a person's genetic make-up may contribute to personality traits associated with criminal behavior. Researchers have hunted in vain for a "crime gene," or a genetic abnormality that could conclusively predict criminal behavior. In 2002, however, British criminologist Terrie Moffitt and several colleagues published results of a study that linked violent behavior to the absence of the gene for a protein called monoamine oxidase-A

AP Photo/Steve Ueckert, Pool

▲ Several years ago, Andrea P. Yates, shown here in a Houston courtroom, methodically drowned her five children, aged six months to seven years, in the family bathtub. Just before the murders, Yates's physician took her off medication to treat postpartum depression, a condition that affects some women following childbirth. In July 2006, a jury found Yates not guilty of murder by reason of insanity. Do you agree that we should punish criminal behavior differently when it may be caused by biochemical conditions?

> "Crime is a fact of the human species, a fact of that species alone, but it is above all the secret aspect, impenetrable and hidden. Crime hides, and by far the most terrifying things are those which elude us."
>
> —*Georges Bataille, French novelist (1965)*

Neurotransmitter A chemical that transmits nerve impulses between nerve cells and from nerve cells to the brain.

Genetics The study of how certain traits or qualities are transmitted from parents to their offspring.

WHAT IS NEUROIMAGING?

Neuroimaging is the process of using technology to create an image of the functioning brain. By placing electrodes on the subject's scalp, for example, scientists can use computerized electroencephalography (CEEG) to measure the brain's electrical response to visual and auditory stimuli. Other neuroimaging measures include positron-emission computer tomography (PET scanning), which produces a computerized image of molecular variations in brain metabolism, and magnetic resonance imaging (MRI), which depicts the form and structure of the brain by bombarding it with magnetic fields and radio waves.

WHAT DOES NEUROIMAGING DO?

Although neuroimaging has not become so familiar that it is accepted as evidence in the vast majority of American courtrooms, the procedure has captured the attention of a number of scientists. Using both CEEG and MRI technology, researchers at the Institute of Living in Hartford, Connecticut, claim to have identified striking abnormalities in the brain activity of repeat violent offenders. Specifically, the scientists found that the brains of those with violent tendencies respond differently from those of "normal" subjects when processing emotion. In one experiment, the researchers showed members of each subset a photograph of a distraught woman holding a dead child. While the image triggered heightened activity in the amygdala region of most people's brains, the violent criminals did not respond to the picture on a subconscious level any differently

than they would have responded to any inanimate object. Neuroimaging has also been effective in identifying *attention-deficit/hyperactivity disorder*, a condition that is believed to affect between 3 and 5 percent of this nation's children and has been linked with high risks of substance abuse, learning disabilities, and delinquency.

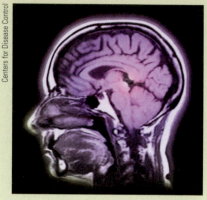

▲ An MRI scan showing the human brain.

THINKING ABOUT NEUROIMAGING

Suppose, for argument's sake, that at some time in the future neuroimaging allows scientists to determine, with a reasonable degree of certainty, which children are most likely to exhibit violent behavior as adults. What would be the implications of this technology? How would it help law enforcement officials prevent crimes? What might be some of the drawbacks of the ability to "predict" crime in this manner?

For more information on neuroimaging and other CJ technologies, click on *Crime and Technology* under *Book Resources* at **www.cjinaction.com.**

(MAOA).[20] This protein helps adjust a person's mood by regulating the molecules that carry "command signals" from one cell to another. Following more than five hundred men in New Zealand from birth to their late twenties, Moffitt and her team found that 12 percent of these males had *both* low levels of MAOA and had been abused as children. This group of 12 percent accounted for 85 percent of the entire sample who showed signs of overly aggressive behavior and 44 percent of those who had been convicted of violent crimes.

Because people who have been abused as children generally exhibit higher levels of antisocial behavior than those who have not—regardless of their MAOA supply—these findings are hardly decisive. Nor will they affect the consistent view of the courts that medical evidence has not been able to establish a causal relationship between genetic defects and criminal behavior.[21] Nevertheless, the efforts of Moffitt and her colleagues have spurred interest in the possibility that a "crime gene" does exist.

Twin Studies Because genes are inherited, some researchers have turned to *twin studies* to determine the relationship between genetics and criminal behavior. If the two are linked, then twins should exhibit similar antisocial tendencies. The problem with twin studies is that most twins grow up in the same environment, so it is difficult to determine whether their behavior is influenced by their genes or by their surroundings. To overcome this difficulty, criminologists compare identical twins, known as MZ twins, and fraternal twins of the same sex, known as DZ twins. Because MZ twins are genetically identical while DZ twins share only half of their genes, the latter should be less likely to have similar behavior patterns than the former.

Indeed, some studies seem to support this hypothesis. Researcher Karl Christiansen, for example, examined nearly four thousand male twin pairs and found that 52 percent of MZ pairs exhibited similar behavior patterns compared to only 22 percent for DZ pairs.[22] As is often the frustrating case in criminology, however, other studies seem to refute the idea that genetics is more important than environment in determining delinquent behavior. Research by criminologist David Rowe shows that nontwin siblings resemble each other in terms of delinquency to the same extent as twins do.[23] Consequently, though twin studies have contributed much to the discussion of trait theories, they have not proved conclusive in determining the effect of genetics on criminal behavior.[24]

Psychology and Crime For all of his accomplishments in the field of psychology, Sigmund Freud (1856–1939) rarely turned his attention to the causes of crime. His followers, however, have proposed a *psychoanalytic theory* for criminal behavior. This theory rests on the belief that the human personality is made up of three parts:

1. The *id,* which controls sexual urges.
2. The *ego,* which controls behavior that leads to the fulfillment of the id.
3. The *superego,* which is directly related to the conscience and determines which actions are right and wrong, in the context of a person's environment.

Psychoanalytic theorists contend that people who exhibit criminal behavior have an overdeveloped ego or an underdeveloped superego. A strong ego leads to such feelings of guilt that a person commits a crime in order to be punished; alternatively, a weak superego means that a person cannot control his or her violent urges.

Antisocial Personality Disorder (ASPD) Because such impressions are often based on observations rather than a testable prediction, some criminologists resist psychoanalytic theories of crime. Even so, the study of extreme disturbances in a person's behavior, or **personality disorders,** has found a place in the study of crime. During the middle of the twentieth century, the concept of the criminal as *psychopath* (used interchangeably with the term *sociopath*) gained a great deal of credence. The psychopath was seen as a person who had somehow lost her or his "humanity" and was unable to experience human emotions such as love or regret, to control criminal impulses, or to understand the consequences of her or his decisions.[25]

Although some criminologists continue to adhere to the concept of the psychopath, the term has fallen out of favor. In its place, many researchers have turned to the designation of **antisocial personality disorder (ASPD).** A person is diagnosed with ASPD if he or she is at least eighteen years old and exhibits three or more of the following characteristics:

1. Repeated unlawful behavior.
2. Deceitfulness, defined as persistent lying for personal profit or pleasure.
3. Impulsiveness or failure to plan for the future.
4. Reckless disregard to one's own safety or the safety of others.
5. Irresponsibility, as indicated by chronic unemployment and indebtedness.
6. Lack of remorse with regard to mistreatment of others.
7. Aggressiveness in the form of repeated physical fights or assaults.[26]

Personality Disorder A mental disorder characterized by deeply ingrained and maladjusted patterns of behavior.

Antisocial Personality Disorder (ASPD) A mental illness that is characterized by antisocial behavior and meets specific criteria established by the American Psychiatric Association.

According to one estimate, 40 percent of all convicted criminals suffer from ASPD.[27]

Other Personality Disorders ASPD is not the only personality disorder associated with crime. *Post-traumatic stress disorder,* a condition that occurs after a person has been exposed to a terrifying physical or emotional event, is relatively common in repeat violent criminals and sex offenders. People with *borderline personality disorder* suffer severe mood swings and often act aggressively, though

Drug Abuse The use of
drugs that results in physical
or psychological problems for
the user, as well as disruption
of personal relationships and
employment.

this more often results in self-injury than harm of others. Childhood conditions such as *attention-deficit/hyperactivity disorder,* mentioned in the *CJ and Technology* feature on page 42, are strongly correlated with juvenile delinquency.

Substance Abuse Disorders As we shall see throughout this textbook, no mental disorder is more closely linked with crime and violence than substance abuse and dependency. One study found that about half of all state prisoners and one-third of all federal prisoners admitted to being under the influence of either drugs or alcohol when they committed the crime for which they were arrested.[28]

Drug Abuse versus Drug Use There is little conclusive evidence that biological or psychological factors can explain initial experimentation with drugs. As we shall soon see, that behavior is probably learned from external actors. Science has, however, provided a great deal of insight into patterns of drug use. In particular, it has aided in understanding the difference between drug *use* and drug *abuse.* **Drug abuse** can be defined as the use of any drug—licit or illicit—that causes either physiological or psychological harm to the abuser or to third parties. Just as most people who drink beer or wine avoid abusing that drug, most users of controlled substances are not abusers. For most drugs, only between 7 and 20 percent of all users suffer from compulsive abuse.[29]

Addiction Basics The most extreme abusers are addicted, or physically dependent on a drug. To understand the basics of addiction and physical dependence, one must understand the role of dopamine in the brain.[30] As noted earlier, dopamine is responsible for delivering pleasure signals to brain nerve endings in response to behavior—such as eating good food or engaging in sex—that makes us feel good. The bloodstream delivers drugs to the area of the brain that produces dopamine, thereby triggering a large amount of the neurotransmitter. Over time, the continued use of drugs physically changes the nerve endings, called receptors. To continue operating in the presence of large amounts of dopamine, the receptors become less sensitive, meaning that greater amounts of any particular drug are required to create the amount of dopamine needed for the same level of pleasure. When the supply of the drug is cut off, the brain strongly feels the lack of dopamine stimulation, and the abuser will suffer symptoms of withdrawal until the receptors readjust.

▼ Boxer Mike Tyson, left, in a Phoenix, Arizona, court on January 22, 2007, following his arrest for drug possession and driving under the influence of drugs. Two weeks later, Tyson checked himself into an inpatient treatment program for "various addictions." What do you think of the idea that the criminal justice system should recognize drug addiction as a disease and try to rehabilitate criminal addicts rather than punish them?

Addiction and physical dependence are interrelated, though not exactly the same. Those who are physically dependent on a drug suffer withdrawal symptoms when they stop using it, but after a certain time period, they are generally able to emerge without further craving. Addicts, in contrast, continue to feel a need for the drug long after withdrawal symptoms have passed. Though some evidence suggests that certain people are genetically predisposed to alcoholism,[31] researchers are still striving to determine whether some people are more likely to become addicts than others for biological reasons.

The Models of Addiction Since the late nineteenth century, the treatment and rehabilitation of addiction have played a role in determining the attitude society takes toward criminal drug abusers. Those who followed, and follow, the **medical model of addiction** believe that addicts are not criminals, but mentally or physically ill individuals who are forced into acts of petty crime to "feed their habit." Those who believe in the "enslavement theory of addiction" advocate treating addiction as a disease and hold that society should not punish addicts but attempt to rehabilitate them, as would be done for any other patients.[32] Although a number of organizations, including the American Medical Association, recognize alcoholism and other forms of drug dependence as diseases, the criminal justice system tends to favor the **criminal model of addiction** over the medical model. The criminal model holds that drug abusers and addicts endanger society with their behavior and should be treated the same as any other citizens who commit crimes.[33]

Trait Theory and Public Policy Whereas choice theory justifies punishing wrongdoers, biological and psychological views of criminality suggest that antisocial behavior should be identified and treated before it manifests itself in first-time or further criminal activity. Though the focus on treatment diminished somewhat in the 1990s, rehabilitation practices in corrections have made somewhat of a comeback over the past few years. The primary motivation for this new outlook is the pressing need to divert nonviolent offenders from the nation's overburdened prison and jail system.

SOCIOLOGICAL THEORIES OF CRIME

The problem with trait theory, many criminologists contend, is that it falters when confronted with certain crime patterns. Why is the crime rate in Detroit, Michigan, twenty-five times that of Sioux Falls, South Dakota? Do high levels of air pollution cause an increase in abnormal brain activity or higher levels of testosterone? As no evidence has been found that would suggest that biological factors can be so easily influenced, several generations of criminologists have instead focused on social and physical environmental factors in their study of criminal behavior.

The Chicago School The importance of sociology in the study of criminal behavior was established by a group of scholars who were associated with the Sociology Department at the University of Chicago in the early 1900s. These sociologists, known collectively as the Chicago School, gathered empirical evidence from the slums of the city that showed a correlation between conditions of poverty, such as inadequate housing and poor sanitation, and high rates of crime. Chicago School members Ernest Burgess (1886–1966) and Robert Ezra Park (1864–1944) argued that neighborhood conditions, be they of wealth or poverty, had a much greater determinant effect on criminal behavior than ethnicity, race, or religion.[34] The methods and theories of the Chicago School, which stressed that humans are social creatures whose behavior reflects their environment, have had a profound effect on criminology over the past century.

The study of crime as correlated to social structure revolves around three specific theories: (1) social disorganization theory, (2) strain theory, and (3) cultural deviance theory.

Social Disorganization Theory Park and Burgess introduced an *ecological* analysis of crime to criminology. Just as ecology studies the relationships between animals and their environments, the two Chicago School members studied the relationship between inner-city residents and their environment. In addition, Clifford Shaw and Henry McKay, contemporaries of the Chicago School and researchers in juvenile crime, popularized the idea of ecology in criminology through **social disorganization theory**. This theory states that crime is largely a product of unfavorable conditions in certain communities.[35]

Disorganized Zones Studying juvenile delinquency in Chicago, Shaw and McKay discovered certain "zones" that exhibited high rates of crime. These zones were

See **Crime Times** for an online publication dedicated to understanding the role brain dysfunction plays in criminal behavior. Find this Web site by clicking on *Web Links* under *Chapter Resources* at **www.cjinaction.com**.

Medical Model of Addiction An approach to drug addiction that treats drug abuse as a mental illness and focuses on treating and rehabilitating offenders rather than punishing them.

Criminal Model of Addiction An approach to drug abuse that holds that drug offenders harm society by their actions to the same extent as other criminals and should face the same punitive sanctions.

Social Disorganization Theory The theory that deviant behavior is more likely in communities where social institutions such as the family, schools, and the criminal justice system fail to exert control over the population.

characterized by "disorganization," or a breakdown of the traditional institutions of social control such as family, school systems, and local businesses. In contrast, in the city's "organized" communities, residents had developed certain agreements about fundamental values and norms. Shaw and McKay found that residents in high-crime neighborhoods had to a large degree abandoned these fundamental values and norms. Also, a lack of social controls had led to increased levels of antisocial, or criminal, behavior.[36] According to social disorganization theory, ecological factors that lead to crime in these neighborhoods are perpetuated by continued elevated levels of high school dropouts, unemployment, deteriorating infrastructures, and single-parent families. (See ■ Figure 2.1 to better understand social disorganization theory.)

Fading Neighborhoods Some criminologists have questioned the usefulness of conventional social disorganization theory. As Robert J. Sampson, a sociologist from Harvard University, has pointed out, the "ideal typical neighborhoods" characterized by close-knit ties between residents on which Shaw and McKay based their research are no longer common in the United States.[37] Social bonds between people who live in the same area are weakening, meaning that members of any given community have less influence on each other than in the past. Furthermore, the concept of the neighborhood as a distinct place, separate and different from other neighborhoods, is no longer helpful in most contemporary cities.[38] Sampson and those who agree with him do not think the ideas of the Chicago School should be abandoned, but rather feel that they should not be limited by reliance on traditional notions of neighborhood and community.

Strain Theory Another self-perpetuating aspect of disorganized neighborhoods is that once residents gain the financial means to leave a high-crime community, they usually do so. This desire to escape the inner city is related to the second branch of social structure theory: **strain theory.** Most Americans have similar life goals, which include gaining a certain measure of wealth and financial freedom. The means of attaining these goals, however, are not universally available. Many

■ **Figure 2.1** The Stages of Social Disorganization Theory

Social disorganization theory holds that crime is related to the environmental pressures that exist in certain communities or neighborhoods. These areas are marked by the desire of many of their inhabitants to "get out" at the first possible opportunity. Consequently, residents tend to ignore the important institutions in the community, such as business and education, causing further erosion and an increase in the conditions that lead to crime.

The Problem: Poverty
The Consequences: Formation of isolated impoverished areas, racial and ethnic discrimination, lack of legitimate economic opportunities.

Leads to

The Problem: Social Disorganization
The Consequences: Breakdown of institutions such as school and the family.

Leads to

The Problem: Breakdown of Social Control
The Consequences: Peer groups replace family and educators as primary influences on youth; formation of gangs.

Leads to

The Problem: Criminal Areas
The Consequences: Rise of crime in poverty-stricken neighborhood; delinquent behavior becomes socially acceptable for youths; outside investment and support shun the area.

Leads to

The Problem: Cultural Transmission
The Consequences: The younger juveniles inherit the values of delinquency and crime from their older siblings and friends, establishing a deep-rooted impoverished-area culture.

Leads to

The Problem: Criminal Careers
The Consequences: The majority of youths "age out" of crime, start families, and, if they can, leave the neighborhood. Those who remain still adhere to the values of the impoverished-area culture and become career criminals.

Source: Adapted from Larry J. Siegel, *Criminology,* 9th ed. (Belmont, CA: Thomson/Wadsworth, 2005), 184.

citizens do not have access to the education or training necessary for financial success. This often results in frustration and anger, or *strain*.

Strain theory has its roots in the works of French sociologist Emile Durkheim (1858–1917) and his concept of **anomie** (derived from the Greek word for "without norms"). Durkheim believed that *anomie* resulted when social change threw behavioral norms into a flux, leading to a weakening of social controls and an increase in deviant behavior.[39] Another sociologist, American Robert K. Merton, expanded on Durkheim's ideas in his own theory of strain. Merton believed that *anomie* was caused by a social structure in which all citizens have similar goals without equal means to achieve them.[40] One way to alleviate this strain is to gain wealth by the means that are available to the residents of disorganized communities: drug trafficking, burglary, and other criminal activities.

In the 1990s, Robert Agnew of Emory University in Atlanta, Georgia, updated this line of criminology with his *general strain theory*, or GST.[41] Agnew reasoned that of all "strained" individuals, very few actually turn to crime to relieve the strain. GST tries to determine what factors, when combined with strain, actually lead to criminal activity. By the early 2000s, Agnew and other criminologists settled on the factor of *negative emotionality*, a term used to cover personality traits of those who are easily frustrated, quick to lose their tempers, and disposed to blame others for their own problems.[42] Thus, GST mixes strain theory with aspects of psychological theories of crime.

Cultural Deviance Theory Combining, to a certain extent, social disorganization and strain theories, **cultural deviance theory** asserts that people adapt to the values of the subculture to which they belong. A **subculture** (a subdivision that exists within the dominant culture) has its own standards of behavior, or norms. By definition, a disorganized neighborhood is isolated from society at large, and the strain of this isolation encourages the formation of subcultures within the slum. According to cultural deviance theory, members of low-income subcultures are more likely to conform to value systems that celebrate behavior, such as violence, that directly confronts the value system of society at large and therefore draws criminal sanctions.

Social Structure Theory and Public Policy If criminal behavior can be explained by the conditions in which certain groups of people live, then it stands to reason that changing those conditions can prevent crime. Indeed, government programs to decrease unemployment, reduce poverty, and improve educational facilities in low-income neighborhoods have been justified to a degree as part of large-scale attempts at crime prevention.

FAMILY, FRIENDS, AND THE MEDIA: SOCIAL PROCESSES OF CRIME

Some criminologists find class theories of crime overly narrow. Surveys that ask people directly about their criminal behavior have shown that the criminal instinct is pervasive in middle- and upper-class communities, even if it is expressed differently. Anybody, these criminologists argue, has the potential to act out criminal behavior, regardless of class, race, or gender.

Psychologist Philip Zimbardo conducted a well-known, if rather unscientific, experiment to make this point. Zimbardo placed an abandoned automobile with its hood up on the campus of Stanford University. The car remained in place, untouched, for a week. Then, the psychologist smashed the car's window with a sledgehammer. Within minutes, passersby had joined in the destruction of the automobile, eventually stripping its valuable parts.[43] **Social process theories** function on the same basis as Zimbardo's "interdependence of decisions experiment": the potential for criminal behavior exists in everyone and will be realized depending on an individual's interaction with various institutions and processes of society. Social process theory has three main branches: (1) learning theory, (2) control theory, and (3) labeling theory.

Anomie A condition in which the individual suffers from the breakdown or absence of social norms. According to this theory, this condition occurs when a person is disconnected from these norms or rejects them as inconsistent with his or her personal goals.

Cultural Deviance Theory A branch of social structure theory based on the assumption that members of certain subcultures reject the values of the dominant culture through deviant behavior patterns.

Subculture A group exhibiting certain values and behavior patterns that distinguish it from the dominant culture.

Social Process Theories A school of criminology that considers criminal behavior to be the predictable result of a person's interaction with his or her environment. According to these theories, everybody has the potential for wrongdoing. Those who act on this potential are conditioned to do so by family or peer groups, or institutions such as the media.

I had no plans to become a criminologist when I began my Ph.D. program in sociology at the University of North Carolina. In fact, I never took a course in criminology during my undergraduate days. The turning point came when I had to pick my dissertation subject. I discovered a survey that had some excellent measures of the relationship between a person's social environment and later delinquent behavior. I had my topic: the impact of social environment on delinquency.

Courtesy of Robert Agnew

STUMBLING UPON STRAIN THEORY My research led to the "strain" or *anomie* theories that said when a person stumbles in achieving financial success or middle-class status due to social factors beyond his or her control, he or she may turn to crime. That is, if you didn't have access to a good education because your local school was poor, or perhaps your parents just didn't have the money to send you to college, or you couldn't land a good job because of your background, you might respond to these kinds of frustrations by turning to crime. While strain theory made a lot of sense to me, I felt that the theory was incomplete.

When I looked around me, it was easy to spot other sources of frustration and anger, such as harassment by peers, conflict with parents or romantic partners, poor grades in school, or poor working conditions. In addition, strain theory did not explain why some people reacted to strain by turning to crime, while others did not.

My dissertation proposed additional sources of strain besides failure to achieve monetary success. I continued to

L05 **Learning Theory** Popularized by Edwin Sutherland in the 1940s, **learning theory** contends that criminal activity is a learned behavior. In other words, a criminal is taught both the practical methods of crime (such as how to pick a lock) and the psychological aspects of crime (how to deal with the guilt of wrongdoing). Sutherland's *theory of differential association* held that individuals are exposed to values from family and peers such as school friends or co-workers. If the dominant values one is exposed to favor criminal behavior, then that person is more likely to mimic such behavior.[44] Sutherland concentrated particularly on familial relations, believing that a child was more likely to commit crimes if she or he saw an older sibling or a parent doing so.

More recently, learning theory has been expanded to include the growing influence of the media. In the latest in a long series of studies, psychologists at the University of Michigan's Institute for Social Research released data in 2003 showing that exposure to high levels of televised violence erodes a natural aversion to violence and increases aggressive behavior among young children.[45] Such findings have spurred a number of legislative attempts to curb violence on television.[46] (The controversy surrounding the violent attributes of another medium—video games—is the subject of the *Criminal Justice in Action* feature at the end of this chapter.)

Learning Theory The hypothesis that delinquents and criminals must be taught both the practical and emotional skills necessary to partake in illegal activity.

Control Theory A series of theories that assume that all individuals have the potential for criminal behavior, but are restrained by the damage that such actions would do to their relationships with family, friends, and members of the community. Criminality occurs when these bonds are broken or nonexistent.

Control Theory Criminologist Travis Hirschi focuses on the reasons why individuals *do not* engage in criminal acts, rather than why they do. According to Hirschi, social bonds promote conformity to social norms. The stronger these social bonds—which include attachment to, commitment to, involvement with, and belief in societal values—the less likely that any individual will commit a crime.[47] **Control theory** holds that although we all have the potential to commit crimes, most of us are dissuaded from doing so because we care about the opinions of our family and peers. (See ■ Figure 2.2 on page 50 to better understand the role that various theories, including control theory, play in criminological explanations for why people abuse drugs.) James Q. Wilson and George Kelling describe control theory in terms of the "broken windows" effect. Neighborhoods in poor condition are filled with cues of lack of social control (for example, broken windows) that invite further vandalism and other deviant behavior.[48] If these cues are removed,

research this topic after I joined the faculty at Emory University. I drew on strain theory, social psychology, and my own experiences to develop a new "general strain theory" [see note 41].

SOURCES OF STRAIN I outlined sources of strain as the loss of "positively valued stimuli" such as romantic relationships, or the threat of "negatively valued stimuli" such as an insult or physical assault. I also pointed out that monetary success was just one among many "positively valued goals" that might cause strain when not achieved.

Finally, I noted that people who experience strain may turn to crime for several reasons—crime might allow them to achieve their monetary and status goals, protect positively valued stimuli, escape negative stimuli, achieve revenge against wrongs, or simply to deal with the strain (such as taking drugs to forget problems).

I think that general strain theory is important because it significantly expands the scope of strain theory and—in doing so—it has helped generate new interest in strain theories of crime.

I've explored a number of factors that influence whether a person will respond to strain by turning to crime, including coping skills and resources, social support, and association with delinquent peers [see note 42].

DO-IT-YOURSELF CRIMINOLOGY If you are planning to do research on strain theory or on the causes of crime more generally, first familiarize yourself with relevant literature. Ask yourself whether a particular theory or argument makes sense—does it jibe with your experiences and your observations of others? If not, you may want to suggest an extension or revision in the theory.

Likewise, ask yourself whether the empirical tests of the theory make sense—are adequate samples employed, are all major concepts measured, and the like. It is not as difficult to make an original contribution as you might think.

Go to the **Careers in Criminal Justice Interactive CD** for more profiles in the field of criminal justice.

according to Wilson and Kelling, so is the implied acceptance of crime within a community.

Janet Lauritsen, a criminologist at the University of Missouri–St. Louis, contends that familial control is more important than run-down surroundings in predicting whether crime will occur. Lauritsen found that adolescents residing in two-parent households were victims of crime at similar rates, regardless of the levels of disadvantage in the neighborhoods in which they lived. By contrast, adolescents from single-parent homes who lived in highly disorganized neighborhoods were victimized at much higher rates than their counterparts in more stable locales. In Lauritsen's opinion, the support of a two-parent household offers crucial protection for children, whatever the condition of their neighborhood.[49]

Labeling Theory A third social process theory, **labeling theory**, focuses on perceptions of criminal behavior rather than the behavior itself. Labeling theorists study how being labeled a criminal—a "whore," or a "junkie," or a "thief"—affects that person's future behavior. Sociologist Howard Becker contends that deviance is

> a consequence of the application by others of rules and sanctions to an offender. The deviant is one to whom that label has successfully been applied; deviant behavior is behavior that people so label.[50]

Such labeling, some criminologists believe, becomes a self-fulfilling prophecy. Someone labeled a "junkie" will begin to consider himself or herself a deviant and continue the criminal behavior for which he or she has been labeled. Following this line of reasoning, the criminal justice system is engaged in artificially creating a class of criminals by labeling victimless crimes such as drug use, prostitution, and gambling as "criminal."

Social Process Theory and Public Policy Because adult criminals are seen as too "hardened" to unlearn their criminal behavior, crime prevention policies associated with social process theory focus on juvenile offenders. Many youths, for example, are diverted from the formal juvenile justice process to keep them from being labeled "delinquent." Furthermore, many schools have implemented programs

Labeling Theory The hypothesis that society creates crime and criminals by labeling certain behavior and certain people as deviant. The stigma that results from this social process excludes a person from the community, thereby increasing the chances that she or he will adopt the label as her or his identity and engage in a pattern of criminal behavior.

At first glance, the reason people use drugs is obvious: the substances give the user pleasure and provide a temporary escape for those who may feel tension or anxiety. Ultimately, however, such explanations are unsatisfactory because they fail to explain why some people use drugs while others do not. Earlier in this chapter, we noted how trait theory accounts for the problem of drug abuse. Here, we see how other theories discussed in this chapter explain why people begin to use drugs in the first place.

Social Disorganization Theory

Hypothesis: The breakdown of community rules and norms can cause people to become disaffiliated from mainstream society, leading to drug use as a means of rejecting that society

Control Theory

Hypothesis: Lack of the social control provided by the family or school leads to unregulated behavior and antisocial activity such as drug use.

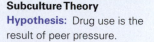

Subculture Theory

Hypothesis: Drug use is the result of peer pressure.

Learning Theory

Hypothesis: Experienced drug users teach beginners (1) the techniques of drug use, (2) how to perceive the pleasurable effects of drug use, and (3) how to enjoy the social experience of taking drugs.

that attempt to steer children away from crime by encouraging them to "just say no" to drugs and stay in school. As we shall see in Chapter 6, implementation of Wilson and Kelling's "broken windows" principles has been credited with lowering the violent crime rate in New York and a number of other major cities.

SOCIAL CONFLICT THEORIES

A more recent movement in criminology focuses not on psychology, biology, or sociology, but on *power*. Those who identify power—seen as the ability of one person or group of persons to control the economic and social positions of other people or groups—as the key component in explaining crime entered the mainstream of American criminology during the 1960s. These theorists saw social ills such as poverty, racism, sexism, and destruction of the environment as the "true crimes," perpetrated by the powerful, or ruling, classes. Burglary, robbery, and even violent crimes were considered reactions by the powerless against laws that were meant to repress, not protect, them. Supporters of these ideas aligned themselves with Marxist, radical, conflict, and feminist schools of criminology. Collectively, they have constructed the **social conflict theories** of crime causation.

Marxism versus Capitalism The genesis of social conflict theory can be found in the political philosophy of Karl Marx (1818–1883). Though he did not concentrate on crime in his writings, Marx's belief that a capitalist economic system necessarily produces income inequality and leads to exploitation of the working classes has been adopted by social conflict theorists.[51] These criminologists generally hold that crime is the natural result of class inequality as identified by Marx.

For this reason, social conflict theory is often associated with a critique of our capitalist economic system. Capitalism is seen as leading to high levels of violence and crime because of the disparity of income that results. The poor commit property crimes for reasons of need and because, as members of a capitalist society, they desire the same financial rewards as everybody else. They commit violent crimes because of the frustration and rage they feel when these rewards seem unattainable. Laws, instead of reflecting the values of society as a whole, reflect only the values of the segment of society that has achieved power and is willing to use the criminal justice system as a tool to keep that power.[52] Thus, the harsh penalties for "lower-class" crimes such as burglary can be seen as a means of protecting the privileges of the "haves" from the aspirations of the "have-nots."

The Social Reality of Crime It is important to note that, according to social conflict theory, power is not synonymous with wealth. Women and members of minority groups can be wealthy and yet still be disassociated from the benefits of

Social Conflict Theories A school of criminology that views criminal behavior as the result of class conflict. Certain behavior is labeled illegal not because it is inherently criminal, but because the ruling class has an economic or social interest in restricting such behavior in order to protect the status quo.

◄ Cincinnati police prepare to confront street protesters following the fatal shooting of a nineteen-year-old African American named Timothy Thomas. The police officer who killed Thomas was attempting to arrest him for an outstanding warrant involving traffic violations. If you were a proponent of social conflict theory, how would you interpret Thomas's death?

The Cincinnati Enquirer/Steven M. Herppich

power in our society. Richard Quinney, one of the most influential social conflict theorists of the past thirty years, encompasses issues of race, gender, power, and crime in a theory known as the **social reality of crime**.[53] For Quinney, along with many of his peers, criminal law does not reflect a universal moral code, but instead is a set of "rules" through which those who hold power can control and subdue those who do not. Any conflict between the "haves" and the "have-nots," therefore, is bound to be decided in favor of the "haves," who make the law and control the criminal justice system. Following this reasoning, Quinney sees violations of the law not as inherently criminal acts, but rather as political ones—as revolutionary acts against the power of the state.

> "The common argument that crime is caused by poverty is a kind of slander on the poor."
>
> —H. L. Mencken, American journalist (1956)

Thinking along racial lines, many observers would assert that African Americans as a group have been "have-nots" since the colonial period. Today, the median income of an African American family is nearly $20,000 less than that of a non-Hispanic Caucasian family.[54] In 2007, only four of the nation's five hundred most profitable companies had a black chief executive. Similarly, women have run up against what has been called the "glass ceiling" as they attempt to assume positions of power in corporations: only nine major U.S. corporations have a female chief executive. Furthermore, those women most likely to be arrested and imprisoned have exactly the characteristics—low income, often raising children without the aid of a partner—that social conflict theorists would predict.

Those who perceive the criminal justice system as an instrument of social control point to a number of historical studies and statistics to support their argument. In the nineteenth century, nearly three-quarters of female inmates had been incarcerated for sexual misconduct; they were sent to institutions such as New York's Western House of Refuge at Albion to be taught the virtues of "true" womanhood.[55] Today, approximately 90,000 women are arrested each year for prostitution. After the Civil War, many African Americans were driven from the South by "Jim Crow laws" designed to keep them from attaining power in the postwar period. Today, the criminal justice system performs a similar function. One out of every eight black men in their twenties is in prison or jail on any given day, and African American males are incarcerated at more than six times the rate of white males.[56]

Social Reality of Crime The theory that criminal laws are designed by those in power (the rich) to help them keep power at the expense of those who do not have power (the poor).

Social Conflict Theory and Public Policy Given its radical nature, social conflict theory has had a limited impact on public policy. Even in the aftermath of situations in which class conflict has had serious and obvious repercussions, such as the Los Angeles riots of 1991, few observers feel that enough has been accomplished to improve the conditions that led to the violence. Indeed, many believe that the best hope for a shift in the power structure is the employment of more women and minorities in the criminal justice system itself.

LOOKING BACK TO CHILDHOOD: LIFE COURSE THEORIES OF CRIME

LO6 Over the past decade, a number of criminologists have begun to fill a gaping hole in the study of the causes of crime. As Francis T. Cullen and Robert Agnew put it, "throughout much of the history of American criminology, scholars simply ignored the fact that humans have a childhood."[57] Instead, the bulk of research on youthful offending has focused on teenagers.

This emphasis on adolescents has occurred for two very good reasons. First, because adolescents and young adults commit proportionally more crimes than any other age groups, criminologists have tended to focus on what happens during these years. Second, studying the behavior patterns of juveniles into adulthood is difficult enough. Extending these studies back to childhood is an even more daunting task.

Nevertheless, childhood may hold the key to many questions criminologists have been asking for years. The other theories we have studied in this chapter tend to attribute criminal behavior to factors—such as unemployment or poor educational performance—that take place long after an individual's personality has been established. Practitioners of **life course criminology** believe that lying, stealing, bullying, and other conduct problems that occur in childhood are the strongest predictors of future criminal behavior and have been seriously undervalued in the examination of why crime occurs.[58]

Self-Control Theory Focusing on childhood behavior raises the question of whether conduct problems established at a young age can be changed as one grows toward adulthood. Michael Gottfredson and Travis Hirschi, whose 1990 publication *A General Theory of Crime* is one of the foundations of life course criminology, think not.[59] Gottfredson and Hirschi believe that criminal behavior is linked to "low self-control," a personality trait that is formed before a child reaches the age of ten and can usually be attributed to poor parenting.[60]

Someone with low self-control is generally impulsive, thrill seeking, and likely to solve problems with violence rather than his or her intellect. Gottfredson and Hirschi think that once low self-control has been established, it will persist; that is, childhood behavioral problems are not "solved" by positive developments later in life, such as healthy personal relationships or a good job.[61] Thus, these two criminologists ascribe to what has been called the *continuity theory of crime,* which essentially says that once negative behavior patterns have been established, they cannot be changed.

The Possibility of Change Not all of those who practice life course criminology follow the continuity theory. Terrie Moffitt, for example, notes that youthful offenders can be divided into two groups. The first group are life-course-persistent offenders; they are biting playmates at age five, skipping school at ten, stealing cars at sixteen, committing violent crimes at twenty, and perpetrating fraud and child abuse at thirty.[62] The second group are adolescent-limited offenders; as the name suggests, their "life of crime" is limited to the teenage years.[63]

So, according to Moffitt, change is possible, if not for the life-course-persistent offenders (who are saddled with psychological problems that lead to continued social failure and misconduct), then for the adolescent-limited offenders. Robert Sampson and John Laub take this line of thinking one step further. While acknowledging that "antisocial behavior is relatively stable" from childhood to old age, Sampson and Laub have gathered a great deal of data showing, in their

Life Course Criminology The study of crime based on the belief that behavioral patterns developed in childhood can predict delinquent and criminal behavior later in life.

opinion, that offenders may experience "turning points" when they are able to veer off the road to a life of crime.[64]

Life Course Criminology and Public Policy As we will see in Chapter 15, the American public often seems of two minds as to how to treat juvenile offenders. The American juvenile justice system was created with an eye toward rehabilitating wayward youths, but in recent years it has become more of an instrument to punish them. Though it is too early to determine how life course criminology will affect public policy in this area, certain patterns are rather predictable. On the one hand, politicians who want to continue to "get tough" with juvenile delinquents will point to continuity theories to promote the view that "once a criminal, always a criminal"—no matter what the age. On the other hand, those who favor rehabilitation will use research such as that done by Sampson and Laub to argue that the juvenile justice system's primary purpose should be to provide the "turning points" that these troubled youths so badly need. (See *Mastering Concepts* on the following page for a review of the theories discussed so far in this chapter.)

EMERGING THEORIES IN CRIMINOLOGY

The six theories described so far form the bedrock of criminological study, but the field is in no way limited to these basic principles. Criminologists such as Anthony Walsh, a professor of criminal justice at Boise State University, are constantly challenging accepted theories on crime with new insights and research. Walsh believes that "biological factors do not operate in an environmental vacuum, nor do environmental factors operate in a biological vacuum."[65] Consequently, he advocates a "biosocial" model of crime, combining aspects of trait and sociological theories to explain antisocial behavior. Other emerging theories in criminology include racial threat theory, convict criminology, and environmental criminology.

Racial Threat Theory Sometimes, criminological theories result from dramatic developments in the broader society. Over the past few decades, for example, increased arrest and incarcertaion rates of African Americans have sparked a renewed interest in *racial threat theory*. First developed to describe the reaction of many whites to the growing social, economic, and political power of blacks in the 1960s,[66] today the theory focuses on the relationship between modern racism and the amount of control the criminal justice system exerts on the African American community. Criminologists have used racial threat theory to explain police use of force against blacks,[67] disproportionate African American representation on death row,[68] and state laws that *disenfranchise* (deprive of the right to vote) those who have been convicted of a crime.[69]

"It is not racism that makes whites uneasy about blacks moving into their neighborhoods . . . it is fear. Fear of crime, of drugs, of gangs, of violence."

—James Q. Wilson, criminologist (1992)

Racial threat theory is based on the hypothesis that as the size of a minority group increases, members of the majority group will perceive a threat to their position and take steps to reduce the competition.[70] This hypothesis has found support in a number of studies that link increases in the proportion of black residents to increases in the size and funding of local police departments, as well as higher arrest and incarceration rates for African Americans in those areas.[71] Recently, however, Karen F. Parker, Brian J. Stults, and Stephen K. Rice produced data that showed the opposite effect: increases in the black population in an area generally lead to *decreases* in black arrest rates. Upsurges in arrests of African Americans occur only when members of this minority group are disadvantaged. Thus, the researchers concluded, majority populations are more likely to enforce social control against poor blacks than against those who have achieved a measure of economic success.[72]

CHOICE THEORIES

Crime is the result of rational choices made by those who decide to engage in criminal activity for the rewards it offers. The rewards may be financial or they may be psychological—criminals enjoy the "rush" that comes with committing a crime. According to choice theorists, the proper response to crime is harsh penalties, which force potential criminals to weigh the benefits of wrongdoing against the costs of punishment if they are apprehended.

BIOLOGICAL AND PSYCHOLOGICAL TRAIT THEORIES

Criminal behavior is explained by biological and psychological attributes of the individual. Those who support biological theories of crime believe that the secret to crime is locked in the human body: in genes, brain disorders, reaction to improper diet or allergies, and the like. Psychological attempts to explain crime are based on the study of personality and intelligence and the development of a person's behavioral patterns during infancy.

SOCIOLOGICAL THEORIES

Crime is not something a person is "born to do." Instead, it is the result of the social conditions under which a person finds himself or herself. Those who are socially disadvantaged— because of poverty or other factors such as racial discrimination—are more likely to commit crimes because other avenues to "success" have been closed off. High-crime areas will develop their own cultures that are in constant conflict with the dominant culture and create a cycle of crime that claims the youths who grow up in the area and go on to be career criminals.

SOCIAL PROCESS THEORIES

The major influence on any individual is not society in general, but the interactions that dominate everyday life. Therefore, individuals are drawn to crime not by general factors such as "society" or "community," but by family, friends, and peer groups. Crime is "learned behavior"; the "teacher" is usually a family member or friend. Everybody has the potential to become a criminal. Those who form positive social relationships instead of destructive ones have a better chance of avoiding criminal activity. Furthermore, if a person is labeled "delinquent" or "criminal" by the authority figures or organizations in his or her life, there is a greater chance he or she will create a personality and actions to fit that label.

SOCIAL CONFLICT THEORIES

Criminal laws are a form of social control. Through these laws, the dominant members of society control the minority members, using institutions such as the police, courts, and prisons as tools of oppression. Crime is caused by the conflict between the "haves" and "have-nots" of society. The poor commit crimes because of the anger and frustration they feel at being denied the benefits of society.

LIFE COURSE THEORIES

Even though criminal behavior usually begins after the age of fourteen, the factors that lead to that behavior start much earlier. Thus, to fully understand why crime occurs, criminologists must better understand conduct problems of early childhood and how those problems lead to or predict later wrongdoing. The most pressing question becomes whether early misbehavior necessarily leads to a life of crime, or whether it can be used as a warning signal to prevent such a future from taking place.

Convict Criminology A second "new" criminology highlights the messenger as much as the message. A group of nearly thirty criminology professors and graduate students who have served prison time are promoting the benefits of *convict criminology* research. These former inmates reject what they see as the antiseptic approach of mainstream criminology in favor of an approach that relies on experience and a comfort level with those elements of society who have committed crimes and served time in correctional facilities.[73] Daniel S. Murphy, a criminology professor at Appalachian State University in Boone, North Carolina, who spent five years in federal prison for a drug offense, thinks that he and other convict criminologists feel more at ease with inmates than traditional researchers do and therefore are more likely to engage them on a one-on-one level. "In some ways it's easier to sit in your office and look at government statistics," he says.[74]

This school of research is primarily concerned with corrections issues, such as the use—or overuse—of incarceration as a crime-fighting tool and the dehumanizing conditions in many prisons and jails. Some critics of the movement find the convict criminologists *too* focused on prisons and prison life, to the exclusion of the other facets of the field that have been discussed in this chapter. In general, though, the consensus appears to be that the unique insights of ex-inmates can only enrich the body of criminological knowledge.[75]

Environmental Criminology What motivates someone to commit a crime? Proponents of *environmental criminology* answer this question by saying, in effect, "Who cares?" Discussions of motivations may be of interest to academics and researchers, but the topic does little to help law enforcement agencies prevent crime. Environmental criminologists focus on the places where crime occurs and the characteristics of those places that make those areas susceptible to criminal activity. They believe that if there is an opportunity to commit crime, someone will eventually take advantage of that opportunity, whatever his or her motivation.[76]

Environmental criminology relies heavily on the *opportunity theory*, which holds that opportunity is a crucial and often overlooked cause of crime. In this context, the opportunity for a potential criminal to become an actual criminal is created by environmental factors such as the effort needed to commit the crime and the risk of being detected and apprehended.[77] So, for example, taking a relatively simple step such as increasing the number of streetlights in a dark neighborhood should reduce the opportunity for crime. According to opportunity theory, a potential criminal seeing the well-lighted streets would doubt that he or she could offend without being noticed.

© Mark Lyons

▲ Criminology professor Stephen C. Richards of Northern Kentucky University is a self-described "convict criminologist." During the 1980s, Richards spent three years in prison after being found guilty of conspiracy to distribute marijuana. He feels his time behind bars provided a "sort of crash course in studying the reality of prisons." What other kinds of "real-life" backgrounds do you think would be helpful in researching and teaching criminal justice topics?

Self Check Fill in the Blanks

Criminologists employ _____, or explanations based on observations and reasoning, to explain the possible causes of crime. _____ theory holds that criminals make a deliberate decision to commit a crime after weighing the possible rewards and punishments of the act. _____ theories of crime suggest that the origins of crime can be found in the body, while _____ theories focus on the disorders of the mind. A criminologist who studies the effect of community or neighborhood conditions on criminal activity is testing _____ theories of crime, while one who concentrates on the influence of friends and family is analyzing _____ theories of criminal behavior. Check your answers on page 65.

Victimology and Victims of Crime

Since its founding days, criminology has focused almost exclusively on one-half of the crime equation: the offender. If you review our discussion of criminology up to this point, you will find little mention of the other half: the victim. Indeed, it was not until after World War II (1939–1945) that the scientific study of crime victims began to appeal to academicians, and only in the last several decades has **victimology** become an essential component of criminology.[78] The growing emphasis on the victim has had a profound impact on the police, the courts, and corrections administrators in this country. Accordingly, Andrew Karmen, a professor of sociology at the John Jay College of Criminal Justice in New York City, has defined *victimology* as the study of "relationships between victims and offenders [and] the interactions between victims and the criminal justice system."[79]

THE EXPERIENCE OF BEING A VICTIM

L07 Although he never used the term *victimology* to describe his work, the German criminologist Hans von Hentig (1887–1974) has been credited with introducing the notion that increased attention needed to be paid to the victim's role in crime.[80] In his 1948 book, *The Criminal and His Victim*, von Hentig described the victim as one of the "causative elements" of the crime, consciously or unconsciously provoking the criminal act through his or her behavior.[81] The theory that the victim played an active role in his or her own victimization continued to dominate victimology for several decades.[82] Starting in the 1970s, however, the "art of blaming the victim" came under heavy criticism, and criminologists began to concentrate on the physical, emotional, and economic damages suffered by individuals as a result of crime.

Taking into account factors ranging from lost wages to medical costs to psychological trauma, Ross Macmillan of the University of Minnesota has estimated that an adolescent victim of crime will lose about $240,000 over the course of her or his lifetime.[83] A number of studies have also shown that victimization results in mental health problems and substance abuse, as crime victims struggle to deal with the psychological aftermath of the experience.[84] Furthermore, data show that the same persons tend to be both victims and offenders, suggesting that being a victim may lead to future criminal wrongdoing.[85]

THE RISKS OF VICTIMIZATION

Anybody can be a victim of crime. This does not mean, however, that everybody is at an equal risk of being victimized. In the late 1970s, criminologists Larry Cohen and Marcus Felson devised the *routine activities theory* to explain the circumstances surrounding victimization. According to Cohen and Felson, most criminal acts require the following:

1. A likely offender.
2. A suitable target (a person or an object).
3. The absence of a capable guardian—that is, any person (not necessarily a law enforcement agent) whose presence or proximity prevents a crime from happening.[86]

When these three factors are present, the likelihood of crime rises. Cohen and Felson believe that routine activities often contribute to this "perfect storm" of criminal opportunity. For example, when a person leaves for work, her or his home becomes a suitable target for a likely offender because the guardian is absent.

Repeat Victimization Cohen and Felson also hypothesize that offenders attach "values" to suitable targets, and the higher the value, the more likely that target is going to be the subject of a crime.[87] A gold watch, for example, would obviously have a higher value for a thief than a plastic watch and therefore is more likely to be stolen. Similarly, people who are perceived to be weak or unprotected can have high value for criminals. Law enforcement officials in southern Florida, for

Victimology A school of criminology that studies why certain people are the victims of crimes and the optimal role for victims in the criminal justice system.

◀ Lisa Elek argues with her mother, Shelly Court, on the porch of their Elyria, Ohio, home. Earlier, one such confrontation turned violent when Lisa struck Shelly. Nearly one thousand teens are charged with domestic violence in Cuyahoga County, which includes the town of Elyria, each year. Why might the actual rate of juvenile domestic violence be even higher than this official number?

example, believe that illegal immigrants in the area have high victimization rates because criminals know they are afraid to report crimes to authorities for fear of being deported.

Resources such as the National Crime Victimization Survey, which you will learn more about in the next chapter, provide "victimologists" with an important tool for determining which types of people are most valued as potential victims. The data clearly show that a small percentage of victims are involved in a disproportionate number of crimes. This statistic has led many observers to champion an approach to crime analysis known as **repeat victimization.** This theory is based on the premise that certain people are more likely to be victims of crimes than others and, therefore, past victimization is a strong predictor of future victimization.[88]

Factors of Victimization As ■ Figure 2.3 on the following page shows, certain demographic groups—particularly young, low-income African Americans—are statistically more vulnerable than others. Without suggesting that these groups cause their own victimization, criminologists can explore how aspects of an individual's life affect the possibility of being a crime victim. In this section, we will expand on the raw data of Figure 2.3 by looking closer at three factors of victimization: family, alcohol, and gender.

Family and Victimization According to the federal government, **domestic violence**—or violence that occurs between family members or members of the same household—accounts for about 11 percent of all violent crime.[89] Even though these figures take unreported crimes into account, the figure is probably still too low. Because of the shame and stigma that come with domestic violence, its victims are often reluctant to report its incidence to the authorities.

Certain family relationships create a high risk for victimization. Children in homes where one parent or guardian batters the other are more likely to be physically abused themselves, either within or outside the home. Furthermore, the emotional trauma of living in a violent household increases the probability that these children will develop personality disorders associated with victimization. In

Repeat Victimization The theory that certain people and places are more likely to be subject to criminal activity and that past victimization is therefore a valuable crime prevention tool because it is a strong indicator of future victimization.

Domestic Violence The act of willful neglect or physical violence that occurs within a familial or other intimate relationship.

■ Figure 2.3 Crime Victims in the United States

According to the U.S. Department of Justice, African Americans, households with annual incomes of less than $7,500, and young people between the ages of twelve and fifteen are most likely to be victims of violent crime in this country.

Source: Bureau of Justice Statistics, *Criminal Victimization, 2005* (Washington, D.C.: U.S. Department of Justice, September 2006), 4, 6.

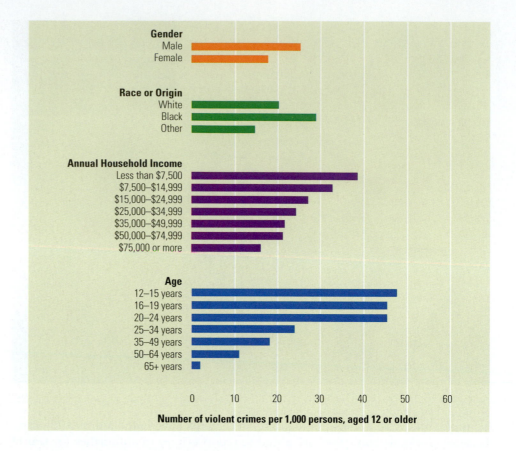

keeping with control theory, discussed earlier in the chapter, households that are characterized by a lack of supervision also create an unsafe environment for the children who live there.[90]

Alcohol and Victimization In the introduction to this chapter, we discussed the differences between correlations and causes. Due to the complexities of their field, criminologists are usually reluctant to declare that any one factor causes a certain result. Richard B. Felson and Keri B. Burchfield of Penn State University, however, believe that alcohol consumption has a causal effect on victimization under certain circumstances.[91] After examining victimization surveys, Felson and Burchfield found that "frequent and heavy drinkers" are at a great risk of assault when they are drinking, but do not show abnormal rates of victimization when they are sober. The authors hypothesize that drinking causes aggressive and offensive behavior, particularly in intoxicated men, which in turn triggers violent reactions in those around them.

Women and Victimization The discipline of victimology has been particularly informative in expanding the knowledge of female victims of crime. Although female offending rates are on the rise, the vast majority of offenders are men. Consequently, traditional criminology has centered primarily on male criminal behavior. As Figure 2.3 shows, however, victimization rates of men and women are comparable. In certain circumstances, women are more at risk: nearly three-fourths of domestic violence victims are women.[92] As a consequence, criminologists have produced a wide range of studies concerning female victims.

The research conducted by Felson and Burchfield, for example, shows that the relationship between alcohol and sexual assault is unaffected by the gender of the victim.[93] These findings are somewhat at odds with a tenet of social conflict

LO8

theory, which holds that men are motivated to rape drunk women to punish them for socially unacceptable ("unladylike") behavior such as drinking heavily. Rather, alcohol affects judgment and leads to risky behavior by both male and female victims of sexual assault.

A study published by Janet L. Lauritsen and Robin J. Schaum of the University of Missouri–St. Louis has similarly expanded our understanding of women at risk of violent crime.[94] Though much research has focused on the victim's race, ethnicity, or economic status, Lauritsen and Schaum believe that family structure and the family composition of a community may provide more consistent clues to the actual threat of violence faced by women. They found that young women who are raising children without the help of a partner and who live in communities with a higher concentration of other single-mother households suffer consistently elevated victimization rates, regardless of their race or income level. Lauritsen and Schaum's results may be partly explained by the difficulty these women have in forming the community ties that, in the eyes of social disorganization theorists, help protect individuals against crime.

▲ Nell Rankins, whose daughter was murdered, holds a candle at the Victims of Crime and Leniency vigil on the steps of the Public Safety Building in Montgomery, Alabama. What have been some of the results of these kinds of efforts to give victims and their families a greater voice in the criminal justice system?

PROTECTING VICTIMS' RIGHTS

L09 Female victims of crime, particularly sexual assault, have been integral to perhaps the most remarkable aspect of victimology: its transformation from a solely academic discipline to the basis for a political movement.[95] Historically, victims of crime were virtually absent from the criminal justice system. Once the crime was committed, the victim's role in the process was generally limited to appearing as a witness for the prosecution. In criminal trials, the state brings charges against the defendant "in the name of the people," effectively reducing the victim to an afterthought. "[T]he purpose of the criminal trial is not to stand by the victim," says Stephen J. Schulhofer, a professor at the New York University School of Law. "The purpose of the trial is to determine whether the defendant is factually and legally responsible for an offense."[96]

The Victims' Rights Movement A large number of Americans, particularly victims themselves, do not agree with Schulhofer. Advocates of victims' rights speak of *system revictimization,* a term used to describe the frustration of victims.[97] "The system saw me as a piece of evidence, like a fingerprint or a photograph, not as a feeling, thinking human being," said one rape victim.[98] Indeed, the modern victims' rights movement began with the opening of rape-crisis centers by feminist groups in the early 1970s. Since then, hundreds of grassroots organizations have been formed to deal with the needs of victims. Some, such as Parents of Murdered Children, are primarily concerned with the emotional state of victims. Others, such as Mothers Against Drunk Driving, concentrate on lobbying legislators for victims' rights laws.

State Laws Much of this effort has focused on state-level protection, and the impact has been impressive. State legislators have passed nearly 30,000 victim-related laws over the past twenty years, and thirty-two state constitutions now include protections for the rights of crime victims.[99] These laws generally focus on three areas:

- Enabling the victim to receive restitution from the person who committed the crime.
- Allowing the victim to participate in the criminal prosecution and sentencing of the offender (a topic we will explore in Chapters 9 and 11).

See the **National Organization for Victim Assistance,** an advocacy organization for victims' rights. Find its Web site by clicking on *Web Links* under *Chapter Resources* at **www.cjinaction.com**.

- Protecting the victim from harassment or abuse from the criminal justice process (such as intrusive interviews by the police).[100]

This legislation often gives the victim a legal ground on which to challenge the actions of police, judges, and corrections officials. In Arizona, for example, a state parole board granted a rapist parole without notifying his victim of the parole hearing. The woman challenged the decision, noting that the state constitution gave her the right to be present at any such proceeding. Citing this failure to notify the victim, the Arizona Supreme Court ordered a new parole hearing at which she was given a chance to tell her "side of the story." The parole decision was reversed, and the offender was sent back to prison.[101]

Federal Laws Despite decisions such as the Arizona parole board's reversal, many observers feel that state laws do not go far enough in protecting victims' rights. A large-scale study carried out by federal government researchers found that these laws are not consistently observed. Even in states with "strong" legislative protections for victims, 62 percent of victims were not notified when their offender was released from jail before trial, and 45 percent were not notified of their offender's sentencing hearing. In states with "weak" protections, the percentages were significantly higher.[102]

Many victims' advocates feel that the U.S. Constitution is at the root of the problem. Though the Constitution provides numerous rights for criminal defendants, its articles and amendments never mention crime victims. A long and intense effort to insert a Victims' Rights Amendment into the Constitution was finally abandoned in 2004, defeated by concerns that the amendment would place "enormous new burdens" on law enforcement agencies and possibly make it more difficult for the criminal justice system to effectively punish wrongdoers.[103] Even those who favor more rights for victims also worried that an amendment would impinge on the constitutional rights of the accused to a fair trial, a subject we will study in more detail in Chapter 10.

Instead, supporters of the amendment had to settle for new federal legislation that President George W. Bush signed into law on October 31, 2004.[104] The statute gives victims of violent crime a core set of procedural rights in federal courts, including the right to be "reasonably protected" from the accused offender, the right to be involved in all public proceedings concerning the victim, and the right to "be treated with fairness and with respect for the victim's dignity and privacy." (For a discussion of how one European country has dealt with this issue, see the feature *International CJ—Victims' Rights in Germany.*)

Self Check Fill in the Blanks

According to statistics, _____ are victims of crime more frequently than members of other races, teenagers are _____ likely to be victimized than those over the age of twenty, and wealthy citizens are _____ likely to be victimized than poorer ones. The _____ movement is a political campaign with a goal of improving treatment of victims in the criminal justice system. The movement's efforts to insert a _____ into the U.S. Constitution have been _____. Check your answers on page 65.

Criminology from Theory to Practice

You have almost completed the only chapter in this textbook that deals primarily with theory. What follows will concentrate on the more practical and legal aspects of the criminal justice system: how law enforcement agencies fight crime, how our court systems determine guilt or innocence, and how we punish those who are found guilty. As our discussion of victimology's influence on victims' rights legislation shows, however, criminology can play a crucial role in the criminal justice

American supporters of victims' rights might well look with envy at the criminal justice system of Germany. According to one German official, the aim of victim protection laws in his country is to "stop a person aggrieved because of a criminal act from being a mere object of the proceedings." Rather, in Germany the victim is "made a player in the proceedings with rights he [or she] can assert [in court]."

Specifically, Chapter Two of the German Federal Code of Criminal Procedure codifies the victim's right to "join a public prosecution as a private accessory prosecutor." In essence, this means that a victim (or, in the case of murder, a victim's parents, children, siblings, and/or spouse) can choose to become a "secondary accuser" in a German criminal trial and receive treatment equal to the defendant's. The victim is permitted to use a "victim attorney," or *Opferanwalt,* and this attorney has the same access to evidence and the same ability to obtain information regarding the crime as the state's attorney and the defense attorney. If the victim is unable to afford an *Opferanwalt,* the government will provide one at no cost.

Initially, critics of this system, known as *Nebenklager,* worried that its costs would be too burdensome for German society. The procedure is, however, limited by two factors. First, it is available only to victims of serious, violent crimes such as murder, assault, kidnapping, and rape. Second, the procedure is optional. So far, only sexual-assault victims have decided to invoke *Nebenklager* in large numbers. In fact, it is now standard practice for German police to inform rape victims of their right to participate in the trial.

FOR CRITICAL ANALYSIS

Why do you think victims of sexual assault have been more likely than victims of other violent crimes to take advantage of the opportunities provided by the *Nebenklager* procedure? In general, could such a system operate effectively in the United States?

---

system. "A lot of my colleagues just want to write scholarly articles for scholarly journals," notes Professor James Alan Fox. "But I think if you're in a field with specialized knowledge that can be useful to the community, you should engage the public and policymakers."[105]

CRIMINOLOGY AND THE CHRONIC OFFENDER

Perhaps the most useful criminological contribution to crime fighting in the past half century was *Delinquency in a Birth Cohort,* published by the pioneering trio of Marvin Wolfgang, Robert Figlio, and Thorsten Sellin in 1972. This research established the idea of the **chronic offender,** or career criminal, by showing that a small group of juvenile offenders—6 percent—was responsible for a disproportionate amount of the violent crime attributed to a group of nearly 10,000 young males: 71 percent of the murders, 82 percent of the robberies, 69 percent of the aggravated assaults, and 73 percent of the rapes.[106]

Further research has supported the idea of a "chronic 6 percent,"[107] and law enforcement agencies and district attorneys' offices have devised specific strategies to apprehend and prosecute repeat offenders, with dozens of local police agencies forming career criminal units to deal with the problem. Legislators have also reacted to this research: habitual offender laws that provide harsher sentences for repeat offenders have become quite popular. We will discuss these statutes, including the controversial "three-strikes-and-you're-out" laws, in Chapter 11.

CRIMINOLOGY AND THE CRIMINAL JUSTICE SYSTEM

There is a sense, however, that criminology has not done enough to make our country a safer place. Eminent criminologist James Q. Wilson, for one, has criticized his peers for trying to understand crime rather than reduce it.[108] Many criminal justice practitioners also argue that too much of the research done by criminologists is inaccessible for them. As Sarah J. Hart, director of the National Institute of Justice, has noted, an overwhelmed police chief simply does not have

Chronic Offender A delinquent or criminal who commits multiple offenses and is considered part of a small group of wrongdoers who are responsible for a majority of the antisocial activity in any given community.

► A police officer keeps watch over a murder victim in the South End of Boston, a city experiencing increased crime rates and gun violence. Studies conducted by the Boston Police Department show that nearly a third of all persons arrested in the city for firearms charges had one or more prior arrests. Considering the theory of the chronic offender, what steps could Boston law enforcement officials take to reduce their violent crime rate?

the time or patience to wade through the many scientific journals in which crime research appears.[109]

These criticisms notwithstanding, John H. Laub of the American Society of Criminology defends modern criminology's practical benefits.[110] He points out that the work of Clifford Shaw and Henry McKay (see page 45) focused law enforcement efforts on the community, while Travis Hirshi's research in the 1960s on the root causes of delinquency has had a wide impact on the juvenile justice system. As we will discuss further in Chapter 6, Wilson himself (in collaboration with George Kelling) developed the "broken windows" theory, which reshaped police strategy in the 1990s and 2000s. Indeed, in the opinion of many observers, researchers know more today about "what works" in criminology than at any other time in our nation's history.[111]

Self Check Fill in the Blanks

In 1972, Marvin Wolfgang and his colleagues established the idea of the _____ offender, by showing that a _____ percentage of offenders is often responsible for a disproportionately _____ amount of crime. Research on this subject has led law enforcement agencies to focus resources on _____ offenders. Check your answers on page 65.

THE LINK BETWEEN VIOLENT VIDEO GAMES AND CRIME

According to a blog that he kept on VampireFreaks.com, Kimveer Gill enjoyed playing *Super Columbine Massacre,* an Internet-based video game based on the 1999 rampage by Dylan Klebold and Eric Harris at a Colorado high school that left thirteen people dead. On September 13, 2006, the twenty-five-year-old Gill, wearing a black trench coat (as did Klebold and Harris), walked into Montreal's Dawson College and opened fire in the cafeteria (as did Klebold and Harris), killing one person and wounding nineteen others. Gill followed Klebold and Harris, who were aficionados of the first-person shooter video game *Doom,* in one other way. His actions sparked controversy over the possible links between violent video games and violent crime, a topic we now address in this chapter's *Criminal Justice in Action* feature.

THE M GENERATION

Video games—now representing a $13 billion industry—have saturated American youth culture. A recent study by the National Institute on Media and the Family found that 87 percent of all eight- to seventeen-year-olds surveyed played video games. Almost half of this group claimed to have purchased games rated "M" (Mature) for excessive sex and violence, a category supposedly restricted for sale to those over the age of seventeen.[112] Such statistics worry those, including many scientists and criminologists, who believe that exposure to violent video games increases aggressiveness in certain players, leading to antisocial and criminal behavior. This concern is fueled by anecdotal evidence of the link between video games and crime, provided by the actions of offenders such as Klebold, Harris, and Gill.

The Case for a Link between Violent Video Games and Crime

- Magnetic resonance imaging (MRI; see page 42) studies show that, immediately after playing a violent video game, teenagers exhibit increased brain activity in the areas of the brain related to aggressive behavior and decreased brain activity in the areas of the brain related to self-control.[113]

- Research has found that violent video games, especially those of the first-person shooter type, not only desensitize players to real violence, but also train them to commit real acts of violence.[114]

- A consortium of health organizations has concluded that "well over 1,000 studies . . . point overwhelmingly to a causal connection between media violence and aggressive behavior in some children."[115]

The Case against a Link between Violent Video Games and Crime

- No legal authority has found that any of the studies cited above prove that violent video games actually cause crime. At best, they show a correlation between the games and aggressiveness, which does not always lead to violence.

- The studies cited cast video games as an easy scapegoat, failing to account for the many other possible factors in criminal behavior, such as parental control, socioeconomic status, and hormonal imbalance, that have been discussed in this chapter.

- Over the past decade, as sales of violent video games have skyrocketed, arrests for juvenile violent crimes have plummeted.[116]

Your Opinion—Writing Assignment

Since 2000, more than forty states and municipalities have introduced legislation that attempts to restrict a minor's access to violent video games. The courts, however, have stuck down these laws on the ground that video games are protected under the First Amendment to the U.S. Constitution. Therefore, to restrict the sale and use of these games, a government entity must prove a causal connection between the games and real-life aggression by minors. As noted earlier, no researcher has been able to do that.

Do you think that the correlation between video games and violent behavior is strong enough to support laws that restrict a minor's ability to purchase or play them? If so, what issues would you make sure were addressed in the legislation? If not, why do you think such a law is unnecessary? Furthermore, what role should parental responsibility play in this debate? Before responding, you can review our discussion in this chapter concerning:

- The difference between cause and correlation (page 37).

- Social process theories of crime, particularly learning theory and control theory (pages 47–48).

- Life course theories of crime (pages 52–53).

Your answer should take at least three full paragraphs.

www.xbox.com

LO1 **Explain why classical criminology is based on choice theory.** Choice theory holds that those who commit crimes choose to do so. Classical criminology is based on a model of a person rationally making a choice before committing a crime—weighing the benefits against the costs.

LO2 **Contrast positivism with classical criminology.** Whereas classical theorists believe criminals make rational choices, those of the positivist school believe that criminal behavior is determined by psychological, biological, and social forces that the individual cannot control.

LO3 **Contrast the medical model of addiction with the criminal model of addiction.** Those who support the former believe that addicts are not criminals but rather are mentally or physically ill individuals who are forced into acts of petty crime to "feed their habit." Those in favor of the criminal model of addiction believe that abusers and addicts endanger society with their behavior and should be treated like any other citizens who commit crimes.

LO4 **List and describe the three theories of social structure that help explain crime.** Social disorganization theory states that crime is largely a product of unfavorable conditions in certain communities, or zones of disorganization. The strain theory argues that most people seek increased wealth and financial security and that the strain of not being able to achieve these goals legally leads to criminal behavior. Finally, cultural deviance theory asserts that people adapt to the values of the subculture—which has its own standards of behavior—to which they belong.

LO5 **List and briefly explain the three branches of social process theory.** (a) Learning theory, which contends that people learn to be criminals from their family and peers. (b) Control theory, which holds that most of us are dissuaded from a life of crime because we place importance on the opinions of family and peers. (c) Labeling theory, which holds that a person labeled a "junkie" or a "thief" will respond by remaining whatever she or he is labeled.

LO6 **Describe how life course criminology differs from the other theories addressed in this chapter.** The five other theories addressed in this chapter

link criminal behavior to factors—such as unemployment or poor schools—that affect an individual long after his or her personality has been established. Life course theories focus on behavioral patterns of childhood such as bullying, lying, and stealing as predictors of future criminal behavior.

LO7 **Discuss the evolution of victimology from its beginnings in the 1940s until today.** When criminologists first began studying the victims of crimes after World War II, they theorized that the victim played an active role in her or his victimization. This line of thinking remained popular for several decades. In the 1970s, however, victims' rights groups began to criticize the "blame the victim" tendency in criminology, and researchers turned their attention to the experience of being a victim and the victim's role in the criminal justice system.

LO8 **Explain why some criminologists believe the connection between alcohol and victimization is unique.** In general, criminologists are unwilling to say that a factor causes victimization or crime. Rather, they focus on correlations between data and actions. Research has shown, however, that people who abuse alcohol are much more likely to be the victim of an assault when they are drinking than when they are sober. Thus, some criminologists suggest that victimization may be a direct result of alcohol intake.

LO9 **List the arguments for and against greater legal protection of victims' rights.** (a) Those who have been the target of crimes also suffer from "system revictimization" due to the thoughtlessness of the criminal justice system. Even though the majority of state constitutions contain provisions to protect victims' rights, these laws are not consistently observed. Only federal legislation, in the form of an amendment to the U.S. Constitution or otherwise, will adequately protect a victim's interests. (b) Victims are excluded from the trial process because it is designed to determine the guilt or innocence of the accused. Because the defendant is in an adversarial relationship with the government, he or she needs the legal protections provided in the Constitution and elsewhere. The victim is not "on trial," so providing equal protection would only "bog down" the criminal justice system.

Key Terms

Self Check Answer Key

Page 55 i. theories, ii. Choice (or Rational choice), iii. Biological, iv. psychological, v. sociological, vi. social process

Page 60 i. African Americans, ii. more, iii. less, iv. victims' rights, v. Victims' Rights Amendment, vi. unsuccessful.

Page 62 i. chronic, ii. small, iii. large, iv. repeat or habitual

Questions for Critical Analysis

1. What is one possible reason for higher crime rates in low-income communities?

2. If you believe that fear of punishment can have a deterrent effect on criminal activity, to what view of human behavior are you subscribing?

3. If you believe that criminals learn how to be criminals, to what theory are you subscribing?

4. Why have social conflict theories had a limited impact on public policy in the United States?

5. Why is it important for criminologists to study the behavior of preadolescents?

6. Why do some convict criminologists believe they have an advantage over their mainstream colleagues?

7. In what ways does environmental criminology rely on rational choice theory?

8. How can law enforcement agencies employ the premise of the repeat victimization theory to devise crime prevention strategies?

9. What factors contributed to the victims' rights movement becoming politically successful?

10. What is a chronic offender, and why is this sort of person of interest to criminologists?

Maximize Your Best Possible Outcome for Chapter 2

1. **Maximize Your Best Chance for Getting a Good Grade on the Exam.** ThomsonNOW Personalized Study is a diagnostic study tool containing valuable text-specific resources—and because you focus on just what you don't know, you learn more in less time to get a better grade. How do you get ThomsonNOW? If your textbook does not include an access code card, go to **thomsonedu.com** to get ThomsonNOW before your next exam!

2. Get the Most Out of Your Textbook by going to the book companion Web site at **www.cjinaction.com** to access one of the tutorial quizzes, use the flash cards to master key terms, and check out the many other study aids you'll find there. Under chapter resources you will also be able to access the Stories from the Street feature and Web links mentioned in the textbook.

3. Learn about Potential Criminal Justice Careers discussed in this chapter by exploring careers online at **www.cjinaction.com**. You will find career descriptions and information about job requirements, training, salary and benefits, and the application process. You can also watch video profiles featuring criminal justice professionals.

Notes

1. Bureau of Labor Statistics, *National Census of Fatal Occupational Injuries in 2005* (Washington, D.C.: U.S. Department of Labor, 2007), 7.
2. Amy D. Whitten and Deanne M. Mosley, "Caught in the Crossfire: Employer's Liability for Workplace Violence," *Mississippi Law Journal* (2000), 506.
3. Quoted in Anne Fisher, "How to Prevent Violence at Work," *USA Today* (July 15, 2004), 2A.
4. Thomas Capozzoli and Steve McVey, *Managing Violence in the Workplace* (Delray Beach, FL: St. Lucie Press, 1996), 23–24, 26–27.
5. James Q. Wilson and Richard J. Hernstein, *Crime and Human Nature: The Definitive Study of the Causes of Crime* (New York: Simon & Schuster, 1985), 515.
6. Jeremy Bentham, *An Introduction to the Principles of Morals and Legislation,* ed. W. Harrison (Oxford: Basil Blackwell, 1948).

7. Wilson and Hernstein, 44.
8. Jack Katz, *Seductions of Crime: Moral and Sensual Attractions of Doing Evil* (New York: Basic Books, 1988).
9. Quoted in Tim Cahill, *Buried Dreams: Inside the Mind of a Serial Killer* (New York: Bantam Books, 1986), 349.
10. David C. Rowe, *Biology and Crime* (Los Angeles: Roxbury, 2002), 2.
11. "Ex-Supervisor Held Unable to Tell Right from Wrong," *New York Times* (May 8, 1979), A16.
12. L. E. Kreuz and R. M. Rose, "Assessment of Aggressive Behavior and Plasma Testosterone in a Young Criminal Population," *Psychosomatic Medicine* 34 (1972), 321–332.
13. H. Persky, K. Smith, and G. Basu, "Relation of Psychological Measures of Aggression and Hostility to Testosterone Production in Men," *Psychosomatic Medicine* 33 (1971), 265, 276.
14. Katherine L. Wisner, Barbara L. Parry, and Catherine M. Piontek, "Postpartum Depression," *New England Journal of Medicine* (July 18, 2002), 194–199.
15. Robert J. Meadows and Julie Kuehnel, *Evil Minds: Understanding and Responding to Violent Predators* (Upper Saddle River, NJ: Pearson Prentice Hall, 2005), 156–157.
16. *Ibid.*, 157, 169.
17. D. Williams, "Neural Factors Related to Habitual Aggression," *Brain* 92 (1969), 503.
18. Leda Cosmides and John Tooby, "Cognitive Adaptations for Social Exchange," in *The Adapted Mind: Evolutionary Psychology and the Generation of Culture*, ed. Jerome H. Berkow, Leda Cosmides, and John Tooby (New York: Oxford University Press, 1992).
19. Lee Ellis and Anthony Walsh, "Gene-Based Evolutionary Theories in Criminology," *Criminology* 35 (May 1997), 229–276.
20. Avshalom Caspi, Joseph McClay, Terrie E. Moffitt, and Jonathan Mill, "Role of Genotype in the Cycle of Violence in Maltreated Children," *Science* (August 2, 2002), 851–854.
21. *State v. Roberts*, 14 Wash.App. 733–744, 544 P.2d 758 (1976).
22. Sarnoff A. Mednick and Karl O. Christiansen, eds., *Biosocial Bases in Criminal Behavior* (New York: Gardner Press, 1977).
23. David C. Rowe, "Genetic and Environmental Components of Antisocial Behavior: A Study of 265 Twin Pairs," *Criminology* 24 (1986), 513–532.
24. Alison Pike and Robert Plomin, "Importance of Nonshared Environmental Factors for Childhood and Adolescent Psychopathology," *Journal of the American Academy of Child and Adolescent Psychopathology* 35 (May 1996), 560.
25. Hervey M. Cleckley, *The Mask of Sanity*, 4th ed. (St. Louis: Mosby, 1964.)
26. American Psychiatric Association, *Diagnostic and Statistical Manual of Mental Disorders—IV* (Washington, D.C.: APA, 2000).
27. David Gottlieb, "Preventative Detention of Sex Offenders," *University of Kansas Law Review* (2002), 1040.
28. Bureau of Justice Statistics, *Substance Abuse and Treatment, State and Federal Prisoners* (Washington, D.C.: U.S. Department of Justice, January 1999), Table 1, page 3.
29. Peter B. Kraska, "The Unmentionable Alternative: The Need for and the Argument against the Decriminalization of Drug Laws," in *Drugs, Crime, and the Criminal Justice System*, ed. Ralph Weisheit (Cincinnati, OH: Anderson Publishing, 1990).
30. Anthony A. Grace, "The Tonic/Phasal Model of Dopamine System Regulation," *Drug and Alcohol Dependence* 37 (1995), 111.
31. Lawrence K. Altman, "Scientists See a Link between Alcoholism and a Specific Gene," *New York Times* (April 18, 1990), A1.
32. James A. Inciardi, *The War on Drugs: Heroin, Cocaine, and Public Policy* (Palo Alto, CA: Mayfield, 1986), 148.
33. *Ibid.*, 106.
34. Robert Park, Ernest Burgess, and Roderic McKenzie, *The City* (Chicago: University of Chicago Press, 1929).
35. Clifford R. Shaw, Henry D. McKay, and Leonard S. Cottrell, *Delinquency Areas* (Chicago: University of Chicago Press, 1929).
36. Clifford R. Shaw and Henry D. McKay, *Report on the Causes of Crime*, vol. 2: *Social Factors in Juvenile Delinquency* (Washington, D.C.: National Commission on Law Observance and Enforcement, 1931).
37. Robert. J. Sampson, "Transcending Tradition: New Directions in Community Research, Chicago Style," *Criminology* (May 2002), 216–217.
38. Jeffrey D. Morenoff, Robert J. Sampson, and Stephen W. Raudenbush, "Neighborhood Inequality, Collective Efficacy, and the Spatial Dynamics of Urban Violence," *Criminology* (August 2001), 517–560.
39. Emile Durkheim, *The Rules of Sociological Method*, trans. Sarah A. Solovay and John H. Mueller (New York: Free Press, 1964).
40. Robert K. Merton, *Social Theory and Social Structure* (New York: Free Press, 1957). See the chapter on "Social Structure and Anomie."
41. Robert Agnew, "Foundation for a General Strain Theory of Crime and Delinquency," *Criminology* 30 (1992), 47–87.
42. Robert Agnew, Timothy Brezina, John Paul Wright, and Francis T. Cullen, "Strain, Personality Traits, and Delinquency: Extending General Strain Theory," *Criminology* (February 2002), 43–71.
43. Philip G. Zimbardo, "The Human Choice: Individuation, Reason, and Order versus Deindividuation, Impulse, and Chaos," in *Nebraska Symposium on Motivation*, ed. William J. Arnold and David Levie (Lincoln, NE: University of Nebraska Press, 1969), 287–293.
44. Edwin H. Sutherland, *Criminology*, 4th ed. (Philadelphia: Lippincott, 1947).
45. L. Rowell Huesmann, Jessica Moise-Titus, Cheryl-Lynn Podolski, and Leonard D. Eron, "Longitudinal Relations between Children's Exposure to TV Violence and Their Aggressive and Violent Behavior in Young Adulthood: 1977–1992," *Developmental Psychology* (March 2003), 201.
46. Telecommunications Act of 1996, 47 U.S.C. Section 303 (1999).
47. Travis Hirschi, *Causes of Delinquency* (Berkeley: University of California Press, 1969).
48. James Q. Wilson and George L. Kelling, "Broken Windows," *Atlantic Monthly* (March 1982), 29.
49. Janet L. Lauritsen, *How Families and Communities Influence Youth Victimization* (Washington, D.C.: Office of Juvenile Justice and Delinquency Prevention, 2003).
50. Howard S. Becker, *Outsiders: Studies in the Sociology of Deviance* (New York: Free Press, 1963).
51. Lawrence L. Shornack, "Conflict Theory and the Family," *International Social Science Review* 62 (1987), 154–157.
52. Robert Meier, "The New Criminology: Continuity in Criminology Theory," *Journal of Criminal Law and Criminology* 67 (1977), 461–469.
53. Richard Quinney, *The Social Reality of Crime* (Boston: Little, Brown, 1970).
54. Carmen DeNavas-Walt, Bernadette D. Proctor, and Cheryl Hill Lee, *Income, Poverty, and Health Insurance Coverage in the United States: 2005* (Washington, D.C.: U.S. Census Bureau, August 2006), 5.
55. Nicole Hahn Rafter, *Partial Justice: Women, Prisons, and Social Control* (New Brunswick, NJ: Transaction Publishers, 1990).
56. The Sentencing Project, at **www.sentencingproject.org/ IssueAreaHome.aspx?IssueID=3**.
57. Francis T. Cullen and Robert Agnew, *Criminological Theory, Past to Present: Essential Readings*, 2d ed. (Los Angeles: Roxbury Publishing Co., 2003), 12.
58. *Ibid.*, 443.
59. Michael R. Gottfredson and Travis Hirschi, *A General Theory of Crime* (Stanford, CA: Stanford University Press, 1990).
60. *Ibid.*, 90.
61. *Ibid.*
62. Terrie Moffitt, "Adolescent-Limited and Life-Course-Persistent Antisocial Behavior: A Developmental Taxonomy," *Psychological Review* 100 (1993), 679–680.
63. *Ibid.*, 674.
64. Robert J. Sampson and John H. Laub, *Crime in the Making: Pathways and Turning Points through Life* (Cambridge, MA: Harvard University Press, 1993), 11.
65. Anthony Walsh, *Biosocial Criminology: Introduction and Integration* (Cincinnati, OH: Anderson, 2002), vii.
66. Hubert M. Blalock, *Toward a Theory of Minority-Group Relations* (New York: Capricorn Books, 1967).
67. Mitchell B. Chamlin, "Conflict Theory and Police Killings," *Deviant Behavior* (1989), 353–368.
68. David Jacobs and Jason T. Carmichael, "The Political Sociology of the Death Penalty: A Pooled Time-Series Analysis," *American Sociology Review* (February 2002), 109–131.
69. Angela Behrens, Christopher Uggen, and Jeff Manza, "Ballot Manipulations and the 'Menace of Negro Domination': Racial Threat and Felon Disenfranchisement in the United States, 1850–2002," *American Journal of Sociology* (November 2003), 559–605.
70. Blalock.
71. These studies are discussed in Ted Chiricos, Kelly Welch, and Marc Gertz, "Racial Typification of Crime and Support for Punitive Measures," *Criminology* (May 1, 2004), 359–390.

72. Karen F. Parker, Brian J. Stults, and Stephen K. Rice, "Racial Threat, Concentrated Disadvantage and Social Control: Considering the Macro-Level Sources of Variation in Arrests," *Criminology* (November 2005), 1111–1134.

73. Jeffrey Ian Ross and Stephen C. Richards, *Convict Criminology* (Belmont, CA: Wadsworth, 2003), 6.

74. Quoted in John Railey, "ASU Professor Has Insider's Insight on Criminology," *Winston-Salem Journal* (September 28, 2003), 1.

75. Warren St. John, "Professors with a Past," *New York Times* (August 9, 2003), B7.

76. Francis T. Cullen, John E. Eck, and Christopher Lowenkamp, "Environmental Corrections—A New Paradigm for Effective Probation and Parole Supervision," in Lynn S. Branham, *Cases and Materials on the Law and Policy of Sentencing and Corrections,* 7th ed. (St. Paul, MN: West Group, August 2005), 236–239.

77. Ronald V. Clarke and Ross Homel, "A Revised Classification of Situational Crime Prevention Techniques," *Crime Prevention at the Crossroads,* ed. Stephen P. Lab (Cincinnati, OH: Anderson Publishing Co., 1997), 17–30.

78. Ezzat A. Fattah, "Victimology: Past, Present, and Future," *Criminologie* (2000), 18.

79. Andrew Karmen, *Crime Victims: An Introduction to Victimology* (Belmont, CA: Wadsworth, 2003).

80. Fattah, 22.

81. Hans von Hentig, *The Criminal and His Victim* (New Haven, CT: Yale University Press, 1948), 436.

82. Emilio C. Viano, "Victimology: The Study of the Victim," *Victimology* (1976), 1.

83. Ross Macmillan, "Adolescent Criminalization and Income Deficits in Adulthood," *Criminology* (May 2000), 574.

84. Scott Menard, *Short- and Long-Term Consequences of Adolescent Victimization* (Washington, D.C.: Office of Juvenile Justice and Delinquency Prevention, February 2002), 2.

85. Robert J. Sampson and Janet L. Lauritsen, "Deviant Lifestyles, Proximity to Crime, and the Offender-Victim Link in Personal Violence," *Journal of Research in Crime and Delinquency* 27 (1990), 110–139.

86. Larry Cohen and Marcus Felson, "Social Change and Crime Rate Trends: A Routine Activity Approach," *American Sociological Review* (1979), 588–608.

87. *Ibid.*

88. Ron W. Glensor, Ken J. Peak, and Mark E. Correia, "Focusing on Prey Rather Than Predators," in *Contemporary Policing: Controversies, Challenges, and Solutions,* ed. Quint C. Thurman and Jihong Zhao (Los Angeles: Roxbury Publishing Co., 2004), 91–92.

89. Bureau of Justice Statistics, *Family Violence Statistics: Including Statistics on Strangers and Acquaintances* (Washington, D.C.: U.S. Department of Justice, June 2005), 1.

90. Meadows and Kuehnel, 13–14.

91. Richard B. Felson and Keri B. Burchfield, "Alcohol and the Risk of Physical and Sexual Assault Victimization," *Criminology* (November 1, 2004), 837.

92. Bureau of Justice Statistics, *Family Violence Statistics,* 1.

93. Felson and Burchfield.

94. Janet L. Lauritsen and Robin J. Schaum, "The Social Ecology of Violence against Women," *Criminology* (May 1, 2004), 323.

95. Fattah, 25.

96. Stephen J. Schulhofer, "The Trouble with Trials; the Trouble with Us," *Yale Law Journal* (1995), 840.

97. Victor-Hugo Schulze, "In the Cold No Longer: A Primer on Victims' Rights," *Nevada Lawyer* (April 2001), 14, 15.

98. Prepared Testimony of Christine Long before the House Judiciary Committee's Constitution Subcommittee, February 10, 2000.

99. David Beatty and Trudy Gregorie, "Implementing Victims' Rights," *Corrections Today* (August 1, 2003), 81.

100. Gessner H. Harrison, "The Good, the Bad, and the Ugly: Arizona's Courts and the Crime Victims' Bill of Rights," *Arizona State Law Journal* (Summer 2002), 531.

101. *Ibid.*

102. U.S. Senate Crime Victims' Rights Amendment Report 108-91 [to accompany Senate Joint Resolution 1], November 7, 2003, 14.

103. Kelly McMurry, "Victims' Rights Movement Rises in Power," *Trial* (July 1, 1997), 12.

104. Justice for All Act of 2004, Pub. L. No. 108-405, Title I, Section 102.

105. Quoted in Timothy Egan, "After 7 Deaths, Digging for an Explanation," *New York Times* (June 25, 2006), 12.

106. Marvin Wolfgang, Robert Figlio, and Thorsten Sellin, *Delinquency in a Birth Cohort* (Chicago: University of Chicago Press, 1972).

107. Lawrence W. Sherman, "Attacking Crime: Police and Crime Control," in *Modern Policing,* ed. Michael Tonry and Norval Morris (Chicago: University of Chicago Press, 1992), 159.

108. James Q. Wilson, "What to Do about Crime," *Commentary* (September 1994), 25–34.

109. Sarah J. Hart, "A New Way of Doing Business at the NIJ," *Law Enforcement News* (January 15/31, 2002), 9.

110. John H. Laub, "The Life Course of Criminology in the United States: The American Society of Criminology 2003 Presidential Address," *Criminology* (February 1, 2004), 1.

111. Richard Rosenfeld, "Book Review: *The Limits of Crime Control,*" *Journal of Criminal Law and Criminology* (Fall 2002).

112. David Walsh *et al.,* "Tenth Annual MediaWise Video Game Report Card" (2005), at **www.mediafamily.org/research/report_vgrc_2005.shtml**.

113. Lee Bowman, "A Way to Lose Self-Control? Violent Games Shown to Have Effects on Brain," *Chicago Sun-Times* (December 4, 2006), 14.

114. David Grossman and Gloria DeGaetano, *Stop Teaching Our Kids to Kill: A Call to Action against TV, Movie and Video Game Violence* (New York: Crown, 1999), 4.

115. Quoted in Kevin Saunders, "A Disconnect between Law and Neuroscience: Modern Brain Science, Media Influences, and Juvenile Justice," *Utah Law Review* (2005), 705.

116. Karen Sternheimer, "Do Video Games Kill?" *Contexts* (Winter 2007), at **www.contextsmagazine.org/content_sample_v6-1.php**.

CHAPTER 3

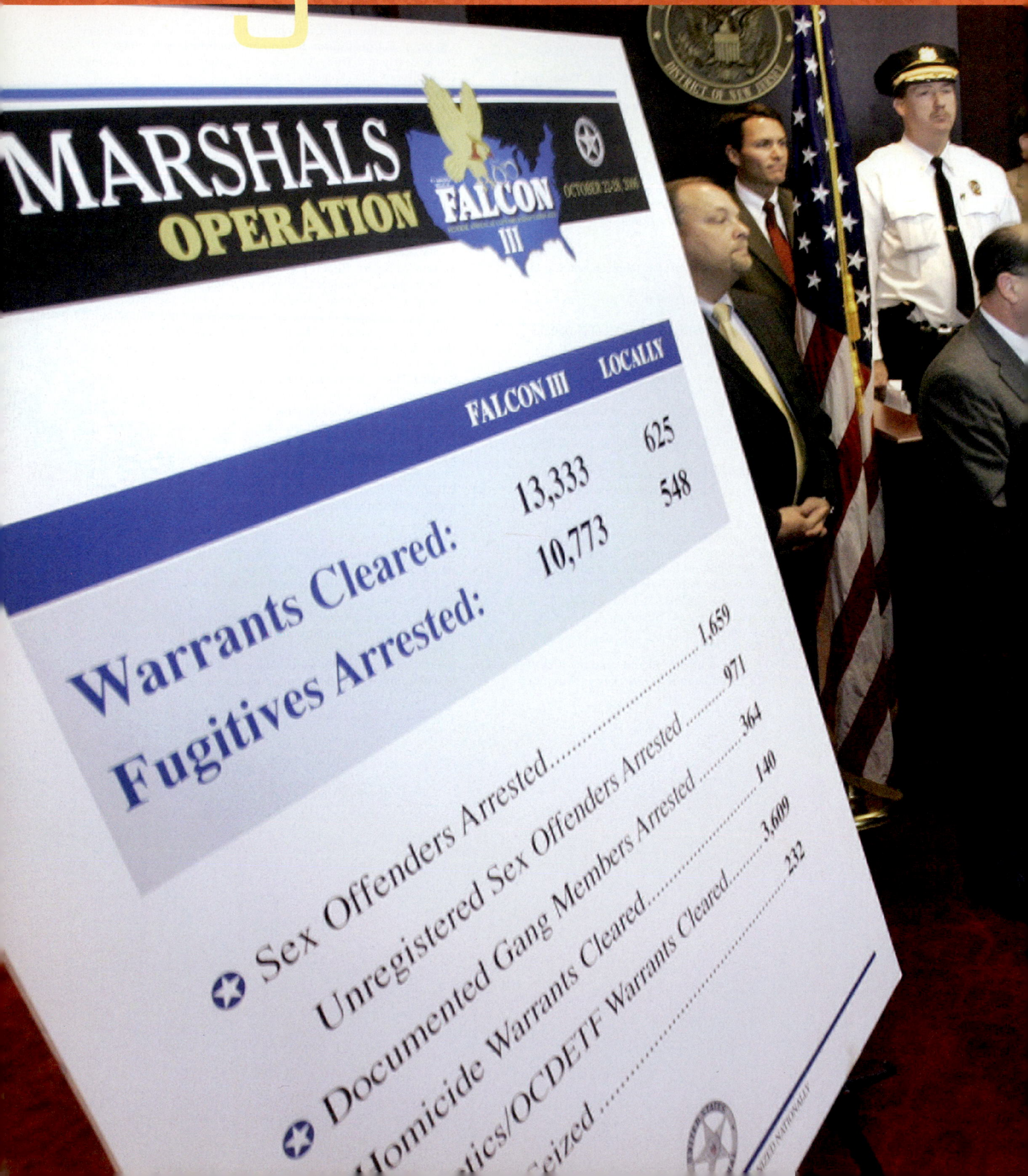

MARSHALS
OPERATION
FALCON
III
FALCON III
LOCALLY
Warrants Cleared: 13,333 625
Fugitives Arrested: 10,773 548
Sex Offenders Arrested 1,659
Unregistered Sex Offenders Arrested 971
Documented Gang Members Arrested 364
Homicide Warrants Cleared 140

Defining and
Measuring Crime

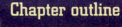

Chapter outline

- Classification of Crimes
- The Uniform Crime Report
- Alternative Measuring Methods
- Crime Trends Today
- Criminal Justice in Action—Legalizing Drugs

Learning objectives

After reading this chapter, you should be able to:

L01 Discuss the primary goals of civil law and criminal law and explain how these goals are realized.

L02 Explain the differences between crimes *mala in se* and *mala prohibita*.

L03 Identify the publication in which the FBI reports crime data and list the three ways it does so.

L04 Distinguish between Part I and Part II offenses as defined in the Uniform Crime Report (UCR).

L05 Describe some of the shortcomings of the UCR as a crime-measuring tool.

L06 Distinguish between the National Crime Victimization Survey and self-reported surveys.

L07 Identify some of the reasons given to explain the high rate of delinquent and criminal behavior by adolescents and young adults.

L08 Explain some of the links between income level and crime.

L09 Discuss how crime statistics explain the rising number of women incarcerated in the United States.

"How often did you think about your family?" Oprah Winfrey asked fifteen-year-old Shawn Hornbeck. "Every day," replied the boy. In the autumn of 2002, Hornbeck, then eleven years old, had disappeared while riding his bicycle in Richwoods, Missouri. On January 12, 2007, while searching for another missing child, police stumbled on Hornbeck in an apartment complex in Kirkwood, Missouri, a suburb of St. Louis. Hornbeck had been kidnapped and held captive by a man named Michael Devlin, and his rescue set off a firestorm of media attention, including the appearance on *The Oprah Winfrey Show*.

"Did you ever write or try to call them?" Winfrey inquired, gently. "No," said Hornbeck. This four-year silence was one aspect of the case that fascinated the public. Another was how Hornbeck and Devlin's Kirkwood neighbors could have failed to notice something suspicious about the pair's strange relationship. Speculation on these matters clogged the nation's airwaves and newspapers. Newscasters and columnists offered helpful hints on "how to keep this from happening to *your* child," and, for the most part, succeeded in scaring America's parents out of their wits.

Lost in the commotion was one significant detail: child abductions such as Shawn Hornbeck experienced are exceedingly rare. Just how rare, however, is a bit of a mystery. Even though such cases dominate the headlines whenever they occur, the federal government does not classify child abduction or kidnapping as a major criminal offense. Consequently, no authoritative national statistics on these crimes exist.

▲ Shawn Hornbeck, right, and his mother Pam Akers speak to reporters at a news conference on January 13, 2007, following his rescue from kidnapper Michael Devlin.

Criminal Justice ⚖ Now™

Maximize your study time by using ThomsonNOW's Personalized Study plan to help you review this chapter and prepare for examination. The Study Plan will

• Help you identify areas on which you should concentrate

• Provide interactive exercises to help you master the chapter concepts; and

• Provide a post-test to confirm you are ready to move on to the next chapter information.

Every year the Federal Bureau of Investigation (FBI) gathers data on crimes ranging from murder and sexual assault to curfew violations and drunkenness. In contrast, over the past two decades the federal government has released only one report on kidnappings, a 2002 study that put the annual number of *stereotypical kidnappings*, or lengthy abductions by a complete stranger, at 115.[1] During the media storm following Shawn Hornbeck's liberation, many observers expressed dismay at this situation. "You only have to think about a comparable situation in public health," said University of New Hampshire sociologist David Finkelhor, who worked on the 2002 study. "If there were some disease killing even a few hundred kids a year, and parents were anxious, you know the Centers for Disease Control would have good statistics."[2]

What difference would "good statistics" make in keeping children safe? In fact, the data that have been collected on child abductions show that a young person is vastly more likely to be kidnapped by a family member or friend than by someone he or she does not know.[3] Therefore, parents would be well advised to supplement the "don't talk to strangers" lessons for their children with advice on how to recognize and avoid specific threatening behaviors and situations. As we will see in this chapter, definitions and measurements of crime are tools that both the police and other members of the community can use to help fight crime. We will start our examination of these subjects with an overview of how crimes are classified, move on to the various methods of measuring crime, and end with a discussion of some statistical trends that give us a good idea of the "state of crime" in the United States today.

Classification of Crimes

The huge body of the law may be broken down according to various classifications. Three of the most important distinctions can be made between (1) civil law and criminal law, (2) felonies and misdemeanors, and (3) crimes *mala in se* and *mala prohibita*.

CIVIL LAW AND CRIMINAL LAW

All law can be divided into two categories: civil law and criminal law. As U.S. criminal law has evolved, it has diverged from U.S. civil law. The two categories of law are distinguished by their primary goals. The criminal justice system is concerned with protecting society from harm by preventing and prosecuting crimes. A crime is an act so reprehensible that it is considered a wrong against society as a whole, as well as against the individual victim. Therefore, the state prosecutes a person who commits a criminal act. If the state is able to prove that a person is guilty of a crime, the government will punish her or him with imprisonment or fines, or both.

▲ On December 30, 2006, actress/singer Brandy failed to notice that traffic had slowed in front of her on a Los Angeles freeway. Her inattention caused the accident shown here, in which Awatef Aboudihaj was killed. While the district attorney's office was determining whether to charge Brandy with the crime of vehicular manslaughter, Aboudihaj's family filed a $50 million wrongful-death civil suit against her. How does this case highlight the differences between civil law and criminal law?

Civil law, which includes all types of law other than criminal law, is concerned with disputes between private individuals and between entities. Proceedings in

L01 civil lawsuits are normally initiated by an individual or a corporation (in contrast to criminal proceedings, which are initiated by public prosecutors). Such disputes may involve, for example, the terms of a contract, the ownership of property, or an automobile accident. Under civil law, the government provides a forum for the resolution of torts—or private wrongs—in which the injured party, called the **plaintiff,** tries to prove that a wrong has been committed by the accused party, or the **defendant.** (Note that the accused party in both criminal and civil cases is known as the *defendant*.)

Guilt and Responsibility   A criminal court is convened to determine whether the defendant is *guilty*—that is, whether the defendant has, in fact, committed the offense charged. In contrast, civil law is concerned with *responsibility*, a much more flexible concept. For example, after seventeen-year-old Benjamin White stabbed thirteen-year-old Casey Hilmer in 2005, a Cincinnati civil jury partially blamed White's parents. Lance and Diane White, the jury ruled, were **liable,** or legally responsible, for their son's actions because they failed to properly supervise or control him.

Most civil cases involve a request for monetary damages to compensate for the wrong that has been committed. Thus, the Cincinnati jurors ordered the Whites to pay Hilmer and her family $6.5 million for medical bills and the "pain and suffering" caused by her injuries. (See *Mastering Concepts* on the following page for a comparison of civil and criminal law.)

The Burden of Proof   Although criminal law proceedings are completely separate from civil law proceedings in the modern legal system, the two systems do have some similarities. Both attempt to control behavior by imposing sanctions on those who violate the law. Furthermore, criminal and civil law often supplement each other. In certain instances, a victim may file a civil suit against an individual who is also the target of a criminal prosecution by the government.

Civil Law The branch of law dealing with the definition and enforcement of all private or public rights, as opposed to criminal matters.

Plaintiff The person or institution that initiates a lawsuit in civil court proceedings by filing a complaint. In doing so, this party seeks a legal remedy to the matter in question.

Defendant In a civil court, the person or institution against whom the action is brought. In a criminal court, the person or entity who has been formally accused of violating a criminal law.

Liability In a civil court, legal responsibility for one's own or another's actions.

ISSUE	CIVIL LAW	CRIMINAL LAW
Area of concern	Rights and duties between individuals	Offenses against society as a whole
Wrongful act	Harm to a person or business entity	Violation of a statute that prohibits some type of activity
Party who brings suit	Person who suffered harm (plaintiff)	The state (prosecutor)
Party who responds	Person who supposedly caused harm (defendant)	Person who allegedly committted a crime (defendant)
Standard of proof	Preponderance of the evidence	Beyond a reasonable doubt
Remedy	Damages to compensate for the harm	Punishment (fine or incarceration)

Beyond a Reasonable Doubt The degree of proof required to find the defendant in a criminal trial guilty of committing the crime. The defendant's guilt must be the only reasonable explanation for the criminal act before the court.

Felony A serious crime, usually punishable by death or imprisonment for a year or longer.

Because the burden of proof is much greater in criminal trials than civil ones, it is usually easier to win monetary damages than a criminal conviction. In March 2005, for example, a California jury acquitted actor Robert Blake of murdering or soliciting someone else to murder his wife, Bonny Lee Bakley. Six months after the criminal trial, however, Bakley's children from a previous marriage won a $30 million civil lawsuit against Blake. In this case, the government had been unable to prove **beyond a reasonable doubt** (the burden of proof in criminal cases) that Blake was responsible for Bakley's 2001 shooting death in a car outside a restaurant where the couple had just dined. Nevertheless, the civil trial established by a *preponderance of the evidence* (the burden of proof in civil cases) that Blake was behind the killing.

FELONIES AND MISDEMEANORS

Depending on their degree of seriousness, crimes are classified as *felonies* or *misdemeanors*. **Felonies** are serious crimes punishable by death or by imprisonment in a federal or state penitentiary for one year or longer (though some states, such as North Carolina, consider felonies to be punishable by at least two years' incarceration). The Model Penal Code, a general guide for criminal law that you will learn more about in the next chapter, provides for four degrees of felony:

1. Capital offenses, for which the maximum penalty is death.
2. First degree felonies, punishable by a maximum penalty of life imprisonment.
3. Second degree felonies, punishable by a maximum of ten years' imprisonment.
4. Third degree felonies, punishable by a maximum of five years' imprisonment.[4]

> "Crime, like virtue, has its degrees."
>
> —Jean Racine, French playwright (1639–1699)

Degrees of Murder Though specifics vary from state to state, some general rules apply when grading crimes. For example, most jurisdictions punish a burglary that involves a nighttime forced entry into a home more seriously than one that takes place during the day and involves a nonresidential building or structure. Murder in the first degree occurs under two circumstances:

1. When the crime is *premeditated*, or considered beforehand by the offender, instead of being a spontaneous act of violence.
2. When the crime is *deliberate*, meaning that it was planned and decided on after a process of decision making. Deliberation does not require a lengthy planning process; a person can be found guilty of first degree murder even if she or he made the decision to murder only seconds before committing the crime.

Second degree murder occurs when no premeditation or deliberation was present, but the offender did have *malice aforethought* toward the victim. In other words,

◀ Police officers sort through the debris of The Station, a nightclub in West Warwick, Rhode Island, that burned down in 2003. One hundred patrons died in the fire, which started when a pyrotechnics display ignited the highly flammable soundproofing foam that lined the establishment's walls and ceiling. In May 2006, Daniel Biechele, the rock-band manager who set off the indoor fireworks, pleaded guilty to one hundred counts of involuntary manslaughter. Why was involuntary manslaughter the proper charge in this instance?

the offender acted with wanton disregard of the consequences of his or her actions. The difference between first and second degree murder is clearly illustrated in a case involving a California man who beat a neighbor to death with a partially full brandy bottle. The crime took place after Ricky McDonald, the victim, complained to Kazi Cooksey, the offender, about the noise coming from a late-night barbecue Cooksey and his friends were holding. The jury could not find sufficient evidence that Cooksey's actions were premeditated, but he certainly acted with wanton disregard of his victim's safety. Therefore, the jury convicted Cooksey of second degree murder rather than first degree murder.

Types of Manslaughter   A homicide committed without malice toward the victim is known as *manslaughter* and is usually punishable by up to fifteen years in prison. **Voluntary manslaughter** occurs when the intent to kill may be present, but malice was lacking. Voluntary manslaughter covers crimes of passion, in which the emotion of an argument between two friends may lead to a homicide. Voluntary manslaughter can also occur when the victim provoked the offender to act violently. **Involuntary manslaughter** covers incidents in which the offender's acts may have been careless, but she or he had no intent to kill. In 2007, for example, Kevin Eckenrode of Philadelphia was convicted of involuntary manslaughter for his role in his girlfriend's fatal fall from a twenty-third-story apartment window. Even though there was no evidence that Eckenrode intended for his girlfriend to slip from his grasp while he was playfully dangling her out the window, a jury felt that he was responsible for her death nonetheless.

Degrees of Misdemeanor   Under federal law and in most states, any crime that is not a felony is considered a **misdemeanor**. Misdemeanors are crimes punishable by a fine or by confinement for up to a year. If imprisoned, the guilty party goes to a local jail instead of a penitentiary. Disorderly conduct and trespassing are common misdemeanors. Like felonies, misdemeanors are graded by level of seriousness. In Illinois, for example, misdemeanors are either Class A (confinement for up to a year), Class B (not more than six months), or Class C (not more than thirty days).

Most states similarly distinguish between *gross misdemeanors*, which are offenses punishable by thirty days to a year in jail, and *petty misdemeanors*, or

Voluntary Manslaughter A homicide in which the intent to kill was present in the mind of the offender, but malice was lacking. Most commonly used to describe homicides in which the offender was provoked or otherwise acted in the heat of passion.

Involuntary Manslaughter A negligent homicide, in which the offender had no intent to kill his or her victim.

Misdemeanor A criminal offense that is not a felony, usually punishable by a fine and/or a jail term of less than one year.

offenses punishable by fewer than thirty days in jail. The least serious form of crime is a *violation* (such as a traffic offense), which is punishable only by a small fine and does not appear on the wrongdoer's criminal record. Whether a crime is a felony or a misdemeanor can also determine whether the case is tried in a magistrate's court (for example, by a justice of the peace) or in a general trial court (for example, superior court).

Probation and community service are often imposed on those who commit misdemeanors, especially juveniles.[5] Also, most states have decriminalized all but the most serious traffic offenses. These infractions are treated as civil proceedings, and civil fines are imposed. In many states, the violator has "points" assessed against her or his driving record.

MALA IN SE AND MALA PROHIBITA

Criminologists often express the social function of criminal law in terms of *mala in se* or *mala prohibita* crimes. A criminal act is referred to as **mala in se** if it would be considered wrong even if there were no law prohibiting it. *Mala in se* crimes are said to go against "natural laws"—that is, against the "natural, moral, and public" principles of a society. Murder, rape, and theft are examples of *mala in se* crimes. These crimes are generally the same from country to country or culture to culture. In contrast, the term **mala prohibita** refers to acts that are considered crimes only because they have been codified as such through statute— "human-made" laws. A *mala prohibita* crime is considered wrong only because it has been prohibited; it is not inherently a wrong, though it may reflect the moral standards of a society at a given time. Thus, the definition of a *mala prohibita* crime can vary from country to country or even from state to state. Bigamy could be considered a *mala prohibita* crime.

A Difficult Distinction   Some observers believe that the distinction between *mala in se* and *mala prohibita* is problematic. In many instances, it is difficult to define a "pure" *mala in se* crime; that is, it is difficult to separate a crime from the culture that has deemed it a crime.[6] Even murder, in certain cultural circumstances, is not considered a criminal act. In a number of poor, traditional areas of the Middle East and Asia, for example, the law excuses "honor killings" in which men kill female family members suspected of sexual indiscretion. Our own legal system excuses homicide in extreme situations, such as self-defense or when a law enforcement agent kills in the course of upholding the law. Therefore, all "natural" laws can be seen as culturally specific. Similar difficulties occur in trying to define a "pure" *mala prohibita* crime.[7] (For an example of how different cultures have different views on crime, see the feature *International CJ—The World's Oldest Profession.*)

The Drug Dilemma   In certain circumstances, however, the *mala in se/mala prohibita* split can be useful in explaining seeming contradictions in criminal law. Take the law's treatment of *stimulants,* which are drugs that act on the nervous system to produce feelings of well-being and euphoria. *Nicotine,* a naturally occurring substance in the tobacco plant, and *caffeine,* found in coffee, tea, and soft drinks, are both stimulants. So are *cocaine,* an active ingredient in the South American coca plant, and *amphetamine,* developed in the 1920s to treat asthma sufferers. Nicotine and caffeine are considered **licit drugs,** or socially acceptable substances, if used in moderation and not by children. In contrast, cocaine and many amphetamines are considered **illicit drugs,** or drugs whose sale and use have been made illegal. The most widely used drug in the United States is *alcohol,* consumed, at least occasionally, by approximately two-thirds of adult Americans.[8]

Mala in Se A descriptive term for acts that are inherently wrong, regardless of whether they are prohibited by law.

Mala Prohibita A descriptive term for acts that are made illegal by criminal statute and are not necessarily wrong in and of themselves.

Licit Drugs Legal drugs or substances, such as alcohol, coffee, and tobacco.

Illicit Drugs Certain drugs or substances whose use or sale has been declared illegal.

Bridgette does not think that prostitution should exist. "I know there are a lot of women suffering in that business," she says. Her opinion might come as a surprise to her clients, given that Bridgette, who lives and works in Belgium, is herself a prostitute. "I'm making good money," she admits. Part of the reason for her success is that prostitution is legal in Belgium. In fact, about 80,000 people pay for sex every day there, more than go to the movies.

The situation in Belgium is hardly unique. According to the Protection Project (www.protectionproject.org), prostitution is legal (though often heavily regulated) in more than 150 countries, including most members of the European Union. Indeed, in the past several years, both Germany and the Netherlands have passed legislation that treats prostitutes like any other workers, collecting taxes on their sex profits in return for health care, unemployment insurance, and pensions.

In the United States, state laws have made the buying and selling of sex illegal almost everywhere. In part, these laws are designed to prevent the

illegal activities that are said to go along with prostitution, such as organized crime, drug use, trafficking in women from other countries, and the spread of sexually transmitted diseases. The main driving force behind the legislation, however, is public morality: prostitution is widely believed to go against America's "social fabric." Indeed, in the seven Nevada counties that have legalized prostitution, criminal problems associated with the practice are almost nonexistent, and thanks to strict testing regulations, the rate of AIDS and other sexually transmitted diseases among registered prostitutes in the state is practically zero.

FOR CRITICAL ANALYSIS

Is prostitution a *mala in se* crime or a *mala prohibita* crime? Explain your answer, and discuss whether the practice should be legalized more broadly in the United States. How does the fact that illicit trafficking in women who are forced into the sex trade is much more common in countries such as the Netherlands and Germany than in the United States affect your argument?

REUTERS/Manuela Hartling/Landov

▲ Molly Luft has been a prostitute for thirty years and operates one of the best-known legal brothels in Berlin, Germany.

Distinguishing between Licit and Illicit Drugs   Why has society prohibited the use of certain drugs, while allowing the use of others? The answer cannot be found in the risk of harm caused by the substances. Both licit and illicit drugs, if abused, can have serious consequences for the health of the user. As many as 450 Americans die of acute liver failure each year because of overuse of the nonprescription pain reliever Tylenol (acetaminophen).[9] Hospital emergency rooms are reporting a dramatic increase in the number of children who overdose on common, over-the-counter cold medicines such as Robitussin, which contain an ingredient (dextromethorphan) that can produce hallucinations and loss of motor control.[10] About 2,300 young people between the ages of fifteen and twenty die each year from alcohol-related motor vehicle accidents.[11]

Nor is illegality linked to the addictive quality of the drug. According to the American Medical Association, nicotine is the most addictive substance, with over two-thirds of people who smoke cigarettes becoming addicted.[12] The next most addictive drug is heroin, followed by cocaine, alcohol, amphetamines, and marijuana, in that order. The drug most widely associated with violent behavior, especially domestic violence, is alcohol.[13] One professor of preventive medicine

■ **Figure 3.1** **Schedules of Narcotics as Defined by the Federal Controlled Substances Act**

The Comprehensive Drug Abuse Prevention and Control Act of 1970 continues to be the basis for the regulation of drugs in the United States. Substances named by the act were placed under direct regulation of the Drug Enforcement Administration (DEA). The act "ranks" drugs from I to V, with Schedule I drugs being the most heavily controlled and carrying the most severe penalties for abuse.

	Criteria	Examples
SCHEDULE I	Drugs with high abuse potential that are lacking therapeutic utility or adequate safety for use under medical supervision.	Marijuana, heroin, LSD, peyote, PCP, mescaline
SCHEDULE II	Drugs with high abuse potential that are accepted in current medical practice despite high physical and psychological dependence potential.	Opium, cocaine, morphine, Benezedrine, methadone, methamphetamine
SCHEDULE III	Drugs with moderate abuse protential that are utilized in current medical practice despite dependence potential.	Barbiturates, amphetamine
SCHEDULE IV	Drugs with low abuse potential that are accepted in current medical practice despite limited dependence potential.	Valium, Darvon, phenobarbital
SCHEDULE V	Drugs with minimal abuse potential that are used in current medical practice despite limited dependence potential.	Cough medicine with small amounts of narcotic

Source: The Comprehensive Drug Abuse Prevention and Control Act of 1970.

has concluded that "there are no scientific . . . or medical bases on which the legal distinctions between various drugs are made."[14]

Society and the Law   If drug laws are not based on science or medicine, on what are they based? The answers lies in the concept of *mala prohibita:* certain drugs are characterized as illicit while others are not because of presiding social norms and values. The general attitude of American society toward drugs has changed dramatically over the past century and a half. With the notable exception of alcohol, many drugs were considered useful, medicinal substances in the 1800s. Cocaine was promoted as a remedy for dozens of ailments. Coca-Cola, introduced in 1886, was marketed as providing the benefits of cocaine without the dangers of alcohol.[15]

As these attitudes have changed, the law has changed as well. Today, licit and illicit drugs are regulated under the Controlled Substances Act (**CSA**), which is part of the Comprehensive Drug Abuse Prevention and Control Act of 1970.[16] The CSA specifies five hierarchical categories for drugs and the penalties for the manufacture, sale, distribution, possession, or consumption of these drugs, based on the substances' medical use, potential for abuse, and addictive qualities (see ■ Figure 3.1). The CSA explicitly excludes "distilled spirits, wine, malt beverages, and tobacco" from the legal definition of a "controlled substance."[17] Therefore, alcohol and tobacco are legal not because they have pharmacological effects that are considerably different, or safer, than those of illicit drugs, but rather because the law, as supported by society, says so.[18]

Self Check Fill in the Blanks

_____ law is concerned with disputes between private individuals and other entities, whereas criminal law involves the _____'s duty to protect society by preventing and prosecuting crimes. A _____ is a serious crime punishable by more than a year in prison or the death penalty, while a person found guilty of a _____ will usually spend less than a year in jail or pay a fine. _____ occurs when a homicide is premeditated and deliberate. If there is no premeditation or malice on the part of the offender toward the victim, the homicide is classified as _____. Check your answers on page 95.

The Uniform Crime Report

Suppose that a firefighter dies while fighting a fire at an office building. Later, police discover that the building manager intentionally set the fire. All of the elements of the crime of arson are certainly met, but can the manager be charged with murder? In some jurisdictions, the act might be considered a form of manslaughter, but according to the U.S. Department of Justice, arson-related deaths and injuries of police officers and firefighters due to the "hazardous natures of their professions" are not murders.[19]

The distinction is important because the Department of Justice provides the most far-reaching and oft-cited set of national crime statistics. Each year, the department releases the **Uniform Crime Report (UCR).** Since its inception in 1930, the UCR has attempted to measure the overall rate of crime in the United States by organizing "offenses known to the police."[20] To produce the UCR, the FBI relies on the voluntary participation of local law enforcement agencies. These agencies—approximately 17,500 in total, covering 95 percent of the population—base their information on three measurements:

1. The number of persons arrested.
2. The number of crimes reported by victims, witnesses, or the police themselves.
3. The number of officers and support law enforcement specialists.[21]

Once this information has been sent to the FBI, the agency presents the crime data in three ways:

1. As a *rate* per 100,000 people. In 2006, for example, the crime rate was 3,808. In other words, for every 100,000 inhabitants of the United States, 3,808 *Part I offenses* (explained below) were reported to the FBI. This statistic is known as the *crime rate* and is often cited by media sources when discussing the level of crime in the United States.
2. As a *percentage* change from the previous year or other time periods. From 2005 to 2006, there was a 1 percent rise in the violent crime rate and a 2.8 percent decrease in the property crime rate.
3. As an *aggregate*, or total, number of crimes. In 2006, the FBI recorded 1,417,745 violent crimes and 9,938,568 property crimes.[22]

The Department of Justice publishes these data annually in *Crime in the United States*. Along with the basic statistics, this publication offers an exhaustive array of crime information, including breakdowns of crimes committed by city, county, and other geographic designations and by the demographics (gender, race, age) of the individuals who have been arrested for crimes.

PART I OFFENSES

The UCR divides the criminal offenses it measures into two major categories: Part I and Part II offenses. **Part I offenses** are those crimes that, due to their seriousness and frequency, are recorded by the FBI to give a general idea of the "crime picture" in the United States in any given year. For a description of the seven Part I offenses, see ■ Figure 3.2 on the following page.

The Part I offense rate is hardly constant. As you can see in ■ Figure 3.3 on the next page, the last two decades have witnessed "peaks" (the early and late 1980s) and "valleys" (the mid-1980s and early 2000s) in the Part I offense rate. As we discussed in Chapter 2, the reasons for these fluctuations are a matter of great debate among those who study crime in the United States; some point to social conditions such as poverty and education, while others see the rates as a reflection of criminal laws and the efforts of law enforcement agencies.

Part I offenses are those most likely to be covered by the media and, consequently, inspire the most fear of crime in the population. These crimes have come to dominate

The **Federal Bureau of Investigation** posts many of its statistical findings, including the Uniform Crime Report. Find its Web site by clicking on *Web Links* under *Chapter Resources* at **www.cjinaction.com**.

Uniform Crime Report (UCR) An annual report compiled by the FBI to give an indication of criminal activity in the United States. The FBI collects data from local, state, and federal law enforcement agencies in preparing this report.

Part I Offenses Those crimes reported annually by the FBI in its Uniform Crime Report. Part I offenses include murder, rape, robbery, aggravated assault, burglary, larceny, and motor vehicle theft.

Every month local law enforcement agencies voluntarily provide information on serious offenses in their jurisdiction to the FBI. These serious offenses, known as Part I offenses, are defined here. The FBI collects data on Part I offenses in order to present an accurate picture of criminal activity in the United States. Arson is not included in national crime rate figures, but it is sometimes considered a Part I offense nonetheless, so it is included here.

Criminal Homicide.
a. Murder and nonnegligent manslaughter: the willful (nonnegligent) killing of one human being by another. Deaths caused by negligence, attempts to kill, assaults to kill, suicides, accidental deaths, and justifiable homicides are excluded. Justifiable homicides are limited to (1) the killing of a felon by a law enforcement officer in the line of duty; and (2) the killing of a felon, during the commission of a felony, by a private citizen.
b. Manslaughter by negligence: the killing of another person through gross negligence. Traffic fatalities are excluded. Although manslaughter by negligence is a Part I offense, it is not included in the national crime rate figures.

Forcible rape. The carnal knowledge of a female forcibly and against her will. Included are rapes by force and attempts or assaults to rape. Statutory offenses (no force used—victim under age of consent) are excluded.

Robbery. The taking or attempting to take anything of value from the care, custody, or control of a person or persons by force or threat of force or violence and/or by putting the victim in fear.

Aggravated assault. An unlawful attack by one person on another for the purpose of inflicting severe or aggravated bodily injury. This type of assault is usually accompanied by the use of a weapon or by means likely to produce death or great bodily harm. Simple assaults are excluded.

Burglary—breaking or entering. The unlawful entry of a structure to commit a felony or a theft. Attempted forcible entry is included.

Larceny-theft (except motor vehicle theft). The unlawful taking, carrying, leading, or riding away of property from the possession or constructive possession of another. Examples are thefts of bicycles or automobile accessories, shoplifting, pocket picking, or the stealing of any property or article that is not taken by force and violence or by fraud. Attempted larcenies are included. Embezzlement, "con" games, forgery, worthless checks, and the like, are excluded.

Motor vehicle theft. The theft or attempted theft of a motor vehicle. A motor vehicle is self-propelled and runs on the surface and not on rails. Specifically excluded from this category are motorboats, construction equipment, airplanes, and farming equipment.

Arson. Any willful or malicious burning or attempt to burn, with or without intent to defraud, a dwelling house, public building, motor vehicle or aircraft, personal property of another, and the like.

Source: Federal Bureau of Investigation, *Crime in the United States, 2006* (Washington, D.C.: U.S. Department of Justice, 2007), at **www.fbi.gov/ucr/2006cius/about/offense_definitions.html**.

crime coverage to such an extent that, for most Americans, the first image that comes to mind at the mention of "crime" is one person physically attacking another person or a robbery taking place with the use or threat of force.[23] Furthermore, in the stereotypical crime, the offender and the victim usually do not know each other.

Given the trauma of violent crimes, this perception is understandable. It is not, however, accurate. According to UCR statistics, a relative or other acquaintance of the victim commits at least 42 percent of the homicides in the United States.[24] Furthermore, as is evident from ■ Figure 3.4, the majority of Part I offenses committed are property crimes. Notice that 58.1 percent of all reported Part I offenses are larceny-thefts, and nearly another 19.1 percent are burglaries.[25]

PART II OFFENSES

L04 Not only do violent crimes represent the minority of Part I offenses, but Part I offenses are far outweighed by **Part II offenses,** or those crimes that can be designated as either misdemeanors or felonies. While information gathered

Part II Offenses All crimes recorded by the FBI that do not fall into the category of Part I offenses. Include both misdemeanors and felonies.

■ **Figure 3.3**
Part I Offense Rates

These data chart the rate of Part I offenses per 100,000 inhabitants in the United States from 1978 to 2006.

Source: Federal Bureau of Investigation, *Crime in the United States, 2006* (Washington, D.C.: U.S. Department of Justice, 2007), at **www.fbi.gov/ucr/cius2006/data/table_01.html**.

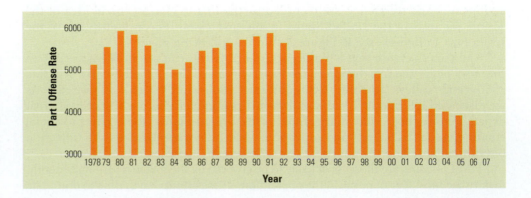

on Part I offenses reflects those offenses "known," or reported to the FBI by local agencies, Part II offenses are measured only by arrest data. In 2006, the FBI recorded more than 2.1 million arrests for Part I offenses in the United States. That same year, more than 12.2 million arrests for Part II offenses took place.[26] In other words, a Part II offense was about six times more common than a Part I offense (for a description of Part II offenses and their rates, see ■ Figure 3.5 on the following page). Such statistics have prompted Marcus Felson, a professor at Rutgers University School of Criminal Justice, to comment that "most crime is very ordinary."[27]

THE UCR: A FLAWED METHOD?

Even though the UCR is the predominant source of crime data in the country, there are numerous questions about the accuracy of its findings. These criticisms focus on the methods by which the UCR statistics are collected by local law enforcement agencies and reported to the FBI.

L05

Discretionary Distortions For the UCR to be accurate, citizens must report criminal activity to the police, and the police must then pass this information on to the FBI. Criminologists have long been aware that neither can be expected to perform these roles with consistency.[28] Citizens may not report a crime for any number of reasons, including fear of reprisal, embarrassment, or a personal bias in favor of the offender. Many also feel that police cannot do anything to help them in the aftermath of a crime, so they do not see the point of involving law enforcement agents in their lives. Surveys of crime victims reveal that only 47 percent of violent crimes and 40 percent of property crimes were reported to the police in 2006.[29] Studies have also shown that police underreport crimes in certain instances, such as when the offense has occurred within a family or the victim does not want the offender to be charged.[30] Also, some police departments may have unofficial policies that keep crime rates artificially low.

Furthermore, the FBI and local law enforcement agencies do not always interpret Part I offenses in the same manner. FBI guidelines, for example, define forcible rape as the "carnal knowledge" of a woman "forcibly and against her will." Although some local agencies may strictly adhere to this definition, others may define rape more loosely—listing any assault on a woman as a rape. Furthermore, different jurisdictions have different definitions of rape. In Alabama, rape occurs only in cases where the woman offers "earnest resistance" to sexual intercourse,[31] and in a number of other jurisdictions, the courts require proof that the victim physically opposed her attacker's advances. A number of jurisdictions have also expanded their definition of the crime to include the possibility that males can be raped.

Clearance Distortions These factors influence the arrest decision, as police officers are more likely to make arrests that can be *cleared*. **Clearance of an arrest** occurs when the suspect is charged with a particular crime and turned over to the court for trial. With law enforcement agents in different jurisdictions operating under different definitions of rape, or any other crime, their reports to the FBI for UCR purposes may be misleading. Indeed, when a police department in Alabama and a police department in Oregon both report a rape to the federal agency, they may not be describing the same act. Given that the UCR incorporates reports from 17,000 different local agencies, varying methods of defining offenses could have a significant effect on the overall outcome.

Overreporting Violent Crime Many observers also believe that the UCR overreports violent crime and underreports Part II offenses. This is partially due to human nature; a triple murder will certainly get more attention from a police department

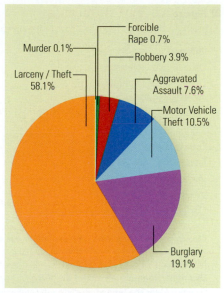

■ **Figure 3.4** Composition of Part I Offenses

Source: Federal Bureau of Investigation, *Crime in the United States, 2006* (Washington, D.C.: U.S. Department of Justice, 2007), at **www.fbi.gov/ucr/cius2006/data/table_01.html**.

Clearance of an Arrest For crime-reporting purposes, occurs when the arrested suspect is charged with a crime and handed over to a court for prosecution.

■ Figure 3.5 Part II Offenses

Offense	Estimated Annual Arrests	Offense	Estimated Annual Arrests
Drug abuse violations	1,889,810	Offenses against family and children	131,491
Driving under the influence	1,460,498	Stolen property	122,722
Other assaults	1,305,757	Runaways	114,179
Disorderly conduct	703,504	Forgery and counterfeiting	108,823
Liquor laws	645,734	Sex offenses (except forcible rape and prostitution)	87,252
Drunkenness	533,188	Prostitution and commercialized vice	79,673
Fraud	280,693	Vagrancy	36,471
Vandalism	300,679	Embezzlement	20,012
Weapons	200,782	Gambling	12,307
Curfew and loitering law violations	152,907	Suspicion	2,482

Curfew and loitering laws (persons under age eighteen)—Offenses relating to violations of local curfew or loitering ordinances where such laws exist.

Disorderly conduct—Breach of the peace.

Driving under the influence—Driving or operating any vehicle or common carrier while drunk or under the influence of liquor or narcotics.

Drug abuse violations—State and/or local offenses relating to the unlawful possession, sale, use, growing, and manufacturing of narcotic drugs. The following drug categories are specified: opium or cocaine and their derivatives (morphine, heroin, codeine); marijuana; synthetic narcotics—manufactured narcotics that can cause true addiction (Demerol, methadone); and dangerous nonnarcotic drugs (barbiturates, Benzedrine).

Drunkenness—Offenses relating to drunkenness or intoxication. Excluded is "driving under the influence."

Embezzlement—Misappropriation or misapplication of money or property entrusted to one's care, custody, or control.

Forgery and counterfeiting—Making, altering, uttering, or possessing, with intent to defraud, anything false in the semblance of that which is true. Attempts are included.

Fraud—Fraudulent conversion and obtaining money or property by false pretenses. Included are confidence games and bad checks, except forgeries and counterfeiting.

Gambling—Promoting, permitting, or engaging in illegal gambling.

Liquor laws—State and/or local liquor law violations, except "drunkenness" and "driving under the influence." Federal violations are excluded.

Offenses against the family and children—Nonsupport, neglect, desertion, or abuse of family and children.

Other assaults (simple)—Assaults and attempted assaults where no weapon is used and that do not result in serious or aggravated injury to the victim.

Prostitution and commercialized vice—Sex offenses of a commercialized nature, such as prostitution, keeping a bawdy house, procuring, or transporting women for immoral purposes. Attempts are included.

Runaways (persons under age eighteen)—Limited to juveniles taken into protective custody under provisions of local statutes.

Sex offenses (except forcible rape, prostitution, and commercialized vice)—Statutory rape and offenses against chastity, common decency, morals, and the like. Attempts are included.

Stolen property: buying, receiving, possessing—Buying, receiving, and possessing stolen property, including attempts.

Suspicion—No specific offense; suspect released without formal charges being placed.

Vagrancy—Vagabondage, begging, loitering, and the like.

Vandalism—Willful or malicious destruction, injury, disfigurement, or defacement of any public or private property, real or personal, without consent of the owner or persons having custody or control.

Weapons: carrying, possessing, and the like—All violations of regulations or statutes controlling the carrying, using, possessing, furnishing, and manufacturing of deadly weapons or silencers. Included are attempts.

Source: Federal Bureau of Investigation, *Crime in the United States, 2006* (Washington, D.C.: U.S. Department of Justice, 2007), at **www.fbi.gov/ucr/2006cius/data/table_29.html** and **www.fbi/gov/ucr/2006cius/about/offense_definitions.html**.

than the theft of a bicycle. There is evidence, however, that FBI instructions to local law enforcement agencies contribute to this situation as well. For example, if police cannot distinguish the aggressors from the victims in a multiparty physical dispute, the *Uniform Crime Reporting Handbook* advises that officers report the number of persons involved as the number of Part I offenses.[32] A barroom brawl involving five people, therefore, may be reported as five incidents of aggravated assault.

The manner of reporting multiple crimes committed by a single offender also skews results toward violent Part I offenses. Under the so-called hierarchy rule, the UCR handbook instructs local agencies to report only the most serious crime if an individual has committed a number of crimes in a single crime "spree." So, if a person steals an automobile, robs a convenience store, and then kills the store clerk, only the murder will be recorded for the UCR.

THE NATIONAL INCIDENT-BASED REPORTING SYSTEM

In the 1980s, well aware of the various criticisms of the UCR, the Department of Justice began seeking ways to revise its data-collecting system. The result was the

■ Figure 3.6 NIBRS Offense Categories

The NIBRS collects data of each single incident and arrest within twenty-two offense categories made up of these forty-six specific crimes, called Group A offenses.

1. **Arson**
2. **Assault Offenses**—Aggravated Assault, Simple Assault, Intimidation
3. **Bribery**
4. **Burglary/Breaking and Entering**
5. **Counterfeiting/Forgery**
6. **Destruction/Damage/Vandalism of Property**
7. **Drug/Narcotic Offenses**—Drug/Narcotic Violations, Drug Equipment Violations
8. **Embezzlement**
9. **Extortion/Blackmail**
10. **Fraud Offenses**—False Pretenses/Swindle/Confidence Game, Credit Card/ATM Fraud, Impersonation, Welfare Fraud, Wire Fraud
11. **Gambling Offenses**—Betting/Wagering, Operating/Promoting/Assisting Gambling, Gambling Equipment Violations, Sports Tampering
12. **Homicide Offenses**—Murder and Nonnegligent Manslaughter, Negligent Manslaughter, Justifiable Homicide

13. **Kidnapping/Abduction**
14. **Larceny/Theft Offenses**—Pocket Picking, Purse Snatching, Shoplifting, Theft from Building, Theft from Coin-Operated Machine or Device, Theft from Motor Vehicle, Theft of Motor Vehicle Parts or Accessories, All Other Larceny
15. **Motor Vehicle Theft**
16. **Pornography/Obscene Material**
17. **Prostitution Offenses**—Prostitution, Assisting or Promoting Prostitution
18. **Robbery**
19. **Sex Offenses, Forcible**—Forcible Rape, Forcible Sodomy, Sexual Assault with an Object, Forcible Fondling
20. **Sex Offenses, Nonforcible**—Incest, Statutory Rape
21. **Stolen Property Offenses (Receiving and the like)**
22. **Weapon Law Violations**

Source: The Federal Bureau of Investigation.

National Incident-Based Reporting System (NIBRS). In the NIBRS, local agencies collect data on each single crime occurrence within twenty-two offense categories made up of forty-six specific crimes called Group A offenses (see ■ Figure 3.6 for a list of NIBRS offense categories). These data are recorded on computerized record systems provided—though not completely financed—by the federal government.

Though the NIBRS became available to local agencies in 1989, eighteen years later only 31 states had been NIBRS certified, with 9 other states in the process of testing the new process.[33] Even in its still-limited form, however, criminologists have responded enthusiastically to the NIBRS because the system provides information about four "data sets"—offenses, victims, offenders, and arrestees—unavailable through the UCR. The NIBRS also presents a more complete picture of crime by monitoring all criminal "incidents" (including kidnappings and abductions, as discussed in the opening to this chapter) reported to the police, not just those that lead to an arrest.[34] Furthermore, because jurisdictions involved with the NIBRS must identify bias motivations of offenders, the procedure is very useful in studying hate crimes, a topic we will address in the next chapter.

Self Check Fill in the Blanks

To produce its annual _____, the FBI relies on the cooperation of law enforcement agencies across the nation. The FBI often presents its findings to the public in terms of a crime _____, or the frequency with which offenses occur for every 100,000 inhabitants of the United States. Although _____ offenses are more likely to be covered by the media, _____ offenses are much more commonplace in the American crime landscape. Check your answers on page 95.

Alternative Measuring Methods

The shortcomings of the UCR have led to other attempts to collect data that better measure crime in the United States. Two of the most highly regarded methods, along with their shortcomings, are discussed below.

VICTIM SURVEYS

Victim Surveys A method of gathering crime data that directly surveys participants to determine their experiences as victims of crime.

Dark Figure of Crime A term used to describe the actual amount of crime that takes place. The "figure" is "dark," or impossible to detect, because a great number of crimes are never reported to the police.

One alternative source of data collecting attempts to avoid the distorting influence of the "intermediary," or the local police agencies. In **victim surveys,** criminologists or other researchers ask the victims of crime directly about their experiences, using techniques such as interviews or electronic mail and phone surveys. The first large-scale victim survey took place in 1966, when members of 10,000 households answered questionnaires as part of the President's Commission on Law Enforcement and the Administration of Justice. The results indicated a much higher victimization rate than had been previously expected, and researchers felt the process gave them a better understanding of the **dark figure of crime,** or the actual amount of crime that occurs in the country.

The National Crime Victimization Survey   Criminologists were so encouraged by the results of the 1966 experiment that the federal government decided to institute an ongoing victim survey. The result was the National Crime Victimization Survey (NCVS), which started in 1972. Conducted by the U.S. Bureau of the Census in cooperation with the Bureau of Justice Statistics of the Justice Department, the NCVS conducts an annual survey of more than 40,000 households with nearly 75,000 occupants over twelve years of age. Participants are interviewed twice a year concerning their experiences with crimes in the prior six months. As you can see in ■ Figure 3.7, the questions cover a wide array of possible victimization.

Supporters of the NCVS highlight a number of aspects in which the victim survey is superior to the UCR:

1. It measures both reported and unreported crime.
2. It is unaffected by police bias and distortions in reporting crime to the FBI.
3. It does not rely on victims directly reporting crime to the police.[35]

Most important, some supporters say, is that the NCVS gives victims a voice in the criminal justice process.

■ **Figure 3.7 Sample Questions from the NCVS (National Crime Victimization Survey)**

36a. **Was something belonging to YOU stolen, such as:**

   a. Things that you carry, like luggage, a wallet, purse, briefcase, book—
   b. Clothing, jewelry, or cell phone—
   c. Bicycle or sports equipment—
   d. Things in your home—like a TV, stereo, or tools—
   e. Things from outside your home, such as a garden hose or lawn furniture—
   f. Things belonging to children in the household—
   g. Things from a vehicle, such as a package, groceries, camera, or CDs—
   h. Did anyone ATTEMPT to steal anything belonging to you?

41a. **Has anyone attacked or threatened you in any of these ways:**

   a. With any weapon, for instance, a gun or knife—
   b. With anything like a baseball bat, frying pan, scissors, or stick—
   c. By something thrown, such as a rock or bottle—
   d. Include any grabbing, punching, or choking,
   e. Any rape, attempted rape, or other type of sexual attack—
   f. Any face-to-face threats—OR
   g. Any attack or threat or use of force by anyone at all? Please mention it even if you are not certain it was a crime.

42a. **People often don't think of incidents committed by someone they know. Other than the incidents already mentioned, did you have something stolen from you OR were you attacked or threatened by:**

   a. Someone at work or school—
   b. A neighbor or friend—
   c. A relative or family member—
   d. Any other person you've met or known?

43a. **Incidents involving forced or unwanted sexual acts are often difficult to talk about. Have you been forced or coerced to engage in unwanted sexual activity by—**

   a. someone you didn't know before—
   b. a casual acquaintance—OR
   c. someone you know well?

44a. **During the last 6 months (other than any incidents already mentioned), did you call the police to report something that happened to YOU which you thought was a crime?**

45a. **During the last 6 months (other than any incidents already mentioned), did anything which you thought was a crime happen to YOU, but you did NOT report to the police?**

Source: U.S. Department of Justice, *National Crime Victimization Survey 2006* (Washington, D.C.: Bureau of Justice Statistics, 2007).

Reliability of the NCVS Even supporters of the NCVS would not, however, claim that the process is infallible. For one thing, there is no guarantee that those who answer the questionnaire will do so accurately. For reasons of shame, forgetfulness, or fear of reprisal, a participant may not give a completely true picture of her or his recent history. Also, as with any survey research, the manner in which the questions are asked can have a distorting effect on the answers.[36] Consider the following two questions:

1. Have you ever been the victim of a rape?
2. Were you knifed, shot, or attacked with some other weapon? Did someone try to attack you in some other way?

The second question is, in fact, one that the NCVS has used in the past to measure rape. Surveyors expected, or hoped, that victims of rape would answer accordingly, as they had been "attacked in some other way." On the one hand, the first question was more direct and may have elicited more "yes" answers. On the other hand, because of the stigma attached to the word *rape*, it may have discouraged participants from answering truthfully. As a result of complaints that the vagueness of the second question led rape to be seriously underreported in the NCVS, in the early 1990s the surveyors altered their methods of gaining information concerning sexual assaults (see Question 43a of the revised version in Figure 3.7).

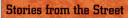
Stories from the Street
Go to the Stories from the Street feature at **www.cjinaction.com** to hear Larry Gaines tell insightful stories related to this chapter and his experiences in the field.

Further Drawbacks of Victim Surveys Victim surveys also present a number of other potential problems. Many citizens are not well versed in the terminology of criminal justice, and a person may not know, for example, that a break-in that occurred at her home while she was at the movies is a burglary and not a robbery. (Remember that *burglary* refers to breaking into a structure with the intention to commit a felony, whereas *robbery* is the illegal taking of property using force or the threat of force.) There are also a number of crimes that victim surveys cannot record, such as drug use or gambling, for legal reasons, and murder, for more obvious ones.

SELF-REPORTED SURVEYS

Based on many of the same principles as victim surveys, but focusing instead on offenders, **self-reported surveys** are a third source of data for criminologists. In this form of data collection, persons are asked directly—through personal interviews or questionnaires, or over the telephone—about specific criminal activity to which they may have been a party. Though not implemented on the scale of the UCR or NCVS, self-reported surveys are most useful in situations in which the group to be studied is already gathered in an institutional setting, such as a juvenile facility or a prison. One of the most widespread self-reported surveys in the United States, the Drug Use Forecasting Program, collects information on narcotics use from arrestees who have been brought into booking facilities. These kinds of surveys can often get forthright information from students, as can be seen in ■ Figure 3.8 on the next page.

Such studies can also be particularly helpful in finding specific information about groups of subjects. When professors Peter B. Wood, Walter R. Grove, James A. Wilson, and John K. Cochran wanted to learn how criminals "felt" when committing crimes, for example, they used self-reported surveys. By comparing these results to those gathered from a group of male students at a state university, the researchers were able to draw conclusions on the "high" a criminal experiences during a crime.[37] Another advantage is that self-reported surveys allow researchers to control aspects of the data collection themselves, thereby assuring that race, class, and gender will not bias the results.

Self-Reported Survey A method of gathering crime data that relies on participants to reveal and detail their own criminal or delinquent behavior.

Excerpts from the Wisconsin Youth Risk Behavior Survey

As part of a national effort to monitor health-risk behaviors of high school students, the Wisconsin Department of Public Instruction administers a self-reported survey each year. Some of the questions (without the corresponding multiple-choice answers) from that survey are reprinted here.

- During the past 30 days, on how many days did you carry a weapon such as a gun, knife, or club on school property?
- During the past 12 months, how many times were you in a physical fight on school property?
- How much do you approve or disapprove of people using violence against another person?
- During the past 12 months, did you ever seriously consider attempting suicide?
- During the past 30 days, how did you usually get your own cigarettes?
- During the past 30 days, on how many days did you have at least one drink of alcohol?
- How old were you when you tried marijuana for the first time?
- During your life, how many times have you used any form of cocaine, including powder, crack, or freebase?

Source: Wisconsin Youth Risk Behavior Survey, at **dpi.state.wi.us/sspw/pdf/yrbs05survey.pdf**.

A "Giant" Dark Figure Because there is no penalty for admitting to criminal activity in a self-reported survey, subjects tend to be more forthcoming in discussing their behavior. The researchers mentioned above found that a significant number of the students interviewed admitted to committing minor crimes for which they had never been arrested. This fact points to the most striking finding of self-reported surveys: the dark figure of crime, referred to earlier in the chapter as the *actual* amount of crime that takes place, appears to be much larger than the UCR or NCVS would suggest.

The first major self-reported survey, conducted by James S. Wallerstein and Clement J. Wyle in 1947, queried 1,020 men and 678 women from a wide spectrum of different backgrounds on their participation in a number of crimes. Ninety-nine percent of the participants admitted to committing at least one of the crimes referenced by Wallerstein and Wyle.[38] When alcohol offenses, recreational drug use, truancy, and petty theft are factored in, self-reported surveys consistently show that almost everybody has committed at least one crime in their lifetime.[39]

Reliability of Self-Reported Surveys Again, despite these advantages there are a number of perceived disadvantages with self-reported surveys. A subject's personality or beliefs often affect the manner in which he or she answers questions. If a person sees criminal behavior as something to be ashamed of, he or she may downplay such behavior. In contrast, a person who sees criminal behavior as positive may exaggerate the truth to impress the questioner.

For the same reason that a participant has nothing to lose by telling the truth, she or he has nothing to gain by telling the truth, either. The effects of lying on self-reported surveys can be dramatic. In a self-reported survey of juveniles, researchers Thomas Gray and Eric Walsh tested their subjects with urinalysis as well as asking them about their drug use. Less than 33 percent of the juveniles who tested positive for marijuana also admitted to using the drug, and only 15 percent of those who tested positive for cocaine were truthful about their habits.[40] These types of results have led many criminologists to conclude that self-reported surveys are skewed by many of the same inaccuracies that plague the other collection methods.

Self Check Fill in the Blanks

_____ surveys rely on those who have been the subject of criminal activity to discuss the incidents with researchers. _____ surveys ask participants to detail their own criminal behavior. Both methods show that the _____ of crime, or the actual amount of crime that takes place in this country, is much _____ than official crime data would suggest. Check your answers on page 95.

Crime Trends Today

The UCR, NCVS, and other statistical measures we have discussed so far in this chapter, though important, represent only the tip of the iceberg of crime data. Thanks to the efforts of government law enforcement agencies, educational institutions, and private individuals, more information on crime is available today than at any time in the nation's history. These figures provide a crucial litmus test for the criminological theories discussed in the previous chapter and help us establish a detailed picture of crime trends in the United States. In recent years, they have been pointing in a troubling direction: toward the return of violent crime.

VIOLENT CRIME REBOUNDS

The late 1990s and early 2000s were something of a golden era for anticrime efforts. With only a few exceptions, both the UCR and the NCVS showed consistently dropping crime rates, and, at least statistically, most Americans were as safe as they had been in decades. For nonviolent offenses, this trend has continued. According to the NCVS, in 2005 property crime rates hit a thirty-two-year low.[41] The same good news does not apply, however, to violent crime rates, which have recently experienced their largest increases in fifteen years (see ■ Figure 3.9).

A Potentially Dangerous Situation   As Figure 3.9 shows, our violent crime rates are still relatively low, and a return to the astronomically high rates of the early 1990s is unlikely. Still, as criminologist James Alan Fox of Northeastern University warns, "the potential does exist" that this country could be heading toward a sustained period of increased violent crime.[42]

Some criminal justice experts see this trend as a natural result of a massive law enforcement shift in focus following the terrorist attacks of September 11, 2001. Federal agencies such as the FBI are concentrating on fighting terrorism rather than conventional crime, putting more pressure on state and local police departments. At the same time, resources for those departments have been reduced: in 2006, state and local police received $890 million in federal aid, compared to $2.5 billion in 2001.[43] Consequently, law enforcement agents are struggling to combat three of the primary culprits behind rising violence: guns, gangs, and illegal drugs.

Guns and Crime   In 2006, the Police Executive Research Forum (PERF) released a report detailing the growing violent crime problem in America's cities. The report is awash with information on how guns are fueling a resurgence of violence in this country. Specifically, PERF researchers found that aggravated assaults with a firearm increased 10 percent between 2004 and 2006. In that same time period, the number of homicides rose 10.2 percent and robberies went up 12.3 percent.[44] According to the most recent FBI statistics, firearms are used in about two-thirds of murders and 42 percent of robberies in this country.[45] NCVS data also point to

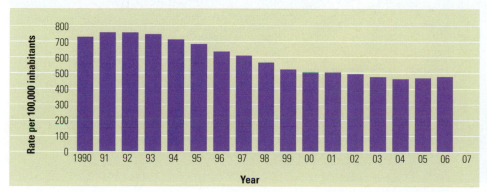

■ Figure 3.9 Violent Crime Rates, 1990–2006

The Uniform Crime Report's violent crime statistics cover murders, forcible rapes, robberies, and aggravated assaults. As you can see, after a steady decline, these rates have begun to head upward.

Source: Federal Bureau of Investigation, *Crime in the United States, 2006* (Washington, D.C.: U.S. Department of Justice, 2007), at **www.fbi.gov/ucr/cius2006/data/table_01.html**.

The issue of guns and crime is widely debated on the Internet. The **Coalition to Stop Gun Violence** offers the pro–gun control view, while the **National Rifle Association** provides arguments against gun control. Find their Web sites by clicking on *Web Links* under *Chapter Resources* at **www.cjinaction.com**.

increased illegal gun use, with the number of victims reporting a violent gun crime rising 43 percent between 2004 and 2005.[46]

For many law enforcement officials, the true impact of guns on the street goes beyond the bare statistics. Boston authorities believe that the city's recent upswing in violence is at least partly attributable to an influx of firearms from Maine, New Hampshire, and Vermont—neighboring states where the gun laws are less strict than in Massachusetts. Philadelphia Police Commissioner Sylvester Johnson says that his city's murder problem is, in essence, a gun problem, also caused by lax regulations.[47] In general, law enforcement officials believe that fewer and fewer murders are premeditated. Rather, these crimes are the result of quick anger and frustration that turn deadly only because a weapon is involved. "We seem to be dealing with an awful lot of people who have zero-conflict resolution skills," says Chris Magnus, police chief of Richmond, California, a city that recorded a 20 percent rise in homicides and a 65 percent surge in aggravated assaults with a firearm in the PERF report.[48]

Gangs and Crime   Gangs, in particular, are known for settling disputes with bullets. Although national statistics on gang violence remain elusive, local statistics highlight the problem. In Houston, for example, officials attribute a 15 percent raise in homicides in 2006 to gang members who moved to the city after evacuating New Orleans after Hurricane Katrina. In Los Angeles, which is enjoying a decline in its overall murder rate, nearly half of all homicides are gang related, as are 84 percent of homicides with victims age thirty-five or younger. The trend extends to smaller cities as well. In Palm Beach County, Florida, 55 to 75 percent of all violent crimes are the result of gang activity.

Like other upsurges in gang violence over the past several decades, particularly in the late 1980s, the latest activity is closely related to the illegal drug trade and the use of firearms to protect that trade. Today, one of every three gangs runs drug-dealing operations, and according to a spokesperson for the Chicago Police Department, the modern street gang is "much more violent than the Mafia ever was."[49] The difference, say some experts, is that more people are becoming

▶ Friends comfort Linda Holmes, second from the right, at the scene of her son's murder in New Orleans, Louisiana. The city experienced 161 homicides in 2006, making it, by most measures, the murder capital of the country. What are some of the factors contributing to a recent upswing in violent crime in many American cities?

Lee Celano/*The New York Times*

involved in gangs for purely economic reasons, rather than for the cultural or territorial motives that have historically driven gang membership.[50] (We will look at why young people join gangs as part of the larger discussion of juvenile crime in Chapter 15.) In addition, the major gangs appear to have "weapons superiority" over most police forces, making it very difficult for law enforcement to control their illegal operations.[51]

Illegal Drugs and Crime   Many observers blamed the explosion for violent crime that shook this country in the late 1980s and early 1990s on the widespread use and sale of crack cocaine. Today, rising murder rates are still seen as a reflection of illegal drug activity. Indeed, Baltimore crime statistics show that about 90 percent of the city's homicide victims have criminal records, typically for drug-related convictions. In other words, as one official commented, "Baltimore is actually a very safe city if you are not involved in the drug trade."[52] Nationally, about 4 percent of all homicides are drug related.[53] In 2006, police made nearly 1.9 million arrests for drug violations in the United States, up from about 581,000 in 1980.[54]

The impact of illegal drug use is much greater than even these statistics would indicate. Drug use appears to be an intricate part of criminal culture. About one-third of all state prisoners and a quarter of federal prisoners were under the influence of illegal drugs at the time they committed the offense that landed them behind bars.[55] Furthermore, 53 percent of state inmates and 45 percent of federal prisoners are dependent on illegal drugs, using the criteria we discussed in Chapter 2.[56]

The Drug-Crime Relationship   Epidemiologist Paul Goldstein has devised three models to explain the relationship between drugs and crime:

- The *psychopharmacological model* holds that individuals act violently or criminally as a direct result of the drugs they have ingested.
- The *economically impulsive model* holds that drug abusers commit crimes to get the funds to purchase drugs. According to the U.S. Department of Justice, 16 percent of jail inmates said that they committed the crimes for which they were incarcerated in order to get funds to buy drugs.[57]
- The *systemic model* suggests that violence is a by-product of the interpersonal relationships within the drug-using community, such as when a dealer is assaulted by a buyer for selling "bad" drugs.[58]

The strength of the drug-crime relationship has provided justification for increased law enforcement efforts to criminalize drug use to punish offenders of controlled substance laws.

Some observers, however, have questioned the conclusion that drug use causes crime. Instead, they believe that the violent and property crimes associated with illicit drugs take place "not because the drugs are drugs [but because] the drugs are illegal."[59] Seventy years ago, when alcohol was illegal in this country, the criminal gangs that controlled the alcohol trade used methods of violence similar to those associated with today's drug gangs. The fact that we

> no longer have drive-by shooting, turf wars and "cement shoes" in the alcohol business [is due to the fact that] alcohol today is legal—not because alcohol no longer intoxicates people, not because alcohol is no longer addicting, and not because alcohol dealers have suddenly developed a social conscience.[60]

The controversial issue of how the criminal justice system should respond to illegal drug use and abuse is the subject of the *Criminal Justice in Action* feature at the end of this chapter.

The Methamphetamine Scourge.   As ■ Figure 3.10 on the following page shows, more arrests take place for the sale and use of marijuana than for any other drug. According to the most recent survey of law enforcement officials, however,

Approximately XX million arrests for drug abuse violations were made in the United States in 2006. As you can see, more of these arrests concerned marijuana than any other illegal drug.

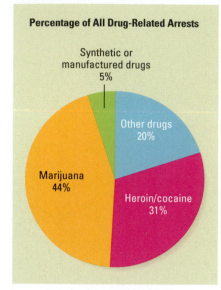

Percentage of All Drug-Related Arrests

Synthetic or manufactured drugs 5%

Other drugs 20%

Marijuana 44%

Heroin/cocaine 31%

Source: Federal Bureau of Investigation, *Crime in the United States, 2006* (Washington, D.C.: U.S. Department of Justice, 2007), at **www.gov. fbi/ucr/cius2006/arrests/index.html**.

Methamphetamine (meth) A synthetic stimulant that creates a strong feeling of euphoria in the user and is highly addictive.

■ Figure 3.11 **Percentage of Arrests by Age**

As this graph shows, the majority of those persons arrested for property crimes in the United States are under twenty-five years old, and more violent crimes are committed by eighteen- to twenty-four-year-olds than by any other age group.

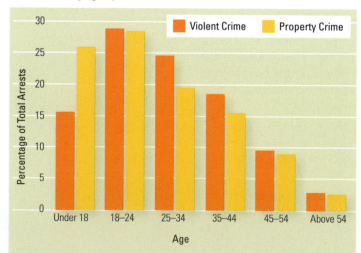

Source: Federal Bureau of Investigation, *Crime in the United States, 2006* (Washington, D.C.: U.S. Department of Justice, 2007), at **www.fbi.gov/ucr/ cius2006/data/table_38.html**.

methamphetamine (meth) is the most serious drug problem in the United States.[61] The substance—also known as speed or crank—is a highly addictive stimulant to the central nervous system. Meth, which can be smoked, swallowed, or injected, produces feelings of increased energy and euphoria but also leads to violent behavior, anxiety, and confusion. It is cheap and easy to make in a home laboratory using the ingredients of common cold medicines and farm chemicals. Consequently, it has become a "scourge" in the nation's poor rural areas.

At the height of the recent epidemic, in 2003, law enforcement agencies seized more than 10,000 meth labs in this country.[62] That number has dropped considerably, as law enforcement efforts against production and sale of the drug have intensified. Nevertheless, rural police forces still strain to combat the crimes associated with meth use such as robbery and assault. In addition, the spread of the drug has had significant secondary effects. Children who have been taken away from parents caught using or making the substance, known as "meth orphans," are overwhelming foster homes and social services in many states.

AGE AND CRIME: THE PEAK YEARS

Officials in Boston partly attribute the recent rise in murders in that city (23 percent increase from 2005 to 2007) to the growing number of young people involved in drug-related gang activity.[63] In fact, the strongest statistical determinant of criminal behavior appears to be age. Criminal behavior peaks during the teenage years. For most offenses, rates are at their highest between the ages of eighteen and twenty-four. As ■ Figure 3.11 shows, criminal activity begins to decline as a person grows older; 85 percent of former delinquents are no longer involved in wrongdoing by the time they reach age twenty-eight.[64]

Criminological Explanations Why is the crime rate dramatically higher for young people? There is no single, simple answer. As already noted, biological theories of crime point to high testosterone levels in young males, which increase levels of aggression and violence (see page 40). Adolescents are also more susceptible to peer pressure, and sociological and social process theories of crime in this area are backed by studies showing that juvenile delinquents tend to socialize with other juvenile delinquents.[65] A recent survey conducted by researchers from Columbia University found that juveniles who were frequently bored were 50 percent more likely than other teenagers to abuse illegal drugs and alcohol, and those who received more than $25 a week in spending money were twice as likely to get high or drunk as those who received less than that amount.[66]

Risk Factors Criminologists call possible sources of juvenile delinquency such as boredom and too much pocket money *risk factors*. Common risk factors cited by those who study juvenile delinquency include poor parental supervision, poor academic achievement, weapon carrying, gang membership, and low intelligence. No single risk factor can predict delinquency, and the consensus seems to be that the more risk factors that are present in the life of any juvenile, the better are his or her chances of offending.[67] As we saw in Chapter 2, life course theories of crime have convinced a number of criminologists to begin searching for risk factors in early childhood, without waiting until a person has reached adolescence and entered the juvenile justice system. We will take a comprehensive look at juvenile delinquency and crime in Chapter 15.

CRIME, RACE, AND POVERTY

Homicide data also produce disturbing results when race is taken into account. According to government statistics, African Americans are about six times more likely to be murder victims than Caucasians, and blacks are about seven times more likely to commit murder than whites.[68] In general, poor people and members of minority groups commit more crimes—and are more often the victims of crimes—than wealthier people and whites. But the relationship among race, income level, and crime is much more complicated than any generalization.

L08 Studies have shown that, even in low-income neighborhoods, the rate of violent crime is associated much more strongly with family disorganization (lack of a father in the household, family members committing crimes) than with race.[69]

▲ Drug Enforcement Administration agents photograph evidence at a meth lab in Liverpool, Ohio. Meth labs cause more than 200 explosions and fires each year, and the federal government spends nearly $30 million annually to dispose of the dangerous waste materials generated by the drug's production. Why has this particular drug flourished in poor, rural areas?

Class and Crime The highest crime rates in the United States are consistently recorded in the low-income, urban neighborhoods with the highest unemployment rates. Lack of education, another handicap most often faced by low-income citizens, also seems to correlate with criminal activity. Forty-one percent of all inmates in state and federal prisons failed to obtain a high school diploma, compared to 18 percent in the population at large.[70]

It might seem logical that those who believe they lack a legal opportunity to gain the consumer goods and services that dominate American culture would turn to illegal methods to do so. But, logic aside, many criminologists are skeptical of such an obvious class-crime relationship. After all, poverty does not *cause* crime; the majority of residents in low-income neighborhoods are law abiding. Furthermore, higher-income citizens are also involved in all sorts of criminal activities and are more likely to commit white-collar crimes, which are not included in statistics on violent crime.

In addition, self-reported surveys have shown that as far as less serious crimes are concerned, the behavior of lower-, middle-, and upper-class criminals differs very little.[71] These findings tend to support the theory that high crime rates in low-income communities are at least partly the result of a greater willingness of police to arrest poor citizens, and of the court system to convict them.

Race and Crime The class-crime relationship and the class-race relationship are invariably linked. Official crime data seem to indicate a strong correlation between minority status and crime: African Americans—who make up 13 percent of the population—constitute 39 percent of those arrested for violent crimes and 29 percent of those arrested for property crimes.[72] Furthermore, although less than half of those arrested for violent crimes are African American, blacks account for just over half of all convictions and approximately 60 percent of prison admissions.[73]

Subculture Wars The racial differences in the crime rate are one of the most controversial areas of the criminal justice system (see the feature *Myth versus Reality— Race Stereotyping and Crime* on the next page). At first glance, crime statistics seem to support the idea that the subculture of African Americans in the United States is disposed toward criminal behavior. Not all of the data, however, support that assertion. Among inmates in state and federal prisons, for example, whites were at least twenty times more likely than African Americans to report recent methamphetamine

Myth *versus* Reality

Race Stereotyping and Crime

In an effort to study the effect of race on perception, Birt Duncan gathered 104 white undergraduate students at the University of California and had them observe an argument between two people in which one person shoved the other. The undergraduates were randomly assigned to view one of four different conditions: (1) white shover/African American victim, (2) white shover/white victim, (3) African American shover/white victim, and (4) African American shover/African American victim. The students were then asked to rate the behavior of the person who did the shoving.

Duncan found that when the shover was African American and the victim was white, 75 percent of the students considered the shove to be "violent behavior" and 6 percent saw it as "playing around." In contrast, when the shover was white and the victim black, only 17 percent characterized the shove as violent while 42 percent saw it as playful.

THE MYTH The results of Duncan's study are not, in the end, surprising. Racial stereotyping is not an aberration in our society. Negative stereotypes of minorities, especially African Americans, label them as prone to violence and more likely to be criminals or members of gangs than others.

THE REALITY According to the University of Maryland's Katheryn K. Russell, the best-kept secret in criminology is that the United States has a "white crime" problem. Whites, Russell points out, are the subject of about two-thirds of the arrests in this country each year. Russell believes that public and academic obsession with "black crime" has severely limited discussion of "white crime." This fascination can be explained, at least from a criminological standpoint, by the different *proportional* involvement of racial minorities in crime. As ■ Figure 3.12 shows, although white involvement in crime is high, it is "relatively" low given the percentage of the American population that is of white, European descent. In contrast, minorities have a disproportionate involvement in crime—especially as a percentage of prison and jail inmates—based on their population statistics.

FOR CRITICAL ANALYSIS

According to Figure 3.12, although African Americans are arrested at less than half the rate of whites, they comprise almost 30 percent more of the prison population. How might this statistical anomaly be explained?

■ **Figure 3.12** **Crime and Race in the United States**

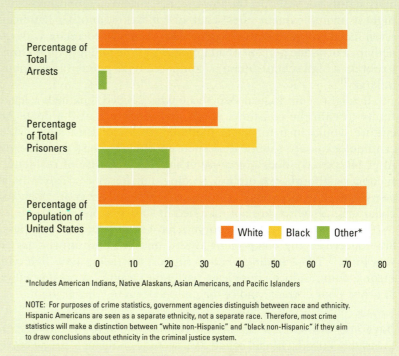

*Includes American Indians, Native Alaskans, Asian Americans, and Pacific Islanders

NOTE: For purposes of crime statistics, government agencies distinguish between race and ethnicity. Hispanic Americans are seen as a separate ethnicity, not a separate race. Therefore, most crime statistics will make a distinction between "white non-Hispanic" and "black non-Hispanic" if they aim to draw conclusions about ethnicity in the criminal justice system.

Sources: U.S. Census, U.S. Department of Justice, Federal Bureau of Investigation.

use.[74] A number of other crime-measuring surveys show consistent levels of crime and drug abuse across racial lines.[75] In addition, a 2002 study of nearly 900 African American children (400 boys and 467 girls) from neighborhoods with varying income levels showed that, regardless of the different factors often cited by criminologists, family income level had the only significant correlation with violent behavior. The authors of the study were so impressed by the results that they called on their colleagues to make greater efforts to include African American families living outside urban neighborhoods in future research in order to give a more complete—and perhaps less stereotypical—picture of race and crime in this country.[76]

More recently, a research project led by sociologist Robert J. Sampson of Harvard University collected extensive data on more than 11,000 residents living in 180 Chicago neighborhoods. Sampson and his colleagues found that 60 percent of the "gap" in levels of violence between whites and African Americans could be attributed to neighborhood and family conditions. In other words, regardless of race, a person would have a much higher risk of violent behavior if he or she lived in a poverty-stricken, disorganized neighborhood or in a household run by a single parent.[77]

Ethnicity and Crime Another point to remember when reviewing statistical studies of minority offenders and victims is that they tend to focus on *race*, which distinguishes groups based on physical characteristics such as skin color, rather than *ethnicity*, which denotes national or cultural background. Thus, the bulk of criminological research in this area has focused on the differences between European Americans and African Americans, both because the latter have been the largest minority group in the United States for most of its history and because the racial differences between the two groups are easily identifiable. Americans of Hispanic descent have either been excluded from many crime studies or been linked with whites or blacks based on racial characteristics. Other minority groups, such as Asian Americans, Native Americans, and immigrants from the South Pacific or Eastern Europe, have been similarly underreported in crime studies.

This state of affairs will more than likely change over the next few decades. Just as Hispanics are the fastest-growing minority group in the U.S. population at large, they are also the fastest-growing minority group in the U.S. prison population.[78] Indeed, criminologists have already begun to focus on issues of Hispanic criminality. For example, Robert Sampson's research project, mentioned earlier, found lower rates of violence among Mexican Americans than among either whites or blacks living in Chicago. The authors theorize that strong social ties in immigrant populations create an environment that is antithetical to crime.[79]

WOMEN AND CRIME

To put it bluntly, crime is an overwhelmingly male activity. More than 65 percent of all murders involve a male victim and a male perpetrator; in only 2.4 percent of homicides are both the offender and the victim female.[80] Only 13 percent of the **L09** national jail population and 7 percent of the national prison population are female, and in 2006 only 24 percent of all arrests involved women.[81] These statistics, however, fail to convey the startling rate at which the female presence in the criminal justice system has been increasing. In 1970, there were about 6,000 women in federal and state prisons; today, there are more than 107,000.[82] As you can see in ■ Figure 3.13 on the next page, the rate of arrests for women has also risen much more quickly than that for men over the past decade.

Equal in Crime? Given that the basic nature of American women is unlikely to have changed over the past thirty years, criminologists have looked for other explanations of these statistics. Freda Adler, a professor of criminal justice at Rutgers University, uses the "liberation hypothesis" to partially explain the increase in female arrestees and inmates.[83] This theory holds that as women become more and more equal in society as a whole, their opportunities to commit crimes will increase as well. "You can't embezzle if you're not near funds," Professor Adler notes. "You can't get

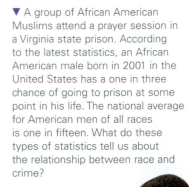

▼ A group of African American Muslims attend a prayer session in a Virginia state prison. According to the latest statistics, an African American male born in 2001 in the United States has a one in three chance of going to prison at some point in his life. The national average for American men of all races is one in fifteen. What do these types of statistics tell us about the relationship between race and crime?

© Andrew Lichtenstein/Corbis

■ Figure 3.13 Arrest Rates by Gender, 1996–2006

Over the past ten years, arrest rates in the United States have fluctuated a great deal. The only consistent trend, as shown here, is that the change in arrest rates for women from year to year has been higher than the change in arrest rates for men.

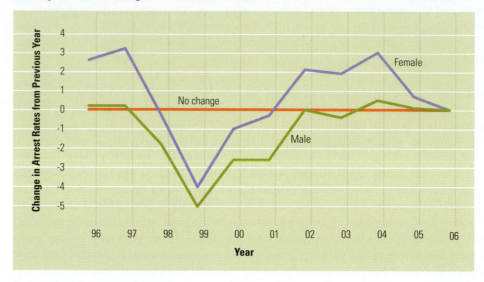

Source: Federal Bureau of Investigation.

involved in a fight at the bar if you're not allowed in the bar."[84] Criminologist Meda Chesney-Lind believes that the "get tough" attitude among politicians and law enforcement agencies has been the main contributor to increased rates of female criminality. "Simply put," she says, "it appears that the criminal justice system is now more willing to incarcerate women."[85]

Women and the "War on Drugs" A closer look at the offenses for which women are sent to prison and jail supports Chesney-Lind's thesis. The vast majority of women are prosecuted for nonviolent crimes, usually drug-related offenses. In fact, drug offenses account for nearly two-thirds of the women sent to federal prison each year (violent crimes account for less than 2 percent).[86] The habitual offender statutes and mandatory sentences for drug crimes that have accompanied the "war on drugs," which we will discuss in Chapter 11, have been particularly influential. In the 1980s, many of the women now in prison would not have been arrested or would have received light sentences for their drug-related wrongdoing.

When women commit violent crimes, the patterns are distinct as well. Research conducted by social psychologists Angela Browne and Kirk R. Williams shows that when women do kill, the victim is usually an intimate male partner. Moreover, a woman is likely to kill in response to physical aggression or threats of physical aggression by her partner.[87]

Self Check Fill in the Blanks

According to many crime experts, the upsurge in gang violence over the past few years is closely related to the gangs' need to protect their _____ trade with _____. In fact, the pattern may have more to do with demographics, as _____ is the strongest statistical determinant of criminal behavior. Despite perceptions, self-reported surveys show that criminal behavior is _____ among people of different income levels and racial backgrounds. It is clear, however, that women commit many _____ total crimes than do men. Check your answers on page 95.

LEGALIZING DRUGS

"It helps you stop thinking," says the thirty-seven-year-old mother of two of her twice-a-week marijuana habit. "I either can't sleep at night because I'm restless, or I can't get in the mood with my husband because my mind is spinning."[88] The Denver resident was one of nearly sixty thousand voters who supported their city's successful push to legalize the possession of small amounts of marijuana. The vote was mostly symbolic—Denver police can still arrest offenders under Colorado or federal antidrug laws—but when it comes to the legalization of drugs, the subject of this chapter's *Criminal Justice in Action* feature, even symbolic measures are bound to stir up controversy.

NO TREND

The term *legalization* refers to the removal of all criminal sanctions on the sale and production of an illegal drug, with the exception of restrictions on sales to children. After Denver's success in this area, supporters of the idea of liberalizing America's often-harsh drug laws hoped to see the start of a new trend, but these hopes have not been realized. In 2006, voters in Colorado and Nevada failed to support measures that would have allowed adults to possess less than an ounce of marijuana. Alaska remains the only state to have legalized possession of small amounts of the drug—a situation that state officials are desperately trying to change.

The Case for Legalization

- The "peace dividend" would be substantial. On the one hand, law enforcement agencies could eliminate costly drug-control programs, which cost U.S. taxpayers more than $40 billion annually.[89] On the other hand, the country would reap a windfall in taxes on the controlled sale of previously illegal drugs. One Harvard University economist has estimated that the net economic gain to the United States for legalizing marijuana alone would be between $10.1 billion and $13.9 billion a year.[90]

- The end of the "war on drugs" would mark the end of violent crime associated with drug dealing, as black market organizations would be put out of business or forced to rely on less profitable criminal activities.

- Legalization would result in a more efficient criminal justice system, as scarce law enforcement resources would be diverted away from drug offenses and the pressure on both overloaded courts and overcrowded prisons would be alleviated.[91]

The Case against Legalization

- If drugs such as marijuana, cocaine, and heroin were legalized, more people would use and abuse them, with serious health consequences for the nation.

- Minors can often easily obtain legal but controlled drug products such as cigarettes and alcohol. If other drugs were legalized, we can expect that minors would have greater access to them as well.

- The United States already has a problem with alcohol-related violence. Although some illegal drugs, notably marijuana, do not provoke aggressive behavior, others such as cocaine and certain hallucinogens do.[92]

Your Opinion—Writing Assignment

One commentator has compared the debate over what to do about illegal drugs to the problem that Goldilocks faced on entering the house of the Three Bears.[93] The first bed that Goldilocks tried, Mama Bear's bed, was too soft. The second, Papa Bear's bed, was too hard. Only the third, Baby Bear's bed, was just right. Surely, some suggest, there is a "Baby Bear's bed" way for America to regulate drugs—something between the "too soft" option of legalization and the "too hard" system under which we now function.

What would be your "Baby Bear" solution to the issue of drug legalization? Or, do you think that our current strict antidrug laws are adequate and might even benefit from being strengthened? Or, conversely, do you think that legalization would be the proper policy to follow? Before responding, you can review our discussions in this chapter concerning

- *Mala in se* and *mala prohibita* crimes on pages 74–76.
- Self-reported surveys and the dark figure of crime on pages 83–84.
- Illegal drugs and crime on pages 87–88.

Your answer should take at least three full paragraphs.

Getty Images

L01 **Discuss the primary goals of civil law and criminal law and explain how these goals are realized.** Civil law is designed to resolve disputes between private individuals and other entities such as corporations. In these disputes, one party, called the plaintiff, tries to gain monetary damages by proving that the accused party, or defendant, is to blame for a tort, or wrongful act. In contrast, criminal law exists to protect society from criminal behavior. To that end, the government prosecutes defendants, or persons who have been charged with committing a crime.

L02 **Explain the differences between crimes *mala in se* and *mala prohibita*.** A criminal act is *mala in se* if it is inherently wrong, while a criminal act *mala prohibita* is illegal only because it goes against the "natural, moral, and public" principles of society. It is sometimes difficult to distinguish between these two sorts of crimes because what may be considered a *mala in se* crime in one culture may not go against the "natural laws" of another.

L03 **Identify the publication in which the FBI reports crime data and list the three ways it does so.** Every year the FBI releases the Uniform Crime Report (UCR), in which it presents different crimes as (a) a rate per 100,000 people; (b) a percentage change from the previous year; and (c) an absolute, or aggregate, number.

L04 **Distinguish between Part I and Part II offenses as defined in the Uniform Crime Report (UCR).** Part I offenses are always felonies and include the most violent crimes. Part II offenses can be either misdemeanors or felonies and constitute the majority of crimes committed.

L05 **Describe some of the shortcomings of the UCR as a crime-measuring tool.** To collect its data, the Uniform Crime Report (UCR) relies on citizens reporting crimes to the police and the police passing this information on to the FBI. If either fails to do so, the UCR will not accurately reflect criminal activity in the United States. Furthermore, the FBI and local law enforcement agencies do not always define crimes in the same manner,

leading to inconsistencies in the data. Finally, the UCR tends to overreport violent crimes and underreport more common offenses.

L06 **Distinguish between the National Crime Victimization Survey and self-reported surveys.** The NCVS involves an annual survey of more than 40,000 households conducted by the Bureau of the Census along with the Bureau of Justice Statistics. The survey queries citizens on crimes that have been committed against them. As such, the NCVS includes crimes not necessarily reported to police. Self-reported surveys, in contrast, involve asking individuals about criminal activity to which they may have been a party.

L07 **Identify some of the reasons given to explain the high rate of delinquent and criminal behavior by adolescents and young adults.** (a) Young males have high levels of testosterone, which increases aggression; (b) adolescents are more susceptible to peer pressure and, therefore, can be convinced to misbehave by friends and peers; (c) teenagers often seek the "thrill" of crime or delinquency to alleviate boredom; and (d) risk factors such as lack of parental supervision, poor academic achievement, weapon carrying, and gang membership increase the likelihood of criminal behavior.

L08 **Explain some of the links between income level and crime.** Statistically, poor people commit more crimes, and are victims of more crimes, than those in the middle- and upper-income levels. Evidence shows, however, that income is not as important as other factors such as family disorganization, lack of education, and lack of employment. Indeed, the vast majority of all residents in low-income neighborhoods are law abiding.

L09 **Discuss how crime statistics explain the rising number of women incarcerated in the United States.** Experts believe that many women are arrested and given harsh punishments for activity that would not have placed them behind bars several decades ago. For the most part, this activity is nonviolent: drug-related offenses account for about two out of every three women sent to prison every year. Only about 2 percent of women are incarcerated for violent crimes.

Key Terms

beyond a reasonable doubt   72
civil law   71
clearance of an arrest   79
dark figure of crime   82
defendant   71
felony   72
illicit drugs   74

involuntary manslaughter   73
liability   71
licit drugs   74
mala in se   74
mala prohibita   74
methamphetamine (meth)   88
misdemeanor   73

Part I offenses   77
Part II offenses   78
plaintiff   71
self-reported surveys   83
Uniform Crime Report (UCR)   77
victim surveys   82
voluntary manslaughter   73

Questions for Critical Analysis

1. Give an example of how one person could be involved in a civil lawsuit and a criminal lawsuit for the same action.

2. What is the difference between a felony and a misdemeanor?

3. Two fathers, John and Phil, get in a heated argument following a dispute between their sons in a Little League baseball game. They come to blows and John strikes Phil in the temple, killing him. Will John be charged with voluntary manslaughter or involuntary manslaughter? What other details might you need to be sure of your answer?

4. Why is murder considered a *mala in se* crime? What argument can be made that murder is not a *mala in se* crime?

5. What is the distinction between the crime rate and crime in America?

6. Although Part II offenses constitute the bulk of crimes, Part I offenses get the most publicity. Is this necessarily irrational? Why or why not?

7. Why might self-reported surveys be the best method of learning the dark figure of crime?

8. What are some of the ways that drug use increases the amount of criminal activity in the United States besides the actual use or possession of illegal substances?

9. How do self-reported surveys give lie to the stereotype that someone from a low-income neighborhood is more likely to engage in criminal activity than someone from a high-income neighborhood?

10. Why do some experts feel that female crime rates increase as women become more nearly equal to men in our society?

Maximize Your Best Possible Outcome for Chapter 3

1. **Maximize Your Best Chance for Getting a Good Grade on the Exam.** ThomsonNOW Personalized Study is a diagnostic study tool containing valuable text-specific resources—and because you focus on just what you don't know, you learn more in less time to get a better grade. How do you get ThomsonNOW? If your textbook does not include an access code card, go to **thomsonedu.com** to get ThomsonNOW before your next exam!

2. **Get the Most Out of Your Textbook** by going to the book companion Web site at **www.cjinaction.com** to access one of the tutorial quizzes, use the flash cards

to master key terms, and check out the many other study aids you'll find there. Under chapter resources you will also be able to access the Stories from the Street feature and Web links mentioned in the textbook.

3. **Learn about Potential Criminal Justice Careers** discussed in this chapter by exploring careers online at **www.cjinaction.com**. You will find career descriptions and information about job requirements, training, salary and benefits, and the application process. You can also watch video profiles featuring criminal justice professionals.

Notes

1. Andrea J. Sedlak, David Finkelhor, Heather Hammer, and Dana J. Schultz, *National Incidence Studies of Missing, Abducted, Runaway, and Thrownaway Children* (Washington, D.C.: Office of Juvenile Justice and Delinquency Prevention, October 2002), 7.
2. David Cray, "Solid Data Scarce for Child Abductions," *Associated Press* (January 19, 2007).
3. Sedlak, Finkelhor, Hammer, and Schultz, 6.
4. Model Penal Code Section 1.04 (2).
5. Advisory Task Force on the Juvenile Justice System, *Final Report* (Minneapolis, MN: Minnesota Supreme Court, 1994), 5–11.
6. Johannes Andenaes, "The Moral or Educative Influence of Criminal Law," *Journal of Social Issues* 27 (Spring 1971), 17, 26.
7. Stuart P. Green, "Why It's a Crime to Tear the Tag Off a Mattress," *Emory Law Journal* 46 (Fall 1997), 1533–1614.

8. National Center for Health Statistics, *Health, United States, 2006* (Washington, D.C.: Centers for Disease Control and Prevention, 2006), Table 68, page 276.

9. Aimee Heckel, "A Shelf Full of Options, but Are They the Right Choices for You?" *Boulder (Colo.) Daily Camera* (March 6, 2007), B1.

10. Karen Kaplan and Seema Mehta, "Teens Try Cough Medicine for a High," *Los Angeles Times* (December 5, 2006), 1.

11. MADD, "Fatalities and Alcohol-Related Fatalities among 15–20 year olds—2003 v. 2002," at **www.madd.com/stats/9659**.

12. John Slade, "Health Consequences of Smoking: Nicotine Addiction," *Hearings before the Subcommittee on Health and the Environment of the House Committee on Energy and Commerce* (Washington, D.C.: U.S. Government Printing Office, 1988), 163–164.

13. Ethan Nadelmann, "Should We Legalize Drugs? History Answers: Yes," *Hofstra Law Review* 18 (1990), 41.

14. Steven Jonas, "Solving the Drug Problem: A Public Health Approach to the Reduction of the Use and Abuse of Both Legal and Recreational Drugs," *Hofstra Law Review* 18 (1990), 753.

15. David F. Musto, *The American Disease: Origins of Narcotic Control* (New York: Oxford University Press, 1987), 1.

16. Codified as amended at 21 U.S.C. Sections 801–966 (1994).

17. Uniform Controlled Substances Act (1994), Section 201(h).

18. Douglas N. Husak, *Drugs and Rights* (New York: Cambridge University Press, 2002), 21.

19. Federal Bureau of Investigation, *Uniform Crime Reporting Handbook* (Washington, D.C.: U.S. Department of Justice, 2004), 74.

20. Federal Bureau of Investigation, *Crime in the United States, 2006* (Washington, D.C.: U.S. Department of Justice, 2007), at **www.fbi. gov/ucr/cius2006/about/index.htm**.

21. *Ibid.*

22. *Ibid.*, at **www.fbi.gov/ucr/cius2006/data/table_01.html**.

23. Jeffery Reiman, *The Rich Get Richer and the Poor Get Prison*, 4th ed. (Boston: Allyn & Bacon, 1995), 59–60.

24. *Crime in the United States, 2006*, at **www.fbi.gov/ucr/cius2006/ offenses/expanded_information/data/shrtable_09.html**.

25. *Ibid.*, at **www.fbi.gov./ucr/cius2006/data/table_01.html**.

26. *Ibid.*, at **www.fbi.gov./ucr/cius2006/arrests/index.html**.

27. Marcus Felson, *Crime in Everyday Life* (Thousand Oaks, CA: Pine Forge Press, 1994), 3.

28. Donald J. Black, "Production of Crime Rates," *American Sociological Review* 35 (1970), 733–748.

29. Bureau of Justice Statistics, *Crime Victimization, 2005* (Washington, D.C.: U.S. Department of Justice, 2006), 1.

30. Victoria W. Schneider and Brian Weirsma, "Limits and Use," in Doris Layton MacKenzie, Phyllis Jo Baunach, and Roy R. Robergs, eds., *Measuring Crime: Large-Scale, Long-Range Efforts* (Albany, NY: State University of New York Press, 1990), 21–27.

31. Alabama Code Sections 13A-6-60(8), 13A-6-61(a)(1) (1994).

32. William Chambliss, *Exporting Criminology* (New York: Macmillan, 1988), 30.

33. *Crime in the United States, 2006*, at **www.fbi.gov/ucr/cius2006/about/ about_ucr.html**.

34. Lisa Stolzenberg, Stewart J. D'Alessio, and David Eitle, "A Multilevel Test of Racial Threat Theory," *Criminology* (August 1, 2004), 680.

35. Victor E. Kappeler, Mark Blumberg, and Gary W. Potter, *The Mythology of Crime and Criminal Justice*, 2d ed. (Prospect Heights, IL: Waveland Press, 1993), 31.

36. Alfred D. Biderman and James P. Lynch, *Understanding Crime Statistics: Why the UCR Diverges from the NCVS* (New York: Springer-Verlag, 1991).

37. Peter B. Wood, Walter R. Grove, James A. Wilson, and John K. Cochran, "Nonsocial Reinforcement and Criminal Conduct: An Extension of Learning Theory," *Criminology* 35 (May 1997), 335–366.

38. James S. Wallerstein and Clement J. Wyle, "Our Law-Abiding Law Breakers," *Probation* 35 (April 1947), 107–118.

39. Michael Hindelang, "Causes of Delinquency: A Partial Replication and Extension," *Social Problems* 20 (1973), 471–487.

40. Thomas Gray and Eric Walsh, *Maryland Youth at Risk: A Study of Drug Use in Juvenile Detainees* (College Park, MD: Center for Substance Abuse Research, 1993).

41. Bureau of Justice Statistics, *Crime Victimization, 2005* (Washington, D.C.: U.S. Department of Justice, 2006), 1.

42. Quoted in Maria Newman, "Violent Crimes Rose in '05, with Murders Up by 4.8 Percent," *New York Times* (June 13, 2006), A16.

43. Richard B. Schmidt, "FBI Reports Rise in Violent Crime," *Los Angeles Times* (December 19, 2006), 13.

44. *Violent Crime in America: 24 Months of Alarming Trends* (Washington, D.C.: Police Executive Research Forum, 2007), 1.

45. *Crime in the United States, 2005*, at **www.fbi.gov/ucr/cius2006/ offenses/violent_crime/index.html**.

46. *Crime Victimization, 2005*, 10.

47. Kate Zernike, "Violent Crime Rising Sharply in Some Cities," *New York Times* (February 12, 2006), 28.

48. Quoted in Kate Zernike, "Violent Crime in Cities Shows Sharp Surge, Reversing Trend," *New York Times* (March 9, 2007), A1; and *Violent Crime in America*, 10.

49. "The Growing Gang Problem," *Economist* (February 26, 2005), 80.

50. H. Mitchell Caldwell and Daryl Fisher-Ogden, "Stalking the Jets and Sharks: Exploring the Constitutionality of the Gang Death Penalty Enhancer," *George Mason Law Review* (Spring 2004), 601.

51. Jeffrey Fagan, "Gangs, Drugs, and Neighborhood Change," in *Gangs in America*, 2d ed., ed. Ronald Huff (Thousand Oaks, CA: Sage Publications, 1996), 61.

52. James Dao, "Baltimore Streets Meaner," *New York Times* (February 9, 2005), A1.

53. Bureau of Justice Statistics, *Drug Use and Crime*, at **www.ojp.usdoj. gov/bjs/dcf/duc.htm**.

54. *Crime in the United States, 2006*, at **www.fbi.gov/ucr/cius2006/data/ table_29.html**.

55. Bureau of Justice Statistics, *Drug Use and Dependence, State and Federal Prisoners, 2004* (Washington, D.C.: U.S. Department of Justice, October 2006), 1.

56. *Ibid.*

57. Bureau of Justice Statistics, *Substance Dependence, Abuse, and Treatment of Jail Inmates, 2002* (Washington, D.C.: U.S. Department of Justice, July 2005), 7.

58. Paul J. Goldstein, "The Drug/Violence Nexus: A Tripartite Conceptual Framework," *Journal of Drug Issues* 15 (1985), 493–506.

59. Daniel K. Benjamin and Roger LeRoy Miller, *Undoing Drugs: Beyond Legalization* (New York: Basic Books, 1991), 110.

60. *Ibid.*, 110–111.

61. Sam Hananel, "Meth Still No. 1 Drug Problem, Study Finds," *Associated Press* (July 18, 2006).

62. National Drug Intelligence Center, *National Drug Threat Assessment, 2006* (Washington, D.C.: U.S. Department of Justice, 2006), 10.

63. Suzanne Smalley, "Hub's Rise in Deadly Violence Reflects Disturbing U.S. Change," *Boston Globe* (March 9, 2007), 3B.

64. Avshalom Caspi and Terrie Moffitt, "The Continuity of Maladaptive Behavior: From Description to Understanding in the Study of Antisocial Behavior," in Dante Cicchetti and Donald J. Cohen, eds., *Manual of Developmental Psychology* (New York: John Wiley, 1995), 493.

65. Delbert S. Elliot and Scott Menard, "Delinquent Friends and Delinquent Behavior: Temporal and Developmental Patterns," in Rolf Loeber and David P. Farrington, eds., *Delinquency and Crime: Current Theories* (Thousand Oaks, CA: Sage Publications, 1996), 47–66.

66. *National Survey of American Attitudes on Substance Abuse VIII: Teens and Parents* (New York: National Center on Addiction and Substance Abuse at Columbia University, August 2003), 2.

67. Rolf Loeber, David P. Farrington, and David Petechuk, *Child Delinquency: Early Intervention and Prevention* (Washington, D.C.: Office of Juvenile Justice and Delinquency Prevention, May 2003), 6–9.

68. See **www.ojp.usdoj.gov/bjs/homicide/race.htm**.

69. James Q. Wilson, "The Family Way," *The Wall Street Journal* (January 7, 2003), A12.

70. Caroline Wolf Harlow, *Education and Correctional Populations* (Washington, D.C.: Bureau of Justice Statistics, January 2003), 1.

71. Charles Tittle and Robert Meier, "Specifying the SES/Delinquency Relationship," *Criminology* 28 (1990), 270–301.

72. *Crime in the United States, 2006*, at **www.fbi.gov/ucr/cius2006/data/ table_43.html**.

73. Robert M. A. Johnson, "Racial Bias in the Criminal Justice System and Why We Should Care," *Criminal Justice* (Winter 2007), 1.

74. *Drug Use and Dependence, State and Federal Prisoners, 2004*, 1.

75. Arthur H. Garrison, "Disproportionate Minority Arrests: A Note on What Has Been Said and How It Fits Together," *New England Journal on Criminal and Civil Confinement* (Winter 1997), 29.

76. Eric A. Stewart, Ronald L. Simons, and Rand D. Donger, "Assessing

Neighborhood and Social Psychological Influences on Childhood Violence in an African American Sample," *Criminology* (November 2002), 801–829.

77. Robert J. Sampson, Jeffrey Morenoff, and Stephen W. Raudenbush, "Social Anatomy of Racial and Ethnic Disparities in Violence," *American Journal of Public Health* 95 (2005), 224–232.

78. Bureau of Justice Statistics, *Prisoners in 2005* (Washington, D.C.: U.S. Department of Justice, 2006), 8.

79. Sampson, Morenoff, and Raudenbush. 231.

80. See **www.ojp.usdoj.gov/bjs/homicide/gender.htm**.

81. Bureau of Justice Statistics, *Prison and Jail Inmates, Midyear 2006*, (Washington, D.C.: U.S. Department of Justice, June 2007), Table 8, page 5, and Table 9, page 5; and *Crime in the United States, 2006*, at **www.fbi.gov/ucr/cius2006/arrests/index.html**.

82. *Prisoners in 2005*, 4.

83. Freda Adler, *Sisters in Crime: The Rise of the New Female Criminal* (New York: McGraw-Hill, 1975), 95.

84. Quoted in Barry Yeoman, "Violent Tendencies: Crime by Women Has Skyrocketed in Recent Years," *Chicago Tribune* (March 15, 2000), 3.

85. Meda Chesney-Lind, "Patriarchy, Prisons, and Jails: A Critical Look at Trends in Women's Incarceration," *Prison Journal* (Spring/Summer 1991), 57.

86. Bureau of Justice Statistics, *Sourcebook of Criminal Justice Statistics* (Washington, D.C: U.S. Department of Justice, 2004), Table 6.53.

87. Angela Browne and Kirk R. Williams, "Exploring the Effect of Resource Availability and the Likelihood of Female-Perpetrated Homicides," *Law and Society Review 23* (1989), 75–94.

88. Quoted in Douglas Brown, "Grass Roots," *Denver Post* (December 27, 2005), F1.

89. Jonathan Caulkins and Robert MacCoun, "Analyzing Illicit Drug Markets When Dealers Act with Limited Rationality," in *The Law and Economics of Irrational Behavior*, Francesco Parisi and Vernon L. Smith, ed. (Stanford, CA: Stanford University Press, 2005), 315.

90. Jeffrey A. Miron, "The Budgetary Implications of Marijuana Prohibition" (June 2005), at **www.prohibitioncosts.org/mironreport.html**.

91. James A. Inciardi and Duane C. McBride, "Debating the Legalization of Drugs," in *Handbook of Drug Control in the United States*, ed. James A. Inciardi (New York: Greenwood Press, 1990), 285–289.

92. *Ibid.*, 289–294.

93. Stephen Mudford, "Drug Legalization and the 'Goldilocks' Problem: Thinking about Costs and Control of Drugs," in *Searching for Alternatives: Drug Control Policy in the United States*, ed. Melvin B. Krauss and Edward P. Lazear (Stanford, CA: Hoover Institution Press, 1991), 31.

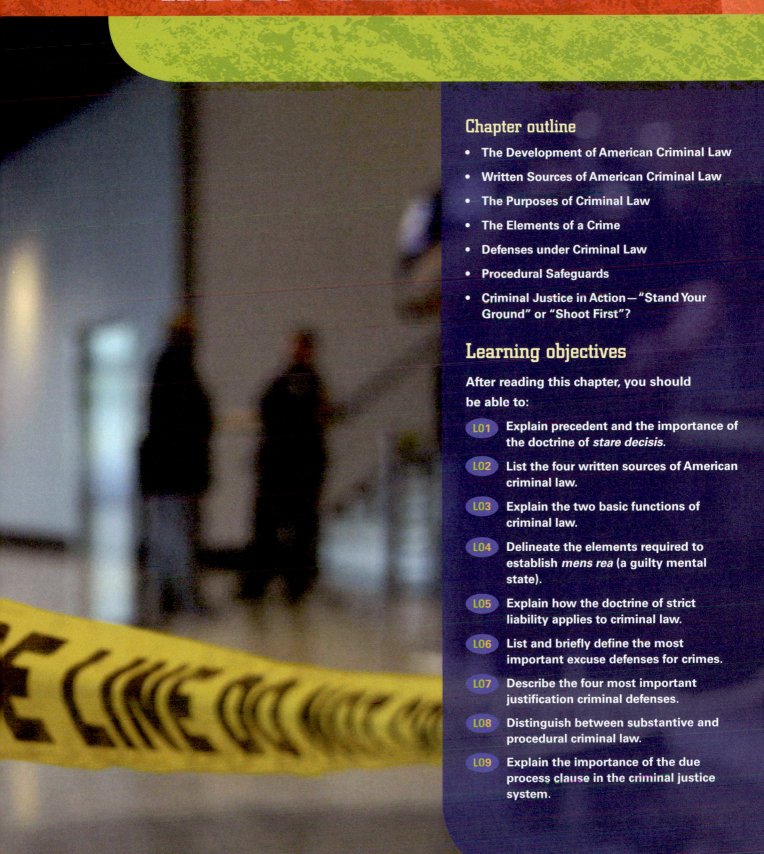

Inside Criminal Law

Learning objectives

After reading this chapter, you should be able to:

LO1 Explain precedent and the importance of the doctrine of *stare decisis*.

LO2 List the four written sources of American criminal law.

LO3 Explain the two basic functions of criminal law.

LO4 Delineate the elements required to establish *mens rea* (a guilty mental state).

LO5 Explain how the doctrine of strict liability applies to criminal law.

LO6 List and briefly define the most important excuse defenses for crimes.

LO7 Describe the four most important justification criminal defenses.

LO8 Distinguish between substantive and procedural criminal law.

LO9 Explain the importance of the due process clause in the criminal justice system.

When Matthew Koso was twenty-two years old and Crystal Guyer was fourteen, the Nebraska couple produced irrefutable evidence that Matthew had committed a crime: a baby daughter named Samara. In Nebraska, as in most American jurisdictions, intercourse between an adult and a minor is considered statutory rape. "We don't want grown men having sex with young girls," said state attorney general John Bruning, explaining his decision to bring charges against Matthew.

Even though a crime had clearly taken place, disapproval of Bruning's course of action was widespread. Critics focused on two factors. First, Crystal had, by all appearances, consented to any sex she had with Matthew. Second, the couple married before Samara's birth. One protester wrote a letter to Bruning in which she declared, "I'm sure your time can be better spent putting away real criminals." For his part, Matthew called the attorney general a "homewrecker" who was trying to "rip a father away from a child and a husband away from a wife."

Matthew eventually pleaded guilty to first degree sexual assault, a felony that carries the possible punishment of fifty years behind bars. In 2006, Judge Daniel E. Bryan, Jr., sentenced him to a term of eighteen to thirty months, with a possibility of early release. Although Matthew's family decried the sentence as overly harsh, Bruning had no problem with the judge's penalty. "It recognizes the seriousness of the act and gives him a chance, if he behaves well in prison, to be out in nine months and get on with his life," he said.

AP Photo/Nati Harnik

▲ Crystal Koso, the fifteen-year-old wife of Matthew Koso, waits in a Nebraska courtroom before her husband's sentencing for first degree sexual assault.

Was the law fair to Matthew Koso? In this chapter, we will learn that a defendant usually must have a guilty state of mind, or *mens rea*, to have committed a crime. The criminal code of Nebraska, however, declares that a person is guilty of a felony if he or she is "19+" years of age and "engages in sexual penetration with any person under 16 years old."[1] No provision is made for the offender's intent, which is why statutory rape is a *strict liability crime* (another concept we will discuss later in the chapter). Under statutory rape laws, a criminal act has occurred even if the adult was unaware of the minor's age or was misled to believe that the minor was older. In fact, the sexual contact is criminal even if the minor consents because, being underage, she or he is considered incapable of making a rational decision on the matter.

Generally, of course, consensual sexual behavior is not a criminal offense. In this case, however, Crystal Guyer's tender years meant that the state of Nebraska was going to protect her whether she wanted it or not. As the *Koso* case suggests, criminal law must be flexible enough to encompass behavior that is not marked by criminal intent yet still poses a threat to society and therefore, in the eyes of some, merits punishment. In this chapter, we will examine how these "threats to society" are identified and focus on the guidelines that determine how the criminal justice system resolves and punishes criminal guilt.

The Development of American Criminal Law

Given its various functions, a single definition of *law* is difficult to establish. To the Greek philosopher Aristotle (384–322 B.C.E.), law was a "pledge that citizens of a state will do justice to one another." Aristotle's mentor, Plato (427–347 B.C.E.),

Criminal Justice ⚖ Now™

Maximize your study time by using ThomsonNOW's Personalized Study plan to help you review this chapter and prepare for examination. The Study Plan will

- Help you identify areas on which you should concentrate
- Provide interactive exercises to help you master the chapter concepts; and
- Provide a post-test to confirm you are ready to move on to the next chapter information.

saw the law as primarily a form of social control. The British jurist Sir William Blackstone (1723–1780) described law as "a rule of civil conduct prescribed by the supreme power in a state, commanding what is right, and prohibiting what is wrong." In the United States, jurist Oliver Wendell Holmes, Jr. (1841–1935), contended that law was a set of rules that allowed one to predict how a court would resolve a particular dispute.

See the **Legal Information Institute** for an overview of criminal law and links to an extensive number of documents relating to criminal justice. Find its Web site by clicking on *Web Links* under *Chapter Resources* at **www.cjinaction.com**.

THE CONCEPTION OF LAW

Although these definitions vary in their particulars, they are all based on the following general observation: *law* consists of enforceable rules governing relationships among individuals and between individuals and their society.[2] Searching back into history, several sources for modern American law can be found in the rules laid out by ancient societies. One of the first known sets of written law was created during the reign of Hammurabi (1792–1750 B.C.E.), the sixth king of the ancient empire of Babylon. The Code of Hammurabi set out crimes and their punishments based on *lex Talionis,* or "an eye for an eye." This concept of retribution is still important and will be discussed in Chapter 11.

Another ancient source of law can be found in the Mosaic Code of the Israelites (1200 B.C.E.). According to tradition, Moses—acting as an intermediary for God—presented the code to the tribes of Israel. The two sides entered into a covenant, or contract, in which the Israelites agreed to follow the code and God agreed to protect them as the chosen people. Besides providing the basis for Judeo-Christian teachings, the Mosaic Code is also reflected in modern American law, as evident by similar prohibitions against murder, theft, adultery, and perjury.

"Justice?—You get justice in the next world, in this world you have the law."

—*William Gaddis, American novelist*

Modern law also owes a debt to the Code of Justinian, promulgated throughout the Roman Empire in the sixth century. This code collected many of the laws that Western society had produced. It was influential in the development of the civil law systems of the European continent. To some extent, it also influenced the common law of England.

ENGLISH COMMON LAW

The English system of law as it stands today was solidified during the reign of Henry II (1154–1189). Henry sent judges on a specific route throughout the country known as a *circuit.* These circuit judges established a **common law** in England; that is, they solidified a national law in which legal principles applied to all citizens equally, no matter where they lived or what the local customs had dictated in the past. When confusion about any particular law arose, the circuit judges could draw on English traditions, or they could borrow from legal decisions made in other European countries. Once a circuit judge made a ruling, other circuit judges faced with similar cases generally followed that ruling. Each interpretation became part of the law on the subject and served as a legal **precedent**—a decision that furnished an example or authority for deciding subsequent cases involving similar legal principles or facts. Over time, a body of general rules that prescribed social conduct and that was applied throughout the entire English realm was established, and subsequently it was passed on to British colonies, including those in the New World that would eventually become the thirteen original states.

What is important about the formation of the common law is that it developed from the customs of the people rather than simply the will of a ruler. As such, the common law came to reflect the social, religious, economic, and cultural values of the people. All the while, a system of sheriffs, courts, juries, and lawyers accompanied the development of the common law.

L01

Common Law The body of law developed from custom or judicial decisions in English and U.S. courts and not attributable to a legislature.

Precedent A court decision that furnishes an example of authority for deciding subsequent cases involving similar facts.

The United States was not the only country to adopt the basics of English common law and *stare decisis*. Many of Britain's former colonies have assimilated elements of common law to complement their traditional legal practices. As this figure shows, however, a number of countries operate under civil legal systems (not to be confused with the classification of civil versus criminal law, which was explained in Chapter 3). Civil law systems rely primarily on legislation (usually called codes) rather than case law and *stare decisis*. In a country with a civil law system, the courts normally refer only to legislation on the subject. The decisions of civil law judges do not necessarily set precedents for later cases.

Civil Law		Common Law	
Argentina	Japan	Australia	United States
Austria	Mexico	Bangladesh	Zambia
Brazil	Poland	Canada	
Chile	South Korea	Ghana	
China	Sweden	India	
Egypt	Tunisia	Israel	
Finland	Venezuela	Jamaica	
France		Kenya	
Germany		Malaysia	
Greece		New Zealand	
Indonesia		Nigeria	
Iran		Singapore	
Italy		United Kingdom	

STARE DECISIS

The practice of deciding new cases with reference to precedents is the basis for a doctrine called *stare decisis* ("to stand on decided cases"). Under this doctrine, judges are obligated to follow the precedents established within their jurisdictions.[3] For example, any decision of a particular state's highest court will control the outcome of future cases on that issue brought before all of the lower courts within that same state (unless preempted by the federal Constitution). All United States Supreme Court decisions on issues involving the U.S. Constitution are normally binding on *all* courts because the U.S. Constitution is the supreme law of the land and the Court is its final interpreter.

Controlling precedents in a jurisdiction are referred to as *binding authorities*, as are statutes or other laws that must be followed. In contrast, in civil law systems, which rely primarily on legislation and custom rather than case law, precedent is not binding. (To see the extent to which common law and the doctrine of *stare decisis* have been adopted in other countries, see ■ Figure 4.1.)

The doctrine of *stare decisis* helps the court system to be more efficient because if other courts have carefully examined a similar case, their legal reasoning and opinions can serve as a guide. This does not mean, however, that the system is rigid. The United States Supreme Court, for example, will sometimes rule against precedent set in a previous Court decision. It does so when there have been sufficient changes in society to warrant departing from the doctrine of *stare decisis*. In general, however, the judicial system is slow to change, and courts rarely alter major points of law. The doctrine of *stare decisis* leads to stability in the law, allowing people to predict how the law will be applied in given circumstances.

Stare Decisis (pronounced *ster*-ay dih-*si-ses*). A common law doctrine under which judges are obligated to follow the precedents established under prior decisions.

Self Check Fill in the Blanks

American law has its roots in English _____ law, which represents a set of legal principles that apply equally to all citizens. Under this legal system, once a judge made a ruling, other judges faced with similar cases followed this _____ . Today, the doctrine of _____ reflects the tradition of relying on decided cases to settle new ones. Check your answers on page 130.

Written Sources of American Criminal Law

Originally, common law was *uncodified;* that is, it relied primarily on judges following precedents, and the body of the law was not written down in any single place. Uncodified law, however, presents a number of drawbacks, not the least being that citizens have difficulty learning which acts are illegal and understanding the procedures that must be followed to establish innocence or guilt. Consequently, U.S. history has seen the development of several written sources of American criminal law, also known as "substantive" criminal law. These sources include:

L02

1. The U.S. Constitution and the constitutions of the various states.
2. Statutes, or laws, passed by Congress and by state legislatures, plus local ordinances.
3. Regulations, created by regulatory agencies, such as the federal Food and Drug Administration.
4. Case law (court decisions).

We describe each of these important written sources of law in the following pages. (Most, but not all, modern societies rely on written sources of criminal law. To learn about one region whose law has remained uncodified for centuries, see the feature *International CJ—The Pushtun Way* on the following page.)

CONSTITUTIONAL LAW

The federal government and the states have separate written constitutions that set forth the general organization and powers of, and the limits on, their respective governments. **Constitutional law** is the law as expressed in these constitutions.

The U.S. Constitution is the supreme law of the land. As such, it is the basis of all law in the United States. Any law that violates the Constitution, as ultimately determined by the United States Supreme Court, will be declared unconstitutional and will not be enforced. The Tenth Amendment, which defines the powers and limitations of the federal government, reserves to the states all powers not granted to the federal government. Under our system of federalism (see Chapter 1), each state also has its own constitution. Unless they conflict with the U.S. Constitution or a federal law, state constitutions are supreme within their respective borders. (You will learn more about how constitutional law applies to our criminal justice system in later chapters.)

Constitutional Law Law based on the U.S. Constitution and the constitutions of the various states.

Statutory Law The body of law enacted by legislative bodies.

STATUTORY LAW

Statutes enacted by legislative bodies at any level of government make up another source of law, which is generally referred to as **statutory law.** *Federal statutes* are laws that are enacted by the U.S. Congress. *State statutes* are laws enacted by state legislatures, and statutory law also includes the ordinances passed by cities and counties. A federal statute, of course, applies to all states. A state statute, in contrast, applies only within that state's borders. City or county ordinances (statutes) apply only to those jurisdictions where they are enacted. As mentioned, statutory law found by the Supreme

The Granger Collection

▲ George Washington, standing at right, presided over the Constitutional Convention of 1787. The convention resulted in the U.S. Constitution, the source of a number of laws that continue to form the basis of our criminal justice system today.

Pakistan's North-West Frontier Province (NWFP), which runs along the country's northwestern border with Afghanistan, is one of the most remote regions in the world. It is the home of about 28 million Pushtuns, also known as Pathans or Pakhtuns. With a well below average literacy rate and a population spread thin over vast mountain ranges and steppes, the Pushtuns have showed little interest in written, codified criminal law. Instead, for millennia they have relied on a tribal code of ethics known as *Pushtunwali* to regulate behavior in their society.

The basic value of *Pushtunwali* is *nang,* or honor. A person who loses *nang* is effectively rejected by the community. A Pushtun's *nang* is closely related to his property—that is, his money, his land, and his women. If any of these are dishonored, the Pushtun is required by the code to take revenge. In one recent example, a Pushtun businessman's daughter eloped against his wishes, fleeing to the Afghan capital of Kabul with her boyfriend. The businessman sold his land, tracked the couple to Kabul, and killed his daughter's lover. He promised to do the same

to his daughter, who sought refuge with a Western human rights organization.

Under the rules of *Pushtunwali*, tribal councils called *jirga* are convened on a semiregular basis to moderate disputes. *Jirga* consist of *spingeeri* ("white beards"), who make their decisions based on history, custom, and their own experience. At a recent *jirga,* after a Pushtun named Khan admitted to killing every male member of a rival family, the *spingeeri* decided that his punishment would be the destruction of two of his homes and a fine of 500,000 rupees (about $8,500).

FOR CRITICAL ANALYSIS

The *Pushtunwali* code has come under severe criticism from Western human rights groups for its treatment of women, who are considered to be the property of their male relatives and are often traded from family to family to settle disputes. What are the possible drawbacks when representatives from one culture try to change the traditions of another culture? Do you think that foreign governments should pressure the Pushtuns to modify their criminal laws so that they are more in keeping with "modern" values?

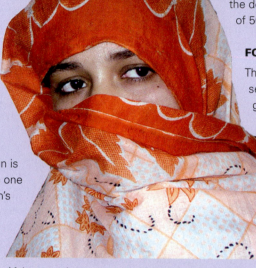

▲ Afsheen, a nineteen-year-old Pashtun woman, was married at the age of nine as compensation for a murder committed by her father.

© Ali Imam/Reuters/Corbis

Court to violate the U.S. Constitution will be overturned. In the late 1980s, for example, the Court ruled that any state laws banning the burning of the American flag were unconstitutional because they impinged on the individual's right to freedom of expression.[4]

Common Law and State Statutes   Even though the body of statutory law has expanded greatly since the beginning of this nation, thus narrowing the applicability of common law doctrines, there is significant overlap between statutory law and common law. For example, many statutes essentially codify existing common law rules. Therefore, the courts, when interpreting the statutes, often rely on the common law as a guide to what the legislators intended. In some instances, statutory law has brought common law principles more in line with modern criminal theory. Under common law, for example, the law of rape applied only when the victim was a female. Today, many states recognize that both genders may be the targets of sexual assault. Under common law, burglary was defined as the breaking into and entering of a dwelling during the nighttime. State legislatures, in contrast, generally have defined burglary as occurring at any time. They have extended it to apply to structures beyond dwellings and even to automobiles.

Model Penal Code   Until the mid-twentieth century, state statutes were disorganized, inconsistent, and generally inadequate for modern society. In 1952, the American Law Institute began to draft a uniform penal code in hopes of solving this problem. The first **Model Penal Code** was released ten years later and has had a broad effect on state statutes.[5] Though not a law itself, the code defines the general principles of criminal responsibility and codifies specific offenses; it is the source for many of the definitions of crime in this textbook. The majority of the states have adopted parts of the Model Penal Code into their statutes, and some states, such as New York, have adopted a large portion of the Code.[6]

It is important to keep in mind that there are essentially fifty-two different criminal codes in this country—one for each state, the District of Columbia, and the federal government. Even if a state has adopted a large portion of the Model Penal Code, there may be certain discrepancies. Indeed, a state's criminal code often reflects specific values of its citizens, which may not be in keeping with those of the majority of other states. New Mexico and Louisiana, for example, are the only states where cockfighting is still legal. Sometimes, old laws remain on the books even though they are clearly anachronistic and are rarely, if ever, enforced: in Oklahoma, a person can be sentenced to thirty days in jail for "injuring fruit," and a hundred counties in North Carolina prohibit swearing.[7]

■ **Figure 4.2** *Sources of American Law*

1 **Constitutional law** The law as expressed in the U.S. Constitution and the various state constitutions. The U.S. Constitution is the supreme law of the land. State constitutions are supreme within state borders to the extent that they do not violate the U.S. Constitution or a federal law.

2 **Statutory law** Laws or ordinances created by federal, state, and local legislatures and governing bodies. None of these laws can violate the U.S. Constitution or the relevant state constitution. Uniform laws, when adopted by a state legislature, become statutory law in that state.

3 **Administrative law** The rules, orders, and decisions of federal or state government administrative agencies. Federal administrative agencies are created by enabling legislation enacted by the U.S. Congress. Agency functions include rulemaking, investigation and enforcement, and adjudication.

4 **Case law and common law doctrines** Judge-made law, including interpretations of constitutional provisions, of statutes enacted by legislatures, and of regulations created by administrative agencies. The common law— the doctrines and principles embodied in case law— governs all areas not covered by statutory law (or agency regulations issued to implement various statutes).

ADMINISTRATIVE LAW

A third source of American criminal law consists of **administrative law**—the rules, orders, and decisions of *regulatory agencies*. A regulatory agency is a federal, state, or local government agency established to perform a specific function. The Occupational Safety and Health Administration (OSHA), for example, oversees the safety and health of American workers; the Environmental Protection Agency (EPA) is concerned with protecting the natural environment; and the Food and Drug Administration (FDA) regulates food and drugs produced in the United States. Disregarding certain laws created by regulatory agencies can be a criminal violation. Many modern federal statutes, such as the Federal Food, Drug and Cosmetic Act, designate authority to a specific regulatory agency, such as the FDA, to promulgate regulations to which criminal sanctions are attached. So, after tainted spinach killed one person and sent ninety-eight more to the hospital in 2006, the FDA opened a criminal investigation into the safety practices of several California spinach growers and distributors.

CASE LAW

As is evident from the earlier discussion of the common law tradition, another basic source of American law consists of the rules of law announced in court decisions. These rules of law include interpretations of constitutional provisions, of statutes enacted by legislatures, and of regulations created by administrative agencies. Today, this body of law is referred to variously as the common law, judge-made law, or **case law.**

Case law relies to a certain extent on how courts interpret a particular statute. If you wanted to learn about the coverage and applicability of a particular statute, for example, you would need to locate the statute and study it. You would also need to see how the courts in your jurisdiction have interpreted the statute—in other words, what precedents have been established in regard to that statute. The use of precedent means that judge-made law varies from jurisdiction to jurisdiction. (For a summary of the four different sources of American law, see ■ Figure 4.2.)

Model Penal Code A statutory text created by the American Law Institute that sets forth general principles of criminal responsibility and defines specific offenses. States have adopted many aspects of the Model Penal Code, which is not itself a law, into their criminal codes.

Administrative Law The body of law created by administrative agencies (in the form of rules, regulations, orders, and decisions) in order to carry out their duties and responsibilities.

Case Law The rules of law announced in court decisions. Case law includes the aggregate of reported cases that interpret judicial precedents, statutes, regulations, and constitutional provisions.

Self Check Fill in the Blanks

The U.S. _____ is the supreme law of this country. Any law that violates this document will be declared _____ by the United States Supreme Court. Laws enacted by legislative bodies are known as _____, while the body of law created by judicial decisions is known as _____ law. Check your answers on page 130.

The Purposes of Criminal Law

Why do societies need laws? Many criminologists believe that criminal law has two basic functions: one relates to the legal requirements of a society, and the other pertains to its need to maintain and promote social values.

LO3

PROTECT AND PUNISH: THE LEGAL FUNCTION OF THE LAW

The primary legal function of the law is to maintain social order by protecting citizens from *criminal harm*. This term refers to a variety of harms that can be generalized to fit into two categories:

1. Harms to individual citizens' physical safety and property, such as the harm caused by murder, theft, or arson.
2. Harms to society's interests collectively, such as the harm caused by unsafe foods or consumer products, a polluted environment, or poorly constructed buildings.[8]

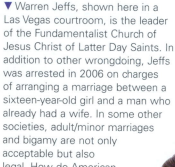

▼ Warren Jeffs, shown here in a Las Vegas courtroom, is the leader of the Fundamentalist Church of Jesus Christ of Latter Day Saints. In addition to other wrongdoing, Jeffs was arrested in 2006 on charges of arranging a marriage between a sixteen-year-old girl and a man who already had a wife. In some other societies, adult/minor marriages and bigamy are not only acceptable but also legal. How do American prohibitions against such practices reflect the social function of criminal law?

The first category is self-evident, although even murder has different degrees, or grades, of offense to which different punishments are assigned. The second, however, has proved more problematic, for it is difficult to measure society's "collective" interests. Often, laws passed to reduce such harms seem overly intrusive and marginally necessary. An extreme example would seem to be the Flammable Fabrics Act, which makes it a crime for a retailer to willfully remove a precautionary instruction label from a mattress that is protected with a chemical fire retardant.[9] Yet even in this example, a criminal harm is conceivable. Suppose a retailer removes the tags before selling a large number of mattresses to a hotel chain. Employees of the chain then unknowingly wash the mattresses with an agent that lessens their flame-resistant qualities. After the mattresses have been placed in rooms, a guest falls asleep while smoking a cigarette, starting a fire that burns down the entire hotel and causes several deaths.[10]

MAINTAIN AND TEACH: THE SOCIAL FUNCTION OF THE LAW

If criminal laws against acts that cause harm or injury to others are almost universally accepted, the same cannot be said for laws that criminalize "morally" wrongful activities that may do no obvious, physical harm outside the families of those involved. Why criminalize gambling or prostitution if the participants are consenting?

Expressing Public Morality The answer lies in the social function of criminal law. Many observers believe that the main purpose of criminal law is to reflect the values and norms of society, or at least of those segments of society that hold power. Legal scholar Henry Hart has stated that the only justification for criminal law and punishment is "the judgment of community condemnation."[11]

Take, for example, the misdemeanor of bigamy, which occurs when someone knowingly marries a second person without terminating her or his marriage to an original husband or wife. Apart from moral considerations, there would appear to be no victims in a bigamous relationship, and indeed many societies have allowed and continue to allow bigamy to exist. In the American social tradition, however, as John L. Diamond of the University of California's Hastings College of the Law points out:

> Marriage is an institution encouraged and supported by society. The structural importance of the integrity of the family and a monogamous marriage requires unflinching enforcement of the criminal laws against bigamy. The immorality is not in choosing to do wrong, but in transgressing, even innocently, a fundamental social boundary that lies at the core of social order.[12]

When discussing the social function of criminal law, it is important to remember that a society's views of morality change over time. Puritan New England society not only had strict laws against adultery, but also considered lying and idleness to be criminal acts.[13] Today, such acts may carry social stigmas, but only in certain extreme circumstances do they elicit legal sanctions. Furthermore, criminal laws aimed at minority groups, which were once widely accepted in the legal community as well as society at large, have increasingly come under question. (See the feature *Landmark Cases*—Lawrence v. Texas on the following page.)

Teaching Societal Boundaries   Some scholars believe that criminal laws not only express the expectations of society, but "teach" them as well. Professor Lawrence M. Friedman of Stanford University thinks that just as parents teach children behavioral norms through punishment, criminal justice "'teaches a lesson' to the people it punishes, and to society at large." Making burglary a crime, arresting burglars, placing them in jail—each step in the criminal justice process reinforces the idea that burglary is unacceptable and is deserving of punishment.[14]

This teaching function can also be seen in traffic laws. There is nothing "natural" about most traffic laws; Americans drive on the right side of the street, the British on the left side, with no obvious difference in the results. These laws, such as stopping at intersections, using headlights at night, and following speed limits, do lead to a more orderly flow of traffic and fewer accidents—certainly socially desirable goals. Various forms of punishment for breaking traffic laws teach drivers the social order of the road.

Self Check Fill in the Blanks

The _____ function of the law is to protect citizens from _____ harm by assuring their physical safety.

The _____ function of the law is to teach citizens proper behavior and express public _____ by codifying the norms and values of the community. Check your answers on page 130.

The Elements of a Crime

In fictional accounts of police work, the admission of guilt is often portrayed as *the* crucial element of a criminal investigation. Although an admission is certainly useful to police and prosecutors, it alone cannot establish the innocence or guilt of a suspect. Criminal law normally requires that the *corpus delicti,* a Latin phrase for "the body of the crime," be proved before a person can be convicted of wrongdoing.[15] *Corpus delicti* can be defined as "proof that a specific crime has actually been committed by someone."[16] It consists of the basic elements of any

Corpus Delicti The body of circumstances that must exist for a criminal act to have occurred.

Landmark Cases *Lawrence v. Texas*

Police officers in Houston arrested John Geddes Lawrence and Tyron Garner for violating a Texas law that prohibits individuals of the same sex from engaging in "deviate sexual intercourse." Lawrence and Garner challenged the law as unconstitutional because it banned sexual practices—in this case, sodomy—by homosexual couples that are lawful when performed by a man and a woman. The Texas Supreme Court upheld the statute, relying on the United States Supreme Court's decision in *Bowers v. Hardwick* (1986), which preserved a similar state law (since repealed) in Georgia. Lawrence and Garner appealed to the Supreme Court, in essence telling the highest court in the land that it had been mistaken when it ruled on the *Bowers* case and asking it to reconsider.

Lawrence v. Texas
United States Supreme Court
522 U.S. 1064 (2003)
laws.findlaw.com/US/000/02-102.html

IN THE WORDS OF THE COURT . . .

Justice Kennedy, majority opinion

* * * *

The laws involved in *Bowers* and here are, to be sure, statutes that purport to do no more than prohibit a particular sexual act. Their penalties and purposes, though, have more far-reaching consequences, touching upon the most private human conduct, sexual behavior, and in the most private of places, the home. The statutes do seek to control a personal relationship that, whether or not entitled to formal recognition in the law, is within the liberty of persons to choose without being punished as criminals.

This, as a general rule, should counsel against attempts by the State, or a court, to define the meaning of the relationship or to set its boundaries absent injury to a person or abuse of an institution the law protects. It

suffices for us to acknowledge that adults may choose to enter upon this relationship in the confines of their homes and their own private lives and still retain their dignity as free persons. * * * The liberty protected by the Constitution allows homosexual persons the right to make this choice.

* * * *

When homosexual conduct is made criminal by the law of the State, that declaration in and of itself is an invitation to subject homosexual persons to discrimination both in the public and in the private spheres. The central holding of *Bowers* has been brought in question by this case, and it should be addressed. Its continuance as precedent demeans the lives of homosexual persons.

* * * *

The petitioners are entitled to respect for their private lives. The State cannot demean their existence or control their destiny by making their private sexual conduct a crime.

DECISION

Overturning its earlier *Bowers* decision, the Court ruled that the Texas antisodomy law was unconstitutional, at the same time invalidating similar statutes in three other states—Kansas, Missouri, and Oklahoma.

FOR CRITICAL ANALYSIS

Nine states still have laws on the books that make sodomy illegal for both heterosexual and homosexual partners. How do you think one of these laws would fare if brought before the Supreme Court today? Have the morals of American society changed to the point where any law criminalizing consensual sexual conduct between adults is outdated?

For more information and activities related to this case, click on Landmark Cases *under* Book Resources *at* **www.cjinaction.com**.

crime, which include (1) *actus reus,* or a guilty act; (2) *mens rea,* or a guilty intent; (3) concurrence, or the coming together of the criminal act and the guilty mind; (4) a link between the act and the legal definition of the crime; (5) any attendant circumstances; and (6) the harm done, or result of the criminal act. (See *Mastering Concepts* for an example showing some of the various elements of a crime.)

CRIMINAL ACT: *ACTUS REUS*

Suppose Mr. Smith walks into a police department and announces that he just killed his wife. In and of itself, the confession is insufficient for conviction unless the police find Mrs. Smith's corpse, for example, with a bullet in her brain and establish through evidence that Mr. Smith fired the gun. (This does not mean that an actual dead body has to be found in every homicide case. Rather, it is the fact of the death that must be established in such cases.)

Carl Robert Winchell walked into the SunTrust Bank in Volusia County, Florida, and placed a bag containing a box on a counter. Announcing that the box held a bomb, he demanded to be given an unspecified amount of money. After being provided with several thousand dollars in cash, Winchell fled, leaving the box behind. A Volusia County Sheriff's Office bomb squad subsequently determined that the box did not in fact contain any explosive device. Winchell was eventually arrested and charged with robbery.

Winchell's actions were criminal because they satisfy the three elements of a crime:

1. ACTUS REUS

The physical act of a crime took place. In this case, Winchell committed bank robbery.

2. MENS REA

The offender must intentionally, knowingly or willingly commit the criminal act. In this case, Winchell obviously planned to rob the SunTrust Bank using the false threat of a bomb.

3. A CONCURRENCE of actus reus and mens rea

The criminal act must be the result of the offender's intention to commit that particular criminal act. In this case, the robbery was the direct result of Winchell's intent to take property using the threat of the fake bomb. If, in addition, a bank customer had died of a heart attack during the robbery attempt, Winchell could not have been charged

with first degree murder because he did not intend to harm anyone.

Note that the fact that there was no bomb in the box has no direct bearing on the three elements of the crime. It could, however, lead to Winchell receiving a lighter punishment than if he had used a real bomb.

Most crimes require an act of *commission;* that is, a person must *do* something in order to be accused of a crime. The prohibited act is referred to as the **actus reus,** or guilty act. Furthermore, the act of commission must be voluntary. For example, if Mr. Smith had an epileptic seizure while holding a hunting rifle and accidentally shot his wife, he normally would not be held criminally liable for her death. (See *You Be the Judge—A Voluntary Act?* on the next page)

A Legal Duty   In some cases, an act of *omission* can be a crime, but only when a person has a legal duty to perform the omitted act. One such legal duty is assumed to exist based on a "special relationship" between two parties, such as a parent and child, adult children and their aged parents, and spouses.[17] Those persons involved in contractual relationships with others, such as physicians and lifeguards, must also perform legal duties to avoid criminal penalty. Rhode Island, Vermont, and Wisconsin have even passed "duty to aid" statutes requiring their citizens to report criminal conduct and help victims of such conduct if possible.[18] Another example of a criminal act of omission is failure to file a federal income tax return when required by law to do so.

A Plan or Attempt   The guilty act requirement is based on one of the premises of criminal law—that a person is punished for harm done to society. Planning to kill someone or to steal a car may be wrong, but the thoughts do no harm and are therefore not criminal until they are translated into action. Of course, a person can be punished for *attempting* murder or robbery, but normally only if he or she took substantial steps toward the criminal objective and the prosecution can prove that the desire to commit the crime was present. Furthermore, the punishment for an **attempt** normally is less severe than if the act had succeeded.

MENTAL STATE: MENS REA

A wrongful mental state—*mens rea*—is as necessary as a wrongful act in establishing guilt. The mental state, or requisite *intent*, required to establish guilt of a crime is indicated in the applicable statute or law. For theft, the wrongful act is the taking of another person's property, and the required mental state involves both the awareness that the property belongs to another and the desire to deprive the owner of it.

Actus Reus (pronounced *ak*-tus *ray*-uhs). A guilty (prohibited) act. The commission of a prohibited act is one of the two essential elements required for criminal liability, the other element being the intent to commit a crime.

Attempt   The act of taking substantial steps toward committing a crime while having the ability and the intent to commit the crime, even if the crime never takes place.

Mens Rea (pronounced *mehns* ray-uh). Mental state, or intent. A wrongful mental state is as necessary as a wrongful act to establish criminal liability.

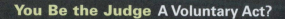

You Be the Judge A Voluntary Act?

THE FACTS On a bright, sunny afternoon, Emil was driving on Delaware Avenue in Buffalo, New York. As he was making a turn, Emil suffered an epileptic seizure and lost control of his automobile. The car careened onto the sidewalk and struck a group of six schoolgirls, killing four of them. Emil knew that he was subject to epileptic attacks that rendered him likely to lose consciousness.

THE LAW An "act" committed while one is unconscious is in reality not an act at all. It is merely a physical event or occurrence over which the defendant has no control; that is, such an act is involuntary. If the defendant voluntarily causes the loss of consciousness by, for example, using drugs or alcohol, however, then he or she will usually be held criminally responsible for any consequences.

YOUR DECISION Emil was charged in the deaths of the four girls. He asked the court to dismiss the charges, as he was unconscious at the time of the accident and therefore had not committed a voluntary act. In your opinion, is there an *actus reus* in this situation, or should the charges against Emil be dismissed?

[To see how the appellate court in New York ruled in this case, go to Example 4.1 in Appendix B.]

The Categories of *Mens Rea* A guilty mental state includes elements of purpose, knowledge, negligence, and recklessness.[19] A defendant is said to have *purposefully* committed a criminal act when he or she desires to engage in certain criminal conduct or to cause a certain criminal result. For a defendant to have *knowingly* committed an illegal act, he or she must be aware of the illegality, must believe that the illegality exists, or must correctly suspect that the illegality exists but fail to do anything to dispel (or confirm) his or her belief. Criminal **negligence** involves the mental state in which the defendant grossly deviates from the standard of care that a reasonable person would use under the same circumstances. The defendant is accused of taking an unjustified, substantial, and foreseeable risk that resulted in harm. In Texas, for example, a parent commits a felony if she or he fails to secure a loaded firearm or leaves it in such a manner that it could easily be accessed by a child.[20]

A defendant who commits an act *recklessly* is more blameworthy than one who is criminally negligent. The Model Penal Code defines criminal **recklessness** as "consciously disregard[ing] a substantial and unjustifiable risk."[21] Some courts, particularly those adhering to the Model Penal Code, will not find criminal recklessness on the part of a defendant who was subjectively unaware of the risk when she or he acted.

Criminal Liability Intent plays an important part in allowing the law to differentiate among varying degrees of criminal liability for similar, though not identical, guilty acts. The role of intent is clearly seen in the different classifications of homicide, defined generally as the willful killing of one human being by another. It is important to emphasize the word *willful*, as it precludes deaths caused by accident or negligence and those deemed justifiable. A death that results from negligence or accident normally is considered a private wrong and a matter for civil law, although some statutes allow for culpable negligence, which permits certain negligent homicides to be criminalized. As we saw in Chapter 3, when the act of killing is willful, deliberate, and premeditated (planned beforehand), it is considered first degree murder. When premeditation does not exist but intent does, the act is considered second degree murder. (See ■ Figure 4.3 for an example of the different homicide statutes in Florida.)

Negligence A failure to exercise the standard of care that a reasonable person would exercise in similar circumstances.

Recklessness The state of being aware that a risk does or will exist and nevertheless acting in a way that consciously disregards this risk.

■ **Figure 4.3** Florida Homicide Statutes (Excerpts)

782.02 Justifiable use of deadly force.
The use of deadly force is justifiable when a person is resisting any attempt to murder such person or to commit any felony upon him or her or upon or in any dwelling house in which such person shall be.

782.03 Excusable homicide.
Homicide is excusable when committed by accident and misfortune in doing any lawful act by lawful means with usual ordinary caution, and without any unlawful intent, or by accident and misfortune in the heat of passion, upon any sudden and sufficient provocation, or upon a sudden combat, without any dangerous weapon being used and not done in a cruel or unusual manner.

782.04 Murder.
(1)(a) The unlawful killing of a human being:

1. When perpetrated from a premeditated design to effect the death of the person killed or any human being;

2. When committed by a person engaged in the perpetration of, or in the attempt to perpetrate, any: [such acts as arson, robbery, burglary, etc.]; . . .

is murder in the first degree and constitutes a capital felony, ...

(2) The unlawful killing of a human being, when perpetrated by any act imminently dangerous to another and evincing a depraved mind regardless of human life, although without any premeditated design to effect the death of any particular individual, is murder in the second degree and constitutes a felony of the first degree, punishable by imprisonment for a term of years not exceeding life . . . .

782.07 Manslaughter; aggravated manslaughter of an elderly person or disabled adult; aggravated manslaughter of a child.
(1) The killing of a human being by the act, procurement, or culpable negligence of another, without lawful justification according to the provisions of Chapter 776 and in cases in which such killing shall not be excusable homicide or murder, according to the provisions of this chapter, is manslaughter, a felony of the second degree, ...

Different degrees of criminal liability for various categories of homicide lead to different penalties. The distinction between murder and manslaughter was evident in the punishment given to Kevin Kelly, a resident of Manassas, Virginia, who left his twenty-one-month-old daughter buckled in the family van for more than seven hours. With the temperature inside the car rising to 140 degrees, the child eventually died of heatstroke. Local prosecutors had the option of charging Kelly with murder, but could find no indication that he had *intentionally* killed his daughter. Instead, the evidence showed that Kelly, who has twelve other children, forgot where he had placed the girl. Kelly was charged with involuntary manslaughter; found guilty, he was sentenced to spend one day in jail each year for seven years. A murder conviction, in contrast, could have brought the death penalty.

Strict Liability Crimes Certain crimes, such as traffic violations, in which the defendant is guilty regardless of her or his state of mind at the time of the act.

Strict Liability For certain crimes, criminal law holds the defendant to be guilty even if intent to commit the offense is lacking. These acts are known as **strict liability crimes** and generally involve endangering the public welfare in some way.[22] Drug-control statutes, health and safety regulations, and traffic laws are all strict liability laws. To a certain extent, the concept of strict liability is inconsistent with the traditional principles of criminal

L05 law, which hold that *mens rea* is required for an act to be criminal. The goal of strict liability laws is to protect the public by eliminating the possibility that wrongdoers could claim ignorance or mistake to absolve themselves of criminal responsibility.[23] Thus, a person caught dumping waste in a protected pond or driving 70 miles per hour in a 55 miles-per-hour zone cannot plead a lack of intent in his or her defense.

▶ Tamara Schmidt is handcuffed in a Las Vegas, Nevada, courtroom. She had pleaded guilty to charges of child neglect after leaving her two young daughters home alone in a trailer. Disgruntled methamphetamine customers of Schmidt attacked the two girls, killing one and leaving the other paralyzed. Even though she had no intent to see her children harmed, why did Schmidt still deserve punishment?

AP Photo/Jae C. Hong

One of the most controversial strict liability crimes is **statutory rape,** in which an adult engages in a sexual relationship with a minor. As discussed in the introduction to this chapter, in most states, even if the minor consents to the sexual act, the crime still exists because, being underage, he or she is considered incapable of making a rational decision on the matter.[24] Therefore, statutory rape has been committed even if the adult was unaware of the minor's age or was misled to believe that the minor was older.

Accomplice Liability

Under certain circumstances, a person can be charged with and convicted of a crime that he or she did not actually commit. This occurs when the suspect has acted as an *accomplice* to a crime; that is, he or she has helped another person commit the crime. Generally, to be found guilty as an accomplice a person must have the "dual intent" (1) to aid the person who committed the crime and (2) that such aid would lead to the commission of the crime.[25] As for the *actus reus*, the accomplice must have helped the primary actor in either a physical sense (for example, by providing the getaway car) or a psychological sense (for example, by encouraging her or him to commit the crime).[26]

In some states, a person can be convicted as an accomplice even without intent if the crime was a "natural and probable consequence" of his or her actions.[27] Suppose that Jim and Mary enter Frank's home with the goal of burglary. Frank walks in on them while they are carrying out his television, and Jim shoots and kills Frank with a shotgun. Mary could be charged as an accomplice to murder because it is reasonably foreseeable that if one illegally enters another's home with a dangerous weapon, a homicide could occur.

CONCURRENCE

According to criminal law, there must be *concurrence* between the guilty act and the guilty intent. In other words, the guilty act and the guilty intent must occur together.[28] Suppose, for example, that a woman intends to murder her husband with poison in order to collect his life insurance. Every evening, this woman drives her husband home from work. On the night she plans to poison him, however, she swerves to avoid a cat crossing the road and runs into a tree. She survives the accident, but her husband is killed. Even though her intent was realized, the incident would be considered an accidental death because she had not planned to kill him by driving the car into a tree.

CAUSATION

Criminal law also requires that the criminal act cause the harm suffered. In Michigan, for example, two defendants were convicted of murder even though their victim died several years after the initial crime. In the course of that robbery, the defendants had shot the victim in the heart and abdomen and abandoned him in a sewer. Though the victim survived, his heart remained very weak. Four years later, the victim collapsed during a basketball game and died. Medical examination established that his heart failed as a direct result of the earlier injury, and the Michigan Supreme Court ruled that, despite the passing of time, the defendants' criminal act had been the cause of the man's death.[29] (Can a person cause a crime by failing to control her or his pets? See *You Be the Judge—Beware of Dog.*)

ATTENDANT CIRCUMSTANCES

In certain crimes, **attendant circumstances**—also known as accompanying circumstances—are relevant to the *corpus delicti*. Most states, for example, differentiate between simple assault and the more serious offense of aggravated assault depending on whether the defendant used a weapon such as a gun or a knife while committing the crime. Criminal law also classifies degrees of property crimes

You Be the Judge Beware of Dog

THE FACTS Dorothy, an eighty-two-year-old widow, was walking her Shih Tzu, Buttons, in her backyard when both were attacked and killed by three large pit bulls. Deana, who owned the pit bulls, had been warned on several occasions by neighbors and animal-control officers to keep her dangerous pets under control. In previous incidents, Deana's dogs had killed a kitten and a German shepherd.

THE LAW Prosecutors in Spotsylvania County, Virginia, charged Deana with involuntary manslaughter for Dorothy's death. Under state law, a person is guilty of involuntary manslaughter if he or she shows a reckless disregard of human life and knows or should know the probable consequences of his or her conduct.

YOUR DECISION "It's not something that Deana did, but something the dogs did," says Deana's defense attorney. In your opinion, did Deana show a reckless disregard of human life to the extent that she can be held responsible for the actions of her pets? (You can review the definition of recklessness on page 110.) In other words, did Deana *cause* Dorothy's death? Keep in mind that no person in Virginia history has ever been found guilty of involuntary manslaughter because of the violent behavior of his or her dog.

[To see how a Virginia jury decided this case, go to Example 4.2 in Appendix B.]

---

based on the amount stolen. According to federal statutes, the theft of less than $1,000 from a bank is a misdemeanor, while the theft of any amount over $1,000 is a felony.[30]

Requirements of Proof and Intent Attendant circumstances must be proved beyond a reasonable doubt, just like any other element of a crime.[31] Furthermore, the *mens rea* of the defendant regarding each attendant circumstance must be proved as well. Consider, for example, the Portland (Oregon) City Code provision stating that it is "unlawful for any person on a public street or in a public place to carry a firearm upon his [or her] person . . . unless all ammunition has been removed from the chamber."[32] The requirement that the firearm be loaded is an attendant circumstance to the crime of carrying the weapon in a public place and must be proved beyond a reasonable doubt. If the gun is not loaded, then there can be no crime. Furthermore, the prosecution must prove that the defendant *knew* that the gun was loaded.[33] If a legislature wants to remove such knowledge from the definition of the crime, it must say so in the statute, thus making the "loadedness" of the gun a *strict liability* (see the previous discussion) attendant circumstance.

Hate Crime Laws In most cases, a person's motive for committing a crime is irrelevant—a court will not try to read the accused's mind. Over the past few decades, however, nearly every state and the federal government have passed *hate crime laws* that make the suspect's motive an important attendant circumstance to his or her criminal act. In general, **hate crime laws** provide for greater sanctions against those who commit crimes motivated by bias against a person based on race, ethnicity, religion, gender, sexual orientation, disability, or age (see ■ Figure 4.4 on the following page).

In 2006, for example, three white men drove a Navajo man named William Blackie to a secluded area near Farmington, New Mexico, and beat him for refusing to buy them beer. Because the three men, charged with kidnapping, robbery, and assault, shouted racial slurs at Blackie during the beating, they were prosecuted

Hate Crime Law A statute that provides for greater sanctions against those who commit crimes motivated by bias against an individual or a group based on race, ethnicity, religion, gender, sexual orientation, disability, or age.

■ Figure 4.4 Offenses Motivated by Bias

In 2005, the Federal Bureau of Investigation reported 8,380 bias-motivated offenses. This chart shows the percentage distribution of the motivating factors.

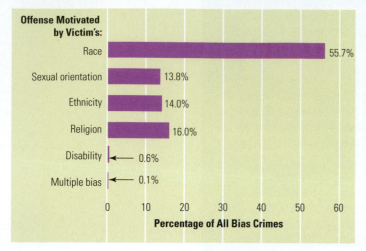

Offense Motivated by Victim's:

- Race — 55.7%
- Sexual orientation — 13.8%
- Ethnicity — 14.0%
- Religion — 16.0%
- Disability — 0.6%
- Multiple bias — 0.1%

Percentage of All Bias Crimes

Source: Adapted from Federal Bureau of Investigation, *Crime in the United States, 2005* (Washington, D.C.: U.S. Department of Justice, 2006), at **www.fbi.gov/ucr/hc2005/table1.htm**.

under the state's hate crimes act. According to this law, the punishment for most felonies can be increased by one year if the prosecution can prove that the crime was motivated by bias.[34]

Supreme Court Support The concept of a hate crime as a measurable, definable criminal act, separate from other acts, is a relatively new one. The Uniform Crime Report did not start measuring hate crimes until 1992, and the National Crime Victimization Survey did not ask questions relating to crimes of "bigotry" and prejudice" until 1997.[35] Most state hate crime laws are based on a model created by the Anti-Defamation League (ADL) in 1981. The ADL model was centered around the concept of "penalty enhancement": just as someone who robs a convenience store using a gun will face a greater penalty than if he or she had been unarmed, so will someone who commits a crime because of prejudice against her or his victim or victims.[36]

The United States Supreme Court signaled its acceptance of hate crime laws when it refused to strike down Wisconsin's penalty enhancement statute in *Wisconsin v. Mitchell* (1993).[37] The case involved Todd Mitchell, a nineteen-year-old African American who incited his friends to attack a white teenager after viewing the film *Mississippi Burning*. The victim was left in a coma for two days, and Mitchell was convicted of felony aggravated battery and sentenced to two years in prison, plus an additional two years under the state's hate crime law. The Supreme Court upheld the statute, reasoning that the results of hate crimes, such as community fear, justify harsher punishments. The Court clarified this ruling in *Apprendi v. New Jersey* (2000),[38] holding that motive must be specifically listed as an attendant circumstance in the language of any hate crime law and that, like other elements of a crime, it must be proved beyond a reasonable doubt.

Questioning Hate Laws Many of those who question the validity of hate crime legislation do so because of the First Amendment, which states that the government shall make no law "abridging the freedom of speech." Punish Todd Mitchell for his acts, they say, but not his beliefs, which he has a constitutional right to hold, no matter how unpleasant they may be. Some also question laws that seem to indicate that some victims are worthy of more protection than others. They find it disturbing that Mitchell would have received a lesser sentence if his friends had beaten an African American youth instead of a white youth.[39]

HARM

For most crimes to occur, some harm must have been done to a person or to property. A certain number of crimes are actually categorized depending on the harm done to the victim, regardless of the intent behind the criminal act. Take two offenses, both of which involve one person hitting another in the back of the head with a tire iron. In the first instance, the victim dies, and the offender is charged with murder. In the second, the victim is only knocked unconscious, and the offender is charged with battery. Because the harm in the second instance was less severe, so was the crime with which the offender was charged, even though the act was exactly the same. Furthermore, most states have different degrees of battery depending on the extent of the injuries suffered by the victim.

Many acts are deemed criminal if they could do harm that the laws try to prevent. Such acts are called **inchoate offenses.** They exist when only an attempt at a criminal act was made. If Jenkins solicits Peterson to murder Jenkins's business partner, this is an inchoate offense on the part of Jenkins, even though Peterson fails to carry out the act. Conspiracies also fall into the category of inchoate offenses; in 2003, the United States Supreme Court ruled that a person could be convicted of criminal conspiracy even though police intervention made the completion of the illegal plan impossible.[40]

> ### Self Check Fill in the Blanks
>
> Proof that a crime has been committed is established through the elements of the crime, which include the _____, or the physical act of the crime; the _____, or the intent to commit the crime; and the _____ of the guilty act and the guilty intent. With _____ crimes, the law determines that a defendant is guilty even if he or she lacked the _____ to perform a criminal act. _____ circumstances are those circumstances that accompany the main criminal act in a criminal code, and they must be proved _____, just like any other elements of a crime. Check your answers on page 130.

Defenses under Criminal Law

On Halloween night, 2005, a writer named Peter Braunstein dressed in a firefighter's uniform and set two small fires in the lobby of a New York residential building. He then forced his way into the apartment of a thirty-four-year-old woman, tied her to a bed, drugged her, and sexually molested her for thirteen hours. At trial, his lawyers claimed that Braunstein's actions were part of an elaborate fantasy life over which he had no control.

In 2007, a New York jury refused to accept Braunstein's overactive imagination as a reasonable excuse for his behavior and convicted him of kidnapping, robbery, sexual assault, and several other felonies. A number of other defenses for wrongdoing, however, can be raised in the course of a criminal trial. These defenses generally rely on one of two arguments: (1) the defendant is not responsible for the crime, or (2) the defendant was justified in committing the crime.

CRIMINAL RESPONSIBILITY AND THE LAW

The idea of responsibility plays a significant role in criminal law. In certain circumstances, the law recognizes that even though an act is inherently criminal, society will not punish the actor because he or she does not have the requisite mental condition. In other words, the law "excuses" the person for his or her behavior. Insanity, intoxication, and mistake are the most important excuse defenses today, but we start our discussion of the subject with one of the first such defenses recognized by American law: infancy.

Infancy Under the earliest state criminal codes of the United States, children younger than seven years of age could never be held legally accountable for crimes. Those between seven and fourteen years old were presumed to lack the capacity for criminal behavior, while anyone over the age of fourteen was tried as an adult. Thus, early American criminal law recognized **infancy** as a defense in which the accused's wrongdoing is excused because he or she is too young to fully understand the consequences of his or her actions.

With the creation of the juvenile justice system in the early 1900s, the infancy defense became redundant, as youthful delinquents were automatically treated differently from adult offenders. Today, most states either designate an age (sixteen or eighteen) under which wrongdoers are sent to juvenile court or allow prosecutors to decide whether a minor will be charged as an adult on a case-by-case basis. We will explore the concept of infancy as it applies to the modern American juvenile justice system in much greater detail in Chapter 15.

Insanity After Dena Schlosser killed her infant daughter Maggie by severing the child's arms, she told police officers that the voice of God had ordered her to do so. In 2006, Texas District Judge Chris Oldner found that Schlosser's severe mental problems kept her from knowing that her actions were wrong. As a result, Schlosser was sent to a mental hospital rather than to prison. Thus, **insanity** may be a defense to a criminal charge when the defendant's state of mind is such that she or he cannot claim legal responsibility for her or his actions.

Measuring Sanity Although criminal law has accepted the idea that an insane person cannot be held responsible for criminal acts, society has long debated what standards should be used to measure sanity for the purposes of a criminal trial. One of the oldest tests for insanity resulted from a case in 1843 in which Daniel M'Naghten shot and killed Edward Drummond in the belief that Drummond was Sir Robert Peel, the British prime minister. At trial, M'Naghten claimed that he was suffering from delusions at the time of the murder, and he was found not guilty by reason of insanity. In response to public outcry over the decision, the British court established the **M'Naghten rule.** Also known as the right-wrong test, the *M'Naghten rule* states that a person is legally insane and therefore not criminally responsible if, at the time of the offense, he or she was not able to distinguish between right and wrong.[41]

As ■ Figure 4.5 shows, twenty-two states still use a version of the *M'Naghten* rule. Several other jurisdictions, reacting to criticism of the *M'Naghten* rule as too narrow, have supplemented it with the less restrictive **irresistible-impulse test.** Under this combined approach, a person may be found insane even if he or she was aware that a criminal act was "wrong," provided that some "irresistible impulse" resulting from a mental deficiency drove him or her to commit the crime.[42] Under the **Durham rule,** established by the District of Columbia Federal Court of Appeals in 1954, a jury is expected to decide whether the criminal act was the product of a mental defect or disease.[43] For this reason, the rule is referred to as the *products test.* The *Durham* rule fell out of favor, however, as judges struggled to determine exactly what constituted a "mental defect or disease," and today all federal courts and about two-fifths of the states use the **substantial-capacity test** to determine sanity. Characterized as a modern improvement on the *M'Naghten* test, substantial-capacity guidelines state:

> A person is not responsible for criminal conduct if at the time of such conduct as a result of mental disease or defect he [or she] lacks substantial capacity either to appreciate the wrongfulness of his [or her] conduct or to conform his [or her] conduct to the requirements of the law.[44]

The key element of this rule is that it requires only a lack of "substantial capacity" to release a defendant from criminal responsibility. This standard is considerably easier to meet than the "right-wrong" requirements of the *M'Naghten* rule or the irresistible-impulse test.

Determining Competency In 1981, John Hinckley was found not guilty of the attempted murder of President Ronald Reagan by reason of insanity.

◀ In 2006, a West Palm Beach judge found former professional baseball player Jeff Reardon, pictured here, not guilty by reason of insanity of robbing a jewelry store. At the time of the crime, Reardon was severely depressed because of his son's recent death from a drug overdose and was taking a dozen prescription drugs to help recover from an angioplasty. What does it mean to say that an offender such as Reardon is "not responsible" for his criminal act due to mental illness?

© Palm Beach County Sheriff/ZUMA/Corbis

Due to the media attention garnered by this and other high-visibility cases, many Americans see the insanity defense as an easy means for violent criminals to "cheat" the criminal justice system. In fact, this public perception is faulty. The insanity defense is rarely entered and is even less likely to result in an acquittal, as it is difficult to prove.[45] (See the feature *Myth versus Reality—Are Too Many Criminals Found Not Guilty by Reason of Insanity?* on pages 118–119.) Psychiatry is far more commonly used in the courtroom to determine the "competency" of a defendant to stand trial. If a judge believes that the defendant is unable to understand the nature of the proceedings or to assist in his or her own defense, the trial will not take place. When **competency hearings** (which may also take place after the initial arrest and before sentencing) reveal that the defendant is in fact incompetent, the court may decide to place the defendant under treatment. Once competency has been restored to the defendant, the proceedings may recommence.[46]

Guilty but Mentally Ill Nevertheless, public backlash against the insanity defense caused seven state legislatures to pass "guilty but mentally ill" statutes. Under these laws, a defendant is guilty but mentally ill if

> at the time of the commission of the act constituting the offense, he [or she] had the capacity to distinguish right from wrong . . . but because of mental disease or defect he [or she] lacked sufficient capacity to conform his [or her] conduct to the requirements of the law.[47]

In other words, the laws allow a jury to determine that a defendant is "mentally ill," though not insane, and therefore criminally responsible for her or his actions. Defendants found guilty but mentally ill generally spend the early years of their sentences in a psychiatric hospital and the rest of the time in prison, or they receive treatment while in prison.

Intoxication The law recognizes two types of **intoxication,** whether from drugs or from alcohol: *voluntary* and *involuntary*. Involuntary intoxication occurs when a person is physically forced to ingest or is injected with an intoxicating substance, or is unaware that a substance contains drugs or alcohol. Involuntary intoxication is a viable defense to a crime if the substance leaves the person unable to form the mental state necessary to understand that the act committed while under the influence was wrong.[48] In Colorado, for example, the murder conviction of a man who shot a neighbor was overturned on the basis that the jury in the initial trial was not informed of the possibility of involuntary intoxication. At the time of the crime, the man had been taking a prescription decongestant that contained phenylpropanolamine, which has been known to cause psychotic episodes.

Voluntary drug or alcohol intoxication is also used to excuse a defendant's actions, though it is not a defense in itself. Rather, it is used when the defense attorney wants to show that the defendant was so intoxicated that *mens rea* was negated. In other words, the defendant could not possibly have had the state of mind that a crime requires. Many courts are reluctant to allow voluntary intoxication arguments to be presented to juries, however. After all, the defendant, by definition, voluntarily chose to enter an intoxicated state.

Twelve states have eliminated voluntary intoxication as a possible defense, a step that has been criticized by many legal scholars but was upheld by the United States Supreme Court in *Montana v. Egelhoff* (1996).[49] The case concerned a double

■ **Figure 4.5 Insanity Defenses**

■ *M'Naghten*
"Didn't know what he was doing or didn't know it was wrong."

■ No insanity defense
■ No standard to determine mental illness

■ *M'Naghten* plus Irresistible impulse
"Could not control his conduct."

■ Substantial capacity
"Lacks substantial capacity to appreciate the wrongfulness of his conduct or to control it."

Source: Bureau of Justice Statistics, *State Court Organization, 1998* (Washington, D.C.: U.S. Department of Justice, 2000), 257–259.

Competency Hearing A court proceeding to determine whether the defendant is mentally well enough to understand the charges filed against him or her and cooperate with a lawyer in presenting a defense. If a judge believes the defendant to be incompetent, the trial cannot take place.

Intoxication A defense for criminal liability in which the defendant claims that the taking of intoxicants rendered him or her unable to form the requisite intent to commit a criminal act.

murder committed by James Allen Egelhoff, who was extremely drunk at the time of the crime. Egelhoff was convicted on two counts of deliberate homicide, which is defined by Montana law as "knowingly" or "purposefully" causing the death of another human being.[50] Egelhoff appealed his conviction, arguing that the state statute prohibiting evidence of voluntary intoxication kept his attorneys from showing the jury that he was too inebriated to "knowingly" or "purposefully" commit the murders.[51] The Court allowed Egelhoff's conviction, ruling that states were constitutionally within their rights to abolish the voluntary intoxication defense.

Mistake Everyone has heard the saying, "Ignorance of the law is no excuse." Ordinarily, ignorance of the law or a *mistaken idea* about what the law requires is not a valid defense.[52] A few years ago, for example, Gilbert A. Robinson appealed his conviction for possession of sexually explicit photographs of teenage boys, claiming he did not know that such an act had become illegal. Chief Judge Juan R. Torruella del Valle of the Fifth Circuit Court of Appeals upheld Robinson's conviction, stating that child pornography is "inherently deleterious" and that the "probability of regulation is so great that anyone who is aware that he is in possession of [it] . . . must be presumed to be aware of the regulation."[53]

Mistake of Law In some states, however, that rule has been modified to allow for a mistake-of-law defense. People who claim that they honestly did not know that they were breaking a law may have a valid defense if (1) the law was not published or reasonably known to the public or (2) the person relied on an official statement of the law that was erroneous.[54]

Mistake of Fact A *mistake of fact,* as opposed to a *mistake of law,* operates as a defense if it negates the mental state necessary to commit a crime. If, for example, Oliver mistakenly walks off with Julie's briefcase because he thinks it is his, there is no theft. Theft requires knowledge that the property belongs to another. The mistake-of-fact defense has proved very controversial in rape and sexual assault cases, in which the accused claims that the sex was consensual while the alleged victim claims it was coerced.

Incidentally, a defendant would have a difficult time proving that he or she made a mistake of fact because of insanity. Several years ago, Eric Clark was charged with first degree murder for killing a police officer named Jeffrey Moritz in Flagstaff, Arizona. According to state law, prosecutors had to prove that Clark "intentionally or knowingly" killed a "law enforcement officer acting in the line

Myth *versus* Reality

Are Too Many Criminals Found Not Guilty by Reason of Insanity?

To many Americans, it seems likely that any person who commits a gruesome murder or any other sort of violent crime has psychological problems. The question, then, is, how do we balance the need to punish such a person with the possibility that he or she may be seriously ill?

THE MYTH The American system of criminal justice answers this question by stating that a person may not be tried for an offense if that person cannot be held legally responsible for her or his actions. Because of the publicity surrounding the insanity defense, many people are under the impression that it is a major loophole in our system, allowing criminals to be "let off" no matter how heinous their crimes.

THE REALITY In fact, the insanity defense is raised in only about 1 percent of felony trials, and it is successful only one out of every four times it is raised. The reason: it is extremely difficult to prove insanity under the law. For example, after drowning her three young sons in San Francisco Bay, LaShaun Harris entered a plea of

of duty."[55] Clark's attorneys argued that their client could not be guilty of the crime because, as the result of his mental illness, he did not realize that Moritz was a "police officer acting in the line of duty." (Clark claimed that he thought that Moritz was a space alien trying to kill him.) In 2006, the United States Supreme Court rejected this argument. The Court ruled that although a defendant has a constitutional right to present evidence of insanity as a defense to a criminal act, he or she does not have the right to present evidence of insanity to support a mistake-of-fact defense.[56]

JUSTIFICATION CRIMINAL DEFENSES AND THE LAW

In certain instances, a defendant will accept responsibility for committing an illegal act, but contend that—given the circumstances—the act was justified. In other words, even though the guilty act and the guilty intent are present, the particulars of the case relieve the defendant of criminal liability. In 2006, for example, there were 617 "justified" killings of those who were in the process of committing a felony: 376 were killed by law enforcement officers, and 241 by private citizens.[57] Four of the most important justification defenses are duress, self-defense, necessity, and entrapment.

L07

Duress   **Duress** exists when the *wrongful* threat of one person induces another person to perform an act that she or he would otherwise not perform. In such a situation, duress is said to negate the *mens rea* necessary to commit a crime. For duress to qualify as a defense, the following requirements must be met:

1. The threat must be of serious bodily harm or death.
2. The harm threatened must be greater than the harm caused by the crime.
3. The threat must be immediate and inescapable.
4. The defendant must have become involved in the situation through no fault of his or her own.[58]

When ruling on the duress defense, courts often examine whether the defendant had the opportunity to avoid the threat in question. Two narcotics cases illustrate this point. In the first, the defendant claimed that an associate threatened to kill him and his wife unless he participated in a marijuana deal. Although this contention was proved true during the course of the trial, the court rejected the duress defense because the defendant made no apparent effort to escape, nor did he report his dilemma to the police. In sum, the drug deal was avoidable—the defendant could have made an effort to extricate himself, but he did not, thereby surrendering the protection of the duress defense.[59]

Duress Unlawful pressure brought to bear on a person, causing the person to perform an act that he or she would not otherwise perform.

not guilty by reason of insanity. The success of this strategy seemed inevitable to many observers, who felt that only an insane woman could systematically kill her children as Harris had done. Indeed, in a videotaped confession Harris claimed that she had been following the orders of God. Nonetheless, prosecutors were able to convince a California jury that Harris understood that her actions were "wrong," and she was found guilty of second degree murder. Even if Harris had succeeded with the insanity defense, she would not have been "let off" in the sense that she would have been set free.

Many defendants found not guilty by reason of insanity spend more time in mental hospitals than criminals who are convicted of similar acts spend in prison.

FOR CRITICAL ANALYSIS

What do the relatively limited use and success rate of the insanity defense indicate about the impact of public opinion on criminal law?

▲ Special agents examine the body of Brian Douglas Wells, who was killed after robbing a bank in Summit Township, Pennsylvania, when a bomb attached to his neck detonated. Before his death, Wells told state troopers that the explosive device was used to force him to commit the crime. If this is true, and he had survived, would Wells have been able to claim duress as a defense?

In the second case, a taxi driver in Bogotá, Colombia, was ordered by a passenger to swallow cocaine-filled balloons and take them to the United States. The taxi driver was warned that if he refused, his wife and three-year-old daughter would be killed. After a series of similar threats, the taxi driver agreed to transport the drugs. On arriving at customs at the Los Angeles airport, the defendant consented to have his stomach X-rayed, which led to discovery of the contraband and his arrest. During trial, the defendant told the court that he was afraid to notify the police in Colombia because he believed them to be corrupt. The court accepted his duress defense, on the grounds that it met the four requirements listed above and the defendant had notified American authorities when given the opportunity to do so.[60]

Justifiable Use of Force—Self-Defense   A person who believes he or she is in danger of being harmed by another is justified in defending himself or herself with the use of force, and any criminal act committed in such circumstances can be justified as **self-defense.** Other situations that also justify the use of force include the defense of one's dwelling, the defense of other property, and the prevention of a crime. In all these situations, it is important to distinguish between deadly and nondeadly force. Deadly force is likely to result in death or serious bodily harm.

Reasonable Belief   Generally speaking, people can use the amount of nondeadly force that seems necessary to protect themselves, their dwellings, or other property or to prevent the commission of a crime. Deadly force can be used in self-defense if there is a *reasonable belief* that imminent death or bodily harm will otherwise result, if the attacker is using unlawful force (an example of lawful force is that exerted by a police officer), if the defender has not initiated or provoked the attack, and if there is no other possible response or alternative way out of the life-threatening situation.[61] Deadly force normally can be used to defend a dwelling only if the unlawful entry is violent and the person believes deadly force is necessary to prevent imminent death or great bodily harm or—in some jurisdictions—if the person believes deadly force is necessary to prevent the commission of a felony (such as arson) in the dwelling.

When a person is outside the home or in a public space, the rules for self-defense change somewhat. In almost thirty states, someone who is attacked under these circumstances has a duty to "retreat to the wall" before fighting back. In other words, under this **duty to retreat** one who is being assaulted may not resort to deadly force if she or he has a reasonable opportunity to "run away" and thus avoid the conflict. Once this person has run into a "wall," literally or otherwise, then deadly force may be used in self-defense. A recent trend in this area of the law has been to remove the duty to retreat requirement from deadly confrontations in public spaces, a topic we will discuss in the *Criminal Justice in Action* feature at the end of this chapter.

The Battered Woman Defense   About four hundred men are killed each year by a female intimate partner (wife, ex-wife, or girlfriend).[62] In many of these

Self-Defense The legally recognized privilege to protect one's self or property from injury by another. The privilege of self-defense covers only acts that are reasonably necessary to protect one's self or property.

Duty to Retreat The requirement that a person claiming self-defense prove that she or he first took reasonable steps to avoid the conflict that resulted in the use of deadly force. Generally, the duty to retreat (1) applies only in public spaces and (2) does not apply when the force used in self-defense was nondeadly.

AP Photo/Duane A. Laverty, Pool

◄ Waco, Texas, prosecutor Crawford Long shows Carolyn Thomas the handgun used by an abusive boyfriend to kill her mother and critically wound her. In the United States, intimate partners kill about 1,300 women and injure 2 million more each year. What role does a history of domestic violence play in the "battered woman defense"?

instances, the offender was subject to domestic abuse at the hands of the victim. Traditionally, however, it has been difficult, if not impossible, for women to claim self-defense in these situations for two reasons. First, domestic abuse is generally a pattern of behavior that rarely rises to the level of deadly force, so the defendant has had a difficult time proving that she faced "an immediate or imminent threat of death or serious injury." Second, juries and judges would question why the defendant did not simply leave her abuser instead of killing him.[63]

Today, most states allow defendants in this situation to present evidence of *battered woman syndrome* (BWS). Developed in the early 1970s, BWS describes the psychological changes that take place within a woman who has suffered extended abuse. These changes make it difficult for the woman to consider leaving her abuser and cause her to be in constant fear for her life—meaning that, in her mind, the threat of death or serious injury is always "immediate or imminent."[64] The majority of states now allow BWS evidence to be presented in court, not as a defense in itself, but rather as a means to satisfy the "imminence" requirement of self-defense and, less commonly, duress justifications. Despite its prevalence, BWS has come under a great deal of criticism as "junk science" that provides battered women with a handy excuse for premeditated murder.[65] The controversy has heightened with the inevitable expansion of BWS to include male victims of domestic abuse who find themselves in court on murder charges.[66]

Necessity   In 2006, Jim Stevenson was charged with felony animal cruelty for shooting the feral cats that live among the sand dunes near Galveston, Texas. He claimed that the cats needed to die to protect the local bird population, a popular tourist draw for the area. Local authorities may have been unimpressed by Stevenson's justification, but the **necessity** defense is valid under other circumstances.

According to the Model Penal Code, the necessity defense is justifiable if "the harm or evil sought to be avoided by such conduct is greater than that sought to be prevented by the law defining the offense charged."[67] For example, in one case a convicted felon was threatened by an acquaintance with a gun. The felon grabbed the gun and fled the scene, but subsequently he was arrested under a statute that prohibits convicted felons from possessing firearms. In this situation, the necessity defense was valid because the defendant's crime avoided a "greater evil."[68] The one crime for which the necessity defense is not viable is murder.[69]

Necessity A defense against criminal liability in which the defendant asserts that circumstances required her or him to commit an illegal act.

Entrapment Entrapment is a justification defense that criminal law allows when a police officer or government agent deceives a defendant into wrongdoing. Although law enforcement agents can legitimately use various forms of subterfuge—such as informants or undercover agents—to gain information or apprehend a suspect in a criminal act, the law places limits on these strategies. Police cannot persuade an innocent person to commit a crime, nor can they coerce a suspect into doing so, even if they are certain she or he is a criminal.

Stories from the Street

Go to the Stories from the Street feature at www.cjinaction.com to hear Larry Gaines tell insightful stories related to this chapter and his experiences in the field.

The Whiskey Case The guidelines for determining entrapment were established in the 1932 case of *Sorrells v. United States*.[70] The case, which took place during Prohibition when the sale of alcoholic beverages was illegal, involved a federal law enforcement agent who repeatedly urged the defendant to sell him bootleg whiskey. The defendant initially rejected the agent's overtures, stating that he "did not fool with whiskey." Eventually, however, he sold the agent a half-gallon of the substance and was summarily convicted of violating the law. The United States Supreme Court held that the agent had improperly induced the defendant to break the law and reversed his conviction.

The Pornography Case In the *Sorrells* case, the Supreme Court set the precedent for taking a "subjective" view of entrapment. In other words, the Court decided that entrapment occurs if a defendant who is not predisposed to commit a crime is enticed to do so by an agent of the government.[71] In the 1992 case of *Jacobson v. United States*,[72] for example, the U.S. Postal Inspection Service targeted the defendant as a potential purchaser of child pornography. Over a period of more than two years, postal agents sent the defendant seven letters inquiring about his sexual preferences, two sex catalogues, and two sexual-attitude surveys, all from fictitious persons and organizations. Eventually, the defendant ordered a publication called "Boys Who Love Boys" and was arrested and convicted for breaking child-pornography laws.[73] The Court overturned the conviction, ruling that entrapment had taken place because the defendant had shown no predisposition to order the illicit publication in the absence of the government's efforts. (For an overview of justification and excuse defenses, see ■ Figure 4.6.)

Self Check Fill in the Blanks

Criminal law recognizes that a defendant may not be _____ for a criminal act if her or his mental state was impaired, by either _____—the psychological inability to separate right from wrong—or _____ due to drugs or alcohol. Defendants may also claim that they were _____ in committing an act either because they were under _____ to perform an act that they would not otherwise have performed or because they were acting in _____ to protect themselves from deadly harm. _____ occurs when a government agent deceives a defendant into committing a crime. Check your answers on page 130.

Entrapment A defense in which the defendant claims that he or she was induced by a public official—usually an undercover agent or police officer—to commit a crime that he or she would otherwise not have committed.

Substantive Criminal Law Law that defines the rights and duties of individuals with respect to each other.

Procedural Criminal Law Rules that define the manner in which the rights and duties of individuals may be enforced.

Procedural Safeguards

To this point, we have focused on **substantive criminal law**, which defines the acts that the government will punish. We will now turn our attention to **procedural criminal law**. (The section that follows will provide only a short overview of criminal procedure. In later chapters, many other constitutional issues will be examined in more detail.) Criminal law brings the force of the state, with all

L08

After Hurricane Katrina swept through New Orleans, Louisiana, in late August 2005, the city needed a hero. Captain Timothy Bayard was just the cop for the job. While much of the New Orleans Police Department (NOPD) seemed ill prepared to meet the storm's challenges, Bayard turned his narcotics-vice squad into a floating rescue unit. The forty-five officers commandeered all the motorboats they could find and spread out through the inundated city. Bayard, who coordinated the effort from a casino parking lot, estimates that the men and women under his command retrieved ten thousand people from the floodwaters.

Barely a year later, Bayard was stuck behind a desk, his career jeopardized because of what he called a "boneheaded move." In July 2006, Bayard authorized an undercover operation against Bangkok Spa, a downtown New Orleans massage parlor suspected of providing sex for its clients. During the ensuing raid, his officers arrested two spa employees who happened to be witnesses in a federal corruption case against two ex-NOPD officers. Under the circumstances, it appeared as though Bayard was trying to intimidate the witnesses to keep them from testifying against his former colleagues.

A subsequent joint investigation by the NOPD and the Federal Bureau of Investigation (FBI) cleared Bayard of unlawful intent regarding the bust. Nonetheless, NOPD Police Superintendent Warren Riley relieved Bayard of his command and transferred him to a job where his main task is reviewing reports of arrests, not making them. Bayard's allies on the force have no doubt that Riley was using the Bangkok Spa incident to punish Bayard for perceived disloyalty: in January, Bayard had appeared before the U.S. Senate and harshly criticized the NOPD's reaction to Hurricane Katrina. "Taking a man of Timmy Bayard's talent and experience off the street and putting him behind a desk . . . is a total disservice to all the citizens of this city," complained one retired NOPD detective.

▲ New Orleans Police Department Captain Timothy Bayard, back to the camera, coordinates search efforts in the aftermath of Hurricane Katrina.

For the citizens of New Orleans, Timothy Bayard's suspicious demotion was just another example of their police department's ineptitude. Frustrated by a frightening post-Katrina rise in the city's murder rate, three thousand of them took to the streets in January 2007. Superintendent Warren Riley, in particular, was a target of the crowd's rage. "You have really let us down," one protester told Riley and other city officials. "You have failed

The acrimony directed at N_____ enforcement agencies receive much _____leans's finest comes as no surprise. Law in this country is good, and the bulk _____credit when the news concerning crime are the most visible representatives of _____blame when it is bad. Police officers symbolize the system for many Americ_____minal justice system; indeed, they courtroom or a prison cell. The police are en_____may never see the inside of a and protect the public good: the power to use _____ith immense power to serve But that same power alarms many citizens, who_____and the power to arrest. trarily against them. The role of the police is cons_____ut it may be turned arbi- primary mission to fight crime, or should they also_____ted as well. Is their conditions that presumably lead to crime?

This chapter will lay the foundation for our study of_____d with the social and the work that they do. A short history of policing will be _____ nation of the many different agencies that make up the Americ_____ment agen_____ _____n exam_____

■ Figure 4.6 Justification and Excuse Defenses

JUSTIFICATION DEFENSES: Based on a defendant admitting that he or she committed the particular criminal act, but asserting that, under the cricumstances, the criminal act was justified.

	The defendant must prove that:	Example
DURESS	She or he performed the criminal act under the use or threat of use of unlawful force against her or his person that a reasonable person would have been unable to resist.	A mother assists her boyfriend in committing a burglary after he threatens to kill her children if she refuses to do so.
SELF-DEFENSE	He or she acted in a manner to defend himself or herself, others, or property, or to prevent the commission of a crime.	A husband awakes to find his wife standing over him, pointing a shotgun at his chest. In the ensuing struggle, the firearm goes off, killing the wife.
NECESSITY	The criminal act he or she committed was necessary in order to avoid a harm to himself or herself or another that was greater than the harm caused by the act itself.	Four people physically remove a friend from her residence on the property of a religious cult, arguing that the crime of kidnapping was justified in order to remove the victim from the damaging influence of cult leaders.
ENTRAPMENT	She or he was encouraged by agents of the state to engage in a criminal act she or he would not have engaged in otherwise.	The owner of a boat marina agrees to allow three federal drug enforcement agents, posing as drug dealers, to use his dock to unload shipments of marijuana from Colombia.

EXCUSE DEFENSES: Based on a defendant admitting that she or he committed the criminal act, but asserting that she or he cannot be held criminally responsible for the act due to lack of criminal intent.

	The defendant must prove that:	Example
INFANCY	Because he or she was under a statutorily determined age, he or she did not have the maturity to make the decisions necessary to commit a criminal act.	A fourteen-year-old takes a handgun from his backpack at school and begins shooting at fellow students, killing three. (In such cases, the offender is often processed by the juvenile justice system rather than the criminal justice system.)
INSANITY	At the time of the criminal act, he or she did not have the necessary mental capacity to be held responsible for his or her actions.	A man with a history of mental illness pushes a woman in front of an oncoming subway train, which kills her instantly.
INTOXICATION	She or he had diminished control over her or his actions due to the influence of alcohol or drugs.	A woman who had been drinking malt liquor and vodka stabs her boyfriend to death after a domestic argument. She claims to have been so drunk as to not remember the incident.
MISTAKE	He or she did not know that his or her actions violated a law (this defense is very rarely even attempted), or that he or she violated the law believing a relevant fact to be true when, in fact, it was not.	A woman, thinking that her divorce in another state has been finalized when it was not, marries for a second time, thereby committing bigamy.

its resources, to bear against the individual. Criminal procedures, drawn from the ideals stated in the Bill of Rights, are designed to protect the constitutional rights of individuals and to prevent the arbitrary use of power by the government.

THE BILL OF RIGHTS

For various reasons, proposals related to the rights of individuals were rejected during the framing of the U.S. Constitution in 1787. In fact, the original constitution contained only three provisions that referred to criminal procedure. Article I, Section 9, Clause 2 states that the "Privilege of the Writ of Habeas Corpus shall not be suspended." As will be discussed in Chapter 10, a writ of *habeas corpus* is an order that requires jailers to bring a person before a court or judge and explain why the person is being held in prison. Article I, Section 9, Clause 3 holds that

▲ As part of heightened airport security following the September 11, 2001, terrorist attacks, a police officer leads a bomb-sniffing dog through Boston's Logan Airport. Other measures included increased scrutiny of luggage, a ban on customer parking within three hundred feet of a terminal, and not allowing anyone without a ticket past airline checkpoints. Despite the Fourth Amendment, the courts consider these actions to be reasonable, given the need to maintain airport security.

⊙ The **American Civil Liberties Union** defines its mission with the slogan, "Defending the Bill of Rights." To find its Web site, click on *Web Links* under *Chapter Resources* at **www.cjinaction.com**.

Bill of Rights The first ten amendments to the U.S. Constitution.

no "Bill of Attainder or ex post facto Law shall be passed." A bill of attainder is a legislative act that targets a particular person or group for punishment without a trial, while an *ex post facto* law operates retroactively, making an event or action illegal though it took place before the law was passed. Finally, Article III, Section 2, Clause 3 maintains that the "Trial of all Crimes" will be by jury and "such Trial shall be held in the State where the said crimes shall have been committed."

Amending the Constitution The need for a written declaration of rights of individuals eventually caused the first Congress to draft twelve amendments to the Constitution and submit them for approval by the states. Ten of these amendments, commonly known as the **Bill of Rights,** were adopted in 1791. Since then, seventeen more amendments have been added.

The Bill of Rights, as interpreted by the United States Supreme Court, has served as the basis for procedural safeguards of the accused in this country. These safeguards include the following:

1. The Fourth Amendment protection from unreasonable searches and seizures.
2. The Fourth Amendment requirement that no warrants for a search or an arrest can be issued without probable cause.
3. The Fifth Amendment requirement that no one can be deprived of life, liberty, or property without "due process" of the law.
4. The Fifth Amendment prohibition against *double jeopardy* (trying someone twice for the same criminal offense).
5. The Fifth Amendment guarantee that no person can be required to be a witness against (incriminate) himself or herself.
6. The Sixth Amendment guarantees of a speedy trial, a trial by jury, a public trial, the right to confront witnesses, and the right to a lawyer at various stages of criminal proceedings.
7. The Eighth Amendment prohibitions against excessive bails and fines and cruel and unusual punishments. (For the full text of the Bill of Rights, see Appendix A.)

Expanding the Constitution The Bill of Rights offered citizens protection only against the federal government. Shortly after the end of the Civil War, in 1868, three-fourths of the states ratified the Fourteenth Amendment to expand the protections of the Bill of Rights. For our purposes, the most important part of the amendment reads:

> No State shall make or enforce any law which shall abridge the privileges or immunities of citizens of the United States, nor shall any State deprive any person of life, liberty, or property, without due process of the law; nor deny to any person within its jurisdiction the equal protection of the laws.

The United States Supreme Court did not immediately interpret the Fourteenth Amendment as extending the procedural protections of the Bill of Rights to people who had been charged with breaking state criminal law. Indeed, it would be nearly a hundred years before those accused of crimes on the state level would enjoy all the same protections as those accused of breaking federal laws.[74] As these protections are crucial to criminal justice procedures in the United States, they will be afforded much more attention in Chapter 6, with regard to police action, and in Chapter 10, with regard to the criminal trial.

DUE PROCESS

Both the Fifth and Fourteenth Amendments provide that no person should be deprived of "life, liberty, or property without due process of the law." This **due process clause** basically requires that the government not act unfairly or arbitrarily. In other words, the government cannot rely on individual judgment and impulse when making decisions, but must stay within the boundaries of reason and the law. Of course, disagreements as to the meaning of these provisions have plagued courts, politicians, and citizens since this nation was founded, and will undoubtedly continue to do so.

To understand due process, it is important to consider its two types: procedural due process and substantive due process.

Photo by Mario Tama/Getty Images

▲ After the destruction caused by Hurricane Katrina in 2005, suspects arrested by the New Orleans Police Department such as the ones shown here were held for long periods of time before being informed of the charges against them. Two years later, the city's jails were still full of inmates who had not formally been charged with a crime. What procedural due process concerns does this situation raise?

L09 **Procedural Due Process** According to **procedural due process,** the law must be carried out by a *method* that is fair and orderly. It requires that certain procedures be followed in administering and executing a law so that an individual's basic freedoms are never violated.

For example, the United States Supreme Court requires that schools follow certain procedures before suspending students for misconduct. The Court has held that a student facing a suspension of ten days or less must be given oral or written notice of the charges against him or her. Furthermore, if the student denies the charges, he or she must be given an explanation of the evidence of misconduct and an opportunity to present his or her side of the story.[75] In criminal law, procedural due process prevents a host of unfair practices, such as forced confessions, denial of counsel, and unreasonable searches.

Substantive Due Process Fair procedures would obviously be of little use if they were used to administer unfair laws. For example, suppose a law requires everyone to wear a red shirt on Mondays. You wear a blue shirt on Monday, and you are arrested, convicted, and sentenced to one year in prison. The fact that all proper procedures were followed and your rights were given their proper protections would mean very little because the law that you broke was unfair and arbitrary.

Thus, **substantive due process** requires that the laws themselves be reasonable. The idea is that if a law is unfair or arbitrary, even if properly passed by a legislature, it must be declared unconstitutional. In the 1930s, for example, Oklahoma instituted the Habitual Criminal Sterilization Act. Under this statute, a person who had been convicted of three felonies could be "rendered sexually sterile" by the state (that is, the person would no longer be able to produce children). The United States Supreme Court held that the law was unconstitutional, as there are "limits to the extent which a legislatively represented majority may conduct biological experiments at the expense of the dignity and personality and natural powers of a minority."[76]

Due Process Clause The provisions of the Fifth and Fourteenth Amendments to the Constitution that guarantee that no person shall be deprived of life, liberty, or property without due process of law. Similar clauses are found in most state constitutions.

Procedural Due Process A provision in the Constitution that states that the law must be carried out in a fair and orderly manner.

Substantive Due Process The constitutional requirement that laws used in accusing and convicting persons of crimes must be fair.

The Supreme Court's Role in Due Process As the last example suggests, the United States Supreme Court often plays the important role of ultimately deciding when due process has been violated and when it has not. (See ■ Figure 4.7 for a list of important Supreme Court due process cases.) This is not a role that the Court has always embraced. As noted earlier, for much of its history the Court did not apply the Bill of Rights to criminal procedures in state trials. Until relatively recently most justices have felt that due process rights were not violated if state procedures were fair and, therefore, there was no need to burden the states with the Bill of Rights.[77]

This line of thinking changed in the early 1960s, when the Court—presided over by Chief Justice Earl Warren—began to *incorporate* the procedural safeguards in the Bill of Rights, meaning that they were now applicable to the states. Between 1961 and 1968, the Warren Court incorporated the right to a jury trial,[78] the right of the accused to confront witnesses at trial,[79] the right against self-incrimination,[80] the right to counsel,[81] and the right to be free from cruel and unusual punishment, among others.[82]

Challenges to Due Process The due process clause does not, however, automatically doom laws that may infringe on procedural or substantive rights. In certain circumstances, the lawmaking body may be able to prove that its interests are greater than the due process rights of the individual, and in those cases the statute may be upheld. Several years ago, for example, a U.S. appeals court upheld the immediate suspension of a kindergarten student who said, "I'm going to shoot you," to classmates during recess. Although, as we saw earlier, in most cases a school must follow certain steps before suspending a student, the court in this instance felt that the kindergarten's interest in limiting this kind of violent speech was more important than the student's due process rights.[83] (For a better understanding of the tension between procedural and substantive rights, see the feature *A Question of Ethics—Forced Competency*.)

The U.S. court system, including the Supreme Court, is more likely to defer to the government in times of national crisis. The Court was powerless in 1861,

■ **Figure 4.7** Important United States Supreme Court Due Process Decisions

Year	Issue	Amendment Involved	Court Case
1948	Right to a public trial	VI	*In re Oliver*, 333 U.S. 257
1949	No unreasonable searches and seizures	IV	*Wolf v. Colorado*, 338 U.S. 25
1961	Exclusionary rule	IV	*Mapp v. Ohio*, 367 U.S. 643
1963	Right to a lawyer in all criminal felony cases	VI	*Gideon v. Wainwright*, 372 U.S. 335
1964	No compulsory self-incrimination	V	*Malloy v. Hogan*, 378 U.S. 1
1964	Right to have counsel when taken into police custody and subject to questioning	VI	*Escobedo v. Illinois*, 378 U.S. 478
1965	Right to confront and cross-examine witnesses	VI	*Pointer v. Texas*, 380 U.S. 400
1966	Right to an impartial jury	VI	*Parker v. Gladden*, 385 U.S. 363
1966	Confessions of suspects not notified of due process rights ruled invalid	V	*Miranda v. Arizona*, 384 U.S. 436
1967	Right to a speedy trial	VI	*Klopfer v. North Carolina*, 386 U.S. 21
1967	Juveniles have due process rights, too	V	*In re Gault*, 387 U.S. 1
1968	Right to a jury trial ruled a fundamental right	VI	*Duncan v. Louisiana*, 391 U.S. 145
1969	No double jeopardy	V	*Benton v. Maryland*, 395 U.S. 784

A Question of Ethics Forced Competency

THE SITUATION Hessam Ghane has been arrested in Kansas City, Missouri, for possessing cyanide in an amount capable of "killing 800 to 1,000 people," in the words of one law enforcement official. It seems that only one aspect of the case can keep Ghane out of prison: his mental health. Ghane suffers from a severe delusional disorder that prevents him from understanding the nature of the charges against him. Hence, Ghane is unlikely to be found competent to stand trial, as he cannot meaningfully participate in the court proceedings. Missouri officials have requested that Dr. Robert McGuinn medicate Ghane with antipsychotic drugs that are otherwise harmless and will render him competent to take part in his own defense. Ghane has refused the drugs, so Dr. McGuinn would have to medicate him by force. Ghane's lawyers argue that this would violate their client's due process rights.

THE ETHICAL DILEMMA A major ethical tenet of the medical profession is that physicians should do no harm to a patient, no matter what that patient has done. Physicians are also, however, required to follow the law. As already mentioned, there are two types of due process rights: substantive and procedural. The nation's courts have consistently held that a person has a constitutionally protected, substantive "liberty interest" from unwanted bodily intrusions by the government, including being forced to take antipsychotic medication. Under procedural due process law, however, this liberty interest must always be balanced against the state's interest—here, in trying a person who as been charged with a very serious offense and may pose a great danger to the community.

WHAT IS THE SOLUTION? Should Dr. McGuinn participate in Ghane's involuntary medication? In 2003, the United States Supreme Court ruled that forced medication in these circumstances is allowed only if the government can prove that the defendant committed a "serious" crime and that successful use of the drugs will not cause any harmful side effects. Does this case meet these criteria? Even if Dr. McGuinn has legal justification for forcing competency, is such an act justified under medical ethics? Can one argue that because criminal punishment is always "harmful," no physician should aid in forcing an accused to stand trial? How does the argument change if the defendant has committed a crime that would expose her or him to the death penalty?

---

when President Abraham Lincoln suspended constitutional guarantees of *habeas corpus* at the start of the Civil War.[84] During World War II, in perhaps its most widely criticized decision of the twentieth century, the Court gave its approval to the federal government's rounding up of Japanese American citizens and confining them in "relocation" camps.[85] At the same time, thousands of Italian Americans and German Americans were also interned. Finally, since the September 11, 2001, terrorist attacks, the U.S. Department of Justice has moved to limit the due process rights of suspected terrorists and certain types of immigrants. Some observers feel that the federal government is overstepping the bounds of the Constitution by limiting access to counsel, the right to confront hostile witnesses, and a number of other due process rights. These issues will be explored in more detail in Chapter 16.

Self Check Fill in the Blanks

The basis for procedural safeguards for the accused is found in the _____ of the U.S. Constitution. According to these safeguards, no person shall be deprived of life or liberty without _____ of the law. This means that the _____ by which the law is carried out must be fair and orderly and the laws themselves must be _____. The _____ ultimately decides whether these rights have been violated. Check your answers on page 130.

"STAND YOUR GROUND" OR "SHOOT FIRST"?

Jacqueline Galas was a prostitute. On June 11, 2006, one of Galas's regular clients, a man named Frank Labiento, pointed a .357 Magnum at her in his Port Richie, Florida, home and threatened to kill her. Galas managed to calm Labiento down, and when the telephone rang, he went to answer it, leaving his handgun on a table. Galas picked up the gun and fatally shot Labiento. The prostitute's judgment may have been shaky, but her timing was impeccable. Had the shooting occurred eight months earlier, Galas would certainly have been charged with murder. Under a new self-defense law, however, Galas was not prosecuted for Labiento's death. This legislation—called a "stand your ground" law by supporters and a "shoot first" law by opponents—is the subject of this chapter's *Criminal Justice in Action* feature.

OUT WITH THE OLD

Florida's new self-defense law, called the Protection of Persons Act,[86] went into effect on October 1, 2005. Under the state's old statute, a person was justified in using deadly force in self-defense only if he or she "reasonably believed" that such force was "necessary to prevent imminent death or great bodily harm."[87] Furthermore, a person had a duty to retreat (see page 120) rather than use deadly force if the attack took place outside the home.[88]

The new "stand your ground" law changes the picture dramatically. Now, a person can automatically use deadly force against someone who unlawfully intrudes into her or his house (or vehicle), regardless of whether she or he fears for her or his safety.[89] Furthermore, the new law does away with the "duty to retreat" outside the home, stating that citizens have "the right to stand [their] ground and meet force with force, including deadly force" if they "reasonably" fear for their safety.[90] Thus, even though Jacqueline Galas could have fled Labiento's house, she acted within her rights when she picked up the gun and killed him. As of April 2007, fourteen other states had passed "stand your ground" laws with provisions similar to those found in Florida's statute.

The Case for "Stand Your Ground" Laws

- The laws give citizens more rights when it comes to making difficult, split-second decisions to protect themselves. Without such laws, a person could be criminally prosecuted or sued in civil court for shooting an intruder if he or she could not prove to the satisfaction of a judge or jury that the intruder presented an imminent danger of death or bodily harm.

- The duty to retreat increases the possibility that an attacker will harm the person who is in the process of retreating. These laws make the position of the law clear: one can stand his or her ground when attacked.

- The laws are very popular among voters in the states where they are on the books.

The Case against "Stand Your Ground" Laws

- The laws are unnecessary. Even without them, a person can use deadly force under any circumstances when there is a "reasonable" belief of deadly harm. Consequently, very few people have been successfully prosecuted or sued when they used deadly self-defense in a reasonable manner.

- Under the laws, a person who kills an intruder need not prove that the intruder posed a threat. He or she need only prove that the intruder entered the dwelling or car. This essentially gives people a "license to kill" for any reason, including spite or revenge.

- Prosecutors and police believe the laws will inevitably lead to an increase in accidental and vigilante murders.

Writing Assignment—Your Opinion

On March 28, 2006, Michael Frazzini was hiding in his mother's backyard in North Fort Myers, Florida. Wearing a ski mask and brandishing a fourteen-inch mini baseball bat, he was trying to videotape a neighbor whom he believed was harassing his mother. Todd Rasmussen, another neighbor, spotted Frazzini and, not recognizing him in the ski mask, shot and killed him.

Under Florida's old self-defense law, would Rasmussen be charged with murder? What do you think will be the consequences for Rasmussen under the new "stand your ground" law? Which outcome do you think is preferable, both in this individual case and for

Getty Images

the community as a whole? Before responding, you can review our discussions in this chapter concerning

- The purpose of criminal law (pages 106–107).
- *Mens rea* and criminal acts (pages 109–112).
- The justifiable use of self-defense (pages 120–121).

Your answer should take at least three full paragraphs.

L01 **Explain precedent and the importance of the doctrine of *stare decisis*.** Precedent is a common law concept in which one decision becomes the example or authority for deciding future cases with similar facts. Under the doctrine of *stare decisis,* judges in a particular jurisdiction are bound to follow precedents of that same jurisdiction. The doctrine of *stare decisis* leads to efficiency in the judicial system.

L02 **List the four written sources of American criminal law.** (a) The U.S. Constitution and state constitutions; (b) statutes passed by Congress and state legislatures (plus local ordinances); (c) administrative agency regulations; and (d) case law.

L03 **Explain the two basic functions of criminal law.** The primary function is to protect citizens from harms to their safety and property and from harms to society's interest collectively. The second function is to maintain and teach social values as well as social boundaries; for example, laws against bigamy and speed limits.

L04 **Delineate the elements required to establish *mens rea* (a guilty mental state).** (a) Purpose, (b) knowledge, (c) negligence, or (d) recklessness.

L05 **Explain how the doctrine of strict liability applies to criminal law.** Strict liability crimes do not allow the alleged wrongdoer to claim ignorance or mistake to avoid criminal responsibility; for example, exceeding the speed limit and statutory rape.

L06 **List and briefly define the most important excuse defenses for crimes.** Insanity—different tests of insanity can be used including (a) the *M'Naghten* rule (right-wrong test); (b) the irresistible-impulse test; (c) the *Durham* rule, also called the products test, in which the criminal act was the product of a mental defect or disease; and (d) the substantial-capacity test. **Intoxication**—voluntary and involuntary, the latter being a possible criminal defense. **Mistake**—sometimes valid if the law was not published or reasonably known or if the alleged offender relied on an official statement of the law that was erroneous. Also, a mistake of fact may negate the mental state necessary to commit a crime.

L07 **Describe the four most important justification criminal defenses. Duress**—requires that (a) the threat is of serious bodily harm or death, (b) the harm is greater than that caused by the crime; (c) the threat is immediate and inescapable; and (d) the defendant became involved in the situation through no fault of his or her own. **Justifiable use of force**—the defense of one's person, dwelling, or property, or the prevention of a crime. **Necessity**—justifiable if the harm sought to be avoided is greater than that sought to be prevented by the law defining the offense charged. **Entrapment**—that the criminal action was induced by certain governmental persuasion or trickery.

L08 **Distinguish between substantive and procedural criminal law.** The former concerns questions about what acts are actually criminal. The latter concerns procedures designed to protect the constitutional rights of individuals and to prevent the arbitrary use of power by the government.

L09 **Explain the importance of the due process clause in the criminal justice system.** The due process clause acts to limit the power of government. In the criminal justice system, the due process clause requires that certain procedures be followed to ensure the fairness of criminal proceedings and that all criminal laws be reasonable and in the interest of the public good.

Key Terms

actus reus   109
administrative law   105
attempt   109
attendant circumstances   112
Bill of Rights   124
case law   105
common law   101
competency hearing   117
constitutional law   103
corpus delicti   107
due process clause   125
duress   119
Durham rule   116

duty to retreat   120
entrapment   122
hate crime law   113
inchoate offenses   115
infancy   115
insanity   116
intoxication   117
irresistible-impulse test   116
mens rea   109
M'Naghten rule   116
Model Penal Code   105
necessity   121
negligence   110

precedent   101
procedural criminal law   122
procedural due process   125
recklessness   110
self-defense   120
stare decisis   102
statutory law   103
statutory rape   112
strict liability crimes   111
substantial-capacity test   116
substantive criminal law   122
substantive due process   125

Questions for Critical Analysis

1. Why is the common law said to be uncodified?

2. How does *stare decisis* contribute to the efficiency of a court system?

3. What is the Model Penal Code, and how has it contributed to criminal law in the United States?

4. Give an example of how the criminal justice system teaches societal boundaries.

5. Many people are careless. At what point can such carelessness be deemed criminal negligence?

6. Assume you are planning to pay someone to set fire to an old barn (arson) for the insurance money. Before you get a chance to carry out your plan, you accidentally drop a tool on another metal object, creating a spark that ignites some dry hay and burns the barn down. What essential element of a crime is missing in your actions?

7. Why do you suppose that motive usually is not considered in criminal law? Why might determining motive be difficult when prosecuting a hate crime?

8. What test is most often used for insanity, and how does it differ from other tests?

9. Why would a defense attorney admit that a client had voluntarily gotten drunk before an accident in which she hit and killed a pedestrian?

10. How has the United States Supreme Court incorporated the due process clause?

Maximize Your Best Possible Outcome for Chapter 4

1. **Maximize Your Best Chance for Getting a Good Grade on the Exam.** ThomsonNOW Personalized Study is a diagnostic study tool containing valuable text-specific resources—and because you focus on just what you don't know, you learn more in less time to get a better grade. How do you get ThomsonNOW? If your textbook does not include an access code card, go to **thomsonedu.com** to get ThomsonNOW before your next exam!

2. **Get the Most Out of Your Textbook** by going to the book companion Web site at **www.cjinaction.com** to access one of the tutorial quizzes, use the flash cards to master key terms, and check out the many other study aids you'll find there. Under chapter resources you will also be able to access the Stories from the Street feature and Web links mentioned in the textbook.

3. **Learn about Potential Criminal Justice Careers** discussed in this chapter by exploring careers online at **www.cjinaction.com**. You will find career descriptions and information about job requirements, training, salary and benefits, and the application process. You can also watch video profiles featuring criminal justice professionals.

Notes

1. Nebraska Revised Statutes Sections 28-318 and 28-319 (Supp. 2004).
2. Roger LeRoy Miller and Gaylord A. Jentz, *Business Law Today, Comprehensive Edition,* 7th ed. (St. Paul, MN: West Publishing Co., 2007), 2–3.
3. *Neff v. George,* 364 Ill. 306, 4 N.E.2d 388, 390, 391 (1936).
4. *Texas v. Johnson,* 491 U.S. 397 (1989).
5. Joshua Dressler, *Understanding Criminal Law,* 2d ed. (New York: Richard D. Irwin, 1995), 22–23.
6. *Ibid.,* 23.
7. Jim Yardley, "Unmarried and Living Together, Till the Sheriff Do Us Part," *New York Times* (March 25, 2000), A7.
8. Joel Feinberg, *The Moral Limits of the Criminal Law: Harm to Others* (New York: Oxford University Press, 1984), 221–232.
9. Flammable Fabrics Act, 15 U.S.C. Section 1196 (1994).
10. Stuart P. Green, "Why It's a Crime to Tear the Tag Off a Mattress," *Emory Law Journal* 46 (Fall 1997), 1533–1614.

11. Henry M. Hart, Jr., "The Aims of the Criminal Law," *Law & Contemporary Problems* 23 (1958), 405–406.
12. John L. Diamond, "The Myth of Morality and Fault in Criminal Law Doctrine," *American Criminal Law Review* 34 (Fall 1996), 111.
13. Lawrence M. Friedman, *Crime and Punishments in American History* (New York: Basic Books, 1993), 34.
14. *Ibid.*, 10.
15. Thomas A. Mullen, "Rule without Reason: Requiring Independent Proof of the *Corpus Delicti* as a Condition of Admitting Extrajudicial Confession," *University of San Francisco Law Review* 27 (1993), 385.
16. *Hawkins v. State*, 219 Ind. 116, 129, 37 N.E.2d 79 (1941).
17. David C. Biggs, "'The Good Samaritan Is Packing': An Overview of the Broadened Duty to Aid Your Fellowman, with the Modern Desire to Possess Concealed Weapons," *University of Dayton Law Review* 22 (Winter 1997), 225.
18. Rhode Island General Laws Section 11-56-1 (1956); Vermont Statutes Annotated Title 12, Section 519 (2000); and Wisconsin Statutes Section 940.34 (West 2000).
19. Model Penal Code Section 2.02.
20. Texas Penal Code Section 46.13 (1995).
21. Model Penal Code Section 2.02(c).
22. *Black's Law Dictionary*, 1423.
23. *United States v. Dotterweich*, 320 U.S. 277 (1943).
24. *State v. Stiffler*, 763 P.2d 308, 311 (Idaho Ct.App. 1988).
25. *State v. Harrison*, 425 A.2d 111 (1979).
26. Richard G. Singer and John Q. LaFond, *Criminal Law: Examples and Explanations* (New York: Aspen Law & Business, 1997), 322.
27. *State v. Linscott*, 520 A.2d 1067 (1987).
28. *Morissette v. United States*, 342 U.S. 246, 251–252 (1952).
29. *People v. Harding*, 443 Mich. 699–703, 506 N.W.2d 486–487 (1994).
30. Federal Bank Robbery Act, 18 U.S.C.A. Section 2113.
31. *In re Winship*, 397 U.S. 358, 364, 368–369 (1970).
32. Portland (Oregon) City Code, 14.32.010(C).
33. *Oregon v. Andrews*, 27 P.3d 137 (Or.Ct.App. 2001).
34. New Mexico Statutes Annotated Section 31-18B-3(A) (2003).
35. "Statement of the Anti-Defamation League on Bias-Motivated Crime and H.R. 1082—The Hate Crimes Prevention Act," *Chicago-Latino Law Review* (Spring 2000), 56.
36. Steve M. Freeman, "Hate Crime Laws: Punishment Which Fits the Crime," *Annual Survey of American Law* 4 (1992/1993), 581–585.
37. 508 U.S. 476 (1993).
38. 530 U.S. 466 (2000).
39. Nat Hentoff, "Letting Loose the Hate Crimes Police," *The Village Voice* (July 13, 1993).
40. *United States v. Jiminez Recio*, 537 U.S. 270 (2003).
41. *M'Naghten's Case*, 10 Cl.&F. 200, Eng.Rep. 718 (1843). Note that the name is also spelled M'Naughten and McNaughten.
42. Joshua Dressler, *Cases and Materials on Criminal Law*, 2d ed. (St. Paul, MN: West Group, 1999), 599.
43. 214 F.2d 862 (D.C.Cir. 1954).
44. Model Penal Code Section 401 (1952).
45. Stephen Lally, "Making Sense of the Insanity Plea," *Washington Post Weekly Edition* (December 1, 1997), 23.
46. Bruce J. Winick, "Presumptions and Burdens of Proof in Determining Competency to Stand Trial: An Analysis of *Medina v. California* and the Supreme Court's New Due Process Methodology in Criminal Cases," *University of Miami Law Review* 47 (1993), 817.
47. South Carolina Code Annotated Section 17-24-20(A) (Law. Co-op. Supp. 1997).
48. Lawrence P. Tiffany and Mary Tiffany, "Nosologic Objections to the Criminal Defense of Pathological Intoxication: What Do the Doubters Doubt?" *International Journal of Law and Psychiatry* 13 (1990), 49.
49. 518 U.S. 37 (1996).
50. Montana Code Annotated Section 45-5-102 (1997).
51. Montana Code Annotated Section 45-2-203 (1997).
52. Kenneth W. Simons, "Mistake and Impossibility, Law and Fact, and Culpability: A Speculative Essay," *Journal of Criminal Law and Criminology* 81 (1990), 447.
53. *United States v. Robinson*, 119 F.3d 1205 (5th Cir. 1997).
54. *Lambert v. California*, 335 U.S. 225 (1957).
55. Arizona Revised Statutes Section 13-1105(A)(3).
56. *Clark v. Arizona*, 126 S.Ct. 2709 (2006).
57. Federal Bureau of Investigation, *Crime in the United States, 2006* (Washington, D.C.: U.S. Department of Justice, 2007), at **www.fbi.gov/ucr/cius2006/offenses/expanded_information/data/shrtable_13.html**, and **www.fbi.gov/ucr/cius2006/offenses/expanded_information/data/shrtable_14.html**.
58. Craig L. Carr, "Duress and Criminal Responsibility," *Law and Philosophy* 10 (1990), 161.
59. *United States v. May*, 727 F.2d 764 (1984).
60. *United States v. Contento-Pachon*, 723 F.2d 691 (1984).
61. *People v. Murillo*, 587 N.E.2d 1199, 1204 (Ill.App.Ct. 1992).
62. Bureau of Justice Statistics, "Homicide Trends in the U.S.: Intimate Homicides," at **www.ojp.usdoj.gov/bjs/homicide/intimates.htm**.
63. Jennifer Gentile Long and Dawn Doran Wilsey, "Understanding Battered Women Syndrome and Its Application to the Duress Defense," *Prosecutor* (March/April 2006), 36.
64. Lenore E. Walker, *The Battered Woman* (New York: HarperPerennial, 1979).
65. David L. Faigman and Amy J. Wright, "The Battered Woman Syndrome in the Age of Science," *Arizona Law Review* 39 (1997), 67, 106.
66. Melody M. Crick, "Access Denied: The Problem of Abused Men in Washington," *Seattle University Law Review* (Spring 2004), 1035–1061.
67. Model Penal Code Section 3.02.
68. *United States v. Paolello*, 951 F.2d 537 (3d Cir. 1991).
69. *People v. Petro*, 56 P.2d 984 (Cal.Ct.App. 1936); and *Regina v. Dudley and Stephens*, 14 Q.B.D. 173 (1884).
70. 287 U.S. 435 (1932).
71. Kenneth M. Lord, "Entrapment and Due Process: Moving toward a Dual System of Defenses," *Florida State University Law Review* 25 (Spring 1998), 463.
72. 503 U.S. 540 (1992).
73. Fred Warren Bennett, "From *Sorrells* to *Jacobson:* Reflections on Six Decades of Entrapment Law and Related Defenses in Federal Court," *Wake Forest Law Review* 27 (1992), 829.
74. Henry J. Abraham, *Freedom and the Court: Civil Liberties in the United States*, 7th ed. (New York: Oxford University Press, 1998), 38–41.
75. *Goss v. Lopez*, 419 U.S. 565 (1975).
76. *Skinner v. Oklahoma*, 316 U.S. 535, 546–547 (1942).
77. William J. Stuntz, "The Substantive Origins of Criminal Procedure," *Yale Law Journal* 105 (1995), 440.
78. *Duncan v. Louisiana*, 391 U.S. 145 (1968).
79. *Pointer v. Texas*, 380 U.S. 400 (1965).
80. *Malloy v. Hogan*, 378 U.S. 1 (1964).
81. *Gideon v. Wainwright*, 372 U.S. 335 (1963).
82. *Robinson v. California*, 370 U.S. 660 (1962).
83. "*S.G.V. Sayreville Board of Education et al.*, No. 02-2384," *New Jersey Law Journal* (July 14, 2003), 139.
84. Alfred H. Kelley and Winfred A. Harbison, *The American Constitution: Its Origins and Developments*, 7th ed. (New York: Norton, 1991), 441–448.
85. *Korematsu v. United States*, 323 U.S. 214 (1944).
86. H.B. 249, 107th Legislature (Fla. 2005).
87. Florida Statutes Section 776.012 (2004).
88. *Weiand v. State*, 732 So.2d 1044 (Fla. 1999).
89. Florida Statutes Section 776.013 (2005).
90. *Ibid.*

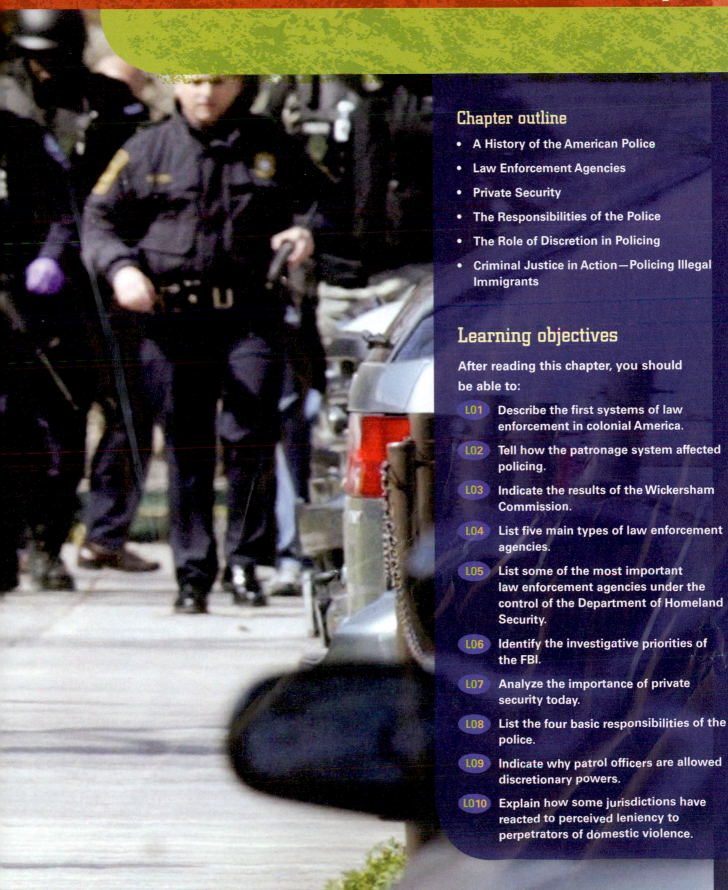

CHAPTER 5

Law Enforcement Today

Chapter outline

- A History of the American Police
- Law Enforcement Agencies
- Private Security
- The Responsibilities of the Police
- The Role of Discretion in Policing
- Criminal Justice in Action—Policing Illegal Immigrants

Learning objectives

After reading this chapter, you should be able to:

LO1 Describe the first systems of law enforcement in colonial America.

LO2 Tell how the patronage system affected policing.

LO3 Indicate the results of the Wickersham Commission.

LO4 List five main types of law enforcement agencies.

LO5 List some of the most important law enforcement agencies under the control of the Department of Homeland Security.

LO6 Identify the investigative priorities of the FBI.

LO7 Analyze the importance of private security today.

LO8 List the four basic responsibilities of the police.

LO9 Indicate why patrol officers are allowed discretionary powers.

LO10 Explain how some jurisdictions have reacted to perceived leniency to perpetrators of domestic violence.

After Hurricane Katrina swept through New Orleans, Louisiana, in late August 2005, the city needed a hero. Captain Timothy Bayard was just the cop for the job. While much of the New Orleans Police Department (NOPD) seemed ill prepared to meet the storm's challenges, Bayard turned his narcotics-vice squad into a floating rescue unit. The forty-five officers commandeered all the motorboats they could find and spread out through the inundated city. Bayard, who coordinated the effort from a casino parking lot, estimates that the men and women under his command retrieved ten thousand people from the floodwaters.

Barely a year later, Bayard was stuck behind a desk, his career jeopardized because of what he called a "boneheaded move." In July 2006, Bayard authorized an undercover operation against Bangkok Spa, a downtown New Orleans massage parlor suspected of providing sex for its clients. During the ensuing raid, his officers arrested two spa employees who happened to be witnesses in a federal corruption case against two ex-NOPD officers. Under the circumstances, it appeared as though Bayard was trying to intimidate the witnesses to keep them from testifying against his former colleagues.

A subsequent joint investigation by the NOPD and the Federal Bureau of Investigation (FBI) cleared Bayard of unlawful intent regarding the bust. Nonetheless, NOPD Police Superintendent Warren Riley relieved Bayard of his command and transferred him to a job where his main task is reviewing reports of arrests, not making them. Bayard's allies on the force have no doubt that Riley was using the Bangkok Spa incident to punish Bayard for perceived disloyalty: in January, Bayard had appeared before the U.S. Senate and harshly criticized the NOPD's reaction to Hurricane Katrina. "Taking a man of Timmy Bayard's talent and experience off the street and putting him behind a desk . . . is a total disservice to all the citizens of this city," complained one retired NOPD detective.

▲ New Orleans Police Department Captain Timothy Bayard, back to the camera, coordinates search efforts in the aftermath of Hurricane Katrina.

For the citizens of New Orleans, Timothy Bayard's suspicious demotion was just another example of their police department's ineptitude. Frustrated by a frightening post-Katrina rise in the city's murder rate, three thousand of them took to the streets in January 2007. Superintendent Warren Riley, in particular, was a target of the crowd's rage. "You have really let us down," one protester told Riley and other city officials. "You have failed us."[1]

The acrimony directed at New Orleans's finest comes as no surprise. Law enforcement agencies receive much of the credit when the news concerning crime in this country is good, and the bulk of the blame when it is bad. Police officers are the most visible representatives of our criminal justice system; indeed, they symbolize the system for many Americans who may never see the inside of a courtroom or a prison cell. The police are entrusted with immense power to serve and protect the public good: the power to use weapons and the power to arrest. But that same power alarms many citizens, who fear that it may be turned arbitrarily against them. The role of the police is constantly debated as well. Is their primary mission to fight crime, or should they also be concerned with the social conditions that presumably lead to crime?

This chapter will lay the foundation for our study of law enforcement agents and the work that they do. A short history of policing will be followed by an examination of the many different agencies that make up the American law enforcement

Criminal Justice ⚖ Now™

Maximize your study time by using ThomsonNOW's Personalized Study plan to help you review this chapter and prepare for examination. The Study Plan will

- Help you identify areas on which you should concentrate

- Provide interactive exercises to help you master the chapter concepts; and

- Provide a post-test to confirm you are ready to move on to the next chapter information.

system. We will also look at the various responsibilities of police officers and discuss the crucial role of discretion in law enforcement.

A History of the American Police

Although modern society relies on law enforcement officers to control and prevent crime, in the early days of this country police services had little to do with crime control. The policing efforts in the first American cities were directed toward controlling certain groups of people (mostly slaves and Native Americans), delivering goods, regulating activities such as buying and selling in the town market, maintaining health and sanitation, controlling gambling and vice, and managing livestock and other animals.[2] Furthermore, these police services were for the most part performed by volunteers, as a police force was an expensive proposition. Most communities simply could not afford to pay a group of law enforcement officers.[3]

> "Every society gets the kind of criminal it deserves. What is equally true is that every community gets the kind of law enforcement it insists on."
>
> —Robert Kennedy, U.S. attorney general (1964)

Eventually, of course, as the populations of American cities grew, so did the need for public order and the willingness to devote resources to the establishment of formal police forces. Policing in the United States and in England evolved along similar lines, and many of our policing institutions have their roots in English tradition. Consequently, we will begin our discussion of the history of American police with a look back at its English beginnings.

ENGLISH ROOTS

Before William the Conqueror invaded the island in 1066, the dominant system of law enforcement in Anglo-Saxon England was the **tithing system.** Every male was enrolled in a group of ten families, which was called a *tithing*. If one person in the tithing committed a crime, then every person in the group was responsible for paying the fine. The theory was that this obligation would be an incentive for the tithing to engage in collective community policing. Later, ten tithings were joined together to form a *hundred*, whose top law official was the *reeve*. Finally, the hundreds were consolidated into *shires* (the equivalent of modern counties), and the law enforcement official became known as the **shire-reeve.** As the phonetics suggest, this official is the earliest example of what is now the county sheriff.

The Role of the Constable In 1326, the office of the **justice of the peace** was established to replace the shire-reeve. Over the next centuries, in most English cities the justice of the peace, with the help of a constable, came to oversee various law enforcement activities, including organizing the night watch, investigating crimes, and securing criminals for trial. In the countryside, the hundred was replaced by the parish, which corresponded to the territory served by a particular church and included its members. Under the *parish constable system*, the parish hired a person to oversee criminal justice for its parishioners.

The London Experiments By the mid-1700s, London, England—one of the largest cities in the Western world—still did not have an organized system of law enforcement. Crime was endemic to city life, and the government's only recourse was to *read the riot act* (call in the military when the lawbreaking became unbearable). Such actions were widely unpopular, as the townspeople did not appreciate being disciplined (and fired on) by soldiers whose salaries they were paying. Furthermore, the soldiers proved unreliable peacemakers, as they were hesitant to use force against their fellow London citizens. Despite rampant crime in the city, most Londoners were not in favor of a police force under the control of the city government. English history is rife with instances in which the king or some other

Tithing System In Anglo-Saxon England, a system of law enforcement in which groups of ten families, known as tithings, were collectively responsible for law and order within their groups.

Shire-Reeve The chief law enforcement officer in an early English shire, or county. The forerunner of the modern sheriff.

Justice of the Peace Established in fourteenth-century England, a government official who oversaw various aspects of local law enforcement. The post eventually became strictly identified with judicial matters.

The first modern police force was established in London by the Metropolitan Police Act of 1829. Sir Robert Peel, the politician who pushed through the legislation, wanted a police force that would provide citizens with "the full and complete protection of the law" and "check the increase of crime." To fulfill these objectives, Peel's early police were guided by the basic principles listed here.

1. The police force must be organized along military lines.
2. Police administrators and officers must be under government control.
3. Emphasis must be placed on hiring qualified persons and training them properly.
4. New police officers must complete a probationary period; if they fail to meet standards during this time, they will not be hired as permanent officers.
5. Police personnel should be assigned to specific areas of the city for a specific time period.
6. Police headquarters must be centrally located in the city.
7. Police officers must maintain proper appearances at all times in order to gain and keep the respect of citizens.
8. Individual police officers should be able to control their temper and refrain from violence whenever possible.
9. Police records must be kept in order to measure police effectiveness.

government official abused military power by turning it against the citizens. Therefore, the citizenry were wary of any formal, armed organization that could restrict their individual liberties.

This mistrust began to ebb in 1829, when British Home Secretary Sir Robert "Bobbie" Peel pushed the Metropolitan Police Act through Parliament. This legislation has had a lasting impact, as many of its operating goals were similar to those of modern police forces (see ■ Figure 5.1 for a summary of the act). Under the terms of this act, the London Metropolitan Police was formed. One thousand strong at first, the members of this police force were easily recognizable in their uniforms that included blue coats and top hats. Under Peel's direction, the "bobbies," as the police were called in honor of their founder, had four specific operating philosophies:

1. To reduce tension and conflict between law enforcement officers and the public.
2. To use nonviolent means (they did not carry firearms) in keeping the peace, with violence to be used only as a last resort. This point was crucial because, as mentioned earlier, the English were suspicious of armed government military organizations. Being unarmed, the bobbies could hardly be confused with soldiers.
3. To relieve the military from certain duties, such as controlling urban violence. (Peel specifically hoped that his police would be less inclined to use excessive force than the military had been.)
4. To be judged on the absence of crime rather than through high-visibility police action.[4]

London's police operation was so successful that it was soon imitated in smaller towns throughout England and, eventually, in the United States.

THE EARLY AMERICAN POLICE EXPERIENCE

In colonial America and immediately following the American Revolution (1775–1783), law enforcement virtually mirrored the English system. Constables and night watchmen were taken from the ranks of ordinary citizens. The governor of each colony hired a sheriff in each county to oversee the formal aspects of law enforcement, such as selecting juries and managing jails and prisons.[5] These colonial appointees were not always of the highest moral character. In 1730, the Pennsylvania colony felt the need to pass laws specifically prohibiting sheriffs from extorting money from prisoners or selling "strong liquors" to "any person under arrest."[6]

The First Police Department In 1801, Boston became the first American city to acquire a formal night watch; the watchmen were paid 50 cents a night. For the next three decades, most major cities went no further than the watch system. Finally, facing the same pressures as London, major American metropolitan areas began to form "reactive patrol units" geared toward enforcing the law and preventing crime.[7] In 1833, Philadelphia became the first city to employ both day and night watchmen. Five years later, working from Sir Robert Peel's model, Boston formed the first organized police department, consisting of six full-time officers. In 1844, New York City set the foundation for the modern police department by combining its day and night watches under the control of a single police chief. By the onset of the Civil War in 1861, a number of American cit-

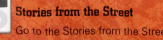

Stories from the Street
Go to the Stories from the Street feature at **www.cjinaction.com** to hear Larry Gaines tell insightful stories related to this chapter and his experiences in the field.

ies, including Baltimore, Boston, Chicago, Cincinnati, New Orleans, and Philadelphia, had similarly consolidated police departments, modeled on the Metropolitan Police of London.

Like their modern counterparts, many early police officers were hard working, honest, and devoted to serving and protecting the public. On the whole, however, in the words of historian Samuel Walker, "The quality of American police service in the nineteenth century could hardly have been worse."[8] This poor quality can be attributed to the fact that the recruitment and promotion of police officers were intricately tied into the politics of the day. Police officers received their jobs as a result of political connections, not because of any particular skills or knowledge. Whichever political party was in power in a given city would hire its own cronies to run the police department; consequently, the police were often more concerned with serving the interests of the political powers than with protecting the citizens.[9]

▲ A horse-drawn police wagon used by the New York City Police Department, circa 1886. In the 1880s a number of American cities introduced patrol wagons, which transported prisoners and drunks and also performed ambulance duties. Along with signal service, or "call boxes," the police wagon represented a "revolution" in police methods. If a patrol officer made an arrest far from headquarters, he could now call the station and request a police wagon to pick up and deliver the arrested person (instead of having to deliver the arrestee himself).

The Spoils System Corruption was rampant during this *political era* of policing, which lasted roughly from 1840 to 1930. (See ■ Figure 5.2 on the next page for an overview of the three eras of policing, which are discussed in this chapter and referred to throughout the book.) Police salaries were relatively low; thus, many police officers saw their positions as opportunities to make extra income through any number of illegal activities. Bribery was common, as police would use their close proximity to the people to request "favors," which went into the police officers' own pockets or into the coffers of the local political party as "contributions."[10] This was known as the **patronage system,** or the "spoils system," because to the political victors went the spoils.

L02

The political era also saw police officers take an active role in providing social services for their bosses' constituents. In many instances, this role even took precedence over law enforcement duties. Politicians realized that they could attract more votes by offering social services to citizens than by arresting them, and they required the police departments under their control to act accordingly.

THE MODERNIZATION OF THE AMERICAN POLICE

The abuses of the political era of policing did not go unnoticed. Nevertheless, it was not until 1929 that President Herbert Hoover appointed the national Commission on Law Observance and Enforcement to assess the American criminal justice system. The Wickersham Commission, named after its chairman, George Wickersham, focused on two areas of American policing that were in need of reform: (1) police brutality and (2) "the corrupting influence of politics." According to the commission, this reform should come about through higher personnel standards, centralized police administrations, and the increased use of technology.[11] Reformers of the time took the commission's findings as a call for the professionalization of American police and initiated the progressive (or *reform*) era in American policing.

L03

Professionalism In truth, the Wickersham Commission was not groundbreaking. Many of its recommendations echoed the opinions of one of its contributors—August Vollmer, the police chief of Berkeley, California, from 1905 until 1932. Known as "the father of modern police administration," Vollmer pioneered the training of potential police officers in institutions of higher learning. The first

Patronage System A form of corruption in which the political party in power hires and promotes police officers, receiving job-related "favors" in return.

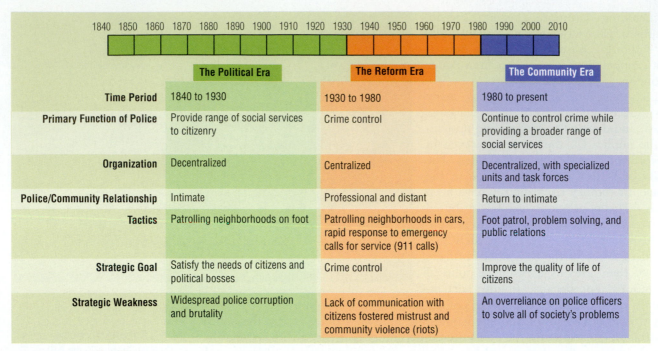

	The Political Era	The Reform Era	The Community Era
Time Period	1840 to 1930	1930 to 1980	1980 to present
Primary Function of Police	Provide range of social services to citizenry	Crime control	Continue to control crime while providing a broader range of social services
Organization	Decentralized	Centralized	Decentralized, with specialized units and task forces
Police/Community Relationship	Intimate	Professional and distant	Return to intimate
Tactics	Patrolling neighborhoods on foot	Patrolling neighborhoods in cars, rapid response to emergency calls for service (911 calls)	Foot patrol, problem solving, and public relations
Strategic Goal	Satisfy the needs of citizens and political bosses	Crime control	Improve the quality of life of citizens
Strategic Weakness	Widespread police corruption and brutality	Lack of communication with citizens fostered mistrust and community violence (riots)	An overreliance on police officers to solve all of society's problems

■ **Figure 5.2** **The Three Eras of American Policing**

George L. Kelling and Mark H. Moore have separated the history of policing in the United States into three distinct periods. Above is a brief summarization of these three eras.

Source: Adapted from George L. Kelling and Mark H. Moore, "From Political to Reform to Community: The Evolving Strategy of Police," in *Community Policing: Rhetoric or Reality,* ed. Jack R. Greene and Stephen D. Mastrofski (New York: Praeger Publishers, 1991), 14–15, 22–23; plus authors' updates. Reproduced with permission of Greenwood Publishing Group, Inc., Westport, Connecticut.

Professional Model A style of policing advocated by August Vollmer and O. W. Wilson that emphasizes centralized police organizations, increased use of technology, and a limitation of police discretion through regulations and guidelines.

program to grant a degree in law enforcement, at San Jose State College (now a university), was developed under Vollmer.

Along with increased training, Vollmer also championed the use of technology in police work. His Berkeley police department became the first in the nation to use automobiles to patrol city streets and to hire a scientist to assist in solving crimes.[12] Furthermore, Vollmer believed that police could prevent crime by involving themselves in the lives of *potential* criminals, which led to his establishing the first juvenile crime unit in the nation.

Vollmer's devotion to modernism was also apparent in the career of his most successful protégé, police reformer O. W. Wilson, who promoted a style of policing known as the **professional model.** In an attempt to remove politics from police work, Wilson stressed the need for efficiency through bureaucracy and technology.

Administrative Reforms Under the professional model, police chiefs, who had been little more than figureheads during the political era, took more control over their departments. A key to these efforts was the reorganization of police departments in many major cities. To improve their control over operations, police chiefs began to add midlevel positions to the force. These new officers, known as majors or assistant chiefs, could develop and implement crime-fighting strategies and more closely supervise individual officers. Police chiefs also tried to consolidate their power by bringing large areas of a city under their control so that no local ward, neighborhood, or politician could easily influence a single police department.

Finally, police chiefs set up special units such as criminal investigation, vice, and traffic squads with jurisdiction-wide power. Previously, all police powers within a precinct were controlled by the politicians in that precinct. By creating specialized units that worked across all precincts, the police chiefs increased their own power at the expense of the political bosses.

Technology Technological innovations on all fronts—including patrol cars, radio communications, public records systems, fingerprinting, toxicology (the study of poisons), and forensics (the application of chemistry to the examination of physical evidence)—allowed police operations to move even more quickly toward O. W. Wilson's professional model. By the 1950s, America prided itself on having the most modern and professional police force in the world. (The pace of technological innovation continues to this day, as you can see in the feature *CJ and Technology—Project*

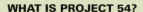

CJ and Technology

Project 54

WHAT IS PROJECT 54?

Project 54 is a voice-recognition system developed by researchers at the University of New Hampshire for installation in police cars. The system features four Andrea digital array microphones that are positioned in the cab of the automobile to cancel all noise except the sound of the police officer's voice.

WHAT DOES PROJECT 54 DO?

To a certain extent, the increased number of "gadgets" found in most police cars has become problematic. An average police cruiser contains a radio with as many as 250 channels, communication and radar devices, a computer-operated mobile data terminal, and siren and light controls. It can be difficult for a patrol officer to "multitask," particularly during pursuits. Project 54 software allows officers to control this technology without having to divert their attention from the road or take a hand off the steering wheel. The officer simply pushes a button, and the equipment becomes voice operated. So, for example, if the officer sees a hit-and-run accident, he or she can switch on the automobile's siren and flashing lights, call for an ambulance, and run a check on the offender's license plate—all by voice command.

THINKING ABOUT PROJECT 54

The next step for Project 54 is to give patrol officers voice control over video cameras positioned on their car's exterior. In Chicago, law enforcement authorities have already had considerable success with this kind of technology. In the first six weeks of operation, a database and camera system that automatically reads and checks the license plates of every car it passes led to the recovery of forty-eight stolen vehicles and two stolen handguns. What might be some of the drawbacks of having police cars equipped with such powerful video cameras?

For more information on Project 54 and other CJ technologies, click on *Web Links* under *Chapter Resources* at **www.cjinaction.com**.

54.) As efficiency became the goal of the reform-era police chief, however, relations with the community suffered. Instead of being members of the community, police officers were now seen almost as intruders, patrolling the streets in the anonymity of their automobiles. The drawbacks of this perception—and the professional model in general—would soon become evident.

Turmoil in the 1960s The 1960s was one of the most turbulent decades in American history. The civil rights movement, though not inherently violent, intensified feelings of helplessness and impoverishment in African American communities. These frustrations resulted in civil unrest, and many major American cities experienced race riots in the middle years of the decade.

> "He may be a very nice man. But I haven't got the time to figure that out. All I know is, he's got a uniform and a gun and I have to relate to him that way."
>
> —*James Baldwin, American author (1971)*

Even though police brutality often provided the spark for riots—and there is little question that police departments often overreacted to antiwar demonstrations during the Vietnam era (1964–1975)—it would be simplistic to blame the strife of the 1960s on the police. The rioters were reacting to social circumstances that they found unacceptable. Their clashes with the police were the result rather than the cause of these problems. Many observers, however, believed that the police *contributed* to the disorder. The National Advisory Commission on Civil Disorders stated bluntly that poor relations between the police and African American communities were partly to blame for the violence that plagued many of those communities.[13] In striving for professionalism, the police appeared to have lost touch with the citizens they were supposed to be serving. To repair their damaged relations with a large segment of the population, police would have to rediscover their community roots.

RETURNING TO THE COMMUNITY

The beginning of the third era in American policing, the *community era*, may have started with several government initiatives that took place in 1968. Of primary importance was the Omnibus Crime Control and Safe Streets Act, which was passed that year.[14] Under this act, the federal government provided state and local police departments with funds to create a wide variety of police-community programs. Most large-city police departments established entire units devoted to community relations, implementing programs that ranged from summer recreation activities for inner-city youths to "officer-friendly" referral operations that encouraged citizens to come to the police with their crime concerns.

In the 1970s, as this vital rethinking of the role of the police was taking place, the country was hit by a crime wave. Thus, police administrators were forced to combine efforts to improve community relations with aggressive and innovative crime-fighting strategies. At first, these strategies were *reactive;* that is, they focused on reducing the amount of time the police took to react to crime—how quickly they were able to reach the scene of a crime, for example. Eventually, police departments began to focus on *proactive* strategies—that is, strategies aimed at stopping crimes before they are committed. A dedication to proactive strategies led to widespread acceptance of *community policing* in the 1980s and 1990s. Community policing is based on the notion that meaningful interaction between officers and citizens will lead to a partnership in preventing and fighting crime.[15] Though the idea of involving members of the community in this manner is hardly new—a similar principle was set forth by Sir Robert Peel—innovative tactics in community policing, many of which will be discussed in Chapter 6, have had a significant impact on modern police work.

Law Enforcement Agencies

Another aspect of modern police work is the "multilayering" of law enforcement. For example, a wide network of local, state, and federal law enforcement agencies was involved in the extensive hunt for Richard Lee McNair after he escaped from a Pollock, Louisiana, prison in 2006. McNair had slipped out of the maximum-security facility by hiding in a mailbag. Taking part in the search were hundreds of law enforcement agents from local police and sheriffs' departments in the Pollock area, the Louisiana State Police, the FBI, and the U.S. Marshals Service.

The manhunt illustrates how many agencies can become involved in a single incident. There are over 14,330 law enforcement agencies in the United States, employing nearly 990,000 people.[16] The various agencies include:

- 3,088 sheriffs' departments.
- 1,332 special police agencies, limited to policing parks, schools, airports, and other areas.
- 49 state police departments, with Hawaii being the one exception.
- 70 federal law enforcement agencies.

Each level has its own set of responsibilities, which we shall discuss starting with local police departments.

MUNICIPAL LAW ENFORCEMENT AGENCIES

According to the FBI, there are 2.4 state and local police officers for every 1,000 citizens in the United States.[17] This average somewhat masks the discrepancies between the police forces in urban and rural America. As noted in Chapter 1, the vast majority of all police officers work in small and medium-sized police departments (see ■ Figure 5.3 on the next page). While the New York City Police Department has more than 35,000 employees, some 560 small towns have only one police officer.[18]

Of the three levels of law enforcement, municipal agencies have the broadest authority to apprehend criminal suspects, maintain order, and provide services to the community. Whether the local officer is part of a large force or the only law enforcement officer in the community, he or she is usually responsible for a wide spectrum of duties, from responding to noise complaints to investigating homicides. Much of the criticism of local police departments is based on the belief that local police are too underpaid or poorly trained to handle these various responsibilities. Reformers have suggested that residents of smaller American towns would benefit from greater statewide coordination of local police departments.[19]

SHERIFFS AND COUNTY LAW ENFORCEMENT

A vestige of the English shire-reeve discussed earlier in the chapter, the **sheriff** is still an important figure in American law enforcement. Almost every one of the more than three thousand counties in the United States (except those in Alaska) has a sheriff. In every state except Rhode Island and Hawaii, sheriffs are elected by members of the community for two- or four-year terms and are paid a salary set by the state legislature or county board. As elected officials who do not necessarily need a background in law enforcement, modern sheriffs resemble their counterparts from the political era of policing in many ways. Simply stated, the sheriff is also a politician. When a new sheriff is elected, she or he will sometimes repay political debts by appointing new deputies or promoting those who have given her or him support. This high degree of instability and personnel turnover in many states is seen as one of the weaknesses of county law enforcement.[20]

Size and Responsibility of Sheriffs' Departments
Like municipal police forces, sheriffs' departments vary in size. The largest is the Los Angeles County Sheriff's Department, with more than 8,600 full-time employees. Of the 3,061 sheriffs' departments in the country, thirteen employ more than 1,000 officers, while nineteen have only one.[21]

The image of the sheriff as a powerful figure patrolling vast expanses is not entirely misleading. Most sheriffs' departments are assigned their duties by state law. About 80 percent of all sheriffs' departments have the primary responsibility for

Sheriff The primary law enforcement officer in a county, usually elected to the post by a popular vote.

▼ A local police officer operates a roadblock as part of the search for Jason Lee Wheeler, who killed a Lake County (Florida) sheriff's deputy and wounded two others in 2005. The search for Wheeler, which ended successfully later that day, involved members of the U.S. Marshals Service, the Orlando Police Department, and the Seminole, Orange, and Brevard County Sheriff's Departments. Why would local law enforcement agencies seek the aid of federal law enforcement agencies in a situation such as this one?

AP Photo/Phil Sandlin

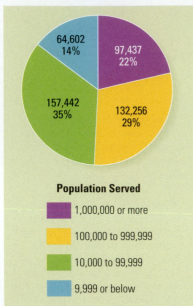

Population Served

- 1,000,000 or more
- 100,000 to 999,999
- 10,000 to 99,999
- 9,999 or below

64,602
14%

97,437
22%

157,442
35%

132,256
29%

■ **Figure 5.3 Full-Time Police Personnel, by Size of Population Served**

Source: Matthew J. Hickman and Brian A. Reaves, *Local Police Departments, 2003* (Washington, D.C.: U.S. Department of Justice, May 2006), Table 3, p. 3.

Coroner The medical examiner of a county, usually elected by popular vote.

investigating violent crimes in their jurisdictions. Other common responsibilities of a sheriff's department include:

- Investigating drug crimes.
- Maintaining the county jail.
- Carrying out civil and criminal processes within county lines, such as serving eviction notices and court summonses.
- Keeping order in the county courthouse.
- Collecting taxes.
- Enforcing orders of the court, such as overseeing the sequestration of a jury during a trial.[22]

It is easy to confuse sheriffs' departments and local police departments. As ■ Figure 5.4 shows, both law enforcement agencies are responsible for many of the same tasks, including crime investigation and routine patrol. There are differences, however, also evident in Figure 5.4: sheriffs' departments are more likely to be involved in county court and jail operations and to perform certain services such as search and rescue. Local police departments, for their part, are more likely to perform traffic-related functions than are sheriffs' departments.

The County Coroner Another elected official on the county level is the **coroner,** or medical examiner. Duties vary from county to county, but the coroner has a general mandate to investigate "all sudden, unexplained, unnatural, or suspicious deaths" reported to the office. The coroner is ultimately responsible for determining the cause of death in these cases. Coroners also perform autopsies and assist other law enforcement agencies in homicide investigations.[23] In certain rare circumstances, such as when the sheriff is arrested or otherwise forced to leave his or her post, the coroner becomes the leading law enforcement officer of the county.

STATE POLICE AND HIGHWAY PATROLS

The most visible state law enforcement agency is the state police or highway patrol agency. Historically, state police agencies were created for four reasons:

1. To assist local police agencies, which often did not have adequate resources or training to handle their law enforcement tasks.
2. To investigate criminal activities that crossed jurisdictional boundaries (such as when bank robbers committed a crime in one county and then fled to another part of the state).
3. To provide law enforcement in rural and other areas that did not have local or county police agencies.
4. To break strikes and control labor movements.

The first statewide police organization was the Texas Rangers. When this organization was initially created in 1835, the Rangers' primary purpose was to patrol the border with Mexico as scouts for the Republic of Texas Army. The Rangers evolved into a more general-purpose law enforcement agency, and in 1874 they were commissioned as police officers and given law enforcement duties. The Arizona Rangers (created in 1901) and the New Mexico Mounted Police (1905) were formed in a similar manner.

The Difference between the State Police and Highway Patrols Today, there are twenty-three state police agencies and twenty-six highway patrols in the United States. State police agencies have statewide jurisdiction and are authorized to perform a wide variety of law enforcement tasks. Thus, they provide the same services as city or county police departments and are limited only by the boundaries of the state. In contrast, highway patrols have limited authority. They are limited either by their jurisdiction or by the specific types of offenses they have the authority to control. As their name suggests, most highway patrols concentrate

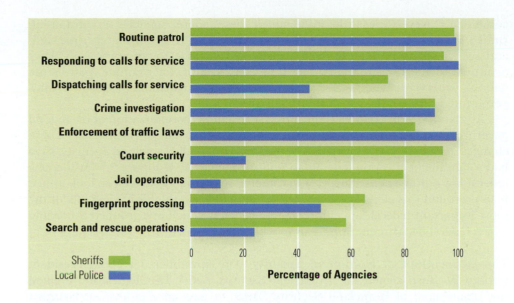

■ **Figure 5.4** The Functions of Sheriffs' and Local Police Departments

Sheriffs' and local police departments perform many of the same functions. As you see here, however, the emphasis is often different. Sheriffs' departments are much more involved in operating local jails, while police departments are more likely to deal with traffic control.

Source: Bureau of Justice Statistics, *Sheriffs' Departments, 1997* (Washington, D.C.: U.S. Department of Justice, February 2000), 14.

primarily on regulating traffic; specifically, they enforce traffic laws and investigate traffic accidents. Furthermore, they usually limit their activity to patrolling state and federal highways.

Trying to determine what state agency has which duties can be confusing. The Washington State Highway Patrol, despite its name, also has state police powers. In addition, thirty-five states have investigative agencies that are independent of the state police or highway patrol. Such agencies are usually found in states with highway patrols, and they have the primary responsibility of investigating criminal activities. For example, in addition to its highway patrol, Oklahoma runs a State Bureau of Investigation and a State Bureau of Narcotics and Dangerous Drugs. Each state has its own methods of determining the jurisdictions of these various organizations.

For the most part, however, state police are complementary to local law enforcement agencies. They maintain crime labs to assist in local investigations and also keep statewide intelligence files. State officers in some instances also provide training to local police and will assist local forces when needed.[24]

Limited-Purpose Law Enforcement Agencies Even with the agencies just discussed, a number of states have found that certain law enforcement areas need more specific attention. As a result, a wide variety of limited-purpose law enforcement agencies have sprung up in the fifty states. For example, most states have an alcoholic beverage control commission (ABC), or a similarly named organization, which monitors the sale and distribution of alcoholic beverages. The ABC monitors alcohol distributors to assure that all taxes are paid on the beverages and is responsible for revoking or suspending the liquor licenses of establishments that have broken relevant laws.

Many states have fish and game warden organizations that enforce all laws relating to hunting and fishing. Motor vehicle compliance (MVC) agencies monitor interstate carriers or trucks to make sure that they are in compliance with state and federal laws. MVC officers generally operate the weigh stations that are commonly found on interstate highways. Other limited-purpose law enforcement agencies deal with white-collar and computer crime, regulate nursing homes, and provide training to local police departments.

FEDERAL LAW ENFORCEMENT AGENCIES

Statistically, employees of federal agencies do not make up a large part of the nation's law enforcement force. In fact, the New York City Police Department has about one-third as many employees as all of the federal law enforcement agencies

⊘ Nearly every law enforcement agency hosts a Web site. To find the home pages of the **Pennsylvania State Police** and the **Washington State Highway Patrol,** click on *Web Links* under *Chapter Resources* at **www.cjinaction.com**.

combined.[25] Nevertheless, the influence of these federal agencies is substantial. Unlike local police departments, which must deal with all forms of crime, federal agencies have been authorized, usually by Congress, to enforce specific laws or attend to specific situations. The U.S. Coast Guard, for example, patrols the nation's waterways, while U.S. Postal Inspectors investigate and prosecute crimes perpetrated through the use of the U.S. mails.

As mentioned in Chapter 1, the most far-reaching reorganization of the federal government since World War II took place in the first half of this decade. These changes, particularly the formation of the Department of Homeland Security, have had a significant effect on federal law enforcement. (See ■ Figure 5.5 for the new federal law enforcement "lineup.") In Chapter 16, we will take a close look at just how profound this effect has been. Here, you will learn the basic elements of the most important federal law enforcement agencies, which are grouped according to the federal department or bureau to which they report.

The Department of Homeland Security On November 25, 2002, President George W. Bush signed the Homeland Security Act.[26] This legislation created the Department of Homeland Security (DHS), a new cabinet-level department designed to coordinate federal efforts to protect the United States against international and domestic terrorism. The new department has no new agencies; rather, twenty-two existing agencies were shifted under the control of the secretary of homeland security, a post now held by Michael Chertoff. For example, the Transportation Security Administration, which was formed in 2001 to revive the Federal Air Marshals program placing undercover federal agents on commercial flights, was moved from the Department of Transportation to the DHS. U.S. Customs and Border Protection, U.S. Immigration and Customs Enforcement, and the U.S. Secret Service are the three most visible agencies under the direction of the DHS.

U.S. Customs and Border Protection (CBP) One of the most important effects of the Homeland Security Act was the termination of the Immigration and Naturalization Service (INS), which had monitored and policed the flow of immigrants into the United States since 1933. Many of the INS's duties have been transferred to U.S. Customs and Border Protection (CBP), which polices the flow of goods and people across the United States' international borders. In general terms, this means that the agency has two primary goals: (1) to keep illegal immigrants (particularly terrorists), drugs, and drug traffickers from crossing

⊘ See the **U.S. Department of Homeland Security** for information on how this branch of federal law enforcement is fighting terrorism. Find its Web site by clicking on *Web Links* under *Chapter Resources* at **www.cjinaction.com**.

L05

■ **Figure 5.5** Federal Law Enforcement Agencies

A number of federal agencies employ law enforcement officers who are authorized to carry firearms and make arrests. The most prominent ones are under the control of the U.S. Department of Homeland Security, the U.S. Department of Justice, or the U.S. Department of the Treasury.

Source: Bureau of Justice Statistics, *Federal Law Enforcement Officers, 2004* (Washington, D.C.: U.S. Department of Justice, July 2006), Table 4, page 6.

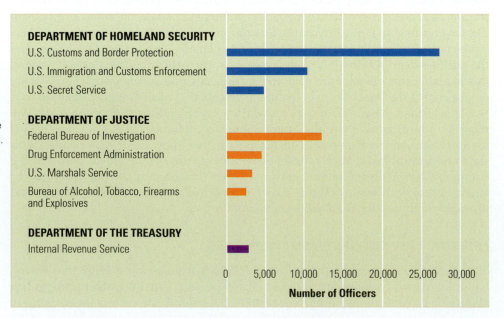

our borders, and (2) to facilitate the smooth flow of legal trade and travel. Consequently, CBP officers are stationed at every port of entry and exit to the United States. The officers have widespread authority to investigate and search all international passengers, whether they arrive on airplanes, ships, or other forms of transportation.

The U.S. Border Patrol, a branch of the CBP, has the burden of policing both the Mexican and Canadian borders between official ports of entry. In 2005, Border Patrol agents caught nearly 1.2 million people entering the country illegally and confiscated more than $1.4 billion worth of narcotics.[27] Today, about 12,000 Border Patrol agents guard 19,000 miles of land and sea borders, about double the number of ten years earlier.

U.S. Immigration and Customs Enforcement (ICE) The CBP shares responsibility for locating and apprehending those persons illegally in the United States with special agents from U.S. Immigration and Customs Enforcement (ICE). While the CBP focuses almost exclusively on the nation's borders, ICE has the broader mandate to investigate and to enforce our country's immigration and customs laws. Simply stated, the CBP covers the borders, and ICE covers everything else. The latter agency's duties include detaining illegal aliens and deporting (removing) them from the United States, ensuring that those without permission do not work or gain other benefits in this country, and disrupting human trafficking operations. In 2006, ICE deported 186,000 illegal immigrants from this country and seized $42 million in smuggling operation assets.[28] As we shall see in Chapter 16, both the CBP and ICE are crucial elements of the nation's antiterrorism strategy.

▲ Border Patrol agents make their rounds of the United States' shared boundary with Mexico on all-terrain vehicles (ATVs). What is the difference between U.S. Customs and Border Protection, which oversees the Border Patrol, and U.S. Immigration and Customs Enforcement?

The U.S. Secret Service When created in 1865, the Secret Service was primarily responsible for combating currency counterfeiters. In 1901, the agency was given the added responsibility of protecting the president of the United States, the president's family, the vice president, the president-elect, and former presidents. These duties have remained the cornerstone of the agency, with several expansions. After a number of threats against presidential candidates in the 1960s and early 1970s, including the shootings of Robert Kennedy and Governor George Wallace of Alabama, in 1976 Secret Service agents became responsible for protecting those political figures as well.

In addition to its special plainclothes agents, the agency also directs two uniformed groups of law enforcement officers. The Secret Service Uniformed Division protects the grounds of the White House and its inhabitants, and the Treasury Police Force polices the Treasury Building in Washington, D.C. This responsibility includes investigating threats against presidents and those running for presidential office.

To aid its battle against counterfeiters and forgers of government bonds, the agency has the use of a laboratory at the Bureau of Engraving and Printing in the nation's capital.

The Department of Justice The U.S. Department of Justice, created in 1870, is still the primary federal law enforcement agency in the country. With the responsibility of enforcing criminal law and supervising the federal prisons, the Justice Department plays a leading role in the American criminal justice system. To carry out its responsibilities to prevent and control crime, the department has a number of law enforcement agencies, including the Federal Bureau of Investigation, the federal Drug Enforcement Administration, the Bureau of Alcohol, Tobacco, Firearms and Explosives, and the U.S. Marshals Service.

The Federal Bureau of Investigation (FBI) Initially created in 1908 as the Bureau of Investigation, this agency was renamed the **Federal Bureau of Investigation (FBI)** in 1935. One of the primary investigative agencies of the federal government, the FBI has jurisdiction over nearly two hundred federal crimes, including sabotage, espionage (spying), kidnapping, extortion, interstate transportation of stolen property, bank robbery, interstate gambling, and civil rights violations. Note that the FBI is not considered a "national" police force. In general, law enforcement is seen as the responsibility of state and local governments. There is no doubt, however, that the agency plays a crucial role in today's law enforcement landscape. With its network of agents across the country and the globe, the FBI is uniquely positioned to combat worldwide criminal activity such as terrorism and drug trafficking. Furthermore, in times of national emergency the FBI is the primary arm of federal law enforcement. Within hours after the terrorist attacks on September 11, 2001, more than 7,000 FBI employees in 57 different countries had begun an intense search for those responsible.

Today, the FBI has more than 30,000 employees and an annual budget of over $6.4 billion. The agency's investigative priorities include (1) terrorism, (2) foreign intelligence operations in the United States (3) cyber crime, (4) public corruption, (5) civil rights violations, (6) white-collar crime, and (7) violent crime.[29] The agency also provides valuable support to local and state law enforcement agencies. The FBI's Identification Division maintains a large database of fingerprint information and offers assistance in finding missing persons and identifying the victims of fires, airplane crashes, and other disfiguring disasters. The services of the FBI Laboratory, the largest crime laboratory in the world, are available at no charge to other agencies. Finally, the FBI's National Crime Information Center (NCIC) provides lists of stolen vehicles and firearms, missing license plates, vehicles used to commit crimes, and other information to local and state law enforcement officers who may access the NCIC database.

The Drug Enforcement Administration (DEA) With a $2.4 billion budget and more than 5,300 special agents, the Drug Enforcement Administration (DEA) is one of the fastest-growing law enforcement agencies in the country. The mission of the DEA is to enforce domestic drug laws and regulations and to assist other federal and foreign agencies in combating illegal drug manufacture and trade on an international level. The agency also enforces the provisions of the Controlled Substances Act, which governs the manufacture, distribution, and dispensing of legal drugs, such as prescription drugs.

The federal government has had a role in policing the manufacture and sale of illicit drugs since 1914. The first federal drug agency, the Federal Bureau of Narcotics (FBN), was established in 1930 under President Herbert Hoover. The FBN's main priorities were cocaine and opiates such as heroin. As the level of illegal drug use expanded over the decades, and international trafficking became a more pressing problem, several additional agencies were formed to deal with drug enforcement. Then, in 1970 Congress passed the comprehensive Drug Abuse Prevention and Control Act,[30] which gave Congress the authority to regulate interstate commerce of legal drugs. With the Bureau of Narcotics and Dangerous Drugs (a successor to the FBN), the U.S. Customs Service, the FBI, and hundreds of state and local law enforcement agencies all working to enforce drug laws—as well as the government's new responsibility with regard to legal drugs—it was evident that a new "superagency" was needed. In 1973, by order of President Richard Nixon, the DEA was formed.

Today, DEA agents often work in conjunction with local and state authorities to prevent illicit drugs from reaching communities. The agency also conducts

Federal Bureau of Investigation (FBI) The branch of the Department of Justice responsible for investigating violations of federal law. The bureau also collects national crime statistics and provides training and other forms of aid to local law enforcement agencies.

extensive operations with law enforcement entities in other drug-producing countries. In 2007, for example, DEA coordination with Mexican law enforcement authorities led to the seizure of $200 million in U.S. currency from methamphetamine producers in Mexico City. Mexican officials called it the largest drug cash seizure in the country's history.[31] Like the FBI, the DEA operates a network of six regional laboratories used to test and categorize seized drugs. Local law enforcement agencies have access to the DEA labs and often use them to ensure that information about particular drugs that will be presented in court is accurate and up to date. In recent years Congress has given the FBI more authority to enforce drug laws, and the two agencies now share a number of administrative controls.

The Bureau of Alcohol, Tobacco, Firearms and Explosives (ATF) As its name suggests, the Bureau of Alcohol, Tobacco, Firearms and Explosives (ATF) is primarily concerned with the illegal sale, possession, and use of firearms and the control of untaxed tobacco and liquor products. The Firearms Division of the agency has the responsibility of enforcing the Gun Control Act of 1968, which sets the circumstances under which firearms may be sold and used in this country. The bureau also regulates all gun trade between the United States and foreign nations and collects taxes on all firearm importers, manufacturers, and dealers. In keeping with these duties, the ATF is also responsible for policing the illegal use and possession of explosives. Furthermore, the ATF is charged with enforcing federal gambling laws.

Because it has jurisdiction over such a wide variety of crimes, especially those involving firearms and explosives, the ATF is a constant presence in federal criminal investigations. Since 1982, for example, the agency has been working in conjunction with the FBI to prevent the bombing of abortion clinics. Recently, the agency, along with the FBI, has begun to place undercover informants inside antiabortion groups to gain information about proposed bombings. The ATF has also formed multijurisdictional drug task forces with other federal and local law enforcement agencies to investigate drug crimes involving firearms.

The U.S. Marshals Service The oldest federal law enforcement agency is the U.S. Marshals Service. In 1789, President George Washington assigned thirteen U.S. Marshals to protect his attorney general. That same year, Congress created the office of the U.S. Marshals and Deputy Marshals. Originally, the U.S. Marshals acted as the main law enforcement officers in the western territories. Following the Civil War (1861–1865), when most of these territories had become states, these agents were assigned to work for the U.S. district courts, where federal crimes are tried. The relationship between the U.S. Marshals Service and the federal courts continues today and forms the basis for the officers' main duties, which include:

1. Providing security at federal courts for judges, jurors, and other courtroom participants.
2. Controlling property that has been ordered seized by federal courts.
3. Protecting government witnesses who place themselves in danger by testifying against the targets of federal criminal investigations. This protection is sometimes accomplished by relocating the witnesses and providing them with different identities.

▼ Bureau of Alcohol, Tobacco, Firearms and Explosives (ATF) agent Doug Moore observes the remains of a warehouse in Salt Lake City, Utah. Officials suspected ecoterrorism as the cause of the suspicious fire. Why might the ATF be involved in investigating this sort of crime?

AP Photo/Douglas C. Pizac

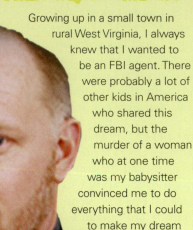

Courtesy of Jim Rice

Growing up in a small town in rural West Virginia, I always knew that I wanted to be an FBI agent. There were probably a lot of other kids in America who shared this dream, but the murder of a woman who at one time was my babysitter convinced me to do everything that I could to make my dream of becoming a law enforcement officer come true.

TRAINING DAYS Following college, I went to work for the West Virginia State Police (WVSP) as a forensic toxicologist, a job that prepared me well for my current position with the FBI. These four years were well spent, because it was an interesting and challenging job and also because the FBI seeks to attract candidates who are competitive and who bring a specialty or work experience to the job.

I joined the FBI as a Special Agent in 1988 and spent the first sixteen weeks of my Bureau career at the FBI Academy in Quantico, Virginia, as do all new agents. The FBI Academy is similar to a small college campus, with classrooms, dormitories, a cafeteria, and a gymnasium, with hundreds of students in residence at any given time, including new agents, experienced agents who are back for a week or two of specialized training, and police officers from all over the country and the world.

GETTING STARTED Following graduation from the FBI Academy, agents are subject to transfer to one of the fifty-six field offices in the United States for their first assignment. I was

4. Transporting federal prisoners to detention institutions.
5. Investigating violations of federal fugitive laws.[32]

The Department of the Treasury   The Department of the Treasury, formed in 1789, is mainly responsible for all financial matters of the federal government. It pays all the federal government's bills, borrows money, collects taxes, mints coins, and prints paper currency. The largest bureau of the Treasury Department, the Internal Revenue Service (IRS), is concerned with violations of tax laws and regulations. The bureau has three divisions, only one of which is involved in criminal investigations. The examination branch of the IRS audits the tax returns of corporations and individuals. The collection division attempts to collect taxes from corporations or citizens who have failed to pay the taxes they owe. Finally, the criminal investigation division investigates cases of tax evasion and tax fraud. Criminal investigation agents can make arrests. The IRS has long played a role in policing criminal activities such as gambling and selling drugs for one simple reason: those who engage in such activities almost never report any illegally gained income on their returns. Therefore, the IRS is able to apprehend them for tax evasion. The most famous instance of this took place in the 1920s, when the IRS finally arrested famed crime boss Al Capone—responsible for numerous violent crimes—for not paying his taxes.

THE MILITARY AND LAW ENFORCEMENT

The distinction between federal law enforcement agencies and the U.S. military is an important one. By law, the U.S. military cannot participate in domestic criminal law investigations. According to the Posse Comitatus Act (PCA) of 1878, anyone who uses a branch of the military to carry out criminal law may be punished by a fine or two years' imprisonment.[33] The statute reflects the wishes of lawmakers, both at the time it was passed and today, that armed soldiers never be used to oppress the citizenry. The act does, however, allow the use of the military in law enforcement when authorized by the U.S. Congress. To fight the "war

sent to the Indianapolis (Indiana) office, where I was assigned to a "reactive squad," which handled violent criminal violations, such as bank robberies, fugitives, kidnappings, and extortions.

It was during my time in Indianapolis that I worked on a case that had a major impact on me and reaffirmed that the FBI was the right career choice for me. A young boy was kidnapped by an adult family friend and driven cross-country in the subject's truck. The FBI had surveillances on a number of locations in the Midwest, including the home of the subject's relatives in Indianapolis. After many long hours of surveillance in the cold and rain, our team found a truck that matched the description of the subject's truck, parked beside a house in a desolate part of the city. We continued the surveillance on the truck, and finally, the subject and the victim emerged from the house. As they drove off in the truck, our team followed discreetly at a distance until the order came from the lead agent to move in and conduct a tactical car stop. The subject was arrested and the boy was rescued, frightened but unharmed, and reunited with his parents.

TERRORISM TASK FORCE A rotational transfer brought me to the Washington, D.C., field office in 1992, where I joined the SWAT team and worked on a "safe streets gang task force" and then on a cold case homicide squad. Soon thereafter, a joint terrorism task force was formed to address domestic terrorism matters in the nation's capital, an area filled with symbolic targets for would-be terrorist activities.

I volunteered to be part of this task force in late 1992 and was promoted to the position of Supervisory Special Agent of the squad in 1998. My duties include the operational and emergency response to incidents of domestic terrorism; bombings and bomb threats; chemical, biological, and nuclear incidents; and security for special events, such as presidential inaugurations.

Go to the **Careers in Criminal Justice Interactive CD** for more profiles in the field of criminal justice.

on drugs," for example, in 1981 Congress created an exception to the PCA and encouraged the military to share equipment and information with law enforcement agencies fighting the illegal drug trade in Central and South America and Southeast Asia.[34]

Militarism in Police Culture   Some believe that American law enforcement has already adopted a "culture of paramilitarism."[35] As we will see in the next chapter, most police departments in the United States are organized according to a military structure of command. Police officers who operate near military bases often train with soldiers, and military equipment is becoming more widely available to law enforcement agencies. In addition, almost every police department that serves a population of more than 250,000 operates a **Special Weapons and Tactics (SWAT) team**.[36] These special operational units are more heavily armed than regular police squads and use military tactics to respond to particularly dangerous circumstances such as hostage situations, barricaded suspects, and drug raids.

The National Guard   One organization affiliated with the U.S. military can perform law enforcement duties under certain circumstances—the **National Guard**, which consists of the reserve forces of the U.S. Army and the U.S. Air Force. Members of these forces also serve their respective states by being "on call" to respond to natural disasters, civil disturbances, and other emergency situations. When National Guard units are acting on the order of their state governor, the Posse Comitatus Act does not apply to their duties.[37]

So, for example, in 2006 then-governor Kathleen Blanco was able to order three hundred members of the Louisiana National Guard into New Orleans to help combat the crime wave discussed in this chapter's introduction. In contrast, when the National Guard is "federalized," or acting under the orders of the president, such law enforcement duties would be unconstitutional. (Proposals to neutralize the Posse Comitatus Act in the event of terrorist attacks will be discussed in Chapter 16.)

Special Weapons and Tactics (SWAT) Team A specialized squad of police officers who have been trained to handle violent and dangerous situations using advanced weaponry and technology.

National Guard Military reserve units of the U.S. Army and U.S. Air Force controlled by each state of the United States and subject to deployment by both the federal and state executive branches in times of emergency.

Self Check Fill in the Blanks

Municipal police departments and _____ departments are both considered "local" organizations and have many of the same responsibilities. On the state level, the authority of the _____ is usually limited to enforcing traffic laws. Nationally, the _____ has jurisdiction over all federal crimes, while the _____ focuses on federal drug laws and the _____ regulates the illegal sale and possession of guns. Check your answers on page 159.

Private Security

Even with increasing numbers of local, state, and federal law enforcement officers, the police do not have the ability to prevent every crime. Recognizing this, many businesses and citizens have decided to hire private guards for their properties and homes. In fact, more than $100 billion a year is spent worldwide on **private security.** In the United States, estimates put the figure at $39 billion.[38] More than 10,000 firms employing around 2 million people provide private security services in the United States, compared to about 700,000 public law enforcement agents.

PRIVATIZING LAW ENFORCEMENT

Private Security The practice of private corporations or individuals offering services traditionally performed by police officers.

In the eyes of the law, a private security guard is the same as any other private person when it comes to police powers such as being able to arrest or interrogate a person suspected of committing a crime. Ideally, a security guard—lacking the training of a law enforcement agent—should only observe and report criminal activity unless use of force is needed to prevent a felony.[39]

Citizens' Arrests Any private citizen (including private security guards) may perform a "citizen's arrest" under certain circumstances. The California Penal Code, for example, allows a private person to arrest another:

- For a public offense committed in his or her presence.
- When the person arrested has committed a felony, even if it was not in the arrester's presence, if he or she has reasonable cause to believe that the person committed the felony.[40]

Obviously, these are not very exacting standards, and, in reality, private security guards have many, if not most, of the same powers to prevent crime that a police officer does.

The Deterrence Factor As a rule, however, private security is not designed to "replace" law enforcement. It is intended to deter crime rather than stop it.[41] A uniformed security guard patrolling a shopping mall parking lot or a bank lobby has one primary function—to convince a potential criminal to search out a shopping mall or bank that does not have private security. For the same reason, many citizens hire security

▼ A private security guard on duty in a Costa Mesa, California, mall. Today, about 2 million Americans find employment in the private security industry. How is this security guard doing his job by simply standing in a visible area of a shopping center?

© Spencer Grant/PhotoEdit

personnel to drive marked cars through their neighborhoods, making them a less attractive target for burglaries, robberies, vandalism, and other crimes.

PRIVATE SECURITY TRENDS

Despite the proliferation of private security, many questions remain about this largely unregulated industry. Several years ago, four security guards accidentally asphyxiated Peter James Lawrence to death outside a nightclub in Las Vegas, Nevada. The security guards were trying to subdue Lawrence, who reacted violently when he was asked to stop bothering an ex-girlfriend.[42] The only requirement for becoming a security guard in Nevada is four hours of training.[43]

Lack of Standards   As there are no federal regulations regarding private security, each state has its own rules for employment as a security guard. In several states, including California and Florida, prospective guards must have at least forty hours of training. Twenty-nine states, however, have no specific training requirements, and ten states do not regulate the private security industry at all. By comparison, Spain mandates 160 hours of theoretical training, 20 hours of practical training, and 20 hours of annual continuing education for anybody hoping to find employment as a security guard.[44]

The quality of employees is also a problem for the U.S. private security industry. Given the low pay (see ■ Figure 5.6) and lack of benefits such as health insurance, paid vacation time, and sick days, the industry does not always attract highly qualified and motivated recruits.[45] "At those wages," notes one industry specialist, "you're competing with McDonald's."[46] To make matters worse, fewer than half of the states require a fingerprint check for applicants, making it relatively easy for a person with a criminal record in one state to obtain a security guard position in another.[47]

The security industry is finding it much easier to uncover past convictions of employees and job applicants thanks to the Private Security Officer Employment Authorization Act of 2004.[48] The legislation, which authorizes the FBI to provide background checks for security firms, was spurred by congressional concern over possible terrorist attacks on shipping ports, water treatment facilities, telecommunications facilities, power plants, and other strategic targets that are often secured by private guards. In the first year of this program, the FBI found that 990,000 of the estimated 9 million applicants for private security positions (about 11 percent) had criminal records.[49]

Continued Growth in the Industry   Issues surrounding private security promise to gain even greater prominence in the criminal justice system, as indicators point to higher rates of growth for the industry. The Hallcrest Report II, a far-reaching overview of private security trends funded by the National Institute of Justice, identifies four factors driving this growth:

1. An increase in fear on the part of the public triggered by the growing rate of crime, either real or perceived.
2. The problem of crime in the workplace.
3. Budget cuts in states and municipalities that have forced reductions in the number of public police, thereby raising the demand for private ones.

■ **Figure 5.6** Average Salaries in Law Enforcement

In New York City, servers in restaurants, landscapers, hotel desk clerks, and domestic workers all earn more than private security guards. Nationwide, as this figure shows, security guards are the lowest paid of the "protective service occupations."

Source: Bureau of Labor Statistics.

Occupation

- Police and sheriff's patrol
- All other occupations
- Correctional officers
- Parking enforcement
- Airport screeners
- Security guards (staff)
- Security guards (contract)
- Minumum wage

0   $10,000 $20,000 $30,000 $40,000 $50,000

Average Annual Salary

4. A rising awareness of private security products (such as home burglar alarms) and service as cost-effective protective measures.[50]

Another reason is fear of terrorism. The U.S. Bureau of Labor Statistics reported that nearly 15,000 new security guards were hired between September 11, 2001, and October 11, 2001.[51] According to the industry-research group Freedonia, spending on private security services will continue to grow by 4.3 percent each year for the rest of this decade, reaching almost $50 billion by 2010.[52]

Self Check Fill in the Blanks

Private security is designed to _____ crime rather than to prevent it. The majority of states require _____ hours of training and _____ background checks before a person can become a security guard. Despite this situation, the industry is poised to see _____ rates of growth in the near future. Check your answers on page 159.

The Responsibilities of the Police

Some law enforcement officials welcome the massive influx of private security. Private firms, they believe, may be able to relieve the constant budget and staffing pressures that public police forces face.[53] The problem with this theory, however, is that public and private police have different basic functions. For a private security firm, the primary goal is to protect property. As noted earlier, that often means persuading a criminal to choose an alternative target for a burglary or some other crime. As a manager at one private security company noted, "We're a business, not a law enforcement agency."[54]

The goal of public law enforcement, in contrast, is to stop crimes, not simply shift them from one location to another—which is not to say that preventing crime is the only duty of a police officer. For the most part, the incidents that make up a police officer's daily routine would not make it onto television dramas such as *Law and Order*. Besides catching criminals, police spend a great deal of time on such mundane tasks as responding to noise complaints, confiscating firecrackers, and poring over paperwork. Sociologist Egon Bittner warned against the tendency to see the police primarily as agents of law enforcement and crime control. A more inclusive accounting of "what the police do," Bittner believed, would recognize that they provide "situationally justified force in society."[55] In other words, the function of the police is to solve any problem that may *possibly*, though not *necessarily*, require the use of force.

Within Bittner's rather broad definition of "what the police do," we can pinpoint four basic responsibilities of the police:

L08

1. To enforce laws.
2. To provide services.
3. To prevent crime.
4. To preserve the peace.

As will become evident over the next two chapters, there is a great deal of debate among legal and other scholars and law enforcement officers over which responsibilities deserve the most police attention and what methods should be employed by the police in meeting those responsibilities.

ENFORCING LAWS

In the public mind, the primary role of the police is to enforce society's laws—hence, the term *law enforcement officer*. In their role as "crime fighters," police officers have a clear mandate to seek out and apprehend those who have violated the law. The crime-fighting responsibility is so dominant that all police activity—from the purchase of new automobiles to a plan to hire more minority officers—must often be justified in terms of its law enforcement value.[56]

Police officers also primarily see themselves as crime fighters, or "crook catchers," a perception that often leads people into what they believe will be an exciting career in law enforcement. Although the job certainly offers challenges unlike any other, police officers normally do not spend the majority of their time in law enforcement duties. After surveying a year's worth of dispatch data from the Wilmington (Delaware) Police Department, researchers Jack Greene and Carl Klockars found that officers spent only about half of their time enforcing the law or dealing with crimes. The rest of their time was taken up with order maintenance, providing services, traffic patrol, and medical assistance.[57] Furthermore, information provided by the Uniform Crime Report shows that most arrests are made for "crimes of disorder" or public annoyances rather than violent or property crimes.[58] In 2006, for example, police made more than 12 million arrests for drunkenness, liquor law violations, disorderly conduct, vagrancy, loitering, and other minor offenses, but only about 610,000 arrests for violent crimes.[59]

▲ Police officers struggle to capture one of nine American bison that escaped from a farm in Stevenson, Maryland, in April 2005. Law enforcement agents provide a number of services to the community that have little to do with fighting crime.

PROVIDING SERVICES

The popular emphasis on crime fighting and law enforcement tends to overshadow the fact that a great deal of a police officer's time is spent providing services for the community. The motto "To Serve and Protect" has been adopted by thousands of local police departments, and the *Law Enforcement Code of Ethics* recognizes the duty "to serve the community" in its first sentence.[60] The services that police provide are numerous—a partial list would include directing traffic, performing emergency medical procedures, counseling those involved in domestic disputes, providing directions to tourists, and finding lost children. Along with firefighters, police officers are among the first public servants to arrive at disaster scenes to conduct search and rescue operations. This particular duty adds considerably to the dangers faced by law enforcement agents (discussed in more detail in Chapter 6). In the aftermath of Hurricane Katrina, New Orleans police officers had to dodge snipers' bullets as they tried to restore order to the beleaguered city. As mentioned earlier, a number of police departments have adopted the strategy of community policing, and as a consequence, many officers find themselves providing assistance in areas that have not until recently been their domain.[61] For example, police are required to deal with the problems of the homeless and the mentally ill to a greater extent than in past decades.

PREVENTING CRIME

Perhaps the most controversial responsibility of the police is to *prevent* crime. According to Jerome Skolnick of the University of California at Berkeley, there are two predictable public responses when crime rates begin to rise in a community. The first is to punish convicted criminals with stricter laws and more severe penalties. The second is to demand that the police "do something" to prevent crimes from occurring in the first place. Is it, in fact, possible for the police to "prevent" crimes? The strongest response that Professor Skolnick is willing to give to this question is "maybe."[62]

On a limited basis, police can certainly prevent some crimes. If a rapist is dissuaded from attacking a solitary woman because a patrol car is cruising the area, then the police officer behind the wheel has prevented a crime. Furthermore, exemplary police work can have an effect. Observers credit the Los Angeles Police Department's focus on "gangs, guns, and drugs" for that city's five straight years of dropping violent crime rates, which went against the national trend we discussed in Chapter 2.[63] In general, however, the deterrent effects of police presence are unclear. Carl Klockars has written that the "war on crime" is a war that the police cannot win because they cannot control the factors—such as unemployment, poverty, immorality, inequality, political change, and lack of educational opportunities—that lead to criminal behavior in the first place.[64] As we shall see in the next chapter, many police stations have adopted the idea of community policing in an attempt to better prevent crime.

PRESERVING THE PEACE

To a certain extent, the fourth responsibility of the police, that of preserving the peace, is related to preventing crime. Police have the legal authority to use the power of arrest, or even force, in situations in which no crime has yet occurred, but might occur in the immediate future.

In the words of James Q. Wilson, the police's peacekeeping role (which Wilson believes is the most important role of law enforcement officers) often takes on a pattern of simply "handling the situation."[65] For example, when police officers arrive on the scene of a loud late-night house party, they may feel the need to disperse the party and even arrest some of the party goers for disorderly conduct. By their actions, the officers have lessened the chances of serious and violent crimes taking place later in the evening. The same principle is often used when dealing with domestic disputes, which, if escalated, can lead to homicide. Such situations are in need of, to use Wilson's terminology again, "fixing up," and police can use the power of arrest, or threat, or coercion, or sympathy, to do just that.

The basis of Wilson and George Kelling's zero-tolerance theory is similar: street disorder—such as public drunkenness, urination, and loitering—signals to both law-abiding citizens and criminals that the law is not being enforced and therefore leads to more violent crime. Hence, if police preserve the peace and "crack down" on the minor crimes that make up street disorder, they will in fact be preventing serious crimes that would otherwise occur in the future.[66] (Some believe that the police should take on even greater responsibilities—see the *Criminal Justice in Action* feature at the end of this chapter.)

Self Check Fill in the Blanks

Both the public and law enforcement officers themselves believe that the police's primary job is to _____ laws. A large and crucial part of policing, however, involves providing _____ such as directing traffic. The ability of the police to actually _____ crime is a matter of great debate, and some experts believe that the most important role of a police officer is to _____ the peace. Check your answers on page 159.

The Role of Discretion in Policing

Though the responsibilities just discussed provide a helpful overview of "what police do," they also highlight the ambiguity of a police officer's duties. To say, for example, that highway patrol officers have a responsibility to enforce speed laws is to oversimplify their "real" job. In fact, most highway patrol officers would not find it feasible to hand out speeding tickets to every driver who exceeds the posted speed limit. Furthermore, depending on the circumstances, a patrol officer may decide not to issue a ticket to a driver who has been pulled over. Rather, most officers selectively enforce speed laws, ticketing only those who significantly exceed the limit or drive so recklessly that they endanger other drivers. As noted in Chapter 1, when police officers use their judgment in deciding which offenses to punish and which to ignore, they are said to be using *discretion*. Whether this discretion applies to speed limits or any other area of the law, it is a crucial aspect of policing.

JUSTIFICATION FOR POLICE DISCRETION

One of the ironies of law enforcement is that patrol officers—often the lowest-paid members of an agency with the least amount of authority—have the greatest amount of discretionary power. Part of the explanation for this is practical. Patrol officers spend most of the day on the streets, beyond the control of their supervisors. Usually, only two people are present when a patrol officer must make a decision: the officer and the possible wrongdoer. In most cases, the law enforcement officer has a great deal of freedom to take the action that he or she feels best corresponds to the situation.[67]

L09

This is not to say that police discretion is misplaced. In general, courts have recognized that a patrol officer is in a unique position to be allowed discretionary powers:

- Police officers are considered trustworthy and are therefore assumed to make honest decisions, regardless of contradictory testimony by a suspect.
- Experience and training give officers the ability to determine whether certain activity poses a threat to society, and to take any reasonable action necessary to investigate or prevent such activity.
- Due to the nature of their jobs, police officers are extremely knowledgeable in human, and by extension criminal, behavior.
- Police officers may find themselves in danger of personal, physical harm and must be allowed to take reasonable and necessary steps to protect themselves.[68]

Dr. Anthony J. Pinizzotto, a psychologist with the FBI, and Charles E. Miller, an instructor in the bureau's Criminal Justice Information Services Division, take the justification for discretion one step further, arguing that many police officers have a "sixth sense" that helps them handle on-the-job challenges. Pinizzotto and Miller believe that although "intuitive policing" is often difficult to explain to those outside law enforcement, it is a crucial part of policing and should not be discouraged by civilian administrators.[69]

MAKING THE DECISION

There is no doubt that subjective factors influence police discretion. The officer's beliefs, values, personality, and background all enter into his or her decisions.[70] When it comes to applying the law to any particular situation, however, police officers generally consider three factors. First, and most important, is the nature of the criminal act. The less serious a crime, the more likely a police officer is to ignore it. A person driving 60 miles per hour in a 55-miles-per-hour zone, for example, is much less likely to be ticketed than someone doing 80 miles per hour. A second element often considered is the attitude of the wrongdoer toward the officer. A motorist who is belligerent toward a highway patrol officer is much more likely to be ticketed than one who is contrite and apologetic. Third, departmental policy can place limits on discretion.[71] If a police chief decides that all motorists who exceed the speed limit by 10 miles will be ticketed, that policy will influence the patrol officer's decisions. Indeed, departmental policy has played a large role in shaping the discretionary behavior of police officers in two of the more controversial areas of police work: domestic violence and high-speed chases.

Discretion and Domestic Violence   As we will discuss in more detail in Chapter 7, police have a great deal of discretion in deciding whether to make an arrest. Basically, if a police officer has a good reason (known as *probable cause*) to believe that a person has committed or is about to commit a crime, that officer can arrest the subject. To a certain extent, though, police officers have been hesitant to make arrests when the dispute involves a "family matter," even when faced with strong evidence that domestic violence (see page 57) has taken place.[72]

The Problem: Failure to Arrest   One study of the Chester (Pennsylvania) Police Department found that its officers were less likely to arrest male felony assailants who abused former or present female partners than other males who committed similarly violent acts against strangers. Among the cases that did not lead to arrests were 4 attacks on domestic partners with guns, 38 attacks involving cutting instruments (including one with an ax), and 27 attacks with blunt instruments such as baseball bats or hammers. In one incident that did not result in an arrest, a woman was held by her feet over a second-floor landing and dropped on her head.[73]

A number of factors have been suggested to explain this type of leniency. Many police officers see domestic violence cases as the responsibility of social-service providers, not law enforcement. Officers may also be uncomfortable with the intensely private nature of domestic disputes, causing them to leave the resolution to the parties involved.[74] Finally, even when a police officer does arrest the abuser, the victim often refuses to press charges, and prosecutors are also hesitant to follow through on these cases by taking them to court.[75]

The Response: Mandatory Arrest Policies   Whatever the reason for this reluctance to arrest domestic abusers, many jurisdictions have responded by severely limiting police discretion in domestic violence cases. Today, 87 percent of all police departments have written policies for how officers should handle domestic violence.[76] Sixty-one percent have **mandatory arrest policies,** under which a police officer *must* arrest a person who has battered a spouse or domestic partner. No discretion is involved.[77] (To learn more about what "mandatory" actually means, see the feature *You Be the Judge—Duty Bound?*) The theory behind mandatory arrest policies is relatively straightforward: they act as a deterrent to criminal behavior. Costs are imposed on the person who is arrested. He or she must go to court and face the possibility of time in jail. Arrest may also lead to humiliation, loss of a job, and separation from family and friends. To avoid these unpleasant consequences, the argument goes, potential abusers will not act in a manner that increases the risk they will be arrested.

Discretion and High-Speed Pursuits   Another controversial area of police discretion concerns high-speed pursuits of a suspect who is fleeing in an automobile. Although such drastic action is often neces-

Mandatory Arrest Policy
Requires a police officer to detain a person for committing a certain type of crime as long as probable cause that he or she committed the crime exists.

▼ In 2007, a United States Supreme Court ruling supported a police officer's discretionary use of a ramming technique to end a high-speed chase. Why are courts generally supportive of police discretion as long as it is reasonably applied?

© Martyn Goddard/Corbis

You Be the Judge Duty Bound?

You Be the Judge Duty Bound?

THE FACTS Simon was under court order to stay one hundred yards away from the house of his estranged ex-wife, Jessica. One summer evening, Jessica called the Castle Rock (Colorado) Police Department and reported that Simon had entered her home and abducted their three daughters, ages seven, nine, and ten. A few hours later, Jessica called the police department again with new information: Simon was with the children at a local park. The police failed to take action on either call, and Simon killed the three girls.

THE LAW The preprinted text on the back of Simon's restraining order included the following: "A KNOWING VIOLATION OF A RESTRAINING ORDER IS A CRIME" and "YOU MAY BE ARRESTED WITHOUT NOTICE IF A LAW ENFORCEMENT OFFICER HAS PROBABLE CAUSE TO BELIEVE THAT YOU HAVE KNOWINGLY VIOLATED THIS ORDER."

Your Decision Jessica wants to sue the Castle Rock Police Department in civil court. She claims the language of the restraining order and the circumstances of her case created a situation in which Simon's arrest was mandatory. If you allow her lawsuit to go forward, you are essentially saying that citizens have a right to win monetary awards when police officers fail to use their discretion properly. What is your decision?

[To see how the United States Supreme Court ruled in this case, go to Example 5.1 in Appendix B.]

sary, the results can be tragic: police chases cause about 350 fatalities each year, and one-third of the victims are drivers of other cars or pedestrians who were present merely as innocent bystanders.[78] In response to these deaths, 94 percent of the nation's local police departments have implemented police pursuit policies, with 61 percent restricting the discretion of officers to engage in a high-speed chase.[79] The success of such policies can be seen in the results from Los Angeles, which features more high-speed chases than any other city in the country by a wide margin. In 2003, Los Angeles police officers were ordered to conduct dangerous pursuits only if the fleeing driver was suspected of a serious crime. Within a year, the number of high-speed pursuits decreased by 62 percent, and injuries to third parties dropped by 58 percent.[80]

While police departments are trying to limit the use of high-speed chases, the United States Supreme Court has shown that it will support a police officer's discretionary use of the tactic. In 1998, the Court held that an officer can be sued in civil court for damages caused by a high-speed pursuit only if her or his conduct was so outrageous that it "shocks the conscience."[81] Then, in 2007, the Court ruled in favor of a Georgia police officer who intentionally caused a crash involving the plaintiff, a nineteen-year-old who was trying to avoid arrest by driving 90 miles per hour on a two-lane road. Even though the plaintiff was paralyzed in the accident, the Court held that the officer was justified in his drastic effort to protect other drivers.[82]

Self Check Fill in the Blanks

In general, a law enforcement officer has a great deal of _____ when it comes to his or her duties. When a police administration wants to curtail this freedom of action, it can institute a _____ arrest policy, which requires that certain suspects be arrested for certain behavior. Many police departments are restricting the ability of their officers to engage in _____ so as to better protect the safety of innocent bystanders. Check your answers on page 159.

POLICING ILLEGAL IMMIGRANTS

Victor Cruz, Carlos Rodriguez, Armando Juvenal, and Jose Hernadez gang-raped a New York City woman. Lee Malvo, one of the snipers who terrorized the Washington, D.C., area several years ago, has been linked to sixteen murders. Angel Resendiz is believed to have killed more than a dozen people in four different states to get money for drugs and alcohol. These six men have one thing in common: they were in the United States illegally, and they had been detained and released by the police before committing their crimes.[83] In this *Criminal Justice in Action* feature, we look at the question of whether local and state law enforcement agencies should take on the responsibility—and burden—of helping to enforce our nation's immigration laws.

NEW LEVELS OF COOPERATION

Immigration law determines which non-U.S. citizens may enter this country, how long they can stay, and when they must leave. Basically, people violate immigration law in two ways: by entering the country without proper authorization from the U.S. government or by staying in the country after that authorization is invalid. Because immigration law is part of federal law, its enforcement has traditionally been the domain of federal agencies such as the CBP and ICE and their predecessor, the INS (discussed earlier in this chapter).

After the terrorist attacks of September 11, 2001, however, federal authorities began to seek the help of local and state police departments in immigration matters. Under a previously ignored federal statute, local and state law enforcement officers can be trained and deputized as immigration agents, giving them the power to arrest illegal immigrants who have broken no criminal laws and turn them over to ICE for *deportation* (removal from the country).[84] Most police departments have declined the opportunity to expand their duties in this manner. By the summer of 2007, however, law enforcement agencies in Alabama, Arizona, California, and North Carolina had reached agreements with the federal government that allow them to enforce immigration law.

The Case for Having Local Police Officers Enforce Immigration Law

- Using local police would help prevent crimes such as those listed in the first paragraph of this feature.

- The assistance is badly needed. The federal government has only about 2,000 immigration agents, compared to an estimated 11.5 million illegal immigrants in the United States.[85]

- Arrests for immigration violations are an important part of law enforcement efforts against terrorism and violent criminal gangs. Local police lose the opportunity to apprehend suspects in both areas because they cannot detain them for being in the United States illegally.

The Case against Having Local Police Officers Enforce Immigration Law

- If members of the immigrant community identify local police with federal immigration authorities, they will be much less likely to report crimes and cooperate with criminal investigations, either as witnesses or victims.

- Immigration law is complex and, inevitably, will be misapplied by inexperienced police officers.

- The new duties would be a poor use of scarce law enforcement resources, diverting local police from crime fighting and other responsibilities. "I don't think any of us delight in the idea of becoming immigration officers," said one Arizona sheriff.[86]

Writing Assignment—Your Opinion

With some rare exceptions, those local and state police departments that now cooperate with the federal government are reactive rather than proactive. In other words, they will not apprehend someone simply because they suspect that he or she is an illegal immigrant. Rather, they run a background check to determine immigration status when they come in contact with a person for another reason, such as an arrest or a traffic stop.

At the moment, the violation of an immigration law is a civil infraction. In 2006, the U.S Congress proposed legislation that would have made it a crime. This would have forced all police officers—federal, state, and local—to

Creative Commons

proactively seek out illegal immigrants as they do other criminals. What is your opinion of this proposed legislation? Before responding, you can review our discussions in this chapter concerning:

- Law enforcement agencies (pages 140–149).

- The responsibilities of the police (pages 152–154).

- Justification for police discretion (pages 154–157).

Your answer should be at least three full paragraphs.

Chapter Summary

L01 **Describe the first systems of law enforcement in colonial America.** Constables and night watchmen were drawn from the ranks of ordinary citizens. Each colony had a sheriff in each county who selected juries and managed incarcerations. Local citizens assisted sheriffs in peacekeeping duties.

L02 **Tell how the patronage system affected policing.** During the political era of policing (1840–1930), bribes paid by citizens and business owners often went into the coffers of the local political party. This became known as the patronage system.

L03 **Indicate the results of the Wickersham Commission.** The Wickersham Commission of 1929 called for reform to eliminate police brutality and the corrupting influence of politics. The result was the professionalization of American police, sometimes called the progressive era in American policing. Potential police officers began to be trained in institutes of higher learning. Another result was the increased use of technology in police work.

L04 **List five main types of law enforcement agencies.** (a) Municipal police departments; (b) sheriffs' departments; (c) special police agencies, such as those limited to school protection or airport security; (d) state police departments (in all states except Hawaii); and (e) federal law enforcement agencies.

L05 **List some of the most important law enforcement agencies under the control of the Department of Homeland Security.** (a) U.S. Customs and Border Protection, which polices the flow of goods and people across the United States' international borders and oversees the U.S. Border Patrol; (b) U.S. Immigration and Customs Enforcement, which investigates and enforces our nation's immigration and customs laws; and (c) the U.S. Secret Service, which protects high-ranking federal government officials and federal property.

L06 **Identify the investigative priorities of the FBI.** (a) Terrorism, (b) foreign intelligence operations in the United States, (c) cyber crime, (d) public corruption, (e) civil rights violations, (f) white-collar crime, and (g) violent crime.

L07 **Analyze the importance of private security today.** In the United States, businesses and citizens spend $39 billion a year on private security, more than triple the amount spent on public law enforcement. Heightened fear of crime and increased crime in the workplace have fueled the growth in spending on private security.

L08 **List the four basic responsibilities of the police.** (a) To enforce laws, (b) to provide services, (c) to prevent crime, and (d) to preserve the peace.

L09 **Indicate why patrol officers are allowed discretionary powers.** Police officers are considered trustworthy and able to make honest decisions. They have experience and training. They are knowledgeable in criminal behavior. Finally, they must be able to have the discretion to reasonably protect themselves.

L010 **Explain how some jurisdictions have reacted to perceived leniency to perpetrators of domestic violence.** Some jurisdictions have instituted mandatory arrest policies, requiring a police officer to arrest a person who has battered a spouse or domestic partner. Such policies eliminate police officers' discretion.

Key Terms

coroner 142
Federal Bureau of Investigation (FBI) 146
justice of the peace 135
mandatory arrest policy 156
National Guard 149
patronage system 137
private security 150
professional model 138
sheriff 141
shire-reeve 135
Special Weapons and Tactics (SWAT) team 149
tithing system 135

Self Check Answer Key

Page 140: i. political; ii. patronage; iii. reform; iv. professional; v. community

Page 150: i. sheriffs'; ii. highway patrol; iii. Federal Bureau of Investigation (FBI); iv. Drug Enforcement Administration (DEA); v. Bureau of Alcohol, Tobacco, Firearms and Explosives (ATF)

Page 152: i. deter; ii. zero; iii. no; iv. high

Page 154: i. enforce; ii. services; iii. prevent; iv. preserve

Page 157: i. discretion; ii. mandatory; iii. high-speed pursuits

Questions for Critical Analysis

1. What was the major problem faced by the earliest formal American police departments? Why did it occur?

2. Increased professionalism in police forces has been made possible by two-way radios, telephones, and automobiles. In what way has society *not* benefited from this increased professionalism? Explain your answer.

3. The latest era in policing has been called the community era and dates from the 1980s. How does this "new" era differ from the era of professionalism?

4. To what extent are state police complementary to, rather than substitutes for, local law enforcement agencies?

5. How are the FBI and the DEA different? How are these two federal law enforcement agencies similar?

6. Why do some think that American police forces are becoming increasingly militarized?

7. Why do experts believe that the private security industry will continue to grow for the foreseeable future?

8. Which of the four basic responsibilities of the police do you think is most important? Why?

9. Is it ever possible to completely eliminate discretion in policing? Explain.

10. What are some possible drawbacks of a policy restricting a police officer's ability to engage in high-speed pursuits?

Maximize Your Best Possible Outcome for Chapter 5

1. **Maximize Your Best Chance for Getting a Good Grade on the Exam.** ThomsonNOW Personalized Study is a diagnostic study tool containing valuable text-specific resources—and because you focus on just what you don't know, you learn more in less time to get a better grade. How do you get ThomsonNOW? If your textbook does not include an access code card, go to **thomsonedu.com** to get ThomsonNOW before your next exam!

2. **Get the Most Out of Your Textbook** by going to the book companion Web site at **www.cjinaction.com** to access one of the tutorial quizzes, use the flash cards to master key terms, and check out the many other study aids you'll find there. Under chapter resources you will also be able to access the Stories from the Street feature and Web links mentioned in the textbook.

3. **Learn about Potential Criminal Justice Careers** discussed in this chapter by exploring careers online at **www.cjinaction.com**. You will find career descriptions and information about job requirements, training, salary and benefits, and the application process. You can also watch video profiles featuring criminal justice professionals.

Notes

1. Quoted in Luara Maggi and Gwen Filosa, "Enough! Thousands March to Protest City's Alarming Murder Rate," *New Orleans Times-Picayune* (January 12, 2007), 1.

2. M. K. Nalla and G. R. Newman, "Is White-Collar Crime Policing, Policing?" *Policing and Society* 3 (1994), 304.

3. Richard Maxwell Brown, "Vigilante Policing," in *Thinking about Police*, ed. Carl Klockars and Stephen Mastrofski (New York: McGraw-Hill, 1990), 66.

4. Peter K. Manning, *Police Work* (Cambridge, MA: MIT Press, 1977), 82.

5. Carol S. Steiker, "Second Thoughts about First Principles," *Harvard Law Review* 107 (1994), 820.

6. Lawrence M. Friedman, *Crime and Punishment in American History* (New York: Basic Books, 1993), 29.

7. Mark H. Moore and George L. Kelling, "'To Serve and Protect': Learning from Police History," *Public Interest* 70 (1983), 53.

8. Samuel Walker, *The Police in America: An Introduction* (New York: McGraw-Hill, 1983), 7.

9. Moore and Kelling, 54.

10. Mark H. Haller, "Chicago Cops, 1890–1925," in *Thinking about Police*, ed. Carl Klockars and Stephen Mastrofski (New York: McGraw-Hill, 1990), 90.

11. William J. Bopp and Donald O. Shultz, *A Short History of American Law Enforcement* (Springfield, IL: Charles C Thomas, 1977), 109–110.

12. Roger G. Dunham and Geoffrey P. Alpert, *Critical Issues in Policing: Contemporary Issues* (Prospect Heights, IL: Waveland Press, 1989).

13. National Advisory Commission on Civil Disorders, *Report* (Washington, D.C.: U.S. Government Printing Office, 1968), 157–160.

14. 18 U.S.C.A. Sections 2510–2521.

15. Jayne Seagrave, "Defining Community Policing," *American Journal of Police* 1 (1996), 1–22.

16. Federal Bureau of Investigation, *Crime in the United States, 2006* (Washington, D.C.: U.S. Department of Justice, 2007), at **www.fbi.gov/ucr/cius2006/data/table_74.html**.

17. *Ibid.*, at **www.fbi.gov/ucr/cius2006/police/index/html**.

18. Bureau of Justice Statistics, *Local Police Departments, 2003* (Washington, D.C.: U.S. Department of Justice, May 2006), 2.

19. G. Robert Blakey, "Federal Criminal Law," *Hastings Law Journal* 46 (April 1995), 1175.

20. Vern L. Folley, *American Law Enforcement* (Boston: Allyn & Bacon, 1980), 228.

21. Bureau of Justice Statistics, *Sheriffs' Offices, 2003* (Washington, D.C.: U.S. Department of Justice, May 2006), 2.

22. *Ibid.*, 15–18.

23. *Black's Law Dictionary*, 982.
24. Robert Borkenstein, "Police: State Police," *Encyclopedia of Crime and Justice*, ed. Sanford H. Kadish (New York: Free Press, 1983), 1131.
25. Bureau of Justice Statistics, *Federal Law Enforcement Officers, 2004* (Washington, D.C.: U.S. Department of Justice, July 2006), 1.
26. Pub. L. No. 107-296, 116 Stat. 2135.
27. "CBP Border Patrol Overview," at **www.cbp.gov/xp/cgov/border_ security/border_patrol/overview.xml**.
28. "Fact Sheet: ICE Accomplishments in Fiscal Year 2006," at **www.dhs. gov/xnews/releases/pr_1162228690102.shtm**.
29. Federal Bureau of Investigation, "About Us—Quick Facts," at **www. fbi.gov/quickfacts.htm**.
30. Pub. L. No. 91-513, 84 Stat. 1242, codified as amended at 21 U.S.C. Section 801 (1994).
31. Hector Tober and Carlos Martinez, "Mexico Meth Raid Yields $205 Million in U.S. Cash," *Los Angeles Times* (March 17, 2007), 1.
32. United States Marshals Service, "Fact Sheet," at **www.usmarshals. gov/duties/factsheets/general.pdf**.
33. Army Appropriations Act, Ch. 263, Section 15, 20 Stat. 145 (1878), codified as amended at 18 U.S.C. Section 1385 (2000).
34. Military Cooperation with Law Enforcement Officials Act of 1981, Pub. L. No. 97-86, Section 905, 95 Stat. 115, codified as amended at 10 U.S.C. Section 1385 (1998).
35. Diane Celia Weber, "Warrior Cops: The Ominous Growth of Paramilitarism in American Police Departments," Cato Institute Briefing Paper No. 50 (1999), at **www.cato.org/pubs/briefs/bp-050es.html**.
36. *Local Police Departments, 2003*, Table 38, page 18.
37. *Gilbert v. United States*, 165 F.3d 470, 473 (6th Cir. 1999).
38. *Private Security Services to 2010* (Cleveland, OH: The Freedonia Group, March 2006), 1.
39. John B. Owens, "Westec Story: Gated Communities and the Fourth Amendment," *American Criminal Law Review* (Spring 1997), 1138.
40. California Penal Code Section 837 (West 1995).
41. Bruce L. Benson, "Guns, Crime, and Safety," *Journal of Law and Economics* (October 2001), 725.
42. "Security Guards Won't Face Criminal Charges in Death outside Strip Night Club," *Las Vegas Review-Journal* (January 24, 2005), 2B.
43. See **www.seiu.org/building/security/legislation/ security_report_ card/allstates_report.cfm**.
44. Jeremy Bagott, "Security Standards Putting Public at Risk," *Chicago Tribune* (February 24, 2003), 15.
45. Mimi Hall, "Private Security Guards: Homeland Defense's Weak Link," *USA Today* (January 23, 2003), A1.
46. Brock N. Meeks, "Are 'Rent-a-Cops' Threatening Security?" *MSNBC Online* (March 9, 2005).
47. "Don Walker, CPP, Former President of ASIS International, Testifies before U.S. House of Representatives' Subcommittee on Crime, Terrorism and Homeland Security," *Business Wire* (March 31, 2004).
48. Pub. L. No. 108-458, Section 6402(d)(2) (2004).
49. David Bates, "New Law Allows Nationwide Checks by Security Firms," *Government Security News*, at **www.gsnmagazine.com/feb_ 05/security_checks.html**.
50. William C. Cunningham, John J. Strauchs, and Clifford W. Van Meter, *The Hallcrest Report II: Private Security Trends, 1970 to 2000* (Boston: Butterworth-Heinemann, 1990), 236.
51. Cameron Conant, "Private Security Firms See Improved Status, Job Growth in Recent Months," *Grand Rapids Press* (December 15, 2001), D4.
52. *Private Security Services to 2010*, 1.
53. Ronnie L. Paynter, "Privatization: Something to Think About?" *Law Enforcement Technology* (September 2000), 6.
54. Ronald L. Soble, "Private Firms on Patrol: Security Is Big Business," *Los Angeles Times* (May 21, 1985), Section 1, page 1.
55. Egon Bittner, *The Functions of the Police in a Modern Society*, Public Health Service Publication No. 2059 (Chevy Chase, MD: National Institute of Mental Health, 1970), 38–44.
56. Carl Klockars, "The Rhetoric of Community Policing," in *Community Policing: Rhetoric or Reality*, ed. Jack Greene and Stephen Mastrofski (New York: Praeger Publishers, 1991), 244.
57. Jack R. Greene and Carl B. Klockars, "What Do Police Do?" in *Thinking about Police*, 2d ed., ed. Carl B. Klockars and Stephen B. Mastrofski (New York: McGraw-Hill, 1991), 273–284.
58. John S. Dempsey and Linda S. Forst, *An Introduction to Policing*, 3d ed. (Belmont, CA: Thomson Wadsworth, 2005), 110.
59. *Crime in the United States, 2006*, at **www.fbi.gov/ucr/cius2006/data/ table_29.html**.
60. Reprinted in *Police Chief* (January 1990), 18.
61. Eric J. Scott, *Calls for Service: Citizen Demand and Initial Police Response* (Washington, D.C.: U.S. Government Printing Office, 1981), 28–30.
62. Jerome H. Skolnick, "Police: The New Professionals," *New Society* (September 5, 1986), 9–11.
63. Andrew Blankstein and Garrett Therolf, "Los Angeles Crime Decreases for 5th Year," *Los Angeles Times* (December 27, 2006), 1.
64. Klockars, 250.
65. James Q. Wilson, *Varieties of Police Behavior: The Management of Law and Order in Eight Communities* (Cambridge, MA: Harvard University Press, 1968).
66. James Q. Wilson and George L. Kelling, "Broken Windows," *Atlantic Monthly* (March 1982), 29.
67. A. J. Reiss, Jr., "Police Organization in the Twentieth Century," in *Modern Policing*, ed. Michael Tonry and Norval Morris (Chicago: University of Chicago Press, 1992), 51–98.
68. C. E. Pratt, "Police Discretion," *Law and Order* (March 1992), 99–100.
69. "More than a Hunch," *Law Enforcement News* (September 2004), 1.
70. Geoffrey P. Albert, Roger C. Dunham, and Meghan S. Stroshine, *Policing: Continuity and Change* (Long Grove, IL: Waveland Press, 2006), 134–136.
71. Herbert Jacob, *Urban Justice* (Boston: Little, Brown, 1973), 27.
72. *Scott v. Harris*, 127 S. Ct. 1769 (2007).
73. James J. Fyfe, David A. Klinger, and Jeanne M. Flavin, "Differential Police Treatment of Male-on-Female Spousal Violence," *Criminology* 35 (August 1997), 455–473.
74. L. Craig Parker, Robert D. Meier, and Lynn Hunt Monahan, *Interpersonal Psychology for Criminal Justice* (St. Paul, MN: West Publishing Co., 1989), 113.
75. Paul C. Friday, Vivian B. Lord, M. Lyn Exum, and Jennifer L. Hartman, *Evaluating the Impact of a Specialized Domestic Violence Police Unit* (Charlotte, NC: University of North Carolina, 2006), 6.
76. *Local Police Departments, 2003*, Table 54, page 24.
77. Max Townshend, Dana Hunt, Sarah Kuck, and Caity Baxter, *Law Enforcement Response to Domestic Violence Calls for Service* (Washington, D.C.: National Institute of Justice, 2005), 32.
78. John Mill, "High-Speed Police Pursuits," *Law Enforcement Bulletin* (July 2002), 14; and Frederick Rivara and Chris Mack, "Motor Vehicle Crash Deaths Related to Police Pursuits in the United States," *Injury Prevention* (April 2004), 93–95.
79. *Local Police Departments, 2003*, 24.
80. Jack Richter, "Number of Police Pursuits Drop Dramatically in Los Angeles," *Los Angeles Police Department Press Release* (August 20, 2003).
81. *County of Sacramento v. Lewis*, 523 U.S. 833 (1998).
82. *Harris v. Scott*, CITE TO COME.
83. Daniel Booth, "Federalism on Ice: State and Local Enforcement of Federal Immigration Law," *Harvard Journal of Law and Public Policy* (Summer 2006), 1063.
84. Immigration and Nationality Act, 8 U.S.C. Section 1103(a)(8) (2000).
85. Jeffrey S. Passel, "The Size and Characteristics of the Unauthorized Migrant Population in the United States," Pew Hispanic Center, at **pewhispanic.org/files/reports/61.pdf**.
86. Quoted in Giovana Dell'orto, "Feds Seek Enforcement Help," *Richmond Times-Dispatch* (May 5, 2006), A4.

CHAPTER 6

Challenges to Effective Policing

Chapter outline

- Recruitment and Training: Becoming a Police Officer
- Police Organization
- Law Enforcement in the Field
- Police Strategies: What Works
- "Us versus Them": Issues in Modern Policing
- Police Ethics
- Criminal Justice in Action—The DNA Juggernaut

Learning objectives

After reading this chapter, you should be able to:

LO1 Identify the differences between the police academy and field training as learning tools for recruits.

LO2 Explain some of the benefits of a culturally diverse police force.

LO3 List the three primary purposes of police patrol.

LO4 Indicate some investigation strategies that are considered aggressive.

LO5 Describe how forensic experts use DNA fingerprinting to solve crimes.

LO6 Explain why differential response strategies enable police departments to respond more efficiently to 911 calls.

LO7 Explain community policing and its strategies.

LO8 Determine when police officers are justified in using deadly force.

LO9 Identify the three traditional forms of police corruption.

LO10 Explain what an ethical dilemma is and name four categories of ethical dilemmas typically facing a police officer.

Over the course of a twelve-year career in law enforcement, New York City police detective Michael Oliver had never fired a round in the line of duty. He certainly had no expectation that his streak would be broken on the night of November 25, 2006, when he and the other members of his squad staked out the Club Kalua in Jamaica, Queens.

The early hours of the assignment were spent trying to uncover a sex-for-money trade among the topless dancers, but things got more serious around 4 A.M. when Detective Gescard Isnora, one of Oliver's colleagues, heard a patron say, "Yo, go get my gun." Isnora watched the speaker and two other men get in a Nissan Altima; then he approached the car, flashing his badge. The car swerved at Isnora, and he and the other officers on the scene responded by pouring fifty shots into it—thirty-one of them coming from Oliver's Sig Sauer pistol. When the shooting stopped, Sean Bell, the driver, was dead, and his two passengers were seriously wounded. No firearm was found on them or in the automobile.

The incident attracted attention for two reasons. First, Bell was to be married that evening; he had been at the nightclub for his bachelor party. Second, the three men in the car were African American. Memories of the deaths of Amadou Diallo, a West African immigrant, in 1999 and Ousman Zongo, also from West Africa, in 2004

at the hands of New York police officers remained fresh in the minds of many, and charges of racism were again leveled at the police department. "It's like Little Iraq, I'm sorry, especially toward the blacks in the community," said the pastor who was to have performed Bell's wedding ceremony. "We don't feel protected."

▲ Nicole Paultre sits with her daughter, Jada Bell. On November 25, 2006, Sean Bell, Nicole's fiancé and Jada's father, was killed by undercover New York City police officers..

AP Photo/Richard Drew

A community is in trouble when people start comparing law enforcement efforts to the mayhem in Iraq. Following Sean Bell's death, New York Mayor Michael Bloomberg called the force used against him "excessive,"[1] and in March 2007 Detectives Michael Oliver and Gescard Isnora were charged with first and second degree manslaughter. Accusations of racial motivations for the shootings were somewhat blunted by the fact that two of the four officers who fired into the car were themselves African American. Because of past incidents, however, many of the city's black residents were unwilling to give the police department the benefit of the doubt.

Ideally, police would like to be seen as an integral part of society, with the same goals of crime prevention and public safety as everybody else. When the relationship between police officers and those they serve is marked by ill will and mistrust, these goals become more difficult to reach. Most Americans cannot imagine the on-the-job situations that the average law enforcement officer faces. Detective Isnora's attorney defended his client's actions by stressing how difficult it is "to be out there in the street and have to make a split-second decision."[2] As James Fyfe of Temple University explains, by telling police officers that we expect them to eradicate crime, we are putting them in a "no win war." Like some soldiers in such combat, Fyfe adds, "they commit atrocities."[3] In this chapter, we will examine some of these "atrocities," such as police brutality and corruption. We will also consider the possible causes of police misconduct and review the steps that are being taken to limit these problems. Our discussion begins with a look at how a person becomes a police officer—a process that can have a significant impact on the quality of law enforcement in cities such as New York and in the United States as a whole.

Recruitment and Training: Becoming a Police Officer

In 1961, police expert James H. Chenoweth commented that the methods used to hire police officers had changed little since 1829 when the Metropolitan Police of London was created.[4] The past half-century, however, has seen a number of improvements in the way that police administrators handle the task of **recruitment,** or the development of a pool of qualified applicants from which to select new officers. Efforts have been made to diversify police rolls, and recruits in most police departments undergo a substantial array of tests and screens—discussed below—to determine their aptitude. Furthermore, annual starting salaries that exceed $50,000, along with the opportunities offered by an interesting profession in the public service field, have attracted a wide variety of applicants to police work. (To learn what a police officer can expect to earn in his or her first year on the job, see ■ Figure 6.1.)

BASIC REQUIREMENTS

The selection process involves a number of steps, and each police department has a different method of choosing candidates. Most agencies, however, require at a minimum that a police officer:

- Be a U.S. citizen.
- Not have been convicted of a felony.
- Have or be eligible to have a driver's license in the state where the department is located.
- Be at least twenty-one years of age.
- Meet weight and eyesight requirements.

Beyond these minimum requirements, police departments usually engage in extensive background checks, including drug tests; a review of the applicant's educational, military, and driving records; credit checks; interviews with spouses, acquaintances, and previous employers; and a background search to determine whether the applicant has been convicted of any criminal acts.[5] Police agencies generally require certain physical attributes in applicants: normally, they must be able to pass a physical agility or fitness test. (For an example of one such test, see ■ Figure 6.2 on the next page.)

Age is also a factor, as few departments will accept candidates younger than twenty-one years of

■ **Figure 6.1** Average Annual Salary for Entry-Level Officers by Size of Population Served

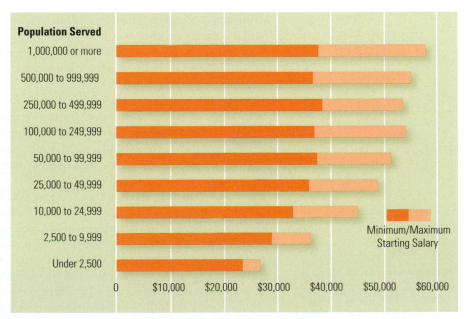

Source: Matthew J. Hickman and Brian A. Reaves, *Local Police Departments 2003* (Washington, D.C.: U.S. Department of Justice, May 2006), Table 20, page 11.

Those applying for the position of police officer must finish this physical agility exam within 3 minutes, 30 seconds. During the test, applicants are required to wear the equipment (with a total weight of between 9 and 13 pounds) worn by patrol officers, which includes the police uniform; leather gun belt; firearm; baton; portable radio; and ballistics vest.

1. Applicant begins test seated in a police vehicle, door closed, seat belt fastened.
2. Applicant must exit vehicle and jump or climb a six-foot barrier.
3. Applicant then completes a one-quarter mile run or walk, making various turns along the way, to simulate a pursuit run.
4. Applicant must jump a simulated five-foot culvert/ditch.
5. Applicant must drag a "human simulator" (dummy) weighing 175 pounds a distance of 50 feet (to simulate a situation in which an officer is required to pull or carry an injured person to safety).
6. Applicant must draw his or her weapon and fire five rounds with the strong hand and five rounds with the weak hand.

age or older than forty-five. In some departments, the applicant must take a polygraph (lie-detector) exam in conjunction with the background check. The results of the polygraph exam are often compared to the information from the background check to ensure that the applicant has not been deceptive.

Educational Requirements One of the most dramatic differences between today's police recruits and those of several generations ago is their level of education. In the 1920s, when August Vollmer began promoting the need for higher education in police officers, few had attended college. Today, 81 percent of all local police departments require at least a high school diploma, and 9 percent require a degree from a two-year college.[6] Recruits with college or university experience are generally thought to have an advantage in hiring and promotion.

Not all police observers believe that education is a necessity for police officers, however. In the words of one police officer, "effective street cops learn their skills on the job, not in a classroom."[7] By emphasizing a college degree, say some, police departments discourage those who would make solid officers but lack the education necessary to apply for positions in law enforcement.

Training If an applicant successfully navigates the application process, he or she will be hired on a *probationary* basis. During this **probationary period,** which can last from six to eighteen months depending on the department, the recruit is in jeopardy of being fired without cause if he or she proves inadequate to the challenges of police work. Almost every state requires that police recruits pass through a training period while on probation. During this time, they are taught the basics of police work and are under constant supervision by superiors. The training period usually has two components: the police academy and field training. On average, local police departments require 954 hours of training—628 hours in the classroom and 326 hours in the field.[8]

Academy Training The *police academy,* run by either the state or a police agency, provides recruits with a controlled, militarized environment in which they receive their introduction to the world of the police officer. They are taught the laws of search, seizure, arrest, and interrogation; how and when to use weapons; the procedures of securing a crime scene and interviewing witnesses; first aid; self-defense; and other essentials of police work. About four in five police academies also provide terrorism-related training to teach recruits how to respond to terrorist incidents including those involving weapons of mass destruction.[9] Academy instructors evaluate the recruits' performance and send intermittent progress reports to police administrators.

> ⊘ The **Oakland Police Academy,** located in Auburn Hills, Michigan, is a full-service police training facility. To visit its Web site, click on *Web Links* under *Chapter Resources* at **www.cjinaction.com**.

LO1

Probationary Period A period of time at the beginning of a police officer's career during which she or he may be fired without cause.

In the Field **Field training** takes place outside the confines of the police academy. A recruit is paired with an experienced police officer known as a field training officer (FTO). The goal of field training is to help rookies apply the concepts they have learned in the academy "to the streets," with the FTO playing a supervisory role to make sure that nothing goes awry. According to many, the academy introduces recruits to the formal rules of police work, but field training gives the rookies their first taste of the informal rules. In fact, the initial advice to recruits from some FTOs is often along the lines of "O.K., kid. Forget everything you learned in the classroom. You're in the real world now." Nonetheless, the academy is a critical component in the learning process, as it provides rookies with a road map to the job.

Field Training The segment of a police recruit's training in which he or she is removed from the classroom and placed on the beat, under the supervision of a senior officer.

RECRUITING MEMBERS OF MINORITY GROUPS AND WOMEN

For many years, the typical American police officer was white and male. As recently as 1968, African Americans represented only 5 percent of all sworn officers in the United States, and the percentage of "women in blue" was even lower.[10] Only within the past thirty years has this situation been addressed, and only within the past fifteen years have many police departments actively tried to recruit women, African Americans, Hispanics, Asian Americans, and other members of minority groups. An estimated 17 percent of the recruits who completed training in 2002 were female, and 27 percent were members of a minority group.[11]

Discrimination and the Law Initially, external pressures drove law enforcement agencies to take these steps. The 1964 Civil Rights Act and its 1972 amendments guaranteed minorities and women equal access to jobs in law enforcement, and the Equal Employment Opportunity Act of 1972 set the stage for affirmative action in hiring and promotion. Court decisions also played a role: in several cases in the 1970s, the United States Supreme Court ruled that police departments could be held in violation of federal law if their hiring and promotion policies were tainted by racial discrimination.[12]

The Benefits of a Culturally Diverse Police Force Not all of the efforts to increase minority representation in law enforcement are simply the result of orders from Congress and the Supreme Court. Many departments, particularly those in urban areas, have realized that a culturally diverse police force can offer a number of benefits, including improved community relations and higher levels of service.[13]

LO2

For example, after a series of racially motivated riots in 1967, Detroit decided to institute quotas to increase its percentage of black police officers—which had been 5 percent in a city that was more than 50 percent African American. In defending itself during a court case that challenged the constitutionality of these quotas, the city argued that it needed a representative police force to fulfill its duties to the citizens of Detroit. The Sixth Circuit Court of Appeals agreed, noting that the presence of a "mostly white police force in minority communities can be a 'dangerous irritant' which can trigger" a destructive response.[14] In 1986, United States Supreme Court Justice John Paul Stevens agreed, stating that police administrators "might reasonably conclude that an integrated police force could develop a better relationship and thereby do a more effective job of maintaining law and order than a force composed of white officers."[15]

As efforts to recruit African Americans, Hispanics, and other minorities have improved, their numbers on the nation's police forces have grown, albeit slowly. Minority representation as a whole increased from 14.6 percent in 1987 to 23.6 percent in 2003 (see ■ Figure 6.3 on the next page). The percentage of police officers who are African American rose from 9.3 to 11.7 percent, and the percentage of Hispanic or Latino officers increased from 4.5 percent to 13 percent.[16] Some recruitment efforts have had a dramatic effect: in 2005, for the first time in New York City's history, a majority of the officers graduating from police academies

▼ Recruits experience a training session at the New York Police Academy. Why are police academies an important part of the learning process for a new police officer?

Piotr Redlinski/Corbis

Female and Minority Police Officers, 1987 and 2003

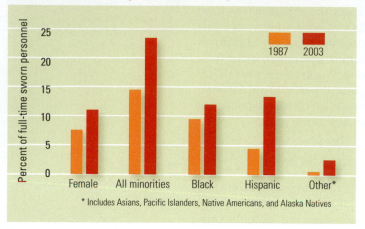

* Includes Asians, Pacific Islanders, Native Americans, and Alaska Natives

Source: Matthew J. Hickman and Brian A. Reaves, *Local Police Departments 2003* (Washington, D.C.: U.S. Department of Justice, May 2006), iii.

were racial minorities.[17] On the whole, however, African Americans, Hispanics, and other minorities are still underrepresented as law enforcement personnel in most jurisdictions, including those metropolitan areas with diverse population bases.[18]

Women in Policing If anything, the barriers against women in law enforcement have been greater than those facing racial and ethnic minorities. As of 1946, only 141 out of 417 American cities had any policewomen at all, and it was not until 1968 that a city—Indianapolis—had two female patrol officers on the force.[19] Today, the percentage of women officers ranges from about 17 percent in metropolitan areas with populations over 1 million to 6 percent in cities with fewer than 10,000 residents.[20] According to a recent survey conducted by the National Center for Women and Policing, in large police agencies women account for only 9.6 percent of supervisory positions (sergeants and lieutenants) and just 7.3 percent of top command posts (captains and above).[21] Over the past few years, however, women have been named to head police departments in several cities including Boston, Detroit, Milwaukee, San Francisco, and Washington, D.C. (See the feature *Myth versus Reality—Women Make Bad Cops.*)

Myth *versus* Reality Women Make Bad Cops

Since the formation of the earliest police departments in the nineteenth century, policing has been seen as "man's work." Only men were considered to have the physical strength necessary to deal with the dangers of the street.

THE MYTH The perception that women are not physically strong enough to be effective law enforcement officers prevails both in the public mind and within police forces themselves. Criminologist Susan Martin has found that policewomen are under "constant pressure to demonstrate their competence and effectiveness vis-à-vis their male counterparts." One female police officer describes her experience:

> I got a call. They send another male officer and then another male officer. The attitude is—get a *guy*. I'm there with the one male officer and when the other guy shows up, the first male officer says to the second, this is right in front of me—"I'm glad you came."

THE REALITY A number of studies have shown, however, that policewomen can be as effective as men in most situations, and often more so. Citizens appear to prefer dealing with a female police officer rather than a male during service calls—especially those that involve domestic violence. In general, policewomen are less aggressive and more likely to reduce the potential for a violent situation by relying on verbal skills rather than their authority as law enforcement agents.

According to a study conducted by the National Center for Women and Policing, payouts in lawsuits for claims of brutality and misconduct involving male officers exceed those involving females by a ratio of 43 to 1.

FOR CRITICAL ANALYSIS

Anecdotal evidence tells us that policewomen continue to face a great deal of bias from male police officers and that sexual harassment still occurs in many departments. What effect might a "male-dominated" police department have on attempts to recruit and keep women as law enforcement officers? What steps can the heads of police departments take to improve the situation?

▲ Two members of the San Francisco (California) Police Department.

Legal Discrimination Unlike with members of minority groups, a law enforcement agency can legally discriminate against women in recruitment and hiring. Often, the instrument of this discrimination is the physical fitness test. In California, for example, by state law all applicants must scale a six-foot wall to be considered for a police job. Officials estimate that this requirement eliminates half the women who apply because they do not possess the physical strength to get over the wall.[22] Overall, agencies without a physical agility test have 31 percent more female police officers than those agencies that require such a test.[23]

In 2002, the Third Circuit Court of Appeals upheld a Pennsylvania law that requires transit police officers to run 1.5 miles in twelve minutes. Even though the effect of this test is to discriminate against female applicants, 93 percent of whom fail the test, the court ruled that the requirement is legal because it represents a reasonable "minimum qualification" that any applicant, regardless of gender, needs to be able to meet to serve the citizens of Pennsylvania.[24] Of course, police departments that value a diverse force may adjust their physical fitness tests to level the playing field. The Champaign (Illinois) Police Department, for example, requires male applicants to run 1.5 miles in thirteen minutes and female applicants to complete the course in sixteen minutes.[25]

Self Check Fill in the Blanks

Most police agencies require that recruits be over _____ years of age and have no history of _____ convictions. During the _____ period, which can last as long as eighteen months, a recruit will attend a _____ to learn the rules of police work in an institutional setting. Then, she or he will leave the classroom and partner with an experienced officer for _____. Check your answers on page 201.

Police Organization

Studies have shown that female police officers are particularly effective in the area of community relations.[26] Consequently, police administrators have an incentive to recruit more women, because "connecting" with the public has become an important objective for law enforcement agencies. Police departments are organizations, and like most organizations in the business world, they have missions, goals, structures, managers, workers, and clients.[27]

The model of the modern police department is bureaucratic. In a **bureaucracy,** formal rules govern an individual's actions and relationships with co-employees. The ultimate goal of any bureaucracy is to reach its maximum efficiency—in the case of a police department, to provide the best service for the community within the confines of its limited resources such as staff and budget. Although some police departments are experimenting with alternative structures based on a partnership between management and the officers in the field,[28] most continue to rely on the hierarchical structure described below.

THE STRUCTURE OF THE POLICE DEPARTMENT

Each police department is organized according to its environment: the size of its jurisdiction, the type of crimes it must deal with, and the demographics of the population it must police. A police department in a racially diverse city often faces different challenges than a department in a homogeneous one. Geographic location also influences police organization. The makeup of the police department in Miami, Florida, for example, is partially determined by the fact that the city is a gateway for illegal drugs from Central and South America. The department directs a high percentage of its resources to special drug-fighting units and has formed

Bureaucracy A hierarchically structured administrative organization that carries out specific functions.

Delegation of Authority The principles of command on which most police departments are based; personnel take orders from and are responsible to those in positions of power directly above them.

Policy A set of guiding principles designed to influence the behavior and decision making of police officers.

cooperative partnerships with federal agencies such as the Federal Bureau of Investigation (FBI) and U.S. Customs and Border Protection in an effort to stop the flow of narcotics and weapons into the South Florida area.

Whatever the size or location of a police department, it needs a clear rank structure and strict accountability to function properly.[29] One of the goals of the police reformers, especially beginning in the 1950s, was to lessen the corrupting influence of politicians. The result was a move toward a militaristic organization of police.[30] As you can see in ■ Figure 6.4, a typical police department is based on a chain of command that leads from the police chief down through the various levels of the department. In this formalized structure, all persons are aware of their place in the chain and of their duties and responsibilities within the organization.

Delegation of authority is a critical component of the chain of command, especially in larger departments. The chief of police delegates authority to division chiefs, who delegate authority to commanders, and on down through the organization. This structure creates a situation in which nearly every member of a police department is directly accountable to a superior. As was the original goal of police reformers, these links encourage discipline and control and lessen the possibility that any individual police employee will have the unsupervised freedom to abuse her or his position.[31] In keeping with the need to delegate authority, police departments in large cities divide their jurisdictions into *precincts*. The precinct commander is then held responsible by his or her superiors at police headquarters for the performance of the officers in the precinct.

POLICY STATEMENTS: RULES FOR POLICING

As we saw at the end of Chapter 5, police administrations often create *policies* for complex situations such as domestic violence and high-speed pursuits. A **policy** is a written set of guiding principles that law enforcement officers must adhere to in

■ **Figure 6.4** **The Command Chain of the Lombard (Illinois) Police Department**

The Lombard (Illinois) Police Department is made up of sixty-eight sworn law enforcement officers and thirty-two civilians. As you can see, the chain of command runs from the chief of police down to crossing guards and part-time clerks.

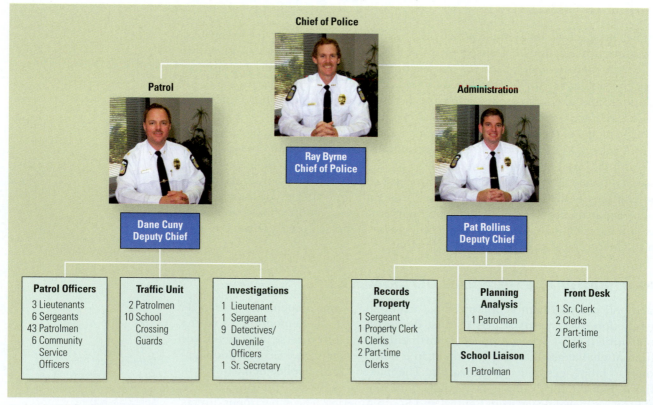

Source: Lombard Police Department.

stated situations. Policies must be flexible enough to allow for officer discretion, but at the same time specific enough to provide the officer with a clear sense of his or her duties and obligations. Consequently, policies often include *rules* that specifically prohibit or require certain behavior.[32]

During the incident described in the opening to this chapter, Detective Michael Oliver and several of his colleagues violated two policies of the New York Police Department. First, officers must not shoot more than three bullets before pausing to reassess the situation. Second, officers are prohibited from firing at a moving vehicle unless deadly force is being used against them by means *other* than the moving vehicle. Professor Eugene O'Donnell of the John Jay College of Criminal Justice explains the reasoning behind the second policy: "[I]f the cops have time to set up a clean shot, then they have time to get out of the way."[33] So, if a person in the car is shooting at the police officer, then the officer can return fire, but if the only threat is from being hit by the vehicle itself, departmental policy requires the police officer to take evasive action.

▲ A lieutenant (in the white shirt) gives instructions to two sergeants. To the extreme left, a patrol officer appears to be awaiting instructions. How do the delegation of authority and the chain of command contribute to police efficiency?

Self Check Fill in the Blanks

As with any other _____, the ultimate goal of a police department is to be efficient. For a police department, this means providing the best possible _____ to the community within the boundaries of limited _____ such as staff and budget. Typically, order and discipline are maintained by a clear _____ of authority through the various levels of the department and by written _____ that set the standards for officer behavior. Check your answers on page 201.

Law Enforcement in the Field

To a large extent, the main goal of any police department is the most efficient organization of its *field services*. Also known as "operations" or "line services," field services include patrol activities, investigations, and special operations. According to Henry M. Wroblewski and Karen M. Hess, most police departments are "generalists"; that is, police officers are assigned to general areas and perform all field service functions within the boundaries of their beats. Larger departments may be more specialized, with personnel assigned to specific types of crime, such as drugs or white-collar crime, rather than geographic locations. Smaller departments, which make up the bulk of local law enforcement agencies, rely almost exclusively on general patrol.[34]

POLICE ON PATROL: THE BACKBONE OF THE DEPARTMENT

One of the great ironies of the police organization is that the people lowest on the hierarchical "stepladder"—the patrol officers—are considered the most valuable members of the force. (Many patrol officers, considering their pay and work hours, would call the situation unjust, not ironic.) As many as two-thirds of the **sworn officers,** or those officers authorized to make arrests and use force, in some large police departments are patrol officers, and every department has a patrol unit.

"Life on the street" is not easy. Patrol officers must be able to handle any number of difficult situations, and experience is often the best and, despite training programs, the only teacher. As one patrol officer commented:

Sworn Officer A law enforcement agent who has been authorized to make arrests and use force, including deadly force, against civilians.

You never stop learning. You never get your street degree. The person who says . . . they've learned it all is the person that's going to wind up dead or in a very compromising position. They've closed their minds.[35]

It may take a patrol officer years to learn when a gang is "false flagging" (trying to trick rival gang members into the open) or what to look for in a suspect's eyes to sense if he or she is concealing a weapon. This learning process is the backdrop to a number of different general functions that a patrol officer must perform on a daily basis.

The Purpose of Patrol In general, patrol officers do not spend most of their shifts chasing, catching, and handcuffing suspected criminals. The vast majority of patrol shifts are completed without a single arrest.[36] Officers spend a great deal of time meeting with other officers, completing paperwork, and patrolling with the goal of preventing crime in general rather than any specific crime or criminal activity.

As Samuel Walker noted, the basic purposes of the police patrol have changed very little since 1829, when Sir Robert Peel founded the modern police department. These purposes include:

1. The deterrence of crime by maintaining a visible police presence.
2. The maintenance of public order and a sense of security in the community.
3. The twenty-four-hour provision of services that are not crime related.[37]

The first two goals—deterring crime and keeping order—are generally accepted as legitimate police functions. The third, however, has been more controversial.

Community Concerns As noted in Chapter 5, the community era has seen a resurgence of the patrol officer as a provider of community services, many of which have little to do with crime. The extent to which noncrime incidents dominate patrol officers' time is evident in the Police Services Study, a survey of 26,000 calls to police in sixty different neighborhoods. The study found that only one out of every five calls involved the report of criminal activity.[38] (See ■ Figure 6.5 for the results of another survey of crime calls.)

There is some debate over whether community services should be allowed to dominate patrol officers' duties. The question, however, remains: If the police do not handle these problems, who will? Few cities have the financial resources to hire public servants to deal specifically with, for example, finding shelter for homeless persons. Furthermore, the police are the only public servants on call twenty-four hours a day, seven days a week, making them uniquely accessible to citizen needs.

Patrol Activities To recap, the purposes of police patrols are to prevent and deter crime and also to provide social services. How can the police best accomplish these goals? Of course, each department has its own methods and strategies, but William Gay, Theodore Schell, and Stephen Schack are able to divide routine patrol activity into four general categories:

1. *Preventive patrol.* By maintaining a presence in a community, either in a car or on foot, patrol officers attempt to prevent crime from occurring. This strategy, which O. W. Wilson called "omnipresence," was a

◄ The most common law enforcement agent is the patrol officer, who is responsible for deterring and preventing crime as well as providing social services. Given that most patrol shifts end without an officer making a single arrest, what activities take up most of a patrol officer's time?

© David Turnley/Corbis

■ **Figure 6.5** Calls for Service

Over a period of two years, the Project on Policing Neighborhoods gathered inormation on calls for service in Indianapolis, Indiana, and St. Petersburg, Florida. As you can see, the largest portion of these calls involved disputes where no violence or threat of violence existed. Be aware also that nearly two-thirds of the nonviolent dispute calls and nearly half of the assault calls answered by police dealt with domestic confrontations.

Description of Violation	Percentage of Total Calls
NONSERIOUS CRIME CALLS	
Nonviolent disputes	41.7
Public disorder (examples: drunk, disorderly, begging, prostitution)	11.1
Assistance (examples: missing persons, traffic accident, damaged property)	9.8
Minor violations (examples: shoplifting, trespassing, traffic/parking offense, refusal to pay)	4.5
SERIOUS CRIME CALLS	
Assaults (examples: using violence against a person, kidnapping, child abuse)	26.0
Serious theft (examples: motor vehicle theft, burglary, purse snatching)	5.1
General disorder (examples: illicit drugs, fleeing police, leaving the scene of an accident)	1.8

Getty Images

Source: Stephen D. Mastrofski, Jeffrey B. Snipes, Roger B. Parks, and Christopher D. Maxwell, "The Helping Hand of the Law: Police Control of Citizens on Request," *Criminology* 38 (May 2000), Table 5, page 328.

cornerstone of policing philosophy and still takes up roughly 40 percent of patrol time.

2. *Calls for service.* Patrol officers spend nearly a quarter of their time responding to 911 calls for emergency service or other citizen problems and complaints.

3. *Administrative duties.* Paperwork takes up nearly 20 percent of patrol time.

4. *Officer-initiated activities.* Incidents in which the patrol officer initiates contact with citizens, such as stopping motorists and pedestrians and questioning them, account for 15 percent of patrol time.[39]

The category estimates made by Gay, Schell, and Schack are not universally accepted. Professor of law enforcement Gary W. Cordner argues that administrative duties account for the largest percentage of patrol officers' time and that when these officers are not consumed with paperwork and meetings, they are either answering calls for service (which takes up 67 percent of the officers' time on the street) or initiating activities themselves (the remaining 33 percent).[40]

"Noise, Booze, and Violence" Indeed, there are dozens of academic studies that purport to answer the question of how patrol officers spend their days and nights. Perhaps it is only fair, then, to give a police officer the chance to describe the duties patrol officers perform. In the words of Anthony Bouza, a former police chief:

[Patrol officers] hurry from call to call, bound to their crackling radios, which offer no relief—especially on summer weekend nights. . . . The cops jump from crisis to crisis, rarely having time to do more than tamp one down sufficiently and leave for the next. Gaps of boredom and inactivity fill the interims, although there aren't many of these in the hot months. Periods of boredom get increasingly longer as the nights wear on and the weather gets colder.[41]

"One night . . . it was so slow that three patrol cars showed up for a dispute between two crackheads over a shopping cart."

—Marcus Laffey, New York police officer

Bouza paints a picture of a routine beat as filled with "noise, booze, violence, drugs, illness, blaring TVs, and human misery." This may describe the situation

A career in law enforcement first entered my mind when I saw a recruitment poster hanging in a very bohemian San Francisco restaurant. It depicted a United Nations of women in uniform and encouraged that I join them. I did. However, the hiring process, inclusive of background checks and written, oral, physical, and polygraph testing, took two years. Concerned with my ability to scale the six-foot wall, I talked my way into a specialized physical prep class designed for female firefighter candidates. To stay motivated, I enrolled in a preacademy study class and I hunkered down for the wait.

INTO THE LIGHT In late June 1994, I received a letter from the San Francisco Police Department: my academy class was to begin in four weeks. By July, my hair was significantly shorter, and I was starching a gray rookie uniform weekly and polishing my brass and shoes daily. Those of us who could write easily were forced to do pushups, and those whose pushup style was one hand behind their backs were compelled to write. After three months, my star was pinned to my navy blue wool uniform by the chief of police, and I was off to four years of midnights before falling into the daylight and community policing.

I credit my fall to Valerie, one of the very first San Francisco community officers, who was about to move to another department when she recruited me to join the Community Police Officer Program, or C.P.O.P., as her replacement. I left the darkness of Mission Police Station's midnight watch, bought a very good pair of sunglasses, and began my adjustment to days. Soon, I was investigating a stalking incident on my beat. The suspect kept eluding us until I went undercover, riding a bicycle. We caught the guy, found he was affected by dementia, and

Courtesy of Lois Perillo

in high-crime neighborhoods, but it certainly does not represent the reality for the majority of patrol officers in the United States. Duties that all patrol officers have in common, whether they work in Bouza's rather nightmarish city streets or in the quieter environment of rural America, include controlling traffic, conducting preliminary investigations, making arrests, and patrolling public events.

POLICE INVESTIGATIONS

Investigation is the second main function of police, along with patrol. Whereas patrol is primarily preventive, investigation is reactive. After a crime has been committed and the patrol officer has gathered the preliminary information from the crime scene, the responsibility of finding "who dunnit" is delegated to the investigator, most commonly known as the **detective.** The most common way for someone to become a detective is to be promoted from patrol officer. Detectives have not been the focus of nearly as much reform attention as their patrol counterparts, mainly because the scope of the detective's job is limited to law enforcement, with less emphasis given to social services or order maintenance.

The job is not a glamorous one, however. Detectives spend much of their time investigating common crimes such as burglaries and are more likely to be tracking down stolen property than a murderer. They must also prepare cases for trial, which involves a great deal of time-consuming paperwork. Furthermore, a landmark Rand Corporation study estimated that more than 97 percent of cases that are "solved" can be attributed to a patrol officer making an arrest at the scene, witnesses or victims identifying the perpetrator, or detectives undertaking routine investigative procedures that could easily be performed by clerical personnel.[42] For example, it was not detective work but an informant's tip in July 2006 that finally led to the arrest of two men responsible for twenty-four random attacks—seven of which resulted in death—over a period of nearly fifteen months in the Phoenix, Arizona, area. "There is no Sherlock Holmes," said one investigator. "The good detective on the street is the one who knows all the weasels and one of the weasels will tell him who did it."[43]

Detective The primary police investigator of crimes.

placed him in mental-health treatment. My career as S.F.P.D.'s first bicycle community officer had begun.

PROBLEM SOLVER At first we rode our personal bicycles with rubber bands around pant legs to protect ourselves from chain snags. After ten years of bicycles on the beat, we are now fully funded with departmental supplies, equipment, and uniforms.

As a bicycle community officer, I don't just lock 'em up and go to court to testify. I am charged to be a problem solver and to stem repeat calls to dispatch. For example, after catching graffiti vandals in the act, I contracted with the teens and their parents that they remove their markings in lieu of facing arrest. I managed a crime alert system that merchants use to share information and hopefully avert criminal activity. I helped organize the community to encourage a judge to compel a once ever-present, panhandling heroin addict to choose drug treatment over jail time. And when Headquarters called me into action, I've switched into cop and robber mode to chase and

catch bike thieves, shoplifters, burglars, and drug dealers on my bike.

Though it doesn't fit on my gun belt like the other tools I carry, the bicycle is an asset to my job and helps me expand my potential; it is a barrier breaker. Children and adults approach me easily, making my duties flow smoothly. My responsibilities include daily bicycle patrol, ongoing contact with residents and merchants, and liaison with other city departments. I frequent community meetings and crime prevention talks. I listen to neighborhood concerns and prioritize my response according to the issues, assisting in residents' empowerment. As with all police officers, I answer radio calls for service, take reports, comfort the aggrieved, bandage wounds, collect evidence, and arrest suspects. I think of myself as an old-fashioned beat officer (with the plus of my bicycle) who was fortunate enough to fall into my life's work.

Go to the **Careers in Criminal Justice Interactive CD** for more profiles in the field of criminal justice.

Clearance Rates Even a cursory glance at **clearance rates,** or the percentages of reported crimes cleared by the arrest and prosecution of the offender, shows that investigations succeed only part of the time. In 2006, more than one-third of homicides and more than half of other violent crimes went unsolved, while police made arrests for only 16 percent of property crimes.[44] To a large extent, the difference in clearance rates for different crimes reflects the resources that a law enforcement agency expends on that crime. In most cases, the police investigate a murder or a rape more vigorously than the theft of a computer or an automobile.

The Detection Function A detective division in the larger police departments usually has a number of sections. These sections often include crimes against persons, such as homicide or sexual assault, and crimes against property, such as burglary and robbery. Many departments have separate detective divisions that deal exclusively with *vice,* a broad term that covers a number of public order crimes such as prostitution, gambling, and pornography. In the past, vice officers have also been primarily responsible for narcotics violations, but many departments now devote entire units to that particular social and legal problem.

The ideal case for any detective, of course, is one in which the criminal stays on the scene of the crime, has the weapon in her or his hands when apprehended, and, driven by an overriding sense of guilt, confesses immediately. Such cases are, needless to say, rare. University of Cincinnati criminal justice professor John E. Eck, in attempting to improve the understanding of the investigative process, concluded that investigators face three categories of cases:

- *Unsolvable cases,* or weak cases that cannot be solved regardless of investigative effort.
- *Solvable cases,* or cases with moderate evidence that can be solved with considerable investigative effort.
- *Already solved cases,* or cases with strong evidence that can be solved with minimum investigative effort.[45]

Eck found that the "unsolvable cases," once identified as such, should not be investigated because the effort would be wasted, and that the "already solved cases" require little additional effort or time on the part of detectives. Therefore,

Clearance Rate A comparison of the number of crimes cleared by arrest and prosecution to the number of crimes reported during any given time period.

During their investigations of crimes, officers with the Rochester (New York) Police Department pay close attention to the solvability factors listed here. Without the answers to at least some of these questions, the chances of determining who committed the crime are minimal.

1.   Are there any eyewitnesses to the crime?

2.   Has the suspect been identified by name or otherwise?

3.   Where did the crime occur?

4.   Is a description of the suspect available?

5.   If the crime is a property crime, does the stolen property have any recognizable marks, numbers, or other identifiable characteristics?

6.   Do the particulars of the crime match any other crimes committed recently?

7.   Is there significant physical evidence (bodily fluids, hair, fingerprints) at the crime scene?

8.   Has a vehicle involved with the crime been identified?

9.   Will additional investigative work or media assistance increase the probabiliy of solving the crime?

10.   Is it possible that someone other than the suspect is responsible for the crime?

Source: Adapted from Ronald F. Becker, *Criminal Investigation*, 2d ed. (Sudbury, MA: Jones and Bartlett Publishers, 2005), 145.

Eck concluded, the investigation resources of a law enforcement agency should primarily be aimed at "solvable cases." Further research by Steven G. Brandl and James Frank found that detectives had relatively high success rates in investigating burglary and robbery cases for which a moderate level of evidence was available.[46] Thus, the Rand study cited above may be somewhat misleading, in that investigators can routinely produce positive results as long as they concentrate on those cases that potentially can be solved. (To learn the factors that help law enforcement agents solve cases, see ■ Figure 6.6.)

AGGRESSIVE INVESTIGATION STRATEGIES

L04 Detective bureaus also have the option of implementing more aggressive strategies. For example, if detectives suspect that a person was involved in the robbery of a Mercedes-Benz parts warehouse, one of them might pose as a "fence"—or purchaser of stolen goods. In what is known as a "sting" operation, the suspect is deceived into thinking that the detective (fence) wants to buy stolen car parts; after the transaction takes place, the suspect can be arrested.

Undercover Operations Perhaps the most dangerous and controversial operation a detective can undertake is to go *undercover*, or to assume a false identity in order to obtain information concerning illegal activities. Though each department has its own guidelines on when undercover operations are necessary, all that is generally required is the suspicion that illegal activity is taking place. (As you may recall from the discussion of entrapment in Chapter 4, police officers are limited in what they can do to convince the target of an undercover operation to participate in the illegal activity.) Today, undercover officers are most commonly used to infiltrate large-scale narcotics operations or those run by organized crime. Undercover operations, though extremely dangerous, can yield impressive results. In February 2007, evidence gathered by an undercover task force led to the arrests of twenty-four drug dealers in Westmoreland County, Pennsylvania.

Confidential Informant (CI) A human source for police who provides information concerning illegal activity in which he or she is involved.

Confidential Informants In some cases, a detective bureau may not want to take the risk of exposing an officer to undercover work or may believe that an outsider cannot infiltrate an organized crime network. When the police need access and information, they have the option of turning to a **confidential informant (CI)**. A CI is a person who is involved in criminal activity and gives information about that activity and those who engage in it to the police. The United States Supreme

Court, in *Rovario v. United States* (1957),[47] held that the state has a confidential informant privilege, which means that it is not required to disclose the identity of an informant unless a court finds that such information is needed to determine the guilt or innocence of a suspect.

FORENSIC INVESTIGATIONS AND DNA

Although the crime scene typically offers a wealth of evidence, much of it is incomprehensible to a patrol officer or detective without assistance. For that aid, law enforcement officers rely on experts in **forensics**, or the practice of using science and technology to investigate crimes. Forensic experts apply their knowledge to items found at the crime scene to determine crucial facts such as:

- The cause of death or injury.
- The time of death or injury.
- The type of weapon or weapons used.
- The identity of the crime victim, if that information is unavailable.
- The identity of the offender (in the best-case scenario).[48]

▲ New York detective Mary Glatzke, wearing a gray wig and the nonthreatening clothes of a civilian, sits on a park bench. By posing as a "Muggable Mary," Detective Glatzke is using herself as bait to lure would-be robbers. This sort of undercover strategy hopes to deter crime as well as catch criminals in the act. What might be some of the deterrent effects of Detective Glatzke's assignment?

To assist forensic experts, many police departments operate or are affiliated with crime laboratories. As we noted in the previous chapter, the FBI also offers the services of its crime lab, the largest in the world, to agencies with limited resources.

Crime Scene Forensics The first law enforcement agent to reach a crime scene has the important task of protecting any **trace evidence** from contamination. Trace evidence is generally very small—often invisible to the naked human eye—and often requires technological aid for detection. Hairs, fibers, blood, fingerprints, broken glass, and footprints are all examples of trace evidence. Police will also search a crime scene for bullets and spent cartridge casings. These items can provide clues as to how far the shooter was from the target, and they can also be compared with information stored in national firearms databases to determine, under some circumstances, the gun used and its most recent owner. The study of firearms and its application to solving crimes goes under the general term **ballistics**.

For more than a century, the most important piece of trace evidence has been the human fingerprint. Because no two fingerprints are alike, they are considered reliable sources of identification. Forensic scientists compare a fingerprint lifted from a crime scene to that of a suspect and declare a match if there are between eight and sixteen "points of similarity." As we will see in Chapter 9, this method of identification is not, however, infallible. It is often difficult to lift a suitable print from a crime scene, and researchers have uncovered numerous incidences in which innocent persons were convicted based on evidence obtained through faulty fingerprinting procedures.[49]

The DNA Revolution The technique of **DNA fingerprinting**, or using a suspect's DNA to match the suspect to a crime, emerged in the mid-1990s and has now all but replaced fingerprint evidence in some types of criminal investigations. The shift has been a boon to crime fighters: one law enforcement agent likened DNA fingerprinting to "the finger of God pointing down" at a guilty suspect.[50]

The Genetic Code DNA, which is the same in each cell of a person's body, provides a "genetic blueprint" or "code" for every living organism. DNA fingerprinting is useful in criminal investigations because no two people, save for identical twins, have the same genetic code. Therefore, lab technicians, using the process described in

Forensics The application of science to establish facts and evidence during the investigation of crimes.

Trace Evidence Evidence such as a fingerprint, blood, or hair found in small amounts at a crime scene.

Ballistics The study of firearms, including the firing of the weapon and the flight of the bullet.

DNA Fingerprinting The identification of a person based on a sample of her or his DNA, the genetic material found in the cells of all living things.

■ Figure 6.7, can compare the DNA sample of a suspect to the evidence found at the crime scene. If the match is negative, it is certain that the two samples did not come from the same source. If the match is positive, the lab will determine the odds that the DNA sample could have come from someone other than

LO5

■ **Figure 6.7** **Unlocking Evidence in DNA**

Deoxyribonucleic acid, or DNA, is the genetic material that carries the code for all living cells. Through DNA profiling, a process explained here, forensic scientists test DNA samples to see if they match the DNA profile of a known criminal or other test subject.

1. Collection of Samples

DNA samples can be taken from a number of sources, including saliva, blood, hair, or skin. These samples are labeled and shipped to a forensic lab.

2. Extraction and Purification

At the lab, the sample is mixed with chemicals that break open the cells and let the DNA seep out. The broken cell fragments are removed from the mixture, and the remains are placed in a test tube. This tube is then spun very quickly, which makes the pure DNA sink to the bottom.

3. Separation and Binding

The double helix is then separated into two single strands. Lab technicians add "probes" to the single strands. These probes are short pieces of single-stranded DNA: A pairs with T, and C pairs with G. Because the probes are tagged with radioactivity, technicians follow them as they form connections, and figure out the strand of the original DNA sample. (For example, whenever a T probe connects, it connects with an A strand, and so on.)

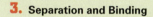

4. Replication

DNA samples are very small and difficult to see. Consequently, scientists have invented a way to "photocopy" them using a process called polymerase chain reaction (PCR). In PCR, when a probe attaches itself to a rung in the original DNA, it very quickly creates a large number of copies of the new pair. (Imagine that the probe acts like a finger pressing the "copy" button on a photocopying machine, producing repeated patterns such as ATGCTAGCAT, and so on.)

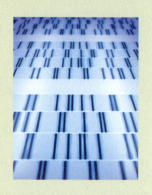

5. Identification

Next, technicians place a drop containing millions of DNA fragments at one end of a sheet of gel. An electric current is then run through the sheet, a process that pulls the DNA fragments across the gel. The larger a fragment is, the slower it will move. In order to measure these movements, the DNA fragments are tagged with dye, and they show up as colored bands when exposed to ultraviolet light.

6. Matching

Normally, a crime lab will analyze thirteen places on a person's DNA in the profiling process. These thirteen markers will be compared with a suspect's DNA profiles that are already on file. If a match is found for each of the thirteen markers, there is almost no chance that the two DNA samples did not come from the same person.

the suspect. Those odds are so high—sometimes reaching 30 billion to one—that a match is practically conclusive.[51]

A Wealth of Evidence The initial use of DNA to establish criminal guilt took place in Britain in 1986; the FBI used it for the first time in the United States two years later. The process begins when forensic technicians gather blood, semen, skin, saliva, or hair from the scene of a crime. Blood cells and sperm are rich in DNA, making them particularly useful in murder and rape cases, but DNA has also been extracted from sweat on dirty laundry, skin cells on eyeglasses, and saliva on used envelope seals. Once a suspect is identified, her or his DNA can be used to determine whether she or he can be placed at the crime scene.

Databases and Cold Hits The ability to "dust" for genetic information on such a wide variety of evidence, as well as that evidence's longevity and accuracy, greatly increases the chances that a crime will be solved (review the solvability factors in Figure 6.6 on page 176). Indeed, police no longer need a witness or even a suspect in custody to solve crimes. What they do need is a piece of evidence and a database. In 2006, for example, Bridgeport (Connecticut) police issued an arrest warrant for Emmanuel Webb in connection with a series of murders that had taken place in the late 1980s and early 1990s. Webb had been convicted of murder in Georgia in 1994, and his DNA was entered into the National Combined DNA Index System (CODIS) at that time. When Bridgeport officials plugged DNA samples from semen and cigarette butts discovered at their crimes scenes into CODIS, Webb's name came up.

Operated by the FBI since 1998, CODIS gives local and state law enforcement agencies access to the DNA profiles of a wide variety of persons who have been convicted of murder and sexual assault. Today, CODIS contains DNA records of more than 4.5 million people. Emmanuel Webb's arrest is an example of what police call a **cold hit,** which occurs when they "find a suspect out of nowhere" by randomly comparing DNA evidence from a crime scene against the contents of a database. As of February 2007, CODIS had produced almost 45,400 cold hits nationwide.[52]

Information Overload The investigative uses of DNA fingerprinting are expanding rapidly. Because relatives have similar DNA, law enforcement agents are conducting "familial searches" to gain more information about suspects. Furthermore, although CODIS was designed to help police solve murders and rapes, it is becoming increasingly useful in identifying suspects in burglaries and other property crimes. This, in turn, has led authorities to start collecting DNA samples from those convicted of nonviolent crimes and, in rare instances, from those who have merely been arrested for a crime but not convicted. (We will examine the controversy surrounding that practice in the *Criminal Justice in Action* feature at the end of the chapter.) At this time, the main problem with DNA fingerprinting is that many law enforcement agencies do not have the resources to store and analyze all of the DNA data coming into their possession.[53]

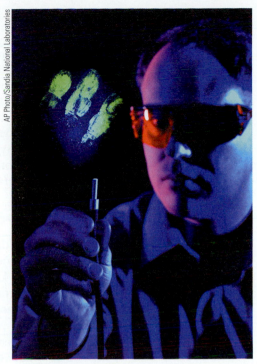

▲ A special light designed to illuminate fingerprints is tested at Sandia National Laboratories in Livermore, California. Fingerprints—the result of sweat and grease from the pores of the skin—bloodstains, footprints, tire impressions, fiber from clothing, hair and skin samples, and weapons are important types of physical evidence that help police officers investigate crimes and convict offenders.

Cold Hit The establishment of a connection between a suspect and a crime, often through the use of DNA evidence, in the absence of an ongoing criminal investigation.

Self Check Fill in the Blanks

_____ officers make up the backbone of a police department. One of their primary functions is to _____ crime by maintaining a visible _____ in the community. _____, in contrast, investigate crimes that have already occurred. In the past decade, _____, or the science of crime investigation, has been revolutionized by the technique of _____, in which crime labs use samples of a person's genetic material to match suspects to crimes. Check your answers on page 201.

Police Strategies: What Works

No matter how "miraculous" DNA fingerprinting may appear, the technology does have its limitations. Being evidence, DNA can only help the police solve a crime that has already taken place. It does little to prevent crime that has yet to occur. Needless to say, police experts have come up with numerous crime prevention strategies, and a great deal of research has been done to determine their effectiveness. Lawrence W. Sherman, director of the Jerry Lee Center of Criminology at the University of Pennsylvania, has turned a critical eye on the most popular crime prevention strategies.[54] His conclusion, as we shall see in this section, is that some work better than others.

MORE POLICE OFFICERS, LESS CRIME

When William Bratton took over the Los Angeles Police Department in the early 2000s, one of his stated goals was to increase the size of his force from about 9,300 to 12,500. When asked how he came up with this figure, Bratton admitted, "Quite frankly, some of it is guesstimate."[55] Indeed, even though the premise that adding police officers reduces crime is quite popular among police administrators and politicians, research backing this assumption is inconsistent, according to Professor Sherman.[56] On the one hand, crime rates in New York City dropped dramatically in the 1990s after the city added 13,000 new police officers. On the other hand, Washington, D.C., experienced its lowest crime levels in twenty-five years in 2006 even though its police force had shrunk by 4,000 officers in the previous eight years.[57]

A study conducted by Thomas Marvell and Carlisle Moody in the 1990s concluded that large cities with high crime rates do benefit from an infusion of more police officers.[58] Furthermore, increasing the police presence in a very small, high-crime area can be highly beneficial. Compton, California, for example, experienced seventy-two murders in 2005. In response, law enforcement officials doubled the number of sheriff's deputies, detectives, and other personnel assigned to the crime-plagued city. The result: during the first three months of 2006, the officers seized 129 guns, made 330 felony arrests, and served thirty-six major search warrants. Homicides in the city dropped to three compared to twenty-two during the same time period the previous year, and gang-related weapons assaults were down by about 50 percent.[59] In general, however, "nobody knows what the precise formula [for the number of police officers] should be," says Jerome Skolnick, a criminologist at New York University.[60]

RESPONSE TIME TO 911 CALLS

One of the perceived benefits of a larger police force is that it will reduce the response time to 911 calls. Even though law enforcement officers do not like to think of themselves as being at the "beck and call" of citizens, that is the operational basis of much police work. All police departments practice **incident-driven policing**, in which calls for service are the primary instigators of action. Between 40 and 60 percent of police activity is the result of 911 calls or other citizen requests, which means that police officers in the field initiate only about half of such activity.[61]

Response Time and Efficiency The speed with which the police respond to calls for service has traditionally been seen as a crucial aspect of crime fighting and crime prevention. In incident-driven policing, the ideal scenario is as follows: a citizen sees a person committing a crime and calls 911; then the police arrive quickly and catch the perpetrator in the act. Alternatively, a citizen who is the victim of a crime, such as a mugging, calls 911 as soon as possible, and the police arrive to catch the mugger before she or he can flee the immediate area of

Incident-Driven Policing A reactive approach to policing that emphasizes a speedy response to calls for service.

the crime. Although such scenarios are quite rare in real life, **response time,** or the time elapsed between the instant a call for service is received and the instant the police arrive on the scene, has become a benchmark for police efficiency.

As Professor Sherman points out, however, one of the most wide-reaching and respected research efforts ever conducted on police work, the Kansas City Preventive Patrol Experiment of 1972 and 1973, raised serious questions about focusing on response time. The Kansas City researchers found absolutely no correlation between arrest probability and response time when citizens waited longer than 9 minutes before reporting a crime. In Kansas City, the average reporting time was 41 minutes.[62] Furthermore, cutting response time in half would require a doubling of the police force, with almost no improvement in the odds of making an arrest.[63]

▲ Rosemary Wilson takes a 911 call at the Sumter City–County Law Enforcement Center in Sumter, South Carolina. What does the importance of 911 systems tell us about the way that much police activity is initiated?

Differential Response Many police departments have come to realize that overall response time is not as critical as response time for the most important calls. In Los Angeles, for example, the response time for "emergencies"—including shootings, knifings, and robberies—is 6.7 minutes. Urgent nonemergency calls such as those reporting car break-ins and other property crimes that do not involve any danger to life are answered in 10.5 minutes, and calls considered routine have a response time of almost half an hour.[64]

The Los Angeles Police Department has instituted a **differential response** strategy, in which the police distinguish among different calls for service so that they can respond more quickly to the most serious incidents. Suppose, for example, that a police department receives two calls for service at the same time. The first caller reports that a burglar is in her house, and the second says that he has returned home from work to find his automobile missing. If the department employs differential response, the burglary in progress—a "hot" crime—will receive immediate attention. The missing automobile—a "cold" crime that could have been committed several hours earlier—will receive attention "as time permits," and the caller may even be asked to make an appointment to come to the police station to formally report the theft. (See ■ Figure 6.8 on the following page for possible responses to calls to a 911 operator.)

PATROL STRATEGIES

Earlier in this chapter, we noted that the majority of police officers are assigned to patrol duties. Most of these officers work **general patrol,** making the rounds of a specific area with the purpose of carrying out the various patrol functions. Every police department in the United States patrols its jurisdiction using automobiles; in addition, 59 percent utilize foot patrols, 38 percent bicycle patrols, 14 percent motorcycle patrols, 4 percent boat patrols, and 2 percent horse patrols.[65]

General patrols are *random* because the officers spend a substantial amount of their shifts hoping to notice any crimes that may be occurring. In contrast, **directed patrols** are specifically designed to deal with crimes that commonly occur in certain locations and under circumstances that provide police with opportunity for preparation. The police response to high crime rates in Compton, California, discussed earlier is a good example of a directed patrol.

Response Time The rapidity with which calls for service are answered; used as a measurement of police efficiency.

Differential Response A strategy for answering calls for service in which response time is adapted to the seriousness of the call.

General Patrol A patrol strategy that relies on police officers monitoring a certain area with the goal of detecting crimes in progress or preventing crime due to their presence; also known as *random* or *preventive patrol.*

Directed Patrol A patrol strategy that is designed to focus on a specific type of criminal activity at a specific time.

■ Figure 6.8 Putting the Theory of Differential Response into Action

Differential response strategies are based on a simple concept: treat emergencies like emergencies and nonemergencies like nonemergencies. As you see, calls for service that involve "hot crimes" will be dealt with immediately, while those that report "cold crimes" will be deal with at some point in the future.

"HOT" CALLS FOR SERVICE — IMMEDIATE RESPONSE	
Complaint to 911 Officer	**Rationale**
"I just got home from work and I can see someone in my bedroom through the window."	Possibility that the intruder is committing a crime.
"My husband has a baseball bat, and he says he's going to kill me."	Crime in progress
"A woman in a green jacket just grabbed my purse and ran away."	Chances of catching the suspect are increased with immediate action.

"COLD" CALLS FOR SERVICE — ALTERNATIVE RESPONSE	
"I got to my office about two hours ago, but I just noticed that the fax machine was stolen at some point during the night."	The crime occurred at least two hours earlier.
"The guy in the apartment above me has been selling pot for years, and I'm sick and tired of it."	Not an emergency situation.
"My husband came home late two nights ago with a black eye, and I finally got him to admit that he didn't run into a doorknob. Larry Smith smacked him."	Past crime with a known suspect who is unlikely to flee.

Source: Adapted from John S. Dempsey, *An Introduction to Policing*, 2d ed. (Belmont, CA: West/Wadsworth Publishing, 1999), Table 8.1, page 175.

Testing General Patrol Theories in Kansas City Some observers have compared a patrol officer to a scarecrow because of the hope that the officer's presence alone will deter any would-be criminals from attempting a crime.[66] This theory was tested in the Kansas City experiment mentioned on the previous page. With the cooperation of the local police department, a team of researchers chose three areas, each comprising five *beats* with similar crime statistics. (A *beat*, in this instance, is the area that a police officer or group of police officers regularly patrol.) Over the course of twelve months, the police applied different patrol strategies to each designated area:

- On the *control* beats, normal preventive measures were taken, meaning that a single automobile drove the streets when not answering a call for service.
- On the *proactive* beats, the level of preventive measures was increased, with automobile patrols being doubled or tripled.
- On the *reactive* beats, preventive patrol was eliminated entirely, and patrol cars only answered calls for service.

Before, during, and after the experiments, the researchers also interviewed residents of the three designated areas to determine their opinion of police service and fear of crime.

The results of the Kansas City experiment were somewhat shocking. Researchers found that increasing or decreasing preventive patrol had little or no impact on crimes, public opinion, the effectiveness of the police, police response time, traffic accidents, or reports of crime to police.[67]

Interpreting the Kansas City Experiment Criminologists were, and continue to be, somewhat divided on how to interpret these results. For some, the Kansas City experiment and other similar data prove that patrol officers, after a certain threshold, are not effective in preventing crime and that scarce law enforcement resources should therefore be diverted to other areas. "It makes about as much sense to have police patrol routinely in cars to fight crime as it does to have firemen patrol routinely in fire trucks to fight fire," said University of Delaware professor Carl Klockars.[68]

Others saw the experiment as proving only one conclusion in a very specific set of circumstances and were unwilling to accept the results as universal.

Professor James Q. Wilson, for example, argues that the study showed only that random patrols in marked police cars were of questionable value and that it proved nothing about other types of police presence such as foot patrols or patrols in unmarked vehicles.[69]

Directed Patrols and "Hot Spots" For his part, Professor Sherman believes that while the evidence on the effectiveness of general patrol may be inconclusive, the evidence for the effectiveness of directed patrol is quite strong.[70] The target areas of directed patrols are often labeled **hot spots** because of their high levels of criminal activity.

Several studies attest to the positive results of focusing on hot spots. Minneapolis police discovered, for example, that 100 percent of robberies in a certain year occurred in only 2 percent of the city's ZIP codes. Similarly, law enforcement officials in Jersey City, New Jersey, found that fifty-six hot spots of drug activity, occupying 4.4 percent of the city's street sections, accounted for 45 percent of the city's narcotics sales and 46 percent of emergency calls for service. In both cases, the city's police department undertook experiments in which extra patrol coverage—in brief bursts of activity—was directed to the hot spots. In Minneapolis, robbery rates in targeted areas fell by more than 20 percent, and in both cities calls for service reporting public disorder also decreased.[71]

One criticism leveled at directed patrols is that they do not reduce overall crime but simply move criminals to other areas, or "scatter" them "like cockroaches in the light," as one observer puts it.[72] A group of researchers recently returned to Jersey City to see if this had indeed happened. They found that, at least for drug offenses and prostitution, crime does not simply "move around the corner." Instead, the benefits of directed patrols are spread to areas surrounding the hot spot.[73] (Many police departments are using *crime-mapping* technology to locate and identify hot spots. To learn more about the impact of this strategy, see the feature *CJ and Technology—CompStat* on the following page.)

ARREST STRATEGIES

The connection between arrest rates and crime seems clear enough. The more arrests a police department makes, the fewer the number of criminals on the streets. Again, however, practice does not necessarily follow theory. The amount of crime is not a function of arrest rates; self-reported surveys show that many, if not most, criminal acts do not lead to arrests. Perhaps arrest rates and crime rates would prove more consistent if all arrests were made for serious crimes. As we discussed in Chapter 2, though, this is not the case. Most arrests are for misdemeanors, not felonies. Furthermore, arrests are poor predictors of incarceration: one study found that nearly sixty times more Americans are arrested than are sent to prison each year.[74]

Types of Arrests Like patrol strategies, arrest strategies can be broken into two categories that reflect the intent of police administrators. **Reactive arrests** are those arrests made by police officers, usually on general patrol, who observe a criminal act or respond to a call for service. **Proactive arrests** occur when the police take the initiative to target a particular type of criminal or behavior. As you might expect, Professor Sherman has little confidence in the overall impact of reactive arrest strategies in preventing crime, but finds evidence that proactive arrests can be effective if implemented properly.[75]

Indeed, Sherman calls proactive arrest policies that focus on drunk driving "one of the great success stories of world policing."[76] The efforts of law enforcement authorities in Fresno, California, are just one example. The Fresno Police Department routinely runs "bar stings" by posting undercover officers in the parking lots of bars to stop obviously inebriated patrons from getting into their cars. The city operates nearly a hundred DUI (driving under the influence) checkpoints every year, the most of any metropolitan area in the United States. Fresno police

Hot Spots Concentrated areas of high criminal activity that draw a directed police response.

Reactive Arrests Arrests that come about as part of the ordinary routine of police patrol and responses to calls for service.

Proactive Arrests Arrests that occur because of concerted efforts by law enforcement agencies to respond to a particular type of criminal or criminal behavior.

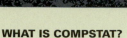
WHAT IS COMPSTAT?

CompStat is a computerized crime-mapping system first launched in New York City in 1994. William Bratton, the city's police commissioner at the time, modeled the earliest version of the system after England's use of radar to target and shoot down German Luftwaffe bombers during World War II.

WHAT DOES COMPSTAT DO?

CompStat starts with patrol officers reporting the exact location of crimes and other crime-related information to department officials. These reports are then fed into a computer, which prepares grids of a particular city or neighborhood and highlights areas with a high incidence of violent crime, drug dealing, and other serious offenses (see ■ Figure 6.9). In New York and many other cities, the police department holds "Crime Control Strategy Meetings," during which precinct commanders are held accountable for CompStat's data-based reports on their districts. In theory, this system provides the police with accurate information about patterns of crime and gives them the ability—and the incentive—to shift resources to those areas with the most crime prevention needs.

THINKING ABOUT COMPSTAT

After New York experienced record-breaking crime lows in the late 1990s, the "gospel" of CompStat spread throughout the nation, as other cities were eager to replicate the Big Apple's successes. Today, CompStat is used by police departments in dozens of cities, including Baltimore, Los Angeles, and Philadelphia. Statistics show, however, that crime decreased

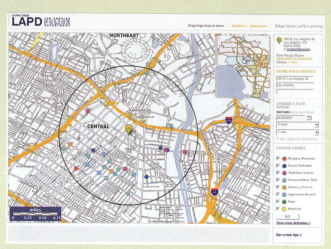

■ **Figure 6.9**
This crime map shows the incidence of burglaries, robberies, aggravated assaults, and other crimes over a three-day period in Los Angeles.

everywhere in the United States in the late 1990s and early 2000s, regardless of the presence of CompStat. What does this suggest about CompStat's effectiveness? Do you think that police departments that have instituted CompStat are better prepared to prevent crime than those that have not?

For more information on CompStat and other CJ technologies, click on *Crime and Technology* under *Book Resources* at **www.cjinaction.com**.

---

officers sometimes even plant satellite tracking devices on the automobiles of convicted drunk drivers. As a result, deaths from drunken driving in the city have plummeted over the past decade.[77]

The Broken Windows Effect Proactive arrest policies were given a boost with the popularity of a magazine article that James Q. Wilson and George L. Kelling wrote in 1982.[78] In their piece, entitled "Broken Windows," Wilson and Kelling argued that reform-era policing strategies focused on violent crime to the detriment of the vital police role of promoting the quality of life in neighborhoods. As a result, many communities, particularly in large cities, had fallen into a state of disorder and disrepute, with two very important consequences. First, these neighborhoods—with their broken windows, dilapidated buildings, and lawless behavior by residents—send out "signals" that criminal activity is tolerated. Second, this disorder spreads fear among law-abiding citizens, dissuading them from leaving their homes or attempting to improve their surroundings.

Thus, the **broken windows theory** is based on "order maintenance" of neighborhoods by cracking down on "quality-of-life" crimes such as panhandling, public drinking and urinating, loitering, and graffiti painting. Only by encouraging directed arrest strategies with regard to these quality-of-life crimes, the two professors argued, could American cities be rescued from rising crime rates. Their advice has been followed by numerous police departments in this country and has even influenced public policy in other countries includ-

Broken Windows Theory
Wilson and Kelling's theory that a neighborhood in disrepair signals that criminal activity is tolerated in the area. Thus, by cracking down on quality-of-life crimes, police can reclaim the neighborhood and encourage law-abiding citizens to live and work there.

ing Mexico and Honduras. The strategy has, however, drawn protests from two groups: (1) civil libertarians, who claim that its "zero tolerance" for minor crimes in low-income neighborhoods discriminates against the poor and minority groups, and (2) criminologists, who point out that little evidence supports a causal connection between crackdowns on quality-of-life crimes and reductions in violent crime rates.[79]

COMMUNITY POLICING

In "Broken Windows," Wilson and Kelling insisted that, to reduce fear and crime in high-risk neighborhoods, police had to rely on the cooperation of citizens. For all its drawbacks, the political era of policing (see Chapter 5) did have characteristics that observers such as Wilson and Kelling have come to see as advantageous. During the nineteenth century, the police were much more involved in the community than they were after the reforms. Officers performed many duties that today are associated with social services, such as operating soup kitchens and providing lodging for homeless people. They also played a more direct role in keeping public order by "running in" drunks and intervening in minor disturbances.[80] To a certain extent, **community policing** advocates a return to this understanding of the police mission.

Return to the Community Community policing can be defined as an approach that promotes community-police partnerships, proactive problem solving, and community engagement to address issues such as fear of crime and the causes of such fear in a particular area.[81] During the reform era, police were more detached from the community. They did their jobs to the best of their ability but were more concerned with making arrests or speedily answering calls for service than learning about the problems or concerns of the citizenry.

L07 In their efforts to eliminate police corruption, administrators put more emphasis on segregating the police from the public than on cooperatively working with citizens to resolve community problems. Under community policing, patrol officers have much more freedom to improvise. They are expected to develop personal relationships with residents and to encourage those residents to become involved in making the community a safer place. (See *Mastering Concepts—The Professional Model versus Community Policing* on the next page.)

Thinking Locally The strategy of increasing police presence in the community has been part of, in the words of George Kelling, a "quiet revolution" in American law enforcement.[82] Today, nearly two-thirds of police departments mention community policing in their mission statements, and a majority of the departments in large cities offer community policing training for employees.[83] Neighborhood Watch, the oldest and best-known community policing project, has partnered with more than five thousand police and sheriffs' agencies to connect officers with the communities in which they work.

Local police departments have come up with innovative ways to involve

▼ Redlands (California) police officer Stephen Crane takes part in a one-legged jumping race with neighborhood children. The race was sponsored by Redlands's Risked Focus Policing Program, which works to reduce juvenile delinquency in the community. How can establishing friendly relations with citizens help law enforcement agencies reduce crime?

AP Photo/Damian Dovarganes

The past sixty years have seen two dominant trends in the style of American policing. The first was the professional model, designed to reduce corruption and improve performance by emphasizing efficiency. The second, community policing, was a reaction against the professional model, which many thought went too far in relying on statistics and technology. The main characteristics of these two trends are summarized below.

PROFESSIONAL MODEL OF POLICING	COMMUNITY POLICING
• The separation of policing from politics. • Reduced emphasis on the social-service function of police, with limited resources and strategies directed toward crime control. • Limits placed on police discretion; emphasis placed on following guidelines and respecting the authority of the law. • Centralized, bureaucratic police departments. • The promotion of a certain distance between police officers and citizens, also the result of increased use of automobile patrols as opposed to foot patrols.	• Although professionalism is still valued, it is tempered by recognition that police serve the community and its citizens, as well as the ideal of the law. • Decentralized, less bureaucratic police departments, allowing more authority and discretion to rest in the hands of police officers. • Recognition that crime control is only one function of law enforcement, to be included with crime prevention and the provision of social services. • A more intimate relationship between police and citizens, which comes from understanding that police officers can do only so much to fight crime; ultimately, they need the cooperation of the community to be successful.
Main strategies: 1. Rapid response to calls for service, made possible by technological innovations such as the two-way radio. 2. Preventive patrol, which attempts to use police presence to deter criminal activity.	**Main strategies:** 1. Return to foot patrol to "reconnect" with the community. 2. Problem solving, which treats crimes not just as isolated incidents but as "problems" that can be "solved" with innovative, long-term approaches.

themselves with citizens. The Columbia (South Carolina) Police Department, for example, has adopted the Japanese *koban* system. A *koban* is a mini-police station where police officers live as well as work. Police officers stay rent-free in the upper floor of the building, while the lower floor is a police station/community center. Residents are encouraged to come to the *koban* to report crimes, and it also serves as a work station for social and educational services.[84]

Evaluating Community Policing Despite, or maybe because of, its "feel good" associations, community policing has been the target of several criticisms. First, more than half of the police chiefs and sheriffs in a survey conducted by the National Institute of Justice were unclear about the actual meaning of "community policing,"[85] leading one observer to joke that Professor Kelling's revolution is even quieter than expected.[86] Second, since its inception, community policing has been criticized—not the least by police officials—as having more to do with public relations than with actual crime fighting.[87]

The third, and most damning, criticism of community policing is that it may not have much of an impact on the community it is trying to help. After evaluating the body of research on this police strategy, Professor Sherman called the crime prevention benefits of community policing "promising" at best.[88] Sherman did find a measurable increase of citizen satisfaction in areas where police are more visibly a part of the community, but he has yet to find this perception reflected in concrete statistical data showing reduced crime.[89]

PROBLEM-ORIENTED POLICING

Professor Sherman is more optimistic about the success of **problem-oriented policing,** which was introduced by Herman Goldstein of the Police Executive Research Forum in the late 1970s.[90] Goldstein's basic premise was that police departments were devoting too many of their resources to reacting to calls for service and too few to "acting on their own initiative to prevent or reduce community problems."[91] To rectify this situation, problem-oriented policing moves beyond simply responding to incidents and attempts instead to control or even solve the root causes of criminal behavior.

Finding a Long-Term Solution Goldstein's theory encourages police officers to stop looking at their work as a day-to-day proposition. Rather, they should try to shift the patterns of criminal behavior in a positive direction. For example, instead of responding to a 911 call concerning illegal drug use by simply arresting the offender—a short-term response—the patrol officers should also look at the long-term implications of the situation. They should analyze the pattern of similar arrests in the area and interview the arrestee to determine the reasons, if any, that the site was selected for drug activity.[92] Then additional police action should be taken to prevent further drug sales at the identified location. (For an example of problem-oriented policing in action, see ■ Figure 6.10 on the next page.)

Different Terms, Same Approach Because both approaches appear to include aspects of community involvement and problem solving, a great deal of confusion has arisen concerning the extent to which community policing and problem-oriented policing are separate strategies. Actually, according to criminologists David Kennedy and Mark Moore, the two tend to merge into one, regardless of the angle by which a police department approaches them. Community policing forces police administrators to take a fresh look at tactics, which often involves some form of long-term problem solving. At the same time, problem-oriented policing inevitably requires that law enforcement agents engage members of the community to determine just what the problem may be.[93]

Problem-Oriented Policing A policing philosophy that requires police to identify potential criminal activity and develop strategies to prevent or respond to that activity.

Self Check Fill in the Blanks

Without exception, modern police departments practice _____-driven policing, in which officers respond to _____ such as 911 phone calls after a crime has occurred. Along the same lines, most patrol officers work _____ patrols, in which they cover designated areas and react to the incidents they encounter. _____ patrols, which often focus on "hot spots" of crime, and _____ arrest policies, which target a particular type of criminal behavior, have both been shown to be very effective. Under the popular strategy of _____ policing, officers are encouraged to develop partnerships with _____ to reduce crime.

Check your answers on page 201.

Proponents of problem-oriented policing often use the acronym SARA (scanning, analysis, response, assessment) to describe how the strategy works. Here is an example of how SARA can be applied to a particular situation.

S (Scanning): The (fictional) city of Nash Bay has a burglary problem. In *scanning* the problem, the Nash Bay Police Department discovers something interesting about its burglary patterns. The burglaries that occurred in Nash Bay's inner city took place during the day, from the front of the dwelling, and usually involved easy-to-carry items, such as cash and jewelry. In Nash Bay's wealthier suburbs, however, the burglaries occurred at night, involved rear entries, and targeted electronic devices, such as computers and televisions.

A (Analysis): By *analyzing* this information, the police concluded that the inner-city burglaries were probably committed mostly by juveniles and young adults who (1) would not invite suspicion if seen on the streets and (2) knew who was away at work during the day. Furthermore, these criminals operated on foot. In contrast, the suburban burglaries involved outsiders who needed automobiles to reach their targets and to carry away their loot. These criminals were most likely targeting homes with no lights, suggesting that the owners were absent.

R (Response): Nash Bay's police administrators *responded* by increasing levels of foot patrols in the inner city during daylight hours and ordered the officers to keep an eye out for suspicious groups of loitering young people. The suburbs received increased numbers of police cruisers, with the officers on the lookout for slow-moving automobiles. In both areas, police officers went door to door to educate residents on the burglary threats and suggest the purchase of burglar alarms.

A (Assessment) Three months after these steps, an *assessment* showed that burglary rates had dropped significantly in both sections of Nash Bay, an unlikely result if the police had responded similarly to what turned out do be two different problems.

Source: Adapted from Ronald V. Clarke, "Defining Police Strategies," in Quint C. Thurman and Jihong Zhao, eds., *Contemporary Policing: Controversies, Challenges, and Solutions* (Los Angeles: Roxbury Publishing Co., 2004), 18–24.

"Us versus Them": Issues in Modern Policing

Several years ago, Richard Herzog, a King's County (Washington) sheriff's deputy, was killed trying to restrain a man who had been running naked in traffic. When the man, named Ronald Matthews, turned and attacked, Herzog pulled out his pepper spray instead of his firearm. Matthews knocked Herzog to the ground, grabbed his holstered handgun, and shot him several times. In the days following his death, the question on the minds of the law enforcement community in Seattle was, "Why didn't Herzog draw his gun?" The answer, for many, came down to racial politics. County Executive Ron Sims, the highest-ranking African American in the city, had no doubt that Herzog had been inhibited in using his weapon because he was white and Matthews was black. Several killings of black suspects by white police officers in the months before Herzog's death—and the ensuing criticism—had, Sims said, made police officers afraid to protect themselves in situations involving African Americans.[94]

Racial tension is one of the many on-the-job issues that make law enforcement such a challenging and often difficult career. When faced with these issues, sometimes police officers make the right decisions, and sometimes they make the wrong ones. In the worst-case scenario, as with Deputy Herzog, even a seemingly "right" decision may have an unexpected outcome.

POLICE SUBCULTURE

At a press conference after Richard Herzog's death, King County Sheriff Dave Reichert vented his frustrations. "We are sick and tired of being nitpicked about decisions we make every day," said Reichert.[95] His words encapsulate the bitterness toward civilians that often marks **police subculture,** a broad term used to describe the basic assumptions and values that permeate law enforcement agencies and are taught to new members of a law enforcement agency as the proper way to think, perceive, and act.[96] Every organization has a subculture, with values shaped by the particular aspects and pressures of that organization. In the police subculture, those values are formed in an environment characterized by danger, stress, boredom, and violence.

> "The police subculture permits and sometimes demands deception of courts, prosecutors, defense attorneys, and defendants."
>
> —Jerome Skolnick, criminologist

The Core Values of Police Subculture From the first day on the job, rookies begin the process of **socialization,** in which they are taught the values and rules of police work. This process is aided by a number of rituals that are common to the law enforcement experience. Police theorist Harry J. Mullins believes that the following rituals are critical to the police officer's acceptance, and even embrace, of police subculture:

- Attending a recruit academy.
- Working with a senior officer, who passes on the "lessons" of police work and life to the younger officer.
- Making the initial felony arrest.
- Using force to make an arrest for the first time.
- Using or witnessing deadly force for the first time.
- Witnessing major traumatic incidents for the first time.[97]

Each of these rituals makes it clear to the police officer that this is not a "normal" job. The only other people who can understand the stresses of police work are fellow officers, and consequently law enforcement officers tend to insulate themselves from civilians. Eventually, the insulation breeds mistrust, and the police officer develops an "us versus them" outlook toward those outside the force.[98] In turn, this outlook creates what sociologist William Westly called the **blue curtain,** also known as the "blue wall of silence" or simply "the code."[99] This curtain separates the police from the civilians they are meant to protect.

Police Cynicism A cynic is someone who universally distrusts human motives and expects nothing but the worst from human behavior. **Police cynicism** is characterized by a rejection of the ideals of truth and justice—the very values that an officer is sworn to uphold.[100] As cynical police officers lose respect for the law, they replace legal rules with those learned in the police subculture, which are believed to be more reflective of "reality." The implications for society can be an increase in police misconduct, corruption, and brutality.[101]

Police cynicism is exacerbated by a feeling of helplessness—to report another officer's wrongdoing is a severe breach of the blue wall of silence. As one officer said:

> If you were to challenge somebody for something that was going on, they would say: "Listen, if the supervisor isn't saying anything, what the hell are you interjecting for? What are you, a rat?" You've gotta work with a lot of these guys. You go on a gun job, the next thing you know, you got nobody following you up the stairs.[102]

The officer's statement highlights one of the reasons why the police subculture resonates beyond department walls—he has basically admitted that he will not report wrongdoing by his peers. In this manner, the police subculture influences

Police Subculture The values and perceptions that are shared by members of a police department and, to a certain extent, by all law enforcement agents. These values and perceptions are shaped by the unique and isolated existence of the police officer.

Socialization The process through which a police officer is taught the values and expected behavior of the police subculture.

Blue Curtain A metaphorical term used to refer to the value placed on secrecy and the general mistrust of the outside world shared by many police officers.

Police Cynicism The suspicion that citizens are weak, corrupt, and dangerous. This outlook is the result of a police officer being constantly exposed to civilians at their worst and can negatively affect the officer's performance.

the actions of police officers, sometimes to the detriment of society. In the next two sections, we will examine two areas of the law enforcement work environment that help create the police subculture and must be fully understood if the cynical nature of the police subculture is ever to be changed: (1) the danger of police work and (2) the need for police officers to establish and maintain authority.[103]

THE PHYSICAL AND MENTAL DANGERS OF POLICE WORK

Police officers face the threat of physical harm every day. According to the U.S. Department of Justice, police have the most dangerous job in the United States.[104] In the two-year period 2005–2006, almost 300 police officers were killed in the line of duty, and officers are the target of approximately 60,000 attacks each year.[105]

In addition to physical dangers, police work entails considerable mental pressure and stress. Any number of factors can contribute to chronic stress for a police officer, including the rigors of the job, constant fear for personal safety, depressing on-the-job conditions, and excessive paperwork.[106] Stress, in turn, leads to other problems. Police officers suffer abnormally high levels of diabetes, headaches, hypertension, and heart disease.[107] According to one study, the rate of alcohol abuse among police officers is twice that of the population at large.[108] Sadly, police officers are also twice as likely to commit suicide as the average American.[109]

AUTHORITY AND THE USE OF FORCE

If the police subculture is shaped by the dangers of the job, it often finds expression through authority. The various symbols of authority that decorate a police officer—including the uniform, badge, nightstick, and firearm—establish the power she or he holds over civilians. For better or for worse, both police officers and civilians tend to equate terms such as *authority* and *respect* with the ability to use force. Near the turn of the twentieth century, a police officer stated that his job was to "protect the good people and treat the crooks rough."[110] Implicit in the officer's statement is the idea that to do the protecting, he had to do some roughing up as well. This attitude toward the use of force is still with us today. Indeed, it is generally accepted that not only is police use of force inevitable, but that police officers who are unwilling to use force in certain circumstances cannot do their jobs effectively.

▼ Fairfax County (Virginia) Police Honor Guard pallbearers salute the casket during funeral services for detective Vicky O. Armel, shot and killed by a carjacking subject on May 8, 2006. About 150 police officers die on duty each year, most from gunfire, automobile accidents, and vehicular assault. What are some of the other occupational threats that police officers face on a daily basis?

AP Photo/Mary F. Calvert, Pool

The "Misuse" of Force In general, the use of physical force by law enforcement personnel is very rare, occurring in only about 1 percent of police-public encounters.[111] Still, the Department of Justice estimates that law enforcement officers threaten to use force or use force in encounters with about 665,000 Americans a year.[112] (See ■ Figure 6.11.) Of course, police officers are often justified in using force to protect themselves or other citizens. At the same time, few observers would be naïve enough to believe that police are *always* justified in the use of force. How, then, is "misuse" of force to be defined?

One attempt to qualify excessive force that has been lauded by legal scholars, if not necessarily by police officers, was offered by the Christopher Commission.

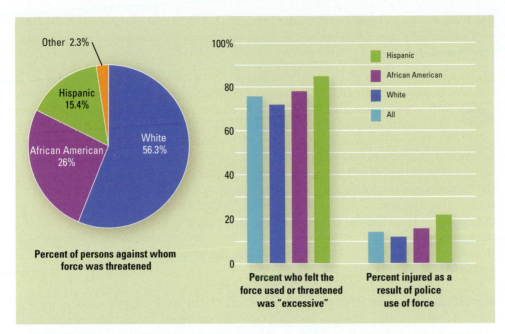

Figure 6.11 The Use of Force by Police against Suspects

Of the approximately 45 million Americans who came into contact with police officers in a typical year, about 1.5 percent reported the use or threat of force. As you can see, whites had more total forceful contacts with the police, but minorities were more likely to suffer "excessive" force and injuries.

Source: Bureau of Justice Statistics, *Contacts between Police and the Public* (Washington, D.C.: U.S. Department of Justice, February 2005), 16, 18.

Established in Los Angeles in 1991 after the beating of African American motorist Rodney King, the commission advised that "an officer may resort to force only where he or she faces a credible threat, and then may only use the minimum amount necessary to control the subject."[113]

The Phoenix Study Terms such as *credible* and *necessary* are, of course, quite subjective, rendering these definitions too vague to be practical. To better understand the subject, the Phoenix (Arizona) Police Department, in partnership with Rutgers University and Arizona State University, conducted a study to measure how often police officers used force. The results showed that police used some form of "physical force"—defined as any "weaponless tactic" (such as kicking or shoving) or the threatened or actual use of any weapon—in 22 percent of the surveyed arrests.[114] The study also examined the predictors of force; that is, the factors that were present in the situations in which force was used. As one might expect, the study found that the best predictor of police use of force was the suspect's use of force.[115]

Types of Force To comply with the various, and not always consistent, laws concerning the use of force, a police officer must understand that there are two kinds of force: *nondeadly force* and *deadly force*. Most force used by law enforcement is nondeadly force. In most states, the use of nondeadly force is regulated by the concept of **reasonable force,** which allows the use of nondeadly force when a reasonable person would assume that such force was necessary. In contrast, **deadly force** is force that an objective police officer realizes will place the subject in direct threat of serious injury or death.

The United States Supreme Court and Use of Force The United States Supreme Court set the limits for the use of deadly force by law enforcement officers in *Tennessee v. Garner* (1985).[116] The case involved an incident in which Memphis police officer Elton Hymon shot and killed a suspect who was trying to climb over a fence after stealing ten dollars from a residence. Hymon testified that he had been trained to shoot to keep a suspect from escaping, and indeed Tennessee law at the time allowed police officers to apprehend fleeing suspects in this manner.

In reviewing the case, the Court focused not on Hymon's action but on the Tennessee statute itself, ultimately finding it unconstitutional:

Reasonable Force The degree of force that is appropriate to protect the police officer or other citizens and is not excessive.

Deadly Force Force applied by a police officer that is likely or intended to cause death.

When the suspect poses no immediate threat to the officer and no threat to others, the use of deadly force is unjustified. . . . It is not better that all felony suspects die than that they escape.[117]

The Court's ruling forced twenty-three states to change their fleeing felon rules. It did not, however, completely eliminate police discretion in such situations; police officers may use deadly force if they have probable cause to believe that the fleeing suspect poses a threat of serious injury or death to the officers or others. (We will discuss the concept of probable cause in the next chapter.) In essence, the Court recognized that police officers must be able to make split-second decisions without worrying about the legal ramifications. Four years after the *Garner* case, the Court tried to clarify this concept in *Graham v. Connor* (1989), stating that the use of any force should be judged by the "reasonableness of the moment."[118] In 2004, the Court modified this rule by suggesting that an officer's use of force could be "reasonable" even if, by objective measures, the force was not needed to protect the officer or others in the area.[119] (See *You Be the Judge—Justified Force?*)

Nonlethal Weapons Regardless of any legal restrictions, violent confrontations between officers and suspects are inevitable. To decrease the likelihood that such confrontations will result in death or serious injury, many police departments use *nonlethal weapons,* which are designed to subdue but not seriously harm suspects. An estimated 99 percent of local police departments authorize the use of Oleoresin capsicum, or OC pepper spray.[120] An organic substance that combines ingredients such as resin and cayenne pepper, OC causes a sensation "similar to having sand or needles" in the eyes when sprayed into a suspect's face. Other common nonlethal weapons include tear gas, water cannons, and 37-mm pistols that fire

You Be the Judge Justified Force?

THE FACTS Officer Brosseau of the Puyallup (Washington) Police Department answered a 911 call reporting that Haugen and two other men were fighting in front of Haugen's mother's home. Brosseau knew that a warrant was out for Haugen's arrest on drug charges. When Brosseau arrived on the scene, Haugen fled. After a forty-five-minute chase, Haugen managed to circle around and jump in his Jeep Cherokee, which was parked in front of the house. He locked the doors and began fumbling for the keys as Brosseau approached the vehicle. Believing that Haugen was searching for a weapon, Brosseau smashed the driver's side window of the Jeep with her handgun and tried to grab the keys out of Haugen's hands, striking him on the head with her weapon in the process. Despite the officer's efforts, Haugen succeeded in starting the car and began to drive away. Brosseau then fired a shot through the car window, hitting Haugen in the back and puncturing his lung. Brosseau later testified that she shot Haugen because she feared for the safety of other police officers and citizens in the area.

THE LAW The United States Supreme Court has ruled that cases involving the use of police force should be decided by observing all the circumstances surrounding the incident and then determining whether the police officer was "reasonable" in the use of force. In other words, would a reasonable police officer in this officer's shoes have been justified in using force?

YOUR DECISION Haugen has sued Officer Brosseau for using excessive and unnecessary force. Under the circumstances, was Brosseau justified in firing at Haugen?

[To see how the United States Supreme Court decided this case, go to Example 6.1 in Appendix B.]

wood, rubber, beanbags, or polyure-thane bullets.

Even nonlethal weapons can raise safety concerns, and these have intensified with the increased use of Tasers—handheld electronic stun guns that fire blunt darts up to twenty-five feet, delivering 50,000 volts into their targets for a span of about five seconds. More than 7,000 local police departments employ Tasers, and many law enforcement agents credit Taser use with reducing the number of fatal shootings by police in their jurisdictions.[121] Nevertheless, a study conducted by the *Arizona Republic* identified 167 Taser-related deaths in the United States and Canada between 1999 and 2006.[122] Critics of the Taser insist that it poses a deadly threat to any person with a weak heart and are calling for further research to be done on the stun gun's safety. To date, no federal or state law enforcement agencies have adopted the Taser, though the U.S. military employs the device.

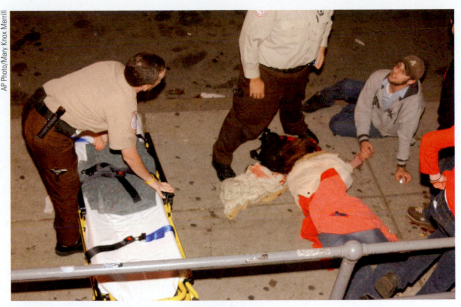

▲ Twenty-one-year-old college student Victoria Snelgrove lies unconscious on Lansdowne Street in downtown Boston after being struck in the eye by a projectile designed to disperse pepper spray on impact. A Boston police officer had fired the object to help break up a crowd of unruly Boston Red Sox fans who were celebrating their team's playoff victory over the New York Yankees on October 21, 2004. How can the use of supposedly "nonlethal" weapons increase the risk that police officers will accidentally kill or seriously injure a civilian?

RACIAL AND ETHNIC BIASES IN POLICING

In its guidelines for the use of deadly force by undercover officers, the New York Police Department warns its officers not to be victims of symbolic opponent syndrome, defined as a "preconceived notion that places suspects into a 'BAD GUY' category because of race, nationality, grooming, or mode of dress."[123] The warning may seem self-evident, but it addresses a clear problem in law enforcement today. A Department of Justice study reports that police officers are almost three times more likely to use force when coming into contact with African Americans than with whites and more than twice as likely with Hispanics as with whites.[124] Furthermore, Malcolm D. Holmes of the University of Wyoming has determined that in some of the nation's largest cities blacks and Hispanics are significantly more likely than whites to file civil rights complaints alleging police brutality.[125]

The "Just Us" System These experiences have led some to believe that the United States has, in practice, not a justice system but a "just us" system. Around the time of Sean Bell's shooting, described in the opening of this chapter, New York's African American community was further outraged to learn that 55 percent of all police "stops and frisks" in their city involved black citizens.[126] In the next chapter's discussion of racial profiling, we will see that many African Americans believe that they are often targeted for a particular "offense"—DWB, or "driving while black." Since the September 11, 2001, terrorist attacks, Muslims living in the United States have also felt that they are being singled out for law enforcement attention. This perception is strengthened by such actions as the FBI directive in 2003 ordering field supervisors to investigate the Muslim populations in their areas as part of their antiterrorism duties.

Race and the War on Drugs Such attitudes lead many to think that law enforcement in the United States is plagued by racism, particularly when it comes to the "war on drugs." These suspicions are hardly alleviated by statistics and surveys showing that African Americans are disproportionately charged and incarcerated for drug offenses. Researchers from the University of Washington recently found, for example, that the majority of Seattle drug dealers who traffic in methamphetamine, ecstasy, powder cocaine, and heroin are white. Blacks dominate only one area of the city's drug trade—crack cocaine. Nevertheless, 64 percent of those arrested for delivering one of these five banned substances are black.[127]

Stories from the Street
Go to the Stories from the Street feature at
www.cjinaction.com to hear Larry Gaines tell insightful stories related to this chapter and his experiences in the field.

The apparent targeting of African Americans for drug arrests may, however, be the result of economic disparities and selective enforcement rather than overt racism. When blacks in the inner city are arrested, they are unlikely to be able to afford expensive legal help to contest the police action. A faulty drug arrest in a middle-class or wealthy neighborhood is apt to earn the police an expensive and embarrassing lawsuit by the wronged individual. The same mistake inflicted on the resident of an inner city will likely produce little more than a futile vocal complaint. Quite simply, the inner city is an expedient locale for police to rack up impressive arrest numbers, with little fear for consequences if mistakes are made.[128]

Police Attitudes and Discretion A greater police presence in minority neighborhoods is not necessarily automatic evidence of law enforcement bias either. As we learned earlier in the chapter, the primary operational tactic of all metropolitan police forces is responding to calls for service. According to research by law enforcement expert Richard J. Ludman, the greater police presence in these communities is mainly the result of calls for service from residents, which, in turn, are caused by higher local crime rates. Indeed, Randall Kennedy believes that such "selective law enforcement" should be, and for the most part is, welcomed by those who live in high-crime areas and appreciate the added protection.[129]

Furthermore, as several experts point out, cultural differences often exist between police officers and the residents of the neighborhoods they patrol. One survey found that police working in minority areas perceived higher levels of abuse and less respect from those citizens than from those in nonminority areas.[130] In looking at police abuse in Inglewood, California, the *Los Angeles Times* found that most of the victims claimed they were assaulted after "contempt of cop" incidents, such as not immediately following orders or verbally challenging the officer.[131] Judging someone's demeanor is often a subjective task and can be influenced by a lack of communication between two people of different backgrounds—another reason why it is so important for police departments to attract members of minority groups, as noted in our discussion of recruiting strategies.

POLICE CORRUPTION

Police *corruption* has been a concern since the first organized American police departments. As you recall from Chapter 5, a desire to eradicate, or at least limit, corruption was one of the motivating factors behind the reform movement of policing. For general purposes, **police corruption** can be defined as the misuse of authority by a law enforcement officer "in a manner designed to produce personal gain."

In the 1970s, a police officer named Frank Serpico went public about corruption in the New York Police Department. City authorities responded by establishing the Knapp Commission to investigate Serpico's claims. The inquiry uncovered widespread institutionalized corruption in the department. In general, the Knapp Commission report divided corrupt police officers into two categories: "grass eaters" and "meat eaters." "Grass eaters" are involved in passive corruption; they simply accept the payoffs and opportunities that police work can provide. As the name implies, "meat eaters" are more aggressive in their quest for personal gain, initiating and going to great lengths to carry out corrupt schemes.[132]

Police Corruption The abuse of authority by a law enforcement officer for personal gain.

Types of Corruption Specifically, the Knapp Commission's investigation identified three basic, traditional types of police corruption:

1. *Bribery,* in which the police officer accepts money or other forms of payment in exchange for "favors," which may include allowing a certain criminal activity to continue or misplacing a key piece of evidence before a trial. Related to bribery are *payoffs,* in which an officer demands payment from an individual or a business in return for certain services.

2. *Shakedowns,* in which an officer attempts to coerce money or goods from a citizen or criminal.

3. *Mooching,* in which the police officer accepts free "gifts" such as cigarettes, liquor, or services in return for favorable treatment of the gift giver.[133]

▲ Atlanta police officers Gregg Junnier, left, and J. R. Smith pled guilty to involuntary manslaughter for their involvement in the fatal shooting of 92-year-old Kathryn Johnston during a botched drug raid in April 2007. The investigation into Johnston's shooting uncovered evidence that Atlanta police officers lied to obtain the search warrant to her home and planted marijuana on the premises following her death. How does this kind of activity differ from traditional forms of police corruption such as bribery and shakedowns?

About twenty years after the Knapp Commission, the arrest of six Brooklyn police officers for their involvement in an illegal drug ring led to the creation of the Mollen Commission. This commission's final report, issued in 1992, showed that police corruption had changed dramatically since the 1970s. No longer were corrupt law enforcement agents content with "accommodating" criminal activity through bribes and shakedowns. The officers had begun to engage directly in criminal activity, particularly narcotics trafficking. Furthermore, they were more likely to use brutality and to commit perjury to protect their activities.[134]

Corruption in Police Subculture There is no single reason that police corruption occurs. In covering corrupt behavior by a group of Miami police officers known as the Miami River Cops, journalist John Dorschner highlighted some of the factors that lead to unethical behavior, including a lack of proper training, a lack of supervision, and the fact that most officers can double or triple their salaries through corrupt activities.[135]

Lawrence Sherman identifies several stages in the moral decline of police officers.[136] In the first stage, the officers accept minor gratuities, such as the occasional free meal from a restaurant on their beats. These gratuities gradually evolve into outright bribes, in which the officers receive the gratuity for overlooking some violation. For example, a law officer may accept pay from a bar owner to ensure that the establishment is not investigated for serving alcohol to minors. In the final stage, officers no longer passively accept bribes, but actively seek them out, to the point where the officers may even force the other party to pay for unwanted police services. This stage often involves large amounts of money and may entail protection of or involvement in drug, gambling, or prostitution organizations.

POLICE ACCOUNTABILITY

Even in a police department with excellent recruiting methods, state-of-the-art ethics and discretionary training programs, and a culturally diverse workforce that nearly matches the makeup of the community, the problems discussed earlier in this chapter are bound to occur. The question then becomes—given the inevitability of excessive force, corruption, and other misconduct—*who shall police the police?*

Internal Affairs Unit (IAU) A division within a police department that receives and investigates complaints of wrongdoing by police officers.

Citizen Oversight The process by which citizens review complaints brought against individual police officers or police departments. The citizens often do not have the power to discipline misconduct, but can recommend that action be taken by police administrators.

Ethics The rules or standards of behavior governing a profession; aimed at ensuring the fairness and rightness of actions.

Internal Investigations "The minute the public feels that the police department is not investigating its own alleged wrongdoing well, the police department will not be able to function credibly in even the most routine of matters," says Sheldon Greenberg, a professor of police management at Johns Hopkins University.[137] The mechanism for these investigations within a police department is the **internal affairs unit (IAU)**. In many smaller police departments, the police chief conducts internal affairs investigations, while midsized and large departments have a team of internal affairs officers.

As much as police officers may resent internal affairs units, most realize that it is preferable to settle disciplinary matters in house. The alternatives may be worse. Police officers are criminally liable for any crimes they might commit, and city and state governments can be held civilly liable for wrongdoing by their police officers. Over the past decade, drug dealers and gang members filed more than 200 lawsuits in connection with a spate of wrongdoing by an elite Los Angeles anti-gang unit. As a result of the police corruption, which included planting evidence and physically abusing criminal suspects, the courts eventually overturned 100 convictions. By 2007, the city of Los Angeles had paid an estimated $80 million to settle the lawsuits.

Citizen Oversight Despite the large sums involved, such civil suits are unlikely to deter police corruption for two reasons. First, the misbehaving officers do not pay the damages out of their own pockets. Second, in the vast majority of cases, the offending officers do not face disciplinary measures within the department.[138] Mounting frustration over this lack of accountability has led many communities to turn to an external procedure for handling citizens' complaints known as **citizen oversight**. In this process, citizens—people who are not sworn officers and, by inference, not biased in favor of law enforcement officers—review allegations of police misconduct or brutality. According to Samuel Walker, nearly one hundred cities now operate some kind of review procedure by an independent body.[139] For the most part, citizen review boards can only recommend action to the police chief or other executive. They do not have the power to discipline officers directly. Police officers generally resent this intrusion by civilians, and most studies have shown that civilian review boards are not widely successful in their efforts to convince police chiefs to take action against their subordinate officers.[140]

Self Check Fill in the Blanks

Laws regulating police use of force rely on two concepts: _____ force, which is the amount of force that a rational person would consider necessary in a given situation, and _____ force, which is a level of force that the officer realizes will place the subject in grave bodily danger. According to the United States Supreme Court, the latter type of force is _____ if there is no immediate threat to the officer or anyone else. Misconduct such as accepting bribes or shaking down citizens is known as police _____, and such behavior is investigated by _____units within police departments. Check your answers on page 201.

Police Ethics

Police corruption is intricately connected with the ethics of law enforcement officers. **Ethics** has to do with fundamental questions of the fairness, justice, rightness, or wrongness of any action. Given the significant power that police officers hold, society expects very high standards of ethical behavior from them. These expectations are summed up in the *Police Code of Conduct*, which was developed by the International Association of Chiefs of Police in 1989.

To some extent, the *Police Code of Conduct* is self-evident: "A police officer will not engage in acts of corruption or bribery." In other aspects, it is idealistic, perhaps unreasonably so: "Officers will never allow personal feelings, animosities, or friendships to influence official conduct." The police working environment—rife with lying, cheating, lawbreaking, and violence—often does not allow for such ethical absolutes.

Samuel Walker, professor of criminal justice at the University of Nebraska, is one of the nation's leading experts on the **Best Practices in Police Accountability.** Click on *Web Links* under *Chapter Resources* at **www.cjinaction.com** for access to his Web site.

ETHICAL DILEMMAS

Some police actions are obviously unethical, such as the behavior of a Pennsylvania officer who paid a woman he was dating $500 to pretend to be an eyewitness in a murder trial. The majority of ethical dilemmas that a police officer will face are

LO10 not so clear-cut. Joycelyn M. Pollock and Ronald F. Becker, both members of the Criminal Justice Department at Southwest Texas State University, define an ethical dilemma as a situation in which law enforcement officers:

- Do not know the right course of action;
- Have difficulty doing what they consider to be right; and/or
- Find the wrong choice very tempting.[141]

These ethical dilemmas can occur often in police work, and it is how an officer deals with them that determines to what extent he or she is behaving ethically. (For a closer look at one difficult ethical situation that police officers may face, see the feature *A Question of Ethics—Testilying*.)

ELEMENTS OF ETHICS

Pollock and Becker, both of whom have extensive experience as ethics instructors for police departments, further identify four categories of ethical dilemmas, involving discretion, duty, honesty, and loyalty.[142]

A Question of Ethics Testilying

THE SITUATION Officer Oliva is sitting in his police cruiser at the corner of Main Street and Second Avenue. A green pickup truck approaches from the west. According to Oliva's speed gun, the car is traveling under the speed limit. When the driver of the pickup truck sees the police car, he slows down dramatically. This makes Oliva suspicious, so he pulls the pickup truck over. Oliva sees a shotgun sitting in the truck's passenger seat and arrests the driver, a man named Jacobs, for possessing an unregistered firearm. As it turns out, twenty minutes earlier Jacobs had killed his wife and young daughter with this very weapon.

THE ETHICAL DILEMMA As you will see in the next chapter, Officer Oliva had no proper reason to pull over the green pickup truck. Under these circumstances, "driving too slow" does not warrant a traffic stop. Therefore, any evidence that he found following the improper stop is inadmissible in court, meaning that Jacobs probably would be released even though he committed a double murder. If, however,

Oliva testifies in court that Jacobs was speeding, then the police officer's actions were within the law, and the shotgun can be used as evidence to convict Jacobs.

WHAT IS THE SOLUTION? Lying by police officers to ensure the conviction of suspects they know to be guilty is so common in some jurisdictions that officers have come up with a name for it: "testilying." Indeed, this type of subterfuge is strongly in keeping with the police subculture's mistrust of the court system. Nonetheless, the practice does great damage to the credibility of the trial process, which relies on participants telling the truth under oath. Furthermore, testilying rests on the assumption that police are qualified to determine a suspect's guilt, which is not their role in our criminal justice system. What advice would you give Officer Oliva in this situation?

▶ Chicago Police Superintendent Philip Cline announced his retirement on April 2, 2007. He stepped down amid furor over a highly publicized brutal videotaped beating of a bartender by Anthony Abbate, an off-duty police officer. Cline's administration waited a month before ordering the arrest of Abbate, and initially charged him with only a misdemeanor. What ethical issues are involved in a situation such as this one, and how should it have been handled?

AP Photo/Charles Rex Arbogast

- *Discretion.* The law provides rigid guidelines for how police officers must act and how they cannot act, but it does not offer guidelines for how officers *should* act in many circumstances. As mentioned in Chapter 5, police officers often use discretion to determine how they should act, and ethics plays an important role in guiding discretionary actions.
- *Duty.* The concept of discretion is linked with **duty,** or the obligation to act in a certain manner. Society, by passing laws, can make a police officer's duty more clear and, in the process, help eliminate discretion from the decision-making process. But an officer's duty will not always be obvious, and ethical considerations can often supplement "the rules" of being a law enforcement agent.
- *Honesty.* Of course, honesty is a critical attribute for an ethical police officer. A law enforcement agent must make hundreds of decisions in a day, and most of them require him or her to be honest in order to properly do the job.
- *Loyalty.* What should a police officer do if he or she witnesses a partner using excessive force on a suspect? The choice often sets loyalty against ethics, especially if the officer does not condone the violence.

Although there is no easy "formula" to guide police officers through ethical challenges, Linda S. Miller of the Midwest Regional Community Policing Institute and Karen M. Hess of Normandale Community College have come up with three questions that can act as personal "checks" for police officers. Miller and Hess suggest that officers, when considering a particular action, ask themselves:

1. Is it legal?
2. Is it balanced?
3. How does it make me feel about myself?[143]

Duty The moral sense of a police officer that she or he should apply authority in a certain manner.

Self Check Fill in the Blanks

Given the authority they command, police officers are held to high standards of _____ behavior by society. A police officer is often guided by his or her sense of _____, which obliges him or her to act in a certain manner depending on the circumstances. Feelings of _____ for a partner who is acting improperly can keep a police officer from reporting the partner's behavior to a superior. Check your answers on page 201.

THE DNA JUGGERNAUT

Despite his nasty personal history, which included arrests for stalking and attempted murder, Louisiana officials had no reason to link Derrick Lee Todd to the serial killings of five women in Baton Rouge in the early 2000s. After learning that Todd was a suspect in the disappearance of two other women five years earlier, authorities obtained a warrant to test his DNA against samples found at the scene of the first murder. A match was made, leading to Todd's arrest for murder. In hindsight, Louisiana officials bemoaned the fact that Todd's DNA was not collected at the time of any of his previous arrests. Collecting DNA from a person who has been arrested but not convicted of a crime is controversial, however, as we discuss in this chapter's *Criminal Justice in Action*.

Photodisc/Getty Images, Inc.

EXPANDING DNA SAMPLING

In the early days of DNA fingerprinting, government agencies stored only DNA samples taken from offenders who had been convicted of serious felonies such as murder and sexual assault. The theory was that these felons were most likely to be repeat offenders and to leave behind DNA evidence (such as semen, blood, and hair) at the scene of their crimes. As DNA fingerprinting proved to be a particularly effective crime-fighting tool, sampling policies changed, and today forty-three states collect DNA from *all* persons convicted of a felony.[144] In addition, thirty-eight states gather DNA from those found guilty of a misdemeanor, and twenty-eight do the same for juvenile felony offenders.[145]

Five states—including Louisiana, in the wake of the Derrick Lee Todd situation—and the federal government are taking the process one step further. They have passed legislation that allows for DNA fingerprinting of those who have not been convicted of a felony but have merely been arrested.[146] Supporters of this strategy see it as similar, if not identical, to the common practice of recording the actual fingerprints of all arrestees. Opponents counter that, unlike fingerprints, DNA provides information of family relationships, possible physical diseases and mental disorders, and other intimate matters that should be kept private whenever possible.

The Case for Collecting DNA from Arrestees

- The more comprehensive our DNA data banks, the higher the number of cold hits and other matches by law enforcement agencies. As a Virginia prosecutor puts it, "enhanced databases increase the chances of solving crimes."[147]
- Such measures are preventive, as they increase the odds that individuals who have committed violent crimes and are subsequently arrested on separate, less serious charges will wind up behind bars.
- The public interest in law enforcement is more important than the privacy interests of individuals who have been arrested for criminal behavior.

The Case against Collecting DNA from Arrestees

- Our criminal justice system is based on the premise that someone is innocent until proved guilty. An arrest does not equal guilt, and a person should not suffer the consequences of guilt until it has been proved in court. In California alone, each year approximately 50,000 people are arrested for felonies and never charged with a crime, and thousands more are tried and not convicted.[148]
- Crime labs are already overwhelmed by growing DNA databases. Under these new laws, these databases will be deluged with millions of samples, costing taxpayers billions of dollars and causing delays in getting lab results to police—a process that already takes as long as six months in some states.[149]
- Members of minority groups are already disproportionately arrested in this country, particularly for drug crimes. This system would increase the presence of African American and Hispanic DNA in crime databases, exacerbating the perception by many that our criminal justice system is inherently biased.

Your Opinion—Writing Assignment

Although most states would limit DNA fingerprinting to those arrested for felonies, South Carolina is considering applying the procedure to people arrested for any crime, including misdemeanors such as shoplifting, vandalism, and jaywalking.[150] What is your opinion of collecting DNA from arrestees, in general? What do you think of South Carolina's proposed law? From what you have learned about police strategies and the police subculture, what impact do you think the spread of these laws would have on criminal investigations in this country? Before responding, you can review our discussions in this chapter concerning:

- Police strategies, particularly arrest strategies (pages 183–185) and problem-oriented policing (pages 187–188).
- Detective investigations and DNA (pages 174–179).
- Police ethics (pages 196–198).

Your answer should be at least three full paragraphs.

L01 **Identify the differences between the police academy and field training as learning tools for recruits.** The police academy is a controlled environment where police recruits learn the basics of policing from instructors in classrooms. In contrast, field training takes place in the "real world": the recruit is taken on patrol with an experienced police officer. In the field, the recruit learns to apply the lessons he or she received at the academy.

L02 **Explain some of the benefits of a culturally diverse police force.** Members of an integrated police force are more likely to develop strong relationships with the community, which may allow them to do a more effective job of maintaining law and order. Specifically, a predominantly white department can be a "dangerous irritant" in minority neighborhoods during times of crisis.

L03 **List the three primary purposes of police patrol.** (a) The deterrence of crime, (b) the maintenance of public order, and (c) the provision of services that are not related to crime.

L04 **Indicate some investigation strategies that are considered aggressive.** Using undercover officers is considered an aggressive (and often dangerous) investigative technique. The use of informants is also aggressive, but involves danger for those who inform.

L05 **Describe how forensic experts use DNA fingerprinting to solve crimes.** Law enforcement agents gather trace evidence such as blood, semen, skin, or hair from the crime scene. Because these items are rich in DNA, which provides a unique genetic blueprint for every living organism, crime labs can create a DNA profile of the suspect and test it against other such profiles of known criminals stored in databases. If the profiles match, then law enforcement agents have found a strong suspect for the crime.

L06 **Explain why differential response strategies enable police departments to respond more efficiently to 911 calls.** A differential response strategy allows a police department to distinguish among calls for service so that officers may respond to important calls more quickly. Therefore, a "hot" crime, such as a burglary in progress, will receive more immediate attention than a "cold" crime, such as a missing automobile that disappeared several days earlier.

L07 **Explain community policing and its strategies.** Community policing involves proactive problem solving and a community-police partnership in which the community engages itself along with the police to address crime and the fear of crime in a particular geographic area. Strategies include sending police officers to schools, opening community intervention offices for high-risk youths, and encouraging police officers to live in high-crime neighborhoods.

L08 **Determine when police officers are justified in using deadly force.** Police officers must make a reasonable judgment in determining when to use force that will place the suspect in threat of injury or death; that is, given the circumstances, the officer must reasonably assume that the use of such force is necessary to avoid serious injury or death to the officer or someone else.

L09 **Identify the three traditional forms of police corruption.** The three traditional forms are bribery, shakedowns, and mooching.

L09 **Explain what an ethical dilemma is and name four categories of ethical dilemmas typically facing a police officer.** An ethical dilemma is a situation in which police officers (a) do not know the right course of action; (b) have difficulty doing what they consider to be right; and/or (c) find the wrong choice very tempting. The four types of ethical dilemmas involve (a) discretion, (b) duty, (c) honesty, and (d) loyalty.

Key Terms

ballistics 177	directed patrol 181	policy 170
blue curtain 189	DNA fingerprinting 177	proactive arrests 183
broken windows theory 184	duty 198	probationary period 166
bureaucracy 169	ethics 196	problem-oriented policing 187
citizen oversight 196	field training 167	reactive arrests 183
clearance rate 175	forensics 177	reasonable force 191
cold hit 179	general patrol 181	recruitment 165
community policing 185	hot spots 183	response time 181
confidential informant (CI) 176	incident-driven policing 180	socialization 189
deadly force 191	internal affairs unit (IAU) 196	sworn officer 171
delegation of authority 170	police corruption 194	trace evidence 177
detective 174	police cynicism 189	
differential response 181	police subculture 189	

Questions for Critical Analysis

1. In what sense have police departments' physical standards been used to discriminate against women?

2. What are the benefits of delegation of authority within the organizational structure of a police department?

3. Under what circumstances does an increase in the number of police officers on the streets seem to have the most positive effect on crime rates?

4. The Kansas City Preventive Patrol Experiment involved control beats, proactive beats, and reactive beats. Did the results of that experiment show any benefits to increasing preventive police patrol? If yes, how? If not, why not?

5. Relate the concept of "broken windows" to high-crime neighborhoods and potential ways to combat crime in such neighborhoods.

6. Contrast the community policing model with the professional policing model.

7. What are the various experiences that rookie police officers undergo that make them aware they are not in a "normal" job?

8. How does the police subculture affect police officers?

9. Under what circumstances can a police officer legally shoot a suspect who is trying to escape a crime scene?

10. How does the police subculture contribute to police corruption?

Maximize Your Best Possible Outcome for Chapter 6

1. **Maximize Your Best Chance for Getting a Good Grade on the Exam.** ThomsonNOW Personalized Study is a diagnostic study tool containing valuable text-specific resources—and because you focus on just what you don't know, you learn more in less time to get a better grade. How do you get ThomsonNOW? If your textbook does not include an access code card, go to **thomsonedu.com** to get ThomsonNOW before your next exam!

2. **Get the Most Out of Your Textbook** by going to the book companion Web site at **www.cjinaction.com** to access one of the tutorial quizzes, use the flash cards

to master key terms, and check out the many other study aids you'll find there. Under chapter resources you will also be able to access the Stories from the Street feature and Web links mentioned in the textbook.

3. **Learn about Potential Criminal Justice Careers** discussed in this chapter by exploring careers online at **www.cjinaction.com**. You will find career descriptions and information about job requirements, training, salary and benefits, and the application process. You can also watch video profiles featuring criminal justice professionals.

Notes

1. Quoted in Diane Cardwell and Sewell Chan, "New York Mayor Calls 50 Shots by Police 'Unacceptable,'" *New York Times* (November 28, 2006), A1.

2. Quoted in Erika Hayasaki, "3 Officers Charged in N.Y.'s Sean Bell Shooting," *Los Angeles Times* (March 17, 2007), 12.

3. Quoted in Gordon Witkin, "When the Bad Guys Are Cops," *U.S. News and World Report* (September 11, 1995), 22.

4. James H. Chenoweth, "Situational Tests: A New Attempt at Assessing Police Candidates," *Journal of Criminal Law, Criminology and Police Science* 52 (1961), 232.

5. Bureau of Justice Statistics, *Local Police Department, 2003* (Washington, D.C.: U.S. Department of Justice, May 2006), 8.

6. *Local Police Departments, 2003*, Table 16, page 9.

7. D. P. Hinkle, "College Degree: An Impractical Prerequisite for Police Work," *Law and Order* (July 1991), 105.

8. *Local Police Departments, 2003*, 11.

9. Bureau of Justice Statistics, *State and Local Law Enforcement Training Academies, 2002* (Washington, D.C.: U.S. Department of Justice, January 2005), 18.

10. National Advisory Commission on Civil Disorder, *Report* (Washington, D.C.: U.S. Government Printing Office, 1968), Chapter 11.

11. *State and Local Law Enforcement Training Academies, 2002*, 8.

12. *Griggs v. Duke Power Co.*, 401 U.S. 424 (1971); and *Abermarle Paper Co. v. Moody*, 422 U.S. 405 (1975).

13. Corrine Streit, "Recruiting Minority Officers," *Law Enforcement Technology* (February 2001), 70–75.
14. *Detroit Police Officers' Association v. Young,* 608 F.2d 671, 675 (6th Cir. 1979).
15. *Wygant v. Jackson Board of Education,* 476 U.S. 314 (1986).
16. *Local Police Departments, 2003,* 7.
17. Jennifer Lee, "In Police Class, Blue Comes in Many Colors," *New York Times* (July 8, 2005), B2.
18. David Alan Sklansky, "Not Your Father's Police Department: Making Sense of the New Demographics of Law Enforcement," *Journal of Criminal Law and Criminology* (Spring 2006), 1209–1244.
19. Lawrence M. Friedman, *Crime and Punishment in American History* (New York: Basic Books, 1993), 364–365.
20. *Local Police Departments, 2003,* 7.
21. National Center for Women and Policing, *Equality Denied: The Status of Women in Policing, 2001* (Los Angeles: National Center for Women and Policing, April 2002), 7.
22. Liz Tascio, "Women Recruits Meet High Standard," *Contra Costa Times* (March 16, 2003), 4.
23. Kimberly A. Lonsway, "Tearing Down the Wall: Problems with Consistency, Validity, and Adverse Impact of Physical Agility Testing in Police Selection," *Police Quarterly* (2003), 237.
24. *Lanning v. SEPTA,* No. 01-1040 (3d Cir. 2002).
25. "DOJ Decides Suit Is a Bad Fit," *Law Enforcement News* (October 31, 2001), 1.
26. Penny E. Harrington, *Recruiting and Retaining Women: A Self-Assessment Guide for Law Enforcement* (Los Angeles: National Center for Women and Policing, 2001), 22–27.
27. Larry K. Gaines and Gary W. Cordner, *Policing Perspectives: An Anthology* (Los Angeles: Roxbury Publishing Co., 1999), 351.
28. H. Nees, "Policing 2001," *Law and Order* (January 1990), 257–264.
29. Peter K. Manning, *Police Work: The Social Organization of Policing,* 2d ed. (Prospect Heights, IL: Waveland Press, 1997), 96.
30. Samuel Walker, *The Police in America: An Introduction,* 2d ed. (New York: McGraw-Hill, 1992), 16.
31. George L. Kelling and Mark H. Moore, "From Political to Reform to Community: The Evolving Strategy of Police," in *Community Policing: Rhetoric or Reality,* ed. Jack Greene and Stephen Mastrofski (New York: Praeger Publishers, 1988), 13.
32. Geoffrey P. Alpert, Roger C. Dunham, and Meghan S. Stroshine, *Policing: Continuity and Change* (Long Grove, IL: Waveland Press, 2006), 91.
33. Quoted in Cara Buckley and William K. Rashbaum, "Officer Who Opened Fire Suspected Men in Car Had a Gun," *New York Times* (November 27, 2006), A20.
34. Henry M. Wrobleski and Karen M. Hess, *Introduction to Law Enforcement and Criminal Justice,* 7th ed. (Belmont, CA: Wadsworth/Thomson Learning, 2003), 119.
35. Connie Fletcher, "What Cops Know," *On Patrol* (Summer 1996), 44–45.
36. David H. Bayley, *Police for the Future* (New York: Oxford University Press, 1994), 20.
37. Walker, 103.
38. Eric J. Scott, *Calls for Service: Citizens Demand an Initial Police Response* (Washington, D.C.: National Institute of Justice, 1981), 28–30.
39. William G. Gay, Theodore H. Schell, and Stephen Schack, *Routine Patrol: Improving Patrol Productivity,* vol. 1 (Washington, D.C.: National Institute of Justice, 1977), 3–6.
40. Gary W. Cordner, "The Police on Patrol," in *Police and Policing: Contemporary Issues,* ed. Dennis Jay Kenney (New York: Praeger Publishers, 1989), 60–71.
41. Anthony V. Bouza, *The Police Mystique: An Insider's Look at Cops, Crime, and the Criminal Justice System* (New York: Plenum Press, 1990), 27.
42. Peter W. Greenwood and Joan Petersilia, *The Criminal Investigation Process: Summary and Policy Implications* (Santa Monica, CA: Rand Corporation, 1975).
43. Fletcher, 46.
44. Federal Bureau of Investigation, *Crime in the United States, 2006* (Washington, D.C.: U.S. Department of Justice, 2007), at **www.fbi.gov/ucr/cius2006/data/table_25.html**.
45. John E. Eck, *Solving Crimes: The Investigation of Burglary and Robbery* (Washington, D.C.: Police Executive Research Forum, 1983).
46. Steven G. Brandl and James Frank, "The Relationship between Evidence, Detective Effort, and the Disposition of Burglary and Robbery Investigations," *American Journal of Police* 1 (1994), 149–168.
47. 353 U.S. 53 (1957).
48. Ronald F. Becker, *Criminal Investigation,* 2d ed. (Sudbury, MA: Jones and Bartlett, 2004), 7.
49. Simon A. Cole, "More than Zero: Accounting for Error in Latent Fingerprinting Identification," *Journal of Criminal Law and Criminology* (Spring 2005), 985–1078.
50. Quoted in "New DNA Database Helps Crack 1979 N.Y. Murder Case," *Miami Herald* (March 14, 2000), 18A.
51. Judith E. Lewter, "The Use of Forensic DNA in Criminal Cases in Kentucky as Compared with Other Selected States," *Kentucky Law Journal* (1997–1998), 223.
52. CODIS statistics, at **www.fbi.gov/hq/lab/codis/success.htm**.
53. Vesna Jaksic, "DNA Databases May Be Growing Too Quickly," *National Law Journal* (January 15, 2007), 6.
54. Lawrence W. Sherman, "Policing for Crime Prevention," in Quint C. Thurman and Jihong Zhao, eds., *Contemporary Policing: Controversies, Challenges, and Solutions* (Los Angeles: Roxbury Publishing Co., 2004), 57–76.
55. Quoted in Sewell Chan, "Counting Heads along the Thin Blue Line," *New York Times* (March 26, 2006), Section 4, page 4.
56. Sherman, 59.
57. Chan.
58. Thomas B. Marvell and Carlisle E. Moody, "Specification Problems, Police Levels, and Crime Rates," *Criminology* (November 1996), 609–646.
59. Richard Winton and Hector Becerra, "Deputies Slash Compton Crime," *Los Angeles Times* (March 22, 2006), A1.
60. Quoted in Chan.
61. Wrobleski and Hess, 173.
62. Lawrence Sherman, *Response Time Analysis,* vol. 2 (Kansas City, MO: Kansas City Police Department, 1977), 23, 39.
63. Sherman, "Policing for Crime Prevention," 61.
64. Patrick McGreevy, "LAPD's Response Time Gauged," *Los Angeles Times* (February 16, 2005), B3.
65. *Local Police Departments, 2003,* 13.
66. Dale O. Cloninger, "Enforcement Risks and Deterrence: A Reexamination," *Journal of Socio-Economics* 23 (1994), 273.
67. George L. Kelling, Tony Pate, Duane Dieckman, and Charles Brown, *The Kansas City Preventive Patrol Experiment: A Summary Report* (Washington, D.C.: The Police Foundation, 1974), 3–4.
68. Carl B. Klockars and Stephen D. Mastrofski, "The Police and Serious Crime," in *Thinking about Police,* ed. Carl B. Klockars and Stephen Mastrofski (New York: McGraw-Hill, 1990), 130.
69. James Q. Wilson, *Thinking about Crime* (New York: Basic Books, 1983), 65–66.
70. Sherman, "Policing for Crime Prevention," 62.
71. Lawrence W. Sherman, Patrick R. Gartin, and Michael E. Buerger, "Hot Spots of Predatory Crime: Routine Activities and the Criminology of Place," *Criminology* 27 (1989), 27–55; and National Institute of Justice Research Preview, *Policing Drug Hot Spots* (Washington, D.C.: Office of Justice Programs, January 1996.)
72. Brian J. Taylor, "The Screening of America," *Reason* (May 1, 1997), 44.
73. David Weisburd, Laura A. Wyckoff, Justin Ready, John E. Eck, Joshua C. Hinkle, and Frank Gajewski, "Does Crime Just Move around the Corner? A Controlled Study of Spatial Displacement and Diffusion of Crime Control Benefits," *Criminology* (August 2006), 549–592.
74. Lawrence W. Sherman, "Attacking Crime: Police and Crime Patrol," in *Modern Policing,* ed. Michael H. Tonry and Norval Morris, vol. 16 of *Crime and Justice: A Review of Research* (Chicago: University of Chicago Press, 1992), 335.
75. Sherman, "Policing for Crime Prevention," 63–66.
76. *Ibid.,* 65.
77. Larry Copeland, "Some See Fresno's DUI Crackdown as a Model," *USA Today* (November 6, 2006), 1A.
78. James Q. Wilson and George L. Kelling, "Broken Windows," *Atlantic Monthly* (March 1982), 29–38.
79. Bernard E. Harcourt and Jens Ludwig, "Broken Windows: New Evidence from New York City and a Five City Social Experiment," *University of Chicago Law Review* (Winter 2006), 271–320.
80. Mark H. Moore and George L. Kelling, "'To Serve and Protect': Learning from Police History," *Public Interest* (Winter 1983), 54–57.
81. A. Steven Deitz, "Evaluating Community Policing: Quality Police Service and Fear of Crime," *Policing: An International Journal of Police Strategies and Management* 20 (1997), 83–100.

82. George Kelling, "Police and Community: The Quiet Revolution," in *Perspectives in Policing* (Washington, D.C.: National Institute of Justice, 1988).
83. *Local Police Departments, 2003*, 19.
84. See **www.columbiasc.net/index.php?pageid=20**.
85. National Institute of Justice Preview, *Community Policing Strategies* (Washington, D.C.: Office of Justice Programs, November 1995), 1.
86. Jihong Zhao and Quint C. Thurman, "Community Policing: Where Are We Now?" *Crime and Delinquency* (July 1997), 345–357.
87. Robert C. Trojanowicz and David Carter, "The Philosophy and Role of Community Policing," at **www.cj.msu.edu/~people/cp/cpphil. html**.
88. Sherman, "Policing for Crime Prevention," 66–68.
89. *Ibid.*, 67.
90. *Ibid.*, 68.
91. Herman Goldstein, "Improving Policing: A Problem-Oriented Approach," *Crime and Delinquency* 25 (1979), 236–258.
92. Bureau of Justice Assistance, *Problem-Oriented Drug Enforcement: A Community-Based Approach for Effective Policing* (Washington, D.C.: Office of Justice Programs, 1993), 5.
93. David Kennedy and Mark Moore, "Underwriting the Risky Investment in Community Policing: What Social Science Should Be Doing to Evaluate Community Policing," *Justice System Journal* 17 (1995), 273.
94. Timothy Egan, "Killing of White Deputy Quiets Protests over Police Shootings of 2 Blacks," *New York Times* (July 13, 2002), A7.
95. *Ibid.*
96. Edgar H. Schein, *Organizational Culture and Leadership* (San Francisco: Jossey-Bass, 1985), 9.
97. Harry J. Mullins, "Myth, Tradition, and Ritual," *Law and Order* (September 1995), 197.
98. John Van Maanen, "Observations on the Making of a Policeman," *Human Organization* 32 (1973), 407–418.
99. William Westly, *Violence and the Police: A Sociological Study of Law, Custom, and Morality* (Cambridge, MA: MIT Press, 1970).
100. Wallace Graves, "Police Cynicism: Causes and Cures," *FBI Law Enforcement Bulletin* (June 1996), 16–21.
101. Robert Regoli, *Police in America* (Washington, D.C.: R. F. Publishing, 1977).
102. Bob Herbert, "A Cop's View," *New York Times* (March 15, 1998), 17.
103. Jerome H. Skolnick, *Justice without Trial: Law Enforcement in a Democratic Society* (New York: Wiley, 1966), 44.
104. Detis T. Duhart, *Violence in the Workplace, 1993–99* (Washington, D.C.: U.S. Department of Justice, December 2001), 1.
105. National Law Enforcement Memorial Fund, "Deaths, Assaults, and Injuries—1996–2006," at **www.nleomf.org/TheMemorial/Facts/ daifacts.htm**.
106. Alpert, Dunham, and Stroshine, 163.
107. *Ibid.*, 170.
108. John M. Violanti, "Alcohol Abuse in Policing: Prevention Strategies," *FBI Law Enforcement Bulletin* (January 1999), 16–18.
109. Audrey L. Honig and Elizabeth K. White, "By Their Own Hand: Suicide among Law Enforcement Personnel," *Police Chief* (October 2000), 156–160.
110. Friedman, 362.
111. Bureau of Justice Statistics, *Citizen Complaints about Police Use of Force* (Washington, D.C.: U.S. Department of Justice, June 2006), 6.
112. Bureau of Justice Statistics, *Contacts between Police and the Public* (Washington, D.C.: U.S. Department of Justice, February 2005), v.
113. Independent Commission on the Los Angeles Police Department, *Report of the Independent Commission on the Los Angeles Police Department* (1991), ix.
114. Joel Garner, John Buchanan, Tom Schade, and John Hepburn, *Research in Brief: Understanding the Use of Force by and against the Police* (Washington, D.C.: Office of Justice Programs, November 1996), 5.
115. *Ibid.*, 1.
116. 471 U.S. 1 (1985).
117. 471 U.S. 1, 11 (1985).
118. 490 U.S. 386 (1989).
119. *Brosseau v. Haugen*, 543 U.S. 194 (2004).
120. *Local Police Departments, 2003*, iv.
121. Kris Axtman, "On Trial: The Safety of Taser Stun Guns," *Christian Science Monitor* (December 5, 2005), 4.
122. Robert Anglen, "167 Cases of Death Following Stun-Gun Use," at **www.azcentral.com/specials/special43/articles/1224taserlist24-0N.html**.
123. Cited in Peter Noel, "I Thought He Had a Gun," *Village Voice* (July 13, 1998), 41.
124. *Contacts between Police and the Public*, 16.
125. Malcolm D. Holmes, "Minority Threat and Police Brutality: Determinants of Civil Rights Criminal Complaints in U.S. Municipalities," *Criminology* (May 2000), 361.
126. Nahal Toosi, "Critics Say Data Show Racial Bias by N.Y. City Police," *Buffalo News* (February 9, 2007), A6.
127. Katherine Beckett, Kris Nyrop, and Lori Pfingst, "Race, Drugs, and Policing: Understanding Disparities in Drug Delivery Arrests," *Criminology* (February 2006), 129.
128. Daniel K. Benjamin and Roger LeRoy Miller, *Undoing Drugs: Beyond Legalization* (New York: Basic Books, 1991), 21.
129. Randall L. Kennedy, "*McClesky v. Kemp*, Race, Capital Punishment, and the Supreme Court," *Harvard Law Review* 101 (1988), 1436–1438.
130. Douglas A. Smith, "Minorities and the Police: Attitudinal and Behavioral Questions," *Race and Criminal Justice*, ed. Michael J. Lynch and E. Britt Patterson (New York: Harrow & Heston, 1991), 28–30.
131. Matt Lait and Scott Glover, "Inglewood Police Accused of Abuse in Other Cases," *Los Angeles Times* (July 15, 2002), A1.
132. Bouza, 72.
133. Knapp Commission, *Report on Police Corruption* (New York: Brazilier, 1973).
134. *Commission to Investigate Allegations of Police Corruption and the Anti-Corruption Procedures of the Police Department* (New York: The Commission, 1994), 36.
135. J. Dorschner, "Police Deviance: Corruption and Controls," in *Critical Issues in Policing, Contemporary Readings*, ed. Roger G. Dunham and Geoffrey P. Albert (Prospect Heights, IL: Waveland Press, 1989), 249–285.
136. Lawrence W. Sherman, "Becoming Bent: Moral Careers of Corrupt Policemen," in *Police Corruption: A Sociological Perspective*, ed. Lawrence W. Sherman (Garden City, NY: Doubleday, 1974), 191–208.
137. Quoted in Jennifer Dukes and Loren Keller, "Can Police Be Police to Selves?" *Omaha World-Herald* (February 22, 1998), 1A.
138. National Research Council of the National Academies, *Fairness and Effectiveness in Policing: The Evidence* (Washington, D.C.: National Academies Press, 2004), 279, 289.
139. "Roster of Civilian Oversight Agencies in the U.S.," National Association for Civilian Oversight of Law Enforcement, at **www. nacole.org**.
140. Hazel Glenn Beh, "Municipal Liability for Failure to Investigate Citizen Complaints against Police," *Fordham Urban Law Journal* 23 (Winter 1998), 209.
141. Jocelyn M. Pollock and Ronald F. Becker, "Ethics Training Using Officers' Dilemmas," *FBI Law Enforcement Bulletin* (November 1996), 20–28.
142. *Ibid.*
143. Linda S. Miller and Karen M. Hess, *Police in the Community: Strategies for the 21st Century*, 2d ed. (Belmont, CA: Wadsworth Publishing, 1998), 81.
144. Seth Axelrad, "Survey of State DNA Database Statutes," American Society of Law, Medicine and Ethics, at **www.aslme.org**.
145. Rick Weiss, "Vast DNA Bank Pits Policing against Privacy," *Washington Post* (June 3, 2006), A1.
146. *Ibid.*
147. Quoted in Ellen Sorokin, "Attorney General Hopefuls Favor More DNA Collection," *Washington Times* (August 7, 2001), C1.
148. Tania Simoncelli and Barry Steinhardt, "California's Proposition 69: A Dangerous Precedent for Criminal DNA," *Journal of Law, Medicine, and Ethics* (Summer 2006), 208.
149. Brandon Bailey, "Crime Sleuths Hampered by DNA Delays," *San Jose Mercury News* (February 22, 2007), A1.
150. Yvonne M. Wenger, "Proposal Expands DNA Use by Police," *Post and Courier (Charleston, South Carolina)* (January 3, 2007), 1.

CHAPTER 7

Police and the Constitution:

The Rules of Law Enforcement

Learning objectives

After reading this chapter, you should be able to:

L01 Outline the four major sources that may provide probable cause.

L02 Explain the exclusionary rule and the exceptions to it.

L03 Distinguish between a stop and a frisk, and indicate the importance of the case *Terry v. Ohio.*

L04 List the four elements that must be present for an arrest to take place.

L05 List the four categories of items that can be seized by use of a search warrant.

L06 Explain when searches can be made without a warrant.

L07 Describe how the Patriot Act of 2001 changed the guidelines for electronic surveillance of suspected terrorists.

L08 Recite the *Miranda* warning.

L09 Indicate situations in which a *Miranda* warning is unnecessary.

L010 List the three basic types of police identification.

Janet Randolph was furious with her husband, Scott. Months of marital tension had reached a boiling point, and he had just disappeared from the family home in Americus, Georgia, with their young son. Janet promptly called the police. A few minutes after two officers arrived at the house, Scott returned home and explained that he had left his son with neighbors because he was concerned that his wife would take the boy to Canada. Janet insisted that Scott used drugs and that "items of drug evidence" could be found in the house. The officers asked for permission to search the home. Janet said, "yes." Scott said "no."

Eventually, Janet led the police to her husband's bedroom, where they found a straw covered with a powdery substance that turned out to be cocaine. This discovery led to Scott's eventual arrest and indictment for possession of a banned substance. His lawyers claimed that the cocaine could not be used as evidence. According to the United States Supreme Court, unless police have an order from a judge called a *warrant*, under most circumstances they cannot enter a home without the consent of the occupant. In this case, argued Scott's attorneys, the police did not have a warrant, so the search was improper. Prosecutors countered that Janet's consent made the search legal, as she was occupying the home at the time of the incident.

In 2006, the Supreme Court agreed with Scott and held that the search was invalid. "We have, after all, lived our whole national history with an understanding of the ancient adage that a man's home is his castle," wrote Justice David H. Souter. "Disputed permission is thus no match for this central value" of the Constitution.

▲ According to the United States Supreme Court, in most circumstances law enforcement agencies cannot conduct a warrantless search of a home without the consent of the occupant.

N ote that the Supreme Court's decision was not unanimous.[1] Three justices thought that the search of Scott Randolph's bedroom was reasonable, with Chief Justice John G. Roberts, Jr., arguing that because Scott had agreed to "share" his "castle" with his wife, both had the ability to consent to a police search against the wishes of the other.[2] In effect, each member of the Court had the task of weighing Scott's personal freedoms against the ability of Georgia law enforcement to combat illegal drugs. This balance between the need for effective law enforcement and the rights of American citizens under the U.S. Constitution has been, and remains, a controversial issue. Many observers feel that courts go too far in protecting the rights of the accused, but others believe that police have been given a dangerous amount of leeway in using their powers. In this chapter we will examine the extent to which police behavior is controlled by the law, starting with a discussion of the constitutional principles on which such control is grounded.

The Fourth Amendment

In *Georgia v. Randolph*, the Supreme Court did not address the defendant's illegal activity. Rather, it ruled that the police officers had overstepped the boundaries of their authority in searching his bedroom. To understand these boundaries, law enforcement officers must understand the Fourth Amendment, which reads as follows:

> The right of the people to be secure in their persons, houses, papers, and effects, against unreasonable searches and seizures, shall not be violated, and no Warrants shall issue, but upon probable cause, supported by Oath or affirmation, and particularly describing the place to be searched, and the persons or things to be seized.

This amendment contains two critical legal concepts: a prohibition against *unreasonable* **searches and seizures** and the requirement of *probable cause* to issue a warrant (see ■ Figure 7.1).

REASONABLENESS

Law enforcement personnel use searches and seizures to look for and collect the evidence they need to convict individuals suspected of crimes. As you have just read, when police are conducting a search or seizure, they must be *reasonable*. Though courts have spent innumerable hours scrutinizing the word, no specific meaning for "reasonable" exists. A thesaurus can provide useful synonyms—logical, practical, sensible, intelligent, plausible—but because each case is different, those terms are relative.

In the *Randolph* case, the Supreme Court accepted the argument that the search had been so unreasonable as to violate the Fourth Amendment's prohibition against unreasonable searches and seizures. That does not mean that the police officers' actions would have been unreasonable under any circumstances. What if Scott Randolph had not yet returned home when Janet agreed to the search? In this situation, the officers' conduct would almost certainly have been considered reasonable. More than thirty years ago, the Court held that a co-occupant of a home can consent to a search when the other occupant is not present.[3]

PROBABLE CAUSE

The concept of reasonableness is linked to **probable cause.** The Supreme Court has ruled, for example, that any arrest or seizure is unreasonable unless it is supported by probable cause.[4] The burden of probable cause requires more than mere suspicion on a police officer's part; that officer must know of facts and circumstances that would reasonably lead to "the belief that an offense has been or is being committed."[5]

Sources of Probable Cause If no probable cause existed when a police officer took a certain action, it cannot be retroactively applied. If, for example, a police officer stops a person for jaywalking and then (without the help of a drug-

Searches and Seizures The legal term, as found in the Fourth Amendment of the U.S. Constitution, that generally refers to the searching for and the confiscating of evidence by law enforcement agents.

Probable Cause Reasonable grounds to believe the existence of facts warranting certain actions, such as the search or arrest of a person.

■ **Figure 7.1** **The Meaning of Unreasonable Searches and Seizures and Probable Cause**

Corbis

UNREASONABLE SEARCHES AND SEIZURES The Fourth Amendment provides that individuals have the right to be "secure in their persons" against "unreasonable searches and seizures" conducted by government agents. In practice, this means that law enforcement officers are required to obtain a search warrant prior to any search and seizure. Basically, the search warrant is the acknowledgment by a judge that probable cause exists for law enforcement officers to search for or take a person or property. In other words, the search and seizure must be "reasonable."

PROBABLE CAUSE Before a search can take place or an individual can be arrested, the requirement of probable cause must be met. Probable cause exists if there is a substantial likelihood that (1) a crime was committed and (2) the individual committed the crime. Note that probable cause involves a *likelihood*—not just a possibility—that the suspect committed the crime. Probable cause must exist before police can get an arrest warrant or a search warrant from a judge.

sniffing dog) finds several ounces of marijuana in that person's pocket, the arrest for marijuana possession would probably be disallowed. Remember, suspicion does not equal probable cause. If, however, an informant had tipped the officer off that the person was a drug dealer, probable cause might exist and the arrest could be valid. Informants are one of several sources that may provide probable cause. Others include:

1. *Personal observation.* Police officers may use their personal training, experience, and expertise to infer probable cause from situations that may not be

   L01 obviously criminal. If, for example, a police officer observes several people in a car slowly circling a certain building in a high-crime area, that officer may infer that the people are "casing" the building in preparation for a burglary. Probable cause could be established for detaining the suspects.

2. *Information.* Law enforcement officers receive information from victims, eyewitnesses, informants, and official sources such as police bulletins or broadcasts. Such information, as long as it is believed to be reliable, is a basis for probable cause.

3. *Evidence.* In certain circumstances, which will be examined later in this chapter, police have probable cause for a search or seizure based on evidence—such as a shotgun—in plain view.

4. *Association.* In some circumstances, if the police see a person with a known criminal background in a place where criminal activity is openly taking place, they have probable cause to stop that person. Generally, however, association is not adequate to establish probable cause.[6]

(To see how El Salvador has expanded the concept of probable cause to combat violent gangs, see the feature *International CJ—Telltale Tattoos.*)

The Probable Cause Framework In a sense, the concept of probable cause allows police officers to do their job effectively. Most arrests are made without a warrant because most arrests are the result of quick police reaction to the commission of a crime. Indeed, it would not be practical to expect a police officer to obtain a warrant before making an arrest on the street. Thus, probable cause provides a framework that limits the situations in which police officers can make arrests, but also gives officers the freedom to act within that framework. In 2003, the Supreme Court reaffirmed this freedom by ruling that Baltimore (Maryland) police officers acted properly when they arrested all three passengers of a car in which cocaine had been hidden in the back seat. "A reasonable officer," wrote then Chief Justice William H. Rehnquist, "could conclude that there was probable cause to believe" that the defendant, who had been sitting in the front seat, was in "possession" of the illicit drug despite his protestations to the contrary.[7]

Once an arrest is made, the arresting officer must prove to a judge that probable cause existed. In *County of Riverside v. McLaughlin* (1991),[8] the Supreme Court ruled that this judicial determination of probable cause must be made within forty-eight hours after the arrest, even if this two-day period includes a weekend or holiday.

THE EXCLUSIONARY RULE

Exclusionary Rule A rule under which any evidence that is obtained in violation of the accused's rights under the Fourth, Fifth, and Sixth Amendments, as well as any evidence derived from illegally obtained evidence, will not be admissible in criminal court.

Historically, the courts have looked to the Fourth Amendment for guidance in regulating the activity of law enforcement officers, as the language of the Constitution does not expressly do so. The courts' most potent legal tool in this endeavor is the **exclusionary rule,** which prohibits the use of illegally seized evidence. According to this rule, any evidence obtained by an unreasonable search or seizure is inadmissible (may not be used) against a defendant in a criminal trial.[9] Even

   L02 highly incriminating evidence, such as a knife stained with the victim's blood, usually cannot be introduced at a trial if illegally obtained. Furthermore,

The Mara Salvatrucha (MS-13), which translates to "Gang of Salvadoran Guys," operates in thirty-four states as well as the District of Columbia. Considered one of the most dangerous gangs in the United States by the Federal Bureau of Investigation, MS-13 has its roots in the civil wars of El Salvador in the 1980s. To escape the violence, thousands of immigrants fled to this country, particularly to Los Angeles. Their children found themselves easy prey for the established local gangs and formed MS-13 as a protective measure. The gang soon became involved in criminal activity of its own, and American authorities responded by deporting the members—and their violent gang culture—back to El Salvador.

A country with limited resources, El Salvador struggled for years to contain the wave of violent crime caused by these transplanted criminals. Finally, in 2003, the government passed Ley Anti Mara (LAM-1), a "law against gangs" that essentially made gang membership illegal. Under the LAM-1, Salvadoran police were given the power to arrest suspected gang members for a wide variety of behavior, including wandering into the wrong neighborhood or having *mara* tattoos. Human rights activists criticized LAM-1 for its arbitrary focus on behavior that is, by itself, harmless. For example, the police could arrest a group of teenagers loitering in an empty field if they had gang tattoos, while the same group of teenagers absent the tattoos would be deemed innocent of any wrongdoing.

AP Photo/Rodrigo Abd

▲ Gang tattoos cover the face of MS-13 member Fernando Garcia Torres, also known as "El Coco."

FOR CRITICAL ANALYSIS

In 2004, El Salvador repealed LAM-1 and replaced it with LAM-2. The new law prohibits police from making arrests based on tattoos alone but still allows the markings to be used as evidence of gang membership. Given the probable cause requirements of American criminal law, can you imagine any circumstances under which a gang tattoo, by itself, could provide cause for arrest? Before answering, consider one fact about MS-13 body art: a tattoo of a teardrop is a symbol that the gang member has committed murder.

any physical or verbal evidence police are able to acquire by using illegally obtained evidence is known as the **fruit of the poisoned tree** and is also inadmissible. For example, if the police use the existence of the bloodstained knife to get a confession out of a suspect, that confession will be excluded as well.

One of the implications of the exclusionary rule is that it forces police to gather evidence properly. If they follow appropriate procedures, they are more likely to be rewarded with a conviction. If they are careless or abuse the rights of the suspect, they are unlikely to get a conviction. Critics of the exclusionary rule, however, argue that its strict application may permit guilty people to go free because of police carelessness or innocent errors.

Establishing the Exclusionary Rule The exclusionary rule is applied to all evidence presented in federal courts as a result of the decision in *Weeks v. United States*.[10] For almost fifty years after this 1914 case, however, state courts continued to allow illegally obtained evidence, and federal courts could do so if the evidence had been obtained by state officers. This practice was known rather sarcastically as the *silver platter doctrine*, because such evidence handed the prosecution a conviction "on a silver platter." The only exception to the silver platter doctrine was when police actions were so extreme that they "shocked the conscience" of the court.

The "shocks the conscience" standard was established in *Rochin v. California* (1952).[11] In this case, police officers entered Rochin's home without a warrant and

Fruit of the Poisoned Tree Evidence that is acquired through the use of illegally obtained evidence and is therefore inadmissible in court.

FindLaw has a handy summary of the many laws regarding police procedure that can be traced to the Fourth Amendment. Find its Web site by clicking on *Web Links* under *Chapter Resources* at **www. cjinaction.com**.

saw him place what they thought were narcotics in his mouth. The police tried to forcibly expel the items from Rochin. When this failed, they took him to the hospital and had his stomach pumped. This action produced two tablets of morphine. Rochin was convicted of possession of illegal drugs and sentenced to sixty days in jail. The Supreme Court overturned his conviction on the ground that the police officers' actions violated Rochin's Fourth Amendment due process rights; Justice Felix Frankfurter compared the police's methods to the "rack and screw."

Extending the Exclusionary Rule The *Rochin* decision did not make the exclusionary rule applicable to all state cases. Instead, the Supreme Court ruled that it applied only in cases that involved serious police misconduct. The silver platter doctrine was finally eliminated nine years later by the Court's decision in *Mapp v. Ohio* (1961).[12] This case involved an illegal search and seizure conducted by Cleveland (Ohio) police officers. Whereas the Court had previously been hesitant to apply the exclusionary rule to a decision made in state courts, the *Mapp* case signaled a new willingness to apply the Fourth Amendment to both federal and state law enforcement officers.[13]

Exceptions to the Exclusionary Rule Critics of the exclusionary rule have long maintained that the costs to society of losing critical evidence are higher than the benefits of deterring police misconduct. A number of Supreme Court decisions have mirrored this view and provided exceptions to the exclusionary rule. The **"inevitable discovery" exception** was established in the wake of the disappearance of ten-year-old Pamela Powers of Des Moines, Iowa, on Christmas Eve, 1968. The primary suspect in the case, a religious fanatic named Robert Williams, was tricked by a detective into leading police to the site where he had buried Powers. Specifically, the detective convinced Williams that if he did not lead police to the body, he would soon forget where it was buried. This would deny his victim a "Christian burial." Initially, in *Brewer v. Williams* (1977),[14] the Court ruled that the evidence (Powers's body) had been obtained illegally because Williams's attorney had not been present during the interrogation that led to his admission. The state of Iowa appealed this decision. In *Nix v. Williams* (1984),[15] the Court reversed itself, ruling that the evidence was admissible because the body would have eventually ("inevitably") been found by lawful means.

The scope of the exclusionary rule was further diminished in the wake of the Supreme Court's ruling in *United States v. Leon* (1984).[16] The case involved evidence that had been seized by police on the authority of a search warrant that had been improperly issued by a magistrate. In allowing the evidence, the Court created a **"good faith" exception** to the exclusionary rule. Under this exception, evidence acquired by a police officer using a technically incorrect search warrant is admissible if the officer was unaware of the error. In this situation, the officer is said to have acted in "good faith." By the same token, if police officers use a search warrant that they know to be technically incorrect, the good faith exception does not apply and the evidence can be suppressed.

Self Check Fill in the Blanks

The Fourth Amendment contains two critically important restrictions on police authority: a prohibition against _____ searches and seizures and a requirement of _____ that a crime has been committed before a warrant for a search or seizure can be issued. Judges rely on the _____ rule to keep _____ that has been improperly obtained by the police out of criminal courts. Check your answers on page 237.

Stops and Frisks

Several years ago, an off-duty Miami–Dade County police officer named Aaron Campbell was driving on the Florida turnpike when he was pulled over by two Orange County deputies, allegedly for changing lanes without properly signaling. A fistfight ensued. At the resulting trial, Campbell claimed that he was stopped because he fit a drug courier profile in use by the deputies; he was an African American and had South Florida license plates. A circuit judge agreed, ruling that Campbell had been stopped illegally.[17]

The problem was not that the deputies had stopped Campbell. Law enforcement officers are expected to stop and question people if there is a suspicion of illegal behavior. The problem was that the Orange County deputies did not have a "reasonable" suspicion that Campbell was breaking the law. Instead, they had only a "mere" suspicion based on the drug courier profile—without any other specific facts. When reasonable suspicion exists, police officers are well within their rights to *stop and frisk* a suspect. In a stop and frisk, law enforcement officers (1) briefly detain a person they reasonably believe to be suspicious, and (2) if they believe the person to be armed, proceed to pat down, or "frisk," that person's outer clothing.[18]

THE ELUSIVE DEFINITION OF REASONABLE SUSPICION

Like so many elements of police work, the decision of whether to stop a suspect is based on the balancing of conflicting priorities. On the one hand, a police officer feels a sense of urgency to act when he or she believes that criminal activity is occurring or is about to occur. On the other hand, law enforcement agents do not want to harass innocent individuals, especially if doing so runs afoul of the U.S. Constitution. In stop-and-frisk law, this balancing act rests on the fulcrum of reasonable suspicion.

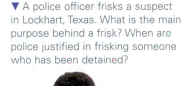
▼ A police officer frisks a suspect in Lockhart, Texas. What is the main purpose behind a frisk? When are police justified in frisking someone who has been detained?

Terry v. Ohio The precedent for the ever-elusive definition of a "reasonable" suspicion in stop-and-frisk situations was established in *Terry v. Ohio* (1968).[19] In that case, a detective named McFadden observed two men (one of whom was Terry) acting strangely in downtown Cleveland. The men would walk past a certain store, peer into the window, and then stop at a street corner and confer. While they were talking, another man joined the conversation and then left quickly. Several minutes later the three men met again at another corner a few blocks away. Detective McFadden believed the trio was planning to break into the store. He approached them, told them who he was, and asked for identification. After receiving a mumbled response, the detective frisked the three men and found handguns on two of them, who were tried and convicted of carrying concealed weapons.

L03

The Supreme Court upheld the conviction, ruling that Detective McFadden had reasonable cause to believe that the men were armed and dangerous and that swift action was necessary to protect himself and other citizens in the area.[20] The Court accepted McFadden's interpretation of the unfolding scene as based on objective facts and practical conclusions. It therefore concluded that his suspicion was reasonable. In the Florida case described above, the deputies' reasons for stopping Campbell—his race and place of car registration—were not seen as reasonable.

John Boykin/PhotoEdit

The "Totality of the Circumstances" Test For the most part, the judicial system has refrained from placing restrictions on police officers' ability to make stops. In the *Terry* case, the Supreme Court did say that an officer must have "specific and articulable facts" to support the decision to make a stop, but added that the facts may be "taken together with rational inferences."[21] The Court has consistently ruled that because of their practical experience, law enforcement agents are in a unique position to make such inferences and should be given a good deal of freedom in doing so.

In the years since the *Terry* case was decided, the Court has settled on a "totality of the circumstances" test to determine whether a stop is based on reasonable suspicion.[22] In 2002, for example, the Court ruled that a U.S. Border Patrol agent's stop of a minivan in Arizona was reasonable.[23] On being approached by the Border Patrol car, the driver had stiffened, slowed down his van, and avoided making eye contact with the agent. Furthermore, the children in the van waved at the officer in a mechanical manner, as if ordered to do so. The agent pulled over the van and found 128 pounds of marijuana. In his opinion, Chief Justice William Rehnquist pointed out that such conduct might have been unremarkable on a busy city highway, but on an unpaved road thirty miles from the Mexican border it was enough to reasonably arouse the agent's suspicion.[24] The justices also made clear that the need to prevent terrorist attacks is part of the "totality of the circumstances" and, therefore, law enforcement agents will have more leeway to make stops near U.S. borders. (For another example of how the "totality of the circumstances" test works, see the feature *You Be the Judge—The Wrong-Handed Beer Drinker*.)

Stories from the Street

Go to the Stories from the Street feature at **www.cjinaction.com** to hear Larry Gaines tell insightful stories related to this chapter and his experiences in the field.

You Be the Judge — The Wrong-Handed Beer Drinker

THE FACTS It is 2:00 A.M., and Officers Perry and Medrano are on routine motor vehicle patrol in a high-crime neighborhood of El Paso, Texas. As they pass Alacran's Lounge, a bar known for its rough clientele, Perry sees a man run behind the building at the sight of the police car. The officers decide to investigate and find three men milling about behind the bar, including Johnny, the one who had fled moments before. Johnny has an open beer can in his left hand, and his right hand is in his right pants pocket. This raises Perry's suspicion because "most people are right-handed." Perry also notes that although Johnny "was calm, he seemed a little bit cocky" and "we made eye contact, but then he looked away and acted as though I was not there and tried to walk by." Thus alerted, Perry searched Johnny and found a .22 caliber pistol in his right pants pocket. Johnny was convicted of unlawful possession of a firearm by a convicted felon and sentenced to thirty-three months in prison.

THE LAW Police officers may stop and frisk individuals even though there is no probable cause to arrest them if the officers have a reasonable suspicion that illegal activity is taking place. The police officers cannot rely on a mere hunch to make the stop and frisk decision but must be acting reasonably given the "totality of the circumstances."

YOUR DECISION Do the circumstances surrounding Officer Perry's stop and frisk support a reasonable suspicion that Johnny was illegally carrying a firearm or committing some other crime? Alternatively, was Perry merely acting on a hunch that he then tried to "dress up" for the court by talking about a beer in the wrong hand and Johnny's suspicious attitude? Explain your answer.

[To see how the U.S. Court of Appeals for the Fifth Circuit ruled in this case, go to Example 7.1. in Appendix B.]

Informants and Reasonable Suspicion A "bare-bones" anonymous tip is at the opposite end of the reasonable suspicion spectrum from a situation that meets the "totality of the circumstances" test. In 2000, the Supreme Court overturned a conviction based on such a "bare-bones" tip. An anonymous caller had told the Miami–Dade County (Florida) police that a young African American male standing at a bus stop was illegally carrying a handgun. Even though the information was correct, the police officer who made the stop and subsequent arrest had no reason other than the anonymous tip to suspect criminal activity.[25]

This restriction does not prevent tips from informants from being valuable resources for police officers. The Court has held that a tip from a *known* informant who had provided reliable information in the past is sufficient to justify a *Terry* stop, even if there is no other supporting evidence to make the stop.[26] Furthermore, an anonymous tip can pass the "totality of the circumstances" test if it is specific enough and the police verify it with their own observations.[27]

▲ Walter J. Oliver of Fall River, Massachusetts, is ticketed for driving 40 m.p.h. in a 35 m.p.h. zone. Some observers believe that traffic laws are often enforced more harshly against African Americans. Why would an American criminal court consider any police stop and frisk that is based solely on the race of the suspect to be unconstitutional?

Race and Reasonable Suspicion As we have already seen, a person's race or ethnicity alone cannot provide reasonable suspicion for stops and frisks. Some statistical measures, however, show that race plays a troubling role in this area of the law. A few years ago in Milton, Massachusetts, for example, minorities received 58 percent of the traffic tickets even though they made up only 16 percent of the drivers.[28] Another study found that San Diego police searched almost 50 percent of vehicles with Hispanic drivers after a traffic stop, compared to about 29 percent for whites.[29]

These and many other similar studies are seen as proof that police use **racial profiling** in deciding which motorists to stop and search. Racial profiling occurs when a police action is initiated by the race, nationality, or national origin of the suspect, rather than by evidence or information that the suspect has broken the law. Although no law enforcement agencies have official policies that support the practice, many observers feel that racial profiling is widespread. We will take a closer look at the subject in the *Criminal Justice in Action* feature at the end of this chapter.

A STOP

The terms *stop* and *frisk* are often used in concert, but they describe two separate acts. A **stop** takes place when a law enforcement officer has reasonable suspicion that a criminal activity is about to take place. Because an investigatory stop is not an arrest, there are limits to the extent police can detain someone who has been stopped. For example, in one situation an airline traveler and his luggage were detained for ninety minutes while the police waited for a drug-sniffing dog to arrive. The Supreme Court ruled that the initial stop of the passenger was constitutional, but that the ninety-minute wait was excessive.[30]

Racial Profiling The practice of targeting members of minority groups for police stops based solely on their race, ethnicity, or national origin.

Stop A brief detention of a person by law enforcement agents for questioning. The agents must have a reasonable suspicion of the person before making a stop.

David Kamerman/The Boston Globe/Redux

In 2004, the Court held that police officers could require suspects to identify themselves during a stop that is otherwise valid under the *Terry* ruling.[31] The case involved a Nevada rancher who was fined $250 for refusing to give his name to a police officer investigating a possible assault. The defendant argued that such requests force citizens to incriminate themselves against their will, which is prohibited, as we shall see later in the chapter, by the Fifth Amendment. Justice Anthony Kennedy wrote, however, that "asking questions is an essential part of police investigations" that would be made much more difficult if officers could not determine the identity of a suspect.[32] The ruling validated "stop-and-identify" laws in twenty states and numerous cities and towns.

A FRISK

The Supreme Court has stated that a **frisk** should be a protective measure. Police officers cannot conduct a frisk as a "fishing expedition" simply to try to find items besides weapons, such as illegal narcotics, on a suspect.[33] A frisk does not necessarily follow a stop and in fact may occur only when the officer is justified in thinking that the safety of police officers or other citizens may be endangered.

Again, the question of reasonable suspicion is at the heart of determining the legality of frisks. In the *Terry* case, the Court accepted that Detective McFadden reasonably believed that the three suspects posed a threat. The suspects' refusal to answer McFadden's questions, though within their rights because they had not been arrested, provided him with sufficient motive for the frisk.

Self Check Fill in the Blanks

A police officer can make a _____ , which is not the same as an arrest, if she or he has _____ suspicion that a criminal act is taking place or is about to take place. Then, the officer has the ability to _____ the suspect for weapons as a protective measure. Check your answers on page 237.

Arrests

As in the *Terry* case, a stop and frisk may lead to an **arrest.** An arrest is the taking into custody of a citizen for the purpose of detaining him or her on a criminal charge. It is important to understand the difference between a stop and an arrest. In the eyes of the law, a stop is a relatively brief intrusion on a citizen's rights, whereas an arrest—which involves a deprivation of liberty—is deserving of a full range of constitutional protections, which we shall discuss throughout the chapter (see *Mastering Concepts—The Difference between a Stop and an Arrest*). Consequently, while a stop can be made based on reasonable suspicion, a law enforcement officer needs probable cause, as defined earlier, to make an arrest.[34]

ELEMENTS OF AN ARREST

When is somebody under arrest? The easy—and incorrect—answer would be whenever the police officer says so. In fact, the state of being under arrest is dependent not only on the actions of the law enforcement officers but also on the perception of the suspect. Suppose Mr. Jones is stopped by plainclothes detectives, driven to the police station, and detained for three hours for questioning. During this time, the police never tell Mr. Jones he is under arrest, and in fact, he is free to leave at any time. But if Mr. Jones or any other reasonable person *believes* he is not free to leave, then, according to the Supreme Court, that person is in fact under arrest and should receive the necessary constitutional protections.[35]

Frisk A pat-down or minimal search by police to discover weapons; conducted for the express purpose of protecting the officer or other citizens, and not to find evidence of illegal substances for use in a trial.

Arrest To take into custody a person suspected of criminal activity. Police may use only reasonable levels of force in making an arrest.

Both stops and arrests are considered seizures because both police actions involve the restriction of an individual's freedom to "walk away." Both must be justified by a showing of reasonableness as well. You should be aware, however of the differences between a stop and an arrest.

The stop is an important part of police activity. Police officers therefore have the right to stop and frisk a person if they suspect that a crime is about to be committed. Police may stop those who are acting strangely, do not "fit" the time or place, are known to associate with criminals, or are loitering. They may also stop a person who reasonably fits a description of a person who is wanted in conjunction with a crime. **During a stop,** police can interrogate the person and make a limited search of his or her outer clothing. If anything occurs during the stop, such as the discovery of an illegal weapon, then officers may arrest the person. **If an arrest is made,** the suspect is now in police custody and is protected by the U.S. Constitution in a number of ways that will be discussed later in the chapter.

	STOP	ARREST
Justification	Reasonable suspicion	Probable cause
Warrant	None	Required in some, but not all, situations
Intent of Officer	To investigate suspicious activity	To make a formal charge against the suspect
Search	May frisk, or "pat down" for weapons	May conduct a full search for weapons or evidence
Scope of Search	Outer clothing only	Area within the suspect's immediate control or "reach"

Criminal justice professor Rolando V. del Carmen of Sam Houston State University has identified four elements that must be present for an arrest to take place:

1. The *intent* to arrest. In a stop, though it may entail slight inconvenience and a short detention period, there is no intent on the part of the law enforcement officer to take the person into custody. Therefore, there is no arrest. As intent is a subjective term, it is sometimes difficult to determine whether the police officer intended to arrest. In situations when the intent is unclear, courts often rely—as in our hypothetical case of Mr. Jones—on the perception of the arrestee.[36]

2. The *authority* to arrest. State laws give police officers the authority to place citizens under custodial arrest, or take them into custody. Like other state laws, the authorization to arrest varies among the fifty states. Some states, for example, allow off-duty police officers to make arrests, while others do not.

3. *Seizure or detention.* A necessary part of an arrest is the detention of the subject. Detention is considered to have occurred as soon as the arrested individual submits to the control of the officer, whether peacefully or under the threat or use of force.

4. The *understanding* of the person that she or he has been arrested. Through either words—such as "you are now under arrest"—or actions, the person taken into custody must understand that an arrest has taken place. If a subject has been forcibly subdued by the police, handcuffed, and placed in a patrol car, that subject is believed to understand that an arrest has been made. This understanding may be lacking if the person is intoxicated, insane, or unconscious.[37]

ARRESTS WITH A WARRANT

When law enforcement officers have established probable cause to arrest an individual who is not in police custody, they obtain an **arrest warrant** for that person. An arrest warrant contains information such as the name of the person suspected and the crime he or she is suspected of having committed. (See ■ Figure 7.2 for

Arrest Warrant A written order, based on probable cause and issued by a judge or magistrate, commanding that the person named on the warrant be arrested by the police.

United States District Court

_____ DISTRICT OF _____

UNITED STATES OF AMERICA
V.

WARRANT FOR ARREST

CASE NUMBER:

To: The United States Marshal
and any Authorized United States Officer

YOU ARE HEREBY COMMANDED to arrest _____
_____
 name

and bring him or her forthwith to the nearest magistrate to answer a(n)

☐ Indictment ☐ Information ☐ Complaint ☐ Order of Court ☐ Violation Notice ☐ Probation Violation Petition

charging him or her with (brief description of offense)

in violation of Title _____ United States Code, Section(s) _____

Name of Issuing Officer   Title of Issuing Officer

Signature of Issuing Officer   Date and Location

Bail fixed at $ _____ by _____
     Name of Judicial Officer

RETURN

This warrant was received and executed with the arrest of the above-named defendant at _____

DATE RECEIVED   NAME AND TITLE OF ARRESTING OFFICER   SIGNATURE OF ARRESTING OFFICER

DATE OF ARREST

an example of an arrest warrant.) Judges or magistrates issue arrest warrants after first determining that the law enforcement officers have indeed established probable cause.

There is a perception that an arrest warrant gives law enforcement officers the authority to enter a dwelling without first announcing themselves. This is not accurate. In _Wilson v. Arkansas_ (1995),[38] the Supreme Court reiterated the common law requirement that police officers must knock and announce their identity and purpose before entering a dwelling. Under certain conditions, known as **exigent circumstances,** law enforcement officers need not announce themselves. These circumstances include situations in which the officers have a reasonable belief of any of the following:

- The suspect is armed and poses a strong threat of violence to the officers or others inside the dwelling.
- Persons inside the dwelling are in the process of destroying evidence or escaping because of the presence of the police.
- A felony is being committed at the time the officers enter.[39]

The Supreme Court severely weakened the practical impact of the "knock and announce" rule with its recent decision in _Hudson v. Michigan_ (2006).[40] In that case, Detroit police did not knock before entering the defendant's home with a warrant. Instead, they announced themselves and then waited only three to five seconds before making their entrance, not the fifteen to twenty seconds suggested by a prior Court ruling.[41] Hudson argued that the drugs found during the subsequent search were inadmissible because the law enforcement agents did not follow proper procedure. By a 5–4 margin, the Court disagreed. In his majority opinion, Justice Antonin Scalia stated that an improper "knock and announce" is not unreasonable enough to provide defendants with a "get-out-of-jail-free card" by disqualifying evidence uncovered on the basis of a valid search warrant.[42] Thus, the exclusionary rule, discussed earlier in this chapter, would no longer apply under such circumstances. Legal experts still advise, however, that police observe a reasonable waiting period after knocking and announcing to be certain that any evidence found during the subsequent search will stand up in court.[43]

ARRESTS WITHOUT A WARRANT

Arrest warrants are not always required, and in fact, most arrests are made on the scene without a warrant.[44] A law enforcement officer may make a **warrantless arrest** if:

1. The offense is committed in the presence of the officer; or
2. The officer has knowledge that a crime has been committed and probable cause to believe the crime was committed by a particular suspect.[45]

The type of crime also comes to bear in questions of arrests without a warrant. As a general rule, officers can make a warrantless arrest for a crime they did not see if they have probable cause to believe that a felony has been committed. For misdemeanors, the crime must have been committed in the presence of the officer for a warrantless arrest to be valid. According to a 2001 Supreme Court ruling involving a Texas mother who was handcuffed, taken away from her two young children, and placed in jail for failing to wear her seat belt, even an arrest for a misdemeanor that involves "gratuitous humiliations" imposed by a police officer "exercising extremely poor judgment" is valid as long as the officer can satisfy probable cause requirements.[46]

Exigent Circumstances
Situations that require extralegal or exceptional actions by the police. In these circumstances, police officers are justified in not following procedural rules, such as those pertaining to search and arrest warrants.

Warrantless Arrest An arrest made without first seeking a warrant for the action; permitted under certain circumstances, such as when the arresting officer has witnessed the crime or has probable cause that the suspect has committed a felony.

In certain situations, warrantless arrests are unlawful even though a police officer can establish probable cause. In *Payton v. New York* (1980),[47] for example, the Supreme Court held that when exigent circumstances do not exist and the suspect does not give consent to enter a dwelling, law enforcement officers cannot force themselves in for the purpose of making a warrantless arrest. The *Payton* ruling was expanded to cover the homes of third parties when, in *Steagald v. United States* (1981),[48] the Court ruled that if the police wish to arrest a criminal suspect in another person's home, they cannot enter that home to arrest the suspect without first obtaining a search warrant, a process we will discuss in the following section.

Lawful Searches and Seizures

How far can law enforcement agents go in searching and seizing private property? Consider the steps taken by Jenny Stracner, an investigator with the Laguna Beach (California) Police Department. After receiving information that a suspect, Greenwood, was engaged in drug trafficking, Stracner enlisted the aid of the local trash collector in procuring evidence. Instead of taking Greenwood's trash bags to be incinerated, the collector agreed to give them to Stracner. The officer found enough drug paraphernalia in the garbage to obtain a warrant to search Greenwood's home. Subsequently, he was arrested and convicted on narcotics charges.[49]

Search The process by which police examine a person or property to find evidence that will be used to prove guilt in a criminal trial.

Remember, the Fourth Amendment is quite specific in forbidding unreasonable searches and seizures. Were Stracner's search of Greenwood's garbage and her seizure of its contents "reasonable"? The Supreme Court thought so, holding that Greenwood's garbage was not protected by the Fourth Amendment.[50]

THE ROLE OF PRIVACY IN SEARCHES

A crucial concept in understanding search and seizure law is *privacy*. By definition, a **search** is a governmental intrusion on a citizen's reasonable expectation of privacy. The recognized standard for a "reasonable expectation of privacy" was established in *Katz v. United States* (1967).[51] The case dealt with the question of whether the defendant was justified in his expectation of privacy in the calls he made from a public phone booth. The Supreme Court held that "the Fourth Amendment protects people, not places," and Katz prevailed.

▼ Michigan state and federal law enforcement officers take part in a predawn raid of a Detroit residence. Before taking such action, the officers must receive permission from a judge or magistrate in the form of a search warrant. Ideally, the judicial official will issue such a warrant only if the law enforcement agency involved can provide probable cause that an illegal activity is taking place in the dwelling. How does the need to provide probable cause in such instances limit police power?

AP Photo, *Detroit News*/Charles V. Tines

In his concurring opinion, Justice John Harlan, Jr., set a two-pronged test for a person's expectation of privacy:

1. The individual must prove that she or he expected privacy, and
2. Society must recognize that expectation as reasonable.[52]

Accordingly, the Court agreed with Katz's claim that he had a reasonable right to privacy in a public phone booth. (Remember, however, that the *Terry* case allows for conditions under which a person's privacy rights are superseded by a reasonable suspicion on the part of a law enforcement officer that a threat to public safety is present.)

In contrast, in *California v. Greenwood* (1988),[53] described on the previous page, the Court did not believe that the suspect had a reasonable expectation of privacy when it came to his garbage bags. The Court noted that when we place our trash on a curb, we expose it to any number of intrusions by "animals, children, scavengers, snoops, and other members of the public."[54] In other words, if Greenwood had truly intended for the contents of his garbage bags to remain private, he would not have left them on the side of the road. To give another example, the Court also upheld the search in a case in which a drug-sniffing dog was used to detect marijuana in the trunk of a car after the driver was stopped for speeding. The Court ruled that no one has a legitimate privacy interest in possessing illegal drugs or other contraband such as explosives in the trunk of his or her car.[55]

SEARCH AND SEIZURE WARRANTS

To protect against charges that they have unreasonably infringed on privacy rights during a search, law enforcement officers can obtain a **search warrant**. (See ■ Figure 7.3 for an example of a search warrant.) Similar to an arrest warrant, a search warrant is a court order that authorizes police to search a certain area. Before a judge or magistrate will issue a search warrant, law enforcement officers must provide:

- Information showing probable cause that a crime has been or will be committed.
- Specific information on the premises to be searched, the suspects to be found and the illegal activities taking place at those premises, and the items to be seized.

The purpose of a search warrant is to establish, before the search takes place, that a *probable cause to search* justifies infringing on the suspect's reasonable expectation of privacy.

Particularity of Search Warrants The members of the First Congress specifically did not want law enforcement officers to have the freedom to make "general, exploratory" searches through a person's belongings.[56] Consequently, the Fourth Amendment requires that a warrant describe with "particularity" the place to be searched and the things—either people or objects—to be seized.

This "particularity" requirement places a heavy burden on law enforcement officers. Before going to a judge to ask for a search warrant, they must prepare an **affidavit** in which they provide specific, written information on the property that they wish to search and seize. They must know the specific address of any place they wish to search; general addresses of apartment buildings or office complexes are not sufficient. Furthermore, courts generally frown on vague descriptions of goods to be seized. "Stolen goods" would most likely be considered unacceptably imprecise; "1 MacBook Pro laptop computer" would be preferred.

A **seizure** is the act of taking possession of a person or property by the government because of a (suspected) violation of the law. In general, four categories of items can be seized by use of a search warrant:

1. Items that resulted from the crime, such as stolen goods.

Search Warrant A written order, based on probable cause and issued by a judge or magistrate, commanding that police officers or criminal investigators search a specific person, place, or property to obtain evidence.

Affidavit A written statement of facts, confirmed by the oath or affirmation of the party making it and made before a person having the authority to administer the oath or affirmation.

Seizure The forcible taking of a person or property in response to a violation of the law.

L05

2. Items that are inherently illegal for anybody to possess (with certain exceptions), such as narcotics and counterfeit currency.
3. Items that can be called "evidence" of the crime, such as a bloodstained sneaker or a ski mask.
4. Items used in committing the crime, such as an ice pick or a printing press used to make counterfeit bills.[57]

Reasonableness during a Search and Seizure No matter how "particular" a warrant is, it cannot provide for all the conditions that are bound to come up during its service. Consequently, the law gives law enforcement officers the ability to act "reasonably" during a search and seizure in the event of unforeseeable circumstances. For example, if a police officer is searching an apartment for a stolen MacBook Pro laptop computer and notices a vial of crack cocaine sitting on the suspect's bed, that contraband is considered to be in "plain view" and can be seized. (See the feature *You Be the Judge—A Valid Search?*)

Note that if law enforcement officers have a search warrant that authorizes them to search for a stolen laptop computer, they would *not* be justified in opening small drawers. Because a computer could not fit in a small drawer, an officer would not have a basis for reasonably searching one. Officers are restricted in terms of where they can look by the items they are searching for.

Anticipatory Search Warrants In 2006, the United States Supreme Court further clarified this area of criminal law by approving the use of *anticipatory search warrants*.[58] The case involved Jeffrey Grubbs who purchased a child-pornography videotape from a Web site that had been set up as an undercover operation by the U.S. Postal Inspection Service. As part of a plan to arrest Grubbs as soon as the video arrived in the mail, a government agent submitted an affidavit for a warrant stating that the search would not take place "unless and until the parcel has been received [and] physically taken

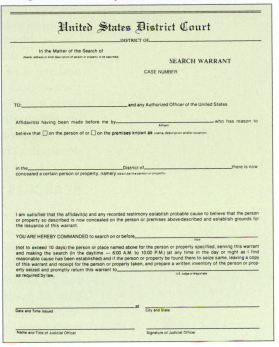

■ Figure 7.3 **Example of a Search Warrant**

You Be the Judge A Valid Search?

THE FACTS Baltimore police officers obtained a valid warrant to search Larry's apartment for marijuana. Larry's address, as described on the warrant, was "the premises known as 2036 Park Avenue third floor apartment." When the officers conducted the search, they reasonably believed that there was only one apartment on the third floor of the building. In fact, the third floor was divided into two apartments, the second one rented by Harold. Before the officers became aware that they were actually searching Harold's apartment, for which they had no warrant, they discovered illegal drugs there. Harold was eventually charged with possession of heroin with intent to distribute.

THE LAW To prevent general searches, the Fourth Amendment requires warrants to describe with particularity "the place to be searched." Police officers are required to make a "reasonable effort" to make sure that the place they are searching is the place specified in the warrant.

YOUR DECISION Harold claims that the evidence against him is invalid, because "the officers, not having a warrant for [his] apartment, had no right to go into that apartment." Do you agree?

[To see how the United States Supreme Court ruled in this case, go to Example 7.2 in Appendix B.]

into the residence."[59] Grubbs's wife received the parcel and took it into their home, and Grubbs was arrested and charged with "receiving a visual depiction of a minor engaged in sexually explicit conduct."

Grubbs argued that the search warrant was invalid because no probable cause existed at the time it was issued. In other words, the federal agents had to wait and see if he would take the video into his home. The Supreme Court ruled that the warrant was valid because the government did establish a "fair probability" that Grubbs would accept the package, given that he had placed the order. Thus, an **anticipatory search warrant** is constitutional if it is "based upon an affidavit showing probable cause that at some future time (but not presently) certain evidence of a crime will be located at a specific place."[60]

SEARCHES AND SEIZURES WITHOUT A WARRANT

Although the Supreme Court has established the principle that searches conducted without warrants are *per se* (by definition) unreasonable, it has set "specifically established" exceptions to the rule.[61] In fact, most searches, like most arrests, take place in the absence of a judicial order. Warrantless searches and seizures can be lawful when police are in "hot pursuit" of a subject or when they search bags of trash left at the curb for regular collection. Because of the magnitude of smuggling activities in "border areas" such as airports, seaports, and international boundaries, a warrant normally is not needed to search property in those places. Furthermore, in 2006 the Court held unanimously that police officers do not need a warrant to enter a private home in an emergency, such as when they reasonably fear for the safety of the inhabitants.[62] The two most important circumstances in which a warrant is not needed, though, are (1) searches incidental to an arrest and (2) consent searches.

Searches Incidental to an Arrest The most frequent exception to the warrant requirement involves **searches incidental to arrests,** so called because nearly every time police officers make an arrest, they also search the suspect. As long as the original arrest was based on probable cause, these searches are valid for two reasons, established by the Supreme Court in *United States v. Robinson* (1973):

1. The need for a police officer to find and confiscate any weapons a suspect may be carrying.
2. The need to protect any evidence on the suspect's person from being destroyed.[63]

Law enforcement officers are, however, limited in the searches they may make during an arrest. These limits were established by the Supreme Court in *Chimel v. California* (1969).[64] In that case, police arrived at Chimel's home with an arrest warrant but not a search warrant. Even though Chimel refused their request to "look around," the officers searched the entire three-bedroom house for nearly an hour, finding stolen coins in the process. Chimel was convicted of burglary and appealed, arguing that the evidence of the coins should have been suppressed.

The Supreme Court held that the search was unreasonable. In doing so, the Court established guidelines as to the acceptable extent of searches incidental to an arrest. Primarily, the Court ruled that police may search any area within the suspect's "immediate control" to confiscate any weapons or evidence that the suspect could destroy. The Court found, however, that there was no justification

> for routinely searching rooms other than that in which the arrest occurs—or, for that matter, for searching through all desk drawers or other closed or concealed areas in that room itself. Such searches, in the absence of well-recognized exceptions, may be made only under the authority of a search warrant.[65]

The exact interpretation of the "area within immediate control" has been left to individual courts, but in general it has been taken to mean the area within the

Anticipatory Search Warrant A search warrant based on the premise that specific evidence of a crime will be located at a named place in the future, though the evidence is not necessarily at that place when the warrant is issued.

Searches Incidental to Arrests Searches for weapons and evidence of persons who have just been arrested. The fruit of such searches is admissible if any items found are within the immediate vicinity or control of the suspect.

L06

reach of the arrested person. Thus, the Court is said to have established the "arm's reach doctrine" in its *Chimel* decision.

Searches with Consent As we saw with the *Randolph* case in this chapter's introduction, **consent searches**, the second most common type of warrantless searches, take place when individuals give law enforcement officers permission to search their persons, homes, or belongings. (For an overview of the circumstances under which warrantless searches are allowed, see *Mastering Concepts—Exceptions to the Requirement That Officers Have a Search Warrant* on the next page.) The consent must, however, be *voluntary*. If a person has been physically threatened or otherwise coerced into giving consent, the search is invalid.[66]

▲ Ohio State Highway Patrol troopers talk with motorists at a sobriety checkpoint designed to deter drivers who drink or use drugs. The United States Supreme Court has ruled that such stops do not constitute illegal searches and seizures bcause the public interest in reducing drunk driving is sufficient to justify brief intrusions. What argument could be made that these sobriety checkpoints—which allow police to stop *all* drivers on a certain road—constitute unreasonable searches and seizures?

The Citizen's Decision The standard for consent searches was set in *Schneckcloth v. Bustamonte* (1973),[67] in which, after being asked, the defendant told police officers to "go ahead" and search his car. A packet of stolen checks found in the trunk was ruled valid evidence because the driver consented to the search. Numerous court decisions have also supported the "knock and talk" strategy, in which the law enforcement agent simply walks up to the door of a residence, knocks, and asks to come in and talk to the resident.[68] The officer does not need reasonable suspicion or probable cause that a crime has taken place in this situation because the decision to cooperate rests with the civilian.

The Intimidation Factor Critics of consent searches hold that such searches are rarely voluntary because most citizens are intimidated by police and will react to a request for permission to make a search as if it were an order.[69] Furthermore, most citizens are unaware that they have the option *not* to comply with a request for a search. Thus, if a police officer asks to search a citizen's car after issuing a speeding ticket, the citizen is well within her or his rights to refuse. According to the United States Supreme Court in *Florida v. Bostick* (1991),[70] as long as police officers do not improperly coerce a suspect to cooperate, they are not *required* to inform the person that he or she has a choice in the matter.

Consequently, in *Ohio v. Robinette* (1996),[71] the Court held that police officers do *not* need to notify citizens that they are "free to go" after an initial stop when no arrest is involved. Similarly, in 2002, the Court ruled that the inside of a bus is not an inherently coercive environment and thus officers do not need to advise passengers that they can refuse to be searched.[72] The significance of this line of cases is underscored by data presented in connection with the *Robinette* ruling: in the two years leading up to that case, four hundred Ohio drivers were convicted of narcotics offenses that resulted directly from search requests that could have been denied but were not.[73]

SEARCHES OF AUTOMOBILES

Though the *Chimel* case limited the scope of searches and seizures incident to an arrest in most circumstances, the Supreme Court has not been as restrictive concerning searches in arrests involving automobile passengers. In *New York v. Belton* (1981),[74] the Supreme Court held that when police officers lawfully arrest a person driving a car, they can legally make a warrantless search of the car's entire front and back compartments. This expansive interpretation of "the area within

Consent Searches Searches by police that are made after the subject of the search has agreed to the action. In these situations, consent, if given of free will, validates a warrantless search.

In many circumstances, it would be impractical for police officers to leave a crime scene, go to a judge, and obtain a search warrant before conducting a search. Therefore, under a number of circumstances, a search warrant is not required.

INCIDENT TO LAWFUL ARREST

Police officers may search the area within immediate control of a person after they have arrested him or her.

CONSENT

Police officers may search a person without a warrant if that person voluntarily agrees to be searched and has the legal authority to authorize the search.

STOP AND FRISK

Police officers may frisk, or "pat down," a person if they suspect that the person may be involved in criminal activity or pose a danger to those in the immediate area.

HOT PURSUIT

If police officers are in "hot pursuit" or chasing a person they have probable cause to believe committed a crime, and that person enters a building, the officers may search the building without a warrant.

AUTOMOBILE EXCEPTION

If police officers have probable cause to believe that an automobile contains evidence of a crime, they may, in most instances, search the vehicle without a warrant.

PLAIN VIEW

If police officers are legally engaged in police work and happen to see evidence of a crime in "plain view," they may seize it without a search warrant.

ABANDONED PROPERTY

Any property, such as a hotel room that has been vacated or contraband that has been discarded, may be searched and seized by police officers without a warrant.

BORDER SEARCHES

Law enforcement officers on border patrol do not need a warrant to search vehicles crossing the border.

INEVITABLE DISCOVERY

Evidence that has been illegally obtained (without the necessary warrant) may be admitted as evidence if the prosecution can prove that it would have "inevitably" been found by lawful means.

---

immediate control" is indicative of the Supreme Court's lenient view of automobile searches.

The "Movable Vehicle" Exception In *Carroll v. United States* (1925),[75] the Supreme Court ruled that the law would distinguish among automobiles, homes, and persons in questions involving police searches. In the years since *Carroll*, the Court has established that the Fourth Amendment does not require police to obtain a warrant to search automobiles or other movable vehicles when they have probable cause to believe that a vehicle contains contraband or evidence of criminal activity.[76] The reasoning behind such leniency is straightforward: requiring a warrant to search an automobile places too heavy a burden on police officers. By the time the officers could communicate with a judge and obtain the warrant, the suspects could drive away and destroy any evidence. Consequently, the Court has consistently held that someone in a vehicle does not have the same reasonable expectation of privacy as someone at home or even in a phone booth.

A number of rulings have increased police powers in these situations. In *Whren v. United States* (1996),[77] the Supreme Court ruled that the "true" motivation of police officers in making traffic stops was irrelevant as long as they had probable cause to believe that a traffic law had been broken. In other words, police may stop a car they believe to be transporting drugs in order to issue a speeding citation. The fact that the officers are using the speeding ticket as a pretext to search for drugs (and would not have stopped the driver otherwise) does not matter, as long as the driver actually was speeding. One year later, in *Maryland v. Wilson* (1997),[78] the Court further expanded police power by ruling that an officer may order passengers as well as the driver out of a car during a traffic stop; the Court reasoned that the danger to an officer is increased when there is a passenger in the automobile. Then, in 2005, the Court held that, following a valid traffic stop, police officers could use a drug-sniffing dog to search the car even if they had no reason to suspect that the driver was transporting contraband.[79]

Containers within a Vehicle In keeping with the principles of the "movable vehicle" exception, the Supreme Court has also provided law enforcement agents with a great deal of leeway for warrantless searches of containers within a vehicle. In one case, Washington, D.C., detectives received a reliable tip that a man known as the "Bandit" was selling drugs from his car. Without first getting a warrant, the detectives searched the Bandit's trunk and found heroin in a closed paper bag. The Court refused to suppress the evidence, ruling that in such situations police officers can search every part of the vehicle that might contain the items they are seeking, as long as they have probable cause to believe that the items are somewhere in the car.[80] Nevertheless, there are limits to what can be searched. As Justice John Paul Stevens stated in his opinion, "probable cause to believe that undocumented aliens are being transported in a van will not justify a warrantless search of a suitcase" in that van.[81] By the same token, if the tipster had told the police specifically that "Bandit has a bag of heroin in his trunk," they would not have been justified in searching the front area of the car without a warrant or probable cause.[82]

THE PLAIN VIEW DOCTRINE

The Constitution, as interpreted by our courts, provides very little protection to contraband *in plain view*. For example, suppose a traffic officer pulls over a person for speeding, looks in the driver's side window, and clearly sees what appears to be a bag of heroin resting on the passenger seat. In this instance, under the **plain view doctrine,** the officer would be justified in seizing the drugs without a warrant.

▲ A police officer searches a car in front of the Capitol building in Washington, D.C. According to the United States Supreme Court, under some circumstances the Fourth Amendment to the U.S. Constitution does not require police officers to obtain a warrant before searching an automobile. What is the reasoning behind this "movable vehicle" exception?

The plain view doctrine was first enunciated by the Supreme Court in *Coolidge v. New Hampshire* (1971).[83] The Court ruled that law enforcement officers may make a warrantless seizure of an item if four criteria are met:

1. The item is positioned so as to be detected easily by an officer's sight or some other sense.
2. The officer is legally in a position to notice the item in question.
3. The discovery of the item is inadvertent; that is, the officer had not intended to find the item.
4. The officer immediately recognizes the illegal nature of the item. No interrogation or further investigation is allowed under the plain view doctrine.

(For a discussion of how the plain view doctrine is being tested by new technology, see *CJ and Technology—The Thermal Imager* on the following page.)

ELECTRONIC SURVEILLANCE AND THE FIGHT AGAINST TERRORISM

During the course of a criminal investigation, law enforcement officers may decide to use **electronic surveillance,** or electronic devices such as wiretaps or hidden microphones ("bugs"), to monitor and record conversations, observe movements, and trace or record telephone calls.

Basic Rules: Consent and Probable Cause Given the invasiveness of electronic surveillance, the Supreme Court has generally held that the practice is prohibited by the Fourth Amendment. In *Burger v. New York* (1967),[84] however, the Court ruled that it was permissible under certain circumstances. That same year, *Katz v. United States* (discussed earlier) established that recorded conversations are inadmissible as evidence unless certain procedures are followed.

In general, law enforcement officers can use electronic surveillance only if:

1. Consent is given by one of the parties to be monitored; or
2. There is a warrant authorizing the use of the devices.[85]

Plain View Doctrine The legal principle that objects in plain view of a law enforcement agent who has the right to be in a position to have that view may be seized without a warrant and introduced as evidence.

Electronic Surveillance The use of electronic equipment by law enforcement agents to record private conversations or observe conduct that is meant to be private.

CJ and Technology

The Thermal Imager

WHAT IS THE THERMAL IMAGER?

Every object with a temperature above absolute zero emits infrared radiation, which cannot be seen by the naked eye. A thermal imager, however, can detect this radiation and project a reading of it onto a screen.

WHAT DOES THE THERMAL IMAGER DO?

Thermal imagers have most commonly been used in searches for missing persons—humans' high body temperatures are readily detected. Only recently have the devices been put to use by law enforcement agencies Thermal imagers can be particularly effective in detecting marijuana grown indoors because of the heat thrown off by the "grow lights" the plants need to survive.

THINKING ABOUT THE THERMAL IMAGER

With regard to searches involving a thermal imager, the question for courts has been whether, in the absence of a warrant, an infrared search of a dwelling violates Fourth Amendment protections of privacy. In one case in which police used a helicopter fitted with a thermal imager to detect marijuana growing in a house, a Hawaii court ruled that that no reasonable expectation of privacy was involved. The court held that the thermal imaging device measured only heat emanating from the defendants' home and that this "abandoned heat" was not subject to privacy protections because they had not tried to prevent its escape. Subsequently, however, the United States Supreme Court ruled that an item is not in plain view if law enforcement agents need the aid of technology to "see" it. Thus, information from a thermal imager is not by itself justification for a warrantless search. In his dissent from the majority's opinion in this case, Justice John Paul Stevens wrote, "Heat waves, like aromas that are generated in a kitchen, or in a laboratory or opium den, enter the public domain if and when they leave a building." What is your opinion of the use of technology such as thermal imagers to search buildings without a warrant?

For more information on thermal imaging and other CJ technologies, click on *Crime and Technology* under *Book Resources* at **www.cjinaction.com**.

Note that the consent of only one of the parties being monitored is needed to waive the reasonable expectation of privacy. The Court has ruled that people whose conversations have been recorded by supposed friends who turn out to be police informers have not been subjected to an unreasonable search.[86] Therefore, at least theoretically, a person always assumes the risk that whatever he or she says to someone else may be monitored by the police. A number of states do, however, have statutes that forbid private citizens from tape-recording another person's conversation without her or his knowledge. In Maryland, for example, such an act is a felony.

If consent exists, then law enforcement officers are not required to obtain a warrant before engaging in electronic surveillance. In most other instances, however, a warrant is required. For the warrant to be valid, it must:

1. Detail with "particularity" the conversations that are to be overheard.
2. Name the suspects and the places that will be under surveillance.
3. Show with probable cause that a specific crime has been or will be committed.[87]

Once the specific information has been gathered, the law enforcement officers must end the electronic surveillance immediately.[88] In any case, the surveillance cannot last more than thirty days without a judicial extension.

Electronic Surveillance and National Security The federal government has long struggled with how to apply the basic rules for electronic surveillance to the area of national security. In the late 1970s, responding to concerns that the Federal Bureau of Investigation (FBI) had too much power to "spy" on domestic religious and political groups, Congress passed legislation restricting this power. Under the Foreign Intelligence Surveillance Act (FISA), government agents could wiretap or otherwise bug a target only if there was probable cause that the target was a foreign infiltrator.[89]

New Rules The Patriot Act of 2001 amended the FISA. This new legislation, as noted earlier in this textbook, was a legislative response to the terrorist attacks of September 11, 2001. It effectively did away with the probable cause requirements of the FISA, allowing agents to procure a warrant for electronic surveillance as long as the surveillance serves a "significant purpose" in gathering foreign intelligence.[90] Under the old rules, for example, an FBI agent could not randomly surf the Internet looking for signs of wrongdoing because there was no "particularity" to support a showing of probable cause that terrorist activity was taking place. Under the new guidelines, the agent can search Web sites and chat rooms randomly because this activity might serve the significant purpose of providing leads to future terrorist attacks.[91]

The "Sneak and Peak" Provision Opponents of the Patriot Act have focused on Section 213 of the legislation. This provision allows law enforcement agents to search a person's home and seize property without immediately notifying the target of the search if the agents have "reasonable" cause to believe that notification would (1) endanger public safety, (2) lead to destruction of evidence, or (3) jeopardize an ongoing investigation.[92] By removing the traditional "probable cause" requirement for search warrants, Section 213 provides police officers with greater leeway to conduct secret, or "sneak and peak," searches of a person's home or property without that person being aware of the search.

Another controversial aspect of Section 213 is that it applies to *all* federal criminal investigations, not just those involving terrorism.[93] Between April 2003 and January 2005, the U.S. Department of Justice used Section 213 delayed-notification warrants 108 times to investigate not only terrorist activities but also drug trafficking, organized crime, and child-pornography operations.[94] In one instance, Drug Enforcement Administration (DEA) agents were following a van they knew to be transporting large amounts of marijuana and ecstasy. When the drivers stopped at a roadside restaurant, the DEA agents "stole" the van using a duplicate key. They spread broken glass in the parking space to create the impression that the drug runners had been the victims of an auto theft.[95]

The government defends delayed-notification warrants as a valuable crime-fighting tool that keeps suspects from fleeing or destroying evidence.[96] In the example just given, Section 213 allowed the DEA agents to seize a large cache of drugs without tipping off their targets to the larger operation that eventually led to 130 arrests.[97] Critics, however, contend that the legislation has "severely undermined the protections guaranteed by the Fourth Amendment" for a wide range of criminal suspects.[98]

National Security Letters The Patriot Act also expanded the ability of the FBI to issue *national security letters*. These documents allow the FBI to request bank account numbers, credit-card records, and information about Internet use without first securing a search warrant. In the twelve months following September 11, 2001, the FBI sent national security letters to almost 550 libraries seeking information on their patrons. Other recipients have included Internet service providers, Las Vegas hotels, and major airlines.[99]

In 2005, press reports of a large, domestic spying program run by the National Security Agency (NSA) refocused attention on the Patriot Act and its relationship to the Fourth Amendment. We will take a detailed look at this controversy, along with other issues involving searches, seizures, and homeland security, in Chapter 16.

▼ Reports that the National Security Agency (NSA) had been secretly collecting the phone call records of millions of American citizens caused a great deal of controversy and led to numerous protests.

Charles Dharapak/AP Photo

A search is a governmental intrusion on the _____ of an individual. To protect these rights, law enforcement agents must procure a _____ before examining a suspect's home or personal possessions. During a properly executed search, officers may _____ any items that may be used as evidence or that are inherently illegal to possess. Law enforcement agents do not need a judge's prior approval to conduct a search incidental to an _____ or when the subject of the search gives his or her _____. Check your answers on page 237.

The Interrogation Process and *Miranda*

After the Pledge of Allegiance, there is perhaps no recitation that comes more readily to the American mind than the *Miranda* warning:

> You have the right to remain silent. If you give up that right, anything you say can and will be used against you in a court of law. You have the right to speak with an attorney and to have the attorney present during questioning. If you so desire and cannot afford one, an attorney will be appointed for you without charge before questioning.

The *Miranda* warning is not a mere prop. It strongly affects one of the most important aspects of any criminal investigation—the **interrogation,** or questioning of a suspect from whom the police want to get information concerning a crime and perhaps a confession.

THE LEGAL BASIS FOR *MIRANDA*

The Fifth Amendment guarantees protection against self-incrimination. A defendant's choice *not* to incriminate himself or herself cannot be interpreted as a sign of guilt by a jury in a criminal trial. A confession, or admission of guilt, is by definition a statement of self-incrimination. How, then, to reconcile the Fifth Amendment with the critical need of law enforcement officers to gain confessions? The answer lies in the concept of *coercion*. When torture or brutality is involved, it is relatively easy to determine that a confession was improperly coerced and is therefore invalid.

Setting the Stage for *Miranda* The Supreme Court first recognized that a confession could not be physically coerced in a 1936 case concerning a defendant who was beaten and whipped until confessing to a murder.[100] It was not until 1964, however, that the Court specifically recognized that the accused's due process rights should be protected during interrogation. That year, the Court heard the case of *Escobedo v. Illinois*,[101] which involved a convicted murderer who had incriminated himself during a four-hour questioning session at a police station. Police officers ignored the defendant's requests to speak with his lawyer, who was actually present at the station while his client was being interrogated. The Court overturned the conviction, setting forth a five-pronged test that essentially established that if police are interrogating a suspect in custody, they cannot deny the suspect's request to speak with an attorney and must warn the suspect of his or her constitutional right to remain silent under the Fifth Amendment. If any one of the five prongs was not satisfied, the suspect had effectively been denied his or her right to counsel under the Sixth Amendment.[102]

The *Miranda* Case The limitations of the *Escobedo* decision quickly became apparent. All five of the prongs had to be satisfied for the defendant to enjoy the Sixth Amendment protections it offered. In fact, the accused rarely request counsel, rendering the *Escobedo* test irrelevant no matter what questionable interroga-

Interrogation The direct questioning of a suspect to gather evidence of criminal activity and try to gain a confession.

tion methods the police used to elicit their confessions. Consequently, two years later, the Supreme Court handed down its *Miranda* decision,[103] establishing the *Miranda* **rights** and introducing the concept of what University of Columbia law professor H. Richard Uviller called *inherent coercion;* that is, even if a police officer does not lay a hand on a suspect, the general atmosphere of an interrogation is in and of itself coercive.[104]

Though the *Miranda* case is best remembered for the procedural requirement it spurred, at the time the Supreme Court was more concerned about the treatment of suspects during interrogation. (See the feature *Landmark Cases*—Miranda v. Arizona on pages 228–229.) The Court found that routine police interrogation strategies, such as leaving suspects alone in a room for several hours before questioning them, were inherently coercive. Therefore, the Court reasoned, every suspect needed protection from coercion, not just those who had been physically abused. The *Miranda* warning is a result of this need. In theory, if the warning is not given to a suspect before an interrogation, the fruits of that interrogation, including a confession, are invalid.

WHEN A *MIRANDA* WARNING IS REQUIRED

As we shall see, a *Miranda* warning is not necessary under several conditions, such as when no questions are asked of the suspect. Generally, *Miranda* requirements apply only when a suspect is in **custody.** In a series of rulings since *Miranda*, the Supreme Court has defined custody as an arrest or a situation in which a reasonable person would not feel free to leave.[105] Consequently, a **custodial interrogation** occurs when a suspect is under arrest or is deprived of her or his freedom in a significant manner. Remember, a *Miranda* warning is only required *before* a custodial interrogation takes place.

WHEN A *MIRANDA* WARNING IS NOT REQUIRED

A *Miranda* warning is not necessary in a number of situations:

1. When the police do not ask the suspect any questions that are *testimonial* in nature. Such questions are designed to elicit information that may be used against the suspect in court. "Routine booking questions," such as the suspect's name, address, height, and eye color, however, are an exception to this rule. Even though answering these questions may provide incriminating evidence (especially if the person answering is a prime suspect), the Supreme Court has held that they are absolutely necessary if the police are to do their jobs.[106] (Imagine the officer not being able to ask a suspect her or his name.)
2. When the police have not focused on a suspect and are questioning witnesses at the scene of a crime.
3. When a person volunteers information before the police have asked a question.
4. When the suspect has given a private statement to a friend or some other acquaintance. *Miranda* does not apply to these statements as long as the government did not orchestrate the situation.
5. During a stop and frisk, when no arrest has been made.
6. During a traffic stop.[107]

Furthermore, suspects can *waive* their Fifth Amendment rights and speak to a police officer, but only if the waiver is made voluntarily. Silence on the part of a suspect does not mean that his or her *Miranda* protections have been relinquished. To waive their rights, suspects must state—either in writing or orally—that they understand those rights and that they will voluntarily answer questions without the presence of counsel.

To ensure that the suspect's rights are upheld, prosecutors are required to prove by a preponderance of the evidence that the suspect "knowing and intelligently"

LO9

Miranda Rights The constitutional rights of accused persons taken into custody by law enforcement officials. Following the United States Supreme Court's decision in *Miranda v. Arizona*, on taking an accused person into custody, the arresting officer must inform the person of certain constitutional rights, such as the right to remain silent and the right to counsel.

Custody The forceful detention of a person, or the perception that a person is not free to leave the immediate vicinity.

Custodial Interrogation The questioning of a suspect after that person has been taken in custody. In this situation, the suspect must be read his or her *Miranda* rights before interrogation can begin.

waived his or her *Miranda* rights.[108] To make the waiver perfectly clear, police will ask suspects two questions in addition to giving the *Miranda* warning:

1. Do you understand your rights as I have read them to you?
2. Knowing your rights, are you willing to talk to another law enforcement officer or me?

If the suspect indicates that she or he does not want to speak to the officer, thereby invoking her or his right to silence, the officer must *immediately* stop any questioning.[109] Similarly, if the suspect requests a lawyer, the police can ask no further questions until an attorney is present.[110] The suspect must be clear about this intention, however. In *Davis v. United States* (1994),[111] the Supreme Court upheld the interrogation of a suspect after he said, "Maybe I should talk to a lawyer." The Court found that this statement was too ambiguous, stating that it did not want to force police officers to "read the minds" of suspects who make vague declarations.

THE LAW ENFORCEMENT RESPONSE TO *MIRANDA*

When the *Miranda* decision was first handed down, many people, particularly police officials, complained that it distorted the Constitution by placing the rights of criminal suspects above the rights of society as a whole.[112] In the four decades since the ruling, however, law enforcement agents have adapted to the *Miranda* restrictions, and strategies to work within their boundaries have become a standard part of police training.

Policing around *Miranda* After an extensive on-site study of police interrogation tactics, Richard A. Leo, a criminologist from the University of California at Irvine,

Landmark Cases *Miranda v. Arizona*

AP/Wide World

Ernesto Miranda

Ernesto Miranda, a produce worker, was arrested in Phoenix, Arizona, in 1963 and charged with kidnapping and rape. After being identified by the victim in a lineup, Miranda was taken into an interrogation room and questioned for two hours by detectives. At no time was Miranda informed that he had a right to have an attorney present. When the police emerged from the session, they had a signed statement by Miranda confessing to the crimes. He was subsequently convicted and sentenced to twenty to thirty years in prison. After the conviction was confirmed by the Arizona Supreme Court, Miranda appealed to the United States Supreme Court, claiming that he had not been warned that any statement he made could be used against him, and that he had a right

to counsel during the interrogation. The *Miranda* case was one of four examined by the Court that dealt with the question of coercive questioning.

Miranda v. Arizona
United States Supreme Court
384 U.S. 436 (1966)
laws.findlaw.com/US/384/436.html

IN THE WORDS OF THE COURT . . .
Chief Justice WARREN, majority opinion

* * * *

The cases before us raise questions which go to the roots of our concepts of American criminal jurisprudence: the restraints society must observe consistent with the Federal Constitution in prosecuting individuals for crime. More specifically, we deal with the admissibility of statements obtained from an individual who is subjected to custodial police interrogation and the necessity for procedures which assure that the individual is accorded his privilege under the Fifth Amendment to the Constitution not to be compelled to incriminate himself.

* * * *

As for the procedural safeguards to be employed, unless other fully effective means are devised to inform accused

noted a pattern of maneuvers that officers use to convince suspects to voluntarily waive their *Miranda* rights. Leo identifies three such strategies:

- The *conditioning* strategy is geared toward creating an environment in which the suspect is encouraged to think positively of the interrogator and thus is conditioned to cooperate. The interrogator will offer the suspect coffee or a cigarette and make pleasant small talk. These steps are intended to lower the suspect's anxiety level and generate a sense of trust that is conducive to a *Miranda* waiver and confession.
- The *deemphasizing* strategy tries to downplay the importance of *Miranda* protections, giving the impression that the rights are unimportant and can be easily waived. For example, one officer told a suspect, "I need to advise you of your rights. It's a formality. I'm sure you've watched television with the cop shows and you hear them say their rights so you can probably recite this better than I can, but it's something I need to do and we can get this out of the way before we talk about what happened."
- When using the *persuasion* strategy, an officer will explicitly try to convince the suspect to waive her or his rights. Commonly, the detective will tell suspects that waiving the rights is the only way they will be able to get their side of the story out. Otherwise, the detective continues, only the victim's side of the story will be considered during the trial.[113]

Sometimes, officers go too far with their interrogation strategies and infringe on a suspect's rights. In 2006, for example, a Florida court threw out incriminating statements made by John Evander Couey because detectives had not allowed him to consult with a lawyer as he had requested. In these statements, Couey admitted that he had kidnapped, raped, and murdered nine-year-old Jessica Marie Lunsford and told the detectives where he had buried her body. Despite

persons of their right of silence and to assure a continuous opportunity to exercise it, the following measures are required. Prior to any questioning, the person must be warned that he has a right to remain silent, that any statement he does make may be used as evidence against him, and that he has a right to the presence of an attorney, either retained or appointed. The defendant may waive effectuation of these rights, provided the waiver is made voluntarily, knowingly and intelligently. * * * The mere fact that he may have answered some questions or volunteered some statements on his own does not deprive him of the right to refrain from answering any further inquiries until he has consulted with an attorney and thereafter consents to be questioned.

* * * *

It is obvious that such an interrogation environment is created for no purpose other than to subjugate the individual to the will of his examiner. This atmosphere carries its own badge of intimidation. To be sure, this is not physical intimidation, but it is equally destructive of human dignity. The current practice of incommunicado interrogation is at odds with one of our Nation's most cherished principles—that the individual may not be compelled to incriminate himself. Unless adequate protective devices are employed to dispel the compulsion inherent in custodial surroundings, no statement obtained from the defendant can truly be the product of his free choice.

DECISION

The Court overturned Miranda's conviction, stating that police interrogations are, by their very nature, coercive and therefore deny suspects their constitutional right against self-incrimination by "forcing" them to confess. Consequently, any person who has been arrested and placed in custody must be informed of his or her right to be free from self-incrimination and to be represented by counsel during any interrogation. In other words, suspects must be told that they *do not have to* answer police questions. To accomplish this, the Court established the *Miranda* warning, which must be read prior to questioning a suspect in custody.

FOR CRITICAL ANALYSIS

What is meant by the phrase "coercion can be mental as well as physical"? What role does the concept of "mental coercion" play in Chief Justice Warren's opinion?

For more information and activities related to this case, click on Landmark Cases under Book Resources at **www.cjinaction.com**.

A Los Angeles police officer reads a handcuffed "suspect" his *Miranda* rights during a training exercise. Does a police officer need to take this action every time he or she arrests a suspect? If not, under what circumstances must an officer administer the *Miranda* warning?

this error, the judge allowed the case to proceed because, in his opinion, law enforcement agents would have found Lunsford's remains even without Couey's confession. (See the discussion of the "inevitable discovery" exception to the exclusionary rule on page 210.) Couey was eventually convicted and sentenced to be executed.

The Problem of False Confessions In a number of instances, the police appear to have become *too* skilled at gaining confessions. In the early 2000s, the reopening of the Central Park jogger case focused national attention on the phenomenon of false confessions. Thirteen years after an investment banker was raped and severely beaten while jogging in New York City, a judge overturned the convictions of four young men who had confessed to attacking the woman. DNA evidence showed that another person was responsible for the crime.

A number of studies have found that between 14 and 25 percent of all *wrongful convictions* (discussed in Chapter 10) can be attributed to false confessions.[114] Experts point to a number of reasons why people admit to a crime they did not commit. Saul Kassin, a professor of psychology at Williams College, suggests that the police tactics described above amount to a form of legal coercion, with some suspects more susceptible than others. Many times, a person will confess in the absence of any wrongdoing because he or she is hungry, frightened, or exhausted.[115] In the Central Park jogger case, several "risk factors" for a false confession were present, including the age of the subjects (the five defendants were between fourteen and sixteen years old) and the interrogation methods (they had been in custody for between fourteen and thirty hours). In Chapter 16, we

> "The psychological games that are played during an interrogation . . . are difficult at best to understand: assured by authorities you don't remember things, being led to doubt your own memory, having things suggested to you only to have those things pop up in a conversation a short time later but from your own lips."
>
> —*Peter Reilly, who confessed while under police interrogation to having murdered his mother*

will address the question of whether government agents should be allowed to use "any means necessary," including torture, to get information from suspected terrorists. (To consider this question in a law enforcement context, see the feature *A Question of Ethics—The "Dirty Harry" Problem*.)

THE FUTURE OF *MIRANDA*

In 2001, the Supreme Court made a strong ruling in favor of the continued importance of *Miranda*. In *Dickerson v. United States*,[116] the Court rejected the application of a little-known law passed by Congress in 1968 that allowed police in federal cases to use incriminatory statements even if the suspect had not been read the warning. "*Miranda* has become embedded in routine police practice to the point where the warnings have become part of our national culture," wrote Chief Justice William Rehnquist in his opinion. The chief justice added that *Miranda* was a "constitutional rule" that Congress could not overturn by passing a law.[117]

The Erosion of *Miranda* Despite these strong words, many legal scholars believe that a series of Supreme Court rulings have eroded *Miranda*'s protections. According to legal scholar Alan M. Dershowitz, the Court has carved "out so many exceptions that [*Miranda*] is falling of its own weight."[118] (See ■ Figure 7.4 on the following page for a rundown of the Court rulings that have weakened *Miranda* over the past several decades.)

The latest such decision, issued in 2004, involved a Colorado case in which the defendant had voluntarily told the police the location of his gun (which, being an ex-felon, he was not allowed to possess) without being read his rights.[119] The Court upheld the conviction, finding that *Miranda* warnings are merely *prophylactic*. In other words, they are only intended to prevent violations of the Fifth Amendment. Because only the gun, and not the defendant's testimony, was presented at trial, the police had not violated his constitutional rights. In essence, the Court was ruling that the "fruit of the poisoned tree" doctrine, discussed earlier in this chapter, does not ban the admission of physical evidence that is discovered based on voluntary statements by a suspect who has not been "Mirandized."[120]

Recording Confessions *Miranda* may eventually find itself obsolete regardless of any decisions made in the courts. A relatively new trend in law enforcement has been for agencies to record interrogations and confessions either on videotape or digitally. Eight states and approximately 450 police departments now require that all interrogations of those who are suspected of committing serious felonies be recorded.[121] In many instances, these policies were established as a result of faulty interrogations. The Detroit Police Department, for example, implemented its video-taping policy after a mentally ill man spent seventeen years in prison after having confessed to a rape that he did not commit. Some scholars have suggested that recording all custodial interrogations would satisfy the Fifth Amendment's prohibition against coercion and thus render the *Miranda* warning unnecessary.

When Thomas P. Sullivan, a former U.S. attorney, and his staff interviewed members of several hundred police departments, they found almost universal support for the recording of custodial interrogations.[122] The officers praised the technology for saving money and time, creating valuable evidence to use in court, and making it more difficult for defense attorneys to claim that their clients were illegally coerced. In contrast, the FBI has resisted the practice on

A Question of Ethics
The "Dirty Harry" Problem

THE SITUATION A young girl has been kidnapped by a psychotic killer named Scorpio. Demanding a $200,000 ransom, Scorpio has buried the girl alive, leaving her with just enough oxygen to survive for a few hours. Detective Harry Callahan manages to find Scorpio, but the kidnapper stubbornly refuses to reveal the location of the girl. Callahan comes to the conclusion that the only way he can get this information from Scorpio in time is to beat it out of him.

THE ETHICAL DILEMMA The U.S. Constitution, as interpreted by the United States Supreme Court, forbids the torture of criminal suspects. Following proper procedure, Callahan should arrest Scorpio and advise him of his *Miranda* rights. If Scorpio requests an attorney, Callahan must comply. If the attorney then advises Scorpio to remain silent, there is nothing Callahan can do. Of course, after all this time, the girl will certainly be dead.*

WHAT IS THE SOLUTION? What should Detective Callahan do? According to the late Carl B. Klockars of the University of Delaware, "Each time a police officer considers deceiving a suspect into confessing by telling him that his [or her] fingerprints were found at the scene or that a conspirator has already confessed, each time a police officer considers adding some untrue details to his [or her] account of a probable cause to legitimate a crucial stop or search [that police officer] faces" the same problem as Detective Callahan. Are police ever justified in using unlawful methods, no matter what good may ultimately be achieved?

* This scenario is taken from *Dirty Harry* (1971), one of the most popular police dramas of all time. In the film, Detective Callahan, played by Clint Eastwood, shoots Scorpio and then tortures him. Although Callahan eventually gets the information he needs, it is too late to save the girl.

■ Figure 7.4 Supreme Court Decisions Eroding *Miranda* Rights

Rhode Island v. Innis (446 U.S. 291 [1980]). **In this case the Supreme Court clarified its definition of an interrogation,** which it said could extend only to "actions or words" that the police "should have known were reasonably likely to elicit an incriminating response." In making this ruling, the Court allowed as evidence an admission made by a suspect as to where a shotgun he had used in a crime was hidden. The suspect confessed after police mentioned that there was a possibility that a handicapped child might find the firearm, given that a home for such children was nearby. This was not, the Court ruled, an interrogation and therefore *Miranda* rights were not necessary.

New York v. Quarles (467 U.S. 649 [1984]). **This case established the "public-safety" exception to the *Miranda* rule.** It concerned a police officer who, after feeling an empty shoulder holster on a man he had just arrested, asked the suspect the location of the gun without informing him of his *Miranda* rights. The Court ruled that the gun was admissible as evidence and that the need for police officers to protect the public is more important than a suspect's *Miranda* rights.

Moran v. Burbine (475 U.S. 412 [1986]). **This case established that police officers are not required to tell suspects undergoing custodial interrogation that their attorney is trying to reach them.** The Court ruled that events that the suspect could have no way of knowing about have no bearing on his ability to waive his *Miranda* rights.

Illinois v. Perkins (496 U.S. 292 [1990]). Perkins was a suspected murderer in prison on an unrelated drug charge who admitted to the murder in order to impress his cellmate, who happened to be an undercover police officer. The Court ruled that even though the undercover officer goaded Perkins into making the admission, the defendant was not being subjected to a custodial interrogation; indeed, he eagerly bragged to his cellmate, describing the murder in detail in order to impress. ***Miranda* does not protect suspects from their own foolishness.**

Arizona v. Fulminante (499 U.S. 279 [1991]). **In this very important ruling, the Court held that a conviction is not automatically overturned if the suspect was coerced into making a confession.** If the other evidence introduced at the trial is strong enough to justify a conviction without the confession, then the fact that the confession was illegally gained can be, for all intents and purposes, ignored.

Davis v. United States (512 U.S. 452 [1994]). This case involved a suspect who, instead of demanding that he be provided with his *Miranda* right to an attorney, said, "Maybe I should talk to a lawyer" during his custodial interrogation. **The Court ruled that a suspect must unequivocally and assertively state his right to counsel in order to stop police questioning.** Furthermore, police officers are not required to try and decipher the suspect's intentions in such cases.

Texas v. Cobb (532 U.S. 162 [2001]). When a suspect refuses to waive his or her *Miranda* rights, a police officer cannot lawfully continue the interrogation until the suspect's attorney arrives on the scene. In this case, however, **the Court held that a suspect may be questioned without having a lawyer present if the interrogation does not focus on the crime for which he or she was arrested,** even though it does touch on another, closely related, offense.

the theory that it would cause jurors to sympathize with the suspect. One internal FBI document warned, "Perfectly lawful and acceptable interviewing techniques do not always come across in recorded fashion to laypersons as proper means of obtaining information from defendants."[123]

Self Check Fill in the Blanks

Miranda requirements apply only when law enforcement agents have the suspect in _____. The *Miranda* warning is only required _____ a custodial interrogation takes place. A suspect can _____ his or her *Miranda* rights, but this must be done "knowingly and intentionally." If the suspect indicates that he or she does not wish to speak, the police officer must _____ stop any questioning. The suspect can also end questioning any time by requesting the presence of an _____. Check your answers on page 237.

The Identification Process

A confession is a form of self-identification; the suspect has identified herself or himself as the guilty party. If police officers are unable to gain a confession, they must use other methods to link the suspect with the crime. In fact, to protect against false admissions, police must do so even if the suspect confesses.

ESSENTIAL PROCEDURES

Unless police officers witness the commission of the crime themselves, they **L010** must establish the identity of the suspect using three basic types of identification procedures:

1. *Showups,* which occur when a suspect who matches the description given by witnesses is apprehended near the scene of the crime within a reasonable amount of time after the crime has been committed. The suspect is usually returned to the crime scene for possible identification by witnesses.
2. *Photo arrays,* which occur when no suspect is in custody but the police have a general description of the person. Witnesses and victims are shown "mug shots" of people with police records that match the description. Police will also present witnesses and victims with pictures of people they believe might have committed the crime.
3. *Lineups,* which entail lining up several physically similar people, one of whom is the suspect, in front of a witness or victim. The police may have each member of the lineup wear clothing similar to that worn by the criminal and say a phrase that was used during the crime. These visual and oral cues are designed to help the witness identify the suspect.

As with the other procedures discussed in this chapter, constitutional law governs the identification process, though some aspects are more tightly restricted than others. The Sixth Amendment right to counsel, for example, does not apply during showups or photo arrays. In showups, the police often need to establish a suspect quickly, and it would be unreasonable to expect them to wait for an attorney to arrive. According to the Supreme Court in *United States v. Ash* (1973),[124] however, the police must be able to prove this need for immediate identification, perhaps by showing that it was necessary to keep the suspect from fleeing the state. As for photo arrays, courts have found that any procedure that does not require the suspect's presence does not require the presence of his or her attorney.[125] The lack of an attorney does not mean that police can "steer" a witness toward a positive identification with statements such as "Are you sure this isn't the person you saw robbing the grocery store?" Such actions would violate the suspect's due process rights.

> See **Officer.com** for a wealth of information on the identification process and other law enforcement issues. Find this Web site by clicking on *Web Links* under *Chapter Resources* at **www.cjinaction.com**.

James Shaffer/PhotoEdit

◀ Lineups are one of the primary means police have of identifying suspects. As you can see, in a lineup several people with similar appearances are placed together so that a victim or witness can study them. The victim or witness is then asked to point out the one that most closely resembles the person who committed the crime. Lineup identifications are generally considered most valuable if they take place within several hours after the crime has been committed. Why is timing so important with regard to a lineup?

NONTESTIMONIAL EVIDENCE

Some observers feel that the standard **booking** procedure—the process of recording information about the suspect immediately after arrest—infringes on a suspect's Fifth Amendment rights. During booking, the suspect is photographed and finger-printed, and blood samples may be taken. If these samples lead to the suspect's eventual identification, according to some, they amount to self-incrimination. In *Schmerber v. California* (1966),[126] however, the Supreme Court held that such tests are not the equivalent of *testimonial* self-incrimination (where the suspect testifies verbally against himself or herself) and therefore do not violate the Fifth Amendment.

Using similar legal reasoning, the Court has also determined that voice and handwriting samples gathered by police may be used to identify a suspect.[127] The Court has, however, set some limits on the use of nontestimonial evidence. In the early 1980s, Ralph Watkinson of Richmond, Virginia, shot a man who had assaulted him and then fled the scene of the crime. Police found Rudolph Lee a few blocks away bleeding from a bullet wound beneath his collarbone. Watkinson identified Lee as the assailant, and the local prosecutor tried to get a court order to remove the bullet from Lee's body to match it with Watkinson's gun. In *Winston v. Lee* (1985),[128] the Court ruled that the surgery required was "highly intrusive" and was offensive to Lee's "human dignity." Therefore, the bullet was not allowed as nontestimonial evidence in the trial.

Self Check Fill in the Blanks

Police employ several methods to _____ a suspect, or link that suspect to the crime. They will show witnesses a _____ of suspect "mug shots" or present a number of physically similar persons, one of whom is the suspect, in a _____. The United States Supreme Court has determined that standard _____ procedures, during which police record information on the suspect, do not violate the Fifth Amendment. Check your answers on page 237.

RACIAL PROFILING AND THE CONSTITUTION

When confronted with data showing that his officers targeted nonwhite motorists when searching automobiles for illegal drugs, Colonel Carl A. Williams, superintendent of the New Jersey State Police, seemed undisturbed. "Two weeks ago, the president of the United States went to Mexico to talk about drugs," he replied. "He didn't go to Ireland. He didn't go to England."[129] Williams (who subsequently resigned) was defending the practice of racial profiling, in which law enforcement officers focus on race in their decisions to stop, question, or arrest suspects. In this *Criminal Justice in Action* feature, we will explore the difficult question of whether this police tactic can be justified.

Getty Images

THE *WHREN* EFFECT

As noted earlier in the chapter, the Fourth Amendment protects persons against "unreasonable searches and seizures." Intuitively, it would seem that when the police search or detain a person because of his or her race, an unreasonable search or seizure has taken place. The United States Supreme Court, however, made it practically impossible to prove "racist intent" on the part of law enforcement agents with its decision in *Whren v. United States* (1996),[130] discussed on page 222.

In that case, the Court ruled that the subjective intentions of the police, including any motives based on racial stereotyping or bias, are irrelevant as far as the Fourth Amendment is concerned.[131] As long as police have objective probable cause to believe a traffic violation or other wrongdoing has occurred, any other reasons for the stop should be ignored. Thus, if a suspect was driving over the speed limit or was not wearing a seat belt, then a police officer's decision to stop that driver is constitutional, even if the "real" reason for the stop was the driver's race. Thus, if racial profiling is to be eradicated, America's lawmakers must pass legislation banning the practice. Should they do so?

The Case for Racial Profiling

- Crime rates are racially disproportionate. Young African American males are more likely than other age and racial groups to commit drug-related crimes. Hispanics are more likely than other ethnic groups to have violated immigration laws. To ignore such evidence in the name of cultural sensitivity does a disservice to law-abiding citizens of all races.[132]

- Racial profiling can work. In the late 1990s, New York's Street Crime Unit was disbanded after racking up 45,000 stops and frisks, only 22 percent of which led to arrests and 90 percent of which involved members of a minority group.[133] The unit's actions did, however, result in the seizure of 2,500 illegal guns, leading some to argue that the "hassle factor" was offset by "great gains."[134]

- Racial profiling is necessary to protect against terrorist acts, which, at present, have mostly been committed by men of Middle Eastern background. "We're at war with a terrorist network," says one commentator. "Are we really supposed to ignore the one identifiable fact that we know about them?"[135]

The Case against Racial Profiling

- Racial profiling is indistinguishable from racism and subjects thousands of innocent people to unfair stress, humiliation, and indignity.

- If members of minority groups are more likely to be carrying drugs than are whites, then police should find drugs more often on them than on whites after a stop and search. In fact, such "hit rates" are remarkably consistent among the races.[136]

- Racial profiling is poor strategy. If terrorist groups know in advance that law enforcement agencies are focusing on certain races or ethnic groups, they will simply select individuals of different races or ethnic groups for future attacks.

Your Opinion—Writing Assignment

On November 20, 2006, Minneapolis airport police removed six Muslim religious leaders from a US Airways flight because of suspicious behavior that included shouting "Allah" in prayer, switching seats, and requesting seat belt extensions. In all probability, though, the Muslims' most suspicious "behavior" was their appearance. Earlier in this chapter, you learned that law enforcement agents need reasonable suspicion to conduct a stop and frisk and probable cause to make an arrest. Do you think that there are any circumstances, such as those that existed in Minneapolis, when a suspect's race or ethnicity can be used to establish reasonable suspicion or probable cause? Or, do you think that law enforcement should always be "color blind"? Before responding, you can review our discussions in this chapter concerning

- Probable cause (pages 207–208).
- The definition of reasonable suspicion (pages 211–213).
- Arrests (pages 214–217).

Your answer should be at least three full paragraphs.

L01 Outline the four major sources that may provide probable cause. (a) Personal observation, usually due to an officer's personal training, experience, and expertise; (b) information, gathered from informants, eyewitnesses, victims, police bulletins, and other sources; (c) evidence, which often has to be in plain view; and (d) association, which generally must concern a person with a known criminal background who is seen in a place where criminal activity is openly taking place.

L02 Explain the exclusionary rule and the exceptions to it. This rule, established federally in *Weeks v. United States* and at the state level in *Mapp v. Ohio*, prohibits the use of illegally seized evidence, or evidence obtained by an unreasonable search and seizure in an inadmissible way. Exceptions to the exclusionary rule are the "inevitable discovery" exception established in *Nix v. Williams* and the "good faith" exception established in *United States v. Leon*.

L03 Distinguish between a stop and a frisk, and indicate the importance of the case *Terry v. Ohio*. Though the terms *stop* and *frisk* are often used in concert, a stop is the separate act of detaining a suspect when an officer reasonably believes that a criminal activity is about to take place. A frisk is the physical "pat-down" of a suspect. In *Terry v. Ohio*, the Supreme Court ruled that an officer must have "specific and articulable facts" before making a stop, but those facts may be "taken together with rational inferences."

L04 List the four elements that must be present for an arrest to take place. (a) Intent, (b) authority, (c) seizure or detention, and (d) the understanding of the person that he or she has been arrested.

L05 List the four categories of items that can be seized by use of a search warrant. (a) Items resulting from a crime, such as stolen goods; (b) inherently illegal items; (c) evidence of the crime; and (d) items used in committing the crime.

L06 Explain when searches can be made without a warrant. Searches and seizures can be made without a warrant if they are incidental to an arrest (but they must be reasonable); when they are made with voluntary consent; when they involve the "movable vehicle" exception; when property has been abandoned; and when items are in plain view, under certain restricted circumstances (see *Coolidge v. New Hampshire*).

L07 Describe how the Patriot Act of 2001 changed the guidelines for electronic surveillance of suspected terrorists. Under the old surveillance guidelines, law enforcement agents needed probable cause of a crime to engage in counterterrorism. Under the Patriot Act of 2001, agents are free to search for leads or clues to terrorist activities if such surveillance serves a "significant purpose." The "significant purpose" standard is much easier to meet than "probable cause."

L08 Recite the *Miranda* warning. You have the right to remain silent. If you give up that right, anything you say can and will be used against you in a court of law. You have the right to speak with an attorney and to have the attorney present during questioning. If you so desire and cannot afford one, an attorney will be appointed for you without charge before questioning.

L09 Indicate situations in which a *Miranda* warning is unnecessary. (a) When no questions that are testimonial in nature are asked of the suspect; (b) when there is no suspect and witnesses in general are being questioned at the scene of a crime; (c) when a person volunteers information before the police ask anything; (d) when a suspect has given a private statement to a friend without the government orchestrating it; (e) during a stop and frisk when no arrests have been made; and (f) during a traffic stop.

L010 List the three basic types of police identification. (a) Showups, (b) photo arrays, and (c) lineups.

Key Terms

Questions for Critical Analysis

1. What are the two most significant legal concepts contained in the Fourth Amendment, and why are they important?

2. Suppose that a police officer stops a person who "looks funny." The person acts strangely, so the police officer decides to frisk him. The officer feels a bulge in the suspect's coat pocket, which turns out to be a bag of cocaine. Would the arrest for cocaine possession hold up in court? Why or why not?

3. What continues to be the best indicator of probable cause in the face of no hard-and-fast definitions?

4. How does the expression "fruit of the poisoned tree" relate to the issue of searches and seizures?

5. Is it possible for a person legally to be under arrest without an officer indicating to that person that she or he is in fact under arrest? Explain.

6. Are there any circumstances in which an officer can make a warrantless arrest for a crime that is a misdemeanor? Explain.

7. What is the difference between an arrest warrant and a search warrant?

8. "A person always assumes the risk that her or his conversation may be monitored by the police." Is there any truth to this statement? Why or why not?

9. Describe some of the interrogation strategies that police officers use to gain confessions within the guidelines set down by the Supreme Court's *Miranda* decision.

10. What circumstances have led some states to videotape interrogations, and why have some jurisdictions decided not to do so?

Maximize Your Best Possible Outcome for Chapter 7

1. **Maximize Your Best Chance for Getting a Good Grade on the Exam.** ThomsonNOW Personalized Study is a diagnostic study tool containing valuable text-specific resources—and because you focus on just what you don't know, you learn more in less time to get a better grade. How do you get ThomsonNOW? If your textbook does not include an access code card, go to **thomsonedu.com** to get ThomsonNOW before your next exam!

2. **Get the Most Out of Your Textbook** by going to the book companion Web site at **www.cjinaction.com** to access one of the tutorial quizzes, use the flash cards to master key terms, and check out the many other study aids you'll find there. Under chapter resources you will also be able to access the Stories from the Street feature and Web links mentioned in the textbook.

3. **Learn about Potential Criminal Justice Careers** discussed in this chapter by exploring careers online at **www.cjinaction.com**. You will find career descriptions and information about job requirements, training, salary and benefits, and the application process. You can also watch video profiles featuring criminal justice professionals.

Notes

1. *Georgia v. Randolph,* 126 S.Ct. 1515 (2006).
2. *Ibid.,* 1531.
3. *United States v. Matlock,* 415 U.S. 164 (1974).
4. *Michigan v. Summers,* 452 U.S. 692 (1981).
5. *Brinegar v. United States,* 338 U.S. 160 (1949).
6. Rolando V. del Carmen, *Criminal Procedure for Law Enforcement Personnel* (Monterey, CA: Brooks/Cole Publishing Co., 1987), 63–64.
7. *Maryland v. Pringle,* 540 U.S. 366 (2003).
8. 500 U.S. 44 (1991).
9. *United States v. Leon,* 468 U.S. 897 (1984).
10. 232 U.S. 383 (1914).
11. 342 U.S. 165 (1952).
12. 367 U.S. 643 (1961).
13. Potter Stewart, "The Road to *Mapp v. Ohio* and Beyond: The Origins, Development, and Future of the Exclusionary Rule in Search-and-Seizure Cases," *Columbia Law Review* 83 (October 1983), 1365.
14. 430 U.S. 387 (1977).
15. 467 U.S. 431 (1984).
16. 468 U.S. 897 (1984).
17. "Jury's Mixed Verdict in Cop Trial," *UPI Online* (April 3, 1998).
18. Karen M. Hess and Henry M. Wrobleski, *Police Operation: Theory and Practice* (St. Paul, MN: West Publishing Co., 1997), 122.
19. 392 U.S. 1 (1968).
20. *Ibid.,* 20.
21. *Ibid.,* 21.

22. See *United States v. Cortez*, 449 U.S. 411 (1981); and *United States v. Sokolow*, 490 U.S. 1 (1989).
23. *United States v. Arvizu*, 534 U.S. 266 (2002).
24. *Ibid.*, 270.
25. *Florida v. J.L.*, 529 U.S. 266, 274 (2000).
26. *Adams v. Williams*, 407 U.S. 143 (1972).
27. *Alabama v. White*, 496 U.S. 325 (1990).
28. "Nationwide, Profiling Controls Still Rankle," *Law Enforcement News* (June 2004), F1.
29. Gary Cordner, Brian Williams, and Alfredo Valasco, *Vehicle Stops in San Diego: 2001* (San Diego, CA: San Diego Police Department, 2002), 34.
30. *United States v. Place*, 462 U.S. 696 (1983).
31. *Hibel v. Sixth Judicial District Court*, 542 U.S. 177 (2004).
32. *Ibid.*, 182.
33. *Minnesota v. Dickerson*, 508 U.S. 366 (1993).
34. Rolando V. del Carmen and Jeffrey T. Walker, *Briefs of Leading Cases in Law Enforcement*, 2d ed. (Cincinnati, OH: Anderson, 1995), 38–40.
35. *Florida v. Royer*, 460 U.S. 491 (1983).
36. See also *United States v. Mendenhall*, 446 U.S. 544 (1980).
37. del Carmen, *Criminal Procedure*, 97–98.
38. 514 U.S. 927 (1995).
39. Linda J. Collier and Deborah D. Rosenbloom, *American Jurisprudence*, 2d ed. (Rochester, NY: Lawyers Cooperative Publishing, 1995), 122.
40. 126 S.Ct. 2159 (2006).
41. *United States v. Banks*, 540 U.S. 31, 41 (2003).
42. *Hudson v. Michigan*, 126 S.Ct. 2159, 2163 (2006).
43. Tom Van Dorn, "Violation of Knock-and-Announce Rule Does Not Require Suppression of All Evidence Found in Search," *Police Chief* (October 2006), 10.
44. Wayne R. LeFave and Jerold H. Israel, *Criminal Procedure* (St. Paul, MN: West Publishing Co., 1985), 141–144.
45. David Orlin, Jacob Thiessen, Kelli C. McTaggart, Lisa Toporek, and James Pearl, "Warrantless Searches and Seizures," in "Twenty-sixth Annual Review of Criminal Procedure," *Georgetown Law Journal* 85 (April 1997), 847.
46. *Atwater v. City of Lago Vista*, 532 U.S. 318, 346–347 (2001).
47. 445 U.S. 573 (1980).
48. 451 U.S. 204 (1981).
49. *California v. Greenwood*, 486 U.S. 35 (1988).
50. *Ibid.*
51. 389 U.S. 347 (1967).
52. *Ibid.*, 361.
53. 486 U.S. 35 (1988).
54. *Ibid.*
55. *Illinois v. Caballes*, 543 U.S. 405 (2005).
56. *Coolidge v. New Hampshire*, 403 U.S. 443, 467 (1971).
57. del Carmen, *Criminal Procedure*, 158.
58. *United States v. Grubbs*, 547 U.S. ____ (2006).
59. Reprinted in David C. Mount, "Case Law Alert: U.S. Supreme Court Approves the Use of Anticipatory Search Warrants," *Police Chief* (July 2006), 8.
60. *Grubbs*, at ____.
61. *Katz v. United States*, 389 U.S. 347, 357 (1967).
62. *Brigham City v. Stuart*, 547 U.S. ____ (2006).
63. 414 U.S. 234–235 (1973).
64. 395 U.S. 752 (1969).
65. *Ibid.*, at 763.
66. *Bumper v. North Carolina*, 391 U.S. 543 (1968).
67. 412 U.S. 218 (1973).
68. Jayme W. Holcomb, "Knock and Talks," *FBI Law Enforcement Bulletin* (August 2006), 22–32.
69. Ian D. Midgley, "Just One Question before We Get to Ohio v. Robinette: 'Are You Carrying Any Contraband . . . Weapons, Drugs, Constitutional Protections . . . Anything Like That?'" *Case Western Reserve Law Review* 48 (Fall 1997), 173.
70. 501 U.S. 429 (1991).
71. 519 U.S. 33 (1996).
72. *United States v. Drayton*, 536 U.S. 194 (2002).
73. Linda Greenhouse, "Supreme Court Upholds Police Methods in Vehicle Drug Searches," *New York Times* (November 19, 1996), A23.
74. 453 U.S. 454 (1981).
75. 267 U.S. 132 (1925).
76. *United States v. Ross*, 456 U.S. 798, 804–809 (1982); and *Chambers v. Maroney*, 399 U.S. 42, 44, 52 (1970).
77. 517 U.S. 806 (1996).
78. 519 U.S. 408 (1997).
79. *Illinois v. Caballes*, 543 U.S. 405 (2005).
80. *United States v. Ross*, 456 U.S. 798 (1982).
81. *Ibid.*, at 824.
82. *California v. Acevedo*, 500 U.S. 565 (1991).
83. 403 U.S. 443 (1971).
84. 388 U.S. 42 (1967).
85. 18 U.S.C. Sections 2510(7), 2518(1)(a), 2516 (1994).
86. *Lee v. United States*, 343 U.S. 747 (1952).
87. Christopher K. Murphy, "Electronic Surveillance," in "Twenty-Sixth Annual Review of Criminal Procedure," *Georgetown Law Journal* (April 1997), 920.
88. *United States v. Nguyen*, 46 F.3d 781, 783 (8th Cir. 1995).
89. Foreign Intelligence Surveillance Act of 1978, Pub. L. No. 95-511, 92 Stat. 1783, codified at 50 U.S.C. Sections 1801–1811 (2000).
90. Uniting and Strengthening America by Providing Appropriate Tools Required to Interrupt and Obstruct Terrorism Act of 2001, Pub. L. No. 107-56, 115 Stat. 272, codified as amended at 50 U.S.C.A. Sections 1801–1811 (West 2000 & Supp. 2002).
91. David Hardin, "The Fuss over Two Small Words: The Unconstitutionality of the USA Patriot Act Amendments to FISA under the Fourth Amendment," *George Washington Law Review* (April 2003), 291.
92. 18 U.S.C. Section 3103a (2003).
93. *Ibid.*
94. Nathan H. Seltzer, "Still Sneaking and Peaking," *Criminal Law Bulletin* (May/June 2006), 290–292.
95. *Delayed-Notice Search Warrant: A Vital and Time Honored Tool for Fighting Crime* (Washington, D.C.: U.S. Department of Justice, September 2004), 5.
96. *Ibid.*, 1–8.
97. *Ibid.*, 5–6.
98. Nathan H. Seltzer, "When History Matters Not: The Fourth Amendment in the Age of the Secret Search," *Criminal Law Bulletin* (March/April 2004), 143.
99. Laura K. Donohue, "Anglo-American Privacy and Surveillance," *Journal of Criminal Law and Criminology* (Spring 2006), 1109–1111.
100. *Brown v. Mississippi*, 297 U.S. 278 (1936).
101. 378 U.S. 478 (1964).
102. *Ibid.*, at 490–491.
103. *Miranda v. Arizona*, 384 U.S. 436 (1966).
104. H. Richard Uviller, *Tempered Zeal* (Chicago: Contemporary Books, 1988), 188–198.
105. *Orozco v. Texas*, 394 U.S. 324 (1969); *Oregon v. Mathiason*, 429 U.S. 492 (1977); and *California v. Beheler*, 463 U.S. 1121 (1983).
106. *Pennsylvania v. Muniz*, 496 U.S. 582 (1990).
107. del Carmen, *Criminal Procedure*, 267–268.
108. *Moran v. Burbine*, 475 U.S. 412 (1986).
109. *Michigan v. Mosley*, 423 U.S. 96 (1975).
110. *Fare v. Michael C.*, 442 U.S. 707, 723–724 (1979).
111. 512 U.S. 452 (1994).
112. Patrick Malone, "You Have the Right to Remain Silent: *Miranda* after Twenty Years," *American Scholar* 55 (1986), 367.
113. Richard A. Leo, "The Impact of *Miranda* Revisited," *Journal of Criminal Law and Criminology* 86 (Spring 1996), 621–692.
114. Steven A. Drizin and Richard A. Leo, "The Problem of False Confessions in the Post DNA World," *North Carolina Law Review* (March 2004), 891–1007.
115. Saul Kassin, "False Confessions and the Jogger Case," *New York Times* (November 1, 2002), A31.
116. 530 U.S. 428 (2000).
117. *Ibid.*, 443.
118. Alan M. Dershowitz, "A Requiem for the Exclusionary Rule," in *Taking Liberties: A Decade of Hard Cases, Bad Laws, and Bum Raps* (Chicago: Contemporary Books, 1988), 10.
119. *United States v. Patane*, 542 U.S. 630 (2004).
120. *Ibid.*, 640.
121. Eric Lipton and Jennifer Steinhauer, "Battle over F.B.I. Policy against Taping of Suspects Comes to Light in Firing Inquiry," *New York Times* (April 2, 2007), A18.
122. Thomas P. Sullivan, *Police Experiences with Recording Custodial Interrogations* (Chicago: Northwestern University School of Law Center on Wrongful Convictions, Summer 2004), 4.
123. Quoted in Lipton and Steinhauer.
124. 413 U.S. 300 (1973).

125. *United States v. Barker,* 988 F.2d 77, 78 (9th Cir. 1993).
126. 384 U.S. 757 (1966).
127. *United States v. Dionisio,* 410 U.S. 1 (1973); and *United States v. Mara,* 410 U.S. 19 (1973).
128. 470 U.S. 753 (1985).
129. Quoted in Jackson Toby, "'Racial Profiling' Doesn't Prove Cops Are Racist," *Wall Street Journal* (March 11, 1999), A22.
130. 517 U.S. 806 (1996).
131. *Ibid.,* 813.
132. Dinesh D'Souza, *The End of Racism: Principles for a Multicultural Society* (New York: Free Press, 1995), 260–261.
133. Melanie Lefkowitz, "Policy Set on the Street," *Newsday* (March 14, 2002), A3.
134. James Q. Wilson and Heather Mac Donald, "Profiles in Courage," *Wall Street Journal* (January 10, 2002), A12.
135. Michael Kinsley, "When Is Racial Profiling Okay?" *Washington Post* (September 30, 2001), A1.
136. David Cole and John Lamberth, "The Fallacy of Racial Profiling," *New York Times* (May 13, 2001), 133.

Courts and the
Quest for Justice

Learning objectives

After reading this chapter, you should be able to:

L01 Define and contrast the four functions of the courts.

L02 Define *jurisdiction* and contrast geographic and subject-matter jurisdiction.

L03 Explain the difference between trial and appellate courts.

L04 Outline the several levels of a typical state court system.

L05 Outline the federal court system.

L06 Explain briefly how a case is brought to the Supreme Court.

L07 List the actions that a judge might take prior to an actual trial.

L08 Explain the difference between the selection of judges at the state level and at the federal level.

L09 List and describe the members of the courtroom work group.

L010 Explain the consequences of excessive caseloads.

Campus Controversy

The crowd that had gathered on the campus of North Carolina Central University (NCCU) in Durham was angry. A month earlier, on March 13, 2006, a captain of the Duke University lacrosse team had called an escort service and hired two "exotic" dancers to perform at a party. Early the next morning, one of the dancers wound up in the emergency room of a local hospital. The woman, a twenty-seven-year-old African American NCCU student, told local police that she had been raped, sodomized, and choked by three white men in a bathroom at the house where the party took place. Why, someone in the crowd asked Durham County district attorney Michael Nifong, had no charges been filed yet? "My presence here means that this case is not going away," promised Nifong.

Nifong kept his vow, eventually charging three Duke lacrosse players—senior David Evans and sophomores Colin Finnerty and Reade Seligmann—with first degree rape, sexual assault, and kidnapping. The three defendants, who had been identified from a photo array by the alleged victim, faced thirty years behind bars for each charge. In December 2006, however, Nifong dropped the rape charges against the suspects after the alleged victim changed her story, saying that she could not be certain about exactly what had happened that night. Then, on April 11, 2007, the North Carolina attorney general threw out the entire case, citing the woman's "faulty and unreliable" accusations.

By this time, Nifong himself had, contrary to his promise, "gone away." North Carolina officials removed him from the case after the state bar opened an ethics investigation concerning his prosecutorial strategy. Eventually, he lost his license to practice law. Nifong expressed remorse for "judgments that ultimately proved to be incorrect," but the defendants were having none of it. "You can accept an apology from someone who knows all the facts and simply makes an error," said Reade Seligmann's attorney. "If a person refuses to know all the facts and then makes a judgment, that's far worse—particularly when that judgment destroys lives."

▲ Durham County (North Carolina) district attorney Mike Nifong, faced heavy criticism for his handling of the so-called Duke rape case.

Criminal Justice Now™

Maximize your study time by using ThomsonNOW's Personalized Study plan to help you review this chapter and prepare for examination. The Study Plan will

- Help you identify areas on which you should concentrate
- Provide interactive exercises to help you master the chapter concepts; and
- Provide a post-test to confirm you are ready to move on to the next chapter information.

Did the three Duke lacrosse players suffer unfairly at the hands of the criminal justice system? Certainly, Michael Nifong made a number of serious legal and ethical miscalculations. He told the media that the suspects were a "bunch of hooligans" who felt contempt for the alleged victim "based on her race." He tried to hide the results of a DNA test that found no match between any Duke lacrosse player and genetic material found on the young woman's underwear and body. He pressed on with the charges even though medical records showed no physical evidence of rape. Furthermore, the photo array used to identify the suspects was highly suspect, and Reade Seligmann's cell phone logs showed that he had left the party before the time of the alleged criminal activity.[1]

After the case was dismissed, Colin Finnerty said, "I knew justice would prevail [because] I had the truth on my side." In a wry aside, however, he added, "There seem to be some flaws in the legal system."[2] Famed jurist Roscoe Pound characterized "justice" as society's demand "that serious offenders be convicted and punished," while at the same time "the innocent and unfortunate are not oppressed."[3] We can expand on this noble, if idealistic, definition. Citizens expect their courts to discipline the guilty, provide deterrents for illegal activities, protect civil liberties, and rehabilitate criminals—all simultaneously. Over the course of the next four chapters, we shall examine these lofty goals and the extent to which they can be reached, keeping in mind Finnerty's warning about the inevitable "flaws in the system." We start with a discussion of how courts in the United States work.

Functions of the Courts

Simply stated, a court is a place where arguments are settled. The argument may be between the federal government and a corporation accused of violating environmental regulations, between business partners, between a criminal and the state, or between any other number of parties. The court provides an environment in which the basis of the argument can be decided through the application of the law.

Courts have extensive powers in our criminal justice system: they can bring the authority of the state to seize property and to restrict individual liberty. Given that the rights to own property and to enjoy personal freedom are enshrined in the U.S. Constitution, a court's *legitimacy* in taking such measures must be unquestioned by society. This legitimacy is based on two factors: impartiality and independence.[4] In theory, each party involved in a courtroom dispute must have an equal chance to present its case and must be secure in the belief that no outside factors are going to influence the decision rendered by the court. In reality, as we shall see over the next four chapters, it does not always work that way.

DUE PROCESS AND CRIME CONTROL IN THE COURTS

As mentioned in Chapter 1, the criminal justice system has two sets of underlying values: due process and crime control. Due process values focus on protecting the rights of the individual; crime control values stress the punishment and repression of criminal conduct.[5] The competing nature of these two value systems is often evident in the nation's courts.

The Due Process Function The primary concern of early American courts was to protect the rights of the individual against the power of the state. Memories of

L01 injustices suffered at the hands of the British monarchy were still strong, and most of the procedural rules that we have discussed in this textbook were created with the express purpose of giving the individual a "fair chance" against the government in any courtroom proceedings. Therefore, the due process function of the courts is to protect individuals from the unfair advantages that the government—with its immense resources—automatically enjoys in legal battles. Seen in this light, constitutional guarantees such as the right to counsel, the right to a jury trial, and protection from self-incrimination are equalizers in the "contest" between the state and the individual. The idea that the two sides in a courtroom dispute are adversaries is, as we shall discuss in the next chapter, fundamental in American courts.

The Crime Control Function Advocates of crime control distinguish between the court's obligation to be fair to the accused and its obligation to be fair to society.[6] The crime control function of the courts emphasizes punishment and retribution—criminals must suffer for the harm done to society, and it is the courts' responsibility to see that they do so. Given this

▼ McNairy County (Tennessee) Circuit Court Judge Weber McCraw presided over the high-profile 2007 criminal trial in which a minister's wife, Mary Winkler, was found guilty of voluntary manslaughter in the death of her husband. Judge McCraw kept reporters out of the courtroom during jury selection—just one of the many decisions that judges make as "gatekeepers" of the American court system.

AP Photo/Russell Ingle

responsibility to protect the public, deter criminal behavior, and "get criminals off the streets," the courts should not be concerned solely with giving the accused a fair chance. Rather than using due process rules as "equalizers," the courts should use them as protection against blatantly unconstitutional acts. For example, a detective who beats a suspect with a tire iron to get a confession has obviously infringed on the suspect's constitutional rights. If, however, the detective uses trickery to gain a confession, the court should allow the confession to stand because it is not in society's interest that law enforcement agents be deterred from outwitting criminals.

THE REHABILITATION FUNCTION

A third view of the court's responsibility is based on the "medical model" of the criminal justice system. In this model, criminals are analogous to patients, and the courts perform the role of physicians who dispense "treatment."[7] The criminal is seen as sick, not evil, and therefore treatment is morally justified. Of course, treatment varies from case to case, and some criminals require harsh penalties such as incarceration. In other cases, however, it may not be in society's best interest for the criminal to be punished according to the formal rules of the justice system. Perhaps the criminal can be rehabilitated to become a productive member of society and thus save taxpayers the costs of incarceration or other punishment.

THE BUREAUCRATIC FUNCTION

To a certain extent, the crime control, due process, and rehabilitation functions of a court are secondary to its bureaucratic function. In general, a court may have the goal of protecting society or protecting the rights of the individual, but on a day-to-day basis that court has the more pressing task of dealing with the cases brought before it. Like any bureaucracy, a court is concerned with speed and efficiency, and loftier concepts such as justice can be secondary to a judge's need to wrap up a particular case before six o'clock so that administrative deadlines can be met. Indeed, many observers feel that the primary adversarial relationship in the courts is not between the two parties involved but between the ideal of justice and the reality of bureaucratic limitations.[8]

Self Check Fill in the Blanks

The _____ function of American courts is to protect _____ from the unfair advantages that the government enjoys during legal proceedings. In contrast, the _____ function of the courts emphasizes punishment—criminals must suffer for the harm they do to _____. A third view of the court system focuses on the need to _____ a criminal, in much the same way as a doctor would treat a patient.

Check your answers on page 270.

The Basic Principles of the American Judicial System

One of the most often cited limitations of the American judicial system is its complex nature. In truth, the United States does not have a single judicial system, but fifty-two different systems—one for each state, the District of Columbia, and the federal government. As each state has its own unique judiciary with its own set of rules, some of which may be in conflict with the federal judiciary, it is helpful at this point to discuss the basics—jurisdiction, trial and appellate courts, and the dual court system.

JURISDICTION

In Latin, *juris* means "law," and *diction* means "to speak." Thus, **jurisdiction** literally refers to the power "to speak the law." Before any court can hear a case, it must have jurisdiction over the persons involved in the case or its subject matter. The jurisdiction of every court, even the United States Supreme Court, is limited in some way.

Geographic Jurisdiction One limitation is geographic. Generally, a court can exercise its authority over residents of a certain area. A state trial court, for example, normally has jurisdictional authority over crimes committed in a particular

L02 area of the state, such as a county or a district. A state's highest court (often called the state supreme court) has jurisdictional authority over the entire state, and the United States Supreme Court has jurisdiction over the entire country. For the most part, criminal jurisdiction is determined by legislation. The U.S. Congress or a state legislature can determine what acts are illegal within the geographic boundaries it controls, thus giving federal or state courts jurisdiction over those crimes. What happens, however, when more than one court system has jurisdiction over the same criminal act?

Federal versus State Jurisdiction Under the principles of federalism (see pages 11–12), crime is considered a state and local issue. The United States Supreme Court has long held that state governments have the "principal responsibility for defining and prosecuting crimes."[9] Indeed, according to the U.S. Constitution, the federal government has no specific jurisdiction over criminal law. The Constitution does, however, allow the U.S. Congress to make laws that are "necessary and proper" to carry out its other duties. Congress has deemed it "necessary and proper" that the federal courts have jurisdiction over about four thousand crimes, including drug trafficking, kidnapping, bank robbery, and illegal gambling.[10]

Many acts that are illegal under federal law are also illegal under state law. As a general rule, when Congress "criminalizes" behavior that is already prohibited under a state criminal code, the federal and state courts both have jurisdiction over that crime unless Congress states otherwise in the initial legislation. Thus, **concurrent jurisdiction,** which occurs when two different court systems have simultaneous jurisdiction over the same case, is quite common. (See the feature *You Be the Judge—Medical Marijuana* on the following page for an example of what can happen when federal and state laws contradict each other.)

Sorting Out Concurrent Jurisdiction Because neither the federal nor the state courts have unlimited resources, it would be impractical for every case in which concurrent jurisdiction exists to be prosecuted in both court systems. Therefore, federal and state prosecutors have the discretion to abandon cases that are already being tried in other courts. Generally, this decision is based on practical considerations, but politics can also play a role. Take the saga of John Allen Muhammad and John Lee Malvo. Although media attention focused on their sniper activities in the Washington, D.C., area in the fall of 2002, the two were ultimately charged with killing fourteen people and injuring several others in Alabama, Georgia, Louisiana, and Washington State, as well as in the District of Columbia, Maryland, and Virginia.

Once Muhammad and Malvo were arrested, the question became, where would they stand trial? Technically, each state in which they had committed a crime had a jurisdictional claim, as did the federal courts because one of the murders took place in the nation's capital. The decision lay with the U.S. Department of Justice, which had custody of the suspects. Maryland authorities argued that because more people were killed in their state—six—than in any other jurisdiction, they should have "first crack" at the alleged snipers. Federal officials, however, wanted Muhammad and Malvo to receive the death penalty if found guilty and felt Virginia had, in the words of then U.S. Attorney General John Ashcroft, "the

Jurisdiction The authority of a court to hear and decide cases within an area of the law or a geographic territory.

Concurrent Jurisdiction The situation that occurs when two or more courts have the authority to preside over the same criminal case.

best law, the best facts, and the best range of possible penalties."[11] Both suspects were eventually found guilty in Virginia courts, with Muhammad being sentenced to death and Malvo—a juvenile and therefore not eligible for execution—receiving two life sentences.

State versus State Jurisdiction As the "D.C. sniper" case shows, two states can claim jurisdiction over the same defendant. They can even have concurrent jurisdiction over the same crime under certain circumstances, depending on state legislation. For example, if Billy is standing in State A and shoots Frances, who is standing in State B, the two states could have concurrent jurisdiction to try Billy for murder. Similarly, if a property theft takes places in State A but police recover the stolen goods in State B, concurrent jurisdiction could exist. Some states have also passed laws stating that they have jurisdiction over their own citizens who commit crimes in other states, even if there is no other connection between the home state and the criminal act.[12]

When concurrent jurisdiction occurs, state officials become negotiators. In 2006, for example, police in Las Vegas, Nevada, arrested polygamist sect leader Warren Jeffs after a traffic stop. Jeffs had been on the run for almost a year and was facing charges that he arranged marriages of underage girls to older men in both Utah and Arizona. Because Jeffs would face harsher punishment if convicted in Utah, officials from the two states agreed that he should stand trial there. Subsequently, Nevada law enforcement agents *extradited* Jeffs to Utah. **Extradition** is the formal process by which one legal authority such as a state or a nation transfers a fugitive to another legal authority that has a claim on the suspect.

Extradition The process by which one jurisdiction surrenders a person accused or convicted of violating another jurisdiction's criminal law to the second jurisdiction.

You Be the Judge Medical Marijuana

THE FACTS California resident Angie has been diagnosed with a number of serious medical conditions, including an inoperable brain tumor and a seizure disorder. After determining that no conventional drugs could help her, Angie's physician prescribed medical marijuana to ease her chronic pain. One day, federal agents raided Angie's home, destroyed her six marijuana plants, and arrested her for violating federal drug laws.

THE LAW As we saw in Chapter 3, the federal Controlled Substances Act (CSA) regulates the nation's drug laws. According to the CSA, marijuana has "no accepted medical use" and its possession is illegal under all circumstances. Under California's Compassionate Use Act (CUA), however, seriously ill Californians such as Angie "have the right to obtain and use marijuana for medical purposes where that medical use is deemed appropriate and has been recommended by a physician." When a federal law and a state law contradict each other, as is the case with the CSA and California's CUA, the federal law preempts the state law if that was the intent of Congress when passing the federal law.

YOUR DECISION When the U.S. Congress enacted the CSA, it said nothing about whether the law should preempt contradictory state statutes. Federal law enforcement officials argue, however, that allowing some citizens in some states to grow their own medical marijuana would make it impossible to control the illegal marijuana market. Do you think that Angie should be protected by the CUA, or should she be arrested for marijuana possession as required by the CSA? In general, what is your opinion of allowing states to pass statutes that contradict federal criminal laws?

[To see how the United States Supreme Court ruled in a case similar to this one, go to Example 8.1 in Appendix B.]

Multiple Prosecutions By allowing Utah to prosecute Warren Jeffs, Arizona officials did not relinquish their own jurisdiction over the case. Even if Jeffs is eventually found guilty in Utah, an Arizona court will still be able to try him for the crimes committed in Arizona. Indeed, this is what happened to John Allen Muhammad, the "D.C. sniper" discussed earlier. After being sentenced to death by a Virginia court, he was transferred to Maryland. A jury in that state found him guilty on six counts of first degree murder, and he received an additional six consecutive life sentences in prison. Critics called the second trial an expensive exercise in futility, but state officials insisted that the families of Muhammad's Maryland victims deserved the same "sense of closure" as their Virginia counterparts.[13] In addition, as we will see in Chapter 10, guilty verdicts can be appealed and reversed, and the Maryland convictions would serve as "insurance" against that possibility in Virginia. In most situations, however, conviction in one jurisdiction ends prosecution of the same case in another jurisdiction.

International Jurisdiction Under international law, each country has the right to create and enact criminal law for its territory. Therefore, the notion that a nation has jurisdiction over any crimes committed within its borders is well established. The situation becomes more delicate when one nation feels the need to go outside its own territory to enforce its criminal law. (We will see just how delicate these situations can become when we discuss the International Criminal Court in the *Criminal Justice in Action* feature at the end of this chapter.)

Extradition Treaties In the early 1990s, the Drug Enforcement Administration (DEA) hired bounty hunters to go into Mexico and abduct Dr. Humberto Alvarez-Machain, a Mexican physician that American law enforcement agents believed had been involved in the murder of a DEA agent. DEA officials felt this drastic action was necessary because Mexican officials had failed to cooperate in capturing the doctor. Needless to say, the kidnapping action outraged Mexican government officials and caused a diplomatic crisis between the two countries.

Such conflicts can be avoided by an extradition treaty, in which nations agree to extradite fugitives to each other following a formal request. Between July 2006 and January 2007, the Mexican government extradited sixty-three fugitives to the United States, where they were wanted on murder, rape, and drug trafficking charges.[14] In that same time period, the United States extradited a pedophile suspect to Mexico to stand trial for heading a child-abuse operation.

The Long Arm of the Law Historically, American criminal law has been based on the premise that where a crime took place was the most important factor in determining a court's jurisdiction over that crime. Today, limiting the law by such territorial concerns is as outdated as it is impractical. How could such notions of jurisdiction apply to, say, the case of Ludwig Feinberg, an American citizen living in Russia who arranged to

▼ In 2006, Neil Entwistle, right, was charged with first degree murder in the deaths of his wife, Rachel, and their nine-year-old daughter, Lillian. Before law enforcement agents even found the two bodies, Entwistle had fled to his native England. Once there, however, he was apprehended and extradited to Massachusetts to stand trial. What reasons might a country have for granting an extradition request under such circumstances?

REUTERS/Neal Hamberg/Landov

sell a diesel submarine to drug runners so that they could deliver illegal narcotics from Panama to the West Coast of the United States? Or to a terrorist who plans to launch an attack on the United States without setting foot on American soil?

International law has provided the United States and other countries with several bases for expanding their jurisdiction across international borders. For example, antiterrorism efforts have been aided by the principle that acts committed outside a jurisdiction but intended to produce detrimental effects within that jurisdiction can be treated as if they were committed within national boundaries.[15] Furthermore, a nation can arrest one of its citizens for breaking its criminal laws when the act takes place on foreign soil.[16] Thus, the PROTECT (Prosecuting Remedies and Tools Against the Exploitation of Children Today) Act of 2003 makes it a crime for any U.S. citizen to travel abroad and have sex with a minor.[17] The legislation explicitly allows American courts to exercise jurisdiction when the prohibited behavior—the sex act itself—occurs in a foreign country.[18]

Subject-Matter Jurisdiction Jurisdiction over subject matter also acts as a limitation on the types of cases a court can hear. State court systems include courts of *general* (unlimited) *jurisdiction* and courts of *limited jurisdiction.* Courts of general jurisdiction have no restrictions on the subject matter they may address, and therefore deal with the most serious felonies and civil cases. Courts of limited jurisdiction, also known as lower courts, handle misdemeanors and civil matters under a certain amount, usually $1,000. To alleviate caseload pressures in lower courts, many states have created special subject-matter courts that only dispose of cases involving a specific crime. For example, a number of jurisdictions have established drug courts to handle an overload of illicit narcotics arrests, and California has created twelve courts that deal specifically with domestic violence offenders.

TRIAL AND APPELLATE COURTS

Another distinction is between courts of original jurisdiction and courts of appellate, or review, jurisdiction. Courts having *original jurisdiction* are courts of the first instance, or **trial courts.** Almost every case begins in a trial court. It is in this court that a trial (or a guilty plea) takes place, and the judge imposes a sentence if the defendant is found guilty. Trial courts are primarily concerned with *questions of fact;* that is, they are designed to determine exactly what events occurred that are relevant to questions of the defendant's guilt or innocence.

Courts having *appellate jurisdiction* act as reviewing courts, or **appellate courts.** In general, cases can be brought before appellate courts only on appeal by one of the parties in the trial court. (Note that because of constitutional protections against being tried twice for the same crime, prosecutors who lose in *criminal* trial court *cannot* appeal the verdict.) An appellate court does not use juries or witnesses to reach its decision. Instead, its judges make a decision on whether the case should be *reversed* and *remanded,* or sent back to the court of original jurisdiction for a new trial. Appellate judges present written explanations for their decisions, and these **opinions** of the court are the basis for a great deal of the precedent in the criminal justice system.

It is important to understand that appellate courts do not determine the defendant's guilt or innocence—they only make judgments on questions of procedure. In other words, they are concerned with *questions of law* and normally accept the facts as established by the trial court. Only rarely will an appeals court question a jury's decision. Instead, the appellate judges will review the manner in which the facts and evidence were provided to the jury and rule on whether errors were made in the process.

THE DUAL COURT SYSTEM

Like many other aspects of American government, the structure of the judicial system was the result of a compromise. During the framing of the U.S. Constitution, two camps emerged with different views on the courts. The Anti-Federalists, inter-

Trial Courts Courts in which most cases usually begin and in which questions of fact are examined.

Appellate Courts Courts that review decisions made by lower courts, such as trial courts; also known as *courts of appeals.*

Opinions Statements by the court expressing the reasons for its decision in a case.

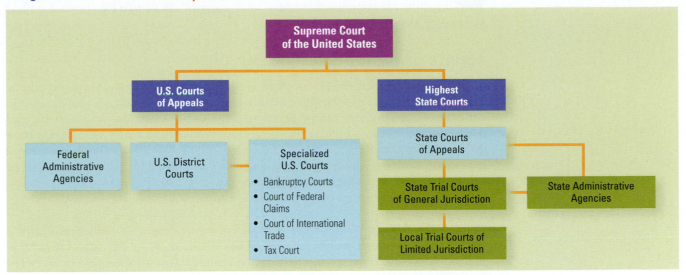

ested in limiting the power of the federal government, wanted the Supreme Court to be the only *national* court, with the states handling the majority of judicial work. The Federalists, dedicated to ensuring that the states did not have too much power, wanted all cases to be heard in federal courts. Both sides eventually made concessions, and the outcome is reflected in the **dual court system** that we have today (see ■ Figure 8.1).[19]

Federal and state courts both have limited jurisdiction. Generally, federal courts deal with acts that violate federal law, and state courts deal with acts that violate state law. The distinction is not, however, always clear. A number of crimes—such as kidnapping and transportation of narcotics—are deemed illegal by both federal and state statutes, and persons accused of such crimes can be tried in either court system. In these instances, federal and state prosecutors must decide among themselves who will handle the case—a decision based on a number of factors, including the notoriety of the crime and the relative caseloads of the respective court systems. As we saw earlier in the chapter, the prosecutors will often "steer" a suspect toward the harsher penalty. Thus, if the punishment for a particular crime is more severe under federal law than state law, then law enforcement officials may decide to try the defendant in federal court (and vice versa).

Self Check Fill in the Blanks

Before any court can hear a case, it must have _____ over the persons involved or the _____ of the dispute. Almost every case begins in a _____ court, which is primarily concerned with determining the facts of the dispute. After this first trial, the participants can, under some circumstances, ask an _____ court to review the proceedings for errors in applying the law. The American court system is called a _____ court system because _____ courts address violations of federal law and _____ courts address violations of state law. Check your answers on page 270.

State Court Systems

Typically, a state court system includes several levels, or tiers, of courts. State courts may include (1) lower courts, or courts of limited jurisdiction; (2) trial courts of general jurisdiction; (3) appellate courts; and (4) the state's highest court. As previously mentioned, each state has a different judicial structure, in

Dual Court System The separate but interrelated court system of the United States, made up of the courts on the national level and the courts on the state level.

LO4 which different courts have different jurisdictions, but there are enough similarities to allow for a general discussion. ■ Figure 8.2 shows a typical state court system.

COURTS OF LIMITED JURISDICTION

Most states have local trial courts that are limited to trying cases involving minor criminal matters, such as traffic violations, prostitution, and drunk and disorderly conduct. Although these minor courts usually keep no written record of the trial proceedings and cases are decided by a judge rather than a jury, defendants have the same rights as those in other trial courts. The majority of all minor criminal cases are decided in these lower courts. Courts of limited jurisdiction can also be responsible for the preliminary stages of felony cases. Arraignments, bail hearings, and preliminary hearings often take place in these lower courts.

Magistrate Courts One of the earliest courts of limited jurisdiction was the *justice court*, presided over by a *justice of the peace*, or JP. In the early days of this nation, JPs were found everywhere in the country. One of the most famous JPs was Judge Roy Bean, the "hanging judge" of Langtry, Texas, who presided over his court at the turn of the twentieth century. Today, more than half the states have

■ **Figure 8.2 A Typical State Court System**

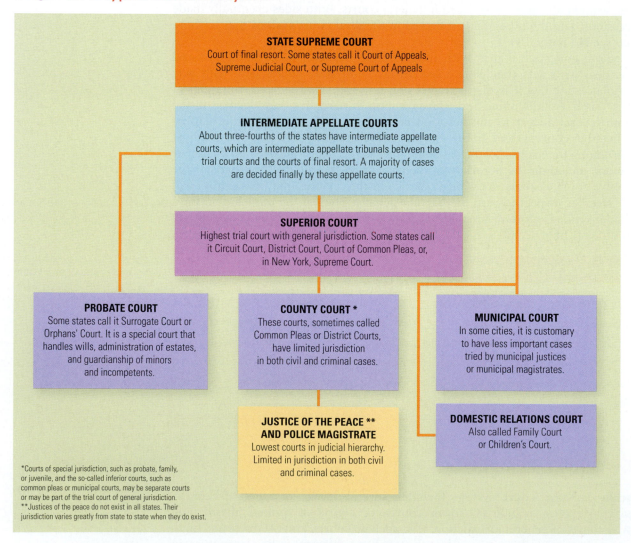

STATE SUPREME COURT
Court of final resort. Some states call it Court of Appeals, Supreme Judicial Court, or Supreme Court of Appeals

INTERMEDIATE APPELLATE COURTS
About three-fourths of the states have intermediate appellate courts, which are intermediate appellate tribunals between the trial courts and the courts of final resort. A majority of cases are decided finally by these appellate courts.

SUPERIOR COURT
Highest trial court with general jurisdiction. Some states call it Circuit Court, District Court, Court of Common Pleas, or, in New York, Supreme Court.

PROBATE COURT
Some states call it Surrogate Court or Orphans' Court. It is a special court that handles wills, administration of estates, and guardianship of minors and incompetents.

COUNTY COURT *
These courts, sometimes called Common Pleas or District Courts, have limited jurisdiction in both civil and criminal cases.

MUNICIPAL COURT
In some cities, it is customary to have less important cases tried by municipal justices or municipal magistrates.

JUSTICE OF THE PEACE **
AND POLICE MAGISTRATE
Lowest courts in judicial hierarchy. Limited in jurisdiction in both civil and criminal cases.

DOMESTIC RELATIONS COURT
Also called Family Court or Children's Court.

*Courts of special jurisdiction, such as probate, family, or juvenile, and the so-called inferior courts, such as common pleas or municipal courts, may be separate courts or may be part of the trial court of general jurisdiction.
**Justices of the peace do not exist in all states. Their jurisdiction varies greatly from state to state when they do exist.

abolished justice courts, though JPs still serve a useful function in some cities and rural areas, notably in Texas. The jurisdiction of justice courts is limited to minor disputes between private individuals and to crimes punishable by small fines or short jail terms. The equivalent of a county JP in a city is known as a **magistrate** or, in some states, a municipal court judge. Magistrate courts have the same limited jurisdiction as do justice courts in rural settings. In most jurisdictions, magistrates are responsible for providing law enforcement agents with search and seizure warrants, discussed in Chapter 7.

Specialty Courts   Many states have created **specialty courts** that have jurisdiction over very narrowly defined areas of criminal justice. Not only do these courts remove many cases from the existing court systems, but they also allow court personnel to become experts in a particular subject. Specialty courts include:

1. Drug courts, which deal only with illegal substance crimes.
2. Gun courts, which have jurisdiction over crimes that involve the illegal use of firearms.
3. Juvenile courts, which specialize in crimes committed by minors. (We will discuss juvenile courts in more detail in Chapter 15.)
4. Domestic courts, which deal with crimes of domestic violence, such as child and spousal abuse.
5. Elder courts, which focus primarily on the special needs of the elderly victims rather than the offenders.

As we will see in Chapter 12, many state and local governments are searching for cheaper alternatives to locking up nonviolent offenders in prison or jail. Because specialty courts offer a range of treatment options for wrongdoers, these courts are becoming increasingly popular in today's more budget-conscious criminal justice system. For example, about two thousand drug courts are now operating in the United States, a number that is expected to increase as the financial benefits of diverting drug law violators from correctional facilities become more evident.

TRIAL COURTS OF GENERAL JURISDICTION

State trial courts that have general jurisdiction may be called county courts, district courts, superior courts, or circuit courts. In Ohio, the name is the court of common pleas and in Massachusetts, the trial court. (The name sometimes does not correspond with the court's functions. For example, in New York the trial court is called the supreme court, whereas in most states the supreme court is the state's highest court.) Courts of general jurisdiction have the authority to hear and decide cases involving many types of subject matter, and they are the setting for criminal trials (discussed in Chapter 10).

STATE COURTS OF APPEALS

Every state has at least one court of appeals (known as an appellate, or reviewing, court), which may be an intermediate appellate court or the state's highest court. About three-fourths have intermediate appellate courts. The highest

Magistrate A public civil officer or official with limited judicial authority within a particular geographic area, such as the authority to issue an arrest warrant.

Specialty Courts Lower courts that have jurisdiction over one specific area of criminal activity, such as illegal drugs or domestic violence.

▼ Randy Williams collects trash as part of his participation in the Albany County (Wyoming) Drug Court. Such courts allow certain offenders to opt out of the traditional court system in favor of a treatment-based sentencing process. What are the benefits of drug courts and other specialty courts?

AP Photo/Laramie Boomerang, AAron Ontiveroz

appellate court in a state is usually called the supreme court, but in both New York and Maryland, the highest state court is called the court of appeals. The decisions of each state's highest court on all questions of state law are final. Only when issues of federal law or constitutional procedure are involved can the United States Supreme Court overrule a decision made by a state's highest court.

Self Check Fill in the Blanks

State court systems include several levels of courts. Lower courts, or courts of _____ jurisdiction, hear only cases involving minor criminal matters or narrowly defined areas of crime such as domestic violence. Trial courts of _____ jurisdiction hear cases involving many different subject matters. The state courts of _____ make the final decisions on all questions of state law. Check your answers on page 270.

The Federal Court System

The federal court system is basically a three-tiered model consisting of (1) U.S. district courts (trial courts of general jurisdiction) and various courts of limited jurisdiction, (2) U.S. courts of appeals (intermediate courts of appeals), and (3) the United States Supreme Court.

L05

Unlike state court judges, who are usually elected, federal court judges—including the justices of the Supreme Court—are appointed by the president of the United States, subject to the approval of the Senate. All federal judges receive lifetime appointments (because under Article III of the Constitution they "hold their offices during Good Behavior").

U.S. DISTRICT COURTS

On the lowest tier of the federal court system are the U.S. district courts, or federal trial courts. These are the courts in which cases involving federal laws begin, and a judge or jury decides the case (if it is a jury trial). Every state has at least one federal district court, and there is one in the District of Columbia. The number of judicial districts varies over time, primarily owing to population changes and corresponding caseloads. At the present time, there are ninety-four judicial districts. The federal system also includes other trial courts of limited jurisdiction, such as the tax court and the court of international trade.

U.S. COURTS OF APPEALS

In the federal court system, there are thirteen U.S. courts of appeals—also referred to as U.S. circuit courts of appeals. The federal courts of appeals for twelve of the circuits hear appeals from the district courts located within their respective judicial circuits (see ■ Figure 8.3). The Court of Appeals for the Thirteenth Circuit, called the Federal Circuit, has national appellate jurisdiction over certain types of cases, such as cases involving patent law and cases in which the U.S. government is a defendant. The decisions of the circuit courts of appeals are final unless a further appeal is pursued and granted; in that case, the matter is brought before the Supreme Court.

THE UNITED STATES SUPREME COURT

Alexander Hamilton, writing in *Federalist Paper* No. 78 (1788), predicted that the United States Supreme Court would be the "least dangerous branch" of the federal government because it had neither the power of the purse nor the power

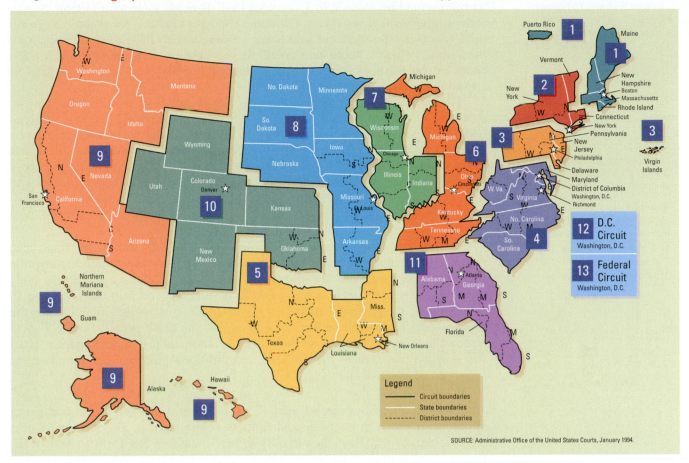

SOURCE: Administrative Office of the United States Courts, January 1994.

of the sword (that is, it could not raise any revenue, and it lacked an enforcement agency).[20] Unless the other two branches of the government—the president and Congress—would accept its decisions, the Court would be superfluous.

In the Supreme Court's earliest years, it appeared that Hamilton's prediction would come true. The first chief justice of the Supreme Court, John Jay, resigned to become governor of New York because he thought the Court would never play an important role in American society. The next chief justice, Oliver Ellsworth, quit to become an envoy to France. In 1801, when the federal capital was moved to Washington, no one remembered to include the Supreme Court in the plans. It did not have its own meeting space until 1835.[21]

Interpreting and Applying the Law Despite these early bouts of inconsequence, the Supreme Court has come to dominate the country's legal culture. Although it reviews fewer than 0.5 percent of the cases decided in the United States each year, the decisions of the Supreme Court profoundly affect our lives. The impact of Court decisions on the criminal justice system is equally far

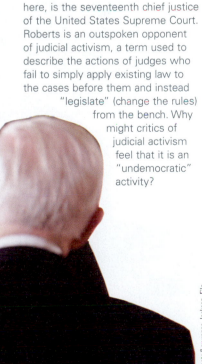

▼ John G. Roberts, Jr., pictured here, is the seventeenth chief justice of the United States Supreme Court. Roberts is an outspoken opponent of judicial activism, a term used to describe the actions of judges who fail to simply apply existing law to the cases before them and instead "legislate" (change the rules) from the bench. Why might critics of judicial activism feel that it is an "undemocratic" activity?

AP Photo/Lawrence Jackson, File

reaching: *Gideon v. Wainwright* (1963)[22] established every American's right to be represented by counsel in a criminal trial; *Miranda v. Arizona* (1966)[23] transformed pretrial interrogations; *Furman v. Georgia* (1972)[24] ruled that the death penalty was unconstitutional; and *Gregg v. Georgia* (1976)[25] spelled out the conditions under which it could be allowed. As you have no doubt noticed from references in this textbook, the Court has addressed nearly every important facet of criminal law.

The Supreme Court "makes" criminal justice policy in two important ways: through *judicial review* and through its authority to interpret the law. **Judicial review** refers to the power of the Court to determine whether a law or action by the other branches of the government is constitutional. For example, in the late 1980s Congress and several state legislatures passed laws criminalizing the act of burning the U.S. flag. In two separate decisions—*Texas v. Johnson* (1989)[26] and *United States v. Eichman* (1990)[27]—the Court invalidated these laws as unconstitutional on the ground that they violated First Amendment protections of freedom of expression.

As the final interpreter of the Constitution, the Supreme Court must also determine the meaning of certain statutory provisions when applied to specific situations. Deciding what the framers of the Constitution or a legislative body meant by a certain phrase or provision is never easy, and inevitably, at least to some extent, the personal attributes of the justices come into play during the process. For example, those justices who oppose the death penalty for ideological reasons have tended to interpret the Eighth Amendment prohibition against "cruel and unusual punishment" as sufficient constitutional justification to outlaw the execution of criminals by the state.[28]

Jurisdiction of the Supreme Court

The United States Supreme Court consists of nine justices—a chief justice and eight associate justices. The Supreme Court has original, or trial, jurisdiction only in rare instances (set forth in Article III, Section 2, of the Constitution). In other words, only rarely does a case originate at the Supreme Court level. Most of the Court's work is as an appellate court. It has appellate authority over cases decided by the U.S. courts of appeals, as well as over some cases decided in the state courts when federal questions are at issue.

Which Cases Reach the Supreme Court?

There is no absolute right to appeal to the United States Supreme Court. Although thousands of cases are filed with the Supreme Court each year, in 2006–2007 the Court heard only seventy-five. With a **writ of *certiorari*** (pronounced sur-shee-uh-*rah*-ree), the Supreme Court orders a lower court to send it the record of a case for review. A party can petition the Supreme Court to issue a writ of *certiorari*, but whether the Court will do so is entirely within its discretion.

LO6

More than 90 percent of the petitions for writs of *certiorari* (or "certs," as they are popularly called) are denied. A denial is not a decision on the merits of a case, nor does it indicate agreement with the lower court's opinion. Therefore, the denial of the writ has no value as a precedent.[29] The Court will not issue a writ unless at least four justices approve of it. This is called the **rule of four**. Although the justices are not required to give their reasons for refusing to hear a case,

▼ Attorney Seth Waxman addresses the media in front of the U.S. Supreme Court building in Washington, D.C. Waxman had just presented his oral arguments before the Court in a case involving patent infringement.

Chris Greenberg/Bloomberg News/Landov

most often the discretionary decision is based on whether the legal issue involves a "substantial federal question." Political considerations aside, if the justices do not feel the case addresses an important federal law or constitutional issue, they will vote to deny the writ of *certiorari*.

Supreme Court Decisions Like all appellate courts, the Supreme Court normally does not hear any evidence. The Court's decision in a particular case is based on the written record of the case and the written arguments (briefs) that the attorneys submit. The attorneys also present **oral arguments**—arguments presented in person rather than on paper—to the Court, after which the justices discuss the case in *conference*. The conference is strictly private—only the justices are allowed in the room.

When the Court has reached a decision, the chief justice, if in the majority, assigns the task of writing the Court's opinion to one of the justices. When the chief justice is not in the majority, the most senior justice voting with the majority assigns the writing of the Court's opinion. The opinion outlines the reasons for the Court's decision, the rules of law that apply, and the decision.

Often, one or more justices who agree with the Court's decision may do so for different reasons than those outlined in the majority opinion. These justices may write **concurring opinions** setting forth their own legal reasoning on the issue. Frequently, one or more justices disagree with the Court's conclusion. These justices may write **dissenting opinions** outlining the reasons why they feel the majority erred. Although a dissenting opinion does not affect the outcome of the case before the Court, it may be important later. In a subsequent case concerning the same issue, a justice or attorney may use the legal reasoning in the dissenting opinion as the basis for an argument to reverse the previous decision and establish a new precedent.

⊗ The **Supreme Court of the United States** provides an up-to-date record of its decisions and the most important issues that it considers. Visit the Court's Web site by clicking on *Web Links* under *Chapter Resources* at **www.cjinaction.com**.

Self Check Fill in the Blanks

The lowest tier of the federal court system contains U.S. _____ courts, also known as federal trial courts. Appeals from this lower tier are heard in the thirteen U.S. _____ courts of appeals. A decision handed down by a court in this second tier is final unless the United States _____ Court issues a writ of _____, indicating that it has agreed to review the case. Check your answers on page 270.

Judges in the Court System

Supreme Court justices are the most visible and best-known American jurists, but in many ways they are unrepresentative of the profession as a whole. Few judges enjoy three-room office suites fitted with a fireplace and a private bath, as do the Supreme Court justices. Few judges have four clerks to assist them. Few judges get a yearly vacation that stretches from July through September. Most judges, in fact, work at the lowest level of the system, in criminal trial courts, where they are burdened with overflowing caseloads and must deal daily with the detritus of society.

One thing a Supreme Court justice and a criminal trial judge in any small American city do have in common is the expectation that they will be just. Of all the participants in the criminal justice system, no single person is held to the same high standards as the judge. From her or his lofty perch in the courtroom, the judge is counted on to be "above the fray" of the bickering defense attorneys and prosecutors. When the other courtroom contestants rise at the entrance of the judge, they are placing the burden of justice squarely on the judge's shoulders.

Oral Arguments The verbal arguments presented in person by attorneys to an appellate court. Each attorney presents reasons why the court should rule in his or her client's favor.

Concurring Opinions Separate opinions prepared by judges who support the decision of the majority of the court but who want to make or clarify a particular point or to voice disapproval of the grounds on which the decision was made.

Dissenting Opinions Separate opinions in which judges disagree with the conclusion reached by the majority of the court and expand on their own views about the case.

THE ROLES AND RESPONSIBILITIES OF TRIAL JUDGES

One of the reasons that judicial integrity is considered so important is the amount of discretionary power a judge has over the court proceedings. As you can see in ■ Figure 8.4, nearly every stage of the trial process includes a decision or action to be taken by the presiding judge.

Before the Trial A great deal of the work done by a judge takes place before the trial even starts, free from public scrutiny. These duties, some of which you have seen from a different point of view in the section on law enforcement agents, include determining the following:

1. Whether there is sufficient probable cause to issue a search or arrest warrant.
2. Whether there is sufficient probable cause to authorize electronic surveillance of a suspect.
3. Whether enough evidence exists to justify the temporary incarceration of a suspect.
4. Whether a defendant should be released on bail, and if so, the amount of the bail.
5. Whether to accept pretrial motions by prosecutors and defense attorneys.
6. Whether to accept a plea bargain.

During these pretrial activities, the judge takes on the role of the *negotiator*.[30] As most cases are decided through plea bargains rather than through trial proceedings, the judge often offers his or her services as a negotiator to help the prosecution and the defense "make a deal." The amount at which bail is set is often negotiated as well. Throughout the trial process, the judge usually spends a great deal of time in his or her *chambers*, or office, negotiating with the prosecutors and defense attorneys. (To learn about the surprising pretrial responsibilities of judges in France, see the feature *International CJ*—Le Juge d'Instruction.)

■ **Figure 8.4** **The Role of the Judge in the Criminal Trial Process**

In the various stages of a felony case, judges must undertake the actions described here.

1. Pre-Arrest
- Decide whether law enforcement officers have provided sufficient probable cause to justify a search or arrest warrant.

2. Initial Appearance
- Inform the suspect of the charges against him or her and of his or her rights.
- Review the charges to see if probable cause exists that the suspect committed the crime; if not, the judge will dismiss the case.
- Set the amount of bail (or deny bail) and determine any other conditions of pretrial release.

3. Preliminary Hearing
- Based on evidence provided by the prosecution and defense, decide whether there is probable cause that the suspect committed the crime.
- Continue to make sure that the defendant's constitutional rights are not being violated.

4. Arraignment
- Ensure that the defendant has been informed of the charges against him or her.
- Ensure that the defendant understands the plea choices before him or her (to plead guilty, not guilty, or *nolo contendere* [no contest]).

5. Plea Bargain
- Assist with the plea bargaining process, if both sides are willing to "make a deal."
- If the defendant decides to plead guilty in return for charges being lessened, ensure that the defendant understands the nature of the plea bargain and has not been pressured into pleading guilty by his or her attorney.

6. Pretrial Motions
- Rule on pretrial motions presented by the defense.
- Decide whether to grant continuances (the postponement of the trial to allow more time for gathering evidence).

7. Trial
- Ensure that proper procedure is followed in jury selection.
- "Officiate" at the trial, making sure that both the prosecutor and the defense follow procedural rules in presenting evidence and questioning witnesses.
- Explain to the jury points of law that affect the case.
- Provide jury instructions, or instruction to jurors on the meaning of the laws applicable to the case.
- Receive the jury's final verdict of guilty or not guilty.

8. Sentencing
- If the verdict is "guilty," impose the sentence on the defendant.

The American judge is a stationary creature. She or he rarely needs to leave the safe haven of the courthouse, and eager attorneys deliver much of the material required for judicial decision making directly to the judge. This is not the system in France, home of the investigating judge, or *le juge d'instruction.* After a public prosecutor determines that charges should be brought against the accused, the case is handed over to *le juge,* a completely independent figure whose only responsibility is get to the bottom of the situation.

Le juge's investigation is carried out in secret. Her or his powers include the ability to (1) order searches of premises and seizures of goods; (2) interrogate suspects and witnesses; (3) arrange face-to-face meetings between the defendant and witnesses; (4) visit the crime scene; (5) make inquiries into the social, family, and financial circumstances of the defendant; (6) order medical or psychological examinations; and (7) keep the suspect in pretrial detention for up to ten days, during which time he or she may not communicate with others, including defense lawyers. If *le juge* believes that there are grounds for the accused to stand trial, she or he will refer the case to the criminal court, providing a *dossier* with the results of the investigation. *Le juge* is not allowed to attend the trial and, in fact, is prohibited from investigating future crimes involving the same defendant.

FOR CRITICAL ANALYSIS

The purpose of *le juge d'instruction* is to provide an impartial investigator who is on the "side" of neither the prosecution nor the defense. Because of this presumed impartiality, *le juge* faces few of the restraints that, as we saw in Chapter 7, are imposed on criminal investigations in the United States. In what ways, if any, do you think our criminal justice system would benefit from a figure like *le juge d'instruction*?

During the Trial   When the trial starts, the judge takes on the role of *referee*. In this role, she or he is responsible for seeing that the trial unfolds according to the dictates of the law and that the participants in the trial do not overstep any legal or ethical bounds. In this role, the judge is expected to be neutral, determining the admissibility of testimony and evidence on a completely objective basis. The judge also acts as a *teacher* during the trial, explaining points of law to the jury. If the trial is not a jury trial, then the judge must also make decisions concerning the guilt or innocence of the defendant. If the defendant is found guilty, the judge must decide on the length of the sentence and the type of sentence. (Different types of sentences, such as incarceration, probation, and other forms of community-based corrections, will be discussed in Chapters 11 and 12.)

The Administrative Role   Judges are also *administrators;* that is, they are responsible for the day-to-day functioning of their courts. A primary administrative task of a judge is scheduling. Each courtroom has a **docket,** or calendar of cases, and it is the judge's responsibility to keep the docket current. This entails not only scheduling the trial, but also setting pretrial motion dates and deciding whether to grant attorneys' requests for *continuances,* or additional time to prepare for a case. Judges must also keep track of the immense paperwork generated by each case and manage the various employees of the court. In some instances, judges are even responsible for the budgets of their courtrooms.[31] In 1939, Congress, recognizing the burden of such tasks, created the Administrative Office of the United States Courts to provide administrative assistance for federal court judges.[32] Most state court judges, however, do not have the luxury of similar aid, though they are supported by a court staff.

SELECTION OF JUDGES

L08

In the federal court system, all judges are appointed by the president and confirmed by the Senate. It is difficult to make a general statement about how judges are selected in state court systems, however, because the procedure varies widely from state to state. In some states, such as New Jersey, all judges are appointed by the governor and confirmed by the upper chamber of the state

Docket The list of cases entered on a court's calendar and thus scheduled to be heard by the court.

legislature. In other states, such as Alabama, all judges are elected on a partisan ballot, meaning they must be affiliated with a political party and that affiliation is noted on the ballot. In still other states, such as Kentucky, all judges are elected on a nonpartisan ballot, where no party affiliation is required. Finally, some states, such as Missouri, select judges based on a subjective definition of merit. ■ Figure 8.5 shows the variety in the procedures for selecting judges.

The two key concepts in discussing methods of selecting judges are *independence* and *accountability*.[33] Those who feel that judicial fairness is dependent on the judges' belief that they will not be removed from office as the result of an unpopular ruling support methods of selection that include appointment.[34] In contrast, some observers feel that judges are "politicians in robes" who make policy decisions every time they step to the bench. Following this line of thought, judges should be held accountable to those who are affected by their decisions and therefore should be chosen through elections, as legislators are.[35] The most independent, and therefore least accountable, judges are those who hold lifetime appointments. They are influenced neither by the temptation to make popular decisions to impress voters nor by the need to follow the ideological or party line of the politicians who provided them with their posts.

Appointment of Judges   Article II, Section 2, of the Constitution authorizes the president to appoint the justices of the Supreme Court with the advice and consent of the Senate. Subsequent laws enacted by Congress provide that the same procedure is used for appointing judges to the lower federal courts as well.

On paper, the appointment process is relatively simple. After selecting a nominee, the president submits the name to the Senate for approval. The Senate Judiciary Committee then holds hearings and makes its recommendation to the Senate, where a majority vote is needed to confirm the nomination. In practice, the process does not always proceed smoothly. If the members of the minority party in the Senate consider the political views of a nominee too "extreme," they can block a vote on that nominee by instituting a *filibuster*—a procedural device in which senators refuse to give up the floor during debate. The filibuster has become a more common method of blocking judicial nominees in recent years. Whereas the Senate confirmed 92 percent of the federal circuit court nominees of President Jimmy Carter (1977–1981), President Bill Clinton (1991–1999) had only a 70 percent success rate, and, as of President George W. Bush's fifth year in office, only 69 percent of his nominees were confirmed.[36]

Three states, as well as Puerto Rico, employ similar selection methods, with the governor offering nominees for the approval of the state legislature. Judges in these states, as would be expected, serve longer terms than their counterparts in nonappointment judicial systems.[37] They are also regarded as products of *patronage*, as are

■ **Figure 8.5 Methods of Judicial Selection in the Fifty States**

Most states use a variety of methods to select their judges, with different procedures in different jurisdictions. The information presented here, therefore, identifies the predominant method in each state.

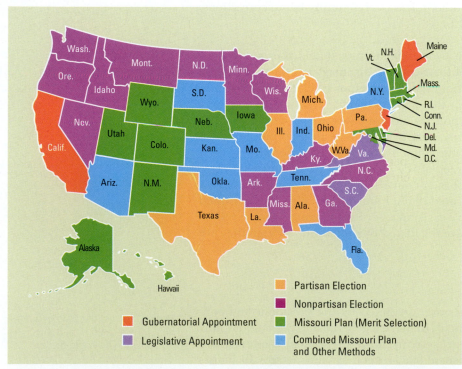

Partisan Election
Nonpartisan Election
Gubernatorial Appointment
Missouri Plan (Merit Selection)
Legislative Appointment
Combined Missouri Plan and Other Methods

Source: American Judicature Society.

judges appointed to federal positions by the president. In other words, appointed judges often obtain their positions because they belong to the same political party as the president (or governor, at the state level) and also have been active in supporting the candidates and ideology of the party in power. One of the most prevalent criticisms of appointing judges is that the system is based on "having friends in high places" rather than on merit.[38]

Election of Judges   Most states moved from an appointive to an elective system for judges in the mid-nineteenth century. The reasoning behind the move was to make judges more representative of the communities in which they served. Today, elections are the dominant method of selecting judges in twenty-one states. Of these, eight states rely primarily on **partisan elections,** in which the judicial candidate is openly supported and endorsed by a political party. The other thirteen states conduct mostly **nonpartisan elections,** in which the candidate is not affiliated with a political party.

Proponents of elections insist that unless judges are regularly forced to submit themselves to the will of the electorate, there is no way to hold them accountable for their actions. Critics, such as Judge Hans A. Linde of the Oregon Supreme Court, counter:

> "Judicial accountability" has a virtuous ring to it, until one asks, accountability for what? For judging fairly and impartially, for conscientious attention to law and facts, for staying awake, sober, and courteous to the parties, witnesses, and court personnel—in short, for performing according to the classic model of judging? Or does it mean accountability for decisions in controversial cases?[39]

The answer to Judge Linde's rhetorical question, at least in his mind, is that the public will hold a judge accountable for making popular rulings, not "correct" ones. In recent years, many elected judges have felt pressure to hand out harsher sentences to convicted criminals in order to appear "tough on crime."

Merit Selection   In 1940, Missouri became the first state to combine appointment and election in a single merit selection. When all jurisdiction levels are counted, twenty-four states and the District of Columbia now utilize the **Missouri Plan,** as merit selection has been labeled. The Missouri Plan consists of three basic steps:

- When a vacancy on the bench arises, candidates are nominated by a nonpartisan committee of citizens.
- The names of the three most qualified candidates are sent to the governor or executive of the state judicial system, and that person chooses who will be the judge.
- A year after the new judge has been installed, a "retention election" is held so that voters can decide whether the judge deserves to keep the post.[40]

The goal of the Missouri Plan is to eliminate partisan politics from the selection procedure, while at the same time giving the citizens a voice in the process. One noted drawback of the merit system—and indeed of any elective method of selecting judges—is that voters may lack knowledge not only of the issues of a judicial election, but of who the candidates are in the first place. A poll in Michigan found that nine out of ten voters could not identify any sitting state supreme court justice, and an equal number did not know how many justices served on the state's highest court or the length of their term in office.[41] (For a review of the selection processes, see *Mastering Concepts—The Selection of State and Federal Judges* on the next page.)

DIVERSITY ON THE BENCH

Another criticism of the Missouri Plan is that the members of the selection committees, who are mostly white, upper-class attorneys, nominate mostly white, upper-class attorneys.[42] Similar criticisms, however, have been leveled at the

> **Justice at Stake** is an organization dedicated to fair and impartial courts in the United States. Find its Web site by clicking on *Web Links* under *Chapter Resources* at **www.cjinaction.com**.

Partisan Elections Elections in which candidates are affiliated with and receive support from political parties; the candidates are listed in conjunction with their party on the ballot.

Nonpartisan Elections Elections in which candidates are presented on the ballot without any party affiliation.

Missouri Plan A method of selecting judges that combines appointment and election. Under the plan, the state governor or another government official selects judges from a group of nominees chosen by a nonpartisan committee. After a year on the bench, the judges face a popular election to determine whether the public wishes to keep them in office.

FEDERAL JUDGES	STATE JUDGES	
1. The president nominates a candidate to the U.S. Senate. 2. The Senate Judiciary Committee holds hearings concerning the qualifications of the candidate and makes its recommendation to the full Senate. 3. The full Senate votes to confirm or reject the president's nominee.	**Partisan Elections** • Judicial candidates, supported by and affiliated with political parties, place their names before the voters for consideration for a particular judicial seat. • The electorate votes to decide who will retain or gain the seat. **Executive Apointment** • The governor nominates a candidate to the state legislature. • The legislature votes to confirm or reject the governor's nominee.	**Nonpartisan Elections** • Judicial candidates, not supported by or affiliated with political parties, place their names before the voters for consideration for a particular judicial seat. • The electorate votes to decide who will retain or gain the seat. **Missouri Plan** • A nominating commission provides a list of worthy candidates. • An elected official (usually the governor) chooses from the list submitted by the commission. • A year later, a "retention election" is held to allow voters to decide whether the judge will stay on the bench.

federal judiciary and at judges in states that do not use the Missouri Plan. Indeed, of the nearly 900 federal judges, only about 10 percent are African American, 7 percent are Hispanic, and 1 percent are Asian American.[43] Of the 110 justices who have served on the United States Supreme Court, only two have been African American: Thurgood Marshall (1970–1991) and Clarence Thomas (1991–present).

State judiciaries show similar patterns. The discrepancy is particularly striking in areas with diverse populations. In California, where members of minority groups make up 56 percent of the population, 15 percent of the state court judges are Hispanic, African American, Asian, or Native American. In Texas, a 50 percent minority population translates to only 17 percent of state judgeships.[44] Women are also underrepresented on the bench. Only about one in five federal judges is a woman.[45] Only two women have been appointed to the Supreme Court: Sandra Day O'Connor (1981–2005) and Ruth Bader Ginsburg (1993–present).

THE IMPACT OF PAST DISCRIMINATION

Edward Chen, a federal magistrate judge for the Northern District of California, identifies a number of reasons for the low minority representation on the bench. Past discrimination in law schools has limited the pool of experienced minority attorneys who have the political ties, access to "old boy" networks, and career opportunities that lead to judgeships.[46] Only recently, as increased numbers of minorities have graduated from law schools, have rates of minority judges begun to creep slowly upward.

The Benefits of Diversity   Traditionally, efforts to diversify American judges by race, ethnicity, and gender have been met with resistance from those who argue that because judges must be impartial, it makes no difference whether a judge is black, Asian, Hispanic, or white.[47]

Sherrilyn A. Ifill of the University of Maryland School of Law rejects this argument. She believes that "diversity on the bench" can only enrich our judiciary by introducing a variety of voices and perspectives into what are perhaps the most powerful positions in the criminal justice system. By the same token, Ifill credits the

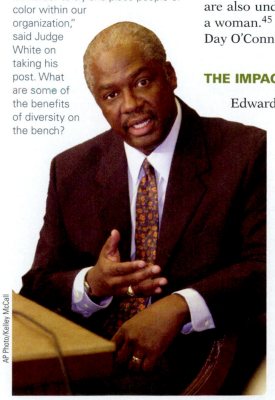

▼ Ronnie L. White became the first African American to hold the post of chief justice of the Missouri Supreme Court in 2003. "I truly believe that within the judicial department, we need to work a little bit harder to try and place people of color within our organization," said Judge White on taking his post. What are some of the benefits of diversity on the bench?

lack of diversity in many trial and appeals courts with a number of harmful consequences, such as more severe sentences for minority youths than for white youths who have committed similar crimes, disproportionate denial of bail to minority defendants, and the disproportionate imposition of the death penalty on minority defendants accused of killing white victims.[48]

JUDICIAL CONDUCT

The question of judicial accountability is further complicated by the gulf between what the public expects of judges and what the law expects of judges. The public wants judges to administer justice, while the law demands that they make sure proper legal procedures and rules have been followed. Sometimes, proper judicial conduct leads to what we would call injustice—setting a guilty person free. For example, a judge may know that a conviction is justified but overturn it anyway because tainted evidence contributed to the jury's finding. Consequently, for judges, proper behavior does not necessarily lead to justice, a concept many citizens have a difficult time accepting.

Judicial Ethics During the nineteenth century, the American public showed little enthusiasm for formal regulation of judicial conduct—as long as judges were competent, their ethics and honesty were of secondary concern.[49] It was not until the 1920s, when the entire criminal justice system was being reformed, that the American Bar Association (ABA) created the first code to regulate judicial behavior. The ABA's Canons of Judicial Ethics was updated in 1972 and 1990, and today the Model Code of Judicial Conduct forms the basis for judicial conduct codes in forty-seven states and the District of Columbia.[50]

The main goal of the Code of Judicial Conduct is to prevent conduct that would "tend to reduce public confidence in the integrity and impartiality of the judiciary."[51] Consequently, the judicial ethics codes disfavor not only obviously illegal and corrupt activities such as bribery but also personal conduct that is lawful yet gives the appearance of impropriety. Rhode Island, for example, saw two successive state supreme court chief justices resign because of **judicial misconduct**. The first, Chief Justice Thomas Fay, stepped down because of allegations that he used his position to help a relative and friends, and the second, Chief Justice Joseph Bevilacqua, was under investigation for associating with organized crime figures.

The Recusal Requirement To prevent any appearance of partiality in the courtroom, the Code of Judicial Conduct, federal law, and nearly all of the states require judges to *recuse*, or disqualify, themselves from court proceedings when any sort of prejudice or personal involvement would cloud their judgment In general, these **recusal** requirements apply to situations in which:

- The judge has a personal bias or prejudice concerning one of the parties to the trial.
- Prior to entering the judiciary, the judge served as a lawyer or worked as a government employee on the matter in controversy.
- The judge or a member of his or her family has a financial or other interest in the subject matter of the trial.
- The judge or a member of his or her family is likely to be called as a witness during the trial.[52]

Even though the parties to a court proceeding can request a recusal, the final decision is left to the discretion of the judge. The standard for this decision is rather vague—recusal must take place if a reasonable person knowing all the facts would think it necessary.[53] Furthermore, it is very difficult for attorneys to argue after the trial has ended that the judge *should* have opted for recusal. An appeals court will generally affirm a judge's decision not to recuse herself or himself unless

Judicial Misconduct A general term describing behavior that diminishes public confidence in the judiciary. This behavior includes obviously illegal acts, such as bribery, and conduct that gives the appearance of impropriety, such as consorting with known felons.

Recusal The withdrawal of a judge from legal proceedings when her or his impartiality might reasonably be questioned.

I began my legal career as a law clerk in the Delaware Court of Chancery. Observing many good trial lawyers that year, I decided I would like to do trial practice, or litigation as it's called. My first position was as a deputy attorney general in Delaware's Department of Justice. There I prosecuted criminal cases as well as defending the state in civil actions. I left the Justice Department and became Delaware's chief deputy public defender. In that role, I defended serious criminal charges, including murder. After a short time in private law practice I was elected Delaware Attorney General in 1978. After returning to private practice, I was appointed by the governor to my current position as a superior court judge. I was reappointed to a second twelve-year term in 1996.

JUDICIAL WORK As a superior court judge, I try both civil and criminal cases as well as hear appeals from administrative boards and agencies. I am currently assigned to do primarily criminal work. The large majority of all criminal cases are resolved by pleas so a large part of my work is taking those pleas, assuring that the defendant knows what he or she is doing, and then sentencing the defendant. In superior court these are usually serious felony charges. In those cases where there is no plea, it is my job to ensure that the defendant receives a fair trial. That means I rule on evidence issues and instruct the jury as to the law to be applied in the case. In some cases the jury will be waived, and then I must decide the facts as well as the law.

Our criminal justice system depends on the lawyers and the judge performing their different functions fairly and effectively. Thus, the responsibilities of each participant are great. Our system only works if each participant actively and aggressively fulfills the duties of his or her office.

Courtesy R. S. Gebelein

it was an obvious abuse of discretion that affected the outcome of the trial.[54] (To see why some judges have come under criticism for their recusal decisions, see the feature *A Question of Ethics—Getting Personal.*)

The Removal of Judges The ABA's Code of Judicial Conduct is not a binding document; it merely offers a model of judicial ethics. As the states adopted aspects of the code, however, they also developed procedures for removing those guilty of judicial misconduct from office. Nearly every state has a *judicial conduct commission*, which consists of lawyers, judges, and other prominent citizens and is often a branch of the state's highest court. This commission investigates charges of judicial misconduct and may recommend removal if warranted by the circumstances. The final decision to discipline a judge must generally be made by the state supreme court.[55]

On average, about ten state judges are removed from office each year. Recent examples include St. Joseph County (Michigan) Circuit Judge James Noecker, who lost his seat after driving his car into the side of a convenience store while intoxicated, fleeing the scene, and lying to investigators about the accident. Such transgressions, however deplorable, would be unlikely to result in a similar outcome if committed by a federal judge. Appointed under Article II of the U.S. Constitution, federal judges can be removed from office only if found guilty of "Treason, Bribery, or other high Crimes and Misdemeanors." Before a federal judge can be **impeached,** the U.S. House of Representatives must be presented with specific charges of misconduct and vote on whether these charges merit further action. If the vote passes in the House by a simple majority (more than 50 percent), the U.S. Senate—presided over by the chief justice of the United States Supreme Court—holds a trial on the matter. At the conclusion of this trial, a two-thirds majority vote is required in the Senate for the removal of a federal judge.

Impeach To charge a public official with misconduct. As authorized by Article I of the Constitution, the House of Representatives votes on impeachment; if the measure passes, the matter is sent to the Senate for a vote to remove the president, vice president, or civil officers (such as federal judges) of the United States.

THE CASE OF THE SERIAL KILLER The seriousness and reality of those duties came home to me several years ago when I was assigned to try the case of Delaware's first serial killer. The case was an extremely high profile case that resulted in almost daily headlines. It was not an easy case in that there were many difficult evidence issues. These included the attempt to use DNA identification for the first time in Delaware as well as an evidence suppression issue involving the key evidence that broke the case. Luckily, both the prosecutors and the defense lawyers were excellent and did their jobs professionally. After a long trial and lengthy jury deliberations, the defendant was convicted of two counts of first degree murder. The jury could not reach a verdict on the third count of murder. A penalty trial was held, and the jury could not reach a unanimous recommendation of death, thereby causing a life sentence to be imposed by law.

But this was not the end of the case, as evidence was developed during the trial to link the defendant directly to a fourth murder. He was reindicted for that murder as well as the undecided murder from the first trial. The defendant waived a jury trial for this second case, and I had to try the case as to both facts and law. After conviction, I then had to hear the penalty phase. Nothing in my training prepared me to make the solitary decision that his crimes demanded the death penalty. Nothing really can prepare you to announce in front of the defendant's family, mother, wife, and child that he is to die by lethal injection.

This one hard decision, this one hard act makes it crystal clear why it is absolutely essential that good, bright, and ethical people participate as lawyers and judges in our criminal justice system. It is critical that every defendant be assured a fair trial, and that means a good, energetic effective defense lawyer; an ethical, effective prosecutor; and a fair judge. These are not easy jobs, but if they are done right, you can feel satisfaction that you are doing your part to ensure justice in America.

Go to the **Careers in Criminal Justice Interactive CD** for more profiles in the field of criminal justice.

This disciplinary action is extremely rare: only eleven federal judges have been impeached and convicted in the nation's history. In 1989, federal judges Alcee Hastings and Walter Nixon were both removed from office—Hastings for accepting a $150,000 bribe and lying to a grand jury and Nixon for lying to a grand jury. More recently, in 1993, Judge Robert Collins resigned before he could be impeached for receiving a $100,000 bribe from a marijuana smuggler.

A Question of Ethics Getting Personal

THE SITUATION Sixteen-year-old Terra, who lives in Memphis, wants to get an abortion. Under Tennessee law, a minor in Terra's situation has two options: (1) she must obtain permission from her parents, or (2) she must obtain permission from a judge. Terra does not want her parents to know that she is pregnant, so she goes to the courthouse and appears before Judge McCord of the Shelby County District Court. Because of his religious beliefs, Judge McCord believes that "taking the life of an innocent human being is contrary to the moral order."

THE ETHICAL DILEMMA The Code of Judicial Conduct states that a judge who has a "personal bias against a party" must recuse herself or himself. Judge McCord's personal bias in Terra's case is clear: under no condition can he in good conscience allow any minor to proceed with an abortion.

WHAT IS THE SOLUTION? If a judge's decision is based on religious beliefs rather than the facts of the case, then that judge is not acting impartially. Nevertheless, religious beliefs generally are not considered to be the kind of personal bias that requires recusal. As a panel of judicial ethics experts told the Tennessee Supreme Court, "Unwillingness to follow the law is not a legitimate ground for recusal." What should a judge do if his or her moral or religious beliefs conflict with the law? Why might participants in the proceedings want a judge to recuse himself or herself in these situations? In which areas of criminal law might a judge's moral or religious beliefs be an issue?

Self Check Fill in the Blanks

In the federal court system, judges are appointed by the _____ and confirmed by the _____. In state court systems, however, the selection process varies. Some states mirror the federal system, with the _____ making judicial appointments with the approval of the legislature. Others conduct either _____ elections, in which political parties openly support judicial candidates, or _____ elections, in which the candidate is not affiliated with any political group. Finally, almost half of the states rely on _____ selection, which combines appointment and election. Federal judges can be removed only through the process of _____, while state judges face removal if they engage in serious _____. Check your answers on page 270.

The Courtroom Work Group

Television dramas often depict the courtroom as a battlefield, with prosecutors and defense attorneys spitting fire at each other over the loud and insistent protestations of a frustrated judge. Consequently, many people are somewhat disappointed when they witness a real courtroom at work. Rarely does anyone raise his or her voice, and the courtroom professionals appear—to a great extent—to be cooperating with each other. In Chapter 6, we discussed the existence of a police subculture, based on the shared values of law enforcement agents. A courtroom subculture exists as well, centered on the **courtroom work group.** The most important feature of any work group is that it is a *cooperative* unit, whose members establish shared values and methods that help the group efficiently reach its goals. Though cooperation is not a concept usually associated with criminal courts, it is in fact crucial to the adjudication process.[56]

MEMBERS OF THE COURTROOM WORK GROUP

The courtroom work group is made up of those individuals who are involved with
L09 the defendant from the time she or he is arrested until sentencing. The most prominent members are the judge, the prosecutor, and the defense attorney (the latter two will be discussed in detail in the next chapter). Three other court participants complete the work group:

1. The *bailiff of the court* is responsible for maintaining security and order in the judge's chambers and the courtroom. Bailiffs lead the defendant in and out of the courtroom and attend to the needs of the jurors during the trial. A bailiff, often a member of the local sheriff's department but sometimes an employee of the court, also delivers summonses in some jurisdictions.
2. The *clerk of the court* has an exhausting list of responsibilities. Any plea, motion, or other matter to be acted on by the judge must go through the clerk. The large amount of paperwork generated during a trial, including transcripts, photographs, evidence, and any other records, is maintained by the clerk. The clerk also issues subpoenas for jury duty and coordinates the jury selection process. In the federal court system, judges select clerks, while state clerks are either appointed or, in nearly a third of the states, elected.
3. *Court reporters* record every word that is said during the course of the trial. They also record any *depositions*, or pretrial question-and-answer sessions in which a party or a witness answers an attorney's questions under oath.

FORMATION OF THE COURTROOM WORK GROUP

The premise of the work group is based on constant interaction that fosters relationships among the members. As legal scholar David W. Neubauer describes:

Courtroom Work Group The social organization consisting of the judge, prosecutor, defense attorney, and other court workers. The relationships among these persons have a far-reaching impact on the day-to-day operations of any court.

Every day, the same group of courthouse regulars assembles in the same courtroom, sits or stands in the same places, and performs the same tasks as the day before. The types of defendants and the nature of the crimes they are accused of committing also remain constant. Only the names of the victim, witnesses, and defendants are different.[57]

After a period of time, the members of a courtroom work group learn how the others operate. The work group establishes patterns of behavior and norms, and cooperation allows the adjudication process to function informally and smoothly.[58] In some cases, the members of the work group may even form personal relationships, which only strengthen the courtroom culture.

One way in which the courtroom work group differs from a traditional work group at a company such as Microsoft Corporation is that each member answers to a different sponsoring organization. Although the judge has ultimate authority over a courtroom, he or she is not the "boss" of the attorneys. The prosecutor is hired by the district attorney's office; the defense attorney by a private individual or the public defender's office; the judge by the court system itself.

Each member of the work group is under pressure from his or her sponsoring organization to carry out certain tasks.[59] A judge, for example, needs to take care of the cases on her or his docket, or else a backlog will accumulate. A defense attorney—under constant pressure to attain the best results—usually has many clients and often cannot spend too much time on a single case. A prosecutor must win convictions. Within the courtroom work group, each member relies on the others to help alleviate these pressures. If a defense attorney disrupts the trial routine with unnecessary motions or unreasonably rejects sentence bargains for his or her clients, all members of the work group become less efficient in performing their roles. (See ■ Figure 8.6 on the following page for an overview of the relationships among the main participants in the courtroom work group.)

▲ A stenotype machine, such as the one shown in use here, allows court reporters to press more than one key at a time to keep up with the often fast-paced action of the courtroom. Why do you think it is necessary for court reporters to produce written records of criminal trials?

THE JUDGE IN THE COURTROOM WORK GROUP

The judge is the dominant figure in the courtroom and therefore exerts the most influence over the values and norms of the work group. A judge who runs a "tight ship" follows procedure and restricts the freedom of attorneys to deviate from regulations, while a *laissez-faire* judge allows more leeway to members of the work group. A judge's personal philosophy also affects the court proceedings. If a judge has a reputation for being "tough on crime," both prosecutors and defense attorneys will alter their strategies accordingly. In fact, a lawyer may be able to manipulate the system to "shop" for a judge whose philosophy best fits the attorney's goals in a particular case.[60] If a lawyer is caught trying to influence the assignment of judges, however, she or he is said to be "corrupting judicial independence" and may face legal proceedings.

"A judge is not supposed to know anything about the facts . . . until they have been presented in evidence and explained to him at least three times."

—*Lord Chief Justice Parker, British judge (1961)*

Although preeminent in the work group, a judge must still rely on other members of the group. To a certain extent, the judge is the least informed member of the trio; like a juror, the judge learns the facts of the case as they are presented by the attorneys. If the attorneys do not properly present the facts, then the judge is hampered in making rulings. Furthermore, if a judge deviates from the norms of the work group—by, for example, refusing to grant continuances—the other members of the work group can "discipline" the judge. Defense attorneys and prosecutors can request further continuances, fail to produce witnesses in a timely matter, and slow down the proceeding through a general lack of preparedness. The delays

■ **Figure 8.6** The Courtroom Work Group and Incentives to Cooperate

The major figures of the courtoom work group—judges, prosecutors, and defense attorneys—benefit from a certain degree of cooperation. As you can see, one of the primary considerations of each of the three principals is to dispose of cases as quickly as possible.

Defense Attorney's obligations to the Judge
- Be prepared
- Negotiate pleas when justified
- Refrain from engaging in time-consuming arguments with prosecutor
- Refrain from filing time-consuming motions

Judge's obligation to the Defense Attorney
- Grant continuances when extra time is needed to get client to pay fees

Judge's obligation to the Prosecutor
- Grant continuances when extra time is needed to prepare case

Prosecutor's obligations to the Judge
- Be prepared
- Negotiate pleas when justified
- Refrain from engaging in time-consuming arguments with defense attorney

JUDGE

Official Responsibility: To make sure that proper legal procedure is followed before, during, and after a trial

Job Pressures: Large caseloads, little time; the administrative burden of managing case dockets

DEFENSE ATTORNEY

Official Responsibility: To advocate for the client's innocence

Job Pressures: Earning a living by having a large number of clients; get best outcome for client with limited resources

PROSECUTOR

Official Responsibility: To convict those guilty of crimes against society

Job Pressures: More cases than time to dispose of all of them; satisfy public expectations that criminals will be punished

Defense Attorney's obligations to the Prosecutor
- Persuade clients to accept "reasonable" plea bargains
- Negotiate a sentence that is favorable to client

Prosecutor's obligations to the Defense Attorney
- Provide access to witnesses, police reports, and other information that is unavailable due to limited resources
- Be accommodating when extra time is needed to prepare case

caused by such acts can ruin a judge's calendar—especially in large courts—and bring pressure from the judge's superiors.

ASSEMBLY-LINE JUSTICE

In discussing the goals of the courtroom work group, several general concepts figure prominently—efficiency, cooperation, rapidity, and socialization. One aim of the work group, however, is glaring in its absence: justice. One of the main criticisms of the American court system is that it has sacrificed the goal of justice for efficiency. Some observers claim that only the wealthiest can afford to receive justice as promised by the Constitution, while the rest of society is left with a watered-down version of *assembly-line justice*.

The Impact of Excessive Caseloads Given the caseloads that most courts face, some degree of assembly-line justice seems inevitable. A quick survey of the nation's court system provides clear examples of the extent of the problem and its consequences. Approximately two out of every three state courts are consistently behind on their dockets. In Clark County, Nevada, 83,271 cases were filed in one district court in 2006, meaning that each of the court's judges handled 2,523 cases. The county's municipal judges were even busier that year, overseeing an average of 5,277 cases.[61] In Dallas, lack of available courtrooms means that defendants charged with murder can spend up to five years free on bail waiting for a jury trial. On August 31, 2006, one such murder suspect whose day in court had been delayed twenty-three months shot a woman he had taken hostage, a Dallas police officer trying to rescue her, and finally, and fatally, himself.[62]

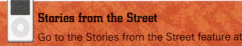

Stories from the Street

Go to the Stories from the Street feature at **www.cjinaction.com** to hear Larry Gaines tell insightful stories related to this chapter and his experiences in the field.

The federal court system faces many of the same problems. Criminal caseloads in U.S. district courts quadrupled between 1980 and 2005, spurred by a nearly 500 percent increase in drug cases.[63] The lack of resources to deal with excessive caseloads is generally recognized as one of the most critical issues facing both federal and state law enforcement agencies and courtrooms.[64]

The Courtroom Work Group and Overloaded Courts A judge's worth is increasingly measured by her or his ability to keep the "assembly line" of cases moving, rather than by the quality of her or his judicial work. Consequently, the judicial process is accused of being "careless and haphazard" and of routinely supporting decisions made on the basis of incomplete information. Though definitive statistics on the subject have never been adequately gathered, many observers feel that assembly-line justice affects the actions of others in the criminal justice system as well:

LO10

- Beyond filling out a crime report, police officers often do not investigate misdemeanors and less serious felonies unless the offender was caught in the act.
- Police officers often are encouraged to obtain confessions—using whatever means necessary—from defendants, rather than find incriminating evidence, because a confession is more likely to lead to conviction.
- Prosecutors often press charges for misdemeanors and nonviolent felonies only when the case is a "slam dunk"—that is, when conviction is certain.
- To wrap up cases quickly, prosecutors generally bargain reduced sentences for guilty verdicts; as a result, criminals spend less time in prison than is in society's best interests.[65]

If the public is under the impression that police, judges, and lawyers are more interested in speed than in justice, the pressure of caseloads may also lead to loss of respect for the criminal justice system as a whole.

Self Check Fill in the Blanks

The three most prominent members of the courtroom work group are the _____, the _____, and the _____. As a rule, these professionals must _____ with each other to ensure the smooth functioning of the court system. A condition known as _____ exists when courtroom work groups sacrifice justice for the sake of efficiency. Check your answers on page 270.

Criminal Justice in Action

THE INTERNATIONAL CRIMINAL COURT

The United States has a long history of supporting international prosecution of the most heinous crimes. In 1946, the United States was the guiding force behind the Nuremberg Trials, which established that individuals could be convicted for war crimes and crimes against humanity. (The trials resulted in Nazi leaders being found guilty of the mass murder of millions of Jews.) More recently, the United States has provided funds to international tribunals set up to punish the instigators of genocide (the deliberate extermination of a national, racial, or cultural group) in Rwanda and the Balkans. Nevertheless, when the International Criminal Court (ICC)—the subject of this *Criminal Justice in Action* feature—was created in 2002, the United States was nowhere to be found.

JURISDICTIONAL ISSUES

The problem, for American politicians and military leaders, has to do with jurisdiction. The ICC assumes jurisdiction over persons responsible for acts of genocide, crimes against humanity, and war crimes. This jurisdiction applies when (1) the criminal act takes place in a nation that has signed the treaty that created the ICC or (2) the individual responsible for the criminal act is a citizen of one of these nations.[66] An independent prosecutor has the power to initiate investigations into those acts that fall under the jurisdiction of the ICC at his or her own discretion.

In theory, this means that the independent prosecutor could accuse any American, from a high-ranking government official to a soldier in the field, of committing a war crime as long as the act took place in a country that is a signatory to the ICC. Because the United States has military operations in dozens of countries at any one time, the administration of President George W. Bush worried that Americans would be easy targets for frivolous accusations. Therefore, the administration demanded that it be given veto power over any ICC prosecutions involving U.S. citizens. When the other member countries refused to grant this proviso, the United States refused to support the venture.[67]

The Case for U.S. Involvement in the International Criminal Court

- As of April 2007, 145 countries, including most of the United States' allies, have signed the treaty that created the ICC. By not participating, the United States has damaged its reputation in the international community.

- Without U.S. financial and military backing, the ICC will be much less effective at protecting human rights around the globe.

- The chances of an American citizen being prosecuted in the ICC are extremely remote. According to its rules, the ICC will prosecute a case only if the accused's home government is unable or unwilling to do so itself.[68]

The Case against U.S. Involvement in the International Criminal Court

- Allowing an international court to have jurisdiction over American citizens without the permission of the U.S. government would be contrary to our legal principles.

- The ICC does not provide for a trial by jury and does not protect against unreasonable searches and seizures, as guaranteed to any American charged with committing a crime by our Bill of Rights.[69]

- Because of the unpopularity of American military operations, U.S. citizens would be likely targets for politically motivated prosecutions before the ICC.

Your Opinion—Writing Assignment

According to an Afghan human rights group, in March 2007 U.S. Marines reacted to a bomb ambush in the Nangarhar province of Afghanistan by going on a rampage that left twelve civilians dead, including a sixteen-year-old girl and an infant. U.S. officials are investigating the incident, and their findings could lead to criminal charges in military court.[70]

This is precisely the sort of incident that would fall under the jurisdiction of the ICC as a war crime. If the United States belonged to the ICC, how likely do you think it is that the Marines would wind up before the

Courtesy ICC

international court? How would the U.S. public react to seeing American soldiers tried by non-U.S. prosecutors and judges? What is your opinion of this prospect, and how does that influence your feelings concerning future U.S. acceptance of the ICC? Before responding, you can review our discussions in this chapter concerning

- The legitimacy of a court (page 243).
- Jurisdiction (pages 245–248).
- Judicial ethics and recusal (pages 261–262).

Your answer should take at least three full paragraphs.

L01 **Define and contrast the four functions of the courts.** The four functions are (a) due process, (b) crime control, (c) rehabilitation, and (d) bureaucratic. The most obvious contrast is between the due process and crime control functions. The former is mainly concerned with the procedural rules that allow each accused individual to have a "fair chance" against the government in a criminal proceeding. For crime control, the courts are supposed to impose enough "pain" on convicted criminals to deter criminal behavior. For the rehabilitation function, the courts serve as "doctors" who dispense "treatment." In their bureaucratic function, courts are more concerned with speed and efficiency.

L02 **Define *jurisdiction* and contrast geographic and subject-matter jurisdiction.** Jurisdiction relates to the power of a court to hear a particular case. Courts are typically limited in geographic jurisdiction—for example, to a particular state. Some courts are restricted in subject matter, such as a small claims court, which can hear only cases involving civil matters under a certain amount.

L03 **Explain the difference between trial and appellate courts.** Trial courts are courts of the first instance, where a case is first heard. Appellate courts review the proceedings of a lower court. Appellate courts do not have juries.

L04 **Outline the several levels of a typical state court system.** (a) At the lowest level are courts of limited jurisdiction, (b) next are trial courts of general jurisdiction, (c) then appellate courts, and (d) finally, the state's highest court.

L05 **Outline the federal court system.** (a) At the lowest level are the U.S. district courts in which trials are held, as well as various minor federal courts of limited jurisdiction; (b) next are the U.S. courts of appeals, otherwise known as circuit courts of appeal; and (c) finally, the United States Supreme Court.

L06 **Explain briefly how a case is brought to the Supreme Court.** Cases decided in U.S. courts of appeals, as well as cases decided in the highest state courts (when federal questions arise), can be appealed to the Supreme Court. If at least four justices approve of a case filed with the Supreme Court, the Court will issue a writ of *certiorari*, ordering the lower court to send the Supreme Court the record of the case for review.

L07 **List the actions that a judge might take prior to an actual trial.** Trial judges may do the following before an actual trial: (a) issue search or arrest warrants, (b) authorize electronic surveillance of a suspect, (c) order the temporary incarceration of a suspect, (d) decide whether a suspect should be released on bail and the amount of that bail, (e) accept or reject pretrial motions by prosecutors and defense attorneys, and (f) accept or reject a plea bargain.

L08 **Explain the difference between the selection of judges at the state level and at the federal level.** The president nominates all judges at the federal level, and the Senate must approve the nominations. A similar procedure is used in some states. In other states, all judges are elected on a partisan ballot or on a nonpartisan ballot. Some states use merit selection, or the Missouri Plan, in which a citizen committee nominates judicial candidates, the governor or executive of the state judicial system chooses among the top three nominees, and a year later a "retention election" is held.

L09 **List and describe the members of the courtroom work group.** (a) The judge; (b) the prosecutor, who brings charges in the name of the people (the state) against the accused; (c) the defense attorney; (d) the bailiff, who is responsible for maintaining security and order in the judge's chambers and the courtroom; (e) the clerk, who accepts all pleas, motions, and other matters to be acted on by the judge; and (f) court reporters, who record what is said during a trial as well as at depositions.

L10 **Explain the consequences of excessive caseloads.** Excessive caseloads have led to assembly-line justice. Such a criminal justice system increases the possibility that (a) police officers will not investigate crimes unless the offender was caught in the act; (b) officers will seek only confessions, rather than spending time finding incriminating evidence; (c) prosecutors will press charges in criminal cases only when conviction is certain; and (d) plea bargaining will be common.

Key Terms

appellate courts 248
concurrent jurisdiction 245
concurring opinions 255
courtroom work group 264
dissenting opinions 255
docket 257
dual court system 249
extradition 246

impeach 262
judicial misconduct 261
judicial review 254
jurisdiction 245
magistrate 251
Missouri Plan 259
nonpartisan elections 259
opinions 248

oral arguments 255
partisan elections 259
recusal 261
rule of four 254
specialty courts 251
trial courts 248
writ of *certiorari* 254

Questions for Critical Analysis

1. "The primary adversarial relationship in the courts is not between the plaintiff (prosecutor, or state) and defendant, but rather between the ideal of justice and the reality of bureaucratic limitations." Explain why you agree or disagree with this statement.

2. Which court has virtually unlimited geographic and subject-matter jurisdiction? Why is this so?

3. In the late 1990s, American citizen John Walker Lindh converted to Islam and traveled to the Middle East to engage in terrorist training alongside Taliban and al Qaeda operatives. In 2002, U.S. troops captured Lindh in Afghanistan and brought him back to the United States to face charges for aiding terrorist organizations and conspiring to kill Americans. Why do American courts have jurisdiction over Lindh?

4. How did we end up with a dual court system?

5. Federal judges and justices typically hold office for many years. Why is this so?

6. What effect does the Supreme Court's refusal to issue a writ of *certiorari* have on lower courts' decisions?

7. What are some of the various functions that a judge undertakes during a trial? What function does a judge assume when presiding over a trial that is not a jury trial?

8. Many states, even those using the merit system, elect their judges. What is the main drawback of using elections to select or maintain judges in office?

9. How does a courtroom work group differ from the management of a corporation?

Maximize Your Best Possible Outcome for Chapter 8

1. **Maximize Your Best Chance for Getting a Good Grade on the Exam.** ThomsonNOW Personalized Study is a diagnostic study tool containing valuable text-specific resources—and because you focus on just what you don't know, you learn more in less time to get a better grade. How do you get ThomsonNOW? If your textbook does not include an access code card, go to **thomsonedu.com** to get ThomsonNOW before your next exam!

2. **Get the Most Out of Your Textbook** by going to the book companion Web site at **www.cjinaction.com** to access one of the tutorial quizzes, use the flash cards to master key terms, and check out the many other study aids you'll find there. Under chapter resources you will also be able to access the Stories from the Street feature and Web links mentioned in the textbook.

3. **Learn about Potential Criminal Justice Careers** discussed in this chapter by exploring careers online at **www.cjinaction.com.** You will find career descriptions and information about job requirements, training, salary and benefits, and the application process. You can also watch video profiles featuring criminal justice professionals.

Notes

1. Duff Wilson and Jonathan D. Glater, "Files from Duke Rape Case Give Details but No Answers," *New York Times* (August 25, 2006), A1.
2. Quoted in David Zucchino, "All Charges Dropped in Duke Athletes' Sex Case," *Los Angeles Times* (April 12, 2007), A1.
3. Roscoe Pound, "The Administration of Justice in American Cities," *Harvard Law Review* 12 (1912).
4. Russell Wheeler and Howard Whitcomb, *Judicial Administration: Text and Readings* (Englewood Cliffs, NJ: Prentice Hall, 1977), 3.
5. Herbert Packer, *The Limits of the Criminal Sanction* (Stanford, CA: Stanford University Press, 1968), 154–173.
6. Herbert Packer, "The Courts, the Police and the Rest of Us," *Criminal Law, Criminology & Political Science* 57 (1966), 238–239.
7. Larry J. Siegel, *Criminology: Instructor's Manual,* 6th ed. (Belmont, CA: West/Wadsworth Publishing Co., 1998), 440.
8. Gerald F. Velman, "Federal Sentencing Guidelines: A Cure Worse than the Disease," *American Criminal Law Review* 29 (Spring 1992), 904.
9. *Malloy v. Hogan*, 378 U.S. 1, 84 (1964).
10. Stephanie Martz, "Verbatim," *Champion* (July 2006), 42.
11. "State, Feds Should Help Pay Costs of Sniper Trials," *Virginian-Pilot & Ledger Star* (September 30, 2002), B8.

12. Wayne R. LaFave, "Section 4.6. Multiple Jurisdiction and Multiple Prosecution," *Substantive Criminal Law*, 2d ed. (C.J.S. Criminal Section 254), 2007.
13. William Wan, "Snipers to Be Tried in Maryland," *Baltimore Sun* (May 11, 2005), 1A.
14. Jerry Seper, "Drug Gang Revolt Feared in Mexico," *Washington Times* (January 28, 2007), A2.
15. *Strassheim v. Daily*, 221 U.S. 280 (1911).
16. *Jones v. United States*, 137 U.S. 202 (1890).
17. Pub. L. No. 108-21, 117 Stat. 650 (2003).
18. 18 U.S.C. Section 2423(c) (2005).
19. David W. Neubauer, *America's Courts and the Criminal Justice System*, 5th ed. (Belmont, CA: Wadsworth Publishing Co., 1996), 41.
20. Alexander Hamilton, *Federalist Paper* No. 78 in Clinton Rossier, ed., *The Federalist Papers* (New York: New American Library, 1961), 467–470.
21. G. Edward White, *History of the Supreme Court*, vols. 3–4: *The Marshall Court and Cultural Change* (New York: Oxford University Press, 1988), 157–200.
22. 372 U.S. 335 (1963).
23. 384 U.S. 436 (1966).
24. 408 U.S. 238 (1972).
25. 428 U.S. 153 (1976).
26. 491 U.S. 397 (1989).
27. 496 U.S. 310 (1990).
28. Mark Alan Ozimek, "The Case for a More Workable Standard in Death Penalty Jurisprudence: *Atkins v. Virginia* and Categorical Exemptions under the Imprudent 'Evolving Standards of Decency' Doctrine," *University of Toledo Law Review* (Spring 2003), 651.
29. *Singleton v. Commissioner of Internal Revenue*, 439 U.S. 940 (1978).
30. Barry R. Schaller, *A Vision of American Law: Judging Law, Literature, and the Stories We Tell* (Westport, CT: Praeger, 1997).
31. Harlington Wood, Jr., "Judiciary Reform: Recent Improvements in Federal Judicial Administration," *American University Law Review* 44 (June 1995), 1557.
32. Pub. L. No. 76-299, 53 Stat. 1223, codified as amended at 28 U.S.C. Sections 601–610 (1988 & Supp. V 1993).
33. Patrick Emery Longan, "Judicial Professionalism in a New Era of Judicial Selection," *Mercer Law Review* (Spring 2005), 913.
34. Andrew F. Hanssen, "Learning about Judicial Independence: Institutional Change in the State Courts," *Journal of Legal Studies* (2004), 431–474.
35. Brian P. Anderson, "Judicial Elections in West Virginia," *West Virginia Law Review* (Fall 2004), 243.
36. Bob Deans, "Senate Showdown: Nominee Fights May Diminish Faith in Courts," *Atlanta Journal-Constitution* (May 19, 2005), A12.
37. Daniel R. Deja, "How Judges Are Selected: A Survey of the Judicial Selection Process in the United States," *Michigan Bar Journal* 75 (September 1996), 904.
38. Edmund V. Ludwig, "Another Case against the Election of Trial Judges," *Pennsylvania Lawyer* 19 (May/June 1997), 33.
39. Quoted in Daniel Burke, "Code of Judicial Conduct Canon 7B(1)(c): Toward the Proper Regulation of Speech in Judicial Campaigns," *Georgetown Journal of Legal Ethics* 81 (Summer 1993), 181.
40. James E. Lozier, "The Missouri Plan a.k.a. Merit Selection Is the Best Solution for Selecting Michigan's Judges," *Michigan Bar Journal* 75 (September 1996), 918.
41. William Ballenger, "In Judicial Wilderness, Even Brickley's Not Safe," *Michigan Politics* 28 (1996), 1–3.
42. Richard A. Watson and Rondal G. Downing, *The Politics of the Bench and Bar: Judicial Selection under the Missouri Nonpartisan Court Plan* (New York: John Wiley & Sons, 1969).
43. "Demographic Overview of the Federal Judiciary," Alliance for Justice, at **www.afj.org/judicial/judicial_selection_resources/selection_database/byCourtRaceGender.asp**.
44. American Bar Association, "National Database on Judicial Diversity in State Courts," at **www.abanet.org/judind/diversity/national.html**.
45. "Demographic Overview of the Federal Judiciary."
46. Edward M. Chen, "The Judiciary, Diversity, and Justice for All," *California Law Review* (July 2003), 1109.
47. Theresa B. Beiner, "The Elusive (but Worthwhile) Quest for a Diverse Bench in the New Millennium," *University of California at Davis Law Review* (February 2003), 599.
48. Sherrilyn A. Ifill, "Racial Diversity on the Bench: Beyond Role Models and Public Confidence," *Washington and Lee Law Review* (Spring 2000), 405.
49. Shirley S. Abrahamson, *Foreword to Judicial Conduct and Ethics* (Charlottesville, VA: Michie Co., 1990), vi–vii.
50. American Bar Association, *Model Code of Judicial Conduct* (Chicago: ABA, August 1990).
51. ABA Commission on Ethics and Professional Responsibility, Informal Opinion 1468 (1981).
52. 28 U.S.C.A. Sections 445(a), (b), and (c).
53. 28 U.S.C.A. Section 455(a).
54. *United States v. Howard*, 218 F.3d 556 (6th Cir. 2000).
55. John Gardiner, "Preventing Judicial Misconduct: Defining the Role of Conduct Organizations," *Judicature* 70 (1986), 113–121.
56. Roy B. Fleming, Peter F. Nardulli, and James Eisenstein, *The Craft of Justice: Politics and Work in Criminal Court Communities* (Philadelphia: University of Pennsylvania Press, 1992).
57. Neubauer, 41.
58. Alissa P. Worden, "The Judge's Role in Plea Bargaining: An Analysis of Judges' Agreement with Prosecutors' Sentencing Recommendations," *Justice Quarterly* 10 (1995), 257–278.
59. Neubauer, 72.
60. Kimberly Jade Norwood, "Shopping for Venue: The Need for More Limits," *University of Miami Law Review* 50 (1996), 295–298.
61. Sam Skolnik, "Looking in on: The Courts," *Las Vegas Sun* (January 6, 2007), A1.
62. Robert Tharp and Jason Trahan, "Gunman Wounds Officer, Hostage at Dallas Hotel: Shooter Kills Himself," *Dallas Morning News* (August 31, 2006), 1A.
63. *Sourcebook of Criminal Justice Statistics Online*, 2007, at **www.albany.edu/sourcebook/pdf/t592005.pdf and www.albany.edu/sourcebook/pdf/t5372005.pdf**.
64. *2004 Annual Report to the Director* (Washington, D.C.: The Administrative Office of the U.S. Courts, 2005), 3.
65. Malcolm Feeley, *Felony Arrests: Their Prosecutions and Disposition in New York Courts* (New York: Vera Institute, 1981), xii.
66. "Rome Statute of the International Criminal Court," U.N. Doc. A/CONF.183/9, 37 I.L.M. 999, July 17, 1998, available at **www.un.org/law/icc/statute/romefra.htm**.
67. Remigius Chibueze, "United States Objections to the International Criminal Court: A Paradox of 'Operation Enduring Freedom,'" *Annual Survey of International and Comparative Law* (2003), 19–31.
68. "Rome Statute of the International Criminal Court," *Article* 17(1)(a)-(b).
69. David M. Baronoff, "Unbalance of Powers: The International Criminal Court's Potential to Upset the Founders' Checks and Balances," *University of Pennsylvania Journal of Constitutional Law* (May 2002), 800, 804.
70. Carlotta Gall, "Report Faults Marine Attack," *Albany (New York) Times Union* (April 15, 2007), A1.

Pretrial Procedures:

The Adversary System in Action

Chapter outline

- The Prosecution
- The Defense Attorney
- Truth, Victory, and the Adversary System
- Pretrial Detention
- Establishing Probable Cause
- The Prosecutorial Screening Process
- Pleading Guilty
- Going to Trial
- Criminal Justice in Action—The Plea Bargain Puzzle

Learning objectives

After reading this chapter, you should be able to:

LO1 List the different names given to public prosecutors and indicate the general powers that they have.

LO2 Contrast the prosecutor's roles as an elected official and as a crime fighter.

LO3 Delineate the responsibilities of defense attorneys.

LO4 Indicate the three types of defense allocation programs.

LO5 List the three basic features of an adversary system of justice.

LO6 Identify the steps involved in the pretrial criminal process.

LO7 Indicate the three influences on a judge's decision to set bail.

LO8 Explain how a prosecutor screens potential cases.

LO9 List and briefly explain the different forms of plea bargaining agreements.

LO10 Indicate the ways that both defense attorneys and prosecutors can induce plea bargaining.

Above all else, Shasta Groene's family wanted to keep the young girl off the witness stand. They felt she had suffered enough since the day, fifteen months earlier, when Joseph E. Duncan kidnapped then eight-year-old Shasta and her nine-year-old brother Dylan from their home in Coeur d'Alene, Idaho. Before taking the children, Duncan had bludgeoned their older brother, their mother, and her boyfriend to death with a framing hammer. He then hid Shasta and Dylan at a primitive campsite deep in Montana's Lolo National Forest, raping and molesting them while making sex and torture videos. The ordeal lasted seven weeks until law enforcement agents managed to rescue Shasta. Sadly, Duncan had apparently killed Dylan with a shotgun before the officers arrived.

Steve Groene, Shasta's father, lobbied Kootenai County (Idaho) prosecutors to spare his daughter the hardship of testifying at Duncan's state trial for the murders of her three family members in Coeur d'Alene. Finally, on October 15, 2006, just days before the trial was scheduled to begin, the prosecutors and Duncan's defense attorneys made a deal. Duncan pleaded guilty to three counts of first degree murder and first degree kidnapping. He also agreed to give one of his defense attorneys the password of his encrypted computer files, which were suspected to contain evidence of other, unsolved crimes. In return, Duncan was spared the death penalty, at least for the time being, and sentenced to three life terms in prison.

Duncan's plea bargain meant that no trial in Idaho court was necessary. To Shasta's family, it also meant that the girl would never have to face her tormentor again, and vice versa. "We felt it [would have been] a privilege for him to be able to see her one more time," said Sam Doble, Shasta's aunt. "We didn't want that."

AP Photo/Kootenai County Sheriff Department.

▲ Eight-year-old Shasta Groene recovers at the Kootenai Medical Center in Coeur d'Alene, Idaho, after seven weeks of captivity by sex offender Joseph E. Duncan.

Criminal Justice Now™

Maximize your study time by using ThomsonNOW's Personalized Study plan to help you review this chapter and prepare for examination. The Study Plan will

- Help you identify areas on which you should concentrate
- Provide interactive exercises to help you master the chapter concepts; and
- Provide a post-test to confirm you are ready to move on to the next chapter information.

Soon after announcing Joseph Duncan's plea bargain, Kootenai County Prosecutor Bill Douglas cleared up some misconceptions about the agreement. First, it was still possible that Shasta Groene migh have to testify in court, although the chances were "extremely remote."[1] Douglas's deal with the defendant applied only to the murders of the three people in Coeur d'Alene, which fell within the jurisdiction of the Idaho court system. Shasta and Dylan's kidnapping and Dylan's murder were federal crimes because Duncan had transported the children over state lines. Therefore, those crimes fell within the jurisdiction of the federal courts, and federal prosecutors could call Shasta to the witness stand as part of Duncan's upcoming federal criminal trial. (For a review of jurisdiction basics, go to page 245.)

Furthermore, although Duncan had handed his encryption code over to Roger Peven, his defense attorney, Peven was under no obligation to reveal the contents of those files to law enforcement agents. Indeed, Peven told the media that he planned to use the files as a bargaining chip to spare his client the death penalty in federal court.[2] Given the brutal nature of Duncan's crimes and Shasta's unimaginable suffering, all this bartering may strike some as inappropriate and somewhat distasteful. In fact, prosecutors and defendants are constantly "making deals" just like the one between Duncan and Kootenai County. The *formal* adversary process of the trial is the exception rather than the rule in American courts. More than

95 percent of those charged with a felony in this country opt, as Duncan did, for the *informal* process. In other words, they plead guilty, thereby avoiding a trial and serving, in almost all instances, a lighter sentence. Indeed, most prosecutors, defense attorneys, and judges could not imagine a system in which plea bargaining was not the predominant means of resolving cases.

Given, then, that the vast majority of cases never go to trial, is it realistic to claim that the United States even has an adversary system? In this chapter, we will attempt to answer this question by examining the actions of the courtroom work group with regard to plea bargaining, bail, and other pretrial procedures. We will start with a discussion of the two main combatants of the adversary system: the prosecutor and the defense attorney.

The Prosecution

Criminal cases are tried by **public prosecutors,** who are employed by the government. The public prosecutor in federal criminal cases is called a U.S. attorney. In cases tried in state or local courts, the public prosecutor may be referred to as a *prosecuting attorney, state prosecutor, district attorney, county attorney,* or *city attorney.* Given their great autonomy, prosecutors are generally considered the most dominant figures in the American criminal justice system. In some jurisdictions, the district attorney is the chief law enforcement officer, with broad powers over police operations. Prosecutors have the power to bring the resources of the state against the individual and hold the legal keys to meting out or withholding punishment.[3] Ideally, this power is balanced by a duty of fairness and a recognition that the prosecutor's ultimate goal is not to win cases, but to see that justice is done. In *Berger v. United States* (1935), Justice George Sutherland called the prosecutor

> in a peculiar and very definite sense the servant of the law, the twofold aim of which is that guilt shall not escape or innocence suffer. He may prosecute with earnestness and vigor—indeed, he should do so. But, while he may strike hard blows, he is not at liberty to strike foul ones. It is as much his duty to refrain from improper methods calculated to produce a wrongful conviction as it is to use every legitimate means to bring about a just one.[4]

THE OFFICE OF THE PROSECUTOR

When he or she is acting as an *officer of the law* during a criminal trial, there are limits on the prosecutor's conduct, as we shall see in the next chapter. During the pretrial process, however, prosecutors hold a great deal of discretion in deciding the following:

1. Whether an individual who has been arrested by the police will be charged with a crime.
2. The level of the charges to be brought against the suspect.
3. If and when to stop the prosecution.[5]

There are more than eight thousand prosecutor's offices around the country, serving state, county, and municipal jurisdictions. Even though the **attorney general** is the chief law enforcement officer in any state, she or he has limited (and in some states, no) control over prosecutors within the state's boundaries.

Each jurisdiction has a chief prosecutor who is sometimes appointed but more often elected. As an elected official, he or she typically serves a four-year term, though in some states, such as Alabama, the term is six years. In smaller jurisdictions, the chief prosecutor has several assistants, and they work closely together. In larger ones, the chief prosecutor may have numerous *assistant prosecutors,* many of whom he or she rarely meets. Assistant prosecutors—for the most part young

Public Prosecutors Individuals, acting as trial lawyers, who initiate and conduct cases in the government's name and on behalf of the people.

Attorney General The chief law officer of a state; also, the chief law officer of the nation.

■ Figure 9.1 The Baltimore City State's Attorney's Office

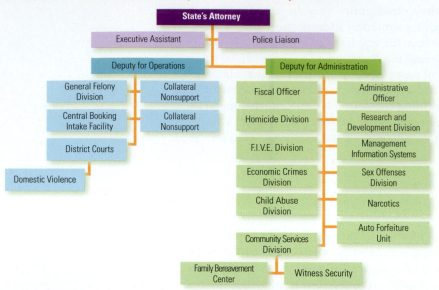

Source: Baltimore City State's Attorney's Office.

attorneys recently graduated from law school—may be assigned to particular sections of the organization, such as criminal prosecutions in general or areas of *special prosecution*, such as narcotics or gang crimes. (See ■ Figure 9.1 for the structure of a typical prosecutor's office.)

THE PROSECUTOR AS ELECTED OFFICIAL

The chief prosecutor's autonomy is not complete: as an elected official, she or he must answer to the voters. (There are exceptions: U.S. attorneys are nominated by the president and approved by the Senate, and chief prosecutors in Alaska, Connecticut, New Jersey, Rhode Island, and the District of Columbia are either appointed or hired as members of the attorney general's office.) The prosecutor may be part of the political machine; in many jurisdictions the prosecutor must declare a party affiliation and is expected to reward fellow party members with positions in the district attorney's office if elected. The post is often seen as a "stepping-stone" to higher political office, and many prosecutors have gone on to serve in legislatures or as judges. Arlen Specter, a Republican senator from Pennsylvania; Ron Castille, who sits on the state's supreme court; and Ed Rendell, a former mayor of Philadelphia and now governor of the state, all served as Philadelphia district attorneys early in their careers.

L02 Prosecutors are also subject to community pressures. Prosecutor Michael Nifong brought rape charges against three Duke University lacrosse players, as discussed in the introduction to Chapter 8, in the midst of his bid to hold onto his post as Durham County's district attorney. Many observers believe that Nifong's aggressive stance against the defendants, despite a lack of evidence, was a political ploy to win votes from the county's large African American population, who for the most part sympathized with the alleged victim.[6] If this was Nifong's plan, it worked only to a certain extent. He won the election, but his many missteps during the investigation eventually cost him his license to practice law in North Carolina.

THE PROSECUTOR AS CRIME FIGHTER

One of the reasons the prosecutor's post is a useful first step in a political career is that it is linked to crime fighting. Thanks to savvy public relations efforts and television police dramas such as *Law and Order*—with its opening line, "In the criminal justice system, the people are represented by two separate yet equally important groups: the police who investigate crime and the district attorneys who prosecute the offenders"—prosecutors are generally seen as law enforcement agents. Indeed, the prosecutors and the police do have a symbiotic relationship. Prosecutors rely on police to arrest suspects and gather sufficient evidence, and police rely on prosecutors to convict those who have been apprehended.

Police-Prosecutor Conflict Despite, or perhaps because of, this mutual dependency, the relationship between the two branches of law enforcement is often strained. Part of this can be attributed to different backgrounds. Most prosecutors come from middle- or upper-class families, while police are often recruited from the working class. Furthermore, prosecutors are required to have a level of education that is not attained by most police officers.

More important, however, is a basic divergence in the concept of guilt. For a police officer, a suspect is guilty if he or she has in fact committed a crime. For a prosecutor, a suspect is guilty if enough evidence can be legally gathered to prove such guilt in a court of law. In other words, police officers often focus on *factual guilt*, whereas prosecutors are ultimately concerned with *legal guilt*.[7] Thus, police officers will feel a great deal of frustration when a suspect they "know" to be guilty is set free. Similarly, a prosecutor may become annoyed when police officers do not follow the letter of the law in gathering evidence, thereby effectively ruining the chances of conviction.

Attempts at Cooperation Tension arising from these grievances can hamper crime control efforts. As a result, a number of jurisdictions are trying to achieve better police-prosecutor relations. A key step in the process seems to be improving communications between the two groups. In San Diego, for example, the district attorney has a permanent office in the police department for the express purpose of counseling officers on legal questions. From the office, a deputy district attorney (DDA) acts as a human legal reference book, advising police officers on how to write a search warrant, what steps they can take to help solidify a prosecutor's case, and other issues. The DDA will even sit in on morning briefings, giving updates on how changes in the law may affect police work.

AP Photo/Paul Sancya

▲ In 2006, the U.S. Department of Justice accused former federal prosecutor Richard Convertino of wrongdoing for misleading the jury in the first terrorism trial to result from investigations surrounding the September 11, 2001, attacks. Why is it harmful to the criminal justice system when a prosecutor breaks the rules of the court to gain a conviction, even if the defendant is ultimately guilty?

Self Check Fill in the Blanks

Public prosecutors initiate and conduct cases on behalf of the _____ against the defendant. During the pretrial process, prosecutors must decide whether to _____ an individual with a particular crime. Ideally, a prosecutor's ultimate goal is not to _____ cases, but rather to see _____ done. Check your answers on page 303.

The Defense Attorney

The media provide most people's perception of defense counsel: the idealistic public defender who nobly serves the poor, the "ambulance chaser," or the celebrity attorney in the $3,000 suit. These stereotypes, though not entirely fictional, tend to obscure the crucial role that the **defense attorney** plays in the criminal justice system. Most persons charged with crimes have little or no knowledge of criminal procedure. Without assistance, they would be helpless against a government prosecutor. By acting as a staunch advocate for her or his client, the defense attorney (ideally) assures that the government proves every point against that client beyond a reasonable doubt, even for cases that do not go to trial. In sum, the defense attorney provides a counterweight against the state in our adversary system. (See the feature *Myth versus Reality—Are Fingerprint Matches Foolproof?* on pages 280–281 to learn more about how defense attorneys fight for their clients.)

THE RESPONSIBILITIES OF THE DEFENSE ATTORNEY

The Sixth Amendment right to counsel is not limited to the actual criminal trial. In a number of instances, the United States Supreme Court has held that defendants are entitled to representation as soon as their rights may be denied, which, as we

Defense Attorney The lawyer representing the defendant.

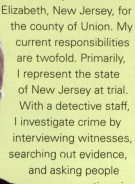

Careers in CJ   John Esmerado
Assistant Prosecutor

My name is John G. Esmerado. I am an assistant prosecutor in Elizabeth, New Jersey, for the county of Union. My current responsibilities are twofold. Primarily, I represent the state of New Jersey at trial. With a detective staff, I investigate crime by interviewing witnesses, searching out evidence, and asking people questions in court to establish beyond a reasonable doubt that a defendant

committed a crime. Trial work is incredibly fun. It requires vast amounts of pretrial preparation. Once it starts, however, it moves at lightning speed. Trials are strategic chess games of facts and law as well as all-out mental combat, a blitzkrieg of sorts, to find the truth. My secondary responsibility is to act as legal adviser to the police. Many times during the week and periodically in the early morning hours while the world sleeps, detectives call to discuss problematic cases. They arrest someone and are not clear what the appropriate charges are. I listen to the facts and authorize certain complaints and ask the detectives to pursue additional facts to help make the case stronger for trial.

CAPITAL QUESTIONS Recently, I was confronted with a moral dilemma. I was asked to participate as the second prosecutor in a death penalty trial. As a Catholic, I was ambivalent at best about the use of the death penalty by the state. I consulted the *Gospel of Life* and other Church teachings on the topic as well as my own conscience. The defendant was charged with hiring a hit man to kill his longtime girlfriend. The defendant had served a previous state prison sentence for threatening the

Courtesy of John Esmerado

have seen, includes the custodial interrogation and lineup identification procedures.[8] Therefore, an important responsibility of the defense attorney is to represent the defendant at the various stages of the custodial process, such as arrest, interrogation, lineup, and arraignment. Other responsibilities include:

- Investigating the incident for which the defendant has been charged.
- Communicating with the prosecutor, which includes negotiating plea bargains.
- Preparing the case for trial.
- Submitting defense motions, including motions to suppress evidence.
- Representing the defendant at trial.
  - Negotiating a sentence, if the client has been convicted.
  - Determining whether to appeal a guilty verdict.[9]

L03

DEFENDING THE GUILTY

"Look at the stakes. In civil law, if you screw up, it's just money. Here, it's the client—his life, his time in jail—and you never know how much time people have in their life."

—*Criminal defense attorney Stacey Richman*

At one time or another in their careers, all defense attorneys will face a difficult question: Must I defend a client whom I know to be guilty? According to the American Bar Association's code of legal ethics, the answer is almost always, "yes."[10] The most important responsibility of the criminal defense attorney is to be an advocate for her or his client. As such, the attorney is obligated to use all ethical and legal means to achieve the client's desired goal, which is usually to avoid or lessen punishment for the charged crime. As Supreme Court Justice Byron White once noted, defense counsel has no "obligation to ascertain or present the truth." Rather, our adversarial system insists that the defense attorney "defend the client whether he is innocent or guilty."[11] Indeed, if defense attorneys refused to represent clients whom they believed to be guilty, the Sixth Amendment guarantee to a criminal trial for all accused persons would be rendered meaningless.

same woman in the past. The defendant was no angel and had a lengthy criminal record. After much soul searching, I consented to work on the case with the premier assistant prosecutor in the office, Regina Caulfield. After a three-week trial, we secured a conviction for first degree murder for hire. The guilt phase of the trial was over. We had one week off to prepare for the penalty phase. I began to have doubts about the whole process. Was this really fair to both the defendant and the victim's family? Is death a legitimate tool in the prosecutor's arsenal of justice? After a four-day hearing and a day and a half of deliberation, the jury returned a verdict for life and not for death. The victim's family was disappointed. I was relieved.

As a prosecutor, I have always sought to do what is right and just. Incoming data support the conclusion that the current system with all its Byzantine rules cannot function properly. Jurors disregard legal instructions, while defense attorneys engender emotional sympathy for the defendant's upbringing, and victims are offered little, if any, opportunity to place their loss before the jury. Death must be reevaluated by the entire criminal justice community.

Immediately after this trial, I took some time off, grew a beard, and gained weight. I was depressed. For the first time in my career I had participated in something I did not wholly believe in. Since that time, I found my razor, exercise consistently, and have firmly resolved not to participate in another capital case.

THE "GREATEST JOB IN THE WORLD" In summary, I am glad to have a job that provides an outlet for my desire to do good. Sometimes, when I am working late at night, for free, on a case, I say to myself, "This is the greatest job in the world." I receive a salary to find the truth. I help people in crisis, people subject to violence, confront their attackers and ultimately bring some form of closure. Truth, justice, and the American way, a job far too important to leave to Superman cartoons, is the job of the prosecutor every day in and out of court.

Go to the **Careers in Criminal Justice Interactive CD** for more profiles in the field of criminal justice.

THE PUBLIC DEFENDER

Generally speaking, there are two different types of defense attorneys: (1) private attorneys, who are hired by individuals, and (2) **public defenders,** who work for the government. The distinction is not absolute, as many private attorneys hire out as public defenders, too. The modern role of the public defender was established by the Supreme Court's interpretation of the Sixth Amendment in *Gideon v. Wainwright* (1963).[12] In that case, the Court ruled that no defendant can be "assured a fair trial unless counsel is provided for him," and therefore the state must provide a public defender to those who cannot afford to hire one for themselves. Subsequently, the Court extended this protection to juveniles in *In re Gault* (1967)[13] and those faced with imprisonment for committing misdemeanors in *Argersinger v. Hamlin* (1972).[14] The impact of these decisions has been substantial: about 90 percent of all criminal defendants in the United States are represented by public defenders or other appointed counsel.[15]

Eligibility Issues   Although the Supreme Court's *Gideon* decision obligated the government to provide attorneys for poor defendants, it offered no guidance on just how poor the defendant needs to be to qualify for a public defender. In theory, counsel should be provided for those who are unable to hire an attorney themselves without "substantial hardship."[16] In reality, each jurisdiction has its own guidelines, and a defendant refused counsel in one area might be entitled to it in another. A judge in Kittitas County, Washington, to give an extreme example, frequently denies public counsel for college student defendants. This judge believes that any person who chooses to go to school rather than work automatically falls outside the *Gideon* case's definition of indigence.[17]

Defense Counsel Programs   In most areas, the county government is responsible for providing indigent defendants with attorneys. Three basic types of programs are used to allocate defense counsel:

Public Defenders Court-appointed attorneys who are paid by the state to represent defendants who are unable to hire private counsel.

1. *Assigned counsel programs,* in which local private attorneys are assigned clients on a case-by-case basis by the county.
2. *Contracting attorney programs,* in which a particular law firm or group of attorneys is hired to regularly assume the representative and administrative tasks of indigent defense.
3. *Public defender programs,* in which the county assembles a salaried staff of full-time or part-time attorneys and creates a public (taxpayer-funded) agency to provide services.[18]

Jurisdictions can use several of these programs concurrently. In the most recent published survey, 63 percent of state court prosecutors' offices used assigned counsel, 29 percent contracted out their defense counsel, and 68 percent had public defender programs.[19]

The **National Association of Criminal Defense Lawyers** represents more than ten thousand lawyers and advocates on a number of issues relating to the criminal justice system. To find its Web site, click on *Web Links* under *Chapter Resources* at **www.cjinaction.com**.

Effectiveness of Public Defenders   Under the U.S. Constitution, a defendant who is paying for her or his defense attorney has a right to choose that attorney without interference from the court.[20] This right of choice does not extend to indigent defendants. According to the United States Supreme Court, "a defendant may not insist on an attorney he cannot afford."[21] In other words, an indigent defendant must accept the public defender provided by the court system. (Note that, unless the presiding judge rules otherwise, a person can waive her or his Sixth Amendment rights and act as her or his own defense attorney.) This lack of control contributes to the widespread belief that public defenders do not provide an acceptable level of defense to indigents. "If you are the average poor person, you are going to be herded through the criminal justice system about like an animal is herded through the stockyards," says Stephen Bright, director of the Southern Center for Human Rights in Atlanta, Georgia.[22]

Overworked and Underpaid   In Missouri, a public defender often must hold the initial meeting with an indigent defendant just before the first court appearance, while the defendant is still shackled to another inmate.[23] This situation highlights the caseload pressures facing many public counsel systems across the country. The American Bar Association recommends that public defenders handle no more than 150 felony cases and 400 misdemeanor cases each year. For Dallas County

Myth *versus* Reality
Are Fingerprint Matches Foolproof?

For nearly a century, police and prosecutors have relied on fingerprint evidence as a powerful tool to link suspects to crimes. Today, however, defense attorneys are challenging this traditional weapon of forensic science, saying that it is not really "science" at all.

THE MYTH No true fingerprints are alike. Therefore, when law enforcement agents match a print taken from a crime scene to a print from a suspect, the suspect must have been at the crime scene.

THE REALITY When forensic scientists compare a fingerprint lifted from a crime scene with one taken from a suspect, they are looking for points of similarity. These experts will usually declare a match if there are between eight and sixteen points of similarity between the two samples. Many defense attorneys claim that this method is flawed, however. First, prints found at crime scenes tend to be incomplete, which means that examiners generally compare fragments of fingerprints rather than whole fingerprints. Two fingerprints that clearly are not alike when viewed in their entirety may appear to be identical when only fragments are compared. Second, fingerprint evidence found at crime scenes requires ultraviolet light to make it clear enough to process. Is it scientifically acceptable to compare this "altered" print with a "clean" one obtained from a suspect in controlled circumstances?

An internal audit by the Federal Bureau of Investigation (FBI) has found a 0.8 percent error rate for fingerprint matches—a seemingly small number, until one realizes that crime labs handle about 250,000 latent print analyses each year. Thus, there could be as many as

(Texas) public defenders, the average felony caseload is about 380, and the average misdemeanor caseload is more than 1,000.[24]

Public defender systems also struggle to attract qualified lawyers because of substandard budgets and salaries. Massachusetts, for example, limits the compensation paid to court-appointed attorneys to $30 an hour for district court cases, $39 an hour for superior court cases, and $54 an hour for murder cases.[25] When the fees from private clients that these lawyers lose every hour they work for the state are taken into account, a Massachusetts public defender who spends a reasonable amount of time preparing for a murder case is being paid less than the national minimum wage. In Shawnee County, Kansas, the salary of a public defender hovers around $40,000, compared to average pay of nearly $90,000 for other attorneys in the region.[26]

The Strickland Standard In a recent Louisiana murder trial, not only did the court-appointed defense attorney spend only eleven minutes preparing for trial on a charge that carries a mandatory life sentence, but she also represented the victim's father and had been representing the victim at the time of his death. Not surprisingly, her defendant was found guilty.[27] Such behavior raises a critical question: When a lawyer does such a poor job, has the client essentially been denied his or her Sixth Amendment right to assistance of counsel? In *Strickland v. Washington* (1984),[28] the Supreme Court set up a two-pronged test to determine whether constitutional requirements have been met. To prove that prior counsel was not sufficient, a defendant must show (1) that the attorney's performance was deficient *and* (2) that this deficiency *more likely than not* caused the defendant to lose the case.

In practice, it has been very difficult to prove the second prong of this test. A prosecutor can always argue that the defendant would have lost the case even if his or her lawyer had not been inept. For example, in 2006, the U.S. Court of Appeals for the Sixth Circuit declined to overturn the death sentence of Jeffrey Leonard even though his public defender's investigation of the case was so superficial that it did not even uncover Leonard's real name. Despite the court's finding that the public defender's performance was so lax as to violate the Constitution, it held that the evidence against Leonard was strong enough that he would have suffered the same fate even if he had enjoyed the services of a relatively competent defense attorney.[29]

▲ What's wrong with this picture? Because of an incompetent public defender, the true identity of Jeffrey Leonard, shown here under the false name of "James Earl Slaughter," was unknown to the jury that sentenced him to death. Why did a court of appeals uphold Leonard's punishment, even though his defense attorney badly bungled the case?

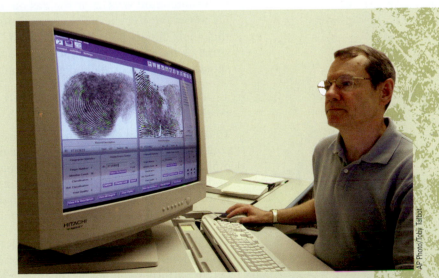

2,000 false matches annually. Consequently, the FBI has decided to review the cases of all state and federal prisoners scheduled for execution whose convictions were based on testimony by its fingerprint examiners. Defense attorneys are taking advantage of this recent uncertainty regarding the technique to challenge the fail-safe reputation of fingerprint matches as evidence. In 2004, after spending six years in prison, a Massachusetts man became the first person to be convicted by fingerprint evidence and then exonerated by DNA evidence.

FOR CRITICAL ANALYSIS

Despite these concerns, fingerprint matching is still a widespread and critical tool for law enforcement. Each year, thousands of guilty persons are linked to specific crimes because of fingerprints they left at the crime scene. Is a small error rate acceptable given the large number of criminals who are justly convicted based on fingerprint matches?

Public versus Private Counsel Although there is certainly a great deal of anecdotal evidence to support the contention that the public defender system routinely fails its clients, a recent study by researchers Roger A. Hanson, Brian J. Ostrom, and Ann A. Jones suggests that the outcome of a criminal case is not greatly affected by the private or public nature of the defense attorney. In the courts covered by the study, 95 percent of the defendants with public counsel and 91 percent of those with private counsel resolved their cases via a guilty plea.[30] Additional research by the U.S. Department of Justice revealed that, if found guilty, defendants with private counsel were 10 percent more likely to be sent to prison than those represented by public counsel.[31]

THE ATTORNEY-CLIENT RELATIONSHIP

The implied trust between an attorney and her or his client is not usually in question when the attorney has been hired directly by the defendant—as an "employee," the attorney well understands her or his duties. Relationships between public defenders and their clients, however, are often marred by suspicion on both sides. As Northwestern University's Jonathan D. Casper discovered while interviewing indigent defendants, many of them feel a certain amount of respect for the prosecutor. Like police officers, prosecutors are just "doing their job" by trying to convict the defendant. In contrast, the defendants' view of their own attorneys can be summed up in the following exchange between Casper and a defendant:

> Did you have a lawyer when you went to court the next morning?
> No, I had a public defender.[32]

This attitude is somewhat understandable. Given the caseloads that most public defenders carry, they may have as little as five or ten minutes to spend with a client before appearing in front of a judge. How much, realistically, can a public defender learn about the defendant in that time? Furthermore, the defendant is well aware that the public defender is being paid by the same source as the prosecutor and the judge. About a decade ago, "Unabomber" Ted Kaczynski acted on impulses felt by many defendants when he requested the right to defend himself, complaining that his public counsel was "supping from the same trough" as the prosecution.[33]

The situation handcuffs the public defenders as well. With so little time to spend on each case, they cannot validate the information provided by their clients. If the defendant says he or she has no prior offenses, the public defender often has no choice but to believe the client. Consequently, many public defenders later find that their clients have deceived them. In addition to the low pay and high pressures of the job, a client's lack of cooperation and disrespect can limit whatever satisfaction a public defender may find in the profession.

ATTORNEY-CLIENT PRIVILEGE

To defend a client effectively, a defense attorney must have access to all the facts concerning the case, even those that may be harmful to the defendant. To promote the unrestrained flow of information between the two parties, legislatures and lawyers themselves have constructed rules of **attorney-client privilege.** These rules require that communications between a client and his or her attorney be kept confidential, unless the client consents to the disclosure.

The Privilege and Confessions Attorney-client privilege does not stop short of confessions.[34] Indeed, if, on hearing any statement that points toward guilt, the defense attorney could alert the prosecution or try to resign from the case, attorney-client privilege would be rendered meaningless. Even if the client says, "I have just killed seventeen women. I selected only pregnant women so I could torture them and kill two people at once. I did it. I liked it. I enjoyed it," the defense attorney must continue to do his or her utmost to serve that client.[35]

▼ Defense attorney Thomas Mesereau, Jr., has represented a number of celebrities, including Michael Jackson, Robert Blake, and Mike Tyson, and often appears on national television to discuss high-profile cases. What are some of the responsibilities of a defense attorney?

AP Photo/Carlo Allegri, Pool

Without attorney-client privilege, observes legal expert John Kaplan, lawyers would be forced to give their clients the equivalent of *Miranda* warnings before representing them.[36] In other words, lawyers would have to make clear what clients could or could not say in the course of preparing for trial, because any incriminating statement might be used against the client in court. Such a development would have serious ramifications for the criminal justice system.

The Exception to the Privilege   The scope of attorney-client privilege is not all encompassing. In *United States v. Zolin* (1989),[37] the Supreme Court ruled that lawyers may disclose the contents of a conversation with a client if the client has provided information concerning a crime that has yet to be committed. This exception applies only to communications involving a crime that is ongoing or will occur in the future. If the client reveals a past crime, the privilege is still in effect, and the attorney may not reveal any details of that particular criminal act.

Therefore, in the situation discussed in the opening to this chapter, public defender Roger Peven could not disclose any information about past crimes that he found in Joseph Duncan's computer files without Duncan's agreement. If, however, the files revealed the location of another child that Duncan was keeping locked in a basement, Peven could share that information with authorities. (To learn more about the difficult situations that result from attorney-client privilege, see the feature *A Question of Ethics—Keeping a Secret* on the next page.)

Self Check Fill in the Blanks

The _____ Amendment states that every person accused of a crime has a right to counsel. There are two types of defense attorneys: (1) _____ attorneys hired by individuals and (2) _____ defenders, provided to _____ defendants by the government. Because of attorney-client _____, any admissions of guilt for past crimes that a client makes to her or his defense attorney are _____, unless the client _____ to their disclosure. Check your answers on page 303.

Truth, Victory, and the Adversary System

In strictly legal terms, three basic features characterize the **adversary system:**

1. A neutral and passive decision maker, either the judge or the jury.
2. The presentation of evidence from both parties.
3. A highly structured set of procedures (in the form of constitutional safeguards) that must be followed in the presentation of that evidence.[38]

Some critics of the American court system believe that it has been tainted by overzealous prosecutors and defense attorneys. Gordon Van Kessel, a professor at Hastings College of Law in California, complains that American lawyers see themselves as "prize fighters, gladiators, or, more accurately, semantic warriors in a verbal battle," and bemoans the atmosphere of "ritualized aggression" that is endemic to the courts.[39]

Our discussion of the courtroom work group in the last chapter, however, seems to belie this image of "ritualized aggression." As political scientists Herbert Jacob and James Eisenstein have written, "pervasive conflict is not only unpleasant; it also makes work more difficult."[40] The image of the courtroom work group as "negotiators" rather than "prize fighters" seems to be supported by the fact that more than nine out of every ten cases conclude with negotiated "deals" rather than trials. Jerome Skolnick of the University of California at Berkeley has found that work group members grade each other according to "reasonableness"[41]—a concept criminal justice scholar Abraham S. Blumberg has embellished by labeling

Adversary System A legal system in which the prosecution and defense are opponents, or adversaries, and present their cases in the light most favorable to themselves. The court arrives at a just solution based on the evidence presented by the contestants and determines who wins and who loses.

Initial Appearance An accused's first appearance before a judge or magistrate following arrest; during the appearance, the defendant is informed of the charges, advised of the right to counsel, told the amount of bail, and given a date for the preliminary hearing.

the defense attorney a "double agent." Blumberg believes that a defense attorney is likely to cooperate with the prosecutor in convincing a client to accept a negotiated plea of guilty because the defense attorney's main object is to finish the case quickly so as to collect the fee and move on.[42]

Perhaps, then, the most useful definition of the adversary process tempers Professor Van Kessel's criticism with the realities of the courtroom work group. University of California at Berkeley law professor Malcolm Feeley observes:

> In the adversary system the goal of the advocate is not to determine truth but to win, to maximize the interests of his or her side within the confines of the norms governing the proceedings. This is not to imply that the theory of the adversary process has no concern for the truth. Rather, the underlying assumption of the adversary process is that truth is most likely to emerge as a by-product of vigorous conflict between intensely partisan advocates, each of whose goal is to win.[43]

Blumberg takes a more cynical view when he calls the court process a "confidence game" in which "victory" is achieved when a defense attorney—with the implicit aid of the prosecutor and judge—is able to persuade the defendant to plead guilty.[44] As you read the rest of the chapter, which deals with pretrial procedures, keep in mind Feeley's and Blumberg's contentions concerning "truth" and "victory" in the American courts.

Pretrial Detention

After an arrest has been made, the first step toward determining the suspect's guilt or innocence is the **initial appearance** (for an overview of the entire process, see **LO6** ■ Figure 9.2). During this brief proceeding, a magistrate (see Chapter 8) informs the defendant of the charges that have been brought against him or her and explains his or her constitutional rights—particularly, the right to remain silent (under the Fifth Amendment) and the right to be represented by counsel (under the Sixth Amendment). At this point, if the defendant cannot afford to hire a private attorney, a public defender may be appointed, or private counsel may be hired by the state to represent the defendant. As the U.S. Constitution does not specify how soon a

that in most instances an attorney does not face criminal penalties for breaking these rules. At most, an attorney who betrays the confidence of a client needs to worry about a civil lawsuit brought by the client and a reprimand from his or her state bar association (which could include the loss of the attorney's license to practice law in that state).

A Question of Ethics Keeping a Secret

THE SITUATION Factory manager Leo Frank is arrested for raping and killing a young woman named Mary Phagan with whom he worked. Frank is convicted of murder and sentenced to life behind bars. After Frank is imprisoned, a client of attorney Arthur Powell admits to Powell that he, and not Frank, killed Phagan.

THE ETHICAL DILEMMA According to the rules of attorney-client privilege, a defense attorney has an ethical duty not to reveal past crimes committed by a client if the client confesses to those crimes in confidence. Note, however,

WHAT IS THE SOLUTION? Should Arthur Powell disclose his client's confession and possibly exonerate Leo Frank? What are the arguments for and against taking this action? In the actual case, which occurred early in the twentieth century, Powell did not disclose his client's confession, and Frank was subsequently lynched by other inmates in prison. Afterward, an anguished Powell said, "I could not have revealed the information the client had given me in the confidential relationship without violating my oath as an attorney. Such is the law; I did not make the law, but it is my duty and the court's duty to obey the law, so long as it stands."

Booking   After arrest, at the police station, the suspect is searched, photographed, finger-printed, and allowed at least one telephone call. After the booking, charges are reviewed, and if they are not dropped, a complaint is filed and a judge or magistrate examines the case for probable cause.

Initial Appearance   The suspect appears before the judge, who informs the suspect of the charges and of his or her rights. If the suspect requests a lawyer, one is appointed. The judge sets bail (conditions under which a suspect can obtain release pending disposition of the case).

Grand Jury   A grand jury determines if there is probable cause to believe that the defendant committed the crime. The federal government and about one-third of the states require grand jury indictments for at least some felonies.

Preliminary Hearing   A preliminary hearing is a court proceeding in which the prosecutor presents evidence and the judge determines whether there is probable cause to hold the defendant over for trial.

Indictment   An indictment is the charging instrument issued by the grand jury.

Information   An information is the charging instrument issued by the prosecutor.

Arraignment   The suspect is brought before the trial court, informed of the charges, and asked to enter a plea.

Plea Bargain   A plea bargain is a prosecutor's promise of concessions (or promise to seek concessions) in return for the defendant's guilty plea. Concessions include a reduced charge and/or a lesser sentence.

Guilty Plea   In most jurisdictions, most cases that reach the arraignment stage do not go to trial but are resolved by a guilty plea, often as the result of a plea bargain. The judge sets the case for sentencing.

Trial   If the defendant refuses to plead guilty, he or she proceeds to either a jury trial (in most instances) or a bench trial.

defendant must be brought before a magistrate after arrest, it has been left to the judicial branch to determine the timing of the initial appearance. The Supreme Court has held that the initial appearance must occur "promptly," which in most cases means within forty-eight hours of booking.[45]

In misdemeanor cases, a defendant may decide to plead guilty and be sentenced during the initial appearance. Otherwise, the magistrate will usually release those charged with misdemeanors on their promise to return at a later date for further proceedings. For felony cases, however, the defendant is not permitted to make a plea at the initial appearance because a magistrate's court does not have jurisdiction to decide felonies. Furthermore, in most cases the defendant will be released only if she or he posts **bail**—an amount paid by the

Bail The amount or conditions set by the court to ensure that an individual accused of a crime will appear for further criminal proceedings. If the accused person provides bail, whether in cash or by means of a bail bond, then she or he is released from jail.

defendant to the court and retained by the court until the defendant returns for further proceedings. Defendants who cannot afford bail are generally kept in a local jail or lockup until the date of their trial, though many jurisdictions are searching for alternatives to this practice because of overcrowded incarceration facilities.

THE PURPOSE OF BAIL

Bail is provided for under the Eighth Amendment. The amendment does not, however, guarantee the right to bail. Instead, it states that "excessive bail shall not be required." This has come to mean that in all cases except those involving a capital crime (where bail is prohibited), the amount of bail required must be reasonable compared with the seriousness of the wrongdoing. It does *not* mean that the amount of bail must be within the defendant's ability to pay.

The vagueness of the Eighth Amendment has encouraged a second purpose of bail: to protect the community by preventing the defendant from committing another crime before trial. To achieve this purpose, a judge can simply set bail at a level the suspect cannot possibly afford. As we shall see, several states and the federal government have passed laws that allow judges to detain suspects deemed a threat to the community without going through the motions of setting relatively high bail.

SETTING BAIL

There is no uniform system for pretrial detention; each jurisdiction has its own *bail tariffs,* or general guidelines concerning the proper amount of bail. For misdemeanors, the police usually follow a preapproved bail schedule created by local judicial authorities. In felony cases, the primary responsibility to set bail lies with the judge. ■ Figure 9.3 shows typical bail amounts for various offenses.

The Judge and Bail Setting Bail tariffs can be quite extensive. In Illinois, for example, a judge is required to take thirty-eight different factors into account when setting bail: fourteen involve the crime itself, two refer to the evidence gathered, four to the defendant's record, nine to the defendant's flight risk and immigration status, and nine to the defendant's general character.[46] For the most part, however, judges are free to use such tariffs as loose guidelines, and they have a great deal of discretion in setting bail according to the circumstances in each case.

Extralegal factors may also play a part in bail setting. University of New Orleans political scientist David W. Neubauer has identified three contexts that may influence a judge's decision-making process:[47]

1. *Uncertainty.* To a certain extent, predetermined bail tariffs are unrealistic, given that judges are required to set bail within forty-eight hours of arrest. It is often difficult to get information on the defendant in that period of time, and even if a judge can obtain a "rap sheet," or list of prior arrests ("priors"), she or he will probably not have an opportunity to verify its accuracy. Due to this uncertainty, most judges have no choice but to focus primarily on the seriousness of the crime in setting bail.

2. *Risk.* There is no way of knowing for certain whether a defendant released on bail will return for his or her court date, or whether he or she will commit a crime while free. Judges are aware of

■ **Figure 9.3** Average Bail Amounts for Various Felonies

These figures represent the median bail figures for the seventy-five largest counties in the nation.

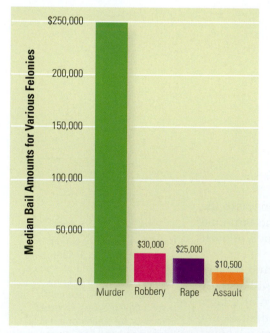

Source: Adapted from Bureau of Justice Statistics, *Felony Defendants in Large Urban Counties, 2002* (Washington, D.C.: U.S. Department of Justice, February 2006), Table 16, page 18.

the criticism they will come under from police groups, prosecutors, the press, and the public if a crime is committed during that time. Consequently, especially if she or he is up for reelection, a judge may prefer to "play it safe" and set a high bail to detain a suspect or refuse outright to offer bail when legally able to do so. In general, risk aversion also dictates why those who are charged with a violent crime such as murder are usually less likely to be released prior to trial than those who are charged with property crimes such as larceny or motor vehicle theft (see ■ Figure 9.4).

L07

3. *Overcrowded jails.* As we will discuss in detail in Chapter 13, many of the nation's jails are overcrowded. This may force a judge to make a difficult distinction between those suspects she or he believes must be detained and those who might need to be detained. To save jail space, a judge might be more lenient in setting bail for members of the latter group.[48]

Prosecutors, Defense Attorneys, and Bail Setting Though the judge has ultimate discretion in setting bail, the prosecutor and, to a lesser extent, the defense attorney can influence his or her decision. If the two sides disagree on the question of bail, a judge will usually side with the prosecutor. In many cases, given the uncertainty mentioned above, a trusted prosecutor can be a useful source of information for the judge. A hearing in Brigham City, Utah, provides a fairly typical example of the extent of the adversary process in determining pretrial detention. The defense attorney for a man charged with rape and sexual abuse asserted that his client was not a risk to the community. The prosecutor countered that the defendant had been accused of an average of one sexual offense every ten days over a three-month period. Not surprisingly, the judge denied bail.

Defense attorneys have a number of incentives for wanting their clients to be free on bail before a trial. A defendant who shows that she or he can function in the community without committing any further crimes may reduce her or his chances of conviction or at least impress on the judge the feasibility of a lighter sentence. Furthermore, a defendant free on bail is able to assist in the preparation for her or his defense by helping to gather evidence and personally steering the defense attorney toward favorable witnesses. Finally, a client free on bail is more likely to be able to earn income to pay legal bills.

The Benefits of Bail In a classic study of Philadelphia conviction rates, legal scholar Caleb Foote found that 67 percent of those suspected of violent crimes who had been released on bail were acquitted, compared to 25 percent of those who had been jailed before their trials.[49] More recent research by Marian R. Williams of the Criminal Justice Program at Bowling Green State University also shows that convicted offenders who have been denied bail are more likely to be incarcerated and to receive longer sentences.[50] (Critics of these types of studies point out, though, that they rarely control completely for the fact that those not released on bail were likely to be more violent and to have more extensive prior criminal records than those granted bail.)

Given these benefits, one would think that defense attorneys would fight vigorously for low bail for their clients. This is not the case, however. Most courtroom work groups establish "rules of the game"

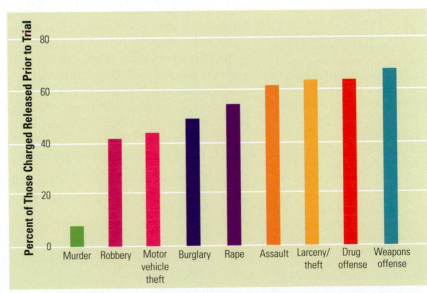

■ **Figure 9.4** **The Likelihood of Pretrial Release**

Source: Bureau of Justice Statistics, *Felony Defendants in Large Urban Counties, 2002* (Washington, D.C.: U.S. Department of Justice, February 2006), Table 13, page 16.

that determine the levels at which bail will be set for particular crimes, and judges, prosecutors, and defense attorneys do not spend a great deal of time contesting the matter.[51]

▲ Although bail bonds businesses provide a service for which there is a demand, several states have abolished bail bonding for profit. The reasoning behind such measures is that economic motives should have no place in any decision concerning the suspect's pretrial release. What other ethical issues are raised by the bail system?

GAINING PRETRIAL RELEASE

Earlier, we mentioned that many jurisdictions are looking for alternatives to the bail system. One of the most popular options is **release on recognizance (ROR).** This is used when the judge, based on the advice of trained personnel, decides that the defendant is not at risk to "jump" bail and does not pose a threat to the community. The defendant is then released at no cost with the understanding that he or she will return at the time of the trial. The Vera Institute, a nonprofit organization in New York City, introduced the concept of ROR as part of the Manhattan Bail Project in the 1960s, and such programs are now found in nearly every jurisdiction. When properly administered, ROR programs seem to be successful, with less than 5 percent of the participants failing to show for trial.[52]

Posting Bail Those suspected of committing a felony, however, are rarely released on recognizance. These defendants may post, or pay, the full amount of the bail in cash to the court. The money will be returned when the suspect appears for trial. Given the large amount of funds required, and the relative lack of wealth of many criminal defendants, a defendant can rarely post bail in cash. Another option is to use personal property as collateral. These **property bonds** are also rare because most courts require property valued at double the bail amount. Thus, if bail is set at $5,000, the defendant (or the defendant's family and friends) will have to produce property valued at $10,000.

Bail Bondspersons If unable to post bail with cash or property, a defendant may arrange for a **bail bondsperson** to post a bail bond on the defendant's behalf. The bondsperson, in effect, promises the court that he or she will turn over to the court the full amount of bail if the defendant fails to return for further proceedings. The defendant usually must give the bondsperson a certain percentage of the bail (often 10 percent) in cash. This amount, which is often not returned to the defendant later, is considered payment for the bondsperson's assistance and assumption of risk. Depending on the amount of the bail bond, the defendant may also be required to sign over to the bondsperson rights to certain property (such as a car, a valuable watch, or other asset) as security for the bond.

Although bail bondspersons obviously provide a service for which there is demand, several states have abolished bail bonding for profit.[53] The rationale for such reform focuses on two perceived problems with the practice.

1. Bail bondspersons provide opportunities for corruption, as they may bribe officials who are involved in setting bail (police and the like) to inflate the bail.
2. Because they can refuse to post a bail bond, bail bondspersons are, in essence, making a business decision concerning a suspect's pretrial release. This is considered the responsibility of a judge, not a private individual with a profit motive.[54]

The states that have banned bail bondspersons have established an alternative known as **ten percent cash bail.** This process, pioneered in Chicago in the

Release on Recognizance (ROR) A judge's order that releases an accused from jail with the understanding that he or she will return for further proceedings of his or her own will; used instead of setting a monetary bond.

Property Bond An alternative to posting bail in cash, in which the defendant gains pretrial release by providing the court with property valued at the bail amount as assurance that he or she will return for trial.

Bail Bondsperson A businessperson who agrees, for a fee, to pay the bail amount if the accused fails to appear in court as ordered.

Ten Percent Cash Bail An alternative to traditional bail in which defendants may gain pretrial release by posting 10 percent of their bond amount to the court instead of seeking a bail bondsperson.

early 1960s, requires the court, in effect, to take the place of the bondsperson. An officer of the court will accept a deposit of 10 percent of the bail amount, refundable when the defendant appears at the assigned time.[55] A number of jurisdictions allow for both bail bondspersons and ten percent cash bail, with the judge deciding whether a defendant is eligible for the latter.

Bounty Hunters Supreme Court Justice Robert Jackson once called the possibility that an accused person would not return to face trial "a calculated risk which the law takes as the price of our system of justice."[56] This risk is often taken by bail bondspersons, who suffer a monetary loss if a suspect skips bail. To protect their financial interests, bail bondspersons sometimes hire a *bounty hunter* to retrieve a client who has skipped bail. Under a Supreme Court decision issued in 1873, bounty hunters have almost unlimited power to apprehend someone who has signed a bail contract, including imprisoning the fugitive and breaking and entering into his or her house.[57]

Despite the police powers involved, bounty hunting is essentially unregulated in most of the United States. Only seven states require that bounty hunters be licensed, while another seven states restrict their activities and four (Illinois, Kentucky, Oregon, and Wisconsin) have banned the practice outright. This lack of control becomes an issue when a bounty hunter uses deadly force improperly, as occurred in 2004 when Mark Smith killed Michael Robinson in Butler County, Pennsylvania. Smith shot Robinson after the fugitive swiped at him with a "shiny silver object" that turned out to be a toenail clipper. Following the incident, the Pennsylvania legislature considered, but did not pass, a bill that would require all state bounty hunters to be licensed and take lethal weapons training.[58]

BAIL REFORM AND PREVENTIVE DETENTION

Release on recognizance programs and ten percent cash bail were the result of a movement in the 1960s to reform the bail system. As various researchers produced empirical proof that pretrial detention increased the odds of conviction and led to longer sentences, reformers began to point out that this created an imbalance of justice between the wealthy and the poor.[59] Those who could afford to post bail were convicted less frequently and spent less time in jail than those who could not. Furthermore, the conditions in pretrial detention centers were considerably worse than the conditions in prison, and the cost of maintaining these centers was becoming prohibitive.

The Bail Reform Acts In response to these concerns, Congress passed the Bail Reform Act of 1966.[60] Though the new law did not place statutory restrictions on the discretionary powers of federal judges, it did strongly suggest that judges implement a wide range of "conditions of release" for suspects who qualified.[61]

The Bail Reform Act of 1966 was criticized for concentrating on ways of increasing pretrial release, while failing to give judges the ability to detain suspects who posed a danger to the community.[62] Although judges have always had the *de facto* power to do just that by setting prohibitively high bails for dangerous defendants, thirty states have passed **preventive detention** laws that allow judges to deny bail to suspects with prior records of violence or nonappearance for trial. The Bail Reform Act of 1984 similarly states

See the **Professional Bail Agents of the United States** for a wealth of information about how bail bondspersons operate. Find its Web site by clicking on *Web Links* under *Chapter Resources* at **www.cjinaction.com**.

Preventive Detention The retention of an accused person in custody due to fears that she or he will commit a crime if released before trial.

▼ In Macon, Georgia, bounty hunter Cedric Miller takes aim at Stan Bernard Rouse. Miller, a former Macon narcotics cop, is often paid substantial sums by bail bondspersons to capture bond-jumping clients.

Beau Cabell, *The Macon Telegraph*

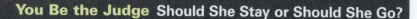

You Be the Judge Should She Stay or Should She Go?

THE FACTS While Christopher and Reina were living together, Christopher subjected his two children, four-year-old Ariana and five-year-old Tyler, to extreme physical abuse. Eventually, he killed both of them. Police found Ariana's body in a self-storage unit and have been unable to locate Tyler's remains. Christopher has been charged with two murders. Prosecutors in Tucson, Arizona, have charged Reina with a single count of child abuse with death or serious injury likely to occur. Reina's attorneys are requesting that their client be released from jail before her trial.

THE LAW In Arizona, judges consider the following factors in making the pretrial release determination: (1) the seriousness of the offense; (2) the past criminal record of the defendant; (3) the defendant's employment record; (4) any drug, alcohol, and mental health issues (and possible treatment); and (5) the wishes of the prosecutors and the victims.

YOUR DECISION Reina has no previous criminal record and claims that Christopher never told her where he hid Tyler's body. Her defense attorneys point out that she is not a flight risk, has strong family support, and poses no danger to the community. Also, she is fighting to regain custody of the two-year-old son that she shares with Christopher. Prosecutors, who do not want Reina released before her trial, argue that she faces a ten-year prison sentence, has a history of substance abuse, and could accrue additional charges, including first degree murder. They add that instead of reporting Ariana's death, Reina fled from her home and checked into a local hotel with Christopher under an assumed name. If you were the judge, would you grant Reina pretrial release? If so, what bail amount would you require? What are the most important factors in your decision?

[To see how a Pima County (Arizona) Superior Court judge ruled in this case, go to Example 9.1 in Appendix B.]

that federal offenders can be held without bail to assure "the safety of any other person and the community."[63]

The Constitutionality of Bail Critics of the 1984 act believe that it violates the U.S. Constitution by allowing the freedom of a citizen to be restricted before he or she has been proved guilty in a court of law. For many, the act also brings up the troubling issue of *false positives*—erroneous predictions that defendants, if given pretrial release, would commit a crime, when in fact they would not. In *United States v. Salerno* (1987),[64] however, the Supreme Court upheld the act's premise. Then Chief Justice William Rehnquist wrote that preventive detention was not a "punishment for dangerous individuals" but a "potential solution to a pressing social problem." Therefore, "there is no doubt that preventing danger to the community is a legitimate . . . goal." In fact, about 18 percent of released defendants are rearrested before their trials begin, 12 percent for violent felonies.[65] (See the feature *You Be the Judge—Should She Stay or Should She Go?*)

Self Check Fill in the Blanks

During the _____, a magistrate informs the defendant of the charges brought against her or him and explains her or his _____ rights. Following this proceeding, the defendant will be detained until trial unless he or she can post _____, the amount of which is determined by the _____. Even if the defendant can afford to pay this amount, he or she may be kept in jail until trial under a _____ detention statute if the court decides that he or she poses a risk to the community. Check your answers on page 303.

Establishing Probable Cause

Once the initial appearance has been completed and bail has been set, the prosecutor must establish *probable cause;* that is, the prosecutor must prove that a crime was committed and link the defendant to that crime. There are two formal procedures for establishing probable cause at this stage of the pretrial process: preliminary hearings and grand juries.

THE PRELIMINARY HEARING

During the **preliminary hearing,** the defendant appears before a judge or magistrate who decides whether the evidence presented is sufficient for the case to proceed to trial. Normally, every person charged by warrant has a right to this hearing within a reasonable amount of time after his or her initial arrest[66]—typically, no later than ten days if the defendant is in custody or within thirty days if he or she has gained pretrial release.

The Preliminary Hearing Process The preliminary hearing is conducted in the manner of a mini-trial. Typically, a police report of the arrest is presented by a law enforcement officer, supplemented with evidence provided by the prosecutor. Because the burden of proving probable cause is relatively light (compared to proving guilt beyond a reasonable doubt), prosecutors rarely call witnesses during the preliminary hearing, saving them for the trial. During this hearing, the defendant has a right to be represented by counsel, who may cross-examine witnesses and challenge any evidence offered by the prosecutor. In most states, defense attorneys can take advantage of the preliminary hearing to begin the process of **discovery,** in which they are entitled to have access to any evidence in the possession of the prosecution relating to the case. Discovery is considered a keystone in the adversary process, as it allows the defense to see the evidence against the defendant prior to making a plea.

Waiving the Hearing The preliminary hearing often seems rather perfunctory, although in some jurisdictions it replaces grand jury proceedings. It usually lasts no longer than five minutes, and the judge or magistrate rarely finds that probable cause does not exist. In one study, only 2 percent of the cases were dismissed by the judicial official at this stage in the process.[67] For this reason, defense attorneys commonly advise their clients to waive their right to a preliminary hearing. Once a judge has ruled affirmatively on probable cause, the defendant is bound over to the grand jury in many jurisdictions. If the grand jury believes there are grounds for a trial, it issues an *indictment.* In other jurisdictions, the government prosecutor issues an **information,** which replaces the police complaint as the formal charge against the defendant for the purposes of a trial.

THE GRAND JURY

The federal government and about one-third of the states require a grand jury to make the decision as to whether a case should go to trial. **A grand jury** is a group of citizens called to decide whether probable cause exists. Grand juries are *impaneled,* or created, for a period of time usually not exceeding three months. During that time, the grand jury sits in closed (secret) session and hears only evidence presented by the prosecutor—the defendant cannot present evidence at this hearing. The prosecutor presents to the grand jury whatever evidence the state has against the defendant, including photographs, documents, tangible objects, the testimony of witnesses, and other items. If the grand jury finds that probable cause exists, it issues an **indictment** (pronounced in-*dyte*-ment) against the defendant. Like an information in a preliminary hearing, the indictment becomes the formal charge against the defendant. As ■ Figure 9.5 on the next page shows, some states require a grand jury to indict for

Preliminary Hearing An initial hearing in which a magistrate decides if there is probable cause to believe that the defendant committed the crime with which he or she is charged.

Discovery Formal investigation prior to trial. During discovery, the defense uses various methods to obtain information from the prosecution to prepare for trial.

Information The formal charge against the accused issued by the prosecutor after a preliminary hearing has found probable cause.

Grand Jury The group of citizens called to decide whether probable cause exists to believe that a suspect committed the crime with which she or he has been charged.

Indictment A charge or written accusation, issued by a grand jury, that probable cause exists to believe that a named person has committed a crime.

As you can see, in some states a grand jury indictment is required to charge an individual with a crime, while in others it is either optional or prohibited. When a grand jury is not used, the discretion of whether to charge is left to the prosecutor, who must then present his or her argument at the preliminary hearing (discussed earlier in the chapter).

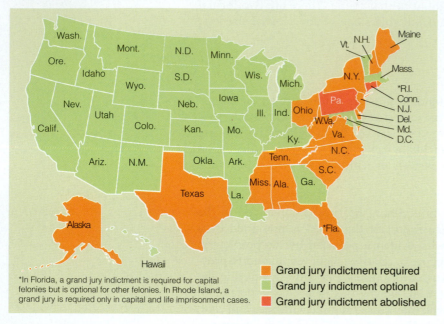

*In Florida, a grand jury indictment is required for capital felonies but is optional for other felonies. In Rhode Island, a grand jury is required only in capital and life imprisonment cases.

Grand jury indictment required
Grand jury indictment optional
Grand jury indictment abolished

Source: Bureau of Justice Statistics, *State Court Organization, 2004* (Washington, D.C.: U.S. Department of Justice, August 2006), 215–217.

certain crimes, while in other states a grand jury indictment is optional.

The "Shield" and the "Sword" The grand jury has a long history in the United States, having been brought over from England by the colonists and codified in the Fifth Amendment to the U.S. Constitution. Historically, it has acted as both a "shield" and a "sword" in the criminal justice process. By giving citizens the chance to review government charges of wrongdoing, it "shields" the individual from the power of the state. At the same time, the grand jury offers the government a "sword"— the opportunity to provide evidence against the accused—in its efforts to fight crime and protect society.[68]

A "Rubber Stamp" Today, the protective function of the grand jury is in doubt—critics say that the "sword" aspect works too well and the "shield" aspect not at all. Statistically, the grand jury is even more prosecutor friendly than the preliminary hearing. Defendants are indicted at a rate of more than 99 percent,[69] leading to the common characterization of the grand jury as little more than a "rubber stamp" for the prosecution. Certainly, the procedural rules of the grand jury favor prosecutors. The exclusionary rule (see Chapter 7) does not apply in grand jury investigations, so prosecutors can present evidence that would be disallowed at any subsequent trial. Furthermore, because the grand jury is given only one version of the facts—the prosecution's—it is likely to find probable cause. In the words of one observer, a grand jury would indict a "ham sandwich" if the government asked it to do so.[70] As a result of these concerns, more than half of the jurisdictions have abolished grand juries.

Self Check Fill in the Blanks

If a case is to proceed to trial, the prosecutor must establish _____ that the defendant committed the crime in question. One way of doing this involves a _____ hearing, in which a judge or magistrate rules whether the prosecutor has met this burden. In the other method, the decision rests with a group of citizens called a _____ who will hand down an _____ if they believe the evidence is sufficient to support the charges. Check your answers on page 303.

The Prosecutorial Screening Process

Some see the high government success rates in pretrial proceedings as proof that prosecutors successfully screen out weak cases before they get to a grand jury or preliminary hearing. If, however, grand juries have indeed abandoned their traditional duties in favor of "rubber stamping" most cases set in front of them, and preliminary hearings are little better, what is to keep prosecutors from using their charging powers indiscriminately? Nothing, say many

Prosecutors in the United States are generally believed to have a great deal of charging discretion. The discretionary power of American prosecutors, however, does not equal that of their Japanese counterparts. With the ability to "cherry pick" their cases, prosecutors in Japan routinely have annual conviction rates of over 99.9 percent.

THE "CONFESSION MILL"

One observer described the Japanese courts as a "confession mill." Unlike the American system, Japan has no arraignment procedure during which the accused can plead guilty or innocent. Instead, the focus of the Japanese criminal justice system is on extracting confessions of guilt: police can hold and question suspects for up to twenty-three days without pressing charges. Furthermore, the suspect has no absolute right to counsel during the interrogation, and police are often able to get confessions that make for open-and-shut convictions. The prosecutor also has the "benevolent" discretion to drop the case altogether if the suspect expresses remorse.

The extraordinarily high conviction rate is also a product of Japanese culture. To fail in an attempt to convict results in a loss of face, not only for the individual prosecutor but also for the court system as a whole. The Japanese Justice Ministry

estimates that, to avoid the risk of losing, prosecutors decline to press charges against 35 percent of indictable suspects each year. Japanese judges—there are no juries—contribute to the high conviction rate by rarely questioning the manner in which prosecutors obtain confessions.

NO PLEA BARGAINING

Interestingly, given the amount of prosecutorial discretion, the Japanese criminal justice system does not allow for plea bargaining. The Japanese see the practice of "trading" a guilty plea for a lesser sentence as counterproductive, as a defendant may be tempted to confess to crimes she or he did not commit if the prosecution has a strong case. For the Japanese, a confession extracted after twenty-three days of interrogation may be "voluntary," but a confession gained through a promise of leniency is "forced" and therefore in conflict with the system's goals of truth-seeking and accuracy.

FOR CRITICAL ANALYSIS

Explain the fundamental differences between the American and Japanese criminal justice systems. Do you think the lack of a comparable adversarial system weakens or strengthens the Japanese system in comparison with the American one?

---

observers. Once the police have initially charged a defendant with committing a crime, the prosecutor can prosecute the case as it stands, reduce or increase the initial charge, file additional charges, or dismiss the case. In a system of government and law that relies on checks and balances, asked legal expert Kenneth Culp Davis, why should the prosecutor be "immune to review by other officials and immune to review by the courts?"[71] (For information on another prosecutor-friendly system, see the feature *International CJ—Japan's All-Powerful Prosecutors.*)

Though American prosecutors have far-ranging discretionary charging powers, it is not entirely correct to say that they are unrestricted. Controls are indirect and informal, but they do exist.

> "Let me tell you, you can paint pictures and get people indicted for just about anything."
>
> —Alfonse D'Amato, former U.S. senator from New York

CASE ATTRITION

Prosecutorial discretion includes the power *not* to prosecute cases. In 2006, for example, federal prosecutors declined to bring charges in 87 percent of the terrorism cases referred to them by the Federal Bureau of Investigation.[72] ■ Figure 9.6 on the following page depicts the average outcomes of one hundred felony arrests in the United States. As you can see, of the sixty-five adult arrestees brought before the district attorney, only thirty-five are prosecuted, and only eighteen of these prosecutions lead to incarceration. Consequently, fewer than one in three adults arrested for a felony sees the inside of a prison or jail cell. This phenomenon is known as **case attrition**, and it is explained in part by prosecutorial discretion.

Case Attrition The process through which prosecutors, by deciding whether to prosecute each person arrested, effect an overall reduction in the number of persons prosecuted. As a result, the number of persons convicted and sentenced is much smaller than the number of persons arrested.

■ Figure 9.6 **Following One Hundred Felony Arrests: The Criminal Justice Funnel**

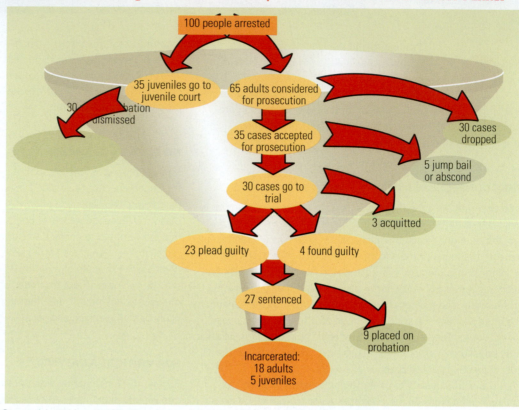

Source: Adapted from Todd R. Clear, George F. Cole, and Michael D. Reisig, *American Corrections,* 7th ed. (Belmont, CA: Thomson Wadsworth, 2006), 129.

Scarce Resources About half of those adult felony cases brought to prosecutors by police are dismissed through a *nolle prosequi* (Latin for "unwilling to pursue"). Why are these cases "nolled," or not prosecuted by the district attorney? In the section on law enforcement, you learned that the police do not have the resources to arrest every lawbreaker in the nation. Similarly, district attorneys do not have the resources to prosecute every arrest. They must choose how to distribute their scarce resources. In some cases, the decision is made for them, such as when police break procedural law and negate important evidence. This happens rarely— less than 1 percent of felony arrests are dropped because of the exclusionary rule, and almost all of these are the result of illegal drug searches.[73]

Screening Factors Most prosecutors have a *screening process* for deciding when to prosecute and when to "noll." This process varies a bit from jurisdiction to jurisdiction, but most prosecutors consider several factors in making the decision:

- The most important factor in deciding whether to prosecute is not the prosecutor's belief in the guilt of the suspect, but whether there is *sufficient evidence for conviction.*[74] If prosecutors have strong physical evidence and a number of reliable and believable witnesses, they are quite likely to prosecute.

  L08

- Prosecutors also tend to establish *case priorities.* In other words, everything else being equal, a district attorney will prosecute a rapist instead of a jaywalker because the former presents a greater threat to society than does the latter. A prosecutor will also be more likely to prosecute someone with an extensive record of wrongdoing than a first-time offender. Often, in coordination with the police, a district attorney's office will target a single area of crime, such as drug use or drunk driving.

- Sometimes a case is dropped even when it involves a serious crime and a wealth of evidence exists against the suspect. These situations usually involve *uncooperative victims*. Domestic violence cases are particularly difficult to prosecute because the victims may want to keep the matter private, fear reprisals, or have a strong desire to protect their abuser.[75] In some jurisdictions, as many as 80 percent of domestic violence victims refuse to cooperate with the prosecution.[76]
- *Unreliability of victims* can also affect a charging decision. If the victim in a rape case is a crack addict and a prostitute, while the defendant is the chief executive officer of a large corporation, prosecutors may be hesitant to have a jury decide which one is more trustworthy.
- A prosecutor may be willing to drop a case, or reduce the charges, against a *defendant who is willing to testify against other offenders*. Federal law encourages this kind of behavior by offering sentencing reductions to defendants who provide "substantial assistance in the investigation or prosecution of another person who has committed an offense."[77]

Despite their recently enhanced status in the criminal justice system discussed earlier in this textbook, crime victims have no ability to control the prosecutorial screening process. This does not mean that victim attitudes are not a factor in charging decisions. A victim's wishes can have a moral and political influence on prosecutors, who are, after all, public officials. The parents of two children killed in a hit-and-run accident in Danville, California, for example, were instrumental in convincing the district attorney to charge the driver, a nanny named Jimena Barreto with a history of drunken driving convictions, with second degree murder instead of manslaughter. In 2005, a jury found the defendant guilty, and a judge sentenced her to thirty years to life in prison.

PROSECUTORIAL CHARGING AND THE DEFENSE ATTORNEY

For the most part, there is little the defense attorney can do when the prosecutor decides to charge a client. If a defense attorney feels strongly that the charge has been made in violation of the defendant's rights, he or she can, however, submit *pretrial motions* to the court requesting that a particular action be taken to protect his or her client. Pretrial motions include the following:

1. Motions to suppress evidence obtained illegally.
2. Motions for a change of venue because the defendant cannot receive a fair trial in the original jurisdiction.
3. Motions to invalidate a search warrant.
4. Motions to dismiss the case because of a delay in bringing it to trial.
5. Motions to obtain evidence that the prosecution may be withholding.

As we shall soon see, defense attorneys sometimes use these pretrial motions to pressure the prosecution into offering a favorable deal for their client.

AP Photo/Dennis Schroeder, Pool

▲ On August 26, 2006, Boulder County (Colorado) District Attorney Mary Lacy explains the dismissal of charges against John Mark Karr, who had been arrested after admitting to killing child beauty queen JonBenet Ramsey a decade earlier. Lacy came under a great deal of criticism after DNA tests proved that Karr could not have been at the murder scene. Why might a prosecutor be more likely to charge a suspect on the basis of weak evidence if the case is high profile?

Self Check Fill in the Blanks

On average, of sixty-five adult arrestees, a district attorney will prosecute only thirty-five. This process, which is known as case _____, requires that the prosecutor _____ all potential cases and dismiss the ones where the likelihood of _____ is weakest. The most important factor in this decision is whether there is sufficient _____ to find the defendant guilty. Check your answers on page 303.

Chapter 9 Pretrial Procedures: The Adversary System in Action   **295**

Pleading Guilty

Based on the information (delivered during the preliminary hearing) or indictment (handed down by the grand jury), the prosecutor submits a motion to the court to order the defendant to appear before the trial court for an **arraignment.** Due process of law, as guaranteed by the Fifth Amendment, requires that a criminal defendant be informed of the charges brought against her or him and be offered an opportunity to respond to those charges. The arraignment is one of the ways in which due process requirements are satisfied by criminal procedure law.

At the arraignment, the defendant is informed of the charges and must respond by pleading not guilty or guilty. In some but not all states, the defendant may also enter a plea of *nolo contendere*, which is Latin for "I will not contest it." The plea of *nolo contendere* is neither an admission nor a denial of guilt. (The consequences for someone who pleads guilty and for someone who pleads *nolo contendere* are the same in a criminal trial, but the latter plea cannot be used in a subsequent civil trial as an admission of guilt.) Most frequently, the defendant pleads guilty to the initial charge or to a lesser charge that has been agreed on through *plea bargaining* between the prosecutor and the defendant. If the defendant pleads guilty, no trial is necessary, and the defendant is sentenced based on the crime he or she has admitted committing.

PLEA BARGAINING IN THE CRIMINAL JUSTICE SYSTEM

Plea bargaining usually takes place after the arraignment and before the beginning of the trial. In its simplest terms, it is a process by which the accused, represented by the defense counsel, and the prosecutor work out a mutually satisfactory disposition of the case, subject to court approval. Plea bargaining agreements can take several different forms:

- *Charge bargaining.* In charge bargaining, the defendant pleads guilty in exchange for a reduction of the charges. A felony burglary charge, for example, could be reduced to the lesser offense of breaking and entering. The more serious the initial charge, the more an accused has to gain by bargaining: pleading guilty to second degree murder can save the defendant from the risk of being convicted of first degree murder, which carries the death penalty in some states.

- *Sentence bargaining.* In sentence bargaining, the defendant pleads guilty in exchange for a lighter sentence, which may include a shorter prison term or probation. In most jurisdictions, the judge makes the final decision on whether to accept this agreement; the prosecutor can only recommend a lighter sentence. The prosecutor may also suggest that the defendant be placed in a counseling program, such as a drug rehabilitation center, in return for the guilty plea.

- *Count bargaining.* A person can be charged with multiple counts, either for committing multiple crimes or for different aspects of a single incident. A person who goes on a killing spree that results in seven deaths, for example, would be charged with seven counts of first degree murder. A person who breaks into a home, sexually assaults the inhabitants, and then takes their credit cards could be charged with counts of rape, aggravated burglary, misdemeanor theft, felony theft, and criminal use of a credit card. In count bargaining, a defendant pleads guilty in exchange for a reduction in the counts against him or her.

Arraignment A court proceeding in which the suspect is formally charged with the criminal offense stated in the indictment. The suspect enters a plea (guilty, not guilty, *nolo contendere*) in response.

Nolo Contendere Latin for "I will not contest it." A criminal defendant's plea, in which he or she chooses not to challenge, or contest, the charges brought by the government. Although the defendant may still be sentenced or fined, the plea neither admits nor denies guilt.

Plea Bargaining The process by which the accused and the prosecutor work out a mutually satisfactory conclusion to the case, subject to court approval. Usually, plea bargaining involves the defendant's pleading guilty to a lesser offense in return for a lighter sentence.

L09

In a sense, count bargaining is a form of sentence bargaining. If a person is convicted of multiple counts, her or his prison time is calculated by combining the attendant sentence of each count (which is why some criminals are sentenced to a seemingly ridiculously long prison term, well past their life expectancies). If a count is dropped, so is the prison time that goes with it.

In *Santobello v. New York* (1971),[78] the Supreme Court held that plea bargaining "is not only an essential part of the process but a highly desirable part for many reasons." Some observers would agree, but with ambivalence. They understand that plea bargaining offers the practical benefit of saving court resources, but question whether it is the best way to achieve justice.[79] We will address the question of whether plea bargaining is an acceptable means of determining the defendant's fate in the *Criminal Justice in Action* feature at the end of the chapter.

MOTIVATIONS FOR PLEA BARGAINING

Given the high rate of plea bargaining—accounting for 95 percent of criminal convictions in state courts[80]—it follows that the prosecutor, defense attorney, and defendant each have strong reasons to engage in the practice.

Prosecutors and Plea Bargaining In most cases, a prosecutor has a single goal after charging a defendant with a crime: conviction. If a case goes to trial, no matter how certain a prosecutor may be that the defendant is guilty, there is always a chance that a jury or judge will disagree. Plea bargaining removes this risk. Furthermore, the prosecutorial screening process described earlier in the chapter is not infallible. Sometimes, a prosecutor will find that the evidence against the accused is weaker than first thought or will uncover new information that changes the complexion of the case. In these situations, the prosecutor may decide to drop the charges or, if he or she still feels that the defendant is guilty, turn to plea bargaining to "save" a questionable case.

The prosecutor's role as an administrator also comes into play. She or he may be interested in the quickest, most efficient manner to dispose of caseloads, and plea bargains reduce the time and money spent on each case. Personal philosophy can affect the proceedings as well. A prosecutor who feels that a mandatory minimum sentence for a particular crime, such as marijuana possession, is too strict may plea bargain in order to lessen the penalty. Similarly, some prosecutors will consider plea bargaining only in certain instances—for burglary and theft, for example, but not for more serious felonies such as rape and murder.[81]

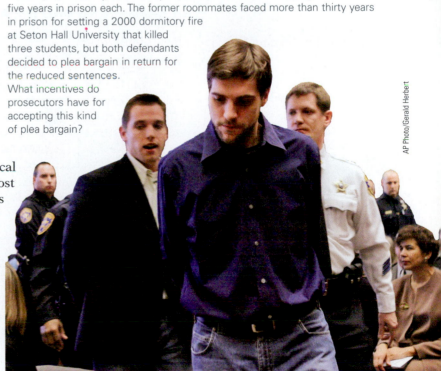

▼ Joseph T. LePore, right, and Sean Ryan, both 26, are led from a courtroom in Newark, New Jersey, on January 26, 2007, moments after being sentenced to five years in prison each. The former roommates faced more than thirty years in prison for setting a 2000 dormitory fire at Seton Hall University that killed three students, but both defendants decided to plea bargain in return for the reduced sentences. What incentives do prosecutors have for accepting this kind of plea bargain?

AP Photo/Gerald Herbert

Defense Attorneys and Plea Bargaining Political scientist Milton Heumann has said that the most important thing that a defense attorney learns is that "most of his [or her] clients are guilty."[82] Given this stark reality, favorable plea bargains are often the best a defense attorney can do for clients, aside from helping them to gain acquittals. Some have suggested that defense attorneys have other, less savory motives for convincing a client to plead guilty, such as a desire to increase profit margins by quickly disposing of cases[83] or a wish to ingratiate themselves with the other members of the courtroom work group by showing their "reasonableness."[84] In other cases, a defense attorney may want to go to trial, even though it is not in the client's best interest, to win publicity or gain work experience.[85]

Defendants and Plea Bargaining The plea bargain allows the defendant a measure of control over his or her fate. When Joseph Duncan accepted the deal offered by prosecutors discussed in the introduction to this chapter, he greatly increased the possibility that he would not be executed and could live out the rest of his years in prison. The benefits of plea bargaining are tangible. As ■ Figure 9.7 shows, defendants who plea bargain receive significantly lighter sentences on average than those who are found guilty at trial.

Victims and Plea Bargaining One of the major goals of the victims' rights movement, discussed in Chapter 2, has been to increase the role of victims in the plea bargaining process. In recent years, the movement has had some success in this area. About half of the states now allow for victim participation in plea bargaining. Many have laws similar to North Carolina's statute that requires the district attorney's office to offer victims "the opportunity to consult with the prosecuting attorney" and give their views on "plea possibilities."[86] On the federal level, the Crime Victims' Rights Act (see page 60) grants victims the right to be "reasonably heard" during the process.[87]

If they choose, prosecutors can provide victims with more of a voice. After Alfonso Rodriguez, Jr., was arrested for kidnapping Dru Sjodin, a twenty-two-year-old University of North Dakota student, in 2003, federal prosecutors consulted closely with the young woman's family. In early 2004, Sjodin's parents agreed to a deal that prosecutors presented to the suspect: if Rodriguez would plead guilty to kidnapping and murder and tell law enforcement agents the location of Sjodin's body, the government would not seek his execution. Rodriguez spurned the proposition. Eventually, volunteers found Sjodin's remains in a ravine near Crookston, Minnesota. Two years into the federal trial, Rodriguez changed his mind and offered to plead guilty in return for a life sentence. Sjodin's family, speaking through the prosecutors, said, in effect, "too little, too late."[88] On February 8, 2007, Rodriguez received the death penalty for his crimes.

PLEA BARGAINING AND THE ADVERSARY SYSTEM

One criticism of plea bargaining is that it subverts the adversary system, the goal of which is to determine innocence or guilt. Although plea bargaining does value negotiation over conflict, it is important to remember that it does so in a context in which legal guilt has already been established. Even within this context, plea bargaining is not completely divorced from the adversary process.

Strategies to Induce a Plea Bargain Earlier, we pointed out that the most likely reason why a prosecutor does not bring charges is the lack of a strong case. This is also the most common reason why a prosecutor agrees to a plea bargain once charges have been brought. Defense attorneys are well aware of this fact and often file numerous pretrial

■ **Figure 9.7** Sentencing Outcomes for Guilty Pleas

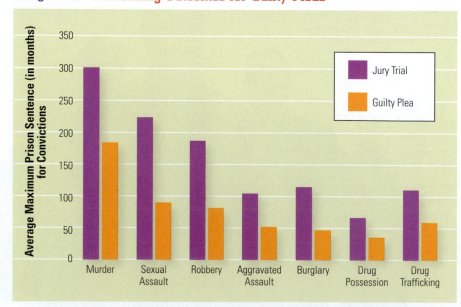

Source: Adapted from Bureau of Justice Statistics, *State Court Sentencing of Convicted Felons, 2002* (Washington, D.C.: U.S. Department of Justice, May 2005), Table 4.5.

motions in an effort to weaken the state's case. Even if the judge does not accept the motions, the defense may hope that the time required to process them will wear on the prosecutor's patience. As one district attorney has said, "the usual defense strategy today is to bring in a stack of motions as thick as a Sunday newspaper; defense attorneys hope that we won't have the patience to ride them out."[89]

Prosecutors have their own methods of inducing a plea bargain. The most common is the ethically questionable practice of *overcharging*—that is, charging the defendant with more counts than may be appropriate. There are two types of overcharging:

1. In *horizontal overcharging*, the prosecutor brings a number of different counts for a single criminal incident.
2. In *vertical overcharging*, the prosecutor raises the level of a charge above its proper place. For example, the facts of the case warrant a charge of battery, but the prosecutor charges the defendant with attempted murder.

After overcharging, prosecutors allow themselves to be "bargained down" to the correct charge, giving the defense attorney and the defendant the impression that they have achieved some sort of victory.

Protecting the Defendant Watching the defense attorney and the prosecutor maneuver in this manner, the defendant often comes to the conclusion that the plea bargaining process is a sort of game with sometimes incomprehensible rules.[90] The Supreme Court is also aware of the potential for taking advantage of the defendant in plea bargaining and has taken steps to protect the accused. (For a summary of notable Supreme Court cases involving plea bargaining procedures, see ■ Figure 9.8.) Until *Boykin v. Alabama* (1969),[91] judges would often accept the defense counsel's word that the defendant wanted to plead guilty. In that case, the Court held that the

■ **Figure 9.8** **Notable United States Supreme Court Decisions on Plea Bargaining**

The constitutional justification of the plea bargain as an accepted part of the criminal justice process has been fortified by these Supreme Court rulings.

Brady v. United States (397 U.S. 742 [1970]). In this case the defendant entered a guilty plea in order to avoid the death penalty. In allowing this action, the Court ruled that **plea bargains are a legitimate part of the adjudication process as long as they are entered into voluntarily and the defendant has full knowledge of the consequences of pleading guilty.**

North Carolina v. Alford (400 U.S. 25 [1970]). Although maintaining he was innocent of the first degree murder for which he was charged, Alford pleaded guilty to second degree murder in order to avoid the possibility of the death penalty that came with the original charges. After being sentenced to thirty years in prison, Alford argued that he was forced to plea bargain because of the threat of the death penalty. The Court refused to invalidate Alford's guilty plea, stating that **plea bargains are valid even if the defendant claims innocence, as long as the plea was entered into voluntarily.**

Santobello v. New York (404 U.S. 257 [1971]). This case focused on the prosecutor's role in the plea bargain process. The Court ruled that **if a prosecutor promises a more lenient sentence in return for the defendant's guilty plea, the promise must be kept.**

Bordenkircher v. Hayes (434 U.S. 357 [1978]). A Kentucky prosecutor told Hayes that if he entered a guilty plea, the prosecutor would recommend a light sentence. If not, he would indict Hayes under the state's habitual offender act, which carried the possibility of life imprisonment. The Court ruled that **prosecutors are within their rights to threaten defendants with harsher sentences in order to induce a guilty plea.**

Ricketts v. Adamson (483 U.S. 1 [1987]). In return for a reduction of charges, Ricketts agreed to plead guilty and to testify against a codefendant in a murder

case. When the codefendant's conviction was reversed on appeal, Ricketts refused to testify a second time. Therefore, the prosecutor rescinded the offer of leniency. The Court ruled that the prosecutor's action was justified, and that **defendants must uphold their side of the plea bargain in order to receive its benefits.**

United States v. Mezzanatto (513 U.S. 196 [1995]). The Court ruled that a prosecutor can refuse to plea bargain with a defendant unless the defendant agrees that any statements made by him or her during the bargaining process can be used against him or her in a possible trial. In other words, **if the defendant admits to committing the crime during plea bargain negotiations, and then decides to plead not guilty, the prosecution can use the admission as evidence during the trial.**

Boykin Form A form that must be completed by a defendant who pleads guilty; the defendant states that she or he has done so voluntarily and with full comprehension of the consequences.

defendant must make a clear statement that he or she accepts the plea bargain. As a result, many jurisdictions now ask the accused to sign a *Boykin* form waiving his or her right to a trial. A statement in which the defendant admits exactly what crime he or she committed must accompany this guilty plea.

Self Check Fill in the Blanks

A _____ occurs when the prosecution and the defense work out an agreement that resolves the case. Generally, a defendant will plead guilty in exchange for a reduction of the _____ against him or her or a lighter _____, or both. To ensure that the defendant understands the terms of the plea, he or she must sign a _____ form waiving his or her right to a _____. Check your answers on page 303.

Going to Trial

The pretrial process does not inexorably lead to a guilty plea. Just as prosecutors, defense attorneys, and defendants have reasons to negotiate, they may also be motivated to take a case to trial. If either side is confident in the strength of its arguments and evidence, it will obviously be less likely to accept a plea bargain. Both prosecutors and defense attorneys may favor a trial to gain publicity, and sometimes public pressure after an extremely violent or high-profile crime will force a chief prosecutor (who is, remember, normally an elected official) to take a weak case to trial. Also, some defendants may insist on their right to a trial, regardless of their attorneys' advice. In the next chapter, we will examine what happens to the roughly 5 percent of indictments that do lead to the courtroom.

▶ In late August 2007, Michael Vick, shown here being escorted into federal court in Richmond, Virginia, entered a guilty plea to dog-fighting conspiracy charges. A month earlier, the Atlanta Falcons quarterback had pleaded not guilty and vowed to take his case to criminal court to prove his innocence. However, after three co-defendants in the dog-fighting operation pleaded guilty and appeared willing to testify against Vick in court, he changed his mind and decided to forego the court proceedings. What are the risks that Vick would have run had he engaged in a criminal trial?

AP Photo/Ed Murray, Pool

THE PLEA BARGAIN PUZZLE

The Shelby County, Tennessee, district attorney's office has a "no deals" policy, meaning that prosecutors will not enter into plea bargains with criminal defendants—unless, of course, they have to. In April 2007, five years after charging Brian Young with first degree murder and promising the mother of his victim that they would seek the death penalty, prosecutors allowed the defendant to plead guilty to second degree murder and a twenty-three-year prison sentence. "We did the best we could with what we had, but it just didn't pan out," said district attorney Karen Cook.[92] In this *Criminal Justice in Action* feature, we will examine why criminal cases fail to "pan out" more often than not and whether this is a good thing for our system of justice.

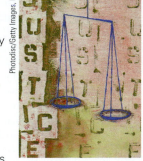

Photodisc/Getty Images, Inc.

ADVERSARIAL AND INEVITABLE

Plea bargaining is a natural outgrowth of the American adversarial criminal justice system. For most of the nineteenth century, when many criminal prosecutions took place without lawyers, plea bargains were rare.

As prosecutors and defense attorneys began to infuse themselves into the process, the incidence of plea bargaining increased. By the 1960s, when a crime wave combined with a population boom began to flood criminal courts with cases, plea bargaining had become an integral component of criminal justice procedures in the United States.[93]

Those who support plea bargaining often do so because they cannot imagine life without it. In 1970, Supreme Court Chief Justice Warren Burger warned that "a reduction from 90 percent to 80 percent in guilty pleas requires the assignment of twice the judicial manpower and facilities—judges, court reporters, bailiffs, clerks, jurors, and courtrooms." Burger added, "A reduction to 70 percent trebles this demand."[94] This practicality bothers some observers. "Because of plea bargaining, I guess we can say, 'Gee, the trains run on time,'" notes criminologist Franklin Zimring. "But do we like where they're going?"[95]

The Case for Plea Bargaining

- Plea bargaining provides prosecutors and defense attorneys with the flexibility to quickly dispose of some cases while allocating scarce resources to the cases that require them.

- Because of mandatory minimum sentencing, which we will study in Chapter 11, criminal defendants who go to trial risk very harsh punishment if they lose.

Plea bargaining allows them to mitigate that risk and accept a lesser sentence.

- As we saw in the opening to this chapter, the practice spares victims such as Shasta Groene from reliving the horrors of their victimization as courtroom witnesses.

The Case against Plea Bargaining

- Plea bargaining gives innocent people an incentive to plead guilty if they feel that there is even a slight chance that a jury or judge might decide against them.

- Plea bargaining gives prosecutors too much power to coerce defendants, either by overcharging (see page 299) or by bluffing by claiming to have evidence that

the prosecutor knows would actually be inadmissible at trial, such as contraband gained by an illegal search.

- The practice allows dangerous criminals to "beat the system" by negotiating for lighter sentences than they deserve. Consequently, it undermines the deterrent effects of punishment and the public's confidence in the criminal justice system.

Your Opinion—Writing Assignment

When Kathleen Rice took office as district attorney for Nassau County, New York, she was dismayed to see that one-third of the people arrested for drunken driving in the county had previous convictions for the same offense. "The message was that you can do this as many times as you want and you're always going to be given the option to plead out to the equivalent of a traffic infraction," said Rice.[96] As a result, she instituted a "no deals" policy of her own for drinking-and-driving charges. Not surprisingly, Nassau County's defense attorneys have not reacted positively to Rice's plan. "People need some degree of hope, and under [her] policies, they're not getting it," complained one.[97]

What is your opinion of "no deals" policies for specific crimes? What impact do such policies have on prosecutors, defense attorneys, and defendants? If you agree with this strategy, to which crimes would you apply it and why? Before responding, you can review our discussions in this chapter concerning

- Defense attorneys (pages 277–283).
- Case attrition (pages 293–295).
- Plea bargaining (pages 296–300).

Your answer should take at least three full paragraphs.

L01 **List the different names given to public prosecutors and indicate the general powers that they have.** At the federal level, the prosecutor is called the U.S. attorney. In state and local courts, the prosecutor may be referred to as the prosecuting attorney, state prosecutor, district attorney, county attorney, or city attorney. Prosecutors in general have the power to decide when and how the state will pursue an individual suspected of criminal wrongdoing. In some jurisdictions, the district attorney is also the chief law enforcement officer, holding broad powers over police operations.

L02 **Contrast the prosecutor's roles as an elected official and as a crime fighter.** In most instances, the prosecutor is elected and therefore may feel obliged to reward members of her or his party with jobs. To win reelection or higher political office, the prosecutor may feel a need to bow to community pressures. As a crime fighter, the prosecutor is dependent on the police, and indeed prosecutors are generally seen as law enforcement agents. Prosecutors, however, generally pursue cases only when they believe there is sufficient legal guilt to obtain a conviction.

L03 **Delineate the responsibilities of defense attorneys.** (a) Representation of the defendant during the custodial process; (b) investigation of the supposed criminal incident; (c) communication with the prosecutor (including plea bargaining); (d) preparation of the case for trial; (e) submission of defense motions; (f) representation of the defendant at trial; (g) negotiation of a sentence after conviction; and (h) appeal of a guilty verdict.

L04 **Indicate the three types of defense allocation programs.** (a) Assigned counsel programs, which use local private attorneys; (b) contracting attorney programs; and (c) public defender programs.

L05 **List the three basic features of an adversary system of justice.** (a) A neutral decision maker (judge or jury); (b) presentation of evidence from both parties; and (c) a highly structured set of procedures that must be used when evidence is presented.

L06 **Identify the steps involved in the pretrial criminal process.** (a) Suspect taken into custody or arrested; (b) initial appearance before a magistrate, at which time the defendant is informed of his or her constitutional rights and a public defender may be appointed or private counsel may be hired by the state to represent the defendant; (c) the posting of bail or release on recognizance; (d) preventive detention, if deemed necessary to ensure the safety of other persons or the community, or regular detention, if the defendant is unable to post bail; (e) preliminary hearing (mini-trial), at which the judge rules on whether there is probable cause and the prosecutor issues an information; or in the alternative (f) grand jury hearings, after which an indictment is issued against the defendant if the grand jury finds probable cause; (g) arraignment, in which the defendant is informed of the charges and must respond by pleading not guilty or guilty (or in some cases *nolo contendere*); and (h) plea bargaining.

L07 **Indicate the three influences on a judge's decision to set bail.** (a) Uncertainty about the character and past criminal history of the defendant; (b) the risk that the defendant will commit another crime if out on bail; and (c) overcrowded jails, which may influence a judge to release a defendant on bail.

L08 **Explain how a prosecutor screens potential cases.** (a) Is there sufficient evidence for conviction? (b) What is the priority of the case? The more serious the alleged crime, the higher the priority. The more extensive the defendant's criminal record, the higher the priority. (c) Are the victims cooperative? Violence against family members often yields uncooperative victims; therefore, these cases are rarely prosecuted. (d) Are the victims reliable? (e) Might the defendant be willing to testify against other offenders?

L09 **List and briefly explain the different forms of plea bargaining agreements.** (a) Charge bargaining, in which the charge is reduced to a lesser crime; (b) sentence bargaining, in which a lighter sentence is obtained; (c) count bargaining, in which a certain number or most of the multiple counts are eliminated.

L010 **Indicate the ways that both defense attorneys and prosecutors can induce plea bargaining.** Defense attorneys can file numerous pretrial motions in an effort to weaken the state's case. Prosecutors can engage in horizontal or vertical overcharging so that they can be "bargained down" in the process of plea bargaining.

Key Terms

adversary system 283
arraignment 296
attorney general 275
attorney-client privilege 282
bail 285
bail bondsperson 288
Boykin form 300
case attrition 293

defense attorney 277
discovery 291
grand jury 291
indictment 291
information 291
initial appearance 284
nolo contendere 296
plea bargaining 296

preliminary hearing 291
preventive detention 289
property bond 288
public defenders 279
public prosecutors 275
release on recognizance (ROR) 288
ten percent cash bail 288

Questions for Critical Analysis

1. Why are public prosecutors considered the most dominant figures in the American criminal justice system?

2. Why is it difficult for a defendant to have her or his conviction overturned on the ground of inadequate counsel even though the defense attorney was clearly ineffective during trial?

3. Is it true that there is no concern for truth in our adversary system of justice? Explain your answer.

4. During an initial appearance, can defendants plead guilty of having committed a felony? Why or why not?

5. What are the arguments against preventive detention?

6. What is the distinction between a preliminary hearing and an initial appearance?

7. If grand juries indict almost all criminal defendants brought before them, why do we use grand juries?

8. What is case attrition, and why does it occur?

9. Whom does a *Boykin* form protect, and how does it do so?

Maximize Your Best Possible Outcome for Chapter 9

1. **Maximize Your Best Chance for Getting a Good Grade on the Exam.** ThomsonNOW Personalized Study is a diagnostic study tool containing valuable text-specific resources—and because you focus on just what you don't know, you learn more in less time to get a better grade. How do you get ThomsonNOW? If your textbook does not include an access code card, go to **thomsonedu.com** to get ThomsonNOW before your next exam!

2. **Get the Most Out of Your Textbook** by going to the book companion Web site at **www.cjinaction.com** to access one of the tutorial quizzes, use the flash cards to master key terms, and check out the many other study aids you'll find there. Under chapter resources you will also be able to access the Stories from the Street feature and Web links mentioned in the textbook.

3. **Learn about Potential Criminal Justice Careers** discussed in this chapter by exploring careers online at **www.cjinaction.com**. You will find career descriptions and information about job requirements, training, salary and benefits, and the application process. You can also watch video profiles featuring criminal justice professionals.

Notes

1. Taryn Brodwater, "Shasta Key to Duncan Plea Deal: Chance She May Testify at Federal Trial Called 'Remote,'" *Spokane (Washington) Spokesman-Review* (October 19, 2006), 1A.

2. *Ibid.*

3. Bennett L. Gershman, "Abuse of Power in the Prosecutor's Office," in *Criminal Justice 92/93*, ed. John J. Sullivan and Joseph L. Victor (Guilford, CT: The Dushkin Publishing Group, 1991), 117–123.

4. 295 U.S. 78 (1935).

5. Celesta Albonetti, "Prosecutorial Discretion: The Effects of Uncertainty," *Law and Society Review* 21 (1987), 291–313.

6. Stuart K. Taylor, Jr., and K. C. Johnson, "A Dirty Game," *Wall Street Journal* (December 27, 2006), A8.

7. Herbert Packer, *Limits of the Criminal Sanction* (Stanford, CA: Stanford University Press, 1968), 166–167.

8. *Gideon v. Wainwright*, 372 U.S. 335 (1963); *Massiah v. United States*, 377 U.S. 201 (1964); *United States v. Wade*, 388 U.S. 218 (1967); *Argersinger v. Hamlin*, 407 U.S. 25 (1972); and *Brewer v. Williams*, 430 U.S. 387 (1977).

9. Larry Siegel, *Criminology*, 6th ed. (Belmont, CA: West/Wadsworth Publishing Co., 1998), 487–488.

10. Center for Professional Responsibility, *Model Rules of Professional Conduct* (Washington, D.C.: American Bar Association, 2003), Rules 1.6 and 3.1.
11. *United States v. Wade,* 388 U.S. 218, 256–258 (1967).
12. 372 U.S. 335 (1963).
13. 387 U.S. 1 (1967).
14. 407 U.S. 25 (1972).
15. Peter A. Joy and Kevin C. McMunigal, "Client Autonomy and Choice of Counsel," *Criminal Justice* (Fall 2006), 57.
16. American Bar Association, "Providing Defense Services," Standard 5-7.1, at **www.abanet.org/crimjust/standards/defsvcs_blk.html#7.1**.
17. Robert C. Boruchowitz, "The Right to Counsel: Every Accused Person's Right," *Washington State Bar Association Bar News* (January 2004), at **www.wsba.org/media/publications/barnews/2004/jan-04-boruchowitz.htm**.
18. Bureau of Justice Statistics, *State Funded Indigent Defense Services, 1999* (Washington, D.C.: U.S. Department of Justice, September 2001), 3.
19. *Ibid.,* 4.
20. *United States v. Gonzalez-Lopez,* 548 U.S. ____ (2006).
21. *Wheat v. United States,* 486 U.S. 153, 159 (1988).
22. Quoted in Bob Herbert, "Cheap Justice," *New York Times* (March 1, 1998), 15.
23. "Justice in Missouri: Public Defender System Needs Help," *Kansas City Star* (April 1, 2006), B6.
24. Kevin Krause, "Judges Rely on Costlier Lawyers," *Dallas Morning News* (April 3, 2007), 1A.
25. Jonathan Saltzman, "Suit Seeks Pay Raise for Public Defenders," *Boston Globe* (June 29, 2004), B1.
26. Michael Hooper, "Out of College, Out of Money," *Topeka (Kansas) Capital Journal* (June 4, 2006), 1.
27. Catherine Bean, "Indigent Defense: Separate and Unequal," *Champion* (May 2004), 54.
28. 466 U.S. 668 (1984).
29. Adam Liptak, "Despite Flawed Defense, a Death Sentence Stands," *New York Times* (November 2, 2006), A17.
30. Roger A. Hanson, Brian J. Ostrom, and Ann A. Jones, "Effective Adversaries for the Poor," in *The Japanese Adversary System in Context,* ed. Malcolm M. Feeley and Setsuo Miyazawa (New York: Palgrave Macmillan, 2002), 89, 102.
31. Bureau of Justice Statistics, *Defense Counsel in Criminal Cases* (Washington, D.C.: U.S. Department of Justice, November 2000), 3–4.
32. Jonathan D. Casper, *American Criminal Justice: The Defendant's Perspective* (Englewood Cliffs, NJ: Prentice Hall, 1972), 101.
33. William Finnegan, "Defending the Unabomber," *New Yorker* (March 16, 1998), 61.
34. *Model Rules of Professional Conduct,* Rule 1.2(c)–(d).
35. Randolph Braccialarghe, "Why Were Perry Mason's Clients Always Innocent?" *Valparaiso University Law Review* (Fall 2004), 65.
36. John Kaplan, "Defending Guilty People," *University of Bridgeport Law Review* (1986), 223.
37. 491 U.S. 554 (1989).
38. Johannes F. Nijboer, "The American Adversary System in Criminal Cases: Between Ideology and Reality," *Cardozo Journal of International and Comparative Law* 5 (Spring 1997), 79.
39. Gordon Van Kessel, "Adversary Excesses in the American Criminal Trial," *Notre Dame Law Review* 67 (1992), 403.
40. James Eisenstein and Herbert Jacob, *Felony Justice* (Boston: Little, Brown, 1977), 24.
41. Jerome Skolnick, "Social Control in the Adversary System," *Journal of Conflict Resolution* 11 (1967), 52–70.
42. Abraham S. Blumberg, "The Practice of Law as Confidence Game: Organizational Cooption of a Profession," *Law and Society Review* 4 (June 1967), 115–139.
43. Malcolm Feeley, "The Adversary System," in *Encyclopedia of the American Judicial System,* ed. Robert J. Janosik (New York: Scribners, 1987), 753.
44. Blumberg, 115.
45. *Riverside County, California v. McLaughlin,* 500 U.S. 44 (1991).
46. Illinois Annotated Statutes Chapter 725, Paragraph 5/110-5.
47. David W. Neubauer, *America's Courts and the Criminal Justice System,* 5th ed. (Belmont, CA: Wadsworth Publishing Co., 1996), 179–181.
48. Roy Flemming, C. Kohfeld, and Thomas Uhlman, "The Limits of Bail Reform: A Quasi Experimental Analysis," *Law and Society Review* 14 (1980), 947–976.
49. Caleb Foote, "Compelling Appearance in Court: Administration of Bail in Philadelphia," *University of Pennsylvania Law Review* 102 (1954), 1031–1052.
50. Marian R. Williams, "The Effect of Pretrial Detention on Imprisonment Decisions," *Criminal Justice Review* (Autumn 2003), 299–300, 313.
51. Frederic Suffet, "Bail Setting: A Study of Courtroom Interaction," *Crime and Delinquency* 12 (1966), 318.
52. Wayne H. Thomas, Jr., *Bail Reform in America* (Berkeley, CA: University of California Press, 1976), 4.
53. Andrew D. Patrick, "Running from the Law," *Vanderbilt Law Review* (January 1999), 172.
54. John S. Goldkamp and Michael R. Gottfredson, *Policy Guidelines for Bail: An Experiment in Court Reform* (Philadelphia: Temple University Press, 1985), 18.
55. Thomas, 7.
56. *Stack v. Boyle,* 342 U.S. 1, 7–8 (1951).
57. *Taylor v. Taintor,* 83 U.S. (16 Wall.) 366 (1873).
58. Jeremy Boren, "Bill Would Set Rules for Bounty Hunters," *Pittsburgh Tribune Review* (March 21, 2005), A1.
59. Esmond Harmsworth, "Bail and Detention: An Assessment and Critique of the Federal and Massachusetts Systems," *New England Journal on Criminal and Civil Confinement* 22 (Spring 1996), 213.
60. 18 U.S.C. Section 3146(b) (1966).
61. Harmsworth, 213.
62. Thomas C. French, "Is It Punitive or Is It Regulatory?" *University of Toledo Law Review* 20 (Fall 1988), 189.
63. 18 U.S.C. Sections 3141–3150 (Supp. III 1985).
64. 481 U.S. 739 (1987).
65. Bureau of Justice Statistics, *Felony Defendants in Large Urban Counties, 2002* (Washington, D.C.: U.S. Department of Justice, February 2006), 22.
66. *Gerstein v. Pugh,* 420 U.S. 103 (1975).
67. David W. Neubauer, *Criminal Justice in Middle America* (Morristown, NJ: General Learning Press, 1974).
68. Andrew D. Leipold, "Why Grand Juries Do Not (and Cannot) Protect the Accused," *Cornell Law Review* 80 (January 1995), 260.
69. Robert L. Misner, "In Partial Praise of *Boyd:* The Grand Jury as Catalyst for Fourth Amendment Change," *Arizona State Law Review* (Fall 1997), 805.
70. New York Court of Appeals Judge Sol Wachtler, quoted in David Margolik, "Law Professor to Administer Courts in State," *New York Times* (February 1, 1985), B2.
71. Kenneth C. Davis, *Discretionary Justice: A Preliminary Inquiry* (Baton Rouge, LA: Louisiana State University Press, 1969), 189.
72. Transactional Records Access Clearinghouse, "FBI: National Profile and Enforcement Trends over Time," at **trac.syr.edu/tracfbi/newfindings/current**.
73. Milton Hirsh and David Oscar Markus, "Fourth Amendment Forum," *Champion* (December 2002), 42.
74. Barbara Boland, Paul Mahanna, and Ronald Scones, *The Prosecution of Felony Arrests, 1988* (Washington, D.C.: Bureau of Justice Statistics, 1992).
75. Richard Felson and Paul-Philippe Pare, *The Reporting of Domestic Violence and Sexual Assault by Nonstrangers to the Police* (Washington, D.C.: U.S. Department of Justice, March 2005), 6.
76. Tom Lininger, "Evidentiary Issues in Federal Prosecutions of Violence against Women," *Indiana Law Review* 36 (2003), 709.
77. 18 U.S.C. Section 3553(e) (2006).
78. 404 U.S. 257 (1971).
79. Fred C. Zacharias, "Justice in Plea Bargaining," *William and Mary Law Review* 39 (March 1998), 1121.
80. Bureau of Justice Statistics, *State Court Sentencing of Convicted Felons, 2002* (Washington, D.C.: U.S. Department of Justice, May 2005), Table 4.1, page 44.
81. Albert W. Alschuler, "The Prosecutor's Role in Plea Bargaining," *University of Chicago Law Review* 36 (1968), 52.
82. Milton Heumann, *Plea Bargaining: The Experiences of Prosecutors, Judges, and Defense Attorneys* (Chicago: University of Chicago Press, 1978), 58.
83. Albert W. Alschuler, "The Defense Attorney's Role in Plea Bargaining," *Yale Law Journal* 84 (1975), 1200.
84. Stephen J. Schulhofer, "Plea Bargaining as Disaster," *Yale Law Journal* 101 (1992), 1987.

85. Kevin Cole and Fred C. Zacharias, "The Agony of Victory and the Ethics of Lawyer Speech," *Southern California Law Review* 69 (1996), 1660–1663.

86. North Carolina General Statutes Section 15A-832(f) (2003).

87. 18 U.S.C. Section 3771 (2004).

88. Chuck Haga, "Killer Rejected Life-Sentence Plea Bargain," *(Minneapolis, Minnesota) Star Tribune* (February 18, 2007), 1B.

89. Alschuler, "The Prosecutor's Role in Plea Bargaining," 53.

90. Casper, 77–81.

91. 395 U.S. 238 (1969).

92. Quoted in Alex Doniach, "Plea Bargain in Boy's Killing Shakes Family," *Commercial Appeal* (Memphis, Tennessee) (April 21, 2007), B3.

93. Lawrence M. Friedman, "Plea Bargaining in Historical Perspective," *Law and Society Review* 13 (1978), 247–259.

94. Warren Burger, "Address to the American Bar Association Annual Convention," *New York Times* (August 11, 1970), 24.

95. Quoted in "Is Plea Bargaining a Cop-Out?" *Time* (August 28, 1978), at **www.time.com/time/magazine/article/0,9171,916340-3,00.html**.

96. Quoted in Frank Eltman, "D.A. Gets Tough on DWIs," *Grand Rapids (Michigan) Press* (October 1, 2006), A10.

97. *Ibid.*

The Criminal Trial

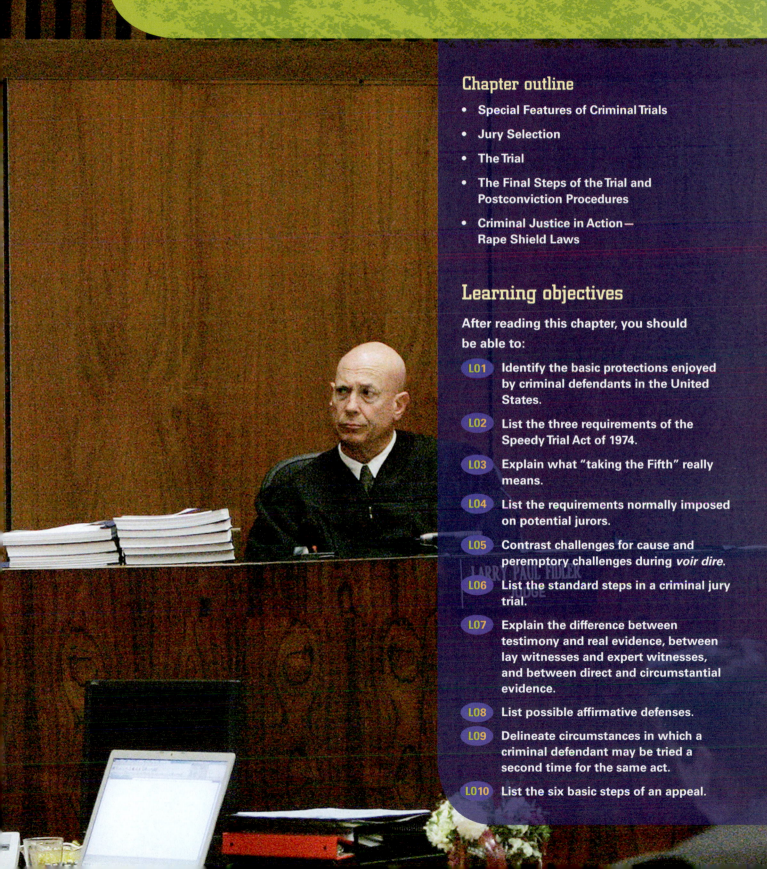

Learning objectives

After reading this chapter, you should be able to:

LO1 Identify the basic protections enjoyed by criminal defendants in the United States.

LO2 List the three requirements of the Speedy Trial Act of 1974.

LO3 Explain what "taking the Fifth" really means.

LO4 List the requirements normally imposed on potential jurors.

LO5 Contrast challenges for cause and peremptory challenges during *voir dire*.

LO6 List the standard steps in a criminal jury trial.

LO7 Explain the difference between testimony and real evidence, between lay witnesses and expert witnesses, and between direct and circumstantial evidence.

LO8 List possible affirmative defenses.

LO9 Delineate circumstances in which a criminal defendant may be tried a second time for the same act.

LO10 List the six basic steps of an appeal.

Susan Polk had good reason to worry. She was on trial in Contra Costa Superior Court for the brutal murder of her husband, Felix, who had been stabbed twenty-seven times and left for dead in the couple's Orinda, California, pool house. Over five days of often rambling testimony in the spring of 2006, Susan tried to convince the jury of her innocence. By her account, on the night of the crime she and Felix had a violent argument that started when she accused him of being an Israeli spy and failing to warn the U.S. government of the September 11, 2001, terrorist attacks. After Felix struck her with an ottoman, Susan said, she retaliated with a blast of pepper spray. Undeterred, he tried to rub the greasy spray into her eyes and then came at her with a knife. Susan testified that she kicked Felix in the groin, grabbed the knife, and stabbed him in the side and the back. Then, suddenly, according to Susan, he stood straight up, said, "Oh my God, I think I'm dead," and suffered a fatal heart attack.

Assistant District Attorney Paul Sequiera must have been enjoying Susan's performance. First, crime scene investigators had found no traces of pepper spray in the pool house. Second, a pathologist testified that Felix had suffered numerous stab wounds to the chest, arms, and hands—not his side and back. Third, and most damning, Susan admitted that she told no one, not even the couple's teenage son, Gabriel, about Felix's death so that she could continue to "take care of my dogs." She even

drove her husband's car to the train station to deceive her son into thinking Felix was at work. When Gabriel finally found his father's body the next evening and called the police, Susan denied any knowledge of the death. In all, Susan's testimony did great damage to her credibility. If she had had a defense attorney, the professional probably would have tried to keep her off the stand, but Susan represented herself throughout the proceedings.

AP Photo/Ben Margot

▲ Speaking from behind a Plexiglass window in the visiting room of the West County Detention Center in Richmond, California, Susan Polk proclaims that she is innocent of the violent stabbing death of her husband, Felix.

When Susan Polk informed Judge Laurel Brady that she wished to act as her own defense counsel, the judge agreed—with reservations. "It's a risky way to proceed," warned Brady. "It's certainly not recommended, [but] it's your choice."[1] Daniel Horowitz, relieved from his position as Polk's defense attorney, wished his client the best and said, "I hope she can get a fair trial."[2] After the criminal trial, which one observer called "a train wreck every day,"[3] the jury convicted Polk of second degree murder, and on February 24, 2007, Brady gave her the maximum sentence of sixteen years to life in state prison. "It was distressing to me to see her represent herself," said Charlie Hoehn, a defense attorney who agreed to stand at Polk's side during the punishment phase of the proceedings. "From speaking with her, it sounds like she didn't have a fair trial."[4]

Fairness is, of course, a crucial component of the criminal trial. Protection against the arbitrary abuse of power is at the heart of the U.S. Constitution, and the right to a criminal trial before a jury is one means of assuring this protection. In this chapter, we will examine the fairness of the criminal trial in the context of the current legal environment. Because "fairness" can only be defined subjectively, we will also make an effort to look into the effect human nature has on the adversary process. Trials may be based on fact finding, but as Judge Jerome Frank once sardonically asserted, when it comes to a jury, "facts are guesses."[5]

Special Features of Criminal Trials

Civil trials (see Chapter 4) and criminal trials have many similar features. In both types of trials, attorneys from each side select a jury, make their opening statements to the court, examine and cross-examine witnesses, and summarize their positions in closing arguments. The jury is charged (instructed), and if it reaches a verdict, the trial comes to an end.

The principal difference is that in civil trials, the adversaries are persons (including corporations, which are legal persons, and businesses), one of whom often is seeking a remedy in the form of damages from the other. In a criminal trial, it is the state, not the victim of the crime, that brings the action against an alleged wrongdoer. Criminal trial procedures reflect the need to protect criminal defendants against the power of the state by providing them with a number of rights. Many of the significant rights of the accused are spelled out in the Sixth Amendment, which reads, in part, as follows:

> **L01** In all criminal prosecutions, the accused shall enjoy the right to a speedy and public trial, by an impartial jury of the State and the district wherein the crime shall have been committed, . . . and to be informed of the nature and cause of the accusation; to be confronted with the witnesses against him; to have compulsory process for obtaining witnesses in his favor; and to have the Assistance of Counsel for his defense.

In this section, we will examine the aspects of the criminal trial that make it unique, beginning with two protections explicitly stated in the Sixth Amendment: the right to a speedy trial by an impartial jury.

A "SPEEDY" TRIAL

As you have just read, the Sixth Amendment requires a speedy trial for those accused of a criminal act. The reason for this requirement is obvious: depending on various factors, the defendant may lose his or her right to move freely and may be incarcerated prior to trial. Also, the accusation that a person has committed a crime jeopardizes that person's reputation in the community. If the defendant is innocent, the sooner the trial is held, the sooner his or her innocence can be established in the eyes of the court and the public.

Reasons for Delay As the preceding chapter made clear, there are numerous reasons for delay in bringing a defendant to trial. In defending the rights of the accused, a defense attorney may use a number of legal tactics, including pretrial motions and plea negotiations. Court congestion also contributes to the problem; many jurisdictions do not have enough judges and courtroom space to meet the needs of the system. This situation has been aggravated by the increase in drug-related arrests, which threatens to create judicial "gridlock" in certain metropolitan courthouses.[6]

The Definition of a Speedy Trial The Sixth Amendment does not specify what is meant by the term *speedy*. The United States Supreme Court has refused to quantify "speedy" as well, ruling instead in *Barker v. Wingo* (1972)[7] that only in situations in which the delay is unwarranted and proved to be prejudicial can the accused claim a violation of Sixth Amendment rights.

▼ Two U.S. marshals lead former Ku Klux Klan member James Ford Seale, 81, from the federal courthouse in Jackson, Mississippi. In 2007, a jury convicted Seale of two counts of kidnapping and one count of conspiracy for his role in the killing of two African American teenagers forty-three years earlier. Why do statutes of limitations (see the next page) not apply to serious crimes such as those involving murder? What are some of the drawbacks of prosecuting a crime more than four decades after it occurred?

AP Photo/Rogelio V. Solis

Speedy-Trial Laws As a result, all fifty states have their own speedy-trial statutes. For example, the Illinois Speedy Trial Act states that a defendant must be tried within 120 days of arrest unless both the prosecution and the defense agree otherwise.[8] Keep in mind, however, that a defendant does not automatically go free if her or his trial is not "speedy" enough. There must be judicial action. Several years ago, for example, a Philadelphia judge ordered the release of seven men, some of whom had been charged with murder and kidnapping, because they had spent six or more years in jail awaiting trial. According to Pennsylvania law, trials must start within one year of arrest.[9]

At the national level, the Speedy Trial Act of 1974[10] (amended in 1979) specifies the following time limits for those in the federal court system

1. No more than thirty days between arrest and indictment.
2. No more than ten days between indictment and arraignment.
3. No more than sixty days between arraignment and trial.

Federal law allows extra time for hearings on pretrial motions, mental competency examinations, and other procedural actions.

Statutes of Limitations Note that the Sixth Amendment's guarantee of a speedy trial does not apply until a person has been accused of a crime. Citizens are protected against unreasonable delays before accusation because of **statutes of limitations,** which are legislative time limits that require prosecutors to charge a defendant with a crime within a certain amount of time after the illegal act took place. If the statute of limitations on a particular crime is ten years, and the police do not identify a suspect until ten years and one day after the criminal act occurred, then that suspect cannot be charged with that particular offense.

In general, prosecutions for murder and other offenses that carry the death penalty do not have a statute of limitations. Therefore, in 2007, when the Arapahoe County (Colorado) Sheriffs' Department uncovered new evidence that Herbert Frye had killed his wife on June 9, 1973, the county attorney was able to bring fresh murder charges against the eighty-one-year-old suspect. The problem with prosecuting such cases, of course, is that so much time has passed since the criminal act that witnesses may be missing or dead, memories may be unreliable, and other evidence may have been lost.

THE ROLE OF THE JURY

The Sixth Amendment also states that anyone accused of a crime shall be judged by "an impartial jury." In *Duncan v. Louisiana* (1968),[11] the Supreme Court solidified this right by ruling that in all felony cases, the defendant is entitled to a **jury trial.** The Court has, however, left it to the individual states to decide whether juries are required for misdemeanor cases.[12] If the defendant waives her or his right to trial by jury, a **bench trial** takes place in which a judge decides questions of legality and fact, and no jury is involved.

Jury Size The predominant American twelve-person jury is not the result of any one law—the Constitution does not require that the jury be a particular size. Historically, the number was inherited from the size of English juries, which was fixed at twelve during the fourteenth century.

In 1970, responding to a case that challenged Florida's practice of using a six-person jury in all but capital cases, the Supreme Court ruled that the accused did not have the right to be tried by a twelve-person jury. Indeed, the Court labeled the number twelve "a historical accident, wholly without significance except to mystics."[13] In *Ballew v. Georgia* (1978),[14] however, the Court did strike down attempts to use juries with fewer than six members, stating that a jury's

---

Statute of Limitations A law limiting the amount of time prosecutors have to bring criminal charges against a suspect after the crime has occurred.

Jury Trial A trial before a judge and a jury.

Bench Trial A trial conducted without a jury, in which a judge makes the determination of the defendant's guilt or innocence.

effectiveness was severely hampered below that limit. About half the states allow fewer than twelve persons on criminal juries, though only for misdemeanor cases. In federal courts, defendants are entitled to have the case heard by a twelve-member jury unless both parties agree in writing to a smaller jury.

Unanimity In most jurisdictions, jury verdicts in criminal cases must be *unanimous* for **acquittal** or conviction. As will be explained in more detail later, if the jury cannot reach unanimous agreement on whether to acquit or convict the defendant, the result is a *hung jury,* and the judge may order a new trial.

Again, the Supreme Court has not held that unanimity is a rigid requirement. It has declared that jury verdicts must be unanimous in federal criminal trials, but has given states leeway to set their own rules.[15] Five states—Louisiana, Montana, Oklahoma, Oregon, and Texas—permit nonunanimous trial verdicts, though none allow more than three dissenting votes for convictions by twelve-person juries.

THE PRIVILEGE AGAINST SELF-INCRIMINATION

In addition to the Sixth Amendment, which specifies the protections we have just discussed, the Fifth Amendment to the Constitution also provides important safeguards for the defendant. The Fifth Amendment states that no person "shall be compelled in any criminal case to be a witness against himself." Therefore, a defendant has the right *not* to testify at a trial if to do so would implicate him or her in the crime. Witnesses may also refuse to testify on this ground. For example, if a witness, while testifying, is asked a question and the answer would reveal her or his own criminal wrongdoing, the witness may "take the Fifth." In other words, she or he can refuse to testify on the ground that such testimony may be self-incriminating. This rarely occurs, however, as witnesses are often granted *immunity* before testifying, meaning that no information they disclose can be used to bring criminal charges against them. Witnesses who have been granted immunity cannot refuse to answer questions on the basis of self-incrimination.

It is important to note that not only does the defendant have the right to "take the Fifth," but also that the decision to do so should not prejudice the jury in the prosecution's favor. The Supreme Court came to this controversial decision while reviewing *Adamson v. California* (1947),[16] a case involving the convictions of two defendants who had declined to testify in their own defense against charges of robbery, kidnapping, and murder. The prosecutor in *Adamson* frequently and insistently brought this silence to the notice of the jury in his closing argument, insinuating that if the pair had been innocent, they would not have been afraid to testify. The Court ruled that such tactics effectively invalidated the Fifth Amendment by using the defendants' refusal to testify against them. Now judges are required to inform the jury that an accused's decision to remain silent cannot be held against him or her.

THE PRESUMPTION OF A DEFENDANT'S INNOCENCE

The presumption in criminal law is that a defendant is innocent until proved guilty. The burden of proving guilt falls on the state (the public prosecutor). Even if a defendant did in fact commit the crime, she or he will be "innocent" in the eyes of the law unless the prosecutor can substantiate the charge with sufficient evidence to convince a jury (or judge in a bench trial) of the defendant's guilt.[17] Sometimes, especially when a case involves a high-profile violent crime, pretrial publicity may have convinced many members of the community—including potential jurors—that a defendant is guilty. In these instances, a judge has the authority to change the venue of the trial to ensure an unbiased jury. In 2007, for example, the trial of John E. Couey, who had been charged

▼ A billboard in Redwood City, California, asks callers to vote on the guilt or innocence of Scott Peterson, who was eventually convicted of murdering his wife and the couple's unborn son. What impact can pretrial publicity have on a defendant's ability to receive a fair trial?

AP Photo/Paul Sakuma

with raping nine-year-old Jessica Lunsford and burying her alive, was moved three hundred miles from the site of the crime in Citrus County, Florida, to Miami.

A STRICT STANDARD OF PROOF

In a criminal trial, the defendant is not required to prove his or her innocence. As mentioned earlier, the burden of proving the defendant's guilt lies entirely with the state. Furthermore, the state must prove the defendant's guilt *beyond a reasonable doubt;* that is, the prosecution must show that, based on all the evidence, the defendant's guilt is clear and unquestionable. In *In re Winship* (1970),[18] a case involving the due process rights of juveniles, the Supreme Court ruled that the Constitution requires the reasonable doubt standard because it reduces the risk of convicting innocent people and therefore reassures Americans of the law's moral force and legitimacy.

This high standard of proof in criminal cases reflects a fundamental social value—the belief that it is worse to convict an innocent individual than to let a guilty one go free. The consequences to the life, liberty, and reputation of an accused person from an erroneous conviction for a crime are enormous, and this has been factored into the process. Placing a high standard of proof on the prosecutor reduces the margin of error in criminal cases (at least in one direction).

Self Check Fill in the Blanks

The defendant in any felony case is entitled to a trial by _____. If the defendant waives this right, a _____ trial takes place, in which the _____ decides questions of law and fact. Another benefit for the defendant is the privilege against _____, which gives her or him the right to "take the Fifth." Perhaps the most important protection for the defendant, however, is the presumption in criminal law that she or he is _____ until proved _____. Thus, the burden is on the _____ to prove the defendant's culpability beyond a _____. Check your answers on page 338.

Jury Selection

The initial step in a criminal trial involves choosing the jury. The framers of the Constitution ensured that the importance of the jury would not be easily overlooked. The right to a trial by jury is explicitly mentioned no fewer than three times in the Constitution: in Article III, Section 2; in the Sixth Amendment; and again in the Seventh Amendment. The use of a peer jury not only provided safeguards against the abuses of state power that the framers feared, but also gave Americans a chance—and a duty—to participate in the criminal justice system.

In the early years of the country, a jury "of one's peers" meant a jury limited to white, landowning males. Now, as the process has become fully democratized, there are still questions about what "a jury of one's peers" actually means and how effective the system has been in providing the necessary diversity in juries.

INITIAL STEPS: THE MASTER JURY LIST AND *VENIRE*

The main goal of jury selection is to produce a cross section of the population in the jurisdiction where the crime was committed. Sometimes, a defense attorney may argue that his or her client's trial should be moved to another community to protect against undue prejudice. In practice, judges, mindful of the intent of the Constitution, are hesitant to grant such pretrial motions.

A Jury of Peers This belief that trials should take place in the community where the crime was committed is central to the purpose of selecting a jury of the defendant's

◄ To a large extent, the jury selection process is designed to ensure that juries reflect the community in which the trial is held. Why is it important for a defendant to be tried by a jury of her or his "peers"?

"peers." The United States is a large, diverse nation, and the outlook of its citizens varies accordingly. Two very different cases, one tried in rural Maine and the other in San Francisco, illustrate this point.[19] In Maine, the defendant had accidentally shot and killed a woman standing in her backyard; he had mistaken her white mittens for a deer's tail. His attorney argued that it was the responsibility of the victim to wear bright-colored clothing in the vicinity of hunters during hunting season. The jury agreed, and the defendant was acquitted of manslaughter. In the San Francisco case, two people were charged with distributing sterile needles to intravenous drug users. Rather than denying that the defendants had distributed the needles, the defense admitted the act but insisted that it was necessary to stem the transmission of AIDS and, thus, to save lives. The jury voted 11–1 to acquit, causing a mistrial.

These two outcomes may surprise or even anger people in other parts of the country, but they reflect the values of the regions where the alleged crimes were committed. Thus, a primary goal of the jury selection process is to ensure that the defendant is judged by members of her or his community—peers in the true sense of the word.

The Master Jury List Besides having to live in the jurisdiction where the case is being tried, there are very few restrictions on eligibility to serve on a jury. State legislatures generally set the requirements, and they are similar in most states. For the most part, jurors must be

1. Citizens of the United States.
2. Over eighteen years of age.
3. Free of felony convictions.
4. Of the necessary good health to function in a jury setting.
5. Sufficiently intelligent to understand the issues of a trial.
6. Able to read, write, and comprehend the English language.

L04

The **master jury list,** sometimes called the *jury pool,* is made up of all the eligible jurors in a community. This list is usually drawn from voter-registration lists or driver's license rolls, which have the benefit of being easily available and timely.

Increasing Jury List Diversity The drawback of tying master jury lists to voter-registration lists is that the practice has tended historically to exclude the poor, racial minorities, the young, and the uneducated (in other words, the same groups who are less likely to vote). Also, it has been surmised that some people don't vote

Master Jury List The list of citizens in a court's district from which a jury can be selected; often compiled from voter-registration lists, driver's license lists, and other sources.

My first job in the court system was by accident rather than design. After completing a graduate internship with the Essex County government, I had the opportunity to seek permanent employment with the county-funded judiciary. I was first employed in the Trial Court Administrator's Office in Newark, New Jersey, as the court finance officer in 1983. Much of my education in court administration was gained through the Institute for Court Management of the National Center for State Courts. I pursued this program of professional development from 1984 through 1991 when I graduated as a fellow of ICM.

OPPORTUNITY KNOCKS My initial position offered many opportunities to learn about court management and the workings of a large urban court system. My primary concentration was in human resources, budget, and finance. As a state court, funded by the county, we had to continually justify and fight for positions, space, and equipment. Our court was growing rapidly, and we needed additional resources to allow for an effective and efficient operation. In 1985, I was promoted to director of personnel. I had direct responsibility for all personnel programs, policies, and practices. My association with professional organizations, including the National Association for Court Administration, the American Judicature Society, the Mid-Atlantic Association for Court Administration, and the American Society for Public Administration, was critical to my professional development. The knowledge gained combined with experience helped me to successfully seek the position of assistant trial court administrator and my present position as trial court administrator.

As the trial court administrator, I serve principally as the chief administrative officer for the largest trial and municipal

Courtesy Collins E. Ijoma

for the express reason of keeping their names off the master jury list. These people may not be able to afford to miss work at the low pay offered jurors—$40 a day in federal court and often much less in state court—or simply may not want to deal with the inconvenience of jury duty.

A number of states have taken steps to increase the diversity of the master jury list. Both Arizona and New York access welfare and unemployment rolls to find potential jurors, and Arizona also canvasses phone books and water service customer lists for that purpose. California uses Social Security rolls and tax returns as sources of names. In Florida and elsewhere, lists of persons with driver's licenses are also consulted. According to New Mexico's constitution, non-English-speaking citizens cannot be eliminated from jury lists simply because of their lack of language skills.[20] (In every other state, however, potential jurors may be automatically removed if they cannot speak or understand English.)

"A jury consists of twelve persons chosen to decide who has the better lawyer."

—Robert Frost, American poet (1874–1963)

Venire The next step in gathering a jury is to draw together the *venire* (Latin for "to come"). The *venire* is composed of all those people who are notified by the clerk of the court that they have been selected for jury duty. Those selected to be part of the *venire* are ordered to report to the courthouse on the date specified by the notice.

Some people are excused from answering this summons. Persons who do not meet the qualifications listed earlier in this section either need not appear in court or, in some states, must appear only in order to be officially dismissed. Also, people in some professions, including teachers, physicians, and judges, can receive exemptions due to the nature of their work. Each court sets its own guidelines for the circumstances under which it will excuse jurors from service, and these guidelines can be as strict or as lenient as the court desires.

VOIR DIRE

Venire The group of citizens from which the jury is selected.

At the courthouse, prospective jurors are gathered, and the process of selecting those who will actually hear the case begins. This selection process is not haphazard. The court ultimately seeks jurors who are free of any biases that may

court system in New Jersey. We provide technical and managerial support to the court (over sixty superior court judges and thirty-six municipal court judges) on such matters as personnel, program development, case flow, resources, and facilities management. This description may sound "highfalutin" considering that most people can only describe a court in terms of a judge, one or two courtroom staff, and a few other employees associated with the visible activities in the courthouse. Obviously, there is a lot more going on behind the scenes of which the average citizen is not aware. For example, besides directing case flow for the four major divisions (criminal, civil, family, and probation), the work involved in managing personnel programs for more than 1,200 employees, information systems and technology infrastructure, maintaining records of proceedings, coordination of transcription, grand and petit jury operations, and court interpreting, to mention but a few examples, is enormous. The modern court needs dedicated professionals in each of these areas.

ENTHUSIASM AND HOPE One thing that keeps me going and enthused about this profession is the resolve and dedication of our judges and staff. The family division embraces a host of issues, and in some cases those who seek help are hurting and desperate. The court may be their only hope. We are also actively engaged in pursuing new ways to offer and manage dispute resolution. Some of these include drug courts to give nonviolent drug offenders a chance at rehabilitation rather than going to jail, complimentary dispute resolution to reach more satisfactory conclusions in less time and at a lower cost to litigants, and creative uses of volunteers to assist in the work of the court and create a positive connection to the community.

Go to the **Careers in Criminal Justice Interactive CD** for more profiles in the field of criminal justice.

affect their willingness to listen to the facts of the case impartially. To this end, both the prosecutor and the defense attorney have some input into the ultimate makeup of the jury. Each attorney questions prospective jurors in a proceeding known as *voir dire* (French for "to speak the truth"). During *voir dire*, jurors are required to provide the court with a significant amount of personal information, including home address, marital status, employment status, arrest record, and life experiences.

The *voir dire* process involves both written and oral questioning of potential jurors. Attorneys fashion their inquiries in such a manner as to uncover any biases on the parts of prospective jurors and to find persons who might identify with the plights of their respective sides. As one attorney noted, though a lawyer will have many chances to talk to a jury as a whole, *voir dire* is his or her only chance to talk with the individual jurors. (To better understand the specific kinds of questions asked during this process, see ■ Figure 10.1 on the following page.)

Challenging Potential Jurors During *voir dire*, the attorney for each side may exercise a certain number of challenges to prevent particular persons from serving on the jury. Both sides can exercise two types of challenges: challenges "for cause" and peremptory challenges.

If a defense attorney or prosecutor concludes that a prospective juror is unfit to serve, the attorney may exercise a **challenge for cause** and request that that person not be included on the jury. Attorneys must provide the court with a sound, legally justifiable reason for why potential jurors are "unfit" to serve. For example, jurors can be challenged for cause if they are mentally incompetent, do not speak English, or are proved to have a prior link—be it personal or financial—with the defendant or victim.

Jurors can also be challenged if they are outwardly biased in some way that would prejudice them for or against the defendant. Jury selection for the 2007 trial of José Padilla, charged with providing material support to al Qaeda, took more than a month because so many potential jurors had to be dismissed for harboring negative feelings against the defendant. "I try to keep an open mind, but it's difficult with so many Arabs tied to terrorist organizations," wrote one

Voir Dire The preliminary questions that the trial attorneys ask prospective jurors to determine whether they are biased or have any connection with the defendant or a witness.

Challenge for Cause A *voir dire* challenge for which an attorney states the reason why a prospective juror should not be included on the jury.

Sample Juror Questionnaire

In 2007, well-known music producer Phil Spector went on trial for the murder of a nightclub hostess named Lana Clarkson at his home in Los Angeles. The excerpts from the juror questionnaire listed here show how both the prosecution and the defense are interested in gauging the potential jurors' opinions about the treatment of celebrities in our society. The two sides hope that these opinions will provide clues to possible bias for or against the defendant regardless of the facts of the case.

	Strongly Agree	Agree	Disagree	Strongly Disagree	No Opinion
a. Celebrities and high-profile people feel they are entitled to act however they please.	____	____	____	____	____
b. Celebrities and high-profile people tend to have bad tempers and act aggressively.	____	____	____	____	____
c. Celebrities and high-profile people think they can bend the rules.	____	____	____	____	____
d. Celebrities and high-profile people in Los Angeles get away with crimes because of their status.	____	____	____	____	____
e. Police are more lenient with celebrities and high-profile people.	____	____	____	____	____

▲ Phil Spector in a Los Angeles court to face charges for the murder of Lana Clarkson.

©Robert Galbraith/Reuters/Corbis

man on his juror questionnaire,[21] even though Padilla is a U.S. citizen of Puerto Rican birth. The Supreme Court has ruled that individuals may also be legally excluded from a jury in a capital case if they would under no circumstances vote for a guilty verdict if it carried the death penalty.[22] At the same time, potential jurors cannot be challenged for cause if they have "general objections" or have "expressed conscientious or religious scruples" against capital punishment.[23] The final responsibility for deciding whether a potential juror should be excluded rests with the judge, who may choose not to act on an attorney's request.

Peremptory Challenges Each attorney may also exercise a limited number of **peremptory challenges.** These challenges are based solely on an attorney's subjective reasoning; that is, the attorney is usually not required to give any legally justifiable reason for wanting to exclude a particular person from the jury. Because of the rather random nature of peremptory challenges, each state limits the number that an attorney may utilize: between five and ten for felony trials (depending on the state) and ten and twenty for capital trials (also depending on the state). Once an attorney's peremptory challenges are used up, he or she must accept forthcoming jurors, unless a challenge for cause can be used.

An attorney's decision to exclude a juror may sometimes seem whimsical. One state prosecutor who litigated drug cases was known to use a peremptory challenge whenever he saw a potential juror with a coffee mug or backpack bearing the insignia of the local public broadcasting station. The attorney presumed that this was evidence that the potential juror had donated funds to the public station, and that anybody who would do so would be too "liberal" to give the government's case against a drug offender a favorable hearing.[24] Lawyers have been known to similarly reject potential jurors for reasons of demeanor, dress, and posture.

Peremptory Challenges *Voir dire* challenges to exclude potential jurors from serving on the jury without any supporting reason or cause.

RACE AND GENDER ISSUES IN JURY SELECTION

For many years, prosecutors used their peremptory challenges as an instrument of *de facto* segregation in juries. Prosecutors were able to keep African Americans off juries in cases in which an African American was the defendant.

The argument that African Americans—or members of any other minority group—would be partial toward one of their own was tacitly supported by the Supreme Court. Despite its own assertion, made in *Swain v. Alabama* (1965),[25] that blacks have the same right to appear on a jury as whites, the Court mirrored the apparent racism of society as a whole by protecting the questionable actions of many prosecutors.

The *Batson* Reversal The Supreme Court reversed this policy in 1986 with *Batson v. Kentucky.*[26] In this case, the Court declared that the equal protection clause prohibits prosecutors from using peremptory challenges to strike possible jurors on the basis of race. Under *Batson,* the defendant must prove that the prosecution's use of a peremptory challenge was racially motivated. Doing so requires a number of legal steps.[27]

1. First, the defendant must make a *prima facie* case that there has been discrimination during *venire*. (*Prima facie* is Latin for "at first sight"; legally, it refers to a fact that is presumed to be true unless contradicted by evidence.)
2. To do so, the defendant must show that he or she is a member of a recognizable racial group and that the prosecutor has used peremptory challenges to remove members of this group from the jury pool.
3. Then, the defendant must show that these facts and other relevant circumstances raise the possibility that the prosecutor removed the prospective jurors solely because of their race.
4. If the court accepts the defendant's charges, the burden shifts to the prosecution to prove that its peremptory challenges were race neutral. If the court finds against the prosecution, it rules that a *Batson* violation has occurred. (For a closer look at the *Batson* decision, see *Landmark Cases*—Batson v. Kentucky on the next page.)

The Court has revisited the issue of race a number of times in the years since its *Batson* decision. In *Powers v. Ohio* (1991),[28] it ruled that a defendant may contest race-based peremptory challenges even if the defendant is not of the same race as the excluded jurors. In *Georgia v. McCollum* (1992),[29] the Court placed defense attorneys under the same restrictions as prosecutors when making race-based peremptory challenges.

Then, in 2003, the Court stayed the execution of Thomas Miller-El by the state of Texas, giving Miller-El the chance to argue that prosecutors had violated his rights by striking ten of eleven potential black jurors because of their race.[30] (The only African American juror approved by the prosecution had stated that, in his opinion, the correct punishment for murderers was to "pour some honey on them and stake them out over an ant bed.") The Court sent the case back to the Fifth Circuit Court of Appeals to determine whether the jury selection process had been tainted by racial bias. After the appellate court once again let Miller-El's conviction stand, the Court overturned the sentence in 2005.[31] Although this ruling made no new law, it did express the Court's willingness to intervene when the jury selection process is marred by obvious discrimination.

The **Constitutional Rights Foundation of Chicago** has created a Web site dedicated to the American jury and its role in our criminal justice system. Find a link to this site by clicking on *Web Links* under *Chapter Resources* at **www.cjinaction.com**.

Women on the Jury Given the *Batson* precedent, it seemed inevitable that the Supreme Court would eventually address another issue: whether women were constitutionally protected from peremptory challenges based on their gender.[32] The exclusion of women has been more codified than the exclusion of racial groups. At the end of World War II, twenty-one states still prohibited female jurors, and the last state to end this practice—Alabama—did not do so until 1966.

In *J.E.B. v. Alabama ex rel. T. B.* (1994),[33] the Supreme Court extended *Batson* to cover gender bias in jury selection. The case was a civil suit for paternity and child support brought by the state of Alabama. Prosecutors used nine of their ten

Landmark Cases *Batson v. Kentucky*

James Kirkland Batson, an African American, had been charged with second degree burglary and receipt of stolen goods. In the jury selection process for Batson's trial, the prosecutor used his peremptory challenges to strike the only four African Americans in the *venire,* resulting in an all-white jury. Batson was convicted. In appealing his conviction, Batson claimed that by removing the potential jurors on the basis of their race, the prosecution had denied him his right to a jury drawn from a cross section of the community. Previously, the Supreme Court had ruled that racially discriminatory peremptory challenges could not be proved in a single case, but had to be shown as a pattern over a period of time. With *Batson,* however, the Court would reject this ruling.

> *Batson v. Kentucky*
> United States Supreme Court
> 476 U.S. 79 (1986)
> **laws.findlaw.com/US/476/79.html**

IN THE WORDS OF THE COURT . . .

Justice Powell, majority opinion

* * * *

More than a century ago, the Court decided that the State denies a black defendant equal protection of the laws when it puts him on trial before a jury from which members of his race have been purposefully excluded. [*Strauder v. West Virginia,* 100 U.S. 303 (1880).] That decision laid the foundation for the Court's unceasing efforts to eradicate racial discrimination in the procedures used to select the venire from which individual jurors are drawn.

* * * *

Purposeful racial discrimination in selection of the venire violates a defendant's right to equal protection because it denies him the protection that a trial by jury is intended to secure. "The very idea of a jury is a body . . . composed of the peers or equals of the person whose rights it is selected or summoned to determine; that is, of his neighbors, fellows, associates, persons having the same legal status in society as that which he holds."

* * * *

The harm from discriminatory jury selection extends beyond that inflicted on the defendant and the excluded juror to touch the entire community. Selection procedures that purposefully exclude black persons from juries undermine public confidence in the fairness of our system of justice.

* * * *

The reality of [peremptory challenges], amply reflected in many state- and federal-court opinions, shows that the challenge may be, and unfortunately at times has been, used to discriminate against black jurors. By requiring trial courts to be sensitive to the racially discriminatory use of peremptory challenges, our decision enforces the mandate of equal protection and furthers the ends of justice. In view of the heterogeneous population of our Nation, public respect for our criminal justice system and the rule of law will be strengthened if we ensure that no citizen is disqualified from jury service because of his race.

DECISION

The Court overturned Batson's conviction and remanded the case, holding that prosecutors could not constitutionally use peremptory challenges to strike potential jurors based solely on their race. It also rejected the notion that African American jurors, as a whole, are unable to impartially consider a case against an African American defendant. To protect against discrimination, the Court set standards by which a defendant could prove that the jury in his or her trial had been tainted by racially motivated peremptory challenges.

FOR CRITICAL ANALYSIS

In this ruling, the Court (a) states a belief that diverse juries are necessary to ensure fair trials and (b) rejects the notion that a juror's race will influence his or her judgment. Some observers, while noting the obvious drawbacks of discrimination in jury selection, have labeled this the "*Batson* Paradox." How could these two assertions contradict each other when applied to a potential *Batson* violation?

For more information and activities related to this case, click on Landmark Cases under Book Resources at **www.cjinaction.com**.

challenges to remove men from the jury, while the defense made similar efforts to remove women. When challenged, the state defended its actions on what it called the rational belief that men and women might have different views on the issues of paternity and child support. The Court held this to be unconstitutional under the equal protection clause.

Finding a Partial Jury The Sixth Amendment guarantees the right to an *impartial* jury. As researcher Jeremy W. Barber notes, however, it is in the best interests of neither the defense nor the prosecution to seek an impartial jury.[34] In fact, the goal of the attorneys' peremptory challenges is to create a *partial* jury—partial, that is, toward or against the defendant. If the jury turns out to be impartial, it may be that the efforts of the two sides have balanced each other out.

For this reason, many observers believe that the continuing existence of peremptory challenges offsets the protections against discriminatory behavior supposedly created by the *Batson* and *J.E.B.* decisions. According to the Supreme Court, as long as an attorney can provide *any* valid reason for the peremptory challenge in question, a judge *must* uphold it as credible.[35] In his concurrence to the *Batson* ruling, Supreme Court Justice Thurgood Marshall pointed out that this causes a problem—attorneys can always mask a discriminatory removal by calling it a peremptory challenge.[36] (For an example of a dilemma that can arise because of the Court's contradictory rulings, see the feature *A Question of Ethics—The Juror with a Disability*.)

ALTERNATE JURORS

Because unforeseeable circumstances or illness may necessitate that one or more of the sitting jurors be dismissed, the court may also seat several *alternate jurors* who will hear the entire trial. Depending on the rules of the particular jurisdiction, two or three alternate jurors may be present throughout the trial.

A Question of Ethics
The Juror with a Disability

THE SITUATION In Honolulu, Hawaii, public defender Katharine Schwartzmann has been assigned to defend Robert Carter, charged with first degree murder for killing Ahn Min-shik during a robbery of a pizza parlor owned by the victim. The case promises to be a difficult one, and Schwartzmann needs every advantage she can get. The *venire* produces only one potential juror who, like Ahn, is of Korean descent—a woman by the name of Shim Do-yeon. During *voir dire,* Shim states that she has multiple sclerosis and admits that she might have a hard time staying awake during the trial due to the medication she takes.

THE ETHICAL DILEMMA Schwartzmann knows that Honolulu has a very close-knit Korean community, and she worries that Shim might be biased against her client. Although she cannot challenge Shim's inclusion on the jury on the basis of her race, Schwartzmann knows that she has a fallback position: she can justify striking Shim from the juror list because of the woman's disability. According to

case law, group characteristics *other than* race or gender, such as disability, are not protected from peremptory challenges so long as, on review, the attorney can cite another valid reason for the challenge. In this case, Shim's propensity to doze off during trial would certainly be a valid reason. At the same time, however, the state code of legal ethics states that attorneys shall not engage in "adverse discriminatory treatment" of jurors based on a number of characteristics, including disability.

WHAT IS THE SOLUTION? Schwartzmann is faced with competing ethical duties. On the one hand, she has a duty to give her client the best possible chance of acquittal. On the other hand, her state ethics code orders her not to discriminate against people with disabilities. What should she do, and why? How does Schwartzmann's dilemma highlight the problem associated with challenges that was identified by Thurgood Marshall in his concurrence in *Batson?*

If a juror has to be excused in the middle of the trial, an alternate may take his or her place without disrupting the proceedings.

Self Check Fill in the Blanks

The _____ is composed of all those people who have been identified as potential jurors for a particular trial. These people are then gathered for the process of _____, in which the prosecution and defense choose the actual members of the jury. Both sides can remove jurors in two ways: (1) through unlimited challenges for _____, which require the attorney to give a reason for the removal, and (2) through a limited number of _____ challenges, for which no reason is necessary. According to the United States Supreme Court, potential jurors cannot be removed for reasons of _____ or _____, but other characteristics such as disability are not legally protected during jury selection. Check your answers on page 338.

The Trial

Once the jury members have been selected, the judge swears them in and the trial itself can begin. A rather pessimistic truism among attorneys is that every case "has been won or lost when the jury is sworn." This reflects the belief that a juror's values are the major, if not dominant, factor in the decision of guilt or innocence.[37]

In actuality, it is difficult to predict how a jury will go about reaching a decision. Despite a number of studies on the question, researchers have not been able to identify any definitive consistent patterns of jury behavior. Sometimes, jurors in a criminal trial will follow instructions to find a defendant guilty unless there is a reasonable doubt, and sometimes they seem to follow instinct or prejudice and apply the law any way they choose.[38]

L06

OPENING STATEMENTS

Attorneys may choose to open the trial with a statement to the jury, though they are not required to do so. In these **opening statements,** the attorneys give a brief version of the facts and the supporting evidence that they will present during the trial. Because some trials can drag on for weeks or even months, it is extremely helpful for jurors to hear a summary of what will unfold. In short, the opening statement is a kind of "road map" that describes the destination that each attorney hopes to reach and outlines how she or he plans to reach it. The danger for attorneys is that they will offer evidence during the trial that might contradict an assertion made during the opening statement. This may cause jurors to disregard the evidence or shift their own thinking further away from the narrative being offered by the attorney.[39] In *United States v. Dinitz* (1976),[40] the Supreme Court ruled that attorneys are limited in the opening statements to subjects they believe will be presented in the trial itself.

THE ROLE OF EVIDENCE

Once the opening statements have been made, the prosecutor begins the trial proceedings by presenting the state's evidence against the defendant. Courts have complex rules about what types of evidence may be presented and how the evidence may be brought out during the trial. **Evidence** is anything that is used to prove the existence or nonexistence of a fact. For the most part, evidence can be broken down into two categories: testimony and real evidence. **Testimony** consists of statements by competent witnesses. **Real evidence,** presented to the court in the form of exhibits, includes any physical items—such as the murder weapon or a bloodstained piece of clothing—that affect the case.

Opening Statements The attorneys' statements to the jury at the beginning of the trial. Each side briefly outlines the evidence that will be offered during the trial and the legal theory that will be pursued.

Evidence Anything that is used to prove the existence or nonexistence of a fact.

Testimony Verbal evidence given by witnesses under oath.

Real Evidence Evidence that is brought into court and seen by the jury, as opposed to evidence that is described for a jury.

Rules of evidence are designed to ensure that testimony and exhibits presented to the jury are relevant, reliable, and not unfairly prejudicial against the defendant. One of the tasks of the defense attorney is to challenge evidence presented by the prosecution by establishing that the evidence is not reliable. Of course, the prosecutor also tries to demonstrate the irrelevance or unreliability of evidence presented by the defense. The final decision on whether evidence is allowed before the jury rests with the judge, in keeping with his or her role as the "referee" of the adversary system. (See the feature *CJ and Technology—Computer-Generated Evidence* on pages 322–323 to learn more about the role of computerized evidence in a criminal trial.)

Testimonial Evidence A person who is called to testify on factual matters that would be understood by the average citizen is referred to as a **lay witness.** If asked about the condition of a victim of an assault, for example, a lay witness could relate certain facts, such as "she was bleeding from her forehead" or "she was unconscious on the ground for several minutes." A lay witness could not, however, give information about the medical extent of the victim's injuries, such as whether she suffered from a fractured skull or internal bleeding. Coming from a lay witness, such testimony would be inadmissible. When the matter in question requires scientific, medical, or technical skill beyond the scope of the average person, prosecutors and defense attorneys may call an **expert witness** to the stand. The expert witness is an individual who has professional training, advanced knowledge, or substantial experience in a specialized area, such as medicine, computer technology, or ballistics. The rules of evidence state that expert witnesses may base their opinions on three types of information:

1. Facts or data of which they have personal knowledge.
2. Material presented at trial.
3. Secondhand information given to the expert outside the courtroom.[41]

Expert witnesses are considered somewhat problematic for two reasons. First, they may be chosen for their "court presence"—whether they speak well or will appear sympathetic to the jury—rather than their expertise. Second, attorneys pay expert witnesses for their services. Given human nature, the attorneys expect a certain measure of cooperation from an expert they have hired, and an expert witness has an interest in satisfying the attorneys so that he or she will be hired again.[42] Under these circumstances, some have questioned whether the courts can rely on the professional nonpartisanship of expert witnesses.[43]

Direct versus Circumstantial Evidence Two types of testimonial evidence may be brought into court: direct evidence and circumstantial evidence. **Direct evidence** is evidence that has been witnessed by the person giving testimony. "I saw Bill shoot Chris" is an example of direct evidence. **Circumstantial evidence** is indirect evidence that, even if believed, does not establish the fact in question but only the degree of likelihood of the fact. In other words, circumstantial evidence can create an inference that a fact exists.

Suppose, for example, that the defendant owns a gun that shoots bullets of the type found in the victim's body. This circumstantial evidence, by itself, does not establish that the defendant committed the crime. Combined with other circumstantial evidence, however, it may do just that. For instance, if other circumstantial evidence indicates that the defendant had a motive for harming the victim and was at the scene of the crime when the shooting occurred, the jury might conclude that the defendant committed the crime.

Prosecutors take a risk if the *only* evidence they present is circumstantial. In the spring of 2005, prosecutors and many other legal experts were shocked when a California jury acquitted actor Robert Blake of killing his wife, Bonny Lee Bakley. The case against Blake seemed strong: Bakley was shot as she sat in a car outside the restaurant where the couple had just had dinner, two stuntmen testified that

Lay Witness A witness who can truthfully and accurately testify on a fact in question without having specialized training or knowledge; an ordinary witness.

Expert Witness A witness with professional training or substantial experience qualifying her or him to testify on a certain subject.

Direct Evidence Evidence that establishes the existence of a fact that is in question without relying on inference.

Circumstantial Evidence Indirect evidence that is offered to establish, by inference, the likelihood of a fact that is in question.

WHAT IS COMPUTER GENERATED EVIDENCE?

Computer-generated evidence (CGE) takes three forms: (1) computer animation, which usually involves an animated version of witness testimony; (2) computer simulation, which is a computerized reenactment of some event related to the crime or of the crime itself; and (3) enhanced digital photographs, which rely on computer programs to change the appearance of the original photograph.

WHAT DOES COMPUTER-GENERATED EVIDENCE DO?

Numerous studies have shown that people respond more strongly to visual representations than to oral descriptions. As a result, CGE helps a jury better understand and retain the facts introduced during the course of a criminal trial.

THINKING ABOUT COMPUTER-GENERATED EVIDENCE

Because any image that can be created by technology can be manipulated by that same technology, CGE raises questions of reliability. Connecticut's Supreme Court recently addressed this issue in the case of suspected serial killer Alfred Swinton. During his trial for the murder of Carla Terry, the prosecution matched bite marks on the victim's breast to Swinton's teeth using Photoshop overlays and highly detailed computer images.

After Swinton was convicted, he challenged the use of this evidence. The court upheld Swinton's conviction, ruling that CGE is admissible as long as the side presenting it offers expert testimony to vouch for its reliability and to explain to the jury how the technology works.

What is your opinion of this standard, which operates in most jurisdictions? Is it sufficient to safeguard against improper manipulation of CGE?

For more information on computer-generated evidence and other CJ technologies, click on *Crime and Technology* under *Book Resources* at **www.cjinaction.com**.

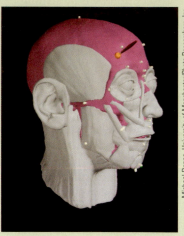
Michael Donne, University of Manchester/Photo Researchers, Inc.

the defendant had asked them to kill his wife two months before her death, and there were no other suspects. All of the evidence against Blake was circumstantial, however. The prosecution did not produce any eyewitnesses and could not link Blake to the murder weapon, a Walther P-38 handgun. In the end, the circumstantial evidence was not enough to convince the jury of Blake's guilt beyond a reasonable doubt.[44]

Relevance Evidence will not be admitted in court unless it is relevant to the case being considered. **Relevant evidence** is evidence that tends to prove or disprove a fact in question. Forensic proof that the bullets found in a victim's body were fired from a gun discovered in the suspect's pocket at the time of arrest, for example, is certainly relevant. The suspect's prior record, showing a conviction for armed robbery ten years earlier, is, as we shall see in the next subsection, irrelevant to the case at hand and in most instances will be ruled inadmissible by the judge.

Prejudicial Evidence Evidence may be excluded if it would tend to distract the jury from the main issues of the case, mislead the jury, or cause jurors to decide the issue on an emotional basis. In American trial courts, this rule precludes prosecutors from using prior purported criminal activities or actual convictions to show that the defendant has criminal propensities or an "evil character."[45]

This concept is codified in the Federal Rules of Evidence, which state that evidence of "other crimes, wrongs, or acts is not admissible to prove the character of a person in order to show action in conformity therewith." Such evidence is allowed only when it does not apply to character construction and focuses instead on "motive, opportunity, intent, preparation, plan, knowledge, identity, or absence of mistake or accident."[46]

Though this legal concept has come under a great deal of criticism, it is consistent with the presumption-of-innocence standards discussed earlier. Presumably, if a prosecutor is allowed to establish that the defendant has shown antisocial or

Relevant Evidence Evidence tending to make a fact in question more or less probable than it would be without the evidence. Only relevant evidence is admissible in court.

even violent character traits, this will prejudice the jury against the defendant. While discussing a 1930 murder case, New York Court of Appeals Chief Judge Benjamin Cardozo addressed the issue thusly:

> With only the rough and ready tests supplied by their experience of life, the jurors were to look into the workings of another's mind, and discover its capacities and disabilities, its urges and inhibitions, in moments of intense excitement. Delicate enough and subtle is the inquiry, even in the most favorable conditions, with every warping influence excluded. There must be no blurring of the issues by evidence illegally admitted and carrying with it in its admission an appeal to prejudice and passion.[47]

(For a better understanding of how issues of evidentiary relevance and prejudice work in a criminal trial, see the feature *You Be the Judge—Bad Education*.)

Authentication of Evidence At trial, an attorney must lay the proper foundation for the introduction of certain evidence, such as documents, exhibits, and other objects, and must demonstrate to the court that the evidence is competent; that is, the evidence is what the attorney claims. The process by which this is accomplished is referred to as **authentication.** The authentication requirement relates to relevance because something offered in evidence is relevant to the case only if it is authentic, or genuine.

Commonly, evidence is authenticated by the testimony of witnesses. For example, if an attorney wants to introduce an autopsy report as evidence in a case, he or she can have the report authenticated by the testimony of the medical examiner who signed it. By the same token, before drugs taken from

Authentication Establishing the genuineness of an item that is to be introduced as evidence in a trial.

You Be the Judge Bad Education

THE FACTS John is a middle-school guidance counselor on the U.S. territory of Guam. He has been charged with sexually abusing seven of the boys under his supervision. During his trial, the prosecution offered into evidence several adult homosexual pornographic magazines taken from John's home. The prosecutor argued that the acts portrayed in the magazines "are acts that, if you look at what the Defendant himself has done, or what he is charged with, that it goes to his knowledge that he's aware of these kinds of acts, that it goes to his intent to engage in these kinds of acts." The jury found John guilty of multiple charges of assault, child abuse, and criminal sexual conduct involving children.

THE LAW Evidence is not considered relevant—and therefore may not be presented in court—if its only purpose is show that the defendant has criminal propensities or an "evil character." Otherwise inadmissible character evidence may be admitted, though, if it is used to prove the motive or intent of the defendant.

YOUR DECISION John's attorneys argue that pornographic magazines are irrelevant to the charges in this case and serve only to "out" their client as a homosexual and prejudice the jury against him. The prosecution contends that the challenged evidence shows that John "intentionally engaged in sexual contact for the purpose of sexual arousal or gratification"; in other words, the pornographic magazines prove his intent. If you were an appeals judge in this case, what would you decide? Keep in mind that if you rule for the defense, John's conviction will be overturned and he will receive a new trial, with no mention of the magazines. Also, be aware that the United States Supreme Court has held that adults have a First Amendment right to keep pornography in their homes.

[To see how U.S. Court of Appeals for the Ninth Circuit ruled in this case, go to Example 10.1 in Appendix B.]

▲ The photo above was shown as an exhibit in the murder trial of John William King, who was charged with dragging an African American named James Byrd, Jr., to his death behind a pickup truck. Jurors were shown a number of photos of images tattooed on King's body, including one that showed a black man hanging from a tree. Do you agree with prosecutors that the intricate racist, satanic, and neo-Nazi tattoos covering King's body helped prove motive, intent, and state of mind? Or do you agree with the defense attorney who said that the tattoos do not make King more likely to have murdered Byrd?

Direct Examination The examination of a witness by the attorney who calls the witness to the stand to testify.

Hearsay An oral or written statement made by an out-of-court declarant that is later offered in court by a witness (not the declarant) concerning a matter before the court. Hearsay usually is not admissible as evidence.

a crime scene can be admitted as evidence, the law enforcement agent who collected them will be required to testify that they are in fact the same drugs.

The rules of evidence require authentication because certain types of evidence, such as exhibits and objects, cannot be cross-examined by opposing counsel, as witnesses can, yet such evidence may have a significant effect on the jury. (The cross-examination process will be examined later in the chapter.) The authentication requirement provides a safeguard against the introduction of nonverified evidence that may strongly influence the outcome of the case.

THE PROSECUTION'S CASE

Because the burden of proof is on the state, the prosecution is generally considered to have a more difficult task than the defense. The prosecutor attempts to establish guilt beyond a reasonable doubt by presenting the *corpus delicti* ("body of the offense" in Latin) of the crime to the jury. The *corpus delicti* is simply a legal term that refers to the substantial facts that show a crime has been committed. By establishing such facts through the presentation of evidence, the prosecutor hopes to convince the jury of the defendant's guilt.

As was mentioned earlier, this evidence must be relevant and nonprejudicial. For example, a prosecutor might not be allowed to show the jury graphic photographs of the victim in a murder trial. Such photographs could elicit emotional responses from jurors and prejudice them against the defendant who is to be presumed innocent.[48] This is not to say, however, that evidence is never used for emotional effect. A prosecutor may, for example, place the murder weapon on a table in plain view of the jury, forcing the jurors to consider that a violent crime has in fact taken place and to focus on their duty to ensure that the guilty party is punished.

Direct Examination of Witnesses Witnesses are crucial to establishing the prosecutor's case against the defendant. The prosecutor will call witnesses to the stand and ask them questions pertaining to the sequence of events that the trial is addressing. This form of questioning is known as **direct examination.** During direct examination, the prosecutor will usually not be allowed to ask *leading questions*—questions that might suggest to the witness a particular desired response. A leading question might be something like "So, Mrs. Williams, you noticed the defendant threatening the victim with a broken beer bottle?" If Mrs. Williams answers "yes" to this question, she has, in effect, been "led" to the conclusion that the defendant was, in fact, threatening with a broken beer bottle. (A properly worded query would be, "Mrs. Williams, please describe the defendant's manner toward the victim during the incident.") The fundamental purpose behind testimony is to establish what actually happened, not what the trial attorneys would like the jury to believe happened.

Hearsay When interviewing a witness, both the prosecutor and the defense attorney will make sure that the witness's statements are based on the witness's own knowledge and not hearsay. **Hearsay** can be defined as any testimony given in court about a statement made by someone else. Literally, it is what someone heard someone else say. For the most part, hearsay is not admissible as evidence. It is excluded because the listener may have misunderstood what the other person said, and without the opportunity of cross-examining the originator of the statement, the misconception cannot be challenged.

There are a number of exceptions to the hearsay rule, and as a result, a good deal of hearsay evidence is allowed before the jury. For example, a hearsay statement is usually admissible if there seems to be little risk of a lie. Therefore, a statement made by someone who believes that his or her death is imminent—a "dying declaration"—is allowed in court even though it is hearsay.[49] The rules of most courts also allow hearsay when the person who made the statement is unavailable to be questioned in court or when the statement is particularly important to the argument being made by one side. Consequently, an admission of guilt by the defendant is often permitted even when it falls under the strict definition of hearsay.[50]

Competence and Reliability of Witnesses The rules of evidence include certain restrictions and qualifications pertaining to witnesses. Witnesses must have sufficient mental competence to understand the significance of testifying under oath. They must also be reliable in the sense that they are able to give a clear and unadulterated description of the events in question. For example, during the murder trial of Robert Blake mentioned earlier, defense attorneys severely damaged the credibility of Ronny "Duffy" Hambleton, who testified that he had been solicited by Blake to kill his wife. Hambleton, as it turned out, had smoked, snorted, and eaten so much of the drug methamphetamine that he experienced hallucinations, a revelation that generally would not instill a jury with confidence in a witness's reliability.[51]

CROSS-EXAMINATION

After the prosecutor has directly examined her or his witnesses, the defense attorney is given the chance to question the same witnesses. The Sixth Amendment states, "In all criminal prosecutions, the accused shall enjoy the right . . . to be confronted with witnesses against him." This **confrontation clause** gives the accused, through his or her attorneys, the right to cross-examine witnesses. **Cross-examination** refers to the questioning of an opposing witness during trial, and both sides of a case are allowed to do so (see ■ Figure 10.2 on the next page).

Cross-examination allows the attorneys to test the truthfulness of opposing witnesses and usually entails efforts to create doubt in the jurors' minds that the witness is reliable. Cross-examination is also linked to the problems presented by hearsay evidence. When a witness offers hearsay, the person making the original remarks is not in the court and therefore cannot be cross-examined. If such testimony were allowed, the defendant's Sixth Amendment right to confront witnesses against him or her would be violated.

After the defense has cross-examined a prosecution witness, the prosecutor may want to reestablish any reliability that might have been lost. The prosecutor can do so by again questioning the witness, a process known as *redirect examination*. Following the redirect examination, the defense attorney will be given the opportunity to ask further questions of prosecution witnesses, or recross-examination. Thus, each side has two opportunities to question a witness. The attorneys need not do so, but only after each side has been offered the opportunity will the trial move on to the next witness or the next stage.

MOTION FOR A DIRECTED VERDICT

After the prosecutor has finished presenting evidence against the defendant, the government will inform the court that it has rested the people's case. At this point, the defense may make a **motion for a directed verdict** (now also known as a *motion for judgment as a matter of law* in federal courts). Through this motion, the defense is basically saying that the prosecution has not offered enough evidence to prove that the accused is guilty beyond a reasonable doubt. If the judge grants this motion, which rarely occurs, then a judgment will be entered in favor of the defendant, and the trial is over.

⊘ **CourtTV** is a cable television channel that offers continuous coverage of the most important criminal trials of the day. Find its Web site, which offers news on current and classic trials, by clicking on *Web Links* under *Chapter Resources* at **www.cjinaction.com**.

Confrontation Clause The part of the Sixth Amendment that guarantees all defendants the right to confront witnesses testifying against them during the criminal trial. In practice, this right entitles the defendant to be present at trial and to cross-examine witnesses for the prosecution.

Cross-Examination The questioning of an opposing witness during trial.

Motion for a Directed Verdict A motion requesting that the court grant judgment in favor of the defense on the ground that the prosecution has not produced sufficient evidence to support the state's claim.

■ Figure 10.2 The Cross-Examination

In the so-called Boston Nanny case, nineteen-year-old British *au pair* Louise Woodward was charged with second degree murder of an infant left in her care. Prosecutors tried to convince the jury that Woodward was a temperamental teenager who became frustrated with caring for a sick child and "snapped." The defense claimed that the brain hemorrhage that killed the child was actually the delayed result of another accident that had occurred several weeks earlier.

Detective Sergeant William Byrne, who interviewed Woodward following the boy's death, testified that she claimed to have dropped the infant on a towel on the bathroom floor, and that the infant "may have banged his head on the floor where it meets the tub." On cross-examination, defense counsel tried to clarify exactly what Woodward, who denied making such statements, had told the police officer.

Defense: You asked her, "What do you mean by 'drop him on the floor'" and her answer was, "I was angry."

Detective Sergeant Byrne: Yes, sir.

Defense: So, she wasn't telling you, according to your testimony, that "I dropped him by accident."

Detective Sergeant Byrne: No, sir.

Defense: She wasn't saying "I tripped and fell."

Detective Sergeant Byrne: No, sir.

Defense: She wan't saying, "He slipped out of my hands."

Detective Sergeant Byrne: No, sir.

Defense: You're saying that she told you that she did this on purpose.

Detective Sergeant Byrne: She was angry, sir.

Defense: Okay. That's what she meant by "angry," according to you, right, that she did this on purpose.

Detective Sergeant Byrne: She didn't say that she did it on purpose.

Defense: But you understood that to mean that she did it on purpose.

Detective Sergeant Byrne: That was my feeling.

In this case, the cross-examination may have hurt the defendant, as Detective Sergeant Byrne was able to reassert his belief that Woodward was responsible for the death. In fact, the Boston jury did convict Woodward, though the trial judge later overturned the conviction.

THE DEFENDANT'S CASE

Assuming that the motion for a directed verdict is denied, the defense attorney may offer the defendant's case. Because the burden is on the state to prove the accused's guilt, the defense is not required to offer any case at all. It can simply "rest" without calling any witnesses or producing any real evidence and ask the jury to judge the merits of the case on what it has seen and heard from the prosecution.

Placing the Defendant on the Stand If the defense does present a case, its first—and often most important—decision is whether the defendant will take the stand in her or his own defense. Because of the Fifth Amendment protection against self-incrimination, the defendant is not required to testify. Therefore, the defense attorney must make a judgment call. He or she may want to put the defendant on the stand if the defendant is likely to appear sympathetic to the jury or is well spoken and able to aid the defense's case. With a less sympathetic or less effective defendant, the defense attorney may decide that exposing the defendant before the jury presents too large a risk. Also, if the defendant testifies, she or he is open to cross-examination under oath from the prosecutor. In any case, remember that the prosecution cannot comment on a defendant's refusal to testify.[52]

Creating a Reasonable Doubt Defense lawyers most commonly defend their clients by attempting to expose weaknesses in the prosecutor's case. Remember that if the defense attorney can create reasonable doubt concerning the client's guilt in the mind of just a single juror, the defendant has a good chance of gaining an acquittal or at least a *hung jury*, a circumstance explained later in the chapter.

Even if the prosecution can present seemingly strong evidence, a defense attorney may succeed by creating reasonable doubt. In an illustrative case, Jason Korey bragged to his friends that he had shot and killed Joseph Brucker in Pittsburgh, Pennsylvania, and a great deal of circumstantial evidence linked Korey to the killing. The police, however, could find no direct evidence: they could not link Korey to the murder weapon, nor could they match his footprints to those found at the crime scene. Michael Foglia, Korey's defense attorney, explained his client's bragging as a ploy to gain attention from his friends. Though this explanation may strike some as unlikely, in the absence of physical evidence it did create doubt in the jurors' minds, and Korey was acquitted.

This strategy is also very effective in cases that essentially rely on the word of the defendant against the word of the victim. In sexual-assault cases, for example, if the defense attorneys can create doubt about the victim's credibility—in other words, raise the possibility that he or she is lying—then they may prevail at trial. According to the Alcohol and Rape Study, carried out by researchers at Rutgers University and the University of New Hampshire, juries acquit about 90 percent of the time when the defendant says the sex was consensual and there is evidence that the alleged victim was drinking alcohol before the incident in question.[53] (The *Criminal Justice in Action* feature at the end of this chapter explores issues concerning evidence in sexual-assault cases in more detail.)

Other Defense Strategies The defense can choose among a number of strategies to generate reasonable doubt in the jurors' minds. It can present an *alibi defense*, by submitting evidence that the accused was not at or near the scene of the crime at the time the crime was committed. Another option is to attempt an *affirmative defense*, by presenting additional facts to the ones offered by the prosecution. Possible affirmative defenses, which we discussed in detail in Chapter 4, include the following:

1. Self-defense   2. Insanity   3. Duress   4. Entrapment

With an affirmative defense strategy, the defense attempts to prove that the defendant should be found not guilty because of extenuating circumstances surrounding the crime. An affirmative strategy can be difficult to carry out because it forces the defense to prove the veracity of its own evidence, not simply disprove the evidence offered by the prosecution.

The defense is often willing to admit that a certain criminal act took place, especially if the defendant has already confessed. In this case, the primary question of the trial becomes not whether the defendant is guilty, but what the defendant is guilty of. In these situations, the defense strategy focuses on obtaining the lightest possible penalty for the defendant. As we saw in the last chapter, this strategy is responsible for the high percentage of proceedings that end in plea bargains.

REBUTTAL AND SURREBUTTAL

After the defense closes its case, the prosecution is permitted to bring new evidence forward that was not used during its initial presentation to the jury. This is called the **rebuttal** stage of the trial. When the rebuttal stage is finished, the defense is given the opportunity to cross-examine the prosecution's new witnesses and introduce new witnesses of its own. This final act is part of the *surrebuttal*. After these stages have been completed, the defense may offer another motion for a directed verdict, asking the judge summarily to find in the defendant's favor. If this motion is rejected, and it almost always is, the case is closed, and the opposing sides offer their closing arguments.

▲ Professional basketball player Kobe Bryant, left, is reassured by defense attorney Pamela Mackey during a hearing in Eagle, Colorado. Bryant was charged with felony sexual assault against a nineteen-year-old; she claimed he forced her to have sex, while Bryant insisted that the sex was consensual. Eventually, all charges against Bryant were dropped.

AP Photo/Gutierrz, Pool

Rebuttal Evidence given to counteract or disprove evidence presented by the opposing party.

■ Figure 10.3 Closing Arguments

AP Photo/Susan Walsh

Lee Boyd Malvo was charged with two counts of capital murder in connection with the sniper attacks that terrified the Washington, D.C., area in the early 2000s. As the trial progressed, it became clear the defense was trying to convince the jury that young Malvo was under the influence of his partner, John Muhammad, and therefore was not responsible for his actions. The prosecution, in contrast, emphasized Malvo's sanity and his reasoned choice to collaborate with Muhammad. These themes are evident in both sides' closing arguments, excerpts of which are provided here. (The jury eventually found Malvo guilty, and he is now serving a life sentence at Red Onion Prison in Southwest Virginia.)

For the defense: Attorney Michael S. Arif: "Understand what [Malvo] told you [in the confessions to police] is not believable. Frankly, it's bull. It's nonsense. It's not real. What he wants to do is take the blame on himself. He's putting it on himself. Why? Why does he want to do that? We've told you he was indoctrinated. We've told you he was protecting his father. Not his real father, but this John Muhammad. Why? Because this was the father he knew."

For the prosecution: Fairfax County Commonwealth Attorney Robert F. Horan, Jr.: "Members of the jury, there can be no doubt, reasonable or otherwise, that [Malvo] is the shooter of both Linda Franklin and Dean Meyers. He said he was. We have the mental-health crowd coming and saying don't believe that. Believe something else. If you believe the mental-health experts the defense presented, they are telling you he's insane, he doesn't know right from wrong, he doesn't know the nature, consequences, and character of his acts, but believe him when he said he was the spotter. Believe this insane man when he said he was the spotter."

CLOSING ARGUMENTS

Closing Arguments Arguments made by each side's attorney after the cases for the plaintiff and defendant have been presented.

In their **closing arguments,** the attorneys summarize their presentations and argue one final time for their respective cases. In most states, the defense attorney goes first, and then the prosecutor. (In Colorado, Kentucky, and Missouri, the order is reversed.) An effective closing argument includes all of the major points that support the government's or the defense's case. It also emphasizes the shortcomings of the opposing party's case. Jurors will view a closing argument with some skepticism if it merely recites the central points of a party's claim or defense without also responding to the unfavorable facts or issues raised by the other side. Of course, neither attorney wants to focus too much on the other side's position, but the elements of the opposing position do need to be acknowledged and their flaws highlighted. (For an example of opposing closing arguments, see ■ Figure 10.3.)

One danger in the closing arguments is that an attorney will become too emotional and make remarks that are later deemed by appellate courts to be prejudicial. Once both attorneys have completed their remarks, the case is submitted to the jury, and the attorneys' role in the trial is, for the moment, complete.

> **Self Check** Fill in the Blanks
>
> Evidence is any object or spoken _____ that can be used in a criminal trial to prove or disprove a _____ related to the crime. Evidence will not be admitted into the trial unless it is _____ and does not unfairly _____ the jury against the defendant by appealing to emotion rather than fact. The prosecution will usually try to build its case through _____ examination of its witnesses, which the defense will counter with a _____ -examination of its own. The defense's main goal is to create _____ concerning the defendant's guilt in the minds of as many jurors as possible. Check your answers on page 338.

The Final Steps of the Trial and Postconviction Procedures

After closing arguments, the outcome of the trial is in the hands of the jury. In this section, we examine the efforts to give jurors the means necessary to make informed decisions about the guilt or innocence of the accused. We will also look at the posttrial motions that can occur when the defense feels that the jurors, prosecution, or trial judge made errors that necessitate remedial legal action.

JURY INSTRUCTIONS

Before the jurors begin their deliberations, the judge gives the jury a **charge,** summing up the case and instructing the jurors on the rules of law that apply to the issues in the case. These charges, also called jury instructions, are usually prepared during a special *charging conference* involving the judge and the trial attorneys. In this conference, the attorneys suggest the instructions they would like to see be sent to the jurors, but the judge makes the final decision as to the charges submitted.[54] If the defense attorney disagrees with the charges sent to the jury, he or she can enter an objection, thereby setting the stage for a possible appeal.

The Judge's Role The judge usually begins by explaining basic legal principles, such as the need to find the defendant guilty beyond a reasonable doubt. Then the jury instructions narrow to the specifics of the case at hand, and the judge explains to the jurors what facts the prosecution must have proved to obtain a conviction. If the defense strategy centers on an affirmative defense such as insanity or entrapment, the judge will discuss the relevant legal principles that the defense must have proved to obtain an acquittal. The final segment of the charges discusses possible verdicts. These always include "guilty" and "not guilty," but some cases also allow for the jury to find "guilt by reason of insanity" or "guilty but mentally ill." Juries are often charged with determining the seriousness of the crime as well, such as deciding whether a homicide is murder in the first degree, murder in the second degree, or manslaughter.

Understanding the Instructions A serious problem with jury instructions is that jurors often do not seem to understand them.[55] This is hardly surprising, as most average Americans do not have the education or legal background to disentangle the somewhat unfathomable jargon of the law. One study came to the unfortunate conclusion that juries that received no instructions whatsoever were basically as well equipped—or poorly equipped, as the case may be—as juries that did receive instructions.[56]

One solution is to simplify the language of the jury instructions. In 2005, California became the first state to move in this direction when state officials approved 2,048 pages of new "plain language" criminal jury instructions. So, for example, a juror in California will no longer read, "The law does not undertake to measure in units of time the length of the period during which the thought must be pondered before it can ripen into an intent to kill which is truly deliberate and premeditated." Instead, he or she will read, "The length of time the person spends considering whether to kill does not alone determine whether the killing is deliberate and premeditated."[57]

JURY DELIBERATION

After receiving the charge, the jury begins its deliberations. Jury deliberation is a somewhat mysterious process, as it takes place in complete seclusion. In extreme cases, the judge will order that the jury be *sequestered,* or isolated from the public, during the trial and deliberation stages of the proceedings. Sequestration is used when deliberations are expected to be lengthy, or the trial is attracting a high amount of interest and the judge wants to keep the jury from being unduly influenced. Juries are usually sequestered in hotels and kept under the watch and guard of officers of the court. The importance of *total* sequestration is reflected in a recent Colorado Supreme Court decision to overturn the death penalty of a man who was sentenced after the jurors consulted a Bible during deliberations. The court held that the Bible constituted an improper outside influence and a reliance on a "higher authority."[58]

Charge The judge's instructions to the jury following the attorneys' closing arguments; the charge sets forth the rules of law that the jury must apply in reaching its decision, or verdict.

Most of what is known about how a jury deliberates comes from mock trials or interviews with jurors after the verdict has been reached. A general picture of the deliberation process can be constructed from this research. It shows that the romantic notion of jurors with high-minded ideals of justice making eloquent speeches is, for the most part, not the reality. In approximately three out of every ten cases, the initial vote by the jury led to a unanimous decision. In 90 percent of the remaining cases, the majority eventually dictated the decision.[59]

THE VERDICT

Once it has reached a decision, the jury issues a **verdict.** The most common verdicts are guilty and not guilty, though, as we have seen, juries may signify different degrees of guilt if instructed to do so. Following the announcement of a guilty or not guilty verdict, the jurors are discharged, and the jury trial proceedings are finished. (See ■ Figure 10.4 for a review of the steps of a jury trial.)

The Hung Jury When a jury in a criminal trial is unable to agree on a unanimous verdict—or a majority in certain states—it returns with no decision. This is known as a **hung jury.** Following a hung jury, the judge will declare a mistrial, and the case will be tried again in front of a different jury if the prosecution decides to pursue the matter a second time. A judge can do little to reverse a hung jury, considering that "no decision" is just as legitimate a verdict as guilty or not guilty. In some states, if there are only a few dissenters to the majority view, a judge can send the jury back to the jury room under a set of rules enunciated more than a century ago by the Supreme Court in *Allen v. United States* (1896).[60] The *Allen* **Charge,** as this instruction is called, asks the jurors in the minority to reconsider the majority opinion. Many jurisdictions do not allow *Allen* Charges on the ground that they improperly coerce jurors with the minority opinion to change their minds.[61]

For all of the attention they receive, hung juries are relatively rare. Juries are unable to come to a decision in only about 6 percent of all cases.[62] Furthermore, juries may be more lenient (or easy to "trick") than is generally perceived; one study found that juries were six times more likely than judges (in bench trials) to acquit a person who turns out to be guilty.[63]

Jury Nullification The last statistic points to a growing concern of a number of criminal justice observers, who question whether jury verdicts are always based on the proper legal principles. Their concern relates to the controversial subject of **jury nullification,** which occurs when jurors "nullify" the law by acquitting a defendant who may be guilty according to the instruction given to them by the court. In other words, the jury acquits *in spite of* the evidence, rather than *because*

Verdict A formal decision made by the jury.

Hung Jury A jury whose members are so irreconcilably divided in their opinions that they cannot reach a verdict.

***Allen* Charge** An instruction by a judge to a deadlocked jury with only a few dissenters that asks the jurors in the minority to reconsider the majority opinion.

Jury Nullification An acquittal of a defendant by a jury even though the evidence presented and the judge's instructions indicate that the defendant is guilty.

■ **Figure 10.4** The Steps of a Jury Trial

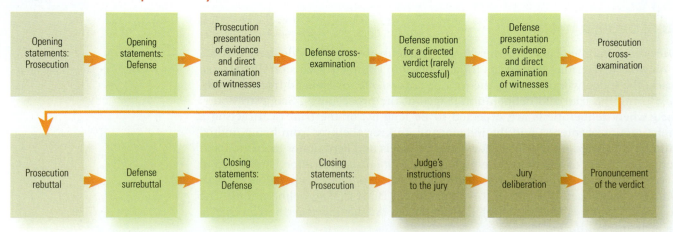

Opening statements: Prosecution → Opening statements: Defense → Prosecution presentation of evidence and direct examination of witnesses → Defense cross-examination → Defense motion for a directed verdict (rarely successful) → Defense presentation of evidence and direct examination of witnesses → Prosecution cross-examination →

Prosecution rebuttal → Defense surrebuttal → Closing statements: Defense → Closing statements: Prosecution → Judge's instructions to the jury → Jury deliberation → Pronouncement of the verdict

of the evidence.[64] The specter of jury nullification is most often raised in cases that involve issues on which jurors may have strong ideological opinions, such as race, the death penalty, assisted suicide, or drug offenses. The not guilty verdict in O. J. Simpson's 1995 criminal trial was widely seen as an example of jury nullification, with jurors swayed by the racially based arguments of the defense rather than the facts of the case.

Many observers believe jury nullification is counter to the principles of American law because it allows a jury to "play by its own rules." Others, however, feel that jurors are within their rights when they question not only the facts in the case before them, but also the merits of the laws that the court is asking them to enforce. This argument has been made since the earliest days of the American legal system, when John Adams (1735–1826) said that a juror has not only a right, but a duty, "to find the verdict according to his own best understanding, judgment, and conscience, though in direct opposition to the direction of the court."[65] By this reasoning, jurors who feel that a particular law is unjust, or that the penalty for a law is too severe, are justified in nullifying a guilty verdict.

▲ On March 10, 2006, John Gotti, Jr., exits a New York courtroom a free man after a jury could not decide whether he ordered an attack on radio personality Curtis Sliwa. For the most part, judges do not have the ability to reverse a hung jury, as the law considers "no decision" a legitimate verdict. Do you think judges should be allowed to force a jury to choose between guilty or not guilty? Explain your answer.

APPEALS

Even if a defendant is found guilty, the trial process is not necessarily over. In our criminal justice system, a person convicted of a crime has a right to appeal. An **appeal** is the process of seeking a higher court's review of a lower court's decision for the purpose of correcting or changing the lower court's judgment. A defendant who loses a case in a trial court cannot automatically appeal the conviction. The defendant normally must first be able to show that the trial court acted improperly on a question of law. Common reasons for appeals include the introduction of tainted evidence by the prosecution or faulty jury instructions delivered by the trial judge. In federal courts, about 16 percent of criminal convictions are appealed.[66]

Double Jeopardy The appeals process is available only to the defense. If a jury finds the accused not guilty, the prosecution cannot appeal to have the decision reversed. To do so would infringe on the defendant's Fifth Amendment rights against multiple trials for the same offense. This guarantee against being tried a second time for the same crime is known as protection from **double jeopardy.**

The Limits of Double Jeopardy The prohibition against double jeopardy means that once a criminal defendant is found not guilty of a particular crime, the government may not reindict the person and retry him or her for the same crime. The basic idea behind the double jeopardy clause, in the words of Supreme Court Justice Hugo Black, is that the state should not be allowed to

> make repeated attempts to convict an individual for an alleged offense, thereby subjecting him to embarrassment, expense, and ordeal and compelling him to live in a continuing state of anxiety and insecurity, as well as enhancing the possibility that though innocent he may be found guilty.[67]

Appeal The process of seeking a higher court's review of a lower court's decision for the purpose of correcting or changing the lower court's judgment or decision.

Double Jeopardy To twice place at risk (jeopardize) a person's life or liberty. The Fifth Amendment to the U.S. Constitution prohibits a second prosecution for the same criminal offense.

The bar against double jeopardy does not preclude a victim from bringing a *civil* suit against the same person to recover damages. For example, in 2007 Gary Dicks was found not guilty of any criminal wrongdoing for an incident in which he drove his tractor-trailer through a malfunctioning traffic light in Columbia, Maryland, and rammed into a car, killing two teenage boys. Two separate $5 million wrongful death lawsuits filed by the victims' parents against Dicks were able to proceed, unaffected by the acquittal. This was not considered double jeopardy because the wrongful death suits involved a civil claim, not a criminal one. Therefore, Dicks was not being tried for the same *crime* more than once.

The Possibility and Risk of Retrial Additionally, a state's prosecution of a crime will not prevent a separate federal prosecution of the same crime, and vice versa; that is, a defendant found not guilty of violating a state law can be tried in federal court for the same act, if the act is also defined as a crime under federal law. Furthermore, as we saw in Chapter 8 with the example of Washington, D.C., area sniper John Allen Muhammad, double jeopardy does not preclude different states from prosecuting the same person for multiple crimes that take place in different jurisdictions.

LO9

Note that a hung jury is *not* an acquittal for purposes of double jeopardy. So, if a jury is deadlocked, the government is free to seek a new trial. The United States Supreme Court reiterated this principle in *Sattazahn v. Pennsylvania* (2003),[68] a case involving a defendant who was convicted of murder but then had a hung jury in the penalty phase of his trial—resulting in an automatic sentence of life in prison rather than execution. The defendant appealed the initial conviction and won a new trial. When he was convicted a second time, the state once again sought the death penalty and succeeded. The Court held that as no acquittal had taken place in the sentencing phase of the first trial, double jeopardy protections were irrelevant.

The Appeal Process There are two basic reasons for the appeal process. The first is to correct an error made during the initial trial. The second is to review policy. Because of this second function, the appellate courts are an important part of the flexible nature of the criminal justice system. When existing law has ceased to be effective or no longer reflects the values of society, an appellate

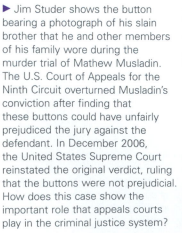

▶ Jim Studer shows the button bearing a photograph of his slain brother that he and other members of his family wore during the murder trial of Mathew Musladin. The U.S. Court of Appeals for the Ninth Circuit overturned Musladin's conviction after finding that these buttons could have unfairly prejudiced the jury against the defendant. In December 2006, the United States Supreme Court reinstated the original verdict, ruling that the buttons were not prejudicial. How does this case show the important role that appeals courts play in the criminal justice system?

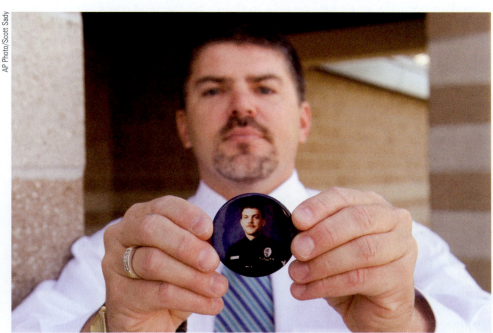

AP Photo/Scott Sady

1. Within a specific period of time—usually between thirty and ninety days—the defendant must file a *notice of appeal.* This is a short written statement outlining the basis of the appeal.

2. The appellant, or losing party in the lower court, must then transfer the trial court record to the appellate court. This record contains items of the case file, including exhibits, and a transcript of the testimony.

3. Next, the briefs must be filed. A *brief* is a written argument that presents the party's legal arguments and precedents to support these arguments. Both the appellant and the winning prosecutorial team must submit briefs to the appellate court.

4. The briefs are followed by *oral arguments,* in which attorneys from both sides appear before the appellate court panel to state their positions. In oral arguments, the judge or judges ask questions of the attorneys to clarify certain points or voice a particular disagreement.

5. After the oral arguments, the judges retire to deliberate the case. After a decision has been made, one or more of the judges prepare the *written opinion.* (This process was described in Chapter 8 in more detail.) A judge who disagrees with the majority opinion may write a *dissenting opinion.*

6. Finally, the court holds a disposition in which it announces the next step for the case. The court can *uphold* the decision of the lower court, or it can *modify* the lower court decision by changing a part of it but not the whole. The lower court's decision may be *reversed,* or set aside, or the appellate court can *reverse* and *remand* the case, meaning that the lower court's decision is overturned and the matter is sent back for further proceedings. Or, the appellate court may simply *remand* the case (send it back for further action) without overturning it.

court can effectively change the law through its decisions and the precedents that it sets.[69] A classic example was the *Miranda v. Arizona* decision, which, although it failed to change the fate of the defendant (he was found guilty on retrial), had a far-reaching impact on custodial interrogation of suspects.

It is also important to understand that once the appeal process begins, the defendant is no longer presumed innocent. The burden of proof has shifted, and the defendant is obligated to prove that her or his conviction should be overturned. The method of filing an appeal differs slightly among the fifty states and the federal government, but the six basic steps are similar enough for summarization in ■ Figure 10.5. For the most part, defendants are not required to exercise their right to appeal. The one exception involves the death sentence. Given the seriousness of capital punishment, the defendant is required to appeal the case, regardless of his or her wishes.

FINALITY AND WRONGFUL CONVICTIONS

In certain instances, particularly with capital cases, the appeals process can seem excessive. In 1991, for example, the state of Maryland sentenced Steve Oken to death for raping, torturing, and killing three young women four years earlier. Even though Oken admitted to his crimes, over the next thirteen years his case was reviewed six times by the Maryland Court of Appeals and nine times by the United States Supreme Court. The legal issues raised by his case were not resolved until thirty minutes before his 2004 execution.[70]

Such scenarios are contrary to the goal of **finality,** which exists when the outcome of a criminal case can no longer be challenged by anyone. The benefits of finality are evident—once a case is over, all of the participants can redirect their energy to other activities. Furthermore, cases that drag on for years or even decades can weaken the public's confidence in the criminal justice system. Several aspects of the criminal justice system discussed in this chapter directly promote finality. Statutes of limitations assure that, after a reasonable amount of time, the government cannot prosecute most crimes. The protection against double jeopardy protects suspects from the "fear and anxiety" of a second trial. Another perspective on finality, though, comes from Judge Sharon Keller of the Texas Court of Criminal Appeals, who says, "We can't give new trials to everyone who establishes, after conviction, that they might be innocent. We would have no finality in the criminal justice system, and finality is important."[71]

Finality The end of a criminal case, meaning that the outcome of the case is no longer susceptible to challenge by prosecutors or the defendant.

Wrongful Conviction The conviction, either by verdict or by guilty plea, of a person who is factually innocent of the charges.

Innocent after Being Proved Guilty Judge Keller's sentiments, though shared by many of her colleagues on the bench and in district attorneys' offices, do seem contrary to one of the basic values of the court system: innocent people do not deserved to be punished. Indeed, Keller seems to be saying that "innocent until proved guilty" applies only before conviction. Once convicted, the person no longer deserves the benefit of the doubt.

For most of American history, finality did have the upper hand over innocence as far as postconviction procedures were concerned. Only during the past fifty years have appeals processes provided significant relief for those who wish to revisit aspects of the criminal trial after a final verdict has been delivered. The most serious threat to the primacy of finality, however, is the same DNA fingerprinting that has been a boon to law enforcement, as we saw in Chapter 6. As these techniques have become more widespread and effective, they have brought the problem of **wrongful convictions,** which occur when an innocent person is found guilty, into the national spotlight.

The DNA Revolution: Part II DNA exonerates potential wrongdoers the same way it identifies them: by matching genetic material found at a crime scene to that of a suspect (or, conversely, by showing that the genetic material does not match the suspect's). For example, in 1981 Jerry Miller was arrested for attacking and raping a woman in a Chicago parking garage. He subsequently spent twenty-five years in prison before being released on parole. In 2007, DNA tests proved that he could not have been the rapist, and a Chicago court cleared him of all charges.

"They say the wheels of justice move slowly, but you know what? The wheels of justice are flat."

—*Roy Brown, who spent fifteen years in prison and was released in 2007 when DNA evidence linked another man to the murder for which he was convicted*

According to the Innocence Project, a New York–based legal group, Miller was the two-hundredth person exonerated by DNA evidence in the United States.[72] Given that state courts convict about one million adults each year,[73] this number may not seem very significant. People convicted of crimes do not have an automatic right to DNA checks of the evidence in their cases, however. In most instances, the trial judge must approve the request, and if it is rejected, the convict has little recourse in the matter.[74] Consequently, the DNA exonerations that have already taken place may represent a "random audit of convictions," meaning that the incidence of wrongful convictions may be a larger problem than the statistics indicate.[75]

▼ James Giles, right, celebrates with family members and Barry Scheck, co-director of the Innocence Project. Giles had spent ten years in a Texas prison for rape before being exonerated with the help of DNA evidence in 2007.

AP Photo/Tim Sharp

Rethinking Finality The availability of DNA fingerprinting for convicted felons will certainly increase as the technology becomes more efficient and less costly. By the spring of 2007, forty states had passed laws making it easier for inmates to access postconviction DNA evidence.[76] These trends may have serious repercussions for present notions of finality. Statutes of limitations, for example, are partly based on the belief that time wears away important facets of evidence, such as witnesses' memories and victims' remains, making them unreliable at trial. DNA evidence, in contrast, retains its validity for decades. The availability of DNA evidence raises another question as well: Should the protections against double jeopardy apply to a

International CJ — A Change of Heart

Like many other aspects of the American criminal justice system, this country's commitment to the principles of double jeopardy was derived from English tradition. The idea that the same person should not be retried for the same crime in the same jurisdiction has been part of English common law for more than eight hundred years. Nevertheless, in 2006, a British court found William Dunlop guilty of murdering Julie Hogg, even though he had been acquitted of the same crime in 1991. In the first trial, Dunlop lied to the court effectively enough about his involvement in Hogg's death to fool a jury and secure his freedom.

Under the 2003 Criminal Justice Act, British law now allows for double jeopardy in very specific circumstances. First, only cases involving serious crimes such as murder, rape, and armed robbery can be reopened. Second, the director of public prosecutions, an appointed official, must agree to a new investigation of the facts surrounding the case. Third, the Court of Appeal must approve the request for a new trial.

Despite misgivings in some sectors of the British legal system, these safeguards seem to have satisfied most critics. Dunlop's conviction, the first under these new procedures, caused little controversy. He had, after all, confessed to the murder several years after his initial acquittal, confident that he had nothing to fear but a charge of perjury for lying to the court.

FOR CRITICAL ANALYSIS In 2006, rumors swirled that O. J. Simpson, who had been acquitted in 1995 of the murders of his ex-wife Nicole Brown Simpson and her friend Ronald Goldman, was going to publish a book in which he admitted to the crimes. Of course, even if this had happened, our prohibitions against double jeopardy would have kept Simpson from facing another trial. How do you think Simpson would have fared under the present British system if he had confessed? Do you think that the United States should follow Britain's lead and modify our laws to allow for retrials under certain circumstances? Explain your answer.

---

person who was acquitted at trial but is subsequently shown by DNA evidence to have been guilty? In Great Britain, the answer to that question may be "no" (see the feature *International CJ—A Change of Heart*).

Habeas Corpus Contrary to many people's belief, an inmate cannot file a *habeas corpus* petition to initiate DNA reviews of her or his case. *Habeas corpus* (Latin for "you have the body") is a judicial order that commands a corrections official to bring a person before a federal court so that the court can hear the person's claims that he or she is being held illegally.

A writ of *habeas corpus* differs from an appeal in several respects. First, it can be filed only by someone who is imprisoned. Second, it can address only constitutional issues, not technical errors. Thus, an inmate can file a *habeas corpus* petition claiming that the conditions of his or her imprisonment constitute cruel and unusual punishment, but not that DNA evidence would prove his or her innocence.

After a dramatic rise in the number of *habeas corpus* petitions, many of them frivolous, in the 1980s and early 1990s, Congress moved to limit this form of review by passing the Antiterrorism and Effective Death Penalty Act in 1996. This legislation imposed a one-year time limit on filing a *habeas corpus* petition after conviction and severely restricted the ability of federal courts to overturn state court criminal convictions.[77] Almost immediately, the United States Supreme Court upheld these *habeas corpus* limits, much to the relief of those who value finality in our criminal justice system.

Habeas Corpus An order that requires correctional officials to bring an inmate before a court or a judge and explain why he or she is being held in prison.

Self Check Fill in the Blanks

Once both the prosecution and the defense have completed their closing arguments, the judge will give the jury a _____ summing up the case and providing instructions on how to proceed. After the jury has _____ and reached a decision, it will announce a _____ of guilty or not guilty. If the jury cannot do so, a _____ jury occurs and the judge will call a mistrial. If a defendant is convicted, he or she has the option of _____ this outcome based on a showing that the trial court acted improperly on a question of _____, not fact, during the proceedings. Check your answers on page 338.

RAPE SHIELD LAWS

Historically, the courtroom has been a hostile environment for victims of sexual assault. Because of a pervasive attitude labeled the "chastity requirement" by Professor Michelle Anderson of the City University of New York School of Law, rape victims who were perceived to be sexually virtuous were much more likely to be believed by jurors than those who had been sexually active.[78] If a woman had consented to sex before, so the line of thought went, she was more likely to do so again. Consequently, defense attorneys invariably and successfully focused on the accuser's sexual past, convincing juries that consent had been given in the present instance by establishing a pattern of consent in past ones. As we close this chapter, we will examine much-debated legislative efforts to make the courtroom "safe" for rape victims.

"UNCHASTITY" EVIDENCE

In 1974, Michigan passed the first *rape shield law* in the United States. The statute keeps specific evidence, including evidence about the victim's reputation and previous sexual conduct, out of the courtroom, except under certain circumstances.[79] Today, every state but Arizona has a rape shield law. (In Arizona, well-established case law, rather than a statute, declares evidence of the accuser's "unchastity" inadmissible.[80]) In 1978, Congress also imposed a rape shield law in federal courts.[81]

Rape shield laws do contain certain exceptions that allow the defense to use evidence of the accuser's prior sexual conduct to undermine the credibility of his or her testimony. For example, Federal Rule 412 states that evidence of "other sexual behavior" or the "sexual disposition" of a rape complainant is inadmissible *unless* it is offered *either* (1) to prove that a person other than the accused was the source of semen, injury, or other physical evidence; *or* (2) to prove consent *and* involves previous sexual behavior by the alleged victim with the defendant. In addition, the defense must show that the exclusion of the evidence would violate the constitutional rights of the defendant.[82]

The Case for Rape Shield Laws

- Without these laws, defense attorneys may subject victims of sexual assault to embarrassing and degrading cross-examination concerning their personal lives. In other words, the rape victim should not be the person on trial.
- These laws ensure that defendants are convicted or acquitted based on the relevant evidence, not the prejudices of jurors more focused on the sexual history of the accuser than on the facts of the case.
- These laws encourage victims to report incidents of sexual assault by protecting their privacy.

The Case against Rape Shield Laws

- The confrontation clause of the Sixth Amendment gives all defendants the right to question their accusers. By limiting this right, rape shield laws leave defendants in sexual-assault cases at the mercy of juries that do not know all the facts surrounding the case.
- In many instances, the victim's prior sexual history is relevant to the issue of whether she or he consented to the incident in question. These facts should not be hidden from the jury simply because they are highly emotional or deal with sexual issues.
- The many exceptions to rape shield laws, listed earlier, have effectively rendered them meaningless. According to the federal government, only 38 percent of those who have been sexually assaulted report the crime to the police.[83]

Your Opinion—Writing Assignment

A woman accuses two men of raping her in the back seat of a car. Both defendants claim that the sexual activity was consensual. At their trial, they want to present the following evidence from that night: (1) a fourth person had witnessed the accuser flirting aggressively with numerous men at a local bar; (2) the accuser had openly tried to seduce the older brother of one of the defendants; and (3) another witness had seen the accuser sitting on a soda crate in front of the defendants, one of whom was zipping up his pants.

Given the goals of rape shield laws and their exceptions discussed in this feature, which evidence, if any, concerning the above incident should be admitted before the jury? In cases such as this one, do you feel that rape shield laws properly balance the rights of the accuser and the rights of the accused? Before responding, you can review our discussions in this chapter concerning

- Relevant and prejudicial evidence (pages 322–323).
- The prosecutor's case (pages 324–325).
- The defendant's case (pages 326–327).

Your answer should take at least three full paragraphs.

L01 Identify the basic protections enjoyed by criminal defendants in the United States. According to the Sixth Amendment, a criminal defendant has the right to a speedy and public trial by an impartial jury in the physical location where the crime was committed. Additionally, a person accused of a crime must be informed of the nature of the crime and be confronted with the witnesses against him or her. Further, the accused must be able to summon witnesses in her or his favor and have the assistance of counsel.

L02 List the three requirements of the Speedy Trial Act of 1974. In federal court, those accused of crimes must experience (a) no more than thirty days between arrest and indictment; (b) no more than ten days between indictment and arraignment; and (c) no more than sixty days between arraignment and trial. Of course, extra time is allowed for hearings on pretrial motions, mental competency examinations, and other procedural actions.

L03 Explain what "taking the Fifth" really means. The Fifth Amendment states that no person "shall be compelled in any criminal case to be a witness against himself." Thus, defendants do not have to testify if their testimony would implicate them in the crime. Witnesses may refuse to testify on this same ground. (Witnesses, though, are often granted immunity and thereafter can no longer take the Fifth.) In the United States, silence on the part of a defendant cannot be used by the jury in forming its opinion about guilt or innocence.

L04 List the requirements normally imposed on potential jurors. They must be (a) citizens of the United States; (b) over eighteen years of age; (c) free of felony convictions; (d) of the necessary health to function on a jury; (e) sufficiently intelligent to understand the issues at trial; and (f) able to read, write, and comprehend the English language.

L05 Contrast challenges for cause and peremptory challenges during *voir dire*. A challenge for cause occurs when an attorney provides the court with a legally justifiable reason why a potential juror should be excluded; for example, the juror does not speak English. In contrast, peremptory challenges do not require any justification by the attorney and are usually limited to a small number. They cannot, however, be based, even implicitly, on race or gender.

L06 List the standard steps in a criminal jury trial. (a) Opening statements by the prosecutor and the defense attorney; (b) presentation of evidence, usually in the form of questioning by the prosecutor, known as direct examination; (c) cross-examination by the defense attorney of the same witnesses; (d) at the end of the prosecutor's presentation of evidence, motion for a directed verdict by the defense (also called a motion for judgment as a matter of law in the federal courts), which is normally denied by the judge; (e) presentation of the defendant's case, which may include putting the defendant on the stand and direct examination of the defense's witnesses; (f) cross-examination by the prosecutor; (g) after the defense closes its case, rebuttal by the prosecution, which may involve new evidence that was not used initially by the prosecution; (h) cross-examination of the prosecution's new witnesses by the defense and introduction of new witnesses of its own, called the surrebuttal; (i) closing arguments by both the defense and the prosecution; (j) the charging of the jury by the judge, during which the judge sums up the case and instructs the jurors on the rules of law that apply; (k) jury deliberations; and (l) presentation of the verdict.

L07 Explain the difference between testimony and real evidence, between lay witnesses and expert witnesses, and between direct and circumstantial evidence. Testimony consists of statements by competent witnesses, whereas real evidence includes physical items that affect the case; a lay witness is an "average person," whereas an expert witness speaks with the authority of one who has professional training, advanced knowledge, or substantial experience in a specialized area; direct evidence is evidence presented by witnesses as opposed to circumstantial evidence, which can create an inference that a fact exists, but does not directly establish the fact.

L08 List possible affirmative defenses. (a) Self-defense, (b) insanity, (c) duress, and (d) entrapment.

L09 Delineate circumstances in which a criminal defendant may be tried a second time for the same act. A defendant who is acquitted in a criminal trial may be sued in a civil case for essentially the same act. When an act is a crime under both state and federal law, a defendant who is acquitted in state court may be tried in federal court for the same act, and vice versa.

L010 List the six basic steps of an appeal. (a) The filing of a notice of appeal; (b) the transfer of the trial court record to the appellate court; (c) the filing of briefs; (d) the presentation of oral arguments; (e) the deliberation of the appellate judges who then prepare a written opinion; and (f) the announcement of the judges—upholding the decision of the lower court, modifying part of the decision, reversing the decision, or reversing and remanding the decision to the trial court.

acquittal 311
Allen Charge 330
appeal 331
authentication 323
bench trial 310
challenge for cause 315
charge 329
circumstantial evidence 321
closing arguments 328
confrontation clause 325
cross-examination 325
direct evidence 321

direct examination 324
double jeopardy 331
evidence 320
expert witness 321
finality 333
habeas corpus 335
hearsay 324
hung jury 330
jury nullification 330
jury trial 310
lay witness 321
master jury list 313

motion for a directed verdict 325
opening statements 320
peremptory challenges 316
real evidence 320
rebuttal 327
relevant evidence 322
statute of limitations 310
testimony 320
venire 314
verdict 330
voir dire 315
wrongful conviction 334

Self Check Answer Key

Page 312: i. jury; ii. bench; iii. judge; iv. self-incrimination; v. innocent; vi. guilty; vii. state/prosecutor; viii. reasonable doubt

Page 320: i. *venire;* ii. *voir dire;* iii. cause; iv. peremptory; v. race; vi. gender

Page 328: i. testimony; ii. fact; iii. relevant; iv. prejudice; v. direct; vi. cross; vii. reasonable doubt

Page 335: i. charge; ii. deliberated; iii. verdict; iv. hung; v. appealing; vi. law

Questions for Critical Analysis

1. If a defendant waives his or her right to a jury trial, what type of trial then takes place?

2. Why is there a higher standard of proof in criminal cases than in civil cases?

3. What danger lies in a defense attorney's or prosecutor's decision to present an opening statement to the jury?

4. Under what circumstances may evidence be excluded?

5. How does an attorney authenticate evidence presented?

6. Are there exceptions to the hearsay rule, and if so, what are they?

7. Why might a defense attorney not want to call the defendant to the stand to testify?

8. What is usually the major problem with the jury instructions that judges present prior to jury deliberations?

9. What steps can a judge take if the jury does not come to a decision on the defendant's guilt or innocence?

10. Under what circumstances can a person ask for *habeas corpus* review of her or his case?

Maximize Your Best Possible Outcome for Chapter 10

1. **Maximize Your Best Chance for Getting a Good Grade on the Exam.** ThomsonNOW Personalized Study is a diagnostic study tool containing valuable text-specific resources—and because you focus on just what you don't know, you learn more in less time to get a better grade. How do you get ThomsonNOW? If your textbook does not include an access code card, go to **thomsonedu.com** to get ThomsonNOW before your next exam!

2. **Get the Most Out of Your Textbook** by going to the book companion Web site at **www.cjinaction.com** to access one of the tutorial quizzes, use the flash cards

to master key terms, and check out the many other study aids you'll find there. Under chapter resources you will also be able to access the Stories from the Street feature and Web links mentioned in the textbook.

3. **Learn about Potential Criminal Justice Careers** discussed in this chapter by exploring careers online at **www.cjinaction.com**. You will find career descriptions and information about job requirements, training, salary and benefits, and the application process. You can also watch video profiles featuring criminal justice professionals.

1. Quoted in Henry K. Lee, "Woman to Defend Herself in Slay Case," *San Francisco Chronicle* (January 21, 2006), B3.
2. *Ibid.*
3. Quoted in Demian Bulwa, "For Gavel Groupies, Polk Trial Is the Best," *San Francisco Chronicle* (May 21, 2006), B1.
4. Quoted in Bruce Gerstman, "Sentence Put Off for Killer of Husband," *San Jose Mercury News* (July 7, 2006), B7.
5. Jerome Frank, *Courts on Trial: Myth and Reality in American Justice* (New York: Atheneum, 1969), 14–33.
6. David L. Cook, Steven R. Schlesinger, Thomas J. Bak, and William T. Rule II, "Criminal Caseload in U.S. District Courts: More than Meets the Eye," *American University Law Review* 44 (June 1995), 44.
7. 407 U.S. 514 (1972).
8. 725 Illinois Compiled Statutes Section 5/103-5 (1992).
9. L. Stuart Ditzen, "Suspects' Release Stuns City Lawyers: Seven Murder Defendants Were Set Free on a Speedy-Trial Violation," *Philadelphia Inquirer* (August 6, 2004), B1.
10. 18 U.S.C. Section 3161.
11. 391 U.S. 145 (1968).
12. *Blanton v. Las Vegas*, 489 U.S. 538 (1989).
13. *Williams v. Florida*, 399 U.S. 102 (1970).
14. 435 U.S. 223 (1978).
15. *Johnson v. Louisiana*, 406 U.S. 356 (1972); and *Apodaca v. Oregon*, 406 U.S. 404 (1972).
16. 332 U.S. 46 (1947).
17. Barton L. Ingraham, "The Right of Silence, the Presumption of Innocence, the Burden of Proof, and a Modest Proposal," *Journal of Criminal Law and Criminology* 85 (1994), 559–595.
18. 397 U.S. 358 (1970).
19. James P. Levine, "The Impact of Local Political Cultures on Jury Verdicts," *Criminal Justice Journal* 14 (1992), 163–164.
20. *State v. Gonzales*, No. CR-99-139 (N.M. January 19, 2000).
21. Quoted in Curt Anderson, "Padilla Trial Trouble," (March 29, 2007), at **www.nysun.com/article/51492?page_no=2**.
22. *Lockhart v. McCree*, 476 U.S. 162 (1986).
23. *Witherspoon v. Illinois*, 391 U.S. 510 (1968).
24. John Kaplan and Jon R. Waltz, *The Trial of Jack Ruby* (New York: Macmillan, 1965), 91–94.
25. 380 U.S. 224 (1965).
26. 476 U.S. 79 (1986).
27. Eric L. Muller, "Solving the *Batson* Paradox: Harmless Error, Jury Representation, and the Sixth Amendment," *Yale Law Journal* 106 (October 1996), 93.
28. 499 U.S. 400 (1991).
29. 502 U.S. 1056 (1992).
30. *Miller-El v. Cockrell*, 537 U.S. 322 (2003).
31. *Miller-El v. Dretke*, 361 F.3d 894 (5th Cir. 2004); and *Miller-El v. Dretke*, 545 U.S. 231 (2005).
32. Karen L. Cipriani, "The Numbers Don't Add Up: Challenging the Premise of *J.E.B. v. Alabama*," *American Criminal Law Review* 31 (Summer 1994), 1253–1277.
33. 511 U.S. 127 (1994).
34. Jeremy W. Barber, "The Jury Is Still Out," *American Criminal Law Review* 31 (Summer 1994), 1225–1252.
35. *Purkett v. Elem*, 514 U.S. 765, 768 (1995).
36. *Batson v. Kentucky*, 476 U.S. 79, 107–108 (1986).
37. Harry Kalven and Hans Zeisel, *The American Jury* (Boston: Little, Brown, 1966), 163–167.
38. Douglas D. Koski, "Testing the Story Model of Juror Decision Making," *Sex Offender Law* (June/July 2003), 53–58.
39. Nancy Pennington and Reid Hastie, "The Story Model for Juror Decision Making," in *Inside the Juror: The Psychology of Juror Decision Making* (Cambridge, MA: Harvard University Press, 1983), 192, 194–195.
40. 424 U.S. 600 (1976).
41. Federal Rule of Evidence 703.
42. Richard A. Epstein, "Judicial Control over Expert Testimony: Of Deference and Education," *Northwestern University Law Review* 87 (1993), 1156.
43. L. Timothy Perrin, "Expert Witnesses under Rules 703 and 803(4) of the Federal Rules of Evidence: Separating the Wheat from the Chaff," *Indiana Law Journal* 72 (Fall 1997), 939.
44. Andrew Blankstein and Jean Guccione, "Actor Robert Blake Acquitted in Shooting Death of His Wife," *Los Angeles Times* (March 17, 2005), A1.
45. Thomas J. Reed, "Trial by Propensity: Admission of Other Criminal Acts Evidenced in Federal Criminal Trials," *University of Cincinnati Law Review* 50 (1981), 713.
46. *Ibid.*
47. *People v. Zackowitz*, 254 N.Y. 192 (1930).
48. Charles McCormick, *Handbook on Evidence* (St. Paul, MN: West Publishing Co., 1987), Chapter 1.
49. Federal Rules of Procedure, Rule 804(b)(2).
50. Arthur Best, *Evidence: Examples and Explanations*, 4th ed. (New York: Aspen Law & Business, 2001), 89–90.
51. Andrew Blankstein, "Blake Witness Meth Use Described," *Los Angeles Times* (February 17, 2005), B5.
52. *Griffin v. California*, 380 U.S. 609 (1965).
53. Douglas D. Koski, "Alcohol and Rape Study," *Criminal Law Bulletin* 38 (2002), 21–159.
54. Roger LeRoy Miller and Mary S. Urisko, *West's Paralegal Today*, 3d ed. (St. Paul, MN: West Publishing Co., 2003), 443.
55. Firoz Dattu, "Illustrated Jury Instructions," *Judicature* 82 (September/October 1998), 79.
56. Walter J. Steele, Jr., and Elizabeth Thornburg, "Jury Instructions: A Persistent Failure to Communicate," *Judicature* 74 (1991), 249–254.
57. Judicial Council of California, *Criminal Jury Instructions* (Eagan, MN: Thomson/West, 2005), no. 521.
58. *People v. Harlan*, 109 P.3d 616 (Colo. 2005).
59. David W. Broeder, "The University of Chicago Jury Project," *Nebraska Law Review* 38 (1959), 744–760.
60. 164 U.S. 492 (1896).
61. *United States v. Fioravanti*, 412 F.2d 407 (3d Cir. 1969).
62. National Center for State Courts, *Are Hung Juries a Problem?* (Washington, D.C.: U.S. Department of Justice, 2002), 1.
63. Joseph L. Gastwirth and Michael D. Sinclair, "Diagnostic Test Methodology in the Design and Analysis of Judge-Jury Agreement Studies," *Jurimetrics Journal* 39 (Fall 1998), 59.
64. Peter Western, "The Three Faces of Double Jeopardy: Reflections on Government Appeals of Criminal Sentences," *Michigan Law Review* 78 (1980), 1001–1002.
65. Quoted in Jeffrey Abramson, *We, the Jury: The Jury System and the Ideal of Democracy* (New York: Basic Books, 1994), 250.
66. Bureau of Justice Statistics, *Federal Criminal Appeals, 1999 with Trends 1985–1999* (Washington, D.C.: U.S. Department of Justice, April 2001), 1.
67. *Green v. United States*, 355 U.S. 184 (1957).
68. 537 U.S. 101 (2003).
69. David W. Neubauer, *America's Courts and the Criminal Justice System*, 5th ed. (Belmont, CA: Wadsworth Publishing Co. 1996), 254.
70. David P. Kennedy, "The End of Finality," *Maryland Bar Journal* (November/December 2004), 24.
71. Quoted in Saad Gul, "The Truth That Dare Not Speak Its Name: The Criminal Justice System's Treatment of Wrongly Convicted Defendants through the Prism of DNA Exonerations," *Criminal Law Bulletin* (November/December 2006), 693.
72. The Innocence Project, "In 200th DNA Exoneration Nationwide, Jerry Miller in Chicago Is Proven Innocent 25 Years after Wrongful Conviction," at **www.innocenceproject.org/Content/530.php**.
73. Bureau of Justice Statistics, *Felony Sentences in State Courts, 2002* (Washington, D.C.: U.S. Department of Justice, December 2004), 1.
74. Gul, 690.
75. Richard A. Rosen, "Innocence and Death," *North Carolina Law Review* (December 2003), 69–70.
76. The Innocence Project, "Access to Post-Conviction DNA Testing," at **www.innocenceproject.org/Content/304.php**.
77. 28 U.S.C. Section 2254(d)(1).
78. Michelle J. Anderson, "From Chastity Requirement to Sexuality License: Sexual Consent and a New Rape Shield Law," *George Washington Law Review* (February 2002), 51.
79. Michigan Compiled Laws Annotated Section 750.520j (West 1991).
80. *State ex rel. Pope v. Superior Court*, 545 P.2d 946, 953 (Ariz. 1996).
81. Federal Rule of Evidence 412(a)(1)–(2).
82. Federal Rule of Evidence 412(b)(1)(A)–(C).
83. Bureau of Justice Statistics, *Criminal Victimization, 2005* (Washington, D.C.: U.S. Department of Justice, September 2006), 10.

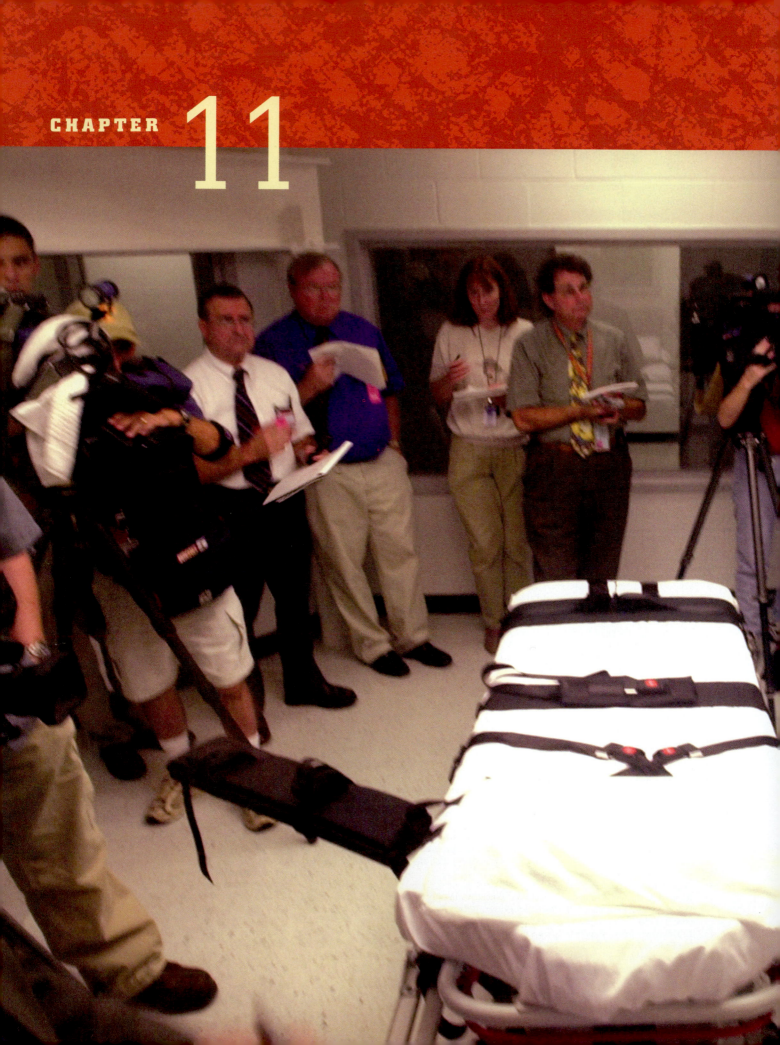

CHAPTER 11

Punishment

and Sentencing

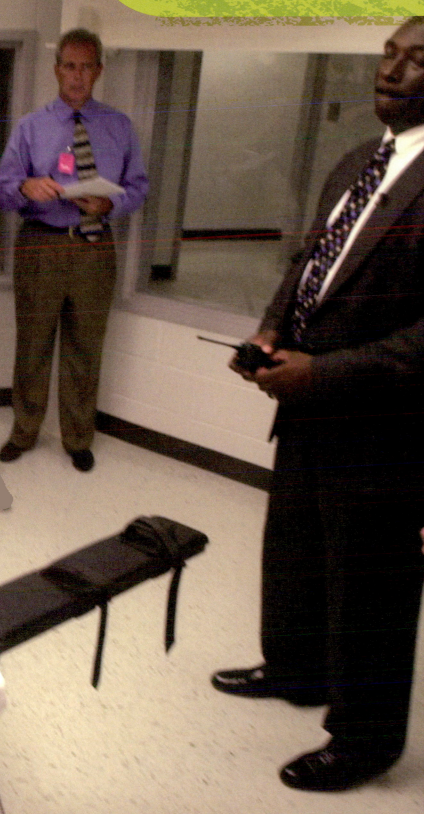

Chapter outline

- The Purpose of Sentencing
- The Structure of Sentencing
- Individualized Justice and the Judge
- Inconsistencies in Sentencing
- Sentencing Reform
- Capital Punishment—The Ultimate Sentence
- Criminal Justice in Action—The Morality of the Death Penalty

Learning objectives

After reading this chapter, you should be able to:

LO1 List and contrast the four basic philosophical reasons for sentencing criminals.

LO2 Contrast indeterminate with determinate sentencing.

LO3 Explain why there is a difference between a sentence imposed by a judge and the actual sentence carried out by the prisoner.

LO4 List the six forms of punishment.

LO5 State who has input into the sentencing decision and list the factors that determine a sentence.

LO6 Explain some of the reasons why sentencing reform has occurred.

LO7 Identify the arguments for and against the use of victim impact statements during sentencing hearings.

LO8 Outline the Supreme Court rulings on capital punishment that led to the bifurcated process for death penalty sentencing.

LO9 Describe the main issues of the death penalty debate.

A Matter of Life or Death

Zacarias Moussaoui is the only person to go on trial in the United States for actions directly related to the terrorist attacks of September 11, 2001. In 2005, the French citizen of Moroccan descent pleaded guilty to taking part in an al Qaeda conspiracy that led to the hijacking of the four airliners. In April 2006, a federal jury in Alexandria, Virginia, concluded that he was responsible for at least some of the nearly 2,972 deaths that occurred on that day. The court's final task was to determine the proper punishment for Moussaoui: Life or death? On May 3, 2006, after seven days of deliberation, the jury decided against execution and sent the defendant to prison for the rest of his days.

The verdict came as somewhat of a surprise. Federal prosecutors had pushed hard for the death penalty, and Moussaoui was hardly a sympathetic witness for his own cause. He openly gloated over the pain of those who had lost family and friends in the attacks. He vowed to continue to try to kill Americans if he lived. He sang, "Burn in the U.S.A.," in court. In addition, the jury heard stirring testimony from victims' family members, as well as tape recordings of 911 calls from inside the burning World Trade Center in New York City and several of the hijacked airplanes.

In the end, however, the jury decided that Moussaoui was not directly responsible for the attacks. Without a finding of direct responsibility, he could not be executed. Prosecutors had argued that by failing to warn law enforcement agents of the terrorist conspiracy, the defendant, in effect, caused the deaths on September 11, 2001. Defense attorneys countered with strong evidence that the government never gave credence to any information offered by Moussaoui, who spent the day of the hijackings in a jail cell in Minneapolis, Minnesota, awaiting deportation. Furthermore, some jurors took the defendant's background, which included a difficult upbringing, into account in choosing to be lenient. After formally sentencing Moussaoui to six life terms without parole, U.S. District Judge Leonie Brinkema called the result an "appropriate ending" to the lengthy and emotional proceedings.

AP Photo/Dana Verkouteren

▲ The 2006 trial of Zacarias Moussaoui (left), who was eventually convicted of conspiring to kill Americans as part of the September 11 terrorist attacks.

On learning his fate, Zacarias Moussaoui shook his fists in the air and yelled, "America, you lost, you lost!"[1] This was not the outcome that some had wanted. "He doesn't deserve any compassion," said one man whose son was killed on September 11, 2001. "It would be better to pay twenty-eight cents and put a round in his head."[2] In general, however, most observers agreed with Judge Brinkema that the jury had done an admirable job in making a difficult decision, and perhaps an "appropriate" penalty was the best anyone could have expected. Punishment and sentencing present some of the most complex issues of the criminal justice system. One scholar has even asserted:

> There is no such thing as "accurate" sentencing; there are only sentences that are more or less just, more or less effective. Nothing in the recent or distant history of sentencing reform suggests that anything approaching perfection is attainable.[3]

In this chapter, we will discuss the various attempts to "perfect" the practice of sentencing over the past century and explore the ramifications of these efforts for the American criminal justice system. Whereas previous chapters have concentrated on the prosecutor and defense attorney, this one will spotlight the judge and his or her role in making the sentencing decision. We will particularly focus on recent national and state efforts to limit judicial discretion in this area, a trend that has had the overall effect of producing harsher sentences for many offenders. Finally, we will examine the issues surrounding the death penalty, a controversial subject that forces us to confront the basic truth of sentencing: the way we punish criminals says a great deal about the kind of people we are.[4]

The Purpose of Sentencing

Professor Herbert Packer has said that punishing criminals serves two ultimate purposes: the "deserved infliction of suffering on evil doers" and "the prevention of crime."[5] Even this straightforward assessment raises several questions. How does one determine the sort of punishment that is "deserved"? How can we be sure that certain penalties "prevent" crime? Should criminals be punished solely for the good of society, or should their well-being also be taken into consideration? Sentencing laws indicate how any given group of people has answered these questions, but do not tell us why they were answered in that manner. To understand why, we must first consider the four basic philosophical reasons for sentencing—retribution, deterrence, incapacitation, and rehabilitation.

RETRIBUTION

L01 The oldest and most common justification for punishing someone is that he or she "deserved it"—as the Old Testament states, "an eye for an eye and a tooth for a tooth." Under a system of justice that favors **retribution,** a wrongdoer who has freely chosen to violate society's rules must be punished for the infraction. Retribution relies on the principle of **just deserts,** which holds that the severity of the punishment must be in proportion to the severity of the crime. Retributive justice is not the same as *revenge*. Whereas revenge implies that the wrongdoer is punished only with the aim of satisfying a victim or victims, retribution is more concerned with the needs of society as a whole.

The *principle of willful wrongdoing* is central to the idea of retribution; that is, society is morally justified in punishing someone only if that person was aware that he or she committed a crime. Therefore, animals, children, and the mentally incapacitated are not responsible for criminal action, even though they may be a threat to the community.[6] Furthermore, the principles of retribution reject any wide-reaching social benefit as a goal of punishment. The philosopher Immanuel Kant, an early proponent of retribution in criminal justice, believed that punishment by a court

> can never be inflicted merely as a means to promote some other good for the criminal himself or for civil society. It must always be inflicted upon him only because he has committed a crime. For a man can never be treated merely as a means to the purposes of another.[7]

In other words, punishment is an end in itself and cannot be justified by any future good that may result from a criminal's suffering.

One problem with retributive ideas of justice lies in proportionality. Whether or not one agrees with the death penalty, the principle behind it is easy to fathom: the punishment (death) fits the crime (death). But what about the theft of an automobile? How does one fairly determine the amount of time the thief must spend in prison? Should the type of car or the wealth of the car owner matter? Theories of retribution often have a difficult time providing answers to such questions.[8]

▼ Mark Hacking wipes away a tear as a Utah judge sentences him to six years to life for the first degree murder of his wife, Lori. Hacking had shot Lori in the head while she was asleep and dumped her body in the trash. Why does society demand that offenders such as Hacking receive harsh punishments?

Douglas C. Pizac/Getty Images

Suppose one were to ask Immanuel Kant and Jeremy Bentham the following question: Is the death penalty a justifiable punishment for illegally selling marijuana? Kant, a proponent of the "principle of equity," would answer no; such a punishment would be too harsh for the crime. Bentham, however, might not agree. If the ultimate goal of punishment is to deter people from committing future crimes, then a literal reading of Bentham's utilitarian theory would seem to support severe penalties for seemingly minor criminal behavior.

Singapore, a nation-city of 3 million people in Southeast Asia, leans toward Bentham rather than Kant in its sentencing theories. According to Singapore law, the selling of any drug—including marijuana—carries a mandatory death sentence by hanging, as do murder and the use of a firearm in committing or attempting to commit a crime. Someone caught smoking marijuana is sentenced to a ten-year prison term. Citizens who litter are fined the equivalent of $1,000, with similar penalties imposed for chewing gum and failing to flush a public toilet. Vandals are sentenced to up to three years in prison and (as American teenager Michael Fay learned in the mid-1990s) are subject to caning.

Many observers criticize Singapore, claiming its strict laws violate human rights. Indeed, according to the human rights group Amnesty International, Singapore has the highest capital punishment rate in the world, with most of the executions taking place for drug trafficking. But Singaporeans point to one of the world's lowest crime rates as justification for their system. The year after robbery with a firearm was deemed punishable by death, for example, not one such incident took place in the city. Singapore officials also point out that the United States—which consistently criticizes human rights abuses in other nations—has the highest violent crime rate and the most citizens in prison of any country in the West.

▲ A funeral portrait of Australian citizen Nguyen Tuong Van, executed by Singaporean authorities on December 2, 2005, for smuggling about 14 ounces of heroin into the country.

FOR CRITICAL ANALYSIS

It is important to note that Singapore is a democracy, and many, if not most, of its citizens support its law enforcement principles. How do you think the American public would react if given the chance to vote on implementing similarly harsh punishments for crime in this country?

DETERRENCE

The concept of **deterrence** (as well as incapacitation and rehabilitation) takes the opposite approach: rather than seeking only to punish the wrongdoer, the goal of sentencing should be to prevent future crimes. By "setting an example," society is sending a message to potential criminals that certain actions will not be tolerated. Jeremy Bentham, a nineteenth-century British reformer who first articulated the principles of deterrence, felt that retribution was counterproductive because it does not serve the community. (See Chapter 2 to review Bentham's utilitarian theories.) He believed that a person should be punished only when doing so was in society's best interests and that the severity of the punishment should be based on its deterrent value, not on the severity of the crime.[9] (See the feature *International CJ—Singapore: A Utilitarian Oasis*.)

General and Specific Deterrence Deterrence can take two forms: general and specific. The basic idea of *general deterrence* is that by punishing one person, others will be dissuaded from committing a similar crime. *Specific deterrence* assumes that an individual, after being punished once for a certain act, will be less likely to repeat that act because she or he does not want to be punished again.[10] Both forms of deterrence have proved problematic in practice. General deterrence assumes that a person commits a crime only after a rational decision-making process, in which he or she implicitly weighs the benefits of the crime against the possible costs of the punishment. This is not necessarily the case, especially for young offenders who tend to value the immediate rewards of crime over the

Deterrence The strategy of preventing crime through the threat of punishment. Assumes that potential criminals will weigh the costs of punishment versus the benefits of the criminal act; therefore, punishments should be severe.

possible future consequences. The argument for specific deterrence is somewhat weakened by the fact that a relatively small number of habitual offenders are responsible for the majority of certain criminal acts.

Low Probability of Punishment Another criticism of deterrence is that for most crimes, wrongdoers are unlikely to be caught, sentenced, and imprisoned. According to the National Crime Victimization Survey, only 47 percent of all violent crimes and 40 percent of all property crimes are even reported to the police.[11] Of those reported, only 45 percent of violent crimes and 16.3 percent of property crimes result in an arrest.[12] Then, as we saw in Chapter 9, case attrition further whittles down the number of arrestees who face trial and the possibility of imprisonment. Thus, in general, potential criminals have less to fear from the criminal justice system than one might expect. Professors Paul H. Robinson of Northwestern University School of Law and John M. Darley of Princeton University note that this low probability of punishment could be offset by making the punishment so severe that even the slightest chance of apprehension could act as a deterrent—for example, an eighty-five-year prison term for shoplifting or the loss of a hand for burglary.[13] Our society is, however, unwilling to allow for this possibility.

> **Incapacitation** A strategy for preventing crime by detaining wrongdoers in prison, thereby separating them from the community and reducing criminal opportunities.

> "Men are not hanged for stealing horses, but that horses may not be stolen."
>
> —*Marquis de Halifax*, Political Thoughts and Reflections *(1750)*

INCAPACITATION

"Wicked people exist," said James Q. Wilson. "Nothing avails except to set them apart from innocent people."[14] Wilson's blunt statement summarizes the justification for **incapacitation** as a form of punishment. As a purely practical matter, incarcerating criminals guarantees that they will not be a danger to society, at least for the length of their prison terms. To a certain extent, the death penalty is justified in terms of incapacitation, as it prevents the offender from committing any future crimes.

The Impact of Incapacitation Several studies do support incapacitation's efficacy as a crime-fighting tool. Criminologist Isaac Ehrlich of the University of Chicago estimated that a 1 percent increase in sentence length will produce a 1 percent decrease in crime rates.[15] Another Chicago professor, Steve Levitt, has noticed a trend that further supports incapacitation. He found that violent crime rates rise in communities where inmate litigation over prison overcrowding has forced the early release of some inmates and a subsequent drop in the prison population.[16]

Incapacitation as a theory of punishment suffers from several weaknesses, however. Unlike retribution, it offers no proportionality with regard to a particular crime. Giving a burglar a life sentence would certainly assure that she or he would not commit another burglary. Does that justify such a severe penalty? Furthermore, incarceration protects society only until the criminal is freed. Many studies have shown that, on release, offenders may actually be more likely to commit crimes than before they were imprisoned.[17] In that case, incapacitation may increase the likelihood of crime, rather than diminish it.

▼ Tyrone Williams hides his face as he is escorted from a Houston courthouse in January 2007. Williams was sentenced to life in prison for his role as driver of a truck in which nineteen illegal immigrants died from dehydration, overheating, and suffocation. How do the theories of deterrence and incapacitation justify Williams's punishment?

AP Photo/Pat Sullivan

Selective and Collective Incapacitation Some observers believe that strategies of *selective incapacitation* should be favored over strategies of *collective incapacitation* to solve this problem. With collective incapacitation, all offenders who have committed a similar crime are imprisoned for the same time period, whereas selective incapacitation provides longer sentences for individuals, such as career criminals, who are judged more likely to commit further crimes if and when they are released. The problem with selective incapacitation, however, lies in the difficulty of predicting just who is at the greatest risk to commit future crimes. Studies have shown that even the most effective methods of trying to predict future criminality are correct less than half of the time.[18]

REHABILITATION

For most of the past century, **rehabilitation** has been seen as the most "humane" goal of punishment. This line of thinking reflects the view that crime is a "social phenomenon" caused not by the inherent criminality of a person, but by factors in that person's surroundings. By removing wrongdoers from their environment and intervening to change their values and personalities, the rehabilitative model suggests, criminals can be "treated" and possibly even "cured" of their proclivities toward crime. Although studies of the effectiveness of rehabilitation are too varied to be easily summarized, it does appear that, in most instances, criminals who receive treatment are less likely to reoffend than those who do not.[19]

For most of the past two decades, the American criminal justice system has been characterized by a notable rejection of many of the precepts of rehabilitation in favor of retributive, deterrent, and incapacitating sentencing strategies that "get tough on crime." Recently, however, more jurisdictions are turning to rehabilitation as a cost-effective (and, possibly, crime-reducing) alternative to punishment, a topic that we will explore more fully in the next chapter. Furthermore, the American public may be more accepting of rehabilitative principles than many elected officials think. A 2006 survey by Zogby International, sponsored by the National Council on Crime and Delinquency, found that 87 percent of respondents favored rehabilitative services for nonviolent offenders, both before and after they leave prison.[20]

RESTORATIVE JUSTICE

It would be a mistake to view the four philosophies we have just discussed as being mutually exlusive. For the most part, a society's overall sentencing direction is influenced by all four theories, with political and social factors determining which one is predominant at any one time. Political and social factors can also support new approaches to punishment. The influence of victims, for example, has contributed to the small but growing *restorative justice* movement in this country.

Rehabilitation The philosophy that society is best served when wrongdoers are provided the resources needed to eliminate criminality from their behavioral pattern rather than simply being punished.

Restorative Justice An approach to punishment designed to repair the harm done to the victim and the community by the offender's criminal act.

Restitution A sum of money paid in compensation for damages done to the victim by the offender's criminal act.

Listening to the Victim Despite the emergence of victim impact statements, which we will discuss later in the chapter, victims have historically been restricted from participating in the punishment process. This policy has found support in the general assumption that victims are focused on vengeance rather than justice. According to criminologists Heather Strang of Australia's Center for Restorative Justice and Lawrence W. Sherman of the University of Pennsylvania, however, this is not always the case. After the initial shock of the crime has worn off, Strang and Sherman have found, victims are most interested in three things that have little to do with revenge: (1) an opportunity to participate in the process, (2) material reparations, and (3) an apology.[21]

Restorative justice strategies focus on these concerns by attempting to repair the damage that a crime does to the victim, the victim's family, and society as a whole. This outlook relies on the efforts of the offender to "undo" the harm caused by the criminal act through an apology and **restitution,** or monetary compensation for losses suffered by the victim(s). Theoretically, the community also participates in the process by providing treatment programs and financial support that allow both offender and victim to reestablish themselves as productive members of society.[22]

■ Figure 11.1 Sentencing Philosophies in Action

In 2007, professional football player Terry "Tank" Johnson pleaded guilty to gun possession charges stemming from a raid on his home that uncovered six illegal firearms and five hundred rounds of ammunition. Cook County (Illinois) Circuit Judge Brian Hughes sentenced him to four months in jail. At sentencing, the judge usually gives reasons for the punishment imposed. Though Judge Hughes did not do so in this instance, here are some of the reasons he might have given, based on the correctional goals we have discussed in this section.

Goal	Judge's Statement
Retribution	I am imposing this sentence on you because you deserve to be punished for breaking our state's gun laws and endangering members of the community. Your criminal behavior in this case is the basis for your punishment. Justice requires me to impose a sanction that reflects the value the community places on lawful conduct.
Deterrence	I am imposing this sentence so that your punishment will serve as an example and deter others who may contemplate similar actions. Also, I hope that the sentence will deter you from ever again breaking this or any other criminal law.
Incapacitation	I am imposing this sentence so that you will be unable to commit a crime while imprisoned.
Rehabilitation	Law enforcement agents found marijuana at your home during the raid. I am imposing this sentence so that you can take advantage of the treatment programs in jail to confront your drug use, which, if continued, will undoubtedly lead to further trouble with the law.
Restorative Justice	I am ordering you to donate $2,500 to the Gurnee Police Department and $2,500 to the Gurnee Exchange Club's child abuse prevention program as restitution to the community for your actions. ("I want to say that I very much regret the mistake in judgment that brought me here today," said Johnson at the end of the hearing.)

Professional football player Terry "Tank" Johnson enters Cook County (Illinois) Court to face gun charges in the spring of 2007.

Source: Based on Todd R. Clear, George F. Cole, and Michael D. Reisig, *American Corrections,* 7th ed. (Belmont, CA: Thomson Wadsworth, 2006), Table 4.1, page 69.

Limited Impact A study of efforts to improve communications between victims and offenders in Indiana found high levels of satisfaction among both parties. Victims appreciated statements of contrition made by the offender, and offenders appreciated the opportunity to express remorse and "make things right."[23] Despite such results, many criminal justice professionals in this country regard restorative justice as too vague and "touchy-feely" to be useful.[24] Furthermore, its practical impact is limited because federal and state sentencing laws do not include it as an option. Therefore, supporters have to rely on sympathetic judges, prosecutors, and defense attorneys to implement restorative justice theories in court. (See ■ Figure 11.1 for a hypothetical example of how the five philosophies of punishment discussed in this section might factor into a sentencing decision.)

Self Check Fill in the Blanks

The saying "an eye for an eye and a tooth for a tooth" reflects the concept of _____ as a justification for punishment. The goal of _____ is to prevent future crimes by "setting an example," while _____ purports to prevent crime by keeping offenders behind bars. Models of _____ suggest that criminals can be "treated" and possibly even "cured." Check your answers on page 378.

The Structure of Sentencing

Philosophy not only is integral to explaining *why* we punish criminals, but also influences *how* we do so. The history of criminal sentencing in the United States has been characterized by shifts in institutional power among the three branches of the government. When public opinion moves toward more severe strategies of retribution, deterrence, and incapacitation, *legislatures* have responded by asserting their power over determining sentencing guidelines. In contrast, periods of rehabilitative justice are marked by a transfer of this power to the *judicial* and *administrative* branches.

LEGISLATIVE SENTENCING AUTHORITY

Because legislatures are responsible for making law, these bodies are also initially responsible for passing the criminal codes that determine the length of sentences.

Indeterminate Sentencing For a good part of the twentieth century, goals of rehabilitation dominated the criminal justice system, and legislatures were more likely to enact **indeterminate sentencing** policies. Penal codes with indeterminate sentences set a minimum and maximum amount of time that a person must spend in prison. For example, the indeterminate sentence for aggravated assault could be three to nine years, or six to twelve years, or twenty years to life. Within these parameters, a judge can prescribe a particular term, after which an administrative body known **L02** as the *parole board* decides at what point the offender is to be released. A prisoner is aware that he or she is eligible for *parole* as soon as the minimum time has been served and that good behavior can further shorten the sentence.

Determinate Sentencing Disillusionment with the ideals of rehabilitation has led to **determinate sentencing,** or fixed sentencing. As the name implies, in determinate sentencing an offender serves exactly the amount of time to which she or he is sentenced (minus "good time," described below). For example, if the legislature deems that the punishment for a first-time armed robber is ten years, then the judge has no choice but to impose a sentence of ten years, and the criminal will serve ten years minus good time before being freed.

"Good Time" and Truth in Sentencing Often, the amount of time prescribed by a judge bears little relation to the amount of time the offender actually spends behind bars. In states with indeterminate sentencing, parole boards have broad powers to release prisoners once they have served the minimum portion of their sentence. Furthermore, all but four states offer prisoners the opportunity to reduce their sentences by doing **"good time"**—or behaving well—as determined by prison administrators. (See ■ Figure 11.2 for an idea of the effects of good-time regulations and other early-release programs on state prison sentences.)

Indeterminate Sentencing An indeterminate term of incarceration in which a judge determines the minimum and maximum terms of imprisonment. When the minimum term is reached, the prisoner becomes eligible to be paroled.

Determinate Sentencing A period of incarceration that is fixed by a sentencing authority and cannot be reduced by judges or other corrections officials.

"Good Time" A reduction in time served by prisoners based on good behavior, conformity to rules, and other positive actions.

■ **Figure 11.2**

Average Sentence Length and Estimated Time to Be Served in State Prison

Source: Bureau of Justice Statistics, *Felony Sentences in State Courts, 2002* (Washington, D.C.: U.S. Department of Justice, December 2004), Table 4, page 5.

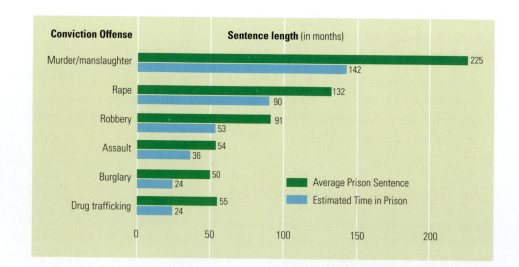

Sentence-reduction programs promote discipline within a correctional institution and reduce overcrowding; therefore, many prison officials welcome them. The public, however, may react negatively to news that a violent criminal has served a shorter term than ordered by a judge and pressure elected officials to "do something." In Illinois, for example, some inmates were serving less than half their sentences by receiving a one-day reduction in their term for each day of "good time." Under pressure from victims' groups, the state legislature passed a **truth-in-sentencing law** that requires murderers and others convicted of serious crimes to complete at least 85 percent of their sentences with no time off for good behavior.[25] As their name suggests, the primary goal of these laws is to provide the public with more accurate information about the actual amount of time an offender will spend behind bars. They have also found support with those who believe that keeping offenders incapacitated for longer periods of time will reduce crime.[26] Today, forty states have instituted some form of truth-in-sentencing laws, though the future of such statutes is in doubt due to the pressure of overflowing prisons.

L03

Truth-in-Sentencing Laws Legislative attempts to assure that convicts will serve approximately the terms to which they were initially sentenced.

JUDICIAL SENTENCING AUTHORITY

Determinate sentencing is a direct encroachment on the long-recognized power of judges to make the final decision on sentencing. Historically, the judge bore most of the responsibility for choosing the proper sentence within the guidelines set by the legislature. In the twentieth century, this power was reinforced by the rehabilitative ethic. Each offender, it was believed, has a different set of problems and should therefore receive a sentence tailored to her or his particular circumstances. Legislators have generally accepted a judge as the most qualified person to choose the proper punishment.

Between 1880 and 1899, seven states passed indeterminate sentencing laws, and in the next dozen years, another twenty-one followed suit. By the 1960s, every state in the nation allowed its judges the freedom of operating under an indeterminate sentencing system.[27] In the 1970s, however, criticism of indeterminate sentencing began to grow. Marvin E. Frankel, a former federal district judge in New York, gained a great deal of attention when he described sentencing authority as "unchecked" and "terrifying and intolerable for a society that professes devotion to a rule of law."[28] As we shall see, the 1980s and 1990s saw numerous attempts on both the state and federal levels to limit this judicial discretion.

ADMINISTRATIVE SENTENCING AUTHORITY

Parole is a condition of early release in which a prisoner is released from a correctional facility but is not freed from the legal custody and supervision of the state. Generally, after an inmate has been released on parole, he or she is supervised by a parole officer for a specified amount of time. The decision of whether to parole an inmate lies with the parole board. Parole is a crucial aspect of the criminal justice system and will be discussed in detail in Chapter 14.

For now, it is important to understand the role rehabilitation theories play in *administrative sentencing authority*. The formation in 1910 of the U.S. Parole Commission and similar commissions in the fifty states implied that the judge, though a legal expert, was not trained to determine when an inmate had been rehabilitated. Therefore, the sentencing power should be given to experts in human behavior, who were qualified to determine whether a convict was fit to return to society.[29] The recent repudiation of rehabilitation principles has not spared these administrative bodies; since 1976, fourteen states and the federal government have abolished traditional parole for their prisoners.[30] (See *Mastering Concepts—Who Has the Responsibility to Determine Sentences?* on the next page.)

▼ On the last day of August 2007, North Carolina Superior Court Judge W. Osmond Smith III, shown here, found former Durham County District Attorney Mike Nifong guilty of criminal contempt of court and sentenced him to one day in jail. As we learned in Chapter 8, Nifong had misrepresented evidence while pursuing rape charges against three falsely accused Duke University lacrosse players in 2006. According to state sentencing guidelines, Judge Smith could have sent Nifong to jail for 30 days for his crime. Do you think that judges should have the freedom to engage in this type of leniency?

REUTERS/Ellen Ozier/Landov

Three different sentencing authorities determine the amount of time a person who has been convicted of a felony will spend in prison: legislatures, judges, and officials of the state executive branch (the governor's office). The ways in which these three groups influence the sentencing process is summarized below.

If lawmakers feel that the other two bodies—judges and officials of the executive branch—are being too lenient in their sentencing decisions, they can pass truth-in-sentencing laws that require convicts to serve the amount of time indicated in criminal codes.

1. First Step: Legislators Pass Laws

Federal and state legislators are responsible for creating and updating the criminal codes that define how the law will punish those who commit crimes. Legislatures specify the terms of imprisonment in two different ways:

- By passing *indeterminate sentencing laws*. These laws designate a maximum and minimum amount of time that a person who commits a specific crime must spend in prison—one to three years, five to ten years, and the like.

- By passing *determinate sentencing law*. These laws designate a fixed amount of time that a person who commits a specific crime must spend in prison—seven years, for example, instead of five to ten.

2. Second Step: Judges Impose Sentences

Judges have the authority to choose among the sentencing options provided by legislatures. They are expected to consider all of the circumstances that surround a case and decide the length of the sentence based on these circumstances. (There are a few exceptions to this judicial authority. Only a jury, for example, can decide whether to impose the death penalty.)

3. Third Step: Executive Officials Set the Date of Release

Although judges impose the sentence, officials of the state executive branch are responsible for deciding the extent to which a prisoner will serve his or her entire sentence. Most prisoners do not serve their maximum possible terms of imprisonment. Parole boards, appointed in most states by the governor, decide whether an inmate is eligible for *parole*—the conditional release of a prisoner before his or her sentence has been served. Executive officials also determine whether an inmate will have his or her sentence reduced because of *"good time,"* which is awarded for good behavior and participation in various treatment, vocational, and educational programs. (Remember, however, that legislatures can restrict parole and good-time provisions.)

Self Check Fill in the Blanks

_____ sentences set a minimum and maximum amount of time a convict must spend in prison or jail, whereas _____ sentences reflect the exact length of incapacitation, minus reductions for _____, or behaving well. Historically, the _____ has had most of the responsibility for making sentencing decisions. Check your answers on page 378.

Individualized Justice and the Judge

During the pretrial procedures and the trial itself, the judge's role is somewhat passive and reactive. She or he is primarily a "procedural watchdog," assuring that the rights of the defendant are not infringed on while the prosecutor and defense attorney dictate the course of action. At a traditional sentencing hearing, however, the judge is no longer an arbiter between the parties. She or he is now called on to exercise the ultimate authority of the state in determining the defendant's fate.

From the 1930s to the 1970s, when theories of rehabilitation held sway over the criminal justice system, indeterminate sentencing practices were guided by the theory of "individualized justice." Just as a physician gives specific treatment to individual patients depending on their particular health needs, the hypothesis goes, a judge needs to consider the specific circumstances of each individual offender in choosing the best form of punishment. Taking the analogy one step further, just as the diagnosis of a qualified physician should not be questioned, a qualified judge should have absolute discretion in making the sentencing decision. *Judicial discretion* rests on the assumption that a judge should be given ample leeway in determining punishments that fit both the crime and the criminal.[31] As we shall see later in the chapter, the growth of determinate sentencing has severely restricted judicial discretion in many jurisdictions.

FORMS OF PUNISHMENT

L04 Within whatever legislative restrictions apply, the sentencing judge has a number of options when it comes to choosing the proper form of punishment. These sentences, or *dispositions*, include:

1. *Capital punishment.* Reserved normally for those who commit first degree murder under aggravated circumstances, capital punishment, or the death penalty, is a sentencing option in thirty-eight states and in federal courts.
2. *Imprisonment.* Whether for the purpose of retribution, deterrence, incapacitation, or rehabilitation, a common form of punishment in American history has been imprisonment. In fact, it is used so commonly today that judges—and legislators—are having to take factors such as prison overcrowding into consideration when making sentencing decisions. The issues surrounding imprisonment will be discussed in Chapters 13 and 14.
3. *Probation.* One of the effects of prison overcrowding has been a sharp rise in the use of probation, in which an offender is permitted to live in the community under supervision and is not incarcerated. (Probation is covered in Chapter 12.) *Alternative sanctions* (also discussed in Chapter 12) combine probation with other dispositions such as electronic monitoring, house arrest, boot camps, and shock incarceration.
4. *Fines.* Fines can be levied by judges in addition to incarceration and probation or independently of other forms of punishment. When a fine is the full extent of the punishment, it usually reflects the judge's belief that the offender is not a threat to the community and does not need to be imprisoned or supervised. In some instances, mostly involving drug offenders, a judge can order the seizure of an offender's property, such as his or her home.
5. *Restitution and community service.* Whereas fines are payable to the government, restitution and community service are seen as reparations to the injured party or to the community. Restitution (see page 346) is a direct payment to the victim or victims of a crime; community service consists of "good works"—such as cleaning up highway litter or tutoring disadvantaged youths—that benefit the entire community.
6. *Apologies.* As we saw earlier in this chapter, when the offender has committed a less serious crime, many judges are turning to restorative justice to provide a remedy. At the heart of restorative justice is the apology. So, for example, a judge in Texas required a teenager who had vandalized thirteen schools to go to each school and apologize to the students and faculty.

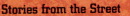

Stories from the Street

Go to the Stories from the Street feature at **www.cjinaction.com** to hear Larry Gaines tell insightful stories related to this chapter and his experiences in the field.

In some jurisdictions, judges have a great deal of discretionary power and can impose sentences that do not fall into any of these categories. This "creative

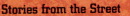

After Jason Householder, left, and John Stockum were convicted of criminal damaging for throwing beer bottles at a car, municipal court judge David Hostetler of Coshocton, Ohio, gave them a choice: jail time or a walk down Main Street in women's clothing. As you can see, they chose the dresses. What reasons might a judge have for handing down this sort of "creative" sentence?

sentencing," as it is sometimes called, has produced some interesting results. In Santa Fe, New Mexico, those convicted of domestic violence and other types of violence participate in New Age anger-management classes. A judge in Coshocton, Ohio, ordered a man who had fled on foot from the scene of a traffic accident to jog around the jail for an hour every other day. In Harris County, Texas, a man who slapped his wife was sentenced to attend yoga class. Though these types of punishments are often ridiculed, for less dangerous offenders many judges see them as a viable alternative to incarceration.

THE SENTENCING PROCESS

The decision of how to punish a wrongdoer is the end result of what Yale Law School professor Kate Stith and federal appeals court judge José A. Cabranes call the "sentencing ritual."[32] The two main participants in this ritual are the judge and the defendant, but prosecutors, defense attorneys, and probation officers also play a role in the proceedings. Individualized justice requires that the judge consider all the relevant circumstances in making sentencing decisions. Therefore, judicial discretion is often tantamount to *informed* discretion—without the aid of the other members of the courtroom work group, the judge would not have sufficient information to make the proper sentencing choice.

L05

The Presentence Investigative Report For judges operating under various states' indeterminate sentencing guidelines, information in the **presentence investigative report** is a valuable component of the sentencing ritual. Compiled by a probation officer, the report describes the crime in question, notes the suffering of any victims, and lists the defendant's prior offenses (as well as any alleged but uncharged criminal activity). The report also contains a range of personal data such as family background, work history, education, and community activities—information that is not admissible as evidence during trial. In putting together the presentence investigative report, the probation officer is supposed to gain a "feel" for the defendant and communicate these impressions of the offender to the judge.

The report also includes a sentencing recommendation. In the past, this aspect has been criticized as giving probation officers too much power in the sentencing process, because less diligent judges would simply rely on the recommendation in determining punishment.[33] Consequently, as we shall see, many jurisdictions have moved to limit the influence of the presentence investigative report.

The Prosecutor and Defense Attorney To a certain extent, the adversary process does not end when the guilt of the defendant has been established. Both the prosecutor and the defense attorney are interviewed in the process of preparing the presentence investigative report, and both will try to present a version of the facts consistent with their own sentencing goals. The defense attorney in particular has a duty to make sure that the information contained in the report is accurate and not prejudicial toward his or her client. Depending on the norms of any particular courtroom work group, prosecutors and defense attorneys may petition the judge directly for certain sentences. Note that this process is not always adversarial. As we saw in Chapter 9, in some instances the prosecutor will advocate leniency and may join the defense attorney in requesting a short term of imprisonment, probation, or some form of intermediate sanction.[34]

Presentence Investigative Report An investigative report on an offender's background that assists a judge in determining the proper sentence.

Sentencing and the Jury Juries also play an important role in the sentencing process. As we will see later in the chapter, it is the jury, and not the judge, who decides whether a convict eligible for the death penalty will in fact be executed. Additionally, six states—Arkansas, Kentucky, Missouri, Oklahoma, Texas, and Virginia—allow juries, rather than judges, to make the sentencing decision even when the death penalty is not an option. In these states, the judge gives the jury instructions on the range of penalties available, and then the jury makes the final decision.[35] Juries have traditionally been assigned a relatively small role in felony sentencing, largely out of concern that jurors' lack of experience and legal expertise leaves them unprepared for the task.[36] When sentencing by juries is allowed, the practice is popular with prosecutors because jurors are more likely than judges to give harsh sentences, particularly for drug crimes, sexual assault, and theft.

FACTORS OF SENTENCING

The sentencing ritual strongly lends itself to the concept of individualized justice. With inputs—sometimes conflicting—from the prosecutor, attorney, and probation officer, the judge can be reasonably sure of getting the "full picture" of the crime and the criminal. In making the final decision, however, most judges consider two factors above all others: the seriousness of the crime and any mitigating or aggravating circumstances.

The Seriousness of the Crime As would be expected, the seriousness of the crime is the primary factor in a judge's sentencing decisions. The more serious the crime, the harsher the punishment, for society demands no less. Each judge has his or her own methods of determining the seriousness of the offense. Many judges simply consider the "conviction offense"; that is, they base their sentence on the crime for which the defendant was convicted.

Other judges—some mandated by statute—focus instead on the **"real offense"** in determining the punishment. The "real offense" is based on the actual behavior of the defendant, regardless of the official conviction. For example, through a plea bargain, a defendant may plead guilty to simple assault when in fact he hit his victim in the face with a baseball bat. A judge, after reading the presentence investigative report, could decide to sentence the defendant as if he had committed aggravated assault, which is the "real" offense. Though many prosecutors and defense attorneys are opposed to "real offense" procedures, which can render a plea bargain meaningless, there is a growing belief in criminal justice circles that they bring a measure of fairness to the sentencing decision.[37]

Mitigating and Aggravating Circumstances When deciding the severity of punishment, judges and juries are often required to evaluate the *mitigating* and *aggravating circumstances* surrounding the case. **Mitigating circumstances** are those circumstances, such as the fact that the defendant was coerced into committing the crime, that allow a lighter sentence to be handed down. In contrast, **aggravating circumstances,** such as a prior record, blatant disregard for the safety of others, or the use of a weapon, can lead a judge or jury to inflict a harsher penalty than might otherwise be warranted (see ■ Figure 11.3 on the next page).

In the case of Zacarias Moussaoui discussed at the beginning of this chapter, the defense asked the jury to consider twenty-four mitigating circumstances. These included Moussaoui's hostile mother and physically abusive father, the racism that he had to face as an African in French society, and his limited knowledge of the September 11, 2001, attack plans. For their part, the prosecutors offered seven aggravating circumstances, including the great death and destruction caused by the terrorist attacks, Moussaoui's desire to harm Americans, and his lack of remorse for the victims. In choosing life imprisonment over the death penalty, the jury decided that the mitigating circumstances surrounding the defendant's crimes outweighed the aggravating circumstances.

"Real Offense" The actual offense committed, as opposed to the charge levied by a prosecutor as the result of a plea bargain. Judges who make sentencing decisions based on the real offense are often seen as undermining the plea bargain process.

Mitigating Circumstances Any circumstances accompanying the commission of a crime that may justify a lighter sentence.

Aggravating Circumstances Any circumstances accompanying the commission of a crime that may justify a harsher sentence.

Figure 11.3 Aggravating and Mitigating Circumstances

Aggravating Circumstances

- An offense involved multiple participants, and the offender was the leader of the group.
- A victim was particularly vulnerable.
- A victim was treated with particular cruelty for which an offender should be held responsible.
- The offense involved injury or threatened violence to others and was committed to gratify an offender's desire for pleasure or excitement.
- The degree of bodily harm caused, attempted, threatened, or foreseen by an offender was substantially greater than average for the given offense.
- The degree of economic harm caused, attempted, threatened, or foreseen by an offender was substantially greater than average for the given offense.
- The amount of contraband materials possessed by the offender or under the offender's control was substantially greater than average for the given offense.

Mitigating Circumstances

- An offender acted under strong provocation or other circumstances in the relationship between the offender and the victim make the offender's behavior less serious and therefore less deserving of punishment.
- An offender player a minor or passive role in the offense or participated under circumstances of coercion or duress.
- An offender, because of youth or physical impairment, lacked substantial capacity for judgment when the offense was committed.

Source: American Bar Association.

Judicial Philosophy Most states spell out mitigating and aggravating circumstances in statutes, but there is room for judicial discretion in applying the law to particular cases. Judges are not uniform, or even consistent, in their opinions concerning which circumstances are mitigating or aggravating. One judge may believe that a fourteen-year-old is not fully responsible for his or her actions, while another may believe that teenagers should be treated as adults. Those judges who support rehabilitative theories of criminal justice have been found to give more lenient sentences than those who subscribe to theories of deterrence and incapacitation.[38] Furthermore, judges can have different philosophies with regard to different crimes, handing down, for example, harsh penalties for domestic abusers while showing leniency toward drug offenders.

> ### Self Check Fill in the Blanks
>
> Judges often rely on information contained in the _____ report when making sentencing decisions. The primary factor in the sentencing process is the _____ of the crime for which the defendant was convicted. _____ circumstances allow a lighter sentence to be handed down, while _____ circumstances can lead to the imposition of a harsher penalty. Check your answers on page 378.

Inconsistencies in Sentencing

For some, the natural differences in judicial philosophies, when combined with a lack of institutional control, raise important questions. Why should a bank robber in South Carolina and a bank robber in Michigan receive different sentences? Even federal indeterminate sentencing guidelines seem overly vague: a bank robber can receive a prison term from one day to twenty years, depending almost entirely on the judge.[39] Furthermore, if judges have freedom to use their discretion, do they not also have the freedom to misuse it?

Purported improper judicial discretion is often the first reason given for two phenomena that plague the criminal justice system: *sentencing disparity* and *sentencing discrimination.* Though the two terms are often used inter-changeably, they describe different statistical occurrences—the causes of which are open to debate.

SENTENCING DISPARITY

Justice would seem to demand that those who commit similar crimes should receive similar punishments. **Sentencing disparity** occurs when this expectation is not met in one of three ways:

1. Criminals receive similar sentences for different crimes of unequal seriousness.
2. Criminals receive different sentences for similar crimes.
3. Mitigating or aggravating circumstances have a disproportionate effect on sentences. Prosecutors, for example, reward drug dealers who inform on their associates with lesser sentences. As a result, low-level drug sellers, who have no information to trade for reduced sentences, often spend more time in prison than their better-informed bosses.[40]

Most of the blame for sentencing disparities is placed at the feet of the judicial profession. Even with the restrictive presence of the sentencing reforms we will discuss shortly, judges have a great deal of influence over the sentencing decision, whether they are making that decision themselves or instructing the jury on how to do so. Like other members of the criminal justice system, judges are individuals, and their discretionary sentencing decisions reflect that individuality. Besides judicial discretion, several other culprits have been offered as explanations for sentencing disparity, including differences between geographic jurisdictions and between federal and state courts.

Geographic Disparities For wrongdoers, the amount of time spent in prison often depends as much on where the crime was committed as on the crime itself. A comparison of the sentences for drug trafficking reveals that someone convicted of the crime in the Northern District of California faces an average of 78 months in prison, whereas a similar offender in northern Iowa can expect an average of 143 months.[41] The average sentences imposed in the Fifth Circuit, which includes Louisiana, Mississippi, and Texas, are considerably harsher than those in the Ninth Circuit, comprising most of the western states: 94 months longer for murder, 21 months longer for robbery, and 8 months longer for firearms violations.[42] Such disparities can be attributed to a number of different factors, including local attitudes toward crime and available financial resources to cover the expenses of incarceration.

Federal versus State Court Disparities Because of different sentencing guidelines, the punishment for the same crime in federal and state courts can also be dramatically different. In North Carolina, for example, a defendant charged with trafficking 50 grams of methamphetamine would face a minimum sentence of 70 months and a maximum sentence of 84 months. A person charged with the exact same crime in a federal court would face a minimum of 120 months and a maximum of life in prison.[43] ■ Figure 11.4 on the following page shows the sentencing disparities for certain crimes in the two systems.

SENTENCING DISCRIMINATION

Sentencing discrimination occurs when disparities can be attributed to extralegal variables such as the defendant's gender, race, or economic standing.

The "Punishment Penalty" At first glance, racial discrimination would seem to be rampant in sentencing practices. Research by Cassia Spohn and David Holleran of the University of Nebraska at Omaha suggests that minorities pay a

Sentencing Disparity A situation in which those convicted of similar crimes do not receive similar sentences.

Sentencing Discrimination A situation in which the length of a sentence appears to be influenced by a defendant's race, gender, economic status, or other factor not directly related to the crime he or she committed.

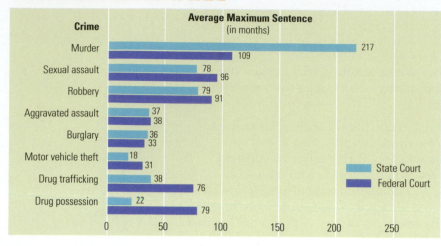

Crime	Average Maximum Sentence (in months)
Murder	State Court: 217 / Federal Court: 109
Sexual assault	State Court: 78 / Federal Court: 96
Robbery	State Court: 79 / Federal Court: 91
Aggravated assault	State Court: 37 / Federal Court: 38
Burglary	State Court: 36 / Federal Court: 33
Motor vehicle theft	State Court: 18 / Federal Court: 31
Drug trafficking	State Court: 38 / Federal Court: 76
Drug possession	State Court: 22 / Federal Court: 79

Source: Bureau of Justice Statistics, *Felony Sentences in State Courts, 2002* (Washington, D.C.: U.S. Department of Justice, December 2004), 3.

▼ Melanie McGuire seeks the comfort of her defense attorney after being convicted of drugging her husband, chopping up his body, and stuffing the remains into a suitcase for disposal. On July 19, 2007, a New Jersey superior court judge sentenced McGuire to the maximum penalty—life in prison—saying that the "depravity of this murder simply shocks the conscience of the courtroom." Is there any reason for McGuire's gender to play a role in the severity of her sentence?

AP Photo/Joe McLaughlin, Pool

"punishment penalty" when it comes to sentencing.[44] In Chicago, Spohn and Holleran found that convicted African Americans were 12.1 percent more likely to go to prison than convicted whites, and convicted Hispanics were 15.3 percent more likely. In Miami, Hispanics were 10.3 percent more likely to be imprisoned than either blacks or whites.[45] Nationwide, about 40 percent of all inmates in state and federal prisons are African American, even though that minority group makes up only about 13 percent of the country's population.[46]

Interestingly, Spohn and Holleran found that the rate of imprisonment rose significantly for minorities who were young and unemployed. This led them to conclude that the disparities between races were not the result of "conscious" discrimination on the part of the sentencing judges. Rather, faced with limited time to make decisions and limited information about the offenders, the judges would resort to stereotypes, considering not just race, but age and unemployment as well.[47] (This research addresses the argument in favor of diversity among judges, discussed in Chapter 8.)

Furthermore, Spohn and Holleran found that none of the offender characteristics (race, age, employment) had an effect on the *length* of the prison sentence,[48] a result that is corroborated by national statistics. According to the Bureau of Justice Statistics, the average prison sentence handed out to blacks and whites in state courts was virtually the same. Indeed, with some crimes, such as murder, whites on average received longer sentences.[49]

Hispanics and Sentencing Unfortunately, the federal data did not include Hispanics. Other studies, such as one conducted in Pennsylvania by Darrell Steffensmeier of Pennsylvania State University and Stephen DeMuth of Bowling Green State University, suggest that Hispanics receive harsher penalties than either whites or blacks.[50] Explanations for this finding vary. Some believe that the harsher sentences result from the "threat" posed by Hispanics as the most recent large immigrant group to change the ethnic outlook of the United States.[51]

Steffensmeier and DeMuth suggest several other possibilities, including language barriers that put Hispanics at a disadvantage in court proceedings, for example, by making it difficult for them to understand what is offered in a plea bargain. A cultural emphasis on loyalty among Hispanics may also limit the number of sentencing "breaks" they get by informing on criminal associates.[52]

Women and Sentencing Few would argue that race or ethnicity should be a factor in sentencing decisions—the system should be "color-blind." Does the same principle apply to women? In other words, should the system be "gender-blind" as well—at least on a policy level? Congress answered that question in the Sentencing Reform Act of 1984, which emphasized the ideal of gender-neutral sentencing.[53] In practice, however, this has not occurred. Women who are convicted of crimes are less likely to go to prison than men, and those who are incarcerated tend to serve shorter sentences. According to government data, the average sentence of a woman for a felony is sixteen months less than that of a man.[54] One study attributes these differences to the elements of female criminality: in property crimes, women are usually accessories, and in violent crimes, women are usually reacting to physical abuse. In both situations, the mitigating circumstances lead to lesser punishment.[55]

Other evidence also suggests that a *chivalry effect*, or the idea that women should be treated more leniently than men, plays a large role in sentencing decisions. Several self-reported studies (see pages 83–84) have shown that judges may treat female defendants more "gently" than males and that judges are influenced by mitigating factors such as marital status and family background with women that they would ignore with men.[56] The leniency of juries is most evident in death penalty cases. Though women account for 10 percent of all murder arrests, only 1.4 percent of the inmates on death row are women. According to jury consultant Karen Jo Koonan, jurors do not want to believe that a woman, in her role as nurturer, could also be a cold-blooded killer.[57]

Self Check Fill in the Blanks

Sentencing _____ occurs when similar crimes are punished with dissimilar sentences, while sentencing _____ is the result of judicial consideration of extralegal variables such as the defendant's race or gender. Check your answers on page 378.

Sentencing Reform

Judicial discretion, then, appears to be a double-edged sword. Although it allows judges to impose a wide variety of sentences to fit specific criminal situations, it appears to fail to rein in a judge's subjective biases, which can lead to disparity and perhaps discrimination. Critics of judicial discretion believe that its costs (the lack of equality) outweigh its benefits (providing individualized justice). As Columbia law professor John C. Coffee noted:

> If we wish the sentencing judge to treat "like cases alike," a more inappropriate technique for the presentation could hardly be found than one that stresses a novelistic portrayal of each offender and thereby overloads the decisionmaker in a welter of detail.[58]

In other words, Professor Coffee feels that judges are given too much information in the sentencing process, making it impossible for them to be consistent in their decisions. It follows that limiting judicial discretion would not only simplify the process but lessen the opportunity for disparity or discrimination. Since the 1970s, this attitude has spread through state and federal legislatures, causing more extensive changes in sentencing procedures than in almost any other area of the American criminal justice system over that time period.

SENTENCING GUIDELINES

In an effort to eliminate the inequities of disparity by removing judicial bias from the sentencing process, many states and the federal government have turned to **sentencing guidelines,** which require judges to dispense legislatively determined sentences based on factors such as the seriousness of the crime and the offender's prior record.

State Sentencing Guidelines In 1978, Minnesota became the first state to create a Sentencing Guidelines Commission with a mandate to construct and monitor the use of a determinate sentencing structure. The Minnesota Commission left no doubt as to the philosophical justification for the new sentencing statutes, stating unconditionally that retribution was its primary goal.[59] Today, about twenty states employ some form of sentencing guidelines with similar goals.

Sentencing Guidelines
Legislatively determined guidelines that judges are required to follow when sentencing those convicted of specific crimes. These guidelines limit judicial discretion.

In general, these guidelines remove discretionary power from state judges by turning sentencing into a mathematical exercise. Members of the courtroom work group are guided by a *grid*, which helps them determine the proper sentence. ■ Figure 11.5 shows the grid established by the Oregon Sentencing Commission. As with the grids used by most states, one axis ranks the type of crime, while the other refers to the offender's criminal history. In Oregon, each of roughly fifty felonies is ranked in seriousness for use with the grid.

■ **Figure 11.5 Oregon's Sentencing Guidelines**

Post-Prison Supervision	Crime		A — Multiple (3+) felony person offender (Three or more person felonies)	B — Repeat (2) felony person offender (Two person felonies, adult or juvenile)	C — Single (1) felony person with felony non-person offender (One person felony, plus one or more adult or juvenile non-person felony)	D — Single (1) felony person offender (One adult or juvenile person felony and no other felony)	E — Multiple (4+) felony non-person offender (Four or more adult non-person felonies)	F — Repeat (2-3) felony non-person offender (Two or three adult non-person felonies)	G — Significant minor criminal record (4 or more adult A misdo's, or 1 adult non-person felony, or 3 or more juvenile non-person felonies)	H — Minor criminal record (No more than 3 adult A misdo's, or no more than 2 juvenile non-person felonies)	I — Minor misdemeanor or no criminal record (No juvenile felony or adult A misdemeanors)	Probation Term
	Murder	11	225–269	196–224	178–194	149–177	149–177	135–148	129–134	122–128	120–121	5 years
3 years	Manslaughter I, Assault I, Rape I, Arson I	10	121–130	116–120	111–115	91–110	81–90	71–80	66–70	61–65	58–60	5 years
	Rape I, Assault I, Kidnapping II, Arson I, Burglary I, Robbery I	9	66–72	61–65	56–60	51–55	46–50	41–45	39–40	37–38	34–36	
	Manslaughter II, Sexual Abuse I, Assault II, Rape II, Using Child in Display of Sexual Conduct, Drugs-Minors, Cult/Mftr/Delivery, Compelling Prostitution, Negligent Homicide	8	41–45	35–40	29–34	27–28	25–26	23–24	21–22	19–20	16–18	Opt probation
	Extortion, Coercion, Supplying Contraband, Escape I	7	31–36	25–30	21–24	19–20	16–18	180 / 90	180 / 90	180 / 90	180 / 90	3 years
2 years	Robbery II, Assault III, Rape III, Bribe Receiving, Intimidation, Property Crimes (more than $50,000), Drug Possession	6	25–30	19–24	15–18	13–14	10–12	180 / 90	180 / 90	180 / 90	180 / 90	
	Robbery II, Theft by Receiving, Trafficking Stolen Vehicles, Property Crimes ($10,000–$49,999)	5	15–16	13–14	11–12	9–10	6–8	180 / 90	120 / 60	120 / 60	120 / 60	2 years
	FTA I, Custodial Interference II, Property Crimes ($5,000–$9,999), Drugs-Cult/Mftr/Delivery	4	10–10	8–9	120 / 60	120 / 60	120 / 60	120 / 60	120 / 60	120 / 60	120 / 60	
1 year	Abandon Child, Abuse of Corpse, Criminal Nonsupport, Property Crimes, ($1,000–$4,999)	3	120 / 60	120 / 60	120 / 60	120 / 60	120 / 60	120 / 60	90 / 30	90 / 30	90 / 30	
	Dealing Child Pornography, Violation of Wildlife Laws, Welfare Fraud, Property Crimes (less than $1,000)	2	90 / 30	90 / 30	90 / 30	90 / 30	90 / 30	90 / 30	90 / 30	90 / 30	90 / 30	18 mos.
	Altering Research, Habitual Offender Violation, Bigamy, Paramilitary Activity, Drugs–Possession	1	90 / 30	90 / 30	90 / 30	90 / 30	90 / 30	90 / 30	90 / 30	90 / 30	90 / 30	

● In light green blocks, numbers are presumptive prison sentences expressed as a range of months.

● In blue blocks, upper number is the maximum number of days of punishment (incarceration or community corrections which may be imposed; lower number is the maximum number of jail days which may be imposed.

For example, Burglary I is assigned a crime seriousness level of 9 if it involved the use of a deadly weapon, level 8 if the dwelling was occupied at the time of the crime, and so on. The state's crime history grid ranks the offender based on prior felonies and misdemeanors, with various points accrued on the basis of the seriousness of the prior crime. Of the ninety-nine cells in Oregon's grid, fifty-three "presume" prison terms and forty-six "presume" probationary sentences. The judge cannot deviate from these guidelines except under certain circumstances, which we will explore shortly.

Federal Sentencing Guidelines In 1984, Congress passed the Sentencing Reform Act (SRA),[60] paving the way for federal sentencing guidelines that went into effect in 1987. Similar in many respects to the state guidelines, the SRA also eliminated parole for federal prisoners and severely limited early release from prison due to good behavior.[61] Furthermore, the act changed the sentencing role of U.S. probation officers. No longer would they be allowed to "suggest" the terms of punishment in presentence investigative reports. Instead, they are simply called on to calculate the presumptive sentence based on the federal sentencing guidelines grid.[62]

The impact of the SRA and the state guidelines has been dramatic. Sentences have become harsher—the average federal prison sentence today is fifty months, more than twice as long as in 1984.[63] Furthermore, much of the discretion in sentencing has shifted from the judge to the prosecutor. Because the prosecutor chooses the criminal charge, she or he can, in effect, present the judge with the range of sentences. Defendants and their defense attorneys realize this and are more likely to agree to a plea bargain, which is, after all, a "deal" with the prosecutor.[64]

Judicial Departures Even in their haste to limit a judge's power, legislators realized that sentencing guidelines could not be expected to cover every possible criminal situation. Therefore, both state and federal sentencing guidelines allow an "escape hatch" of limited judicial discretion known as a **departure**. The SRA includes a proviso that a judge may "depart" from the presumptive sentencing range if a case involves aggravating or mitigating circumstances that are not adequately covered in the guidelines. For example, suppose two men are involved in the robbery of a liquor store, and during court proceedings it becomes clear that one of them forced his partner to take part in the crime by threatening physical harm. In this case, a federal judge could reduce the accomplice's sentence because he committed the crime under "duress," a factor that is not accounted for in the sentencing guidelines.

Judges do not have unlimited freedom to make departures, however. Any such decision must be justified in writing, and both the prosecution and the defense may appeal a judicial departure. In 1989, the U.S. Court of Appeals for the First Circuit ruled that departures must be measured on the basis of the circumstances and facts of the case and the reasonableness of the judge's decision.[65] Still, in 2006, federal judges departed from the sentencing guidelines in almost 40 percent of all cases, showing that they have not completely surrendered their traditional role in the process.[66]

MANDATORY SENTENCING GUIDELINES

In an attempt to close even the limited loophole of judicial discretion offered by departures, politicians (often urged on by their constituents) have passed sentencing laws even more contrary to the idea of individualized justice. These **mandatory (minimum) sentencing guidelines** further limit a judge's power to deviate from determinate sentencing laws by setting firm standards for certain crimes. Forty-six states have mandatory sentencing laws for crimes such as selling drugs, driving under the influence of alcohol, and committing any crime with a dangerous weapon. In Alabama, for example, any person caught selling drugs must spend at least two years in prison, with five years added to the sentence if the sale takes place within three miles of a school or housing project.[67] Similarly, Congress has

⊘ The **United States Sentencing Commission** is an independent agency in the judicial branch that establishes sentencing policies for federal courts. To visit its Web site, click on *Web Links* under *Chapter Resources* at **www. cjinaction.com**.

Departure A stipulation in many federal and state sentencing guidelines that allows a judge to adjust his or her sentencing decision based on the special circumstances of a particular case.

Mandatory Sentencing Guidelines Statutorily determined punishments that must be applied to those who are convicted of specific crimes.

Habitual Offender Laws
Statutes that require lengthy
prison sentences for those
who are convicted of multiple
felonies.

set mandatory minimum sentences for more than one hundred crimes, mostly drug offenses. (See the feature *You Be the Judge—Minimum: Two Hundred Years* to learn about the consequences of mandatory sentencing guidelines.)

Habitual Offender Laws **Habitual offender laws** are a form of mandatory sentencing that has become increasingly popular over the past decade. Also known as "three-strikes-and-you're-out" laws, these statutes require that any person convicted of a third felony must serve a lengthy prison sentence. The crime does not have to be of a violent or dangerous nature. Under Washington's habitual offender law, for example, a "persistent offender" is automatically sentenced to life even if the third felony offense happens to be "vehicular assault" (an automobile accident that causes injury), unarmed robbery, or attempted arson, among other lesser felonies.[68] Today, twenty-six states and the federal government employ "three-strikes" statutes, with varying degrees of severity.

"Three Strikes" in Court The United States Supreme Court paved the way for these three-strikes laws when it ruled in *Rummel v. Estelle* (1980)[69] that Texas's habitual offender statute did not constitute "cruel and unusual punishment" under the Eighth Amendment. Basically, the Court gave each state the freedom to legislate such laws in the manner that it deems proper. Twenty-three years later, in *Lockyer v. Andrade* (2003),[70] the Court upheld California's "three-strikes" law. The California statute allows prosecutors to seek penalties up to life imprisonment without parole on conviction of any third felony, including for nonviolent crimes. Leandro Andrade received fifty years in prison for stealing $153 worth of videotapes, his fourth felony conviction. A federal appeals court overturned the sentence, agreeing with Andrade's attorneys that it met the definition of cruel and unusual punishment.[71]

In a bitterly divided 5–4 decision, the Court reversed. Justice Sandra Day O'Connor, writing for the majority, stated that the sentence was not so "objectively" unreasonable that it violated the Constitution.[72] In his

You Be the Judge Minimum: Two Hundred Years

THE FACTS An Arizona trial court found Morton guilty of twenty counts of sexual exploitation of a minor based on his possession of twenty pornographic images of children. Under the state's mandatory minimum sentencing laws, each count warrants a ten-year prison term, and the terms must be served consecutively. As a result, the trial judge had no choice but to sentence Morton to two hundred years in prison. Morton is appealing the sentence as unconstitutionally cruel and unusual punishment.

THE LAW The Eighth Amendment prohibition against cruel and unusual punishments guarantees individuals the right not to be subjected to excessive sanctions. That right flows from the basic precept of justice that punishment for crime should be proportional to the offense.

YOUR DECISION Morton's lawyers present evidence that in most other states, Morton would be allowed to serve his sentences concurrently and would spend no more than five years behind bars. Had Morton been prosecuted by federal prosecutors, they point out, federal sentencing guidelines would have mandated a five-year sentence. Prosecutors counter by saying, in effect, "the law is the law." If you were a judge hearing Morton's appeal of his sentence, how would you rule? Do you believe that this mandatory minimum sentence is "cruel and unusual" or that it reflects the will of Arizona residents and must be upheld?

[To see how the Arizona Supreme Court ruled in this case, go to Example 11.1 in Appendix B.]

dissent, Justice David H. Souter countered that "[i]f Andrade's sentence is not grossly disproportionate, the principle has no meaning."[73] Basically, the justices who upheld the law said that if the California legislature—and by extension the California voters—felt that the law was reasonable, then the judicial branch was in no position to disagree.

Prosecutors and Determinate Sentencing For all the publicity they receive, three-strikes laws are underused in most jurisdictions. About a decade after the laws went into effect in most jurisdictions, only three states had more than 400 convicts serving terms under habitual offender legislation—California had about 42,000; Florida, 1,600; and Georgia, 7,600.[74] The reason is that although determinate sentencing has given prosecutors more power to influence sentences, it has not removed their discretion in doing so. Prosecutors simply do not have the resources to apply the more draconian aspects of three-strikes laws and other mandatory sentencing guidelines. Even in California, with its large number of habitual offender convictions, prosecutors dismiss felony "strikes" in between 21 and 40 percent of all three-strikes cases.[75]

Judges and Determinate Sentencing As might be expected, judges, for the most part, have not welcomed the reduction in their discretionary powers. University of Minnesota law professor Michael Tonry has written that sentencing guidelines are the most "disliked sentencing reform initiative in the history of the United States" among judges.[76] Federal judges have called the guidelines "a farce," a "dismal failure," and "out of whack."[77] Earlier, we noted that judges have shown their displeasure with the rules by departing from them in about four of every ten sentences they hand out.

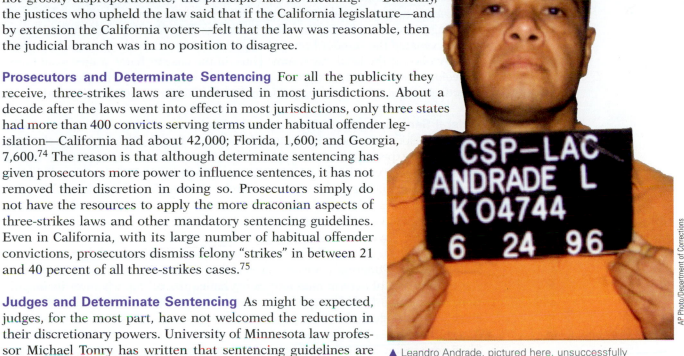

AP Photo/Department of Corrections

▲ Leandro Andrade, pictured here, unsuccessfully challenged California's "three-strikes" law. Under the state law, Andrade was sentenced to fifty years in prison without possibility of parole for stealing $153 worth of videocassettes—the lengthy sentence coming because of his previous convictions for the "serious" felony of residential burglary. What effect do you think the knowledge that a third felony conviction will lead to a long sentence has on those people already found guilty of two such crimes?

THE SUPREME COURT AND SENTENCING

The nine justices who sit on the United States Supreme Court have had a substantial impact on federal and state sentencing policies over the past decade. In addition to the *Lockyer* decision already mentioned, four cases in particular have contributed to what one observer has called a "revolution" in criminal sentencing.[78]

Protecting the Sixth Amendment The Supreme Court fired the first "shot" of this revolution with its ruling in *Apprendi v. New Jersey* (2000),[79] which involved a New Jersey hate crime statute that allowed judges to increase the penalty for any crime if they decided that it was committed with the purpose of intimidating a person because of his or her race. The Court found the law unconstitutional and held that any fact that increases a sentence beyond the legal maximum must be proved beyond a reasonable doubt to the satisfaction of the *jury*, not the judge.

Then, in *Ring v. Arizona* (2002),[80] the Court ruled that Arizona's death penalty procedure was unconstitutional because the judge, and not a jury, decided whether the defendant would be executed. The decision directly voided the death penalty procedures in five states that gave the judge the ultimate power over the "life and death" sentencing decision, a subject we will explore in great detail later in the chapter. Both the *Apprendi* and *Ring* decisions were based on the Court's reading of the Sixth Amendment's guarantee of a trial by *jury*, which the Court interpreted as denying judges the power to make the ultimate decision about the accused's life and liberty.

State Sentencing Guidelines Next, the Supreme Court turned its attention to sentencing guidelines with its unexpected ruling in *Blakely v. Washington* (2004).[81] The case involved a Washington trial judge's decision under state sentencing guidelines to add an extra thirty-seven months to a kidnapping sentence because the defendant acted with "deliberate cruelty." Once again, the Court relied on the Sixth Amendment in ruling that the judge's actions were unconstitutional. By allowing judges to make findings that increase a defendant's penalty, Washington's system violated the standard set in the *Apprendi* case—only the jury can increase a penalty beyond the legal maximum. Thus, in the case at hand, a jury would have to decide whether the accused acted with "deliberate cruelty." The *Blakely* decision effectively nullified sentencing guidelines in Washington and six other states.

Federal Sentencing Guidelines As the federal sentencing guidelines are similar in many respects to the state guidelines nullified by the *Blakely* ruling, the legal community expected that the Supreme Court would have to revisit the federal rules. It did so a year later. In *United States v. Booker* (2005),[82] the Court held that the federal sentencing guidelines were merely "advisory," not "mandatory," in effect restoring to federal judges the individualized discretion they enjoyed before passage of the SRA (see page 359) in 1984. Using legal reasoning based more on convenience than logic, the Court seemed to be saying that all the sentences handed down under the federal guidelines in the past were valid because judges had merely been following Congress's "advice" (even if they did not know it at the time).

Most critics of determinate sentencing hailed the ruling, whatever its inspiration, for shifting the balance of power in the sentencing process back to the judiciary.[83] Nevertheless, the *Booker* decision raised as many questions as it answered. Among the issues left unresolved, two stand out as most important: What does "advisory" mean, and how much discretion do federal judges actually have under the sentencing guidelines? The Court has agreed to hear several cases relating to these concerns, and the legal community hopes that the decisions will clear up this suddenly very muddled area of sentencing law.

VICTIM IMPACT EVIDENCE

The final piece of the sentencing puzzle involves victims and victims' families. As we saw in Chapter 2, crime victims traditionally were banished to the peripheries of the criminal justice system. This situation has changed dramatically with the emergence of the victims' rights movement over the past few decades. Victims are now given the opportunity to testify—in person or through written testimony—during sentencing hearings about the suffering they experienced as the result of the crime. These **victim impact statements (VISs)** have proved extremely controversial, however, and even the Supreme Court has had a difficult time determining whether they cause more harm than good.

Balancing the Process Every state and federal government has some form of victim impact legislation. In general, these laws allow a victim (or victims) to tell his or her "side of the story" to the sentencing body, be it a judge, jury, or parole officer. In nonmurder cases, the victim can personally describe the physical, financial, and emotional impact of the crime. When the charge is murder or manslaughter, relatives or friends can give personal details about the victim and describe the effects of her or his death. In the sentencing phase of the Zacarias Moussaoui trial, discussed in the opening of this chapter, the prosecution called thirty-five witnesses to tell the jury how losing loved ones in the September 11 attacks had affected their lives. (As could have been expected, much of this testimony was heartbreaking, such as that of the Indian-born dentist whose sister hanged herself after her husband perished in one of the hijacked planes.) In almost all instances, the goal of the VIS is to increase the harshness of the sentence.

Most of the debate surrounding VISs centers on their use in the sentencing phases of death penalty cases. Supporters point out that the defendant has always been allowed to present character evidence in the hopes of dissuading a judge or jury from capital punishment. According to some, a VIS balances the equation by giving survivors a voice in the process. Presenting a VIS is also said to have psycho-

Victim Impact Statement (VIS) A statement to the sentencing body (judge, jury, or parole board) in which the victim is given the opportunity to describe how the crime has affected her or him. The general purpose of the statement is to convince the sentencing party to hand down a harsher punishment than might otherwise be the case.

logical benefits for victims, who are no longer forced to sit in silence as decisions that affect their lives are made by others.[84] Finally, on a purely practical level, a VIS may help judges and juries make informed sentencing decisions by providing them with an understanding of all of the consequences of the crime.

The Risks of Victim Evidence Opponents of the use of VISs claim that they interject dangerously prejudicial evidence into the sentencing process, which should be governed by reason, not emotion. The inflammatory nature of VISs, they say, may distract judges and juries from the facts of the case, which should be the only basis for a sentence.[85] Furthermore, critics contend that a VIS introduces the idea of "social value" into the courtroom. In other words, judges and juries may feel compelled to base the punishment on the "social value" of the victim (his or her standing in the community, role as a family member, and the like) rather than the circumstances of the crime.

In 1987, the United States Supreme Court sided with the opponents of VISs, holding that such evidence is "irrelevant to a capital sentencing decision" and "creates a constitutionally unacceptable risk that the jury may impose the death penalty" arbitrarily.[86] Just four years later, however, in *Payne v. Tennessee* (1991),[87] the Court (with several new justices) modified its ruling, finding that a VIS is not *always* inadmissible and that its prejudicial effects must be determined on a case-by-case basis just as with any other type of evidence. (See ■ Figure 11.6 for an example of a VIS that was ruled not to be prejudicial.)

Several years after the *Payne* decision, Bryan Myers of the University of North Carolina at Wilmington and Jack Arbuthnot of Ohio University decided to test the prejudicial impact of the testimony in question. They ran simulated court proceedings with two groups of mock jurors: one group heard a "family member" give a VIS similar to the one presented by the victim's grandmother during Payne's sentencing hearing, while the other group did not. Of those mock jurors who ultimately voted for the death penalty, 67 percent had heard the VIS; in contrast, only 30 percent of those who did not hear it voted to execute the defendant.[88]

■ **Figure 11.6 Victim Impact Statement in Action**

According to the United States Supreme Court, victim impact statements are admissible as long as they are relevant and do not unfairly prejudice the jury against the defendant. In their discretion, however, judges often allow seemingly inflammatory victim impact evidence during sentencing hearings. For example, the Oklahoma Court of Criminal Appeals deemed the following statement, given by the daughter of a murder victim, was admissible.

"I think the only fair punishment for him is he should be confined in a small area. Someone three or four times his size should come into that confined area and beat him, cause him pain. I think he should have to beg for his life. I think he should have to crawl in his own blood. And he should have to crawl to get away from his attacker. I think he should suffer, suffer, suffer. But you know, even if he's put to death, he won't suffer; you know he will have a painless death. We can't do anything to him that will cause him the kind of pain that has been caused to our mother and to us. . . . Mother raised us to be kind and forgiving, but we can't forgive this and we want him killed."

Source: *Williams v. State*, 947 P.2d 1074 (Okla.Crim.App. 1997).

► Claire Hardgrove holds up a picture of her son, Christopher, in a casket, during the sentencing phase of serial killer Charles Cullen's trial in Somerville, New Jersey. Cullen, a nurse, admitted to killing about forty of his patients. Why should victims be given the opportunity to address the court during the sentencing phase of a criminal trial?

AP Photo/Mike Derer, Pool

With the aim of limiting judicial discretion, many states and the federal government have enacted sentencing _____ . These laws have greatly _____ the length of prison sentences in the United States. The trend toward longer prison terms has also been influenced by _____ laws, a form of mandatory sentencing that requires increased punishment for a person convicted of multiple felonies. According to the United States Supreme Court's *Ring* decision, only a _____ can hand down a death sentence.
Check your answers on page 378.

Capital Punishment—The Ultimate Sentence

"You do not know how hard it is to let a human being die," Abraham Lincoln (1809–1865) once said, "when you feel that a stroke of your pen will save him." Despite these misgivings, during his four years in office Lincoln approved the execution of 267 soldiers, including those who had slept at their posts.[89] Our sixteenth president's ambivalence toward **capital punishment** is reflected in America's continuing struggle to reconcile the penalty of death with the morals and values of society. Capital punishment has played a role in sentencing since the earliest days of the Republic and—having survived a brief period of abolition between 1972 and 1976—continues to enjoy public support.

Still, few topics in the criminal justice system inspire such heated debate. Death penalty opponents such as legal expert Stephen Bright wonder whether "there comes a time when a society gets beyond some of the more primitive forms of punishment."[90] They point out that two dozen countries have abolished the death penalty since 1985 and that the United States is the only Western democracy that continues the practice. Critics also claim that a process whose subjects are chosen by "luck and money and race" cannot serve the interests of justice.[91] Proponents believe that the death penalty serves as the ultimate deterrent for violent criminal behavior and that the criminals who are put to death are the "worst of the worst" and deserve their fate.

Today, about 3,400 convicts are living on "death row" in American prisons, meaning they have been sentenced to death and are awaiting execution. In the 1940s, as many as two hundred people were put to death in the United States in one year; as ■ Figure 11.7 shows, the most recent high-water mark was ninety-eight in 1999. Despite declines since then, states and the federal government are currently executing convicts at a rate not seen in six decades. Consequently, the questions that surround the death penalty—Is it fair? Is it humane? Does it deter crime?—will continue to inflame both its supporters and its detractors.

Capital Punishment The use of the death penalty to punish wrongdoers for certain crimes.

■ **Figure 11.7** Executions in the United States, 1976 to 2006

Source: Death Penalty Information Center.

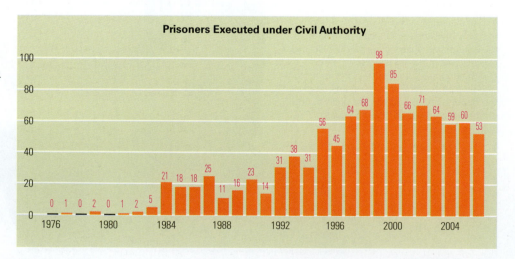

Prisoners Executed under Civil Authority

THE AMERICAN TRADITION OF CAPITAL PUNISHMENT

"Before there were prisons" in the American tradition, points out social psychologist Mark Costanzo, "there was the penalty of death."[92] The first person executed by an American colonial government—taking its cue from the homeland of England, where capital punishment was widespread—was George Kendall, who was shot to death by a firing squad in Virginia for spying for Spain in 1608.[93] Since Kendall, more than 18,000 Americans have been legally executed as punishment for their crimes.

Capital Punishment in the Seventeenth and Eighteenth Centuries In studying capital punishment in the colonies and the early days of the United States, one is struck by two aspects of the practice: the variety of crimes that were punished by death, and the public nature of the executions. During the 1600s, colonists were put to death not only for the crime of murder, but also for witchcraft, blasphemy, sodomy, and adultery. In the 1700s, citizens were executed for robbery, forgery, and illegally cutting down a tree.[94] These executions by hanging, beheading, or firing squad regularly took place in the town square or common area and were attended by the public. In fact, by modern standards the death penalty was often carried out in an overly gruesome manner in an attempt to deter criminal behavior by members of the audience. In 1710, a Virginia court ordered the bodies of two slaves who had been hanged for inciting rebellion to be cut up and displayed in various parts of the colony to keep "other Slaves from entering into such dangerous Conspiracys."[95]

The practice of public executions continued unabated until the 1830s, when reformers instigated the first widespread movement to abolish capital punishment. Government officials in northeastern states, aware that public executions provided death penalty opponents with opportunities to protest, passed a number of laws limiting the number of witnesses at an execution and requiring law enforcement officers to set up enclosures for the event. Furthermore, a desire to "civilize" the execution process moved it indoors, transforming it from a public spectacle to a sober action of the state.[96] The last public execution in the United States took place in Missouri in 1937.

Methods of Execution The desire to civilize executions can also be seen in the evolution of the methods used to carry out the death sentence. Hanging was considered a more humane form of execution than other methods adopted from England, which including drawing and quartering and boiling the subject alive, and was the primary means of carrying out the death sentence in the United States until the end of the nineteenth century. (Indeed, the "long drop" method, in which the subject was hung from a greater height to ensure that death came from breaking the neck rather than strangulation, resulted from the reform movement in the 1830s and 1840s.) The 1890s saw the introduction of electrocution as a less painful method of execution than hanging, and in 1890 in Auburn Prison, New York, William Kemmler became the first American to die in an electric chair.

The "chair" remained the primary form of execution until 1977, when Oklahoma became the first state to adopt lethal injection. Today, thirty-seven of the thirty-eight states that allow the death penalty employ lethal injection; the condemned convict is given a sedative, followed by a combination of drugs administered intravenously. Seventeen states authorize at least two different methods of execution, meaning that electrocution (nine states), lethal gas (four states), hanging (three states), and the firing squad (three states) are still used on rare occasions.[97] Nebraska is the only state that never uses lethal injection, preferring to rely on electrocution as its sole means of execution.

THE DEATH PENALTY AND THE SUPREME COURT

In 1890, William Kemmler challenged his sentence to die in New York's new electric chair (for murdering his mistress) on the grounds that electrocution infringed on his Eighth Amendment rights against cruel and unusual punishment.[98] Kemmler's

See the Web sites of the **Death Penalty Information Center** and **Pro-Death Penalty. com** for opposing views on capital punishment. Find these Web sites by clicking on *Web Links* under *Chapter Resources* at **www.cjinaction.com**.

▼ The Virginia Department of Corrections' electric chair is used only at the request of the inmate facing the death sentence. Why has lethal injection replaced the use of the "chair" in most American executions?

AP Photo/Virginia Department of Corrections

challenge is historically significant in that it did not challenge the death penalty itself as being cruel and unusual, but only the method by which it was carried out. Many constitutional scholars believe that the framers never questioned the necessity of capital punishment, as long as due process is followed in determining the guilt of the suspect.[99] Accordingly, the Supreme Court rejected Kemmler's challenge, stating:

> Punishments are cruel when they involve torture or a lingering death; but the punishment of death is not cruel, within the meaning of that word as used in the Constitution. It implies there something inhuman and barbarous, something more than the mere extinguishment of life.[100]

Thus, the Court set a standard that it has followed to this day. No *method* of execution has ever been found to be unconstitutional by the Supreme Court.

Weems v. United States For nearly eight decades following its decision regarding *Kemmler*, the Supreme Court was silent on the question of whether capital punishment was constitutional. In *Weems v. United States* (1910),[101] however, the Court did make a ruling that would significantly affect the debate on the death penalty. *Weems* concerned a defendant who had been sentenced to fifteen years of hard labor, a heavy fine, and a number of other penalties for the relatively minor crime of falsifying official records. The Court overturned the sentence, ruling that the penalty was too harsh considering the nature of the offense.

L08 Ultimately, in the *Weems* decision, the Court set three important precedents concerning sentencing:

1. Cruel and unusual punishment is defined by the changing norms and standards of society and therefore is not based on historical interpretations.
2. Courts may decide whether a punishment is unnecessarily cruel with regard to physical pain.
3. Courts may decide whether a punishment is unnecessarily cruel with regard to psychological pain.[102]

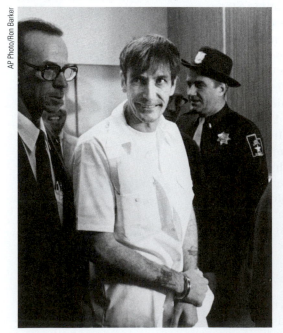

▼ Gary Gilmore is led to a Provo, Utah, court on December 1, 1976. Less than two months later, Gilmore became the first American executed under a new bifurcated system adopted by a number of states in the mid-1970s. How prevalent is the death penalty in the United States today?

AP Photo/Ron Barker

Furman v. Georgia In the 1960s, the Supreme Court, under Chief Justice Earl Warren, became increasingly concerned about what it saw as serious flaws in the way the states administered capital punishment. Finally, in 1967, the Court put a moratorium on executions until it could "clean up" the process. The chance to do so came in 1971, when the Court decided to hear three cases challenging the death penalty. Again, these cases did not question the death penalty itself as cruel and unusual. Instead, they raised the argument that capital punishment was imposed arbitrarily; that is, the death penalty was unconstitutional because there were no recognizable standards under which it could or could not be imposed.

In *Furman v. Georgia* (1972),[103] the lead case, the Supreme Court issued a very complex ruling on this issue. By a 5–4 margin, the Court essentially agreed that the death penalty violated the Eighth Amendment. Only two of those in the majority (Justices Marshall and Brennan), however, were willing to state that capital punishment was blatantly unconstitutional. The other three (Justices Douglas, Stewart, and White) took the narrower view that the sentence was unconstitutional as practiced by the states. Justice Potter Stewart was particularly eloquent on the subject, stating that the sentence of death was so arbitrary as to be comparable to "being struck by lightning."[104] In its decision, therefore, the Court did not rule that the death penalty inherently violated the Eighth Amendment's protection against cruel and unusual punishment or the Fourteenth Amendment's guarantee of due process, only that it did so as practiced by the states. So, although the *Furman* decision invalidated the death penalty for over six hundred offenders on death row at the time, it also provided the states with a window of opportunity to bring their death penalty statutes up to constitutional standards.

The Bifurcated Process By 1976, thirty-five states had done just that, attempting to comply with *Furman* by either making the death penalty mandatory for certain offenses or adopting elaborate procedures to ensure that standards of due process were upheld during the sentencing process. The ten states that attempted the mandatory route found their statutes invalidated for a second time in 1976, when, in *Woodson v. North Carolina*,[105] the Supreme Court ruled that such laws failed to allow for different circumstances in different cases.

The remaining twenty-five states adopted an alternate means of satisfying the questions raised in *Furman* by establishing a two-stage, or *bifurcated*, procedure for capital cases. In the first stage, a jury determines the guilt or innocence of the defendant for a crime that has statutorily been determined to be punishable by death. If the defendant is found guilty, the jury reconvenes in the second stage and considers all aggravating and mitigating factors to decide whether the death sentence is in fact warranted. Therefore, even if a jury were to find the defendant guilty of a crime, such as first degree murder, that *may be* punishable by death, in the second stage it could decide that the circumstances surrounding the crime justified only a punishment of life in prison. The circumstances that justify the death penalty can vary from state to state. In Colorado, for example, the seventeen aggravating factors include deliberately killing a woman knowing that she is pregnant.[106] (See *Mastering Concepts—The Bifurcated Death Penalty Process*.)

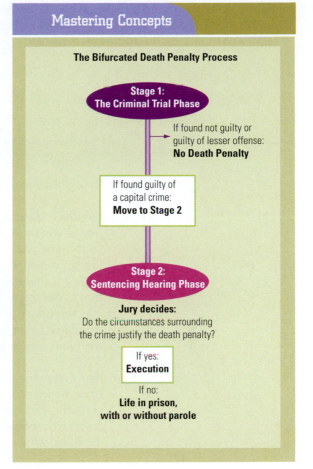

Mastering Concepts

The Bifurcated Death Penalty Process

Stage 1: The Criminal Trial Phase

If found not guilty or guilty of lesser offense:
No Death Penalty

If found guilty of a capital crime:
Move to Stage 2

Stage 2: Sentencing Hearing Phase

Jury decides:
Do the circumstances surrounding the crime justify the death penalty?

If yes:
Execution

If no:
Life in prison, with or without parole

Gregg v. Georgia In *Gregg v. Georgia* (1976),[107] the Supreme Court ruled in favor of Georgia's new bifurcated process, stating that the state's legislative guidelines removed the ability of a jury to "wantonly and freakishly impose the death penalty." The Court upheld similar procedures in Texas and Florida, establishing a model for all states to follow that would assure them protection from lawsuits based on Eighth Amendment grounds. On January 17, 1977, Gary Mark Gilmore became the first American executed (by Utah) under the new laws, and today thirty-eight states and the federal government have capital punishment laws based on the guidelines established by *Gregg*. (Note that state governments are responsible for almost all executions in this country. The executions of Timothy McVeigh and Juan Raul Garza in 2001 were the first death sentences carried out by the federal government since 1963.)

The Court reaffirmed the important role of the jury in death penalties in *Ring v. Arizona* (2002).[108] The case involved Arizona's bifurcated process: after the jury determined a defendant's guilt or innocence, it would be dismissed, and the judge would decide whether execution was warranted. As mentioned earlier, the Court found that this procedure violated the defendant's Sixth Amendment right to a jury trial; juries must be involved in *both* stages of the bifurcated process. The decision invalidated death penalty laws in Arizona, Colorado, Idaho, Montana, and Nebraska, forcing legislatures in those states to hastily revamp their procedures.

Mitigating Circumstances Several mitigating circumstances will prevent a defendant found guilty of first degree murder from receiving the death penalty.

Insanity In 1986, the United States Supreme Court held that the Constitution prohibits the execution of a person who is insane. The Court failed to provide a test for insanity other than Justice Lewis F. Powell's statement that the Eighth Amendment "forbids the execution only of those who are unaware of the punishment they are about to suffer and why they are to suffer it."[109] Consequently, each state must come up with its own definition of "insanity" for death penalty purposes. A state may also force convicts on death row to take medication that will make them sane enough to be aware of the punishment they are about to suffer and why they are about to suffer it.[110]

Mentally Handicapped The Supreme Court's recent change of mind on the question of whether a mentally handicapped convict may be put to death underscores the continuing importance of the *Weems* test (see page 366). In 1989, the Court rejected the argument that execution of a mentally handicapped person was "cruel and unusual" under the Eighth Amendment.[111] At the time, only two states barred execution of the mentally handicapped. Thirteen years later, eighteen states had such laws, and the Court decided that this increased number reflected "changing norms and standards of society." In *Atkins v. Virginia* (2002),[112] the Court used the *Weems* test as the main rationale for barring the execution of the mentally handicapped.

Age Following the *Atkins* case, many observers, including four Supreme Court justices, hoped that the same reasoning would be applied to the question of whether convicts who committed the relevant crime when they were juveniles may be executed. These hopes were realized in 2005 when the Court issued its *Roper v. Simmons* decision, which effectively ended the execution of those who committed crimes as

Landmark Cases *Roper v. Simmons*

When he was seventeen years old, Christopher Simmons abducted Shirley Crook, used duct tape to cover her eyes and mouth and bind her hands, and threw her to her death in a river. Although he bragged to his friends that he would "get away with it" because he was a minor, he was found guilty of murder and sentenced to death by a Missouri court. After the United States Supreme Court held, in *Atkins v. Virginia* (2002), that "evolving standards of decency" rendered the execution of mentally retarded persons unconstitutional, Simmons appealed his own sentence on similar grounds, pointing to his juvenile status at the time of the crime. The Missouri Supreme Court agreed and overturned his death sentence, stating that, in light of the *Atkins* ruling, the United States Supreme Court's support for juvenile executions in *Stanford v. Kentucky* (1989) was no longer valid. On appeal, the high court had to decide whether to follow its own precedent or that of the Missouri Supreme Court.

Roper v. Simmons
United States Supreme Court
543 U.S. 551 (2005)
laws.findlaw.com/US/543/551.html

IN THE WORDS OF THE COURT . . .
Justice KENNEDY, majority opinion

* * * *

The evidence of national consensus against the death penalty for juveniles is similar, and in some respects parallel, to the evidence *Atkins* held sufficient to demonstrate a national consensus against the death penalty for the mentally retarded. * * * [I]n this case, thirty States prohibit the juvenile death penalty, comprising twelve that have rejected the death penalty altogether and eighteen that maintain it but, by express provision or judicial interpretation, exclude juveniles from its reach. * * * In the present case, too, even in the twenty States without a formal prohibition on executing juveniles, the practice is infrequent.

* * * *

Three general differences between juveniles under 18 and adults demonstrate that juvenile offenders cannot with reliability be classified among the worst offenders. First, as any parent knows and as the scientific and sociological studies * * * tend to confirm, "[a] lack of maturity and an underdeveloped sense of responsibility are found in youth more often than in adults and are

juveniles.[113] As in the *Atkins* case, the Court relied on the "evolving standards of decency" test, noting that a majority of the states, as well as every other civilized nation, prohibited the execution of offenders who committed their crimes before the age of eighteen. (See the feature *Landmark Cases:* Roper v. Simmons.) The *Roper* ruling required that seventy-two convicted murderers in twelve states be resentenced and took the death penalty "off the table" for dozens of pending cases in which prosecutors were seeking capital punishment for juvenile criminal acts.

DEBATING THE SENTENCE OF DEATH

Of the topics covered in this textbook, few inspire such passionate argument as the death penalty. Many advocates believe that execution is "just deserts" for those who commit heinous crimes. In the words of Ernest van den Haag, death is the "only fitting retribution for murder that I can think of."[114] Opponents worry that retribution is simply another word for vengeance and that "the use of the death penalty by the state will increase the acceptance of revenge in our society and will give official sanction to a climate of violence."[115] As the debate over capital punishment continues, it tends to focus on several key issues: deterrence, incapacitation, fallibility, arbitrariness, constitutionality, and discrimination.

L09

Deterrence Those advocates of the death penalty who wish to show that the practice benefits society often turn to the idea of deterrence. In other words, they believe that by executing convicted criminals, the criminal justice system discourages potential criminals from committing similar violent acts. (When people speak of "deterrence" with regard to the death penalty, they are usually referring to general deterrence rather than specific deterrence.) Deterrence was the primary justification for the frequent public executions carried out in this country before the 1830s and for the brutality of those events.

more understandable among the young. These qualities often result in impetuous and ill-considered actions and decisions * * * ." In recognition of the comparative immaturity and irresponsibility of juveniles, almost every State prohibits those under eighteen years of age from voting, serving on juries, or marrying without parental consent.

The second area of difference is that juveniles are more vulnerable or susceptible to negative influences and outside pressures, including peer pressure. * * * The third broad difference is that the character of a juvenile is not as well formed as that of an adult. The personality traits of juveniles are more transitory, less fixed.

These differences render suspect any conclusion that a juvenile falls among the worst offenders. * * * Retribution is not proportional if the law's most severe penalty is imposed on one whose culpability or blameworthiness is diminished, to a substantial degree, by reason of youth and immaturity.

DECISION

The Court found that, applying the Eighth Amendment in light of "evolving standards of decency," the

execution of offenders who were under the age of eighteen when their crimes were committed was cruel and unusual punishment and therefore unconstitutional. The Missouri Supreme Court's decision to overturn Simmons's death penalty was, therefore, upheld.

FOR CRITICAL ANALYSIS

In the majority decision, Justice Kennedy noted that since 1990 Iran, Pakistan, Saudi Arabia, Yemen, Nigeria, the Democratic Republic of Congo, and China have disavowed the death penalty for juveniles, leaving the United States "alone in a world that has turned its face" against the practice. What effect, if any, should international customs have on American criminal law?

For more information and activities related to this case, click on *Landmark Cases* under *Book Resources* at **www.cjinaction.com**.

In 1975, Isaac Ehrlich, an economist at the University of Chicago, attempted to find statistical proof of the deterrent effect of capital punishment by focusing on the relationship between different jurisdictions' homicide rates and the percentage of those convicted of murder who were actually executed. According to Ehrlich, each additional execution that would have taken place between 1933 and 1967 could have saved the lives of as many as eight murder victims.[116] A number of reports released in the 2000s have given credence to Ehrlich's findings. These studies, which rely for the most part on statistical comparisons of death sentences, executions, and homicide rates in particular geographic areas, claim that for each convict executed by the state, between three to eighteen future homicides are deterred.[117]

At the same time, each study that "proves" the deterrent effect of the death penalty seems be matched by one that "disproves" the same premise.[118] In 2004, for example, criminal justice professors Lisa Stolzenberg and Stewart J. D'Alessio of Florida International University found no evidence that the number of executions had any effect on the incidence of murder in the Houston, Texas, area over a five-year period.[119] In the end, the deterrence debate follows a familiar pattern. Opponents of the death penalty claim that murderers rarely consider the consequences of their act, and therefore it makes no difference whether capital punishment exists or not. Proponents counter that this proves the death penalty's deterrent value, because if the murderers *had* considered the possibility of execution, they would *not* have committed their crimes. (For a discussion of the moral component to this argument, see the feature *Criminal Justice in Action* at the end of the chapter.)

Incapacitation In one sense, capital punishment acts as the ultimate deterrent by rendering those executed incapable of committing further crimes. A study done by Paul Cassell and Stephen Markman analyzed the records of 52,000 state inmates doing time for murder and found that 810 of them had been previously convicted for the same crime. These 810 recidivists had killed 821 people after being released from prison the first time.[120] If, hypothetically, the death penalty was mandatory for those convicted of murder, then 821 innocent lives would have been saved in Cassell and Markman's example, and thousands of others among the general population. Such projections seem to show that by incapacitating dangerous criminals, capital punishment could provide society with measurable benefits.

Of course, the benefits of incapacitation are also available for those offenders sentenced to life without parole as an alternative to execution. Recent studies have found that the repeat murder rate of death-eligible convicts who live the remainder of their lives behind bars is about .002 percent. In the rare instance when one of these offenders is involved in a homicide, the victim is almost always another inmate.[121]

Fallibility Furthermore, the incapacitation justification for capital punishment rests on two questionable assumptions: (1) every convicted murderer is likely to recidivate, and (2) the criminal justice system is *infallible*. In other words, the system never convicts someone who is actually not guilty. According to the Death Penalty Information Center, however, between 1976, when the

AP Photo/John Raoux

▲ Death penalty supporters cheer moments after the 2006 execution of Danny Rolling, also known as the "Gainesville Ripper." Rolling had confessed to murdering five University of Florida students in August 1990. What are some of the emotional reasons for popular support of the death penalty?

Supreme Court reinstated capital punishment, and November 2006, 123 American men and women who had been convicted of capital crimes and sentenced to death were later found to be innocent. Over that same time period, 1,056 executions took place, meaning that for every eight convicts put to death since *Gregg*, about one death row inmate has been found innocent.

Problems with the Prosecution There are several explanations for this relatively high rate of error in capital cases. Police and prosecutors are often under a great deal of public pressure to solve violent crimes and may be overzealous in arresting and prosecuting suspects. Such was the case with Rolando Cruz, who spent a decade on Illinois's death row for the rape and murder of a ten-year-old girl. Even after another man named Brian Dugan confessed to the crime and DNA testing linked Dugan to the crime scene, prosecutors still insisted that Cruz was the culprit. Only after a police officer admitted that he lied under oath concerning Cruz's "confession" was Cruz declared not guilty.[122]

Outright lying by persons involved in capital cases contributes to false convictions as well. In 2006, for example, Jack Leonard Garcia faced the death penalty after New Mexico prosecutors charged him with contributing to the rape and murder of a seventy-year-old grandmother. Only one piece of evidence connected Garcia to the crime: statements made by Arturo Alvarado, who had fought with Garcia at a homeless shelter a few days before implicating him and who also happened to be the prime suspect in the case. After nine months in jail, Garcia was finally released when DNA tests failed to link him to the crimes. Professors Hugo Bedau of Tufts University and Michael Radelet of the University of Florida found that one-third of wrongful capital convictions resulted from "jailhouse snitches" who perjured themselves by telling the court that they overheard a confession by the defendant. In addition, false confessions and faulty eyewitness identifications were found to be responsible for two of every seven wrongful convictions.[123]

Problems with the Defense The single factor that contributes the most to the criminal justice system's fallibility in this area, however, is widely believed to be unsatisfactory legal representation. Many states and counties cannot or will not allocate adequate funds for death penalty cases, meaning that indigent capital defendants are often provided with a less-than-vigorous defense. The state of Alabama even fails to provide indigent death row inmates with attorneys, meaning that, in many instances, the convicts must act as their own lawyers as they try to navigate the complicated appeals process discussed in the last chapter.

The case of convicted murderer Ronald Rompilla highlights the consequences of poor counsel in a capital case. During the sentencing phase of his trial, Rompilla's lawyers made two serious errors. First, they failed to challenge the prosecution's characterization of Rompilla's previous conviction for rape and assault. In fact, they never even looked at the file of that case. Second, they failed to provide the Pennsylvania jury with mitigating factors that would argue against a death sentence, such as their client's troubled childhood, severe alcoholism, and other mental illnesses. Not surprisingly, the jury ordered Rompilla's execution, a sentence that was eventually overturned by the United States Supreme Court due to ineffective counsel.[124]

Arbitrariness One of the reasons it is so difficult to determine the deterrent effect of the death penalty is that it is rarely meted out. Despite the bifurcated process required by the Supreme Court's *Furman* ruling (see page 366), a significant amount of arbitrariness appears to remain in the system. Only 2 percent of all defendants convicted of murder are sentenced to death, and, as we have seen, relatively few of those on death row are ever executed.[125]

The chances of a defendant in a capital trial being sentenced to death seem to depend heavily on, as we have just seen, the quality of the defense counsel and the jurisdiction where the crime was committed. A Columbia University study, headed by Professor James Liebman, reported that of the 4,578 death

■ **Figure 11.8** Executions by State, 1976–2006

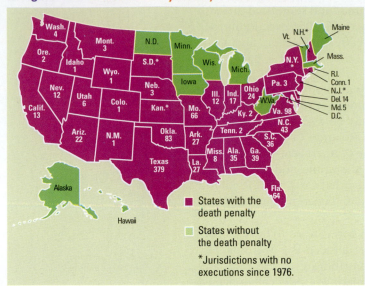

Wash. 4
Mont. 3
N.D.
Minn.
Vt. N.H.*
Maine
Ore. 2
Idaho 1
S.D.*
Wis.
Mich.
N.Y.*
Mass.
Wyo. 1
Neb. 3
Iowa
R.I.
Conn. 1
N.J.*
Nev. 12
Utah 6
Colo. 1
Ill. 12
Ind. 17
Ohio 24
Pa. 3
Del. 14
Md. 5
D.C.
Calif. 13
Kan.*
Mo. 66
Ky. 2
W.Va.
Va. 98
Ariz. 22
N.M. 1
Okla. 83
Ark. 27
Tenn. 2
N.C. 43
Texas 379
La. 27
Miss. 8
Ala. 35
Ga. 39
S.C. 36
Fla. 64
Alaska
Hawaii

■ States with the death penalty

■ States without the death penalty

*Jurisdictions with no executions since 1976.

sentences handed down between 1973 and 1995, two-thirds were reversed on appeal. About 37 percent of the reversals occurred because of incompetent lawyering.[126] Furthermore, as ■ Figure 11.8 shows, a convict's chances of being executed are strongly influenced by geography. Six states (Texas, Virginia, Oklahoma, Missouri, Florida, and North Carolina) account for more than two-thirds of all executions, while twelve states and the District of Columbia do not provide for capital punishment within their borders. Thus, a person on trial for first degree murder in New Mexico has a much better chance of avoiding execution than someone who has committed the same crime in Texas. Dramatic differences can even exist within the same state. Those convicted of death-eligible crimes in Baltimore County, Maryland, are twenty-three times more likely to be sentenced to death than are similarly situated defendants in neighboring Baltimore City.[127] Accordingly, Professor Hugo Bedau compares those who are executed to "losers in an arbitrary lottery."[128]

Not all observers of the criminal justice system agree with Professor Bedau's assessment. In responding to the Columbia University study mentioned above, James Q. Wilson points out that its authors do not claim that any innocent people have actually been executed.[129] Instead, Wilson suggests, the system is designed to give convicted murderers every chance to prove their innocence. In the *Gregg* case, the Supreme Court interpreted the Fourteenth Amendment as requiring "meaningful appellate review" for anybody found guilty of a capital crime.[130] In other words, the case of any defendant sentenced to death must automatically be reviewed by a higher court. To decrease the chances that the death sentence will be imposed "in a freakish manner," to use the Court's phrase, the appeals process in capital cases usually lasts twelve years. Thus, Wilson notes, the death penalty is actually quite rare: of the 4,578 death sentences considered in the Columbia University study, only 313 led to executions.[131]

Still Cruel and Unusual Finally, many observers believe that the Supreme Court should revisit the idea of the death penalty as cruel and unusual punishment, given the changing standards of society provided for in the *Weems* decision discussed earlier. Although the Court has given no indication that it plans do so, in 2006 it did rule that inmates sentenced to death could ask judges to postpone their executions, pending an investigation of death penalty procedures in their jurisdictions.[132] As a result, legal challenges to lethal injections, the dominant form of execution in this country, have been filed in nearly every state that engages in the practice.[133]

The Problem with Lethal Injections Over the past thirty years, lethal injections have been used to put nearly nine hundred inmates to death. Most states employ the same three-drug process. First, the sedative sodium thiopental is administered to deaden pain. Then pancuronium bromide, a paralytic, immobilizes the prisoner. Finally, a dose of potassium chloride stops the heart. Members of the law enforcement and medical communities have long claimed that, if performed correctly, this procedure kills the subject quickly and painlessly.

A flurry of lawsuits filed in the mid-2000s shows, however, that lethal injection is often performed incorrectly. When the state of Florida executed Angel Diaz in December 2006, for example, personnel accidentally injected the painkiller into his soft tissue rather than one of his veins. This caused foot-long chemical burns on his arms and surely made the experience—which lasted more than half an hour—extremely uncomfortable for Diaz, who could be seen grimacing in pain during the procedure. Testifying as part of a California lawsuit involving faulty lethal injection procedures, a member of the state's execution team answered a question about the team's level of training by admitting, "Training? We don't have training, really." Another described execution mistakes thusly: "[Expletive] does happen."[134]

Moreover, a recent study of lethal injections in North Carolina and California found that the dose of sodium thiopental administered to subjects is rarely sufficient to keep them unconscious throughout the procedure.[135] Consequently, the inmate may feel excruciating pain during the execution but be unable to express the sensation because she or he is paralyzed.

A Ready Solution? By the summer of 2007, twelve of the thirty-eight states that administer the death penalty—including California, Florida, and North Carolina—had issued temporary bans on lethal injections to address procedural concerns. These steps were not taken with an eye toward abolishing capital punishment, but rather toward "fixing" it. Generally, the remedies involve stricter guidelines for carrying out lethal injections, better training for the personnel, and oversight by a certified medical authority.[136]

Ironically, most experts agree that a suitable alternative method of lethal injection is readily available: an overdose of only the sedative sodium thiopental, which is how veterinarians euthanize animals. The procedure would cause inmates to lose consciousness and stop breathing without pain. This method does have one drawback, however. The subject, though unconscious, does not appear to die peacefully, and the process can take up to forty-five minutes to complete, four times longer than the present three-step procedure. When, in 2006, a federal judge gave California officials a choice between ensuring that a physician was present at all "three-step" lethal injections and performing executions using the "one-step" method, the officials chose the first option. To many observers, California seemed to be giving more consideration to the comfort of those watching the execution than to the suffering of the inmates experiencing it.[137]

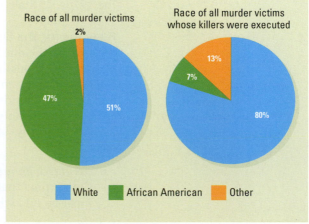

AP Photo/Florida Department of Corrections

▲ Convicted murderer Angel Diaz was executed by the state of Florida on December 13, 2006. Diaz remained alive for 34 minutes following the initial lethal injection, and could be seen gasping for air before a second dose of chemicals finally stopped his heart. Why should society care about the suffering of an inmate during the execution process?

DISCRIMINATORY EFFECT AND THE DEATH PENALTY

Whether or not capital punishment is imposed arbitrarily, some observers claim that it is not done without bias. Of the 1,078 prisoners executed in the United States between 1976 and the spring of 2007, 34 percent were African American, even though that minority group made up only about 12 percent of the national population during that time span.[138] Today, 42 percent of all inmates on death row are black; thus, the black proportion of the death row population is more than triple the black proportion of the population.

The Race of the Victim Another set of statistics also continues to be problematic. In 214 cases involving interracial murders in which the defendant was executed between 1976 and 2007, the defendant was African American and the victim was white. Over that same time period, only 15 cases involved a white defendant and a black victim.[139] Furthermore, a recent study of death penalty cases in California found that persons of any race convicted of murdering a white victim were four times more likely to be sentenced to death than if the victim was Hispanic and three times more likely to get the death sentence than if the victim was an African American.[140] In fact, although only slightly more than half of murder victims are white, four out of every five executions involve white victims (see ■ Figure 11.9). More recent data also suggest that minority defendants charged with murdering white victims

■ **Figure 11.9** **Race and the Death Penalty**

As these two graphs show, a disproportionate percentage of executed murderers had white victims.

Race of all murder victims
- 2%
- 47%
- 51%

Race of all murder victims whose killers were executed
- 13%
- 7%
- 80%

■ White   ■ African American   ■ Other

Source: U.S. Bureau of Justice Statistics.

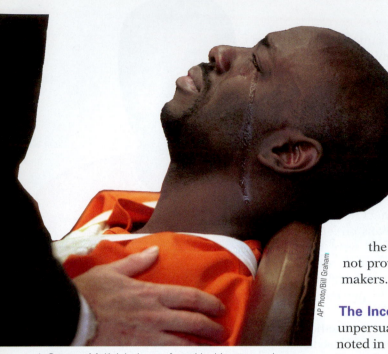

▲ Gregory McKnight is comforted by his attorney in a Vinton County (Ohio) common pleas court. Even though McKnight was convicted of aggravated murder, which is punishable by execution, the judge in his case initially ruled that McKnight was not eligible for the death penalty because Vinton County did not have the funds to provide him with an adequate defense. The judge later rescinded this ruling, and McKnight was sentenced to death. Why might the inability to hire a private attorney increase a death row inmate's chances of being executed?

are much more likely than others to be erroneously convicted of capital offenses.[141]

In *McCleskey v. Kemp* (1987),[142] the defense attorney for an African American sentenced to death for killing a white police officer used similar statistics to challenge Georgia's death penalty law. A study of two thousand Georgia murder cases showed that although African Americans were the victims of six out of every ten murders in the state, more than 80 percent of the cases in which death was imposed involved murders of whites.[143] In a 5–4 decision, the United States Supreme Court rejected the defense's claims, ruling that statistical evidence did not prove discriminatory intent on the part of Georgia's lawmakers.

The Income of the Victim One of the reasons the study was unpersuasive in the *McKleskey* case is that statistics, as we noted in Chapter 3, are often imperfect tools to measure trends. Even though the studies mentioned above show that race has an effect on the probability of receiving the death penalty, to prove discrimination from a legal standpoint, race must be the *only* determinant. Thus, a study must show that race, and not other factors such as the severity of the crime, the criminal history of the defendant, and the quality of the defense attorney, was the determining factor.[144]

Furthermore, some experts contend that the wealth, and not the race, of the defendant is the most important factor in death penalty cases. This hypothesis is based on the contention that adequate representation lessens the probability of being sentenced to death, and adequate representation is expensive.[145] Research by William M. Holmes of the Criminal Justice Center at the University of Massachusetts in Boston found that race did not account for wrongful convictions in capital cases. A much more important factor, according to Holmes, was education level, which correlates strongly with income.[146]

THE IMMEDIATE FUTURE OF THE DEATH PENALTY

As Figure 11.7 on page 364 made clear, the number of executions carried out each year in the United States has decreased dramatically since 1999. Other statistics also indicate a decline in death penalty activity. In 2006, only 114 people were sentenced to death, the lowest number since capital punishment was reinstated in the 1970s.[147] State death rows are also shrinking, albeit slowly.[148]

Reasons for the Decline in Executions We have already addressed many of the reasons for the diminishing presence of executions in the criminal justice system. With its decisions in the *Atkins* (2002) and *Roper* (2005) cases, the United States Supreme Court removed the possibility that hundreds of mentally handicapped and juvenile offenders could be sentenced to death. Furthermore, questions about the constitutionality of lethal injections have put capital punishment on hold, at least temporarily, in a number of states. Executions have declined for other reasons as well:

- *The "life without parole" alternative.* More than a decade ago, the Supreme Court ruled that, during the sentencing phase of a capital trial, jurors must be told when the sentence of life in prison without parole is available as an alternative to execution.[149] Thirty-six of the thirty-eight states (the exceptions being New Mexico and Texas) now permit this option, and jurors appear to be selecting it. In federal court, juries choose capital punishment in only about 40 percent of cases in which the defendant has been found guilty of a death-eligible crime.[150] (Remember, the Court's *Ring* decision, discussed on page 361, ensures that juries, not judges, make the death penalty decision.)

- *Prosecutorial discretion.* As juries become more hesitant in applying the death penalty, prosecutors are reacting by being more selective in asking for it. State prosecutors who request the death penalty are successful about half of the time and federal prosecutors about one-third of the time.[151]
- *Economic concerns.* Part of the pressure on prosecutors to be more discriminating in choosing when to press for execution comes from budget-minded supervisors. Because of the costs of intensive investigations, extensive *voir dire* (see pages 314–316), and lengthy appellate reviews, pursuing the death penalty can be very expensive. For example, if Florida prosecutors asked for life without parole in all first degree murder cases and never sought the death penalty, the state would save $51 million a year.[152]

The most important factor in the declining use of the death penalty, however, may be the recognition that the system is susceptible to error.

Fairness Concerns As noted earlier, for all the worry about wrongful convictions, no person who has been executed has been exonerated afterwards. Nearly 130 convicts have, however, been removed from death row because of irregularities in their convictions. With the advent of DNA fingerprinting, many observers believe it is only a matter of time until a posthumous exoneration occurs. To forestall this possibility, in 2006, for the first time, the Supreme Court ordered the reexamination of a death penalty case in Tennessee because of DNA evidence.[153] Taking the strategy further, legislators in New Jersey are considering becoming the first jurisdiction to repeal capital punishment since the *Gregg* decision. "It would eliminate the possibility of executing an innocent person," explains one state lawmaker.[154]

Does this mean society's "standards of decency" are changing to the point that the death sentence is in danger of being abolished? Probably not. Despite its decisions in the first half of the 2000s, the Supreme Court has shown no interest in holding that the death penalty itself is unconstitutional. Although public support for the death penalty has been steadily dropping since the mid-1990s, a Gallup poll taken in 2006 showed that 67 percent of Americans still favor the practice, though that percentage drops to about 50 percent when the choice is between execution and a sentence of life in prison without parole. Indeed, in the 2000s, Americans seem more interested in making the sentence of death fairer than in doing away with it altogether.

Self Check Fill in the Blanks

By a large margin, _____ is the most widespread method of execution in the United States today. According to the United States Supreme Court's *Weems* decision, "cruel and unusual punishment" under the Eighth Amendment is determined by the changing _____ of society. Following these guidelines, in 2002 the Court barred the execution of the _____, and in 2005 it prohibited the execution of persons who were _____ at the time of their crime. Check your answers on page 378.

Criminal Justice in Action

THE MORALITY OF THE DEATH PENALTY

"The argument about whether lethal injection causes pain to the ones on death row has really gone too far," wrote Robert Jackson in a letter to North Carolina Governor Mike Easley.[155] Jackson was undoubtedly thinking about the pain felt by his children twelve years earlier, when Archie Billings raped and killed his eleven-year-old daughter, Amy, and stabbed his son, Bobby, twenty-three times. After numerous appeals, Billings's execution was again delayed in 2007 because of North Carolina's problems administering lethal injections (see page 373). Like many Americans, Jackson does not see the death penalty in terms of the Eighth Amendment, "changing norms and standards," or the bifurcated sentencing process. Rather, he sees it as a matter of right and wrong, a viewpoint we will examine in this *Criminal Justice in Action* feature.

Mike Kemp, Getty

THE "LIFE-LIFE TRADE-OFF"

In academic circles, discussion about the morality of the death penalty has generally focused on two concepts.

Those who take a *utilitarian* approach believe that the "cost" of each execution is acceptable because of the "benefit" to society, usually expressed in terms of deterrence of future crimes. Those who favor the *deontological* approach reject this cost-benefit analysis on the grounds that an individual's right to life should never be sacrificed, not even for the greater good.

Robert Blecker, a professor at New York Law School, sees such arguments as too esoteric to explain our country's somewhat unique relationship with the death penalty. Blecker believes that, for many Americans, capital punishment is an expression of hatred toward the offender and the "wrongness" of his or her crime.[156] Viewed in this light, the idea of a "life-life trade-off" has an appeal that goes beyond its roots in retribution. It positions the death penalty, still popular in the United States, as an expression of society's collective moral judgment on those who commit murder.

The Case for Execution as a Moral Act

- If the death penalty can prevent—through deterrence or incapacitation—even a single future murder, then it is morally justifiable and perhaps even required by the government.
- Some crimes are so horrible that executing the person responsible is the only fitting response.

Our criminal justice system would not be just if it punished murder in the same way as other, less serious crimes.

- The victim's family members often say that a murderer's execution brings them a sense of "closure" by allowing them to come to terms with their grief.

The Case against Execution as a Moral Act

- The death penalty is an inherently cruel and barbaric act, and it is improper for the government of a civilized nation to kill its own citizens.
- Just as we would not permit a physician to remove the organs of a living person to save the lives of others who need organ transplants, we should not

execute a criminal based on the principle that the act would save the lives of others.[157]

- Problems of arbitrariness, discrimination, and wrongful convictions rob the death penalty of any moral justification, leaving it nothing more than the pointless infliction of violence by the state.

Writing Assignment—Your Opinion

In 1977, the United States Supreme Court held that the death penalty could not be imposed for rape, labeling as "cruel and unusual" any punishment that is not proportionate to the crime.[158] In 2003, however, a Louisiana court sentenced Patrick O. Kennedy to be executed for raping an eight-year-old girl. Four other states have also passed legislation allowing the death penalty for certain sex crimes, mostly involving minors.

How do the arguments concerning the morality of the death penalty apply when the punishment extends to other crimes besides murder? In general, do you think an argument can be made that people who rape or

molest children should be executed? Before responding, you can review our discussions in this chapter concerning

- The purposes of sentencing, particularly retribution, deterrence, and incapacitation (pages 343–346).
- The debate over the death penalty, particularly the discussions of fallibility and arbitrariness (pages 370–372).
- Possible discrimination and the death penalty (pages 373–374).

Your answer should take at least three full paragraphs.

L01 **List and contrast the four basic philosophical reasons for sentencing criminals.** (a) Retribution, (b) deterrence, (c) incapacitation, and (d) rehabilitation. Under the principle of retributive justice, the severity of the punishment is in proportion to the severity of the crime. Punishment is an end in itself. In contrast, the deterrence approach seeks to prevent future crimes by setting an example. Such punishment is based on its deterrent value and not necessarily on the severity of the crime. The incapacitation theory of punishment simply argues that a criminal in prison cannot inflict further harm on society. In contrast, the rehabilitation theory believes that criminals can be rehabilitated in the appropriate prison environment.

L02 **Contrast indeterminate with determinate sentencing.** Indeterminate sentencing follows from legislative penal codes that set minimum and maximum amounts of incarceration time; determinate sentencing carries a fixed amount of time, although this may be reduced for "good time."

L03 **Explain why there is a difference between a sentence imposed by a judge and the actual sentence carried out by the prisoner.** Although judges may decide on indeterminate sentencing, thereafter it is parole boards that decide when prisoners will be released after the minimum sentence is served.

L04 **List the six forms of punishment.** (a) Capital (death sentence), (b) imprisonment, (c) probation, (d) fines, (e) restitution and community service, and (f) restorative justice (apologies).

L05 **State who has input into the sentencing decision and list the factors that determine a sentence.** The prosecutor, defense attorney, probation officer, and judge provide inputs. The factors considered in sentencing are (a) the seriousness of the crime, (b) mitigating circumstances, (c) aggravating circumstances, and (d) judicial philosophy.

L06 **Explain some of the reasons why sentencing reform has occurred.** One reason is sentencing disparity, which has been seen both on a geographic basis and on a courtroom basis (due to a particular judge's philosophy). Sentencing discrimination has also occurred on the basis of defendants' gender, race, or economic standing. An additional reason for sentencing reform has been a general desire to "get tough on crime."

L07 **Identify the arguments for and against the use of victim impact statements during sentencing hearings.** Proponents of victim impact statements believe that they allow victims to provide character evidence in the same manner as defendants have always been allowed to do and that they give victims a therapeutic "voice" in the sentencing process. Opponents argue that the statements bring unacceptable levels of emotion into the courtroom and encourage judges and juries to make sentencing decisions based on the "social value" of the victim rather than the facts of the case.

L08 **Outline the Supreme Court rulings on capital punishment that led to the bifurcated process for death penalty sentencing.** In 1967, the Supreme Court placed a hold on all scheduled executions. In 1972, the Court invalidated the death penalty in states that imposed it because the way it was practiced violated the Eighth and Fourteenth Amendments. By 1976, thirty-five states had changed their death penalty statutes to comply with the Supreme Court ruling. The Supreme Court then declared mandatory death penalty statutes invalid, but established a bifurcated process that involves two steps. Today, thirty-eight states have adopted this process and provide for legally acceptable capital punishment.

L09 **Describe the main issues of the death penalty debate.** Many of those who favor capital punishment believe that it is "just deserts" for the most violent of criminals. Those who oppose it see the act as little more than revenge. There is also disagreement over whether the death penalty acts as a deterrent. The relatively high number of death row inmates who have been found innocent has raised questions about the fallibility of the process, while certain statistics seem to show that execution is rather arbitrary. Finally, many observers contend that capital punishment is administered unfairly with regard to members of minority groups.

aggravating circumstances 353	indeterminate sentencing 348	restitution 346
capital punishment 364	just deserts 343	restorative justice 346
departure 359	mandatory sentencing	retribution 343
determinate sentencing 348	guidelines 359	sentencing discrimination 355
deterrence 344	mitigating circumstances 353	sentencing disparity 355
"good time" 348	presentence investigative report 352	sentencing guidelines 357
habitual offender laws 360	"real offense" 353	truth-in-sentencing laws 349
incapacitation 345	rehabilitation 346	victim impact statement (VIS) 362

Questions for Critical Analysis

1. What is the difference between general deterrence and specific deterrence?

2. Why is rehabilitation seen as the most "humane" form of punishment?

3. What are truth-in-sentencing laws, and why are they popular among victims' rights advocates?

4. Why do those who believe in "individualized justice" compare the proper role of a judge in the sentencing process to that of a physician?

5. How do "real offense" procedures effectively render plea bargains meaningless?

6. What is the difference between sentencing disparity and sentencing discrimination?

7. Under what circumstances can a federal judge depart from the federal sentencing guidelines?

8. What is the "bifurcated process," and how did it come to be the standard for state death penalty procedure?

9. What are some of the arguments in favor of the death penalty? What are some of the arguments against it?

10. What is the likelihood that the death penalty will be abolished in the near future? Explain your answer.

Maximize Your Best Possible Outcome for Chapter 11

1. **Maximize Your Best Chance for Getting a Good Grade on the Exam.** ThomsonNOW Personalized Study is a diagnostic study tool containing valuable text-specific resources—and because you focus on just what you don't know, you learn more in less time to get a better grade. How do you get ThomsonNOW? If your textbook does not include an access code card, go to **thomsonedu.com** to get ThomsonNOW before your next exam!

2. **Get the Most Out of Your Textbook** by going to the book companion Web site at **www.cjinaction.com** to access one of the tutorial quizzes, use the flash cards to master key terms, and check out the many other study aids you'll find there. Under chapter resources you will also be able to access the Stories from the Street feature and Web links mentioned in the textbook.

3. **Learn about Potential Criminal Justice Careers** discussed in this chapter by exploring careers online at **www.cjinaction.com**. You will find career descriptions and information about job requirements, training, salary and benefits, and the application process. You can also watch video profiles featuring criminal justice professionals.

Notes

1. Neil A. Lewis, "Moussaoui Given Life Term by Jury over Link to 9/11," *New York Times* (May 4, 2006), A1.

2. Neil A. Lewis, "Moussaoui Jury Hears from Grieving Families and from Victims Themselves," *New York Times* (May 4, 2006), A16.

3. David Yellen, "Just Deserts and Lenient Prosecutors: The Flawed Case for Real Offense Sentencing," *Northwestern University Law Review* 91 (Summer 1997), 1434.

4. Brian Forst, "Prosecution and Sentencing," in *Crime,* ed. James Q. Wilson and Joan Petersilia (San Francisco: ICS Press, 1995), 386.

5. Herbert L. Packer, "Justification for Criminal Punishment," in *The Limits of Criminal Sanction* (Palo Alto, CA: Stanford University Press, 1968), 36–37.

6. Jami L. Anderson, "Reciprocity as a Justification for Retributivism," *Criminal Justice Ethics* (Winter/Spring 1997), 13–14.

7. Immanuel Kant, *Metaphysical First Principles of the Doctrine of Right*, trans. Mary Gregor (Cambridge, UK: Cambridge University Press, 1991), 331.

8. Harold Pepinsky and Paul Jesilow, *Myths That Cause Crime* (Cabin John, MD: Seven Locks Press, 1984).

9. Jeremy Bentham, *An Introduction to the Principles of Morals and Legislation 1789* (New York: Hafner Publishing Corp., 1961).

10. Forst, 376.

11. Bureau of Justice Statistics, *Criminal Victimization, 2005* (Washington, D.C.: U.S. Department of Justice, September 2006), 1.

12. Federal Bureau of Investigation, *Crime in the United States, 2005* (Washington, D.C.: U.S. Department of Justice, 2006), at **www.fbi.gov/ucr/05cius/offenses/clearances/index.html**.

13. Paul H. Robinson and John M. Darley, "The Utility of Desert," *Northwestern University Law Review* 91 (Winter 1997), 453.

14. James Q. Wilson, *Thinking about Crime* (New York: Basic Books, 1975), 235.

15. Isaac Ehrlich, "Participation in Illegitimate Activities: A Theoretical and Empirical Investigation," *Journal of Political Economy* 81 (May/June 1973), 521–564.

16. Steve Levitt, "The Effect of Prison Population Size on Crime Rates," *Quarterly Journal of Economics* 111 (May 1996), 319.

17. Todd Clear, *Harm in Punishment* (Boston: Northeastern University Press, 1980).

18. Jan Chaiken, Marcia Chaiken, and William Rhodes, "Predicting Violent Behavior and Classifying Violent Offenders," in *Understanding and Preventing Violence*, ed. Albert J. Reiss, Jr., and Jeffrey A. Roth (Washington, D.C.: National Academy Press, 1994).

19. Robert J. Meadows and Julie Kuehnel, *Evil Minds: Understanding and Responding to Violent Predators* (Upper Saddle River, NJ: Pearson Prentice Hall, 2005), 256–258.

20. Barry Krisberg and Susan Marchionna, *Attitudes of U.S. Voters toward Prisoner Rehabilitation and Reentry Policies* (Oakland, CA: National Council on Crime and Delinquency, April 2006), 1.

21. Heather Strang and Lawrence W. Sherman, "Repairing the Harm: Victims and Restorative Justice," *Utah Law Review* (2003), 15, 18, 20–25.

22. Todd R. Clear, George F. Cole, and Michael D. Reisig, *American Corrections*, 7th ed. (Belmont, CA: Thomson Wadsworth, 2006), 68–69.

23. Mark S. Umbreit, *Victim Meets Offender: The Impact of Restorative Justice and Mediation* (New York: Criminal Justice Press, 1994), 17–19.

24. Leena Kurki, "Restorative and Community Justice in the United States," in *Crime and Justice: A Review of Research*, vol. 27, ed. Michael Tonry (Chicago: University of Chicago Press, 2000), 253–303.

25. Gregory W. O'Reilly, "Truth-in-Sentencing: Illinois Adds Yet Another Layer of 'Reform' to Its Complicated Code of Corrections," *Loyola University of Chicago Law Journal* (Summer 1996), 986, 999–1000.

26. Marc Mauer, "The Truth about Truth-in-Sentencing," *Corrections Today* (February 1, 1996), 1–8.

27. Marvin Zalman, "The Rise and Fall of the Indeterminate Sentence," *Wayne Law Review* 24 (1977), 45, 52.

28. Marvin E. Frankel, *Criminal Sentences: Law without Order* (New York: Hill & Wang, 1972), 5.

29. Jessica Mitford, *Kind and Usual Punishment* (New York: Alfred A. Knopf, 1973), 80–83.

30. Bureau of Justice Statistics, *Truth in Sentencing in State Prisons* (Washington, D.C.: Department of Justice, 1999).

31. Paul W. Keve, *Crime Control and Justice in America: Searching for Facts and Answers* (Chicago: American Library Association, 1995), 77.

32. Kate Stith and José A. Cabranes, "Judging under the Federal Sentencing Guidelines," *Northwestern University Law Review* 91 (Summer 1997), 1247.

33. Mark M. Lanier and Claud H. Miller III, "Attitudes and Practices of Federal Probation Officers towards Pre-Plea/Trial Investigative Report Policy," *Crime & Delinquency* 41 (July 1995), 365–366.

34. Stith and Cabranes, 1247.

35. Nancy J. King and Rosevelt L. Noble, "Felony Jury Sentencing in Practice: A Three-State Study," *Vanderbilt Law Review* (2004), 1986.

36. Jena Iontcheva, "Jury Sentencing as Democratic Practice," *Virginia Law Review* (April 2003), 325.

37. Julie R. O'Sullivan, "In Defense of the U.S. Sentencing Guidelines Modified Real-Offense System," *Northwestern University Law Review* 91 (1997), 1342.

38. Brian Forst and Charles Wellford, "Punishment and Sentencing: Developing Sentencing Guidelines Empirically from Principles of Punishment," *Rutgers Law Review* 33 (1981).

39. 18 U.S.C. Section 2113(a) (1994).

40. Bob Barr and Eric Sterling, "The War on Drugs: Fighting Crime or Wasting Time?" *American Criminal Law Review* (Fall 2001), 1545.

41. U.S. Sentencing Commission, "Sourcebook for Federal Sentencing Decisions," at **www.ussc.gov/ANNRPT/2006/SBTOC06.htm**.

42. U.S. Sentencing Commission, "Federal Sentencing Statistics by State, District, and Circuit: October 1, 2005, through September 30, 2006," at **www.ussc.gov/JUDPACK/JP2006.htm**.

43. Ronald F. Wright, "Federal or State? Sorting as a Sentencing Choice," *Criminal Justice* (Summer 2006), 17.

44. Cassia Spohn and David Holleran, "The Imprisonment Penalty Paid by Young, Unemployed Black and Hispanic Male Offenders," *Criminology* 35 (2000), 281.

45. *Ibid.*, 297.

46. Bureau of Justice Statistics, *Prisoners in 2005* (Washington, D.C.: U.S. Department of Justice, November 2006), 8.

47. Spohn and Holleran, 301.

48. *Ibid.*, 291.

49. Bureau of Justice Statistics, *State Court Sentencing of Convicted Felons, 2003* (Washington, D.C.: U.S. Department of Justice, May 2005), Table 2.7.

50. Darrell Steffensmeier and Stephen DeMuth, "Ethnicity and Judges' Sentencing Decisions: Hispanic-Black-White Comparisons," *Criminology* 39 (2001), 145.

51. *Ibid.*

52. *Ibid.*, 167.

53. 28 U.S.C. Section 991 (1994).

54. Bureau of Justice Statistics, *State Court Sentencing of Convicted Felons, 2002* (Washington, D.C.: U.S. Department of Justice, May 2005), Table 2.6.

55. Clarice Feinman, *Women in the Criminal Justice System*, 3d ed. (Westport, CT: Praeger, 1994), 35.

56. Darrell Steffensmeier, John Kramer, and Cathy Streifel, "Gender and Imprisonment Decisions," *Criminology* 31 (1993), 411.

57. Quoted in Raymond Smith, "Death Penalty Rise for Women," *Press-Enterprise (Riverside, California)* (July 30, 1998), A12.

58. John C. Coffee, "Repressed Issues of Sentencing," *Georgetown Law Journal* 66 (1978), 987.

59. J. S. Bainbridge, Jr., "The Return of Retribution," *ABA Journal* (May 1985), 63.

60. Pub. L. No. 98-473, 98 Stat. 1987, codified as amended at 18 U.S.C. Sections 3551–3742 and 28 U.S.C. Sections 991–998 (1988).

61. Julia L. Black, "The Constitutionality of Federal Sentences Imposed under the Sentencing Reform Act of 1984 after *Mistretta v. United States*," *Iowa Law Review* 75 (March 1990), 767.

62. Roger Haines, Kevin Cole, and Jennifer Wole, *Federal Sentencing Guidelines Handbook* (New York: McGraw-Hill, 1994), 3.

63. *Fifteen Years of Guidelines Sentencing: An Assessment of How Well the Federal Criminal Justice System Is Achieving the Goals of Sentencing Reform* (Washington, D.C.: U.S. Sentencing Commission, November 2004), 46.

64. Clear, Cole, and Reisig, 86.

65. *United States v. Diaz-Villafane*, 874 F.2d 43, 49 (1st Cir. 1989).

66. U.S. Sentencing Commission, "Statistical Information Packet: Fiscal Year 2006, First Circuit," Table 8, page 11, at **www.ussc.gov/JUDPACK/2006/1c06.pdf**.

67. Alabama Code 1975 Section 20–2–79.

68. Washington Revised Code Annotated Section 9.94A.030.

69. 445 U.S. 263 (1980).

70. 538 U.S. 63 (2003).

71. *Lockyer v. Andrade*, 270 F.3d 743 (9th Cir. 2001).

72. *Lockyer v. Andrade*, 538 U.S. 63, 76 (2003).

73. *Ibid.*, 83.

74. Vincent Schiraldi, Jason Colburn, and Eric Lotke, *Three Strikes and You're Out: An Examination of Three-Strike Laws Ten Years after Their Enactment* (Washington, D.C.: Justice Policy Institute. 2004), 23.

75. *Prosecutor's Perspective on California's Three Strikes Law—A Ten-Year Retrospective* (Sacramento, CA: California District Attorneys Association, Summer 2004), 11.

76. Michael Tonry, "The Failure of the U.S. Sentencing Commission's Guidelines," *Crime & Delinquency* 39 (1993), 131–149.

77. Erik Luna, *Misguided Guidelines: A Critique of Federal Sentencing* (Washington, D.C.: Cato Institute, 2002), 3.

78. Linda Greenhouse, "Supreme Court Constrains Judges' Power in Sentencing," *New York Times* (January 23, 2007), A15.

79. 530 U.S. 466 (2000).

80. 536 U.S. 584 (2002).

81. 542 U.S. 1174 (2004).

82. 543 U.S. 220 (2005).

83. David G. Savage, "Judges Freed from Sentencing Rules," *Los Angeles Times* (January 13, 2005), A1.

84. Edna Erez, "Victim Voice, Impact Statements, and Sentencing: Integrating Restorative Justice and Therapeutic Jurisprudence Principles in Adversarial Proceedings," *Criminal Law Bulletin* (September/October 2004), 495.

85. Bryan Myers and Edith Greene, "Prejudicial Nature of Impact Statements," *Psychology, Public Policy, and Law* (December 2004), 493.

86. *Booth v. Maryland*, 482 U.S. 496, 503 (1987).

87. 501 U.S. 808 (1991).

88. Bryan Myers and Jack Arbuthnot, "The Effects of Victim Impact Evidence on the Verdicts and Sentencing Judgments of Mock Jurors," *Journal of Offender Rehabilitation* (1999), 95–112.

89. Walter Berns, "Abraham Lincoln (Book Review)," *Commentary* (January 1, 1996), 70.

90. Comments made at the Georgetown Law Center, "The Modern View of Capital Punishment," *American Criminal Law Review* 34 (Summer 1997), 1353.

91. David Bruck, quoted in Bill Rankin, "Fairness of the Death Penalty Is Still on Trial," *Atlanta Constitution-Journal* (July 29, 1997), A13.

92. Mark Costanzo, *Just Revenge: Costs and Consequences of the Death Penalty* (New York: St. Martin's Press, 1997), 11.

93. Randall Coyne and Lyn Entzeroth, *Capital Punishment and the Judicial Process* (Durham, NC: Carolina Academic Press, 1994), 2.

94. Jeffrey C. Matura, "When Will It Stop? The Use of the Death Penalty for Non-Homicide Crimes," *Journal of Legislation* 24 (1998), 249.

95. Thorsten Sellin, "The Philadelphia Gibbet Iron," *Journal of Criminal Law, Criminology, and Police Science* 46 (1955), 19.

96. G. Mark Mamantov, "The Executioner's Song: Is There a Right to Listen?" *Virginia Law Review* 69 (March 1983), 373.

97. Bureau of Justice Statistics, *Capital Punishment, 2005* (Washington, D.C.: U.S. Department of Justice, December 2006), 4.

98. Larry C. Berkson, *The Concept of Cruel and Unusual Punishment* (Lexington, MA: Lexington Books, 1975), 43.

99. John P. Cunningham, "Death in the Federal Courts: Expectations and Realities of the Federal Death Penalty Act of 1994," *University of Richmond Law Review* 32 (May 1998), 939.

100. *In re Kemmler*, 136 U.S. 447 (1890).

101. 217 U.S. 349 (1910).

102. Pamela S. Nagy, "Hang by the Neck until Dead: The Resurgence of Cruel and Unusual Punishment in the 1990s," *Pacific Law Journal* 26 (October 1994), 85.

103. 408 U.S. 238 (1972).

104. 408 U.S. 309 (1972) (Stewart, concurring).

105. 428 U.S. 280 (1976).

106. Colorado Revised Statutes Sections 18.1.3-1201(5)(f) and (p) (2003).

107. 428 U.S. 153 (1976).

108. 536 U.S. 584 (2002).

109. *Ford v. Wainwright*, 477 U.S. 399, 422 (1986).

110. Neil A. Lewis, "Judges Let Stand Ruling That Allows Forcibly Drugging an Inmate before Execution," *New York Times* (October 7, 2003), A14.

111. *Penry v. Lynaugh*, 492 U.S. 302 (1989).

112. 536 U.S. 304 (2002).

113. 543 U.S. 551 (2005).

114. Ernest van den Haag, "The Ultimate Punishment: A Defense," *Harvard Law Review* 99 (1986), 1669.

115. *The Death Penalty: The Religious Community Calls for Abolition* (pamphlet published by the National Coalition to Abolish the Death Penalty and the National Interreligious Task Force on Criminal Justice, 1988), 48.

116. Isaac Ehrlich, "The Deterrent Effect of Capital Punishment: A Question of Life and Death," *American Economic Review* 65 (June 1975), 397–417.

117. Hashem Dezhbakhsh, Paul H. Rubin, and Joanna M. Shepherd, "Does Capital Punishment Have a Deterrent Effect? New Evidence from Postmoratorium Panel Data," *American Law and Economics Review* 5 (2003), 344–376; H. Naci Mocan and R. Kaj Gittings, "Getting Off Death Row: Commuted Sentences and the Deterrent Effect of Capital Punishment," *Journal of Law and Economics* 46 (2003), 453–478; Joanna M. Shepherd, "Deterrence versus Brutalization: Capital Punishment's Differing Impact among States," *Michigan Law Review* 104 (2005), 203–255; and Paul R. Zimmerman, "State Executions, Deterrence, and the Incidence of Murder," *Journal of Applied Economics* 7 (2005), 163–193.

118. John J. Donohue and Justin Wolfers, "Uses and Abuses of Empirical Evidence in the Death Penalty Debate," *Stanford Law Review* 58 (2005), 791–845.

119. Lisa Stolzenberg and Stewart J. D'Alessio, "Capital Punishment, Execution Publicity, and Murder in Houston, Texas," *Journal of Criminal Law and Criminology* (Winter 2004), 351–379.

120. Stephen Markman and Paul Cassell, "Protecting the Innocent: A Response to the Bedau-Radelet Study," *Stanford Law Review* 41 (1988), 153.

121. Jonathan R. Sorensen and Rocky L. Pilgrim, "An Actuarial Risk Assessment of Violence Posed by Capital Murder Defendants," *Journal of Criminal Law and Criminology* (Summer 2000), 1251, 1256.

122. Joseph F. Shapiro, "The Wrong Men on Death Row," *U.S. News & World Report* (November 9, 1998), 26.

123. Hugo Adam Bedau and Michael L. Radelet, "Miscarriages of Justice in Potentially Capital Cases," *Stanford Law Review* (1987), 21–23.

124. *Rompilla v. Beard*, 545 U.S. 375 (2005).

125. Adam Liptak, "Geography and the Machinery of Death," *New York Times* (February 5, 2007), A10.

126. James S. Liebman, Jeffrey Fagan, and Valeria West, "A Broken System: Error Rates in Capital Cases, 1973–1995" (2000), at **www2.law.columbia.edu/instructionalservices/liebman**.

127. Raymond Paternoster, Robert Brame, Sarah Bacon, and Andrew Ditchfield, "Justice by Geography and Race: The Administration of the Death Penalty in Maryland 1978–1999," *Maryland's Law Journal on Race, Religion, Gender and Class* (2004), Table 65, page 72.

128. Quoted in Walter Berns and Joseph Bessette, "Why the Death Penalty Is Fair," *Wall Street Journal* (January 9, 1998), A16.

129. James Q. Wilson, "What Death-Penalty Errors?" *New York Times* (July 10, 2000), A19.

130. *Gregg v. Georgia*, 428 U.S. 153, 195 (1976).

131. Wilson, "What Death-Penalty Errors?"

132. *Hill v. McDonough*, 126 S.Ct. 2096 (2006).

133. Death Penalty Information Center, "Death Penalty in Flux," at **www.deathpenaltyinfo.org/article.php?did=2289**.

134. Both quoted in Elizabeth Weil, "The Needle and the Damage Done," *New York Times Magazine* (February 11, 2007), 50.

135. Karen Kaplan, "Reliability of Execution Drugs Is in Question," *Los Angeles Times* (April 24, 2007), A1.

136. Deborah W. Denno, *The Lethal Injection Quandary: How Medicine Has Dismantled the Death Penalty* (working paper) (New York: Fordham University of Law, May 2007), 2-5.

137. Denise Grady, "Doctors See Way to Cut Risks of Suffering in Lethal Injection," *New York Times* (June 23, 2006), A1.

138. Death Penalty Information Center, "Race of Death Row Inmates Executed since 1976," at **www.deathpenaltyinfo.org/article.php?scid=5&did=184**.

139. *Ibid.*

140. Glenn L. Pierce and Michael L. Radelet, "The Impact of Legally Inappropriate Factors on Death Sentencing for California Homicides, 1990–1999," *Santa Clara Law Review* 46 (2005), 1–47.

141. Talia Roitberg Harmon, "Race for Your Life: An Analysis of the Role of Race in Erroneous Capital Convictions," *Criminal Justice Review* (Spring 2004), 76–94.

142. 481 U.S. 279 (1987).

143. David C. Baldus, George Woodworth, and Charles A. Pulaski, *Equal Justice and the Death Penalty: A Legal and Empirical Analysis* (Boston: Northeastern University Press, 1990), 140–197, 306.

144. Laura Argys and Naci Mocan, *Who Shall Live and Who Shall Die? An Analysis of Prisoners on Death Row in the United States* (Cambridge, MA: National Bureau of Economic Research, February 2003), 22.

145. *Ibid.*, 8.

146. William M. Holmes, "Who Are the Wrongly Convicted on Death Row?" in *Wrongly Convicted: When Justice Fails*, ed. Saundra Westervelt and John Humphrey (Piscataway, NJ: Rutgers University Press, 2001).

147. Robert Tanner, "30-Year Low in '06 for Death Sentences," *Chicago Tribune* (January 5, 2007), 3.

148. *Capital Punishment, 2005*, 6.

149. *Simmons v. South Carolina*, 512 U.S. 154 (1994).

150. Adam Liptak, "Moussaoui Case Highlights Where Juries Fear to Tread," *New York Times* (May 5, 2006), A21.

151. *Ibid.*

152. Vivian Berger, "Abolition of the Death Penalty: Prospects Brighten," *National Law Journal* (January 29, 2007), at **www.vberger-mediator.com/death.html**.

153. *House v. Bell*, 126 S.Ct. 2064 (2006).

154. Quoted in Liz Halloran, "Pulling Back from the Brink," *U.S. News & World Report* (May 8, 2006), 36.

155. Quoted in Andrea Weigl, "Father Wants Killer to Die," *Raleigh (North Carolina) News & Observer* (April 23, 2007), A1.

156. Quoted in Weigl, 51.

157. Claire Finkelstein, "A Contractarian Argument against the Death Penalty," *New York University Law Review* (October 2006), 1283.

158. *Coker v. Georgia*, 433 U.S. 584 (1977).

CHAPTER 12

Working at a Satisfactory Rate

Endurance

Communication

Supervision

Competence-
Quality Work

-Problem Solving-
anticipating
consequences

OF MDOC

Probation and Community Corrections

Learning objectives

After reading this chapter, you should be able to:

L01 Explain the justifications for community-based corrections programs.

L02 Indicate when probation started to fall out of favor, and explain why.

L03 Explain several alternative sentencing arrangements that combine probation with incarceration.

L04 Specify the conditions under which an offender is most likely to be denied probation.

L05 Describe the three general categories of conditions placed on a probationer.

L06 Explain why probation officers' work has become more dangerous.

L07 Explain the three stages of probation revocation.

L08 List the five sentencing options for a judge besides imprisonment and probation.

L09 Contrast day reporting centers with intensive supervision probation.

L010 List the three levels of home monitoring.

On a warm summer day in Southern California, eighty-six-year-old George Weller turned his 1992 Buick LeSabre into the Santa Monica Farmers' Market and stepped on the accelerator. Moving at freeway speeds, he plowed through the terrified pedestrian shoppers, killing ten of them and injuring more than sixty others before finally crashing into a barricade. Shortly thereafter, Los Angeles District Attorney Steve Cooley charged Weller with ten counts of felony vehicular manslaughter. During his trial, Weller's defense attorneys claimed that their client had suffered from a phenomenon known as "pedal error," in which the driver becomes disoriented and hits the accelerator when meaning to slam on the brakes.

On October 20, 2006, a jury found Weller guilty of all charges, which carried a possible penalty of eighteen years in prison. Afterwards, one of the jurors said that the decision had been influenced by the defendant's apparent lack of remorse—two witnesses testified that, following the carnage, Weller had said that his victims "should have gotten out of the way." Despite Weller's attitude and the magnitude of his crimes, Judge Michael M. Johnson of the Los Angeles Superior Court decided to spare Weller the trauma of incarceration. Instead, Johnson sentenced him to five years' probation, citing the now-bedridden

eighty-nine-year-old's heart ailment and other health problems. Imprisoning Weller "wouldn't do anybody any good" while saddling taxpayers with the costs of his medical care, said the judge in explaining his decision.

▲ George Weller, left, listens as his defense attorney makes a point during the octogenarian's criminal trial in Los Angeles Superior Court.

Weller's sentence sparked skepticism, as many observers felt that he had been "let off easy" because of his age and infirmity. In fact, Judge Johnson was hardly breaking new ground. Defendants found guilty of crimes as serious as felony manslaughter are routinely given *probation* in this country. A system that initially provided judges with the discretion to show leniency to first-time, minor offenders increasingly allows those who have committed serious crimes to serve their time in the community rather than prison or jail. Nearly one out of every five probationers has been convicted of a violent felony such as assault or rape.[1]

Ironically, the trend toward probation can be partly attributed to the "get tough" approach to crime that has emerged in public policy. Campaigns to crack down on drunk drivers, the "war on drugs," harsher sentencing statutes, and limitations on judicial discretion have placed intense pressure on the American incarceration infrastructure. Even with unprecedented rates of prison and jail construction, there is simply not enough space to lock up all the new criminals. In addition, the rising costs of imprisonment have made it fiscally impossible for many jurisdictions to house their inmates. The result: more than 4.1 million adults are under the supervision of state and federal probation organizations—a figure that has grown at an annual rate of 2.5 percent over the past decade.[2]

In this chapter, we will discuss the strengths and weaknesses of probation and other community sanctions such as intensive probation, fines, boot camps, elec-

Criminal Justice ⚖ Now™

Maximize your study time by using ThomsonNOW's Personalized Study plan to help you review this chapter and prepare for examination. The Study Plan will

- Help you identify areas on which you should concentrate
- Provide interactive exercises to help you master the chapter concepts; and
- Provide a post-test to confirm you are ready to move on to the next chapter information.

tronic monitoring, and home confinement. Given the scarcity of prison resources, decisions made today concerning community-based punishment will affect the criminal justice system for decades to come.

The Justification for Community Corrections

In the court of popular opinion, retribution and crime control take precedence over community-based correctional programs. America, says University of Minnesota law professor Michael Tonry, is preoccupied with the "absolute severity of punishment" and the "widespread view that only imprisonment counts."[3] Mandatory sentencing guidelines and "three-strikes" laws are theoretically opposed to community-based corrections.[4] To a certain degree, correctional programs that are administered in the community are considered a less severe, and therefore less worthy, alternative to imprisonment.

REINTEGRATION

Supporters of probation and intermediate sanctions reject such views as not only shortsighted, but also contradictory to the aims of the corrections system. A very small percentage of all convicted offenders have committed crimes that warrant capital punishment or life imprisonment. Most, at some point, will return to the community. Consequently, according to one group of experts, the task of the corrections system

> includes building or rebuilding solid ties between the offender and the community, integrating or reintegrating the offender into community life—restoring family ties, obtaining employment and an education, securing in the larger sense a place for the offender in the routine functioning of society.[5]

Considering that some studies have shown higher recidivism rates for offenders who are subjected to prison culture, a frequent justification of community-based corrections is that they help to reintegrate the offender into society.

Reintegration has a strong theoretical basis in rehabilitative theories of punishment. An offender is generally considered to be "rehabilitated" when he or she no longer represents a threat to other members of the community and therefore is believed to be fit to live in that community. In the context of this chapter and the two that follow, it will also be helpful to see reintegration as a process through which corrections officials such as probation and parole officers provide the offender with incentives to follow the rules of society. These incentives can be positive, such as enrolling the offender in a drug treatment program. They can also be negative—in particular, the threat of return to prison or jail for failure to comply. In all instances, corrections system professionals must carefully balance the needs of the individual offender against the rights of law-abiding members of the community.

DIVERSION

Another justification for community-based corrections, based on practical considerations, is **diversion.** As you are already aware, most criminal offenses fall into the category of "petty," and it is practically impossible, as well as unnecessary, to imprison every offender for every offense. Community-based corrections are an important means of diverting criminals to alternative modes of punishment so that scarce incarceration resources are consumed by only the most dangerous criminals. In his "strainer" analogy, corrections expert Paul H. Hahn likens this process to the workings of a kitchen strainer. With each "shake" of the corrections "strainer," the less serious offenders are diverted from incarceration. At the end, only the most serious convicts remain to be sent to prison.[6] (The concept of diversion is closely linked to that of selective incapacitation, mentioned in Chapter 11.)

⊘ The **Sentencing Project** is a nonprofit organization that promotes reduced reliance on incarceration and alternative forms of sentencing. To visit its Web site, click on Web Links under Chapter Resources at **www.cjinaction.com**.

Reintegration A goal of corrections that focuses on preparing the offender for a return to the community unmarred by further criminal behavior.

Diversion In the context of corrections, a strategy to divert those offenders who qualify away from prison and jail and toward community-based and intermediate sanctions.

▲ A juvenile prostitute solicits business near MacArthur Park in Los Angeles. Several California police departments have organized task forces designed to identify and help young sex workers change their lifestyles rather than simply putting them in jail. How might society benefit from counseling "sexually exploited children" as they are called by many social workers, rather than punishing them?

The diversionary role of community-based punishments has become more pronounced as prisons and jails have filled up over the past three decades. In fact, probationers now account for nearly two-thirds of all adults in the American corrections systems (see Figure 12.1). According to the U.S. Department of Justice, on any single day, nearly 2 percent of all adult citizens are under probation supervision.[7]

THE "LOW-COST ALTERNATIVE"

Not all of the recent expansion of community corrections can be attributed to acceptance of its theoretical underpinnings. Many politicians and criminal justice officials who do not look favorably on ideas such as reintegration and diversion have embraced programs to keep nonviolent offenders out of prison. The reason is simple: money. The cost of constructing and maintaining prisons and jails, as well as housing and caring for inmates, has placed a great deal of pressure on corrections budgets across the country. Since 2000, thirty-one states have taken significant steps to cut or shift these costs by such measures as reducing staff, closing facilities, and eliminating educational and treatment programs.[8]

Community corrections offer an enticing financial alternative to imprisonment. In the federal corrections system, for example, the annual cost of incarcerating an inmate is just over $23,000, compared to about $3,500 for a year of probation.[9] Governments can also recoup the expenses associated with community-based punishments from the convicts themselves. Oklahoma offenders sentenced to electronic monitoring must pay a monthly fee of $300 for the equipment, while Tennessee charges probationers $45 per month to defray the costs of their own supervision.[10] Washington State collects approximately $25 million in such fees each year.[11] (We will examine one state's efforts to save by keeping offenders on the streets in the *Criminal Justice in Action* feature at the end of this chapter.)

Self Check Fill in the Blanks

The three basic justifications for community corrections are: (1) _____, which focuses on building or rebuilding the offender's ties with the community; (2) _____, a strategy that attempts to allocate scarce jail and prison space to only the most dangerous of criminals; and (3) _____ considerations, as community corrections are generally _____ expensive than incarceration. Check your answers on page 407.

Probation A criminal sanction in which a convict is allowed to remain in the community rather than be imprisoned as long as she or he follows certain conditions set by the court.

Probation: Doing Time in the Community

As ■ Figure 12.1 shows, **probation** is the most common form of punishment in the United States. Although it is administered differently in various jurisdictions, probation can be generally defined as the legal status of an offender who, after being convicted of a crime, has been directed by the sentencing court to remain in the community under the supervision of a probation service for a designated period of time and subject to certain conditions imposed by the court or by law.[12]

The theory behind probation is that certain offenders, having been found guilty of a crime, can be more economically and humanely treated by placing them under controls while still allowing them to live in the community. One of the advantages of probation has been that it provides for the rehabilitation of the offender while saving society the costs of incarceration. Despite probation's widespread use, certain participants in the criminal justice system question its ability to reach its rehabilitative goals. Critics point to the immense number of probationers and the fact that many of them are violent felons as evidence that the system is "out of control." Supporters contend that nothing is wrong with probation in principle, but admit that its execution must be adjusted to meet the goals of modern corrections.[13]

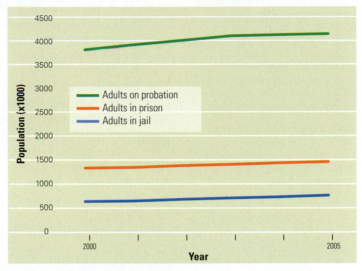

■ **Figure 12.1** **Probation in American Corrections**

As you can see, the number of Americans on probation is considerably larger than the country's prison and jail populations.

Source: Bureau of Justice Statistics, *Probation and Parole in the United States, 2005* (Washington, D.C.: U.S. Department of Justice, November 2006), 1.

THE ROOTS OF PROBATION

In its earliest forms, probation was based on a desire to inject leniency into an often harsh criminal justice system. Nineteenth-century English judges had the power to issue **judicial reprieves,** or to suspend sentences for a certain amount of time, on the condition of continued good behavior on the part of the defendant. This practice was adopted in the United States, albeit in a different form. American judges used their reprieve power to suspend the imposition of a penalty indefinitely, so long as the offender did not commit a second crime. If another crime was committed, the offender could be punished for both crimes.

In *Ex parte United States* (1916),[14] the United States Supreme Court ruled that such indefinite reprieves were unconstitutional because they limited the ability of the legislative and administrative branches to make and enforce sentencing laws. With this diversion option removed, judges increasingly turned to the model of probation first established in Massachusetts eighty years earlier.

John Augustus and the Origins of Probation The roots of probation can be directly traced to a Boston shoemaker named John Augustus. In 1841, Augustus, a religious person with considerable wealth, offered to post bail for a man charged with drunkenness. Augustus persuaded the judge to defer sentencing for three weeks, during which time the offender would be in his custody. At the end of this probationary period, the offender was able to convince the judge that he had been reformed and received a fine instead of incarceration.

During the next eighteen years until his death, Augustus bailed out and supervised nearly 1,800 persons in lieu of confinement in the Boston House of Corrections. He carefully screened potential probationers, researching their personal backgrounds before deciding whether to include them in his caseload. Generally, Augustus accepted only first offenders of otherwise good character. During the probationary period, he helped his charges find employment and lodging and aided them in obtaining an education.[15] Augustus can be credited with nearly every aspect of modern probation, from the name itself (from the Latin term *probatio*, or a "period of governing or trial"), to presentence investigations, to supervision, to revocation.

Judicial Reprieve Temporary relief or the postponement of a sentence on the authority of a judge. In the United States, the judicial power to offer a reprieve has been limited by the Supreme Court.

Augustus's work was continued by a group of volunteer "probation officers" who strived to rescue youths from the dangers of imprisonment. In 1869, the state of Massachusetts passed a law that allowed for probation of juveniles and, nine years later, provided for paid probation officers to be hired by Boston's criminal courts. The law limited probation to "such persons as may reasonably be expected to be reformed without punishment." By 1891, Massachusetts had established the first statewide probation program.[16]

The Evolution of Probation Even as probation systems have been adopted in each of the fifty states and the federal government, the basic conflict between "help" and "punishment" has dominated the context of probation. When both **L02** criminal justice practitioners and the public hold the rehabilitative model in favor, as was the case for most of the first half of the twentieth century, probation is generally considered a valuable aspect of treatment. When, however, retributive goals come to the fore, probation is seen as being in need of reform, as has been the case in the United States since the mid-1970s. (It should be noted, though, that the number of Americans on probation has continued to grow even as its theoretical underpinnings are being challenged.)

SENTENCING CHOICES AND PROBATION

Probation is basically an "arrangement" between sentencing authorities and the offender. In traditional probation, the offender agrees to comply with certain terms for a specified amount of time in return for serving the sentence in the community. One of the primary benefits for the offender, besides not getting sent to a correctional facility, is that the length of the probationary period is usually considerably shorter than the length of a prison term (see ■ Figure 12.2).

The "traditional" form of probation is not, however, the only arrangement that **L03** can be made. A judge can forgo probation altogether by handing down a **suspended sentence.** A descendant of the judicial reprieve discussed earlier, a suspended sentence places no conditions or supervision on the offender. He or she remains free for a certain length of time, but the judge keeps the option of revoking the suspended sentence and remanding the offender to prison or jail if circumstances call for such action.

■ Figure 12.2 *Average Length of Sentence: Prison versus Probation*

As you can see, the average probation sentence is much shorter than the average prison sentence for most crimes.

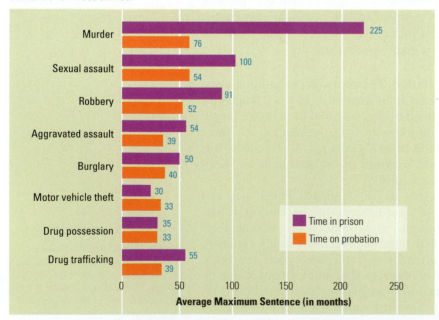

Source: Bureau of Justice Statistics, *Felony Sentences in State Courts, 2002* (Washington, D.C.: U.S. Department of Justice, December 2004), 4.

Alternative Sentencing Arrangements Judges can also combine probation with incarceration. Such sentencing arrangements include:

- *Split sentences.* In **split sentence probation,** also known as *shock probation,* the offender is sentenced to a specific amount of time in prison or jail, to be followed by a period of probation.
- *Shock incarceration.* In this arrangement, an offender is sentenced to prison or jail with the understanding that after a period of time, she or he may petition the court to be released on probation. Shock incarceration is discussed more fully later in the chapter.
- *Intermittent incarceration.* With intermittent incarceration, the offender spends a certain amount of

time each week, usually during the weekend, in a jail, workhouse, or other government institution.

Split sentences have become increasingly popular with judges, as they combine the "treatment" aspects of probation with the "punishment" aspects of incarceration. According to the Department of Justice, nearly 30 percent of all convicted felons receive split sentences.[17]

Eligibility for Probation Not every offender is eligible for probation. In Bell County, Texas, for example, juries can recommend probation only for assessed prison sentences of ten years or less. Generally, research has shown that offenders are most likely to be denied probation if they:

* Are convicted on multiple charges.
* Were on probation or parole at the time of the arrest.
* Have two or more prior convictions.
* Are addicted to narcotics.
* Seriously injured the victim of the crime.
* Used a weapon during the commission of the crime.[18]

Half of all probationers have been found guilty of a misdemeanor, and half have been found guilty of a felony.[19] As might be expected, the chances of a felon being sentenced to probation are highly dependent on the seriousness of the crime he or she has committed. Two out of every three felons on probation have been convicted of a property crime or a drug offense.[20]

CONDITIONS OF PROBATION

As part of the decision to sentence an offender to probation, a judge may also set conditions of probation. These conditions represent a "contract" between the judge and the offender, in which the latter agrees that if she or he does not follow certain rules, probation may be revoked (see ■ Figure 12.3). The probation officer usually recommends the conditions of probation, but judges also have the power to set any terms they believe to be necessary.

Principles of Probation This power is far-reaching, and a judge's personal philosophy is often reflected in the probation conditions that are set. In *In re Quirk* (1998),[21] for example, the Louisiana Supreme Court upheld the ability of a trial judge to impose church attendance as a condition of probation. Though judges have a great deal of discretion in setting the conditions of probation, they do operate under several guiding principles. First, the conditions must be related to the dual purposes of probation, which most federal and state courts define as

■ **Figure 12.3** Conditions of Probation

UNITED STATES DISTRICT COURT
FOR THE
DISTRICT OF COLUMBIA

To: _____ No. 84-417

Address: 1440 N St., N.W., #10, Wash., D.C.

In accordance with authority conferred by the United States Probation Law, you have been placed on probation this date, January 25, 2008 for a period of one year by the Hon. Louis F. Oberdorfer United States District Judge, sitting in and for this District Court at Washington, D.C.

CONDITIONS OF PROBATION

It is the order of the Court that you shall comply with the following conditions of probation:

(1) You shall refrain from violation of any law (federal, state, and local). You shall get in touch immediately with your probation officer if arrested or questioned by a law enforcement officer.

(2) You shall associate only with law-abiding persons and maintain reasonable hours.

(3) You shall work regularly at a lawful occupation and support your legal dependents, if any, to the best of your ability. When out of work you shall notify your probation officer at once. You shall consult him prior to job changes.

(4) You shall not leave the judicial district without permission of the probation officer.

(5) You shall notify your probation officer immediately of any change in your place of residence.

(6) You shall follow the probation officer's instructions.

(7) You shall report to the probation officer as directed.

(8) You shall not possess a firearm (handgun or rifle) for any reason.

The special conditions ordered by the Court are as follows:
Imposition of sentence suspended, one year probation, Fine of $75 on each count.

I understand that the Court may change the conditions of probation, reduce or extend the period of probation, and at any time during the probation period or within the maximum probation period of 5 years permitted by law, may issue a warrant and revoke probation for a violation occurring during the probation period.

I have read or had read to me the above conditions of probation. I fully understand them and I will abide by them.

_____ Date _____
Probationer

You will report as follows: _____ as directed by your Probation Officer

_____ Date _____
U.S. Probation Officer

(1) the rehabilitation of the probationer and (2) the protection of the community. Second, the conditions must not violate the U.S. Constitution; that is, probationers are generally entitled to the same constitutional rights as other prisoners.[22]

Of course, probationers do give up certain constitutional rights when they consent to the terms of probation; most probationers, for example, agree to spot checks of their homes for contraband such as drugs or weapons, and they therefore have a diminished expectation of privacy. In *United States v. Knights* (2001),[23] the United States Supreme Court upheld the actions of deputy sheriffs in Napa County, California, who searched a probationer's home without a warrant or probable cause. The unanimous decision was based on the premise that because those on probation are more likely to commit crimes, law enforcement agents "may therefore justifiably focus on probationers in a way that [they do] not on the ordinary citizen."[24]

Types of Conditions Obviously, probationers who break the law are very likely to have their probation revoked. Other, less serious infractions may also result in revocation. The conditions placed on a probationer fall into three general categories:

⊘ See the **Corrections Connection** for information on the corrections industry, including community corrections. Find its Web site by clicking on *Web Links* under *Chapter Resources* at **www.cjinaction.com**.

- *Standard conditions,* which are imposed on all probationers. These include reporting regularly to the probation officer, notifying the agency of any change of address, not leaving the jurisdiction without permission, and remaining employed.
- *Punitive conditions,* which usually reflect the seriousness of the offense and are intended to increase the punishment of the offender. Such **L05** conditions include fines, community service, restitution, drug testing, and home confinement (discussed later).
- *Treatment conditions,* which are imposed to reverse patterns of self-destructive behavior. Data show that more than 40 percent of probationers were required to undergo drug or alcohol treatment as part of their sentences, and an additional 18 percent were ordered to seek other kinds of treatment such as anger-control therapy.[25]

Some observers feel that judges have too much discretion in imposing overly restrictive conditions that no person, much less one who has exhibited antisocial tendencies, could meet. Citing prohibitions on drinking liquor, gambling, and associating with "undesirables," as well as requirements such as meeting early curfews, the late University of Delaware professor Carl B. Klockars claimed that if probation rules were taken seriously, "very few probationers would complete their terms without violation."[26] As more than eight out of ten federal probationers do complete their terms successfully, Klockars's statement suggests that either probation officers are unable to determine that violations are taking place, or many of them are exercising a great deal of discretion in reporting minor probation violations. Perhaps, the officers realize that violating probationers for every single "slip-up" is unrealistic and would add to the already significant problem of jail and prison overcrowding.

THE SUPERVISORY ROLE OF THE PROBATION OFFICER

The probation officer has two basic roles. The first is investigative and consists of conducting the presentence investigation (PSI), which was discussed in Chapter 11. The second is supervisory and begins as soon as the offender has been sentenced to probation. In smaller probation agencies, individual officers perform both tasks. In larger jurisdictions, the trend has been toward separating the responsibilities, with *investigating officers* handling the PSI and *line officers* concentrating on supervision.

Supervisory policies vary and are often a reflection of whether the authority to administer probation services is *decentralized* (under local, judicial control) or *centralized* (under state, administrative control). In any circumstance, however, certain basic principles of supervision apply. Starting with a preliminary interview, the probation officer establishes a relationship with the offender. This relationship is based on the mutual goal of both parties: the successful completion of the probationary period. Just because the line officer and the offender have the same goal, however, does not mean that probation is necessarily marked by excessive cooperation.

The Use of Authority The ideal probation officer–offender relationship is based on trust. In reality, this trust does not often exist. Any incentive an offender might have to be completely truthful with a line officer is marred by one simple fact: self-reported wrongdoing can be used to revoke probation. Even probation officers whose primary mission is to rehabilitate are under institutional pressure to punish their clients for violating conditions of probation. One officer deals with this situation by telling his clients

> that I'm here to help them, to get them a job, and whatever else I can do. But I tell them too that I have a family to support and that if they get too far off track, I can't afford to put my job on the line for them. I'm going to have to violate them.[27]

In the absence of trust, most probation officers rely on their **authority** to guide an offender successfully through the sentence. An officer's authority, or ability to influence a person's actions without resorting to force, is based not only on her or his power to revoke probation, but also on a number of lesser sanctions. For example, if a probationer fails to attend a required alcohol treatment program, the officer can place him or her in a "lockup," or detention center, overnight. To be successful, a probation officer must establish this authority early in the relationship; it is the primary tool in persuading the probationer to behave in a manner acceptable to the community.[28]

The Offender's Perspective The public perception of probationers is that they are lucky not to be in prison or jail and should be grateful for receiving a "second chance." Although they may not describe their situation in that way, many probationers are willing to comply with the terms of their sentences, if for no other reason than to avoid any further punishments. Such offenders can make a line officer's supervision duties relatively simple.

By the same token, as we discussed in Chapter 2, criminal behavior is often predicated on a lack of respect for authority. This attitude is often incompatible with the supervisory aspects of probation. The average probationer will have eighteen "face-to-face" meetings with her or his probation officer each year. Those under more restrictive probation contracts may see their supervising officers as many as eighty times a year.[29] Furthermore, to follow the conditions of probation, convicts may have to discontinue activities that they find enjoyable, such as going to a bar for a drink on Saturday night. Consequently, some probationers consider supervision as akin to "baby-sitting" and resist the strict controls placed on them by the government.

The Changing Environment of the Probation Officer To some extent, today's probation officers function similarly to John Augustus's volunteers. They spend a great deal of time in the community, working with businesses, churches, schools, and neighborhood groups on behalf of their charges.

▼ Juvenile Court Probation Officer Michael J. Manteria, left, consults with a probationer at the Hampden County Hall of Justice in Springfield, Massachusetts. The ideal probation officer–probationer relationship is based on trust, but often probation officers must rely on their authority to do their jobs correctly. Why is trust often so difficult to achieve between probation officers and offenders?

AP Photo/Springfield Union-News, Michael Gordon

Courtesy Scott T. Ballock

As a federal probation officer, I work for the United States District Court in the District of Nevada (Las Vegas office). U.S. probation officers serve as officers of the court and as agents of the U.S. Parole Commission. We are responsible for the supervision of all persons conditionally released to the community by the courts, the Parole Commission, the Federal Bureau of Prisons, and military authorities. Being released "conditionally" to the community means that in exchange for allowing an offender to remain in the community, the court expects him or her to meet certain standards and goals. These include remaining law abiding and drug free, working, supporting family members, repaying victims, perhaps performing volunteer work for the community, and making other improvements in his or her life.

Supervising offenders in the community, our mission is to execute the court's sentence, control risk, and promote law-abiding behavior. In order to meet these goals, probation officers must become very knowledgeable about an offender's activities and lifestyle. We do so by meeting with him or her on a regular basis in the community, conducting unannounced home inspections, speaking regularly with his or her family, friends, neighbors, and employers, and—when necessary—conducting surveillance or warrantless searches of his or her home and vehicle.

THE ROLE OF THE PROBATION OFFICER I am often asked whether probation officers are law enforcement officers or social workers. We are both. Responsible for protecting the public,

Nevertheless, the profession has seen considerable changes over the past three decades. As noted earlier, probation is being offered to more offenders with violent criminal histories than in the past. Inevitably, this has changed the job description of the probation officer, who must increasingly act as a law enforcement agent rather than concentrating on the rehabilitation of clients. Probation officers now conduct surveillance and search and seizure operations, administer drug tests, and accompany police officers on high-risk law enforcement assignments. Consequently, the work has become more dangerous. According to the National Institute of Corrections, more than half of the probation officers who directly supervise wrongdoers have been victims of a "hazardous incident" that endangered their safety.[30]

As a result, many probation officers are seeking permission to carry guns on the job. Several years ago, for example, the Arizona Probation Officer Association convinced state authorities that probation officers should be able to wield firearms if they so desire. Making a similar argument, Los Angeles probation officer Janis Jones said, "We're not in the '70s anymore. We're not dealing with little dope dealers on the corner selling nickel bags of marijuana." Jones, whose unit collects about a dozen guns a week, added, "These guys are into hard-core, heavy firepower to protect their interests. You feel totally vulnerable [without a gun]."[31] In the federal probation system, eighty-five of the ninety-four federal judicial districts permit their probation officers to carry firearms after receiving proper training, as do thirty-four states.

REVOCATION OF PROBATION

Technical Violation An action taken by a probationer that, although not criminal, breaks the terms of probation as designated by the court; can result in the revocation of probation and a return to prison or jail.

The probation period can end in one of two ways. Either the probationer successfully fulfills the conditions of the sentence, or the probationer misbehaves and probation is revoked, resulting in a prison or jail term. The decision of whether to revoke after a **technical violation**—such as failing to report a change of address or testing positive for drug use—is often a "judgment call" by the probation officer and therefore the focus of controversy.

we are also charged with promoting positive change among our probationers and parolees. Half of our day may be spent following an offender through the city to learn if he is engaged in illegal activities, while the second half is spent counseling offenders, helping them prepare résumés, or referring them to local social-service agencies for further assistance. Our dual role is an especially challenging aspect of the job.

Fortunately, we have the guidance of our boss, the sentencing judge. I used to think that justice was dispensed routinely and methodically with little consideration given to the impact of a sentence. Having worked for several judges, however, I have learned that sentences are carefully crafted and well thought out. Probation officers and judges are genuinely concerned about the welfare of the people who appear before them. If offenders have a substance abuse problem, they'll be offered treatment. If they are lacking in job skills, a judge may order successful completion of a vocational training program.

A HELPING HAND We recognize that a prison sentence is a very costly proposition, to both the offender and the community. A decision to send or return a person to a prison setting is a serious matter, and great lengths are taken to first effect positive change. I think even those we supervise come to realize this. It's not infrequent that a person I've spent months trying to help, and who ultimately fails and is sent back to prison, extends his hand to thank me for trying—even as he's being led away by the U.S. marshals.

Go to the **Careers in Criminal Justice Interactive CD** for more profiles in the field of criminal justice.

Revocation Trends In the past, a technical violation almost always led to revocation. Today, many probation officers will take that step only if they believe the technical violation in question represents a danger to the community. At the same time, the public's more punitive attitude, along with improved drug-testing methods, has increased the number of conditions imposed on probationers and, consequently, the odds that they will violate one of those conditions.

In the 1980s and 1990s, to a certain extent, these two trends negated each other: between 1987 and 1996, there was almost no change in the percentage (between 75 and 80 percent) of offenders who successfully completed their probation terms.[32] In the past few years, however, this rate has dropped. In 2005, only 59 percent of probationers completed their terms without revocation.[33]

The Revocation Process As we have seen, probationers do not always enjoy the same protections under the U.S. Constitution as other members of society. The United States Supreme Court has not stripped these offenders of all rights, however. In *Mempa v. Rhay* (1967),[34] the Court ruled that probationers were entitled to an attorney during the revocation process. Then, in *Morrissey v. Brewer* (1972) and *Gagnon v. Scarpelli* (1973),[35] the Court established a three-stage procedure by which the "limited" due process rights of probationers must be protected in potential revocation situations:

- *The preliminary hearing.* In this appearance before a "disinterested person" (often a judge), the facts of the violation or arrest are presented, and it is determined whether probable cause for revoking probation exists. This hearing can be waived by the probationer.
- *The revocation hearing.* During this hearing, the probation agency presents evidence to support its claim of violation, and the probationer can attempt to refute this evidence. The probationer has the right to know the charges being brought against him or her. Furthermore, probationers can testify on their own behalf and present witnesses in their favor, as well as confront and cross-examine adverse witnesses. A "neutral and detached" body must hear the evidence and rule in favor of the probation agency or the offender.

• *Revocation sentencing.* If the presiding body rules against the probationer, then the judge must decide whether to impose incarceration and for what length of time. In a revocation hearing dealing with technical violations, the judge will often reimpose probation with stricter terms or intermediate sanctions.

In effect, this is a "bare-bones" approach to due process. Most of the rules of evidence that govern regular trials do not play a role in revocation hearings. Probation officers are not, for example, required to read offenders their *Miranda* rights before questioning them about crimes they may have committed during probation. In *Minnesota v. Murphy* (1984),[36] the Supreme Court ruled that a meeting between probation officer and client does not equal custody and, therefore, the Fifth Amendment protection against self-incrimination does not apply.

"I try to get in the field two to three nights a week to see my offenders. It's really the only way to stop trouble before it happens. Otherwise, it's a free-for-all."

—Kevin Dudley, Salt Lake City probation officer

▼ In the spring of 2007, socialite Paris Hilton, shown here arriving at a Los Angeles courtroom, was sentenced to 45 days in jail for violating the conditions of her probation. Hilton, who had received a sentence of thirty-six months' probation in January 2007 for an alcohol-related reckless driving charge, subsequently failed to attend a court-ordered alcohol education program and was twice pulled over for driving with a suspended license. Why is it sometimes necessary to incarcerate probation violators?

AP Photo/Dan Steinberg

DOES PROBATION WORK?

To address the question of whether probation is effective, one must first establish its purpose. Should the probation system be designed to rehabilitate offenders? Is it primarily a method of surveillance and control? Should probation's role in the criminal justice system be to reduce pressure on prison and jail populations? Each of these aspects of probation has its supporters and critics. Indeed, the only consensus among supporters of probation is that the system is severely underfunded. As many states face growing corrections budgets, spending for probation agencies has at best remained stagnant and, in many instances, has been reduced despite increasing probation populations.

The Caseload Dilemma As a result of these financial constraints, say observers, many, if not most, probation officers face the problem of excessive *caseloads.*[37] A **caseload** is the number of clients a probation officer is responsible for at any one time. Though data vary from state to state, Professor Joan Petersilia of the University of California at Irvine estimates that, on average, a probation officer in the United States has a caseload of 175 offenders.[38] Some cities report as many as 1,000 cases per officer.[39]

Heavy probation caseloads seem inevitable: unlike a prison cell, a probation officer can always take "just one more" client." Furthermore, the ideal caseload size is very difficult to determine because different offenders require different levels of supervision. The consequences of unbalanced probation officer–probationer ratios are self-evident, however. When burdened with large caseloads, probation officers find it practically impossible to rigorously enforce the conditions imposed on their clients. Lack of surveillance leads to lack of control, which can undermine the very basis of a probationary system. Several years ago, for example, Dallas County (Texas) probation officers—struggling with high caseloads—"lost track" of more than 10,000 probationers, half of whom had committed felonies.[40]

Risk Assessment Management Many reformers reject the notion that large caseloads are to blame for the inadequacies of the supervision system. These critics believe that probation agencies have failed to direct their limited resources efficiently. In other words, they have failed to devote more supervisory controls to the relatively small percentage of offenders who run the highest risk of recidivism and pose the greatest threat to the community.

In 1981, the National Institute of Corrections developed a "model system" of case management to address these concerns. Based on the notion that some offenders require more attention than others, the model provides probation officers with statistical methods—based on the type of crime committed—to identify these offenders.[41] Within a decade, nearly every probation system in the nation was using similar classification devices to determine the level of supervision based on *risk assessment*.[42]

Basically, risk assessment management strategies determine the offender's threat to the community and the level of supervision required to lessen that threat.[43] In doing so, the probation officer or other officer of the court considers several factors, such as the offender's record of committing violent crimes; previous performance in probation, parole, or other community-based corrections programs; previous experience in jail or prison; and substance abuse or anger-management problems. (See ■ Figure 12.4 for two factors that have proved helpful.) In general, those offenders who are believed to pose the greatest threat to the community are labeled "maximum" risk and subjected to the highest level of supervision. Offenders who have not committed violent crimes or are deemed "medium" or "minimum" risks for other reasons are subjected to less supervision, thus freeing probation officers to deal with their most dangerous clients. This risk assessment model has two benefits: (1) in keeping with "just deserts," those who have committed more serious crimes are subject to more restrictive probationary terms, and (2) it prioritizes community protection.

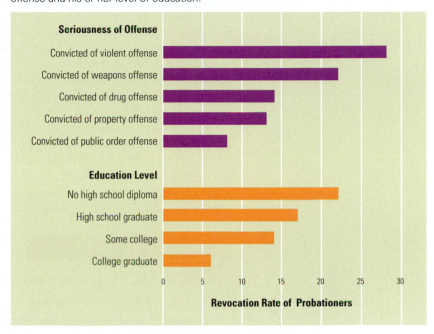

■ **Figure 12.4** Risk Factors for Probation Revocation

Risk assessment management strategies require corrections officials to allocate scarce resources to those probationers who have the greatest chance of revocation. As this figure shows, two helpful indicators are the seriousness of the probationer's initial offense and his or her level of education.

Source: Bureau of Justice Statistics, *Compendium of Federal Justice Statistics, 2004* (Washington, D.C.: U.S. Department of Justice, September 2006), Figures 7.2 and 7.3.

Specialized Caseload Programs Taking risk assessment strategies one step further, some jurisdictions have implemented *specialized caseload programs* for those offenders with specific supervisory needs. These probationers—such as drug offenders, sex offenders, violent and habitual offenders, and mentally ill offenders—are grouped together under the control of a probation officer specially trained in their particular area of criminality. A specialized caseload program for drug offenders, for example, would combine regular urine tests, or *urinalysis*, to determine whether the probationer is "clean" with treatments such as *methadone*, which reduces cravings for heroin.[44] More than 30 percent of the probation agencies in the United States now operate specialized caseload programs.[45]

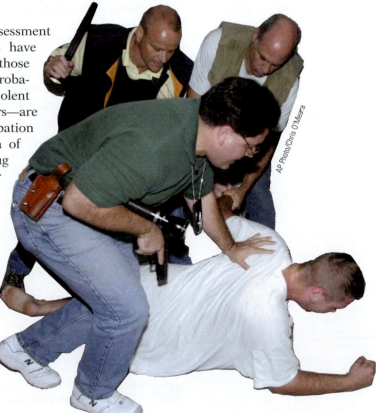

▶ Three probation officers take down a probation violator during a roundup in Tampa, Florida. When an offender violates the terms of probation, his or her status can be revoked, and he or she can be sent to jail or prison. Whether to revoke probation is often a "judgment call" by the probation officer. What might be some reasons that a probation officer would not revoke an offender's probation even though that person has committed a violation?

Recidivism and Probation The majority of probationers complete their terms without being arrested (which does not necessarily mean that they did not commit a new offense). Low rearrest rates are not surprising, given that many of those on probation are first-time, low-risk offenders. Furthermore, a controlled comparison of the recidivism rates of 511 probationers and 511 offenders released from prison found that probation can be at least as effective as incarceration, if not more so. Seventy-two percent of the prisoners were rearrested and 47 percent were imprisoned, while only 38 percent of the probationers were rearrested and 31 percent incarcerated.[46] A more recent study of drug offenders in Kansas City, Missouri, noted that those who went to prison were 2.3 times more likely to be charged with a new offense than those on probation and 2.2 times more likely than the probationers to be sent back to a correctional facility.[47]

By the same token, there is no question that probationers do commit numerous crimes. Researchers John DiIulio, John Walters, and William Bennett contend that convicted offenders living in the community "do tremendous numbers of serious crimes, including a frightening fraction of all murders."[48] They found that, in one year, probation violators were convicted of nearly 6,500 homicides, more than 7,000 rapes, about 10,000 assaults, and 17,000 robberies.[49]

Self Check Fill in the Blanks

Offenders sentenced to probation serve their sentence in the _____ under the supervision of a _____. If a probationer commits a _____ by failing to follow the _____ of his or her probation, it may be revoked. If revocation occurs, the offender will be sent to _____. Check your answers on page 407.

Intermediate Sanctions

Many observers feel that the most widely used sentencing options—imprisonment and probation—fail to reflect the immense diversity of crimes and criminals. **Intermediate sanctions** provide a number of additional sentencing options for those wrongdoers who require stricter supervision than that supplied by probation, but for whom imprisonment would be unduly harsh and counterproductive.[50] The intermediate sanctions discussed in this section are designed to match the specific punishment and treatment of an individual offender with a corrections program that reflects that offender's situation.

Dozens of different variations of intermediate sanctions are handed down each year. To cover the spectrum succinctly, two general categories of such sanctions will be discussed in this section: those administered primarily by the courts and those administered primarily by probation departments, including day reporting centers, intensive supervision probation, shock incarceration, and home confinement. Remember that none of these sanctions are exclusive; they are often combined with imprisonment and probation, and with each other.

JUDICIALLY ADMINISTERED INTERMEDIATE SANCTIONS

The lack of sentencing options is most frustrating for the person who, in the majority of cases, does the sentencing: the judge. Consequently, when judges are given the discretion to "color" a punishment with intermediate sanctions, they will often do so. Besides imprisonment and probation (and, to a lesser extent, other intermediate sanctions), a judge has five sentencing options:

L08
1. Fines
2. Community service

Intermediate Sanctions
Sanctions that are more restrictive than probation and less restrictive than imprisonment. Intended to alleviate pressure on overcrowded corrections facilities and understaffed probation departments.

3. Restitution
4. Forfeiture
5. Pretrial diversion programs

Fines, community service, and restitution were discussed in Chapter 11. In the context of intermediate sanctions, it is important to remember that these punishments are generally combined with incarceration or probation. For that reason, some critics feel the retributive or deterrent impact of such punishments is severely limited. Many European countries, in contrast, rely heavily on fines as the sole sanctions for a variety of crimes. (See *International CJ—Swedish Day-Fines* on the next page.)

▲ Two gang members perform their court-ordered community service under the watchful eye of a supervisor. Community service is one of a number of intermediate sanctions used to punish offenders instead of probation or incarceration. Why might corrections officials support the increased use of intermediate sanctions?

Forfeiture In 1970, Congress passed the Racketeer Influenced and Corrupt Organizations Act (RICO) in an attempt to prevent the use of legitimate business enterprises as shields for organized crime.[51] As amended, RICO and other statutes give judges the ability to implement forfeiture proceedings in certain criminal cases. **Forfeiture** is a process by which the government seizes property gained from or used in criminal activity. For example, if a person is convicted for smuggling cocaine into the United States from South America, a judge can order the seizure of not only the narcotics, but also the speedboat the offender used to deliver the drugs to a pickup point off the coast of South Florida. In *Bennis v. Michigan* (1996),[52] the Supreme Court ruled that a person's home or car could be forfeited even though the owner was unaware that it was connected to illegal activity.

Once property is forfeited, the government has several options. It can sell the property, with the proceeds going to the state and/or federal government law enforcement agencies involved in the seizure. Alternatively, the government agency can use the property directly in further crime-fighting efforts or award it to a third party, such as an informant. Forfeiture has proved highly profitable: federal law enforcement agencies impound close to $1 billion worth of contraband and property from alleged criminals each year.

Pretrial Diversion Programs Not every criminal violation requires the courtroom process. Consequently, some judges have the discretion to order an offender into a **pretrial diversion program** during the preliminary hearing. (Prosecutors can also offer an offender the opportunity to join such a program in return for reducing or dropping the initial charges.) These programs represent an "interruption" of the criminal proceedings and are generally reserved for young or first-time offenders who have been arrested on charges of illegal drug use, child or spousal abuse, or sexual misconduct. Pretrial diversion programs usually include extensive counseling, often in a treatment center. If the offender successfully follows the conditions of the program, the criminal charges are dropped.

Drug Courts With more than two thousand in operation, *drug courts* have become the fasting-growing form of pretrial diversion in the country. Though the specific procedures of drug courts vary widely from jurisdiction to jurisdiction, most follow a general pattern. Either after arrest or on conviction, the offender is given

Forfeiture The process by which the government seizes private property attached to criminal activity.

Pretrial Diversion Program An alternative to trial offered by a judge or prosecutor, in which the offender agrees to participate in a specified counseling or treatment program in return for withdrawal of the charges.

Few ideals are cherished as highly in our criminal justice system as equality. Most Americans take it for granted that individuals guilty of identical crimes should face identical punishments. From an economic perspective, however, this emphasis on equality renders our system decidedly unequal. Take two citizens, one a millionaire investment banker and the other a checkout clerk earning the minimum wage. Driving home from work one afternoon, each is caught by a traffic officer doing 80 miles per hour in a 55-mile-per-hour zone. The fine for this offense is $150. This amount, though equal for both, has different consequences: it represents mere pocket change for the investment banker, but a significant chunk out of the checkout clerk's weekly paycheck.

Restricted by a "tariff system" that sets specific amounts for specific crimes, regardless of the financial situation of the convict, American judges often refrain from using fines as a primary sanction. They either assume that poor offenders cannot afford the fine or worry that a fine will allow wealthier offenders to "buy" their way out of a punishment.

PAYING FOR CRIME

In searching for a way to make fines more effective sanctions, many reformers have seized on the concept of the "day-fine," as practiced in Sweden and several other European countries.

In this system, which was established in the 1920s and 1930s, the fine amount is linked to the monetary value of the offender's daily income. Depending on the seriousness of the crime, a Swedish wrongdoer will be sentenced to between 30 and 150 days or, as combined punishment for multiple crimes, up to 200 days. Each day, the offender is required to pay the equivalent of one-third of her or his daily discretionary income (as established by the Prosecutor General's Office) to the court. Consequently, the day-fine system not only reflects the degree of the crime, but ensures that the economic burden will be equal for those with different means.

Swedish police and prosecutors can levy day-fines without court involvement. Consequently, plea bargaining is nonexistent, and more than 80 percent of all offenders are sentenced to intermediate sanctions without a trial. The remaining cases receive full trials, with an acquittal rate of only 6 percent, compared to roughly 30 percent in the United States.

FOR CRITICAL ANALYSIS

Do you think a "day-fine" system would be feasible in the United States? Why might it be difficult to implement in this country?

---

the option of entering a drug court program or continuing through the standard courtroom process. Those who choose the former come under the supervision of a judge who will oversee a mixture of treatment and sanctions designed to cure their addiction. When offenders successfully complete the program, the drug court rewards them by dropping all charges against them.

Drug courts operate on the assumption that when a criminal addict's drug use is reduced, his or her drug-fueled criminal activity will also decline. To test this assumption, researchers from the Center for Court Innovation focused on New York's drug court system, comparing postrelease behavior of participants and nonparticipants with similar backgrounds. The recidivism rate of the participants was 29 percent lower than that of their nonparticipating counterparts.[53] A larger study conducted by the National Institute of Justice produced almost identical results.[54]

DAY REPORTING CENTERS

Day Reporting Center (DRC) A community-based corrections center to which offenders report on a daily basis for purposes of treatment, education, and incapacitation.

First used in Great Britain, **day reporting centers (DRCs)** are mainly tools to reduce jail and prison overcrowding. Although the offenders are allowed to live in the community rather than jail or prison, they must spend all or part of each day at a reporting center. To a certain extent, being sentenced to a DRC is an extreme form of supervision. With offenders under a single roof, they are much more easily controlled and supervised.

DRCs are instruments of rehabilitation as well. They often feature treatment programs for drug and alcohol abusers and provide counseling for a number of psychological problems, such as depression and anger management. Many of those found guilty in the Roanoke (Virginia) Drug Court, for example, are ordered to participate in a year-long day reporting program. At the center, offenders meet with probation officers, submit to urine tests, and attend counseling and education programs, such as parenting and life-skills classes. After the year has passed, if the offender has completed the program to the satisfaction of the judge and found employment, the charges will be dropped.[55]

Given that each DRC is unique, evaluating the overall success of this particular intermediate sanction can be difficult. In the most successful DRCs, as many as 85 percent of the participants complete the program, while the least successful ones have only a 13 percent completion rate. Similarly, recidivism rates of DRC veterans range from 15 percent (in Maricopa County, Arizona) to 44 percent (in Salt Lake City, Utah).[56] In general, however, the centers appear to have a limited impact on recidivism rates unless they include strong therapeutic programs.[57] The economic benefits of these facilities are more obvious. To give one example, taxpayers pay $12 per day for an offender at the DRC in Morrow, Georgia, compared to $45 a day to house an inmate in a state prison.[58]

▲ Judges and prosecutors may, in certain cases, give offenders the chance to attend pretrial diversion programs. Offered by caregiving facilities such as the community substance abuse center pictured here, these programs provide a chance to treat the causes behind criminal behavior without sending the offender to prison or jail. Do pretrial diversion programs "punish" offenders? If not, can they be justified as part of the corrections system?

INTENSIVE SUPERVISION PROBATION

Intensive supervision probation (ISP) offers a more restrictive alternative to regular probation, with higher levels of face-to-face contact between offenders and officers, drug testing, and electronic surveillance. Different jurisdictions have different methods of determining who is eligible for ISP. In New Jersey, for example, violent offenders may not be placed in the program, while a majority of states limit ISP to those who do not have prior probation violations. The frequency of officer-client contact also varies widely.

Intensive supervision has two primary functions: (1) to *divert* offenders from overcrowded prisons or jails, and (2) to place these offenders under higher levels of *control*, as befits the risk they pose to the community. Researchers have had difficulty, however, in determining whether ISP is succeeding in these two areas. Research conducted by Norval Morris and Michael Tonry rejects the notion that ISP programs divert measurable numbers of would-be inmates from prison.[59] Furthermore, a number of studies have found that ISP clients have higher violation rates than traditional probationers, which means that the practice might well be contributing to prison and jail overcrowding.[60] One theory is that ISP "causes" these high failure rates—greater supervision increases the chances that an offender will be caught breaking conditions of probation.

In addition, as with other intermediate sanctions, the success of ISP programs seems to relate directly to the rigor with which they are carried out. In the New Jersey program, which is considered one of the most effective in the nation, ISP officers are equipped with cell phones, beepers, laptop computers, and automobiles. They have caseloads of only twenty offenders (compared to 115 for other probation officers in the state) and average thirty-one contacts with each client per month. The results have been striking: graduates of the program have only a 10 percent recidivism rate after five years, whereas two-thirds of state prisoners are rearrested within three years of release.[61] Whatever its results, ISP

L09

Intensive Supervision Probation (ISP) A punishment-oriented form of probation in which the offender is placed under stricter and more frequent surveillance and control than in conventional probation by probation officers with limited caseloads.

is viable in today's political landscape because it satisfies the public's desire for stricter controls on convicts, while providing intermediate sanctions options for judges, prosecutors, and corrections administrators.

SHOCK INCARCERATION

As the name suggests, **shock incarceration** is designed to "shock" criminals into compliance with the law. Following conviction, the offender is first sentenced to a prison or jail term. Then, usually within ninety days, he or she is released and resentenced to probation. The theory behind shock incarceration is that by getting a taste of the brutalities of the daily prison grind, the offender will be shocked into a crime-free existence.

The Value of Shock In the past, shock incarceration was targeted primarily toward youthful, first-time offenders, who were thought to be more likely to be "scared straight" by a short stint behind bars. Recent data show, however, that 10 percent of all adults sentenced to probation spend some time in jail or prison before being released into the community.[62] Critics of shock incarceration are dismayed by this trend. They argue that the practice needlessly disrupts the lives of low-level offenders who would not otherwise be eligible for incarceration and exposes them to the mental and physical hardships of prison life (which we will discuss in Chapter 14).[63] Furthermore, there is little evidence that shock probationers fare any better than regular probationers when it comes to recidivism rates.[64]

Boot Camps The *boot camp* is a variation on traditional shock incarceration. Instead of spending the "shock" period of incarceration in prison or jail, offenders are sent to a boot camp. Modeled on military basic training, these camps are generally located within prisons and jails, though some can be found in the community. The programs emphasize strict discipline, manual labor, and physical training. They are designed to instill self-responsibility and self-respect in participants, thereby lessening the chances that they will return to a life of crime. More recently, boot camps have also emphasized rehabilitation, incorporating such components as drug and alcohol treatment programs, anger-management courses, and vocational training.[65]

The first boot camp opened in Georgia in 1983. At the peak of their popularity in the mid-1990s, about 120 local, state, and federal boot camps housed more than seven thousand inmates. Around that time, however, studies began to show that the camps were not meeting their goals of improving rearrest rates while reducing prison populations and corrections budgets.[66] By 2000, nearly one-third of the boot camps had closed, and in 2005 the Federal Bureau of Prisons announced plans to discontinue its boot camp program. Because of their rehabilitative and disciplinarian features, boot camps remain popular in the juvenile corrections system, though not without controversy, as we will see in Chapter 15.

HOME CONFINEMENT AND ELECTRONIC MONITORING

Various forms of **home confinement**—in which offenders serve their sentences not in a government institution but at home—have existed for centuries. It has often served, and continues to do so, as a method of political control, used by totalitarian regimes to isolate and silence dissidents. For example, the military government of Myanmar (Burma) has confined Nobel Peace laureate Aung San Suu Kyi to her home for years at a time since she won an election for leadership of that country in 1990.

For purposes of general law enforcement, home confinement was impractical until relatively recently. After all, one could not expect offenders to "promise" to

Shock Incarceration A short period of incarceration that is designed to deter further criminal activity by "shocking" the offender with the hardships of imprisonment.

Home Confinement A community-based sanction in which offenders serve their terms of incarceration in their homes.

stay at home, and the personnel costs of guarding them were prohibitive. In the 1980s, however, with the advent of **electronic monitoring**, or using technology to "guard" the prisoner, home confinement became more viable. Today, all fifty states and the federal government have home monitoring programs with about 120,000 offenders participating at any one time.[67]

The Levels of Home Monitoring and Their Benefits Home monitoring has three general levels of restriction:

1. *Curfew,* which requires offenders to be in their homes at specific hours each day, usually at night.
2. *Home detention,* which requires that offenders remain home at all times, with exceptions being made for education, employment, counseling, or other specified activities such as the purchase of food or, in some instances, attendance at religious ceremonies.

   L010

3. *Home incarceration,* which requires the offender to remain home at all times, save for medical emergencies.

Under ideal circumstances, home confinement serves many of the goals of intermediate sanctions. It protects the community. It saves public funds and space in correctional facilities by keeping convicts out of institutional incarceration. It meets public expectations of punishment for criminals. Uniquely, home confinement also recognizes that convicts, despite their crimes, play important roles in the community, and allows them to continue in those roles. An offender, for example, may be given permission to leave confinement to care for elderly parents.

Home confinement is also lauded for giving sentencing officials the freedom to match the punishment with the needs of the offender. In Missouri, for instance, the conditions of detention for a musician required him to remain at home during the day, but allowed him to continue his career at night. In addition, he was obliged to make antidrug statements before each performance, to be verified by the manager at the club where he appeared.

Types of Electronic Monitoring According to some reports, the inspiration for electronic monitoring was a *Spiderman* comic book in which the hero was trailed by the use of an electronic device on his arm. In 1979, a New Mexico judge named Jack Love, having read the comic, convinced an executive at Honeywell, Inc., to begin developing similar technology to supervise convicts.[68]

Two major types of electronic monitoring have grown out of Love's initial concept. The first is a "programmed contact" program, in which the offender is contacted periodically by telephone or beeper to verify his or her whereabouts. Verification is obtained via a computer that uses voice or visual identification techniques or by requiring the offender to enter a code in an electronic box when called. The second is a "continuously signaling" device, worn around the convict's wrist, ankle, or neck. A transmitter in the device sends out a continuous signal to a "receiver-dialer" device located in the offender's dwelling. If the receiver device does not detect a signal from the transmitter, it informs a central computer, and the police are notified.[69]

Technological Advances in Electronic Monitoring
As electronic monitoring technology has evolved, the ability of community corrections officials to target specific forms of risky behavior has greatly increased.

Electronic Monitoring A technique of probation supervision in which the offender's whereabouts, though not his or her actions, are kept under surveillance by an electronic device; often used in conjunction with home confinement.

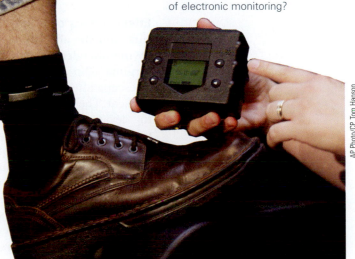

▼ Offenders who are confined to their homes are often monitored by an electronic device that fits around the ankle. A transmitter in the device sends a continuous signal to a receiver known as a personal tracking unit (PTU), also shown here. If this signal is broken—that is, the offender moves outside the range of the PTU—the police are automatically notified. What are some of the drawbacks of this form of electronic monitoring?

AP Photo/CP, Tom Hanson

WHAT IS GPS?

Global positioning system (GPS) technology is a form of tracking technology that relies on twenty-four military satellites orbiting 12,000 miles above the earth. The satellites transmit signals to each other and to a receiver on the ground, allowing a monitoring station to determine the location of the receiving device to within a few feet.

WHAT DOES GPS DO?

GPS provides a much more precise level of electronic monitoring. The offender wears a transmitter, similar to a traditional electronic monitor, around his or her ankle or wrist. This transmitter communicates with a small box called a portable tracking device (PTD), which uses the military satellites to determine the offender's movements.

GPS technology can be used either "actively," to constantly monitor the offender's whereabouts, or "passively," to ensure that the offender is within the confines of his or her limited space. Inclusion and exclusion zones are also very important to GPS supervision. Inclusion zones are areas such as

a home or workplace where the offender is expected to be at certain times. Exclusion zones are areas such as parks, playgrounds, and schools where the offender is not permitted to go. GPS-linked computers can alert officials immediately when a zone has been breached and create a record of all the offender's movements for review at a later time.

THINKING ABOUT GPS

How could GPS technology be used to ensure that a convicted sex offender complies with a judge's order to stay away from areas where large numbers of children are present?

For more information on GPS and other CJ technologies, click on *Crime and Technology* under *Book Resources* at **www.cjinaction.com.**

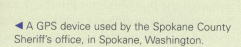

AP Photo/Jeff T. Green

◀ A GPS device used by the Spokane County Sheriff's office, in Spokane, Washington.

A Michigan court, for example, has begun placing black boxes in the automobiles of repeat traffic law violators. Not only do these boxes record information about the offenders' driving habits for review by probation officers, but they also emit a loud beep when the car goes too fast or stops too quickly. Another device—an ankle bracelet—is able to test a person's sweat for alcohol levels and transmit the results over the Internet. The advance with perhaps the greatest potential for transforming electronic monitoring is discussed in the feature *CJ and Technology—Global Positioning System (GPS).*

Effectiveness of Home Confinement As might be expected, technical problems can limit the effectiveness of an electronic monitoring device. So can tampering by the offender. In 2005, for example, a fourteen-year-old girl in Princeton, West Virginia, who was under house arrest on charges of murdering her father, managed to escape after cutting the electronic monitoring device off her ankle and gluing it on a cat. The possibility of such problems will decrease as tamper-resistant monitoring devices are perfected. One such device reacts to the application of heat, which normally loosens some transmitters, by contracting; if enough heat is applied, the offender's circulation will be cut off.[70]

Because most participants in home confinement programs are low-risk offenders, their recidivism rates are quite low. Joan Petersilia found that the majority of home confinement programs report rearrest rates of less than 5 percent.[71] The data are less supportive when measuring how many offenders broke the conditions of confinement. In Indiana, more than 40 percent of participants had at least one violation, and between one-third and one-half failed to complete the program.[72]

One concern about home confinement is that offenders are often required to defray program costs, which can be as high as $100 per week. Consequently, those who cannot afford to pay for electronic monitoring may not be eligible. Furthermore, families of offenders confined to the home can experience high levels of stress and a loss of privacy.[73] In general, however, those who successfully complete a home confinement term seem to benefit in areas such as obtaining and holding employment.[74]

Widen the Net The criticism that intermediate sanctions designed to divert offenders from prison actually increase the number of citizens who are under the control and surveillance of the American corrections system.

WIDENING THE NET

As mentioned above, most of the convicts chosen for intermediate sanctions are low-risk offenders. From the point of view of the corrections official doing the choosing, this makes sense. Such offenders are less likely to commit crimes and attract negative publicity. This selection strategy, however, appears to invalidate one of the primary reasons intermediate sanctions exist: to reduce prison and jail populations. If most of the offenders in intermediate sanctions programs would otherwise have received probation, then the effect on these populations is nullified. Indeed, studies have shown this to be the case.[75]

At the same time, such selection processes broaden the reach of the corrections system. In other words, they increase rather than decrease the amount of control the state exerts over the individual. Suppose a person is arrested for a misdemeanor such as shoplifting and, under normal circumstances, would receive probation. With access to intermediate sanctions, the judge may add a period of home confinement to the sentence. Critics contend that such practices **widen the net** of the corrections system by augmenting the number of citizens who are under the control and surveillance of the state and also *strengthen the net* by increasing the government's power to intervene in the lives of its citizens.[76] (See the feature *You Be the Judge—What's the Sentence?* to make your own decision as to how wide the net should be in a particular instance.)

You be the Judge What's the Sentence?

THE FACTS Marcus, a freshman at Florida College, wanted to join the Kappa Alpha Psi fraternity. Jason and four other fraternity brothers took twenty-seven pledges, including Marcus, to an abandoned warehouse for the initiation rites, in which the pledges were blindfolded, taunted, slapped, punched with boxing gloves, and paddled with wooden canes. The beatings left Marcus with a ruptured eardrum and a hematoma on his buttocks that required surgery. Although Marcus was a willing participant who could have left at any time, a Florida jury found Jason guilty of hazing that resulted in serious bodily injury.

THE LAW Under a new Florida law, hazing that results in serious bodily injury is a third degree felony. As such, it is punishable by penalties ranging from probation to five years in prison.

YOUR DECISION On the one hand, Jason's attorney has requested leniency, pointing out that his client has no previous record of wrongdoing and a fiancée who is four months pregnant. On the other hand, the Florida legislature passed the antihazing law after public outcry over a string of violent incidents on college campuses, including one that resulted in death. Given the range of punishment options you have learned about in the past two chapters, what is your sentence for Jason?

[To see how a Florida judge ruled in a case with similar facts, go to Example 12.1 in Appendix B.]

Self Check Fill in the Blanks

Judicially administered intermediate sanctions include fines, restitution, and _____, a process in which the government seizes property connected to illegal activity. Offenders may also be sentenced to spend part of their time at _____, where they receive treatment and are more easily _____ by corrections officials. _____, or militaristic programs designed to instill self-responsibility, are a form of _____ incarceration. Home confinement, another intermediate sanction, has become more effective in recent years thanks to technology known as _____. Check your answers on page 407.

The Paradox of Community Corrections

Stories from the Street
Go to the Stories from the Street feature at **www.cjinaction.com** to hear Larry Gaines tell insightful stories related to this chapter and his experiences in the field.

Despite their many benefits, including cost savings, treatment options, and the ability to divert hundreds of thousands of nonviolent wrongdoers from prisons and jails, community-based corrections programs suffer from a basic paradox: the more effectively offenders are controlled, the more likely they are to be caught violating the terms of their conditional release. As you may have noticed, the community supervision programs discussed in this chapter are "graded" according to rates of recidivism and revocation, with low levels of each reflecting a successful program. Increased control and surveillance, however, will necessarily raise the level of violations, thus increasing the probability that any single violation will be discovered. Therefore, as factors such as the number of conditions placed on probationers and the technological proficiency of electronic monitoring devices increase, so, too, will the number of offenders who fail to meet the conditions of their community-based punishment.

One observer calls this the "quicksand" effect of increased surveillance. Instead of helping offenders leave the corrections system, increased surveillance pulls them more deeply into it.[77] The quicksand effect can be quite strong, according to researchers Barbara Sims of Sam Houston State University and Mark Jones of East Carolina University. In a study of North Carolina corrections data, Sims and Jones found that 26 percent of the probationers whose probation terms were revoked had been guilty of violations such as failing a single drug test. The researchers believe this strategy is overly punitive—anybody who has tried to quit smoking is aware of the difficulties of breaking an addiction.[78]

CALIFORNIA'S PROPOSITION 36

The California corrections system is a mess. In fact, it is such a mess that in late 2006 Governor Arnold Schwarzenegger declared a state of emergency for the state's prisons and jails. The main culprit is overcrowding, which is so rampant that sixteen thousand inmates sleep on cots in hallways and gyms. The one bright spot, at least according to its supporters, is the Substance Abuse and Crime Prevention Act, or Proposition 36.[79] This controversial diversion program, which treats drug abuse as a medical problem rather than a criminal act, is the subject of this chapter's *Criminal Justice in Action* feature.

DIVERSION DELUXE

In 2000, an overwhelming 61 percent of California voters approved Proposition 36. The initiative led to a change in the state penal code that mandates probation and community-based treatment instead of incarceration for eligible drug offenders. The treatment program is designed to wean drug abusers off self-destructive habits. To be eligible, at the time of arrest the offender must have been in possession of the incriminating drugs for "personal use"—that is, he or she cannot be a drug "dealer."[80] Proposition 36 also excludes those with a prior conviction for a violent felony, those who are

"us[ing] a firearm" at the time of the drug arrest, and those who refuse treatment.[81]

Proposition 36 diverges from the traditional sentencing model in three important ways. First, it *prohibits* judges from sending offenders to prison or jail, severely restricting judicial control over the sentencing process. Second, it makes probation *mandatory* for a certain class of criminals. Third, it limits a judge's ability to *revoke* probation and return offenders to prison or jail as a punishment for failing to follow the terms of a community-based sentence.

AP Photo/Damian Dovarganes

The Case for Proposition 36

- In 2006, a study carried out by the University of California at Los Angeles (UCLA) found that about thirty-five thousand nonviolent drug offenders had successfully completed Proposition 36's treatment program.

- The UCLA researchers calculated that for every dollar spent on Proposition 36, the state has saved $2.50 in incarceration costs, for a total of $140.5 million

in the program's first year and $158.8 million in the second.[82]

- Another study, by the Justice Policy Institute, estimated that the number of inmates in California prisons for drug offenses has dropped by 34 percent since the law took effect.[83]

The Case against Proposition 36

- Only one in four offenders ordered into treatment managed to graduate from the program.

- A quarter of those sentenced under Proposition 36 never showed up for their initial assessment.[84]

- Nearly one-third of the offenders were arrested on drug charges within a year of starting treatment, whereas other diversion programs such as drug courts (see page 397) had much lower recidivism rates.[85]

Your Opinion—Writing Assignment

The problem with Proposition 36, according to some experts, is that it does not require accountability. As we saw earlier in this chapter, most convicts who fail to follow the conditions of their community-based sentence can be incarcerated as punishment. Some California state legislators want to reform Proposition 36 by adding a "flash incarceration" component that would allow judges to send violators caught using drugs to jail for up to ten days.

Do you think that the criminal justice system should offer more pure treatment options similar to Proposition

36 for nonviolent offenders? Or, does even the most treatment-oriented program require the threat of incarceration to protect society's best interests? Before responding, you can review our discussions in this chapter concerning

- The justifications for community corrections (pages 385–386).

- Probation revocation (pages (392–394).

- Shock incarceration (page 400).

Your answer should take at least three full paragraphs.

Chapter Summary

L01 **Explain the justifications for community-based corrections programs.** One justification involves reintegration of the offender into society. Reintegration restores family ties, encourages employment and education, and secures a place for the offender in the routine functioning of society. Another justification involves diversion; by diverting criminals to alternative modes of punishment, further overcrowding of jail and prison facilities can be avoided, as can the costs of incarcerating the offenders.

L02 **Indicate when probation started to fall out of favor, and explain why.** When both criminal justice practitioners and the public held the rehabilitative model in favor, probation was generally considered a valuable aspect of this treatment. Since about the 1950s and more seriously since the mid-1970s, retributive goals have become more important, and probation has fallen out of favor in some criminal justice circles. Nonetheless, two-thirds of those involved in the American corrections system are on probation at any given time.

L03 **Explain several alternative sentencing arrangements that combine probation with incarceration.** In addition to a suspended sentence, which is in fact a judicial reprieve, there are three general types of sentencing arrangements: (a) split sentence probation, in which the judge specifies a certain time in jail or prison followed by a certain time on probation; (b) shock incarceration, in which a judge sentences an offender to be incarcerated, but allows that person to petition the court to be released on probation; and (c) intermittent incarceration, in which an offender spends a certain amount of time each week in jail or in a halfway house or another government institution.

L04 **Specify the conditions under which an offender is most likely to be denied probation.** The offender (a) has been convicted of multiple charges, (b) was on probation or parole when arrested, (c) has two or more prior convictions, (d) is addicted to narcotics, (e) seriously injured the victim of the crime, or (f) used a weapon while committing the crime.

L05 **Describe the three general categories of conditions placed on a probationer.** (a) Standard conditions, such as requiring that the probationer notify the agency of a change of address, not leave the jurisdiction without permission, and remain employed; (b) punitive conditions, such as restitution, community service, and home confinement; and (c) treatment conditions, such as required drug or alcohol treatment.

L06 **Explain why probation officers' work has become more dangerous.** One reason is that probation is increasingly offered to felons, even those who have committed violent crimes. Additionally, because there are more guns on the streets, a probationer is more likely to be armed.

L07 **Explain the three stages of probation revocation.** (a) The preliminary hearing, which usually takes place before a judge, during which the facts of the probation violation are presented; (b) the revocation hearing, during which the claims of the violation are presented as well as any refutation by the probationer; and (c) revocation sentencing, during which a judge decides what to do with the probationer convicted of violating the terms of probation.

L08 **List the five sentencing options for a judge besides imprisonment and probation.** (a) Fines, (b) community service, (c) restitution, (d) forfeiture, and (e) pretrial diversion programs.

L09 **Contrast day reporting centers with intensive supervision probation.** In a day reporting center, the offender is allowed to remain in the community, but must spend all or part of each day at the reporting center. While at the center, offenders meet with probation officers, submit to drug tests, and attend counseling and education programs. In contrast, with intensive supervision probation (ISP), more restrictions are imposed, and there is more face-to-face contact between offenders and probation officers. ISP may also include electronic surveillance.

L010 **List the three levels of home monitoring.** (a) Curfew, which requires that the offender be at home during specified hours; (b) home detention, which requires that the offender be at home except for education, employment, and counseling; and (c) home incarceration, which requires that the offender be at home at all times except for medical emergencies.

Key Terms

Questions for Critical Analysis

1. What is the major reason that probationers account for nearly two-thirds of all adults in the American corrections system?

2. Why have many "tough on crime" politicians embraced community corrections?

3. Why did the Supreme Court rule against indefinite reprieves?

4. Why can law enforcement agents search a probationer's home without a warrant or probable cause?

5. Why do many probation officers feel that they should be allowed to carry firearms on the job?

6. What effect, if any, do large probation officer caseloads have on misconduct (technical violations and criminal acts) by probationers?

7. What happens to property that is forfeited by a convicted criminal?

8. What is the purpose of day reporting centers?

9. How might GPS-enhanced electronic monitoring ease the caseload burden of probation officers?

10. What does the term *widening the net* mean, and why is it important today?

Maximize Your Best Possible Outcome for Chapter 12

1. **Maximize Your Best Chance for Getting a Good Grade on the Exam.** ThomsonNOW Personalized Study is a diagnostic study tool containing valuable text-specific resources—and because you focus on just what you don't know, you learn more in less time to get a better grade. How do you get ThomsonNOW? If your textbook does not include an access code card, go to **thomsonedu.com** to get ThomsonNOW before your next exam!

2. **Get the Most Out of Your Textbook** by going to the book companion Web site at **www.cjinaction.com** to access one of the tutorial quizzes, use the flash cards to master key terms, and check out the many other study aids you'll find there. Under chapter resources you will also be able to access the Stories from the Street feature and Web links mentioned in the textbook.

3. **Learn about Potential Criminal Justice Careers** discussed in this chapter by exploring careers online at **www.cjinaction.com**. You will find career descriptions and information about job requirements, training, salary and benefits, and the application process. You can also watch video profiles featuring criminal justice professionals.

Notes

1. Bureau of Justice Statistics, *Probation and Parole in the United States, 2005* (Washington, D.C.: U.S. Department of Justice, November 2006), Table 3, page 6.

2. *Ibid.*, 1.

3. Michael Tonry, *Sentencing Matters* (New York: Oxford Press, 1996), 28.

4. Todd Clear and Anthony Braga, "Community Corrections," in *Crime,* ed. James Q. Wilson and Joan Petersilia (San Francisco: ICS Press, 1995), 444.

5. Corrections Task Force of the President's Commission on Law Enforcement and Administration of Justice (1967).

6. Paul H. Hahn, *Emerging Criminal Justice: Three Pillars for a Proactive Justice System* (Thousand Oaks, CA: Sage Publications, 1998), 106–108.

7. *Probation and Parole in the United States, 2005*, 5.

8. Jon Wool and Don Stemen, *Changing Fortunes or Changing Attitudes: Sentencing and Corrections Reforms in 2003* (New York: Vera Institute of Justice, March 2004), 2–3.

9. See **www.uscourts.gov/ttb/may05ttb/incarceration-costs/index. html**.

10. Wool and Stemen, 4.

11. Adam Liptak, "Debt to Society Is Least of Costs for Ex-Convicts," *New York Times* (February 23, 2006), A1.

12. Paul W. Keve, *Crime Control and Justice in America* (Chicago: American Library Association, 1995), 183.

13. Andrew R. Klein, *Alternative Sentencing, Intermediate Sanctions and Probation*, 2d ed. (Cincinnati: Anderson Publishing Co., 1997), 72.

14. 242 U.S. 27 (1916).

15. Joan Petersilia, "Probation in the United States," *Perspectives* (Spring 1998), 32–33.

16. Barry A. Krisberg and James F. Austin, "The Unmet Promise of Alternatives to Incarceration," in John Kaplan, Jerome H. Skolnick, and Malcolm M. Feeley, *Criminal Justice*, 5th ed. (Westbury, NY: The Foundation Press, 1991), 537.

17. Bureau of Justice Statistics, *State Court Sentencing of Convicted Felons, 2002* (Washington, D.C.: U.S. Department of Justice, May 2005), Table 3.2.

18. Joan Petersilia and Susan Turner, *Prison versus Probation in California: Implications for Crime and Offender Recidivism* (Santa Monica, CA: Rand Corporation, 1986).

19. *Probation and Parole in the United States, 2005*, 6.

20. *State Court Sentencing of Convicted Felons, 2002*, Table 3.6.

21. 705 So.2d 172 (La. 1997).

22. Neil P. Cohen and James J. Gobert, *The Law of Probation and Parole* (Colorado Springs, CO: Shepard's/McGraw-Hill, 1983), Section 5.01, 183–184; Section 5.03, 191–192.

23. 534 U.S. 112 (2001).

24. *Ibid.*, 113.

25. Bureau of Justice Statistics, *Substance Abuse and Treatment for Adults on Probation, 1995* (Washington, D.C.: U.S. Department of Justice, March 1998), 11.

26. Carl B. Klockars, Jr., "A Theory of Probation Supervision," *Journal of Criminal Law, Criminology, and Police Science* 63 (1972), 550–557.

27. *Ibid.*, 551.

28. Hahn, 116–118.

29. Camille Graham Camp and George M. Camp, *The Corrections Yearbook: 1999* (Middletown, CT: Criminal Justice Institute, 1999).

30. National Institute of Corrections, *New Approaches to Staff Safety* (Washington, D.C.: U.S. Department of Justice, March 2003), 16.

31. Nicholas Riccardi, "Probation Dept. Divided over Rule Prohibiting Guns," *Los Angeles Times* (January 2, 1999), B1.

32. Bureau of Justice Statistics, *Special Report, Federal Offenders under Community Supervisions, 1987–1996* (Washington, D.C.: U.S. Department of Justice, August 1998), Table 6, page 5.

33. *Probation and Parole in the United States, 2005*, 6.

34. 389 U.S. 128 (1967).

35. *Morrissey v. Brewer*, 408 U.S. 471 (1972); and *Gagnon v. Scarpelli*, 411 U.S. 778 (1973).

36. 465 U.S. 420 (1984).

37. Samuel Walker, "Too Many Sticks, Not Enough Carrots: Limits and New Opportunities in American Crime Policy," *University of Saint Thomas Law Journal* (Spring 2006), 430.

38. Joan Petersilia, "Community Corrections," in *Crime: Public Policies for Crime Control*, ed. James Q. Wilson and Joan Petersilia (Oakland, CA: ICS Press, 2002), 483–508.

39. Greg Berman, "Redefining Criminal Courts: Problem Solving and the Meaning of Justice," *American Criminal Law Review* (Summer 2004), 1313.

40. Brooks Egerton, "Losing Track of Crooks," *Dallas Morning News* (August 7, 2005), 1A.

41. James M. Byrne and Linda M. Kelly, *Restructuring Probation as an Intermediate Sanction: An Evaluation of the Massachusetts Intensive Probation Supervision Program* (Washington, D.C.: National Institute of Justice, 1989).

42. Todd R. Clear, George F. Cole, and Michael D. Reisig, *American Corrections*, 7th ed. (Belmont, CA: Thomson Wadsworth, 2006), 205.

43. James Byrne, "Why Assessment 'Matters' in an Evidence-Based Community Corrections System," *Federal Probation* (September 2006), 1.

44. Clear, Cole, and Reisig, 206–207.

45. Brian McKay, "The State of Sex Offender Supervision in Texas," *Federal Probation* (June 2002), 16–20.

46. Petersilia and Turner, vii.

47. Cassia Spohn and David Holleran, "The Effect of Imprisonment on Recidivism Rates of Felony Offenders: A Focus on Drug Offenders," *Criminology* (May 1, 2002), 329–357.

48. William J. Bennett, John J. DiIulio, and John P. Walters, *Body Count: Moral Poverty and How to Win America's War against Crime and Drugs* (New York: Simon & Schuster, 1996), 105.

49. *Ibid.*

50. Norval Morris and Michael Tonry, *Between Prison and Probation: Intermediate Punishments in a Rational Sentencing System* (Oxford, UK: Oxford University Press, 1990).

51. 18 U.S.C. Sections 1961–1968.

52. 516 U.S. 442 (1996).

53. Michael Rempel, Dana Fox-Kralstein, and Amanda Cissner, "Drug Courts: An Effective Treatment Alternative," *Criminal Justice* (Summer 2004), 34–38.

54. John Roman, Wendy Townsend, and Avinash Singh Bhati, *Recidivism Rates for Drug Court Graduates: Nationally Based Estimates, Final Report* (Washington, D.C.: Urban Institute and Caliber Associates, July 2003), 27–42.

55. Model State Drug Court Legislation Committee, *Model State Drug Court Legislation: Model Drug Offender Accountability and Treatment Act* (Alexandria, VA: National Drug Court Institute, May 2004), 42.

56. Sudipto Roy and Shannon Barton, "Convicted Drunk Drivers in Electronic Monitoring Home Detention and Day Reporting Centers: An Exploratory Study," *Federal Probation* (June 2006), 49.

57. Adele Harrell, Ojmarrh Mitchell, Alex Hirst, Douglas Marlowe, and Jeffrey Merrill, "Breaking the Cycle of Drugs and Crime: Findings from the Birmingham BTC Demonstration," *Criminology and Public Policy* (March 2002), 189–216.

58. Kathy Jefcoats, "Criminal Justice Centers: Day Reporting Site Opens," *Atlanta Journal-Constitution* (April 7, 2005), 1.

59. Norval Morris and Michael Tonry, *Between Prison and Probation: Intermediate Punishments in a Rational Sentencing System* (New York: Oxford University Press, 1990).

60. Benjamin Steiner, "Treatment Retention: A Theory of Post-Release Supervision for the Substance Abusing Offender," *Federal Probation* (December 2004), 24.

61. Kate Coscarelli, "A Model Program for Model Prisoners," *(Newark, New Jersey) Star Ledger* (February 24, 2004), 25.

62. *Probation and Parole in the United States, 2005*, Table 3, page 6.

63. Clear, Cole, and Reisig, 229.

64. Ted Palmer, "Programmatic and Nonprogrammatic Aspects of Successful Intervention: New Directions for Research," *Crime and Delinquency* (1995), 100–131.

65. Dale Parent, *Correctional Boot Camps: Lessons from a Decade of Research* (Washington, D.C.: U.S. Department of Justice, June 2003), 6.

66. *Ibid.*, 8, 11–12.

67. Margaret M. Conway, ed., "2002 Electronic Monitoring Survey," in *Journal of Offender Monitoring* (Kingston, NJ: Civic Research Institute, 2002).

68. Josh Kurtz, "New Growth in a Captive Market," *New York Times* (December 31, 1989), 12.

69. Edna Erez, Peter R. Ibarra, and Norman A. Lurie, "Electronic Monitoring of Domestic Violence Cases—A Study of Two Bilateral Programs," *Federal Probation* (June 2004), 15–20.

70. Russell Carlisle, "Electronic Monitoring as an Alternative Sentencing Tool," *Georgia State Bar Journal* 24 (1988), 132.

71. Joan Petersilia, *Expanding Options for Criminal Sentencing* (Santa Monica, CA: Rand Corporation, 1987).

72. Terry Baumer and Robert Mendelsohn, "Electronically Monitored Home Confinement: Does It Work?" in *Smart Sentencing: The Emergence of Intermediate Sanctions*, ed. James M. Byrne, Arthur Lurigio, and Joan Petersilia (Newbury Park, CA: Sage, 1992).

73. Joseph B. Vaughn, "Planning for Change: The Use of Electronic Monitoring as a Correctional Alternative," in *Intermediate Punishments: Intensive Supervision, Home Confinement, and Electronic Surveillance*, ed. Belinda R. McCarthy (Monsey, NY: Criminal Justice Press, 1987), 158.

74. Terry Baumer and Robert Mendelsohn, *The Electronic Monitoring of Nonviolent Convicted Felons* (Washington, D.C.: National Institute of Justice, 1992).

75. Michael Tonry and Mary Lynch, "Intermediate Sanctions," in *Crime and Justice*, vol. 20, ed. Michael Tonry (Chicago: University of Chicago Press, 1996), 99.

76. Dennis Palumbo, Mary Clifford, and Zoann K. Snyder-Joy, "From Net Widening to Intermediate Sanctions: The Transformation of Alternatives to Incarceration from Benevolence to Malevolence," in *Smart Sentencing: The Emergence of Intermediate Sanctions*, ed. James M. Byrne, Arthur Lurigio, and Joan Petersilia (Newbury Park, CA: Sage, 1992), 231.

77. Keve, 207.

78. Barbara Sims and Mark Jones, "Predicting Success or Failure on Probation: Factors Associated with Felony Probation Outcomes," *Crime and Delinquency* (July 1997), 314–327.

79. California Penal Code Sections 1210, 1210.1 (West Supp. 2004); and California Health and Safety Code Sections 11999.4–11999.13 (West Supp. 2004).

80. California Penal Code Section 1210.1(b)(1) (West Supp. 2004).

81. *Ibid.*

82. Douglas Longshore, Angela Hawken, Darren Urada, and M. Douglas Anglin, *Evaluation of the Substance Abuse and Crime Prevention Act: SACPA Cost-Analysis Report (First and Second Years)* (Los Angeles: UCLA Integrated Substance Abuse Programs, 2006), 5.

83. Scott Ehlers and Jason Ziedenberg, *Proposition 36: Five Years Later* (Washington, D.C.: Justice Policy Institute, April 2006), 5.

84. Laura Mecoy, "Drug Law's Failures Spur Get Tough Call," *Sacramento Bee* (February 27, 2006), A1.

85. Longshore, Hawken, Urada, and Anglin, 26.

Prisons and Jails

Learning objectives

After reading this chapter, you should be able to:

LO1 Contrast the Pennsylvania and the New York penitentiary theories of the 1800s.

LO2 List the factors that have caused the prison population to grow dramatically in the last several decades.

LO3 Explain the three general models of prisons.

LO4 List and briefly explain the four types of prisons.

LO5 Describe the formal prison management system, and indicate the three most important aspects of prison governance.

LO6 List the reasons why private prisons can often be run more cheaply than public ones.

LO7 Summarize the distinction between jails and prisons, and indicate the importance of jails in the American correctional system.

LO8 Explain how jails are administered.

LO9 Indicate the difference between traditional jail design and new-generation jail design.

LO10 Indicate some of the consequences of our high rates of incarceration.

Sir Henry Alfred McCardie, the famed English jurist, once said, "Trying a man is easy, as easy as falling off a log, compared with deciding what to do with him when he has been found guilty." In the American criminal justice system, to a certain extent, the decision has been simplified: many of the guilty go behind bars. The United States has the largest corrections system in the world. One out of every 133 Americans is in a federal or state prison or in a local jail. By 2007, the number of inmates in American prisons and jails had surpassed 2.3 million. The United States now locks up six times as many of its citizens as Canada does, and seven times as many as most European democracies. In fact, recent years have seen this country move past Russia to lay claim to the title of "the world's leading incarcerator."

For the most part, this high rate of imprisonment is a product of the past thirty years. From the 1920s until 1970, America's incarceration rate remained fairly stable at 110 per 100,000. Over the past three and a half decades, the jail and prison population of the United States increased by nearly 700 percent. There is, it must be noted, some evidence that the growth rate of the nation's incarcerated population is beginning to slow down. The average annual growth of the nation's prison population dropped from 6.7 percent in 1995 to 2.8 percent in 2007. Some corrections experts believe that this slowed growth is a result of the decline in crime rates in the 1990s: with fewer people committing crimes, fewer people will go to prison. Others point to a number of new state laws under which those convicted of drug possession are sent to treatment programs rather than prison or jail, a trend we discussed in the previous chapter.

AP Photo/Rob Carr

▲ A handful of the approximately 2.35 million inmates incarcerated in the United States wait in line to eat dinner at Alabama's Staton Prison.

A few years of slower growth cannot reverse a decades-long trend, however. The American corrections system remains a massive institution.[1] Throughout the course of this textbook, we have discussed many of the social and political factors that help explain the prison population "boom" of the past thirty years.

In this chapter and the next, we turn our attention to the incarceration system itself. This chapter focuses on the history and organizational structures of prisons (which generally hold those who have committed serious felonies for long periods of time) and jails (which generally hold those who have committed less serious felonies and misdemeanors, and those awaiting trial, for short periods of time). Though the two terms are often used interchangeably, they refer to two very different institutions, each with its own responsibilities and its own set of seemingly unsolvable problems.

A Short History of American Prisons

Today, we view prisons as instruments of punishment; the loss of freedom imposed on inmates is society's retribution for the crimes they have committed. This has not always been the function of incarceration. The prisons of eighteenth-century England, known as "bridewells" after London's Bridewell Palace, actually had little to do with punishment. These facilities were mainly used to hold debtors or those awaiting trial, execution, or banishment from the community. (In many ways, as

Criminal Justice ⊛ Now™

Maximize your study time by using ThomsonNOW's Personalized Study plan to help you review this chapter and prepare for examination. The Study Plan will

- Help you identify areas on which you should concentrate

- Provide interactive exercises to help you master the chapter concepts; and

- Provide a post-test to confirm you are ready to move on to the next chapter information.

shall be made clear, these facilities resemble the modern jail.) English courts generally imposed one of two sanctions on convicted felons: they turned them loose, or they executed them.[2] To be sure, most felons were released, pardoned either by the court or the clergy after receiving a whipping or a branding.

The correctional system in the American colonies differed very little from that of their motherland. If anything, colonial administrators were more likely to use corporal punishment than their English counterparts, and the death penalty was not uncommon in early America. The one dissenter was William Penn, who adopted the "Great Law" in Pennsylvania in 1682. Based on Quaker ideals of humanity and rehabilitation, this criminal code forbade the use of torture and mutilation as forms of punishment; instead, felons were ordered to pay restitution of property or goods to their victims. If the felons did not have sufficient property to make restitution, they were placed in a prison, which was primarily a "workhouse."[3] The death penalty was still allowed under the "Great Law," but only in cases of premeditated murder. Penn proved to be an exception, however, and the path to reform was much slower in the colonies than in England.

WALNUT STREET PRISON: THE FIRST PENITENTIARY

On Penn's death in 1718, the "Great Law" was rescinded in favor of a harsher criminal code, similar to those of the other colonies. At the time of the American Revolution, however, the Quakers were instrumental in the first broad swing of the incarceration pendulum from punishment to rehabilitation. In 1776, Pennsylvania passed legislation ordering that offenders be reformed through treatment and discipline rather than simply beaten or executed.[4] Several states, including Massachusetts and New York, quickly followed Pennsylvania's example.

Pennsylvania continued its reformist ways by opening the country's first **penitentiary** in a wing of Philadelphia's Walnut Street Jail in 1790. The penitentiary operated on the assumption that silence and labor provided the best hope of rehabilitating the criminal spirit. Remaining silent would force the prisoners to think about their crimes, and eventually the weight of conscience would lead to repentance. At the same time, enforced labor would attack the problem of idleness—regarded as the main cause of crime by penologists of the time.[5] Consequently, inmates at Walnut Street were isolated from one another in solitary rooms and kept busy with constant menial chores.

Eventually, the penitentiary at Walnut Street succumbed to the same problems that continue to plague institutions of confinement: overcrowding and excessive costs. As an influx of inmates forced more than one person to be housed in a room, maintaining silence became nearly impossible. By the early 1800s, officials could not find work for all of the convicts, so many were left idle.

THE GREAT PENITENTIARY RIVALRY: PENNSYLVANIA VERSUS NEW YORK

The apparent lack of success at Walnut Street did little to dampen enthusiasm for the penitentiary concept. Throughout the first half of the nineteenth century, a number of states reacted to prison overcrowding by constructing new penitentiaries. Each state tended to have its own peculiar twist on the roles of silence and labor, and two such systems—those of Pennsylvania and New York—emerged to shape the debate over the most effective way to run a prison.

The Pennsylvania System After the failure of Walnut Street, Pennsylvania constructed two new prisons: the Western Penitentiary near Pittsburgh (opened in 1826) and the Eastern Penitentiary in Cherry Hill, near Philadelphia (1829). The Pennsylvania system took the concept of silence as a virtue to new extremes. Based on the idea of **separate confinement**, these penitentiaries were constructed with back-to-back cells facing both outward and inward. (See ■ Figure 13.1 for the lay-

Penitentiary An early form of correctional facility that emphasized separating inmates from society and from each other so that they would have an environment in which to reflect on their wrongdoing and ponder their reformation.

Separate Confinement A nineteenth-century penitentiary system developed in Pennsylvania in which inmates were kept separate from each other at all times, with daily activities taking place in individual cells.

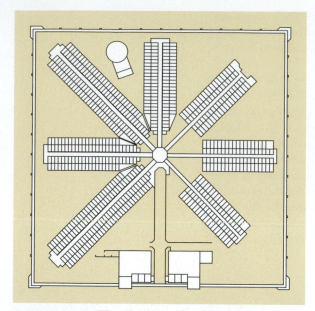

■ Figure 13.1 The Eastern Penitentiary
The Eastern Penitentiary opened in 1829 with the controversial goal of changing the behavior of inmates instead of merely punishing them. An important component of this goal was the layout of the facility. As you can see, the Eastern Penitentiary was designed in the form of a "wagon wheel," known today as the radial style. The back-to-back cells in each "spoke" of the wheel faced outward from the center to limit contact between inmates. About three hundred prisons worldwide have been built based on this design.

out of the original Eastern Penitentiary.) To spare each inmate from the corrupting influence of the others, prisoners worked, slept, and ate alone in their cells. Their only contact with other human beings came in the form of religious instruction from a visiting clergyman or prison official.[6]

The New York System If Pennsylvania's prisons were designed to transform wrongdoers into honest citizens, those in New York focused on obedience. When New York's Newgate Prison (built in 1791) became overcrowded, the state authorized the construction of Auburn Prison, which opened in 1816. Auburn initially operated under many of the same assumptions that guided the penitentiary at Walnut Street. Solitary confinement, however, seemed to lead to an inordinate amount of sickness, insanity, and even suicide among inmates, and it was abandoned in 1822. Nine years later, Elam Lynds became warden at Auburn and instilled the **congregate system,** also known as the Auburn system. Like Pennsylvania's separate confinement system, the congregate system was based on silence and labor. At Auburn, however, inmates worked and ate together, with silence enforced by prison guards.[7]

If either state can be said to have "won" the debate, it was New York. The Auburn system proved more popular, and a majority of the new prisons built during the first half of the nineteenth century followed New York's lead, though mainly for economic reasons rather than philosophical ones. New York's penitentiaries were cheaper to build because they did not require so much space. Furthermore, inmates in New York were employed in workshops, whereas those in Pennsylvania toiled alone in their cells. Consequently, the Auburn system was better positioned to exploit prison labor in the early years of widespread factory production.

THE REFORMERS AND THE PROGRESSIVES

The Auburn system did not go unchallenged. In the 1870s, a group of reformers argued that fixed sentences, imposed silence, and isolation did nothing to improve prisoners; they proposed that penal institutions should offer the promise of early release as a prime tool for rehabilitation. Echoing the views of the Quakers a century earlier, the reformers presented an ideology that would heavily influence American corrections for the next century.

This "new penology" was put into practice at New York's Elmira Reformatory in 1876. At Elmira, good behavior was rewarded by early release and misbehavior was punished with extended time under a three-grade system of classification. On entering the institution, the offender was assigned a grade of 2. If the inmate followed the rules and completed work and school assignments, after six months he was moved up to grade 1, the necessary grade for release. If, however, the inmate broke institutional rules, he was lowered to grade 3. A grade 3 inmate needed to behave properly for three months before he could return to grade 2 and begin to work back toward grade 1 and eventual release.[8]

Although other penal institutions did not adopt the Elmira model, its theories came into prominence in the first two decades of the twentieth century thanks to the Progressive movement in criminal justice. The Progressives—linked to the positivist school of criminology discussed in Chapter 2—believed that criminal behavior was caused by social, economic, and biological factors and, therefore, a corrections system should have a goal of treatment, not punishment. Consequently, they trumpeted a **medical model** for prisons, which held that institutions should offer a variety of programs and therapies to cure inmates of their "ills," whatever the root causes. The

Congregate System A nineteenth-century penitentiary system developed in New York in which inmates were kept in separate cells during the night but worked together in the daytime under a code of enforced silence.

Medical Model A model of corrections in which the psychological and biological roots of an inmate's criminal behavior are identified and treated.

Progressives were greatly responsible for the spread of indeterminate sentences (Chapter 11), probation (Chapter 12), community sanctions (Chapter 12), and parole (Chapter 14) in the first half of the twentieth century.

THE REASSERTION OF PUNISHMENT

Even though the Progressives had a great influence on the corrections system as a whole, their theories had little impact on the prisons themselves, many of which had been constructed in the nineteenth century and were impervious to change. More important, prison administrators usually did not agree with the Progressives and their followers, so the day-to-day lives of most inmates varied little from the congregate system of Auburn Prison.

Academic attitudes began to shift toward the prison administrators in the mid-1960s. Then, in

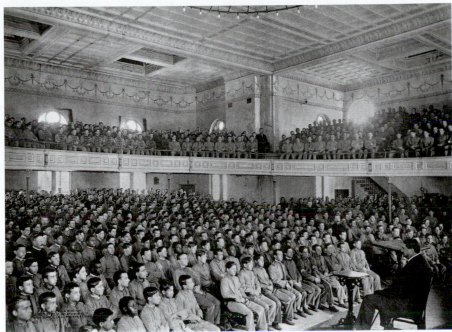

▲ Inmates of Elmira State Prison in New York attend a presentation at the prison auditorium. Zebulon Brockway, the superintendent at Elmira, believed that criminals were an "inferior class" of human being and should be treated as society's defectives. Thus, mental exercises designed to improve the inmates' minds were part of the prison routine at Elmira. To what extent do you believe that treatment should be a part of the incarceration of criminals?

1974, the publication of Robert Martinson's famous "What Works?" essay provided critics of the medical model with statistical evidence that rehabilitation efforts did nothing to lower recidivism rates.[9] This is not to say that Martinson's findings went unchallenged. A number of rebuttals arguing that rehabilitative programs could be successful appeared immediately after the publication of "What Works?"[10] In fact, Martinson himself retracted most of his claims in a little-noticed article published five years after his initial report.[11] Attempts by Martinson and others to "set the record straight" went largely unnoticed, however, as a sharp rise in crime in the early 1970s led many criminologists and politicians to champion "get tough" measures to deal with criminals they now considered "incurable." By the end of the 1980s, the legislative, judicial, and administrative strategies that we have discussed throughout this text had positioned the United States for an explosion in inmate populations and prison construction unparalleled in the nation's history.

Self Check Fill in the Blanks

In the early 1800s, Pennsylvania's _____ confinement strategy and New York's _____ system were the two dominant methods of managing prisons in the United States. Both were based on _____ and labor, but New York's system proved more popular because its institutions were _____ to construct and exploited the demand for prison _____. In the second half of the century, the Progressive movement rejected both systems and introduced the _____ model for prisons, which focused on rehabilitation rather than punishment. Check your answers on page 440.

The Prison Population Bomb

The number of Americans in prison or jail has almost tripled since 1985 and is continuing to rise, though at a slower rate, as mentioned earlier (see ■ Figure 13.2 on the next page). These numbers are not only dramatic, but also, say some observers,

The Inmate Population of the United States

The total number of inmates in custody in the United States has risen from 744,208 in 1985 to nearly 2.4 million in 2006.

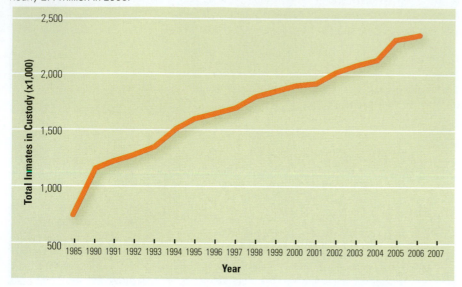

Source: Bureau of Justice Statistics, *Prisoners in 2006* (Washington, D.C.: U.S. Department of Justice, 2007).

inexplicable, given the overall crime picture in the United States. In the 1990s, violent and property crime rates dropped, yet the number of inmates continued to rise. According to accepted theory, rising incarceration rates should be the result of a rise in crime, leaving one expert to comment that America's prison population is "defying gravity."[12] (See the feature *Myth versus Reality: Does Placing Criminals in Prison Reduce Crime?*)

FACTORS IN PRISON POPULATION GROWTH

Much of the growth in the number of Americans behind bars can be attributed to the enhancement and stricter enforcement of the nation's drug laws. There are more people in prison and jail for drug offenses today than there were for

Myth *versus* Reality
Does Placing Criminals in Prison Reduce Crime?

Since the early 1990s until just recently, violent crime rates in the United States have been stable or declining. Yet, during the same period, as ■ Figure 13.3 shows, the rate at which Americans are imprisoned has climbed precipitously. The correlation between these two trends has become the subject of much discussion among crime experts.

THE MYTH A popular view of incarceration is that "a thug in jail can't shoot your sister." Obviously, a prison inmate is incapable of doing any further harm to the community. By extension, then, as the number of criminals behind bars increases, the crime rate should drop accordingly.

THE REALITY Numerous studies have shown that this is not always the case. Between 1985 and 1995, the prison population in the United States almost doubled, yet the number of all major violent crimes also increased. Over the past fifteen years, the rate of imprisonment has risen much more slowly in New York than in California, yet California's crime rate has been significantly higher than New York's during that time period. Some experts believe that these contradictory findings can be attributed to the law of diminishing returns. In other words, if we jailed every person in

an area, the crime rate would be zero. With nobody incarcerated, the crime rate would be very high. At some point between these two extremes, the rate of crime reduction brought about by imprisoning more people begins to slow, or diminish. Accordingly, the goal for the criminal justice system is to find the point at which a further increase in the prison population no longer results in an increase in the rate of crime reduction and then stay below that point. A study released in 2006 placed this point at 3.25 prisoners per 1,000 persons in the general population. Present rates for the United States are double that figure.

Another explanation for the lack of positive correlation between rates of imprisonment and crime focuses on the types of criminals imprisoned. When prison populations are small, as they were until the 1980s, additional inmates tended to be mostly violent and property crime offenders. The data, as well as common sense, tell us that removing these sorts of criminals from the community has a direct impact on violent and property crime rates. When prison populations expanded in the 1990s, most of the new admissions were drug law offenders and probation violators. These types of criminals have a smaller effect on violent and property crime rates. In fact, their absence from their homes may even contribute to

all offenses in the early 1970s.[13] In 1980, about 19,000 drug offenders were incarcerated in state prisons and 4,800 drug offenders were in federal prisons. Two and a half decades later, state prisons contained 250,900 inmates who had been arrested for drug offenses, and the number of drug offenders in federal prisons had risen to almost 87,000 (representing about 50 percent of all inmates in federal facilities).[14]

L02

Other reasons for the growth in incarcerated populations include:

- *Increased probability of incarceration.* Simply stated, the chance of someone who is arrested going to prison today is much greater than it was twenty years ago. Most of this growth took place in the 1980s, when the likelihood of incarceration in a state prison after arrest increased fivefold for drug offenses, threefold for weapons offenses, and twofold for crimes such as sexual assault, burglary, auto theft, and larceny.[15] For federal crimes, the proportion of convicted defendants being sent to prison rose from 54 percent in 1988 to 76 percent in 2003.[16]

- *Inmates serving more time for each crime.* After the Sentencing Reform Act of 1984, the length of time served by federal convicts for their crimes rose significantly. As noted in Chapter 11, in the fifteen years after the law went into effect, the average time served by inmates in federal prisons rose to fifty months—an increase of more than 50 percent.[17] For drug offenders, the average amount of time served in federal prison escalated from 39.3 months to 62.4 months, while the average prison term for weapons offenses grew from 32.4 months to 64.5 months.[18] State sentencing reform statutes

⊙ The **Federal Bureau of Prisons** is the largest incarceration system in the United States. Find its Web site by clicking on *Web Links* under *Chapter Resources* at **www.cjinaction.com**.

criminal activity. As we discussed in Chapter 2, many criminologists believe that widespread family disruption greatly increases the incidence of crime in a community.

FOR CRITICAL ANALYSIS

After a person has been convicted and spent time in prison, it is much more difficult for her or him

to find a job. Many criminologists believe that this situation forces many ex-inmates to rely on criminal activity to support themselves after their release from incarceration. If this theory is correct, what would be the implications for the relationship between crime rates and incarceration rates?

■ **Figure 13.3** Comparing Crime Rates and Incarceration Rates

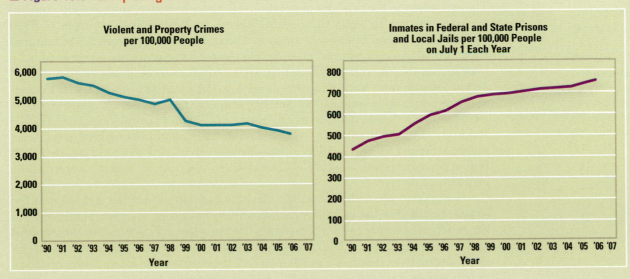

Source: Federal Bureau of Investigation and Bureau of Justice Statistics.

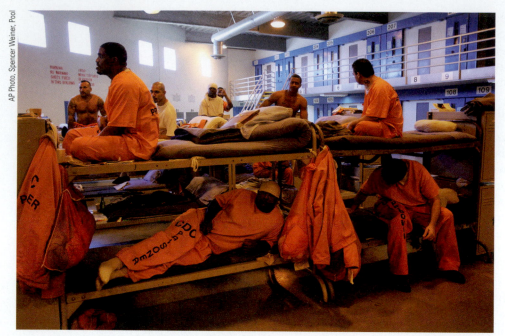

▲ Overcrowding has forced thousands of California inmates, such as those shown here from the state prison in Lancaster, to live in temporary "emergency" sleeping areas in converted dayrooms, gymnasiums, and classrooms. To alleviate the situation, in 2007 California lawmakers approved the construction of 53,000 new prison and jail beds at a cost of more than $7 billion.

and "truth-in-sentencing" laws have had similar consequences. In the thirty-two states that require their inmates to serve at least 85 percent of their sentences, for example, violent offenders are expected to spend an average of fifteen months more in prison than violent offenders in states without such laws.[19]

- *Federal prison growth.* Thanks in part to federal sentencing policy, the federal prison system is now the largest in the country with more than 180,000 inmates. In fact, since 1995 the federal prison population has risen at a rate more than triple that of state prisons (100 percent to 27 percent).[20] Besides the increase in federal drug offenders already mentioned, this growth can be attributed to efforts by Presidents Bill Clinton and George W. Bush to federalize gun possession crimes: from 1995 to 2003, the number of inmates sent to federal prisons for weapons violations jumped by 120 percent.[21] Over that same time period, immigration law offenders increased by almost 400 percent; by 2003, they represented more than 10 percent of all federal inmates.[22]

- *Rising incarceration rates of women.* In 1981, 14,000 women were prisoners in federal and state institutions; by 2005, the number had grown to over 107,518. Women still account for only 7 percent of all prisoners nationwide, but their rates of imprisonment are growing twice as rapidly as those of men.[23]

THE PRISON CONSTRUCTION BOOM

The escalation in the prisoner population has brought with it an increased demand for new prisons. In 1980, the Federal Bureau of Prisons had a budget of $330 million and operated forty-four prisons. Today, its budget exceeds $5 billion and there are 104 federal prisons. Over the past twenty-five years, the number of state prisons has increased from fewer than six hundred to more than one thousand.[24] Today, federal, state, and local governments spend about $65 billion a year to operate their corrections systems—an increase of more than 400 percent since the early 1980s.[25] Eleven states allocate in excess of $1 billion a year on corrections-related services.[26] In 2007, California—which already has the nation's highest annual corrections budget at nearly $5.5 billion—decided it needed to spend another $7.4 billion on new prison and jail construction to alleviate its severe overcrowding problems.

Some observers believe that the increase in prison space has helped spur the inmate population boom, rather than the other way around. As we mentioned earlier, when prison space is limited, judges tend to reserve incarceration for the most violent offenders, sentencing others to probation and the other community corrections alternatives discussed in Chapter 12. If prison space is available, however, judges will be more likely to fill it.[27] Recognizing this, several states have placed

◉ As the name implies, **PrisonSucks.com** is highly critical of what it calls the "crime control industry." Find this Web site by clicking on *Web Links* under *Chapter Resources* at **www.cjinaction.com**.

caps on their prison populations in the hopes of lowering costs by reducing the number of nonviolent offenders behind bars.

Self Check Fill in the Blanks

Of all the factors in the growth of the prison population in the past two decades, stricter enforcement of the nation's _____ laws has had the greatest impact. Other factors in this growth include (1) increased probability of _____, (2) increased _____ of time served in prison, (3) the growth of the _____ prison system, and (4) rising incarceration rates of _____. Check your answers on page 440.

The Role of Prisons in Society

The increase in prison populations also reflects the varied demands placed on penal institutions. As University of Connecticut sociologist Charles Logan once noted, Americans expect prisons to "correct the incorrigible, rehabilitate the wretched . . . restrain the dangerous, and punish the wicked."[28] Basically, prisons exist to make society a safer place. Whether this is to be achieved through retribution, deterrence, incapacitation, or rehabilitation—the four justifications of corrections introduced in Chapter 11—depends on the operating philosophy of the individual penal institution.

> "To assert in any case that a man must be absolutely cut off from society because he is absolutely evil amounts to saying that society is absolutely good, and no one in his right mind will believe this today."
>
> —*Albert Camus, French author (1961)*

Three general models of prisons have emerged to describe the different schools of thought behind prison organization:

- The *custodial model* is based on the assumption that prisoners are incarcerated for reasons of incapacitation, deterrence, and retribution. All decisions within the prison—such as what form of recreation to provide the inmates—are made with an eye toward security and discipline, and the daily routine of the inmates is highly controlled. The custodial model has dominated the most restrictive prisons in the United States since the 1930s.
- The *rehabilitation model* stresses the ideals of individualized treatment that we discussed in Chapter 11. Security concerns are often secondary to the well-being of the individual inmate, and a number of treatment programs are offered to aid prisoners in changing their criminal and antisocial behavior. The rehabilitation model came into prominence during the 1950s and enjoyed widespread popularity until it began to lose general acceptance in the 1970s and 1980s.
- In the *reintegration model*, the correctional institution serves as a training ground for the inmate to prepare for existence in the community. Prisons that have adopted this model give the prisoners more responsibility during incarceration and offer halfway houses and work programs (both discussed in Chapter 14) to help them reintegrate into society. This model is becoming more influential, as corrections officials react to problems such as prison overcrowding.[29]

Competing views of the prison's role in society are at odds with these three "ideal" perspectives. Professor Alfred Blumstein argues that prisons create new criminals, especially with regard to nonviolent drug offenders. Not only do these nonviolent felons become socialized to the criminal lifestyle while in prison, but the stigma of incarceration makes it more difficult for them to obtain employment on release. Their only means of sustenance "on the outside" is to apply the criminal methods they learned in prison.[30] A study by criminal justice professors Cassia

LO3

Figure 13.4 Security Levels of Correctional Facilities in Virginia

The security levels of correctional facilities in Virginia are graded from level 1 to level 6. As you can see, level 1 facilities are for those inmates who pose the least amount of risk to fellow inmates, staff members, and themselves. Level 6 facilities are for those who are considered the most dangerous by the Virginia Department of Corrections.

Level 1-Low

No murder I or II, robbery, sex-related crime, kidnapping/abduction, felonious assault (current or prior), flight/escape history, carjacking, or malicious wounding. No disruptive behavior.

Level 1-High

No murder I or II, sex-related crime, kidnapping/abduction, or flight/escape history. No disruptive behavior for at least past 24 months.

Level 2

For initial assignment only. No escape history for past five years. No disruptive behavior for at least past 24 months prior to transfer to any less secure facility.

Level 3

Single, multiple, and life + sentences. Must have served 20 consecutive years on sentence. No disruptive behavior for at least past 24 months prior to transfer to any less secure facility.

Level 4

Single, multiple, and life + sentences. No disruptive behavior for at least past 24 months prior to transfer to any less secure facility.

Level 5

Same as Level 4.

Level 6

Single, multiple, and life + sentences. PROFILE OF INMATES: disruptive, assaultive, severe behavior problems, predatory-type behavior; escape risks. No disruptive behavior for at least past 24 months prior to transfer to any less secure facility.

Source: Virginia Department of Corrections.

Spohn of the University of Nebraska and David Holleran of East Tennessee State University found that convicted drug offenders who were sentenced to prison were 2.2 times more likely to be incarcerated for a new offense than those sentenced to probation.[31]

Types of Prisons

Prison administrators have long been aware of the need to separate different kinds of offenders. In federal prisons, this led to a system with six levels based on the security needs of the inmates, from level 1 facilities with the lowest amount of security to level 6 with the harshest security measures. (Many states also use the six-level system, an example of which can be seen in ■ Figure 13.4.) To simplify matters, most observers refer to correctional facilities as being one of three levels—minimum, medium, or maximum. A fourth level—the supermaximum-security prison, known as the "supermax"—is relatively rare and extremely controversial due to its hyperharsh methods of punishing and controlling the most dangerous prisoners.

LO4

MAXIMUM-SECURITY PRISONS

In a certain sense, the classification of prisoners today owes a debt to the three-grade system developed at the Elmira Penitentiary, discussed earlier in the chapter. Once wrongdoers enter a corrections facility, they are constantly graded on behavior. Those who serve "good time," as we have seen, are often rewarded with early release. Those who compile extensive misconduct records are usually housed, along with violent and repeat offenders, in **maximum-security prisons.** The names of these institutions—Folsom, San Quentin, Sing Sing, Attica—conjure up foreboding images of concrete and steel jungles, with good reason.

Maximum-security prisons are designed with full attention to security and surveillance. In these institutions, inmates' lives are programmed in a militaristic fashion to keep them from escaping or from harming themselves or the prison staff. About a quarter of the prisons in the United States are classified as maximum security, and these institutions house about 16 percent of the country's prisoners.

Maximum-Security Prison A correctional institution designed and organized to control and discipline dangerous felons, as well as prevent escape, with intense supervision, cement walls, and electronic, barbed wire fences.

The Design Maximum-security prisons tend to be large—holding more than a thousand inmates—and they have similar features. The entire operation is usually surrounded by concrete walls that stand twenty to thirty feet high and have also been sunk deep into the ground to deter tunnel escapes; fences reinforced with razor-ribbon barbed wire that can be electrically charged may supplement or replace these barriers. The prison walls are studded with watchtowers, from which guards armed with shotguns and rifles survey the movement of prisoners below. The designs of these facilities, though similar, are not uniform. Though correctional facilities built using the radial design pioneered by the Eastern State Penitentiary still exist, several other designs have become prominent in more recently constructed institutions. For an overview of these designs, including the radial design, see ■ Figure 13.5.

Inmates live in cells, most of them with similar dimensions to those found in the I-Max maximum-security prison for women in Topeka, Kansas: eight feet by

■ **Figure 13.5** Prison Designs

The Radial Design

The radial design has been utilized since the early nineteenth century. The "wagon wheel"–like form of the structure was created with the dual goals of separation and control. Inmates are separated from each other in their cells on the "spokes" of the wheel, and prison officials can control the activities of the inmates from the control center in the "hub" of the wheel.

The Telephone-Pole Design

The main feature of this design is a long central corridor that serves as a means for transporting inmates from one part of the facility to another. Branching off from this main corridor are the functional areas of the facility: housing, food services, workshops, treatment programs room, and other services. Prison officials survey the entire facility from the central "pole" and can shut off the various "arms" when necessary for security reasons. The majority of maximum-security prisons in the United States were constructed using this design blueprint.

The Courtyard Style

In the courtyard-style prison, a courtyard replaces the transportation function of the "pole" in the telephone-pole prison. The prison buildings form a square around the courtyard, and to get from one part of the facility to another, the inmates go across the courtyard. In a number of these facilities, the recreational area, mess hall, and school are located in the courtyard.

The Campus Style

Some of the newer minimum-security prisons have adopted the campus style, a style that had previously been used in correctional facilities for women and juveniles. Like a college campus, housing units are scattered among functional units such as the dining room, recreation area, and treatment centers. The benefit of the campus style is that individual buildings can be used for different functions, making the operation more flexible. Due to concerns that the campus style provides less security than the other designs discussed, it is used for the most part only for medium- and minimum-security prisons.

Source: Text adapted from Todd R. Clear and George F. Cole, *American Corrections*, 4th ed. (Belmont, CA: Wadsworth Publishing Company, 1997), 255–256.

fourteen feet with cinder block walls.[32] The space contains bunks, a toilet, a sink, and possibly a cabinet or closet. Cells are located in rows of *cell blocks,* each of which forms its own security unit, set off by a series of gates and bars. A maximum-security institution is essentially a collection of numerous cell blocks, each constituting its own prison within a prison.

Inmates' lives are dominated by security measures. Whenever they move from one area of the prison to another, they do so in groups and under the watchful eye of armed correctional guards. Television surveillance cameras may be used to monitor their every move, even when sleeping, showering, or using the toilet. They are subject to frequent pat-downs or strip searches at the guards' discretion. Constant "head counts" assure that every inmate is where he or she should be. Tower guards—many of whom have orders to shoot to kill in the case of a disturbance or escape attempt—constantly look down on the inmates as they move around outdoor areas of the facility.

Technology has added significantly to the power an institution holds over the individual prisoner. Walk-through metal detectors and X-ray body scanners can detect weapons or other contraband hidden on the body of an inmate. Ground-penetrating radar allows the correctional staff to search courtyards for buried items. Prison officials expect that within the next decade, electronic eye scans and noninvasive skin patches will be available to determine whether a prisoner has been using drugs.

Supermax Prisons About thirty states and the Federal Bureau of Prisons (BOP) operate **supermax** (short for supermaximum security) **prisons,** which are supposedly reserved for the "worst of the worst" of America's corrections population. Most of the inmates in these facilities are deemed high risks to commit murder behind bars—about a quarter of the occupants of the BOP's U.S. Penitentiary Administrative Maximum (ADX) in Florence, Colorado, have killed other prisoners or assaulted correctional officers elsewhere. In addition, a growing number are either high-profile individuals who would be at constant risk of attack in a general prison population or convicted terrorists such as Zacarias Moussaoui (see page 342), Ted "the Unabomber" Kaczynski, and Terry Nichols, who was involved in the bombing of the federal building in Oklahoma City in 1995.

▼ Inside the Northern Correctional Institution, the supermax facility in Somers, Connecticut, a correctional officer escorts a prisoner out of a shower, top left. In what ways does the supermax prison represent the ultimate controlled environment for its inmates?

AP Photo, Steve Miller

A Controlled Environment The main purpose of a supermax prison is to strictly control the inmates' movement, thereby limiting (or eliminating) situations that could lead to breakdowns in discipline. The conditions at California's Security Housing Unit (SHU) at Pelican Bay State Prison are representative of most supermax institutions. Prisoners are confined to their one-person cells for twenty-two and a half hours each day under video camera surveillance; they receive meals through a slot in the door. The cells measure eight by ten feet in size and are windowless. No decorations of any kind are permitted on the walls.[33]

To a great extent, supermax prisons operate in a state of perpetual **lockdown,** in which all inmates are confined to their cells and social activities such as meals, recreational sports, and treatment programs are nonexistent. For the ninety minutes of each day that SHU inmates are allowed out of their cells (compared to twelve to sixteen hours in regular maximum-security prisons), they may either shower or exercise in an enclosed, concrete "yard" covered by plastic mesh. Prisoners are strip-searched before and after leaving their cells, and are placed in waist restraints and handcuffs on their way to and from the "yard" and showers.[34]

Supermax Syndrome Many prison officials support the proliferation of supermax prisons because they provide increased security for the most dangerous inmates. Observers believe that the harsh reputation of the facilities will deter convicts from misbehaving for fear of transfer to a supermax. Nevertheless, the supermax has aroused a number of criticisms. Amnesty International and other human rights groups assert that the facilities violate standards for proper treatment of prisoners. At Wisconsin's Supermax Correctional Facility, for example, the cells are illuminated twenty-four hours a day; because they have no air-conditioning or windows, average temperatures during the summer top 100 degrees.[35] Furthermore, while studying prisoners at California's Pelican Bay facility, a Harvard University psychiatrist found that 80 percent suffered from what he called "SHU [security housing unit] syndrome," a condition brought on by long periods of isolation.[36] Further research on SHU syndrome shows that supermax inmates manifest a number of psychological problems, including massive anxiety, hallucinations, and acute confusion.[37] We will take a closer look at the merits and drawbacks of solitary confinement, a method of inmate punishment that extends well beyond supermax prisons, in the *Criminal Justice in Action* feature that ends this chapter.

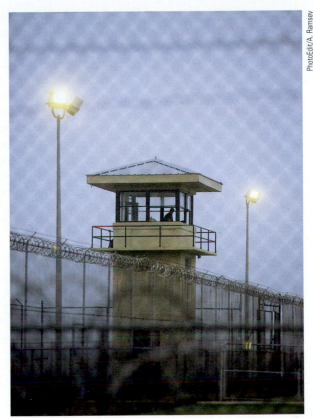

▲ Security measures—including television surveillance, pat-downs, and the constant attention of correctional officers in towers (pictured above)—dominate the lives of inmates in maximum-security prisons. How do guard towers contribute to the overall security of a prison facility? What might be some of the limitations of the guard tower as a security device?

MEDIUM- AND MINIMUM-SECURITY PRISONS

Medium-security prisons hold about 35 percent of the prison population and minimum-security prisons 49 percent. Inmates at **medium-security prisons** have for the most part committed less serious crimes than those housed in maximum-security prisons and are not considered high risks for escaping or causing harm. Consequently, medium-security institutions are not designed for control to the same extent as maximum-security prisons and have a more relaxed atmosphere. These facilities also offer more educational and treatment programs and allow for more contact between inmates. Medium-security prisons are rarely walled, relying instead on high fences. Prisoners have more freedom of movement within the structures, and the levels of surveillance are much lower. Living quarters are less restrictive as well—many of the newer medium-security prisons provide dormitory housing.

A **minimum-security prison** seems at first glance to be more like a college campus than an incarceration facility. Most of the inmates at these institutions are first-time offenders, who are nonviolent and well behaved; a high percentage are white-collar criminals. Indeed, inmates are often transferred to minimum-security prisons as a reward for good behavior in other facilities. Therefore, security measures

Lockdown A disciplinary action taken by prison officials in which all inmates are ordered to their quarters and nonessential prison activities are suspended.

Medium-Security Prison A correctional institution that houses less dangerous inmates and therefore uses less restrictive measures to avoid violence and escapes.

Minimum-Security Prison A correctional institution designed to allow inmates, most of whom pose low security risks, a great deal of freedom of movement and contact with the outside world.

are lax compared even to medium-security prisons. Unlike medium-security institutions, minimum-security prisons do not have armed guards. Prisoners are allowed amenities such as television sets and computers in their rooms, they enjoy freedom of movement, and they are allowed off prison grounds for educational or employment purposes to a much greater extent than those held in more restrictive facilities. (Danbury Women's Prison—where television personality Martha Stewart spent more than five months in the mid-2000s—has a law library, a track, and a gymnasium that is used for Dancersize, Pilates, and yoga classes.) Some critics have likened minimum-security prisons to "country clubs," but in the corrections system, everything is relative. A minimum-security prison may seem like a vacation spot when compared to the horrors of Sing Sing, but it still represents a restriction of personal freedom and separates the inmate from the outside world.

Self Check Fill in the Blanks

Those offenders who have been convicted of violent crimes and repeat offenders are most likely to be sent to _____-security prisons. If a prisoner assaults another inmate or a corrections officer, prison officials may decide to transfer him or her to a _____ prison. Inmates at _____-security prisons have committed less serious felonies and are not considered to pose a serious risk to other prisoners, while _____-security prisons, which resemble college campuses, house mostly first-time, nonviolent offenders. Check your answers on page 440.

Prison Administration

The security level of the institution generally determines the specific methods by which a prison is managed. There are, however, general goals of prison administration, summarized by Charles Logan as follows:

> The mission of a prison is to keep prisoners—to keep them in, keep them safe, keep them in line, keep them healthy, and keep them busy—and to do it with fairness, without undue suffering and as efficiently as possible.[38]

Considering the environment of a prison—an enclosed world inhabited by people who are generally violent and angry and would rather be anywhere else—Logan's mission statement may be highly utopian. A prison staff must supervise the daily routines of hundreds or thousands of inmates, a duty that includes providing them with meals, education, vocational programs, and different forms of leisure. The smooth operation of this supervision is made more difficult—if not, at times, impossible—by budgetary restrictions, overcrowding, and continual inmate turnover.

FORMAL PRISON MANAGEMENT

In some respects, the management structure of a prison is similar to that of a police department, as discussed in Chapter 5. Both systems rely on a hierarchical (top-down) *chain of command* to increase personal responsibility. Both **L05** assign different employees to specific tasks, though prison managers have much more direct control over their subordinates than do police managers. The main difference is that police departments have a *continuity of purpose* that is sometimes lacking in prison organizations. All members of a police force are, at least theoretically, working to reduce crime and apprehend criminals. In a prison, this continuity is less evident. An employee in the prison laundry service and one who works in the visiting center have little in common. In some cases, employees may even have cross-purposes: a prison guard may want to punish an inmate, while a counselor in the treatment center may want to rehabilitate her or him.

Consequently, a strong hierarchy is crucial for any prison management team that hopes to meet Charles Logan's expectations. As ■ Figure 13.6 shows, the **warden** (also known as a superintendent) is ultimately responsible for the operation of a prison. He or she oversees deputy wardens, who in turn manage the various organizational lines of the institution. The custodial employees, who deal directly with the inmates and make up more than half of a prison's staff, operate under a militaristic hierarchy, with a line of command passing from the deputy warden to the captain to the corrections officer.

GOVERNING PRISON POPULATIONS

The implications of mismanagement can be severe. While studying a series of prison riots, sociologists Bert Useem and Peter Kimball found that breakdown in managerial control commonly preceded such acts of mass violence.[39] During the 1970s, for example, conditions at the State Penitentiary in New Mexico deteriorated significantly; inmates were increasingly the targets of random and harsh treatment at the hands of the prison staff, while at the same time a reduction in structured activities left prison life "painfully boring."[40] The result, in 1980, was one of the most violent prison riots in the nation's history.

What sort of prison management is best suited to avoid such situations? Although there is no single "best" form of prison management, political scientist John DiIulio believes that, in general, the sound governance of corrections facilities is a matter of order, amenities, and services:

- *Order* can be defined as the absence of misconduct such as murder, assault, and rape. Many observers, including DiIulio, believe that, having incarcerated a person, the state has a responsibility to protect that person from disorder in the correctional institution.

- *Amenities* are those comforts that make life "livable," such as clean living conditions, decent food, and entertainment. One theory of incarceration holds that inmates should not enjoy a quality of life comparable to life outside prison. Without the basic amenities, however, prison life becomes unbearable, and inmates are more likely to lapse into disorder.

- *Services* include programs designed to improve an inmate's prospects on release, such as vocational training, remedial education, and drug rehabilitation. Again, many feel that a person convicted of a crime does not deserve to participate in these kinds of programs, but they have two clear benefits. First, they keep the inmate occupied and focused during her or his sentence. Second, they reduce the chances that the inmate will go back to a life of crime after he or she returns to the community.[41]

Warden The prison official who is ultimately responsible for the organization and performance of a correctional facility.

According to DiIulio, in the absence of order, amenities, and services, inmates will come to see their imprisonment as not only unpleasant but unfair, and they will become much more difficult to control.[42] Furthermore, weak governance encourages inmates to come up with their own methods of regulating their lives. As we shall see in the next chapter, the result is usually high levels of violence and the expansion of prison gangs and other illicit forms of authority. (The feature *CJ and Technology—Radio Frequency Identification* describes how a new type of monitoring system is helping prison administrators manage and control prison populations.)

Self Check Fill in the Blanks

The management of a prison is hierarchical with the _____ (also known as a superintendent) at the top of the power structure. Unlike other hierarchical systems such as police departments, corrections facilities often lack continuity of _____, meaning that not all employees have the same organizational goals. In general, however, effective governance of a prison requires prison staff to protect prisoners from _____ and provide them with _____ and services. Check your answers on page 440.

The Emergence of Private Prisons

In addition to all the other pressures placed on wardens and other prison administrators, they must operate within a budget assigned to them by an overseeing governmental agency. Today, the great majority of all prisons are under the control of federal and state governments, but government-run prisons have not always been the rule. In the nineteenth century, some correctional facilities were not under the control of the state. In fact, the entire Texas prison system was privately operated from 1872 to the late 1880s. For most of the twentieth century, however, **private prisons,** or prisons run by private business firms to make a profit, could not be found in the United States.

That is certainly not the case today. With corrections exhibiting all appearances of, in the words of one observer, "a recession-proof industry," the American business community has eagerly entered the market. Fourteen private corrections firms operate more than two hundred facilities across the United States. The two largest corrections companies, Corrections Corporation of America (CCA) and the GEO Group, Inc., have contracted to supervise more than 60,000 inmates. In 1997, the Federal Bureau of Prisons (BOP) awarded the first contract paying a private company to operate one of its prisons—the GEO Group received $88 million to run the Taft Correctional Institution in Taft, California. Today, the GEO Group operates twenty-one federal corrections facilities. By 2005, private penal institutions housed more than 107,000 inmates, representing 7 percent of all inmates in the state and federal corrections systems.[43]

WHY PRIVATIZE?

It would be a mistake to automatically assume that private prisons are less expensive to run than public ones. The incentive to privatize is, however, primarily financial.

Private Prisons Correctional facilities operated by private corporations instead of the government and, therefore, reliant on profits for survival.

Cost Efficiency In the 1980s and 1990s, a number of states and cities saved operating costs by transferring government-run services such as garbage collection and road maintenance to the private sector. Similarly, private prisons can often be run more cheaply and efficiently than public ones for the following reasons:

L06

WHAT IS RADIO FREQUENCY IDENTIFICATION?

Radio frequency identification (RFID) is a generic term for technologies that use radio waves to track and identify people or objects.

HOW DOES RADIO FREQUENCY IDENTIFICATION WORK?

In the corrections context, RFID technology works as a high-tech head count: inmates wear bracelets, while corrections officers wear small, pagerlike devices. Guided by a series of radio transmitters and receivers, the system is able to pinpoint the location of inmates and guards within twenty feet. Every two seconds, radio signals "search out" where each inmate and guard is, and relay this information to a central computer. On a grid of the prison, the inmate shows up as a yellow dot and the corrections officer as a blue dot. Administrators can quickly determine the inmate or officer represented by each dot, and all movements are stored in a database for future reference.

Experts predict that RFID systems will soon be customized to fit the needs of specific prison populations. For example, if a prison houses two rival gangs, the RFID system can be programmed to trigger an alarm when individual gang members come in close contact with each other. The bracelets can also be linked to satellite tracking systems, making it easier to locate escaped convicts who manage to get outside the boundaries of the prison's radio transmitters.

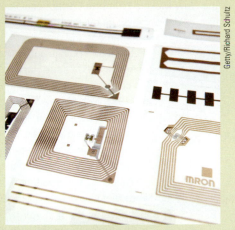

▲ An RFID tag, shown here, is used to identify a person through radio waves.

THINKING ABOUT RADIO FREQUENCY IDENTIFICATION

"[RFID] completely revolutionizes a prison because you know where everyone is—not approximately but exactly where they are," remarked an official at the National Institute of Justice. How might knowing exactly where an inmate is at all times and being able to track that inmate's past movements "revolutionize" prison management?

For more information on radio frequency identification and other CJ technologies, click on *Crime and Technology* under *Book Resources* at **www.cjinaction.com**.

- *Labor costs.* The wages of public employees account for nearly two-thirds of a prison's operating expenses. Although private corrections firms pay base salaries comparable to those enjoyed by public prison employees, their nonunionized staffs receive lower levels of overtime pay, workers' compensation claims, sick leave, and health-care insurance.
- *Competitive bidding.* Because of the profit motive, private corrections firms have an incentive to buy goods and services at the lowest possible price.
- *Less red tape.* Private corrections firms are not part of the government bureaucracy and therefore do not have to contend with the massive amount of paperwork that can clog government organizations.[44]

In 2005, the National Institute of Justice released the results of a five-year study comparing low-security public and private prisons in California. The government agency found that private facilities cost taxpayers between 6 and 10 percent less than public ones.[45] A similar study in Colorado found that housing inmates in private prisons reduced the daily price tag per inmate from $77 to $49—about 36 percent.[46]

Overcrowding and Outsourcing Private prisons are becoming increasingly attractive to state governments faced with the competing pressures of tight budgets and overcrowded corrections facilities. Lacking the funds to alleviate overcrowding by building more prisons, state officials are turning to the private institutions for help. Often, the private prison is out of state, which leads to the "outsourcing"

As warden of the New Mexico Women's Correctional Facility, I have executive oversight of the management and operation of the nation's first privately managed, multicustody state prison. My corrections career began in 1981 with the New Mexico Department of Corrections, where I held a series of progressively more responsible positions, including training officer, ACA accreditation manager, and chief classification officer. In 1985, I became the first woman to be promoted to the rank of assistant warden at a male prison in New Mexico. In order to expand my experience

Courtesy of Penny Lucero

to include juvenile corrections, I took the position of deputy superintendent at the Youth Diagnostic Center and New Mexico Girls' School.

THE CALL OF CORRECTIONS Although I left corrections for a while to manage my own business, I realized that my true career had become corrections. Being my own boss had its "pros," but the "cons" had won my heart; I wanted to dedicate my energy, expertise, and leadership to corrections. Fortunately, Corrections Corporation of America was opening the new women's prison in Grants, and I was quickly recruited as a member of the management team. Joining this team of experienced corrections professionals is what I claim to be the catalyst that propelled me to the highest executive level of institutional leadership. The management team included three well-established professionals: two retired wardens from the New Mexico system and one nationally recognized warden of a female prison. All three

of inmates. California, for example, has adopted this practice to help relieve its overcrowded prisons, which house more than 172,000 prisoners in space designed to hold about 100,000 inmates. Along with the prison construction mentioned earlier in the chapter, in 2007 state officials announced plans to transfer 8,000 inmates to private prisons in other states such as Arizona and Tennessee.[47]

Quality of Service Executives at corrections firms claim that because their contracts can be canceled for poor performance, private prisons have a greater incentive to provide higher-quality service than their public counterparts. At least one study, conducted by Charles Logan, supports this contention. Logan found that, according to statistical data and staff surveys, a private women's prison in New Mexico outperformed a state prison and a federal prison in a number of areas such as security, safety, living conditions, and management.[48] One reason a private prison might be expected to perform better than a public one is that the latter enjoys some immunity from civil liability suits. In other words, an aggrieved inmate can more easily sue a private prison in a civil court.[49]

THE ARGUMENT AGAINST PRIVATE PRISONS

Significantly, in Logan's study mentioned above, the inmates themselves gave the private prison lower scores than did the staff members. Opponents of private prisons worry that, despite the assurances of corporate executives, private corrections companies will "cut corners" to save costs, denying inmates important security guarantees in the process.

Safety Concerns These criticisms find some support in the anecdotal evidence. On April 24, 2007, about five hundred inmates rioted at a medium-security facility operated by the GEO Group in New Castle, Indiana. The disturbance was started by newly transferred inmates from Arizona who were upset at the lack of recreation and other programs at their new "home." In 2004, Arizona recalled some of its inmates from Oklahoma after a racially motivated riot at a CCA facility in Watonga during which hundreds of prisoners attacked each other with fire extin-

became friends and mentors, always encouraging me to excel.

Working with adult female offenders and for a private company were both new experiences for me. The opening of the New Mexico Women's Correctional Facility was the first time the state had provided a purpose-built staffed and programmed facility specifically for female offenders. As program director, I had the opportunity to develop a wide array of state-of-the-art programs and services that would help prepare the women for a successful return to their communities.

A WARDEN'S WORK As warden, I consider my major responsibilities to be maintaining a healthful, positive, safe, and mutually respectful environment for staff and inmates; establishing a working relationship with outside communities in order to assist with public education about offenders and the mutual benefit of working with them on release; participating in civic and professional organizations and encouraging the staff to do so; ensuring that the New Mexico Women's Correctional

Facility meets established national correctional standards; and staying current on new management, program, and technology trends that can assist me in maintaining the standards of excellence established at the facility.

Prisons have changed dramatically over the past two decades. No longer "closed" communities where "outsiders" are unwelcome, they have become an extension of society, welcoming daily interaction with local citizens, elected officials, researchers, student interns, and volunteers in order to create a more normalized environment. Equally important is the commitment to assist offenders in preparing for a lawful return to society. To that end, correctional administrators are eager to recruit and retain creative, thoughtful, and industrious employees for rewarding careers in a lifetime of service to society.

Go to the **Careers in Criminal Justice Interactive CD** for more profiles in the field of criminal justice.

---

guishers and baseball bats. Later that year, a female inmate at a private prison in Nashville, Tennessee, died from a violent head wound—an incident that led to a local police investigation of four CCA employees.

Various studies have also uncovered disturbing patterns of misbehavior at private prisons. For example, officials from the BOP discovered higher levels of serious inmate violence and drug abuse at California's Taft Correctional Institute, operated by the GEO Group, than at three similar government-run prisons.[50] In addition, research conducted by Curtis R. Blakely of the University of South Alabama and Vic W. Bumphus of the University of Tennessee at Chattanooga found that a prisoner in a private corrections facility was twice as likely to be assaulted by a fellow inmate as a prisoner in a public one.[51]

Financial Concerns Furthermore, some observers note, if a private corrections firm receives a fee from the state for each inmate housed in its facility, does that not give management an incentive to increase the amount of time each prisoner serves? Though government parole boards make the final decision on an inmate's release from private prisons, the company could manipulate misconduct and good behavior reports to maximize time served and, by extension, higher profits.[52]

Philosophical Concerns Other critics see private prisons as inherently unjust, even if they do save tax dollars or provide enhanced services. These observers believe that

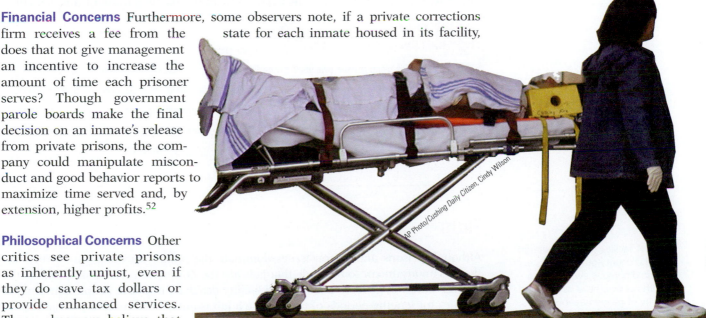

▼ An unidentified prisoner is rushed to the emergency room in Cushing, Oklahoma, after a March 2005 riot at the Cimarron Correction Facility left one inmate dead and thirteen others injured. About fifty gang members at the prison, operated privately by the Corrections Corporation of America, had attacked each other with bats and other gym equipment. What are some of the arguments against sending inmates to a privately run prison?

AP Photo/Cushing Daily Citizen, Cindy Wilson

corrections is not simply another industry, like garbage collection or road maintenance, and that only the government has the authority to punish. In the words of John DiIulio:

> It is precisely because corrections involves the deprivation of liberty, precisely because it involves the legally sanctioned exercise of coercion by some citizens over others, that it must remain wholly within public hands.[53]

Critics of private correctional facilities also believe that private prisons are constitutional contradictions and offer Article I of the U.S. Constitution as support. That passage states that "legislative powers herein granted shall be vested in a Congress of the United States." These powers include the authority to define penal codes and to determine the punishments that will be handed out for breaking federal law. Therefore, a strict interpretation of the Constitution appears to prohibit the passing of this authority from the federal government to a private company.[54]

THE FUTURE OF PRIVATIZATION IN THE CORRECTIONS INDUSTRY

At the beginning of this decade, claims that private incarceration was a "recession-proof industry" hardly seemed prophetic. The reasons for the industry's decline were economic rather than constitutional, however. In 2000, companies such as CCA and the GEO Group (then known as Wackenhut) relied primarily on the states for new business, but for a number of reasons, the states turned out to be poor customers. State corrections officials were reluctant to expend scarce resources on private prison services, and the private facilities themselves were receiving a great deal of negative publicity for inmate violence and poor performance. CCA, the nation's largest private incarceration company, was saddled with thousands of empty prison beds and faced bankruptcy.

Then, the industry found a "source of salvation": the federal government.[55] As noted earlier, tougher enforcement of drug and immigration laws has dramatically increased the number of federal prisoners, and the BOP has turned to private prisons to expand its capacity. Between 2000 and 2005, the number of state inmates in private facilities grew only 7.2 percent, while the number of federal inmates in private facilities rose by 74 percent.[56] The current emphasis on violators of immigration law seems likely to ensure that this trend will continue. The BOP estimates that the number of federal inmates will rise to 226,000 by 2010 (from 180,000 in 2005), and it will rely on private prisons to shoulder much of the burden of this growth.[57]

Self Check Fill in the Blanks

The incentive for using private prisons is primarily _____. Prison officials also feel pressure to send inmates to private prisons to alleviate _____ of public correctional facilities. Critics of private prisons claim that as a result of their cost-cutting measures, inmates are denied important _____ guarantees and thus may be put in physical danger. The industry's future seems assured, however, because of increased demand for prison beds on the part of the _____ government. Check your answers on page 440.

Jails

Although prisons and prison issues dominate the public discourse on corrections, there is an argument to be made that jails are the dominant penal institutions in the United States. In general, a prison is a facility designed to house people convicted of felonies for lengthy periods of time, while a **jail** is authorized to hold pretrial detainees and offenders who have committed misdemeanors. On any given day, about

Jail A facility, usually operated by the county government, used to hold persons awaiting trial or those who have been found guilty of misdemeanors.

L07 735,000 inmates are in jail in this country, and approximately 7 million Americans spend at least a day in jail each year. Furthermore, the jail population increased by 51 percent between 1995 and 2006.[58] Nevertheless, jail funding is often the lowest priority for the tight budgets of local governments, leading to severe overcrowding and other dismal conditions.

Many observers see this negligence as having far-reaching consequences for criminal justice. Jail is often the first contact that citizens have with the corrections system. It is at this point that treatment and counseling have the best chance to deter future criminal behavior.[59] By failing to take advantage of this opportunity, says Professor Frank Zimring of the Earl Warren Legal Institute at the University of California at Berkeley, corrections officials have created a situation in which "today's jail folk are tomorrow's prisoners."[60]

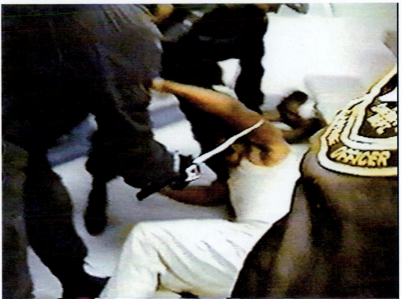

▲ Local sheriffs' deputies strike an inmate of the Brazoria County Detention Center in Clute, Texas, with a baton. After viewing the video from which this scene was taken, the FBI began an investigation into possible civil rights violations at the jail. Guard-on-inmate violence is only one of the problems plaguing the nation's jails, others being inmate-on-inmate violence, poor living conditions, and inadequate health-care facilities. Yet jail problems do not receive nearly the same attention as prison issues. Why might this be the case?

THE FUNCTION OF JAILS

Until the eighteenth century, all penal institutions existed primarily to hold those charged with a crime until their trial. Although jails still serve this purpose, they have evolved to play a number of different roles in the corrections system, including the following:

- Holding those convicted of misdemeanors.
- Receiving individuals pending arraignment and holding them while awaiting trial (if they cannot post bail), conviction, or sentencing.
- Temporarily detaining juveniles pending transfer to juvenile authorities.
- Holding the mentally ill pending transfer to health facilities.
- Detaining those who have violated conditions of probation or parole and those who have "jumped" bail.
- Housing inmates awaiting transfer to federal or state prisons.
- Operating community-based corrections programs such as home confinement and electronic monitoring.

Increasingly, jails are also called on to handle the overflow from saturated state and federal prisons. In Washington State, for example, corrections officials are forced to rent eight hundred jail cells a day to house convicts who have been sent back to prison for violating the terms of their parole.

According to sociologist John Irwin, the unofficial purpose of the jail is to manage society's "rabble," so-called because

> [they] are not well integrated into conventional society, they are not members of conventional social organizations, they have few ties to conventional social networks, and they are carriers of unconventional values and beliefs.[61]

In Irwin's opinion, "rabble" who act violently are arrested and sent to prison. The jail is reserved for merely offensive rabble, whose primary threat to society lies in their failure to conform to its behavioral norms. Nearly seven out of ten jail inmates, for example, are dependent on or abuse alcohol or drugs.[62] This concept has been used by some critics of American corrections to explain the disproportionate number of poor and minority groups who may be found in the nation's jails at any time.

THE JAIL POPULATION

About 87 percent of jail inmates in the United States are male. As in other areas of corrections, however, women are becoming more numerous. Between 2000 and 2006, the adult female jail population increased by 40 percent, compared to a 21 percent increase for males.[63] Jails also follow the general corrections pattern in that, as mentioned, a disproportionate number of their inmates are members of minority groups. (For an overview of the characteristics of the jail population, see ■ Figure 13.7.)

Pretrial Detainees A significant number—about 30 percent—of those detained in jails technically are not prisoners. They are **pretrial detainees** who have been arrested by the police and, for a variety of reasons that we discussed in Chapter 9, are unable to post bail. Pretrial detainees are, in many ways, walking legal contradictions. According to the U.S. Constitution, they are innocent until proven guilty. At the same time, by being incarcerated while awaiting trial, they are denied a number of personal freedoms and are subjected to the poor conditions of many jails. In 1979, the Supreme Court rejected the notion that this situation is inherently unfair by refusing to give pretrial detainees greater legal protections than sentenced jail inmates have.[64] (See the feature *Landmark Cases:* Bell v. Wolfish.)

Sentenced Jail Inmates According to the Department of Justice, 37.9 percent of those in jail have been convicted of their current charges.[65] In other words, they have been found guilty of a crime, usually a misdemeanor, and sentenced to time in jail. The typical jail term lasts between thirty and ninety days, and rarely does a prisoner spend more than one year in jail for any single crime. Often, a judge will credit the length of time the convict has spent in detention waiting for trial—known as **time served**—toward his or her sentence. This practice acknowledges two realities of jails:

Pretrial Detainees Individuals who cannot post bail after arrest or are not released on their own recognizance and are therefore forced to spend the time prior to their trial incarcerated in jail.

Time Served The period of time a person denied bail has spent in jail prior to his or her trial. If the suspect is found guilty and sentenced to a jail or prison term, the judge will often lessen the duration of the sentence based on the amount of time served as a pretrial detainee.

Landmark Cases *Bell v. Wolfish*

In a class-action suit, several pretrial detainees in the Metropolitan Corrections Center in New York City challenged the constitutionality of the conditions under which they were being held. The practices under dispute included placing two inmates in cells designed for one ("double bunking"), restricting books and magazines, and intrusive body searches. The basis of the plaintiffs' argument was that, as pretrial detainees, they should not be subjected to the same terms of confinement as those persons in the jail who had been convicted of crimes. Both the district court and the court of appeals agreed with the plaintiffs. In addressing the case, the Supreme Court focused on whether the Constitution requires different treatment of those who are awaiting trial and those who have been convicted.

Bell v. Wolfish
United States Supreme Court
441 U.S. 520 (1979)
laws.findlaw.com/US/441/520.html

IN THE WORDS OF THE COURT . . .
Justice Rehnquist, majority opinion

* * * *

The presumption of innocence is a doctrine that allocates the burden of proof in criminal trials; * * * . But it has no application to a determination of the rights of a pretrial detainee during confinement before his trial has even begun.

* * * *

[T]he Government concededly may detain [a person] to ensure his presence at trial and may subject him to the restrictions and conditions of the detention facility so long as those conditions and restrictions do not amount to punishment, or otherwise violate the Constitution. * * * Whether it be called a jail, a prison, or a custodial center, the purpose of the facility is to detain. Loss of freedom of choice and privacy are inherent incidents of confinement in such a facility. And the fact that such detention interferes with the detainee's understandable desire to live as comfortably as possible and with as little restraint as possible during confinement does not convert the conditions or restrictions of detention into "punishment."

* * * *

[M]aintaining institutional security and preserving internal order and discipline are essential goals that may require limitation or retraction of the retained

■ **Figure 13.7** **The Characteristics of America's Jail Population**

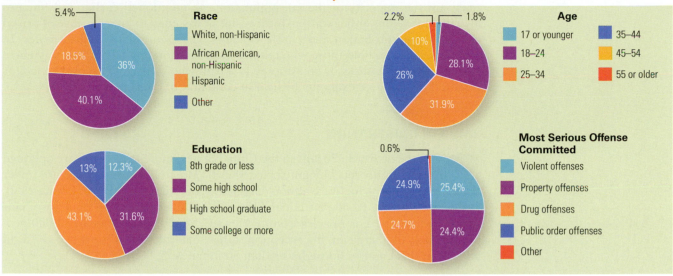

Source: Bureau of Justice Statistics, *Profile of Jail Inmates, 2002* (Washington, D.C.: U.S. Department of Justice, July 2004), 1–4.

1. Terms are generally too short to allow the prisoner to gain any benefit (that is, rehabilitation) from the jail's often limited or nonexistent treatment facilities. Therefore, the jail term can serve no other purpose than to punish the wrongdoer. (Judges who believe jail time can serve purposes of deterrence and incapacitation may not agree with this line of reasoning.)
2. Jails are chronically overcrowded, and judges need to clear space for new offenders.

constitutional rights of both convicted prisoners and pretrial detainees. * * * Prison officials must be free to take appropriate action to ensure the safety of inmates and corrections personnel and to prevent escape or unauthorized entry. Accordingly, we have held that even when an institutional restriction infringes a specific constitutional guarantee, such as the First Amendment, the practice must be evaluated in the light of the central objective of prison administration, safeguarding institutional security.

* * * *

Judges, after all, are human. They, no less than others in our society, have a natural tendency to believe that their individual solutions to often intractable problems are better and more workable than those of the persons who are actually charged with and trained in the running of the particular institution under examination. But under the Constitution, the first question to be answered is not whose plan is best, but in what branch of the Government is lodged the authority to initially devise the plan. This does not mean that constitutional rights are not to be scrupulously observed. It does mean, however, that the inquiry of federal courts into prison management must be limited to the issue of

whether a particular system violates any prohibition of the Constitution or, in the case of a federal prison, a statute. The wide range of "judgment calls" that meet constitutional and statutory requirements are confided to officials outside of the Judicial Branch of Government.

DECISION

The Court reversed the ruling of the court of appeals, holding that the possible innocence of pretrial detainees does not prevent corrections officials from taking any steps necessary to manage jails and maintain security. In a larger sense, the *Bell* decision is seen as giving corrections officials a great deal of freedom in making decisions without interference from the courts.

FOR CRITICAL ANALYSIS

Which constitutional principles apply to the arguments being made in *Bell v. Wolfish?* How much weight does the Court give these principles in light of the need to maintain security in correctional facilities?

For more information and activities related to this case, click on *Landmark Cases* under *Book Resources* at **www. cjinaction.com**.

Other Jail Inmates Pretrial detainees and those convicted of misdemeanors make up the majority of the jail population. As mentioned earlier, jail inmates also include felons either waiting for transfer or assigned to jails because of prison overcrowding, probation and parole violators, the mentally ill, and juveniles. In addition, jails can hold those who require incarceration but do not "fit" anywhere else. A material witness or an attorney in a trial who refuses to follow the judge's instructions may, for example, be held in contempt of court and sent to jail.

JAIL ADMINISTRATION

L08 Of the nearly 3,370 jails in the United States, more than 2,700 are operated on a county level by an elected sheriff. Most of the remainder are under the control of municipalities, although six state governments (Alaska, Connecticut, Delaware, Hawaii, Rhode Island, and Vermont) manage jails. The capacity of jails varies widely. The Los Angeles County Men's Central Jail holds nearly 7,000 people, but jails that large are the exception rather than the rule. Almost two-thirds of all jails in this country house fewer than 50 inmates.[66]

The "Burden" of Jail Administration Given that the public's opinion of jails ranges from negative to indifferent, some sheriffs neglect their jail management duties. Instead, they focus on high-visibility issues such as placing more law enforcement officers on the streets and improving security in schools. In fact, a jail usually receives publicity only after an escape or an incident in which inmates are abused by jailers. Ironically, with their more complex and diverse populations, jails are more difficult to manage than prisons. Jails hold people who have never been incarcerated before, people under the influence of drugs or alcohol at the time of their arrival, the mentally ill, and people who exhibit a range of violent behavior—from nonexistent to extreme—that only adds to the unpredictable atmosphere.[67]

Despite some sheriffs' general apathy toward jails, few would be willing to give up their management duties. As troublesome as they may be, jails can be useful in other ways. The sheriff appoints a jail administrator, or deputy sheriff, to oversee the day-to-day operations of the facility. The sheriff also has the power to hire other staff members, such as deputy jailers. The sheriff may award these jobs to people who helped her or him get elected, and, in return, jail staffers can prove helpful to the sheriff in future elections.

The Challenges of Overcrowding In many ways, the sheriff is placed in an untenable position when it comes to jail overcrowding. He or she has little control over the number of people who are sent to jail; that power resides with prosecutors and judges. Nevertheless, the jail is expected to find space to hold all comers, regardless of its capacity. A sheriff from Kane County, Utah, describes the situation:

> We have people who should get sixty or ninety days, and they just do a weekend and we kick them out. Unless we get a real habitual abuser, we have no choice but to set them free. Most of the time we're pretty sure they will be back in a couple of days with a new offense.[68]

Living Conditions Chronic overcrowding makes the jail experience a miserable one for most inmates. Cells intended to hold one or two people are packed with up to six. Often, inmates are forced to sleep in hallways. In such stressful situations, tempers flare, leading to violent, aggressive behavior. The close proximity and unsanitary living conditions also lead to numerous health problems. In the words of one observer, jail inmates

> share tight space day and night, struggle with human density never before experienced (unless earlier in jail), and search hopelessly for even a moment of solitude. . . . [The

congested conditions offer] inmates next to nothing except a stifling idleness that is almost sure to make them worse for the experience. If hard time in prison or jail is time without meaning, there might be no equal to long periods of time in the seriously overcrowded living areas of jails; for above all else (and clearly in comparison to time in prison), jail time is dead time.[69]

Such conditions also raise basic questions of justice: as we noted earlier, many of the inmates in jail have not yet been tried and must be presumed innocent.

Supply and Demand One way to alleviate overcrowding is to build more jails. The problem, however, is what economists call supply creating its own demand; that is, the number of jail inmates seems to expand to meet the number of available beds. In the twelve months leading up to June 30, 2006, the nation's jails added nearly 22,000 new beds in an effort to meet demand. During that same time period, the jail population in the United States grew by almost that same amount. Today, U.S. jails average 94 percent capacity, and on any given day, depending on arrest patterns, the institutions can reach capacity levels greater than 100 percent.[70] From July 2002 to December 2005, overcrowding in Los Angeles jails forced the sheriff's department to release nearly 150,000 jail inmates before they had served their full terms. More than 15,000 of those convicts were rearrested for crimes they committed during the period when they would otherwise have been locked up—nearly 2,200 for violent crimes such as assault or rape and 16 for murder.[71]

NEW-GENERATION JAILS

The boom in jail construction has been accompanied by a growing realization that simply adding bed space is not sufficient to deal with the problems endemic to the facilities. In other words, *how* the jail is built is just as important as *why* it is built. Over the past thirty years, the trend in jail construction has moved **L09** away from a traditional design toward a structure known as the new-generation jail.

The Traditional Design For most of the nation's history, the architecture of a jail was secondary to its purpose of keeping inmates safely locked away. Consequently, most jails in the United States continue to resemble those from the days of the Walnut Street Jail in Philadelphia. In this *traditional,* or *linear design,* jail cells are located along a corridor (see photo). To supervise the inmates while they are in their cells, correctional staff members must walk up and down the corridor; thus, the number of prisoners they can see at any one time is severely limited. With this limited supervision, inmates can more easily break institutional rules.

The harsh environment and lack of supervision inherent in the traditional design have been found to contribute to inmates' antisocial behavior. The prisoners spend most of their free time isolated and devoid of social control, and they have a tendency to respond with hostility.[72] Given that most jail inmates are released after a short period of confinement, many observers feel that the traditional design can pose a threat to the community by "creating" citizens who are more disposed toward violence on release than when they entered the jail.

Podular Design In the 1970s, the Federal Bureau of Prisons (BOP) decided to upgrade the traditional design based on the motto "If you can't

▼ The linear design is similar to that of a hospital in which long rows of rooms are placed along a corridor. To carry out her or his surveillance duties, the custodial officer must either look down the corridor, or walk down it and peer into the windows of the individual cells. What sorts of risks are inherent in this type of jail design?

Courtesy National Corrections Corporation

▲ In a direct supervision jail, the custodial officer is stationed at an in-pod control terminal. From this point, he or she has visual contact with all inmates and can communicate with inmates quickly and easily. During the day, inmates stay in the open area and are allowed in their cells only when given permission. The officer locks the door to the cells from his or her control terminal. How would the behavior of inmates in a direct supervision jail differ from that of inmates in a traditional, linear jail?

rehabilitate, at least do no harm."[73] The BOP implemented a new management philosophy in designing three Metropolitan Correctional Centers in Chicago, New York, and San Diego. The National Institute of Corrections designated these three facilities **new-generation jails** to distinguish them from the older models.[74]

The new-generation jails differ significantly from their predecessors. The layout of the new facilities makes it easier for the staff to monitor cell-confined inmates. The basic structure of the new-generation jail is based on a **podular design.** Each "pod" contains "living units" for individual prisoners. These units, instead of lining up along a straight corridor, are often situated in a triangle so that a staff member in the center of the triangle has visual access to nearly all the cells. Daily activities such as eating and showering take place in the pod, which also has an outdoor exercise area. Treatment facilities are also located in the pod, allowing greater access for the inmates. A new wing of the Pima County jail in Arizona has even installed two-way video monitors in the rooms so that inmates will not have to leave the pod to receive visitors. Furthermore, the surroundings are not as harsh as in the older jails. Cells have comfortable furniture, rugs, and windows, and a communal "day-room" has televisions, radios, and telephones.[75]

Direct Supervision Approach The podular design also enables a new-generation jail to be managed using a **direct supervision approach.**[76] One or more jail officers are stationed in the living area of the pod and are therefore in constant interaction with all prisoners in that particular pod (see the photo above). Some new-generation jails even provide a desk in the center of the living area, which sends a very different message to the prisoners than the traditional control booth. Theoretically, jail officials who have constant contact with inmates will be able to stem misconduct quickly and efficiently and will also be able to recognize "danger signs" from individual inmates and stop outbursts before they occur.

At first, the new-generation jails provoked a great deal of skepticism, as they were seen as inherently "soft" for criminals. A number of empirical results, however, seem to speak to the success of podular design and direct supervision. One study measured inmate behavior in an adult detention facility before and after it was converted to a direct supervision jail. The researchers found a "dramatic reduction" in the number of assaults, batteries, attempted suicides, sex offenses, possession of weapons, and escapees.[77] Today, nearly two hundred new-generation jails are in operation or under construction.

New-Generation Jail A type of jail that is distinguished architecturally from its predecessors by a design that encourages interaction between inmates and jailers and that offers greater opportunities for treatment.

Podular Design The architectural style of the new-generation jail. Each "pod" consists of between twelve and twenty-four one-person cells and a communal "day-room" to allow for social interaction.

Direct Supervision Approach A process of prison and jail administration in which correctional officers are in continuous physical contact with inmates during the day.

Self Check Fill in the Blanks

About 30 percent of the people in jail are not prisoners, but rather _____ who are unable to post bail and await trial. Another 40 percent have been _____ of their current charges, meaning that the jail sentence is punishment for a crime—usually a _____ and not a felony. Most jails are operated on a local level by the county _____. Check your answers on page 440.

The Consequences of Our High Rates of Incarceration

For many observers, especially those who support the crime control theory of criminal justice, America's high rate of incarceration has contributed significantly to the drop in the country's crime rates.[78] At the heart of this belief is the **LO10** fact, which we discussed in Chapter 2, that most crimes are committed by a relatively small group of repeat offenders. Several studies have tried to corroborate this viewpoint, with varying results—estimates of the number of crimes committed each year by habitual offenders range from 3 to 187.[79] If one accepts the higher estimate, each year a repeat offender spends in prison prevents a significant number of criminal acts.

Criminologists, however, note the negative consequences of America's growing prison and jail population. For one, incarceration can have severe social consequences for communities and the families that make up those communities. When a parent is imprisoned, her or his children will often suffer financial hardships, reduced supervision and discipline, and a general deterioration of the family structure.[80] These factors are used to explain the fact that children of convicts are more likely to become involved in delinquent behavior. Our high rates of incarceration also deny one of the basic rights of American democracy—the right to vote—to about 5.3 million Americans with criminal records.[81] (A number of states and the federal government *disenfranchise*, or take away the ability to vote, from those convicted of felonies. This has a disproportionate impact on minority groups, weakening their voice in the democratic debate.) Today, 8.1 percent of African American men between the ages of twenty-five and twenty-nine are in prison, compared to 2.6 percent of Hispanic men and 1.1 percent of white men in the same age group.[82] With more black men behind bars than enrolled in the nation's colleges and universities, Marc Mauer of the Sentencing Project believes that the "ripple effect on their communities and on the next generation of kids, growing up with their fathers in prison, will certainly be with us for at least a generation."[83]

Whether the American incarceration situation is "good" or "bad" depends to a large extent on one's personal philosophy. In the end, it is difficult to do a definitive cost-benefit analysis for each person incarcerated, weighing the benefits of preventing crimes that might (or might not) have been committed by an inmate against the costs to the convict's family and society. One thing that can be stated with some certainty is that, even with the growing interest in diversion and rehabilitation described in the previous chapter, the increase in prison and jail populations will continue in the foreseeable future.

▼ About half a million children in the United States, including Californian Briana Stevens, pictured below, can see their mothers only by visiting them in prison or jail. What are some of the possible consequences of this separation?

© Tim Rue/Corbis

SOLITARY CONFINEMENT: SENSELESS SUFFERING?

In the 1990s, former New York appellate judge Sol Wachtler, who had been incarcerated for harassing an ex-girlfriend, was stabbed by a fellow inmate. Prison officials confined Wachtler alone in a tiny, windowless cell, for his own protection. One of his neighbors, called "dogman" by the guards, "howled until dawn like a wounded canine." Others "engaged in loud conversations with voices that only they could hear." Finally, "after several weeks of not being able to separate day from night," says Wachtler, "I too began to hallucinate."[84] In this *Criminal Justice in Action* feature, we will examine the widespread practice of solitary confinement, condemned by critics as inhumane but heralded by supporters as an invaluable tool of prison management.

ENFORCED ISOLATION

Although conditions of solitary confinement vary, in general the term refers to the confinement of an inmate alone in a small cell for most or all of the day with minimal environmental stimulation and social interaction.[85] Most solitary confinement cells measure approximately eight feet by six feet. Furnished with only a sink, toilet, and concrete bed, they have no windows or barred doors that would let in natural light.

As a rule, inmates are not sentenced to solitary confinement by a judge, and the assignment has no connection to the severity of the original offense. Rather, these isolation cells are reserved for prisoners who commit disciplinary violations once in prison or, like Sol Wachtler, are deemed a security risk to themselves or others. According to estimates, approximately 60,000 inmates—about 4.5 percent of the American prison population—are in solitary confinement at any given time.[86] In addition, as we saw earlier in this chapter, many states and the federal government operate supermax prisons on the principle of perpetual isolation for all inmates.

The Case for Solitary Confinement

- Prison officials see the threat of solitary confinement as a vital tool in maintaining order and discipline. Because human contact is one of the few privileges that inmates enjoy, they have a strong incentive to conform to the rules of the institution rather than risk losing that privilege.

- Solitary confinement allows prison officials to separate convicts such as violent gang members from the general inmate population if they threaten the safety and security of the institution.

- Solitary confinement can be a form of rehabilitation, as it separates the inmate from negative influences and provides a chance for treatment and other constructive behavior.

The Case against Solitary Confinement

- Solitary confinement causes severe damage to the mental health of prisoners. Researchers have identified a number of resulting symptoms, including intense anxiety, hallucinations, violent fantasies, and reduced impulse control.[87]

- The majority of inmates who suffer the psychological harm of solitary confinement will eventually be returned to society, which will have to bear the burden of their mental illness.

- Because prison officials have unfettered discretion in deciding who gets sent to solitary confinement and for how long, the practice is rife with abuse.

Your Opinion—Writing Assignment

To many observers, the drawbacks of solitary confinement lie in its practice, not its principles. Although it may be useful in controlling inmate populations, solitary confinement procedures suffer from failure to properly monitor the medical and psychological state of those in "the Hole," confinement for trivial offenses like "talking back" to corrections officials, and unacceptably long periods of isolation. The courts have shown no inclination to rein in these abuses, as judges tend to be extremely deferential to the decisions and policies of prison officials.

Today, no federal laws control the use of solitary confinement. Only one state, Washington, places a limit—twenty days—on the length of time an inmate may be kept in isolation.[88] If you were to draft a law regulating the use of solitary confinement, what elements would your law contain? Would you, like the courts, give prison officials a "free hand," or would you restrict their discretion? Would you allow prisoners to challenge their solitary confinement in court? Before responding, you can review our discussions in this chapter concerning

- The three general models of prison organization (page 419).

- Maximum-security and supermax prisons (pages 420–423).

- Prison administration (pages 424–426).

Your answer should take at least three full paragraphs.

L01 **Contrast the Pennsylvania and the New York penitentiary theories of the 1800s.** Basically, the Pennsylvania system imposed total silence on its prisoners. Based on the concept of separate confinement, penitentiaries were constructed with back-to-back cells facing both outward and inward. Prisoners worked, slept, and ate alone in their cells. In contrast, New York used the congregate system; silence was imposed, but inmates worked and ate together.

L02 **List the factors that have caused the prison population to grow dramatically in the last several decades.** (a) The enhancement and stricter enforcement of the nation's drug laws; (b) increased probability of incarceration; (c) inmates serving more time for each crime; (d) federal prison growth; and (e) rising incarceration rates for women.

L03 **Explain the three general models of prisons.** (a) The custodial model assumes the prisoner is incarcerated for reasons of incapacitation, deterrence, and retribution. (b) The rehabilitation model puts security concerns second and the well-being of the individual inmate first. As a consequence, treatment programs are offered to prisoners. (c) The reintegration model sees the correctional institution as a training ground for preparing convicts to reenter society.

L04 **List and briefly explain the four types of prisons.** (a) Maximum-security prisons, which are designed mainly with security and surveillance in mind. Such prisons are usually large and consist of cell blocks, each of which is set off by a series of gates and bars. (b) Medium-security prisons, which offer considerably more educational and treatment programs and allow more contact between inmates. Such prisons are rarely walled, but rather are surrounded by high fences. (c) Minimum-security prisons, which permit prisoners to have television sets and computers and often allow them to leave the grounds for educational and employment purposes. (d) Supermaximum-security (supermax) prisons, in which prisoners are confined to one-person cells for up to twenty-two and a half hours per day under constant video camera surveillance.

L05 **Describe the formal prison management system, and indicate the three most important aspects of prison governance.** A formal system is militaristic with a hierarchical (top-down) chain of command; the warden (or superintendent) is on top, then deputy wardens, and last, custodial employees. Sound governance of a corrections facility requires officials to provide inmates with a sense of order, amenities such as clean living conditions and acceptable food, and services such as vocational training and remedial education programs.

L06 **List the reasons why private prisons can often be run more cheaply than public ones.** (a) Labor costs are lower because private prison employees are nonunionized and receive lower levels of overtime pay, sick leave, and health care. (b) Competitive bidding requires the operators of private prisons to buy goods and services at the lowest possible prices. (c) There is less red tape in a private prison facility.

L07 **Summarize the distinction between jails and prisons, and indicate the importance of jails in the American correctional system.** Generally, a prison is for those convicted of felonies who will serve lengthy periods of incarceration, whereas a jail is for those who have been convicted of misdemeanors and will serve less than a year of incarceration. A jail also (a) receives individuals pending arraignment and holds them while awaiting trial, conviction, or sentencing; (b) temporarily holds juveniles pending transfer to juvenile authorities; (c) holds the mentally ill pending transfer to health facilities; (d) detains those who have violated probation or parole and those who have "jumped" bail; and (e) houses those awaiting transfer to federal or state prisons. Approximately 7 million Americans spend time in jail each year.

L08 **Explain how jails are administered.** Most jails are operated at the county level by an elected sheriff, although about 20 percent are under the control of municipalities and six states manage jails themselves. Sheriffs appoint jail administrators (deputy sheriffs) as well as deputy jailers.

L09 **Indicate the difference between traditional jail design and new-generation jail design.** A traditional design is linear, with jail cells located along a corridor. Such a physical structure is rather cold with an emphasis on iron and steel fixtures that are not easily broken. New-generation jails, in contrast, use a podular design, with the "pods" often arranged in a triangle. Each cell has furniture, rugs, and windows, and there are communal "day-rooms" with televisions, radios, and telephones.

L010 **Indicate some of the consequences of our high rates of incarceration.** Some people believe that the reduction in the country's crime rate is a direct result of increased incarceration rates; others believe that high incarceration rates are having increasing negative social consequences, such as financial hardships, reduced supervision and discipline of children, and a general deterioration of the family structure when one parent is in prison.

Key Terms

congregate system 414
direct supervision approach 436
jail 430
lockdown 423
maximum-security prison 420
medical model 414

medium-security prison 423
minimum-security prison 423
new-generation jails 436
penitentiary 413
podular design 436
pretrial detainees 432

private prisons 426
separate confinement 413
supermax prison 422
time served 432
warden 425

Self Check Answer Key

Page 415: i. separate; ii. congregate; iii. silence; iv. cheaper;
v. labor; vi. medical

Page 419: i. drug; ii. incarceration/imprisonment; iii. length;
iv. federal; v. women

Page 424: i. maximum; ii. supermax; iii. medium;
iv. minimum

Page 426: i. warden; ii. purpose; iii. disorder; iv. amenities

Page 430: i. financial; ii. overcrowding; iii. security/safety;
iv. federal

Page 436: i. pretrial detainees; ii. convicted;
iii. misdemeanor; iv. sheriff

Questions for Critical Analysis

1. Explain the benefit of nonfixed sentences coupled with the possibility of early release.

2. How did the Elmira Reformatory classify prisoners? How did the system work?

3. Overall crime rates are falling, yet prison populations are rising. Why?

4. What are several reasons why prison construction continues to increase?

5. The chain of command in prisons and police departments appears quite similar, yet there is a big difference. What is it?

6. What factor is most responsible for the continuing growth of the private prison industry?

7. Why are jails so important in the American corrections system?

8. Most sheriffs are quite apathetic toward the job of running jails, yet they do not want to give up their management duties. Why not?

Maximize Your Best Possible Outcome for Chapter 13

1. **Maximize Your Best Chance for Getting a Good Grade on the Exam.** ThomsonNOW Personalized Study is a diagnostic study tool containing valuable text-specific resources—and because you focus on just what you don't know, you learn more in less time to get a better grade. How do you get ThomsonNOW? If your textbook does not include an access code card, go to **thomsonedu.com** to get ThomsonNOW before your next exam!

2. **Get the Most Out of Your Textbook** by going to the book companion Web site at **www.cjinaction.com** to access one of the tutorial quizzes, use the flash cards

to master key terms, and check out the many other study aids you'll find there. Under chapter resources you will also be able to access the Stories from the Street feature and Web links mentioned in the textbook.

3. **Learn about Potential Criminal Justice Careers** discussed in this chapter by exploring careers online at **www.cjinaction.com**. You will find career descriptions and information about job requirements, training, salary and benefits, and the application process. You can also watch video profiles featuring criminal justice professionals.

Notes

1. Bureau of Justice Statistics, *Prisoners in 2006* (Washington, D.C.: U.S. Department of Justice, 2007), 1.
2. James M. Beattie, *Crime and the Courts in England, 1660–1800* (Princeton, NJ: Princeton University Press, 1986), 506–507.
3. Samuel Walker, *Popular Justice* (New York: Oxford University Press, 1980), 11.
4. Michael Meranze, *Laboratories of Virtue: Punishment, Revolution, and Authority in Philadelphia, 1760–1835* (Chapel Hill, NC: University of North Carolina Press, 1996), 55.
5. Negley K. Teeters, *The Cradle of the Penitentiary: The Walnut Street Jail at Philadelphia, 1773–1835* (Philadelphia: Pennsylvania Prison Society, 1955), 30.
6. Negley K. Teeters and John D. Shearer, *The Prison at Philadelphia's Cherry Hill* (New York: Columbia University Press, 1957), 142–143.
7. Henry Calvin Mohler, "Convict Labor Policies," *Journal of the American Institute of Criminal Law and Criminology* 15 (1925), 556–557.
8. Zebulon Brockway, *Fifty Years of Prison Service* (Montclair, NJ: Patterson Smith, 1969), 400–401.
9. Robert Martinson, "What Works? Questions and Answers about Prison Reform," *Public Interest* 35 (Spring 1974), 22.
10. See Ted Palmer, "Martinson Revisited," *Journal of Research on Crime and Delinquency* (1975), 133; and Paul Gendreau and Bob Ross, "Effective Correctional Treatment: Bibliotherapy for Cynics," *Crime & Delinquency* 25 (1979), 499.
11. Robert Martinson, "New Findings, New Views: A Note of Caution Regarding Sentencing Reform," *Hofstra Law Review* 7 (1979), 243.
12. Fox Butterfield, "'Defying Gravity,' Inmate Population Climbs," *New York Times* (January 19, 1998), A10.
13. *Ibid.*
14. Bureau of Justice Statistics, *Prisoners in 2005* (Washington D.C.: U.S. Department of Justice, November 2006), 9, 10.
15. Allen J. Beck, "Growth, Change, and Stability in the U.S. Prison Population, 1980–1995," *Corrections Management Quarterly* (Spring 1997), 9–10.
16. Bureau of Justice Statistics, "Sentences Imposed in Cases Terminated in U.S. District Courts," *Sourcebook of Criminal Justice Statistics Online*, Table 5.19, at **www.albany.edu/sourcebook/pdf/ t5192003.pdf**.
17. *Fifteen Years of Guidelines Sentencing: An Assessment of How Well the Federal Criminal Justice System Is Achieving the Goals of Sentencing Reform* (Washington, D.C.: U.S. Sentencing Commission, November 2004), 46.
18. Bureau of Justice Statistics, *Federal Criminal Case Processing, 2002* (Washington, D.C.: U.S. Department of Justice, January 2005), 1.
19. Bureau of Justice Statistics, *Truth in Sentencing in State Prisons* (Washington, D.C.: U.S. Department of Justice, 1999), 7.
20. *Prisoners in 2005*, Table 1, page 2.
21. Bureau of Justice Statistics, *Prisoners in 2005* (Washington, D.C.: U.S. Department of Justice, November 2006), Table 14, page 10.
22. *Prisoners in 2005*, 10.
23. *Ibid.*, 4, 5.
24. Sarah Lawrence and Jeremy Travis, *The New Landscape of Imprisonment: Mapping America's Prison Expansion* (Washington, D.C.: Urban Institute Justice Policy Center, 2004), 2.
25. Bureau of Justice Statistics, *Justice Expenditure and Employment in the United States, 2003* (Washington, D.C.: U.S. Department of Justice, April 2006), 1–2.
26. "Direct Expenditures for Correctional Activities of State Governments," *Sourcebook of Criminal Justice Statistics Online*, at **www.albany.edu/sourcebook/pdf/t1112003.pdf**.
27. Todd R. Clear, George F. Cole, and Michael D. Reisig, *American Corrections*, 7th ed. (Belmont, CA: Thomson Wadsworth, 2006), 463.
28. Charles H. Logan, *Criminal Justice Performance Measures in Prisons* (Washington, D.C.: U.S. Department of Justice, 1993), 5.
29. Todd R. Clear and George F. Cole, *American Corrections*, 4th ed. (Belmont, CA: Wadsworth Publishing Co., 1997), 245–246.
30. Alfred Blumstein, "Prisons," in *Crime*, ed. James Q. Wilson and Joan Petersilia (San Francisco: ICS Press, 1995), 392.
31. Cassia Spohn and David Holleran, "The Effect of Imprisonment on Recidivism Rates of Felony Offenders: A Focus on Drug Offenders," *Criminology* (May 1, 2002), 329–357.
32. Tony Izzo, "I-Max Awaits Green," *Kansas City Star* (May 26, 1996), A1.
33. Charles A. Pettigrew, "Technology and the Eighth Amendment: The Problem of Supermax Prisons," *North Carolina Journal of Law and Technology* (Fall 2002), 195.
34. "Facts about Pelican Bay's SHU," *California Prisoner* (December 1991),
35. *Jones'El et al. v. Berge and Lichter*, 164 F.Supp.2d 1096 (2001).
36. Robert Perkinson, "Shackled Justice: Florence Federal Penitentiary and the New Politics of Punishment," *Social Justice* (Fall 1994), 117–123.
37. Terry Kuppers, *Prison Madness: The Mental Health Crisis behind Bars and What We Must Do about It* (San Francisco: Jossey-Bass, 1999), 56–64.
38. Charles H. Logan, "Well Kept: Comparing Quality of Confinement in a Public and Private Prison," *Journal of Criminal Law and Criminology* 83 (1992), 580.
39. Bert Useem and Peter Kimball, *Stages of Siege: U.S. Prison Riots, 1971–1986* (New York: Oxford University Press, 1989).
40. Bert Useem, "Disorganization and the New Mexico Prison Riot of 1980," *American Sociology Review* 50 (1985), 685.
41. John J. DiIulio, *Governing Prisons* (New York: Free Press, 1987), 12.
42. *Ibid.*
43. *Prisoners in 2005*, 5.
44. "A Tale of Two Systems: Cost, Quality, and Accountability in Private Prisons," *Harvard Law Review* (May 2002), 1872.
45. Douglas C. McDonald and Kenneth Carlson, *Contracting for Imprisonment in the Federal Prison System: Cost and Performance of the Privately Operated Taft Correctional Institution* (Cambridge, MA: Abt Associates, Inc., October 2005), vii.
46. "Keep an Eye on Private Prisons," *Denver Post* (July 10, 2005), E6.
47. Don Thompson, "Governor OKs Adding 53,000 Prison Beds," *San Jose Mercury News* (May 4, 2007), 5B.
48. Logan, "Well Kept," 577.
49. Richard C. Brister, "Changing of the Guard: A Case for Privatization of Texas Prisons," *The Prison Journal* 76 (September 1996), 322–323.
50. Harley G. Lappin *et al.*, *Evaluation of the Taft Demonstration Project: Performance of a Private-Sector Prison and the BOP* (Washington, D.C.: Federal Bureau of Prisons, 2005), 57–59.
51. Curtis R. Blakely and Vic W. Bumphus, "Private and Public Sector Prisons," *Federal Probation* (June 2004), 27.
52. Richard L. Lippke, "Thinking about Private Prisons," *Criminal Justice Ethics* (Winter/Spring 1997), 32.
53. John Dilulio, "Prisons, Profits, and the Public Good: The Privatization of Corrections," in *Criminal Justice Center Bulletin* (Huntsville, TX: Sam Houston State University, 1986).
54. Ira P. Robbins, "Privatization of Prisons, Privatization of Corrections: Defining the Issues," *Vanderbilt Law Review* 40 (1987), 823.
55. Amy Cheung, *Prison Privatization and the Use of Incarceration* (Washington, D.C.: The Sentencing Project, 2002), 3.
56. *Prisoners in 2005*, 5.
57. Quoted in David Crary, "Federal Prisons Bail Out Private Facilities," *Pittsburgh Tribune Review* (July 31, 2005), A4.
58. Bureau of Justice Statistics, *Prison and Jail Inmates at Midyear 2006* (Washington, D.C.: U.S. Department of Justice, June 2007), Table 12, page 8.
59. Arthur Wallenstein, "Jail Crowding: Bringing the Issue to the Corrections Center Stage," *Corrections Today* (December 1996), 76–81.
60. Quoted in Butterfield, "Defying Gravity."
61. John Irwin, *The Jail: Managing the Underclass in American Society* (Berkeley, CA: University of California Press, 1985), 2.
62. Bureau of Justice Statistics, *Substance Dependence, Abuse, and Treatment of Jail Inmates, 2002* (Washington, D.C.: U.S. Department of Justice, July 2005), 1.
63. *Prison and Jail Inmates at Midyear 2006*, Table 9, page 5.
64. 441 U.S. 520 (1979).
65. *Prison and Jail Inmates at Midyear 2006*, Table 11, page 6.
66. Bureau of Justice Statistics, *Bulletin* (Washington, D.C.: U.S. Department of Justice, May 2004), 10.

67. Philip L. Reichel, *Corrections: Philosophies, Practices, and Procedures*, 2d ed. (Boston: Allyn & Bacon, 2001), 283.

68. Quoted in Greg Burton, "Jail Builders Race to Keep Up with Demand," *Salt Lake City Tribune* (May 8, 1998), N31.

69. Robert G. Lawson, "Turning Jails into Prisons—Collateral Damage from Kentucky's 'War on Crime,'" *Kentucky Law Journal* (2006–2007), 1.

70. *Prison and Jail Inmates at Midyear 2006*, 7.

71. Jack Leonard, Megan Garvey, and Doug Smith, "Releasing Inmates Early Has a Costly Human Toll," *Los Angeles Times* (May 14, 2006), A1.

72. John J. Gibbs, "Environmental Congruence and Symptoms of Psychopathology: A Further Exploration of the Effects of Exposure to the Jail Environment," *Criminal Justice and Behavior* 18 (1991), 351–374.

73. Richard Weiner, William Frazier, and Jay Farbstein, "Building Better Jails," *Psychology Today* (June 1987), 40.

74. R. L. Miller, "New Generation Justice Facilities: The Case for Direct Supervision," *Architectural Technology* 12 (1985), 6–7.

75. Gerald J. Bayens, Jimmy J. Williams, and John Ortiz Smykla, "Jail Type and Inmate Behavior: A Longitudinal Analysis," *Federal Probation* (September 1997), 54.

76. Linda L. Zupan, *Jails: Reform and the New Generation Philosophy* (Cincinnati, OH: Anderson Publishing Co., 1991).

77. Bayens, Williams, and Smykla.

78. Dan Seligman, "Lock 'Em Up," *Forbes* (May 23, 2005), 216–217.

79. Franklin E. Zimring and Gordon Hawkins, *Incapacitation: Penal Confinement and the Restraint of Crime* (New York: Oxford University Press, 1995), 38, 40, 145.

80. Todd R. Clear and Dina R. Rose, "A Thug in Jail Can't Shoot Your Sister: The Unintended Consequences of Incarceration," paper presented to the American Sociological Association (August 18, 1996).

81. The Sentencing Project, "Felony Disenfranchisement," at **www.sentencingproject.org/IssueAreaHome.aspx?IssueID=4**.

82. *Prisoners in 2005*, 8.

83. Quoted in Fox Butterfield, "Study Finds 2.6% Increase in U.S. Prison Population," *New York Times* (July 28, 2003), A8.

84. Sol Wachtler, "A Cell of One's Own," *New York Times* (September 24, 2006), 11.

85. Stuart Grassian, "Psychiatric Effects of Solitary Confinement," *Washington University Journal of Law and Policy* (2006), 327.

86. *The Corrections Yearbook, 2000*, ed. Camille Graham Camp and George M. Camp (New York: Criminal Justice Yearbook, 2000), 26.

87. Grassian, 335–337.

88. Washington Revised Code Section 10.64.060 (2005).

CHAPTER 14

Behind Bars:
The Life of an Inmate

Chapter outline

- Prison Culture
- Prison Violence
- Inside a Women's Prison
- Correctional Officers and Discipline
- Protecting Prisoners' Rights
- Parole and Release from Prison
- Reentry into Society
- The Special Case of Sex Offenders
- Criminal Justice in Action—A Second Look at Residency Laws

Learning objectives

After reading this chapter, you should be able to:

L01 Explain the concept of prison as a total institution.

L02 Describe the possible patterns of inmate behavior, which are driven by the inmate's personality and values.

L03 Indicate some of the reasons for violent behavior in prisons.

L04 List and briefly explain the six general job categories among correctional officers.

L05 Contrast the hands-off doctrine of prisoner law with the hands-on approach.

L06 Contrast probation, parole, mandatory release, pardon, and furlough.

L07 Describe truth-in-sentencing laws and their goals.

L08 Describe typical conditions of parole.

L09 Explain the goal of prisoner reentry programs.

L010 Indicate typical conditions for release for a paroled child molester.

"Animal Factories"

James C. Oleson, a professor of sociology and criminal justice at Virginia's Old Dominion University, has come up with a novel solution for the many problems that plague America's prisons and jails. He proposes placing hundreds of thousands of inmates in narcotic comas for the duration of their sentences, turning each "coma bay prisoner," into "a (living) machine, with inputs and outputs." The heavily drugged inmates, kept in full health by liberal doses of antibiotics, would breathe though tubes to their lungs and "eat" through tubes to their stomachs. Resting peacefully on adjustable beds with flotation mattresses, they would be continually monitored by a small staff of corrections officers, all for a fraction of the costs of the present system.

Oleson is not joking to make a point. Rather, his point is that he is not joking. The modern prison, he says, does not work. It has "evolved into an institution that is not only expensive and ineffective, but affirmatively dehumanizing and brutal." Overcrowding has led to high levels of behavioral problems among inmates, which have turned prisons into "breeding grounds for violence, rape, and escalating criminality." According to Oleson, the idea of rehabilitating offenders in the corrections context has largely been abandoned. Most inmates, denied not only meaningful treatment and education programs but even distractions such as weight lifting, radios, adult magazines, and conjugal visits, are left with nothing to do and all of their prison terms to do it.

In essence, Oleson concludes, today's prisons are little more than expensive "animal factories" and must be abolished. His "punitive coma" scheme would end overcrowding, slash costs, and remove the opportunity for violence. As for the inmates themselves, Oleson insists that many of them would prefer to serve their sentences comatose: "For where there is no waking consciousness, there can be neither depression nor aggression, neither suicide nor rape."

▲ A prison tactical team watches over inmates during a drug and weapons sweep at the Big Muddy Correctional Center in Ina, Illinois. Such scenes confirm Professor James C. Oleson's notion that American prisons are "breeding grounds" of "escalating criminality."

AP Photo/Southern Illinoisan

Criminal Justice ⚖ Now™

Maximize your study time by using ThomsonNOW's Personalized Study plan to help you review this chapter and prepare for examination. The Study Plan will

- Help you identify areas on which you should concentrate
- Provide interactive exercises to help you master the chapter concepts; and
- Provide a post-test to confirm you are ready to move on to the next chapter information.

L ife behind bars has long been predicated on the *principle of least eligibility*, which holds that the least advantaged members of outside society should lead a better existence than any person living in prison or jail.[1] The criminal justice system does not seem prepared to follow this principle to the extremes suggested by Professor Oleson.[2] One critic dismissed his "punitive coma" solution on the grounds that it would violate "all human rights" because the prisoner is no longer allowed "to be human."[3] Still, many observers who find Oleson's solution untenable would agree with his assertion that the circumstances in which many inmates exist have become unacceptably inhumane and, indeed, unconstitutional. At one time or another over the past two decades, the federal government, nearly every state government, and countless local authorities have been under court order to improve living conditions in their penal institutions.[4]

In this chapter, we look at some of the factors that influence the quality of life in America's prisons and jails. To that end, we will discuss the ramifications of violence in prison, the role played by correctional officers, efforts by prisoners and prisoners' rights advocates to improve conditions, and several other issues that are at the forefront of prison debate today. To start, we must understand the forces that shape prison culture and how those forces affect the overall operation of the correctional facility.

Prison Culture

Any institution, whether a school, a bank, or a police department, has an organizational culture—a set of values that help the people in the organization understand what actions are acceptable and what actions are unacceptable. According to a theory put forth by the influential sociologist Erving Goffman, prison cultures are unique because prisons are **total institutions** that encompass every aspect of an inmate's life. Unlike a student or a bank teller, a prisoner cannot leave the institution or have any meaningful interaction with outside communities. Others arrange every aspect of daily life, and all prisoners are required to follow this schedule in exactly the same manner.[5]

Inmates develop their own argot, or language (see ■ Figure 14.1). They create their own economy, which, in the absence of currency, is based on the barter of valued items such as food, contraband, and sexual favors. They establish methods of determining power, many of which, as we shall see, involve violence. Isolated and heavily regulated, prisoners create a social world that is, out of both necessity and design, separate from the outside world.

WHO IS IN PRISON?

The culture of any prison is heavily influenced by its inmates; their values, beliefs, and experiences in the outside world will be reflected in the social order that exists behind bars. In Chapter 2, we noted that a majority of Americans commit at least one crime in their lives that could technically send them to prison or jail. In reality, slightly more than 5 percent will be confined in a state or federal prison during their lifetimes. That percentage is considerably higher for male members of minority groups: according to the U.S. Department of Justice, about one in three African American males and one in six Hispanic males, as compared to one in seventeen white males, are likely to go to prison during their lifetimes.[6]

An Ailing Inmate Population The prison population is not static. The past two decades have seen the incarceration rates of women and minority groups rise sharply. Furthermore, the arrest patterns of inmates have changed over that time period. A prisoner today is much more likely to have been incarcerated on drug charges than was the case in the 1980s.[7] Prisons and jails also seem to be housing more people with medical issues. The death rate for state prisoners dying because of poor health increased by 82 percent between 1991 and 2004.[8] More than a third of jail inmates report suffering from at least one illness, the most common being arthritis, hypertension, asthma, and heart problems.[9] Sixty percent of jail inmates and 56 percent of state prisoners suffer from mental illnesses.[10]

Total Institution An institution, such as a prison, that provides all of the necessities for existence to those who live within its boundaries.

■ Figure 14.1 Prison Slang

Ace Another word for "dollar."

Bang A fight to the death, or shoot to kill.

Base head A cocaine addict.

B.G. "Baby gangster," or someone who has never shot another person.

Booty bandit An incarcerated sexual predator who preys on weaker inmates, called "punks."

Bug A correctional staff member, such as a psychiatrist, who is deemed untrustworthy or unreliable.

Bumpin' titties Fighting.

Catch cold To get killed.

Chiva Heroin.

Dancing on the blacktop Getting stabbed.

Diddler Child molester or pedophile.

Green light Prison gang term for a contract killing.

Hacks Correctional officers.

Jug-up Meal-time.

Lugger An inmate who smuggles in and possesses illegal substances.

Punk An inmate subject to rape, usually more submissive than most inmates.

Ride with To perform favors, including sexual favors, for a convict in return for protection or prison-store goods.

Shank Knife.

Tits-up An inmate who has died.

Topped Committed suicide.

Source: **www.insideprison.com/glossary.asp.**

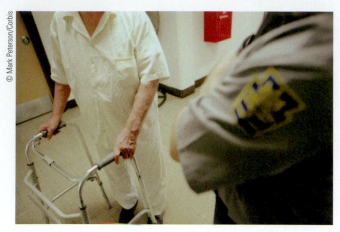

▲ Nearly two out of every five inmates over the age of forty-five, such as this one at the Laurel Highlands facility in Somerset, Pennsylvania, suffer from serious health ailments.

Not surprisingly, corrections budgets are straining under the financial pressures caused by health-care costs. In Ohio, the department of corrections' medical expenses jumped 30 percent—to $180 million—from 2005 to 2007.[11] Though forced to cut back on education and social programs for the population at large, California allocates nearly $2 billion a year for sick inmates.[12] Nationally, spending on prison health care has increased by nearly 80 percent over the past decade. (The feature *A Question of Ethics—The Million-Dollar Man* addresses the issue of whether the government is obliged to provide criminals with expensive medical care at taxpayers' expense.)

The Costs of Growing Old in Prison To a large extent, the growing costs of corrections health care can be attributed to the aging of the prison population, which is the most significant recent shift in the demographics of Americans behind bars. Though the majority of inmates are still under thirty-four years old, as you can see in ■ Figure 14.2 the number of offenders over the age of forty has increased dramatically during the past ten years. Several factors have contributed to this upsurge, including "get tough on crime" measures that impose mandatory terms and longer sentences (discussed in Chapter 11), high rates of recidivism, higher levels of murder and sex crimes committed by older offenders, and the aging of the U.S. population as a whole.[13] According to the best estimates, about 40 percent of jail inmates over the age of forty-five have serious medical problems, including diabetes, emphysema, heart disease, lung cancer, and other cancers.[14]

Given that elderly inmates tend to have the lowest recidivism rates, some criminologists have suggested that the corrections system should institute a form of "medical parole," under which older prisoners with health prob-

A Question of Ethics
The Million-Dollar Man

Prisoner X is serving fourteen years in a California prison for robbery He has fallen ill, and only a heart transplant will save his life. Although many Americans who need organ transplants cannot afford such an expensive procedure, the California Department of Corrections is considering whether to spend the more than $1 million needed to pay for Prisoner X's operation and recovery.

THE ETHICAL DILEMMA At the time Prisoner X fell ill, more than 4,100 names were on the national waiting list for a new heart. Many Californian taxpayers—who would ultimately pay for Prisoner X's operation—were outraged that a convicted criminal could receive a new heart before other, law-abiding patients. In 1976, however, the United States Supreme Court ruled that prisoners have a right to

"adequate" medical care, which has been interpreted to mean the same level of care they would receive if they were not behind bars. According to Michael A. Grodin, director of medical ethics at the Boston University School of Medicine and Public Health, "[B]ecause someone is incarcerated, we have a higher obligation to provide them with health care because we have deprived them of their liberty." As the wife of a patient who was below Prisoner X on the heart transplant waiting list put it, "Since when is it unethical to save someone's life?"

WHAT IS THE SOLUTION? A number of states do not provide their prisoners with organ transplants or will do so only if the prisoner can pay for the operation. What should California do with Prisoner X?* What options do state prison officials have if they decide not to cover the costs of the transplant? Would it be ethical to release Prisoner X or any other inmate simply to avoid the burden of his or her medical bills?

*In the actual case, California did provide Prisoner X with a new heart, but his body rejected the transplanted organ and he died within a year.

lems are released to a form of house arrest. With many of these convicts serving time for violent crimes, however, this option has not proved politically feasible. Instead, a number of states have set up separate facilities to house older and sicker inmates in the hope that providing constant care will prevent more serious, and more expensive, medical emergencies in the future.

ADAPTING TO PRISON SOCIETY

On arriving at prison, each convict attends an orientation session and receives a "Resident's Handbook." The handbook provides information **L02** such as meal and official count times, disciplinary regulations, and visitation guidelines. The norms and values of the prison society, however, cannot be communicated by the staff or learned from a handbook. As first described by Donald Clemmer in his classic 1940 work, *The Prison Community*, the process of **prisonization**—or adaptation to the prison culture—advances as the inmate gradually understands what constitutes acceptable behavior in the institution, as defined not by the prison officials but by other inmates.[15]

In studying prisonization, criminologists have focused on two areas: how prisoners change their behavior to adapt to life behind bars, and how life behind bars has changed because of inmate behavior. Sociologist John Irwin has identified several patterns of inmate behavior, each one driven by the inmate's personality and values:

1. Professional criminals adapt to prison by "doing time." In other words, they follow the rules and generally do whatever is necessary to speed up their release so that they can continue their chosen careers.
2. Some convicts, mostly state-raised youths or those frequently incarcerated in juvenile detention centers, are more comfortable inside prison than outside. These inmates serve time by "jailing," or establishing themselves in the power structure of prison culture.
3. Other inmates take advantage of prison resources such as libraries or drug treatment programs by "gleaning," or working to improve themselves to prepare for a return to society.
4. Finally, "disorganized" criminals exist on the fringes of prison society. These inmates may have mental impairments or low levels of intelligence and find it impossible to adapt to prison culture on any level.[16]

The process of categorizing prisoners has a theoretical basis, but it serves a practical purpose as well, allowing administrators to reasonably predict how different inmates will act in certain situations. An inmate who is "doing time" generally does not present the same security risk as one who is "jailing."

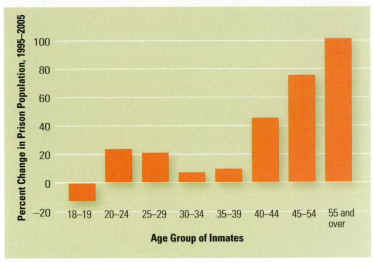

■ **Figure 14.2** **The Aging Prison Population**

Sources: Bureau of Justice Statistics, *Prisoners in 2003* (Washington, D.C.: U.S. Department of Justice, November 2004), Table 10, page 8; Bureau of Justice Statistics, *Prisoners in 2005* (Washington, D.C.: U.S. Department of Justice, November 2006), Table 10, page 8.

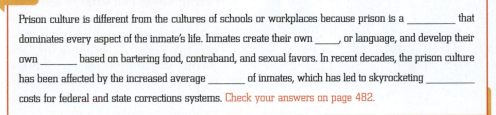

Self Check Fill in the Blanks

Prison culture is different from the cultures of schools or workplaces because prison is a _____ that dominates every aspect of the inmate's life. Inmates create their own _____, or language, and develop their own _____ based on bartering food, contraband, and sexual favors. In recent decades, the prison culture has been affected by the increased average _____ of inmates, which has led to skyrocketing _____ costs for federal and state corrections systems. Check your answers on page 482.

Prisonization The socialization process through which a new inmate learns the accepted norms and values of the prison population.

Prison Violence

Deprivation Model A theory that inmate aggression is the result of the frustration inmates feel at being deprived of freedom, consumer goods, sex, and other staples of life outside the institution.

Relative Deprivation The theory that inmate aggression is caused when freedoms and services that the inmate has come to accept as normal are decreased or eliminated.

Prisons and jails are dangerous places to live. Prison culture is predicated on violence; one observer calls the modern institution an "unstable and violent jungle."[17] Prison guards use the threat of violence (and, at times, its reality) to control the inmate population. Among the prisoners, violence is used to establish power and dominance. Often, this violence leads to death. About fifty-three inmates are murdered by fellow inmates each year, and about 34,000 inmate-on-inmate assaults take place annually. Each year also sees approximately 18,000 inmate-on-staff assaults, of which about five result in death.[18]

VIOLENCE IN PRISON CULTURE

L03 Until the 1970s, prison culture emphasized "noninterference" and did not support inmate-on-inmate violence. Prison "elders" would themselves punish any of their peers who showed a proclivity toward assaulting fellow inmates. Today, in contrast, violence is used to establish the prisoner hierarchy by separating the powerful from the weak. Humboldt State University's Lee H. Bowker has identified several other reasons for violent behavior:

- It provides a deterrent against being victimized, as a reputation for violence may eliminate an inmate as a target of assault.
- It enhances self-image in an environment that does not respect other attributes, such as intelligence.
- In the case of rape, it gives sexual relief.
- It serves as a means of acquiring material goods through extortion or outright robbery.[19]

The **deprivation model** can be used to explain the high level of prison violence. According to this model, the stressful and oppressive conditions of prison life lead to aggressive behavior on the part of inmates. When conditions such as overcrowding worsen, prison researcher Stephen C. Light found that inmate misconduct often increases.[20] In these circumstances, the violent behavior may not have any express purpose—it may just be a means of relieving tension.[21]

RIOTS

The deprivation model is helpful, though less convincing, in searching for the roots of collective violence. As far back as the 1930s, Frank Tannenbaum noted that harsh prison conditions can cause tension to build among inmates until it eventually explodes in the form of mass violence.[22] Living conditions in prisons are fairly constant, however, so how can the seemingly spontaneous outbreak of prison riots be explained?

Loss of Institutional Control Researchers have addressed these inconsistencies with the concept of **relative deprivation,** a theory that focuses on the gap between what is expected in a certain situation and what is achieved. Peter C. Kratcoski has argued that because prisoners enjoy such meager privileges to begin with, any further deprivation can spark disorder.[23] A number of criminologists, including Bert Useem in his studies made in the wake of a major riot at

▼ Several emergency responders leave the New Castle Correctional Facility in New Castle, Indiana, after helping to quell a prison riot that broke out there on April 24, 2007. During the two-hour disturbance, inmates armed with clubs set mattresses and other furniture on fire and smashed windows. According to a spokeswoman, the fracas started because a group of newly transferred prisoners was upset at the facility's no-smoking policy. How does her explanation support the relative deprivation theory of prison violence?

AP Photo/Michael Conroy

the Penitentiary of New Mexico in 1980, have noted that collective violence occurs in response to heightened measures of security at corrections facilities.[24] Thus, the violence occurs in response to an additional reduction in freedom for inmates, who enjoy very little freedom to begin with.

Riots, which have been defined as situations in which a number of prisoners are beyond institutional control for a significant amount of time,[25] are relatively rare. Because of their explosive nature and potential for high casualties, however, riots have a unique ability to focus public attention on prison conditions. The collective violence that took place in 1971 at Attica Prison in upstate New York has been described as a turning point in the history of American corrections because it alerted citizens to the situation in correctional facilities and spurred the prisoners' rights movement.[26]

The Spectrum of Violence The Attica Prison riot lasted five days in September 1971. Nearly half of the institution's 2,500 inmates seized control of most of the prison, holding thirty-eight correctional officers as hostages. In large measure, the riot was a reaction to the punitive atmosphere in Attica; during negotiations to end the standoff, one inmate complained, "We are men, we are not beasts and we will not be beaten or driven as such."[27] The talks ended abruptly when New York state troopers raided the prison grounds, killing thirty-nine inmates and wounding eighty-eight others. In the wake of the riot, however, New York Governor Nelson Rockefeller called for "radical reforms" in the state's corrections system, and twenty-four of the prisoners' original demands for such things as better food, more programs, and due process for disciplinary action were met.

> "I've seen seven stabbings, about six bashings, and three self-mutilations. Two hangings, one attempted hanging, any number of overdoses. And that's only me, in just seventy days."
>
> —*Anonymous jail inmate*

The Attica riot has, however, proved to be the exception to the rule. Most riots are disorganized, and the participants have no political agenda. The incidents are marked by extreme levels of inmate-on-inmate violence and can often be attributed, at least in part, to poor living conditions and inadequate prison administration. The worst disturbance in the past forty years, for example, took place at the Penitentiary of New Mexico in Santa Fe in 1980. Prisoners killed thirty-three of their fellow inmates, and nearly two hundred others were tortured, beaten, and raped. The levels of violence—including the use of blowtorches on genitals—shocked the public. Two weeks *before* the riot, an outside consultant had warned that New Mexico prison officials were playing "Russian roulette with the lives of inmates" by failing to properly staff and train the personnel at the state's penal institutions.[28]

ISSUES OF RACE AND ETHNICITY

The night before the Attica riot erupted, inmates yelled, "[G]et a good night's sleep, whitey. Sleep tight, because tomorrow's the day." Officers in the prison were known to refer to their batons as "nigger sticks."[29] Race plays a major role in prison life, and prison violence is often an outlet for racial tension. As prison populations have changed over the past three decades, with African Americans and Hispanics becoming the majority in many penal institutions, issues of race and ethnicity have become increasingly important to prison administrators and researchers.

Separate Worlds As early as the 1950s, researchers were noticing different group structures in inmate life. At that time, for example, prisoners at California's Soledad Prison informally segregated themselves according to geography as well as race: Tejanos (Mexicans raised in Texas), Chicanos, blacks from California, blacks from the South and Southwest, and the majority whites all formed separate social worlds.[30]

Leo Carroll, professor of sociology at the University of Rhode Island, has written extensively on how today's prisoners are "balkanized," with race determining nearly every aspect of an inmate's life, including friends, job assignments, and cell location.[31] Carroll's research has also shown how minority groups in prison have seized on race to help form their prison identities.[32]

Prison Segregation Severe overcrowding has only worsened racial tensions in the American prison system. In February 2006, more than two thousand African American and Hispanic inmates at the Pitchless Detention Center in Castaic, California, battled each other for several hours, leaving one dead and fifty injured. Corrections officials responded by separating black and Hispanic inmates. Only a year earlier, the United States Supreme Court had struck down the California Department of Corrections' unwritten policy of **prison segregation,** under which prisoners were placed only with those of similar race or ethnicity for their first sixty days of incarceration. The Supreme Court held that such a practice was unconstitutional and might even contribute to race-based violence by reinforcing the idea that members of different racial groups pose a threat to one another.[33]

The Supreme Court did, however, leave prison officials with an "out." They can still segregate prisoners in an "emergency situation."[34] Most observers, including the local branch of the American Civil Liberties Union, agreed that the situation at the Pitchless Detention Center qualified as an emergency. Even so, segregation proved to be only a short-term remedy. A week later Hispanic inmates threw bunk beds and other items at their African American counterparts in a day-room in the nearby Los Angeles Men's Central Jail, sparking a disturbance that resulted in the death of a black inmate. As one observer pointed out, racial segregation "will never solve the underlying problems in L.A. County's jails."[35]

PRISON GANGS AND SECURITY THREAT GROUPS (STGS)

In many instances, racial and ethnic identification is the primary focus of the **prison gang**—a clique of inmates who join together in an organizational structure. In part, the prison gang is a natural result of life in the modern prison. As one expert says of these gangs:

> Their members have done in prison what many people do elsewhere when they feel personally powerless, threatened, and vulnerable. They align themselves with others, organize to fight back, and enhance their own status and control through their connection to a more powerful group.[36]

In addition to their important role in the social structure of corrections facilities, prison gangs participate in a wide range of illegal economic activities within these institutions, including prostitution, drug selling, gambling, and loan sharking. A recent study conducted by the Federal Bureau of Prisons found that gang membership increased all forms of prison misconduct.[37]

The Prevalence of Prison Gangs Recent research places the rate of gang membership at 11.7 percent in federal prisons, 13.4 percent in state prisons, and 15.6 percent in jails.[38] When the National Gang Crime Research Center surveyed prison administrators, however, almost 95 percent said that gang recruitment took place at their institutions, so the overall prevalence of gangs is probably much higher.[39] Los Angeles corrections officials believe that eight out of every ten inmates in their city jails are gang affiliated

In many instances, prison gangs are extensions of street gangs. Indeed, investigators believe leaders of the Mexican Mafia greenlighted the violence in the Los Angeles jails discussed earlier in retaliation for an attack that took place on the city streets. Though the stereotypical gang is composed of African Americans or Hispanics, the majority of large prisons also have white, or "Aryan," gangs. One of the largest federal capital prosecutions in U.S. history, involving thirty-two counts

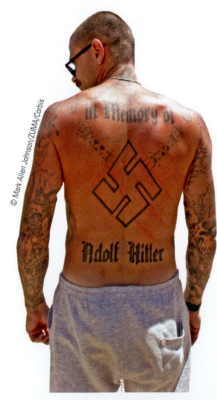

▲ A member of the Aryan Brotherhood in California's Calipatria State Prison. This particular prison gang espouses white supremacy, but for the most part its leadership focuses on illegal activities such as extortion and drug trafficking. Why might an inmate join a prison gang?

Certain prison gangs, such as the Crips and the Bloods, are offshoots of street gangs and gained influence behind bars because so many of their members have been incarcerated. Others, such as the Aryan Brotherhood and the Mexican Mafia, formed in prison and expanded to the streets. Listed here are seven of the most dangerous gangs operating in the American prison system today.

Aryan Brotherhood

White

Origins: Prison gang, formed in San Quentin State Prison in 1967, as white protection against blacks.

Allies: Mexican Mafia

Rivals: Black Guerrilla Family

Signs/Symbols: Swastika, SS Lightning bolts, numbers "666" (satan, evil) and "88" (to signify the eighth letter of the alphabet, or HH), HH for "Heil Hitler," letters "AB," shamrock (a symbol of their original Irish membership), Nordic dagger on shield with lightning bolts.

Black Guerrilla Family

African American

Origins: Prison gang, founded by incarcerated Black Panthers in San Quentin State Prison in the mid-1960s.

Allies: La Nuestra Familia

Rivals: Aryan Brotherhood

Signs/Symbols: Crossed sabers, machetes, rifles, shotguns with the letters "B G F." A black dragon squeezing the life out of a prison guard by a prison tower.

Bloods

African American

Origins: Street gang, formed in Los Angeles in the 1960s, as a defense against the Crips.

Allies: People Nation (Chicago gang), La Nuestra Familia

Rivals: Crips, Aryan Brotherhood

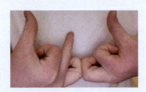

Signs/Symbols: The color red, red bandannas or rags, the word "Piru" (the original Blood gang), crossed out "C" in words as disrespect for Crips, other anti-Crip graffiti, hand signal spells "blood."

Crips

African American

Origins: Street gang, formed in the Central Avenue area of Los Angeles in the late 1960s.

Allies: Black Guerrilla Family, La Nuestra Familia

Rivals: Bloods, Aryan Brotherhood, Vice Lords

Signs/Symbols: The color blue, blue bandannas and rags, use the letter "c" in place of "b" in writing as disrespect for Bloods, calling each other "Cuzz," calling themselves "Blood Killas" (BK), wearing British Knight (BK) tennis shoes.

Mexican Mafia (EMC)

Mexican American/Hispanic

Origins: Prison gang, formed in Los Angeles in the Deuel Vocational Institution in the late 1950s. Foot soldiers and related Southern California street gangs are called Sureños.

Allies: Aryan Brotherhood

Rivals: Black Guerrilla Family, La Nuestra Familia

Signs/Symbols: The national symbol of Mexico, an eagle and a snake, on a flaming circle, lying on crossed knives. The color blue, the number 13.

Mara Salvatrucha 13 (MS-13)

Hispanic

Origins: Largest street gang in North America, originated in El Salvador and formed in Los Angeles in the 1980s.

Allies: Mexican Mafia

Rivals: MS-18 (LA gang)

Yuri Cortez/AFP/Getty Images

Signs/Symbols: Most Mara Salvatrucha members are covered in tattoos, even on their faces. Common markings include "MS," "13," "Salvadorian Pride," the "Devil Horns."

La Nuestra Familia

Mexican American/Hispanic

Origins: Prison gang, formed in Soledad Prison in the late 1960s, as a reaction to the Mexican Mafia. Based in Northern California, foot soldiers outside of prison are called Norteños.

Allies: Black Guerrilla Family, Bloods, Crips

Rivals: Mexican Mafia, Mara Salvatrucha

Signs/Symbols: Large tattoos, often on the entire back. The initials NF, LNF, ENE, and F. The number 14 for "N," the 14th letter in the alphabet stands for Norte or Norteño. The color red, Nebraska cornhuskers' caps with the letter N. A sombrero with a dagger is a common NF symbol.

Sources: "Gangs or Us," at **www.gangsorus.com/index.html**; and "Prison Gang Profiles," at **www. insideprison.com/prison_gang_profiles.asp**.

of murder, focused on a major prison gang known as the Aryan Brotherhood. (See ■ Figure 14.3.)

Combating Prison Gangs In their efforts to combat the influence of prison gangs, over the past decade corrections officials have increasingly turned to the **security threat group (STG)** model. Generally speaking, an STG is an identifiable

Security Threat Group (STG) A group of three or more inmates who engage in activity that poses a threat to the safety of other inmates or the prison staff.

group (three or more) of individuals who pose a threat to the safety of other inmates or members of the corrections community.[40] About two-thirds of all prisons have a corrections officer who acts as an STG coordinator.[41] This official is responsible for determining groups of individuals (not necessarily members of a prison gang) that qualify as STGs and taking appropriate measures. In Arizona, for example, all STGs are eligible to be transferred to one of the state's supermax prisons.[42] In addition, many corrections facilities segregate STGs and gang members from the general prison population, either by solitary confinement or by other methods of separation.

PRISON RAPE

In making his point about the savage and brutal nature of modern prisons, James C. Oleson, whose "punitive coma" theory we discussed in the opening to this chapter, told the story of Michael Blucker. Sent to the Menard Correctional Center in Illinois for car theft, the smallish Blucker was turned into a sex slave by his larger fellow inmates and traded by gang members for cigarettes and drugs. During one of dozens of sexual assaults, ten men raped Blucker in the prison showers. Eventually, Blucker contracted HIV, transforming his seven-year sentence into something far more serious.[43]

▼ Roderick Johnson, pictured below, filed a lawsuit against the Texas Department of Corrections alleging that prison officials refused to protect him when he was sold as a "sex slave" by other inmates and raped hundreds of times at the Allred Unit facility in Iowa Park. Why is it difficult for researchers to gather reliable data on prison rape?

© Brandon McKelvey/Daily Texan

Sexual Assault behind Bars In contrast to riots, the problem of sexual assault in prisons receives very little attention from media sources. This can be partly attributed to the ambiguity of the subject: that rape occurs in prisons and jails is undisputed, but determining exactly how widespread the problem is has proved difficult. Prison officials, aware that any sexual contact is prohibited in most penal institutions, are often unwilling to provide realistic figures for fear of negative publicity. Even when they are willing, they may be unable to do so. Most inmates are ashamed of being rape victims and refuse to report sexual assaults. Consequently, it has been difficult to come up with consistent statistics for sexual assault in prison. Studies that rely primarily on self-reported surveys have estimated that from less than 1 percent to as many as 10 percent of prisoners are forced to engage in sexual activity.[44] Some prison activists claims that as many as 300,000 rapes take place in American prisons each year.[45]

To address the problem of prison rape, in 2003 Congress passed the Prison Rape Elimination Act. The statute requires annual federal and state surveys of sexual assaults in prison, provides federal funds to train and educate corrections staff about rape, and encourages greater prosecution of rapists.[46] Those who hoped that this legislation would shine a light on the darkness that has surrounded sexual violence in prison were somewhat disappointed by the first report released by the U.S. Department of Justice in 2006. Its authors interviewed five hundred inmates, none of whom admitted to having been raped.[47] Another federal government study released that year found only 885 substantiated incidents of sexual violence in American prisons and jails for 2005, meaning that, by this measurement, 0.4 of every 1,000 inmates are the victims of sexual assault behind bars.[48]

The Psychology of Prison Rape Whatever the figures, prison rape, like all rape, is considered primarily an act of violence rather than sex. Inmates subject to rape ("punks") are near the bottom of the prison power structure and, in some instances, may accept rape by one particularly powerful inmate in return for protection from others.[49] Abused inmates often suffer from rape trauma syndrome and a host of other psychological ailments, including suicidal tendencies. Many prisons do not offer sufficient medical treatment for rape victims, nor does the prison staff take the necessary measures to protect obvious targets of rape—young, slightly built, nonviolent offenders. Furthermore, corrections officials are rarely held liable for inmate-on-inmate violence.

Self Check Fill in the Blanks

Some researchers rely on the _____ model, which focuses on the stressful and oppressive conditions of incarceration, to explain general prison violence. The concept of _____, based on the gap between an inmate's expectations and reality, is used to explain the conditions that lead to prison riots. The strategy of prison _____, in which officials assign inmates of different races to separate living areas, has been used at times to control violence started by prison _____, or criminal organizations that operate behind bars. Check your answers on page 482.

Inside a Women's Prison

When the first women's prison in the United States opened in 1839 on the grounds of New York's Sing Sing institution, the focus was on rehabilitation. Prisoners were groomed for a return to society with classes on reading, knitting, and sewing. Early women's reformatories had few locks or bars, and several contained nurseries for the inmates' young children. Today, the situation is dramatically different. "Women's institutions are literally men's institutions, only we pull out the urinals," remarks Meda Chesney-Lind, a criminologist at the University of Hawaii.[50] Given the different circumstances surrounding male and female incarceration, this uniformity can have serious consequences for the women imprisoned in this country.

CHARACTERISTICS OF FEMALE INMATES

Of the nearly 1,700 state and federal correctional facilities in the United States, about 150 house only female prisoners.[51] Consequently, most research concerning the American corrections system focuses on male inmates and men's prisons. Enough data exist, however, to provide a useful portrait of women behind bars. The majority of female inmates are members of racial or ethnic minorities between the ages of thirty and thirty-nine.[52] Most have been incarcerated for a nonviolent drug or property crime[53] (see ■ Figure 14.4). Only four in ten report having had full-time employment at the time of arrest, and nearly 30 percent were on welfare before incarceration, compared to just under 8 percent for male inmates.[54]

A History of Abuse The single factor that most distinguishes female prisoners from their male counterparts is a history of physical or sexual abuse. A self-reported study conducted by the federal government indicates that 55 percent of female jail inmates have been abused at some point in their lives, compared to only 13 percent of male jail inmates.[55] Fifty-seven percent of women in state prisons and 40 percent of women in federal prisons report some form of past abuse; both figures are significantly higher than those for male prisoners.[56] Health experts believe that these levels of abuse are related to the significant amount of drug and/or alcohol addiction that plagues the female prison population, as well as to the mental illness problems that such addictions can cause or exacerbate.[57]

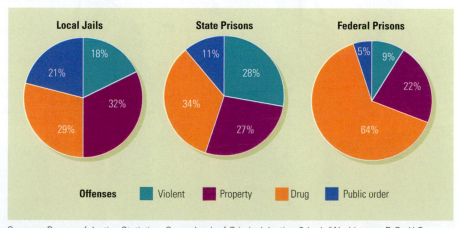

■ **Figure 14.4** **Offenses of Women in Jail and Prison**

Local Jails: 18%, 32%, 29%, 21%

State Prisons: 11%, 28%, 27%, 34%

Federal Prisons: 5%, 9%, 22%, 64%

Offenses ■ Violent ■ Property ■ Drug ■ Public order

Sources: Bureau of Justice Statistics, *Sourcebook of Criminal Justice,* 3d ed. (Washington, D.C.: U.S. Department of Justice, 2003), 495, 519; and Bureau of Justice Statistics, *Special Report: Women Offenders* (Washington, D.C.: U.S. Department of Justice, December 1999), Table 15, page 6.

Other Health Problems In fact, about 25 percent of women in state prisons have been diagnosed with mental disorders such as post–traumatic stress disorder (PTSD), depression, and substance abuse. PTSD, in particular, is found in women who have experienced sexual or physical abuse.[58] Furthermore, more women than men enter prisons and jails with health problems due to higher instances of poverty, inadequate health care, and substance abuse.[59] Women prisoners are 50 percent more likely than men to be HIV positive and are at significantly greater risk for lung cancer; they also have high rates of breast and cervical cancer.[60] The health risks and medical needs are even higher for the 5 percent of the female prison population who enter the correctional facility while pregnant. One study estimates that 20 to 35 percent of women inmates visit the infirmary each day, compared to 7 to 10 percent of male inmates.[61]

THE MOTHERHOOD PROBLEM

Drug and alcohol use within a women's prison can be a function of the anger and depression many inmates experience due to being separated from their children. An estimated seven out of every ten female prisoners have at least one minor child; more than 1.3 million American children have a mother who is under correctional supervision.[62] Given the scarcity of women's correctional facilities, inmates are often housed at great distances from their children. One study found that almost two-thirds of women in federal prison are more than five hundred miles from their homes.[63]

Further research indicates that an inmate who serves her sentence more than fifty miles from her residence is much less likely to receive phone calls or personal visits from family members. For most inmates and their families, the costs of "staying in touch" are too high.[64] This kind of separation can have serious consequences for the children of inmates. When a father goes to prison, his children are likely to live with their mother. When a mother is incarcerated, however, her children are likely to live with other relatives or, in about 10 percent of the cases, be sent to foster care.[65] Only six states—California, Nebraska, New York, Ohio, Washington, and West Virginia—provide facilities where inmates and their infant children can live together, and even in these facilities nursery privileges end once the child is eighteen months old.

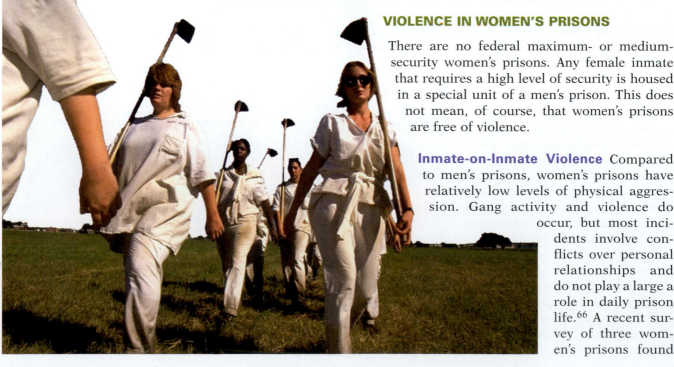

▼ Inmates at a women's prison in Gatesville, Texas, prepare for work detail. Today, nearly 100,000 women are incarcerated in the United States, up from about 70,000 in 1995. About 150 prisons in this country house only female inmates, compared to more than 1,500 male correctional facilities.

Andrew Lichtenstein/Corbis/Sygma

VIOLENCE IN WOMEN'S PRISONS

There are no federal maximum- or medium-security women's prisons. Any female inmate that requires a high level of security is housed in a special unit of a men's prison. This does not mean, of course, that women's prisons are free of violence.

Inmate-on-Inmate Violence Compared to men's prisons, women's prisons have relatively low levels of physical aggression. Gang activity and violence do occur, but most incidents involve conflicts over personal relationships and do not play a large a role in daily prison life.[66] A recent survey of three women's prisons found that the amount of sexual coercion varies greatly from institution to institution and that only one out of every five such incidents could be classified as sexual assault or rape. Most of the unwanted contact involved "forceful sexual touching." This is not to say that female inmates are "better behaved" than male inmates. Researchers find no consistent gender differences in the amount of misbehavior or rules violations, but the type of misbehavior differs.[67] Male prisoners are more likely to commit violent infractions such as assaults on other inmates or on correctional officers. For their part, women prisoners are more likely to be cited for nonviolent rule breaking, such as verbal abuse and stealing.[68]

Sexual Violence and Prison Staff One form of prison violence that continues to plague women prisoners is sexual misconduct by prison staff. The issue came to public attention in 2006, when correctional officers killed an FBI agent during a shootout at the Federal Correctional Institute in Tallahassee, Florida. The officers had been under investigation for running a criminal enterprise that included trading drugs and alcohol for sex with female inmates. Sexual assaults by male correctional officers have led to numerous lawsuits and criminal investigations over the past decade, with the worst offenses taking place in Alabama, Louisiana, Michigan, and New Jersey.

"I know not whether Laws be right
Or whether Laws be wrong;
All that we know who live in gaol
Is that the wall is strong;
And that each day is like a year,
A year whose days are long."

—Oscar Wilde, Irish playwright, author (1898)

Critics of the practice of using male officers to guard female inmates believe that such problems are inevitable, given the potential for abuse of power inherent in staff-prisoner relations.[69] The conditions in most prisons—including lack of privacy, poor grievance procedures, and harsh treatment of "whistleblowers"—exacerbate the problem. Dr. Kerry Kupers, who has studied the effects of sexual assault in these situations, believes that it contributes to the PTSD, depression, anxiety, and other mental illnesses suffered by so many women prisoners.[70]

THE PSEUDO-FAMILY

As in male facilities, a system of prisonization is evident in women's prisons. The adaptation process in the female institution, however, relies on tightly knit cliques of prisoners that mimic the traditional family structure. The more experienced convicts adopt the role of the "father" or "mother" and act as parent figures for younger, inexperienced "sons" or "daughters." Inmates choose their roles depending on appearance, personality, and background. As in "real" families, prison female families restrict sexual contact between members, relying on each other primarily for emotional support.[71]

Homosexuality often manifests itself in a women's prison through the formation of another traditional family model: the monogamous couple. One member of the couple chooses the role of the husband, and the other becomes the wife.[72] In general, sex between inmates plays a different role in women's prisons than in men's prisons. In the latter, rape is considered an act of aggression and power rather than sex, and "true" homosexuals are relegated to the lowest rungs of the social hierarchy. By contrast, women who engage in sexual activity in prison are not automatically labeled homosexual, and lesbians are not hampered in their social-climbing efforts.[73]

Researchers have also found that female inmates share personal belongings a great deal more than their male counterparts. In a men's prison, self-sufficiency and autonomy are valued, whereas in women's prisons members of cliques and families allocate cosmetics, foods, clothes, and other goods.[74] (One observer points out that this greater tendency to share may be attributed to the fact that women are allowed more personal belongings in prison than men are.[75])

Self Check Fill in the Blanks

The majority of female inmates are members of _____ groups who have been arrested for nonviolent _____ or property crimes. On admission to a correctional facility, women report much higher levels of physical and sexual _____ than their male counterparts, and female inmates often suffer from depression because they are separated from their _____. While levels of violence are relatively low in women's prisons, they do face a greater threat of sexual assault from _____ than male inmates do.

Check your answers on page 482.

Correctional Officers and Discipline

Under model circumstances, the presence of correctional officers—the standard term used to describe prison guards—would mitigate the levels of violence in American correctional institutions. To a large extent, this is indeed the case; without correctional officers, the prison would be a place of anarchy. But in the highly regulated, oppressive environment of the prison, correctional officers must use the threat of violence, if not actual violence, to instill discipline and keep order. Thus, the relationship between prison staff and inmates is marked by mutual distrust. Consider the two following statements, the first made by a correctional officer and the second by a prisoner:

> [My job is to] protect, feed, and try to educate scum who raped and brutalized women and children . . . who, if I turn my back, will go into their cell, wrap a blanket around their cellmate's legs, and threaten to beat or rape him if he doesn't give sex, carry contraband, or fork over radios, money, or other goods willingly. And they'll stick a shank in me tomorrow if they think they can get away with it.[76]

> The pigs in the state and federal prisons . . . treat me so violently, I cannot possibly imagine a time I could ever have anything but the deepest, aching, searing hatred for them. I can't begin to tell you what they do to me. If I were weaker by a hair, they would destroy me.[77]

> The **U.S. Department of Labor** offers information about a career as a correctional officer. Find its Web site by clicking on *Web Links* under *Chapter Resources* at **www.cjinaction.com**.

It may be difficult for an outsider to understand the emotions that fuel such sentiments. French philosopher Michael Foucault points out that discipline, both in prison and in the general community, is a means of social organization as well as punishment.[78] Discipline is imposed when a person behaves in a manner that is contrary to the values of the dominant social group. Correctional officers and inmates have different concepts of the ideal structure of prison society, and, as the two quotations above demonstrate, this conflict generates intense feelings of fear and hatred, which often lead to violence.

RANK AND DUTIES OF CORRECTIONAL OFFICERS

L04 After seven convicts escaped from the Connally Unit in Kenedy, Texas, several years ago, much of the blame fell on the custodial staff. Security at the facility had been extremely lax, with officers failing to properly identify visitors before opening gates, leaving prison vehicles unattended on the premises, and allowing unsupervised prisoners to work in a maintenance room. To avoid such problems and promote efficiency, in most prisons each correctional officer has a clearly delineated rank and duty. The custodial staff at most prisons is organized according to four general ranks—captain, lieutenant, sergeant, and officer. In keeping with the militaristic model, captains are primarily administrators who deal directly with the warden on custodial issues. Lieutenants are the disciplinarians of the prison, responsible for policing and transporting the inmates. Sergeants oversee platoons of officers in specific parts of the prison, such as various cell blocks or work spaces.

Lucien X. Lombardo, professor of sociology and criminal justice at Old Dominion University, has identified six general job categories among correctional officers:[79]

1. *Block officers.* These employees supervise cell blocks containing as many as four hundred inmates, as well as the correctional officers on block guard duty. In general, the block officer is responsible for the "well-being" of the inmates. He or she makes sure the inmates do not harm themselves or other prisoners and also acts as something of a camp counselor, dispensing advice and seeing that inmates understand and follow the rules of the facility.

2. *Work detail supervisors.* In many penal institutions, the inmates work in the cafeteria, the prison store, the laundry, and other areas. Work detail supervisors oversee small groups of inmates as they perform these tasks.

3. *Industrial shop and school officers.* These officers perform maintenance and security functions in workshop and educational programs. Their primary responsibility is to make sure that inmates are on time for these programs and do not cause any disturbances during the sessions.

4. *Yard officers.* Officers who work the prison yard usually have the least seniority, befitting the assignment's reputation as dangerous and stressful. These officers must be constantly on alert for breaches in prison discipline or regulations in the relatively unstructured environment of the prison yard.

5. *Tower guards.* These officers spend their entire shifts, which usually last eight hours, in isolated, silent posts high above the grounds of the facility. Although their only means of communication are walkie-talkies or cellular devices, the safety benefits of the position can outweigh the loneliness that comes with the job.

6. *Administrative building assignments.* Officers who hold these positions provide security at prison gates, oversee visitation procedures, act as liaisons for civilians, and handle administrative tasks such as processing the paperwork when an inmate is transferred from another institution.

DISCIPLINE

As Erving Goffman noted in his essay on the "total institution," in the general society adults are rarely placed in a position where they are "punished" as a child would be.[80] Therefore, the strict disciplinary measures imposed on prisoners come as something of a shock and can provoke strong defensive reactions. Correctional officers who must deal with these responses often find that disciplining inmates is the most difficult and stressful aspect of their job.

Sanctioning Prisoners As mentioned earlier, one of the first things that an inmate receives on entering a corrections facility is a manual that details the rules of the prison or jail, along with the punishment that will result from rule violations. These handbooks can be quite lengthy—running one hundred pages in some instances—and specific. Not only will a prison manual prohibit obvious misconduct such as violent or sexual activity, gambling, and possession of drugs or currency, but it also addresses matters of daily life such as personal hygiene, dress codes, and conduct during meals.

Correctional officers enforce the prison rules in much the same way that a highway patrol officer enforces traffic regulations. For a minor violation, the inmate may be "let off easy" with a verbal warning. More serious infractions will result in a "ticket," or a report forwarded to the institution's disciplinary committee.[81] The disciplinary committee generally includes several correctional officers and, in some instances, outside citizens or even inmates. Although, as we shall see, the United States Supreme Court has ruled that an inmate must be given a "fair hearing" before being disciplined,[82] in reality he or she has very little ability to challenge the committee's decision. Depending on the seriousness of the violation, sanctions can range from a loss of privileges such as visits from family members to the unpleasantness of solitary confinement, discussed in the last chapter.

My interest in the corrections field grew out of the need to be involved in solving problems associated with crime and punishment. I began my career as a law enforcement deputy. On completion of my undergraduate studies I sought experience in the counseling and programs aspects of detention. Ultimately, I became interested in the management of jails and decided to become a sworn detention officer. My career path has given me a unique perspective from having experience in three major components of criminal justice: law enforcement, detention, and programs.

Throughout my career I have continued my education as a corrections professional; my accomplishments include a master of arts degree in criminal justice from the University of South Florida, and I am a graduate of the Southern Police Institute's administrative officers course.

COMMAND DUTIES I am currently assigned as a facility commander in a 1,714-bed direct supervision jail. The facility is divided into two factions: housing and central intake. Central intake encompasses all facets of booking as well as the classification and records bureau. There is a combined total of approximately 300 sworn and civilian employees assigned to this multidimensional command and responsible for the processing and booking of over 62,000 inmates a year. Additionally, my command must ensure that inmates make all required court appearances and that all transfers or releases are proper and within established releasing standards. My most important duties are ensuring that staff are properly trained; that staff are assigned to functions that guarantee security is maintained at the highest level; and that all inmates are treated in accordance with local, state, and federal standards.

Courtesy of Robert M. Lucas

Use of Force Most correctional officers prefer to rely on the "you scratch my back and I'll scratch yours" model for controlling inmates. In other words, as long as the prisoner makes a reasonable effort to conform to institutional rules, the correctional officer will refrain from taking disciplinary steps. Of course, the staff-inmate relationship is not always marked by cooperation, and correctional officers often find themselves in situations where they must use force.

Legitimate Security Interests Generally, courts have been unwilling to put too many restrictions on the use of force by correctional officers. Like police officers (see Chapter 5), correctional officers are given great leeway to use their experience to determine when force is warranted. In *Whitley v. Albers* (1986),[83] the Supreme Court held that the use of force by prison officials violates an inmate's Eighth Amendment protections only if the force amounts to "the unnecessary and wanton infliction of pain." Excessive force can be considered "necessary" if the legitimate security interests of the penal institution are at stake. Consequently, an appeals court ruled that when officers at a Maryland prison formed an "extraction team" to remove the leader of a riot from his cell, beating him in the process, the use of force was justified given the situation.[84]

In general, courts have found that the "legitimate security interests" of a prison or jail justify the use of force when the correctional officer is[85]

1. Acting in self-defense.
2. Acting to defend the safety of a third person, such as a member of the prison staff or another inmate.
3. Upholding the rules of the institution.
4. Preventing a crime such as assault, destruction of property, or theft.
5. Preventing an escape effort.

A defining incident in my career was being involved in the mass arrest of 186 individuals as a result of a demonstration. As an assistant tactical commander, I was responsible for remote booking, security, crowd control, and the coordination of inmate transportation to the central jail facility. The incident was significant from two aspects: (1) the dynamics and logistics involved in the arrest, detainment, and booking of a large number of individuals in a short period of time; and (2) the awareness of the importance of a cooperative effort between law enforcement and detention. A number of problems were immediately evident in the arrest and processing of this large number of inmates, including security, site location, feeding, sanitation, and medical care for those in need. As is typical with most agencies, the booking process was normally accomplished in a secure facility separate from any outside disruptive factors. The remote booking exposed the staff to dissidents and necessitated the initial processing of the inmates in a temporary booking area without normal security.

TODAY'S JAIL PRACTITIONER I feel the qualities essential to the corrections field are those common to most fields, such as a desire to perform at a high level of standards, a commitment to personal growth through change and development, and facing each task as a challenge as opposed to a problem. The management and operation of any detention facility is taxing, and it challenges the abilities, knowledge, and experience of those in supervisory roles. Staff are expected to fulfill a number of roles and encounter any number of problems or emergencies daily. The jail practitioner of today must be well versed in all aspects of the jail operation and applicable laws and standards, and be able to address problems associated with expanding inmate populations, construction needs, and specialized inmate categories.

Go to the **Careers in Criminal Justice Interactive CD** for more profiles in the field of criminal justice. .

In addition, most prisons and jails have written policies that spell out the situations in which their employees may use force against inmates.

The "Malicious and Sadistic" Standard The judicial system has not, however, given correctional officers total freedom of discretion to apply force. In *Hudson v. McMillan* (1992)[86] the Supreme Court ruled that minor injuries suffered by a convict at the hands of a correctional officer following an argument did violate the inmate's rights, because there was no security concern at the time of the incident. In other words, the issue is not *how much* force was used, but whether the officer used the force as part of a good faith effort to restore discipline or acted "maliciously and sadistically" to cause harm. This "malicious and sadistic" standard has been difficult for aggrieved prisoners to meet; in the ten years following the *Hudson* decision, only about 20 percent of excessive force lawsuits against correctional officials were successful.[87]

Staffing Problems In recent years, a correctional officer's ability to ensure a safe environment has been greatly affected by a factor beyond his or her control: staffing levels. From 1995 to 2005, the number of prison inmates in this country increased by 51 percent. Over that same time period, the correctional officer rolls grew by only 8 percent.[88] This imbalance inevitably leads to dangerous situations in which a small number of correctional officers may be unable to control a large number of prisoners. During the unrest in the Los Angeles jails discussed earlier in this chapter, for example, the ratio of inmates to officers was 300 to 1. Along with low salaries, the sense of insecurity created by lack of sufficient staffing numbers is often cited by prison experts trying to explain high turnover rates among correctional officers.[89]

▼ Correctional officers report for work at the Oklahoma State Reformatory in Granite, Oklahoma. The state's prisons are suffering staff shortages, a situation some observers blame on low starting salaries of about $24,000 a year. Why are understaffed prisons more likely to suffer from discipline problems and high turnover of correctional guards?

AP Photo

Self Check Fill in the Blanks

Correctional officers known as _____ are responsible for the daily well-being of the inmates in their cells. Perhaps the most stressful and important aspect of a correctional officer's job is enforcing _____ among the inmates. To do so, the officers may use force when a _____ interest is being served, such as preventing an attempted _____. Courts will not, however, accept any force that is "_____ and sadistic." Check your answers on page 482.

Protecting Prisoners' Rights

The general attitude of the law toward inmates is summed up by the Thirteenth Amendment to the U.S. Constitution:

> Neither slavery nor involuntary servitude, except as a punishment for crime whereof the party shall have been duly convicted, shall exist within the United States.

In other words, inmates do not have the same guaranteed rights as other Americans. For most of the nation's history, courts have followed the spirit of this amendment by applying the **"hands-off" doctrine** of prisoner law. This (unwritten) doctrine assumes that the care of inmates should be left to prison officials and that it is not the place of judges to intervene in penal administrative matters.

L05

In the 1960s, as disenfranchised groups from all parts of society began to insist on their constitutional rights, prisoners did so as well. Movement leaders demanded, and received, fuller recognition of prisoners' rights and greater access to American courts. It would be difficult, however, to label the movement a complete success. As one observer notes, "conditions of confinement in many American prisons have deteriorated during the same time period in which judicial recognition and concern for prisoners' legal rights dramatically increased."[90]

THE "HANDS-ON" APPROACH

The end of the "hands-off" period can be dated to the Supreme Court's decision in *Cooper v. Pate* (1964).[91] In this case, Cooper, an inmate at the Illinois State Penitentiary, filed a petition for relief under the Civil Rights Act of 1871, stating that he had a First Amendment right to purchase reading material about the Black Muslim movement. The Court, overturning rulings of several lower courts, held that the act did protect the constitutional rights of prisoners. This decision effectively allowed inmates to file civil lawsuits under Title 42 of the United States Code, Section 1983—known simply as Section 1983—if they felt that a prison or jail was denying their civil rights. An inmate who has been beaten by a correctional officer, for example, can bring a Section 1983 suit against the penal institution for denial of Eighth Amendment protection from cruel and unusual punishment.

A Prisoner's Liberty Interest Symbolically, the Supreme Court's declaration in *Wolff v. McDonnell* (1974)[92] that "[t]here is no iron curtain drawn between the Constitution and the prisons of this country" was just as significant as the *Cooper* ruling. It signaled to civil rights lawyers that the Court would no longer follow the "hands-off" doctrine. The case had practical overtones as well, establishing that prisoners have a right to the following basic due process procedures when being disciplined by a penal institution:

- A fair hearing.
- Written notice at least twenty-four hours in advance of the hearing.
- An opportunity to speak at the hearing (though not to be represented by counsel during the hearing).

"Hands-Off" Doctrine The unwritten judicial policy that favors noninterference by the courts in the administration of prisons and jails.

- An opportunity to call witnesses (unless doing so jeopardizes prison security).
- A written statement detailing the final decision and reasons for that decision.

The main issue in the *Wolff* case was whether a correctional institution had to follow due process procedures when denying a prisoner "good-time" credits, which, as we saw in Chapter 11, take time off a sentence. In its ruling, the Court held that prisoners have a *liberty interest* in receiving these credits and, therefore, they could not be denied without a fair hearing. In the corrections context, a prisoner has a liberty interest when an action by prison officials imposes "atypical or significant hardships in relation to ordinary incidents of prison life."[93]

▲ In general, inmates such as the Muslims pictured here performing daily ritual prayers are allowed to take part in religious activities required by their faith. Numerous American courts have ruled, however, that prison administrators may limit religious activities that threaten the security of the institution or lead to overcrowding or excessive costs. Why might some critics complain that this standard gives officials too much power to infringe on inmates' freedom of religion?

In *Sandin v. Conner* (1995), the Court ruled that solitary confinement is not sufficiently "atypical" to threaten a prisoner's liberty interest and, therefore, prison officials do not need to provide inmates with a hearing before sending them to "the Hole."[94] Thus, the liberty interest standard seems to apply only when a punishment affects the length of a sentence, as with "good-time" credits and parole, a subject we will address in the next section. In 2005, however, the Court did hold that inmates designated for transfer to a supermax prison have the right to a hearing because conditions in those facilities, described in Chapter 13, reach the level of "atypical and significant hardship."[95]

The First Amendment in Prison The First Amendment reads, in part, that the federal government "shall make no law respecting an establishment of religion, or prohibiting the free exercise thereof; or abridging the freedom of speech." In the 1970s, the prisoners' rights movement forced open the "iron curtain" to allow the First Amendment behind bars. In 1974, for example, the Supreme Court held that prison officials can censor inmate mail only if doing so is necessary to maintain prison security.[96] The decade also saw court decisions protecting inmates' access to group worship, instruction by clergy, special dietary requirements, religious publications, and other aspects of both mainstream and nonmainstream religions.[97] Although some of these protections have been modified since then in the interests of prison security,[98] the judicial system's commitment to freedom of speech and religion behind bars remains strong.

LIMITING PRISONERS' RIGHTS

Despite these successes, not all proponents of prisoners' rights feel that the courts have entirely abandoned the "hands-off" doctrine. Instead, they believe that by establishing standards of "deliberate indifference" and "identifiable human needs," court rulings have merely provided penal institutions with legally acceptable methods of denying prisoners' constitutional protections.

"Deliberate Indifference" In the 1976 case *Estelle v. Gamble*,[99] the Supreme Court established the **"deliberate indifference"** standard. Specifically, Justice Thurgood Marshall wrote that prison officials violated a convict's Eighth Amendment rights if they deliberately failed to provide him or her with necessary medical care. At

"Deliberate Indifference" A standard that must be met by inmates trying to prove that their Eighth Amendment rights were violated by a correctional facility. It occurs when prison officials are aware of harmful conditions of confinement but fail to take steps to remedy those conditions.

the time, the decision was hailed as a victory for prisoners' rights, and it continues to ensure that a certain level of health care is provided. Defining "deliberate" has proved difficult, however. Does it mean that prison officials "should have known" that an inmate was placed in harm's way, or does it mean that prison officials purposefully placed the inmate in that position?

The "Purpose" Requirement In subsequent decisions, the Supreme Court appears to have accepted the latter interpretation. In two separate 1986 cases, for example, the Court held that "simple negligence" was not acceptable grounds for a Section 1983 civil suit and that a prison official's behavior was actionable only if it was done "maliciously or sadistically for the very purpose of causing harm."[100] As it is quite difficult to prove in court a person's state of mind, the "deliberate negligence" standard has become a formidable one for prisoners to meet.

In *Wilson v. Seiter* (1991),[101] for example, Pearly L. Wilson filed a Section 1983 suit alleging that certain conditions of his confinement—including overcrowding; excessive noise; inadequate heating, cooling, and ventilation; and unsanitary bathroom and dining facilities—were cruel and unusual. The Supreme Court ruled against Wilson, stating that he had failed to prove that these conditions, even if they existed, were the result of "deliberate indifference" on the part of prison officials. Three years later, in a case concerning a transsexual inmate who was placed in the general population of a federal prison and subsequently beaten and raped, the Court narrowed the definition of "deliberate" even further. Though ruling in favor of the inmate, it held that the prison official must both be aware of the facts that create a potential for harm and also *draw the conclusion* that those facts will lead to harm.[102]

"Identifiable Human Needs" The *Wilson* decision created another standard for determining Eighth Amendment violations that has drawn criticism from civil rights lawyers. It asserted that a prisoner must show that the institution has denied her or him a basic human need such as food, warmth, or exercise.[103] The Court failed, however, to mention any other needs besides these three, forcing other courts to interpret **"identifiable human needs"** for themselves. (Courts must often determine whether prison officials have "gone too far" in regulating inmates' lives, as you can see in the feature *You Be the Judge—Cell Mates*.)

Self Check Fill in the Blanks

When prison officials impose an "atypical or significant" hardship on an inmate, they must follow basic _____ procedures by providing the inmate with, among other things, a fair _____ and the opportunity to call _____ in his or her defense. To prove that prison officials violated the _____ Amendment's prohibitions against cruel and unusual punishment, the inmate must first show that the officials acted with "_____ indifference" in taking, or not taking, an action. Check your answers on page 482.

"Identifiable Human Needs" The basic human necessities that correctional facilities are required by the Constitution to provide to inmates. Beyond food, warmth, and exercise, the court system has been unable to establish exactly what these needs are.

Parole The conditional release of an inmate before his or her sentence has expired. The remainder of the sentence is served in the community under the supervision of correctional (parole) officers, and the offender can be returned to incarceration if he or she breaks the conditions of parole, as determined by a parole board.

Parole and Release from Prison

L06 At any given time, more than 780,000 Americans are living in the community on **parole,** or the *conditional* release of a prisoner after a portion of his or her sentence has been served. Parole allows the corrections system to continue to supervise an offender who is no longer incarcerated. As long as parolees follow the conditions of their parole, they are allowed to finish their terms outside the prison. If parolees break the terms of their early release, however, they face the risk of being returned to a penal institution.

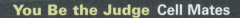

You Be the Judge Cell Mates

THE FACTS Shirley is an inmate at a women's prison in Missouri. Her fiancé, Rilo, is an inmate at a nearby men's maximum-security prison. The Missouri Division of Corrections has promulgated two rules that make Shirley and Rilo's relationship difficult. First, inmates at one state prison are not allowed to send letters to inmates at another state prison. Second, inmates in the Missouri prison system are not permitted to marry each other without permission from the prison superintendent. Shirley and several other Missouri inmates want the two rules to be struck down as unconstitutional.

THE LAW In prison regulation cases, the courts must weigh the rights of the prisoners against the need for prison authorities to promote safety and security. If the regulation is too burdensome on the rights of the inmate without sufficiently promoting the prison system's safety and security, then it must be struck down.

YOUR DECISION Missouri prison officials defend the mail restriction on the basis that letters can be used to communicate escape plans, to discuss assaults and other violent acts, and to further gang activity. They also contend that the marriage ban is necessary to avoid "love triangles" and other romantic liaisons that may lead to confrontations between inmates. Which, if either, of these regulations should be banned, and why? Before you answer, consider that the right to marry is considered "fundamental" by the United States Supreme Court, but no such constitutional importance has been extended to letter writing.

[To see how the United States Supreme Court ruled in a similar case, go to Example 14.1 in Appendix B.]

According to Todd Clear and George F. Cole, parole is based on three concepts:

1. *Grace.* The prisoner has no right to be given an early release, but the government has granted her or him that privilege.
2. *Contract of consent.* The government and the parolee enter into an arrangement whereby the latter agrees to abide by certain conditions in return for continued freedom.
3. *Custody.* Technically, though no longer incarcerated, the parolee is still the responsibility of the state. Parole is an extension of corrections.[104] (The phonetic and administrative similarities between probation and parole can be confusing. See *Mastering Concepts—Probation versus Parole* on the next page for clarification.)

Because of good-time credits and parole, most prisoners do not serve their entire sentence in prison. In fact, the average felon serves only about half of the term handed down by the court.

OTHER TYPES OF PRISON RELEASE

Parole, a conditional release, is the most common form of release, but it is not the only one (see ■ Figure 14.5 on page 467). Prisoners receive an unconditional release when they have completed the terms of their sentence and no longer require incarceration or supervision. One form of unconditional release is **mandatory release** (also known as "maxing out"), which occurs when an inmate has served the maximum amount of time on the initial sentence, minus reductions for good-time credits.

Another, quite rare unconditional release is a **pardon,** a form of executive clemency. The president (on the federal level) and the governor (on the state level) can grant a pardon, or forgive a convict's criminal punishment. Most states have a board of pardons—affiliated with the parole board—which makes

Mandatory Release Release from prison that occurs when an offender has served the full length of his or her sentence, minus any adjustments for good time. Mandatory release occurs as a result of a statutory requirement and, when applicable, negates the possibility of parole.

Pardon An act of executive clemency that overturns a conviction and erases mention of the crime from the person's criminal record.

Probation and parole have many aspects in common. In fact, probation and parole are so similar that many jurisdictions combine them into a single agency. There are, however, some important distinctions between the two systems, as noted below. Because of these differences, many observers believe that probation and parole should not be combined in the same agency, though limited financial resources will assure that many jurisdictions will continue to do so.

	PROBATION	PAROLE
Basic Definition	An alternative to imprisonment in which a person who has been convicted of a crime is allowed to serve his or her sentence in the community subject to certain conditions and supervision by a probation officer.	An early release from a correctional facility as determined by an administrative body (the parole board), in which the convicted offender is given the chance to spend the remainder of his or her sentence under supervision in the community.
Timing	The offender is sentenced to a probationary term in place of a prison or jail term. If the offender breaks the conditions of probation, he or she is sent to prison or jail. Therefore, probation occurs *before* imprisonment.	Parole is a form of early release. Therefore, parole occurs *after* an offender has spent time behind bars.
Authority	Probation falls under the domain of the judiciary. In other words, judges make the decision whether to send a convicted offender to prison or jail or to give her or him a sentence of probation. If a person violates the terms of probation, a judge ultimately decides whether she or he should be sent to a correctional facility as punishment.	Parole falls under the domain of an administrative body (often appointed by an executive such as a state governor) known as the parole board. The parole board determines whether the prisoner is qualified for early release, and under which conditions he or she will be allowed to remain in the community. When a parolee violates the conditions of parole, the parole board must decide whether to send him or her back to prison. (Although they may be asked to make recommendations to the parole board, judges generally are *not* involved in the parole decision.)
Characteristics of Offenders	As a number of studies have shown, probationers are normally less involved in the criminal lifestyle. Most of them are first-time offenders who have committed nonviolent crimes.	Many parolees have spent months or even years in prison and, besides abiding by conditions of parole, must make the difficult transition to "life on the outside."

recommendations to the governor in cases in which it believes a pardon is warranted. Most pardons involve obvious miscarriages of justice, though sometimes a governor will pardon an individual to remove the stain of conviction from his or her criminal record.

Certain *temporary releases* also exist. Some inmates, who qualify by exhibiting good behavior and generally proving that they do not represent a risk to society, are allowed to leave the prison on **furlough** for a certain amount of time, usually between a day and a week. At times, a furlough is granted because of a family emergency, such as a funeral. Furloughs can be particularly helpful for an inmate who is nearing release and can use them to ease the readjustment period.

DISCRETIONARY RELEASE

As you may recall from Chapter 11, corrections systems are classified by sentencing procedure—indeterminate or determinate. Indeterminate sentencing occurs when the legislature sets a range of punishments for particular crimes, and the judge and the parole board exercise discretion in determining the actual length of the prison term. For that reason, states with indeterminate sentencing are said to have systems of **discretionary release.** Until the mid-1970s, all states and the federal government operated in this manner.

Furlough Temporary release from a prison for purposes of vocational or educational training, to ease the shock of release, or for personal reasons.

Discretionary Release The release of an inmate into a community supervision program at the discretion of the parole board within limits set by state or federal law.

Eligibility for Parole Under indeterminate sentencing, parole is not a right but a privilege. This is a crucial point, as it establishes the terms of the relationship between the inmate and the corrections authorities during the parole process. In *Greenholtz v. Inmates of the Nebraska Penal and Correctional Complex* (1979),[105] the Supreme Court ruled that inmates do not have a constitutionally protected right to expect parole, thereby giving states the freedom to set their own standards for determining parole eligibility. In most states that have retained indeterminate sentencing, a prisoner is eligible to be considered for parole release after serving a legislatively determined percentage of the minimum sentence—usually one-half or two-thirds—less any good time or other credits.

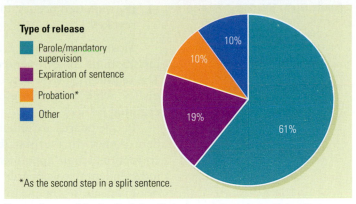

■ **Figure 14.5** **Release from State Correctional Facilities**

Type of release
- Parole/mandatory supervision
- Expiration of sentence
- Probation*
- Other

61%
19%
10%
10%

*As the second step in a split sentence.

Source: Bureau of Justice Statistics, *Probation and Parole in the United States, 2005* (Washington, D.C.: U.S. Department of Justice, November 2006), 8.

Contrary to what is depicted in many films and television shows, a convict does not "apply" for parole. An inmate's case automatically comes up before the parole board a certain number of days—often ninety—before she or he is eligible for parole. The date of eligibility depends on statutory requirements, the terms of the sentence, and the behavior of the inmate in prison. The board has an eligibility report prepared, which provides information on the various factors that must be considered in making the decision. The board also reviews the case file to acquaint itself with the original crime and conducts an interview with the inmate. At some point before the eligibility date, the entire board, or a subcommittee of the board, votes on whether parole will be granted.

Life-Without-Parole Not all convicts are eligible for parole. Many states have a sentencing system in which offenders who have committed the most serious crimes receive life terms without the possibility of early release. In general, life-without-parole is reserved for those offenders who have

- committed capital, or first degree, murder;
- committed serious offenses other than murder; or
- been defined by statute as habitual, or repeat, offenders, such as those sentenced under "three-strikes" laws.[106]

Besides murderers, drug dealers and sex offenders are most commonly targeted for life-without-parole. The sentence is fraught with controversy, as many observers, including inmates, feel serving life-without-parole is a crueler punishment than the death penalty. Furthermore, the Supreme Court has ruled that when a capital defendant who has been convicted of murder will be ineligible for parole, due process requires the jury to be told of this fact.[107] In other words, the jury must know that, in sentencing the defendant, it has a choice between execution and life-without-parole.

The Parole Board The cumulative efforts of the police, the courtroom work group, and correctional officials lead to a single question in most cases: When should an offender be released? This is a difficult question and is often left to the **parole board** to answer. When members of the parole board make what in retrospect was a mistake, they quickly draw the attention of the media, the public, and the courts.

According to the American Correctional Association, the parole board has four basic roles:

1. To decide which offenders should be placed on parole.
2. To determine the conditions of parole and aid in the continuing supervision of the parolee.

Parole Board A body of appointed civilians that decides whether a convict should be granted conditional release before the end of his or her sentence.

3. To discharge the offender when the conditions of parole have been met.
4. If a violation occurs, to determine whether parole privileges should be revoked.[108]

Most parole boards are small, made up of five to seven members. In many jurisdictions, board members' terms are limited to between four and six years. The requirements for board members vary. Nearly half the states have no prerequisites, while others require a bachelor's degree or some expertise in the field of criminal justice.

Parole boards are either affiliated with government agencies or act as independent bodies. In the first instance, board members are usually members of the correctional staff appointed by the state department of corrections. In contrast, independent parole boards are made up of citizens from the community who have been chosen for the post by a government official, usually the governor. Because most states with independent boards have no specific criteria for the members, critics believe that these boards tend to be "politicized" by the appointment of members—who have limited knowledge of the criminal justice system—as a return for political favors.

The Parole Hearing In a system that uses discretionary parole, the actual release decision is made at a **parole grant hearing.** During this hearing, the entire board or a subcommittee reviews relevant information on the convict. Sometimes, but not always, the offender is interviewed. Because the board members have only limited knowledge of each offender, key players in the case are often notified in advance of the parole hearing and asked to provide comments and recommendations. These participants include the sentencing judge, the attorneys at the trial, the victims, and any law enforcement officers who may be involved. After these preparations, the typical parole hearing itself is very short—usually lasting just a few minutes.

If parole is denied, the entire process is replayed at the next "action date," which depends on the nature of the offender's crimes and all relevant laws. In 2006, for example, Leslie Van Houten was denied parole for the sixteenth time. Van Houten was convicted of murder in 1969 for the role she played in the gruesome Beverly Hills, California, killing of pregnant actress Sharon Tate and six others under the direction of Charles Manson. While in prison, Van Houten—who claims that she played a minimal role in the murders—has earned bachelor's and master's degrees and has never had a disciplinary report filed against her. Families of the victims continue to petition the California Board of Prison Terms to keep her incarcerated. Although the board has said Van Houten's chances improve with each hearing, most observers believe she will never be released. (Manson himself has been denied parole eleven times and has stated that he does not want to be released.) In some states, the parole board is required to give written reasons for denying parole, and some jurisdictions give the inmate, prosecution, or victims the option to appeal the board's decision.

▼ Sara Jane Olson spends her days in the Central California Women's Correctional Facility in Chowchilla, California, convicted of murder and other crimes stemming from her links to a band of radicals known as the Symbionese Liberation Army in the early 1970s. Now in her early sixties, Olson recently told a state parole board that she is "incredibly sorry" for her actions. What role, if any, should a convict's contrition have in the decision to grant parole?

AP Photo

THE EMERGENCE OF MANDATORY RELEASE

The legitimacy of discretionary release relies to a certain extent on the perception of parole decisions by offenders, victims, and the general public. Like judicial discretion (as we discussed in Chapter 11), parole board discretion is criticized when the decisions are seen as arbitrary and unfair and lead to rampant disparity in the release dates of similar offenders. Proponents of discretionary release argue that parole boards must tailor their decisions to the individual case, but such protestations seem to be undermined by the raw data: research done by the Bureau of Justice

Statistics has found that most offenders were serving less than a third of their sentences in the early 1990s.[109]

As Michael Tonry noted, such statistics gave the impression that parole board members "tossed darts at a dartboard" to determine who should be released, and when.[110] As a result of this criticism, twenty-seven states have now implemented determinate sentencing systems, which set minimum mandatory terms without possibility of parole. These systems provide for *mandatory release*, in which offenders leave incarceration when their sentences have expired, minus adjustments made for good time.

L07 **Truth in Sentencing** The move toward mandatory release has come partly at the urging of the federal government. The federal sentencing guidelines that went into effect in 1987 required those who were convicted in federal courts to serve at least 85 percent of their terms.[111] Federal crime bills in 1994 and 1995 encouraged states to adopt this truth-in-sentencing (previously mentioned in Chapter 11) approach by making federal aid for prison construction conditional on the passage of such laws.[112] Twenty-nine states have done just that, while fourteen others feature less stringent truth-in-sentencing statutes.[113]

Truth in sentencing is an umbrella term that covers a number of different state and federal statutes. In general, these laws have the following goals:

- To restore "truth" to the sentencing process by eliminating situations in which offenders are released by a parole board after serving less than the minimum term to which they were sentenced.
- To increase the percentage of the term that is actually served in prison, with the purpose of reducing crime by keeping convicts imprisoned for a longer period.
- To control the use of prison space by giving corrections officials the benefit of predictable terms and policymakers advance notice of the impact that sentencing statutes will have on prison populations.[114]

Note that fourteen states and the federal government have officially "abolished" parole. For the most part, however, these states simply emphasize prison terms that are "truthful," not necessarily "longer." Therefore, in Louisiana—noted for its harsh sentencing practices—violent offenders who serve only 50 percent of their term spend more time in prison than do prisoners in many states that have "abolished" parole.

Parole Guidelines One of the most popular methods of ensuring truth in sentencing is the use of **parole guidelines.** Similar to sentencing guidelines (see Chapter 11), parole guidelines attempt to measure a potential parolee's risk of recidivism by considering factors such as the original offense, criminal history, behavior in prison, past employment, substance abuse, and performance under any previous periods of parole or probation. Inmates who score positively in these areas are considered less likely to pose a danger to society and have a better chance of obtaining an early release date.

PAROLE SUPERVISION

The term *parole* has two meanings. The first, as we have seen, refers to the establishment of a release date. The second relates to the continuing supervision of convicted felons after they have been released from prison.

Conditions of Parole Many of the procedures and issues of parole supervision are similar to those of probation supervision. Like probationers, when parolees are granted parole, they are placed under the supervision of correctional officers and required to follow certain conditions. Some of these conditions are fairly uniform. All parolees, for example, must comply with the law, and they are generally responsible for reporting to their parole officer at certain intervals. The

L08

Parole Guidelines Employed to remove discretion from the parole process, these guidelines attempt to measure the risks of an offender recidivating, and then use these measurements to determine whether early release will be granted and under what conditions.

1. Upon my release I will report to my parole officer as directed and follow the parole officer's instructions.

2. I will report to my parole officer in person and in writing whenever and wherever the parole officer directs.

3. I agree that the parole officer has the right to visit my residence or place of employment at any reasonable time.

4. I will seek, obtain, and maintain employment throughout my parole term, or perform community service as directed by my parole officer.

5. I will notify my parole officer prior to any changes in my place of residence, in my place of employment, or of any change in my marital status.

6. I will notify my parole officer within 48 hours if at any time I am arrested for any offense.

7. I will not at any time have firearms, ammunition, or any other weapon in my possession or under my control.

8. I will obey all laws, and to the best of my ability, fulfill all my legal obligations, including payment of all applicable child support and alimony orders.

9. I will not leave the state of _____ without prior permission of my parole officer.

10. I will not at any time, use, or have in my possession or control, any illegal drug or narcotic.

11. I will not at any time have contact or affiliation with any street gangs or with any members thereof.

12. I understand that my release on parole is based upon the conclusion of the parole panel that there is a reasonable probability that I will live and remain at liberty without violating the law and that my release is not incompatible with the welfare of society. In the event that I engage in conduct in the future which renders this conclusion no longer valid, then my parole will be revoked or modified accordingly.

Source: Connecticut Board of Parole.

"Johnny plus alcohol plus women equals trouble."

—*Excerpt from 1976 parole report on Johnny Robert Eggers, who was released on parole five different times before stabbing a female teenager to death in 1994*

---

frequency of these visits, along with the other terms of parole, is spelled out in the **parole contract,** which sets out the agreement between the state and the paroled offender. Under the terms of the contract, the state agrees to release the inmate under certain conditions, and the future parolee agrees to follow these conditions.

Each jurisdiction has its own standard parole contract, although the parole board can add specific provisions if it sees the need (see ■ Figure 14.6). Besides common restrictions, such as no drug use, no association with known felons, and no change of address without notifying authorities, parolees have on occasion been ordered to lose weight and even to undergo chemical castration. The city of Chicago recently instituted a program that requires paroled gang members to agree to stay out of any area controlled by their gang as a condition of their early release.

Positive Reinforcement on Parole Parole plans are not always so one sided. In some instances, prison authorities will agree to help the parolee find employment and a place to live during the supervision period. **Work release programs** are usually available for low-risk prisoners nearing the end of their sentences. Inmates on work release programs must either return to the correctional facility in the evening or live in community residential facilities, known as **halfway houses.** These facilities, also available to other parolees and those who have finished their sentences, are often remodeled hotels or private homes. They provide a less institutional living environment than a prison or jail for a small number of inmates (usually between ten and twenty-five).

Parole Officers The correctional agent assigned the responsibility of supervising parolees is the parole officer. In many respects, the parole officer's relationship with the parolee mirrors that of the probation officer and the probationer (see Chapter 12); in fact, many municipal and state departments of corrections combine the two posts to create probation/parole officers. Parole officers are required to enforce the conditions of parole and initiate revocation hearings when these conditions are not met. Furthermore, a parole officer is expected to help the parolee readjust to life outside the correctional institution by helping her or him find a place to live and a job, and seeing that she or he receives any treatment or rehabilitation that may be necessary.

Parole Contract An agreement between the state and the offender that establishes the conditions under which the latter will be allowed to serve the remainder of her or his prison term in the community.

Work Release Program Temporary release of convicts from prison for purposes of employment. The offenders may spend their days on the job, but must return to the correctional facility at night and during the weekend.

Halfway House A community-based form of early release that places inmates in residential centers and allows them to reintegrate with society.

According to Todd Clear of Florida State University and Edward Latessa of the University of Cincinnati, the major role conflict for parole officers is whether to be a law enforcement officer or a social worker.[115] In other words, parole officers are constantly required to choose between the good of the community and the good of the paroled offender. In one study of parole officer stress and burnout, researchers found that more than 60 percent of the officers interviewed felt uncertain about how to balance these two requirements.[116] To be sure, some parole officers focus entirely on protecting the community and see the welfare of the client as a secondary concern.

A growing number of parole experts, however, believe that parole officers should act as agents of change, meaning that they should try to change the offender's behavior and not simply focus on controlling it. This entails that the parole officer establish strong bonds of trust and commitment with the parolee by taking what could be called a parental attitude to the officer-client relationship.

Parole Revocation If convicts follow the conditions of their parole until the *maximum expiration date*, or the date on which their sentence ends, then they are discharged from supervision. A large number—about 44 percent, according to the latest research—return to incarceration before their maximum expiration date, most because they were convicted of a new offense or had their parole revoked (see ■ Figure 14.7). **Parole revocation** is similar in many aspects to probation revocation. If the parolee commits a new crime, then a return to prison is very likely. If, however, the individual breaks a condition of parole, known as a *technical violation*, the parole authorities have discretion as to whether revocation proceedings should be initiated. An example of a technical violation would be failure to report a change in address to parole authorities. As with probation revocation, many observers believe that those who commit technical violations should not be imprisoned, as they have not committed a crime.

Parole and Due Process Until 1972, parole officers had the power to arbitrarily revoke parole status for technical violations. A parolee who was returned to prison had little or no recourse. In *Morrissey v. Brewer* (1972),[117] the Supreme Court changed this by holding that a parolee has a "liberty interest" in remaining on parole. In other words, before parolees can be deprived of their liberty, they must be afforded a measure of due process at a parole revocation hearing.

Although this hearing does not provide the same due process protections as a criminal trial, the parolee does have the right to be notified of the charges, to present witnesses, to speak in his or her defense, and to question any hostile witnesses (so long as such questioning would not place them in danger). In the first stage of the hearing, the parole board determines whether there is probable cause that a violation occurred. Then, the board decides whether to return the parolee to prison.

Limited Rights of Parolees A parolee's liberty interest in staying out of prison does not mean that he or she always enjoys the same rights as other "free" members of society. Notice in Figure 14.6 that under conditions 3 and 7, parole officers can visit the parolee's home or workplace "at any reasonable time" and apparently can search for weapons or ammunition without a warrant. In contrast, under the rules of search and seizure that we discussed in Chapter 7,

■ **Figure 14.7** **Terminating Parole**

As you can see, about half of all parolees successfully complete their terms of parole. The rest are either returned to incarceration, or have their supervision terminated for administrative reasons such as death or the parole officer's discretion.

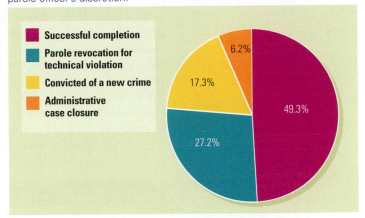

- Successful completion
- Parole revocation for technical violation
- Convicted of a new crime
- Administrative case closure

6.2%
17.3%
49.3%
27.2%

Source: *Sourcebook of Criminal Justice Statistics Online*, "Federal Parole Terminations," Table 6.71.2004, at **www.albany.edu/sosourcebook/pdf/t6712004.pdf**.

Parole Revocation When a parolee breaks the conditions of parole, the process of withdrawing parole and returning the person to prison.

government agents generally must have probable cause before they can take such actions.

The United States Supreme Court resolved this seeming contradiction in *Samson v. California* (2006).[118] The case involved a California law that requires parolees to agree to "search or seizure by a parole officer or other peace officer at any time of the day or night, with or without a search warrant and without probable cause."[119] Parolee Donald Samson challenged this statute after being searched by a parole officer who had no reason to believe that Samson was violating any law. The search uncovered a plastic bag containing methamphetamine, which led to a seven-year sentence for drug possession. The Court upheld both the California law and Samson's conviction, holding that parolees have "severely diminished" expectations of privacy that do not outweigh the government's need to control convicted criminals in the community.[120] (Although this case involved a person on parole, it has been interpreted to apply to any individual in nonincarceration state custody, including probationers.)

Self Check Fill in the Blanks

Parole refers to the _____ release of an inmate from prison before the end of his or her _____. In jurisdictions that have systems of discretionary release, a _____ makes the parole decision. In contrast, under a _____ release system, the inmate will not leave prison until her or his sentence has expired, minus good-time credits. Once an inmate has been released from prison, the terms of his or her release are spelled out in a parole _____, and a _____ violation of these terms or the commission of a new crime will almost certainly result in a return to prison. Check your answers on page 482.

Reentry into Society

L09 After Jerry B. Hobbs was arrested for brutally murdering Laura, his eight-year-old daughter, and her nine-year-old friend on a recent Mother's Day in Zion, Illinois, much was made of the fact that he had been released from prison only weeks before the killings. Hobbs had just completed a two-year sentence stemming from an incident in which he chased Laura's mother around a trailer park with a chain saw. Ex-convicts such as Hobbs present a crucial challenge for the criminal justice system. Each year, about 650,000 persons leave prison and return to the community—six times more than were reentering society in 1970.[121]

What steps can be taken to lessen the possibility that these ex-convicts will continue to harm society following their release? Efforts to answer that question have focused on programs that help inmates make the transition from prison to the "outside." In past years, these programs would have come under the general heading of "rehabilitation," but today corrections officials and criminologists refer to them as part of the strategy of **prisoner reentry**. The concept of reentry has come to mean many things to many people; for our purposes, keep in mind the words of Joan Petersilia of the University of California at Irvine, who defines *reentry* as encompassing "all activities and programming conducted to prepare ex-convicts to return safely to the community and to live as law abiding citizens."[122]

BARRIERS TO REENTRY

Perhaps the largest obstacle to successful prisoner reentry is the simple truth that life behind bars is very different from life on the outside. As one inmate explains, the "rules" of prison survival are hardly compatible with good citizenship:

> An unexpected smile could mean trouble. A man in uniform was not a friend. Being kind was a weakness. Viciousness and recklessness were to be respected and admired.[123]

Prisoner Reentry A corrections strategy designed to prepare inmates for a successful return to the community and to reduce their criminal activity after release.

The prison environment also insulates inmates. They are not required to make the day-to-day decisions that characterize a normal existence beyond prison bars. Depending on the length of incarceration, a released inmate must adjust to an array of economic, technological, and social changes that took place while she or he was behind bars; common acts such as using an ATM or pumping gas may be completely alien to someone who has just completed a long prison term.

Challenges of Release Other obstacles hamper reentry efforts. Housing can be difficult to secure, as many private property owners refuse to rent to someone with a criminal record, and federal and state laws restrict public housing options for ex-convicts. A criminal past also limits the ability to find employment, as does the lack of job skills of someone who has spent a significant portion of his or her life in prison. (■ Figure 14.8 provides a list of rights that are now or have in the past been denied to convicts once they return to the community.) Felix Mata, who works with ex-convicts in Baltimore, Maryland, estimates that the average male prisoner returning to that city has only $50 in his pocket; owes $8,000 in child support; and has no means of transportation, no place to live, and no ability to gain employment.

These economic barriers can be complicated by the physical and mental condition of the freed convict. We have already discussed the high incidence of substance abuse among prisoners and the health-care needs of aging inmates earlier in this chapter. In addition, one study concluded that as many as one in five Americans in jail or prison is seriously mentally ill.[124]

The Threat of Relapse All of these problems conspire to make successful reentry difficult to achieve. Perhaps it is not surprising that research conducted by the Bureau of Justice Statistics found that 67.5 percent of ex-prisoners are rearrested and 51.8 percent are returned to prison or jail within three years of their release dates.[125] These figures highlight the problem of recidivism among those released from incarceration.

Even given the barriers to reentry we have discussed, these rates of recidivism seem improbably high. Regardless of their ability to find a job or housing, it seems that many ex-convicts are fated to run afoul of the criminal justice system. Psychologists Edward Zamble and Vernon Quinsey explain the phenomenon as a *relapse process*.[126] Take the hypothetical example of an ex-convict who gets in a minor automobile accident while driving from his home to his job one morning. The person in the other car gets out and starts yelling at the ex-convict, who "relapses" and reacts just as he would have in prison, by punching the other person in the face. The ex-convict is then convicted of assault and battery and given a harsh prison sentence because of his criminal record.

REENTRY IN ACTION

One ex-inmate compared the experience of being released to entering a "dark room, knowing that there are steps in front of you and waiting to fall."[127] Reentry programs try to shed some light on the more difficult aspects of leaving prison. Although there is no single model for reentry programs, most either (1) specifically focus on the transition from prison to the community or (2) involve a treatment curriculum within the prison that continues after release. The majority of reentry programs include job training and work release programs, continuing education and prerelease "life skills" classes, drug treatment, and a residency period at a halfway house. (A typical "life skills" class includes topics such as finding and keeping a job, locating a residence, understanding family responsibilities, and budgeting.)

■ **Figure 14.8 The Limited Rights of Convicts**

In some states, convicted offenders are denied the right to vote, the reasoning being that they do not have the required honesty and proper values to be allowed to participate in the democratic process. Although such restrictions have been lifted in most states, convicted offenders still face other limits on their rights in some jurisdictions.

In many jurisdictions, convicts do not have the right to:

- Hold public office
- Be employed in the public sector
- Live in public housing
- Own firearms
- Serve on a jury
- Have automobile and life insurance
- Adopt children
- Receive welfare or food stamps
- Be eligible for student loans
- Have custody of their children

▶ Dennis, left, and his sponsor, Jamal, right, are residents of the Walden House, a drug and alcohol treatment center located in San Francisco's Mission District. California officials are increasingly looking to therapeutic communities such as Walden House as reentry options for nonviolent drug offenders. Why are reentry programs generally not created with violent offenders in mind?

A Matter of Time Research has established two truisms with regard to recidivism: (1) persons who have offended in the past are more likely to offend in the future, and (2) the risk of reoffending declines as the amount of time since the last criminal act increases.[128] Criminologists Megan C. Kurlychek and Robert Brame of the University of South Carolina and Shawn D. Bushway of the University of Maryland have taken this research a step further, finding that after six or seven years, the chance that ex-convicts will commit a crime is almost as low as for those who have never done so.[129]

Consequently, the challenge for reentry programs is to get to the ex-convict as soon as possible after release and keep her or him out of trouble for as long as possible. For this reason, the New York City Corrections Departments started a RIDE program that transports inmates released from Riker's Island Jail directly to potential job sites or aftercare programs. Corrections officials hope that the service will keep the ex-convicts from heading directly back to their old neighborhoods and resuming old, risky habits.

A Matter of Place Shadd Maruna, a British expert on reintegrating ex-convicts into society, thinks that reentry programs need to focus on more than treatment programs and job opportunities, as important as those factors may be. Maruna has found that a community support system is also very important. Institutions such as family, schools, and religious organizations play a crucial role in keeping a released prisoner on the right path. Without this support, chances of recidivism increase significantly.[130]

In Chapter 2, we studied sociological theories of crime, which hold that criminal behavior is more likely in communities where businesses, schools, and other social institutions have broken down. It should come as no surprise, then, to learn that such environments also increase the chances of recidivism. In a recently published report, Charis E. Kubrin of George Washington University and Eric A. Stewart of the University of Missouri at St. Louis found that those who return to disadvantaged neighborhoods reoffend at greater rates than do those who return to relatively affluent communities.[131]

Community Centers To compensate for the negative effects of disadvantaged neighborhoods on recidivism rates, many jurisdictions have established "therapeutic communities," or residential treatment programs that house convicts for as long as eighteen months after their release. The therapeutic community offers residents the opportunity to resocialize themselves outside the prison environment while at the same time providing them with drug treatment programs, anger-management classes, and other important resources.

As part of its massive corrections expansion, described in the last chapter, California lawmakers are considering a proposal to create seven thousand new beds for male prisoner in *reentry centers*. Qualified inmates would be sent to these centers during the last year of their sentences and remain for several months after their release date. While at the facility, they would have access to programs ranging from job training to drug treatment. As a further sign of the growing political viability of the reentry movement, in 2007 Congress was considering passage of the Second Chance Act, legislation designed to increase federal funding of reentry programs.

Self Check Fill in the Blanks

Ex-convicts often struggle to succeed after being released from prison because their limited skills make it difficult to find _____. One way in which the corrections system tries to reverse this process is by offering _____ programs that include job training and work release programs, _____ treatment, and continuing _____ classes. Check your answers on page 482.

The Special Case of Sex Offenders

Studies on the impact of reentry programs consistently show that they are beneficial, especially if they are initiated before the convicts leave incarceration.[132] Despite these data, one group of wrongdoers has consistently been denied access to the programs: sex offenders. The eventual return of these prisoners to society causes such high levels of community anxiety that the criminal justice system has not yet figured out what to do with them. (A recent Gallup poll found that 66 percent of the respondents were "very concerned" about child molesters, compared to 52 percent who expressed such concern about violent crime and 36 percent about terrorism.[133])

Part of the problem is that efforts to reform sex offenders have produced inconsistent results. In one of the few long-term studies of the issue, researchers found that sex offenders who took part in therapy programs in California were actually more likely to reoffend than those who received no treatment whatsoever.[134] Thus, corrections officials are caught between public demands for protection from "these monsters" and the insistence of medical professionals that sex offenders represent a public health problem, albeit it one without any ready solution. Not surprisingly, strategies to control sex offenders on their release from prison have frustrated both the public and medical professionals.

> **Parents for Megan's Law** is a nonprofit victims' rights organization dedicated to the prevention and treatment of sexual abuse. It also serves as a warehouse for state sex offender registries. To visit its site, click on *Web Links* under *Chapter Resources* at **www.cjinaction.com**.

SEX OFFENDER NOTIFICATION LAWS

In the summer of 1994, seven-year-old Megan Kanka of Hamilton Township, New Jersey, was raped and murdered by a twice-convicted pedophile (an adult sexually attracted to children) who had moved into her neighborhood after being released from prison on parole. The next year, in response to public outrage, the state passed a series of laws known collectively as the New Jersey Sexual Offender Registration Act, or "Megan's Law."[135] Today, all fifty states and the federal government have their own version of Megan's Law, or a **sex offender notification law,** which requires local law authorities to alert the public when a sex offender has been released into the community.

Sex Offender Notification Law Legislation that requires law enforcement authorities to notify people when convicted sex offenders are released into their neighborhood or community.

■ Figure 14.9 Sex Offender Notification Bulletin

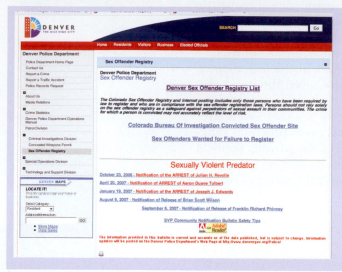

Source: **www.denvergov.org**

Active and Passive Notification No two of these laws have exactly the same provisions, but all are designed with the goal of allowing the public to learn the identities of convicted sex offenders living in their midst. In general, the laws demand that a paroled sexual offender notify local law enforcement authorities on taking up residence in a state. In Georgia, for example, paroled sex offenders are required to present themselves to both the local sheriff and the superintendent of the public school district where they plan to live.[136] This registration process must be renewed every time the parolee changes address.

LO10

The authorities, in turn, notify the community of the sex offender's presence through the use of one of two models. Under the "active" model, the authorities directly notify the community or community representatives. This notification often takes the form of bulletins or posters, distributed and posted within a certain distance from the offender's home. (See ■ Figure 14.9 for an example of such a bulletin on the Internet.) In the "passive" model, information on sex offenders is made open and available for public scrutiny. All fifty states operate Web sites that provide citizens with data on registered sex offenders in their jurisdiction.

Conditions of Release Generally, sex offenders are supervised by parole officers and are subject to the same threat of revocation as other parolees. Paroled child molesters usually have the following conditions of release:

- Must have no contact with children under the age of sixteen.
- Must continue psychiatric treatment.
- Must receive permission from the parole officers to change residence.
- Must stay a certain distance from schools or parks where children are present.
- Cannot own toys that may be used to lure children.
- Cannot have a job or participate in any activity that involves children.

In addition, of course, they are required to register through the proper authorities. Today, more than 600,000 registered sex offenders live throughout the United States.[137]

LEGAL ISSUES WITH NOTIFICATION LAWS

In nearly every jurisdiction, sex offender notification laws have been challenged as unconstitutional. The common theme among these court cases is that Megan's Laws are punitive and, as such, violate state and federal constitutional prohibitions against double jeopardy and cruel and unusual punishment. In other words, by forcing sex offenders to register in expectation of a crime they have yet to commit, these laws operate in opposition to the principle that persons are innocent until proven guilty. Furthermore, because of the scrutiny that is certain to fall on a pedophile whose past crimes have been broadcast to the community, offenders have filed suit claiming that the laws unconstitutionally invade their privacy.[138]

Not Punishment With two recent decisions, the United States Supreme Court has signaled that it is going to give the states a great deal of leeway in managing sex offenders. In *Smith v. Doe* (2003),[139] the Court held that Alaska's sex offender law did not violate the *ex post facto* clause of the Constitution even though it required men who had completed their prison sentences before its passage to register. (For a review of the clause, go to page 124.) The Court noted that even though some of the ramifica-

◄ Heidi Hagen holds up a photo of Jetseta Gage outside the Iowa Supreme Court building in Des Moines. In 2006, Roger Bentley was found guilty of kidnapping, raping, and killing the ten-year-old Gage. Because Bentley was already a convicted sex offender at the time of these crimes, Gage's murder prompted Iowa lawmakers to pass legislation increasing the sentences and community supervision of these types of criminals.

tions of Megan's Laws are punitive, their general purpose is remedial and, therefore, *ex post facto* protections do not apply. In other words, because the laws are designed for treatment and not punishment, the constitutional protections of the rights of criminal defendants have no bearing on the issue.

No Due Process Violation The other case, *Connecticut Department of Public Safety v. Doe* (2003),[140] concerned a convicted sex offender's claim that he was denied his due process rights when the state posted his name and address on the Internet without first holding a hearing to determine if he was a threat to the community. The Court rejected this argument: because Connecticut requires *all* sex offenders to register and places information about *all* of them on the Web, the law is not unfair. In other words, the relative dangerousness of any individual is irrelevant.

"It was just like a hunt for me. I kept choosing children because they were easier prey; they were easier to deal with than women."

—*A male sex offender receiving treatment at California's Atascadero State Hospital*

GETTING TOUGH(ER) ON SEX OFFENDERS

Although Megan's Laws are popular with the public, the reputation of registration efforts has been tarnished by a series of highly publicized crimes committed during the past few years. In 2003, authorities found the body of college student Dru Sjodin in a ravine; she had been abducted and murdered by convicted sex offender Alfonso Rodriguez. In 2005, sex offenders murdered two Florida girls—nine-year-old Jessica Lunsford and thirteen-year-old Sarah Lunde—and ten-year-old Iowan Jetseta Gage. That same year in Idaho, another sex offender, Joseph Duncan, bludgeoned several members of eight-year-old Shasta Groene's family to death before kidnapping the girl who was eventually rescued by law enforcement agents, as described on page 274.

The perpetrators of these crimes had one thing in common: they were all registered sex offenders. John Couey, who killed Jessica Lunsford in Florida, worked on a construction site at his victim's school and failed to inform the state when he moved into her neighborhood. As one Florida lawmaker put it, "The current 'honor system' of having each offender check in with local law enforcement has proven itself ineffective in tracking sexual predators."[141] Indeed, according to victims' rights groups, as many as a quarter of the country's registered sex offenders are "missing"—meaning that local police departments do not know their exact location.[142]

The Legislative Response As a result of these highly publicized failures, many states have tried to "toughen" their sexual offender notification laws. Ohio, for example, is considering legislation that would require convicted sex offenders to place fluorescent green license plates on their cars. Massachusetts authorities now require Level 3 Sex Offenders (those considered the most likely to recidivate) to include the addresses of partners and relatives in their registration information. In 2006, California lawmakers passed legislation prohibiting "high-risk" convicted child molesters from living within half a mile of any school while they are on parole,[143] a controversial strategy that we will look at more closely in the *Criminal Justice in Action* feature at the end of the chapter.

Other states have addressed the problem by changing their criminal codes. In 2005, Florida passed the Jessica Lunsford Act, the strictest sex offender law in the nation. The legislation sets a mandatory sentence of at least twenty-five years for any person convicted of molesting a child under the age of twelve and requires that these offenders wear global satellite tracking devices for the rest of their lives on release from prison.[144] As we saw in Chapter 11, several states are considering making child molesters eligible for the death penalty.

Civil Confinement Despite this flurry of legislative activity, the criminal justice system's failure to identify, treat, and monitor sex offenders has led to frustration among federal and state politicians. "The issue is, what can you do short of putting them all in prison for the rest of their lives?" complained one policymaker.[145]

Indefinite Detention In fact, many jurisdictions have devised a method to keep sex offenders off the streets for, if not their entire lives, then close to it. Eighteen states have passed **civil confinement** laws that allow corrections officials to keep sex offenders locked up in noncorrectional facilities such as psychiatric hospitals at the conclusion of their prison terms. Under these laws, corrections officials can keep sexual criminals confined indefinitely, as long they are deemed a danger to society. Given the recidivism rates of sex offenders, civil confinement laws essentially give the state the power to detain this class of criminal indefinitely. (To learn more about this subject, see the feature *Myth versus Reality—Recidivism Rates of Sex Offenders.*)

Myth *versus* Reality
Recidivism Rates of Sex Offenders

In paving the way for extended confinement of sex offenders beyond the terms of their sentences, the United States Supreme Court focused on the high recidivism rates associated with this class of criminal. According to the Supreme Court, "when convicted sex offenders reenter society they are much more likely than any other type of offender to be arrested for a new rape or sexual assault." The unusually high recidivism rates of sex offenders have been used as justification for a wide range of measures designed to control their movements after release from prison. All of this begs the question: Is the justification justified by the facts?

THE MYTH Sex offenders, more than other criminals, are bound to repeat their crimes.

THE REALITY To a certain extent, the myth is correct, in that the medical health profession has had little success in treating the "urges" that lead to sexually deviant behavior. This has not, however, translated into rampant recidivism among sex offenders when compared to other types of offenders. According to a report published by the U.S. Department of Justice in 2002, the released prisoners with the highest rearrest rates were those who committed property crimes such as possession and sale of stolen goods

In 1997, the United States Supreme Court upheld Kansas's civil confinement law, holding that a "mental abnormality" such as pedophilia could qualify sex offenders for commitment.[146] Four years later, the Court rejected a rapist's claim that Washington officials violated his Fifth Amendment rights against double jeopardy (see pages 331–332) by locking him up for twelve years in a health-care facility after the end of his prison term.[147] In both cases, the Court again differentiated between punishment and treatment, finding that civil confinement statutes are constitutional as long as their goals are therapeutic rather than punitive.

Dubious Results Civil liberty advocates reject the idea that sex offenders are actually receiving treatment in the various civil confinement facilities. Because this form of incarceration is not supposed to be punishment, there is no legal way to compel the "patients" to participate in their own rehabilitation. In California, for example, three-fourths of the civilly confined offenders refuse to attend therapy sessions.[148] At the same time, corrections officials are obliged to keep the sex offenders in custody until they no longer pose a threat to the community. Given the difficulties the health-care community has had in "curing" sexual obsessions, this vague standard is rarely met. Of the 3,000 sex offenders who have been committed since these laws started to appear in 1990, only about 50 have been released.[149]

Despite these problems, the strategy remains popular with the public, as it ensures that violent sex offenders will remain incapacitated beyond the term of their criminal sentences. Public support, of course, translates into political support, which is widespread. Indeed, in 2007, the federal government started its own civil confinement program based on the precedent set by the states.

Self Check Fill in the Blanks

Sex offender _____ laws, also known as Megan's Laws, mandate that law enforcement officials must alert the public when a sex offender has _____. Many of these laws place the burden of _____ with authorities on the sex offender. Megan's Laws have survived numerous constitutional challenges because courts interpret their general purpose as being _____ rather than punitive. Nearly twenty states have made it easier to keep sex offenders locked up at the conclusion of their prison terms through the practice of _____. Check your answers on page 482.

(77.4 percent), larceny (74.6 percent), and burglary (74 percent). The rearrest rates of rapists (46 percent) and those convicted of other forms of sexual assault (41.4 percent) were among the lowest for all crimes. Furthermore, only 2.5 percent of convicted rapists were arrested for another rape within three years of their release.

More recently, Canadian researchers R. Karl Hanson and Kelly Morton-Bourgon analyzed eighty-two recidivism studies on sex offenders and found that 13.7 percent were apprehended for another sex crime after release. On average, the sex offenders were significantly more likely to be rearrested for nonsexual criminal activity, if they were rearrested at all.

FOR CRITICAL ANALYSIS

How do these figures affect your opinion of Megan's Laws and other legal steps taken to monitor and control released sex offenders? Do you think the horrible nature of sex crimes, particularly against children, justifies any measures taken to protect the community against these offenders, regardless of the statistics?

Criminal Justice in Action

A SECOND LOOK AT RESIDENCY LAWS

Rarely do convicts request incarceration, but, for sex offender Kevin Morales, the idea sounded pretty good. "Jail is anytime much better than this, than the life that I'm living here now," he said.[150] In 2007, Morales and several other sex offenders found themselves living homeless under the Julia Tuttle Causeway, a bridge that connects Miami, Florida, with Miami Beach. Morales and the others ended up under the bridge as a result of the city's sexual offender residency law, an increasingly common and popular method for protecting children that, as we will discuss in this *Criminal Justice in Action* feature, may have unexpected consequences.

ZONING RESTRICTIONS FOR SEX OFFENDERS

Since 2000, more than twenty states and hundreds of municipalities have passed residency restrictions for convicted sex offenders. These laws ban sex offenders from living within a certain distance from places where children naturally congregate. In New Jersey, for example, "high-risk" offenders cannot take up residence within 3,000 feet of any school, park or campground,

church, theater, bowling alley, library, or convenience store.[151] (For medium- and low-risk offenders, the distances are 2,500 feet and 1,000 feet, respectively.) The overlapping "off-limits zones" created by residency requirements can dramatically limit where a sex offender can find affordable housing, as was the case with Kevin Morales and the other sex offenders living under the bridge in Miami.

AP Photo/J. Pat Carter

The Case for Sex Offender Residency Restrictions

- Forbidding sex offenders to live near schools and other areas that attract large groups of children decreases their access to these children, thus reducing the risk that they will reoffend. Research conducted by Jeffrey Walker of the University of Arkansas found that child molesters are nearly twice as likely to live near schools as offenders convicted of sexually assaulting adults.[152]

- The residency requirements are reassuring to parents and are generally very popular with the public.

- The right of convicted sex offenders to choose where they live is not more important than the ability of state and local governments to protect law-abiding citizens.

The Case against Sex Offender Residency Restrictions

- The laws push sex offenders into less populated areas or homelessness, which makes it much more difficult for law enforcement and corrections agents to keep tabs on them. "Probation and parole supervisors cannot effectively monitor offenders who are living under bridges, in parking lots, in tents at parks or interstate truck stops," says Elizabeth Barnhill of the Iowa Coalition against Sexual Assault.[153]

- The laws are inadequate. Studies have shown that strangers commit only about 10 percent of all sexual offenses

against children. The perpetrators of such crimes are much more likely to be family members, friends, or other acquaintances.[154]

- The laws create a false sense of security. If a sex offender wants to get to a child, a residency requirement cannot stop him or her from simply getting in a car or walking to find a victim.

Writing Assignment—Your Opinion

The town of Dyersville, Iowa, has one of the strictest residency requirements in the country: no sex offenders can live anywhere within its limits. What is your opinion of this strategy? How do you feel about residency laws in general? Do these regulations constitute extra punishment for convicts who have already, at least in theory, paid their debt for their crimes? As an alternative, should certain sex offenders be sentenced to life in prison without parole, sparing the criminal justice system the need to create awkward laws like

residency requirements and civil confinement? Before responding, you can review our discussions in this chapter concerning

- Parole, particularly the discussion of the reasons for parole (page 465) and life-without-parole (page 467).

- Barriers to reentry (pages (472–473).

- Civil confinement (pages 478–479).

Your answer should take at least three full paragraphs.

L01 **Explain the concept of prison as a total institution.** Though many people spend time in partial institutions—schools, companies where they work, and religious organizations—only in prison is every aspect of an inmate's life controlled, and that is why prisons are called total institutions. Every detail for every prisoner is fully prescribed and managed.

L02 **Describe the possible patterns of inmate behavior, which are driven by the inmate's personality and values.** (a) Professional criminals adapt to prison by "doing time" and follow the rules in order to get out quickly. (b) Those who are "jailing" establish themselves within the power structure of prison culture. These are often veterans of juvenile detention centers and other prisons. (c) Those who are "gleaning" are working to improve themselves for return to society. (d) "Disorganized" criminals have mental impairments or low IQs and therefore are unable to adapt to prison culture.

L03 **Indicate some of the reasons for violent behavior in prisons.** (a) To separate the powerful from the weak and to establish a prisoner hierarchy; (b) to minimize one's own probability of being a target of assault; (c) to enhance one's self-image; (d) to obtain sexual relief; and (e) to obtain material goods through extortion or robbery.

L04 **List and briefly explain the six general job categories among correctional officers.** (a) Block officers, who supervise cell blocks or are on block guard duty; (b) work detail supervisors, who oversee the cafeteria, prison store, and laundry, for example; (c) industrial shop and school officers, who generally oversee workshop and educational programs; (d) yard officers, who patrol the prison yard when prisoners are allowed there; (e) tower guards, who work in isolation; and (f) those who hold administrative building assignments, such as prison gate guards and overseers of visitation procedures.

L05 **Contrast the hands-off doctrine of prisoner law with the hands-on approach.** The hands-off doctrine assumes that the care of prisoners should be left entirely to prison officials and that it is not the place of judges to intervene. In contrast, the hands-on philosophy started in 1964 after the Supreme Court decision in *Cooper v. Pate.* Prisoners have been able to file civil lawsuits, called Section 1983 petitions, when they feel their civil rights have been violated.

L06 **Contrast probation, parole, mandatory release, pardon, and furlough.** Probation is an alternative to incarceration. Parole is an early release program for those incarcerated. Mandatory release occurs when the inmate has served the maximum time for her or his initial sentence minus good-time credits. A pardon can be given only by the president or one of the fifty governors. Furlough is a temporary release while in jail or prison.

L07 **Describe truth-in-sentencing laws and their goals.** Such laws make more transparent the actual time that a convicted criminal will serve in jail or prison. The goals are (a) to restore "truth" to the sentencing process; (b) to increase the percentage of the term that is actually served in prison in order to reduce crime by keeping convicts "off the streets" for a longer period; and (c) to better control the use of prison space by giving corrections officials predictable terms and policymakers advance notice of potential overcrowding.

L08 **Describe typical conditions of parole.** Parolees must not use drugs, not associate with known felons, not change their addresses without notifying authorities, and report to their parole officer at specified intervals. (The latter is usually specified in the parole contract.)

L09 **Explain the goal of prisoner reentry programs.** Based on the ideals of rehabilitation, these programs have two main objectives: (a) to prepare a prisoner for a successful return to the community, and (b) to protect the community by reducing the chances that the ex-convict will continue her or his criminal activity after release from prison.

L010 **Indicate typical conditions for release for a paroled child molester.** (a) Have no contact with children under the age of sixteen; (b) continue psychiatric treatment; (c) obtain permission from a parole officer to change residence; (d) keep away from schools or parks where children are present; (e) cannot own toys that may be used to lure children; and (f) cannot have a job or participate in any activity that involves children.

Key Terms

civil confinement 478
"deliberate indifference" 463
deprivation model 450
discretionary release 466
furlough 466
halfway house 470
"hands-off" doctrine 462
"identifiable human needs" 464
mandatory release 465

pardon 465
parole 464
parole board 467
parole contract 470
parole grant hearing 468
parole guidelines 469
parole revocation 471
prisoner reentry 472
prison gang 452

prisonization 449
prison segregation 452
relative deprivation 450
security threat group (STG) 453
sex offender notification law 475
total institution 447
work release program 470

Questions for Critical Analysis

1. Why is the principle of least eligibility relevant in today's political environment?

2. How does the deprivation model seek to explain prison violence?

3. In 2006, sheriff's deputies ordered one hundred inmates at a Los Angeles County jail to strip naked, removed the mattresses from their cells, and left them with nothing to cover themselves but blankets for twenty-four hours. Are these steps—taken to quell racially motivated violence—acceptable?

4. How does the inmate culture differ in men's prisons and women's prisons?

5. What is the most demanding job assignment in the correctional institution hierarchy?

6. What has caused a reduction in the amount of discretion that parole boards have?

7. Who are some of the individuals asked to provide comments and recommendations for a parole grant hearing?

8. When a parolee is caught committing a crime, what typically tends to happen, and why?

9. How do reentry programs prepare convicts for their return to the community after being released from prison?

10. Why do civil libertarians criticize Megan's Laws?

Maximize Your Best Possible Outcome for Chapter 14

1. **Maximize Your Best Chance for Getting a Good Grade on the Exam.** ThomsonNOW Personalized Study is a diagnostic study tool containing valuable text-specific resources—and because you focus on just what you don't know, you learn more in less time to get a better grade. How do you get ThomsonNOW? If your textbook does not include an access code card, go to **thomsonedu.com** to get ThomsonNOW before your next exam!

2. **Get the Most Out of Your Textbook** by going to the book companion Web site at **www.cjinaction.com** to access one of the tutorial quizzes, use the flash cards to master key terms, and check out the many other study aids you'll find there. Under chapter resources you will also be able to access the Stories from the Street feature and Web links mentioned in the textbook.

3. **Learn about Potential Criminal Justice Careers** discussed in this chapter by exploring careers online at **www.cjinaction.com**. You will find career descriptions and information about job requirements, training, salary and benefits, and the application process. You can also watch video profiles featuring criminal justice professionals.

Notes

1. Edward W. Sieh, "Less Eligibility: The Upper Limits of Penal Policy," *Criminal Justice Policy Review* 3 (1989), 159.
2. James C. Oleson, "The Punitive Coma," *California Law Review* (May 2002), 829–901.
3. Regina E. Rauxloh, "A Thing Called Prisoner," *Criminal Law Bulletin* (2006), 326, 331.
4. Edward L. Rubin and Malcolm M. Feeley, "Judicial Policy Making and Litigation against the Government," *University of Pennsylvania Journal of Constitutional Law* (April 2003), 617.
5. Erving Goffman, "On the Characteristics of Total Institutions," in *Asylums: Essays on the Social Situation of Mental Patients and Other Inmates* (New York: Doubleday, 1961), 6.

6. Bureau of Justice Statistics, *Prevalence of Imprisonment in the U.S. Population, 1974–2001* (Washington, D.C.: U.S. Department of Justice, August 2003), 1.
7. Bureau of Justice Statistics, *Prisoners in 2006* (Washington, D.C.: U.S. Department of Justice, 2007), 9.
8. Bureau of Justice Statistics, *Medical Causes of Death in State Prisons* (Washington, D.C.: U.S. Department of Justice, January 2007), 3.
9. Bureau of Justice Statistics, *Medical Problems of Jail Inmates* (Washington, D.C.: U.S. Department of Justice, November 2006), 1.
10. Bureau of Justice Statistics, *Mental Health Problems of Prison and Jail Inmates* (Washington, D.C.: U.S. Department of Justice, September 2006), 1.
11. Alan Johnson, "Lack of Medical Bills Dogs Prisons," *Columbus (Ohio) Dispatch* (May 22, 2007), 1A.
12. Andy Furillo, "Line Drawn on Prison Health Fixes," *Sacramento Bee* (February 8, 2007), A1.
13. Robert Aday, *Aging Prisoners: Crisis in American Corrections* (Westport, CT: Praeger, 2003), 1–5.
14. Bureau of Justice Statistics, *Medical Problems of Inmates, 1997* (Washington, D.C.: U.S. Department of Justice, January 2001), 8.
15. Donald Clemmer, *The Prison Community* (Boston: Christopher, 1940).
16. John Irwin, *Prisons in Turmoil* (Boston: Little, Brown, 1980), 67.
17. Robert Johnson, *Hard Time: Understanding and Reforming the Prison*, 2d ed. (Belmont, CA: Wadsworth Publishing Co., 1996), 133.
18. Bureau of Justice Statistics, *Census of State and Federal Correctional Facilities, 2000* (Washington, D.C.: U.S. Department of Justice, October 2003), 8.
19. Lee H. Bowker, *Prison Victimization* (New York: Elsevier, 1981), 31–33.
20. Stephen C. Light, "The Severity of Assaults on Prison Officers: A Contextual Analysis," *Social Science Quarterly* 71 (1990), 267–284.
21. Lee H. Bowker, "An Essay on Prison Violence," in *Prison Violence in America*, ed. Michael Braswell, Steven Dillingham, and Reid Montgomery, Jr. (Cincinnati, OH: Anderson Publishing Co., 1985), 7–18.
22. Frank Tannenbaum, *Crime and Community* (Boston: Ginn & Co., 1938).
23. Randy Martin and Sherwood Zimmerman, "A Typology of the Causes of Prison Riots and an Analytical Extension to the 1986 Virginia Riot," *Justice Quarterly* 7 (1990), 711–737.
24. Bert Useem, "Disorganization and the New Mexico Prison Riot of 1980," *American Sociological Review* 50 (1985), 677–688.
25. Bert Useem and Peter Kimball, *State of Siege: U.S. Prison Riots 1971–1984* (New York: Oxford University Press, 1989), 4.
26. Stuart B. Klein, "Prisoners' Rights to Physical and Mental Health Care: A Modern Expansion of the Eighth Amendment's Cruel and Unusual Punishment Clause," *Fordham University Law Journal* 7 (1978), 1.
27. Herman Badillo and Milton Haynes, *A Bill of No Rights: Attica and the American Prison System* (New York: Outerbridge & Lazard, 1972), 42.
28. Michael S. Serrill and Peter Katel, "New Mexico: The Anatomy of a Riot," *Corrections Magazine* (April 1980), 6–7.
29. Badillo and Haynes, 26.
30. Irwin, 47.
31. Leo Carroll, "Race, Ethnicity, and the Social Order of the Prison," in *The Pains of Imprisonment*, ed. R. Johnson and H. Toch (Beverly Hills, CA: Sage, 1982).
32. Leo Carroll, *Hacks, Blacks, and Cons: Race Relations in a Maximum-Security Prison* (Lexington, MA: Lexington Books, 1988), 78.
33. *Johnson v. California*, 543 U.S. 499 (2005).
34. *Ibid.*, at 508.
35. Jody Kent, "Race Walls Won't End Jail Riots," *Los Angeles Times* (February 12, 2006), M3.
36. Craig Haney, "Psychology and the Limits of Prison Pain," *Psychology, Public Policy, and Law* (December 1977), 499.
37. Gerald G. Gaes, Susan Wallace, Evan Gilman, Jody Kein-Saffran, and Sharon Suppa, *The Influence of Gang Affiliation on Violence and Other Prison Misconduct* (Washington, D.C.: Federal Bureau of Prisons, 2001), 25.
38. *A Study of Gangs and Security Threat Groups in America's Adult Prisons and Jails* (Indianapolis: National Major Gang Task Force, 2002).
39. George W. Knox, *The Problem of Gangs and Security Threat Groups (STGs) in American Prisons Today: Recent Research Findings from the 2004 Prison Gang Survey*, available at **www.ngcrc.com/corr2006.html**.

40. David M. Allender and Frank Marcell, "Career Criminals, Security Threat Groups, and Prison Gangs: An Interrelated Threat," *FBI Law Enforcement Bulletin* (June 2003), 8.
41. Knox.
42. Arizona Department of Corrections, Department Order 806, Section 806.07 (1999).
43. Oleson, 859.
44. Cathy Young, "Assault behind Bars," *Reason* (May 2007), 17.
45. *Ibid.*
46. Bureau of Justice Statistics, *Data Collection for the Prison Rape Elimination Act of 2003* (Washington, D.C.: U.S. Department of Justice, June 2004), 1.
47. Mark S. Fleisher and Jessie L. Krienert, *The Culture of Prison Sexual Violence* (Washington, D.C.: U.S. Department of Justice, November 2006).
48. Bureau of Justice Statistics, *Sexual Violence Reported by Correctional Authorities, 2005* (Washington, D.C.: U.S. Department of Justice, July 2006), 1.
49. James E. Robertson, "The Prison Rape Elimination Act of 2003: A Primer," *Criminal Law Bulletin* (May/June 2004), 270–273.
50. Quoted in Alexandra Marks, "Martha Checks in Today," *Seattle Times* (October 8, 2004), A8.
51. James J. Stephan and Jennifer C. Karberg, *Census of State and Federal Correctional Facilities, 2000* (Washington, D.C.: U.S. Department of Justice, 2003), 1.
52. *Prisoners in 2006*, 9.
53. Natasha A. Frost, Judith Greene, and Kevin Pranis, *Hard Hit: The Growth in the Imprisonment of Women, 1977–2004* (New York: Institute on Women & Criminal Justice, May 2006), 10.
54. Bureau of Justice Statistics, *Special Report: Women Offenders* (Washington, D.C.: U.S. Department of Justice, December 1999), 7.
55. Bureau of Justice Statistics, *Profile of Jail Inmates, 2002* (Washington, D.C.: U.S. Department of Justice, July 2004), 10.
56. Bureau of Justice Statistics, *Prior Abuse Reported by Inmates and Probationers* (Washington, D.C.: U.S. Department of Justice, April 1999), 2.
57. *Caught in the Net: The Impact of Drug Policies on Women and Families* (Washington, D.C.: American Civil Liberties Union, 2004), 18–19.
58. Allen J. Beck and Laura M. Maruschak, *Mental Health Treatment in State Prisons, 2000* (Washington, D.C.: U.S. Department of Justice, July 2001), 1.
59. Barbara Bloom, Barbara Owen, and Stephanie Covington, *Gender Responsive Strategies: Research, Practice, and Guiding Principles for Women Offenders* (Washington, D.C.: National Institute of Corrections, 2003), 6.
60. *Ibid.*, 7.
61. *Ibid.*, 6.
62. Bloom, Owen, and Covington, 2.
63. Kelly Bedard and Eric Helland, "Location of Women's Prisons and the Deterrent Effect of 'Harder' Time," *International Review of Law and Economics* (June 2004), 152.
64. *Ibid.*
65. *Caught in the Net*, 49–50.
66. Candace Kruttschnitt and Rosemary Gartner, "Women's Imprisonment," *Crime and Justice* (2003), 1.
67. Rosemary Gartner Kruttschnitt, "Women's Imprisonment," *Crime and Justice* 30 (2003), 1–83.
68. *Ibid.*
69. Kelly Ann Cheesemen and Robert M. Worley, "A 'Captive' Audience: Legal Responses and Remedies to the Sexual Abuse of Female Inmates," *Criminal Law Bulletin* 42 (2006), 440–442.
70. Cited in Bloom, Owen, and Covington, 26.
71. Andi Rierden, *The Farm: Life inside a Women's Prison* (Amherst, MA: University of Massachusetts Press, 1997), 23–26.
72. Esther Heffermn, *Making It in Prison: The Square, the Cool, and the Life* (New York: Wiley, 1972), 91.
73. Leanne F. Alarid, "Female Inmate Subcultures," in *Corrections Contexts: Contemporary and Classical Readings*, ed. James W. Marquart and Jonathan R. Sorenson (Los Angeles: Roxbury Publishing Co., 1997), 136–137.
74. James G. Fox, *Organizational and Racial Conflict in Maximum Security Prisons* (Lexington, MA: Lexington Books, 1982).
75. Lee H. Bowker, "Gender Differences in Prisoner Subcultures," in *Women and Crime in America*, ed. Lee H. Bowker (New York: Macmillan, 1981), 409–419.

76. Quoted in John J. DiIulio, Jr., *No Escape: The Future of American Corrections* (New York: Basic Books, 1991), 268.
77. Jack Henry Abbott, *In the Belly of the Beast* (New York: Vintage Books, 1991), 54.
78. Michael Foucault, *Discipline and Punish: The Birth of the Prison* (New York: Pantheon Books, 1977), 128.
79. Lucien X. Lombardo, *Guards Imprisoned: Correctional Officers at Work* (Cincinnati, OH: Anderson Publishing Co., 1989), 51–71.
80. Goffman, 7.
81. Todd R. Clear, George F. Cole, and Michael D. Reisig, *American Corrections*, 7th ed. (Belmont, CA: Thomson Wadsworth, 2006), 327.
82. *Wolff v. McDonnell*, 418 U.S. 539 (1974).
83. 475 U.S. 312 (1986).
84. *Stanley v. Hejirika*, 134 F.3d 629 (4th Cir. 1998).
85. Christopher R. Smith, *Law and Contemporary Corrections* (Belmont, CA: Wadsworth, 1999), Chapter 6.
86. 503 U.S. 1 (1992).
87. Darrell L. Ross, "Assessing *Hudson v. McMillan* Ten Years Later," *Criminal Law Bulletin* (September/October 2004), 508.
88. Gary Fields, "Bulging Jails and Tight Budgets Make Job of Guard Even Tougher," *Wall Street Journal* (November 2, 2005), A1.
89. *Ibid.*
90. Haney, 499.
91. 378 U.S. 546 (1964).
92. 418 U.S. 539 (1974).
93. *Sandin v. Conner*, 515 U.S. 472, 484 (1995).
94. *Ibid.*, at 472.
95. *Wilkinson v. Austin*, 545 U.S. 209 (2005).
96. *Procunier v. Martinez*, 416 U.S. 396 (1974).
97. *Cruz v. Beto*, 405 U.S. 319 (1972); *Gittlemacker v. Prasse*, 428 F.2d 1 (3d Cir. 1970); and *Kahane v. Carlson*, 527 F.2d 492 (2d Cir. 1975).
98. *Turner v. Safley*, 482 U.S. 78 (1987); and *O'Lone v. Estate of Shabazz*, 482 U.S. 432 (1987).
99. 429 U.S. 97 (1976).
100. *Daniels v. Williams*, 474 U.S. 327 (1986); and *Whitley v. Albers*, 475 U.S. 312 (1986).
101. 501 U.S. 294 (1991).
102. *Farmer v. Brennan*, 511 U.S. 825 (1994).
103. *Wilson v. Seiter*, 501 U.S. 294, 304 (1991).
104. Todd R. Clear and George F. Cole, *American Corrections*, 4th ed. (Belmont, CA: Wadsworth Pubishing Co., 1997), 416.
105. 442 U.S. 1 (1979).
106. Danya W. Blair, "A Matter of Life and Death: Why Life without Parole Should be a Sentencing Option in Texas," *American Journal of Criminal Law* 22 (Fall 1994), 191.
107. *Simmons v. South Carolina*, 512 U.S. 154 (1994).
108. William Parker, *Parole: Origins, Development, Current Practices, and Statutes* (College Park, MD: American Correctional Association, 1972), 26.
109. Bureau of Justice Statistics, *Bulletin* (Washington, D.C.: U.S. Department of Justice, January 1995), 2.
110. Michael Tonry, "Twenty Years of Sentencing Reform: Steps Forward, Steps Backward," *Judicature* 78 (January/February 1995), 169.
111. Comprehensive Crime Control Act of 1984, Pub. L. No. 98-473, Section 217(a), 98 Stat. 1837, 2017 (1984), codified as amended at 28 U.S.C. Sections 991–998 (1988).
112. 42 U.S.C.A. Sections 13701–13709.
113. William J. Sabol, Katherine Rosich, Kamala Malik Kane, David P. Kirk, and Glenn Durbin, *The Influences of Truth-in-Sentencing Reforms on Changes in States' Sentencing Practices and Prison Populations* (Washington, D.C.: National Institute of Justice, April 2002), 8.
114. Marc Mauer, "The Truth about Truth in Sentencing," *Corrections Today* (February 1, 1996), S1.
115. Todd R. Clear and Edward Latessa, "Probation Officer Roles in Intensive Supervision: Surveillance versus Treatment," *Justice Quarterly* 10 (1993), 441–462.
116. J. T. Whitehead and C. A. Lindquist, "Job Stress and Burnout among Probation/Parole Officers: Perceptions and Causal Factors," *International Journal of Offender Therapy and Comparative Criminology* 29 (1985), 109–119.
117. 408 U.S. 471 (1972).
118. 126 S.Ct. 2193 (2006).
119. California Penal Code Section 3067(a) (West 2000).
120. *Samson v. California*, 126 S.Ct. 2193, at 2200–2201, (2006).
121. Joan Petersilia, "What Works in Prisoner Reentry," *Federal Probation* (September 2004), 4.
122. Joan Petersilia, *When Prisoners Come Home: Parole and Prisoner Reentry* (New York: Oxford University Press, 2003), 39.
123. Victor Hassine, *Life without Parole: Living in Prison Today*, ed. Thomas J. Bernard and Richard McCleary (Los Angeles: Roxbury Publishing Co., 1996), 12.
124. *Ill Equipped: U.S. Prisons and Offenders with Mental Illness* (New York: Human Rights Watch, 2003).
125. Bureau of Justice Statistics, *Recidivism of Prisoners Released in 1994* (Washington, D.C.: U.S. Department of Justice, June 2002), 1.
126. Edward Zamble and Vernon Quinsey, *The Criminal Recidivism Process* (Cambridge, England: Cambridge University Press, 1997).
127. Quoted in Kevin Johnson, "After Years of Solitary, Freedom Is Hard to Grasp," *USA Today* (June 9, 2005), 2A.
128. Megan C. Kurlychek, Robert Brame, and Shawn D. Bushway, "Scarlet Letter and Recidivism: Does an Old Criminal Record Predict Future Offending?" *Criminology and Public Policy* (August 2006), 483.
129. *Ibid.*, 483–504.
130. Shadd Maruna, *Making Good: How Ex-Convicts Reform and Rebuild Their Lives* (Washington, D.C.: American Psychological Association, 2001), 83.
131. Charis E. Kurbin and Eric A. Stewart, "Predicting Who Reoffends: The Neglected Role of Neighborhood Context in Recidivism Studies," *Criminology* (February 2006), 165–189.
132. Petersilia, "What Works in Prisoner Reentry," 7.
133. "The Greatest Fear," *The Economist* (August 26, 2006), 25.
134. Janice Marques, Mark Wiederanders, David Day, Craig Nelson, and Alice Ommeren, "Effects of a Relapse Prevention Program on Sexual Recidivism: Final Results from California's Sex Offender Treatment and Evaluation Project (SOTEP)," *Sexual Abuse: A Journal of Research and Treatment* (January 2005), 79–107.
135. New Jersey Revised Statute Section 2C:7-8(c) (1995).
136. Georgia Code Annotated Section 42-9-44.1(b)(1).
137. National Center for Missing and Exploited Children, "Registered Sex Offenders in the United States," at **www.missingkids.com/en_US/documents/sex-offender-map.pdf**.
138. Tara L. Wayt, "Megan's Law: A Violation of the Right to Privacy?" *Temple Political and Civil Rights Law Review* 6 (Fall 1996/Spring 1997), 139.
139. 538 U.S. 84 (2003).
140. 538 U.S. 1 (2003).
141. Quoted in "Problems Still Linger with Megan's Laws," *Law Enforcement News* (May 2004), 12.
142. Abby Goodnough, "After Two Cases in Florida, Crackdown on Molesters," *New York Times* (May 1, 2005), 18.
143. California Penal Code Section 3000(g).
144. Section 1012.465 F.S. (as amended, 2005).
145. Goodnough, 18.
146. *Kansas v. Hendricks*, 521 U.S. 346 (1997).
147. *Selig v. Young*, 531 U.S. 250 (2001).
148. Monica Davey and Abby Goodnough, "Doubts Rise as States Detain Sex Offenders after Prison," *New York Times* (March 4, 2007), 1.
149. *Ibid.*
150. Quoted in John Zarrella and Patrick Oppman, "Florida Housing Sex Offenders under Bridge," CNN.com Law Center, at **www.cnn.com/2007/LAW/04/05/bridge.sex.offenders**.
151. New Jersey Statutes Annotated Section 2C: 7-3.
152. Wendy Kock, "Sex-Offender Residency Laws Get a Second Look," *USA Today* (February 26, 2007), 1A.
153. Quoted in Jenifer Warren, "Sex Crime Residency Laws Exile Offenders," *Los Angeles Times* (October 30, 2006), 1.
154. Bureau of Justice Statistics, *Recidivism of Sex Offenders Released from Prison in 1994* (Washington, D.C.: U.S. Department of Justice, November 2003), 36; and Luis Rosell, "Sex Offenders: Pariahs of the 21st Century?" *William Mitchell Law Review* (2005), 419.

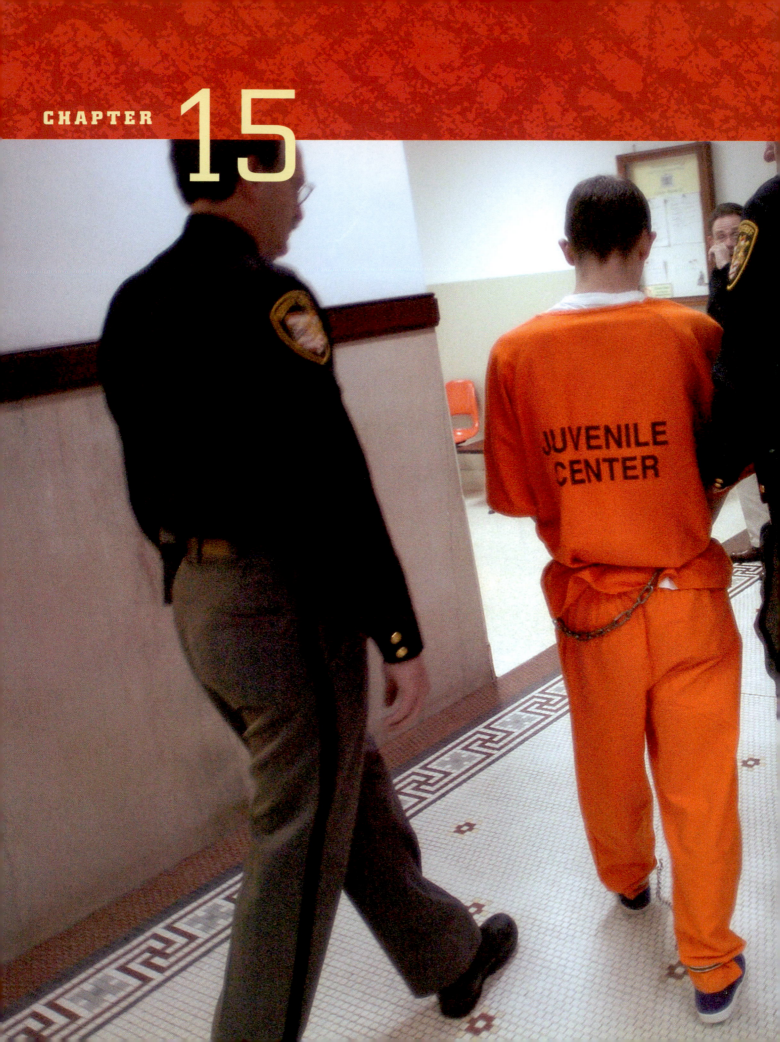

The Juvenile Justice System

Learning objectives

After reading this chapter, you should be able to:

L01 Describe the child-saving movement and its relationship to the doctrine of *parens patriae*.

L02 List the four major differences between juvenile courts and adult courts.

L03 Identify and briefly describe the single most important Supreme Court case with respect to juvenile justice.

L04 List the factors that normally determine what police do with juvenile offenders.

L05 Describe the four primary stages of pretrial juvenile justice procedure.

L06 Explain the distinction between an adjudicatory hearing and a disposition hearing.

L07 List the four categories of residential treatment programs.

L08 Describe the one variable that always correlates highly with juvenile crime rates.

L09 Indicate some of the reasons why youths join gangs.

According to prosecutors, sixteen-year-old Ashley Paige Benton was one cold customer. After taking part in a violent gang brawl during which she allegedly stabbed fifteen-year-old Gabriel Granillo to death, Benton and her friends went to a fast-food restaurant for some chips and salsa. She seemed similarly unperturbed when she was arrested for the murder, telling Houston police officers, "No big deal. Let's go." Perhaps it should have come as no surprise, then, that Benton showed no emotion when informed by Texas District Judge Pat Sheldon that she was going to be tried as an adult for her crime.

It is common practice in Texas for offenders between the ages of fourteen and seventeen who are suspected of committing a serious crime to be transferred to an adult court. Nonetheless, Judge Sheldon did have the option of allowing Benton to be processed through the more informal juvenile system, as the girl's attorneys had requested. After looking at a number of factors, including the seriousness of the incident and Benton's history of misbehavior—which included carrying a knife to school— the judge decided that the "welfare of the community" required an adult trial. So, instead of returning to the relative comfort of the county juvenile lockup, Benton was moved to the Harris County Jail, a facility that had failed three straight inspections because of overcrowding, inadequate health care, and poor sanitation. In January 2007, a grand jury indicted Benton on charges of murder. If found guilty, she would probably spend the rest of her childhood, as well as much of her adult life, in prison.

▲ Sixteen-year-old Ashley Paige Benton appears at a Harris County (Texas) courthouse in January 2007 after being charged with murdering another teenager during a gang brawl.

The judge's decision to try Ashley Paige Benton as an adult underscores a debate that goes to the heart of the American juvenile justice system, which has been both hailed as one of the "greatest social inventions of modern times" and criticized for "failing to protect either the legal rights of the juvenile offenders or the public on whom they prey."[1] The question: Should criminal acts by youths be given the same weight as those committed by adults or be seen as "mistakes" that can be "corrected" by the state?

For most of its century-long history, the system was dominated by the latter philosophy; only recently have opposing views summarized by the sound bite "old enough to do the crime, old enough to do the time" gained widespread acceptance—a change reflected in political trends. Over the past three decades, nearly every state has changed its laws to make it easier to try juveniles as adults, representing a shift toward harsher measures in a juvenile system that generally acts as a "compromise between rehabilitation and punishment, treatment and custody."[2]

In this chapter, we will discuss the successes and failures of this compromise and examine the aspects of the juvenile justice system that differentiate it from the criminal justice system. As you will see, observers on both sides of the "rehabilitation versus punishment" debate find many flaws with the present system; some have even begun to call for its dismantling. Others blame social problems such as racism, poverty, and a culture dominated by images of violence for creating a system that no government agency or policy can effectively control.[3]

AP Photo/Houston Chronicle, Mayra Beltran

The Evolution of American Juvenile Justice

In a recent poll, almost 60 percent of Americans indicated that they favored trying violent youths in adult criminal court instead of juvenile courts, which were perceived as too lenient.[4] To a certain degree, such opinions reflect a desire to return the focus of the American juvenile justice system toward punishment and incapacitation, as was the case at the beginning of the nineteenth century. At that time, juvenile offenders were treated the same as adult offenders—they were judged by the same courts and sentenced to the same severe penalties. This situation began to change in the early 1800s, as urbanization and industrialization created an immigrant underclass that was, at least in the eyes of many reformers, predisposed to deviant activity. Certain members of the Progressive movement, known as the child savers, began to take steps to "save" children from these circumstances, introducing the idea of rehabilitating delinquents in the process.

> "This is a cultural virus. We have to ask ourselves what kind of children we are raising."
>
> —Bill Owens, Colorado governor, following the massacre of fourteen classmates and one teacher by two students at Columbine High School in Littleton, Colorado, on April 20, 1999

THE CHILD-SAVING MOVEMENT

L01

In general, the child savers favored the doctrine of *parens patriae*, which holds that the state has not only a right but a duty to care for children who are neglected, delinquent, or in some other way disadvantaged. Juvenile offenders, the child savers believed, required treatment, not punishment, and they were horrified at the thought of placing children in prisons with hardened adult criminals. In 1967, then Supreme Court Justice Abe Fortas said of the child savers:

> They believed that society's role was not to ascertain whether the child was "guilty" or "innocent," but "What is he, how has he become what he is, and what had best be done in his interest and in the interest of the state to save him from a downward career." The child—essentially good, as they saw it—was made "to feel that he is the object of [the government's] care and solicitude," not that he was under arrest or on trial.[5]

Child-saving organizations convinced local legislatures to pass laws that allowed them to take control of children who exhibited criminal tendencies or had been neglected by their parents. To separate these children from the environment in which they were raised, the organizations created a number of institutions, the best known of which was New York's House of Refuge. Opening in 1825, the House of Refuge implemented many of the same reformist measures popular in the penitentiaries of the time, meaning that its charges were subjected to the healthful influences of hard study and labor. Although the House of Refuge was criticized for its harsh discipline (which caused many boys to run away), similar institutions sprang up throughout the Northeast during the middle of the nineteenth century.

THE ILLINOIS JUVENILE COURT

The efforts of the child savers culminated with the passage of the Illinois Juvenile Court Act in 1899. The Illinois legislature created the first court specifically for juveniles, guided by the principles of *parens patriae* and based on the concepts that children are not fully responsible for criminal conduct and are capable of being rehabilitated.[6]

The Illinois Juvenile Court and those in other states that followed in its path were (and, in many cases, remain) drastically different from adult courts:

L02

- *No juries.* The matter was decided by judges who wore regular clothes instead of black robes and sat at a table with the other participants rather than behind a bench. Because the primary focus of the court

Parens Patriae A doctrine that holds that the state has a responsibility to look after the well-being of children and to assume the role of parent if necessary.

Corbis

THE HOUSE OF REFUGE

▲ An illustration detailing the daily activities in the New York House of Refuge that appeared in *Harper's Weekly* in 1868. The House of Refuge was created in 1825 as a result of reformers' outrage that children who broke the law were treated the same as adults. The purpose of the House was to receive "all such children as shall be taken up or committed as vagrants, or convicted of criminal offenses." As you can see, the children were put to work at a number of different tasks, such as making shoes and hoop skirts. They also attended four hours of school every day. Judging from this illustration, how would you characterize the philosophy behind the House of Refuge?

was on the child and not the crime, the judge had wide discretion in disposing of each case.

- *Different terminology.* To reduce the stigma of criminal proceedings, "petitions" were issued instead of "warrants"; the children were not "defendants," but "respondents"; they were not "found guilty" but "adjudicated delinquent."

- *No adversarial relationship.* Instead of trying to determine guilt or innocence, the parties involved in the juvenile court worked together in the best interests of the child, with the emphasis on rehabilitation rather than punishment.

- *Confidentiality.* To avoid "saddling" the child with a criminal past, juvenile court hearings and records were kept sealed, and the proceedings were closed to the public.

By 1945, every state had a juvenile court system modeled after the first Illinois court. For the most part, these courts were able to operate without interference until the 1960s and the onset of the juvenile rights movement.

JUVENILE DELINQUENCY

After the first juvenile court was established in Illinois, the Chicago Bar Association described its purpose as, in part, to "exercise the same tender solicitude and care over its neglected wards that a wise and loving parent would exercise with reference to his [or her] own children under similar circumstances."[7] In other words, the state was given the responsibility of caring for those minors whose behavior seemed to show that they could not be controlled by their parents. As a result, many **status offenders** found themselves in the early houses of refuge and continue to be placed in state-run facilities today. Also known as "children (or minors, youths, and the like) in need of supervision," status offenders have exhibited behavior—such as violating curfew, truancy (skipping school), and alcohol consumption—that is considered illegal only if an offender is below a specified age (see ■ Figure 15.1).

In contrast, **juvenile delinquency** refers to conduct that would also be criminal if committed by an adult. According to federal law and the laws of most states, a juvenile delinquent is someone who has not yet reached his or her eighteenth birthday, or the age of majority, at the time of the offense in question. In three states (Connecticut, New York, and North Carolina), persons aged sixteen are considered adults, and ten other states (Georgia, Illinois, Louisiana, Massachusetts, Michigan, Missouri, New Hampshire, South Carolina, Texas, and Wisconsin) confer adulthood on seventeen-year-olds. Under certain circumstances, discussed later in this chapter, children below the age of majority can be treated as adults for the purposes of prosecution and trial. Remember that Ashley Paige Benton was sixteen years old when a judge transferred her to adult court to stand trial for the murder of Gabriel Granillo.

CONSTITUTIONAL PROTECTIONS AND THE JUVENILE COURT

Though the ideal of the juvenile court seemed to offer the "best of both worlds" for juvenile offenders, in reality the lack of procedural protections led to many children being arbitrarily punished not only for crimes, but for status offenses.

Status Offender A juvenile who has been found to have engaged in behavior deemed unacceptable for those under a certain, statutorily determined age.

Juvenile Delinquency Behavior that is illegal under federal or state law that has been committed by a person who is under an age limit specified by statute.

Juvenile judges were treating all violators similarly, which led to many status offenders being incarcerated in the same institutions as violent delinquents. In response to a wave of lawsuits demanding due process rights for juveniles, the Supreme Court issued several rulings in the 1960s and 1970s that significantly changed the juvenile justice system.

Kent v. United States The first decision to extend due process rights to children in juvenile courts was *Kent v. United States* (1966).[8] The case concerned sixteen-year-old Morris Kent, who had been arrested for breaking into a woman's house, stealing her purse, and raping her. Because Kent was on juvenile probation, the state sought to transfer his trial for the crime to an adult court (a process to be discussed later in the chapter). Without giving any reasons for his decision, the juvenile judge consented to this judicial waiver, and Kent was sentenced in the adult court to a thirty- to ninety-year prison term. The Supreme Court overturned the sentence, ruling that juveniles have a right to counsel and a hearing in any instance in which the juvenile judge is considering sending the case to an adult court. The Court stated that, in jurisdiction waiver cases, a child receives "the worst of both worlds," getting neither the "protections accorded to adults" nor the "solicitous care and regenerative treatment" offered in the juvenile system.[9]

In re Gault The *Kent* decision provided the groundwork for *In re Gault* one year later. Considered by many the single most important case concerning juvenile justice, *In re Gault* involved a fifteen-year-old boy who was arrested for allegedly making a lewd phone call while on probation.[10] (See the feature *Landmark Cases:* In re Gault on the next page.) In its decision, the Supreme Court held that juveniles are entitled to many of the same due process rights granted to adult offenders, including notice of charges, the right to counsel, the privilege against self-incrimination, and the right to confront and cross-examine witnesses.

Other Important Court Decisions Over the next ten years, the Supreme Court handed down three more important rulings on juvenile court procedure. *In re Winship* (1970)[11] required the government to prove "beyond a reasonable doubt" that a juvenile had committed an act of delinquency, raising the burden of proof from a "preponderance of the evidence." In *Breed v. Jones* (1975),[12] the Court held that the Fifth Amendment's double jeopardy clause prevented a juvenile from being tried in an adult court for a crime that had already been adjudicated in juvenile court. In contrast, *McKeiver v. Pennsylvania* (1971)[13] represented the one instance in which the Court did not move the juvenile court further toward the adult model. It ruled that the Constitution did not give juveniles the right to a jury trial.

■ **Figure 15.1** **Status Offenses**

A status offense is an act that, if committed by a juvenile, is considered grounds for apprehension and perhaps state custody. The same act, if committed by an adult, does not warrant law enforcement action.

1. Smoking cigarettes
2. Drinking alcohol
3. Being truant (skipping school)
4. Disobeying teachers
5. Running away from home
6. Violating curfew
7. Participating in sexual activity
8. Using profane language

Self Check Fill in the Blanks

At its inception, the American juvenile justice system was guided by the principles of _____, which holds that the state has a responsibility to look after children when their parents cannot do so. In general, juveniles are involved in two types of wrongdoing: (1) acts that would not be crimes if committed by adults, or _____, and (2) acts that would be crimes if committed by an adult, or juvenile _____. Check your answers on page 519.

Determining Delinquency Today

In the eyes of many observers, the net effect of the Supreme Court decisions during the 1966–1975 period was to move juvenile justice away from the ideals of the child savers and toward a formalized system that is often indistinguishable from its adult counterpart. But, though the Court has recognized that minors possess certain constitutional rights, it has failed to dictate at what age these rights should be granted and at what age minors are to be held criminally responsible for delinquent actions. Consequently, the legal status of children in the United States varies depending on where they live, with each state making its own policy decisions on the crucial questions of age and competency.

THE AGE QUESTION

In 2006, an eight-year-old Brooklyn boy sneaked onto a school bus and, as a prank, released its parking brake. The vehicle rolled forward and fatally struck second-grader Amber Sadiq. When New York police arrested the boy for criminally negligent homicide, even the victim's family expressed surprise. "[They] don't feel there should be any charges against the boy," said their spokesperson. "He is a baby himself."[14]

Jurisdictions across the country have had various responses to the idea of treating "babies" like criminals. Under common law, a child under the age of seven was considered to lack the requisite *mens rea* to commit a crime (that is, he or she did not possess the mental capacity to understand the consequences of his or her action). Also under common law, a child between the ages of seven and fourteen could use the defense of infancy (being a minor) to plead innocent. On attaining fourteen years of age, the youth was considered an adult and treated accordingly.[15]

Today, as ■ Figure 15.2 shows, twenty-two states and the District of Columbia do not have age restrictions on prosecuting juveniles as adults. Indeed, many states require juveniles who commit violent felonies such as murder, rape, or armed robbery to be waived to adult courts. (Because the Brooklyn boy mentioned earlier did not meet New York's age limit for his offense, he could have been sentenced

Landmark Cases *In re Gault*

In 1964, fifteen-year-old Gerald Gault and a friend were arrested for making lewd telephone calls to a neighbor in Gila County, Arizona. Gault, who was on probation, was placed under custody with no notice given to his parents. The juvenile court in his district held a series of informal hearings to determine Gault's punishment. During these hearings, no records were kept, Gault was not afforded the right to counsel, and the complaining witness was never made available for questioning. At the close of the hearing, the judge sentenced Gault to remain in Arizona's State Industrial School until the age of twenty-one. The defendant filed a writ of *habeas corpus,* claiming that he had been denied due process rights at his hearing. Arizona's Supreme Court affirmed the dismissal of this writ, ruling that the proceedings did not infringe on Gault's due process rights, a matter eventually taken up by the United States Supreme Court.

In re Gault
United States Supreme Court
387 U.S. 1 (1967)
laws.findlaw.com/US/387/1.htm

IN THE WORDS OF THE COURT . . .

Justice FORTAS, majority opinion

* * * *

From the inception of the juvenile court system, wide differences have been tolerated—indeed insisted upon—between the procedural rights accorded to adults and those of juveniles. In practically all jurisdictions, there are rights granted to adults which are withheld from juveniles.

* * * *

Accordingly, the highest motives and most enlightened impulses led to a peculiar system for juveniles, unknown to our law in any comparable context. The constitutional and theoretical basis for this peculiar system is—to say the least—debatable. And in practice, as we remarked in the *Kent* case, the results have not been entirely satisfactory. * * * The absence of substantive standards has not necessarily meant that children receive careful, compassionate, individualized treatment. The absence of procedural rules based upon constitutional principle has not always produced fair, efficient, and effective procedures. Departures from established principles of due process have

to no more than eighteen months in a juvenile facility for his actions. As it turned out, prosecutors declined to press charges.) When juveniles in a state without such a requirement commit a serious crime, they are given a "limited" sentence, usually meaning they cannot remain incarcerated in juvenile detention centers past their eighteenth or twenty-first birthday.

THE CULPABILITY QUESTION

Most researchers believe that by the age of fourteen, an adolescent has the same ability as an adult to make a competent decision.[16] Nevertheless, according to some observers, a juvenile's ability to theoretically understand the difference between "right" and "wrong" does not mean that she or he should be held to the same standards of competency as an adult. A study released in 2003 by the Research Network on Adolescent Development and Juvenile Justice found that 33 percent of juvenile defendants in criminal courts had the same low level of understanding of

■ **Figure 15.2**
The Minimum Age at Which a Juvenile Can Be Tried as an Adult

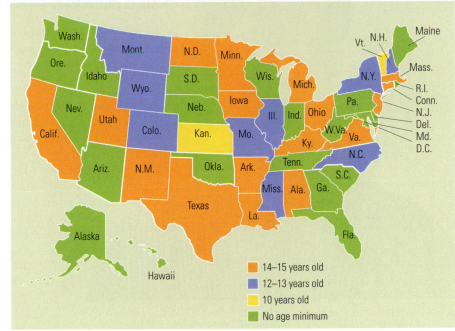

- 🟧 14–15 years old
- 🟪 12–13 years old
- 🟨 10 years old
- 🟩 No age minimum

Source: Howard N. Snyder and Melissa Sickmund, *Juvenile Offenders and Victims: 2006 National Report* (Washington, D.C.: National Center for Juvenile Justice, March 2006), 114.

frequently resulted not in enlightened procedure, but in arbitrariness.

* * * *

Ultimately, however, we confront the reality of that portion of the Juvenile Court process with which we deal in this case. A boy is charged with misconduct. The boy is committed to an institution where he may be restrained of liberty for years. It is of no constitutional consequence—and of limited practical meaning—that the institution to which he is committed is called an Industrial School. The fact of the matter is that, however euphemistic the title, a "receiving home" or an "industrial school" for juveniles is an institution of confinement in which the child is incarcerated for a greater or lesser time. His world becomes "a building with whitewashed walls, regimented routine and institutional hours . . . ." Instead of mother and father and sisters and brothers and friends and classmates, his world is peopled by guards, custodians, state employees, and "delinquents" confined with him for anything from waywardness to rape and homicide. In view of this, it would be extraordinary if our Constitution did not require the procedural regularity and the exercise of care implied in the phrase "due process."

Under our Constitution, the condition of being a boy does not justify a kangaroo court.

* * * *

DECISION

The Court held that juveniles were entitled to the basic procedural safeguards afforded by the Fourteenth Amendment, including the right to advance notice of charges, the right to counsel, the right to confront and cross-examine witnesses, and the privilege against self-incrimination. The decision marked a turning point in juvenile justice in this country: no longer would informality and paternalism be the guiding principles of juvenile courts. Instead, due process would dictate the adjudication process, much as in an adult court.

FOR CRITICAL ANALYSIS

What might be some of the negative consequences of the *In re Gault* decision for juveniles charged with committing delinquent acts?

For more information and activities related to this case, click on *Landmark Cases* under *Book Resources* at **www.cjinaction.com**.

legal matters as mentally ill adults who had been found incompetent to stand trial.[17]

Legal psychologist Richard E. Redding believes that

adolescents' lack of life experience may limit their real-world decision-making ability. Whether we call it wisdom, judgment, or common sense, adolescents may not have nearly enough.[18]

Juveniles are generally more impulsive, more likely to engage in risky behavior, and less likely to calculate the long-term consequences of any particular action. Furthermore, adolescents are far more likely to respond to peer pressure than are adults. The desire for acceptance and approval may drive them to commit crimes; juveniles are arrested as part of a group at much higher rates than adults.[19]

The "diminished culpability" of juveniles was one of the reasons given by the United States Supreme Court in its landmark decision in *Roper v. Simmons* (2005)[20] to forbid the execution of offenders who were under the age of eighteen when they committed their crimes. In his majority opinion, Justice Anthony Kennedy wrote that because minors cannot fully comprehend the consequences of their actions, the two main justifications for the death penalty—retribution and deterrence— do not "work" with juvenile wrongdoers.[21] (To review this important decision, see pages 368–369.)

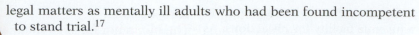

AP Photo/Ted Fitzgerald-Pool

▲ John Odgren was sixteen years old in 2007 when he was charged with stabbing and killing a classmate in a Lincoln-Sudbury Regional High School (Massachusetts) bathroom. Odgren had been taking medication for Asperger's Syndrome, a condition that impairs one's social skills. Before trial, Odgren's defense attorney claimed that his client was not responsible for his actions because of the effects of the medical condition. Should an offender's age also be taken into account when determining his or her ability to form criminal intent?

Self Check Fill in the Blanks

The age at which a child can be held criminally responsible for his or her actions differs from _____ to _____. Many experts believe that minors should not be held to the same level of competency as adults, partially because they are more _____ and more likely to respond to _____ pressure. This "diminished culpability" was one of the reasons the United States Supreme Court gave for prohibiting the _____ for offenders who were under the age of eighteen when they committed their crimes. Check your answers on page 519.

First Contact: Delinquents and the Police

Until recently, most police departments allocated few resources to dealing with juvenile crime. The rise in violent crimes committed by citizens under the age of eighteen has, however, provided a strong incentive for departments to set up special services for children. The standard bearer for these operations is the *juvenile officer,* who operates either alone or as part of a juvenile unit within a department. The initial contact between a juvenile and the criminal justice system is usually handled by a regular police officer on patrol who either apprehends the juvenile while he or she is committing a crime or answers a call for service. (See ■ Figure 15.3 for an overview of the juvenile justice process.) The youth is then passed on to a juvenile officer, who must decide how to handle the case.

POLICE DISCRETION AND JUVENILE CRIME

Police arrest about 1.4 million youths under the age of eighteen each year. In most states, police officers must have probable cause to believe that the minor has committed an offense, just as they would if the suspect was an adult. Police power with

This diagram shows the possible tracks that a young person may take after her or his first contact with the juvenile justice system (usually a police officer).

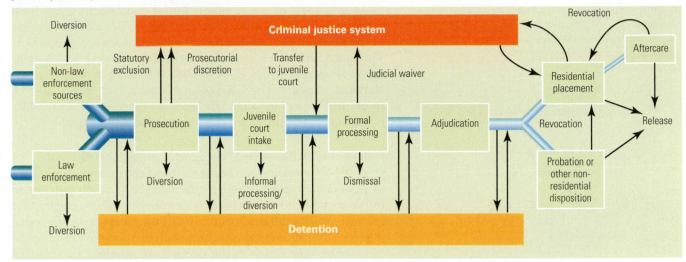

Source: Office of Juvenile Justice and Delinquency Prevention.

regard to juveniles is greater than with adults, however, because police can take youths into custody for status offenses such as possession of alcohol or truancy. In these cases, the officer is acting *in loco parentis,* or in the place of the parent. The officer's role is not necessarily to punish the youths, but to protect them from harmful behavior.

Low-Visibility Decision Making Police officers also have a great deal of discretion in deciding what to do with juveniles who have committed crimes or status

L04 offenses. Juvenile justice expert Joseph Goldstein labels this discretionary power **low-visibility decision making** because it relies on factors that the public is not generally in a position to understand or criticize. When a grave offense has taken place, a police officer may decide to formally arrest the juvenile, send him or her to juvenile court, or place the youth under the care of a social-service organization. In less serious situations, the officer may simply issue a warning or take the offender to the police station and release the child into the custody of her or his parents.

In making these discretionary decisions, police generally consider the following factors:

- The nature of the child's offense.
- The offender's past history of involvement with the juvenile justice system.
- The setting in which the offense took place.
- The ability and willingness of the child's parents to take disciplinary action.
- The attitude of the offender.
- The offender's race and gender.

Law enforcement officers notify the juvenile court system that a particular young person requires its attention through a process known as a **referral.** Anyone with a valid reason, including parents, relatives, welfare agencies, and school officials, can refer a juvenile to the juvenile court. About 85 percent of the cases in juvenile courts, however, are referred by the police.[22]

Arrests and Minority Youths As in other areas of the criminal justice system, members of minority groups are disproportionately represented in juvenile arrests. The violent crime arrest rate for African American juveniles is about four times that for white juveniles, and the property arrest crime rate for black juveniles

Low-Visibility Decision Making A term used to describe the discretionary power police have in determining what to do with misbehaving juveniles. For the most part, this power goes unchallenged and unnoticed by citizens.

Referral The notification process through which a law enforcement officer or other concerned citizen makes the juvenile court aware of a juvenile's unlawful or unruly conduct.

■ **Figure 15.4** Juvenile Arrest Rates by Race, 1980 to the 2000s

Using the FBI's Uniform Crime Report, statisticians can determine the rates of arrest for persons aged ten to seventeen in the United States. As you can see, although the rate of arrests per 100,000 juveniles remains considerably higher for African Americans than for whites, the discrepancy has narrowed since the mid-1990s.

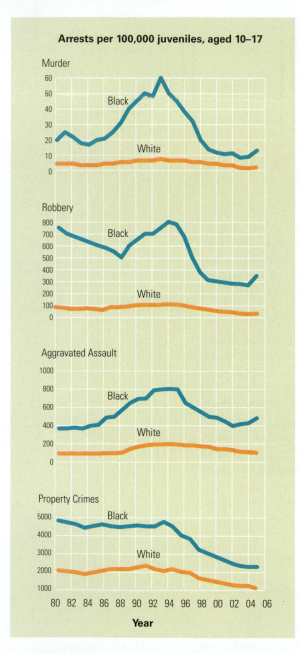

Arrests per 100,000 juveniles, aged 10–17

Murder

Black
White

Robbery

Black
White

Aggravated Assault

Black
White

Property Crimes

Black
White

80 82 84 86 88 90 92 94 96 98 00 02 04 06
Year

Source: Office of Juvenile Justice and Delinquency Prevention, *Statistical Briefing Book*, at **www.jjdp.ncjrs.org/ojstatbb/crime/JAR.asp**.

is double that of whites. Furthermore, African American juveniles are referred to juvenile court twice as often as their white peers.[23]

A great deal of research, much of it contradictory, has been done to determine whether these statistics reflect inherent racism in the juvenile justice system or if social factors are to blame.[24] The latest large-scale study, performed by federal government crime researchers Carl E. Pope and Howard Snyder using the National Incident-Based Reporting System (see pages 80–81), found that nonwhite offenders were no more likely than white offenders to be arrested for the same delinquent behavior.[25]

Failing the "Attitude Test" In general, though, as ■ Figure 15.4 shows, police officers do seem more likely to arrest members of minority groups. Although this may be partially attributed to the social factors discussed in Chapter 2, it also appears that minority youths fail the "attitude test" in interactions with police officers. After the seriousness of the offense and past history, the most important factor in the decision of whether to arrest or release appears to be the offender's attitude. An offender who is polite and apologetic generally has a better chance of being released. If the juvenile is hostile or unresponsive, the police are more likely to place him or her in custody for even a minor offense.[26]

Furthermore, police officers who do not live in the same community with minority youths may misinterpret normal behavior as disrespectful or delinquent and act accordingly.[27] This "culture gap" is of crucial importance to police-juvenile relations and underscores the community-oriented policing goal of having law enforcement agents be more involved in the communities they patrol (see Chapter 6).

JUVENILES AND THE CONSTITUTION

The privacy and *Miranda* rights of juveniles are protected during contact with law enforcement officers, though not to the same extent as for adults. In most jurisdictions, the Fourth Amendment ban against unreasonable searches and seizures and Fifth Amendment safeguards against custodial self-incrimination apply to juveniles. In other words, juvenile court judges cannot use illegally seized evidence in juvenile hearings, and police must read youths their *Miranda* rights after arrest.

Searches and Students Such rights are not absolute, however. In *New Jersey v. T.L.O.* (1985),[28] the Supreme Court held that school officials may search a student on mere "reasonable suspicion" that he or she has violated school regulations or laws. The Court justified this lower standard—most searches require probable cause—on the grounds of maintaining school discipline and the *in loco parentis* doctrine.[29] In 1995, the Court further strengthened school officials' ability to search students by upholding a random drug-testing policy for high school athletes.[30] Seven years later, in *Board of Education v. Earls* (2002),[31] the Court allowed similar testing of students participating in any extracurricular activities.

Miranda Warnings In *Fare v. Michael C.* (1979),[32] the Supreme Court clarified law enforcement officials' responsibilities with regard to *Miranda* warnings and juveniles. The case involved a boy who had been arrested on suspicion of murder. After being read his rights, the youth asked to speak to his probation officer. The request was denied. The boy eventually confessed to the crime. The Court ruled that juveniles may waive their right to protection against self-incrimination and that admissions made to the police in the absence of counsel are admissible. Then, in 2004, the Court seemed to blur any constitutional distinction between juveniles and adults for *Miranda* purposes by ruling that a trial court does not need to consider the defendant's age in determining whether a "reasonable person" would think she or he is in custody.[33] (See pages 226–229 for a review of the *Miranda* procedure.)

This does not mean that juvenile status is completely irrelevant in these situations. Remember that any statement to the police must be given voluntarily. Thus, courts can look at the defendant's age in determining whether he or she was unfairly coerced into speaking.[34] As can be seen in the feature *A Question of Ethics: Interrogating Children* on the following page, police can be taking a chance by relying on the testimony of young suspects and witnesses.

▲ As second-grader Ejuanda Fields exits the school bus that takes her to Indianapolis Public School 84, Indianapolis Public Schools Police Sergeant Kelly Browning checks her backpack for weapons and drugs. Do you believe that students should have the same privacy protections against searches as everybody else? What reasons can be given for denying them those protections?

The Right to a Jury Trial As noted earlier, the Supreme Court has held that juveniles do not have a right to a trial before a jury. In practice, however, only twenty-three states and the District of Columbia fail to provide jury trials for juvenile delinquents under any circumstances. Four states (Alaska, Massachusetts, Michigan, and West Virginia) permit juveniles to request a jury trial for any charges, and the rest allow formal procedure in certain situations.[35] In Idaho, for example, any juvenile over the age of fourteen who is alleged to have committed a violent or drug-related offense has the right to a jury trial.[36]

Self Check Fill in the Blanks

Law enforcement officers have a great deal of _____ in dealing with offending juveniles. If the circumstances are serious enough, the police can formally _____ the juvenile. Otherwise, the officer can _____ the juvenile to the juvenile court system or place her or him in the care of a _____-service organization. In the least serious circumstances, the juvenile may be released into the custody of his or her parents after receiving a stern _____. Check your answers on page 519.

Pretrial Procedures in Juvenile Justice

L05 Once a juvenile offender has been arrested, various decision makers are provided the opportunity to determine how the juvenile justice system will dispose of the case. The offender may be diverted to a social-services program or detained in a juvenile lockup facility. In the most serious cases, the youth may even be transferred to adult court. To ensure due process during pretrial procedures, offenders and their families may retain an attorney or have one appointed by the

Intake Following referral of a juvenile to juvenile court by a police officer or other concerned party, the process by which an official of the court must decide whether to file a petition, release the juvenile, or place the juvenile under some other form of supervision.

Petition The document filed with a juvenile court alleging that the juvenile is a delinquent or a status offender and asking the court to either hear the case or transfer it to an adult court.

court. The four primary stages of this critical period—intake, diversion, waiver, and detention—are discussed below.

INTAKE

As noted earlier, if, following arrest, a police officer feels the offender warrants the attention of the juvenile justice process, the officer will refer the youth to juvenile court. Once this step has been taken, a complaint is filed with a special division of the juvenile court, and the **intake** process begins. During intake, an official of the juvenile court—usually a probation officer, but sometimes a judge—must decide, in effect, what to do with the offender. The intake officer has several options during intake.

1. Simply dismiss the case, releasing the offender without taking any further action.
2. Divert the offender to a social-services program, such as drug rehabilitation or anger management.
3. File a **petition** for a formal court hearing.
4. Transfer the case to an adult court where the offender will be tried as an adult.

The intake process is changing in several very important ways. In particular, the influence of prosecutors on the fate of the juvenile wrongdoer is growing significantly. In the past, the primary responsibility for providing a juvenile judge with a recommendation on how the case should be handled was left to probation personnel. Even though the judge handed down the final decision, in most cases she or he followed the recommendation of a probation officer as to whether the juvenile should take part in a formal court hearing. This approach, indicative of a system that favors rehabilitation, is being replaced in some jurisdictions.

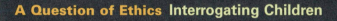

A Question of Ethics Interrogating Children

THE SITUATION The body of an eleven-year-old girl named Ryan Harris has been found in a lot behind an empty building. Evidence shows that Ryan had been beaten and sexually assaulted before her death. Chicago police believe that a seven-year-old boy has knowledge of the circumstances surrounding the murder. Two detectives isolate the boy in an empty room at the police station and ask him if he knows what a lie is. "You should never lie," the boy answers. Each of the detectives takes one of the boy's hands and asks him about Harris. The seven-year-old admits to throwing a brick at the girl and knocking her off her bicycle, and then dragging her body into the weeds with the help of an eight-year-old friend. After corroborating the story with this accomplice, the police detain the boys and classify the case of Ryan Harris as "Cleared/Closed by Arrest."

THE ETHICAL DILEMMA The law allows police to interrogate juvenile of any age without a parent or guardian being present. In these situations, the police must only make a "reasonable attempt" to contact the parents, after which they can question the child. Indeed, as we saw in the text, the rules for interrogating juveniles are almost indistinguishable from those that apply to adults. Police questioning of children does, however, raise ethical and practical questions. How can children as young as the ones involved in this case understand the concept or consequences of waiving their *Miranda* rights, as both boys did? Isn't any situation in which police officers are alone in a room with a child inherently coercive?

WHAT IS THE SOLUTION? How reliable do you consider the statements of juveniles, especially those as young as the boys in the Harris murder? Regardless of the law, how should police approach the interrogation of children who may not fully understand the concept of constitutional rights? In this case, although the police did not break any rules, their strategy backfired. After a forensic examination found semen—which boys so young could not have produced—on the girl's torn underwear, the suspects were immediately released and the investigation reopened.

PRETRIAL DIVERSION

To a certain extent, the juvenile justice system started as a diversionary program with the goal of diverting children from the punitive adult court to the more rehabilitative juvenile court.[37] By the 1960s, many observers felt that juvenile courts had lost sight of this early mandate and were badly in need of reform. One specific target for criticism was the growing number of status offenders—40 percent of all children in the system—who were being punished even though they had not committed a truly delinquent act.

The idea of diverting certain children, including status and first-time offenders, from the juvenile court system to nonjudicial community agencies was encouraged by the President's Commission on Law Enforcement and Administration of Justice in 1967.[38] Seven years later, Congress passed the first Juvenile Justice and Delinquency Prevention (JJDP) Act, which ordered the development of methods "to divert juveniles from the traditional juvenile justice system."[39] Within a few years, hundreds of diversion programs had been put into effect. Today, *diversion* refers to the process of removing low-risk offenders from the formal juvenile justice system by placing them in community-based rehabilitation programs.

Diversion programs vary widely, but fall into three general categories:

1. *Probation.* In this program, the juvenile is returned to the community, but placed under the supervision of a juvenile probation officer. If the youth breaks the conditions of probation, he or she can be returned to the formal juvenile system.
2. *Treatment and aid.* Many juveniles have behavioral or medical conditions that contribute to their delinquent behavior, and many diversion programs offer remedial education, drug and alcohol treatment, and other forms of counseling to alleviate these problems.
3. *Restitution.* In these programs, the offender "repays" her or his victim, either directly or, in the case of community service, symbolically.[40]

Proponents of diversion programs include many labeling theorists (see Chapter 2), who believe that contact with the formal juvenile justice system "labels" the youth a delinquent, which leads to further delinquent behavior.

TRANSFER TO ADULT COURT

One side effect of diversionary programs is that the youths who remain in the juvenile courts are more likely to be seen as "hardened" and less amenable to rehabilitation. This, in turn, increases the likelihood that the offender will be transferred to an adult court, a process in which the juvenile court waives jurisdiction over the youth. As the American juvenile justice system has shifted away from ideals of treatment and toward punishment, transfer to adult court has been one of the most popular means of "getting tough" on delinquents.

Methods of Transfer Juveniles are most commonly transferred to adult court through **judicial waiver.** In all states except New York and Nebraska, the juvenile judge is the official who determines whether jurisdiction over a minor offender should be waived to adult court. The judge formulates this ruling by taking into consideration the offender's age, the nature of the offense, and any criminal history.

Thirty-one states have taken the waiver responsibility out of judicial hands through **automatic transfer,** also known as *legislative waiver.* In these states, the legislatures have designated certain conditions—usually involving serious crimes such as murder and rape—under which a juvenile case is automatically "kicked up" to adult court. In Rhode Island, for example, a juvenile aged sixteen or older with two prior felony adjudications will automatically be transferred on being

Judicial Waiver The process in which the juvenile judge, based on the facts of the case at hand, decides that the alleged offender should be transferred to adult court.

Automatic Transfer The process by which a juvenile is transferred to adult court as a matter of state law. In some states, for example, a juvenile who is suspected of murder is automatically transferred to adult court.

■ Figure 15.5 Felony Arrest Charges for Juveniles Transferred to Adult Criminal Courts

Two out of every three juveniles transferred to adult criminal court under suspicion of committing a felony were charged with a violent offense. The data shown here were collected in criminal courts located in forty of the largest urban counties in the United States.

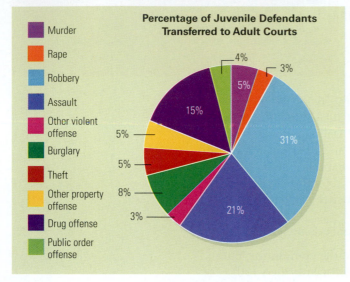

Percentage of Juvenile Defendants Transferred to Adult Courts

Legend:
- Murder
- Rape
- Robbery
- Assault
- Other violent offense
- Burglary
- Theft
- Other property offense
- Drug offense
- Public order offense

Pie chart values: 4%, 3%, 5%, 31%, 21%, 3%, 8%, 5%, 5%, 15%

Source: Bureau of Justice Statistics, *Juvenile Felony Defendants in Criminal Courts* (Washington, D.C.: U.S. Department of Justice, May 2003), Table 2, page 2.

Prosecutorial Waiver A procedure in which juvenile court judges have the discretion to transfer a juvenile case to adult court, when certain predetermined conditions as to the seriousness of the offense and the age of the offender are met.

accused of a third felony.[41] Fourteen states also allow for **prosecutorial waiver,** in which juvenile court judges are allowed to waive jurisdiction when certain age and offense conditions are met. In general, no matter what the process, those juveniles who commit violent felonies are most likely to be transferred to an adult court (see ■ Figure 15.5).

In twenty-four states, criminal court judges also have the freedom to send juveniles who were transferred to adult court back to juvenile court. Known as *reverse transfer* statutes, these laws are designed to provide judges with a measure of discretion even when automatic transfer takes place.

Consequences of Transfer When transfer laws were first enacted, observers worried that judges in adult courts would tend to give juveniles more lenient sentences than adults who had committed the same crime. This "leniency gap" does not appear to exist. Indeed, critics of transfer laws insist that adult courts are *too* severe on juveniles. The most recent study on the subject, carried out by Megan C. Kurlychek of the University of South Carolina and Brian D. Johnson of the University of Maryland, compared the sentencing outcomes of juveniles and young adults over a three-year period in Pennsylvania. The research showed that "transferred" juveniles were more likely to be sent to prison than young adults and received sentences 81 percent longer than the latter.[42]

Furthermore, a number of observers believe that juveniles tried in adult courts have higher recidivism rates than those who are tried in juvenile courts. Comparing juveniles who were transferred to adult prisons for nonviolent crimes and adults in the same facilities for nonviolent crimes, the *Arizona Republic* found that the juvenile inmates were four times more likely than the adults to commit a violent crime after release.[43] Another survey found that, over the short term, 30 percent of transferred offenders were rearrested after release, compared to 19

▼ In April 2007, a Sauk County (Wisconsin) judge decided that sixteen-year-old Eric Hainstock, center, would be tried in adult court. Hainstock had been charged with first degree murder in the shooting death of his high school principal, John Klang. Why would Klang's family, as well as other victims of violent juvenile crime, generally favor a transfer to adult court for defendants in these circumstances?

AP Photo/*Baraboo News Republic*, Christina Beam

percent of those processed in the juvenile court system.[44] "You can learn a whole lot more bad things in here than good," said one juvenile inmate from his cell in an Arizona adult prison.[45]

DETENTION

Once the decision has been made that the offender will face adjudication in a juvenile court, the intake official must decide what to do with him or her until the start of the trial. Generally, the juvenile is released into the custody of parents or a guardian—most jurisdictions favor this practice in lieu of setting money bail for youths. The intake officer may also place the offender in **detention,** or temporary custody in a secure facility, until the disposition process begins. Once a juvenile has been detained, most jurisdictions require that a **detention hearing** be held within twenty-four hours. During this hearing, the offender has several due process safeguards, including the right to counsel, the right against self-incrimination, and the right to cross-examine and confront witnesses.

In justifying its decision to detain, the court will usually address one of three issues:

1. Whether the child poses a danger to the community.
2. Whether the child will return for the adjudication process.
3. Whether detention will provide protection for the child.

The Supreme Court upheld the practice of preventive detention (see Chapter 9) for juveniles in *Schall v. Martin* (1984)[46] by ruling that youths can be detained if they are deemed a "risk" to the safety of the community or to their own welfare.

Self Check Fill in the Blanks

During the _____ process, a judge decides the immediate fate of the juvenile delinquent. One of the judge's options is _____, which keeps low-risk offenders out of juvenile correctional facilities and places them in community rehabilitation programs. If the judge believes that the seriousness of the offense so warrants, he or she can transfer the juvenile into the adult court system through a process called judicial _____. Check your answers on page 519.

Juveniles on Trial

Over the past thirty-five years, the one constant in the juvenile justice system has been change. Supreme Court rulings in the wake of *In re Gault* (1967) have increased the procedural formality and the overriding punitive philosophy of the juvenile court. Diversion policies have worked to remove many status offenders from the juvenile court's jurisdiction, and waiver policies assure that the most violent juveniles are tried as adults. Some observers feel these adjustments have "criminalized" the juvenile court, effectively rendering it indistinguishable both theoretically and practically from adult courts.[47]

Along with a number of his colleagues, law professor Barry C. Feld thinks that the juvenile court has become obsolete and should be abolished. Feld believes the changes noted above have "transformed the juvenile court from its original model as a social-service agency into a deficient second-rate criminal court that provides young people with neither positive treatment nor criminal procedural justice."[48] Indeed, juvenile hearings do proceed along many of the same lines as the adult criminal court, with similar due process protections and rules of evidence (though minors do not enjoy the right to a jury trial). As the *Mastering Concepts* feature on the following page explains, however, juvenile

L06

Detention The temporary custody of a juvenile in a state facility after a petition has been filed and before the adjudicatory process begins.

Detention Hearing A hearing to determine whether a juvenile should be detained, or remain detained, while waiting for the adjudicatory process to begin.

The Juvenile Justice System versus the Criminal Justice System

AP Photo/Columbus Dispatch, James D. DeCamp

When the juvenile justice system first began in the United States, its participants saw it as being separate from the adult criminal justice system. Indeed, the two systems remain separate in many ways. There are, however, a number of similarities between juvenile and adult justice. Here, we summarize both the similarities and the differences.

SIMILARITIES

- The right to receive the *Miranda* warnings.

- Procedural protections when making an admission of guilt.

- Prosecutors and defense attorneys play equally important roles.

- The right to be represented by counsel at the crucial stages of the trial process.

- Access to plea bargains.

- The right to a hearing and an appeal.

- The standard of evidence is proof beyond a reasonable doubt.

- Both can be placed on probation by the judge.

- Both can be held before adjudication if the judge believes them to be a threat to the community.

- Following trial, both can be sentenced to community supervision.

DIFFERENCES

	Juvenile System	Adult System
Purpose	Rehabilitation of the offender.	Punishment.
Arrest	Juveniles can be arrested for acts (status offenses) that are not criminal for adults.	Adults can be arrested only for acts made illegal by the relevant criminal code.
Wrongdoing	Considered a "delinquent act."	A crime.
Proceedings	Informal, closed to public.	Formal and regimented; open to public.
Information	Courts may NOT release information to the press.	Courts MUST release information to the press.
Parents	Play significant role.	Play no role.
Release	Into parent/guardian custody.	May post bail when justified.
Jury trial	In most, but not all, states, juveniles do NOT have this right.	All adults have this right.
Searches	Juveniles can be searched in school without probable cause.	No adult can be searched without probable cause.
Records	Juvenile's record is sealed at age of majority.	Adult's criminal record is permanent.
Sentencing	Juveniles are placed in separate facilities from adults.	Adults are placed in county jails or state prisons.
Death Penalty	No death penalty.	Death penalty for certain serious crimes under certain circumstances.

justice proceedings may still be distinguished from the adult system of criminal justice, and these differences are evident in the adjudication and disposition of the juvenile trial.

ADJUDICATION

During the adjudication stage of the juvenile justice process, a hearing is held to determine whether the offender is delinquent or in need of some form of court supervision. Most state juvenile codes dictate a specific set of procedures that must be followed during the **adjudicatory hearing**, with the goal of providing the respondent with "the essentials of due process and fair treatment." Consequently, the respondent in an adjudicatory hearing has the right to notice of charges, counsel, confrontation and cross-examination, and the privilege against self-incrimination. Furthermore, "proof beyond a reasonable doubt" must be established to find the child delinquent. When the child admits guilt—that is, admits to the charges of the initial petition—the judge must ensure that the admission was voluntary.

Adjudicatory Hearing The process through which a juvenile court determines whether there is sufficient evidence to support the initial petition.

The increased presence of defense attorneys in juvenile courts has had a significant impact on juvenile adjudication. Aspects of the adversarial system have become increasingly apparent in juvenile courts, as has the practice of plea bargaining. To a certain extent, however, juvenile trials have retained the informal atmosphere that characterized pre–*In re Gault* proceedings. At the suggestion of a juvenile probation officer or judge, respondents and their families often waive the due process rights provided by the Supreme Court. One study of Indiana juvenile courts found that no counsel was present in about 50 percent of that state's adjudicatory hearings.[49]

At the close of the adjudicatory hearing, the judge is generally required to rule on the legal issues and evidence that have been presented. Based on this ruling, the judge determines whether the respondent is delinquent or in need of court supervision. Alternatively, the judge can dismiss the case based on a lack of evidence. It is important to remember that finding a child to be delinquent is *not* the same as convicting an adult of a crime. A delinquent does not face the same restrictions, such as those concerning the right to vote and to run for political office, as do adult convicts in some states (discussed in Chapter 14).

DISPOSITION

Once a juvenile has been adjudicated delinquent, the judge must decide what steps will be taken toward treatment and/or punishment. Most states provide for a *bifurcated process* in which a separate **disposition hearing** follows the adjudicatory hearing. Depending on state law, the juvenile may be entitled to counsel at the disposition hearing.

Sentencing Juveniles In an adult trial, the sentencing phase is primarily concerned with the "needs" of the community to be protected from the convict. In contrast, a juvenile judge uses the disposition hearing to determine a sentence that will serve the "needs" of the child. For assistance in this crucial process, the judge will order the probation department to gather information on the juvenile and present it in the form of a **predisposition report.** The report usually contains information concerning the respondent's family background, the facts surrounding the delinquent act, and interviews with social workers, teachers, and other important figures in the child's life.

Judicial Discretion In keeping with the rehabilitative tradition of the juvenile justice system, many judges have a great deal of discretion in choosing one of several disposition possibilities. A judge can tend toward leniency, delivering only a stern reprimand or warning before releasing the juvenile into the custody of parents or other legal guardians. Otherwise, the choice is among incarceration in a juvenile correctional facility, probation, or community treatment. In most cases, seriousness of the offense is the primary factor used in determining whether to incarcerate a juvenile, though history of delinquency, family situation, and the offender's attitude are all relevant. Some research suggests that race plays a significant role in disposition—that minority delinquents are more likely to be incarcerated than their white counterparts.[50]

Further indication of the treatment goals of juvenile courts can be found in the indeterminate sentencing practices that, until recently, dominated disposition. Under this system, correctional administrators were given the freedom to decide when a delinquent had been sufficiently rehabilitated and could be released. In a clear indication of the shift toward the crime control model, today nearly half of the states have enacted determinate or minimum mandatory sentencing laws that cover convicted juvenile offenders. Such statutes shift the focus of disposition from the treatment needs of the delinquent to society's desire to punish and incapacitate.

Disposition Hearing Similar to the sentencing hearing for adults, a hearing in which the juvenile judge or officer decides the appropriate punishment for a youth found to be delinquent or a status offender.

Predisposition Report A report prepared during the disposition process that provides the judge with relevant background material to aid in the disposition decision.

Grandpa had always said I could talk my way out of the electric chair. So when a friend in college suggested applying to law school, I thought, yes, why not? I attended Seton Hall Law in Newark, New Jersey, where I participated in the Juvenile Justice Clinic for two and a half semesters. This experience representing delinquents, coupled with a childhood of being raised on *Perry Mason,* as well as a law clerkship with a Superior Court judge, helped me to recognize my strong interest in criminal law. The forum of pleading my case in open court seemed like the only place to be.

BACK AND FORTH Following my clerkship, I was hired by the office of the public defender. Working for the P.D. is the fastest way to be in command of your own cases and to appear in court on all kinds of matters, particularly trials. My caseload consisted of clients charged with everything from fourth degree theft to armed robbery. The first year and a half, I represented adults. Then I went to the appellate section, where I wrote briefs for two and a half years. I enjoyed the treasure hunt of looking for the cases to support my arguments. I also enjoyed presenting those arguments to the appellate division panels. However, I found I missed being in court on a daily basis and dealing with clients in person. Thus, when the opportunity to transfer to another trial region arose, I grabbed it and began representing juveniles once again.

Every day I enter court prepared to do battle for a youngster who in all likelihood is not cognizant of how at risk his or her freedom is. Initially, my most important responsibility is to interview my client and his family to gain their trust, obtain information about the child, and learn their version of the facts in the case. I gather all the evidence provided by the State, review it carefully, and conduct my own investigations. Following a careful review of all the evidence available, weighing all the strengths and weaknesses in the case, and considering whether any trial would be before a judge rather than a jury, I discuss

Courtesy of Cathy Wasserman

Self Check Fill in the Blanks

A juvenile offender's delinquency is determined during the _____ hearing, which is similar in many ways to an adult trial. If the juvenile is found to be delinquent, her or his sentence is determined during the _____ hearing. In making the sentencing decision, the judge is often aided by a _____ report, compiled by the juvenile probation department. Check your answers on page 519.

Juvenile Corrections

In general, juvenile corrections are based on the concept of **graduated sanctions—** that is, the severity of the punishment should fit the crime. Consequently, status and first-time offenders are diverted or placed on probation, repeat offenders find themselves in intensive community supervision or treatment programs, and serious and violent offenders are placed in correctional facilities.[51] As society's expectations of the juvenile justice system have changed, so have the characteristics of its corrections programs. In some cities, for example, juvenile probation officers join police officers on the beat. Because the former are not bound by the same search and seizure restrictions as other law enforcement officials, this interdepartmental teamwork provides more opportunities to fight youth crime aggressively. Juvenile correctional facilities are also changing their operations to reflect public mandates that they both reform and punish. Also, note that on any given day in 2006, about 6,100 juveniles were in adult jails and another 2,364 were serving time in state prisons.[52]

Graduated Sanctions The practical theory in juvenile corrections that a delinquent or status offender should receive a punishment that matches in seriousness the severity of the wrongdoing.

the options, risks, and penalties with my client. Whether we go to trial or negotiate a plea agreement, my duties are to be an effective attorney for the child. However, once we face a sentence, I must also become a social worker as I attempt to fashion the least restrictive disposition from the myriad of sentencing alternatives. It is this array of options and the court's discretion to impose them which most clearly distinguishes the juvenile system from its adult counterpart.

REHAB OR JAIL? Some of the most challenging cases of my career have involved representing children the State is seeking to have referred to adult court. In New Jersey, there is a presumption of referral where a juvenile is charged with the most serious offenses and is fourteen years of age or older. The discretion to file for referral lies solely in the hands of the prosecutor. There are few tasks more difficult than having to tell a fourteen-year-old, who had a fight in which someone died, that he could be spending the next thirty years of his life in an adult jail. I faced this very scenario a number of years ago. In that particular case, H. T. had no prior involvement with the system and did not inflict the fatal wound. Worse, the confession he gave to the police to "help" himself was the main evidence

against him. Although the State's psychiatrist agreed with the defense expert that the boy could be rehabilitated in the juvenile system, the State pressed on. The pressure and emotional toll on me as counsel was enormous. I struggled to construct arguments out of the jigsaw puzzle of facts and the kid's life. I was confidante, commander, and adviser to not only my client in custody but also to his family. Contrary to the norm in waiver cases, H. T. prevailed. This case helped me to recognize how important my role can be in the life of a child.

I am an impassioned advocate for children because I believe most offenders should be allowed to survive childhood and adolescence without permanently damaging their prospects for a positive future. My skills as an attorney and negotiator give my clients the opportunity to rise above their acts, often committed through poor judgment, due to inexperience, or by succumbing to peer pressure. Occasionally, I make a significant difference in the life of a youngster.

Go to the **Careers in Criminal Justice Interactive CD** for more profiles in the field of criminal justice.

JUVENILE PROBATION

The most common form of juvenile corrections is probation—38 percent of all delinquency cases disposed of by juvenile courts result in conditional diversion. The majority of all adjudicated delinquents (nearly 58 percent) will never receive a disposition more severe than being placed on probation.[53] These statistics reflect a general understanding among juvenile court judges and other officials that removing a child from her or his home should be considered primarily as a last resort.

The organization of juvenile probation is very similar to adult probation (see Chapter 12), and juvenile probationers are increasingly subjected to electronic monitoring and other supervisory tactics. The main difference between the two programs lies in the attitude toward the offender. Adult probation officers have an overriding responsibility to protect the community from the probationer, while juvenile probation officers are expected to take the role of a mentor or a concerned relative in looking after the needs of the child.

CONFINING JUVENILES

About 110,000 American youths (up from 30,000 at the end of the 1970s) are incarcerated in public and private juvenile correctional facilities in the United States.[54] Most of these juveniles have committed crimes against people or property, but a significant number (about 16 percent) have been incarcerated because of other factors, such as familial neglect or mental incapacity. After deciding that a juvenile needs to be confined, the judge has two sentencing options: nonsecure juvenile institutions and secure juvenile institutions.

Nonsecure Confinement Some juvenile delinquents do not require high levels of control and can be placed in **residential treatment programs**. These programs, run

Residential Treatment Programs Government-run facilities for juveniles whose offenses are not deemed serious enough to warrant incarceration in a training school.

▲ Enhanced security videotape shows Martin Lee Anderson, 14, being manhandled by corrections officials at the Bay County Boot Camp in Panama City, Florida, on January 6, 2006. Anderson eventually collapsed and died of suffocation, the result of an effort by the officers to revive him by holding his mouth shut and jamming ammonia tablets up his nose. .

by either probation departments or social-service departments, allow their subjects freedom of movement in the community. Generally, this freedom is predicated on the juveniles following certain rules, such as avoiding alcoholic beverages and returning to the facility for curfew. Residential treatment programs can be divided into four categories:[55]

1. *Foster care programs,* in which the juveniles live with a couple who act as surrogate parents.
2. *Group homes,* which generally house between twelve and fifteen youths and provide treatment, counseling, and education services by a professional staff.
3. *Family group homes,* which combine aspects of foster care and group homes, meaning that a single family, rather than a group of professionals, looks after the needs of the young offenders.
4. *Rural programs,* which include wilderness camps, farms, and ranches where between thirty and fifty children are placed in an environment that provides recreational activities and treatment programs.

L07

Secure Confinement Secure facilities are comparable to the adult prisons and jails we discussed in Chapters 13 and 14. These institutions go by a confusing array of names depending on the state in which they are located, but the two best known are boot camps and training schools.

Boot Camps A **boot camp** is the juvenile variation of shock probation. As we noted in Chapter 12, boot camps are modeled after military training for new recruits. Boot camp programs are based on the theory that by giving wayward youths a taste of the "hard life" of military-like training for short periods of time, usually no longer than 180 days, they will be "shocked" out of a life of offending. New York's Camp Monterey Shock Incarceration Facility is typical of the boot camp experience: inmates are grouped in platoons and live in dormitories; they spend eight hours a day training, drilling, and doing hard labor, and also participate in programs such as basic adult education and job skills training.[56]

Periodically, the boot camp industry has been shaken by a scandal that does severe damage to its reputation. One such incident occurred on January 6, 2006, when several correctional officers at the Bay County Boot Camp for "moderate-risk offenders" in Florida caused the death of fourteen-year-old Martin Lee Anderson. Surveillance cameras showed the officers beating Anderson for nearly half an hour, and an autopsy showed that he died of suffocation as a result of efforts to revive him. Six months later, Florida's legislature responded with a law that replaced the state's boot camps with residential treatment programs. It barred any form of physical discipline at these programs and prohibited state officials from using "harmful psychological intimidation techniques."[57]

Training Schools No juvenile correctional facility is called a "prison." This does not mean they are not prison-like. The facilities that most closely mimic the atmosphere at an adult correctional facility are **training schools,** alternatively known

Boot Camp A variation on traditional shock incarceration in which juveniles (and some adults) are sent to secure confinement facilities modeled on military basic training camps instead of prison or jail. These camps emphasize strict discipline, manual labor, and military training to "shock" inmates out of a life of crime.

Training Schools Correctional institutions for juveniles found to be delinquent or status offenders.

as youth camps, youth development centers, industrial schools, and several other similar titles. Whatever the name, these institutions claim to differ from their adult countparts by offering a variety of programs to treat and rehabilitate the young offenders. In reality, training schools are plagued by many of the same problems as adult prisons and jails, including high levels of inmate-on-inmate violence, substance abuse, gang wars, and overcrowding.

Aftercare Juveniles leave correctional facilities through an early release program or because they have served the length of their sentences. Juvenile corrections officials recognize that many of these children, like adults, need assistance readjusting to the outside world. Consequently, released juveniles are often placed in **aftercare** programs. Based on the same philosophy that drives the prisoner reentry movement (discussed in the last chapter), aftercare programs are designed to offer services for the juveniles, while at the same time supervising them to reduce the chances of recidivism. The ideal aftercare program includes community support groups, aid in finding and keeping employment, and continued monitoring to assure that the juvenile is able to deal with the demands of freedom.

▲ In 2007, the *Dallas Morning News* revealed that supervisors and corrections officers had been sexually abusing juvenile residents of Texas Youth Commission facilities, such as the one in Marlin, Texas, shown above, for years. How might such widespread abuse undermine the purpose of the juvenile justice system?

Self Check Fill in the Blanks

The most common form of juvenile corrections is _____. If the judge decides that the juvenile needs more stringent supervision, he or she can sentence the offender to a _____ facility such as a residential treatment program. If the juvenile's offense has been particularly serious, she or he will most likely be sent to a secure confinement facility such as a _____ camp or a _____ school. Check your answers on page 519.

⊗ The **National Center for Juvenile Justice** is a valuable source for juvenile delinquency information and data. Find its Web site by clicking on *Web Links* under *Chapter Resources* at **www.cjinaction.com**.

Trends in Juvenile Delinquency

When asked, juveniles will admit to a wide range of illegal or dangerous behavior, including carrying weapons, getting involved in physical fights, driving after drinking alcohol, and stealing or deliberately damaging school property.[58] Have juvenile law enforcement efforts, juvenile courts, and juvenile corrections been effective in controlling and preventing this kind of misbehavior, as well as more serious acts?

To answer this question, many observers turn to the Federal Bureau of Investigation's Uniform Crime Report (UCR), initially covered in Chapter 3. Because the UCR breaks down arrest statistics by age of the arrestee, it has been considered the primary source of information on the presence of juveniles in America's justice system. This does not mean, however, that the UCR is completely reliable when it comes to measuring juvenile delinquency. The process measures only those juveniles who were caught and therefore does not accurately reflect all delinquent acts in any given year. Furthermore, it measures the number of arrests but not the number of arrestees, meaning that—due to repeat offenders—the number of juveniles actually in the system could be below the number of juvenile arrests.

DELINQUENCY BY THE NUMBERS

With these cautions in mind, UCR findings are quite clear as to the extent of the juvenile delinquency problem in the United States today. In 2006, juveniles accounted

Aftercare The variety of therapeutic, educational, and counseling programs made available to juvenile delinquents (and some adults) after they have been released from a correctional facility.

for 15.6 percent of violent crime arrests and 15.1 percent of criminal activity arrests in general.[59] According to the 2006 UCR, juveniles were responsible for

- 9.5 percent of all murder arrests;
- 13.1 percent of all aggravated assault arrests;
- 14.8 percent of all forcible rapes;
- 23.4 percent of all weapons arrests;
- 26.4 percent of all robbery arrests;
- 26.5 percent of all property crimes; and
- 10.4 percent of all drug offenses.

IS JUVENILE CRIME LEVELING OFF?

During the mid-1990s, a significant number of criminologists looked at the juvenile crime picture and predicted that it would get much darker in the future. The most famous, or infamous, of these experts was John DiIulio, Jr., of Princeton University, who predicted that a wave of young "superpredators" would take over the streets of America, sending youth crime rates skyrocketing by the mid-2000s.[60] Instead, as Frank E. Zimring of the University of California at Berkeley has pointed out, DiIulio's forecast "wasn't just wrong, it was exactly the opposite of what happened."[61] Indeed, as ■ Figure 15.6 shows, juvenile arrests rates have generally been dropping for about a decade.

Violent Crime Trends Between 1994 and 2005, the juvenile arrest rate for violent crimes dropped 45 percent.[62] Over the same time period, the juvenile murder rate fell below 4 percent, its lowest level since the 1960s.[63] Incidences of juvenile robbery, burglary, and motor vehicle theft have seen similar downturns. Although juvenile arrest rates for some crimes, such as fraud, embezzlement, and driving under the influence, are still relatively high, the overall situation is not nearly as bleak as it was at the height of the youth crime wave in the mid-1990s.

Reasons for the Decline Although the theory is not universally accepted, many observers see the rise and decline of juvenile arrests as mirroring the rise and decline of crack cocaine.[64] When inner-city youths took advantage of the economic opportunities offered by the crack trade in the 1980s, they found they needed to protect themselves against rival dealers. This led to the proliferation of firearms among juveniles, as well as the formation of violent youth gangs. As the crack "epidemic" has slowed in recent years, so have arrest and violent crime rates for juveniles.

Other theories have been put forth as well. Some observers point to the increase in police action against "quality-of-life" crimes such as loitering, which they believe stops juveniles before they have a chance to commit more serious crimes. Furthermore, many schools have adopted "zero-tolerance" policies that punish students harshly for bringing weapons or drugs onto school grounds. Alfred Blumstein, a criminologist at Carnegie Mellon University in Pittsburgh, thinks young Americans learned from the

■ **Figure 15.6 Arrest Rates of Juveniles, 1980 to the 2000s**

After rising dramatically from 1985 to 1994, arrest rates for juveniles began to fall.

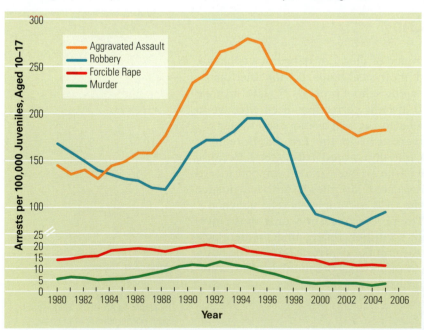

Source: Office of Juvenile Justice and Delinquency Prevention, *Statistical Briefing Book*, at **www.ojjdp.ncjrs.org/ojstatbb/crime/JAR.asp**.

examples of their older acquaintances. "Kids saw what crack was doing to their siblings, friends, and parents and turned away from it," he says.[65]

GIRLS IN THE JUVENILE JUSTICE SYSTEM

Though overall rates of juvenile offending have been dropping, one particular group of juveniles has become more involved in the juvenile justice system than ever before. Just as we saw earlier in this textbook that women are the fasting-growing segment of the adult prison population, girls are becoming more and more visible in the institutions that punish juvenile delinquency and crime.

A Growing Presence Although girls have for the most part been treated more harshly than boys for status offenses,[66] a "chivalry effect" (see page 357) has traditionally existed in other areas of the juvenile justice system. In the past, police were likely to arrest offending boys while allowing girls to go home to the care of their families for similar behavior. This is no longer the case. Between 1996 and 2005, arrests of juvenile boys dropped by twice as much as arrests of juvenile girls.[67] In addition, between 1985 and 2002, the number of delinquency cases in juvenile court involving girls grew at a faster rate than cases involving boys in every offense category.[68] A particular problem area for girls appears to be the crime of assault. In 2006, females accounted for 15 percent of all juvenile arrests for aggravated assault and 25 percent of those arrests for simple assault, far higher percentages than for other violent crimes.[69]

Family-Based Delinquency Criminologists disagree on whether increasing arrest rates for female juveniles reflect a change in behavior or a change in law enforcement practices. A significant amount of data support the latter proposal, especially research showing that police are much more likely to make arrests in situations involving domestic violence than they were even a decade ago. Experts have found that girls are four times more apt to fight with parents or siblings than are boys, who usually engage in violent encounters with strangers. Consequently, a large percentage of female juvenile arrests for assault arise out of family disputes—arrests that until relatively recently would not have been made.[70]

Evidence also shows that law enforcement agents continue to treat girls more harshly for status offenses. More girls than boys are arrested for the status offense of running away from home, for example, even though studies show that male and female juveniles run away from home with equal frequency.[71] Criminologists who focus on issues of gender hypothesize that such behavior is considered normal for boys, but is seen as deviant for girls and therefore more deserving of punishment.[72]

SCHOOL VIOLENCE

During a two-week period in the fall of 2006, the nation's schools experienced a disturbing wave of violence. In Cazenovia, Wisconsin, a fifteen-year-old high school student shot his principal to death. A gunman took five students hostage at Platte Canyon High School in Bailey, Colorado, killing one student and himself before the standoff ended. Five girls were killed and another five injured by a sexual predator at West Nickel Mines Amish School in rural Pennsylvania. Finally, a seventh grader wearing a mask and armed with an MAC-90

Drew Perine, Pool, AP Photo

▼ Douglas Chanthabouly is led from a Tacoma, Washington, courthouse two days after allegedly shooting and killing a classmate at Henry Foss High School in January 2007. How does the intense local and national media attention given to such incidents influence public perception of school violence in the United States?

WHAT IS SAFEWATCH?

Safewatch is a real-time video monitoring system that allows law enforcement officers to see into schools during emergencies.

HOW DOES SAFEWATCH WORK?

First, video cameras are installed in the public areas of the school. The system remains dormant until activated by a trigger such as a 911 call or notification from a school official. Once Safewatch "wakes up," it allows the police to view live feeds from the cameras. Depending on which software is used, public safety officials can have access to images from as many as ten cameras at one time on a Web browser. Because almost all police stations, as well as many police cars, are equipped with computer screens, officers responding to a crisis at a school have the invaluable advantage of an electronic eye within school walls. "We could use the cameras to see inside the buildings before we send in officers," said one police official. "It could save lives."

THINKING ABOUT SAFEWATCH

Safewatch is designed to monitor activities of teachers and students only if there is a crisis situation. It is not in operation on a daily basis to avoid the privacy issues that frequently arise with video monitoring. To protect students' and teachers' privacy, for example, very few security cameras are installed in school bathrooms or classrooms. How does this limit the effectiveness

▲ Students at Beatrice Gilmore School in West Paterson, New Jersey, demonstrate a new security system that relies on video surveillance.

of school video monitoring systems? Do you think security concerns should outweigh privacy concerns in schools?

---

assault rifle opened fire in his school in Joplin, Missouri. Luckily, the weapon jammed before he could injure anyone.

Each one of these incidents received heavy media coverage, suggesting that such violence is pervasive in American schools. As part of a poll taken after the Missouri incident, 35 percent of parents said that they feared for their children's safety at school—10 percent more than had given that response several months earlier.[73] Although this anxiety is understandable, it does not reflect the reality of school violence, which has decreased along with other forms of criminal activity related to juveniles over the past decade.

Security Efforts School-age youths are more than fifty times more likely to be murdered away from school than on a campus.[74] During the 2004–2005 academic year, twenty-one homicides of juveniles took place at school, slightly more than in the previous year but significantly fewer than the average annual toll during the 1990s.[75] Between 1992 and 2004, victimization rates of students for nonfatal crimes at school also declined significantly, meaning that, in general, schools are safer today than they were in the recent past.[76]

To a certain extent, these statistics mirror the downward trend of all criminal activity in the United States since the mid-1990s. In addition, since the fatal shootings of fourteen students and a teacher at Columbine High School near Littleton, Colorado, in 1999, many schools have also improved security measures. Twenty-eight percent of primary schools, 42 percent of middle schools, and 60 percent of high schools use security cameras to monitor their grounds. (To learn more about this strategy, see the feature *CJ and Technology—Safewatch.*) More than 80 percent all public schools control access to school buildings by locking or monitoring their doors.[77]

The Bully Problem Legislators have also become more involved in school safety. In response to research showing that more than half of school shootings are motivated by revenge,[78] eighteen states have passed "antibullying" laws. These measures require local school districts to draw up policies aimed at stopping student bullying and direct officials to notify parents of any such behavior at their child's school.

Some experts criticize these policies for oversimplifying the problem of school violence. One clinical psychologist pointed out that if bullying were the actual cause of such incidents, "we would have millions of school shootings each year."[79] Instead, bullying appears to be only one piece of the puzzle, which includes violence and instability in the home, depression, violence in the culture at large, and the availability of firearms.

Self Check Fill in the Blanks

Contrary to many predictions, the crime rate for juveniles has been _____ for more than a decade. Despite this trend, more _____ are getting involved with the juvenile justice system today than at any time in recent history. _____ violence is another area in which crime rates have dropped since the 1990s, thanks, in part, to greater security measures such as surveillance cameras and locked building doors. Check your answers on page 519.

Factors in Juvenile Delinquency

As we discussed in Chapter 2, an influential study conducted by Professor Marvin Wolfgang and several colleagues in the early 1970s introduced the "chronic 6 percent" to criminology. The researchers found that out of one hundred boys, six will become chronic offenders, meaning that they are arrested five or more times before their eighteenth birthdays. Furthermore, Wolfgang and his colleagues determined that these chronic offenders are responsible for half of all crimes and two-thirds of all violent crimes within any given cohort (a group of persons who have similar characteristics).[80] Does this "6 percent rule" mean that no matter what steps society takes, six out of every hundred juveniles are "bad seeds" and will act delinquently? Or does it point to a situation in which a small percentage of children may be more likely to commit crimes under certain circumstances?

Most criminologists favor the second interpretation. In this section, we will examine the four factors that have traditionally been used to explain juvenile criminal behavior and violent crime rates: age, substance abuse, family problems, and gangs. Keep in mind, however, that the factors influencing delinquency are not limited to these topics (see ■ Figure 15.7). Researchers are constantly interpreting and reinterpreting statistical evidence to provide fresh perspectives on this very important issue. A study released in 2005, for example, focused on immigrant status as a predictor of juvenile violence. According to lead author Robert J. Sampson of Harvard University, youths who are recent immigrants and those who live in neighborhoods with high concentrations of immigrants are

■ **Figure 15.7** Risk Factors for Juvenile Delinquency

The characteristics listed here are generally accepted as "risk factors" for juvenile delinquency. In other words, if one or more of these factors are present in a juvenile's life, he or she has a greater change of exhibiting delinquent behavior—though such behavior is by no means a certainty.

Family
- Broken home/lack of parental role model
- Parental or sibling drug/alcohol abuse
- Extreme economic deprivation
- Family members in a gang

School
- Academic frustration/failure
- Learning disability
- Negative labeling by teachers
- Disciplinary problems

Community
- Social disorganization (refer to Chapter 2)
- Presence of gangs and obvious drug use in the community
- Availability of firearms
- High crime/constant feeling of danger
- Lack of social and economic opportunities

Peers
- Delinquent friends
- Friends who use drugs or are members of gangs
- Lack of "positive" peer pressure

Individual
- Tendency toward aggressive behavior
- Inability to concentrate or focus/easily bored/hyperactive
- Alcohol or drug use
- Fatalistic/pessimistic viewpoint

less likely to commit violent acts than other juveniles from similar racial and economic backgrounds.[81]

THE AGE-CRIME RELATIONSHIP

Crime statistics are fairly conclusive on one point: the older a person is, the less likely he or she will exhibit criminal behavior. Self-reported studies confirm that most people are involved in some form of criminal behavior—however "harmless"—during their early years. In fact, Terrie Moffitt of the University of Wisconsin has said that "it is statistically aberrant to refrain from crime during adolescence."[82] So, why do the vast majority of us not become chronic offenders? According to many criminologists, particularly Travis Hirschi and Michael Gottfredson, any group of at-risk persons—regardless of gender, race, intelligence, or class—will commit fewer crimes at they grow older.[83] This process is known as **aging out** (or, sometimes, *desistance*). Professor Sampson and his colleague John H. Laub believe that this phenomenon is explained by certain events, such as marriage, employment, and military service, which force delinquents to "grow up" and forgo criminal acts.[84]

Another view sees the **age of onset,** or the age at which the youth begins delinquent behavior, as a consistent predictor of future criminal behavior. One study compared recidivism rates between juveniles first judged to be delinquent before the age of fifteen and those first adjudicated delinquent after the age of fifteen. Of the seventy-one subjects who made up the first group, 32 percent became chronic offenders. Of the sixty-five who made up the second group, none became chronic offenders.[85] Furthermore, according to the Office of Juvenile Justice and Delinquency Prevention, the earlier a youth enters the juvenile justice system, the more likely he or she will become a violent offender.[86] This research suggests that juvenile justice resources should be concentrated on the youngest offenders, with the goal of preventing crime and reducing the long-term risks for society.

SUBSTANCE ABUSE

As we have seen throughout this textbook, substance abuse plays a strong role in criminal behavior for adults. The same can certainly be said for juveniles. According to the National Survey on Drug Use and Health (NSDUH), nearly 11 million Americans under the age of twenty consume alcohol on a regular basis, increasing the probability that they will experience academic problems, drop out of school, or commit acts of *vandalism* (the willful destruction of property).[87] The health consequences of this level of underage drinking are staggering: alcohol is a factor in between 50 and 65 percent of all teenage suicides, and nearly 2,500 youths are killed each year in alcohol-related automobile crashes. Furthermore, the NSDUH shows that nearly 10 percent of those between the ages of twelve and seventeen are current drug users, placing them at risk for delinquency.[88]

▼ Female juvenile offenders participate in anger management exercises at the Missouri Division of Youth Services' Rosa Parks Center in Fulton, Missouri. How could such programs help lower recidivism rates among young offenders?

AP Photo/Kelley McCal

Downward Trends There are some signs, however, that use of illegal drugs and alcohol is declining. The Monitoring the Future survey, carried out annually by the University of Michigan's Institute for Social Research, found that cigarette smoking, alcohol intake, and use of illegal drugs by teenagers all decreased in 2002, the first time this had happened in the survey's twenty-seven-year history; furthermore, they continued to drop through 2006.[89] A similar trend can be found in drug- and alcohol-related arrests. From 1997 to 2006, for example, juvenile arrests for drunkenness decreased 29 percent.[90] And, although arrests for drug abuse violations continued to increase until the late 1990s, they declined slightly between 2000 and 2006.[91]

Continued Abuse There is little doubt, however, that substance abuse still plays a major role in juvenile delinquency and crime. Almost 10 percent of all juvenile arrests involve a drug-related crime. About 60 percent of juveniles in correctional facilities admit to regular drug use, and 50 percent say that they were under the influence of drugs or alcohol at the time they committed the offense that led to their incarceration.[92] According to the Arrestee Drug Abuse Monitoring Program, nearly 60 percent of male juvenile detainees and 46 percent of female juvenile detainees test positive for drug use at the time of their offense.[93] Drug use is a particularly strong risk factor for girls: 75 percent of young women incarcerated in juvenile facilities report regular drug and alcohol use—starting at the age of fourteen—and one study found that 87 percent of female teenage offenders need substance abuse treatment.[94]

CHILD ABUSE AND NEGLECT

Abuse by parents also plays a substantial role in juvenile delinquency. **Child abuse** can be broadly defined as the infliction of physical or emotional damage on a child, while **child neglect** refers to deprivations—of love, shelter, food, proper care—children undergo by their parents. A significant portion (estimates can range from 40 percent[95] to 88 percent[96]) of parents who mistreat their children are believed to be under the influence of illegal drugs or alcohol.

Children in homes characterized by violence or neglect suffer from a variety of physical, emotional, and mental health problems at a much greater rate than their peers.[97] This, in turn, increases their chances of engaging in delinquent behavior. A report issued by the Arizona Supreme Court, for example, indicated that 73 percent of children between the ages of fourteen and seventeen whose parents had records of abuse in 2002 had also been sent to juvenile court for delinquency that year.[98] Another survey of violent juveniles showed that 75 percent had suffered severe abuse by a family member and 80 percent had witnessed violence in their homes.[99] Cathy Spatz Widom, a professor of criminal justice and psychology at the State University of New York at Albany, compared the arrest records of two groups of subjects—one made up of 908 cases of substantiated parental abuse and neglect and the other made up of 667 children who had not been abused or neglected. Widom found that those who had been abused or neglected were 53 percent more likely to be arrested as juveniles than those who had not.[100] Simply put, according to researchers Janet Currie of Columbia University and Erdal Tekin of Georgia State University, "child maltreatment roughly doubles the probability that an individual engages in many types of crime."[101]

GANGS

When youths cannot find the stability and support they require in the family structure, they will often turn to their peers. This is just one explanation for why juveniles join **youth gangs.** Although jurisdictions may have varying definitions, for general purposes a youth gang is viewed as a group of three or more persons who (1) self-identify themselves as an entity separate from the community by special

Child Abuse Mistreatment of children by causing physical, emotional, or sexual damage without any plausible explanation, such as an accident.

Child Neglect A form of child abuse in which the child is denied certain necessities such as shelter, food, care, and love. Neglect is justification for a government agency to assume responsibility for a child in place of the parents or legal guardian.

Youth Gangs Self-formed groups of youths with several identifiable characteristics, including a gang name and other recognizable symbols, a geographic territory, a leadership structure, a meeting pattern, and participation in illegal activities.

clothing, vocabulary, hand signals, and names and (2) engage in criminal activity. Although the first gangs may have appeared at the time of the American Revolution in the 1780s, there have been four periods of major gang activity in American history: the late 1800s, the 1920s, the 1960s, and the present. According to an exhaustive survey of law enforcement agencies, there are probably around 22,000 gangs with more than 730,000 members in the United States.[102]

Who Joins Gangs? The average gang member is seventeen to eighteen years old, though members tend to be older in cities with long traditions of gang activity such as Chicago and Los Angeles. Although it is difficult to determine with any certainty the makeup of gangs as a whole, one recent self-reported survey found that 25 percent of all gang members in the United States are Hispanic, 31 percent are African American, 25 percent are white, and 7 percent are Asian, with the remaining 12 percent belonging to other racial or ethnic backgrounds.[103] Though gangs tend to have racial or ethnic characteristics—that is, one group predominates in each gang—many researchers do not believe that race or ethnicity is the dominant factor in gang membership. Instead, gang members seem to come from lower-class or working-class communities, mostly in urban areas but with an increasing number from the suburbs and rural counties. In addition, researchers are finding that adolescents who will eventually join a gang display significantly higher levels of delinquent behavior than those who will never become involved in gang activity.[104]

A very small percentage—less than 10 percent—of youth gang members are female.[105] In many instances, girls associate themselves with gangs, even though they are not considered members. Ashley Paige Benton, for example, whose murder charge is the subject of the introduction to this chapter, was considered by law enforcement officials to be "associated with," but not a member of, a Houston youth gang called Crazy Crew. Generally, girls assume subordinate gender roles in youth gangs, providing emotional, physical, and sexual services for the dominant males.[106] Still, almost half of all youth gangs report having female members, and, as with other areas of juvenile crime and delinquency, involvement of girls in gangs is increasing.[107]

> The **National Youth Gang Center** is a government-sponsored organization that researches the problems caused by gangs and proposes methods of solving them. Find its Web site by clicking on *Web Links* under *Chapter Resources* at **www.cjinaction.com**.

▼ Along with wearing "colors," speaking in code, and "tagging" their turf with graffiti, gangs use hand signals to differentiate themselves from other gangs and to strengthen social bonds within members of their own group. Here, a "gangbanger" in South Central Los Angeles identifies himself as a Crip by his gestures.

© Ted Soqui/Corbis

Why Do Youths Join Gangs? Gang membership often appears to be linked with status in the community. This tends to be true of both males and females. Many teenagers, feeling alienated from their families and communities, join gangs for the social relationships and the sense of identity a gang can provide.[108]

Gang membership is seen as a necessity for a number of youths, especially those who live in high-crime neighborhoods—joining a gang is a form of protection against violence from other gangs. Excitement is another attraction of the gang life, as is the economic incentive of enjoying the profits from illegal gang activities such as dealing drugs or robbery.[109] Finally, some teenagers are literally forced to join gangs by the threat of violence from gang members.

L09

Gangs and Crime To a certain extent, the violent and criminal behavior of youths has been exaggerated by information sources such as the media. In proportion to all gang activities, violence is a rare event; youth gang members spend most of their time "hanging out" and taking part in other normal adolescent behavior.[110] That having been said, gang members are responsible for a disproportionate amount of violent and nonviolent criminal acts by juveniles. As we saw in Chapter 1, traditional gang activities such as using and trafficking in drugs, protecting their territory in "turf battles," and graffiti/vandalism all contribute to high crime rates among members.

Nationwide, youth gang members are responsible for about 1,200 homicides a year, up from fewer than 700 in the late 1990s. Every year, more than half of the murders in Chicago and Los Angeles are attributed to gang violence. Statistics also show high levels of gang involvement in aggravated assault, larceny, and motor vehicle theft, while more than 50 percent of all youth gangs are believed to be involved in drug sales.[111] Furthermore, a study of criminal behavior among juveniles in Seattle found that gang members were considerably more likely to commit crimes than at-risk youths who shared many characteristics with gang members but were not affiliated with any gang (see ■ Figure 15.8).[112] The gang members in Seattle were also much more likely to own firearms or to have friends who owned firearms.

■ **Figure 15.8** **Comparison of Gang and Nongang Delinquent Behavior**

Taking self-reported surveys of subjects aged thirteen to eighteen in the Seattle area, researchers for the Office of Juvenile Justice and Delinquency Prevention found that gang members were much more likely to exhibit delinquent behavior.

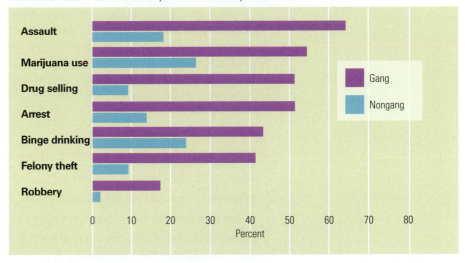

Source: Karl G. Hill, Christina Lui, and J. David Hawkins, *Early Precursors of Gang Membership: A Study of Seattle Youth* (Washington, D.C.: Office of Juvenile Justice and Delinquency Prevention, December 2001), Figure 1, page 2.

GUNS

It is hardly surprising that the gang members in Seattle were much more likely to own firearms or to have friends who did. Studies have shown that youths who are members of gangs are three times as likely to own a handgun as those who are not.[113] Gang members are also much more likely to believe that they need a gun for protection and to be involved in gun-related crimes.[114]

The harmful link between juveniles and guns is hardly limited to gang members, however. Indeed, one explanation for the increase in youth violence in the late 1980s and early 1990s points to the unprecedented access minors had to illegal weapons during that time. According to Carnegie Mellon's Alfred Blumstein:

> [Y]outh have always fought with each other. But when it's a battle with fists, the dynamics run much more slowly. With a gun, it evolves very rapidly, too fast for a third party to intervene. That also raises the stakes and encourages others to arm themselves, thereby triggering a preemptive strike: "I better get him before he gets me."[115]

In fact, the correlation between access to guns and juvenile homicide rates is striking. The juvenile arrest rate for weapons violations doubled between 1987 and 1993. By 1994, 82 percent of all homicides committed by juveniles involved a handgun. Then, as the homicide rate began to drop, so did the arrest rate for weapons offenses, and many experts believe that the downward trend in juvenile homicide arrests can be traced largely to a decline in firearm usage.[116]

Despite these encouraging trends, guns are still widespread in youth culture. A survey by the Josephson Institute of Ethics found that 47 percent of high school and 22 percent of middle school students said they could obtain a gun if they felt the need.[117] Research conducted by H. Naci Mocan of the University of Colorado at Denver and Erdal Tekin of Georgia State University found that 13 percent of juveniles in urban areas and 32 percent of juveniles in suburban and rural areas have access to guns at home—a troubling reality that contributes to several school shootings each year.[118] According to the Centers for Disease Control, 9.9 percent of male students and 0.9 percent of female students will carry a gun at least once during any given year.[119] Nearly 30,000 juveniles were arrested for gun-related crimes in 2006.[120]

Self Check Fill in the Blanks

Criminologists have identified a number of _____ factors that increase the probability of juvenile misbehavior. One is youth—studies of a process called _____ show that children commit fewer offenses as they grow older. One pair of researchers believes that _____ at the hands of parents or guardians doubles the chances of delinquency. Youth who become involved in _____ are also more likely to get involved in criminal activity than those who do not. Check your answers on page 519.

Keeping Juvenile Delinquency under Control

Though the decrease in juvenile crime over the past few years has been welcome, many criminologists and law enforcement officials have expressed concern that this recent drop in youth crime will lead to a sense of complacency among their colleagues. Any such decline, they believe, should be seen in the context of the immense growth in delinquency since 1985. Furthermore, the factors we have just discussed—substance abuse by adults and adolescents, child abuse and neglect, gang membership, and guns—continue to plague juveniles.

Three general strategies are being put in place to deal with juvenile delinquency—and its possible increase—in the near future. The first, transfer to adult court, was discussed earlier and is the subject of this chapter's *Criminal Justice in Action* feature. The second, known as *social-control regulation,* aims to prevent crime by changing behavior without addressing underlying causes. Examples of social-control regulation include

- *Juvenile curfews,* which restrict the movements of minors during certain hours, usually after dark. Over 80 percent of all American municipalities enforce juvenile curfew laws, resulting in more than 60,000 arrests for "staying out too late" in 2006.[121]
- *Parental responsibility statutes,* which make parents responsible in some way for the offenses of their children. At present, forty-four states have enacted these statutes; seventeen of these states hold the parents *criminally* liable for their children's actions, punishing them with fines, community service, and even jail time.

The third method of juvenile delinquency prevention can be found in community-based programs that attempt to improve the chances that at-risk youth will reject a criminal lifestyle. These programs may try to educate children about the dangers of drugs and crime, or they may counsel parents who abuse their children. Today, nearly a thousand private and public groups hold after-school workshops to prevent youth violence. Though the results of community-based efforts are difficult, if not impossible, to measure—it cannot be assumed that children would have become delinquent if they did not participate—they are generally considered a crucial element in keeping youth crime under control.

JUVENILE CRIME, ADULT TIME

In 2002, Congress passed a new version of the Juvenile Justice and Delinquency Prevention Act. Although the language of the act acknowledged that the juvenile violent crime rate was dropping, it concluded that the level of offending by juveniles nationwide was still too high. To solve this problem, the legislation called for "methods for increasing victim satisfaction with respect to the penalties imposed on juveniles for their acts."[122] The most common method for increasing the accountability of violent juvenile offenders is transfer to adult court, a process we first discussed on page 499 and will now examine more closely in this *Criminal Justice in Action* feature.

TOO FAR GONE

In many respects, Congress is behind the curve when it comes to "getting tough" on juvenile offenders. Provisions to waive violent young persons to adult court have existed since the 1960s. At their inception, these procedures were reserved for the most brutal offenders. Increased media attention on violent crimes committed by juveniles changed the political landscape, putting pressure on the criminal justice system to treat all young criminals more harshly. At the same time, a number of experts were claiming that the most violent and chronic juvenile offenders were not amenable to rehabilitation.

The result: in the 1980s and 1990s, states expanded the reach of their waiver programs to include even nonviolent juveniles. While many observers contend that this movement has betrayed the original intent of the juvenile justice system, others have welcomed the new policies. "When you've got a kid in front of you who's done a vicious armed robbery with a beating, it's different than an intellectual argument about what works," said one former prosecuor.[123]

The Case for Transferring Juveniles to the Adult Justice System

- Juvenile courts lack the ability to hand down punishments harsher than limited terms in training schools. Juveniles who commit heinous, violent crimes deserve the more punitive measures available in adult courts.
- The range of penalties available in juvenile courts is so insubstantial as to provide little or no deterrence to other young persons contemplating serious criminal activity.
- Violent juvenile offenders pose a risk to nonviolent offenders in juvenile detention centers. This risk is removed by sending the violent offenders to adult prisons and jails.

The Case against Transferring Juveniles to the Adult Justice System

- Recidivism rates are higher for young offenders incarcerated in adult facilities than for those held in juvenile facilities. One reason for this may be that adult prisons and jails act as "schools of crime" for juveniles.[124]
- The threat of transfer has little deterrent effect on juveniles because they do not appreciate the consequences of their actions to the same extent that adults do.[125]
- Adult prisons do not offer the treatment or rehabilitative services that juvenile offenders need.

Your Opinion—Writing Assignment

In 2005, the United States Supreme Court prohibited the execution of persons who were juveniles when they committed their crimes (see pages 368–369). To justify this controversial decision, the Court explained that juveniles are immature, have "an underdeveloped sense of responsibility" and are "more vulnerable and susceptible to negative influences and outside pressures, including peer pressure."[126] Thus, the Court reasoned, the two main justifications for capital punishment—retribution and deterrence—could not apply to juveniles.

Should this same rationale be used to ban the transfer of juveniles to adult court? Do you think that transfer procedures are in keeping with the goals of the juvenile justice system, or are these goals flawed to begin with, making such procedures necessary? Before responding, you can review our discussions in this chapter concerning

- The traditional principles behind the juvenile justice system (pages 489–490).
- The culpability question (pages (493–494).
- The transfer of juveniles to adult court (pages 499–501).

Your answer should take at least three full paragraphs.

AP Photo/Rogelio Solis

Chapter Summary

L01 **Describe the child-saving movement and its relationship to the doctrine of *parens patriae*.** Under the doctrine of *parens patriae*, the state has a right and a duty to care for neglected, delinquent, or disadvantaged children. The child-saving movement, based on the doctrine of *parens patriae*, started in the 1800s. Its followers believed that juvenile offenders require treatment rather than punishment.

L02 **List the four major differences between juvenile courts and adult courts.** (a) No juries, (b) different terminology, (c) limited adversarial relationship, and (d) confidentiality.

L03 **Identify and briefly describe the single most important Supreme Court case with respect to juvenile justice.** The case was *In re Gault,* decided by the Supreme Court in 1967. In this case a minor was arrested for allegedly making an obscene phone call. His parents were not notified and were not present during the juvenile court judge's decision-making process. In this case, the Supreme Court held that juveniles are entitled to many of the same due process rights granted to adult offenders, including notice of charges, the right to counsel, the privilege against self-incrimination, and the right to confront and cross-examine witnesses.

L04 **List the factors that normally determine what police do with juvenile offenders.** The arresting police officers consider (a) the nature of the offense, (b) the youthful offender's past criminal history, (c) the setting in which the offense took place, (d) whether the parents can take disciplinary action, (e) the attitude of the offender, and (f) the offender's race and gender.

L05 **Describe the four primary stages of pretrial juvenile justice procedure.** (a) Intake, in which an official of the juvenile court engages in a screening process to determine what to do with the youthful offender; (b) pretrial diversion, which may consist of probation, treatment and aid, and/or restitution; (c) jurisdictional waiver to an adult court, in which case the youth leaves the juvenile justice system; and (d) some type of detention, in which the youth is held until the disposition process begins.

L06 **Explain the distinction between an adjudicatory hearing and a disposition hearing.** An adjudicatory hearing is essentially the "trial." Defense attorneys may be present during the adjudicatory hearing in juvenile courts. In many states, once adjudication has occurred, there is a separate disposition hearing that is similar to the sentencing phase in an adult court. At this point, the court, often aided by a predisposition report, determines the sentence that serves the "needs" of the child.

L07 **List the four categories of residential treatment programs.** Foster care, group homes, family group homes, and rural programs such as wilderness camps, farms, and ranches.

L08 **Describe the one variable that always correlates highly with juvenile crime rates.** The older a person is, the less likely he or she will exhibit criminal behavior. This process is known as aging out. Thus, persons in any at-risk group will commit fewer crimes as they get older.

L09 **Indicate some of the reasons why youths join gangs.** Some alienated teenagers join gangs for the social relationships and the sense of identity that gangs can provide. Youths living in high-crime neighborhoods join gangs as a form of protection. The excitement of belonging to a gang is another reason to join.

Key Terms

adjudicatory hearing   502
aftercare   507
age of onset   512
aging out   512
automatic transfer   499
boot camp   506
child abuse   513
child neglect   513
detention   501

detention hearing   501
disposition hearing   503
graduated sanctions   504
intake   498
judicial waiver   499
juvenile delinquency   490
low-visibility decision making   495
parens patriae   489
petition   498

predisposition report   503
prosecutorial waiver   500
referral   495
residential treatment programs   505
status offender   490
training schools   506
youth gangs   513

Questions for Critical Analysis

1. In spite of the constitutional safeguards given to juvenile defendants by the Supreme Court decision in *In re Gault,* only 50 percent of juvenile defendants have lawyers. Why?

2. Why is the discretion given to police officers over juveniles called low-visibility decision making?

3. Is probable cause necessary before a search can legally be conducted in a school setting? Why or why not?

4. Under what conditions in certain states is a juvenile automatically transferred to the adult court system?

5. What changes have resulted from the presence of defense attorneys in juvenile courts? In what way have these changes made juvenile courts resemble adult courts?

6. What distinguishes the sentencing phase in juvenile versus adult courts?

7. Why is the age of onset an important factor in predicting juvenile criminal behavior?

8. What has been the relationship between alcohol and drug abuse and juvenile offenders?

9. What has been the statistical relationship between armed gang members and juvenile violent crime?

Maximize Your Best Possible Outcome for Chapter 15

1. **Maximize Your Best Chance for Getting a Good Grade on the Exam.** ThomsonNOW Personalized Study is a diagnostic study tool containing valuable text-specific resources—and because you focus on just what you don't know, you learn more in less time to get a better grade. How do you get ThomsonNOW? If your textbook does not include an access code card, go to **thomsonedu.com** to get ThomsonNOW before your next exam!

2. **Get the Most Out of Your Textbook** by going to the book companion Web site at **www.cjinaction.com** to access one of the tutorial quizzes, use the flash cards to master key terms, and check out the many other study aids you'll find there. Under chapter resources you will also be able to access the Stories from the Street feature and Web links mentioned in the textbook.

3. **Learn about Potential Criminal Justice Careers** discussed in this chapter by exploring careers online at **www.cjinaction.com**. You will find career descriptions and information about job requirements, training, salary and benefits, and the application process. You can also watch video profiles featuring criminal justice professionals.

Notes

1. Peter W. Greenwood, "Juvenile Crime and Juvenile Justice," in *Crime,* ed. James Q. Wilson and Joan Petersilia (San Francisco: ICS Press, 1995), 91.
2. Jennifer M. O'Connor and Lucinda K. Treat, "Getting Smart about Getting Tough: Juvenile Justice and the Possibility of Progressive Reform," *American Criminal Law Review* 33 (Summer 1996), 1299.
3. Eric K. Klein, "Dennis the Menace or Billy the Kid: An Analysis of the Role of Transfer to Criminal Court in Juvenile Justice," *American Criminal Law Review* 35 (Winter 1998), 371.
4. "Attitudes toward the Treatment of Juveniles Who Commit Violent Crimes," *Sourcebook of Criminal Justice Statistics 2003,* Table 2.48, at **www.albany.edu/sourcebook/pdf/t248.pdf**.
5. *In re Gault,* 387 U.S. 15 (1967).
6. Samuel Davis, *The Rights of Juveniles: The Juvenile Justice System,* 2d ed. (New York: C. Boardman Co., 1995), Section 1.2.
7. Quoted in Anthony Platt, *The Child Savers* (Chicago: University of Chicago Press, 1969), 119.
8. 383 U.S. 541 (1966).

9. *Ibid.*, 556.
10. 387 U.S. 1 (1967).
11. 397 U.S. 358 (1970).
12. 421 U.S. 519 (1975).
13. 403 U.S. 528 (1971).
14. Quoted in Luis Perez and Anthony DeStefano, "A Grieving Mom's Plea," *Newsday* (May 24, 2006), A6.
15. Andrew Walkover, "The Infancy Defense in the New Juvenile Court," *UCLA Law Review* 31 (1984), 509–513.
16. Gary B. Melton, "Toward 'Personhood' for Adolescents: Autonomy and Privacy as Values in Public Policy," *American Psychology* 38 (1983), 99–100.
17. Research Network on Adolescent Development and Juvenile Justice, *Youth on Trial: A Developmental Perspective on Juvenile Justice* (Chicago: John D. & Catherine T. MacArthur Foundation, 2003), 1.
18. Richard E. Redding, "Juveniles Transferred to Criminal Court: Legal Reform Proposals Based on Social Science Research," *Utah Law Review* (1997), 709.
19. Howard N. Snyder and Melissa Sickmund, *Juvenile Offenders and Victims: A National Report* (Washington, D.C.: U.S. Department of Justice, 1995), 47.
20. 543 U.S. 551(2005).
21. *Ibid.*, 567.
22. Office of Juvenile Justice and Delinquency Prevention, *Juveniles in Court* (Washington, D.C.: U.S. Department of Justice, June 2003), 2.
23. *Ibid.*, 15.
24. Carl E. Pope and Howard N. Snyder, *Race as a Factor in Juvenile Arrests* (Washington, D.C.: Office of Juvenile Justice and Delinquency Prevention, April 2003), 1.
25. *Ibid.*, 4.
26. Sarah Lee Browning, "Race and Getting Hassled by the Police: A Research Note," *Police Studies* 17 (1994), 3.
27. George S. Bridges and Sara Steen, "Racial Disparities in Official Assessments of Juvenile Offenders," *American Sociological Review* 63 (1998), 554.
28. 469 U.S. 325 (1985).
29. *Ibid.*, 348.
30. *Vernonia School District v. Acton,* 515 U.S. 646 (1995).
31. 536 U.S. 822 (2002).
32. 422 U.S. 23 (1979).
33. *Yarborough v. Alvarado,* 541 U.S. 652 (2004).
34. *Schneckloth v. Bustamonte,* 412 U.S. 218 (1973).
35. Dean John Champion, *The Juvenile Justice System: Delinquency, Processing, and the Law,* 5th ed. (Upper Saddle River, NJ: Pearson Prentice Hall, 2007), 212–214.
36. *Ibid.*, 214.
37. Frederick Ward, Jr., "Prevention and Diversion in the United States," in *The Changing Faces of Juvenile Justice,* ed. V. Lorne Stewart (New York: New York University Press, 1978), 43.
38. President's Commission on Law Enforcement and Administration of Justice, *Task Force Report: Juvenile Delinquency and Youth Crime* (Washington, D.C.: U.S. Government Printing Office, 1967).
39. 42 U.S.C. Sections 5601–5778 (1974).
40. S'Lee Arthur Hinshaw II, "Juvenile Diversion: An Alternative to Juvenile Court," *Journal of Dispute Resolution* (1993), 305.
41. Rhode Island General Laws Section 14-1-7.1 (1994 and Supp. 1996).
42. Megan C. Kurlychek and Brian D. Johnson, "The Juvenile Penalty: A Comparison of Juvenile and Young Adult Sentencing Outcomes in Criminal Court," *Criminology* (May 2004), 485–517.
43. Judi Villa, "Adult Prisons Harden Teens," *Arizona Republic* (November 14, 2004), A1.
44. Donna Bishop and Charles Frazier, "Consequences of Transfer," in *The Changing Borders of Juvenile Justice: Transfer of Adolescents to Adult Court,* ed. Jeffrey Fagan and Franklin E. Zimring (Chicago: University of Chicago Press, 2000), 237.
45. Villa, A27.
46. 467 U.S. 253 (1984).
47. Barry C. Feld, "Criminalizing the American Juvenile Court," *Crime and Justice* 17 (1993), 227–254.
48. Barry C. Feld, "Abolish the Juvenile Court," *Journal of Criminal Law and Criminology* 88 (Fall 1997), 68.
49. *Assessment of Access to Counsel in Indiana* (Indianapolis: Indiana Juvenile Justice Task Force, 2006), 1.
50. *Juveniles in Court,* 27.
51. Eric R. Lotke, "Youth Homicide: Keeping Perspective on How Many Children Kill," *Valparaiso University Law Review* 31 (Spring 1997), 395.
52. Bureau of Justice Statistics, *Prison and Jail Inmates at Midyear 2006* (Washington, D.C.: U.S. Department of Justice, June 2007), Table 7, page 4, and Table 9, page 5.
53. *Juveniles in Court,* 27.
54. Howard N. Snyder and Melissa Sickmund, *Juvenile Offenders and Victims: 2006 National Report* (Washington, D.C.: National Center for Juvenile Justice, March 2006), 197.
55. Melissa Sickmund and Howard N. Snyder, *Juvenile Offenders and Victims: 1999 National Report* (Washington, D.C.: Office of Juvenile Justice and Delinquency Prevention, 1999), 182.
56. Champion, 581–582.
57. Marc Caputo, "Act May Prevent Other Parents' Pain," *Miami Herald* (June 1, 2006), B1.
58. *Surveillance Summaries: Youth Risk Behavior Surveillance—United States, 2001* (Washington, D.C.: Centers for Disease Control and Prevention, June 28, 2002).
59. Federal Bureau of Investigation, *Crime in the United States, 2006* (Washington, D.C.: U.S. Department of Justice, 2007), at **www.fbi. gov/ucr/cius2006/data/table_36.html**.
60. John J. DiIulio, "The Coming of the Super-Predators," *The Weekly Standard* (November 27, 1995), 23.
61. Quoted in Elizabeth Becker, "As Ex-Theorist on Young 'Superpredators,' Bush Aide Has Regrets," *New York Times* (February 9, 2001), A19.
62. Office of Juvenile Justice and Delinquency Prevention, "Juvenile Arrest Rate Trends," at **ojjdp.ncjrs.org/ojstatbb/crime/JAR_Display. asp?ID=qa05201&text=yes**.
63. Howard N. Snyder, *Juvenile Arrests, 2002* (Washington, D.C.: Office of Juvenile Justice and Delinquency Prevention, December 2004), 12; and Office of Juvenile Justice and Delinquency Prevention, "Juvenile Arrest Rate Trends," at **ojjdp.ncjrs.org/ojstatbb/crime/JAR_Display. asp?ID=qa05202&text=yes**.
64. Alfred Blumstein, "Youth Violence, Guns, and Illicit Drug Markets," *NIJ Research Journal* (Washington, D.C.: National Institute of Justice, 1995).
65. Quoted in Frank Greve, "Teens Not in As Much Trouble," *(Tucson) Arizona Daily-Star* (March 12, 2006), A7.
66. Kimberly Kempf-Leonard and Lisa Sample, "Disparity Based on Sex: Is Gender-Specific Treatment Warranted?" *Justice Quarterly* 17 (2000), 89–128.
67. Federal Bureau of Investigation, *Crime in the United States, 2005* (Washington, D.C.: U.S. Department of Justice, 2006), Table 33, at **www.fbi.gov/ucr/05cius/data/table_33.html**.
68. Anne L. Stahl, *OJJDP Fact Sheet: Delinquency Cases in Juvenile Court, 2002* (Washington, D.C.: November 2006), 1.
69. *Crime in the United States, 2006,* at **www.fbi.gov/ucr/cius2006/data/ table_37.html**.
70. Meda Chesney-Lind, "Are Girls Closing the Gender Gap in Violence?" *Criminal Justice* (Spring 2001), 20.
71. Sickmund and Snyder, 58.
72. Meda Chesney-Lind, *The Female Offender: Girls, Women, and Crime* (Thousand Oaks, CA: Sage Publications, 1997).
73. Leslie Brody, "Why Parents Are Unnerved," *New Jersey Record* (October 11, 2006), A1.
74. National Center for Education Statistics and Bureau of Justice Statistics, *Indicators of School Crime and Safety: 2006* (Washington, D.C.: U.S. Department of Justice, December 2006), 6.
75. *Ibid.*, Figure 1.2, page 7.
76. *Ibid.*, 10–15.
77. *Ibid.*, 58–59.
78. U.S. Secret Service, *The Final Report and Findings of the Safe School Initiative: Implications for the Prevention of School Attacks in the United States* (Washington, D.C.: U.S. Department of Education, May 2002), 24.
79. Michael Janofsky, "Bill on Student Bullying Is Considered in Colorado," *New York Times* (March 19, 2001), A10.
80. Marvin E. Wolfgang, *From Boy to Man, from Delinquency to Crime* (Chicago: University of Chicago Press, 1987).
81. Robert J. Sampson, Jeffrey D. Morenoff, and Stephen Raudenbush, "Social Anatomy of Racial and Ethnic Disparities in Violence," *American Journal of Public Health* (February 2005), 224–232.
82. Quoted in John H. Laub and Robert J. Sampson, "Understanding Desistance from Crime," in *Crime and Justice: A Review of Research* (Chicago: University of Chicago Press, 2001), 6.
83. Travis Hirschi and Michael Gottfredson, "Age and the Explanation of Crime," *American Journal of Sociology* 89 (1982), 552–584.

84. Robert J. Sampson and John H. Laub, "A Life-Course View on the Development of Crime," *Annals of the American Academy of Political and Social Science* (November 2005), 12.

85. David P. Farrington, "Offending from 10 to 25 Years of Age," in *Prospective Studies of Crime and Delinquency*, ed. Katherine Teilmann Van Dusen and Sarnoff A. Mednick (Boston: Kluwer-Nijhoff Publishers, 1983), 17.

86. *Juveniles in Court*, 29.

87. Substance Abuse and Mental Health Services Administration, *Results from the 2005 National Survey on Drug Use and Health: National Findings* (Rockville, MD: Office of Applied Studies, September 2006), 29.

88. *Ibid.*, 17.

89. National Institute on Drug Abuse, *Monitoring the Future: National Results on Adolescent Drug Use: Overview of Key Findings 2006* (Washington, D.C.: U.S. Department of Heath and Human Services, May 2007), 5.

90. *Crime in the United States, 2006*, at **www.fbi.gov/ucr/cius2006/data/table_32.html**.

91. *Ibid.*, at **www.fbi.gov/ucr/cius2006/data/table_34.html**..

92. Lisette Blumhardt, "In the Best Interests of the Child: Juvenile Justice or Adult Retribution?" *University of Hawaii Law Review* (Winter 2000), 341.

93. Arrestee Drug Abuse Monitoring Program, *Preliminary Data on Drug Use and Related Matters among Adult Arrestees and Juvenile Detainees* (Washington, D.C.: National Institute of Justice, 2003).

94. National Mental Health Association, "Mental Health and Adolescent Girls in the Justice System" at **www. nmha.org/children/justjuv/girlsjj.cfm**.

95. *Collaboration, Coordination, and Cooperation: Helping Children Affected by Parental Addiction and Family Violence* (New York: Children of Alcoholics Foundation, 1996).

96. Ching-Tung Lung and Deborah Daro, *Current Trends in Child Abuse Reporting and Fatalities: The Results of the 1997 Annual Fifty-State Survey* (Chicago: National Committee to Prevent Child Abuse, 1998).

97. Kimberly A. Tyler and Katherine A. Johnson, "A Longitudinal Study of the Effects of Early Abuse on Later Victimization among High-Risk Adolescents," *Violence and Victims* (June 2006), 287–291.

98. Joyesha Chesnick, "Child Abuse, Crime Linked," *Arizona Daily Star* (December 3, 2004), B1.

99. Grover Trask, "Defusing the Teenage Time Bombs," *Prosecutor* (March/April 1997), 29.

100. Cathy Spatz Widom, *The Cycle of Violence* (Washington, D.C.: National Institute of Justice, October 1992).

101. Janet Currie and Erdal Tekin, *Does Child Abuse Cause Crime?* (Atlanta: Andrew Young School of Policy Studies, April 2006), 27–28.

102. Office of Juvenile Justice and Delinquency Prevention, *National Youth Gang Survey 1999–2001* (Washington, D.C.: U.S. Department of Justice, July 2006), v.

103. *Ibid.*, 21.

104. Rachel A. Gordon, Benjamin B. Lahey, Eriko Kawai, Rolf Loeber, and Magda Stouthamer-Loeber, "Antisocial Behavior and Youth Gang Membership: Selection and Socialization," *Criminology* (February 2004), 55–89.

105. *National Youth Gang Survey 1999–2001*, 21.

106. National Alliance of Gang Investigators Associates, *2005 National Gang Threat Assessment* (Washington, D.C.: Bureau of Justice Assistance, 2005), 10–11.

107. *National Youth Gang Survey 1999–2001*, 24–25.

108. Marjorie S. Zatz, "Voices from the Barrio: Chicano Gangs, Families, and Communities," *Criminology* (May 31, 2000), 369.

109. Scott H. Decker and B. Van Winkle, *Life in the Gang: Family, Friends, and Violence* (New York: Cambridge University Press, 1996).

110. Sara R. Battin, Karl G. Hill, Robert D. Abbott, Richard F. Catalano, and J. David Hawkins, "The Contribution of Gang Membership to Delinquency beyond Delinquent Friends," *Criminology* 36 (1998), 93–115.

111. *2005 National Gang Threat Assessment*, 23.

112. Karl G. Hill, Christina Lui, and J. David Hawkins, *Early Precursors of Gang Membership: A Study of Seattle Youth* (Washington, D.C.: Office of Juvenile Justice and Delinquency Prevention, December 2001).

113. Joseph F. Sheley and James D. Wright, *In the Line of Fire: Youth, Guns, and Violence in Urban America* (Hawthorne, NY: Aldine De Gruyter, 1995), 100.

114. Beth Bjerregaard and Alan J. Lizotte, "Gun Ownership and Gang Membership," *Journal of Criminal Law and Criminology* 86 (1995), 49.

115. Quoted in Gracie Bond Staples, "Guns in School," *Fort Worth Star-Telegram* (June 3, 1998), 1.

116. Office of Juvenile Justice and Delinquency Prevention, *1999 National Report Series: Juvenile Justice Bulletin—Kids and Guns* (Washington, D.C.: U.S. Department of Justice, March 2000), 4.

117. *Ethics of American Youth* (Marina del Rey, CA: Josephson Institute of Ethics, 2001).

118. H. Naci Mocan and Erdal Tekin, "Guns and Juvenile Crime," *Journal of Law and Economics* (October 2006), 507.

119. Centers for Disease Control and Prevention, "Youth Risk Behavior Surveillance—United States, 2005," *Morbidity and Mortality Weekly Report* (June 9, 2006), 6.

120. *Crime in the United States*, at **www.fbi.gov/ucr/cius2006/data/table_36.html**.

121. David McDowell, "Juvenile Curfew Laws and Their Influence on Crime," *Federal Probation* (December 2006), 58; *ibid*.

122. Juvenile Justice and Delinquency Act of 2002 Section 101, (A)(10)(B), 42 U.S.C. Section 5601 (2004).

123. Quoted in Marilyn Elias, "Is Adult Prison Best for Juveniles?" *USA Today* (September 21, 2006), 9D.

124. Amanda Burgess-Proctor, Kendall Holtrop, and Francisco A. Villarruel, *Youth Transferred to Adult Court: Racial Disparities* (Washington, D.C.: Campaign for Youth Justice, 2006), 4–6.

125. Benjamin Steiner and Emily Wright, "Assessing the Relative Effects of State Direct File Waiver Laws on Violence Juvenile Crime: Deterrence or Irrelevance?" *Journal of Criminal Law and Criminology* (2006), 1451–1470.

126. *Roper v. Simmons*, 543 U.S. 551, 569 (2005).

CHAPTER 16

Homeland Security

Chapter outline

- An Introduction to Terrorism
- The Terrorist Threat
- The Homeland Security Response
- Counterterrorism Challenges and Strategies
- Border Security
- The Double-Edged Sword: Security versus Civil Liberties
- Criminal Justice in Action—Interrogating Terrorists

Learning objectives

After reading this chapter, you should be able to:

L01 Identify five important trends in international terrorism.

L02 Describe the several strains of domestic terrorism.

L03 Compare WMDs and CBERN.

L04 Explain why the Antiterrorism and Effective Death Penalty Act of 1996 (AEDPA) is an important legal tool against terrorists

L05 Describe the primary goals of an intelligence agency and indicate how it differs from an agency that focuses solely on law enforcement.

L06 Explain how American law enforcement agencies have used "preventive policing" to combat terrorism.

L07 Indicate which persons are eligible to be designated enemy combatants and explain the consequences for them.

L08 List the primary duties of first responders following a terrorist attack or other catastrophic event.

L09 Explain how the Patriot Act has made it easier for federal agents to conduct searches during terrorism investigations

L010 Explain how military tribunals differ from federal courts with respect to trials of suspected terrorists.

Down on the Chicken Farm

Russell Defreitas hardly fit the definition of a terrorist mastermind. The sixty-three-year-old U.S. citizen sold books on a Queens, New York, street corner. He would ask his friends for their broken refrigerators and air conditioners, which he would send to a family member in his native Guyana for repair and resale. He boasted of the large settlement he hoped to win as the result of a recent car accident. One acquaintance referred to him as a "two-bit hustler" always out to make a quick buck.

Nonetheless, on June 2, 2007, law enforcement agents arrested Defreitas on charges that he planned to bomb a fuel pipeline leading into New York's John F. Kennedy Airport (JFK). Three accomplices—Guyanians Abdul Kadir and Abdel Nur and Trinidadian Kareem Ibrahim—were eventually apprehended on the Caribbean island of Trinidad. According to federal officials, Defreitas had conducted "precise and extensive" surveillance of JFK, thereby adding to his knowledge of the airport gained over years employed as a cargo worker there. He told an informant that he and several "brothers" from Guyana and Trinidad "wanted to do something bigger than the World Trade Center." To friends and neighbors

in Queens, the plot, called "chicken farm" by the conspirators, seemed ridiculous, as did Defreitas's alleged role as organizer. "He's not smart enough" to have pulled it off, said one. "Very, very silly," said another. "This is like the Three Stooges. Everybody [here] is laughing."

▲ An image taken from a surveillance camera shows Russell Defreitas leaving a New York diner on June 1, 2007, just before his arrest on terrorism-related charges.

E choes of that laughter could be heard in the offices of the Federal Bureau of Investigation (FBI), where many doubted Russell Defreitas's ability to carry out the "chicken farm" plot. One agent even called him a "sad old guy who's got a lot of spit and vinegar in him."[1] Others found no humor, however, in a trip to Trinidad that Defreitas made along with Kareem Ibrahim to visit officials of the radical Islamic group Jamaat al Muslimeen (JAM), which has been linked to the international terrorist organization al Qaeda. If Defreitas "could have gotten the JAM involved," said a federal official, "we wouldn't know where [the plot] could have gone."[2]

Since the attacks of September 11, 2001, the United States has focused most of its international antiterrorism resources on groups and individuals based in the Middle East and South Asia. In contrast, Defreitas's efforts had their roots in Trinidad, the largest of the twenty-three islands that make up the Caribbean nation of Trinidad and Tobago, and nearby Guyana, located on the northeastern coast of South America. "It shows that the threat can come from anywhere," said one expert.[3]

Such unpredictability is one of the most striking, and unnerving, aspects of life in the United States, post–September 11, 2001. Terrorism and its uncertainties have been a constant theme throughout this textbook, and we have seen many instances in which law enforcement, the courts, and corrections have had to evolve to meet the challenge. In this chapter, we will focus solely on the criminal justice system's role in *homeland security*, defined by the federal government as

a concerted national effort to prevent terrorist attacks within the United States, reduce America's vulnerability to terrorism, and minimize the damage and recover from attacks that do occur.[4]

Criminal Justice Now™

Maximize your study time by using ThomsonNOW's Personalized Study plan to help you review this chapter and prepare for examination. The Study Plan will

- Help you identify areas on which you should concentrate

- Provide interactive exercises to help you master the chapter concepts; and

- Provide a post-test to confirm you are ready to move on to the next chapter information.

524   Criminal Justice in Action

We start with a discussion of the phenomenon that has driven the homeland security movement in the United States since September 11: terrorism.

An Introduction to Terrorism

Nonstate Actor An entity that plays a role in international affairs but does not represent any established state or nation.

Relatively speaking, the term *terrorism* has had a short history. In the political context, its birth can be traced to the time during the French Revolution (1789–1799), when the French legislature ordered the public executions of nearly 18,000 "enemies" of the new government. As a result of this *régime de la terreur* (reign of terror), terrorism was initially associated with state-sponsored violence against the people. By the dawn of the twentieth century, this dynamic had shifted. Terrorists had evolved into **nonstate actors,** free of control by or allegiance to any nation, who used violence to further political goals such as the formation or destruction of a particular government.

Today, the dominant strain of terrorism mixes political goals with very strong religious affiliations. Modern terrorism is also characterized by extreme levels of violence: the March 11, 2004, bombing of Madrid's commuter train system resulted in 191 deaths; detonations in and at several Bali nightclubs on October 12, 2002, killed 202 people; and, of course, the September 11, 2001, attacks on New York and Washington, D.C., claimed nearly 3,000 lives. Indeed, the power of terrorism is a direct result of the fear caused by this violence—not only the fear that such atrocities will be repeated, but also that next time, they will be much worse.

DEFINING TERRORISM

Terrorism has always had a subjective quality, summed up by the useful cliché, "one person's terrorist is another person's freedom fighter." Because it means different things to different people in different situations, politicians, academics, and legal experts alike have long struggled to determine which acts of violence qualify as terrorism and which do not. One observer has even compared these efforts to the legendary quest for the Holy Grail, stating, "periodically, eager souls set out, full of purpose, energy and self-confidence, to succeed where so many others before have tried and failed."[5]

The FBI defines terrorism as

> the unlawful use of force or violence against persons or property to intimidate or coerce a government, the civilian population, or any segment thereof, in further of political or social objectives.[6]

This definition is useful for our purposes because it is relatively straightforward and easy to understand. It is inadequate, however, in that is fails to capture the wide scope of international terrorism in the 2000s. Today, many observers are asking whether the state should consider terrorist violence merely "unlawful," as in the FBI definition, or an act of war? The answer is crucial in the homeland security context because, as we shall see later in the chapter, our rules for preventing crimes and fighting a war are markedly different.

Generally, wars are considered military actions undertaken by one state or nation against another. This would seem to remove

▼ Rescue workers sift through a damaged train in Madrid, Spain, on March 11, 2004. A series of coordinated bombings of Madrid's transportation system carried out by an Islamic terrorist group on that day killed 191 people and wounded 2,050. How are such acts of terrorism distinguished from acts of war?

AP Photo/Peter Dejong, File

terrorism from the realm of war, given that its instigators are nonstate actors, as mentioned earlier. Professor David A. Westbrook of the State University of New York at Buffalo points out, however, that the large scale and financial resources of some modern terrorist organizations makes them as powerful as many nations, if not more so. In addition, the high body counts associated with the worst terrorists acts seem better described in terms of war than of crime, which in most cases involves two people—the criminal and the victim.[7] Thus, as we see in ■ Figure 16.1, perhaps the most satisfying, if not the most concise, definition of terrorism describes it as a "supercrime" that incorporates many of the characteristics of warfare.

THE GLOBAL CONTEXT OF TERRORISM

Immediately following the 2004 Madrid train bombings, many Spanish politicians and media outlets blamed Euskadi Ta Askatasuna (ETA), a local paramilitary group that has been using violence for decades in an attempt to force the creation of a Basque homeland in northern Spain. In this context, the attack was decried as an "act of terrorism." Following an investigation, however, the perpetrators were identified as Islamic extremists with links to al Qaeda. Suddenly, the bombings became part of the "war" on terror.[8]

The distinction is basic to understanding international terrorism. One of the ways in which modern terrorism is similar to warfare is that it has created a worldwide feeling of "us" versus "them." For most Americans, the "them" does

■ **Figure 16.1** The "Supercrime" of Terrorism

While Professor George Fletcher of the Columbia University School of Law recognizes the need to define terrorist acts in criminal codes, he is uncomfortable treating terrorism in the same manner as other crimes such as murder or theft. He prefers to think of terrorism as a "different dimension of crime, a higher, more dangerous version, a kind of supercrime incorporating some of the characteristics of warfare." To accommodate this idea of terrorism as a "supercrime," he has devised eight variables that often—though not always—capture the essence of what we think about when we consider terrorism.

1. The violence factor. First and foremost, terrorism is an expression of violence. **Example:** As a result of the September 11, 2001, terrorist attacks on New York City and Washington, D.C., 2,974 people were killed, and another 2,337 were injured.

2. The intention. Just as the purpose of a bank robbery is to get the cash, terrorists have an objective each time they act. In some instances, the very act of violence or destruction fulfills this intent. **Example:** In March 2004, a group of Islamic extremists bombed Madrid's commuter rail system during the final days of Spain's national elections. Many observers believed that the bombings were intended to damage the image of the sitting government, which had sent troops to fight in Iraq.

3. The victims. Terrorist acts generally target civilians or "innocent" persons rather than military personnel. **Example:** In 2005, an al Qaeda suicide bomber detonated himself in the ballroom of a Radisson hotel in Amman, Jordan, during a wedding. Among the thirty-eight people killed in the explosion were the fathers of the bride and groom.

4. The wrongdoers. Similarly, terrorists are fighters outside of a military command structure. **Example:** Ali Hussein Ali al-Shamari, an Iraqi militant, was the suicide bomber at the wedding in Amman. He entered the ballroom with his wife, Sajida Mubarak Atrous al-Rishawi, who was unable to fulfill her role in the attack when her explosive belt failed to detonate.

5. A "just cause." Those who decide to use terror to further their aims believe that the ends justify the often-horrible means. **Example:** From the late 1960s to the 1990s, the Irish Republican Army (IRA) killed hundreds of civilians in its efforts to end British rule in Northern Ireland.

6. Organization. Generally, terrorists act in concert with other like-minded individuals. The solo terrorist, though not unheard of, is rare. **Example:** The Shining Path, a guerrilla group that sought to create a violent revolution in Peru in the 1980s and early 1990s, operated a broad network of "generated organizations" that provided logistical and financial support for thousands of members.

7. Theater. For a terrorist act to be truly effective, it must be dramatic. One expert has even said, "Terrorism is theater." **Example:** On January 23, 2002, al Qaeda operatives kidnapped American journalist Daniel Pearl in Karachi, Pakistan. Several weeks later, the kidnappers released a video on the Internet showing Pearl's throat being slit.

8. The absence of guilt. A terrorist is so certain of the righteousness of the cause that she or he acts without feeling guilt or remorse. **Example:** During a 2007 military trial, al Qaeda operative Khalid Sheik Mohammed bragged, "I decapitated with my blessed right hand the head of the American Jew, Daniel Pearl."

Source: George P. Fletcher, "The Indefinable Concept of Terrorism," *Journal of International Criminal Justice* (November 2006), 894–911.

not refer generally to all terrorists, but instead refers specifically to a brand of radical Islam represented by Osama bin Laden and his al Qaeda terrorist network. To a large extent, the homeland security apparatus that we will discuss in the chapter rests on the same assumption.

Osama bin Laden and al Qaeda Just as there has been some trouble coming up with a useful definition of terrorism, there has been a great deal of confusion concerning the terrorists themselves. To start with, the Arabic term *al Qaeda*, which can be roughly translated as "the base," has two meanings. One alludes to a diffuse, general anti-Western global social movement, while the other refers to a specific organization responsible for the September 11 attacks and numerous other terrorist activities over the past two decades.[9]

Osama bin Laden's al Qaeda organization grew out of a network of volunteers who migrated to Afghanistan in the 1980s to rid that country of its Communist occupiers. (Ironically, in light of later events, bin Laden and these volunteers received significant American financial aid.) For bin Laden, these efforts took the form of *jihad*, a controversial term that, once again, has been the subject of much confusion. *Jihad* does not, as many think, mean "holy war." Rather, it refers to three kinds of struggle, or exertion, required of the Muslim faithful: (1) the struggle against the evil in oneself, (2) the struggle against the evil outside of oneself, and (3) the struggle against nonbelievers.[10] Many Muslims believe that this struggle can be achieved without violence and denounce the form of *jihad* practiced by al Qaeda. Clearly, however, bin Laden and his followers reject the notion that *jihad* can be accomplished through peaceable efforts. (To learn more about this aspect of Muslim law and tradition, see the feature *International CJ—The* Jihad *Loophole* on the following page.)

▲ In the summer of 2007, Osama bin Laden, shown here in a 1998 photo, released a videotaped message to world media outlets. In the video, the leader of al Qaeda warned of his terrorist organization's growing strength and urged all Americans to embrace Islam. He also harshly criticized the governments of the United States, Great Britain, and France, vowing to "continue to escalate the killing and the fighting" in Iraq. How is al Qaeda's resistance to U.S. military operations in Iraq and other parts of the Middle East consistent with the group's notion of *jihad?*

Al Qaeda versus the United States In the 1990s, bin Laden began to turn his attention to the United States. About a year after the September 11, 2001, attacks, he wrote a letter to the American people outlining the reasons behind al Qaeda's opposition to our government. These included American support for Israel, which is widely seen as an enemy to Muslims; U.S. exploitation of Islamic countries for their oil; and the presence of U.S. military forces in the Middle East, "spreading your ideology and thereby polluting the hearts of our people."[11] As it turns out, bin Laden has his own definition of terrorism, which can be either "commendable" or "reprehensible." Terrorism is "reprehensible" only when it is aimed at innocent people, while "terrorizing oppressors and criminals and thieves and robbers is necessary." Not surprisingly, bin Laden considers the terrorism he practices against the United States to be "commendable" because it is "directed at the tyrants and aggressors and the enemies of Allah."[12]

TRENDS IN INTERNATIONAL TERRORISM

One final point must be made about comparisons between modern terrorism and warfare. In practice, wars are "about" something—obtaining land, for example, or removing a military threat. As soon as that goal is reached, or a compromise is negotiated, the warring parties no longer have any incentive to fight. In contrast,

Yemen, a predominantly Arab nation located on the Red Sea, is one of the United States' strongest allies in the Middle East. Since the September 11, 2001, terrorist attacks, the Yemeni government has allowed American forces to search out al Qaeda operatives in that country, and the United States has reciprocated with $8 million a year in antiterrorism aid. Several years ago, Yemen even set up several special courts to handle high-profile terrorist cases.

In 2006, fourteen Yemenis and five Saudi Arabians appeared before one of these courts, charged with traveling to Iraq with the intent to join al Qaeda and kill American soldiers. The defendants freely admitted their guilt, praising Osama bin Laden and showing off battle scars from previous skirmishes with U.S. troops. In response, Judge Mohammed al-Baadani set them free. Despite criticism from American officials stationed in Yemen, Judge al-Baadani felt he had no choice. "Islamic *sharia* law," the judge explained, "permits *jihad* against occupiers" of Muslim lands. Indeed, Yemen law has long recognized the "right of *jihad*," allowing its citizens to battle foreign armies in Afghanistan, Bosnia, and Chechnya.

Five months earlier, Judge al-Baadani had imprisoned fourteen Yemenis for planning to attack U.S. targets within Yemen. In his eyes, the two decisions were perfectly consistent. Because Yemen is not occupied by non-Islamic forces, the dictates of *jihad* do not apply in that country as they do in Iraq. "It is a very tricky concept," the judge admitted. "[However], it is part of the dogma and one cannot just deny its legitimacy."

FOR CRITICAL ANALYSIS

Judge Mohammed al-Baadani has several relatives living in the United States, and he was surprised by their criticism of his decision. "According to American law, isn't it OK to fight with people of your own religion against the occupiers?" he asked, adding that he would "like to visit America to see how the United States handles the issue." If the judge were to pose his question to you, how would you explain the manner in which America "handles" this issue?

Osama bin Laden's global *jihad* does not appear to have any concrete goals. Though he has made certain demands, such as insisting that U.S. military forces leave the Middle East, bin Laden has not indicated that his *jihad* will end if the demands are met. He has never shown any interest in negotiation, nor has he tried to take control of a nation or territory. As we near the end of the 2000s, the modern terrorist movement is motivated by the "struggle" rather than hopes of an as-yet-to-be-defined victory.[13]

With the somewhat disconcerting notion of a perpetual conflict in mind, homeland security expert Brian M. Jenkins has identified five trends in international terrorism:[14]

1. *Terrorism has become progressively bloodier.* In the 1970s, the most deadly
   L01 terrorist incidents caused double-digit fatalities. On September 11, 2001, thousands of people died. As we shall see later in the chapter, the threat posed by a nuclear or a biochemical terrorist attack raises the specter of casualties on a much larger scale.

2. *Terrorists have developed more efficient methods of financing their operations.* Terrorist groups in South America, central Asia, and the Middle East have profited from extensive drug-trafficking operations. Internet fund-raising has also become a lucrative source of funds. A broad network of informal banking systems, cash wire transfers, and money laundering schemes allows terrorist groups to disburse the funds with relative ease.

3. *Terrorists have developed more efficient models of organization.* Bin Laden's al Qaeda has patterned itself on a lean international business model. Different individuals are responsible for different tasks, such as recruiting, planning, logistics, finances, propaganda, and social services including supporting the families of suicide bombers. These "employees" do not answer to a single leader but rather function as a network that is quick to adjust and difficult to infiltrate.

4. *Terrorists are able to mount global campaigns.* These loosely organized and well-financed organizations can attack foreign targets either by crossing

national frontiers themselves or by preying on foreign institutions such as embassies or private companies that are located on their own territory. Consequently, as the U.S. military extends itself to fight terrorism abroad, it becomes more vulnerable to terrorist aggression.

5. *Terrorists have exploited new communication technology.* The Internet allows direct communication between terrorist operatives at minimal cost and with little danger of detection. Terrorist Web sites "get out the message," offer valuable recruiting opportunities, and, in some instances, provide an outlet for the webcast of videotaped violence used for propaganda purposes.

Domestic Terrorism Acts of terrorism that take place within the territorial jurisdiction of the United States without foreign direction or involvement.

Eco-Terrorism Violence or the threat of violence against persons or property for environmental-political reasons.

As you may have noted, each of these trends favors the global terrorism movement. Indeed, Jenkins finds that today's jihadists are dangerous, resilient survivors who have achieved some strategic results and are determined to continue attacking their enemies. "Destroying their terrorist enterprise," he concludes, "will take years."[15]

"Terrorism cannot be 'defeated,' because it is a tactic and not an enemy."

— *Nora Bensahel, political scientist*

DOMESTIC TERRORISM

Because of the magnitude of the events of September 11, 2001, and their far-reaching repercussions, it is easy to forget that, prior to those attacks, an American was responsible for the deadliest act of terrorism ever committed on U.S. soil. On April 19, 1995, Timothy McVeigh set off a truck bomb near the Alfred P. Murrah Federal Building in downtown Oklahoma City, Oklahoma. The blast killed 168 people and left more than 800 injured. The Oklahoma City bombing is an example of **domestic terrorism,** which, as you might suppose, is similar to international terrorism except that its perpetrators are groups or individuals operating entirely within the United States, completely free of foreign influence or direction.[16]

Domestic terrorists hardly represent a cohesive movement. Their political and social objectives vary widely. Timothy McVeigh and his accomplice Terry Nichols represented a strain of domestic terrorism characterized by antipathy toward the U.S government. McVeigh targeted the Alfred P. Murrah Federal Building because it housed agents from the FBI and the Bureau of Alcohol, Tobacco, Firearms and Explosives, representatives of a federal government he believed was turning on its own citizens. Other "fringe" domestic terrorist groups include white supremacists, who promote the idea that whites are racially superior to all other races, and the radical edge of the "pro-life" movement, which is willing to go to extremes to keep physicians from carrying out legal abortions.

According to the FBI, the most active and well-organized form of domestic terrorism is **eco-terrorism,** a movement that commits acts of violence, sabotage, or property damage motivated by a desire to protect animals or the environment.[17] The Animal Liberation Front (ALF), for example, has proclaimed a "long, hard, bloody war" in its efforts to halt "animal exploitation activities" such as scientific research that uses nonhuman subjects.[18] For its part, the Earth Liberation Front (ELF) is a loose organization that encourages acts of sabotage against "enemies of the environment." In 2007, a member of a Eugene, Oregon–based

▼ About a decade ago, the Earth Liberation Front set fire to a number of structures on Colorado's Vail Mountain, including the Two Elks Restaurant shown here. In a communiqué after the incident, the costliest act of eco-terrorism in the nation's history, the group stated, "On behalf of the lynx, five buildings and four ski lifts at Vail were reduced to ashes." What are the general goals of eco-terrorist organizations?

AP Photo/Mark Mobley

ELF splinter group called The Family was sentenced to thirteen years in prison. The Family is believed to be responsible for twenty instances of arson that caused more than $40 million in damage to businesses such as car dealerships and lumber companies.[19] The FBI estimates that, between 1990 and 2004, eco-terrorism groups were responsible for more than 1,200 such crimes.[20]

The Terrorist Threat

On September 18, 2001, just a week after the hijacked airplanes flew into the World Trade Center and the Pentagon, a batch of envelopes containing several grams of *anthrax* powder were sent out to various media outlets from a post office in Trenton, New Jersey. Anthrax is a very dangerous infectious disease transmitted by bacteria so small that a thousand spores would not reach across the thin edge of a dime.[21] On October 5, Robert Stevens, a photo editor for the Florida-based newspaper, *Sun,* died after inhaling some of the powder. Over the next several weeks, several more anthrax-filled envelopes infiltrated the U.S. Postal Service, including two mailed to U.S. senators, and twenty-one other people became infected. Four of them died.

This first-known deliberate use of bacteria to commit murder in the United States was almost completely unexpected. Only eighteen cases of inhaled anthrax spores were recorded in the entire twentieth century. Weapons experts knew that the bacteria could be disseminated from a germ-packed light bulb or a suitcase with holes punched in it, but nobody had considered the post office as an anthrax delivery service.[22] Thus, though the perpetrators and therefore their motives are still unknown, the incident was a very effective act of terrorism. Not only was it unpredictable and random, but it gave people a reason to fear a staple of their daily life—the mail.

THE WEAPONRY OF TERRORISM

While the images and memories of September 11, 2001, remain part of the national psyche, the anthrax mailings have largely been forgotten. For the most part, however, homeland security experts are more concerned about the dangers presented by minuscule bacterium than by the threat posed by two-hundred-ton airplanes. In 2007, Robert Mueller, the director of the FBI, said that "the biggest threat faced by the United States in the counterterrorism arena . . . is [a] WMD in the hands of terrorists."[23] "WMD" is the acronym for **weapons of mass destruction,** a term used to describe a wide variety of deadly instruments that represent significant security challenges for the United States and other targets of international terrorism. Anthrax is considered a WMD because a very small amount of it has the potential to cause a massive amount of destruction, killing and sickening thousands of people.

Types of WMDs WMDs come in four categories: (1) *biological* weapons, (2) *chemical* weapons, (3) *nuclear* weapons, and (4) *radiological* weapons. **Biological weapons** are living organisms such as bacteria, viruses, and other microorganisms such as anthrax that cause disease and death. Because these weapons are "alive," they have unique capabilities to reproduce and spread undetected through large populations of humans, animals, and plants. In con-

Weapons of Mass Destruction (WMDs) A term that describes nuclear, radiological, chemical, or biological weapons that have the capacity to cause large numbers of casualties or do significant property damage.

Biological Weapon Any living organism, such as a bacterium or virus, used to intentionally harm or kill adversaries in war or targets of terrorist attacks.

trast, **chemical weapons** are manufactured for the purpose of causing harm or death. They can be inhaled or ingested, and they can seep into the body though the skin or eyes. (See ■ Figure 16.2 for a description of three of the most dangerous chemical weapons linked to terrorism.)

The true "doomsday" terrorist attack scenario involves **nuclear weapons.** The destructive force of these bombs is caused by the massive release of heat and energy that accompanies their detonation. Only two such bombs have ever been used—by the U.S. military against the Japanese cities of Hiroshima and Nagasaki in August of 1945. About 70,000 people in Hiroshima and 40,000 people in Nagasaki were killed instantly. Adding to the devastating impact of these weapons is the **radiation** that is released following detonation. Radiological material destroys human cells, and exposure to high levels of radiation can lead to immediate death. Exposure to lower levels of radiation is also dangerous, greatly increasing the risk of long-term health problems such as cancer.

Conventional Explosives For all the concern over WMDs, conventional explosives and **improvised explosive devices (IEDs),** created by amateurs rather than

L03 professionally manufactured, are still the dominant type of weapon used in terrorist attacks. They are easy to obtain and to use, with instructions for their assembly readily available on the Internet. Many IEDS can be prepared by mixing chemicals available in common household items. By one estimate,

Chemical Weapon Any weapon that uses a manufactured chemical to intentionally harm or kill adversaries in war or targets of terrorist attacks.

Nuclear Weapon An explosive device that derives its massive destructive power from the release of nuclear energy.

Radiation Harmful energy that is transmitted outward from its source through rays, waves, or particles following the detonation of a nuclear device.

Improvised Explosive Devices (IEDs) Explosive charges created using nonmilitary or nontraditional components, often used by terrorists or other nonstate actors without access to standard weapons training.

Figure 16.2 Chemical Weapons

The Centers of Disease Control and Prevention in Atlanta, Georgia, have identified sixty-five known chemical agents that can be used as weapons. Three—cyanide, ricin, and sarin—are recognized as being particularly well suited for terrorist purposes.

Cyanide

Physical Properties: Naturally present in some plants such as cassava, in its manufactured state cyanide can exist either as a colorless gas or in crystal form.

Symptoms of Exposure: Small amounts of cyanide, whether breathed in, ingested, or absorbed through the skin, can cause dizziness, weakness, headaches, and nausea and vomiting. Large amounts can slow the heart rate, induce convulsions, and cause respiratory failure leading to death.

Link to Terrorism: According to information lifted by government agents off the computer hard drive of a jihadist named Bassam Bokhowa, in 2003 al Qaeda planned to disperse cyanide through New York City's subway system using a remote-controlled device called the mubtakkar. The plot was called off at the last minute, for unknown reasons.

Ricin

Physical Properties: Made from the waste that is left over when castor beans are "mashed" to produce castor oil, ricin is available as a powder, a mist, or a pellet that can be dissolved in water.

Symptoms of Exposure: Ricin attacks the body's cells, denying them the proteins they need to survive. A person who has inhaled a sufficient amount of ricin inevitably experiences difficulty breathing and nausea. Within hours, breathing become more difficult as excess fluid fills the lungs, and the skin turns blue. Swallowed ricin causes bleeding in the stomach and intestines, and eventually the liver, spleen, and kidneys stop functioning. In either case, death can result within forty-eight hours of exposure.

Link to Terrorism: In February 2004, the office of U.S. Senate Majority Leader Bill Frist, a Republican from Tennessee, received a letter containing ricin powder. Several staff members were exposed to the chemical agent, but no injuries resulted.

Sarin

Physical Properties: Originally developed in Germany in the 1930s as a pesticide, sarin is a clear, odorless, and tasteless liquid that can be evaporated into a gas and spread in the environment.

Symptoms of Exposure: Sarin is a nerve agent that prevents the body's glands and muscles from functioning properly. Even a single drop of sarin on the skin can cause muscle twitching at the point of impact. In small doses, it causes eye pain, blurred vision, chest tightness, confusion, and drowsiness. Those exposed to larger doses will lose consciousness, experience paralysis, and run a significant risk of respiratory failure leading to death.

Link to Terrorism: In 1995, using sharp umbrella tips, members of the Japanese cult Aum Shinrikyo punctured eleven pouches filled with sarin in the Tokyo subway system. The vapor caused commuters in the immediate vicinity to suffocate and collapse. Twelve people died and more than one thousand became sick.

Source: Jane A. Bullock, *et al., Introduction to Homeland Security,* 2d. ed (Burlington, MA: Butterworth-Heinemann, 2006), 156–157, 160–163.

more than 70 percent of all terrorist attacks involves these sorts of devices.[24] In law enforcement and military circles, therefore, the different terrorist threats are summarized with another acronym, CBERN, which stands for "chemical, biological, explosive, radiological, and nuclear."

CBERN experts have also begun to recognize that the different categories of weaponry can be "mixed and matched" for greater effect. For example, a significant amount of radiological material is found in hospitals, universities, and other research institutions. If such material is stolen, it can be used in a "dirty bomb," the popular term for radiological dispersion devices (RDDs) that employ conventional explosives rather than nuclear weapons to spread harmful radiation waves. According to one study, an RDD detonated in downtown New York City would kill two thousand people and expose thousands more to severe radiation poisoning.[25]

▲ Baghdad residents gather around the wreckage caused by an improved explosive device (IED). The roadside bomb, detonated from a roadside vehicle, targeted a passing Iraqi police patrol. Why are IEDs still the dominant type of weapon used in terrorist attacks?

THE INCIDENCE OF WMDS

As mentioned earlier, for all the nightmarish possibilities, WMDs have been more a threat than a reality on American soil. Besides the anthrax mailings already discussed, only one instance of bioterrorism has occurred in the United States. In 1984, members of the Rajneesh cult spread salmonella bacteria through supermarkets and restaurants in The Dalles, Oregon, as part of an effort to influence local elections. About 750 residents fell ill, though none fatally. Terrorist attacks using chemical agents have been rare throughout the world, and there have been no nuclear or radiological terrorism incidents.

There are a number of reasons for this situation. The biological agents most appropriate for terrorist attacks are short lived and easily destroyed, so there is no guarantee that they will be effective. The materials needed to carry out a chemical, nuclear, or radiological attack are heavily regulated by the world's governments, and their theft or purchase in significant amounts is likely to set off alarm bells. Furthermore, once a threat has been identified, governments respond by lessening the risks associated with that threat. Within two years of the anthrax scare, for example, U.S. post offices began installing alarm systems designed to detect the presence of anthrax spores in mail-handling facilities.[26]

Self Check Fill in the Blanks

"WMDs" is an acronym for "weapons of _____." These weapons, which have the potential to do significant damage, include (1) _____ weapons, which are living organisms; (2) _____ weapons, which are manufactured to cause great harm; and (3) _____ weapons, whose destructive power comes from their massive release of heat and energy. Despite the attention given to WMD threats, most terrorist attacks feature _____ explosives, which are cheaper and easier to hide and transport.

Check your answers on page 559.

The Homeland Security Response

On September 12, 2001, President George W. Bush made a public promise that the "United States of America will use all our resources to conquer this enemy."[27] In private, he told then Attorney General John Ashcroft, "John, make sure [the September 11 attack] doesn't happen again."[28] Ashcroft responded by issuing a warning to "the terrorists among us":

> If you violate a local law, you will be put in jail and kept in custody as long as possible. We will use every available statute. We will seek every prosecutorial advantage. We will use all our weapons within the law and under the Constitution to protect life and enhance security for America.[29]

So far in this chapter we have concentrated on the nature of terrorism and the threat that it poses. Now we turn our attention to the "weapons within the law and under the Constitution" that the United States has at its disposal to counter this threat. Eventually, this discussion will lead us to an examination of the tactics used by law enforcement agents and other government actors to combat terrorism, along with the controversies that these tactics have sparked. We start, however, with an examination of the "rules" governing counterterrorism and the agencies and individuals that are bound by them.

Antiterrorism and Effective Death Penalty Act of 1996 (AEDPA) Legislation giving law enforcement officers the power to arrest and prosecute any individual who provides "material support or resources" to a "foreign terrorist organization."

THE ANTITERRORISM AND EFFECTIVE DEATH PENALTY ACT

Signed into law by President Bill Clinton on April 24, 1996, the **Antiterrorism and Effective Death Penalty Act (AEDPA)** was passed in response to the 1995 truck bombing of the Alfred P. Murrah Federal Building in Oklahoma City, Oklahoma. The primary goal of the AEDPA is to hamstring terrorist organizations by cutting off their funding from outside sources. The law prohibits persons from "knowingly providing material support or resources" to any group that the United States has designated a "foreign terrorist organization," or FTO.[30] Each year, the U.S. secretary of state is required to provide Congress with a list of these FTOs, loosely defined to cover organizations that are (1) foreign, (2) engage in terrorist activity, and (3) threaten the security of U.S. citizens or the United States itself.[31] The 2007 edition of this list included forty-four such organizations, most of them based in the Middle East.[32]

"Material support" is also defined very broadly in the legislation, covering currency, financial services, lodging, training, expert advice or assistance, communications equipment, transportation, and other physical assets.[33] The "knowingly" requirement applies to all material support except for direct monetary donations to FTOs—this act is a strict liability crime (see Chapter 4). Consequently, even if a person is unaware that the recipient of charitable giving is involved in terrorist activity, he or she can be prosecuted under the AEDPA.[34]

▼ Former attorney Lynne Stewart, shown here at a rally in Manhattan, was found by a New York jury to have passed messages from an imprisoned client, Sheik Omar Abdel-Rahman, to terrorist operatives in Egypt. Convicted of providing material support to terrorists, in October 2006 Stewart was sentenced to twenty-eight months in prison. How does this case show the federal government's broad interpretation of the term "material support"?

AP Photo/Louis Lanzano

THE PATRIOT ACT

The original AEDPA did not include the provision making a donation to an FTO a strict liability crime. This amendment was part of the far-reaching scope of the **Patriot Act,** signed into law by President George W. Bush on October 26, 2001, just six weeks after the September 11, 2001, terrorist attacks.[35]

"Leveling the Playing Field" As we have seen throughout this textbook, particularly in Chapters 6 and 10, the emphasis on the rights of the accused in the American criminal justice system often makes it difficult to arrest and convict suspected criminals. The Patriot Act is the result of a strong impulse in Washington, D.C., and elsewhere to "level the playing field" when it comes to terrorists. The legislation makes it easier for law enforcement agents to collect information about those suspected of committing terrorist acts or having knowledge of terrorist activity and then detain them based on that information. It enhances the power of the federal government to keep noncitizens under suspicion of having terrorist sympathies from entering the United States, and, as we have seen, it targets the fund-raising of terrorist enterprises.

A massive piece of legislation, the Patriot Act is difficult to summarize. Selected aspects are listed here, however, to provide a general idea of the statute's goals, as well as its methods of achieving them.[36]

- The act relaxes restrictions on information sharing between various U.S. law enforcement agencies and other governmental departments concerning suspected terrorists.
- It creates the crime of knowingly harboring a terrorist.
- It allows law enforcement agents greater freedom in seizing the e-mail records of suspected terrorists.
- It authorizes funds to triple the number of border patrol agents, customs inspectors, and immigration enforcement officers along the United States' northern border with Canada.
- It allows the federal government to detain non-U.S. citizens suspected of terrorist activity for up to seven days without informing them of the charges on which they are being held.
- It eliminates the statute of limitations (see page 310) for prosecution of the most serious terrorism-related crimes.

(To learn more about one of many controversial provisions in the Patriot Act, see the feature *You Be the Judge—Free Speech in the Age of Terrorism.*)

Renewing the Patriot Act Partly because of the speed with which the Patriot Act was pieced together and approved, many lawmakers and their constituents were wary of its long-term impact on the civil rights of all Americans and not just those of suspected terrorists. Consequently, a "sunset provision" was added to the initial legislation, meaning that it would expire if not renewed by Congress within four years. After several delays, Congress did just that on March 7, 2006, with a few minor changes.[37] Nevertheless, the Patriot Act remains a target of criticism for many supposed abuses of the U.S. Constitution, which we will examine later in the chapter.

THE DEPARTMENT OF HOMELAND SECURITY

While the Patriot Act transformed the legal landscape of America's counterterrorism efforts, the Homeland Security Act of 2002 had a similar effect on the inner workings of the U.S. government.[38] Prior to this legislation, disaster management at the federal level was primarily the responsibility of the Federal Emergency Management Agency (FEMA). The act placed FEMA, as well as twenty-one other federal agencies, under the control of the Department of Homeland Security (DHS). Descriptions of those agencies within the DHS that have traditionally been oriented toward law enforcement can be found in Chapter 5, and we will not repeat that discussion here. Instead, this section will focus on the DHS's organizational structure, shown in ■ Figure 16.3 on page 536.

Patriot Act Legislation passed in the wake of the September 11, 2001, terrorist attacks that greatly expanded the ability of government agents to monitor and apprehend suspected terrorists.

The Office of the Secretary As you can see in Figure 16.3, at the top of the DHS "totem pole" is the secretary of homeland security, a cabinet-level public servant who reports directly to the president. The current DHS secretary is Michael Chertoff, who replaced the first person to hold the post, former Pennsylvania governor Tom Ridge, in 2003.

A wide variety of federal agencies answer directly to the secretary of homeland security. The Office of Health Affairs, for example, coordinates all the medical activities of the DHS, including preparation for and response to the heath effects of a WMD attack. The Directorate of Science and Technology partners with private companies, national laboratories, universities, and domestic and foreign government agencies to develop counterterrorism technologies. The Office of the Inspector General audits the entire DHS to ensure that its budget—a requested $46 billion in 2008[39]—is spent with efficiency and a minimum of waste.

The Agencies of the DHS The seven agencies lined up across the bottom rung of Figure 16.3 represent the "front line" of the DHS's antiterrorism efforts. The responsibilities of U.S. Customs and Border Protection (CBP), U.S. Immigration and Customs Enforcement (ICE), the U.S. Secret Service, and the U.S. Coast Guard were explained earlier (see pages 144–145). The others, though not

You Be the Judge Free Speech in the Age of Terrorism

THE FACTS Sami is a citizen of Saudi Arabia. He is studying computer science at the University of Idaho when federal law enforcement agents arrest him for violating the Patriot Act. He is accused of helping design several Web sites for the Islamic Assembly of North America, a Michigan-based group that is suspected of having ties with international terrorism. The Web sites contain four *fatwas,* or religious edicts, issued by Muslim clerics that advocate "martyrdom attacks"; one of the *fatwas* specifically endorses crashing airplanes into enemy targets. (Sami's arrest takes place after September 11, 2001.) The sites also include links to the official Web pages of the Palestinian-based terrorist group Hamas and feature messages requesting Muslim members of the U.S. military to provide sensitive information. Federal prosecutors are not claiming that Sami wrote any of the offending material or even that he supports terrorist causes. They insist, however, that he committed a crime by designing the Web sites.

THE LAW Under the Patriot Act, providing "material support" for terrorists includes "advice or assistance derived from scientific, technical or other specialized knowledge." Federal prosecutors claim that Sami violated this provision, and they have charged him with crimes that could lead to a forty-five-year prison sentence. Sami's attorneys admit that he helped set up the Web sites, but claim these actions constitute free speech as protected by the First Amendment to the U.S. Constitution.

YOUR DECISION In the words of U.S. District Court Judge Edward Lodge, the First Amendment protects the expression of beliefs "even if those beliefs advocate the use of force or violation of law," unless the speech is "directed to inciting or producing imminent lawless action." The prosecutors argue that they are not punishing speech, but rather the technical assistance that Sami provided that allowed others to commit illegal acts. They compare Sami's conduct with that of a person who gives his friend a gun, knowing that the friend intends to use the gun to commit armed robbery but not necessarily believing that robbery is the "right thing" to do. Do you think that Sami is guilty of violating the Patriot Act? Even if he is, how can this particular provision of the legislation be reconciled with the First Amendment?

[To see how an Idaho jury ruled in this case, go to Example 16.1 in Appendix B.]

■ **Figure 16.3** U.S. Department of Homeland Security

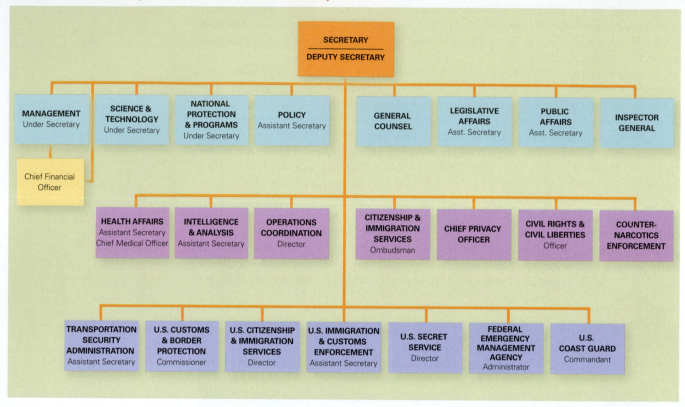

considered law enforcement agencies, play a crucial role in preventing and responding to terrorist-related activity.

- The *Transportation Security Administration (TSA)* is responsible for the safe operation of our airline, rail, bus, and ferry services.
- *United States Citizenship and Immigration Services (USCIS)* handles the "paperwork" side of U.S. immigration law. In other words, it processes the more than 7 million applications made each year by immigrants who want to visit the United States or reside or work in this country.
- *FEMA* retains its position as the lead federal agency in preparing for and responding to disasters such as hurricanes, floods, terrorist attacks, and *infrastructure* concerns. The term **infrastructure** refers to the facilities and systems that provide the daily necessities of modern life such as electric power, food, water, transportation, and telecommunications.

Some critics of the DHS argue that its immense bureaucratic structure has dulled the effectiveness of individual agencies, which must now go through a chain of command rather than relying on their own initiative. FEMA, in particular, was the target of a firestorm of criticism following its less-than-stellar response to Hurricane Katrina, which devastated the Gulf Coast of the United States in 2005. That same year, Secretary Chertoff promised to address these concerns in a six-point reorganization of the DHS, but the very bureaucracy he intends to change has held up many aspects of the plan.[40]

FEDERAL AGENCIES OUTSIDE THE DHS

Infrastructure The services and facilities that support the day-to-day needs of modern life such as electricity, food, transportation, and water.

The DHS does not directly control all federal efforts to combat terrorism. Since September 11, 2001, the Federal Bureau of Investigation (FBI), a branch of the Department of Justice, has been the "lead federal agency" for all terrorism-related matters. Its Strategic Information Operations Center serves as an information clearinghouse for federal, state, and local law enforcement agents who want to share information on terrorism-related matters. Indeed, the agency now lists "protecting the United States from terrorist attack" as its highest organizational priority.[41]

The *intelligence* agencies of the U.S. government also play an important role in antiterrorism efforts. As opposed to a law enforcement agency, which works to solve crimes that have already occurred, an **intelligence agency** works to prevent crimes or other undesirable acts by gathering information, or "intelligence," on potential wrongdoers and stopping the illegal conduct "in the planning stage." Intelligence operations rely on the following strategies to collect information:

1. Electronic surveillance of phone and e-mail communications, as well as advanced recording devices placed on satellites, aircraft, and land-based technology centers.
2. *Human-source collection*, which refers to the recruitment of foreign agents and interviews with people who have particular knowledge about areas of interest.
3. *Open-source collection*, or close attention to "open" data sources such as books, newspapers, radio and television transmissions, and Internet sites.
4. Intelligence sharing with friendly foreign intelligence services.
5. *Counterintelligence*, which involves placing undercover agents in a position to gain information from hostile foreign intelligence services.[42]

In particular, two intelligence agencies are integral to American antiterrorism efforts. The first is the **Central Intelligence Agency (CIA),** which is responsible for gathering and analyzing information on foreign governments, corporations, and individuals, and then passing that information on to the upper echelons of our federal government. The second, the **National Security Agency (NSA),** is also in the business of gathering and analyzing information, but it focuses primarily on communications. NSA agents eavesdrop on foreign "conversations," whatever form they might take, while at the same time working to ensure that sensitive messages sent by the U.S. government are not subjected to similar scrutiny.

STATE AND LOCAL COUNTERTERRORISM EFFORTS

Even with the significant resources of the DHS and the extensive expertise of organizations such as the FBI and the CIA, the federal government cannot effectively protect this nation against terrorism without help. As we pointed out in Chapter 1, the vast majority of law enforcement officers in the United States are members of state and local agencies. These officers are in a much better position than their federal counterparts to notice something out of the ordinary on a local level or to make a low-level arrest that could have homeland security implications. Since September 11, 2001, almost every state law enforcement agency and about a quarter of local law enforcement agencies (primarily in the most-populated municipalities) have formed specialized terrorism units.[43]

Cooperation and Fusion Many experts worry that the nation's state and local police forces have not been properly trained for their new counterterrorism responsibilities.[44] To this end, the FBI increased the number of its Joint Terrorism Task Forces (JTTFs) from thirty-five to more than one hundred between 2001 and 2007. These units are made up of teams of state and local law enforcement officers, FBI agents, and other federal agents who cooperate to investigate and prevent terrorist acts.[45] Ideally, a JTTF should provide benefits for both sides. The FBI can take advantage of the greater numbers of local officers, while the local agencies receive valuable training and assistance from their federal counterparts. In addition, all agencies involved in the JTTF are better able to share information and intelligence with each other.[46]

Intelligence Agency An agency that is primarily concerned with gathering information about potential criminal or terrorist events in order to prevent those acts from taking place.

Central Intelligence Agency (CIA) The U.S. government agency that is responsible for collecting and coordinating foreign intelligence operations.

National Security Agency (NSA) The intelligence agency that is responsible for protecting U.S. government communications and producing intelligence by monitoring foreign communications.

The federal government has made other efforts to include state and local police in its antiterrorism efforts. The FBI's fifty-six Field Intelligence Groups collect and analyze terrorism-related intelligence and dispense their findings to other law enforcement agencies. In almost fifty "fusion centers" scattered across the United States, municipal police are given the opportunity to collaborate with federal agents on terrorist and criminal investigations. The federal government's Terrorist Screening Center (TSC) allows local police officers to check the names of suspicious individuals against a national "watch list" of terrorist suspects.

Dissatisfaction and Confusion Despite these efforts, many state and local administrators are dissatisfied with the aid, or lack thereof, that they have received from the federal government since September 11, 2001. The budgetary and personnel resources of many local police departments have been overwhelmed by their new security demands. A 183-city survey conducted in 2006 by the United States Conference of Mayors found that 80 percent of the respondents lacked sufficient assets to deal with a terrorist attack.[47]

The "Squeeze" on Local Law Enforcement Statistics strongly suggest that the FBI's new focus on terrorism has caused it to turn away from its other crime-fighting duties. A report from the Office of the Inspector General shows that the FBI initiated 67,782 criminal investigations in 2000. By 2004, that number had dropped to 34,451, a reduction of almost 50 percent.[48] These crimes have become the responsibility of local or state police organizations that are already shorthanded because they have diverted resources to homeland security. The Long Beach (California) Police Department, for example, has reassigned officers from its white-collar crime unit, illegal drugs division, and foot patrols to focus on terrorism.

This "squeeze" has had tangible consequences. In Philadelphia, the number of drug-related murders increased 50 percent in the first month after September 11, 2001, a development attributed to the decision to move a number of narcotics division detectives to uniformed patrols of city streets.[49] Some observers feel that the recent increase in violent crime, discussed in Chapter 3, is the result of this shift away from traditional policing. "We need a national movement that recognizes that while homeland security is important, hometown security is equally important," said Doug H. Palmer, mayor of Trenton, New Jersey.[50]

▼ New York City police officers check a passenger's bag at a subway entrance. What kind of strain has homeland security placed on local police departments?

Communication Issues Another area of concern for many local police officials is the lack of communication with federal agencies on terrorism-related subjects. In 2006, for example, the FBI conducted an extensive operation to apprehend Derrick Shareef, a Muslim convert who was planning to set off several grenades at a Rockford, Illinois, shopping center during the holiday season. After Shareef was arrested, Rockford Police Chief Chet Epperson said that his officers had very little involvement or knowledge of the investigation, and admitted that cooperation with the FBI was "not good."[51]

Frustration with such incidents has spurred police chiefs from a dozen of the nation's largest cities to create their own informal information-sharing system. In announcing the new system, Los Angeles Police Chief William Bratton said that most federal agents were more interested in gathering information than in providing local police departments with useful "real-time" intelligence. "We're used to things breaking very quickly and have to respond quickly," said Chief Bratton. "We don't have the luxury of waiting."[52] Federal law enforcement officials, while recognizing the importance of greater cooperation with metropolitan police units, do face a dilemma when it comes to sharing intelligence with them: most local law enforcement agents do not have the security clearance to handle classified information.

INTERNATIONAL COUNTERTERRORISM EFFORTS

American counterterrorism efforts rely not only on cooperation between the various levels of domestic law enforcement agencies, but also on cooperation with international partners. As nonstate actors, terrorists often operate on a global scale: the September 11 hijackers, for example, trained in the Middle East, developed their plans in western Europe, and carried out their attacks in the United States. Consequently, *coalitions*, or alliances between different nations, play a crucial role in the fight against terrorism.

Jurisdictional Restraints Because of *jurisdictional* rules (see pages 247–248), U.S. law enforcement agents are restricted in their ability to operate on foreign soil. Consequently, sometimes they must rely on foreign police to apprehend persons conspiring against American targets from abroad. Police in Trinidad, for example, arrested three of the suspects in the plot to ignite fuel pipelines at New York's JFK Airport, discussed in the introduction to this chapter. Furthermore, the jurisdiction of American courts rarely extends to non-U.S. citizens captured in other countries, even if they are alleged to have committed crimes involving the United States or its citizens. In 2007, a German court sentenced Mounir el-Motassedeq to fifteen years in prison for his role in planning the September 11, 2001, attacks. Motassedeq would probably have received a harsher punishment had he been convicted in the United States, but, having been arrested in Germany, he was under the jurisdiction of the German court system.

Extraditing Terrorist Suspects In Chapter 8, we saw that a country can choose to surrender its jurisdictional rights if it *extradites* a person to a different country. In May 2007, Syed Hashmi became the first terrorism suspect extradited to the United States by Great Britain. British authorities had arrested Hashmi as he boarded a flight from London to Pakistan ten months earlier, and eventually agreed to send him to America to face charges of providing al Qaeda fighters with equipment to be used against U.S. military forces in the Middle East. Previously, Great Britain had refused to extradite terrorist suspects to the United States because of the possibility that they could be subjected to the death penalty.[53]

Self Check Fill in the Blanks

The primary goal of the Antiterrorism and Effective Death Penalty Act (AEDPA) is to prohibit persons from providing _____ support to known terrorists. Passed weeks after September 11, 2001, the _____ Act makes it easier for government agents to monitor terrorist suspects. The Homeland Security Act of 2002 created the Department of _____, which oversees the counterterrorism efforts of twenty-two federal agencies. The National Security Agency is an example of an _____ agency that gathers information used to prevent crimes or other wrongdoing. Check your answers on page 559.

Counterterrorism Challenges and Strategies

On September 4, 2001, someone asked White House counterterrorism expert Richard Clarke, "Is al Qaeda a big deal?" He replied that the federal government had not yet made up its mind.[54] A week later, of course, the question became moot. Clarke's response, however, was indicative of the low priority given to terrorism by federal law enforcement officials before September 11, 2001. The FBI, in particular, has come under withering criticism for its lackadaisical efforts in this area. In 2004, the chair of an independent congressional panel investigating the September 11 attacks (the 9/11 Commission) said of the agency, "It failed and it failed and it failed and it failed."[55]

During the months prior to September 11, the FBI and other government agencies did uncover a number of leads that, in retrospect, pointed to a major terrorist incident:

- In July 2001, an FBI agent based in Phoenix, Arizona, sent a memo to his superiors warning that Osama bin Laden had been sending operatives to flight training schools in the United States. Officials at the FBI headquarters in Washington, D.C., did not see the memo until after several of those American-trained operatives had piloted the airplanes used in the September 11 attacks.

- In August 2001, another FBI agent, this one based in Minneapolis, Minnesota, was unable to persuade his superiors that the French Muslim Zacarias Moussaoui, who had just been arrested on immigration charges, posed a threat. The frustrated agent never was given permission to search Moussaoui's possessions, which included numerous small knives, rosters of flight schools, jet pilot manuals, and other clues. Moussaoui is the only September 11 conspirator to have been convicted in the United States.

- The CIA suspected as early as March 2000 that Khalid al-Midhar and Nawaf Alhazmi had ties to al Qaeda, but the agency did not share this information with the FBI until three weeks before the attacks. Consequently, as the CIA does not operate within U.S. borders, nothing was done to limit the movements of these two men on American soil, and they were both on the plane that crashed into the Pentagon.

In light of the federal government's inability to take advantage of these leads and numerous others, the 9/11 Commission said that the "most important failure" of the nation's leaders prior to the September 11 attacks was "one of imagination."[56] In other words, because our criminal justice and intelligence experts could not imagine such a attack, they were powerless to prevent it. Today, no such imagination is necessary. With memories of the falling towers and a smoldering Pentagon still fresh, the U.S. homeland security apparatus has, as you will see, developed a wide variety of methods to protect America from terrorist activity.

PREVENTIVE POLICING

In December 2005, Narseal Batiste met with a man he believed to be an al Qaeda operative in Miami, Florida. Batiste apparently told this person that he and six other men from a Haitian neighborhood known as Liberty City wanted to bomb the Sears Tower in Chicago and "kill all the devils we can" in an act of destruction that would be "just as good or greater than 9/11."[57] Unfortunately for Batiste, the al Qaeda "contact" was actually an FBI informant. In June 2006, Batiste and his comrades were arrested and charged with conspiracy to provide material support to a foreign terrorist organization, conspiracy to provide material support and resources to terrorists, conspiracy to maliciously damage and destroy by means of an explosive, and conspiracy to levy war against the United States.

LO6

Taking No Chances In Chapter 4, we saw that criminal law generally requires intent and action; that is, a person must have both intended to commit a crime and taken some steps toward doing so. In most cases, criminal law also requires that a harm has been done and that the criminal act caused the harm. According to federal officials, however, no evidence showed that Narseal Batiste and the other members of the "Liberty Seven" had the ingredients or written instructions needed to make explosives. They possessed no details of the layout of the Sears Tower or any other building and had forged no links with any real terrorist group. FBI Deputy Director John Pistole called Batiste and his followers "more aspirational than operational."[58]

The case of the "Liberty Seven" represents a growing trend in the criminal justice system brought about by the new challenges of fighting terrorism. The goal for many law enforcement agencies is no longer to solve crimes after they have occurred, but rather to prevent them from happening in the first place. Even though Narseal Batiste and his followers did not, in the words of one observer, "have a pot to pee in,"[59] federal authorities were not prepared to take the risk that they could evolve into a real threat. Although some observers claim that law enforcement officials are exaggerating the threat posed by many of these accused plotters, the government points to a record of successes to justify this new approach.[60] (See ■ Figure 16.4.)

■ Figure 16.4 Preventive Policing: The Age of the Foiled Plot

Testifying before Congress in 2001, then Attorney General John Ashcroft succinctly outlined the nation's new law enforcement strategy regarding domestic terrorists: "Prevent first, prosecute second." This blueprint has led to dozens of "quick strikes" against alleged terrorists, including the JFK Airport plot discussed in the introduction to this chapter and the five examples listed here.

Attacking Fort Dix
May 2007

The Plot: Six radical Islamists planned to attack New Jersey's Fort Dix military base and "kill as many soldiers as possible."

How Far It Got: The group engaged in weapons training in Pennsylvania and attempted to purchase weapons, including rocket-propelled grenades and AK-47 machine guns, from an FBI informant.

The Result: The six suspects have been charged with conspiring to kill U.S. government employees.

The "Liberty Seven"
June 2006

The Plot: Seven men living in the Liberty City area of Miami, Florida, talked of blowing up the Sears Tower in Chicago and a Miami FBI office.

How Far It Got: The suspects asked an undercover FBI informer posing as an al Qaeda operative for money, weapons, binoculars, and boots. One of the suspects made a video of the FBI office in Miami. The group never established contact with any actual terrorist group.

The Result: The suspects have been charged with conspiracy to support al Qaeda.

Assassinating George W. Bush
February 2005

The Plot: Ahmed Omar Abu Ali, an Arab American student, expressed a desire to join al Qaeda and traveled to Saudi Arabia to study at the Islamic University of Medina.

How Far It Got: Abu Ali is quoted as telling Saudi police, "My idea was . . . I would walk on the street as the President walked by, and I would get close enough to shoot him, or I would use a car bomb." He later claimed that this confession was extracted by torture.

The Result: Abu Ali was sentenced to thirty years in prison in the the United States for conspiracy to commit acts of terrorism.

The "Paintball" Terrorists
June 2003

The Plot: A group of Virginians trained to wage worldwide *jihad* by engaging in paintball games and other training activities.

How Far It Got: Several members of the group traveled to Pakistan to train with the Lashkar-e-Taiba terrorist group, but there was no evidence that the men had concrete plans to take part in a terrorist attack.

The Result: Eleven members of the group were convicted of various terrorism-related crimes and received sentences ranging from four years to life in prison.

The "Lackawanna Six"
September 2002

The Plot: A man named Kamal Derwish recruited six young Muslim men from the small town of Lackawanna, New York, to take part in an al Qaeda training camp in Afghanistan just before September 11, 2001.

How Far It Got: The men were trained in weapons' use and exposed to anti-American propaganda films and lectures at the camp before returning to the United States. Investigators do not know what al Qaeda had in mind for the recruits.

The Result: The six defendants were given sentences ranging from seven to ten years for aiding al Qaeda.

Source: Jane A. Bullock, *et al., Introduction to Homeland Security*, 2d. ed (Burlington, MA: Butterworth-Heinemann, 2006), 156–157, 160–163.

The Criminal Justice Model As noted earlier in the chapter, both the AEDPA and the Patriot Act contain provisions making it illegal to offer "material support" to terrorist organizations. Thus, these laws permit law enforcement agents to arrest suspects even though no crime, in the traditional sense of the word, has taken place and no evident harm has been caused. The AEDPA and the Patriot Act are crucial aspects of America's *criminal justice model* response to terrorism. Under this model, terrorism is treated like any other crime, and the law enforcement, court, and correctional systems work together to deter terrorist activity through the threat of arrest and punishment.

The First Attack on New York Before September 11, 2001, the criminal justice model was our primary response to terrorist activity on American soil. In 1993, for example, a car bomb exploded in the basement of the World Trade Center in New York City, killing six people and injuring more than one thousand. Following an intense investigation, law enforcement agents were able to identify and apprehend the members of the fundamentalist Islamic group responsible for the act. Foreign governments provided aid in the worldwide search for the suspects. In fact, police in Pakistan arrested Ramzi Yousef, who planned the bombing, and extradited him to the United States to stand trial. Though one suspect remains at large, the remaining perpetrators were tried, convicted, and sentenced in the U.S. District Court for the Southern District of New York.[61]

The Criminal Justice Disadvantage There is no doubt that the criminal justice system has been a very active participant in the efforts against terrorism. In 2006 alone, the government prosecuted 194 people for involvement in international terrorism, domestic terrorism, or terrorist financing. Between 2002 and February 2007, federal prosecutors secured nearly 900 convictions for terrorism or terrorist-related activity,[62] including, as we saw in Chapter 11, that of 9/11 co-conspirator Zacarias Moussaoui.

Almost all of these convictions, however, have been for relatively minor acts such as providing material support or conspiracy, rather than actual terrorism. To a certain degree, the criminal justice system is at a disadvantage in the "war" against terrorism because it offers little protection against large-scale attacks, especially when terrorists are willing to commit suicide in the process and are therefore impervious to deterrence. After-the-fact punishment, no matter how harsh, of someone who may be responsible for hundreds of thousands of deaths also strikes many as irrelevant as a response to the damage that has already been done.

THE INTELLIGENCE MODEL

Many experts believe that the *intelligence model*, rather than the criminal justice model, should be the nation's blueprint for combating terrorism. The intelligence model regards terrorist activities as threats to the security of the state rather than as criminal acts.[63] Instead of attempting to deter wrongdoing with the threat of arrest and punishment, the goal of an intelligence investigation, as we have seen, is to gather information that will keep the wrongdoing from happening in the first place.

The "MI5 Solution" A textbook example of a successful intelligence operation occurred in 2006, when an undercover British agent infiltrated a group of terrorists who were in the final stages of a plot to blow up as many as ten airplanes en route from Britain to the United States. MI5, the British intelligence agency, had been tracking the plot, which involved nearly fifty people, for two months before deciding to arrest the suspects.

As a reaction to America's intelligence failures prior to September 11, 2001, a number of politicians and criminal justice experts called for an "MI5 solution": the formation of a single U.S. domestic intelligence agency to replace the inefficient network of federal agencies with intelligence responsibilities. Each one of these organizations—the FBI, the CIA, the U.S. Department of State, the U.S. military, and many others—was capable of gathering valuable intelligence, but they seemed incapable of pooling their knowledge in any meaningful manner. According to the 9/11 Commission, the biggest problem with American intelligence was the "human or systematic resistance to sharing information."[64]

Reforming the FBI The FBI, as we have seen, came under particular criticism for its mishandling of pre–September 11 intelligence. The problem has been that FBI agents see themselves primarily as "door-kicking" crime investigators, not desk-bound intelligence agents sifting through reams of data. Philip D. Zeiklow, the executive director of the 9/11 Commission, observed that FBI agents "don't ask questions the way an intelligence agent would ask questions. The FBI agent is typically interested in the facts of an event [whereas] an intelligence agent is really interested in a person's whole world."[65]

Under severe political pressure, the FBI has made a concerted effort to recast itself as an effective intelligence agency. More than two thousand agents—about 15 percent of the total—have been reassigned from traditional crime-fighting positions to terrorism-related posts since 2001. Hundreds of analysts with backgrounds in areas such as international relations and mathematics have been hired to assess threats identified by agents in the field. Each FBI field office produces a monthly intelligence bulletin that summarizes potential terrorist activity in the region. A 2007 bulletin for the Houston FBI Field Office, for example, contained a report on two Mexican citizens apprehended carrying a large amount of Iraqi currency. It also noted that a man arrested in a bar fight in College Station, Texas, had the word *jihad* show up on his cell phone as part of a text message.[66]

Local Intelligence The degree to which homeland security needs are causing a shift from the criminal justice model to the intelligence model in American law enforcement is evident in the recent emphasis on "intelligence-led" policing throughout the country. Over the past five years, the U.S. Department of Justice and DHS have contributed more than $500 million to state and local police departments for intelligence purposes. This funding has helped create more than one hundred nonfederal police intelligence units, with at least one in every state.[67]

"Intelligence used to be a dirty word" for local police departments, according to David Carter, a professor of criminal justice at Michigan State University.[68] Today, however, cities such as Atlanta, Chicago, Los Angeles, and Las Vegas have as many as eighty officers working the counterterrorism beat. The New York Police Department, in a class by itself, has more than one thousand personnel assigned to homeland security and has stationed agents in six foreign countries. Thanks to the FBI's Joint Terrorism Task Forces and the "fusion" centers discussed earlier in the chapter, state and local police departments also have more opportunities to share intelligence with their federal counterparts.

THE MILITARY MODEL

The American government has made it clear that, besides the criminal justice model and the intelligence model, there is a third response to the terrorist threat: the *military model.* "There are cases in which our criminal justice system is the appropriate way to deliver justice," said then U.S. Attorney General Alberto Gonzales, "but there are also instances in which the national security of the United States requires a military response."[69] Although the scope of this textbook does not include U.S. military actions in Afghanistan, Iraq, and other "hot spots," the militarization of the fight against terrorists has led to several developments with repercussions for the criminal justice system.

Enemy Combatants Within a week of September 11, 2001, the U.S. Congress passed the Authorization for Use of Military Force (AUMF), which gave the president permission to "use all necessary and appropriate force" against those responsible for the attacks.[70] With the AUMF as justification, President Bush ordered the U.S. Department of Defense to designate certain terrorist suspects detained in the course of military operations as **enemy combatants.** According to the federal government, the term refers to a non-U.S. citizen

> who was part of or supporting Taliban [a militant Islamic organization opposed to U.S. troops in Afghanistan] or al Qaeda forces, or associated forces that are engaged in hostilities against the United States or its coalition partners. This includes any person who has committed a belligerent act or has directly supported hostilities in aid of enemy armed forces.[71]

The U.S. government had acted under the assumption that once a person has been designated an enemy combatant, he or she "can be held indefinitely until the end of America's war on terrorism or until the military determines on a case by case basis that the particular detainee no longer poses a threat to the United States or its allies."[72] Nearly eight hundred enemy combatants have been held at the U.S. Naval Base at Guantánamo Bay, Cuba, since the start of U.S. military actions in Afghanistan and Iraq. The methods for determining whether these detainees deserve this designation, as well as their means of eventual release, have generated a great deal of controversy, which we will discuss later in the chapter.

The PCA and Terrorism As we saw in Chapter 5, the Posse Comitatus Act (PCA) prohibits the use of the U.S. military in a law enforcement role unless expressly authorized by a presidential order or an act of Congress.[73] One exception to the PCA is the National Guard (see page 149), a reserve military force that can be called to active duty in "defense of the nation." This vague condition has been applied numerous times in the wake of natural disasters, when the Guard is activated to aid overwhelmed local law enforcement personnel. The Guard has also been used for antiterrorism purposes; after September 11, it provided extra security for commercial airports across the nation.

Many observers wonder how strong the federal government's commitment to the PCA actually is under present circumstances. In 2002, President Bush set up the U.S. Northern Command (NORTHCOM) and ordered it to provide military support for homeland security efforts.[74] Then, three years later, the unacceptable federal, state, and local responses to Hurricane Katrina spurred the president to suggest that the U.S. military be put in charge of natural disaster management, an arrangement that would contradict the PCA.[75] For some, these actions suggest that the president is not completely adverse to the idea of "calling in the troops" should another major disaster—either natural or human-made—strike the United States.[76]

EMERGENCY PREPAREDNESS AND RESPONSE

Several years ago, the Pentagon asked NORTHCOM to develop plans for responding to multiple terrorist attacks on the United States. NORTHCOM officials contemplated a "worst-case scenario"—three simultaneous strikes—and concluded that about 3,000 military troops, including members of the National Guard, would need to be sent to the site of each attack.[77] Such planning, as part of an overall strategy of *preparedness,* is an integral part of homeland security.

Preparedness and Response The White House defines **preparedness** as the "existence of plans, procedures, policies, training, and equipment necessary at

Enemy Combatant A label given to certain persons suspected of terrorist activities by the U.S. government. Persons given this designation can be detained indefinitely without review of their status.

Preparedness An umbrella term for the actions taken by governments to prepare for large-scale catastrophic events such as terrorist attacks or environmental disasters.

the federal, state, and local level to maximize the ability to prevent, respond to, and recover from major events."[78] The term has come to describe a wide variety of actions taken at different governmental levels to protect a community not only against terrorist attacks, but also against natural disasters such as hurricanes, tornadoes, and floods. The Oakland County (Michigan) Emergency Operations Center, for example, combines the contributions of thirty-four different local agencies, each one organized and prepared for a different type of emergency.

A necessary correlate to preparedness is *response*, or the actions taken after an incident has occurred. Because the federal government is usually unable to respond rapidly to any single incident, the burden of response initially falls on local emergency personnel such as police officers, firefighters, and emergency medical technicians. These aptly named **first responders** have several important duties, including the following:

▲ During a training drill in Miami, Florida, trainers check a police officer for nuclear contamination. These exercises are designed to help the officers overcome terrorists using weapons of mass destruction. Why are local police officers so important to emergency preparedness and response strategies?

- Securing the scene of the incident by maintaining order.
- Rescuing and treating any injured civilians.
- Containing and suppressing fires or other hazardous conditions that have resulted from the incident.
- Retrieving those who have been killed.[79]

First responders often show great bravery in carrying out their duties under extremely dangerous circumstances. On September 11, 2001, 343 firefighters and 75 police officers were killed in the line of duty.

Preparedness Concerns Between 2001 and 2007, the federal government provided more than $18 billion in funding to help local and state government preparation and response. Recently, however, the Homeland Security Preparedness Survey, distributed to more than 17,000 state, local, tribal, and federal law enforcement agencies by the International Association of Chiefs of Police, revealed high levels of dissatisfaction. Seventy-one percent of those responding indicated that their agency was either "somewhat" or "not at all" prepared to prevent a terrorist attack. Ninety-four percent identified "critical incident response" training as their most urgent need.[80] In 2007, only six of seventy-five metropolitan areas tested by the DHS received "top" grades for their emergency agencies' ability to communicate with each other during a disaster.[81]

Self Check Fill in the Blanks

Since September 11, 2001, law enforcement agencies have been taking steps to _____ terrorist-related wrongdoing before it gets beyond the planning stage. This strategy is a departure from the _____ model of combating terrorism, which treats a terrorist act like any other crime. Under the intelligence model, the _____, America's leading federal law enforcement agency, has had to adapt to the needs of counterterrorism. The _____ model of antiterrorist strategy is constrained by a federal law that prohibits soldiers from engaging in law enforcement on U.S. soil. Check your answers on page 559.

First Responders Those individuals, such as firefighters, police officers, and emergency medical technicians, who are responsible for the protection and preservation of life and property during the early stages following a disaster.

Border Security

In its final report on the events that led up to September 11, 2001, the 9/11 Commission had plenty of blame to spread around. Poor preparation for a terrorist attack, poor performances by the FBI and other domestic law enforcement agencies, and poor intelligence gathering by the CIA were all highlighted as causes for concern and needed reform. The commission seemed particularly disturbed, however, at the ease with which proven and potential terrorists could enter the United States. "Protecting borders was not a national security issue before 9/11," the report remarked, with more than a hint of disbelief.[82] The protection of our national borders has certainly become an issue since the commission published its report, though questions remain as to whether homeland security has significantly improved as a result.

IMMIGRATION LAW BASICS

An **alien** is someone who is not a citizen of the country in which she or he is found. Somewhere between 11 million and 12 million illegal aliens live in the United States. The vast majority pose no threat to our national security and have come to this country for no other reason than to make a better life for themselves and their families. That having been said, the connection between illegal aliens and terrorism is undeniable. Between 1993 and 2004, 59 of the 94 foreign-born persons either convicted or indicted on terrorism charges had violated federal immigration laws to enter or remain in the United States.[83]

Visa Requirements Most foreign visitors to this country require a valid *visa*. A **visa** is a document issued by the U.S. State Department that indicates the conditions under which the holder can remain within U.S. borders. A person who violates the terms of her or his visa is no longer legally allowed to stay in the country and can be removed by federal officials. Along these same lines, a person who enters the United States without a visa is automatically in violation of immigration law and is considered illegal and removable the instant she or he sets foot on American territory. Generally, if a visa-holder commits a crime while in the United States, he or she is also eligible for immediate removal.

Crucially, immigration law is a form of civil law, *not* criminal law. Therefore, immigration laws offer fewer procedural protections to noncitizens apprehended for immigration violations than are available under criminal law. For example, law enforcement agents do not have to meet the probable cause requirement (discussed in Chapter 7) when stopping a noncitizen for a violation of immigration law.[84] Furthermore, immigration arrestees are not guaranteed court-appointed counsel,[85] and federal law allows a person suspected of violating immigration law to be held for seven days before immigration or criminal charges are filed, and then indefinitely thereafter.[86]

The Role of Immigration Law Officials at the U.S. Immigration and Customs Enforcement (ICE) credit immigration laws for allowing them to apprehend dangerous criminal suspects legally and quickly. In 2003, for example, immigration officials detained Somali-born Nuradin M. Adbi for an immigration violation; a year later, he was indicted for conspiring with an al Qaeda agent to blow up a shopping mall in Columbus, Ohio. Immigration laws also provide federal officials with broad powers to remove suspicious foreigners from the United States without having to prove terrorist connections or criminal charges.

Some critics believe these powers are too broad and allow harsh treatment of illegal aliens who have no connection to terrorist activity. In fact, from 2004 to 2006, federal homeland security agencies initiated 814,073 removal proceedings; only twelve involved terrorist-related charges. Government officials assert that these statistics prove vigilance, not incompetence or bias. "The vast majority of

Alien A person who is not a citizen of the country in which he or she is found and therefore may not enjoy the same rights and protections as a citizen of that country.

Visa Official authorization allowing a person to travel to and within the issuing country.

immigration violations are going to be criminals or economic migrants who arrive illegally, but we're tough for that off-chance [that] one presents a national security concern," explains a DHS spokesperson.[87]

REGULATED PORTS OF ENTRY

People and goods legally enter the United States through checkpoints at airports, seaports, and guarded land stations. At these regulated points of entry, government agents check documentation such as passports and visas and inspect luggage and cargo to ensure compliance with immigration and trade laws. The task is immense: approximately 88 million foreign visitors arrive at America's more than one hundred international airports each year, with millions more passing through patrol stations along our borders with Mexico and Canada.

Legal Loopholes One of the hard lessons of the September 11 attacks was that regulation in this area does not ensure security. Every one of the nineteen hijackers involved in those attacks entered the United States legally—that is, with a valid visa. They were also able to easily board the airplanes that they used as weapons. Consequently, one of the hallmarks of homeland security has been increased scrutiny at points of entry—particularly airports. The DHS's Transportation Security Administration (TSA) has overseen significant changes in the way airports screen passengers, luggage, and cargo. Border personnel have also been trained to look for "terrorist risk factors" in all foreigners entering the United States. In 2003, an official refused entry to a Jordanian named Raed al-Banna at Chicago's O'Hare Airport because of suspicions regarding these risk factors. Two years later, Banna carried out a suicide car bombing that killed 132 people in Hilla, Iraq. (To learn about another way in which the Department of Homeland Security is planning to protect the nation's air travelers, see the feature *CJ and Technology—Project Chloe* on the next page.)

Illegal Presence Another dramatic weakness in America's homeland defenses was exposed by the September 11 plot: an inability to track foreigners who fail to conform to the terms of their visas and are therefore illegally present in the United States. For example, one of the hijackers, the Saudi Arabian Nawaf Alhazmi, entered the country on a B-2 tourist visa on January 15, 2000. Because B-2 visas are valid for only six months, he had already been in the country illegally for more than a year when the attacks occurred. Another, Saudi Arabian Hani Hanjour, was given permission to attend classes at a language center in Oakland, California, on an F-1 student visa in December 2000. By failing to show up for his classes, he also annulled his permission to be in the United States. In total, five of the hijackers had violated their visas—and were therefore eligible for removal from the country—before the attacks occurred. Furthermore, four of the five had had contacts with local police, primarily for traffic violations, before September 11.[88]

To remedy this situation, the DHS created the United States Visitor and Immigrant Status Indicator Technology (US-VISIT) program. Under US-VISIT, which started in 2004, all foreigners entering the United States on visas are subject to fingerprinting and a facial scan using digital photography. Their names are also checked against criminal records and watch lists for suspected terrorists. While the program has been effective in recording the entry of foreigners, it has been less successful in determining their movements once in the United States. In fact, by 2008 US-VISIT still could not determine when, or if, a foreigner had left the country, somewhat defeating its original purpose.

UNREGULATED BORDER ENTRY

Every year approximately 3 million non-U.S. citizens, unable to secure visas, enter the country illegally by crossing the large, unregulated stretches of our borders with Mexico and Canada. Securing these border areas has proved problematic,

WHAT IS PROJECT CHLOE?

For years, the possibility that a hidden terrorist could fire a shoulder-launched missile at a landing or departing commercial airplane has concerned terrorism experts. Project Chloe, named after a character on the television program *24*, is an antimissile system sponsored by the Department of Homeland Security that envisions using remote-controlled spy planes to defend against these sorts of attacks.

HOW DOES PROJECT CHLOE WORK?

An unmanned aerial vehicle (UAV) would hover 65,000 feet above an airport. Once it detected the ultraviolet discharge from a shoulder-fired missile's rocket booster, the UAV would either (1) fire a directed energy weapon such as a high-powered laser or microwave spray at the target or (2) signal a ground-based device to do so. The goal would not be to destroy the missile, but rather to "blind" it by disrupting its heat-seeking sensors and thus sending it off course.

Project Chloe is based, in part, on the success of the U.S. military's remote-controlled Predator drone, which, at an altitude of 2,000 feet, can fire a laser-guided Hellfire missile capable of hitting a target three miles away. The federal government has designated six "airports of interest" to act as testing grounds for Project Chloe and hopes to have the technology operational by 2011.

Department of Homeland Security

THINKING ABOUT PROJECT CHLOE

The airline industry has been testing antimissile laser systems that can be mounted on individual planes since 2002. Researchers have developed viable technology, but its cost—$1 million per plane—and maintenance issues have discouraged airlines from implementing the systems. What is the argument in favor of requiring private companies in the relevant industries to bear some of the costs of homeland security? What is the argument against such an arrangement?

---

if not impossible, for homeland security agencies. Under these conditions, the border areas provide a conduit for illegal drugs, firearms and other contraband, illegal immigrants, and, possibly, terrorists and WMDs to be smuggled into the country.

A Logistical Nightmare The main problem for the U.S. Border Patrol and local law enforcement agents in trying to stem this flow is logistics. The United States has 5,525 miles of border with Canada and 1,989 miles with Mexico. Much of this covers uninhabited plains and woodland to the north and desert and scrubland to the south. Even with almost 13,000 border agents (an increase of 2,000 since September 11, 2001) and physical barriers such as checkpoint stations, tall barbed-wire fences, and roadblocks in the most populous areas, effectively policing this immense expanse of land is practically impossible.

The U.S. Border Patrol makes more than 1 million arrests each year on the U.S.-Mexican border, a figure that is less impressive when one learns that, on average, an illegal immigrant will be arrested six times for crossing the border before being prosecuted. "Let's be honest," says T. J. Bonner, president of the National Border Patrol Council, "there isn't enough jail space to incarcerate everyone."[89]

Stemming the Flow In 2006, President Bush sent 6,000 National Guard troops to the Mexican border amid criticism that the federal government was not doing enough to address security issues in that region. Within three months, the number of arrests for illegal border crossing dropped 45 percent, leading some observers to conclude that the Guard was discouraging many from even trying to make the difficult journey. Others, however, believe that the migrants simply adapted, switching routes to avoid the Guards. "When you crack down in one area, they're going to try to exploit weaknesses in another area," says Bonner.[90]

Technology has strengthened these weaknesses somewhat. In the past few years, the Border Patrol has made use of remote video cameras, underground sensors, unmanned aircraft, and radiation detectors to locate border crossers. Border Patrol agents also have the technological ability to match fingerprints lifted from detained illegal immigrants against the FBI's national criminal database. Between May and December 2004, agents apprehended 30,000 illegal immigrants with U.S. criminal records, up from only 2,600 during the same time period in 2002, before the technology had been made available.[91]

Terrorist Crossings Many national security officials worry that the porous nature of America's borders will prove too tempting for terrorist organizations to resist. In August 2004, after the Border Patrol apprehended two terrorist suspects at a checkpoint along the Mexican border, the FBI issued an alert warning that al Qaeda officials might try to enter the United States through Mexico. "These terrorists are smart," says Richard Schultz, an international security expert at Tufts University in Medford, Massachusetts. "They study these issues and learn from one another. And one way in is right through the southern security perimeter."[92] Despite these worries, as of 2008 no high-level terrorist suspects are known to have taken an illegal land route into the United States.

AP Photo/John Miller

▲ The U.S. Border Patrol's unmanned aerial vehicle (UAV) is shown in flight over the desert of Arizona. The UAV uses thermal and night-vision equipment to detect illegal immigrants trying to sneak into the United States. Why is technology like the UAV so important to the Border Patrol's efforts?

Self Check Fill in the Blanks

Most foreigners who wish to visit the United States are required to obtain a _____ from the Department of State. A person who violates the terms of this document or commits a crime can be immediately _____ from the country by U.S. officials. Approximately 3 million illegal _____ enter the United States each year over its borders with Mexico and Canada, a situation the president has tried to remedy by sending members of the _____ to the Mexican border. Check your answers on page 559.

The Double-Edged Sword: Security versus Civil Liberties

The day after the September 11, 2001, terrorist attacks, President George W. Bush pledged that "we will not allow this enemy to win the war by changing our way of life or restricting our freedoms."[93] There is little doubt, however, that the Bush administration has adopted the crime control model in its approach to the "war" on terrorism. As you may recall from Chapter 1, in the crime control model the criminal justice system must be quick and efficient, with the courts operating on a "presumption of guilt," hampered as little as possible by the protection of individual rights.

RIGHTS DURING WARTIME

In the interests of greater security, Americans appear willing to relinquish some personal freedoms: most have indicated that they favor increased searches of people and their possessions at airports, office buildings, and other public places. At the same time, far smaller percentages are willing to accept monitoring of their phone calls and Internet use.[94] Furthermore, as mentioned earlier, the Patriot Act has acted as a lightning rod for those who oppose the Bush administration's approach to fighting terrorism. Critics of the act, such as Democratic Senator Russell Feingold of Wisconsin, believe that it has allowed the enemies of the United States "to win this battle without firing a shot."[95]

Inevitable Conflicts To a certain extent, the strain on civil liberties that has arisen as government agencies concentrate on homeland security is inevitable. The criminal justice system is designed to err on the side of the defendant; that is, it operates under the assumption that it is better for a guilty person to go free than for an innocent one to be convicted. Further, criminal justice is a deliberative process: no matter how heinous the crime or certain the suspect's guilt, criminal law requires that certain procedures be followed.

These same rules do not apply, however, in a war, even an undeclared one. The goal of a military operation is to destroy the enemy's forces, not to capture them and bring them to justice. The idea that an intelligence officer, having apprehended a terrorist suspect, should be required to read that person his or her *Miranda* rights, which include the right to remain silent and to be represented by counsel, is unrealistic. One senior U.S. military official—stationed in Afghanistan—believes the U.S. counterterrorism strategy should be as follows: "[A]s long as they want to send them here, we will kill them here. If they want to go somewhere else, we will kill them there."[96] Obviously, under the U.S. Constitution, law enforcement officials cannot take a similar view.

The Balancing Act Judges in terrorism-related cases have also felt the pressure of conflicting demands. Magistrate Judge H. Kenneth Schroeder, Jr., who oversaw the "Lackawanna Six" case mentioned in Figure 16.4 on page 541, said he spent "some pretty restless, sleepless nights" trying to "balance the rights of the people of the community to be safe and the rights of the defendants."[97] As we have seen throughout this textbook, the need to balance the rights of society and the rights of the individual is a constant in the criminal justice system. As we will see in this section, nowhere is this challenge more fraught with difficulty than in the "war" against terrorism. (See the *Mastering Concepts* feature for a preview of these difficulties.)

SEARCHES, SURVEILLANCE, AND SECURITY

The Fourth Amendment protects against unreasonable searches and seizures. According to the United States Supreme Court, the purpose of this amendment is to "prevent arbitrary and oppressive interference by enforcement officials with the privacy and personal security of individuals."[98] In practice, this has meant that a "neutral and detached" judge must, in most circumstances, decide whether a search or surveillance of a suspect's person or property is warranted. Law enforcement has often chafed against these restrictions, and this tension has only been exacerbated by the demands of counterterrorism search and surveillance strategies.

The Patriot Act and Searches The case of Zacarias Moussaoui is "Exhibit A" for those who feel that the Fourth Amendment, as interpreted by the courts, is incompatible with homeland security. During the summer of 2001, FBI agents in Minnesota arrested Moussaoui for immigration violations and sought a warrant to

In this section, we examine the tensions between civil liberties and the counterterrorism tactics adopted by the federal government. To help you better understand these conflicts, this *Mastering Concepts* feature focuses on the government's attitude toward the Fourth, Fifth, and Sixth Amendments in the context of its counterterrorism efforts.

	PROVISION	CONSTITUTIONAL BURDEN	THE GOVERNMENT'S ARGUMENT
Fourth Amendment	Individuals have the right to be "secure in their persons" against "unreasonable searches and seizures."	Government agents must obtain a search warrant before any search or seizure. To obtain the warrant, the agent must provide a judge with probable cause that a criminal act has been or is being committed.	Search warrants require specificity—of the premises to be searched, the illegal activities taking place, and the items to be seized. Terrorism investigators often need to move against suspects long before any specific proof of criminal activity exists.
Fifth Amendment	No one can be deprived of life, liberty, or property without due process of law.	The government cannot indefinitely detain a suspect without informing that suspect of the charges against him or her and providing the suspect with the chance to defend himself or herself against those charges.	Terrorists are ideological fighters who, if released for any reason, pose a danger to U.S. troops abroad and civilians at home. Therefore, their indefinite detention is justified, at least until the end of the present conflict.
	No person can be required to incriminate himself or herself.	Any information that is gained from a suspect as a result of improper coercion cannot be used to help convict that suspect of wrongdoing.	Military and intelligence agents are often required to "coerce" crucial information from terrorism suspects to prevent future terrorist activity.
Sixth Amendment	An accused person is guaranteed a speedy and public trial before an impartial jury.	The government must provide the suspect with an open trial in a reasonable amount of time before a jury of her or his peers.	Open trials and rules of evidence make it very difficult to protect "classified information" critical to counterterrorism intelligence operations. Furthermore, an accused terrorist might escape conviction on a "technicality" if tried in a civilian criminal court.
	A suspect has a right to counsel.	The government must provide the suspect with counsel if requested to do so and protect the confidentiality of all attorney-suspect communications.	A terrorist suspect might pass along important information about American counterterrorism strategies to his or her attorney. Therefore, any contact between them should be strictly limited and, if it does occur, should be monitored by government agents.

search his apartment and laptop computer. Because their superiors felt the agents had not established Moussaoui's involvement in terrorist activities, they refused to ask a judge for the necessary search warrant until after the September 11, 2001, attacks. (For a review of these procedures, see pages 218–220.) According to a congressional report, the information on Moussaoui's computer would have helped provide a "veritable blueprint for 9/11."[99]

Addressing these concerns, several sections of the Patriot Act make it easier for law enforcement agents to conduct searches. Previously, to search a suspect's apartment and examine the contents of his or her computer, they needed a court order based on probable cause that a crime had taken place or was about to take place. The Patriot Act amends the law to allow the FBI or other federal agencies to obtain warrants for "terrorism" investigations, "chemical weapons" investigations, or "computer fraud and abuse" investigations as long as agents can prove that such actions have a "significant purpose."[100] In other words, no proof of criminal activity need be provided.

L09

The Patriot Act and Surveillance Even before September 11, 2001, the Foreign Intelligence Surveillance Act of 1978 (FISA), which we first discussed in Chapter 7, had made it easier for intelligence agents to practice surveillance. Under FISA, the Foreign Intelligence Surveillance Court (FISC) would issue a warrant (technically known as a "special court order") without probable cause as long as the "primary purpose" of the document was to investigate foreign espionage and not to engage in criminal law enforcement.[101]

The Patriot Act gives federal agents even more leeway. It amends FISA to allow for searches and surveillance if a "significant purpose" of the investigation is intelligence gathering or any other type of antiterrorist activity.[102] The statute also provides federal agents with "roving surveillance authority," allowing them to continue monitoring a terrorist suspect on the strength of the original warrant even if the suspect moves to another jurisdiction.[103] Furthermore, the Patriot Act makes it much easier for law enforcement agents to avoid the notification requirements of search warrants, meaning that a person whose home has been the target of a search and whose voice mails or computer records have been seized may not be informed of these activities until weeks after they have taken place.[104]

The NSA and Warrantless Wiretaps Many experts worried that the Patriot Act's provisions on searches and surveillance reflected an atmosphere in which the government would take legal "shortcuts" in its intelligence operations. These fears were realized in December 2005, when President Bush admitted that, under his direction, the National Security Agency (NSA) had been conducting warrantless surveillance of communications between suspects on American soil believed to be connected to al Qaeda and their contacts abroad. NSA agents had also gained access to the main telecommunications grids in the United States, looking for telephone and e-mail patterns that might suggest links between terrorists.

While such efforts may have seemed appropriate, they were also, in the eyes of many, illegal because the NSA failed to get court approval for the eavesdropping as required by FISA. President Bush initially defended the NSA's program. "My most important job is to protect the security of the American people," he said during a 2006 speech. "What I'm telling you is we're using all different assets at our disposal to protect you in a different kind of war."[105] In January 2007, however, after months of controversy, the Bush administration reversed course, announcing that the NSA would seek a special court order from the FISC before conducting such surveillance in the future.

▼ Reports that the National Security Agency (NSA) had been secretly collecting the phone call records of millions of American citizens caused a great deal of controversy and led to numerous protests.

DUE PROCESS AND INDEFINITE DETENTION

The Fifth Amendment holds that no *person* shall be deprived of life, liberty, or property without due process of law. More than a century ago, the United States Supreme Court ruled that, because the amendment uses the word *person* and not *citizen*, due process protections extend to non-U.S. citizens under the jurisdiction of the American government.[106] With sensitivities heightened following the attacks of September 11, 2001, however, it seems that crucial aspects of due process have been denied to large numbers of aliens suspected of terrorist sympathies or activities.

"Special Interest" Aliens

Immediately after September 11, the Office of the U.S. Attorney General set forth regulations that allowed homeland security officials to detain aliens of "special interest" without first charging them with any crime. The new rules also allowed for the indefinite detention of such non-U.S. citizens in the event of "emergency or other extraordinary circumstance."[107] The more than seven hundred aliens who were detained on the authority of these regulations were denied due process protections such as notice of the charges against them, access to counsel, and the right to a trial. Instead, most of them were removed from the United States after being subjected to detention periods of as long as two years and secret hearings.[108]

▲ Detainees in orange jumpsuits sit in a holding area at the U.S. Naval Base at Guantánamo Bay, Cuba. The base is serving as a holding facility for hundreds of suspected al Qaeda and Taliban operatives captured during U.S. military operations in Afghanistan. The U.S. government considers the detainees to be "unlawful combatants" and has denied them legal representation and the right to trial. Under what amendment(s) are such rights guaranteed to American citizens? Do you think non-American citizens who are in the custody of the U.S. military should be protected by our Constitution? Why or why not?

Unlawful Combatants For the most part, regulations concerning "special interest" aliens had been rescinded by 2004. The U.S. government's treatment of alien terrorist suspects, however, continued to arouse controversy not only in the United States but also across the globe. Early in the present conflict, the Bush administration decided that any al Qaeda and Taliban operatives captured in foreign lands would be considered *unlawful combatants.* Under international law, *lawful combatants* are those soldiers who belong to a nation's armed forces. According to a series of international treaties known as the Geneva Conventions, to which the United States is a party, captured lawful combatants, or "prisoners of war," cannot be coerced into giving up any information and must be returned to their home countries at the end of hostilities. **Unlawful combatants,** in contrast, are nonstate actors and, therefore, are not covered by the Geneva Conventions.[109]

This unlawful combatant designation provided the United States with the legal justification to detain al Qaeda and Taliban operatives indefinitely without charging them with any wrongdoing. More than six hundred suspected unlawful combatants, most of them captured during the American-led invasion of Afghanistan in 2001, were transferred to a U.S. military detention center at the U.S. Naval Base in Guantánamo Bay, Cuba (GTMO). The detainees were denied access to legal representation or family members and were subjected to harsh interrogation tactics such as waterboarding, sleep and food deprivation, physical stress positions, and isolation.[110] As a result of the conditions at GTMO, the U.S. government has come under a great deal of international criticism, particularly from Arab and Muslim countries and from those non-Muslim nations, such as Australia and Great Britain, whose citizens were being held at the detention center.

The Supreme Court and Indefinite Detention Somewhat impervious to outside condemnation, the Bush administration insisted that it planned to hold the GTMO detainees until the end of hostilities to ensure that they would never pose a future threat to American troops. Give the vague nature of "hostilities" under present

Unlawful Combatant A person who takes part in armed hostilities but who does not belong to the armed forces of a sovereign nation and, therefore, is not afforded protection under the Geneva Conventions.

circumstances, critics point out that those held at GTMO could be detained without being charged and without access to legal representation for years.

The United States Supreme Court weakened the U.S. government's position with its decision in *Rasul v. Bush* (2004).[111] The case involved the authority of American courts to decide whether the noncitizen detainees at GMTO could be held indefinitely without judicial review. The federal government argued that U.S. courts had no jurisdiction over the matter because the detainees were not American citizens and GTMO was not located on American soil. The Court rejected this line of reasoning and ruled that, for due process purposes, the naval base in Cuba was to be considered U.S. territory. The decision opened the door for more than two hundred detainees to file *habeas corpus* petitions challenging their imprisonment. (For a review of *habeas corpus*, see page 335.)

> "As terrible as 9/11 was, it didn't repeal the Constitution."
>
> —Rosemary S. Pooler, U.S. circuit judge

U.S. CITIZENS AS TERRORIST SUSPECTS

Only one American citizen, Yaser Esam Hamdi, has been detained at GTMO. Following his capture in Afghanistan while fighting for the Taliban in 2001, the federal government labeled Hamdi an "enemy combatant" (which is not, as we shall soon see, the same as being labeled an unlawful combatant). Because of this designation, as explained earlier in this chapter, the U.S. military could detain Hamdi indefinitely without charges, a trial, or access to counsel. As an American citizen, however, Hamdi had more legal tools at his disposal than did the average alien enemy combatant. First, the federal government transferred Hamdi from GTMO to a Navy prison in Norfolk, Virginia. Then, Hamdi's father filed a *habeas corpus* petition on his son's behalf, claiming that the government had denied him due process. The Bush administration countered that the president has the right to use extraordinary measures to protect the nation from terrorism.

In 2003, the Fourth Circuit Court of Appeals ruled in favor of the government, stating that courts should defer to the president in a time of "overseas conflict."[112] A year later, in its *Hamdi v. Rumsfeld* decision, the United States Supreme Court reversed, holding that Hamdi, as an American citizen, was entitled to an explanation of the reasoning behind his designation as an enemy combatant and should be given a "fair opportunity" to rebut the status before a neutral decision maker.[113] Rather than provide Hamdi with this opportunity, the Department of Justice released the suspect and sent him to Saudi Arabia.

Padilla's Path Besides Yaser Hamdi, only one other American citizen has been designated an enemy combatant. On May 8, 2002, José Padilla, born in Puerto Rico, was detained at O'Hare International Airport in Chicago on the belief that he was plotting to set off a "dirty bomb" in the United States. Federal authorities refused to let Padilla speak to an attorney for more than two years while holding him in a South Carolina naval prison. In total, Padilla was detained for three and one-half years without having any charges leveled against him.

Like Hamdi, Padilla challenged his designation as an enemy combatant on due process grounds. Although the Supreme Court rejected the claim because of a procedural error by Padilla's attorney,[114] its *Hamdi* ruling set a precedent that seemed to apply to Padilla as well. Consequently, the federal government transferred Padilla from military jurisdiction to the criminal justice system, charging him with conspiring to support terrorist activities in the United States and abroad. In August 2007, a federal jury found Padilla guilty on three counts of terrorism conspiracy, and he faced a sentence of life in prison.

Coercion Tactics Interestingly, the prosecution's case made no mention of the alleged "dirty bomb" plot—the main reason for Padilla's original detention.

Legal experts have speculated that the government dropped these charges to keep certain witnesses from testifying in court. (In Chapter 10, we saw that the Sixth Amendment's confrontation clause allows a defendant to cross-examine all witnesses against him or her.) If the witnesses had been coerced into making incriminating statements about Padilla, details of this coercion might be revealed during the trial—a situation the government would prefer to avoid.[115] The various methods used to interrogate terrorist suspects—including, possibly, torture—have been the subject of much debate, and we will examine the issues surrounding this topic in the *Criminal Justice in Action* feature at the end of the chapter.

Military Tribunal A court that is operated by the military rather than the criminal justice system and is presided over by military officers rather than judges. Often, the tribunals operate in secrecy and do not provide the suspect with the full range of constitutional protections.

MILITARY TRIBUNALS

Perhaps the most controversial step taken by the Bush administration regarding the civil rights of suspected terrorists was a presidential order stating that enemy

LO10 combatants who are not U.S. citizens could be tried in *tribunals* operated by the U.S. military rather than in civilian courts. In these **military tribunals,** there is no right to a trial by jury, as guaranteed by the Sixth Amendment. Instead, a panel of military officers acts in the place of a judge and jury and decides questions of "both fact and law." The traditional rules of evidence (see Chapter 10) do not apply; instead, any evidence is admissible if, in the opinion of the tribunal, it would help a reasonable person decide the issue at hand. Furthermore, only two-thirds of the panel must agree to convict, in contrast to the unanimous jury required in criminal trials.[116]

The Two-Tribunal Process As one would expect, the United States Supreme Court has had a great deal to say about military tribunals. Its *Hamdi* ruling forced the government to provide alien terrorist suspects with a "fair opportunity" to challenge their designation as enemy combatants. Thus, in 2004 the Pentagon began operating Combat Status Review Tribunals (CSRTs) at GTMO. These tribunals are designed to determine whether a detainee is indeed an enemy combatant and therefore eligible to be tried by a military tribunal.

In 2006, the Supreme Court addressed the military tribunals themselves with its decision in *Hamdan v. Rumsfeld*.[117] In this case, the Court found that the tribunals were unconstitutional because they had not been properly authorized by Congress. The Court also ruled that the tribunals violated international law, specifically Common Article 3 of the Geneva Conventions, a treaty signed by the United States. This article requires that prisoners of war be treated humanely and afforded "all the judicial guarantees which are recognized as indispensable by civilized people."[118] (For a review of the important Supreme Court cases dealing with terrorism, see ■ Figure 16.5 on the following page.)

▼ The U.S. military detained José Padilla, center, for three years as an "enemy combatant" because of his supposed terrorist activities. In late 2005, however, federal authorities sought and obtained an indictment of Padilla on charges that he "conspired to murder, kidnap, and maim people overseas," meaning that he would be tried in criminal court. Why would terrorism suspects prefer to have their cases heard in a civilian court rather than a military tribunal?

AP Photo/Alan Diaz

United States Supreme Court Decisions on Terrorism

Historically, American courts have assumed a deferential position toward the government in time of crisis and military action. In the past several years, however, as these cases show, the United States Supreme Court has refused to provide the federal government with a "blank check" when it comes to the issue of civil liberties and the "war" on terrorism.

Rasul v. Bush [542 U.S. 466 (2004)]

The Question: Can noncitizens who have been designated enemy combatants and detained at Guantánamo Bay be denied access to American courts?

The Court's Response: No. American courts have jurisdiction over Guantánamo Bay because it is U.S.-controlled territory; therefore, detainees held there must be allowed to challenge their detention.*

Rumsfeld v. Padilla [542 U.S. 426 (2004)]

The Question: Can an American citizen captured in the United States be denied access to American courts?

The Court's Response: Unclear. Padilla had filed the case in the wrong jurisdiction and would have to refile. Before he could do so, the federal government decided to bring criminal charges against him, thus providing him with the access to the civilian court system he had been seeking all along.

Hamdi v. Rumsfeld [542 U.S. 507 (2004)]

The Question: Can American citizens captured as part of enemy operations in foreign countries be denied access to American courts?

The Court's Response: No. Hamdi had been denied due process and had the right to challenge his detention in court.

Hamdan v. Rumsfeld [126 S.Ct. 2749 (2006)]

The Question: Are the military tribunals set up to try enemy combatants at Guantánamo Bay legal?

The Court's Response: No. The tribunals violate both military and international law.

* In 2006, Congress essentially overturned this decision when it passed legislation denying inmates at Guantánamo the opportunity to challenge their detention.

Unlawful or Not? Two weeks after the *Hamdan* decision, the Bush administration stated, for the first time, that enemy combatants have a right to the protections described in Common Article 3.[119] Then, in February 2007, the Pentagon, as requested by Congress, revised its rules for military tribunals, prohibiting testimony obtained through torture (though testimony obtained through "coercion" is still admissible).[120] Believing that it had addressed all of the constitutional concerns surrounding military tribunals, the administration confidently announced that it would soon be putting seventy-five of the "worst" terrorist offenders detained at GTMO on trial in the near future.

By June 2007, however, the government's plans were again put on hold when a pair of military judges found a flaw in the new system. The regulations governing the new military tribunals gave them jurisdiction over "unlawful enemy combatants." A CSRT, however, determines only whether a detainee at GTMO is an "enemy combatant," making no judgment on whether the detainee is "unlawful." U.S. government lawyers dismissed the discrepancy as a mere technicality, but it is a discrepancy that will have to be resolved before the military tribunals can continue.[121]

Self Check Fill in the Blanks

Under the Patriot Act, government agents no longer need to show _____ cause to obtain warrants for terrorist investigations; rather, they only need to show that their actions have a "_____ purpose." President George W. Bush decided that terrorist operatives captured in foreign lands would be considered _____ combatants and could be detained _____ without notice of any charges against them. The president also decided that enemy combatants could be tried before _____, which offer fewer constitutional protections than do civilian criminal courts. Check your answers on page 559

INTERROGATING TERRORISTS

Abu Zubaydah was in bad shape, feverish and suffering from bullet wounds in his groin and abdomen, but things were about to get worse for the al Qaeda operative. The CIA agents who had detained him in a Thai safehouse in the spring of 2002 were certain that he had information "that could save innocent lives." To get this information, the interrogators stripped Zubaydah naked and then adjusted the air-conditioning until he turned blue with cold. Meanwhile, they blasted him with deafening rock music from bands such as the Red Hot Chili Peppers.[122] The CIA agents also, unwittingly, contributed to the debate that is the subject of this *Criminal Justice in Action* feature: How far should the United States go in interrogating suspected terrorists?

TORTURE LITE

Under U.S. criminal law, it is a crime for any person inside or outside the country to commit torture.[123] President George W. Bush has said that the "United States is committed to the worldwide elimination of torture and we are leading the fight by example."[124] Actions taken by U.S. agents to secure counterterrorism intelligence have, however, skirted the generally accepted definition of torture—the infliction of severe physical or mental pain or suffering on a person in custody. At the Guantánamo Bay military prison in Cuba, for example, detainees were reportedly subjected to "waterboarding," a technique that involves repeatedly pouring water down the throat of a subject to reproduce the feeling of drowning.[125] In Iraq, American military officers authorized twenty-nine "aggressive" interrogation techniques, including isolation, stress positions, sensory and sleep deprivation, and the use of canines to exploit "Arab fear of dogs."[126]

Defenders of these coercive interrogation methods, often known as "torture lite," argue that they do not meet the definition of torture because no actual harm is done to the subject. Critics reject this stance as both disingenuous and untrue. Despite recent federal guidelines designed to eliminate most forms of torture lite, most observers believe that U.S. agents of the "war" on terror still rely on the infliction of mental anguish as an interrogation tool.

The Case for Coercive Interrogation of Terrorist Suspects

- In a number of instances (such as with the aforementioned Abu Zubaydah, who provided detailed information about al Qaeda's organizational strategies), coercive interrogation has produced vital information that has helped disrupt terrorist plots and save lives.

- These methods are not covered by U.S. criminal law because they are done to gather intelligence, not to provide evidence in a criminal trial.

- The methods are justified given the far greater brutality and blatant torture tactics used by many terrorist organizations.

The Case against Coercive Interrogation of Terrorist Suspects

- These methods are immoral and abhorrent. "It's not about the terrorists," says Senator John McCain (Rep.–Ariz.). "It's about us. It's about what kind of country we are."[127]

- Research has shown that confessions made under duress are unreliable, as the subject will "say anything" to avoid further pain.

- The methods backfire by prompting other nations to use similar tactics against captured American military personnel and civilians.

Writing Assignment—Your Opinion

Some observers feel that outright torture is acceptable in a "ticking bomb" situation, when the suspect is known to have knowledge of an extreme danger—such as a "ticking bomb"—and he or she must be persuaded to part with this knowledge immediately to save innocent lives. What should be the rules governing the "ticking bomb" scenario? Where would you draw the line on coercive interrogations of terrorist suspects in general? How does the "torture lite" dilemma reflect the larger challenge of balancing the security interests of the United States as a whole against the civil rights of the individual? Before responding, you can review our discussions in this chapter concerning

AP Photo

- The definition of terrorism (pages 525–526).

- The difference between the criminal justice model and the intelligence model of combating terrorism (pages 542–543).

- Civil rights and terrorism (pages 549–556).

Your answer should take at least three full paragraphs.

LO1 **Identify five important trends in international terrorism.** (a) Terrorist attacks have become more violent, producing larger numbers of casualties; (b) terrorist groups have become more skilled at raising funds to finance their operations; (c) terrorists are organizing themselves as efficient networks; (d) terrorist groups are operating on a global scale; and (e) terrorists are able to take advantage of information technology to improve communications with each other.

LO2 **Describe the several strains of domestic terrorism.** Antigovernment groups commit terrorist acts against the U.S. government, which they believe is working contrary to the interests of the American people. White supremacists promote racial inequality in favor of their own race, and the extreme fringe of the "pro-life" movement uses violent means to block access to legal abortions. Eco-terrorists commit acts of sabotage in an effort to protect animals or the environment.

LO3 **Compare WMDs and CBERN.** WMDs is an acronym for "weapons of mass destruction," which include nuclear, radiological, chemical, and biological weapons with the capacity to do great damage. CBERN, a term favored by the military, stands for "chemical, biological, explosive, radiological, and nuclear"—adding "explosive" because of the threat posed by conventional explosives.

LO4 **Explain why the Antiterrorism and Effective Death Penalty Act of 1996 (AEDPA) is an important legal tool against terrorists.** The AEDPA allows federal law enforcement officials to prosecute those suspected of providing "material support or resources" to any group that the U.S. government has designated a "foreign terrorist organization." The legislation permits the arrest of a suspect who has not yet committed a crime, thereby allowing for preventive measures not usually available under criminal law.

LO5 **Describe the primary goals of an intelligence agency and indicate how it differs from an agency that focuses solely on law enforcement.** The primary goal of an intelligence agency is to prevent crime by gathering information on potential illegal acts before they occur. In contrast, a law enforcement agency devotes its resources to solving crimes that have already occurred and bringing those who committed those crimes to justice.

LO6 **Explain how American law enforcement agencies have used "preventive policing" to combat terrorism.** American law enforcement agencies are no longer willing to take the chance that nascent terrorist plots will develop into significant security threats. Therefore, they are taking steps to stop these plots in the planning stages, even if the dangers posed by the conspirators are minimal.

LO7 **Indicate which persons are eligible to be designated enemy combatants and explain the consequences for them.** An enemy combatant is someone who, in the eyes of the federal government, has actively supported terrorist organizations in hostilities against the United States. By law, enemy combatants can be detained by the U.S. government until the end of the "war" on terrorism or until the military has determined that they no longer pose a threat to America or its allies.

LO8 **List the primary duties of first responders following a terrorist attack or other catastrophic event.** (a) Secure the scene of the incident; (b) rescue and treat any injured civilians; (c) contain fires or other hazardous conditions that may have resulted from the event; (d) and retrieve the dead.

LO9 **Explain how the Patriot Act has made it easier for federal agents to conduct searches during terrorism investigations.** In requesting a search warrant for investigations of terrorism, federal agents no longer need to provide probable cause of wrongdoing. They must only prove that their actions have a "significant purpose," which means that no proof of criminal activity need be provided.

LO10 **Explain how military tribunals differ from federal courts with respect to trials of suspected terrorists.** A defendant before a military tribunal does not enjoy the right to trial by jury; instead, a panel of military officers makes decisions of guilt and innocence. The traditional rules of evidence do not apply in military tribunals, which operate under a much more lenient standard of what evidence is admissible against the defendant. Also, military tribunals do not have to reach a unanimous verdict—only two-thirds of the panel must agree to find guilt.

Key Terms

alien 546
Antiterrorism and Effective Death Penalty Act (AEDPA) 533
biological weapon 530
Central Intelligence Agency (CIA) 537
chemical weapon 531
domestic terrorism 529
eco-terrorism 529

enemy combatant 544
first responders 545
improvised explosive devices (IEDs) 531
infrastructure 536
intelligence agency 537
military tribunal 555
National Security Agency (NSA) 537
nonstate actor 525

nuclear weapon 531
Patriot Act 534
preparedness 544
radiation 531
unlawful combatant 553
visa 546
weapons of mass destruction (WMDs) 530

Self Check Answer Key

Page 530: i. nonstate; ii. *jihad;* iii. international; iv. domestic

Page 532: i. mass destruction; ii. biological; iii. chemical; iv. nuclear; v. conventional

Page 539: i. material; ii. Patriot; iii. Homeland Security; iv. intelligence

Page 545: i. prevent; ii. criminal justice; iii. Federal Bureau of Investigation (FBI); iv. military

Page 549: i. visa; ii. removed; iii. aliens; iv. National Guard

Page 556: i. probable; ii. significant; iii. unlawful; iv. indefinitely; v. military tribunals

Questions for Critical Analysis

1. Why is it difficult to come up with a universally accepted definition of "terrorism"?

2. What is the difference between biological weapons and chemical weapons?

3. Why was a "sunset provision" added to the Patriot Act? What was the result of this "sunset provision"?

4. What are some of the problems that local police departments face in their counterterrorism efforts? In what ways have the federal government's antiterrorism strategies hampered, rather than helped, these efforts?

5. Why does the traditional criminal justice response of punishing a perpetrator for his or her criminal acts seem inadequate when it comes to terrorism?

6. What is the "big cultural change" that the FBI is facing in the aftermath of the September 11, 2001, terrorist attacks?

7. How can law enforcement agents take advantage of the fact that immigration law is a form of civil law, not criminal law?

8. What is the difference between a lawful combatant and an unlawful combatant under international law, and why is this distinction important for America's efforts to combat terrorism?

Maximize Your Best Possible Outcome for Chapter 16

1. **Maximize Your Best Chance for Getting a Good Grade on the Exam.** ThomsonNOW Personalized Study is a diagnostic study tool containing valuable text-specific resources—and because you focus on just what you don't know, you learn more in less time to get a better grade. How do you get ThomsonNOW? If your textbook does not include an access code card, go to **thomsonedu.com** to get ThomsonNOW before your next exam!

2. **Get the Most Out of Your Textbook** by going to the book companion Web site at **www.cjinaction.com** to access one of the tutorial quizzes, use the flash cards

   to master key terms, and check out the many other study aids you'll find there. Under chapter resources you will also be able to access the Stories from the Street feature and Web links mentioned in the textbook.

3. **Learn about Potential Criminal Justice Careers** discussed in this chapter by exploring careers online at **www.cjinaction.com**. You will find career descriptions and information about job requirements, training, salary and benefits, and the application process. You can also watch video profiles featuring criminal justice professionals.

Notes

1. Quoted in Greg Miller and Erika Hayasaki, "Arrests Made in Alleged Plot against JFK Airport," *Los Angeles Times* (June 3, 2007), 1.

2. Quoted in Cara Buckley and William K. Rashbaum, "Four Men Accused of Plot to Blow Up Kennedy Airport Terminals and Fuel Lines," *New York Times* (June 3, 2007), 30.

3. Quoted in Josh Meyer, "Alleged Plot: A Potential Threat Seen in America's Backyard," *Los Angeles Times* (June 3, 2007), 24.

4. *National Strategy for Homeland Security* (Washington, D.C.: Office of Homeland Security, 2002), 2.

5. Geoffrey Levitt, "Is 'Terrorism' Worth Defining?" *Ohio Northern University Law Review* 13 (1986), 97.

6. "Definition of Terrorism," *World Conflict Quarterly,* at **www. globalterrorism101.com/UTdefinition.html**.

7. David A. Westbrook, "Bin Laden's War," *Buffalo Law Review* (December 2006), 981–1012.

8. Ibid.

9. Marc Sageman, "Understanding Al-Qaida Networks," in *The McGraw-Hill Homeland Security Handbook*, ed. David G. Kamien (New York: McGraw-Hill, 2006), 53–54.

10. Ahmed S. Hashim, "Al-Qaida: Origins, Goals, and Grand Strategy," in *The McGraw-Hill Homeland Security Handbook*, ed. David G. Kamien (New York: McGraw-Hill, 2006), 24.

11. Quoted in *ibid.*, 9.
12. "Interview: Osama bin Laden," May 1998, at **www.pbs.org/wgbh/pages/frontline/shows/binladen/who/interview.html**.
13. Westbrook.
14. Brian Michael Jenkins, "The New Age of Terrorism," in *The McGraw-Hill Homeland Security Handbook*, ed. David G. Kamien (New York: McGraw-Hill, 2006), 117–129.
15. *Ibid.*, 128.
16. Statement of James F. Jarboe, Domestic Terrorism Section Chief, Counterterrorism Divisions, Federal Bureau of Investigation, before the House of Representatives Committee on Resources, Subcommittee on Forests and Forest Health, Hearings on Eco-Terrorism and Lawlessness on the National Forests, 107th Congress (February 12, 2002).
17. *Ibid.*
18. Animal Liberation Front, "Animal Liberation—By 'Whatever Means Necessary,'" at **www.animalliberationfront.com/ALFront/Premise_History/alf_ summary.htm**.
19. Jeff Barnard, "Arsonist Sentenced to 13 Years," *Seattle Times* (May 24, 2007), B3.
20. Leslie A. Pappas, "Pa. Considers Outlawing Domestic Terrorism," *Philadelphia Inquirer* (June 5, 2005), B5.
21. Leonard A. Cole, "WMD and Lessons from the Anthrax Attacks," in *The McGraw-Hill Homeland Security Handbook*, ed. David G. Kamien (New York: McGraw-Hill, 2006), 167.
22. *Ibid.*, 168.
23. Quoted in David Cook, "Robert Mueller," *Christian Science Monitor* (May 10, 2007), 25.
24. Jane A. Bullock, George D. Haddow, Damon Coppola, Erdem Ergin, Lissa Westerman, and Sarp Yeletaysi, *Introduction to Homeland Security*, 2d. ed (Burlington, MA: Butterworth-Heinemann, 2006), 153.
25. Terrorism Project, "What If the Terrorists Go Nuclear?" at **www.cdi.org/terrorism/nuclear-pr.cfm**.
26. Cole, 169.
27. Quoted in Jim Lobe, "Nation Girds for War with Unidentified Enemy" (September 12, 2001), at **ipsnews.net/news.asp?idnews=34634**.
28. Quoted in Steven Brill, *After: How America Confronted the September 12 Era* (New York: Simon and Schuster, 2003), 15.
29. Quoted in "Ashcroft Eager to Expand Police Powers," *Newsmax.com Wires* (October 26, 2001), at **www.newsmax.com/archives/articles/2001/10/25/160238.shtml**.
30. 18 U.S.C. Section 2339B(a)(1) (1996).
31. 8 U.S.C. Section 1182(a)(3)(B) (Supp. I 2001); and 8 U.S.C. Section 1189(a)(1)(C) (Supp I 2001).
32. U.S. Department of State, "Country Reports on Terrorism," at **www.state.gov/s/ct/rls/crt/2006/82738.htm**.
33. 18 U.S.C. Section 2339A(b) (Supp I 2001).
34. 8 U.S.C. Section 1182(a)(3)(B)(iv)(VI) (Supp. I 2001), amended by the Patriot Act of 2001, Pub. L. No. 107-56, Section 411(a), 115 Stat. 272.
35. Uniting and Strengthening America by Providing Appropriate Tools Required to Intercept and Obstruct Terrorism Act of 2001, Pub. L. No.107- 56, 115 Stat. 272 (2001).
36. Bullock, *et al.*, 41–42.
37. Charles Babington, "Congress Votes to Renew Patriot Act, with Changes," *Washington Post* (March 8, 2006), A3.
38. Pub. L. No. 107-296, 116 Stat. 2135.
39. U.S. Department of Homeland Security, "Fact Sheet: U.S. Department of Homeland Security Announces Eight Percent Increase in Fiscal Year 2008 Budget Request," at **www.dhs.gov/xnews/releases/pr_1170702193412.shtm**.
40. Stephen Barr, "Report Details Personnel Woes at Homeland Security," *Washington Post* (May 24, 2007), at **mobile.washingtonpost.com/detail.jsp?key=47103&rc=loop_po&p=1&all=1**.
41. Federal Bureau of Investigation, "Facts and Figures: FBI Priorities," at **www.fbi.gov/priorities/priorities.htm**.
42. Bullock, *et al.*, 198.
43. Louis M. Davis, *et al.*, *When Terrorism Hits Home: How Prepared Are State and Local Law Enforcement?* (Santa Monica, CA: RAND Corporation, 2004), 8.
44. K. Jack Riley, Jeremy M. Wilson, Gregory F. Treverton, and Barbara Raymond, "Think Locally, Act Nationally," *RAND Review* (Spring 2006), at **www.rand.org/publications/randreview/issues/spring2006/police.html**.
45. The Council of State Governments and Eastern Kentucky University, *The Impact of Terrorism on State Law Enforcement: Adjusting to New Roles and Changing Conditions* (Washington, D.C.: National Institute of Justice, June 2006), 56.
46. Federal Bureau of Investigation, "A Closer Look at the FBI's Joint Terrorism Task Force," at **www.fbi.gov/page2/dec04/jttf120114.htm**.
47. The United States Conference of Mayors Homeland Security Monitoring Center, *2006 Survey on Homeland Security and Emergency Preparedness: Five Years Post 9/11, One Year Post Katrina* (Washington, D.C.: United States Conference of Mayors, July 26, 2006), 1.
48. Office of the Inspector General, *The External Effects of the Federal Bureau of Investigation's Reprioritization Efforts* (Washington, D.C.: U.S. Department of Justice, 2005), v.
49. Kevin Sack, "Focus on Terrorism Creates Burden for the Police," *New York Times* (October 28, 2001), B4.
50. Quoted in John Files, "Police Chiefs Urge Stronger Effort on Crime," *New York Times* (August 31, 2006), A19.
51. Quoted in Natasha Korecki, Annie Sweeney, and Dan Rozek, "Mall a Terror Target," *Chicago Sun Times* (December 9, 2006), 4.
52. Quoted in John M. Broder, "Police Chiefs Moving to Share Terror Data," *New York Times* (July 29, 2005), A12.
53. Karen J. Greenberg, "Transatlantic Counterterrorism: Some Recommendations," in *The McGraw-Hill Homeland Security Handbook*, ed. David G. Kamien (New York: McGraw-Hill, 2006), 349.
54. Bullock, *et al.*, 82.
55. Quoted in Philip Shenon and Eric Lichtblau, "FBI Assailed for Its Handling of Terror Risks," *New York Times* (April 14, 2004), A1.
56. National Commission on Terrorist Attacks upon the United States, *The 9/11 Commission Report: Executive Summary* (Washington, D.C.: National Commission on Terrorist Attacks upon the United States, 2004), 9.
57. Scott Shane and Andrea Zarrate, "Terror Arrests: Plot against Sears Tower Mostly Just Talk," *Houston Chronicle* (June 24, 2006), A3.
58. Quoted in Larry Lebowitz, Lesely Clark, and Martin Merzer, "Feds' Sting Videotaped Oath to Terrorists," *Miami Herald* (June 24, 2006), A1.
59. *Ibid.*
60. Scott Shane and Lowell Bergman, "Adding Up the Ounces of Prevention," *New York Times* (September 10, 2006), Section 4, page 1.
61. *United States v. Salameh*, 152 F.3d 88 (2d Cir. 1998).
62. Transactional Records Access Clearinghouse, "TRAC Reports: Terrorism Enforcement: International Domestic, and Financial," at **trac.syr.edu/tracreports/terrorism/177**.
63. Arunabha Bhoumik, "Democratic Responses to Terrorism: A Comparative Study of the United States, Israel, and India," *Denver Journal of International Law and Policy* (Spring 2005), 285.
64. National Commission on Terrorist Attacks upon the United States, 11.
65. Quoted in Elsa Walsh, "Learning to Spy," *New Yorker* (November 8, 2004), 96.
66. Richard B. Schmitt, "FBI Races the Clock to Reinvent Itself," *Los Angeles Times* (August 20, 2006), 1.
67. "Spies among Us," *U.S. News & World Report* (May 8, 2006), 41–43.
68. *Ibid.*, 43.
69. Quoted in Michael J. Sniffen and Matthew Baraket, "Moussaoui Trial Not Likely to Be the Norm," Associated Press (May 6, 2006).
70. Authorization for Use of Military Force, Pub. L. No. 107-40, 115 Stat. 224 (2001).
71. Paul Wolfowitz, "Memorandum on Order Establishing Combatant Status of Review Tribunal to the Secretary of the Navy" (July 7, 2004), at **www.defenselink.mil/news/Jul2004/d20040707review.pdf**.
72. *In re Guantánamo Detainee Cases*, 355 F.Supp.2d 443, 447 (D.C.Cir. 2005).
73. 18 U.S.C. Section 1385 (2000).
74. Colonel William F. Kuehn, *The Role of the National Guard in Homeland Security* (Carlisle Barracks, PA: U.S. Army War College, February 2004), 6.
75. Jim VandeHei and Josh White, "Bush Urges Shifts in Relief Responsibilities," *Washington Post* (September 26, 2005), A12.
76. Christopher Ligatti, "The Legality of American Military Troops Engaging in Domestic Law Enforcement in the Event of a Major Terrorist Attack," *New England Law Review* (Fall 2006), 199.

77. Bradley Graham, "War Plans Drafted to Counter Terror Attacks in U.S.: Domestic Effort Is Big Shift for Military," *Washington Post* (August 8, 2005), A1.

78. "Homeland Security Presidential Directive/HSPD-8," at **www.fas.org/ irp/offdocs/nspd/hspd-8.html**.

79. Bullock, *et al.*, 315.

80. "Unanswered Prayers: Police Officials Say Anti-Terror Needs Are Still Unmet," *Law Enforcement News* (September 15–31, 2003), 1.

81. *Tactical Interoperable Communications Scorecards: Summary Report and Findings* (Washington, D.C.: Department of Homeland Security, January 2007).

82. National Commission on Terrorist Attacks upon the United States, 14.

83. Janice L. Kephart, *Immigration and Terrorism: Moving Beyond the 9/11 Staff Report on Terrorist Travel* (Washington, D.C.: Center for Immigration Studies, September 2005), 1.

84. *United States v. Martinez-Fuerte*, 428 U.S. 543, 566–567 (1976).

85. 8 U.S.C. Section 1362 (2000).

86. 8 U.S.C. Section 287.3 (2001).

87. Quoted in Michael J. Sniffen, "Homeland Security Numbers Challenged," *Arizona Daily Star* (May 28, 2007), A4.

88. Kris K. Kobach, "The Quintessential Force Multiplier: The Inherent Authority of Local Police to Make Immigration Arrests," *Albany Law Review* 69 (2005–2006), 179–188.

89. Quoted in "Crossers Rarely Charged, Says Justice Dept. Memo," *Arizona Daily Star* (March 23, 2007), A4.

90. Quoted in Mimi Hall, "Despite New Technology, Border Patrol Overwhelmed," *USA Today* (February 23, 2005), 10A.

91. Richard Marosi, "Criminals at the Border Thwarted by Their Own Hands," *Los Angeles Times* (February 19, 2005), A1.

92. Quoted in Faye Bowers, "U.S.-Mexican Border as a Terror Risk," *Christian Science Monitor* (March 22, 2005), 1.

93. "Remarks by the President in Photo Opportunity with National Security Team," The White House Office of the Press Secretary, at **www.whitehouse.gov/news/releases/2001/09/20010912-4.html**.

94. William E. Gibson, "Privacy Fears Begin to Grow," *South Florida Sun-Sentinel* (May 12, 2006), 10A.

95. Quoted in John Cloud, "Hitting the Wall," *Time* (November 5, 2001), 70.

96. Quoted in Michael Elliott, "Inside the Battle of Shah-i-Kot," *Time* (March 18, 2002), 38–39.

97. Quoted in Susan Sachs, "Murky Lives, Fateful Trip in Buffalo Terrorism Case," *New York Times* (September 20, 2002), A1.

98. *INS v. Delgado*, 466 U.S. 215 (1983).

99. Quoted in Philip Shenon, "Senate Report on Pre-9/11 Failure Tells of Bungling at FBI," *New York Times* (August 28, 2002), A14.

100. USA PATRIOT Act, Pub. L. No. 107-56, Section 201-2-2, 115 Stat. 272, 278 (2001).

101. 50 U.S.C. Section 1803 (2000).

102. Patriot Act, Section 203(d)(1), 115 Stat. 272, 280 (2001).

103. Patriot Act, Section 206, amending Section 105(c)(2)(B) of the Foreign Intelligence Surveillance Act.

104. Patriot Act, Section 213.

105. Quoted in Ron Hutcheson, "Disputing the Powers That Be," *Philadelphia Inquirer* (January 24, 2006), A1.

106. *Wong Wing v. United States*, 163 U.S. 228 (1896).

107. 66 *Federal Register* 48334 (September 20, 2001).

108. Richard M. Pious, *The War on Terrorism and the Rule of Law* (Los Angeles: Roxbury Publishing Co., 2006), 110.

109. *Ibid.*, 165–166.

110. Michael Greenberger, "You Ain't Seen Nothin' Yet: The Inevitable Post-Hamdan Conflict between the Supreme Court and the Political Branches," *Maryland Law Review* 66 (2007), 805, 807.

111. 542 U.S. 466 (2004).

112. *Hamdi v. Rumsfeld*, 316 F.3d 450, 462 (4th Cir. 2003).

113. *Hamdi v. Rumsfeld*, 542 U.S. 507 (2004).

114. *Rumsfeld v. Padilla*, 542 U.S. 426 (2004).

115. Pious, 141–142.

116. *Military Commission Order No. 1* (Washington, D.C.: U.S. Department of Defense, March 21, 2002).

117. 126 S.Ct. 2749 (2006).

118. Protocol Additional to the Geneva Conventions of 12 August 1949, and Relating to the Protection of Victims of International Armed Conflicts (Protocol I), part 1, article 3 (June 8, 1977), available at **www.unhchr.ch/html/menu3/b/93.htm**.

119. Memo to Department of Defense officials from Deputy Defense Secretary Gordon England, printed in Scott Shane, "Terror and Presidential Power: Bush Takes a Step Back," *New York Times* (July 12, 2006), A18.

120. The Military Commissions Act of 2006, Pub. L. No. 109-366, 120 Stat. 2600.

121. William Glaberson, "Military Judges Dismiss Charges for Two Detainees," *New York Times* (June 5, 2007), A1.

122. David Johnston, "At a Secret Interrogation, Dispute Flared over Tactics," *New York Times* (September 10, 2006), A1.

123. 18 U.S.C. Section 2340A (1994).

124. President George W. Bush, Statement by the President at the United Nations International Day in Support of Victims of Torture (June 26, 2003), available at **www.whitehouse.gov/news/releases/2003/06/ 20030626-3.html**.

125. Memorandum from Donald Rumsfeld, Secretary of Defense, U.S. Department of Defense to Commander, U.S. Southern Command, "Counter-resistance Techniques" (January 15, 2003).

126. Major General George R. Fay, "AR 15-6 Investigation of the Abu Ghraib Detention Facility and 205th Military Intelligence Brigade 8 (2004)," at **news.findlaw.com/hdocs/docs/dod/fay82504rpt.pdf**.

127. Quoted in "Do We Use Torture?" *Los Angeles Times* (June 18, 2007), 16.

CHAPTER 17

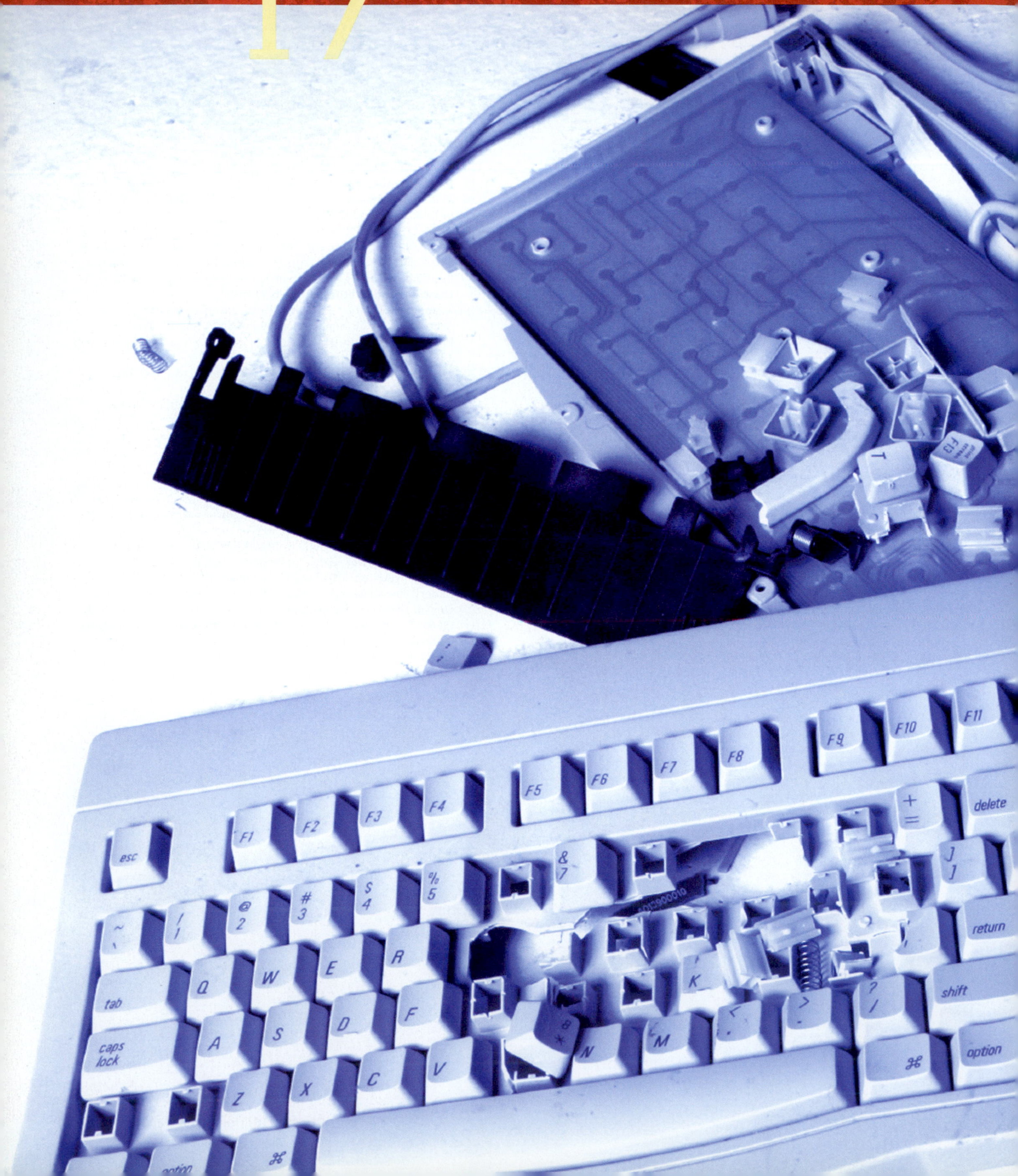

Cyber Crime and the
Future of Criminal Justice

Chapter outline

- **Computer Crime and the Internet**
- **Cyber Crimes against Persons and Property**
- **Cyber Crimes in the Business World**
- **Cyber Crimes against the Community**
- **Fighting Cyber Crime**
- **Freedom of Speech on the Internet**
- **Criminal Justice: Looking to the Future**
- **Criminal Justice in Action—Virtual Child Pornography**

Learning objectives

After reading this chapter, you should be able to:

LO1 Distinguish cyber crime from "traditional" crime.

LO2 Indicate how the Internet has expanded opportunities for identity theft.

LO3 List the three reasons why cyberstalking may be more commonplace than physical stalking.

LO4 Describe the following three forms of malware: (a) botnets, (b) worms, and (c) viruses.

LO5 Outline the three major reasons that the Internet is conducive to juvenile cyber crime.

LO6 Explain how the Internet has contributed to piracy of intellectual property.

LO7 Indicate how encryption programs protect digital data from unauthorized access.

LO8 Explain why the right to free speech on the Internet is not absolute.

LO9 Describe how data mining can be used to combat terrorism.

Internet Baiting

Raymond Merrill was a lonely man. Like millions of other lonely men (and women), the fifty-six-year-old Californian turned to the Internet for solace and hope. Eventually, his surfing led him to a Latin singles Web site, where he met Regina Filomena Crasovich Rachid, a fortyish Brazilian woman who seemed ready, if not eager, to start a new life with him. "I have more kisses for you than there are stars in the sky," Merrill wrote to Rachid in one of hundreds of heartfelt e-mails. "I have more kisses and affection to give you than all the little drops of rain that stay on your window for an entire dark night," she replied.

Rachid had other interests besides "kisses and affection." "Love doesn't pay my bills," she complained in another e-mail detailing her financial woes. After a trip to Brazil during which he bought Rachid a sport utility vehicle, Merrill discovered that $20,000 had been falsely charged to his credit card, with all signs pointing to his new love as the culprit. Undeterred, he planned another visit—to present her with a $5,000 engagement ring.

Merrill left the United States on March 21, 2006, never to return. His charred remains were found several weeks later in a vacant lot twenty-five miles from the beach town of Cabo Frio. Brazilian officials believe that

Rachid and a male accomplice named Nelson Siqueira Neves drugged Merrill and held him captive for six days while they emptied his bank account of $132,000. Then, they strangled him with copper wire, soaked his body with gasoline, and set him alight. "He was very intoxicated with the idea of love and being loved," said Merrill's sister, trying to explain the irrational behavior that led her brother to his demise.

AP Photo/Family of Raymond Merrill

▲ According to Brazilian authorities, Regina Rachid, pictured here, used the Internet to defraud Californian Raymond Merrill and eventually lure him to his death.

Computer Crime Any wrongful act that is directed against computers and computer parts or that involves wrongful use or abuse of computers or software.

Criminal Justice ⚖ Now™

Maximize your study time by using ThomsonNOW's Personalized Study plan to help you review this chapter and prepare for examination. The Study Plan will

- Help you identify areas on which you should concentrate

- Provide interactive exercises to help you master the chapter concepts; and

- Provide a post-test to confirm you are ready to move on to the next chapter information.

Just as the Internet provided Regina Filomena Crasovich Rachid with the means to lure Raymond Merrill to his death, it also provided Brazilian law enforcement officials with the vital clue they needed to crack the case. In the midst of what was proving to be a fruitless search for Nelson Siqueira Neves, investigators decided to scan orkut.com, a social networking Web site popular with Brazilians. Sure enough, Siqueira had recently posted a photo of himself with another man named Evan Celso Augusto Ribiero, who eventually admitted to helping Siqueira and Rachid dispose of Merrill's corpse.[1]

In this final chapter of the textbook, we will examine the various types of crimes that take place in cyberspace and the efforts of law enforcement agencies to combat them. We will also look at private methods of fighting such crimes—just as technology provides opportunities for wrongdoers, it also provides individuals with the means to better protect themselves. Finally, we will explore the impact that the virtual explosion of technological advances has had on the criminal justice system and consider how these developments will affect the immediate future of law enforcement.

Computer Crime and the Internet

The U.S. Department of Justice broadly defines **computer crime** as "any violation of criminal law that involves a knowledge of computer technology for [its] perpetration, investigation, or prosecution."[2] More specifically, computer crimes can be divided into three categories, according to the computer's role in the particular criminal act:

1. The computer is the "object" of a crime, such as when the computer itself or its software is stolen.
2. The computer is the "subject" of a crime, just as a house is the "subject" of a burglary. This type of computer crime occurs, for example, when someone "breaks into" a computer to steal personal information such as a credit-card number.
3. The computer is the "instrument" of a crime, as when Regina Filomena Crasovich Rachid used a computer first to con Raymond Merrill out of a great deal of money and then to facilitate his kidnapping and murder.[3]

A number of the white-collar crimes discussed in Chapter 1, such as fraud, embezzlement, and the theft of intellectual property, are now committed with the aid of computers and are thus considered computer crimes.

In this chapter, we will be using a broader term, **cyber crime,** to describe any criminal activity occurring via a computer in the virtual community of the Internet. It is very difficult, if not impossible, to tell how much cyber crime actually takes place. Often, people never know that they have been the victims of this type of criminal activity. Furthermore, businesses sometimes fail to report such crimes for fear of losing customer confidence. Nonetheless, in June 2007, the Internet Crime Complaint Center (IC3), operated as a partnership between the Federal Bureau of Investigation (FBI) and the National White Collar Crime Center, received its 1 millionth complaint after only seven years of operation.[4] Furthermore, the United States appears to have gained the unwanted distinction of being the world's leader in cyber crime, with more than one-third of all global computer attacks originating in this country.[5]

Cyber Crimes against Persons and Property

Most cyber crimes are not "new" crimes. Rather, they are existing crimes in which the Internet is the instrument of wrongdoing. When, for example, Dr. Anna Maria Santi of Queens, New York, was arrested in 2007 for the illegal sale of steroids and other performance-enhancing drugs over the Internet, she was charged with criminal sale of a controlled substance. The charge would have been the same if she had sold the drugs through the mail or person to person on a street corner. The challenge for law enforcement is to apply traditional laws, which were designed to protect persons from physical harm or to safeguard their physical property, to crimes committed in cyberspace. Here, we look at several types of activity that constitute "updated" crimes against persons and property—online consumer fraud, cyber theft, and cyberstalking.

CYBER CONSUMER FRAUD

The expanding world of e-commerce (buying and selling that takes place in cyberspace) has created many

■ Figure 17.1 Criminal Activities Online

In 2006, the Internet Crime Complaint Center (IC3) received about 200,000 complaints of online criminal behavior. As the graph shows, many of these complaints involved auction fraud.

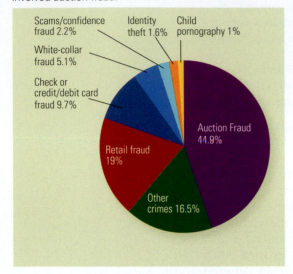

Source: National White Collar Crime Center and Federal Bureau of Investigation, *Internet Crime Report: January 1, 2006–December 31, 2006* (Washington, D.C.: Internet Crime Complaint Center, 2007), Chart 5, page 7.

benefits for consumers. It has also led to some challenging problems, including fraud conducted via the Internet. In general, fraud is any misrepresentation knowingly made with the intention of deceiving another and on which a reasonable person would and does rely to her or his detriment. **Cyber fraud,** then, is fraud committed over the Internet. Scams that were once conducted solely by mail or phone can now be found online, and new technology has led to increasingly more creative ways to commit fraud. In 2007, for example, online advertisements featuring adorable photos of "free" English bulldog puppies began appearing on the Internet. A number of respondents paid close to $1,000 in "shipping fees" (from West Africa), "customs costs," "health insurance," and other bogus charges before realizing that no puppy would be forthcoming.

No one knows the full extent of cyber fraud, but indications are that it is a very common form of cyber crime. In 2006, the IC3 received about 200,000 complaints of online crime involving losses of almost $200 million.[6] As you can see from ■ Figure 17.1, the two most widely reported forms of cyber crime are online auction fraud and online retail fraud.

Online Auction Fraud In its most basic form, online auction fraud is a simple process. A person puts up an expensive item for auction, on either a legitimate or a fake auction site, and then refuses to send the product after receiving payment. Or, as a variation, the wrongdoer may provide the purchaser with an item that is worth less than the one offered in the auction. The larger online auction sites such as eBay try to protect consumers against such schemes by providing warnings about deceptive sellers or offering various forms of insurance. The nature of the Internet, however, makes it nearly impossible to completely block fraudulent auction activity. Because users can assume multiple identities, it is very difficult to pinpoint a fraudulent seller—he or she will simply change his or her screen name with each auction.

Online Retail Fraud Somewhat similar to online auction fraud is online retail fraud, in which consumers pay directly (without bidding) for items that are never delivered. Because most online consumers will purchase items only from reputable, brand-name sites, criminals have had to take advantage of some of the complexities of cyberspace to lure unknowing customers.

Again, though determining the actual extent of online sales fraud is difficult, the anecdotal evidence suggests it is a substantial problem. Virginian Jeremy Jaymes grossed more than $750,000 per week selling nonexistent or worthless products such as "penny stock pickers" and Internet history erasers. By the time he was arrested in 2004, he had amassed an estimated $24 million from his various fraudulent schemes. Perhaps the longest-running Internet fraud is the "Nigerian letter fraud scam." In this scheme, targets are sent e-mails promising them a percentage if they will send funds to help fictitious officials from the African country transfer millions of nonexistent dollars to Western banks. The scam was recently updated to reflect current events, with con artists sending out e-mails asking for financial help in retrieving the fortune of a loved one or associate who had perished as a result of the violent conflict in Iraq.

Cyber Fraud Any misrepresentation knowingly made over the Internet with the intention of deceiving another and on which a reasonable person would and does rely to his or her detriment.

CYBER THEFT

In cyberspace, thieves are not subject to the physical limitations of the "real" world. A thief can steal data stored in a networked computer with network access from anywhere on the globe. Only the speed of the connection and the thief's computer equipment limit the quantity of data that can be stolen.

Identity Theft This freedom has led to a marked increase in **identity theft,** which occurs when the wrongdoer steals a form of identification—such as a name, date of birth, or Social Security number—and uses the information to access the victim's financial resources. This crime existed to a certain extent before widespread use of the Internet. Thieves would "steal" calling-card numbers by watching people using public telephones, or they would rifle through garbage to find bank account or credit-card numbers. The identity thief would then use the calling-card or credit-card number or withdraw funds from the victim's account until the theft was discovered.

The Internet, also known as the "information highway," has provided even easier access to personal data. Frequent Web surfers surrender a wealth of information about themselves without knowing it. Many Web sites use "cookies" to collect data on those who visit their sites. The data can include the areas of the site the user visits and the links the user clicks on. Furthermore, Web browsers often store information such as the consumer's name and e-mail address. Finally, every time a purchase is made online, the item is linked to the purchaser's name, allowing Web retailers to amass a database of who is buying what.

Positive Trends As many consumers are discovering, any information that can be collected can be stolen. About 3 percent of all American households—3.6 million in total—report that at least one member has been the victim of a recent identity theft.[7] Competition among those who traffic in the tools of identity theft has become so fierce that the price of the information has plummeted. Among identity thieves, stolen credit-card numbers are sold for as little as $1 each, while a complete identity, including date of birth, bank account, and government-issued identification numbers, can be purchased for less than $15.[8]

At the same time, the incidence of identity theft appears to be dropping. According to a survey sponsored by the banking and credit-card industries, the percentage of respondents reporting identity theft dropped from 4.7 percent (suffering $54 billion in losses) in 2003 to 3.7 percent (suffering $49 billion in losses) in 2007.[9] The survey's authors attribute this decline to greater consumer awareness of the problem and improved efforts on the part of credit-card companies and banks to protect the data under their control.[10] (See ■ Figure 17.2 for information on how to avoid being the target of identity theft.) In addition, many online criminals are turning to *synthetic identity theft,* in which they use a fabricated identity to gain access to online funds, rather than pilfering a "true" identity.[11]

Phishing A distinct form of identity theft known as *phishing* has added a different wrinkle to the practice. In a phishing attack, the perpetrators "fish" for financial data and passwords from consumers by posing as a legitimate business such as a bank or credit-card company. The "phisher" sends an e-mail asking the recipient to "update" or "confirm" vital information,

■ **Figure 17.2 Eight Steps toward Preventing Identity Theft**

1. **Share information only when necessary.** Make sure that you give out your credit-card number and/or Social Security number only to a trustworthy party that has a legitimate need for this information.

2. **Be cautious about providing identity information in public.** Be on the lookout for "shoulder surfers" when entering account information at an automated teller machine. Also, do not put private information on something that can be easily observed, such as a key chain.

3. **Do not carry unnecessary identification in a purse or wallet.** Thieves can easily gain personal information after stealing these items.

4. **Secure your mailbox.** Thieves can also obtain personal information through stolen mail.

5. **Secure information on your personal computer.** Again, specific information such as credit-card or Social Security numbers should be given out only to legitimate enterprises on the Internet. Also, you should ensure that your hard drive is protected by firewall software that isolates your computer system from the rest of the Internet, thus preventing unauthorized access to personal data.

6. **Shred all nonessential material containing identity information.** Any material with your personal information, such as credit-card statements, canceled checks, bank statements, or even junk mail, should be destroyed before it is placed in the trash.

7. **Remove your name from mailing lists.** This reduces the number of commercial entities with access to your identity information. To opt out of many direct-mail lists, visit the Web site of the Direct Marketing Association at **www.dmaconsumers.org/cgi/offmailing**.

8. **Review financial statements.** Review all credit-card statements, bank account statements, and other personal financial reports for accuracy. Also, pay attention to billing cycles. A missed bill may mean that the document has been stolen.

Source: Office of the United States Attorney.

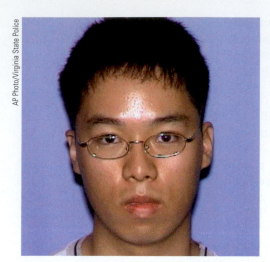

▲ Cho Seung Hui, responsible for the massacre that left 32 dead on the campus of Virginia Tech in April 2007, had been accused of stalking two female students prior to his violent outburst. In one case, his instrument was a cell phone and, in the second, he used text messaging. Do these activities fall under the category of cyberstalking? Why or why not?

> "Reply to my e-mail or you will die."
>
> —*E-mail message sent by a male University of San Diego undergraduate to a female classmate*

Cyberstalking The crime of stalking, committed in cyberspace though the use of the Internet, e-mail, or another form of electronic communication. Generally, stalking involves harassing a person and putting that person in reasonable fear for his or her safety or the safety of the person's immediate family.

often with the threat that an account or some other service will be discontinued if the information is not provided. Once the unsuspecting target enters the information, the phisher can use it to masquerade as the person or to drain his or her bank or credit account. Although the true incidence of phishing is probably incalculable, one study estimates that 57 million people receive at least one fraudulent e-mail each year, and the 3 percent who actually provide their personal data in response lose more than $1 billion annually.[12]

CYBERSTALKING

California passed the first antistalking law in 1990, in response to the murders of six women—including Rebecca Shaeffer, a television star—by stalkers. The law made it a crime to harass or follow a person while making a "credible threat" that puts the person in reasonable fear for her or his safety or the safety of the person's immediate family.[13] Almost every state and the federal government followed with their own antistalking legislation.

By the mid-1990s, it had become clear that these laws, most of which required a "physical act" such as following the victim, were insufficient. They could not protect persons against **cyberstalking**, in which the perpetrator uses the Internet, e-mail, or some other form of electronic communication to carry out his or her harassment. In 1998, California, once again leading the way, amended its stalking statute to include threats made through an electronic communication device.[14] Today, forty-five states and the federal government have their own legislation criminalizing cyberstalking.

The Threat of Cyberstalking The only limitations on a cyberstalker's methods are computer savvy and imagination. He or she may send threatening e-mail messages directly to the victim or menace the victim in a live chat room. Some cyberstalkers deceive other Internet users into harassing or threatening their victim by impersonating that victim while making provocative comments online. In one 1998 California case, Gary Dellapenta, pretending to be an ex-girlfriend, posted Web messages that expressed rape fantasies along with her address. After six different men showed up at the woman's home, Dellapenta was charged under California's updated antistalking law and eventually sentenced to six years in prison.

Jason Russell of Gladstone, Missouri, took advantage of spyware technology to essentially hijack his ex-wife's computer. He sent her an anonymous e-mail that contained a forged e-greeting card. When his ex-wife downloaded the card, she unwittingly transferred and activated Lover-Spy software onto her computer. This software allowed Russell to monitor her online activities from his own home computer. In January 2006, a federal court judge sentenced Russell to three years of probation, including four months of home detention.[15]

An Easier Alternative Although no trustworthy statistics exist, most experts assume that cyberstalking is more commonplace than physical stalking.[16] While it takes a great deal of effort to physically stalk someone, it is relatively easy to harass a victim with electronic messages. Furthermore, the possibility of personal confrontation may discourage a stalker from actually pursuing his or her victim. This disincentive is irrelevant in cyberspace. Finally, physical stalking requires that the stalker and the victim be in the same geographic location. A cyberstalker can carry on his or her activities from anywhere on the planet, as long as he or she has access to a computer.[17]

LO3

Cyber Crimes in the Business World

Just as cyberspace can be a dangerous place for consumers, it presents a number of hazards for businesses that wish to offer their services on the Internet. The same circumstances that enable companies to reach a wide number of consumers also leave them vulnerable to cyber crime. The FBI estimates that all types of computer crime do about $400 billion in damage to American businesses each year.[18]

CREDIT-CARD CRIME ON THE WEB

In the previous section, credit-card theft was mentioned in connection with identity theft. An important point to note, however, is that stolen credit cards are much more likely to hurt merchants than the consumer from whom the card or card number has been appropriated. In most situations, the legitimate holders of credit cards are not held responsible for the costs of purchases made with a stolen number. That means the financial burden must be borne either by the merchant or by the credit-card company. Almost all of these companies require merchants to cover the costs—especially if the address to which the goods are sent does not match the billing address of the credit card.

Companies take further risks by storing their customers' credit-card numbers. In doing so, companies provide quicker service; the consumer can make a purchase by providing a code or clicking on a particular icon without entering the lengthy card number. These electronic warehouses are, however, quite tempting to cyber thieves. Several years ago, an unknown person was able to gain access to computerized records at CardSystems Solutions, a company in Tucson, Arizona, that processes credit-card transactions for small Internet businesses. The breach exposed 40 million credit-card numbers.

HACKERS

The person who "broke into" CardSystems' database to steal the credit-card numbers was a hacker. A **hacker** is someone who uses one computer to break into another. The danger posed by hackers has increased significantly because of **botnets,** or networks of computers that have been appropriated by hackers without the knowledge of their owners. A hacker will secretly install a program on thousands, if not millions, of personal computer "robots," or "bots," that allows him or her to forward transmissions to an even larger number of systems. In 2006, Christoper Maxwell was sentenced to three years in prison for using a botnet to spread unwanted advertising to tens of thousands of computers, including those belonging to a Seattle hospital and the U.S. Department of Defense.

Botnets are one of the latest forms of *malware,* a term that refers to any program that is harmful to a computer or, by extension, a computer user. A **worm,** for example, is a software program that is capable of reproducing itself as it spreads from one computer to the next. A **virus,** another form of malware, is also able to reproduce itself, but must be attached to an "infested" host file to travel from one computer network to another. Worms and viruses can be programmed to perform

Hacker A person who uses one computer to break into another.

Botnet A network of computers that have been appropriated without the knowledge of their owners and used to spread harmful programs via the Internet; short for *robot network*.

Worm A computer program that can automatically replicate itself over a network such as the Internet and interfere with the normal use of a computer. A worm does not need to be attached to an existing file to move from one network to another.

Virus A computer program that can replicate itself over a network such as the Internet and interfere with the normal use of a computer. A virus cannot exist as a separate entity and must attach itself to another program to move through a network.

AP Photo

a number of functions, such as prompting host computers to continually "crash" and reboot, or otherwise infect the system.

The Scope of the Problem Though the hackers and other "techies" who create worms and viruses are often romanticized as youthful rebels, they cause significant damage. A destructive virus can overload a company's computer system, making e-mail and many other functions impossible until it is cleaned out of the system. This cleansing process can cost between $100,000 and $5 million a day, depending on the size of the company affected. Experts estimate that about 10,000 viruses and worms are spreading through the Internet at any given time, with 500 new ones being created every month.[19]

The Computer Crime and Security Survey polled more than 600 U.S. companies and large government institutions and found that 52 percent had suffered security breaches through computer-based means in 2006; correcting the damage cost more than $50 million.[20] These numbers are actually down from previous years, a trend that analysts attribute to three factors: (1) more businesses are taking steps to protect their computer systems; (2) Internet wrongdoers are shifting their focus to identity theft, an easier and more profitable enterprise; and (3) many corporations refuse to report security breaches to law enforcement agencies because of negative publicity and possible loss of customers.[21]

▲ Computers offer juveniles a portal into the world of adult crime. The technological scope of the Internet allows young people to carry out complicated criminal schemes in private and at low cost. How does the anonymity provided by the Internet also encourage juvenile cyber crime?

Juvenile Cyber Crime In the early 2000s, a series of "hack attacks" were launched at some of the largest Internet companies, including Amazon.com and eBay. The sites either froze or significantly slowed down, causing nearly $2 billion in damage for the parent companies. While the FBI was searching for the hacker, one of its investigation chiefs joked that the companies' computer systems were so vulnerable that any fifteen-year-old with technological know-how could break into them.

As it turned out, the FBI agent was only a year off. The culprit was a sixteen-year-old Canadian high school dropout who was employed as a kitchen worker in Montreal when he was arrested. The teenager, who went by the moniker of Mafiaboy, had uploaded software programs on Web sites in Europe and South Korea, from which he bombarded the American companies with e-mails.

Making It Easy According to Assistant U.S. Attorney Joseph V. DeMarco, it should come as no surprise that Mafiaboy could cause so much damage. DeMarco

L05 believes that there are three main reasons why cyber crime is clearly suited to the habits and limitations of juveniles:

- *The enormous technological capacities of personal computers.* Most juvenile delinquents will never commit crimes more serious than shoplifting and other forms of petty theft. Advanced computer equipment and software, however, give these youths the ability to carry out complex criminal fraud and hacking schemes without leaving their bedrooms. Thus, computer technology has given juveniles the ability to "commit offenses that are disproportionate to their age." In addition, about 87 percent of all children have access to the Internet at home, at school, or through a library.[22]
- *The anonymity of the Internet.* The physical world denies juveniles the ability to commit many crimes. It would be very difficult, for example, for a fifteen-year-old to run a fraudulent auction in the flesh. The Internet, however, allows young people to depict themselves as adults, thereby opening up a

number of criminal possibilities that would otherwise be denied to them. Furthermore, the lack of a driver's license or the wealth necessary to travel does not limit a cyber juvenile delinquent's ability to commit far-reaching offenses, as we saw in the case of Mafiaboy.

- *The acceptance of hacking in youth culture.* A poll of nearly 50,000 elementary and middle school students conducted by Scholastic, Inc., found that nearly half of them did not consider hacking to be a crime.[23] Thus, DeMarco believes, there is an "ethical deficit" when it comes to youth and computer crimes: juveniles who would never consider robbery or burglary are not troubled by the prospect of committing cyber crimes.[24]

Schooling Juveniles on Cyber Crime Law enforcement has taken a two-pronged approach to dealing with juvenile cyber crime. First, government officials are becoming more aggressive in prosecuting juveniles who commit such crimes. In 2005, three sixteen-year-old students at Bay High School in Bay County, Florida, were arrested for hacking into the school computer to change grades for friends. In the past, such activity would probably have been seen as a disciplinary matter best handled by school officials. Second, the federal government has started several initiatives to teach children "cyberethics," including one that asks youngsters to "take a btye out of cyber crime" at the behest of McGruff the Crime Dog.[25]

▲ Jeremy Jaymes was the first person in the United States to be convicted of a felony for illegal spamming. In 2005, a Virginia judge sentenced him to nine years in prison for his wrongdoing. Why is spamming a criminal act deserving of such serious punishment?

THE SPREAD OF SPAM

Businesses and individuals alike are targets of **spam,** or unsolicited "junk e-mails" that flood virtual mailboxes with advertisements, solicitations, and other messages. Considered relatively harmless in the early days of the Internet's popularity, by 2006 spam accounted for about 73 percent of all e-mails.[26] Far from being harmless, the unwanted files can wreak havoc on business operations.

Responding to complaints from overwhelmed constituents, a number of jurisdictions have started to pass antispamming laws. In 2003, Congress passed the Controlling the Assault of Non-Solicited Pornography and Marketing Act (CAN-SPAM), which requires all unsolicited e-mails to be labeled and to include opt-out provisions and the sender's physical address.[27] In 2007, federal officials arrested Robert Alan Soloway, considered one of the world's most prolific spammers. Because Soloway had been using botnets, described earlier, to send out hundreds of millions of unwanted e-mails, he was charged under anti-identity theft laws for the appropriation of other people's domain names, among other crimes. Despite these efforts, the flow of spam continues unabated. Even the apprehension of a major spammer like Soloway has little effect—following his arrest, the volume of spam continued at 70 billion messages a day.[28]

PIRATING INTELLECTUAL PROPERTY ONLINE

Most people think of wealth in terms of houses, land, cars, stocks, and bonds. Wealth, however, also includes **intellectual property,** which consists of the products that result from intellectual, creative processes. The government provides various forms of protection for intellectual property such as copyrights and patents. These protections ensure that a person who writes a book or a song or creates a software program is financially rewarded if that product is sold in the marketplace.

Intellectual property such as books, films, music, and software is vulnerable to "piracy"—the unauthorized copying and use of the property. In the past, copying intellectual products was time consuming, and the quality of the pirated copies

Spam Bulk e-mails, particularly of commercial advertising, sent in large quantities without the consent of the recipient.

Intellectual Property Property resulting from intellectual, creative processes.

was clearly inferior. In today's online world, however, things have changed. Simply clicking a mouse can now reproduce millions of unauthorized copies, and pirated duplicates of copyrighted works obtained via the Internet are often exactly the same as the original, or close to it.

L06

The Business Software Alliance estimates that 35 percent of all business software is pirated, costing software makers more than $5 billion in 2006.[29] The International Federation of the Phonographic Industry believes that 37 percent of purchased CDs have been pirated.[30] In the United States, digital pirates can be prosecuted under the No Electronic Theft Act[31] and the Digital Millennium Copyright Act.[32] In 2005, the entertainment industry celebrated the United States Supreme Court's decision in *MGM Studios v. Grokster*.[33] The ruling provided film and music companies with the ability to file piracy lawsuits against Internet file-sharing Web sites that market software used primarily to illegally download intellectual property.

ELECTRONIC BANKING AND ONLINE MONEY LAUNDERING

Few industries have benefited from the convenience of online operation more than the banking industry. Cyberspace connections have allowed banks to transfer more funds in less time and to provide customers with more transfer and withdrawal options.

Cleaning Dirty Money With increased speed and efficiency, however, banks have lost a certain measure of control over the funds that pass through their computer systems. Bank officials have less information about where the funds are coming from or where they are headed. This "blind spot" has made online banking fertile ground for **money laundering.** Tax evaders, drug traffickers, and other criminals seek to "launder" their "dirty" money by moving it through as many bank accounts in as many countries as possible. In the past, uncovering money laundering was much easier for law enforcement agencies because large sums of cash had to be physically transported, often across international borders. Today, when transfers can be completed with the touch of a button, the criminals have the advantage.

U.S. law does require that banks "know their customers"—that is, a bank is required to know the source of a customer's funds.[34] The statute is clearly outdated, however, stemming from a time when bank officials enjoyed face-to-face relations with their customers. Banks can now use software filters to monitor the wire systems for suspicious transfers, but the filters are costly and may slow down legitimate transfers, thereby negating many of the benefits offered by cyber banking.

Digital Currency A number of companies have managed to avoid the regulatory regimes of the banking industry by dealing exclusively in digital currency. If a person wishes to open an account with one of these companies, he or she need only make a credit-card or wire transfer for the amount desired. The "digital dollars" are backed by hard currency, often gold bullion, thereby assuring the client that his or her funds are safe. Clients can use false names for their accounts, and the private companies are not required to monitor the account and report suspicious transactions to the government. Furthermore, clients can "cash out" and trade digital currency for regular money at any time.

Digital currency services seem custom-made for those who want to launder large amounts of ill-gotten money anonymously. In 2007, federal officials charged the directors of e-gold, Ltd., one such digital currency service, with money laundering and illegally "operating a money-transmitting business." According to the company's records, about 40,000 anonymous transactions, totaling as much as $6 million, occurred daily on the e-gold Web site.[35]

Money Laundering The introduction of illegally gained funds into the legal financial system with the goal of covering up the funds' true origin.

CYBERTERRORISM

The U.S. Secret Service agents who spent more than two years investigating e-gold, Ltd., found "hints" that the company's digital currency had been used by terrorist groups to move cash. "It's the perfect system," said one agent. "I can't see why they wouldn't use it."[36] Digital currency is hardly the only aspect of the Internet that worries terrorism experts. Yonah Alexander, director of the International Center for Terrorism Studies in Arlington, Virginia, warns that, with thirty computer experts and a budget of $10 million, a terrorist group could bring the United States "to its knees."[37] Alexander and many of his colleagues believe that the homeland security focus on CBERN terrorism, discussed in the last chapter, should be expanded to "CCBERN," with the extra "C" representing "cyberspace." The threat of **cyberterrorism,** or the use of the Internet to engage in terrorist activities, looms large over U.S. businesses and government operations alike.

A Perfect Fit The qualities of the Internet that make it an ideal environment for criminal behavior apply to cyberterrorism as well. The technology provides terrorist organizations with all of the following:

- Easy access to a potentially huge, worldwide audience.
- Anonymity of communication.
- Little or no regulation or other forms of government control.
- Fast flow of information.
- Inexpensive development and maintenance of a Web presence.[38]

The Internet has been a great boon to transnational terrorist groups such as al Qaeda. The small terrorist organization founded by Osama bin Laden in the 1980s in the remote mountains of Afghanistan has transformed itself into a worldwide web of small cells with no single base of operations, thanks in large part to the communications capabilities of electronic messaging. If any individual leader, including bin Laden himself, were to be killed or apprehended, the operations could continue relatively unhindered.

With *encryption* software, discussed later in the chapter, these groups can create secure communication channels with little cost or effort. Personal contact, long considered essential for recruitment and propaganda efforts, is no longer necessary. Now, potential recruits can download video games such as *Quest for Bush*, with its advanced levels of "Jihad Growing Up" and "Americans' Hell," or browse Web sites featuring graphic photos of dead and injured Muslim women and children, the supposed victims of Western aggression.

Cyber Warfare As an open society, the United States posts a great deal of information about its *infrastructure* on the Internet. (As explained in the last chapter, the term refers to the facilities and systems that provide the daily necessities of modern life, such as electricity, food, water, transportation, and telecommunications.) This information, of course, is just as easily retrieved by someone with criminal or terrorist intentions as by anybody else. While preparing in 2007 for his plot to destroy fuel pipelines to New York's JFK International Airport, Russell Defreitas was able to obtain detailed aerial satellite photos of the facility by visiting the Google Earth Web site. Many

Cyberterrorism The use of the Internet to attack or sabotage businesses and government agencies with the purpose of disrupting infrastructure systems.

▼ Two members of the U.S. Navy watch the action on the Battlescape screen at the Naval War College's War Gaming room. The various branches of the U.S. military have created numerous programs designed to combat terrorists and other potential foes in a "network-centric environment," otherwise known as cyberspace.

AP Photo/Victoria Arocho

observers also believe that the Internet can be used to directly damage our infrastructure. Two-thirds of the approximately 1,300 technology experts polled by the Pew Internet and American Life Project believe that a "devastating" attack will threaten American telecommunications networks, power grids, or air traffic control systems by 2015.[39]

The first such "Digital Pearl Harbor" was launched in the spring of 2007 against the northern European country of Estonia. Following a dispute with neighboring Russia over the treatment of statues honoring Russian war dead on Estonian land, the country's digital infrastructure was bombarded by a data flood from unknown sources. As a result, Web sites of Estonian government agencies were rendered useless, the country's largest bank almost had to shut down operations, and several daily newspapers found they could no longer function online. "This may well turn out to be the watershed in terms of widespread awareness of the vulnerability of modern society," said a U.S. military computer security expert of Estonia's experience. "It has gotten the attention of a lot of people."[40]

Self Check Fill in the Blanks

A _____ is someone who gains illegal access to one computer using another computer. These wrongdoers use _____, or networks of hijacked computers, to carry out a number of different improper online activities, including the illegal spread of junk e-mails known as _____. The Internet has also made it easier for cyber "pirates" to steal and disseminate _____ property, such as movies, music, and software, and for criminal elements to _____ "dirty" money. Check your answers on page 590.

Cyber Crimes against the Community

One of the greatest challenges cyberspace presents for law enforcement is how to enforce laws governing activities that are prohibted under certain circumstances but are not always illegal. Such laws generally reflect the will of the community, which recognizes behavior as acceptable under some circumstances and unacceptable under others. Thus, while it is legal in many areas to sell a pornographic video to a fifty-year-old, it is never legal to sell the same item to a fifteen-year-old. Similarly, placing a bet on a football game with a bookmaker in Las Vegas, Nevada, is legal, but doing the same thing with a bookmaker in Cleveland, Ohio, is not. Of course, in cyberspace it is often impossible to know whether the customer buying porn is aged fifty or fifteen, or if the person placing the bet is from Las Vegas or Cleveland.

ONLINE PORNOGRAPHY

The Internet has been a boon to the pornography industry. According to the Internet Filter Review, 23 percent of all Web sites (some 4.2 million) have pornographic content, and these sites generate $4.9 billion in revenue a year.[41] Though no general figures are available, the Internet has undoubtedly also been a boon to those who illegally produce and sell material depicting sexually explicit conduct involving a child—child pornography. As we have seen with other cyber crimes, the Internet is conducive to child pornography for a number of reasons:

- *Speed.* The Internet is the fastest means of sending visual material over long distances. Child pornographers can deliver their material faster and more securely online than through regular mail.
- *Security.* Any illegal material that is placed in the hands of a mail carrier is inherently in danger of being discovered. This risk is significantly reduced with e-mail. Furthermore, Internet sites that offer child pornography can

protect their customers with passwords, which keep random Web surfers (or law enforcement agents) from stumbling on the site of chat rooms.

- *Anonymity.* Obviously, anonymity is the most important protection offered by the Internet for sellers and buyers of child pornography, as it is for any person engaged in illegal behavior in cyberspace.[42]

Because of these three factors, courts and lawmakers have had a difficult time controlling the dissemination of illegal sexual content via the Internet. In 1996, Congress first attempted to protect minors from pornographic material on the Internet by passing the Communications Decency Act.[43] Later in this chapter, when we examine the issue of civil rights and the Internet, we will discuss the United States Supreme Court's reaction to these congressional efforts.

GAMBLING IN CYBERSPACE

In general, gambling is illegal. All states have statutes that regulate gambling—defined as any scheme that involves the distribution of property by chance among persons who have paid valuable consideration for the opportunity to receive the property. In some states, certain forms of gambling, such as casino gambling or horse racing, are legal. Many states also have legalized state-operated lotteries, as well as lotteries, such as bingo, conducted for charitable purposes. A number of states also allow gambling on Native American reservations.

Legal Confusion In the past, this "mixed bag" of gambling laws has presented a legal quandary: Can citizens in a state that does not allow gambling place bets to a Web site located in a state that does? After all, states have no constitutional authority over activities that take place in other states. Complicating the problem was the fact that many Internet gambling sites are located outside the United States in countries where Internet gambling is legal, and no state government has authority over activities that take place in other countries.

Congress Acts In 2006, Congress, concerned about money laundering stemming from online gambling, the problem of addiction, and underage gambling, passed legislation that greatly strengthened efforts to reduce online gaming. The Unlawful Internet Gambling Enforcement Act of 2006 cuts off the money flow to Internet gambling sites by barring the use of electronic payments, such as credit-card transactions, at those sites.[44]

The reaction by the online gambling industry was swift and dramatic: following the passage of this bill, many of the foreign-based companies suspended the use of real money on the Web sites serving the United States. Without the incentive of playing for cash, the sites have lost their appeal for most clients. In 2005, approximately 12 million Americans wagered $6 billion online,[45] numbers that are expected to plummet given the new landscape for Internet gambling in this country.

▲ On August 16, 2006, David Carruthers, former executive with the British online betting firm BetonSports, leaves a federal courthouse in St. Louis, Missouri. Carruthers had spent a month in jail following his arrest for, among other charges, facilitating gambling across state and national boundaries. The U.S. government claims that operating an online gambling Web site that caters to American citizens is illegal no matter where the establishment may be located—in this case the islands of Costa Rica and Antigua, where online gambling is legal.

Self Check Fill in the Blanks

Nearly a quarter of all Web sites feature _____. Gambling on the Internet was also popular until 2006, fueled by Internet companies located _____ the United States and thus beyond the reach of American law. That year, however, Congress passed legislation to curtail the use of electronic _____ on gambling sites, effectively shutting them down in the process. Check your answers on page 590.

Fighting Cyber Crime

Simply passing a law does not guarantee that the law will be effectively enforced. While the Unlawful Internet Gambling Enforcement Act may reduce visible Internet gambling, few believe that it will stop the practice altogether. "Prohibitions don't work," says Michael Bolcerek, president of the Poker Player's Alliance. "This [legislation] won't stop anything. It will just drive people underground."[46]

As we have already seen in this chapter, the Internet provides an ideal environment for the "underground" of society. With hundreds of millions of users reaching every corner of the globe, transferring unimaginable amounts of information almost instantaneously, the Internet has proved resistant to government regulation. In addition, although a number of countries have tried to "control" the Internet (see the feature *International CJ—The Great Firewall of China*), the U.S. government has generally adopted a "hands-off" attitude to better promote the free flow of ideas and encourage the growth of electronic commerce. Thus, in this country cyberspace is, for the most part, unregulated, making efforts to fight cyber crime all the more difficult.

ON THE CYBER BEAT: CHALLENGES FOR LAW ENFORCEMENT

In trying to describe the complexities of fighting cyber crime, Michael Vatis, former director of the FBI's National Infrastructure Protection Center, imagines a bank robbery during which the police arrive just as "the demand note and fingerprints are vanishing, the security camera is erasing its own images, and the image of the criminal is being erased from the mind of the teller."[47] The difficulty of gathering evidence is just one of the challenges that law enforcement officers face in dealing with cyber crime.

Computer Forensics Police officers cannot put yellow tape around a computer screen or dust a Web site for fingerprints. The best, and often the only, way to fight computer crime is with technology that gives law enforcement agencies the ability to "track" hackers and other cyber criminals through the Internet. But, as Michael Vatis observed, these efforts are complicated by the fact that digital evidence can be altered or erased even as the cyber crime is being committed. In Chapter 5, we discussed *forensics,* or the application of science to find evidence of criminal activity. Within the past two decades, a branch of this science known as **computer forensics** has evolved to gather evidence of cyber crimes.

The practice of computer forensics relies heavily on software that allows law enforcement agents to re-create the activities of a computer user. A program called EnCase, for example, can capture and analyze all the activity on a computer network, providing a set of "electronic fingerprints" that allows investigators to retrace the suspect's digital movements. EnCase and other similar software work by creating a digital duplicate of the targeted hard drive, enabling cyber sleuths to break access codes, determine passwords, and search files.[48] "Short of taking your hard drive and having it run over by a Mack truck," says one expert, "you can't be sure that anything is truly deleted from your computer."[49]

Jurisdictional Challenges Regardless of what type of cyber crime is being investigated, law enforcement agencies are often frustrated by problems of jurisdiction (explained more fully in Chapter 8). Jurisdiction is primarily based on physical geography—each country, state, and nation has jurisdiction, or authority, over crimes that occur within its boundaries. The Internet, however, destroys these traditional notions because geographic boundaries simply do not exist in cyberspace.

Domestic Jurisdiction To see how this can affect law enforcement efforts, let's consider a hypothetical cyberstalking case. Phil, who lives in State A, has been

Computer Forensics The application of computer technology to finding and utilizing evidence of cyber crimes.

The typical Internet café in China bears little resemblance to its American counterpart. Each *wangren,* or Web surfer, must register using a real name before logging on. The government requires that each computer feature spyware called Internet Detective, which records all online activities and immediately reports any suspicious activity, such as viewing pornography or the use of the words *freedom* or *democracy,* to computers at the local police station. Furthermore, several security guards sit in a back room, monitoring each computer to ensure that no banned content appears.

In the United States, the issue of whether the government should regulate the Internet—and, if so, how much—is hotly debated. In China, the question was answered long before the Internet was even imagined. Since the 1950s, the Chinese Communist Party has exercised strict control over all forms of information, including newspapers, television, radio, movies, and books. Today, under the auspices of the Ministry of Information Industry, that control has been extended to the World Wide Web. Under broad laws that prohibit, among other things, "destroying the order of society" and "making falsehoods or distorting

the truth," Chinese censors have free rein to limit the flow of information through government-controlled Internet service providers. The "Great Firewall," as this system is sometimes called, blocks entry to hundreds of "politically sensitive sites," including the Web pages of the *New York Times* and the human rights organization Amnesty International.

Censors known as "big mamas" watch over all official chat rooms in China, and they have the power to delete politically undesirable comments in real time and send a warning to the offender. When such statements go too far, the *wangren* can be arrested. Unlike in the United States, where the anonymity of a user is a given, in China every person with Internet access is required to register with authorities. Thus, "criminal" activity is more easily traced back to the host computer. According to Human Rights Watch, more than sixty Chinese "cyberdissidents" are in prison for expressing political opinions on the Internet.

FOR CRITICAL ANALYSIS

How would China-style Internet censorship affect cyber crime in the United States? Under what circumstances, if any, would Americans accept such levels of Internet control by the government?

---

sending e-mails containing graphic sexual threats to Stephanie, who lives in State B. Where has the crime taken place? Which police department has authority to arrest Phil, and which court system has authority to try him? To further complicate matters, what if State A has not yet added cyberstalking to its criminal code, while State B has? Does that mean that Phil has not committed a crime in his home state, but has committed one in Stephanie's?

The federal government has taken to answering this question by stating that Phil has committed a crime wherever it says he has. The Sixth Amendment to the U.S. Constitution states that federal criminal cases should be tried in the district in which the offense was committed.[50] Because the Internet is "everywhere," the federal government has a great deal of leeway in choosing the venue in which an alleged cyber criminal will face trial. So, for example, British citizen David Carruthers, whose online gambling company operated out of Costa Rica, was charged for taking sports bets in St. Louis, Missouri, because an Internet user accessed his Web site from that area.

International Jurisdiction Issues of jurisdiction are even more pronounced when it comes to international cyber crime. In 2006, U.S. officials charged Dimitry Ivanovich Golubov with a wide-ranging series of cyber crimes, including credit-card fraud. Police had recently arrested Golubov in his home country of Ukraine, and the U.S. government began the process of having him extradited to the United States. These efforts came to a halt when two high-ranking Ukrainian politicians inexplicably arranged for Golubov's release, an act over which the United States had no control because it lacks jurisdiction in Ukraine.

Federal law enforcement officials have worked to avoid such situations by building relationships with police in other countries. In 2007, the FBI used these ties to arrange for the arrest of sixteen Internet credit-card thieves operating out of Poland and Romania. Also in 2007, investigators from thirty-five different countries,

One of the most challenging aspects of my job on the High Technology Crime Task Force in San Diego County is the technological sophistication of the cyber criminals. They use all the tricks imaginable. As a result, it can take tremendous patience to solve a case. For example, I've been working on one case for almost three years that involves a small group of people selling counterfeit software over several states, at a cost to the public of some $20 million.

These kinds of difficult investigations can involve hundreds of legal processes, such as grand jury subpoenas and search warrants. I also have to make sure that I investigate suspect computers and networks in a way that complies with the search and seizure laws, while dealing with evidence that may be encrypted or hidden or protected in some way. For example, evidence may be linked to software time-bombs, Trojan horses, or other destruction devices. Also, the cyber criminals are very hard to find since they resort to aliases, phony addresses, and dead-end cell phone accounts. But the challenges are also what make it especially satisfying to see these individuals standing before a judge and jury.

COMPUTER FORENSICS My first job in law enforcement was with the San Diego County Marshall's office (now in the Sheriff's Department)—and they hired me just after I left the Navy. I eventually moved up the ranks to become a detective with the San Diego Police Department. My interest in computer forensics was just developing when I worked on an assignment with the U.S. Secret Service. That assignment made me realize that this was the area I wanted to pursue.

The case involved a man studying for his master's degree who was accused of plagiarizing his thesis. Apparently, he hid a gun in the lab and when he was brought before a team of

Courtesy of David Hendron

including the United States, identified seven hundred members of an international child-pornography organization that streamed live videos of children being raped. The ringleader was arrested, and more than thirty child victims were rescued. Given the international scope of the Internet, such multinational cooperative investigations are likely to become the rule, rather than the exception.

FEDERAL LAW ENFORCEMENT AND CYBER CRIME

Because of its freedom from jurisdictional restraints, the federal government has traditionally taken the lead in law enforcement efforts against cyber crime. This is not to say that little cyber crime prevention occurs on the local level. Most major metropolitan police departments have created special units to fight cyber crime. In general, however, only a handful of local police and sheriffs' departments have the resources to support a squad of cyber investigators.

Cyberangels is an organization designed to assist people who need help online—whether they are being cyberstalked, harassed, or otherwise victimized by cyber criminals. To visit its Web site, click on *Web Links* under *Chapter Resources* at **www.cjinaction.com**.

The Federal Bureau of Investigation As the primary crime-fighting unit of the federal government, the FBI has taken the lead in law enforcement efforts against cyber crime. The FBI has the primary responsibility for enforcing all federal criminal statutes involving computer crimes. (See ■ Figure 17.3 on page 580 for a rundown of these laws.) In 1998, the Bureau added a Cyber Division dedicated to investigating computer-based crimes. The Cyber Division and its administrators coordinate the FBI's efforts in cyberspace, specifically its investigations into computer crimes and intellectual property theft. The division also has jurisdiction over the Innocent Images National Initiative (IINI), the agency's online child-pornography subdivision. In addition, the FBI has developed several Cyber Action Teams (CATs), which combine the skills of some twenty-five law enforcement agents, digital forensics investigators, and computer programming experts.[51] Today, cyber crime is the FBI's third-highest priority (after counterterrorism and counterintelligence), and each of the bureau's fifty-six field divisions has at least one agent who focuses solely on crimes committed on the Internet.

professors to address their suspicions, he suddenly pulled out the gun and shot all three. Tragically, they all died. As part of the investigation, I did an extensive investigation of the suspect's computer and not only did I find copies of the thesis buried in different spots, but photo scans of the gun used in the shooting. This evidence helped convince jurors that the murders were premeditated, rather than the result of an impulsive rage or temporary insanity.

After this case, I decided I wanted to stay in high tech for the rest of my career in law enforcement. I've learned much on the job, but have also taken additional courses, and have a CRCD certificate (Certified Forensic Computer Examiner) that I earned through the International Association of Computer Investigative Specialists (IACIS).

THE PATIENCE REQUIREMENT A key ingredient to being successful as an investigator of cyber crimes is patience. You need to sift through mountains of data and go down many blind alleys before you can finally piece together the puzzle. Often the

hours are long, and the demands on your time great. In addition, it's important that you can be self-directed and self-motivated because often no one but you is as deeply immersed in an individual case.

If you're interested in this field, you should focus on developing your knowledge and understanding of computers, as well as making sure you have a good background in criminal justice. In particular, you should gain understanding of so-called white-collar crime since that is the foundation of most cyber crime.

Go to the **Careers in Criminal Justice Interactive CD** for a video interview with David Hendron and for other profiles in the field of criminal justice.

The United States Secret Service The Patriot Act greatly increased the Secret Service's role in fighting cyber crime. In the legal arena, the legislation gave the agency jurisidiction over some of the crimes listed in 18 U.S.C. Section 1030 (see Figure 17.3 on the following page).[52] The Secret Service was authorized to develop a national network of electronic crime task forces based on the New York Electronic Crime Task Force, a collaboration among federal, state, and local law enforcement officers and a wide range of corporate sponsors.

PRIVATE EFFORTS TO COMBAT CYBER CRIME

The fact remains, however, that the federal government has very little regulatory oversight over the Internet. Hence, it has little choice but to rely on the voluntary efforts of private companies to secure their computer infrastructures. Although many federal officials do not believe private companies are being sufficiently diligent in this area, the fear of being "hacked" has spurred a billion-dollar industry that helps clients—either individuals or businesses—protect the integrity of their computer systems. Because every computer hooked up to the Internet is a potential security breach, these experts help devise elaborate and ever-changing password systems to ensure that only authorized users access data. They also install protective software such as firewalls and antivirus software, which can limit outside access to a computer or network. Because cyber criminals are constantly updating their technology, cyberspace security firms help their clients do the same with their defensive systems.

Perhaps the most successful and controversial way to protect computer information is to encrypt it. Through **encryption,** a message (plaintext) is transformed into something (ciphertext) that only the sender and receiver can understand. Unless a third party is able to "break the code," the information will stay secure. Encryption is particularly useful in protecting the content of e-mails. The main drawback of this technology is the rate at which it becomes obsolete. As a general rule, computing power doubles every eighteen months, which means that

Encryption The process by which a message is transmitted into a form or code that the sender and receiver intend not to be understandable by third parties.

■ Figure 17.3 Federal Laws and Computer Crime

18 U.S.C. Section 1030—It is a crime to do any of the following to and/or by means of a computer used by a financial institution, used by the federal government, or used in interstate or foreign commerce or communication:

1. gain unauthorized entry into a government computer and thereby discover information which is intended to remain confidential, information which the perpetrator either unlawfully discloses to someone not authorized to receive it or retains in violation of the law;

2. gain unauthorized entry to a computer and thereby gain access to information to which the perpetrator is not entitled to have access;

3. gain unauthorized access to a computer and thereby further the perpetration of a fraud;

4. cause damage to a computer as the result either of gaining unauthorized access to it or of inserting a program, code, or information into the computer;

5. transmit, in interstate or foreign commerce, a threat to cause damage to a computer in order to extort money or property from a person or other legal entity.

6. traffic, with intent to defraud, in passwords which either permit unauthorized access to a government computer or affect interstate or foreign commerce; or

7. transmit in interstate or foreign commerce any threat to cause damage to a protected computer with intent to extort something of value.

18 U.S.C. Section 1462—It is a crime to use a computer to import obscene material into the United States.

18 U.S.C. Section 1463—It is a crime to transport obscene material in interstate or foreign commerce.

18 U.S.C. Section 2251—It is a crime to employ a minor or induce a minor to participate in making a visual depiction of a sexually explicit act if the depiction was created using materials that had been transported (including the transportation by computer) in interstate or foreign commerce.

18 U.S.C. Section 2252—It is a crime to transport child pornography in interstate or foreign commerce.

18 U.S.C. Section 1028—It is a crime to produce, transfer, or possess a device, including a computer, that is intended to be used to falsify identification documents.

Many traditional crimes encompass the use of a computer as well; for example, threatening the president's life or infringing a copyright.

Sources: Susan W. Brenner, "State Cybercrime Legislation in the United States of America: A Survey," *Richmond Journal of Law and Technology* 7 (Winter 2001), 1–5; Heather Jacobson and Rebecca Green, "Computer Crimes," *American Criminal Law Review* (Spring 2002), 280–284; and Computer Fraud and Abuse Act, 18 U.S.C. Section 1030.

programs to break the "latest" encryption code are always imminent. Consequently, those who use encryption must ensure that they update their systems at the same rate as those who would abuse it.

Self Check Fill in the Blanks

The practice of computer _____ is greatly aided by software that allows investigators to retrace a suspect's online activities. In general, however, law enforcement on the Internet is complicated by the lack of geographic boundaries in cyberspace, which leads to problems of _____. Private parties can help protect sensitive information on their computers by installing _____ software, which renders digital text unreadable without the proper code. Check your answers on page 590.

Freedom of Speech on the Internet

As mentioned earlier in this chapter, homeland security authorities are aware that global terrorists take advantage of encryption to engage in illegal activities. For this reason, the U.S. government has tried to restrict the export of encryption codes for fear that they will wind up in the wrong hands. These restrictions have been overturned on the ground that an encryption code is speech and therefore is protected by the First Amendment to the U.S. Constitution. This means that, under most circumstances, any regulations banning its export are unconstitutional.[53]

The open forum for speech that the Internet provides has forced Americans once again to consider this question: How much freedom is *too much* freedom? To date, most of the issues involving civil liberties and the Internet have had to do with efforts to limit freedom of speech, which is hardly surprising considering that the World Wide Web is, first and foremost, a form of communication.

HATE SPEECH ON THE INTERNET

In Chapter 4, we learned that the government can punish a criminal act more severely when the element of "hate" is present. Consequently, *hate crimes* are those crimes in which the victim is intentionally selected because of his or her race, gender, religion, sexual orientation, ethnicity, or disability. Can the government also punish **hate speech,** or words that are used intentionally to offend a person based on these same characteristics? By any measure, the Internet is teeming with Web sites that feature hate speech of every possible type, employing words as well as music, video, and games to spread their message of intolerance.

The Supreme Court and Hate Speech The United States Supreme Court has been vigilant in protecting all types of speech, including hate speech. The Court has consistently ruled that even though such speech may be offensive or harmful to an individual or group, it is still protected under the First Amendment.[54] Speech loses this protection, however, when the speaker intends to "inflict punishment, loss, or pain on another, or to injure another by the commission of some unlawful act."[55] In other words, the speech must be a "true" threat, not just threatening words.

(LO8)

In general, hate speech receives the same protection on the Internet as it does in the "real" world. Therefore, Web sites that advocate violence against African Americans, Jewish people, homosexuals, or any other minority group are generally safe from prosecution because of the First Amendment. This does not mean, however, that "anything goes" on the Internet. In 1999, the American Coalition of Life Activists and Advocates for Life Ministries was required to pay $108 million in damages (later reduced to $5 million) for inciting harm against doctors who performed abortions. The jury in the case found that a list of such doctors posted on the group's Web site was actually a "hit list" that turned the physicians into targets and, therefore, the site represented a true threat rather than just "speech."[56] (For a different look at this issue, see the feature *You Be the Judge—Wanted: Free Speech Protection* on the next page.)

Questions of Regulation A number of observers believe that the government should treat Internet hate speech with more suspicion than other forms of hate speech and that the courts should allow the government to do so regardless of the First Amendment. Before the Internet, extreme racists and other bigots existed in relative isolation. In many instances, they could not communicate with others who shared their beliefs without great effort or cost. Today, extremists can reach a huge audience with the click of a keyboard button, and the Internet has become a highly effective means for various hate groups to spread their ideologies.

Opponents of this idea counter that the Internet is, above all, a forum for the free exchange of ideas and that any sort of "special" hate speech regulation would stifle this freedom. They point out that, just as extremists can post their ideas on the Web, so too can those who disagree with hateful viewpoints.[57] Furthermore, the practical difficulties of policing the millions of potentially hateful Web sites, much less tracking their sources, make the proposition a daunting one for law enforcement agencies.

WEAPON RECIPES ON THE INTERNET

In the late 1990s, when the Internet was still in its relative infancy, two Pittsburgh teenagers built several pipe bombs and placed them on the

▼ The Aryan Nations is an organization that espouses the superiority of the white race and celebrates Nazism, the racist philosophy of Adolf Hitler. Why is it difficult for the government to regulate Aryan Nations Web sites, such as this one, that clearly promote violence and racial hatred?

Aryan Nations Web site

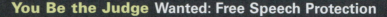

You Be the Judge Wanted: Free Speech Protection

THE FACTS Gary and Sherry are arrested in Alabama for distributing marijuana. To lessen their own penalties, the couple tell government agent DeJohn that a man named Leon hired them to sell drugs. Later that day, DeJohn arrests Leon and charges him with possession of marijuana with intent to distribute. Within a week, Leon sets up a Web site concerning his case. The site features a "WANTED" poster, with pictures of Gary and Sherry below the word "WANTED." Beneath the photos is a statement asking for information about "these informants." The government files a motion asking for the Web site to be shut down on the ground that its unstated purpose is to keep Gary and Sherry from testifying at Leon's trial.

THE LAW To shut down the Web site, the government must prove that Leon knowingly intimidated or threatened Gary and Sherry and that he did so with the intent to prevent them from testifying. Because the Web site is speech and therefore protected by the First Amendment, the government must also show that Leon made a "true" threat, defined as a statement that a reasonable person would construe as a serious expression of an intention to inflict bodily harm.

YOUR DECISION At a pretrial hearing, Sherry testifies that the Web site made her "fearful of what people might do" to her and frightened her into leaving Alabama. She also says that although Leon never threatened her regarding her appearance at his trial, other people had. Gary testifies that the site has "changed his life dramatically" and that he is afraid to let his children leave the house. Agent DeJohn informs the court that three other witnesses have backed out of agreements to testify against Leon since the Web site was posted on the Internet. On the other side, Leon's attorney claims that the fake "WANTED" poster was simply a way for his client to gather more information about the government witnesses for use at trial. Do you think that the Web site is a "true" threat? How does your opinion dictate whether it should be shut down?

[To see how a U.S. district court judge ruled in this case, go to Example 17.1 in Appendix B.]

tracks of a commuter railroad. After being arrested, they claimed that they learned to construct the devices using information provided by a Web site dedicated to the construction of explosives. Instructional materials for explosive devices existed for decades before the spread of the Internet. Nevertheless, as with hate speech, the Web has increased their availability, raising questions about whether sites that provide such materials should be subject to regulation.

No major case involving a Web site of this type has made its way into the courts, but in 1997 the U.S. Court of Appeals for the Fourth Circuit held that the publishers of a book by a "hit man" were not protected by the First Amendment after a reader used the document as a "how to" guide to carry out a murder.[58] Though some observers criticized this decision on the ground that merely publishing an instructional manual does not fulfill the *mens rea* requirements for committing a crime (see Chapter 3 to review *mens rea*), the court found that the publishers should have foreseen the manual's potential to inspire copycat crimes. A similar argument could be made under the "material support" provisions of the Antiterrorism and Effective Death Penalty Act (see Chapter 16), should a link be established between a terrorist act and a Web site that provided, even unintentionally, instructions for the methods used in the attack.[59]

OBSCENITY ON THE INTERNET

Obscenity Speech that is not protected by the First Amendment because it is deemed to be offensive to community standards of decency.

Some observers believe that weapons recipes should be banned from the Internet because they contribute nothing positive to the public good.[60] This argument is crucial to the concept of **obscenity,** a term that covers speech (including images, art, and videos) that is not protected by the First Amendment. A work is obscene if:

1. The average person would find that it causes lascivious or lustful thoughts and desires;
2. The work describes, in an offensive way, sexual conduct as defined by state law; *and*
3. The work "lacks serious literary, artistic, political, or scientific value."[61]

Although, as we have seen, pornographic Web sites on the Internet number in the millions, the images on those sites are protected by a Supreme Court ruling that the First Amendment allows the private possession of adult pornography in the home.[62] Indeed, the Court has stated that a "person's inclinations and 'fantasies'. . . are his own and beyond the reach of the government."[63] This leniency does not, however, extend to obscenity or child pornography, perhaps the most controversial free speech issue in cyberspace and one that we will address further in the *Criminal Justice in Action* feature at the end of this chapter.

Self Check Fill in the Blanks

Most communication on the Internet is protected by the _____ Amendment to the U.S. Constitution. This protection does not, however, extend to speech that represents _____ threats or _____, which is speech that is offensive to community standards of decency. Check your answers on page 590.

Criminal Justice: Looking to the Future

In 1911, the *New York Times*, reacting to reports of a new machine that could determine whether a person was telling the truth, predicted a dazzling future for the criminal justice system:

> [T]here will be no jury, no horde of detectives and witnesses, no charges and counter-charges, and no attorney for the defense. These impediments of our courts will be unnecessary. The State will merely submit all suspects to the tests of scientific instruments.[64]

Almost a century later, the machine—a polygraph—has failed to meet such lofty expectations. Although widely used in the private sector, most evidence from polygraphs, which supposedly read a subject's stress levels during questioning to ascertain if the answers are truthful, is inadmissible in criminal courts.

Today, a new lie-detector machine is causing a similar stir. The fMRI scans changes in the flow of oxygenated blood in the brain and operates on the theory that it takes more effort—and therefore more oxygen—to create a lie than to stick to the facts. Some observers are comparing the potential impact of the fMRI to that of DNA fingerprinting, which, as we saw in Chapter 6, has revolutionized the criminal investigation.[65] In reality, the fMRI, which has yet to survive even the most basic peer review testing, is unlikely to become the miracle device touted by its supporters. We have discussed a number of technologies in this textbook, from infrared sensors that can "see" through walls to satellites that can track criminals from thousands of miles above the earth. For most criminal justice experts, however, the most promising new crime-fighting technology has existed for years: the database.

DATA MINING: "CONNECTING THE DOTS"

In the wake of the September 11, 2001, terrorist attacks on New York City and Washington, D.C., a number of "what if" scenarios emerged. "What if" the FBI and the Central Intelligence Agency (CIA) had shared information about the hijackers living in the United States? "What if" Zacarias Moussaoui's computer had been searched? One of the most intriguing "what if" scenarios involves two messages intercepted by the National Security Agency (NSA) from pay phones in

▲ At the Terrorist Threat Integration Center (TTIC), a special unit at CIA headquarters in Langley, Virginia, government agents data mine, or collect and cross-check large amounts of terrorist-related information. How can data mining be used to protect the United States against terrorist attacks?

al Qaeda–controlled Pakistan on September 10, 2001: "The match begins tomorrow" and "Tomorrow is zero hour."

The messages were not translated until September 12. But given the CIA's knowledge that two of the hijackers were in the United States and had previously been linked to al Qaeda, the messages could conceivably have been a major piece of intelligence. They could have spurred the agency to make computerized cross-references of the two men's credit-card accounts, frequent-flier programs, and cell phone calls. By "connecting the dots," the CIA might have noticed that these two men and seventeen others who had been in close contact with each other were flying on the same day at the same time on four different airplanes.[66]

Better Business Strategy "Connecting the dots" in this way is known as **data mining,** a technique that uses information technology to determine patterns and links in existing data to predict behavior. Corporations have long used data mining to anticipate future buying patterns by consumers based on their past purchases. The technique has a shorter history in law enforcement, but improved data-mining software all but ensures its place in the future of crime fighting.

A simple example of how data mining can work features the Bethlehem (Pennsylvania) Police Department, which was struggling to control a graffiti epidemic several years ago. Officers began collecting information on the graffiti—its location, the words used, the colors used, and the obvious gang affiliations represented in the "street art." By exposing these data, along with the identities of known graffiti offenders and their own behavioral patterns, to data-mining software, Bethlehem police were able to determine who was doing what and make the necessary arrests to "clean up" Bethlehem.[67]

Mining for Terrorists While data mining has been used in many areas of crime fighting (the HBO series *The Wire* showed it helping police track drug dealers via disposable cell phones), the technology's greatest potential seems to be in counterterrorism.

L09 FBI computers are continuously tracking and cross-checking vast quantities of private information on terrorism suspects: e-mails, Internet chat rooms, instant messages, and telephone conversations. Section 215 of the Patriot Act allows the FBI to obtain the records of credit-card companies, telephone companies, businesses, hospitals, Internet service providers (ISPs), and educational institutions when these records are needed for an international terrorism investigation.[68]

The means for obtaining this information is a **national security letter (NSL).** So, for example, if the FBI suspects that a particular terrorist suspect has been using the Internet, it can send an NSL to an ISP requesting data on that suspect's e-mails, Web sites visited, and other personal records. NSLs may be used only in conjunction with "international terrorism cases," meaning that they are unavailable for other criminal investigations.[69] Because they do not require the prior approval of a judge, NSLs have, as we shall see, proved quite popular with federal agents.

IDENTIFICATION ISSUES

Of course, the more data that data-mining programs have to work with, the more valuable these programs are. Throughout this textbook, we have seen the ways in which the government has increased its access to personal information. In

Data Mining The analysis of data to identify patterns of behavior.

National Security Letter (NSL) A document from the FBI directing a third party to provide information concerning customers or patrons.

Chapter 6, we discussed efforts to expand DNA databases by taking samples not only from convicted felons, but also from all those persons arrested merely on the suspicion of committing a crime. In Chapter 16, we learned about the US-VISIT program designed to track all visa holders visiting the United States. Another data-gathering program with far-reaching implications involves the most common form of identification in the United States: the driver's license.

"Smart" Cards of the Near Future In 2005, Congress passed the REAL ID Act, which proposes to create a database that will contain information on every adult American citizen who drives a car.[70] The legislation "requests" that states change the way that they issue driver's licenses. Under the new rules, state licensing offices will have to verify the identity of every person who applies for a new license or renews an old one and ensure that he or she is a U.S. citizen. The new driver's license will include much of the same information as today's version, but each card will also contain a "smart chip" that will allow government officials to retrieve more detailed information, such as fingerprints or employment history. (See ■ Figure 17.4 for more information on these requirements.)

Under the terms of the REAL ID Act, anybody wishing to use federally regulated services such as airplanes, national parks, trains, and federal courthouses will have to possess the new driver's license or a state-issued identification card containing the same information. Each state is also required to create and maintain a database containing all information printed on its driver's licenses and make these records available to other states. The data must also be accessible by police and the federal government. Federal law enforcement officials hope these measures will make it more difficult for illegal aliens to obtain driver's licenses through fraudulent means.

■ **Figure 17.4** The Driver's License of the Future

In 2005, Congress passed the REAL ID Act, which will change the way states issue driver's licenses. Federal officials hope that these changes will make it more difficult for noncitizens wishing to commit terrorist acts on U.S. soil to obtain driver's licenses by fraudulent means.

Before issuing a driver's license, the state must verify the identity of the applicant with the following:
- An identity card that includes the person's full legal name and date of birth.
- Documentation showing the person's date of birth, such as a birth certificate.
- Proof of a person's Social Security number.
- Documentation showing the person's full name and principal residence address.
- Proof that the person (a) is a citizen or national of the United States, or (b) is an alien lawfully admitted to the United States.

Each new driver's license must contain:
- The person's full legal name.
- The person's date of birth.
- The person's gender.
- The person's driver's license or identification card number.
- The person's digital photograph.
- The person's signature.
- Physical security features to prevent tampering, counterfeiting, or duplication.
- Common machine-readable technology with minimum data requirements (a "smart chip").

Source: The REAL ID Act of 2005.

Driver's License Lineups The REAL ID Act requires all Americans to have the new form of identification by 2013. The use of driver's licenses as tools for law enforcement has already begun, however. By 2008, seven states were using databases of driver's license photographs and facial-recognition technology to positively identify "mug shots" of unnamed wrongdoers.[71] In 2007, experts working for the Massachusetts motor vehicles department tested a photo from the Web site of the television show *America's Most Wanted* against the state's database of 9 million drivers. Although they did not intend their actions to be anything more than an experiment, the surprised investigators found a match that led to the arrest of Robert Howell, who had relocated to New York City after being charged with rape in Massachusetts several years earlier.

PRIVACY RIGHTS AND FEARS

Critics of the REAL ID Act doubt that it will provide much protection against forged or fake identification cards. But their primary concerns involve privacy: the system would create a massive database with information on every American over the age of sixteen, accessible by the federal government, possibly by private enterprise, and, in the worst-case scenario, by hackers. As we learned in Chapter 7, even though privacy as a fundamental right is not explicitly mentioned in the U.S. Constitution, the United States Supreme Court has found that some aspects of privacy, including personal information, are constitutionally protected.[72]

Data-Mining Dilemmas "The people of New Hampshire are adamantly opposed to any kind of 'papers-please' society reminiscent of Nazi Germany and Stalinist Russia," complained Neil Kerk, a Republican state representative from New Hampshire during debate over the REAL ID Act. "This is just another effort of the federal government to keep track of all its citizens."[73] While few would go as far as Kerk in comparing our government to those two twentieth-century totalitarian regimes, the force of public opinion has had an impact on federal efforts to use the database as a crime-fighting tool. Several years ago, the federal government started the Computer Assisted Prescreening System, known as CAPPS II. The plan was to create a system that would analyze passengers' past travel reservations, housing information, credit history, and family connections to determine if they represented a pattern that suggested ties to terrorism. Passengers would be color coded green, yellow, or red, depending on the perceived threat.

In 2003, several angry consumers sued JetBlue Airways for violating its privacy policy after the company secretly turned over information on about 1.5 million of its passengers to an agency compiling data for CAPPS II. A year later, in the wake of further evidence that the Transportation Security Administration was improperly collecting information on travelers and then failing to protect that information, the CAPPS II program was discontinued. Furthermore, Congress has refused to fund the U.S. military's Terrorism Awareness Program, which would have created a global data-surveillance system to collect travel, credit-card, medical, and other personal records of U.S. citizens and foreigners alike. Whatever the benefits of database technology, then, it seems that Americans are uncomfortable with data-mining programs that delve into their private lives to find patterns of terrorism.

The National Security Letter Scandal Suspicions of government misuse of expanded data-gathering capabilities were confirmed for many in 2007, when the FBI admitted that it had exceeded its authority with regard to national security letters (NSLs). According to its own records, the FBI violated the rules of NSL use more than a thousand times between 2002 and 2007. Among its transgressions, the FBI issued NSLs as part of investigations that were not connected to international terrorism, made false allegations on many of the documents, and improperly obtained educational records from a North Carolina university. Furthermore, the FBI obtained billing records and subscriber information from telephone companies without even issuing NSLs as required by law.

After the scandal broke, FBI Director Robert S. Mueller III said the abuses were the result of honest mistakes rather than intentional circumvention of the law.[74] That explanation did not sit well with all members of Congress. "What kind of management failures made it possible for the FBI to send out hundreds of [NSLs] containing significant false statements?" Senator Pat Leahy, a Democrat from Vermont, asked Mueller during congressional hearings. Leahy also threatened a reexamination of the "broad authorities we've granted to the FBI" under the Patriot Act,[75] though such threats ring hollow given the continued importance of homeland security in today's political landscape.

DEVELOPMENTS AND TRENDS: PREDICTABLY UNPREDICTABLE

Technology, inevitably, is a mixed blessing. It may improve our daily lives, but it also provides fresh opportunities for crime. Cell phones, for instance, have transformed modern life for many Americans. At the same time, the incidence of viruses, spam, and phishing schemes on cell phones equipped with Internet capabilities has skyrocketed in recent years. Congress has considered a bill that would make the unauthorized photographing of a naked person with a cell phone a crime punishable by a fine of up to $100,000 or one year in prison, or both. In addition, while Wi-Fi technology has freed computer users from the hassle of land-based connections, it has also provided cyber criminals with yet another means to cover their tracks, as they "steal" wireless Internet signals from unsuspecting victims.

As these examples show, the criminal justice system is not static. The landscape of law enforcement, the courts, and corrections is constantly changing and providing new challenges for those who make criminal justice their life's work. In this textbook, we have identified a number of these challenges, with terrorism being the most obvious. Other trends are also having a significant impact, however, including:

- The use of DNA evidence to convict as well as to exonerate.
- The efforts to curb the costs of state prisons and jails, either by providing alternatives to incarceration or through the early release of those already serving time.
- The move to treat juvenile delinquents as adult offenders.
- The use of immigration law to combat drug trafficking and terrorism.

These developments and countless others mean that the criminal justice system ten years from now will not be exactly the same as the one you have learned about in this textbook. This course has, however, provided you with a strong grasp of the fundamentals of criminal justice and hopefully has inspired you to consider a career in one of the most exciting and challenging fields of the twenty-first century.

Stockdisc

▲ According to industry estimates, more than 80 percent of the mobile phones sold in the United States are equipped with cameras. What privacy concerns does this new technology raise? What kind of laws should be passed to make sure that cell phone cameras are not misused?

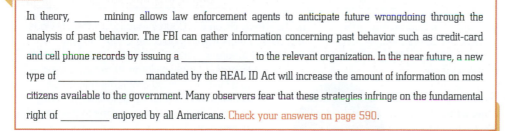

Self Check Fill in the Blanks

In theory, _____ mining allows law enforcement agents to anticipate future wrongdoing through the analysis of past behavior. The FBI can gather information concerning past behavior such as credit-card and cell phone records by issuing a _____ to the relevant organization. In the near future, a new type of _____ mandated by the REAL ID Act will increase the amount of information on most citizens available to the government. Many observers fear that these strategies infringe on the fundamental right of _____ enjoyed by all Americans. Check your answers on page 590.

VIRTUAL CHILD PORNOGRAPHY

In one corner is the United States Congress. In the other corner is the United States Supreme Court. Although the members of both these august bodies are sworn to uphold the Constitution, they come at it from different angles. Members of Congress, as elected representatives, see themselves as carrying out the will of the people. Supreme Court justices, appointed for life, can afford to take a more measured, legalistic approach. When the two institutions grapple with a contentious subject such as virtual child pornography, the results, as we will see in this *Criminal Justice in Action* feature, can have far-reaching implications for American law, society, and culture.

BACK AND FORTH

In its *New York v. Ferber* (1982) decision, the Supreme Court held that the First Amendment does not protect child pornography because (1) the government has a compelling interest in protecting the physical and emotional well-being of those children who might be the subjects of such activity and (2) criminal sanctions for child pornographers would deter such activity and "dry up the market" for child pornography.[76] As part of its ruling, however, the Court noted that depictions of sexual conduct involving children that do not involve "live performances" are still protected by the First Amendment.[77]

In the context of the technological advances of the early 1990s, this statement seemed to form a loophole that allowed for virtual child pornography, or images created by computer software that do not involve "real" children. To remedy this situation, Congress passed the Child Pornography Prevention Act of 1996 (CPPA), which mandated harsh penalties for distribution or possession of computer-generated images or other creative reproductions that *appear* to depict minors engaging in lewd and lascivious behavior.[78] Much to the chagrin of congressional leaders and child-welfare advocates, however, in 2002 the Supreme Court held that the CPPA ran afoul of the First Amendment and was therefore unconstitutional.[79]

The Argument for Banning Virtual Pornography

- In passing the CPPA, Congress found that virtual child pornography is practically indistinguishable from actual child pornography and, therefore, the reasoning of the *Ferber* decision applies equally to both.[80]

- The similarity between the two forms of child pornography would place an unacceptable burden on law enforcement officers and prosecutors to prove that the children depicted are "real."

- Virtual child pornography "whets the desires" of pedophiles and encourages them to engage in illegal conduct.[81]

The Argument against Banning Virtual Photography

- The Supreme Court held that the mere tendency of speech that is not in itself illegal—such as virtual child pornography—to lead to illegal behavior is not sufficient reason to ban it.[82]

- Virtual child pornography offers a legal alternative to the "real thing" and therefore gives its purveyors an incentive to avoid the use of minors in their work.[83]

- By banning any sexually explicit activity that *appears to* include minors, the CPPA could be applied to artistic work of great merit such as William Shakespeare's *Romeo and Juliet*.[84]

Writing Assignment—Your Opinion

In 2003, partly as a response to the Supreme Court's rejection of the CPPA, Congress passed the Child Online Protection Act (COPA), which imposes a $50,000 fine and six months in jail for the posting of *obscene* material that is "harmful to minors" on the Internet.[85] The legislation allows such Web sites only if they restrict access to minors by requiring a credit card, adult access code, or some other shielding mechanism.

The Supreme Court has not yet ruled on the constitutionality of the COPA, but many experts believe it suffers from many of the same flaws as the CPPA. Given the Court's reaction to the previous law, do you think it will uphold the COPA? In your opinion, is Congress justified in limiting obscenity on the Internet to keep children from being exposed to it? What practical problems might there be in enforcing the COPA? Before responding, you can review our discussions in this chapter concerning

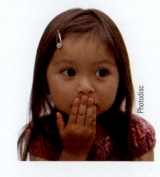

Photodisc

- Online pornography (pages 574–575).
- Jurisdictional challenges in cyberspace (pages 576–578).
- Obscenity on the Internet (pages 582–583).

Your answer should take at least three full paragraphs.

L01 **Distinguish cyber crime from "traditional" crime.** Most cyber crimes are not "new" types of crimes. Rather, they are traditional crimes committed in cyberspace. Perpetrators of cyber crimes are often aided by certain aspects of the Internet, such as its ability to cloak the user's identity and its effectiveness as a conduit for transferring—or stealing—large amounts of information very quickly.

L02 **Indicate how the Internet has expanded opportunities for identity theft.** In cyberspace, thieves can steal data from anywhere in the world as long as they have the necessary expertise and computer equipment. Their task is made easier by the fact that many e-businesses store information such as the consumer's name, e-mail address, and credit-card numbers. Thus, if the wrongdoer can illegally access these online information "warehouses," he or she is immediately in possession of a large amount of the personal data necessary for identity theft.

L03 **List the three reasons why cyberstalking may be more commonplace than physical stalking.** (a) Physically stalking someone takes a great deal of effort on the part of the stalker, whereas harassing someone with electronic messages is fairly easy; (b) there is no possibility of physical confrontation between a cyberstalker and his or her victim, whereas such a possibility is a deterrent to physical stalking; and (c) physical stalking requires that both stalker and victim be in the same geographic location, whereas the reach of the cyberstalker is limitless.

L04 **Describe the following three forms of malware: (a) botnets, (b) worms, and (c) viruses.** (a) A botnet is a network of computers that have been hijacked without the knowledge of their owners and used to spread harmful programs across the Internet; (b) a worm is a damaging software program that reproduces itself as it moves from computer to computer; (c) a virus is a damaging software program that must be attached to an "infested" host file to transfer from one computer to the next.

L05 **Outline the three major reasons that the Internet is conducive to juvenile cyber crime.**

(a) Advanced computer equipment and software allow juveniles to commit crimes without leaving their homes; (b) the anonymity of cyberspace allows young people to commit crimes such as theft that would otherwise be almost impossible, given their limitations of size, money, and experience; and (c) hacking and other cyber crimes are often not recognized as unethical in youth culture.

L06 **Explain how the Internet has contributed to piracy of intellectual property.** In the past, copying intellectual property such as films and music was time consuming, and the quality of the pirated copies was vastly inferior to that of the originals. On the Internet, however, millions of unauthorized copies of intellectual property can be reproduced at the click of a mouse, and the quality of these items is often the same as that of the original, or close to it.

L07 **Indicate how encryption programs protect digital data from unauthorized access.** Through the process of encryption, plaintext data are transformed into ciphertext, which only those who have access to the proper code can read or access. Unless a third party is able to "break" this code, the information will stay secure.

L08 **Explain why the right to free speech on the Internet is not absolute.** The Supreme Court has ruled that the government may regulate certain forms of speech if they create an "imminent danger" for an individual or the community. Therefore, the First Amendment to the U.S. Constitution may not protect information on the Internet that can be proved to have incited dangerous behavior, such as instructions for building a bomb.

L09 **Describe how data mining can be used to combat terrorism.** After government agencies gather information on a suspect's activities, such as his or her e-mails, cell phone calls, and business transactions, they can use data mining to analyze the data to look for patterns of behavior. By tracking and cross-checking this information with that of other terrorist suspects, the government may find patterns that point to a future terrorist attack.

botnet 569
computer crime 564
computer forensics 576
cyber crime 565
cyber fraud 566
cyberstalking 568
cyberterrorism 573

data mining 584
encryption 579
hacker 569
hate speech 581
identity theft 567
intellectual property 571
money laundering 572

national security letter (NSL) 584
obscenity 582
spam 571
virus 569
worm 569

Questions for Critical Analysis

1. Why does the nature of online communication make it difficult to identify and prosecute those who commit cyber crimes?

2. How is online auction fraud carried out, and why is it so difficult to block this activity?

3. Why is credit-card fraud more likely to "hurt" merchants that sell their products online than consumers who purchase those products?

4. What is money laundering, and why has the increased computerization of banking led to an upswing in this practice?

5. Consider the following situation: Melissa Chin is the sheriff of Jackson County, Missouri, population 1,434. Sheriff Chin has only two deputies at her disposal. Mae Brown, a resident of Jackson County, is receiving threatening e-mails from someone who has the cyberspace name of johndoe1313. Mae is certain that the sender is actually Matthew Green, her ex-husband. Matthew lives in Wilson County, Louisiana. What are some of the jurisdictional problems Sheriff Chin may face in investigating Matthew's possible involvement in cyberstalking? What are some of the practical problems Sheriff Chin may encounter? How might she solve these problems?

6. How would the situation in question 5 be different if Matthew Green was living on an island in Indonesia?

7. How has the Internet aided the cause of international terrorism?

8. What is the difference between hate crimes and hate speech? Why is most hate speech on the Internet safe from government regulation?

9. Why have many politicians and citizens resisted the creation of computer databases such as the one mandated by the REAL ID Act?

Maximize Your Best Possible Outcome for Chapter 17

1. **Maximize Your Best Chance for Getting a Good Grade on the Exam.** ThomsonNOW Personalized Study is a diagnostic study tool containing valuable text-specific resources—and because you focus on just what you don't know, you learn more in less time to get a better grade. How do you get ThomsonNOW? If your textbook does not include an access code card, go to **thomsonedu.com** to get ThomsonNOW before your next exam!

2. **Get the Most Out of Your Textbook** by going to the book companion Web site at **www.cjinaction.com** to access one of the tutorial quizzes, use the flash cards to master key terms, and check out the many other study aids you'll find there. Under chapter resources you will also be able to access the Stories from the Street feature and Web links mentioned in the textbook.

3. **Learn about Potential Criminal Justice Careers** discussed in this chapter by exploring careers online at **www.cjinaction.com**. You will find career descriptions and information about job requirements, training, salary and benefits, and the application process. You can also watch video profiles featuring criminal justice professionals.

Notes

1. Patrick J. McDonnell, "Dark End to a Hunt for Love," *Los Angeles Times* (December 13, 2006), 1.

2. National Institute of Justice, *Computer Crime: Criminal Justice Resource Manual* (Washington, D.C.: U.S. Department of Justice, 1989), 2.

3. *Ibid.*

4. Internet Crime Complaint Center, "The Internet Crime Complaint Center Hits 1 Million!" at **www.ic3.gov/media/2007/070613.htm**.

5. *Symantec Internet Security Threat Report: Trends for July–December 06, Executive Summary* (Cupertino, CA: Symantec Corporation, March 2007), 3.

6. National White Collar Crime Center and Federal Bureau of Investigation, *Internet Crime Report: January 1, 2006–December 31, 2006* (Washington, D.C.: Internet Crime Complaint Center, 2007), 4.

7. Bureau of Justice Statistics, *Identity Theft, 2004* (Washington, D.C.: U.S. Department of Justice, April 2006), 1.

8. *Symantec Internet Security Threat Report,* 3.
9. Mary T. Monahan, *2007 Identity Fraud Survey* (Pleasanton, CA: Javelin Strategy & Research, February 2007), 1.
10. John Leland, "Identity Fraud Has Dropped since 2003, Survey Shows," *New York Times* (February 6, 2007), A17.
11. ID Analytics, "ID Analytics Announces New Data Analysis Findings" (February 9, 2005), at **www.idanalytics.com/news_and_events/2005209.html**.
12. Jim Middlemiss, "Gone Phishing," *Wall Street & Technology* (August 2004), 38.
13. California Penal Code Section 646.9.
14. California Penal Code Sections 646.9(g) and (h).
15. "Missouri: Gladstone Man Sentenced for Cyber Stalking," *Cybercrime Law Report* (January 6, 2006), 33.
16. Kimberly Wingteung Seto, "How Should Legislation Deal with Children as the Victims and Perpetrators of Cyberstalking?" *Cardozo Women's Law Journal* 9 (2002), 67.
17. Office of the Attorney General, *Cyberstalking: A New Challenge for Law Enforcement and Industry: A Report to the Vice President* (Washington, D.C.: U.S. Department of Justice, August 1999).
18. "Cybercrime Is Getting Organized," *Wired* (September 15, 2006), at **www.wired.com/techbiz/media/news/2006/09/71793**.
19. "Multimedia Available: One Step Ahead of the Hackers," *Business Wire* (December 13, 2005).
20. Lawrence A. Gordon, Martin P. Loeb, William Lucyshyn, and Robert Richardson, *2006 CSI/FBI Computer Crime and Security Survey* (San Francisco: Computer Security Institute, 2006), 12.
21. *Ibid.,* 22.
22. Amanda Lenhart, Mary Madden, and Paul Hitlin, *Teens and Technology* (Washington, D.C.: Pew Internet and American Life Project, July 2005), ii.
23. Joseph V. DeMarco, *It's Not Just Fun and "War Games"—Juveniles and Computer Crimes* (Washington, D.C.: U.S. Department of Justice, 2001).
24. *Ibid.*
25. See "Ask McGruff," at **www.bytecrime.org/ask_mcgruff/resources.html**.
26. "Increased Spam Levels Fueled through Aggressive Botnet Activities," *Business Wire* (November 2, 2006).
27. 15 U.S.C. Sections 7701–7713 (2003).
28. Anick Jesdanun, "Output Unaffected by Spammer's Arrest," *Charleston (West Virginia) Gazette* (June 1, 2007), 5A.
29. *Fourth Annual BSA and IDC Global Software Piracy Study* (Washington, D.C.: Business Software Alliance, 2007), 2.
30. *The Recording Industry 2006 Commercial Piracy Report* (London: International Federation of the Phonographic Industry, July 2006), 4.
31. 17 U.S.C. Section 23199(c) (1998).
32. 17 U.S.C. Sections 2301 *et seq.* (1998)
33. 545 U.S. 913 (2005).
34. Bank Secrecy Act of 1970, 31 U.S.C. Sections 1051–1709 (2000).
35. James Gordon Meek, "Feds Out to Bust Up 24-Karat Web Worry," *New York Daily News* (June 3, 2007), 29.
36. Quoted in *ibid.*
37. Yonah Alexander, "Terrorism in the Twenty-First Century: Threats and Responses," *DePaul Business Law Journal* 12 (1999/2000), 86.
38. Gabriel Weimann, "Virtual Disputes: The Use of the Internet for Terrorist Debates," *Studies in Conflict & Terrorism* 29 (2006), 624.
39. Susannah Fox, Janna Quitney Anderson, and Lee Rainie, *The Future of the Internet* (Washington, D.C.: Pew Internet and American Life Project, 2005), 14.
40. Quoted in Mark Landler and John Markoff, "After Computer Siege in Estonia, War Fears Turn to Cyberspace," *New York Times* (May 29, 2007), A1.
41. Internet Filter Review, "Internet Pornography Statistics," at **internet-filter-review.toptenreviews.com/internet-pornography-statistics.html#anchor1**.
42. William R. Graham, Jr., "Uncovering and Eliminating Child Pornography Rings on the Internet," *Law Review of Michigan State University Detroit College of Law* (Summer 2000), 466.

43. 47 U.S.C. Sections 230 *et seq.* (1996).
44. 31 U.S.C. Sections 5361 *et seq.* (2006).
45. George Will, "Prohibition II: Good Grief," *Newsweek* (October 23, 2006), 78.
46. Quoted in Michael McCarthy, "Feds Go After Offshore Online Betting Industry," *USA Today* (July 19, 2006), 6C.
47. Quoted in Richard Rapaport, "Cyberwars: The Feds Strike Back," *Forbes* (August 23, 1999), 126.
48. Matthew Boyle, "The Latest Hit: *CSI* in Your Hard Drive," *Fortune* (November 14, 2005), 39.
49. Quoted in "Cybersleuths Find Growing Role in Fighting Crime," *HPC Wire*, at **www.hpcwire.com/hpc-bin/artread.pl?direction=Current&articlenumber=19864**.
50. Laurie P. Cohen, "Internet's Ubiquity Multiplies Venues to Try Web Crimes," *Wall Street Journal* (February 12, 2007), B1.
51. Federal Bureau of Investigation, "Cyber Investigations," at **www.fbi.gov/cyberinvest/cyberhome.htm**.
52. Heather Jacobson and Rebecca Green, "Computer Crimes," *American Criminal Law Review* (Spring 2002), 283.
53. *Junger v. Daley*, 209 F.3d 481, 482 (6th Cir. 2000).
54. *Brandenburg v. Ohio*, 395 U.S. 444 (1969).
55. *R.A.V. v. City of St. Paul*, 505 U.S. 377, 386 (1992).
56. *Planned Parenthood of Columbia/Willamette, Inc. v. American Coalition of Life Activists*, 41 F.Supp.2d 1130 (D.Or. 1999).
57. Peter J. Breckheimer II, "A Haven for Hate: The Foreign and Domestic Implications of Protecting Internet Speech under the First Amendment," *Southern California Law Review* (September 2002), 1493.
58. *Rice v. Paladin*, 128 F.3d 233 (4th Cir. 1997).
59. Liezl I. Pangilinan, " 'When a Nation Is at War': A Context-Dependent Theory of Free Speech for the Regulation of Weapon Recipes," *Cardozo Arts and Entertainment Law Journal* 22 (2004), 683.
60. *Ibid.*
61. *Miller v. California*, 413 U.S. 15, 24 (1973).
62. *Stanley v. Georgia*, 394 U.S. 557 (1969).
63. *Paris Adult Theater I v. Stanton*, 413 U.S. 49, 67 (1973).
64. Quoted in Margaret Talbot, "Duped," *New Yorker* (July 2, 2007), 56.
65. Jonathan Knight, "Lie Detectors: The Truth about Lying," *Nature* (April 2004), 692.
66. Mark Hosenball and Evan Thomas, "Hold the Phone," *Newsweek* (May 22, 2006), 29–30.
67. National Law Enforcement and Corrections Technology Center, "Digging the Connections," *TechBeat* (Washington, D.C.: National Institute of Justice, Summer 2006), 1.
68. 50 U.S.C. Section 1861(b)(2)(A), amended by the USA PATRIOT Improvement and Reauthorization Act of 2005, Section 106(b).
69. USA PATRIOT Act Section 5050(a)(3)(B).
70. Pub. L. No. 109-13 (2005).
71. Adam Liptak, "Driver's License Emerges as Crime Fighting Tool, but Privacy Advocates Worry," *New York Times* (February 17, 2007), A9.
72. *Katz v. United States*, 389 U.S. 347, 350–351 (1967).
73. Quoted in Thomas Frank, "6 States Defy Law Requiring ID Cards," *USA Today* (June 19, 2007), 1A.
74. Quoted in Richard B. Schmitt, "FBI Has Some Explaining to Do," *Los Angeles Times* (March 28, 2007), 12.
75. *Ibid.*
76. 458 U.S. 747, 756–757, 760 (1982).
77. *Ibid.,* at 765.
78. 18 U.S.C. Section 2256 (1996).
79. *Ashcroft v. Free Speech Coalition*, 535 U.S. 234 (2002).
80. Senate Report No. 104-358, 15 (1996).
81. *Ashcroft v. Free Speech Coalition*, at 253.
82. *Ibid.,* at 259.
83. *Ibid.,* at 254.
84. *Ibid.,* at 246.
85. 47 U.S.C. Section 231 (2003).

Appendix A

THE CONSTITUTION OF THE UNITED STATES

PREAMBLE

We the People of the United States, in Order to form a more perfect Union, establish Justice, insure domestic Tranquility, provide for the common defence, promote the general Welfare, and secure the Blessings of Liberty to ourselves and our Posterity, do ordain and establish this Constitution for the United States of America.

ARTICLE I

Section 1. All legislative Powers herein granted shall be vested in a Congress of the United States, which shall consist of a Senate and House of Representatives.

Section 2. The House of Representatives shall be composed of Members chosen every second Year by the People of the several States, and the Electors in each State shall have the Qualifications requisite for Electors of the most numerous Branch of the State Legislature.

No Person shall be a Representative who shall not have attained to the Age of twenty five Years, and been seven Years a Citizen of the United States, and who shall not, when elected, be an Inhabitant of that State in which he shall be chosen.

Representatives and direct Taxes shall be apportioned among the several States which may be included within this Union, according to their respective Numbers, which shall be determined by adding to the whole Number of free Persons, including those bound to Service for a Term of Years, and excluding Indians not taxed, three fifths of all other Persons. The actual Enumeration shall be made within three Years after the first Meeting of the Congress of the United States, and within every subsequent Term of ten Years, in such Manner as they shall by Law direct. The Number of Representatives shall not exceed one for every thirty Thousand, but each State shall have at Least one Representative; and until such enumeration shall be made, the State of New Hampshire shall be entitled to chuse three, Massachusetts eight, Rhode Island and Providence Plantations one, Connecticut five, New York six, New Jersey four, Pennsylvania eight, Delaware one, Maryland six, Virginia ten, North Carolina five, South Carolina five, and Georgia three.

When vacancies happen in the Representation from any State, the Executive Authority thereof shall issue Writs of Election to fill such Vacancies.

The House of Representatives shall chuse their Speaker and other Officers; and shall have the sole Power of Impeachment.

Section 3. The Senate of the United States shall be composed of two Senators from each State, chosen by the Legislature thereof, for six Years; and each Senator shall have one Vote.

Immediately after they shall be assembled in Consequence of the first Election, they shall be divided as equally as may be into three Classes. The Seats of the Senators of the first Class shall be vacated at the Expiration of the second Year, of the second Class at the Expiration of the fourth Year, and of the third Class at the Expiration of the sixth Year, so that one third may be chosen every second Year; and if Vacancies happen by Resignation, or otherwise, during the Recess of the Legislature of any State, the Executive thereof may make temporary Appointments until the next Meeting of the Legislature, which shall then fill such Vacancies.

No Person shall be a Senator who shall not have attained to the Age of thirty Years, and been nine Years a Citizen of the United States, and who shall not, when elected, be an Inhabitant of that State for which he shall be chosen.

The Vice President of the United States shall be President of the Senate, but shall have no Vote, unless they be equally divided.

The Senate shall chuse their other Officers, and also a President pro tempore, in the Absence of the Vice President, or when he shall exercise the Office of President of the United States.

The Senate shall have the sole Power to try all Impeachments. When sitting for that Purpose, they shall be on Oath or Affirmation. When the President of the United States is tried, the Chief Justice shall preside: And no Person shall be convicted without the Concurrence of two thirds of the Members present.

Judgment in Cases of Impeachment shall not extend further than to removal from Office, and disqualification to hold and enjoy any Office of honor, Trust, or Profit under the United States: but the Party convicted shall nevertheless be liable and subject to Indictment, Trial, Judgment, and Punishment, according to Law.

Section 4. The Times, Places and Manner of holding Elections for Senators and Representatives, shall be prescribed in each State by the Legislature thereof; but the Congress may at any time by Law make or alter such Regulations, except as to the Places of chusing Senators.

The Congress shall assemble at least once in every Year, and such Meeting shall be on the first Monday in December, unless they shall by Law appoint a different Day.

Section 5. Each House shall be the Judge of the Elections, Returns, and Qualifications of its own Members, and a Majority of each shall constitute a Quorum to do Business; but a smaller Number may adjourn from day to day, and may be authorized to compel the Attendance of absent Members, in such Manner, and under such Penalties as each House may provide.

Each House may determine the Rules of its Proceedings, punish its Members for disorderly Behavior, and, with the Concurrence of two thirds, expel a Member.

Each House shall keep a Journal of its Proceedings, and from time to time publish the same, excepting such Parts as may in their Judgment require Secrecy; and the Yeas and Nays of the Members of either House on any question shall, at the Desire of one fifth of those Present, be entered on the Journal.

Neither House, during the Session of Congress, shall, without the Consent of the other, adjourn for more than three days, nor to any other Place than that in which the two Houses shall be sitting.

Section 6. The Senators and Representatives shall receive a Compensation for their Services, to be ascertained by Law, and paid out of the Treasury of the United States. They shall in all Cases, except Treason, Felony and Breach of the Peace, be privileged from Arrest during their Attendance at the Session of their respective Houses, and in going to and returning from the same; and for any Speech or Debate in either House, they shall not be questioned in any other Place.

No Senator or Representative shall, during the Time for which he was elected, be appointed to any civil Office under the Authority of the United States, which shall have been created, or the Emoluments whereof shall have been increased during such time; and no Person holding any Office under the United States, shall be a Member of either House during his Continuance in Office.

Section 7. All Bills for raising Revenue shall originate in the House of Representatives; but the Senate may propose or concur with Amendments as on other Bills.

Every Bill which shall have passed the House of Representatives and the Senate, shall, before it become a Law, be presented to the President of the United States; If he approve he shall sign it, but if not he shall return it, with his Objections to the House in which it shall have originated, who shall enter the Objections at large on their Journal, and proceed to reconsider it. If after such Reconsideration two thirds of that House shall agree to pass the Bill, it shall be sent together with the Objections, to the other House, by which it shall likewise be reconsidered, and if approved by two thirds of that House, it shall become a Law. But in all such Cases the Votes of both Houses shall be determined by Yeas and Nays, and the Names of the Persons voting for and against the Bill shall be entered on the Journal of each House respectively. If any Bill shall not be returned by the President within ten Days (Sundays excepted) after it shall have been presented to him, the Same shall be a Law, in like Manner as if he had signed it, unless the Congress by their Adjournment prevent its Return in which Case it shall not be a Law.

Every Order, Resolution, or Vote, to which the Concurrence of the Senate and House of Representatives may be necessary (except on a question of Adjournment) shall be presented to the President of the United States; and before the Same shall take Effect, shall be approved by him, or being disapproved by him, shall be repassed by two thirds of the Senate and House of Representatives, according to the Rules and Limitations prescribed in the Case of a Bill.

Section 8. The Congress shall have Power To lay and collect Taxes, Duties, Imposts and Excises, to pay the Debts and provide for the common Defence and general Welfare of the United States; but all Duties, Imposts and Excises shall be uniform throughout the United States;

To borrow Money on the credit of the United States;

To regulate Commerce with foreign Nations, and among the several States, and with the Indian Tribes;

To establish an uniform Rule of Naturalization, and uniform Laws on the subject of Bankruptcies throughout the United States;

To coin Money, regulate the Value thereof, and of foreign Coin, and fix the Standard of Weights and Measures;

To provide for the Punishment of counterfeiting the Securities and current Coin of the United States;

To establish Post Offices and post Roads;

To promote the Progress of Science and useful Arts, by securing for limited Times to Authors and Inventors the exclusive Right to their respective Writings and Discoveries;

To constitute Tribunals inferior to the supreme Court;

To define and punish Piracies and Felonies committed on the high Seas, and Offenses against the Law of Nations;

To declare War, grant Letters of Marque and Reprisal, and make Rules concerning Captures on Land and Water;

To raise and support Armies, but no Appropriation of Money to that Use shall be for a longer Term than two Years;

To provide and maintain a Navy;

To make Rules for the Government and Regulation of the land and naval Forces;

To provide for calling forth the Militia to execute the Laws of the Union, suppress Insurrections and repel Invasions;

To provide for organizing, arming, and disciplining, the Militia, and for governing such Part of them as may be employed in the Service of the United States, reserving to the States respectively, the Appointment of the Officers, and the Authority of training the Militia according to the discipline prescribed by Congress;

To exercise exclusive Legislation in all Cases whatsoever, over such District (not exceeding ten Miles square) as may, by Cession of particular States, and the Acceptance of Congress, become the Seat of the Government of the United States, and to exercise like Authority over all Places purchased by the Consent of the Legislature of the State in which the Same shall be, for the Erection of Forts, Magazines, Arsenals, dock-Yards, and other needful Buildings;—And

To make all Laws which shall be necessary and proper for carrying into Execution the foregoing Powers, and all other Powers vested by this Constitution in the Government of the United States, or in any Department or Officer thereof.

Section 9. The Migration or Importation of such Persons as any of the States now existing shall think proper to admit, shall not be prohibited by the Congress prior to the Year one thousand eight hundred and eight, but a Tax or duty may be imposed on such Importation, not exceeding ten dollars for each Person.

The privilege of the Writ of Habeas Corpus shall not be suspended, unless when in Cases of Rebellion or Invasion the public Safety may require it.

No Bill of Attainder or ex post facto Law shall be passed.

No Capitation, or other direct, Tax shall be laid, unless in Proportion to the Census or Enumeration herein before directed to be taken.

No Tax or Duty shall be laid on Articles exported from any State.

No Preference shall be given by any Regulation of Commerce or Revenue to the Ports of one State over those of another: nor shall Vessels bound to, or from, one State be obliged to enter, clear, or pay Duties in another.

No Money shall be drawn from the Treasury, but in Consequence of Appropriations made by Law; and a regular Statement and Account of the Receipts and Expenditures of all public Money shall be published from time to time.

No Title of Nobility shall be granted by the United States: And no Person holding any Office of Profit or Trust under them, shall, without the Consent of the Congress, accept of any present, Emolument, Office, or Title, of any kind whatever, from any King, Prince, or foreign State.

Section 10. No State shall enter into any Treaty, Alliance, or Confederation; grant Letters of Marque and Reprisal; coin Money; emit Bills of Credit; make any Thing but gold and silver Coin a Tender in Payment of Debts; pass any Bill of Attainder, ex post facto Law, or Law impairing the Obligation of Contracts, or grant any Title of Nobility.

No State shall, without the Consent of the Congress, lay any Imposts or Duties on Imports or Exports, except what may be absolutely necessary for executing its inspection Laws: and the net Produce of all Duties and Imposts, laid by any State on Imports or Exports, shall be for the Use of the Treasury of the United States; and all such Laws shall be subject to the Revision and Controul of the Congress.

No State shall, without the Consent of Congress, lay any Duty of Tonnage, keep Troops, or Ships of War in time of Peace, enter into any Agreement or Compact with another State, or with a foreign Power, or engage in War, unless actually invaded, or in such imminent Danger as will not admit of delay.

Article II

Section 1. The executive Power shall be vested in a President of the United States of America. He shall hold his Office during the Term of four Years, and, together with the Vice President, chosen for the same Term, be elected, as follows:

Each State shall appoint, in such Manner as the Legislature thereof may direct, a Number of Electors, equal to the whole Number of Senators and Representatives to which the State may be entitled in the Congress; but no Senator or Representative, or Person holding an Office of Trust or Profit under the United States, shall be appointed an Elector.

The Electors shall meet in their respective States, and vote by Ballot for two Persons, of whom one at least shall not be an Inhabitant of the same State with themselves. And they shall make a List of all the Persons voted for, and of the Number of Votes for each; which List they shall sign and certify, and transmit sealed to the Seat of the Government of the United States, directed to the President of the Senate. The President of the Senate shall, in the Presence of the Senate and House of Representatives, open all the Certificates, and the Votes shall then be counted. The Person having the greatest Number of Votes shall be the President, if such Number be a Majority of the whole Number of Electors appointed; and if there be more than one who have such Majority, and have an equal Number of Votes, then the House of Representatives shall immediately chuse by Ballot one of them for President; and if no Person have a Majority, then from the five highest on the List the said House shall in like Manner chuse the President. But in chusing the President, the Votes shall be taken by States, the Representation from each State having one Vote; A quorum for this Purpose shall consist of a Member or Members from two thirds of the States, and a Majority of all the States shall be necessary to a Choice. In every Case, after the Choice of the President, the Person having the greater Number of Votes of the Electors shall be the Vice President. But if there should remain two or more who have equal Votes, the Senate shall chuse from them by Ballot the Vice President.

The Congress may determine the Time of chusing the Electors, and the Day on which they shall give their Votes; which Day shall be the same throughout the United States.

No person except a natural born Citizen, or a Citizen of the United States, at the time of the Adoption of this Constitution, shall be eligible to the Office of President; neither shall any Person be eligible to that Office who shall not have attained to the Age of thirty five Years, and been fourteen Years a Resident within the United States.

In Case of the Removal of the President from Office, or of his Death, Resignation or Inability to discharge the Powers and Duties of the said Office, the same shall devolve on the Vice President, and the Congress may by Law provide for the Case of Removal, Death, Resignation or Inability, both of the President and Vice President, declaring what Officer shall then act as President, and such Officer shall act accordingly, until the Disability be removed, or a President shall be elected.

The President shall, at stated Times, receive for his Services, a Compensation, which shall neither be increased nor diminished during the Period for which he shall have been elected, and he shall not receive within that Period any other Emolument from the United States, or any of them.

Before he enter on the Execution of his Office, he shall take the following Oath or Affirmation: "I do solemnly swear (or affirm) that I will faithfully execute the Office of President of the United States, and will to the best of my Ability, preserve, protect and defend the Constitution of the United States."

Section 2. The President shall be Commander in Chief of the Army and Navy of the United States, and of the Militia of the several States, when called into the actual Service of the United States; he may require the Opinion, in writing, of the principal Officer in each of the executive Departments, upon any Subject relating to the Duties of their respective Offices, and he shall have Power to grant Reprieves and Pardons for Offenses against the United States, except in Cases of Impeachment.

He shall have Power, by and with the Advice and Consent of the Senate to make Treaties, provided two thirds of the Senators present concur; and he shall nominate, and by and with the Advice and Consent of the Senate, shall appoint Ambassadors, other public Ministers and Consuls, Judges of the supreme Court, and all other Officers of the United States, whose Appointments are not herein otherwise provided for, and which shall be established by Law; but the Congress may by Law vest the Appointment of such inferior Officers, as they think proper, in the President alone, in the Courts of Law, or in the Heads of Departments.

The President shall have Power to fill up all Vacancies that may happen during the Recess of the Senate, by granting Commissions which shall expire at the End of their next Session.

Section 3. He shall from time to time give to the Congress Information of the State of the Union, and recommend to their Consideration such Measures as he shall judge necessary and expedient; he may, on extraordinary Occasions, convene both Houses, or either of them, and in Case of Disagreement between them, with Respect to the Time of Adjournment, he may adjourn them to such Time as he shall think proper; he shall receive Ambassadors and other public Ministers; he shall take Care that the Laws be faithfully executed, and shall Commission all the Officers of the United States.

Section 4. The President, Vice President and all civil Officers of the United States, shall be removed from Office on Impeachment for, and Conviction of, Treason, Bribery, or other high Crimes and Misdemeanors.

ARTICLE III

Section 1. The judicial Power of the United States, shall be vested in one supreme Court, and in such inferior Courts as the Congress may from time to time ordain and establish. The Judges, both of the supreme and inferior Courts, shall hold their Offices during good Behaviour, and shall, at stated Times, receive for their Services a Compensation, which shall not be diminished during their Continuance in Office.

Section 2. The judicial Power shall extend to all Cases, in Law and Equity, arising under this Constitution, the Laws of the United States, and Treaties made, or which shall be made, under their Authority;—to all Cases affecting Ambassadors, other public Ministers and Consuls;—to all Cases of admiralty and maritime Jurisdiction;—to Controversies to which the United States shall be a Party;—to

Controversies between two or more States;—between a State and Citizens of another State;—between Citizens of different States;—between Citizens of the same State claiming Lands under Grants of different States, and between a State, or the Citizens thereof, and foreign States, Citizens or Subjects.

In all Cases affecting Ambassadors, other public Ministers and Consuls, and those in which a State shall be a Party, the supreme Court shall have original Jurisdiction. In all the other Cases before mentioned, the supreme Court shall have appellate Jurisdiction, both as to Law and Fact, with such Exceptions, and under such Regulations as the Congress shall make.

The Trial of all Crimes, except in Cases of Impeachment, shall be by Jury; and such Trial shall be held in the State where the said Crimes shall have been committed; but when not committed within any State, the Trial shall be at such Place or Places as the Congress may by Law have directed.

Section 3. Treason against the United States, shall consist only in levying War against them, or, in adhering to their Enemies, giving them Aid and Comfort. No Person shall be convicted of Treason unless on the Testimony of two Witnesses to the same overt Act, or on Confession in open Court.

The Congress shall have Power to declare the Punishment of Treason, but no Attainder of Treason shall work Corruption of Blood, or Forfeiture except during the Life of the Person attainted.

ARTICLE IV

Section 1. Full Faith and Credit shall be given in each State to the public Acts, Records, and judicial Proceedings of every other State. And the Congress may by general Laws prescribe the Manner in which such Acts, Records and Proceedings shall be proved, and the Effect thereof.

Section 2. The Citizens of each State shall be entitled to all Privileges and Immunities of Citizens in the several States.

A Person charged in any State with Treason, Felony, or other Crime, who shall flee from Justice, and be found in another State, shall on Demand of the executive Authority of the State from which he fled, be delivered up, to be removed to the State having Jurisdiction of the Crime.

No Person held to Service or Labour in one State, under the Laws thereof, escaping into another, shall, in Consequence of any Law or Regulation therein, be discharged from such Service or Labour, but shall be delivered up on Claim of the Party to whom such Service or Labour may be due.

Section 3. New States may be admitted by the Congress into this Union; but no new State shall be formed or erected within the Jurisdiction of any other State; nor any State be formed by the Junction of two or more States, or Parts of States, without the Consent of the Legislatures of the States concerned as well as of the Congress.

The Congress shall have Power to dispose of and make all needful Rules and Regulations respecting the Territory or other Property belonging to the United States; and nothing in this Constitution shall be so construed as to Prejudice any Claims of the United States, or of any particular State.

Section 4. The United States shall guarantee to every State in this Union a Republican Form of Government, and shall protect each of them against Invasion; and on Application of the Legislature, or of the Executive (when the Legislature cannot be convened) against domestic Violence.

ARTICLE V

The Congress, whenever two thirds of both Houses shall deem it necessary, shall propose Amendments to this Constitution, or, on the Application of the Legislatures of two thirds of the several States, shall call a Convention for proposing Amendments, which, in either Case, shall be valid to all Intents and Purposes, as part of this Constitution, when ratified by the Legislatures of three fourths of the several States, or by Conventions in three fourths thereof, as the one or the other Mode of Ratification may be proposed by the Congress; Provided that no Amendment which may be made prior to the Year One thousand eight hundred and eight shall in any Manner affect the first and fourth Clauses in the Ninth Section of the first Article; and that no State, without its Consent, shall be deprived of its equal Suffrage in the Senate.

ARTICLE VI

All Debts contracted and Engagements entered into, before the Adoption of this Constitution shall be as valid against the United States under this Constitution, as under the Confederation.

This Constitution, and the Laws of the United States which shall be made in Pursuance thereof; and all Treaties made, or which shall be made, under the Authority of the United States, shall be the supreme Law of the Land; and the Judges in every State shall be bound thereby, any Thing in the Constitution or Laws of any State to the Contrary notwithstanding.

The Senators and Representatives before mentioned, and the Members of the several State Legislatures, and all executive and judicial Officers, both of the United States and of the several States, shall be bound by Oath or Affirmation, to support this Constitution; but no religious Test shall ever be required as a Qualification to any Office or public Trust under the United States.

ARTICLE VII

The Ratification of the Conventions of nine States shall be sufficient for the Establishment of this Constitution between the States so ratifying the Same.

AMENDMENT I [1791]

Congress shall make no law respecting an establishment of religion, or prohibiting the free exercise thereof; or abridging the freedom of speech, or of the press; or the right of the people peaceably to assembly, and to petition the Government for a redress of grievances.

AMENDMENT II [1791]

A well regulated Militia, being necessary to the security of a free State, the right of the people to keep and bear Arms, shall not be infringed.

AMENDMENT III [1791]

No Soldier shall, in time of peace be quartered in any house, without the consent of the Owner, nor in time of war, but in a manner to be prescribed by law.

AMENDMENT IV [1791]

The right of the people to be secure in their persons, houses, papers, and effects, against unreasonable searches and seizures, shall not be violated, and no Warrants shall issue, but upon probable cause, supported by Oath or affirmation, and particularly describing the place to be searched, and the persons or things to be seized.

AMENDMENT V [1791]

No person shall be held to answer for a capital, or otherwise infamous crime, unless on a presentment or indictment of a Grand Jury, except in cases arising in the land or naval forces, or in the Militia, when in actual service in time of War or public danger; nor shall any person be subject for the same offence to be twice put in jeopardy of life or limb; nor shall be compelled in any criminal case to be a witness against himself, nor be deprived of life, liberty, or property, without due process of law; nor shall private property be taken for public use, without just compensation.

AMENDMENT VI [1791]

In all criminal prosecutions, the accused shall enjoy the right to a speedy and public trial, by an impartial jury of the State and district wherein the crime shall have been committed, which district shall have been previously ascertained by law, and to be informed of the nature and cause of the accusation; to be confronted with the witnesses against him; to have compulsory process for obtaining witnesses in his favor, and to have the Assistance of Counsel for his defence.

AMENDMENT VII [1791]

In Suits at common law, where the value in controversy shall exceed twenty dollars, the right of trial by jury shall be preserved, and no fact tried by jury, shall be otherwise reexamined in any Court of the United States, than according to the rules of the common law.

AMENDMENT VIII [1791]

Excessive bail shall not be required, nor excessive fines imposed, nor cruel and unusual punishments inflicted.

AMENDMENT IX [1791]

The enumeration in the Constitution, of certain rights, shall not be construed to deny or disparage others retained by the people.

AMENDMENT X [1791]

The powers not delegated to the United States by the Constitution, nor prohibited by it to the States, are reserved to the States respectively, or to the people.

AMENDMENT XI [1798]

The Judicial power of the United States shall not be construed to extend to any suit in law or equity, commenced or prosecuted against one of the United States by Citizens of another State, or by Citizens or Subjects of any Foreign State.

AMENDMENT XII [1804]

The Electors shall meet in their respective states, and vote by ballot for President and Vice-President, one of whom, at least, shall not be an inhabitant of the same state with themselves; they shall name in their ballots the person voted for as President, and in distinct ballots the person voted for as Vice-President, and they shall make distinct lists of all persons voted for as President, and of all persons voted for as Vice-President, and of the number of votes for each, which lists they shall sign and certify, and transmit sealed to the seat of the government of the United States, directed to the President of the Senate;—The President of the Senate shall, in the presence of the Senate and House of Representatives, open all the certificates and the votes shall then be counted;—The person having the greatest number of votes for President, shall be the President, if such number be a majority of the whole number of Electors appointed; and if no person have such majority, then from the persons having the highest numbers not exceeding three on the list of those voted for as President, the House of Representatives shall choose immediately, by ballot, the President. But in choosing the President, the votes shall be taken by states, the representation from each state having one vote; a quorum for this purpose shall consist of a member or members from two-thirds of the states, and a majority of all states shall be necessary to a choice. And if the House of Representatives shall not choose a President whenever the right of choice shall devolve upon them, before the fourth day of March next following, then the Vice-President shall act as President, as in the case of the death or other constitutional disability of the President.—The person having the greatest number of votes as Vice-President, shall be the Vice-President, if such number be a majority of the whole number of Electors appointed, and if no person have a majority, then from the two highest numbers on the list, the Senate shall choose the Vice-President; a quorum for the purpose shall consist of two-thirds of the whole number of Senators, and a majority of the whole number shall be necessary to a choice. But no person constitutionally ineligible to the office of President shall be eligible to that of Vice-President of the United States.

AMENDMENT XIII [1865]

Section 1. Neither slavery nor involuntary servitude, except as a punishment for crime whereof the party shall have been duly convicted, shall exist within the United States, or any place subject to their jurisdiction.

Section 2. Congress shall have power to enforce this article by appropriate legislation.

AMENDMENT XIV [1868]

Section 1. All persons born or naturalized in the United States, and subject to the jurisdiction thereof, are citizens of the United States and of the State wherein they reside. No State shall make or enforce any law which shall abridge the privileges or immunities of citizens of the United States; nor shall any State deprive any person of life, liberty, or property, without due process of law; nor deny to any person within its jurisdiction the equal protection of the laws.

Section 2. Representatives shall be apportioned among the several States according to their respective numbers, counting the whole number of persons in each State, excluding Indians not taxed. But when the right to vote at any election for the choice of electors for President and Vice President of the United States, Representatives in Congress, the Executive and Judicial officers of a State, or the members of the Legislature thereof, is denied to any of the male inhabitants of such State, being twenty-one years of age, and citizens of the United States, or in any way abridged, except for participation in rebellion, or other crime, the basis of representation therein shall be reduced in the proportion which the number of such male citizens shall bear to the whole number of male citizens twenty-one years of age in such State.

Section 3. No person shall be a Senator or Representative in Congress, or elector of President and Vice President, or hold any office, civil or military, under the United States, or under any State, who having previously taken an oath, as a member of Congress, or as an officer of the United States, or as a member of any State legislature, or as an executive or judicial officer of any State, to support the Constitution of the United States, shall have engaged in insurrection or rebellion against the same, or given aid or comfort to the enemies thereof. But Congress may by a vote of two-thirds of each House, remove such disability.

Section 4. The validity of the public debt of the United States, authorized by law, including debts incurred for payment of pensions and bounties for services in suppressing insurrection or rebellion, shall not be questioned. But neither the United States nor any State shall assume or pay any debt or obligation incurred in aid of insurrection or rebellion against the United States, or any claim for the loss or emancipation of any slave; but all such debts, obligations and claims shall be held illegal and void.

Section 5. The Congress shall have power to enforce, by appropriate legislation, the provisions of this article.

AMENDMENT XV [1870]

Section 1. The right of citizens of the United States to vote shall not be denied or abridged by the United States or by any State on account of race, color, or previous condition of servitude.

Section 2. The Congress shall have power to enforce this article by appropriate legislation.

AMENDMENT XVI [1913]

The Congress shall have power to lay and collect taxes on incomes, from whatever source derived, without apportionment among the several States, and without regard to any census or enumeration.

AMENDMENT XVII [1913]

Section 1. The Senate of the United States shall be composed of two Senators from each State, elected by the people thereof, for six years; and each Senator shall have one vote. The electors in each State shall have the qualifications requisite for electors of the most numerous branch of the State legislatures.

Section 2. When vacancies happen in the representation of any State in the Senate, the executive authority of such State shall issue writs of election to fill such vacancies: *Provided,* That the legislature of any State may empower the executive thereof to make temporary appointments until the people fill the vacancies by election as the legislature may direct.

Section 3. This amendment shall not be so construed as to affect the election or term of any Senator chosen before it becomes valid as part of the Constitution.

AMENDMENT XVIII [1919]

Section 1. After one year from the ratification of this article the manufacture, sale, or transportation of intoxicating liquors within, the importation thereof into, or the exportation thereof from the United States and all territory subject to the jurisdiction thereof for beverage purposes is hereby prohibited.

Section 2. The Congress and the several States shall have concurrent power to enforce this article by appropriate legislation.

Section 3. This article shall be inoperative unless it shall have been ratified as an amendment to the Constitution by the legislatures of the several States, as provided in the Constitution, within seven years from the date of the submission hereof to the States by the Congress.

AMENDMENT XIX [1920]

Section 1. The right of citizens of the United States to vote shall not be denied or abridged by the United States or by any State on account of sex.

Section 2. Congress shall have power to enforce this article by appropriate legislation.

AMENDMENT XX [1933]

Section 1. The terms of the President and Vice President shall end at noon on the 20th day of January, and the terms of Senators and Representatives at noon on the 3d day of January, of the years in which such terms would have ended if this article had not been ratified; and the terms of their successors shall then begin.

Section 2. The Congress shall assemble at least once in every year, and such meeting shall begin at noon on the 3d day of January, unless they shall by law appoint a different day.

Section 3. If, at the time fixed for the beginning of the term of the President, the President elect shall have died, the Vice President elect shall become President. If the President shall not have been chosen before the time fixed for the beginning of his term, or if the President elect shall have failed to qualify, then the Vice President elect shall act as President until a President shall have qualified; and the Congress may by law provide for the case wherein neither a President elect nor a Vice President elect shall have qualified, declaring who shall then act as President, or the manner in which one who is to act shall be selected, and such person shall act accordingly until a President or Vice President shall have qualified.

Section 4. The Congress may by law provide for the case of the death of any of the persons from whom the House of Representatives may choose a President whenever the right of choice shall have devolved upon them, and for the case of the death of any of the persons from whom the Senate may choose a Vice President whenever the right of choice shall have devolved upon them.

Section 5. Sections 1 and 2 shall take effect on the 15th day of October following the ratification of this article.

Section 6. This article shall be inoperative unless

it shall have been ratified as an amendment to the Constitution by the legislatures of three-fourths of the several States within seven years from the date of its submission.

AMENDMENT XXI [1933]

Section 1. The eighteenth article of amendment to the Constitution of the United States is hereby repealed.

Section 2. The transportation or importation into any State, Territory, or possession of the United States for delivery or use therein of intoxicating liquors, in violation of the laws thereof, is hereby prohibited.

Section 3. This article shall be inoperative unless it shall have been ratified as an amendment to the Constitution by conventions in the several States, as provided in the Constitution, within seven years from the date of the submission hereof to the States by the Congress.

AMENDMENT XXII [1951]

Section 1. No person shall be elected to the office of the President more than twice, and no person who has held the office of President, or acted as President, for more than two years of a term to which some other person was elected President shall be elected to the office of President more than once. But this Article shall not apply to any person holding the office of President when this Article was proposed by the Congress, and shall not prevent any person who may be holding the office of President, or acting as President, during the term within which this Article becomes operative from holding the office of President or acting as President during the remainder of such term.

Section 2. This article shall be inoperative unless it shall have been ratified as an amendment to the Constitution by the legislatures of three-fourths of the several States within seven years from the date of its submission to the States by the Congress.

Amendment XXIII [1961]

Section 1. The District constituting the seat of Government of the United States shall appoint in such manner as the Congress may direct:

A number of electors of President and Vice President equal to the whole number of Senators and Representatives in Congress to which the District would be entitled if it were a State, but in no event more than the least populous state; they shall be in addition to those appointed by the states, but they shall be considered, for the purposes of the election of President and Vice President, to be electors appointed by a state; and they shall meet in the District and perform such duties as provided by the twelfth article of amendment.

Section 2. The Congress shall have power to enforce this article by appropriate legislation.

Amendment XXIV [1964]

Section 1. The right of citizens of the United States to vote in any primary or other election for President or Vice President, for electors for President or Vice President, or for Senator or Representative in Congress, shall not be denied or abridged by the United States, or any State by reason of failure to pay any poll tax or other tax.

Section 2. The Congress shall have power to enforce this article by appropriate legislation.

Amendment XXV [1967]

Section 1. In case of the removal of the President from office or of his death or resignation, the Vice President shall become President.

Section 2. Whenever there is a vacancy in the office of the Vice President, the President shall nominate a Vice President who shall take office upon confirmation by a majority vote of both Houses of Congress.

Section 3. Whenever the President transmits to the President pro tempore of the Senate and the Speaker of the House of Representatives his written declaration that he is unable to discharge the powers and duties of his office, and until he transmits to them a written declaration to the contrary, such powers and duties shall be discharged by the Vice President as Acting President.

Section 4. Whenever the Vice President and a majority of either the principal officers of the executive departments or of such other body as Congress may by law provide, transmit to the President pro tempore of the Senate and the Speaker of the House of Representatives their written declaration that the President is unable to discharge the powers and duties of his office, the Vice President shall immediately assume the powers and duties of the office as Acting President.

Thereafter, when the President transmits to the President pro tempore of the Senate and the Speaker of the House of Representatives his written declaration that no inability exists, he shall resume the powers and duties of his office unless the Vice President and a majority of either the principal officers of the executive department or of such other body as Congress may by law provide, transmit within four days to the President pro tempore of the Senate and the Speaker of the House of Representatives their written declaration that the President is unable to discharge the powers and duties of his office. Thereupon Congress shall decide the issue, assembling within forty-eight hours for that purpose if not in session. If the Congress, within twenty-one days after receipt of the latter written declaration, or, if Congress is not in session, within twenty-one days after Congress is required to assemble, determines by two-thirds vote of both Houses that the President is unable to discharge the powers and duties of his office, the Vice President shall continue to discharge the same as Acting President; otherwise, the President shall resume the powers and duties of his office.

Amendment XXVI [1971]

Section 1. The right of citizens of the United States, who are eighteen years of age or older, to vote shall not be denied or abridged by the United States or by any State on account of age.

Section 2. The Congress shall have power to enforce this article by appropriate legislation.

Amendment XXVII [1992]

No law, varying the compensation for the services of the Senators and Representatives, shall take effect, until an election of Representatives shall have intervened.

Appendix B

YOU BE THE JUDGE: THE COURTS' ACTUAL DECISIONS

1.1 State Supreme Court Justice Michael Obus sentenced Dennis Kozlowski, the former CEO of Tyco International, to a maximum of twenty-five years in prison and fined him about $140 million. Although most observers applauded the punishment, Jonathan Simon, a professor of law at the University of California at Berkeley, felt it was too harsh and, in the end, unfruitful. "It would be far more effective to impose a lot of short sentences on a wider group of offenders," says Simon, "rather than the example model of harshly punishing a few celebrity cases while most potential offenders know that they are unlikely ever to get caught and punished." Source: Andrew Ross Sorkin, "How Long to Jail White-Collar Criminals?" *New York Times* (September 16, 2005), C1.

2.1 The judge required Philip to redo his rehabilitation, a twelve-step Sexaholics Anonymous program. Unfettered by his tumor, Philip kept his hands to himself and successfully completed the requirement. Eventually, he returned home to his family. Interestingly, about one year later the headaches returned and Philip resumed collecting child pornography. A brain scan showed that the tumor had begun to reform. As before, doctors removed the tumor, and the deviant behavior ceased. Source: Jeffrey M. Burns and Russell H. Swerdlow, "Right Orbifrontal Tumor with Pedophilia Symptom and Constructional Apraxia Sign," *Archives of Neurology* (March 2003), 437.

4.1 The court refused to throw out the charges. Although Emil was unconscious at the time his car struck the schoolgirls, he had earlier made the decision to get behind the wheel despite the knowledge that he suffered from epileptic seizures. In other words, the *actus reus* in this crime was not Emil's driving into the girls, but his decision to drive in the first place. That decision was certainly voluntary and therefore satisfies the requirements of *actus reus*. Note that if Emil had never had an epileptic seizure before, and had no idea that he suffered from that malady, the court's decision would probably have been different. Source: *People v. Decina*, 138 N.E.2d 799 (1956). A briefed (summarized) version of this case can be found at **www.lectlaw.com/files/lws50.htm**. Scroll down the list to the case title to view the brief.

4.2 In March 2006, a Spotsylvania County, Virginia, jury found Deana Large guilty of involuntary manslaughter in the death of Dorothy Sullivan. The jury said that, given Large's knowledge that her dogs posed a threat to the community, her actions showed a "callous disregard for human life." A judge sentenced Large to three years' imprisonment. That same year, the Virginia legislature passed a law making certain dog attacks that result in injury (not necessarily death) a felony punishable by up to five years in prison and a $2,500 fine. Source: Carlos Santos, "Three-Year Sentence in Dog Attack," *Richmond (Va.) Times-Dispatch* (March 30, 2006), B1.

5.1 The United States Supreme Court ruled that individuals do not have a *right* to protection by law enforcement agencies and, therefore, Jessica could not sue the Castle Rock Police Department. In his majority opinion, Justice Antonin Scalia said that, while the restraining order did seem to mandate an arrest in these circumstances, "a well-established tradition of police discretion has long coexisted with apparently mandatory arrest statutes." Source: *Town of Castle Rock v. Gonzales*, 545 U.S. 748 (2005). The full text of this case can be found online at **supreme.justia.com/us/545/04-278/case.html**.

6.1 The United States Supreme Court, while recognizing that this case belonged in the gray area "between excessive and acceptable force," threw out Haugen's lawsuit against Officer Brosseau. It ruled that even though Brosseau was erroneous in her belief that Haugen (who was unarmed and not wanted for any violent crimes) was a threat to others in the vicinity, her actions were reasonable given the fact that he was a "disturbed felon, set on avoiding capture." The decision signals the Court's desire that judges give police officers the benefit of the doubt in "reasonable force" cases, and makes it very difficult to file a suit against law enforcement agents after questionable shootings. Source: *Brosseau v. Haugen*, 543 U.S. 194 (2004). The full text of this case can be found online at **supreme.justia.com/us/543/03-1261/case.html**.

7.1 The U.S. Court of Appeals for the Fifth Circuit found that El Paso Police Officer George Perry passed the "totality of the circumstances" test for reasonableness in his decision to stop and frisk Johnny Michelletti, and upheld the conviction. The court listed the circumstances that combined to create this reasonableness: the time, the setting, Michelletti's suspicious behavior, and Perry's experience as a police officer. Furthermore, the likelihood that Michelletti was hiding a gun justified the frisk for the protection of the officers and the patrons of the bar. Source: *United States v. Michelletti*, 13 F.3d 838 (5th Cir. 1994). The full text for this case can be found online at **www.ca5.uscourts.gov/opinions/pub/92/92-08274.CR1.wpd.pdf**.

7.2 The United States Supreme Court ruled that the evidence was valid and could be presented against Harold. If the police officers had known, or should have known, that the third floor contained two apartments before they entered Harold's residence, then they would have been required to search only Larry's lodging. But, the Court said, "honest mistakes" by police officers do not equal an "unreasonable search" under the Fourth Amendment. Source: *Maryland v. Garrison*, 480 U.S. 79 (1987). The full text of this case can be found online at **supreme.justia.com/us/480/79/case.html**.

8.1 The United States Supreme Court ruled that the federal government's ability to regulate medical marijuana was "essential" to its efforts to police the drug. Therefore, the federal CSA preempted California's CUA, and Angie could be arrested and prosecuted for violating federal drug laws. The Court expressed sympathy for Angie's medical situation but stated that her ill health did not exempt her from the nation's drug laws. As a practical matter, however, this decision will not have much of an impact. The ruling did not overturn California's CUA, nor did it affect similar laws in eleven other states. Thus, state law enforcement agencies in those jurisdictions are not required to arrest and prosecute patients who use medical marijuana. Those medical users have only federal law enforcement agents to fear, and the likelihood that the Drug Enforcement Administration and other federal agencies will expend resources to combat small-scale marijuana operations remains small. Source: *Gonzales v. Raich*, 545 U.S. 1 (2005). The full text of this case can be found online at **supreme.justia.com/us/545/03-1454/case.html**.

9.1 Pima County Superior Court Judge Richard Fields granted Reina her pretrial release with bail set at $100,000. He ordered her to live with family or friends until the trial and keep out of contact with Christopher, felons, and minors. The judge also ordered Reina to participate in drug and alcohol treatment programs. Source: Kim Smith, "Woman Kept Out of Jail in Killing Case," *Arizona Daily Star* (April 21, 2007), B1.

10.1 The court reversed John's convictions because of the introduction of evidence that he possessed adult gay pornography. According to the court, "The mere possession of reading material that describes a particular type of activity makes it neither more nor less likely that a defendant would intentionally engage in the conduct described and thus fails to meet the test of relevancy" under federal law. In part, the court's decision can be explained as a rejection of the prosecution's obvious attempt to prejudice the jury against John because of his homosexuality. Source: *People of the Territory of Guam v. Shymanovitz*, 157 F.3d 1154 (9th Cir. 1998). A summary of this case can be found online at **www.vlex.com/vid/18499139**.

11.1 The Arizona Supreme Court ruled that the sentence was "not so grossly disproportionate as to constitute cruel and unusual punishment," and upheld Morton's 200-year prison term. While admitting that the sentence might be unusual, the court felt that it was in keeping with the Arizona state legislature's goal of eradicating child pornography. Morton filed a petition for a writ of *certiorari* with the United States Supreme Court, but the Court declined to hear the case. The decision shows how reluctant judges are to strike down sentences as excessive. Source: For the full text of the Arizona Supreme Court's decision, go to **www.cofad1.state.az.us/ opinionfiles/CR/CR030243.pdf**.

12.1 The trial judge sentenced Jason and another fraternity brother who participated in the hazing to two years in prison, followed by three years on probation. The judge also ordered Jason to attend an antihazing class and refrain from communicating with any "Greek" (fraternity) organization while on probation. The judge said that she had considered limiting the sentence to one year, but added a second year to make sure that the punishment was seen as a deterrent. "I want to save the victims who will quietly go along because they want to belong," she said. "I want schools to be furious and mad and upset [and] come down hard on hazing." She added that she wanted other students to say, "Those guys, they got two years, Oh my God." Source: "Judge Sends Frat Brothers to Prison for Hazing," at **www.cnn. com/2007/LAW/01/29/florida.hazing.ap/index. html?eref=rss_topstories**.

14.1 The United States Supreme Court upheld the ban on letter writing and overturned the ban on marriage. On the one hand, it determined that the prohibition of correspondence between Missouri corrections facilities addressed legitimate security concerns and therefore outweighed the inmates' ability to communicate with each other. On the other hand, it rejected the argument that prison marriages posed a threat to prison security significant enough to override the fundamental right of Americans to marry whom they choose. Furthermore, the Court pointed out, the "love triangles" that seemed so worrisome to Missouri prison officials could take place whether the participants were married or not. Source: *Turner v. Safley*, 482 U.S. 78 (1987). The full text of this case can be found online at **supreme.justia.com/us/482/78/case.html**.

16.1 An Idaho jury acquitted Sami Omar Al-Hussayen of the material support charges, and after spending a year in prison, he was released and returned to Saudi Arabia for other, unrelated, immigration violations. One juror remarked that the verdict was based on the idea that in the United States "people could say whatever they want . . . providing it would not cause imminent action." Source: Richard B. Schmitt, "Acquittal in Internet Terrorism Case Is a Defeat for Patriot Act," *Los Angeles Times* (June 11, 2004), 20.

17.1 The judge ruled that Leon's Web site was not a "true" threat and, therefore, it was protected as speech under the First Amendment. He reasoned that there was no explicit threat on the Web site and that there is nothing inherently threatening about asking for information. Although the format of the site— the "WANTED" poster—and the identification of Gary and Sherry as informants did have negative connotations, the judge stated that the First Amendment "does not prohibit name calling." Source: *United States v. Carmichael*, 325 F.Supp.2d 1303 (M.D.Ala. 2004).

Appendix C

TABLE OF CASES

Glossary

Acquittal A declaration following a trial that the individual accused of the crime is innocent in the eyes of the law and thus is absolved from the charges.

Actus Reus (pronounced ak-tus ray-uhs). A guilty (prohibited) act. The commission of a prohibited act is one of the two essential elements required for criminal liability, the other element being the intent to commit a crime.

Adjudicatory Hearing The process through which a juvenile court determines whether there is sufficient evidence to support the initial petition.

Administrative Law The body of law created by administrative agencies (in the form of rules, regulations, orders, and decisions) in order to carry out their duties and responsibilities.

Adversary System A legal system in which the prosecution and defense are opponents, or adversaries, and present their cases in the light most favorable to themselves. The court arrives at a just solution based on the evidence presented by the contestants and determines who wins and who loses.

Affidavit A written statement of facts, confirmed by the oath or affirmation of the party making it and made before a person having the authority to administer the oath or affirmation.

Aftercare The variety of therapeutic, educational, and counseling programs made available to juvenile delinquents (and some adults) after they have been released from a correctional facility.

Age of Onset The age at which a juvenile first exhibits delinquent behavior. The earlier the age of onset, according to some studies, the greater the chance a person will become a career offender.

Aggravating Circumstances Any circumstances accompanying the commission of a crime that may justify a harsher sentence.

Aging Out A term used to explain the fact that criminal activity declines with age.

Alien A person who is not a citizen of the country in which he or she is found and therefore may not enjoy the same rights and protections as a citizen of that country.

Allen **Charge** An instruction by a judge to a deadlocked jury with only a few dissenters that asks the jurors in the minority to reconsider the majority opinion.

Anomie A condition in which the individual suffers from the breakdown or absence of social norms. According to this theory, this condition occurs when a person is disconnected from these norms or rejects them as inconsistent with his or her personal goals.

Anticipatory Search Warrant A search warrant based on the premise that specific evidence of a crime will be located at a named place in the future, though the evidence is not necessarily at that place when the warrant is issued.

Antisocial Personality Disorder (ASPD) A mental illness that is characterized by antisocial behavior and meets specific criteria established by the American Psychiatric Association.

Antiterrorism and Effective Death Penalty Act of 1996 (AEDPA) Legislation giving law enforcement officers the power to arrest and prosecute any individual who provides "material support or resources" to a "foreign terrorist organization."

Appeal The process of seeking a higher court's review of a lower court's decision for the purpose of correcting or changing the lower court's judgment or decision.

Appellate Courts Courts that review decisions made by lower courts, such as trial courts; also known as *courts of appeals.*

Arraignment A court proceeding in which the suspect is formally charged with the criminal offense stated in the indictment. The suspect enters a plea (guilty, not guilty, *nolo contendere*) in response.

Arrest To take into custody a person suspected of criminal activity. Police may use only reasonable levels of force in making an arrest.

Arrest Warrant A written order, based on probable cause and issued by a judge or magistrate, commanding that the person named on the warrant be arrested by the police.

Assault The threat or the attempt to do violence to another person, provided that the other person is aware of the danger.

Attempt The act of taking substantial steps toward committing a crime while having the ability and the intent to commit the crime, even if the crime never takes place.

Attendant Circumstances The facts surrounding a criminal event. With some crimes, these facts must be proved to convict the defendant of the underlying crime. With other crimes, proving these facts can increase the penalty associated with the underlying crime.

Attorney-Client Privilege A rule of evidence requiring that communications between a client and his or her attorney be kept confidential, unless the client consents to disclosure.

Attorney General The chief law officer of a state; also, the chief law officer of the nation.

Authentication Establishing the genuineness of an item that is to be introduced as evidence in a trial.

Authority The power designated to an agent of the law over a person who has broken the law.

Automatic Transfer The process by which a juvenile is transferred to adult court as a matter of state law. In some states, for example, a juvenile who is suspected of murder is automatically transferred to adult court.

B

Bail The amount or conditions set by the court to ensure that an individual accused of a crime will appear for further criminal proceedings. If the accused person provides bail, whether in cash or by means of a bail bond, then she or he is released from jail.

Bail Bondsperson A businessperson who agrees, for a fee, to pay the bail amount if the accused fails to appear in court as ordered.

Ballistics The study of firearms, including the firing of the weapon and the flight of the bullet.

Battery The act of physically contacting another person with the intent to do harm, even if the resulting injury is insubstantial.

Bench Trial A trial conducted without a jury, in which a judge makes the determination of the defendant's guilt or innocence.

Beyond a Reasonable Doubt The degree of proof required to find the defendant in a criminal trial guilty of committing the crime. The defendant's guilt must be the only reasonable explanation for the criminal act before the court.

Bill of Rights The first ten amendments to the U.S. Constitution.

Biological Weapon Any living organism, such as a bacterium or virus, used to intentionally harm or kill adversaries in war or targets of terrorist attacks.

Biology The science of living organisms, including their structure, function, growth, and origin.

Blue Curtain A metaphorical term used to refer to the value placed on secrecy and the general mistrust of the outside world shared by many police officers.

Booking The process of entering a suspect's name, offense, and arrival time into the police log following her or his arrest.

Boot Camp A variation on traditional shock incarceration in which juveniles (and some adults) are sent to secure confinement facilities modeled on military basic training camps instead of prison or jail. These camps emphasize strict discipline, manual labor, and military training to "shock" inmates out of a life of crime.

Botnet A network of computers that have been appropriated without the knowledge of their owners and used to spread harmful programs via the Internet; short for *robot network*.

Boykin **Form** A form that must be completed by a defendant who pleads guilty; the defendant states that she or he has done so voluntarily and with full comprehension of the consequences.

Broken Windows Theory Wilson and Kelling's theory that a neighborhood in disrepair signals that criminal activity is tolerated in the area. Thus, by cracking down on quality-of-life crimes, police can reclaim the neighborhood and encourage law-abiding citizens to live and work there.

Bureaucracy A hierarchically structured administrative organization that carries out specific functions.

Burglary The act of breaking into or entering a structure (such as a home or office) without permission for the purpose of committing a crime. No crime need take place; the key factor is the intent to commit the crime.

C

Capital Punishment The use of the death penalty to punish wrongdoers for certain crimes.

Case Attrition The process through which prosecutors, by deciding whether to prosecute each person arrested, effect an overall reduction in the number of persons prosecuted. As a result, the number of persons convicted and sentenced is much smaller than the number of persons arrested.

Case Law The rules of law announced in court decisions. Case law includes the aggregate of reported cases that interpret judicial precedents, statutes, regulations, and constitutional provisions.

Caseload The number of individual probationers or parolees under the supervision of a probation or parole officer.

Central Intelligence Agency (CIA) The U.S. government agency that is responsible for collecting and coordinating foreign intelligence operations.

Challenge for Cause A *voir dire* challenge for which an attorney states the reason why a prospective juror should not be included on the jury.

Charge The judge's instructions to the jury following the attorneys' closing arguments; the charge sets forth the rules of law that the jury must apply in reaching its decision, or verdict.

Chemical Weapon Any weapon that uses a manufactured chemical to intentionally harm or kill adversaries in war or targets of terrorist attacks.

Child Abuse Mistreatment of children by causing physical, emotional, or sexual damage without any plausible explanation, such as an accident.

Child Neglect A form of child abuse in which the child is denied certain necessities such as shelter, food, care, and love. Neglect is justification for a government agency to assume responsibility for a child in place of the parents or legal guardian.

Choice Theory A school of criminology that holds that wrongdoers act as if they weigh the possible benefits of criminal or delinquent activity against the expected costs of being apprehended. When the benefits are greater than the expected costs, the offender will make a rational choice to commit a crime or delinquent act.

Chronic Offender A delinquent or criminal who commits multiple offenses and is considered part of a small group of wrongdoers who are responsible for a majority of the antisocial activity in any given community.

Circumstantial Evidence Indirect evidence that is offered to establish, by inference, the likelihood of a fact that is in question.

Citizen Oversight The process by which citizens review complaints brought against individual police officers or police departments. The citizens often do not have the power to discipline misconduct, but can recommend that action be taken by police administrators.

Civil Confinement The practice of confining individuals against their will if they present a danger to the community. In the criminal justice context, this term refers to the continued confinement of sex offenders at the conclusion of their prison terms.

Civil Law The branch of law dealing with the definition and enforcement of all private or public rights, as opposed to criminal matters.

Civil Rights The personal rights and protections guaranteed by the Constitution, particularly the Bill of Rights.

Classical Criminology A school of criminology based on the belief that individuals have free will to engage in any behavior, including criminal behavior. To deter criminal behavior, society must hold wrongdoers responsible for their actions by punishing them.

Clearance of an Arrest For crime-reporting purposes, occurs when the arrested suspect is charged with a crime and handed over to a court for prosecution.

Clearance Rate A comparison of the number of crimes cleared by arrest and prosecution to the number of crimes reported during any given time period.

Closing Arguments Arguments made by each side's attorney after the cases for the plaintiff and defendant have been presented.

Cold Hit The establishment of a connection between a suspect and a crime, often through the use of DNA evidence, in the absence of an ongoing criminal investigation.

Common Law The body of law developed from custom or judicial decisions in English and U.S. courts and not attributable to a legislature.

Community Policing A policing philosophy that emphasizes community support for and cooperation with the police in preventing crime. Community policing stresses a police role that is less centralized and more proactive than reform-era policing strategies.

Competency Hearing A court proceeding to determine whether the defendant is mentally well enough to understand the charges filed against him or her and cooperate with a lawyer in presenting a defense. If a judge believes the defendant to be incompetent, the trial cannot take place.

Computer Crime Any wrongful act that is directed against computers and computer parts or that involves wrongful use or abuse of computers or software.

Computer Forensics The application of computer technology to finding and utilizing evidence of cyber crimes.

Concurrent Jurisdiction The situation that occurs when two or more courts have the authority to preside over the same criminal case.

Concurring Opinions Separate opinions prepared by judges who support the decision of the majority of the court but who want to make or clarify a particular point or to voice disapproval of the grounds on which the decision was made.

Confidential Informant (CI) A human source for police who provides information concerning illegal activity in which he or she is involved.

Conflict Model A criminal justice model in which the content of criminal law is determined by the groups that hold economic, political, and social power in a community.

Confrontation Clause The part of the Sixth Amendment that guarantees all defendants the right to confront witnesses testifying against them during the criminal trial. In practice, this right entitles the defendant to be present at trial and to cross-examine witnesses for the prosecution.

Congregate System A nineteenth-century penitentiary system developed in New York in which inmates were kept in separate cells during the night but worked together in the daytime under a code of enforced silence.

Consensus Model A criminal justice model in which the majority of citizens in a society share the same values and beliefs. Criminal acts are those acts that conflict with these values and beliefs and are deemed harmful to society.

Consent Searches Searches by police that are made after the subject of the search has agreed to the action. In these situations, consent, if given of free will, validates a warrantless search.

Constitutional Law Law based on the U.S. Constitution and the constitutions of the various states.

Control Theory A series of theories that assume that all individuals have the potential for criminal behavior, but are restrained by the damage that such actions would do to their relationships with family, friends, and members of the community. Criminality occurs when these bonds are broken or nonexistent.

Coroner The medical examiner of a county, usually elected by popular vote.

Corpus Delicti The body of circumstances that must exist for a criminal act to have occurred.

Courtroom Work Group The social organization consisting of the judge, prosecutor, defense attorney, and other court workers. The relationships among these persons have a far-reaching impact on the day-to-day operations of any court.

Crime An act that violates criminal law and is punishable by criminal sanctions.

Crime Control Model A criminal justice model that places primary emphasis on the right of society to be protected from crime and violent criminals. Crime control values emphasize speed and efficiency in the criminal justice process; the benefits of lower crime rates outweigh any possible costs to individual rights.

Criminal Model of Addiction An approach to drug abuse that holds that drug offenders harm society by their actions to the same extent as other criminals and should face the same punitive sanctions.

Criminal Justice System The interlocking network of law enforcement agencies, courts, and corrections institutions designed to enforce criminal laws and protect society from criminal behavior.

Criminologist A specialist in the field of crime and the causes of criminal behavior.

Criminology The scientific study of crime and the causes of criminal behavior.

Cross-Examination The questioning of an opposing witness during trial.

Cultural Deviance Theory A branch of social structure theory based on the assumption that members of certain subcultures reject the values of the dominant culture through deviant behavior patterns.

Custodial Interrogation The questioning of a suspect after that person has been taken in custody. In this situation, the suspect must be read his or her *Miranda* rights before interrogation can begin.

Custody The forceful detention of a person, or the perception that a person is not free to leave the immediate vicinity.

Cyber Crime A crime that occurs online, in the virtual community of the Internet, as opposed to in the physical world.

Cyber Fraud Any misrepre-sentation knowingly made over the Internet with the intention of deceiving another and on which a reasonable person would and does rely to his or her detriment.

Cyberstalking The crime of stalking, committed in cyberspace though the use of the Internet, e-mail, or another form of electronic communication. Generally, stalking involves harassing a person and putting that person in reasonable fear for his or her safety or the safety of the person's immediate family.

Cyberterrorism The use of the Internet to attack or sabotage businesses and government agencies with the purpose of disrupting infrastructure systems.

D

Dark Figure of Crime A term used to describe the actual amount of crime that takes place. The "figure" is "dark," or impossible to detect, because a great number of crimes are never reported to the police.

Data Mining The analysis of data to identify patterns of behavior.

Day Reporting Center (DRC) A community-based corrections center to which offenders report on a daily basis for purposes of treatment, education, and incapacitation.

Deadly Force Force applied by a police officer that is likely or intended to cause death.

Defendant In a civil court, the person or institution against whom the action is brought. In a criminal court, the person or entity who has been formally accused of violating a criminal law.

Defense Attorney The lawyer representing the defendant.

Delegation of Authority The principles of command on which most police departments are based; personnel take orders from and are responsible to those in positions of power directly above them.

"Deliberate Indifference" A standard that must be met by inmates trying to prove that their Eighth Amendment rights were violated by a correctional facility. It occurs when prison officials are aware of harmful conditions of confinement but fail to take steps to remedy those conditions.

Departure A stipulation in many federal and state sentencing guidelines that allows a judge to adjust his or her sentencing decision based on the special circumstances of a particular case.

Deprivation Model A theory that inmate aggression is the result of the frustration inmates feel at being deprived of freedom, consumer goods, sex, and other staples of life outside the institution.

Detective The primary police investigator of crimes.

Detention The temporary custody of a juvenile in a state facility after a petition has been filed and before the adjudicatory process begins.

Detention Hearing A hearing to determine whether a juvenile should be detained, or remain detained, while waiting for the adjudicatory process to begin.

Determinate Sentencing A period of incarceration that is fixed by a sentencing authority and cannot be reduced by judges or other corrections officials.

Deterrence The strategy of preventing crime through the threat of punishment. Assumes that potential criminals will weigh the costs of punishment versus the benefits of the criminal act; therefore, punishments should be severe.

Deviance Behavior that is considered to go against the norms established by society.

Differential Response A strategy for answering calls for service in which response time is adapted to the seriousness of the call.

Directed Patrol A patrol strategy that is designed to focus on a specific type of criminal activity at a specific time.

Direct Evidence Evidence that establishes the existence of a fact that is in question without relying on inference.

Direct Examination The examination of a witness by the attorney who calls the witness to the stand to testify.

Direct Supervision Approach A process of prison and jail administration in which correctional officers are in continuous physical contact with inmates during the day.

Discovery Formal investigation prior to trial. During discovery, the defense uses various methods to obtain information from the prosecution to prepare for trial.

Discretion The ability of individuals in the criminal justice system to make operational decisions based on personal judgment instead of formal rules or official information.

Discretionary Release The release of an inmate into a community supervision program at the discretion of the parole board within limits set by state or federal law.

Disposition Hearing Similar to the sentencing hearing for adults, a hearing in which the juvenile judge or officer decides the appropriate punishment for a youth found to be delinquent or a status offender.

Dissenting Opinions Separate opinions in which judges disagree with the conclusion reached by the majority of the court and expand on their own views about the case.

Diversion In the context of corrections, a strategy to divert those offenders who qualify away from prison and jail and toward community-based and intermediate sanctions.

DNA Fingerprinting The identification of a person based on a sample of her or his DNA, the genetic material found in the cells of all living things.

Docket The list of cases entered on a court's calendar and thus scheduled to be heard by the court.

Domestic Terrorism Acts of terrorism that take place within the territorial jurisdiction of the United States without foreign direction or involvement.

Domestic Violence The act of willful neglect or physical violence that occurs within a familial or other intimate relationship.

Double Jeopardy To twice place at risk (jeopardize) a person's life or liberty. The Fifth Amendment to the U.S. Constitution prohibits a second prosecution for the same criminal offense.

Drug Any substance that modifies biological, psychological, or social behavior; in particular, an illegal substance with those properties.

Drug Abuse The use of drugs that results in physical or psychological problems for the user, as well as disruption of personal relationships and employment.

Dual Court System The separate but interrelated court system of the United States, made up of the courts on the national level and the courts on the state level.

Due Process Clause The provisions of the Fifth and Fourteenth Amendments to the Constitution that guarantee that no person shall be deprived of life, liberty, or property without due process of law. Similar clauses are found in most state constitutions.

Due Process Model A criminal justice model that places primacy on the right of the individual to be protected from the power of the government. Due process values hold that the state must prove a person's guilt within the confines of a process designed to safeguard personal liberties as enumerated in the Bill of Rights.

Duress Unlawful pressure brought to bear on a person, causing the person to perform an act that he or she would not otherwise perform.

***Durham* Rule** A test of criminal responsibility adopted in a 1954 case: "an accused is not criminally responsible if his unlawful act was the product of mental disease or mental defect."

Duty to Retreat The requirement that a person claiming self-defense prove that she or he first took reasonable steps to avoid the conflict that resulted in the use of deadly force. Generally, the duty to retreat (1) applies only in public spaces and (2) does not apply when the force used in self-defense was nondeadly.

Duty The moral sense of a police officer that she or he should apply authority in a certain manner.

E

Eco-Terrorism Violence or the threat of violence against persons or property for environmental-political reasons.

Electronic Monitoring A technique of probation supervision in which the offender's whereabouts, though not his or her actions, are kept under surveillance by an electronic device; often used in conjunction with home confinement.

Electronic Surveillance The use of electronic equipment by law enforcement agents to record private conversations or observe conduct that is meant to be private.

Encryption The process by which a message is transmitted into a form or code that the sender and receiver intend not to be understandable by third parties.

Enemy Combatant A label given to certain persons suspected of terrorist activities by the U.S. government. Persons given this designation can be detained indefinitely without review of their status.

Entrapment A defense in which the defendant claims that he or she was induced by a public official—usually an undercover agent or police officer—to commit a crime that he or she would otherwise not have committed.

Ethics The rules or standards of behavior governing a profession; aimed at ensuring the fairness and rightness of actions.

Evidence Anything that is used to prove the existence or nonexistence of a fact.

Exclusionary Rule A rule under which any evidence that is obtained in violation of the accused's rights under the Fourth, Fifth, and Sixth Amendments, as well as any evidence derived from illegally obtained evidence, will not be admissible in criminal court.

Exigent Circumstances Situations that require extralegal or exceptional actions by the police. In these circumstances, police officers are justified in not following procedural rules, such as those pertaining to search and arrest warrants.

Expert Witness A witness with professional training or substantial experience qualifying her or him to testify on a certain subject.

Extradition The process by which one jurisdiction surrenders a person accused or convicted of violating another jurisdiction's criminal law to the second jurisdiction.

F

Federal Bureau of Investigation (FBI) The branch of the Department of Justice responsible for investigating violations of federal law. The bureau also collects national crime statistics and provides training and other forms of aid to local law enforcement agencies.

Federalism A form of government in which a written constitution provides for a division of powers between a central government and several regional governments. In the United States, the division of powers between the federal government and the fifty states is established by the Constitution.

Felony A serious crime, usually punishable by death or imprisonment for a year or longer.

Field Training The segment of a police recruit's training in which he or she is removed from the classroom and placed on the beat, under the supervision of a senior officer.

Finality The end of a criminal case, meaning that the outcome of the case is no longer susceptible to challenge by prosecutors or the defendant.

First Responders Those individuals, such as firefighters, police officers, and emergency medical technicians, who are responsible for the protection and preservation of life and property during the early stages following a disaster.

Forensics The application of science to establish facts and evidence during the investigation of crimes.

Forfeiture The process by which the government seizes private property attached to criminal activity.

Frisk A pat-down or minimal search by police to discover weapons; conducted for the express purpose of protecting the officer or other citizens, and not to find evidence of illegal substances for use in a trial.

Fruit of the Poisoned Tree Evidence that is acquired through the use of illegally obtained evidence and is therefore inadmissible in court.

Furlough Temporary release from a prison for purposes of vocational or educational training, to ease the shock of release, or for personal reasons.

G

General Patrol A patrol strategy that relies on police officers monitoring a certain area with the goal of detecting crimes in progress or preventing crime due to their presence; also known as *random* or *preventive patrol.*

Genetics The study of how certain traits or qualities are transmitted from parents to their offspring.

"Good Faith" Exception The legal principle, established through court decisions, that evidence obtained with the use of a technically faulty search warrant is admissible during trial if the police acted in good faith when they sought the warrant from a judge.

"Good Time" A reduction in time served by prisoners based on good behavior, conformity to rules, and other positive actions.

Graduated Sanctions The practical theory in juvenile corrections that a delinquent or status offender should receive a punishment that matches in seriousness the severity of the wrongdoing.

Grand Jury The group of citizens called to decide whether probable cause exists to believe that a suspect committed the crime with which she or he has been charged.

Gun Control Efforts by a government to regulate or control the sale of guns.

H

Habeas Corpus An order that requires correctional officials to bring an inmate before a court or a judge and explain why he or she is being held in prison.

Habitual Offender Laws Statutes that require lengthy prison sentences for those who are convicted of multiple felonies.

Hacker A person who uses one computer to break into another.

Halfway House A community-based form of early release that places inmates in residential centers and allows them to reintegrate with society.

"Hands-Off" Doctrine The unwritten judicial policy that favors noninterference by the courts in the administration of prisons and jails.

Hate Crime Law A statute that provides for greater sanctions against those who commit crimes motivated by bias against an individual or a group based on race, ethnicity, religion, gender, sexual orientation, disability, or age.

Hate Speech Speech that is intended to offend an individual on the basis of her or his race, gender, religion, sexual orientation, ethnicity, or disability.

Hearsay An oral or written statement made by an out-of-court declarant that is later offered in court by a witness (not the declarant) concerning a matter before the court. Hearsay usually is not admissible as evidence.

Home Confinement A community-based sanction in which offenders serve their terms of incarceration in their homes.

Homeland Security A concerted national effort to prevent terrorist attacks within the United States and reduce the country's vulnerability to terrorism.

Hormone A chemical substance, produced in tissue and conveyed in the bloodstream, that controls certain cellular and bodily functions such as growth and reproduction.

Hot Spots Concentrated areas of high criminal activity that draw a directed police response.

Hung Jury A jury whose members are so irreconcilably divided in their opinions that they cannot reach a verdict.

I

"Identifiable Human Needs" The basic human necessities that correctional facilities are required by the Constitution to provide to inmates. Beyond food, warmth, and exercise, the court system has been unable to establish exactly what these needs are.

Identity Theft The theft of identity information, such as a person's name, driver's license number, or Social Security number. The information is then usually used to access the victim's financial resources.

Illicit Drugs Certain drugs or substances whose use or sale has been declared illegal.

Impeach To charge a public official with misconduct. As authorized by Article I of the Constitution, the House of Representatives votes on impeachment; if the measure passes, the matter is sent to the Senate for a vote to remove the president, vice president, or civil officers (such as federal judges) of the United States.

Improvised Explosive Devices (IEDs) Explosive charges created using nonmilitary or nontraditional components, often used by terrorists or other nonstate actors without access to standard weapons training.

Incapacitation A strategy for preventing crime by detaining wrongdoers in prison, thereby separating them from the community and reducing criminal opportunities.

Inchoate Offenses Conduct deemed criminal without actual harm being done, provided that the harm that would have occurred is one the law tries to prevent.

Incident-Driven Policing A reactive approach to policing that emphasizes a speedy response to calls for service.

Indeterminate Sentencing An indeterminate term of incarceration in which a judge determines the minimum and maximum terms of imprisonment. When the minimum term is reached, the prisoner becomes eligible to be paroled.

Indictment A charge or written accusation, issued by a grand jury, that probable cause exists to believe that a named person has committed a crime.

"Inevitable Discovery" Exception The legal principle that illegally obtained evidence can be admitted in court if police using lawful means would have "inevitably" discovered it.

Infancy A condition that, under early American law, excused young wrongdoers of criminal behavior because they could not understand the consequences of their actions.

Information The formal charge against the accused issued by the prosecutor after a preliminary hearing has found probable cause.

Infrastructure The services and facilities that support the day-to-day needs of modern life such as electricity, food, transportation, and water.

Initial Appearance An accused's first appearance before a judge or magistrate following arrest; during the appearance, the defendant is informed of the charges, advised of the right to counsel, told the amount of bail, and given a date for the preliminary hearing.

Insanity A defense for criminal liability that asserts a lack of criminal responsibility. According to the law, a person cannot have the requisite state of mind to commit a crime if she or he did not know at the time of the act that it was wrong, or did not know the nature and quality of the act.

Intake Following referral of a juvenile to juvenile court by a police officer or other concerned party, the process by which an official of the court must decide whether to file a petition, release the juvenile, or place the juvenile under some other form of supervision.

Intellectual Property Property resulting from intellectual, creative processes.

Intelligence Agency An agency that is primarily concerned with gathering information about potential criminal or terrorist events in order to prevent those acts from taking place.

Intensive Supervision Probation (ISP) A punishment-oriented form of probation in which the offender is placed under stricter and more frequent surveillance and control than in conventional probation by probation officers with limited caseloads.

Intermediate Sanctions Sanctions that are more restrictive than probation and less restrictive than imprisonment. Intended to alleviate pressure on overcrowded corrections facilities and understaffed probation departments.

Internal Affairs Unit (IAU) A division within a police department that receives and investigates complaints of wrongdoing by police officers.

Interrogation The direct questioning of a suspect to gather evidence of criminal activity and try to gain a confession.

Intoxication A defense for criminal liability in which the defendant claims that the taking of intoxicants rendered him or her unable to form the requisite intent to commit a criminal act.

Involuntary Manslaughter A negligent homicide, in which the offender had no intent to kill his or her victim.

Irresistible-Impulse Test A test for the insanity defense under which a defendant who knew his or her action was wrong may still be found insane if he or she was nonetheless unable, as a result of a mental deficiency, to control the urge to complete it.

J

Jail A facility, usually operated by the county government, used to hold persons awaiting trial or those who have been found guilty of misdemeanors.

Judicial Misconduct A general term describing behavior that diminishes public confidence in the judiciary. This behavior includes obviously illegal acts, such as bribery, and conduct that gives the appearance of impropriety, such as consorting with known felons.

Judicial Reprieve Temporary relief or the postponement of a sentence on the authority of a judge. In the United States, the judicial power to offer a reprieve has been limited by the Supreme Court.

Judicial Review The power of a court—particularly the United States Supreme Court—to review the actions of the executive and legislative branches and, if necessary, declare those actions unconstitutional.

Judicial Waiver The process in which the juvenile judge, based on the facts of the case at hand, decides that the alleged offender should be transferred to adult court.

Jurisdiction The authority of a court to hear and decide cases within an area of the law or a geographic territory.

Jury Nullification An acquittal of a defendant by a jury even though the evidence presented and the judge's instructions indicate that the defendant is guilty.

Jury Trial A trial before a judge and a jury.

Just Deserts A sanctioning philosophy based on the assertion that criminals deserve to be punished for breaking society's rules. The severity of the punishment should be determined only by the severity of the crime without considering any other factors.

Justice of the Peace Established in fourteenth-century England, a government official who oversaw various aspects of local law enforcement. The post eventually became strictly identified with judicial matters.

Juvenile Delinquency Behavior that is illegal under federal or state law that has been committed by a person who is under an age limit specified by statute.

L

Labeling Theory The hypothesis that society creates crime and criminals by labeling certain behavior and certain people as deviant. The stigma that results from this social process excludes a person from the community, thereby increasing the chances that she or he will adopt the label as her or his identity and engage in a pattern of criminal behavior.

Larceny The act of taking property from another person without the use of force with the intent of keeping that property.

Lay Witness A witness who can truthfully and accurately testify on a fact in question without having specialized training or knowledge; an ordinary witness.

Learning Theory The hypothesis that delinquents and criminals must be taught both the practical and emotional skills necessary to partake in illegal activity.

Liability In a civil court, legal responsibility for one's own or another's actions.

Licit Drugs Legal drugs or substances, such as alcohol, coffee, and tobacco.

Life Course Criminology The study of crime based on the belief that behavioral patterns developed in childhood can predict delinquent and criminal behavior later in life.

Lockdown A disciplinary action taken by prison officials in which all inmates are ordered to their quarters and nonessential prison activities are suspended.

Low-Visibility Decision Making A term used to describe the discretionary power police have in determining what to do with misbehaving juveniles. For the most part, this power goes unchallenged and unnoticed by citizens.

M

***M'Naghten* Rule** A common law test of criminal responsibility derived from *M'Naghten's* Case in 1843 that relies on the defendant's inability to distinguish right from wrong.

Magistrate A public civil officer or official with limited judicial authority within a particular geographic area, such as the authority to issue an arrest warrant.

Mala in Se A descriptive term for acts that are inherently wrong, regardless of whether they are prohibited by law.

Mala Prohibita A descriptive term for acts that are made illegal by criminal statute and are not necessarily wrong in and of themselves.

Mandatory Arrest Policy Requires a police officer to detain a person for committing a certain type of crime as long as probable cause that he or she committed the crime exists.

Mandatory Release Release from prison that occurs when an offender has served the full length of his or her sentence, minus any adjustments for good time. Mandatory release occurs as a result of a statutory requirement and, when applicable, negates the possibility of parole.

Mandatory Sentencing Guidelines Statutorily determined punishments that must be applied to those who are convicted of specific crimes.

Master Jury List The list of citizens in a court's district from which a jury can be selected; often compiled from voter-registration lists, driver's license lists, and other sources.

Maximum-Security Prison A correctional institution designed and organized to control and discipline dangerous felons, as well as prevent escape, with intense supervision, cement walls, and electronic, barbed wire fences.

Medical Model of Addiction An approach to drug addiction that treats drug abuse as a mental illness and focuses on treating and rehabilitating offenders rather than punishing them.

Medical Model A model of corrections in which the psychological and biological roots of an inmate's criminal behavior are identified and treated.

Medium-Security Prison A correctional institution that houses less dangerous inmates and therefore uses less restrictive measures to avoid violence and escapes.

Mens Rea (pronounced *mehns* ray-uh). Mental state, or intent. A wrongful mental state is as necessary as a wrongful act to establish criminal liability.

Methamphetamine (meth) A synthetic stimulant that creates a strong feeling of euphoria in the user and is highly addictive.

Military Tribunal A court that is operated by the military rather than the criminal justice system and is presided over by military officers rather than judges. Often, the tribunals operate in secrecy and do not provide the suspect with the full range of constitutional protections.

Minimum-Security Prison A correctional institution designed to allow inmates, most of whom pose low security risks, a great deal of freedom of movement and contact with the outside world.

***Miranda* Rights** The constitutional rights of accused persons taken into custody by law enforcement officials. Following the United States Supreme Court's decision in *Miranda v. Arizona,* on taking an accused person into custody, the arresting officer must inform the person of certain constitutional rights, such as the right to remain silent and the right to counsel.

Misdemeanor A criminal offense that is not a felony, usually punishable by a fine and/or a jail term of less than one year.

Missouri Plan A method of selecting judges that combines appointment and election. Under the plan, the state governor or another government official selects judges from a group of nominees chosen by a nonpartisan committee. After a year on the bench, the judges face a popular election to determine whether the public wishes to keep them in office.

Mitigating Circumstances Any circumstances accompanying the commission of a crime that may justify a lighter sentence.

Model Penal Code A statutory text created by the American Law Institute that sets forth general principles of criminal responsibility and defines specific offenses. States have adopted many aspects of the Model Penal Code, which is not itself a law, into their criminal codes.

Money Laundering The introduction of illegally gained funds into the legal financial system with the goal of covering up the funds' true origin.

Motion for a Directed Verdict A motion requesting that the court grant judgment in favor of the defense on the ground that the prosecution has not produced sufficient evidence to support the state's claim.

Murder The unlawful killing of one human being by another.

N

National Guard Military reserve units of the U.S. Army and U.S. Air Force controlled by each state of the United States and subject to deployment by both the federal and state executive branches in times of emergency.

National Security Agency (NSA) The intelligence agency that is responsible for protecting U.S. government communications and producing intelligence by monitoring foreign communications.

National Security Letter (NSL) A document from the FBI directing a third party to provide information concerning customers or patrons.

Necessity A defense against criminal liability in which the defendant asserts that circumstances required her or him to commit an illegal act.

Negligence A failure to exercise the standard of care that a reasonable person would exercise in similar circumstances.

Neurotransmitter A chemical that transmits nerve impulses between nerve cells and from nerve cells to the brain.

New-Generation Jail A type of jail that is distinguished architecturally from its predecessors by a design that encourages interaction between inmates and jailers and that offers greater opportunities for treatment.

Nolo Contendere Latin for "I will not contest it." A criminal defendant's plea, in which he or she chooses not to challenge, or contest, the charges brought by the government. Although the defendant may still be sentenced or fined, the plea neither admits nor denies guilt.

Nonpartisan Elections Elections in which candidates are presented on the ballot without any party affiliation.

Nonstate Actor An entity that plays a role in international affairs but does not represent any established state or nation.

Nuclear Weapon An explosive device that derives its massive destructive power from the release of nuclear energy.

O

Obscenity Speech that is not protected by the First Amendment because it is deemed to be offensive to community standards of decency.

Opening Statements The attorneys' statements to the jury at the beginning of the trial. Each side briefly outlines the evidence that will be offered during the trial and the legal theory that will be pursued.

Opinions Statements by the court expressing the reasons for its decision in a case.

Oral Arguments The verbal arguments presented in person by attorneys to an appellate court. Each attorney presents reasons why the court should rule in his or her client's favor.

Organized Crime A conspiratorial relationship among any number of persons engaged in the market for illegal goods or services, such as illicit drugs or firearms.

P

Pardon An act of executive clemency that overturns a conviction and erases mention of the crime from the person's criminal record.

Parens Patriae A doctrine that holds that the state has a responsibility to look after the well-being of children and to assume the role of parent if necessary.

Parole The conditional release of an inmate before his or her sentence has expired. The remainder of the sentence is served in the community under the supervision of correctional (parole) officers, and the offender can be returned to incarceration if he or she breaks the conditions of parole, as determined by a parole board.

Parole Board A body of appointed civilians that decides whether a convict should be granted conditional release before the end of his or her sentence.

Parole Contract An agreement between the state and the offender that establishes the conditions under which the latter will be allowed to serve the remainder of her or his prison term in the community.

Parole Grant Hearing A hearing in which the entire parole board or a subcommittee reviews information, meets the offender, and hears testimony from relevant witnesses to determine whether to grant parole.

Parole Guidelines Employed to remove discretion from the parole process, these guidelines attempt to measure the risks of an offender recidivating, and then use these measurements to determine whether early release will be granted and under what conditions.

Parole Revocation When a parolee breaks the conditions of parole, the process of withdrawing parole and returning the person to prison.

Part I Offenses Those crimes reported annually by the FBI in its Uniform Crime Report. Part I offenses include murder, rape, robbery, aggravated assault, burglary, larceny, and motor vehicle theft.

Part II Offenses All crimes recorded by the FBI that do not fall into the category of Part I offenses. Include both misdemeanors and felonies.

Partisan Elections Elections in which candidates are affiliated with and receive support from political parties; the candidates are listed in conjunction with their party on the ballot.

Patronage System A form of corruption in which the political party in power hires and promotes police officers, receiving job-related "favors" in return.

Penitentiary An early form of correctional facility that emphasized separating inmates from society and from each other so that they would have an environment in which to reflect on their wrongdoing and ponder their reformation.

Peremptory Challenges *Voir dire* challenges to exclude potential jurors from serving on the jury without any supporting reason or cause.

Personality Disorder A mental disorder characterized by deeply ingrained and maladjusted patterns of behavior.

Petition The document filed with a juvenile court alleging that the juvenile is a delinquent or a status offender and asking the court to either hear the case or transfer it to an adult court.

Plaintiff The person or institution that initiates a lawsuit in civil court proceedings by filing a complaint. In doing so, this party seeks a legal remedy to the matter in question.

Plain View Doctrine The legal principle that objects in plain view of a law enforcement agent who has the right to be in a position to have that view may be seized without a warrant and introduced as evidence.

Plea Bargaining The process by which the accused and the prosecutor work out a mutually satisfactory conclusion to the case, subject to court approval. Usually, plea bargaining involves the defendant's pleading guilty to a lesser offense in return for a lighter sentence.

Podular Design The architectural style of the new-generation jail. Each "pod" consists of between twelve and twenty-four one-person cells and a communal "day-room" to allow for social interaction.

Police Corruption The abuse of authority by a law enforcement officer for personal gain.

Police Cynicism The suspicion that citizens are weak, corrupt, and dangerous. This outlook is the result of a police officer being constantly exposed to civilians at their worst and can negatively affect the officer's performance.

Police Subculture The values and perceptions that are shared by members of a police department and, to a certain extent, by all law enforcement agents. These values and perceptions are shaped by the unique and isolated existence of the police officer.

Policy A set of guiding principles designed to influence the behavior and decision making of police officers.

Positivism A school of the social sciences that sees criminal and delinquent behavior as the result of biological, psychological, and social forces. Because wrongdoers are driven to deviancy by external factors, they should not be punished but treated to lessen the influence of those factors.

Precedent A court decision that furnishes an example of authority for deciding subsequent cases involving similar facts.

Predisposition Report A report prepared during the disposition process that provides the judge with relevant background material to aid in the disposition decision.

Preliminary Hearing An initial hearing in which a magistrate decides if there is probable cause to believe that the defendant committed the crime with which he or she is charged.

Preparedness An umbrella term for the actions taken by governments to prepare for large-scale catastrophic events such as terrorist attacks or environmental disasters.

Presentence Investigative Report An investigative report on an offender's background that assists a judge in determining the proper sentence.

Pretrial Detainees Individuals who cannot post bail after arrest or are not released on their own recognizance and are therefore forced to spend the time prior to their trial incarcerated in jail.

Pretrial Diversion Program An alternative to trial offered by a judge or prosecutor, in which the offender agrees to participate in a specified counseling or treatment program in return for withdrawal of the charges.

Preventive Detention The retention of an accused person in custody due to fears that she or he will commit a crime if released before trial.

Prisoner Reentry A corrections strategy designed to prepare inmates for a successful return to the community and to reduce their criminal activity after release.

Prison Gang A group of inmates who band together within the corrections system to engage in social and criminal activities.

Prisonization The socialization process through which a new inmate learns the accepted norms and values of the prison population.

Prison Segregation The practice of separating inmates based on a certain characteristic, such as age, gender, type of crime committed, or race. The United States Supreme Court has held that prison officials may not segregate inmates based on race or ethnicity except in response to an emergency situation.

Private Prisons Correctional facilities operated by private corporations instead of the government and, therefore, reliant on profits for survival.

Private Security The practice of private corporations or individuals offering services traditionally performed by police officers.

Proactive Arrests Arrests that occur because of concerted efforts by law enforcement agencies to respond to a particular type of criminal or criminal behavior.

Probable Cause Reasonable grounds to believe the existence of facts warranting certain actions, such as the search or arrest of a person.

Probation A criminal sanction in which a convict is allowed to remain in the community rather than be imprisoned as long as she or he follows certain conditions set by the court.

Probationary Period A period of time at the beginning of a police officer's career during which she or he may be fired without cause.

Problem-Oriented Policing A policing philosophy that requires police to identify potential criminal activity and develop strategies to prevent or respond to that activity.

Procedural Criminal Law Rules that define the manner in which the rights and duties of individuals may be enforced.

Procedural Due Process A provision in the Constitution that states that the law must be carried out in a fair and orderly manner.

Professional Model A style of policing advocated by August Vollmer and O. W. Wilson that emphasizes centralized police organizations, increased use of technology, and a limitation of police discretion through regulations and guidelines.

Property Bond An alternative to posting bail in cash, in which the defendant gains pretrial release by providing the court with property valued at the bail amount as assurance that he or she will return for trial.

Prosecutorial Waiver A procedure in which juvenile court judges have the discretion to transfer a juvenile case to adult court, when certain predetermined conditions as to the seriousness of the offense and the age of the offender are met.

Psychoactive Drugs Chemicals that affect the brain, causing changes in emotions, perceptions, and behavior.

Psychology The scientific study of mental processes and behavior.

Public Defenders Court-appointed attorneys who are paid by the state to represent defendants who are unable to hire private counsel.

Public Order Crime Behavior that has been labeled criminal because it is contrary to shared social values, customs, and norms.

Public Prosecutors Individuals, acting as trial lawyers, who initiate and conduct cases in the government's name and on behalf of the people.

R

Racial Profiling The practice of targeting members of minority groups for police stops based solely on their race, ethnicity, or national origin.

Radiation Harmful energy that is transmitted outward from its source through rays, waves, or particles following the detonation of a nuclear device.

Reactive Arrests Arrests that come about as part of the ordinary routine of police patrol and responses to calls for service.

Real Evidence Evidence that is brought into court and seen by the jury, as opposed to evidence that is described for a jury.

"Real Offense" The actual offense committed, as opposed to the charge levied by a prosecutor as the result of a plea bargain. Judges who make sentencing decisions based on the real offense are often seen as undermining the plea bargain process.

Reasonable Force The degree of force that is appropriate to protect the police officer or other citizens and is not excessive.

Rebuttal Evidence given to counteract or disprove evidence presented by the opposing party.

Recklessness The state of being aware that a risk does or will exist and nevertheless acting in a way that consciously disregards this risk.

Recruitment The process by which law enforcement agencies develop a pool of qualified applicants from which to select new members.

Recusal The withdrawal of a judge from legal proceedings when her or his impartiality might reasonably be questioned.

Referral The notification process through which a law enforcement officer or other concerned citizen makes the juvenile court aware of a juvenile's unlawful or unruly conduct.

Rehabilitation The philosophy that society is best served when wrongdoers are provided the resources needed to eliminate criminality from their behavioral pattern rather than simply being punished.

Reintegration A goal of corrections that focuses on preparing the offender for a return to the community unmarred by further criminal behavior.

Relative Deprivation The theory that inmate aggression is caused when freedoms and services that the inmate has come to accept as normal are decreased or eliminated.

Release on Recognizance (ROR) A judge's order that releases an accused from jail with the understanding that he or she will return for further proceedings of his or her own will; used instead of setting a monetary bond.

Relevant Evidence Evidence tending to make a fact in question more or less probable than it would be without the evidence. Only relevant evidence is admissible in court.

Repeat Victimization The theory that certain people and places are more likely to be subject to criminal activity and that past victimization is therefore a valuable crime prevention tool because it is a strong indicator of future victimization.

Residential Treatment Programs Government-run facilities for juveniles whose offenses are not deemed serious enough to warrant incarceration in a training school.

Response Time The rapidity with which calls for service are answered; used as a measurement of police efficiency.

Restitution A sum of money paid in compensation for damages done to the victim by the offender's criminal act.

Restorative Justice An approach to punishment designed to repair the harm done to the victim and the community by the offender's criminal act.

Retribution The philosophy that those who commit criminal acts should be punished based on the severity of the crime and that no other factors need be considered.

Robbery The act of taking property from another person through force, threat of force, or intimidation.

Rule of Four A rule of the United States Supreme Court that the Court will not issue a writ of *certiorari* unless at least four justices approve of the decision to hear the case.

S

Search The process by which police examine a person or property to find evidence that will be used to prove guilt in a criminal trial.

Searches and Seizures The legal term, as found in the Fourth Amendment of the U.S. Constitution, that generally refers to the searching for and the confiscating of evidence by law enforcement agents.

Searches Incidental to Arrests Searches for weapons and evidence of persons who have just been arrested. The fruit of such searches is admissible if any items found are within the immediate vicinity or control of the suspect.

Search Warrant A written order, based on probable cause and issued by a judge or magistrate, commanding that police officers or criminal investigators search a specific person, place, or property to obtain evidence.

Security Threat Group (STG) A group of three or more inmates who engage in activity that poses a threat to the safety of other inmates or the prison staff.

Seizure The forcible taking of a person or property in response to a violation of the law.

Self-Defense The legally recognized privilege to protect one's self or property from injury by another. The privilege of self-defense covers only acts that are reasonably necessary to protect one's self or property.

Self-Reported Survey A method of gathering crime data that relies on participants to reveal and detail their own criminal or delinquent behavior.

Sentencing Discrimination A situation in which the length of a sentence appears to be influenced by a defendant's race, gender, economic status, or other factor not directly related to the crime he or she committed.

Sentencing Disparity A situation in which those convicted of similar crimes do not receive similar sentences.

Sentencing Guidelines Legislatively determined guidelines that judges are required to follow when sentencing those convicted of specific crimes. These guidelines limit judicial discretion.

Separate Confinement A nineteenth-century penitentiary system developed in Pennsylvania in which inmates were kept separate from each other at all times, with daily activities taking place in individual cells.

Sex Offender Notification Law Legislation that requires law enforcement authorities to notify people when convicted sex offenders are released into their neighborhood or community.

Sexual Assault Forced or coerced sexual intercourse (or other sexual act) against the will of the victim.

Sheriff The primary law enforcement officer in a county, usually elected to the post by a popular vote.

Shire-Reeve The chief law enforcement officer in an early English shire, or county. The forerunner of the modern sheriff.

Shock Incarceration A short period of incarceration that is designed to deter further criminal activity by "shocking" the offender with the hardships of imprisonment.

Social Conflict Theories A school of criminology that views criminal behavior as the result of class conflict. Certain behavior is labeled illegal not because it is inherently criminal, but because the ruling class has an economic or social interest in restricting such behavior in order to protect the status quo.

Social Disorganization Theory The theory that deviant behavior is more likely in communities where social institutions such as the family, schools, and the criminal justice system fail to exert control over the population.

Socialization The process through which a police officer is taught the values and expected behavior of the police subculture.

Social Process Theories A school of criminology that considers criminal behavior to be the predictable result of a person's interaction with his or her environment. According to these theories, everybody has the potential for wrongdoing. Those who act on this potential are conditioned to do so by family or peer groups, or institutions such as the media.

Social Reality of Crime The theory that criminal laws are designed by those in power (the rich) to help them keep power at the expense of those who do not have power (the poor).

Spam Bulk e-mails, particularly of commercial advertising, sent in large quantities without the consent of the recipient.

Specialty Courts Lower courts that have jurisdiction over one specific area of criminal activity, such as illegal drugs or domestic violence.

Special Weapons and Tactics (SWAT) Team A specialized squad of police officers who have been trained to handle violent and dangerous situations using advanced weaponry and technology.

Split Sentence Probation A sentence that consists of incarceration in a prison or jail, followed by a probationary period in the community.

Stare Decisis (pronounced *ster*-ay dih-*si-ses*). A common law doctrine under which judges are obligated to follow the precedents established under prior decisions.

Status Offender A juvenile who has been found to have engaged in behavior deemed unacceptable for those under a certain, statutorily determined age.

Statute of Limitations A law limiting the amount of time prosecutors have to bring criminal charges against a suspect after the crime has occurred.

Statutory Law The body of law enacted by legislative bodies.

Statutory Rape A strict liability crime in which an adult engages in a sexual act with a minor. The difference in age between the two participants automatically criminalizes the behavior of the older participant, regardless of whether the younger one consented.

Stop A brief detention of a person by law enforcement agents for questioning. The agents must have a reasonable suspicion of the person before making a stop.

Strain Theory The assumption that crime is the result of frustration felt by individuals who cannot reach their financial and personal goals through legitimate means.

Street Gang A group of people, usually three or more, who share a common identity and engage in illegal activities.

Strict Liability Crimes Certain crimes, such as traffic violations, in which the defendant is guilty regardless of her or his state of mind at the time of the act.

Subculture A group exhibiting certain values and behavior patterns that distinguish it from the dominant culture.

Substantial-Capacity Test From the Model Penal Code, a test that states that a person is not responsible for criminal behavior if when committing the act "as a result of mental disease or defect he [or she] lacks substantial capacity either to appreciate the wrongfulness of his [or her] conduct or to conform his [or her] conduct to the requirements of the law."

Substantive Criminal Law Law that defines the rights and duties of individuals with respect to each other.

Substantive Due Process The constitutional requirement that laws used in accusing and convicting persons of crimes must be fair.

Supermax Prison A correctional facility reserved for those inmates who have extensive records of misconduct in maximum-security prisons; characterized by extremely strict control and supervision over the inmates, including extensive use of solitary confinement.

Suspended Sentence A judicially imposed condition in which an offender is sentenced after being convicted of a crime, but is not required to begin serving the sentence immediately. The judge may revoke the suspended sentence and remit the offender to prison or jail if he or she does not comply with certain conditions.

Sworn Officer A law enforcement agent who has been authorized to make arrests and use force, including deadly force, against civilians.

T

Technical Violation An action taken by a probationer that, although not criminal, breaks the terms of probation as designated by the court; can result in the revocation of probation and a return to prison or jail.

Ten Percent Cash Bail An alternative to traditional bail in which defendants may gain pretrial release by posting 10 percent of their bond amount to the court instead of seeking a bail bondsperson.

Terrorism The use or threat of violence to achieve political objectives.

Testimony Verbal evidence given by witnesses under oath.

Testosterone The hormone primarily responsible for the production of sperm and the development of male secondary sex characteristics such as the growth of facial and pubic hair and the change of voice pitch.

Theory A testable method of explaining certain behavior or circumstances, based on observation, experimentation, and reasoning.

The Patriot Act Legislation passed in the wake of the September 11, 2001, terrorist attacks that greatly expanded the ability of government agents to monitor and apprehend suspected terrorists.

Time Served The period of time a person denied bail has spent in jail prior to his or her trial. If the suspect is found guilty and sentenced to a jail or prison term, the judge will often lessen the duration of the sentence based on the amount of time served as a pretrial detainee.

Tithing System In Anglo-Saxon England, a system of law enforcement in which groups of ten families, known as tithings, were collectively responsible for law and order within their groups.

Total Institution An institution, such as a prison, that provides all of the necessities for existence to those who live within its boundaries.

Trace Evidence Evidence such as a fingerprint, blood, or hair found in small amounts at a crime scene.

Training Schools Correctional institutions for juveniles found to be delinquent or status offenders.

Trial Courts Courts in which most cases usually begin and in which questions of fact are examined.

Truth-in-Sentencing Laws Legislative attempts to assure that convicts will serve approximately the terms to which they were initially sentenced.

U

Uniform Crime Report (UCR) An annual report compiled by the FBI to give an indication of criminal activity in the United States. The FBI collects data from local, state, and federal law enforcement agencies in preparing this report.

Unlawful Combatant A person who takes part in armed hostilities but who does not belong to the armed forces of a sovereign nation and, therefore, is not afforded protection under the Geneva Conventions.

Utilitarianism An approach to ethical reasoning in which the "correct" decision is the one that results in the greatest amount of good for the greatest number of people affected by that decision.

V

Venire The group of citizens from which the jury is selected.

Verdict A formal decision made by the jury.

Victim Impact Statement (VIS) A statement to the sentencing body (judge, jury, or parole board) in which the victim is given the opportunity to describe how the crime has affected her or him. The general purpose of the statement is to convince the sentencing party to hand down a harsher punishment than might otherwise be the case.

Victimology A school of criminology that studies why certain people are the victims of crimes and the optimal role for victims in the criminal justice system.

Victim Surveys A method of gathering crime data that directly surveys participants to determine their experiences as victims of crime.

Virus A computer program that can replicate itself over a network such as the Internet and interfere with the normal use of a computer. A virus cannot exist as a separate entity and must attach itself to another program to move through a network.

Visa Official authorization allowing a person to travel to and within the issuing country.

Voir Dire The preliminary questions that the trial attorneys ask prospective jurors to determine whether they are biased or have any connection with the defendant or a witness.

Voluntary Manslaughter A homicide in which the intent to kill was present in the mind of the offender, but malice was lacking. Most commonly used to describe homicides in which the offender was provoked or otherwise acted in the heat of passion.

W

Warden The prison official who is ultimately responsible for the organization and performance of a correctional facility.

Warrantless Arrest An arrest made without first seeking a warrant for the action; permitted under certain circumstances, such as when the arresting officer has witnessed the crime or has probable cause that the suspect has committed a felony.

Weapons of Mass Destruction (WMDs) A term that describes nuclear, radiological, chemical, or biological weapons that have the capacity to cause large numbers of casualties or do significant property damage.

"Wedding Cake" Model A wedding cake–shaped model that explains why different cases receive different treatment in the criminal justice system. The cases at the "top" of the cake receive the most attention, while those cases at the "bottom" are disposed of quickly and virtually ignored by the media.

White-Collar Crime Nonviolent crimes committed by corporations and individuals to gain a personal or business advantage.

Widen the Net The criticism that intermediate sanctions designed to divert offenders from prison actually increase the number of citizens who are under the control and surveillance of the American corrections system.

Work Release Program Temporary release of convicts from prison for purposes of employment. The offenders may spend their days on the job, but must return to the correctional facility at night and during the weekend.

Worm A computer program that can automatically replicate itself over a network such as the Internet and interfere with the normal use of a computer. A worm does not need to be attached to an existing file to move from one network to another.

Writ of *Certiorari* A request from a higher court asking a lower court for the record of a case. In essence, the request signals the higher court's willingness to review the case.

Wrongful Conviction The conviction, either by verdict or by guilty plea, of a person who is factually innocent of the charges.

Y

Youth Gangs Self-formed groups of youths with several identifiable characteristics, including a gang name and other recognizable symbols, a geographic territory, a leadership structure, a meeting pattern, and participation in illegal activities.

Index

Concurrence, 109, 112
Concurrent jurisdiction, 245–246
Concurring opinions, 255
Conditional release. *See* Parole
Confession(s), 328
    attorney-client privilege and, 282–283
    false, 230
    in Japan, 293
    recording, 231–232
    waiver and, 229
Confidential informant (CI), 176–177
Conflict model, 6
Confrontation clause, 124, 126, 325, 336, 491, 501, 502, 555
Congo, Democratic Republic of, death penalty for juveniles disavowed by, 369
Congregate (Auburn) system, 414, 415
Connolly, Patrick, 14–15
Consensus model, 5–6
Consent
    to electronic surveillance, 223–224
    search with, 221, 222
Constable, 135
Constitution
    state, 103
    United States. *See* United States Constitution
Constitutional Convention of 1787, 103
Constitutional law, 103. *See also* United States Constitution
Containers within vehicle, 222–223
Continuances, 257
Continuity of purpose, 424
Continuity theory of crime, 52
Control theory, 48–49, 50, 58
Controlled Substances Act (CSA)(1970), 246
    enforced by DEA, 146
    schedules of narcotics as defined by, 76
Controlling the Assault of Non-Solicited Pornography and Marketing Act (CAN-SPAM)(2003), 571
Convertino, Richard, 277
Convict criminology, 55
Conviction
    evidence sufficient for, 294
    jury unanimity and, 310–311
    wrongful, 230, 333–335
Cook, Karen, 301
Cooksey, Kazi, 73
Cooley, Steve, 384
COPA (Child Online Protection Act)(2003), 588
Cordner, Gary W., 173
Coroner, 142
Corpus delicti (the body of the crime), 107–108, 112, 324
Correctional officer(s), 458–462
    discipline and, 459–461
    duties of, 458–459, 460–461
    job categories among, 459
    rank of, 458–459
    staffing problems and, 461
Corrections, 13–14
    community-based. *See* Community corrections
    medical model of, 414
    prisons and. *See* Prison(s)
    probation and. *See* Probation
Corrections Corporation of America (CCA), 426, 428–429, 430
Cosmides, Leda, 41
Costa Rica, Internet gambling establishment in, 575, 577
Costanzo, Mark, 365
Couey, John Evander, 17, 229–230, 311–312, 477
Count bargaining, 296–297
Counterintelligence, 537
Counterterrorism
    challenges and strategies in, 540–545
    data mining and, 583–586
    efforts in
    international, 539
    state and local, 537–539
    emergency preparedness and response and, 544–545
    foiled plots and, 540–541

intelligence model for, 542–543
    "MI5 solution" to, 542–543
    military model for, 543–544
    preventive policing and, 540–542
County attorney. *See* Prosecutor(s)
County coroner, 142
Court(s)
    of appeals. *See* Appellate court(s)
    appellate. *See* Appellate court(s)
    assembly-line justice and, 266–267
    bailiff of, 264
    basic principles of American judicial system and, 244–252
    as bureaucracy, 244
    clerk of, 264
    crime control in, 243–244
    criminal. *See* Criminal court(s)
    docket of, 257
    domestic, 251
    drug. *See* Drug courts
    dual system of. *See* Dual court system
    due process in. *See* Due process
    elder, 251
    excessive caseloads of, impact of, 266–267
    function(s) of, 243–244
    gun, 251
    judges in. *See* Judge(s)
    jurisdiction of. *See* Jurisdiction
    justice, 135, 250–251
    juvenile. *See* Juvenile court(s)
    legitimacy of, 243
    magistrate, 250–251, 285
    national. *See* United States Supreme Court
    quest for justice and, 242–271
    rehabilitation and, 244
    reviewing. *See* Appellate court(s)
    specialty, 251
    supreme
    state, 13, 102, 245, 251–252
    United States. *See* United States Supreme Court
    trial. *See* Trial court(s)
    work group of. *See* Courtroom work group
Court, Shelly, 57
Court reporters, 264, 265
Courtroom work group, 264–267
    adversary system and, 283–284
    defined, 264
    formation of, 264–265
    and incentives to cooperate, 266
    judge in, 265–266
    members of, 264
    overloaded courts and, 267
    sentencing and, 352
Courtyard style of prison, 421
CPPA (Child Pornography Prevention Act)(1996), 588
Crack cocaine, 6, 194, 508
Crane, Stephen, 185
Crank, 88. *See also* Methamphetamine
Crazy Crew, 514
"Creative sentencing," 351–352
Credit-card crime, 569, 577
Crenshaw, Fran, 36
Crime(s)
    age and, 88–89, 512
    biochemical conditions and, 39–41
    body of (*corpus delicti*), 107–108, 112, 324
    cause(s) of, 36–67. *See also* Crime(s), theory(ies) of
    exploring, 37–55
    summarized, 54
    theory(ies) of. *See* Theory(ies) of crime
    class and, 89
    classification of, 71–76
    computer. *See* Computer crime; Cyber crime(s)
    controlling, 11
    credit-card, 569, 577
    cyber. *See* Cyber crime(s)
    dark figure of, 82, 84
    defined, 5–10
    deliberate, 72
    deviance versus, 7
    elements of, 107–115
    ethnicity and, 91

evidence of. *See* Evidence
    free will and, 37–39
    gangs and, 23, 86–87, 515. *See also* Gang(s)
    genetics and, 41–43
    guns and, 23, 85–86, 515–516
    hate, 113–114, 361, 581
    high-tech, 10
    illegal drugs and, 87–88
    inmates serving more time for each, 417–418
    mala in se, 74–76
    mala prohibita, 74–76
    measuring, 77–92
    ongoing or to occur in the future, 283
    organized, 9–10
    premeditated, 72
    prevention of, 11, 153–154, 172–173
    strategies in, 180–183
    property, 8, 112–113, 345, 478–479
    psychology and, 43–44
    public order, 8
    punishment and, 24–25. *See also* Punishment
    race and, 89–91
    rates of, increased incarceration's effect on, 416, 417
    reduction in, with more police officers, 180
    same, trials in both state and federal courts for, 332
    seduction of, 39, 41
    seriousness of, sentencing and, 353
    social reality of, 50–51
    strict liability, 100, 111–112, 533
    subculture wars and, 89–91
    super, terrorism as, 526. *See also* Terrorism
    theory(ies) of. *See* Theory(ies) of crime
    trends in, today, 85–92
    types of, 7–10
    victimless, 8
    victims of. *See* Victim(s); Victimology
    video games and, 63
    violent. *See* Violent crime(s)
    white-collar. *See* White-collar crime(s)
    women and, 91–92
Crime control model, 549
    courts and, 243–244
    defined, 19
    due process model versus, 20
    in present day, 20–22
"Crime gene," 41–42
Crime in the United States (DOJ), 77
Crime statistics
    dangerous jobs and, 190
    felons receiving split sentences and, 389
    jail inmates and, 433
    National Crime Victimization Survey (NCVS) and, 82, 85
    prisons and, 416, 417
    probation and, 387
    rearrest of ex-prisoners and, 473
    recidivism and, 473, 478–479
    trends today and, 85–92
Crime Victims' Rights Act, 298
Crime-mapping technology, 183, 184
The Criminal and His Victim (von Hentig), 56
Criminal court(s)
    bailiff of, 264
    clerk of, 264
    defined, 13
    docket of, 257
    excessive caseloads of, impact of, 266–267
    judge in. *See* Criminal court judge(s)
    overloaded, 267
    specialty, 251
    transfer from juvenile court to, 499–501, 516, 517
    work group of. *See* Courtroom work group
Criminal court judge(s)
    bail setting and, 286–287
    individualized justice and, 350–354
    intermediate sanctions administered by, 396–398
    judicial reprieves and, 387
    philosophy of, 354
    responsibilities of, 256–257
    role(s) of, 256–257. *See also* Criminal trial(s)

Evans, David, 242
Evidence
    authentication of, 323–324
    circumstantial, 321–322
    computer-generated, 322
    defined, 320
    direct, 321–322
    discovery process and, 291
    excluded. See Exclusionary rule
    fingerprint, 280–281
    nontestimonial, 234
    prejudicial, 322–323
    probable cause based upon, 208
    real, 320
    relevant, 322
    role of, during trial, 320–324
    rules of, 321, 322, 501
    sufficient for conviction, 294
    testimonial, 321
    trace, 177
    victim impact, 362–363
Ex post facto law, 124, 476–477
Examination of witness. See Witness(es),
        examination of
Exclusionary rule, 208–210, 216, 294
    defined, 208
    establishing, 209–210
    exceptions to, 210, 222, 230
    extending, 210
    grand jury investigations and, 292
Exigent circumstances, 216, 217
Expert witness, 321
Extradition, 246, 247, 539
Eye scanning, 27

F

Face-recognition systems, 27
Fact
    mistake of, 118–119
    questions of, 248
Factual guilt, 277
Fairfax County (Virginia) Police Department,
        190
Fallibility, criminal justice system and, 370–371
False confessions, 230
"False flagging," 172
False positives, 290
Family, victimization and, 57–58
The Family, 530
Family group homes, 506
Fatwas, 535
Fay, Michael, 344
Fay, Thomas, 261
FBI. See Federal Bureau of Investigation
FBI Academy, 14, 148
FBI Laboratory, 146
FBN (Federal Bureau of Narcotics), 146
FDA (Food and Drug Administration), 103, 105
Federal Air Marshals program, 144
Federal Bureau of Investigation (FBI), 13, 134,
        529
    abortion clinic bombings and, 147
    background searches conducted by, for
            private security firms, 151
    CIA and, information sharing and, 25, 537
    civil rights violations investigated by, 431
    CODIS (Combined DNA Index System)
            operated by, 179
    cooperation of, with Miami to stop flow of
            narcotics and weapons into U.S., 170
    creation and functions of, 146
    crime data gathered by, 70
    Criminal Justice Information Services
            Division of, 155
    Cyber Action Teams (CATs) developed by,
            578
    death penalty convictions based upon
            fingerprints to be reviewed by, 281
    defined, 146
    drug law enforcement and, 146
    FBI Academy and, 14, 148
    FBI Laboratory of, 146
    Field Intelligence Groups of, 538
    fighting cyber crime and, 576, 578
    fighting terrorism and, 85, 146, 149, 193,
            293, 536–537

fingerprint match error rate and, 280–281
    FISA and, 225
    Identification Division of, 146
    Innocent Images National Initiative (IINI)
            and, 578
    Internet Crime Complaint Center (IC3)
            and, 565
    lack of communication with local police
            and, 538–539
    manhunt and, 140
    National Crime Information Center (NCIC)
            of, 146
    National Infrastructure Protection Center
            and, 576
    National Joint Terrorism Task Forces
            (JTTFs) and, 14–15, 537, 543
    national security letters issued by, 225, 584,
            588–589
    Patriot Act and, 21, 225, 586–587
    power of, legislation restricting, 224
    pre-September 11, 2001 antiterrorism
            performance by, 540, 543, 546, 583
    recording interrogations and, 231–232
    reforming, 543
    "squeeze" on local law enforcement and,
            538
    Strategic Information Operations Center of,
            536–537
    terrorism defined by, 525
    Uniform Crime Report published by. See
            Uniform Crime Report
Federal Bureau of Narcotics (FBN), 146
Federal Bureau of Prisons (BOP), 392, 400
    budget of, 418
    gang study conducted by, 452
    jail design upgraded by, 435–436
    private company paid to operate one of its
            prisons, 426
    supermax prisons operated by, 422
Federal Correctional Institute in Tallahassee,
        Florida, 457
Federal court system, 252–255
    appellate courts of, 252, 253. See also
            United States Supreme Court
    judges of
    appointment(s) of, 257, 258–259, 260
        lifetime, 252
        past discrimination in, 260–261
    diversity among, 260–261
    impeachment and, 262–263
    minorities as, 260
    removal of, 262–263
    jurisdiction and, 245–246. See also
            Jurisdiction
    as part of dual court system, illustrated,
            249
    sentencing in, disparities between state
            court sentencing and, 355. See also
            Sentencing
    trial courts of, 252
    United States courts of appeals of, 252, 253
    United States district courts of, 252
    United States Supreme Court of. See United
            States Supreme Court
    work group of. See Courtroom work group
Federal Emergency Management Agency
        (FEMA), 534, 536
Federal Food, Drug and Cosmetic Act, 105
Federal government
    courts of. See Federal court system
    intelligence agencies of, 537
    law enforcement agencies of, 13, 143–148
    Terrorist Screening Center (TSC) of, 538
    traditional parole abolished by, 349, 359,
            469
    victim-related laws and, 60, 298
Federal Rules of Evidence, 322
Federal statutes, as source of American
        criminal law, 103
Federalism, 11–12, 103, 245
Federalist Paper No. 78, 252–253
Federalists, 249
Feeley, Malcolm, 284
Feinberg, Ludwig, 247–248
Feingold, Russell, 550
Feld, Barry C., 501

Felony(ies)
    defined, 17
    degrees of, 72–73
Felson, Marcus, 56
Felson, Richard B., 58–59
FEMA (Federal Emergency Management
        Agency), 534, 536
Field services, 171
Field training, 167
Field training officer (FTO), 167
Fields, Ejuanda, 497
Fifth Amendment, 124, 125, 214, 226, 227, 231,
        234, 284, 292, 311, 331, 394, 479, 491,
        496, 551
    due process clause of, 124, 296. See also
            Due process
Fight Club gang, 297
Figlio, Robert, 61
Filibuster, 258
Finality
    defined, 333
    rethinking, 334–335
    wrongful convictions and, 333–335
Fines
    as form of punishment, 351
    as judicially administered intermediate
            sanction, 396, 397, 398
    Swedish day-fines and, 398
Fingerprinting
    booking procedure and, 234
    DNA. See DNA profiling
    "electronic," 576
    myth regarding, 280–281
    as physical evidence, 179, 199
Finkelhor, David, 70
Finnerty, Colin, 242, 243
Firearms. See Gun(s)
First Amendment, 114, 254, 462, 535, 580, 581,
        582, 588. See also Freedom of speech
    in prison, 463
First responders, 545
FISA (Foreign Intelligence Surveillance Act),
        224–225, 552
FISC (Foreign Intelligence Surveillance Court),
        552
Fixed sentencing. See Determinate sentencing
Flammable Fabrics Act, 106
Fleeing felon rules, 192
Fletcher, George, 526
Foglia, Michael, 327
Folsom Prison, 420
Food and Drug Administration (FDA), 103, 105
Foote, Caleb, 287
Force
    deadly, 191, 192
    "misuse" of, 190–191, 193
    nondeadly, 191
    nonlethal weapons and, 192–193
    reasonable, 191
    use of
    justifiable (self-defense), 120–121
    by police officers, 190–193
    by prison officials, 460–461
Foreign Intelligence Surveillance Act (FISA),
        224–225, 552
Foreign Intelligence Surveillance Court (FISC),
        552
Foreign terrorist organization (FTO), 533
Forensics
    computer, 576
    defined, 177
    investigations using, 177–179
Forfeiture, 397
Fort Dix, planned terrorist attack at, 541
Fortas, Abe, 489, 492–493
Foster care programs, 506
Foucault, Michael, 458
Fourteenth Amendment, 124–125, 210, 367
Fourth Amendment, 124, 206–210, 217–226,
        235, 496, 550, 551
Fox, James Alan, 36, 61, 85
France
    criminal offense to deny Holocaust in, 5
    French Revolution and, 525
    investigating judge (*le juge d'instruction*)
            in, 257

response to September 11, 2001
    attacks and, 533–539. *See also*
    Counterterrorism
Homeland Security Act (2002), 144, 534
Homeland Security Preparedness Survey, 545
Honduras, broken windows theory used in,
    184–185
Honesty, police ethics and, 198
Honeywell, Inc., 401
"Honor killings," 74
Hoover, Herbert, 137, 146
Horan, Robert F., Jr., 328
Horizontal overcharging, 299
Hormones, 40
Hornbeck, Shawn, 70
Horowitz, Daniel, 308
Hostetler, David, 352
Hughes, Brian, 347
Human-source collection, 537
Hung jury, 311, 326, 330, 331
Hurricane Katrina, 13, 86, 125, 134, 149, 153,
    536, 544
Hymon, Elton, 191–192

I

IAU (internal affairs unit), 196
Ibrahim, Kareem, 524
IC3 (Internet Crime Complaint Center), 565, 566
ICE. *See* United States Immigration and
    Customs Enforcement
"Identifiable human needs," 464
Identification
    data mining and, 584–586
    lineups and, 233, 278
    photo arrays and, 233
    process of, 232–234
    showups and, 233
Identity theft
    cost of, to victims in 2006, 28
    defined, 27–28, 567
    preventing, 567
    synthetic, 567
IEDs (improvised explosive devices), 531–532
Ifill, Sherrilyn A., 260–261
IINI (Innocent Images National Initiative), 578
Ijoma, Collins E., 314–315
Illegal drug(s). *See also* Illicit drugs;
    Psychoactive drug(s)
    crime and, 87–88
    DEA and, 146–147
    legalizing, 93
    Miami as gateway for, from Central and
        South America, 169–170
    problems with, 23–24
    trafficking in, 23, 344, 515
    use of, in the United States, 24, 146–147
    war against
        race and, 193–194
        women and, 92
Illegal immigrants
    deportation of, 145, 158, 546–547
    DNA samples from, 26
    laws regarding, 546–547
    number of, in United States, 546
    policing, 158
Illicit drugs. *See also* Illegal drug(s)
    defined, 74
    licit drugs and, distinguishing between,
        75–76
Illinois Juvenile Court, 489–490
I-Max maximum-security prison for women in
    Topeka, Kansas, 421–422
Immigrants, illegal. *See* Illegal immigrants
Immigration and Naturalization Service (INS),
    158
    terminated by Homeland Security Act, 144
Immigration law, 546–547
Immunity, granted to witness, 311
Impeachment, 262–263
Imprisonment, 351. *See also* Incarceration
Improvised explosive devices (IEDs), 531–532
In loco parentis doctrine, 495, 496

Incapacitation
    capital punishment and, 370
    collective, 346
    defined, 345
    selective, 346
    sentencing and, 345–346, 347
Incarceration. *See also* Jail(s); Prison(s)
    home, 401
    increased probability of, 417
    intermittent, 388–389
    rates of
        high, consequences of, 437
        rising, of women, 24, 91, 92, 418, 432
    shock. *See* Shock incarceration
    in United States. *See* United States,
        incarceration in
Inchoate offenses, 115
Incident-driven policing, 180
Income of victim, death sentences and, 374
Independence, selecting judges and, 258
Indeterminate sentencing, 348, 350, 415, 467
Indianapolis (Indiana) police department,
    Project on Policing Neighborhoods and,
    173
Indictment, 291–292
Indonesia, Bali, terrorist bombings in, 525
Industrial shop officers, 459
"Inevitable discovery" exception to exclusionary
    rule, 210, 222, 230
Infancy, as defense under criminal law,
    115–116, 492–493. *See also* Children;
    Juvenile(s)
Informant
    confidential (CI), 176–177
    known, 213
    reasonable suspicion and, 213
Information
    issued by prosecutor, 291
    probable cause based upon, 208
Informed discretion, 352
Infrastructure, 536, 573–574
Inherent coercion, 227
Initial appearance, 284–286
Inmate. *See* Prisoner(s)
Innocence
    after being proved guilty, 334–335
    of defendant, presumption of, 311–312,
        322, 432, 476
Innocence Project, 334
Innocent Images National Initiative (IINI), 578
INS. *See* Immigration and Naturalization
    Service
Insanity
    capital punishment and, 368
    as defense under criminal law, 116–117,
        118–119, 327
Institute for Social Research, 48, 513
Institute of Living, 42
Intake, 498
Intellectual property
    defined, 571
    online pirating of, 571–572
Intelligence agency, 537
Intelligence model, 542–543
Intensive supervision probation (ISP), 396,
    399–400
Intent. *See* Mens rea
Intermediate sanction(s), 396–404
    day reporting centers (DRCs) and, 396,
        398–399
    defined, 396
    forfeiture and, 397
    intensive supervision probation (ISP) and,
        396, 399–400
    judicially administered, 396–398
    pretrial diversion programs and, 397
    shock incarceration and. *See* Shock
        incarceration
    in Sweden, 398
    widening the net and, 403
Intermittent incarceration, 388–389
Internal affairs unit (IAU), 196
Internal investigations, 196
Internal Revenue Service (IRS), 148
International Association of Chiefs of Police,
    196, 545

International Center for Terrorism Studies, 573
International Criminal Court, 268
International Federation of the Phonographic
    Industry, 572
Internet
    anonymity of, 570–571
    baiting on, 564
    computer crime and, 564–565
    credit-card crime on, 569
    criminal activities on, 566
    criminal activity and, 27–28
    cyber crime and. *See* Cyber crime(s)
    fraud via, 564, 565–566
    freedom of speech on, 580–587
    gambling via, 575, 576, 577
    obscenity on, 582–583
    pornography on, 574–575, 578, 583, 588
    weapon recipes on, 581–582
Internet Crime Complaint Center (IC3), 565, 566
Interrogation(s)
    of children, 498
    coercion and, 226, 227, 557
    custodial, 227, 231, 278
    defined, 226
    Miranda rights and, 226–232
    recording, 231–232
    of terrorists, 557
Intoxication
    as defense under criminal law, 117–118
    defined, 117
    involuntary, 117
    voluntary, 117, 118
Investigation(s)
    forensic, 177–179
    police. *See* Police investigation(s)
    presentence, 352, 359, 390
Involuntary intoxication, 117
Involuntary manslaughter, 73, 195
IRA (Irish Republican Army), 526
Iran, death penalty for juveniles disavowed
    by, 369
Iraq
    IEDs (improvised explosive devices) used
        in, 532
    suicide car bombing in, 547
Irish Republican Army (IRA), 526
Irresistible-impulse test, 116
IRS (Internal Revenue Service), 148
Irwin, John, 431, 449
Islamic Assembly of North America, 535
Isnora, Gescard, 164
ISP (intensive supervision probation), 396,
    399–400
Israel
    American support for, 527
    ancient, Mosaic Code of, 101
Italian Americans, confinement of, in
    "relocation" camps during World
    War II, 127

J

Jackson, Amy, 376
Jackson, Bobby, 376
Jackson, Michael, 282
Jackson, Robert, 289, 376
Jacob, Herbert, 283
Jail(s), 430–436. *See also* Prison(s)
    administration of, 434–435
    defined, 13, 430
    design of, 435–436
    direct supervision approach and, 436
    function of, 431
    legitimate security interests of, 460–461
    new-generation, 435–436
    population in, 431, 432–434
        characteristics of, 433
    overcrowding and, 287, 405, 433, 434–435,
        488
    pretrial detainees and, 432, 434
    sentenced inmates in, 432–434
    staffing problems and, 461
    women in, offenses of, 455
Jamaat al Muslimeen (JAM), 524
Japan
    nuclear bombs used against in World
        War II, 531

Newgate Prison, 414
New-generation jails, 435–436
Nguyen Tuong Van, 344
NIBRS (National Incident-Based Reporting
     System), 80–81, 496
Nichols, Terry, 422, 529
Nicotine, 74, 75
Nielsen, Christian, 7
Nifong, Michael, 242, 276, 349
Nigeria, death penalty for juveniles disavowed
     by, 369
9/11 Commission, 540, 543, 546
Nixon, Richard, 146
Nixon, Walter, 263
No Electronic Theft Act, 572
Noecker, James, 262
Nolle prosequi, 294
Nolo contendere plea, 296
Nondeadly force, 191
Nonlethal weapons, 192–193
Nonpartisan elections, 259, 260
Nonsecure confinement, 505–506
Nonstate actors, 525
Nontestimonial evidence, 234
NOPD. *See* New Orleans Police Department
Norepinephrine, 41
NORTHCOM (United States Northern
     Command), 544
Northern Correctional Institution, 422
Northern Ireland, 526
NSA. *See* National Security Agency
NSDUH (National Survey on Drug Use and
     Health), 23–24, 512
Nuclear weapons, 531. *See also* Weapons of
     mass destruction
Nur, Abdel, 524
Nuremberg Trials, 268
NYPD. *See* New York Police Department

O

Obscenity, 582–583
Observation, personal, probable cause based
     upon, 208, 235
OC (Oleoresin capsicum) pepper spray, 192
Occupational Safety and Health Administration
     (OSHA), 105
O'Connor, Sandra Day, 260, 360–361
Odgren, John, 494
O'Donnell, Eugene, 171
Offender(s)
     chronic, 61, 62
     sex. *See* Sex offender(s)
     status, 490, 491, 495
Offenses
     inchoate, 115
     status, 491, 495
Office of Health Affairs of DHS, 535
Office of Juvenile Justice and Delinquency
     Prevention, 512
Office of the Inspector General, 535, 538
Officer of the law, prosecutor as, 275
Ohio State Highway Patrol, 221
Oken, Steve, 333
Oklahoma City bombing, 422, 529, 533
Oklahoma State Reformatory, 461
Oldner, Chris, 116
Oleoresin capsicum (OC) pepper spray, 192
Oleson, James C., 446, 454
Oliver, Michael, 164, 171
Oliver, Walter J., 213
Olson, Sara Jane, 468
Omission, act of, 109
Omnibus Crime Control and Safe Streets Act
     (1968), 139–140
Online auction fraud, 566
Online retail fraud, 566
Opening statements, 320
Open-source collection, 537
Opiates, 146
Opinion(s)
     concurring, 255
     defined, 248
     dissenting, 255
Opportunity theory, 55
The Oprah Winfrey Show, 70
Oral arguments, 255

Orange County (Florida) Sheriff's Department,
     141, 211
Organized crime, 9–10
Original jurisdiction, 248, 254
Orlando Police Department, 141
OSHA (Occupational Safety and Health
     Administration), 105
Ostrom, Brian J., 282
Overcharging, 299
Owens, Bill, 489

P

Packer, Herbert, 15–16, 18–19, 343
Padilla, José, 315–316, 554–555
Pain, pleasure and, 38
"Paintball" terrorists, 541
Pakistan, 104
     death penalty for juveniles disavowed by, 369
Palmer, Doug H., 538
Pardon, 465–466
Parens patriae, 489
Parental responsibility statutes, 516
Parents of Murdered Children, 59
Parish constable system, 135
Park, Robert Ezra, 45
Parker, Karen F., 53
Parole, 348, 415, 464–465
     concepts based on, 465
     conditions of, 469–470
     defined, 14, 349, 464
     eligibility for, 467
     halfway houses and, 470, 473
     life-without-, 374–375, 467
     limited rights of parolees and, 471–472
     maximum expiration date and, 471
     parole board and. *See* Parole board
     parole contract and, 470
     parole grant hearing and, 468
     parole guidelines and, 469
     parole officer and, 349, 470–471, 476
     probation versus, 466
     revocation of, 471
     of sex offenders. *See* Sex offender(s)
     supervision and, 349, 469–472, 476
     terminating, 471
     traditional, abolished by federal
          government, 349, 359, 469
     work release programs and, 470
Parole board, 348, 349, 350, 465, 467–468
     defined, 467
     parole hearing and, 468
     roles of, 467–468
Parole contract, 470
Parole grant hearing, 468
Parole guidelines, 469
Parole officers, 349, 470–471, 476
Parole revocation, 471
Part I offenses, 77–78
     composition of, 79
     defined, 77
     listed, 78
     rates of, 78
Part II offenses, 78–79
     defined, 78
     listed, 80
Partisan elections, 259, 260
Patriot Act (2001), 27, 533–534, 542, 550, 579,
     584, 586–587
     defined, 535
     FISA amended by, 225, 552
     goals of, 534
     key provisions of, 21, 535
     renewal of, 534
     searches and, 550–551
     "sneak and peak" provision of, 225
     surveillance and, 551
Patrol(s), 171–174
     activities of, 172–173
     directed, 181, 183
     general, 181, 182
     preventive, 172–173
     purpose of, 172
     random, 181, 183
     strategies in, 181–183
Patronage system ("spoils system"), 137,
     258–259

Paultre, Nicole, 164
Payoffs, 195
PCA (Posse Comitatus Act)(1878), 148–149, 544
Peace
     justice of (JP), 135, 250–251
     preservation of, 154
Pearl, Daniel, 526
Peel, Sir Robert "Bobbie," 116, 136, 140, 172
Peers, jury of, 312–313
Pelican Bay State Prison, 422, 423
Penitentiary
     defined, 413
     first, 413
     Pennsylvania system versus New York
          system and, 413–414
Penitentiary of New Mexico at Santa Fe, riot
     at, 450–451
Penn, William, 413
Pentagon, terrorist attack on, 26, 530. *See also*
     September 11, 2001 attacks; Terrorism
Percival, Robert V., 17
Peremptory challenges, 316, 317, 318, 319
PERF (Police Executive Research Forum),
     85–86, 187
Perillo, Lois, 174–175
Perry Mason, 504
Personal observation, probable cause based
     upon, 208
Personality disorders, 43–44
Peru, terrorism in, 526
Petersilia, Joan, 394, 402, 472
Peterson, Scott, 311
Petition, 498
Petty misdemeanors, 73–74
Peven, Roger, 274, 283
Pew Internet and American Life Project, 574
Philadelphia police department, 137
     CompStat and, 184
Phillips, William, 36, 37
Phishing, 567–568
Phoenix (Arizona) Police Department, 191
Phoenix Study, 191
Photo arrays, 233
Photoshop, 322
Physical agility tests, 165, 166, 169
Physician-assisted suicide, 6
Pinizzotto, Anthony J., 155
Pistole, John, 541
Pitchless Detention Center, 452
Plain view doctrine, 222, 223, 224
Plaintiff, 71
Plato, 100–101
Plea bargaining, 274–275, 327
     absence of, in Japan, 293
     adversary system and, 298–300, 301
     Boykin form and, 300
     in criminal justice system, 296–297, 301
     death penalty avoided by, 274, 298
     defined, 296
     inducing, 298–299
     in juvenile justice system, 503
     motivations for, 297–298
     Supreme Court decisions on, 299–300
Pleading guilty, 296–300. *See also* Plea
     bargaining
     sentencing outcomes for, 298
Pleasure, pain and, 38
Podular design, 435–436
Poker Player's Alliance, 576
Poland, credit-card thieves operating out of,
     577
Police
     accountability and, 195–196
     American, history of, 135–140
     the community and, 139–140
     early American experience and, 136–137
     English roots and, 135–136
     first department and, 136–137
     police modernization and, 137–139
     three eras of American policing and, 138
     turmoil of the 1960s and, 139
     corruption and. *See* Police corruption
     ethics and. *See* Police ethics
     interrogation by. *See* Interrogation(s)
     juvenile delinquents and, 494–497
     officers of. *See* Law enforcement officer(s)

cooperation of, with Miami to stop flow of narcotics and weapons into U.S., 170
functions of, 144–145
United States Department of Homeland Security (DHS), 534–536
agencies of
law enforcement, 144–145, 535
non law enforcement, 534, 535, 536
creation of, 13, 144
Federal Emergency Management Agency (FEMA) of, 534, 536
organizational structure of, illustrated, 536
Project Chloe antimissile system sponsored by, 548
terrorism-combating agencies outside of, 536–537
United States Visitor and Immigrant Status Indicator Technology (US-VISIT) program created by, 547, 585
United States Department of Justice (DOJ), 277
Bureau of Justice Statistics of, 82, 356. See also Crime statistics
computer crime defined by, 564
delayed-notification warrants used by, 225
Federal Bureau of Investigation an agency of. See Federal Bureau of Investigation
Federal Bureau of Prisons of. See Federal Bureau of Prisons
law enforcement agencies of, 145–148
limitation of due process rights of suspected terrorists sought by, 127
sniper case jurisdiction and, 245–246
study by, 193
Uniform Crime Report published by. See Uniform Crime Report
United States Department of State
pre-September 11, 2001 antiterrorism performance by, 543
visas issued by, 546
United States Department of Transportation, 144
United States Department of the Treasury, 148
United States district courts, 252
United States Immigration and Customs Enforcement (ICE), 144, 158
drug law enforcement and, 146
functions of, 145
powers of, 546–547
United States Marshals Service, 146
history and functions of, 147–148
manhunt and, 140, 141
United States Northern Command (NORTHCOM), 544
United States Parole Commission, 349, 392
United States Penitentiary Administrative Maximum (ADX) in Florence, Colorado, 422
United States Postal Inspection Service, 122, 144, 219
United States Postal Service, 530, 532
United States probation officers, 359, 392–393
United States Secret Service, 13, 144, 535, 573, 578
creation and primary functions of, 145
role of, in fighting cyber crime, 579
Secret Service Uniformed Division of, 145
United States Supreme Court, 13, 252–255
cases which reach, 254–255
decision(s) of, 102, 255
eroding Miranda rights, 232
regarding capital punishment, 365–369, 374–375, 467, 517
regarding due process, 126
regarding hate speech, 581
regarding indefinite detention, 553–554
regarding juvenile justice system, 491
regarding plea bargaining, 299–300
regarding police use of force, 191–192
regarding sentencing, 361–362
regarding terrorism, 553–554, 556
regarding the exclusionary rule, 210
Earl Warren's tenure and, 21, 126, 366
interpretation and application of the law by, 253–254

judicial review and, 254
jurisdiction of, 245, 254
as the only national court, 249
oral arguments before, 255
rule of four of, 254
stare decisis and, 102
writ of certiorari and, 254–255
United States Visitor and Immigrant Status Indicator Technology (US-VISIT) program, 547, 585
Unlawful combatants, 553
Unlawful Internet Gambling Enforcement Act (2006), 575, 576
USCIS (United States Citizenship and Immigration Services), 536
Useem, Bert, 425, 450–451
US-VISIT (United States Visitor and Immigrant Status Indicator Technology) program, 547, 585
Utilitarianism, 38, 344, 376
Uviller, H. Richard, 227

V

Van den Haag, Ernest, 369
Van Houton, Leslie, 468
Van Kessel, Gordon, 283
Vandalism, 512
Vatis, Michael, 576
Vehicle(s). See also Automobile
containers within, 222–223
high-speed pursuits and, 156–157
Venire, 314, 317, 318
Venue, change of, 311–312
Vera Institute, 288
Verdict
defined, 330
directed, 325
jury, 310–311, 330–331
unanimous, 311
Vertical overcharging, 299
Vick, Michael, 300
Victim(s), 55–60, 298
civil lawsuit brought by, 332
experience of being, 56
factors of victimization and, 57–59
income of, death sentences and, 374
plea bargaining and, 298. See also Plea bargaining
race of, death sentences and, 373–374
rights of. See Victims' rights
risks of victimization and, 56–59
of sexual assault, "chastity requirement" and, 336
surveys of, 82–83
uncooperative, 295
unreliability of, 295
victim impact statements (VIS) by, 346, 362–363
Victim impact evidence, 362–363
Victim impact statements (VIS), 346, 362–363
Victim surveys, 82–83
Victimization
factors of, 57–59
repeat, 56–57
risks of, 56–59
Victimless crimes, 8
Victimology, 55–60
defined, 56
factors of victimization and, 56–59, 57–59
Victims of Crime and Leniency, 59
Victims' rights
in Germany, 61
movement supporting, 59
protecting, 59–60, 298
Victims' Rights Amendment, 60
Victory, adversary system and, 283–284
Video games, crime and, 63
Vietnam era, police overreaction to antiwar demonstrations and, 139
Violations, 74
Violence
domestic. See Domestic violence
prison, 450–455
in prison culture, 450
in schools. See School violence
in women's prisons, 456–457

Violent crime(s)
categories of, 7
defined, 7
degree and, 7
overreporting of, 79–80
rates of, 1990-2006, 85
rebound in, 85–88
statistics regarding, 22–24, 85–88
trends in, 508–509
underreporting of, 345
Virginia Tech (Virginia Polytechnic Institute) shootings, 4–5, 36, 568
Virtual child pornography, 588
Virus, 569–570
VIS (victim impact statements), 346, 362–363
Visas, 546, 547
Voir dire, 314–316, 319, 375
Vollmer, August, 137–138, 166
Voluntary intoxication, 117, 118
Voluntary manslaughter, 73, 243
von Hentig, Hans, 56
Voting right lost by convicted felon, 53, 437

W

Wachtler, Sol, 438
Wackenhut. See GEO Group, Inc.
Waiver, 227, 229
judicial, 499
of jury trial, 310
legislative, 499
of preliminary hearing, 291, 393
prosecutorial, 500
of Sixth Amendment right to counsel, 280
Walden House, 474
Walker, Jeffrey, 480
Walker, Samuel, 137, 172, 195
Wallace, George, 145
Wallerstein, James S., 84
Walnut Street Prison, 413, 435
Walsh, Anthony, 41, 53
Walsh, Eric, 84
Walters, John, 396
War on terrorism
constitutional rights of Americans during, 550
crime control model approach to, 549
electronic surveillance and, 223–225, 550–552
FBI and, 85, 146, 149, 193, 293
Warden
defined, 425
of women's prison, 428–429
Warrant(s)
arrest. See Arrest warrant
delayed-notification, 225
electronic surveillance and, 223–224
search. See Search warrant(s)
searches and seizures without, 220–221
Warrantless arrest, 124, 214, 216–217
Warren, Earl, 21, 126, 366
Washington, D.C. police department
decrease in force size and, 180
woman as head of, 168
Washington, George, 103, 147
Washington State Highway patrol, 143
Wasserman, Cathy, 504–505
Watkinson, Ralph, 234
Watt, William W., 24
Waxman, Seth, 254
Weapon(s)
biological, 530
chemical, 531
of mass destruction. See Weapons of mass destruction
nonlethal, 192–193
nuclear, 531
Weapons of mass destruction (WMDs)
defined, 530
emergency preparedness and response and, 545
incidence of, 532
types of, 530–531
Web. See Internet
Webb, Emanuel Lovell, 26, 179
"Wedding cake" model, 16–18
Weller, George, 384

CRIMINAL JUSTICE IN ACTION

Students! Tell us about your "unsung heroes" and you could win a

$500 Student Scholarship

Gaines Scholarship Competition

Do you know an "Unsung Hero?" . . . someone who influenced your decision to study criminal justice? If so, submit a brief essay (or express yourself in any other media, such as photography, digital media, etc), telling us your story. Author Larry K. Gaines will judge the entries. The winning student will receive a $500 scholarship for his/her upcoming term. Last year's winning essay tells of a childhood experience that left a lasting impression on Emily Cavalieri, who is now pursuing a career in Criminal Justice.

To Whom It May Concern:

I would like to tell you about my childhood heroes and how these people have directed me into a Criminal Justice career. When I was younger, I had always heard to never talk to strangers, but I never thought it would be of any concern. My parents always told me to stay with my friends or brother and never to wander off. I thought they were just being paranoid.

One day I was watching the evening news with my parents, and there was a news flash about a missing girl from the area. My parents got all worried and so did I. I realized that something bad could actually happen to someone my age. The police were doing everything they could, from searching the near-by fields to interviewing all the close neighbors. Nothing was of any use and she was still missing.

A few months later, after the snow had melted, they found her body in a nearby field. She was so young and never got to live the life that she wanted. From that point on I knew that I wanted to be in Law Enforcement, because they worked so hard to find her. They put all of the clues together and caught the perpetrators.

All of the people that helped solve her case, my parents, and my teachers are my heroes. I realized that day that bad things can happen to all sorts of people, including children like me. The parents and teachers were just looking out for all of us, when they told us of their concerns. I chose Criminal Justice, so I can make a difference in this world and to show my respect to all of my heroes.

Thank you for your time and consideration.
Sincerely,

Emily Cavalieri

Entries must be received by May 30, 2008.
The winner will be announced on June 30, 2008.
Please send entries, questions, and requests for rules to:
Terra Schultz
Marketing Manager, Criminal Justice
10 Davis Drive, Belmont CA 94002
terra.schultz@cengage.com

Selected Criminal Justice Careers

POSITION	PRIMARY RESPONSIBILITIES	REQUIREMENTS	FOR MORE INFORMATION
F.B.I. Special Agent	Activities include investigating organized and white collar crime, public corruption, civil rights violations, bank robberies, air piracy, terrorism, and other federal statute violations.	> Four year degree from a U.S. accredited college or university > U.S. citizen > 23 years of age, but not older than 36 > Able to relocate > Good vision > Good health > Valid driver's license	**www.fbi.gov**
Federal Police	Enforce federal laws through patrol, apprehension of criminals, and investigation of crimes. Respond to incidents and emergencies and assist state and local police as needed.	> Valid driver's license > U.S. citizen > Pass background screening and physical exam. > Must have a bachelor's degree, or experience in law enforcement.	**www.usajobs.opm.gov**
United States Marshal	Enforce all federal laws that aren't covered by other federal agencies, administer federal court proceedings, and apprehend fugitives.	> U.S. citizen > Between the ages of 21–37 > Physically fit > Bachelor's degree or three years work experience or a combination.	**www.usdoj.gov/marshals/careers/career.html**
Sheriff	Responsibilities vary according to size of county. In addition to law enforcement responsibilities, sheriff's departments typically perform court-related functions such as providing court security.	> High school diploma or equivalent > U.S. citizen > Valid driver's license > Between the ages of 21–37 > Good physical condition (meet vision, hearing standards, and height/weight ratio)	
Municipal Police	Uphold laws, promote public safety, provide services, maintain order. Typical duties include evidence gathering when responding to incidents, reporting suspicious activities, communicating with community to promote safety, apprehending suspects.	> Police Academy is typically three to seven months, > Most departments require continuing education.	**www.officer.com**
Private Investigator	Generally employed by private and public organizations to protect their businesses and employees.	> Education and licensing varies by state > Minimum: High school diploma > Some jobs require college > Screening can include background investigation, fingerprinting, aptitude test.	**www.bls.gov/oco/ocos157.htm**